A DICTIONARY OF THE UGARITIC LANGUAGE IN THE ALPHABETIC TRADITION

SECOND REVISED EDITION

HANDBOOK OF ORIENTAL STUDIES
HANDBUCH DER ORIENTALISTIK

SECTION ONE

THE NEAR AND MIDDLE EAST

EDITED BY

H. ALTENMÜLLER · B. HROUDA · B.A. LEVINE · R.S. O'FAHEY
K.R. VEENHOF · C.H.M. VERSTEEGH

VOLUME SIXTY-SEVEN

A DICTIONARY OF
THE UGARITIC LANGUAGE
IN THE ALPHABETIC TRADITION
PART ONE

A DICTIONARY OF THE UGARITIC LANGUAGE IN THE ALPHABETIC TRADITION

Part One: [ʾ(a/i/u) – k]

BY

GREGORIO DEL OLMO LETE AND JOAQUÍN SANMARTÍN

English Version Edited and Translated
by Wilfred G.E. Watson

SECOND REVISED EDITION

BRILL
LEIDEN · BOSTON
2004

This book is printed on acid-free paper.

Library of Congress Cataloging-in-Publication Data

LC Control Number 2003065472

ISSN 0169-9423
ISBN 90 04 13694 0 (set)
ISBN 90 04 13695 9 (part one)
ISBN 90 04 13696 7 (part two)

PRINTED IN THE NETHERLANDS

CONTENTS

FOREWORD

1. Ugaritic lexicography was under way, paradoxical though it may seem, even before the complete and satisfactory decipherment of the alphabetic cuneiform sign-list: there had been several guesses about the probable existence of Semitisms in the tablets which made it possible to read them.

The pioneering days of H. Bauer, E. Dhorme, C. Virolleaud and R. Dussaud already lie in the distant past, as do those of the generation of W.F. Albright, A. Alt, G.R. Driver, O. Eissfeldt, Th.H. Gaster, A. Jirku and many others, whose work culminated in the significant compilations by J. Aistleitner, (*Wörterbuch der ugaritischen Sprache*, Berlin 1963, 1965²) and by C. H. Gordon (*Ugaritic Textbook*, Rome 1965, photomechanical reprint 1967; revised reprint 1998). All of us working in this field have had to have these two dictionaries re-bound time and again, the greatest praise a book can receive. In their own day, Aistleitner and Gordon marked a divide, at once the close of the heroic age and the starting point for new and more ambitious tasks.

The task of this type of a dictionary, that is to say, a dictionary of a dead language, is to indicate the stage reached by lexical description and to serve as a reference work for later study. The publication of the lexicographic compendia of Aistleitner and Gordon had at least this beneficial outcome, and in fact the venerable names of the first generation of 'Ugaritologists' were virtually all relegated to footnotes. A similar effect was produced also by the publication of the *Akkadisches Handwörterbuch* (vols. I-III, Wiesbaden, 1965-1981; 1985²) by W. von Soden and by the *Chicago Assyrian Dictionary* (Chicago, since 1956).

The works of Aistleitner and Gordon were what they were: the leaven of new lexicographic production. Also, their publication either coincided with the publication of important compilations of texts such as *PRU 5* and *Ugaritica V* etc., or preceded them by some years, so that a considerable part of the lexical material was missing from their lists. Once again a period of lexicographical unrest began, inhabited by many many names which we all know and are included in the pages that follow, habitués of the specialist periodicals, of which *Ugarit-Forschungen* (Münster, since 1969) must be mentioned as the overall archetype. The archaeological campaigns at Ras Shamra were not always as generous as epigraphers wished and philologists hoped. However, the texts in alphabetic cuneiform recovered after the seventies, in Ugarit and elsewhere can be numbered in their hundreds, as is clearly shown by the two editions of *KTU*, in 1976 and 1995.

2. In the mid-eighties, the authors of these pages began to exchange card-indices, particularly on lexicographical problems, with the intention of editing a Ugaritic Dictionary. The task has been slow and frequently thankless. During the work of defining and describing the various complete or lexical units it became clear that a large output of lexicographic studies on a particular entry is rarely a sign of near certainty and that - given the nature of the material - much of what in their time Aistleitner and Gordon stated as being lexically uncertain continued to be so twenty years later.

This *Dictionary* is to some degree a collective work. In the bibliography the voices of colleagues past and present are heard continually, with their doubts and their certainties: to a large extent our work was simply to harvest the fruit from trees which others have planted and - with some success, we hope - to put a little order into the granaries. It has not always been possible to harmonise the opinions, to reach a consensus. In such cases we have considered that our final responsibility as authors was to make decisions and to establish a distinction between the certain and the plausible, the plausible and the probable or the probable and the merely possible. Sometimes - though rarely - in the case of readings with no bibliography at all, it was necessary to act alone. In the one case as in the other, the responsibility for successes or mistakes is ours alone. Otherwise, in the dictionary, only Ugaritic words are included, including those which occur in Hurrian contexts.

3. In order to be included in the Dictionary, the following are considered as lexical units* in their own right:

(a) independent morphemes ("words", e.g. *ab (I)*), and

*That is, 'headword', 'entrada', 'Lemma', 'entreé'; cf. W. Wolski, in F.J. Hausmann, ed., *Wörterbücher, ein internationales Handbuch der Lexicographie (= Dictionaries / Dictionnaires)*, vol. I, Berlin-New York 1989, pp. 360ff.).

(b) attached morphemes ("affixes", e.g. *-h (I), l (I)*) typical of Semitic.

We have thought it appropriate to mention the following also:

(c) proper names of people (PN), places (TN), deities (DN), months (MN), etc., considering that the user, in a corpus as small as the texts in alphabetic Ugaritic, would welcome such information on their lexical nature, especially in obscure or uncertain contexts. They are strictly morphological and semantic elements, often from non-Semitic or representing earlier linguistic stages (palaeo-Semitic); therefore, apart from their identification as proper names and - in the case of personal names - their attribution to a particular linguistic group (Semitic, Hurrian, Anatolian, etc.) here there is no insistence on linguistic explanations nor is the material made use of as a lexicographic resource, since in each and every case reference is being made to the secondary bibliographical information. In a way, therefore, what follows is a combination of a bilingual dictionary and an onomastic list. The possible lexical connection between both aspects can be checked indirectly in the sections which close some entries.

The Dictionary is based on the readings of the alphabetic texts as in *KTU: second enlarged edition*, Münster 1995. The very few discrepancies are marked by the sign (!). In general, we do not insist on the purely epigraphic dimension of the text and reconstructions which are supported by parallel passages or for obvious reasons which we think are certain, are not marked by square brackets ([ ]), use of which is limited to cases where their omission might affect the certainty of interpretation. The portions of text omitted in quotations are marked by (...). Names of persons or deities which do not affect the comprehension of a passage are usually given as *PN* or *DN* both in the text and in the translation.

Transliteration follows the standard system used since C.H. Gordon (UT) with the addition of the sign ⊕ used in KTU (cf. *KTU*, p. XI). For the verbal stems an abstract pattern of the root structure: */C-C-C/*, */C-C-(C)/* or */C-C/* has been chosen. The nominal lexical units (nouns and adjectives) are cited in the singular form of the absolute state, either attested or hypothetical. Sometimes, forms postulated or suggested by various lexicographical studies are listed, although in our judgement they lack enough proof; these proposals appear in parentheses ( ), with reference to the lexical unit or form we consider as the most plausible.

4. The macrostructure of the Dictionary is a list of lexical units in the order of the Latin alphabet, with the necessary adjustments for special graphemes or graphemes with diacritics: the alphabetic sequence chosen isas follows: *(ʔ)a/i/u*, ʕ, *b, d, ḏ, g, ǵ, h, ḥ, ḫ, k, l, m, n, p, q, r, s/ś, ṣ, š/s̀, t, ṭ, ṯ/⊕, w, y, z, ẓ*. The three signs for ʔalif (a, i and u) are considered as equivalent for the purposes of the sequence; for verbal roots with ʔalif as first, second or third radical, the graphemic abstractions */ʔ-C_2-(C_3)/*, */C_1-ʔ(-C_3)/* or */C_1-C_2-ʔ/* have been created. From all these, sequences such as */ʔ-r/*, *a/ir*, *ar*, *ir*, *ur*, *irab*, *arb*ʕ etc. originate. For the graphemes *ś*, *s̀*, and ⊕, which require special treatment, we have adopted a largely pragmatic approach based on convenience and on the need to look up lexemes quickly rather than on strictly phonological considerations. Accordingly, the lexical items beginning with *ś* have been included under *s*; those beginning with *s̀*, an allophone of */š/ or */ṯ/, but an allograph of *š*, are listed under *š*, and those beginning with ⊕ are listed under *ṯ* (see Tropper UG 15f. [21.222]). Hence the respective headings *s/ś*, *š/s̀* and *ṯ/⊕*. The special graphemes of the 'short alphabets' are arranged according to their outward appearance and not according to their special allophonic values or 'internal forms'.

The decision to adopt the order of the Latin alphabet is based on pragmatic reasons, but not exclusively. Ugaritic is not Hebrew and the sequence which takes the Hebrew aphabet as its model is as alien to Ugaritic and as conventional as any other; simply compare the treatment in J. Aistleitner (*Wörterbuch der ugaritischen Sprache*, p. XVI) and C.H. Gordon (*Ugaritic Textbook*, pp. 13 ff.) with regard to their respective signs no. 28 (WuS: $\check{s}_2$) and no. 7 (UT: *ḏ*). On the other hand, the Latin sequence - standard in Assyriology since the publication of CAD Ḫ in 1956 and of AHw 1/1 in 1959 - has proved its usefulness to the full.

5. The **microstructure** of each lexical unit comprises two sections: the heading, which is chiefly descriptive, and the body, which is chiefly a definition. In both cases this Dictionary is intended to be a tool for research rather than for (precise) definition. To a large extent, its function is to direct the scholar in his or her (re)search and smooth the way rather than providing him or her with a single definitive choice which in many cases does not exist.

5.1. The **heading** includes the following elements:

5.1.1. The lexical unit is given in bold together with a description of its grammatical function or **lexical class** (verb, noun, adjective, adverb, functor, preposition, conjunction, etc.). In proper names, this position is occupied by the sigla PN, TN, DN, MN, etc.

5.1.2. The **translation** or lexical meaning, which is in quotation marks whenever we consider it to be unequivocal. For obvious reasons, it has only rarely been possible to distinguish everything as well as might have wished between denotation, connotation and the possible cases of lexical restraints on an entry (cf. L. Zgusta, *Manual of Lexicography*, Prague/The Hague/Paris 1971, 27ff.). Frequently, and when it was not possible to provide a more or less unequivocal translation, generic descriptions have been used: a type of, a kind of, etc. On the other hand, scholars have not hesitated in placing a question mark (?) after meanings which do not reach the degree of certainty wished for. This sign usually replaces adverbs which run from 'perhaps' to 'probably'. In a certain number of cases we have been unable to provide any moderately plausible translation; such entries are translated by "?".

5.1.3. As a general rule, the translation is followed by the list of **isolexemes** and some **bibliographical** references (all between parentheses).

5.1.3.1. The **isolexemes** have been treated with due caution. The bibliography includes a large number of etymological references, almost always following neo-grammatical rules: in collecting these references or providing new ones, we have taken care to avoid the extremes and prejudices which have helped to discredit the discipline (art or science?) of etymology (Y. Malkiel, *Etymology*, Cambridge 1993, 169). We could be criticised for the synchronic presentation of this section, but a diachronic approach would have increased the size of the volume and made this Dictionary into a kind of 'Herkunftswörterbuch' which never entered into our calculations.

We have not attempted to prepare an 'etymological' dictionary of Ugaritic in the strict sense, but instead to provide a set of comparative data which makes likely the interpretation that, in the first instance, emerges from the immediate linguistic context. The phonological equivalents of the lexeme are always respected, avoiding any daring, while the semantic correspondence which can link the Ugaritic lexeme with those of cognate languages is determined, above all, within the frame of 'strong semantic relationship'. In the case of 'weak semantic relationship', the correlation is qualified by **cf.** in an attempt to denote a lesser degree of likelihood in the equivalence, which does not exclude that possibly the lexemes are in fact 'etymologically' related. It should not be forgotten that, even within strict phonological correlation of roots, each lexeme acquires a semantic meaning only within the frame of a system of oppositions which defines that language. If, ultimately, we insist on this comparative approach, which in a living language could be merely illuminating or learned, this is because it is both an 'ancient' and a 'dead' language, and so lacks any ratification of meaning through spoken usage, and in addition is very limited in terms of texts. The comparative approach tries to make up the lack of context and reconstruct the square of semantic oppositions by using options from cognate language and cultures.

In any case, the very existence of supposedly isolexical morphemes is usually justitified by the quotation of the more common dictionaries, although the translation provided in them are not included. We thought that was enough and that the user is the best person to exercise control over this kind of data by means of lexicographical reference. The isolexical map basically covers three linguistic areas from which the data allow a diachronic reading, i.e. North Semitic and East Semitic (especially for palaeo-Semitic), Northwest Semitic (for standard Semitic) and South Semitic (for late Semitic). These areas are as follows:

Hebrew, substantiated by *HALOT*.

The data from Northwest *Semitic epigraphy* (basically, Phoenician, Punic, Aramaic [ancient Aramaic or if unavailable, Imperial Aramaic], Nabataean and Palmyrene), substantiated by Hoftijzer - Jongeling [*DNWSI*].

Jewish Aramaic (following Levy [*WTM*], Jastrow or Sokoloff [*DJPA*]) and Syriac (following Brockelmann [*LS*]), when there are no data from ancient or imperial Aramaic.

Eblaite, very often qualified by the restrictive abbreviation **cf.**, however, we have opted not to refer to the recently published *Thesaurus inscriptionum eblaicarum, Volume A, Parte Prima* (Rome 1995) by G. Pettinato and to wait instead until later volumes of this work increase the comparative material. Various bibliographical sources have been cited that provide lexicographical material.

Amorite, normalized between /slashes/ using material generally from Huffmon [*APNMT*], Buccellati [*Amorites*], Gelb [*CAAA*] and Hess [*AmPN*].

Akkadian, following *AHw* and *CAD* ; forms from peripheral Akkadian (basically Nuzi, Alalakh, Boğazköy, Emar or El Amarna) are also cited.

Classical Arabic is given where possible according to Lane's dictionary, and ancient *Epigraphic South Arabic* is represented by the Sabaean dialect described by Biella [*DOSA*].

Ethiopic, generally *Geʕez* as documented by Leslau in *CDG*; otherwise, but rarely, reference is made to *Tigrē* [*WTS*].

References to Semitic loans in *Egyptian* are usually cited according to the transcriptions given in Erman - Grapow [*WäS*], the 'group writings' in Helck [*Bez.*] and the transcriptions in Hoch [*SWET*]. The few references to *Greek* are usually based on Liddell - Scott.

5.1.3.2. In the **bibliographical** references an attempt has been made to include everything we considered to be essential or important for understanding the problem. This Dictionary is not a bibliographical reference work. It implies the omission of very valuable opinions which have been mentioned later and discussed, with preference given to the most recent publications. Publications which support the lexical choice made by the Dictionary are listed as well as alternative choices, which are preceded by **diff.** [different(ly)], followed by the solution 'within single inverted commas' in the original language of the publication.

5.1.4. Where necessary, data related to syllabic Ugaritic [**syll. Ug.**], and to the Akkadian of Ras Shamra [**RS Akk.**] are included, and the context of parallel lexemes [**par.**].

5.1.5. The section labelled **Forms** in the heading gives a list of the various morphological forms attested, including allographs and allophones.

5.2. The **body** of the entry repeats the lexical definition given in the heading and justifies its translation in the context. The transliteration is given in *italics*; in poetic passages mention is made of the parallel morphemes using the sign //. Included are all the passages which we consider important for the lexical definition of the morpheme, though not every occurrence is always included. In other words, this Dictionary is not a *Thesaurus* and it cannot replace a *Concordance*. The abbreviation **Cf.** at the end of an entry refers to other entries which are etymologically related.

6. We would like to express our thanks, first and foremost, to Dr Wilfred G. E. Watson. Right from the beginning Dr Watson has collaborated closely in the preparation of the first (Spanish) edition, constantly contributing numerous ideas and constructive criticism. Now we have had the good fortune of being able to make use of his collaboration in editing and translating the English version, since Dr Watson is not only a well-known Semitist but also knows -and is an aficionado of- the Spanish language. His contributions to the foundation and formation of the *Dictionary* have been decisive and as a result DUL is, in large measure, also his work.

Our thanks also go, in a very special way, to P. Bordreuil and D. Pardee, who generously allowed us to include in the *Dictionary* the rich epigraphic material from the 1986-1992 campaings (RS 86.-RS 92.) that will be published in RSOu 14, and to Dr J. Belmonte Marín, who kindly put at our disposal his material on toponymy, recently published (*Die Orts- und Gewässernamen der Texte aus Syrien im 2. Jt. v. Chr.* [RGTC 12/2], Wiesbaden 2001). Others who had a very active part in the preparation of the original Spanish edition are Dr Ignacio Márquez Rowe, Dr Adelina Millet and María J. Domènech. Our thanks go to all of these as well as to those sent us directly their comments on Volumes I and II of the Spanish edition, and to the reviewers - mostly favourable - who were kind enough to present the work to its readers.

The *Dictionary* was started in 1984 as a research project with the title "Lexicografía cananea del II milenio. Materiales para la edición de un Diccionario Ugarítico", financed by the Comisión Asesora de Investigación Científica y Técnica del Ministerio de Educación y Ciencia (ref. no. 3418-83-C02-01-2) and to some extent its publication is due to an Acción de Política Cientifica granted by the same institution (ref. no. APC94-0023). This twofold official support, which merits due acknowledgement, enabled a task to be begun and completed that has taken almost twenty years, a task that in 1988 we promised to complete 'within a reasonably short space of time' (*AuOr* 6 [1988] 255ff). Clearly lexicography proceeds at a pace that is entirely its own.

Barcelona, May 2002

G. del Olmo Lete - J. Sanmartín

FOREWORD TO THE SECOND EDITION

Due to the magnificent welcome given to our Dictionary of the Ugaritic Language, the first edition was sold out sooner than expected. The second edition is essentially the same as the first, although we have used the opportunity to insert some minor improvements and correct the more obvious mistakes. We hope that we can continue to rely on the support of our colleagues and users of the Dictionary and would be grateful for their suggestions and criticisms. Learning a language is always an endless task: "Verba [...] admonent tantum, ut quaeramus res; non exhibent, ut norimus" (S. Agustín, De magistro 36).

Barcelona, September 2003

G. del Olmo Lete – J. Sanmartín

LIST OF ABBREVIATIONS

I. Sigla

< >	graphemes omitted by mistake
{ }	superfluous graphemes
[ ]	reconstructed text
[[ ]]	erased text
(...)	text of varying length, shortened or omitted in the quotation
(nn)	unspecified amounts in the quotation
(!)	correction of erroneous grapheme(s)
(?)	character with very uncertain reading
<	derives etymologically, morphologically or semantically from
>	becomes etymologically, morphologically or semantically
//	parallel lexeme, morpheme or text segment
/	graphical, phonological or morphological alternative
/xxx/	/transcription/
/C-C-C/	verbal root
+	sequence of graphemes or morphemes
±	optional element
≃	similar or very like
=	separation of morphemes into transcribed segments

II. General sigla

abs.	absolute state
abstr.	abstract
acc.	accusative
act.	active
adj.	adjective
agent.	agentive (case, Hurr.)
admin.	administration, administrative
adv.	adverb, adverbial
afform.	afformative
Akk.	Akkadian

Alal.Akk.	Akkadian (docum. in the texts) from Alalakh (cf. AT)
Alal.	Alalakh
allogr.	allograph, allographic
alph.	alphabetic
alt.	alternative(ly)
Amh.	Amharic
Amm.	Ammonite
Amor.	Amorite, Amurrite
anat.	anatomy, anatomically
Anat.	Anatolian
ant.	antecedent
aph.	ʔaphʕel (Syr.-Aram).
appos.	apposition
Arab.	Arabic
Aram.	Aramaic
astron.	astronomical
AT	number of tablet from Alalakh
BAram.	Biblical Aramaic
Bo	Boğazköy
Can.	Canaanite
cf.	see, compare
cj.	conjecture
coll.	collective
com.	common, commonly
cond.	conditional
conj.	conjunction
c.Sem.	common Semitic
cstr.	construct state, construction
ctx.	context
D	triconsonantal verbal stem with long second radical
defect.	defective spelling
del.	*delendum*, to be deleted
dem.	demonstrative
denom.	denominative
deriv.	derivative(s)
det.	determined, determination (Hurr. *-n*)
diff.	different(ly)
dir.	direct (compl.), directive (case, Hurr. *-d*)
disj.	disjunctive
dittog.	dittography
DN(N)	divine name(s)

Dpass.	verbal stem D passive
Dt	verbal stem D with infixed -t-
du.	dual
e.	edge
EA Akk.	Akkadian (documented in the texts) from El Amarna (cf. EA, EAT)
EA	Akkadian of Tell el Amarna; tablet number in Knutdzon
EAT	El Amarna Text
Ebla.	Eblaite
econ.	economic
Edom.	Edomite
Eg.	Egyptian
elem.	element
Emar Akk.	Akkadian (documented in the texts) from Emar
encl.	enclitic
espec.	especially
ESA	Epigraphic South Arabic
ET	English translation.
Eth.	Ethiopic
etym.	etymology, etymological(ly)
ext.	extension, extended, lengthened
f.	feminine
f(f).	following
fin.	finite
freq.	frequent(ly)
G	basic (ground) verbal stem
ge.	genitive
gen.	general
Gpass.	G passive
Gk	Greek
GN(N)	gentilic(s)
graph.	graphic
Gt	verbal G stem with -t- infix
Hb.	Hebrew
HH	Hieroglyphic Hittite
hif.	hifʕil
Hitt.	Hittite
ho.	hofʕal
Hurr.	Hurrian
hypoc.	hypocoristicon

i.a.	*inter alia*
ibid.	*ibidem*, the same citation
I-E	Indo-European
impv.	imperative
inf.	infinitive
interj.	interjection
interr.	interrogative
JAram.	Jewish Aramaic
juss.	jussive
Kass.	Kassite
l.e.	left edge.
L	biconsonantal verbal stem with lengthened second radical
lang.	language
LB	Late Babylonian
lex.	lexical
lex. l.	lexical list(s)
lit.	literary, literally
ln.	line
lr.e.	lower edge
Lt	verbal L stem with infix -t-
Luw.	Luwian
m.	masculine
MA	Middle Assyrian
MB	Middle Babylonian
Mesop.	Mesopotamian
metath.	metathesis
meton.	metonymy
MHb.	Middle Hebrew
MN	month name
Moab.	Moabite
mod.	modern
morph.	morphology, morphological(ly)
MSA	Modern South Arabian
MT	received (consonantal) Masoretic Text
mult.	multiplicative
Myc.	Mycenaean
n.	name
n.	note [in bibliographical reference]
N	verbal stem with n-prefix
NA	Neo-Assyrian
Nab.	Nabataean

NB	Neo-Babylonian
NC	Nominal clause
neg.	negative, negation
NH	modern Hebrew
ni.	nifʕal
NN	common noun which has become a proper name (e.g.: *gt dprn* > *gt NN*)
nom.	nominative
NPun.	Neo-Punic
num.	numeral
OAkk.	Old Akkadian
OAram.	Old Aramaic
OAss.	Old Assyrian
OB	Old Babylonian
obl.	oblique
obv.	obverse (of tablet)
OInd.	Old Indian
ord.	ordinal
p.	person, personal
p(p).	pages(s) [in bibliographical reference]
Palm.	Palmyrene
par.	parallel
pass.	passive
periph.	peripheral
Ph.	Phoenician
pi.	piʕʕel
pl. t.	*plurale tantum*
pl.	plural
pn.	pronoun
PN(N)	personal name(s)
PNF	feminine personal name
pos.	positive
poss.	possible, possibly
pre-Sarg.	Pre-Sargonic
precat.	precative
prefc.	prefix conjugation
prep.	preposition
probl.	probable, probably
ptc.	participle
pu.	puʕʕal
Pun.	Punic

Q	qal
Qpass.	qal passive
r.e.	right edge.
R	reduplicated verbal biconsonantal stem
rdg	reading
rel.	relative
relig.	religious
rev.	reverse (of tablet)
RN	royal name
RS	Ras Shamra
RS Akk.	Akkadian (documented in the texts) from Ras Shamra
Š	verbal stem with š-prefix
Samal.	Samalian
SB	Standard Babylonian
Sem.	Semitic
sg.	singular
Št	verbal stem with š-prefix and infixed -t-
stat.	stative
subst.	substantive, substantivized
suff.	suffix, suffixed
suffc.	suffix conjugation
Sum.	Sumerian
s. v.	*sub voce*
syll.	syllabic
syll. Ug.	Ugaritic written in the syllabic tradition
Syr.	Syriac
tD	verbal D stem with t-prefix
Tigr.	Tigrē
tL	verbal L stem with t-prefix
TN(N)	place name(s), toponym(s)
trad.	tradition(ally), traditional (translation or explanation)
txt	text(s)
u.e.	upper edge
Ug.	Ugaritic written in the alphabetic tradition
Urart.	Urartian
unc.	uncertain
unpub.	unpublished
vb	verb
var.	variant
VC	verbal clause
verb.	verbal

WS	West Semitic
Yaud.	Yaudic

III. Bibliographical abbreviations

A1CILSChS	A. Caquot - D. Cohen, eds., Actes du Premier Congrès Int. de Linguistique Sémitique et Chamito-Sémitique, Paris 16-19 juillet 1969, The Hague/Paris 1974.
A1CISFP	Atti del I Congresso Internazionale di Studi Fenici e Punici (Roma 1979), Rome 1983.
A2CISFP	Atti del II Congresso Internazionale di Studi Fenici e Punici (Roma, 9-14 Novembre 1987), I-III, Rome 1991.
AaG	R. Degen, Altaramäische Grammatik der Inschriften des 10.-8. Jh. v. Chr., Wiesbaden 1969.
AAN 1	E. Cassin - J.-J. Glassner, Anthroponymie et Anthropologie de Nuzi. 1. Les anthroponymes, Malibu 1977.
ABAW NF	Abhandlungen des Bayerischen Akademie der Wissenschaften, München.
AC	P. Garelli, Les Assyriens à Cappadoce, Paris 1963.
ACF	Annuaire du Collège de France, Paris.
ACIP 1993	M. Yon - M. Sznycer - P. Bordreuil, Le pays d'Ougarit autour de 1200 av. J.-C. Histoire et archéologie. Actes du Colloque International Paris [...] 1993, Paris 1995.
AcOrHun	Acta Orientalia Hungarica, Budapest.
AD	J.-L. Cunchillos, Cuando los ángeles eran dioses, Salamanca 1978.
Adonis	S. Ribichini, ed., Adonis. Relazioni del colloquio in Roma, 22-23 maggio 1981, Rome 1984.
AdS	G. Wilhelm, Das Archiv des Silwa-Tessup, Hefte 2ff., Wiesbaden 1980ff.
AE	Ṣ. Rin, *ʕlylwt hʔlym. kl šyrwt ʔwgryt*, Jerusalem 1968.
AED	T.L. Kane, Amharic-English Dictionary, Wiesbaden 1990.
AEO	A.H. Gardiner, Ancient Egyptian Onomastica, 1-3, London 1947.
AfO	Archiv für Orientforschung, Vienna.
AGI	Archivio Glottologico Italiano, Florence.
AHw	W. von Soden, Akkadisches Handwörterbuch, I-III, Wiesbaden 1965-1981.

AIA	St. Kaufman, The Akkadian Influences on Aramaic, Chicago, IL 1974.
AION	Annali. Istituto Universitario Orientale, Naples.
AJBI	Annual of the Japanese Biblical Institute, Tokyo.
AKDT	I. Gelb - B. Kienast, Altakkadische Königsinschriften des dritten Jahrtausends, Stuttgart 1990. Cf. GlAKI.
AkkUg	J. Huehnergard, The Akkadian of Ugarit, Atlanta, GA 1989.
ALASP	Abhandlungen zur Literatur Alt-Syrien-Palästinas und Mesopotamiens, Münster.
ALM	A. Finet, L'Accadien des lettres de Mari, Brussels 1956.
AmAk	Sh. Izreʔel, Amurru Akkadian: a Linguistic Study, vol. 1-2, Atlanta, GA 1991.
AmL	W.L. Moran, The Amarna Letters, Baltimore / London 1992. Cf. LEA.
Amorites	G. Buccellati, The Amorites of the Ur III period, Naples 1966.
AmPN	R.S. Hess, Amarna Personal Names, Winona Lake, IN 1993.
Anat	N. H. Walls, The Goddess Anat in Ugaritic Myth, Atlanta GA 1992.
AnBib	Analecta Biblica, Rome.
ANET	J.B. Pritchard, ed., Ancient Near Eastern Texts Relating to the Old Testament, Princeton, NJ 1955.
ANH	G. Dalman, Aramäisch-Neuhebräisches Handwörterbuch zu Targum, Talmud und Midrasch, Göttingen 1938.
AntSém	Antiquités Sémitiques, Paris.
AOAT	Alter Orient und Altes Testament, Kevelaer/ Neukirchen-Vluyn.
AOATT	K.R. Veenhof, Aspects of Old Assyrian Trade and its Terminology, Leiden 1972.
AoF	Altorientalische Forschungen, Berlin.
ÄP	H. Ranke, Die ägyptischen Personennamen, I-III, Glückstadt 1935-1977.
APNMT	H.B. Huffmon, Amorite Personal Names in the Mari Texts: A Structural and Lexical Study, Baltimore, MD 1965.
ArchEbl	G. Pettinato, The Archives of Ebla. An Empire Inscribed in Clay, with an Afterword by Mitchell

	Dahood, S.J., Garden City, NY 1981 (ET of Ebla(1)).
ARES	Archivi reali di Ebla, Studi, Rome.
ARET	Archivi reali di Ebla, Testi, Rome.
ARM	Archives royales de Mari, Paris.
ARMT	Archives royales de Mari. Textes, Paris.
ArOr	Archiv Orientální, Prague.
Arrapḫe	G. Dosch, Struktur der Gesellschaft des Königsreichs Arrapḫe, Heidelberg 1993.
ARTU	J.C. de Moor, An Anthology of Religious Texts from Ugarit, Leiden 1987.
AS	Assyriological Studies, Chicago.
Assur	Assur, Malibu CA.
AT	H.H. Dressler, The Aqht-Text. A New Transcription, Translation, Commentary, and Introduction (Cambridge Univ. Ph.D. Diss.), 1976.
AUL	M.A. Merlis, Akkadian and Ugaritic Lexicography (Yeshiva Univ., NY, Ph.D. Diss.) 1983.
AULS	F. Renfroe, Arabic-Ugaritic Lexical Studies, Münster 1992.
AuOr	Aula Orientalis, Sabadell (Barcelona).
AuOrS	Aula Orientalis Supplementa, Sabadell (Barcelona).
BA	K. Spronk, Beatific Afterlife in Ancient Israel and in the Ancient Near East, Kevelaer/Neukirchen-Vluyn 1986.
Baal	P.J. Van Zijl, Baal. A Study of Texts in Connexion with Baal in the Ugaritic Epics, Kevelaer/Neukirchen-Vluyn 1972.
BÄBÄ	W. Helck, Die Beziehungen Ägyptens und Vorderasiens zur Ägäis bis ins 7. Jahrhundert v. Chr., Darmstadt 1979.
BAfO	Beiheft(e). Archiv für Orient-Forschung, Graz/Berlin.
BASOR	Bulletin of the American Schools of Oriental Research, New Haven, CT.
BC	M. Smith, The Ugaritic Baal Cycle, I, Leiden / New York / Köln, 1994.
BDB	Fr. Brown - S.R. Driver - Ch.A Briggs, Hebrew and English Lexicon of the Old Testament, Oxford 1966.
Beitr.	J.J. Stamm, Beiträge zur hebräischen und aramäischen Namenkunde. Zu seinem 70. Geburtstag eds. E. Jenni and M. A. Klopfenstein, Freiburg-Schweiz/Göttingen 1980.

Berytus	Archaeological Studies, Copenhagen/Beirut.
Bez.	W. Helck, Die Beziehungen Ägyptens zu Vorderasien im 3. und 2. Jahrtausend v. Chr., Wiesbaden [2]1971.
BFE	M. Krebernik, Die Beschwörungen aus Fara und Ebla, Hildesheim 1984.
BGUL	St. Segert, A Basic Grammar of the Ugaritic Language, Berkeley 1984.
Bib	Biblica. Commentarii trimestres a Facultate Biblica P.I.B., Rome.
BH	P. Xella, Baal Hammon. Recherches sur l'identité el l'histoire d'un dieu phénico-punique, Rome 1991.
BHL	E. Ullendorff, Is Biblical Hebrew a Language?, Wiesbaden 1977.
Bible World	G. Rendsburg etc. (eds.), The Bible World. Essays in Honor of C. Gordon, New York 1980.
BibMes	Bibliotheca Mesopotamica, Malibu, CA.
Biling.	L. Cagni, ed., Il bilinguismo a Ebla. Atti del convegno internazionale (Napoli, 19-22 aprile 1982), Naples 1984.
BiOr	Bibliotheca Orientalis, Leiden.
BK	U. Rüterswörden, Die Beamten der israelitischen Königszeit, Neukirchen-Vluyn 1988.
BL	H. Bauer - P. Leander, Historische Grammatik der hebräischen Sprache, I, Halle 1922.
BN	Biblische Notizen, Bamberg.
BOS	U. Cassuto, Biblical and Oriental Studies, I-II, Jerusalem 1973/75.
BSA	Bulletin of Sumerian Agriculture, Cambridge.
CAAA	I. Gelb, Computer-aided Analysis of Amorite, Chicago 1980.
CAD	The Assyrian Dictionary of the Oriental Institute of the University of Chicago, Chicago/Glückstadt 1956ff.
CAME	K. Conti Rossini, Chrestomathia arabica meridionalis epigraphica, Rome 1931.
Caphtor	J. Strange, Caphtor/Keptiu. A New Investigation, Leiden 1980.
CARTU	J.C. de Moor - K. Spronk, A Cuneiform Anthology of Religious Texts from Ugarit, Leiden 1987.
CAT	A.F. Rainey, Canaanite in the Amarna Tablets. A Linguistic Analysis of the Mixed Dialect Used by

	Scribes from Canaan, I-IV, Leiden / New York / Köln, 1996.
CBQ	The Catholic Biblical Quarterly, Washington, DC.
CC	M.E. Cohen, The Cultic Calendars of the Ancient Near East, Bethesda, MD 1993.
CDG	W. Leslau, Comparative Dictionary of Geʕez, Wiesbaden 1987.
CEB	U. Oldenburg, The Conflict Between El and Baal in Canaanite Religion, Leiden 1969.
Chadwick	J. Chadwick(- M. Ventris), Documents in Mycenaean Greek (second edition), Cambridge 1973.
Cities	G. Buccellati, Cities and Nations of Ancient Syria, Rome 1967.
CMC	R.J. Clifford, The Cosmic Mountain in Canaan and the Old Testament, Cambridge, MA 1972.
CMHE	F.M. Cross, Canaanite Myths and Hebrew Epics. Essays in the History of the Religion of Israel, Cambridge, MA 1973.
CML	J.C.L. Gibson, Canaanite Myths and Legends, Edinburgh 1978.
Council	M.T. Mullen, The Divine Council in Canaanite and Early Hebrew Literature, Chico, CA 1980.
CPHPB	J. Cors i Meya, A Concordance of The Phoenician History of Philo of Byblos, Sabadell (Barcelona) 1995.
CR	G. del Olmo Lete, Canaanite Religion According to the Liturgical Texts of Ugarit, Bethesda MD 1999 (= ET of RC).
CRAIBL	Académie des Inscriptions et Belles-Lettres, Comptes rendus des séances de l'année ..., Paris.
CRANE	T. Mikasa ed., Cult and Ritual in the Ancient Near East, Wiesbaden 1992.
CRRA	Compte(s) rendue(s) de la ... Rencontre Assyriologique Internationale.
CS	W.W. Hallo - K. Lawson - D.E. Orton (eds.), The Context of Scripture, I. Canonical Compositions from the Biblical World, Leiden / New York / Köln, 1997.
CU	J.-M. de Tarragon, Le culte à Ugarit d'après les textes de la pratique en cunéiforme alphabétiques, Paris 1980.
Culto	G. Pettinato, Il culto ufficiale ad Ebla durante el regno di Ibbi-Sipiš, Rome 1979.
Cults	T. Lewis, Cults of the Dead in Ancient Israel and

Ugarit, Atlanta GA 1989.

Cyprominoica O. Masson, Cyprominoica. Répertoires, Documents de Ras Shamra, Essais d'interprétation, Göteborg 1974.

DA Ch. Virolleaud, La déesse ʕAnat. Poème de Ras Shamra, Paris 1938.

DAFA R. Blachère - M. Chouémi - Cl. Denizeau, Dictionnaire arabe-français-anglais, vol. 1ff., Paris 1967ff.

Das Hurritische
E. Neu, Das Hurritische: Eine altorientalische Sprache in neuem Licht, Mainz/Stuttgart 1988.

Das Sumerische
A. Falkenstein, Das Sumerische, Leiden 1959.

DDD K. van der Toorn - B. Becking - P.W. van der Horst (eds.), Dictionary of Deities and Demons in the Bible, Leiden 1995; ^{2}1999.

DJPA M. Sokoloff, A Dictionary of the Jewish Palestinian Aramaic of the Byzantine Period, Ramat Gan 1990.

DMic Fr. Aura Jorro, Diccionario Micénico (Diccionario Griego-Español, Anejo I-II), vols. I-II, Madrid 1985/1993.

DMT I. Nakata, Deities in the Mari Texts, Ann Arbor, MI 1974.

DNWSI J. Hoftijzer - K.Jongeling, Dictionary of the North-West Semitic Inscriptions. Parts One/Two, Leiden 1995.

DOSA J.C. Biella, Dictionary of Old South Arabic. Sabaean Dialect, Chico, CA 1982.

Dozy R. Dozy, Supplément aux dictionnaires arabes, Leyde ^{2}1927.

DUA J. Healey, Underworld and Afterlife in the Ugaritic Texts (London PhD. Diss.), 1977.

EAR E. Ashley, The "Epic of AQHT" and the "RPUM Texts": A Critical Interpretation (New York Univ. Ph. D. Diss.), 1977.

EAT J.A. Knudtzon (- O. Weber - E. Ebeling), Die El-Amarna Tafeln, I-II, Aalen 1964 / A.F. Rainey, El Amarna Tablets. Supplement to J.A. Knudtzon Die El-Amarna-Tafeln (2nd edition, revised), Kevelaer/ Neukirchen-Vluyn 1978.

Ebla(1) G. Pettinato, Ebla, un impero inciso nell'argilla, Milan 1979.

Ebla(2)	G. Pettinato, Ebla. Nuovi orizzonti della storia, Milan 1986.
Eblaitica	C.H. Gordon et al. (eds.), Eblaitica. Studies on the Ebla Archives and Eblaitic Language, 1-3, Winona Lake, IN 1987/1990/1992.
EC	R. Lebrun, Ebla et les civilisations du Proche-Orient Ancien, Louvain-La-Neuve 1984.
EDA	L. Cagni, ed., Ebla 1975-1985. Dieci anni di studi linguistici e filologici. Atti del Convegno Internazionale (Napoli, 9-11 ottobre 1985), Naples 1987.
EDP	R. Du Mesnil du Buisson, Études sur les dieux phéniciens hérités par l'empire romain, Leiden 1970.
EEU	J.-L. Cunchillos-Ilarri, Estudios de epistolografía ugarítica, Valencia 1989.
EHS 1	H. Kronasser, Etymologie der hethitischen Sprache, 1, Wiesbaden 1966; 2: Ausführliche Indices zu Bd. 1 zusammengestellt von E. Neu, Wiesbaden 1987.
EI	Eretz Israel, Jerusalem.
EL	P. Fronzaroli, Eblaic Lexicon, QuSe 13, 1984, 117-157.
Emar	D. Arnaud, Recherches au pays d'Aštata. Emar VI. 1-2: Texts sumériens et accadiens. Planches. 3: Textes sumériens et accadiens. Texte. 4: Textes de la bibliotèque: transcriptions et traductions, Paris 1985/1986/1987.
EML	C.H. Gordon, Evidence for the Minoan Language, Ventnor, NJ 1966.
EPHEA	École Pratique des Hautes Études, Annuaire, Paris.
ER	A.-M. Blondeau - K. Schipper (eds.), Essais sur le rituel, I, II, Leuven 1990.
Erg.	Ergänzungsheft
ESP	J.J.M. Roberts, The Earliest Semitic Pantheon, Baltimore/London 1972.
ESTU	M. Dietrich - O. Loretz, Die Elfenbeininschriften und S-Texte aus Ugarit, Kevelaer-Neukirchen/Vluyn 1976.
ETL	Ephemerides Theologicae Lovanienses, Leuven.
EU	J.-P. Vita, El ejército de Ugarit, Madrid 1995.
EV	Extracts from the Vocabulary of Ebla, in MEE 4. Cf. VE.
Faulkner	R.O. Faulkner, A Concise Dictionary of Middle Egyptian, Oxford 1981.
FoOr	Folia Orientalia, Kraków.

Forte G. Deiana, LʔJ = essere forte nel semitico del nord-ovest e nella bibbia masoretica (suppl. nº 48 a AION), Naples 1984.

Freilassung E. Neu, Das hurritische Epos der Freilassung, I, Wiesbaden 1996.

Fs. Bakoš AA.VV., Studia J. Bakoš, Bratislava 1965.

Fs. Baumgartner Hebräische Wortforschung. Festschrift zum 80. Geburtstag von W. Baumgartner, Leiden 1967.

Fs. Bergerhof M. Dietrich - O. Loretz (eds.), Mesopotamica-Ugaritica-Biblica. Festschrift für K. Bergerhof zur Vollendung seines 70. Lebensjahres, Kevelaer / Neukirchen-Vluyn 1993.

Fs. Birot J.-M. Durand - J.-R. Kupper, eds., Miscellanea Babylonica, Paris 1985.

Fs. Bittel R.M. Boehmer - H. Hauptmann, eds., Beiträge zur Altertumskunde Kleinasiens. Festschrift für K. Bittel, 1. Text, Mainz 1983.

Fs. Cazelles A. Caquot - M. Delcor, eds., Mélanges bibliques et orientaux en l'honneur de M. Henri Cazelles, Kevelaer/Neukirchen-Vluyn 1981.

Fs. Civil Velles paraules. Ancient Near Eastern Studies in Honor of Miguel Civil on the Occasion of his Sixty-Fifth Birthday, Sabadell (Barcelona) 1991.

Fs. Cotsen G. Buccellati - M. Kelly-Buccellati, eds., Urkesh and the Hurrians. Studies in Honor of Lloyd Cotsen, Malibu CA, 1983.

Fs. Craigie L. Eslinger - G. Taylor, eds., Ascribe to the Lord. Biblical & other studies in memory of Peter C. Craigie, Sheffield 1988.

Fs. Delcor A. Caquot - S. Legasse - M. Tardieu, eds., Mélanges bibliques et orientaux en l'honneur de M. Mathias Delcor, Kevelaer/Neukirchen-Vluyn 1985.

Fs. Díez Macho D. Muñoz León, ed., Salvación en la Palabra. Targum - Derash - Berith. En memoria del profesor Alejandro Díez Macho, Madrid 1986.

Fs. Elliger H. Gese - H.P. Rüger, eds., Wort und Geschichte, Kevelaer/Neukirchen-Vluyn 1973.

Fs. Fecht J. Osing - G. Dreyer, eds., Form and Mass, Festschrift für G. Fecht, Wiesbaden 1987.

Fs. Finkelstein
M. deJong Ellis, ed., Essays on the Ancient Near East in Memory of Jacob Joel Finkelstein, Hamden, CT 1977.

Fs. Fitzmyer M.P. Horgan - P.J. Kobelski, eds., To Touch the Text. Biblical and Related Studies in Honor of Joseph A. Fitzmyer, S.J., Crossroad, NY 1989.

Fs. Fleury J.-M. Durand, ed., Florilegium marianum. Recueil d'études en l'honneur de M. Fleury, Tours-Paris 1992.

Fs. Fohrer J.A. Emerton ed., Prophecy. Essays presented to G. Fohrer, Berlin 1980.

Fs. Garelli D. Charpin - F. Joannès, eds., Marchands, diplomates et empereurs. Études sur la civilisation mésopotamienne offertes à P. Garelli, Paris 1991.

Fs. Gispen AA.VV., Schrift en uitleg. Studies van oud-leerlingen, collega's en vrieden aangeboden aan Prof. Dr. W.H. Gispen, Kampen 1970.

Fs. Gordon cf. Bible World.

Fs. Gordon 1973
H.A. Hoffner, ed., Orient and Occident. Essays presented to C.H. Gordon on the Occasion of his Sixty-fifth Birthday, Kevelaer / Neukirchen-Vluyn 1973.

Fs. Gordon 1998
M. Lubetski - C. Gootlieb - Sh. Keller, eds., Boundaries of the Ancient Near Eastern World. A Tribute to Cyrus H. Gordon, Sheffield 1998.

Fs. Helck H. Altenmüller - D. Wildung, eds., Festschrift Wolfgang Helck zu seinem 70. Geburtstag (Studien zur altägyptischen Kuktur, Bd. 11), Hamburg 1984.

Fs. Landsberger
H. Güterbock *et al.*, eds., Studies in Honor of Benno Landsberger on His Seventy-Fifth Birthday April 21, 1965, Chicago, IL 1965.

Fs. Loretz 1998
M. Dietrich - I. Kottsieper, eds., "Und Mose schrieb dieses Lied auf". Studien zum Alten Testament und zum Alten Orient, Münster 1998.

Fs. Pope J.H. Marks - R.M. Good, eds., Love & Death in the Ancient Near East. Essays in Honor of Marvin H. Pope, Guilford, CT 1987.

Fs. Prado L. Álvarez Verdes - E.J. Alonso Hernández, eds.,

	Homenaje a Juan Prado. Miscelánea de estudios bíblicos y hebraicos, Madrid 1975.
Fs. Röllig	B. Pongratz-Leisten - H. Kühne - P. Xella, eds., Ana šadî Labnāni lū allik. Beiträge zu altorientalischen und mittelmeerischen Kulturen. Festschrift Wolfgang Röllig, Kevelaer / Neukirchen-Vluyn 1997.
Fs. Thomas	P. Kosta, ed., Studia indogermanica et slavica. Festgabe für Werner Thomas zum 65 Geburtstag, München 1988.
Fs. Volterra	Studi in onore di E. Volterra, 6, Milan 1971.
Fs. Von Soden 1995	M. Dietrich - O. Loretz, eds., Vom Alten Orient zum Alten Testament. Festschrift für W. Freiherr von Soden zum 85. Geburtstag, Kevelaer / Neukirchen - Vluyn 1995.
Fs. Vööbus	R.H. Fisher, ed., A Tribute to Arthur Vööbus: Studies in Early Christian Literature and its Environment, Primarily in the Syrian East, Chicago 1977.
Fs. Wessetzky	AA.VV., Receuil d'études dédiés à Vilmos Wessetzky à l'occasion de son 65e anniversaire, Budapest 1974.
Fs. Williams	G.E. Kadish - G. E. Freeman, eds, Studies in Philology. Festschrift Ronald James Williams, Toronto 1982.
FU	P. Fronzaroli, La fonetica ugaritica, Rome 1955.
FuF	Forschungen und Forschritten, Berlin.
GA	U. Cassuto, The Goddess Anath, Jerusalem 1971.
GAG	W. von Soden (unter Mitarbeit von W.R. Mayer), Grundriss der akkadischen Grammatik, Rome ^{3}1995.
GAGl	D. Sivan, Grammatical Analysis and Glossary of the Northwest Semitic Vocables in Akkadian Texts of the 15th-13th C.B.C. from Canaan and Syria, Kevelaer/ Neukirchen-Vluyn 1984.
GAR	E. Neu, Glossar zu den althethitischen Ritualtexten, Wiesbaden 1983.
Gardiner	Hieroglyphic sign in the catalogue of A. Gardiner, Egyptian Grammar being an Introduction to the Study of Hieroglyphs, Oxford 1982.
GBM	M. Wakeman, God's Battle with the Monster. A Study in Biblical Imagery, Leiden 1973.
General's Letter	S. Izre'el - I. Singer, The General's Letter from Ugarit: A Linguistic and Historical Reevaluation of RS 20.33 (Ugaritica V, No. 20), Tel Aviv 1990.

GeSyr	H. Klengel, Geschichte Syriens im 2. Jahrtausend v.u.Z., Teile 1, 2, 3, Berlin 1965 / 1969 / 1970.
GG	C.M. Foley, The Gracious Gods and The Royal Ideology of Ugarit (McMaster Univ., Ph.D. Diss.), 1980.
GGA	Göttingische Gelehrte Anzeigen, Göttingen.
GHB	P. Joüon, Grammaire de l'hébreu biblique, Rome 1947.
GHL	F.W. Bush, A Grammar of the Hurrian Language (Brandeis Univ. Ph.D. Diss.), 1964.
Giacumakis	G. Giacumakis, The Akkadian of Alalaḫ, The Hague 1970.
GKT	W. Hecker, Grammatik der Kültepe-Texte, Rome 1968.
GlAKI	B. Kienast - W. Sommerfeld, Glossar zu den altakkadischen Königsinschriften, Stuttgart 1994. Cf. AKDT.
GLECS	Comptes Rendues du Groupe Linguistique d'Études Chamito-Sémitiques, Paris.
GLH	E. Laroche, Glossaire de la langue hourrite, Paris 1980.
GPOTU	M. Heltzer, Goods, prices and the organization of Trade in Ugarit, Wiesbaden 1978.
GUL	D. Sivan, A Grammar of the Ugaritic Language, Leiden 1997, 2001[2].
GvG	C. Brockelmann, Grundriss der vergleichenden Grammatik der semitischen Sprachen in zwei Bänden, Hildesheim 1961.
Harris	Z.S. Harris, A Grammar of the Phoenician Language, New Haven, CT 1936.
Habiru	O. Loretz, Habiru - Hebräer. Eine soziolinguistische Studie über die Herkunft des Gentiliziums ʕibrî vom Apellativum ḫabiru, Berlin/New York 1984.
Ḫabiru	J. Bottéro, ed., Le problème des ḫabiru à la 4e. Rencontre Assyriologique Internationale, Paris 1954.
HAH	W. Gesenius, Hebräisches und aramäisches Handwörterbuch über das Alte Testament, bearb. von Frants Buhl. Unveränderter Neudruck der 1915 erschienenen 17. Auflage, Berlin-Göttingen-Heidelberg 1950.
HäK	J. von Beckerath, Handbuch der ägyptischen Königsnamen, München 1984.
HAL	L. Koehler - W. Baumgartner, Hebräisches und aramäisches Lexikon zum Alten Testament, Leiden 1967-1990.

HALOT The Hebrew and Aramaic Lexicon of the Old Testament, vols. I-V (revised ET of HAL by M.E J. Richardson), Leiden 1994 ff.
HAM A. Salonen, Die Hausgeräte der alten Mesopotamien nach sumerisch-akkadischen Quellen, I, Helsinki 1965; II, Helsinki 1966.
Hava J.G. Hava, Al-faraid Arabic-English dictionary, Beirut 1964.
HBHS V. Haas, Hethitische Berggötter und hurritische Steindämonen. Riten, Kulte und Mythen, Mainz am Rhein 1982.
HDBS J. Obermann, How Daniel was blessed with a son. An incubation scene in Ugarit, New Haven, CT 1946.
HdO Handbuch der Orientalistik, Leiden.
HED J. Puhvel, Hittite Etymological Dictionary, Iff., Berlin 1984ff.
HEG J. Tischler, Hethitisches etymologisches Glossar, Iff., Innsbruck 1983ff.
HH V. Haas, ed., Hurriter und Hurrisch, Konstanz 1988.
HHA A.D. (Draffkorn-)Kilmer, Hurrians and Hurrian at Alalaḫ. An Ethno-Linguistic Analysis (Univ. of Pennsylvania Ph. D.), Philadelphia 1959.
Hipp. A. Kammenhuber, Hippologia hethitica, Wiesbaden 1961.
HU I.M. Diakonoff, Hurrisch und Urartäisch, München 1971.
HUCA Hebrew Union College Annual, Cincinnati, OH.
Hurrians G. Wilhelm, The Hurrians, Warminster 1989 (ET of Grundzüge der Geschichte und Kultur der Hurriter, Darmstadt 1982).
HUS W. G. E. Watson - N. Wyatt, eds., Handbook of Ugaritic Studies, Leiden 1999.
HW J. Friedrich, Hethitisches Wörterbuch. Kurzgefasste Kritische Sammlung der deutungen hethitischer Wörter, Heildelberg 1952ff.
HW^2 J. Friedrich - A. Kammenhuber, Hethitisches Wörterbuch (Zweite, völlig neubearbeitete Auflage), Iff., Heidelberg 1975ff.
HZL C. Rüster - E. Neu, Hethitisches Zeichenlexikon. Inventar und Interpretation der Keilschriftzeichen aus den Boğazköy-Texten, Wiesbaden 1989.

ICE — Th.O. Lambdin, Introduction to Classical Ethiopic (Geʕez), Missoula, MT 1978.
ICGSL — S. Moscati, ed., An Introduction to the Comparative Grammar of the Semitic Languages, Wiesbaden 1964.
IEJ — Israel Exploration Journal, Jerusalem.
Ilku — I. Márquez Rowe, El ilku en Ugarit. Estudio contextual acerca del sistema tributario territorial (Univ. of Barcelona, doctoral thesis in history 1995).
IMC — G. del Olmo Lete, Interpretación de la mitología cananea. Estudios de semántica ugarítica, Valencia 1984.
IncGr — Incunabula Graeca, Rome. Cf. SMEA.
Indo-Arier — M. Mayrhofer, Die Indo-Arier im Alten Vorderasien, Wiesbaden 1966..
IOKU — M. Heltzer, Internal Organization of the Kingdom of Ugarit, Wiesbaden 1982.
IOS — Israel Oriental Studies, Jerusalem.
Ishtar — J.C. Oliva, Ishtar Syria. La deidad semítico-occidental en los textos acadios del Oeste (Univ. of Murcia, doctoral thesis in history 1994).
JA — M. Dietrich - O. Loretz, "Jahwe und seine Ashera". Anthropomorphes Kultbild in Mesopotamien, Ugarit und Israel. Das Biblische Bilderverbot, Münster 1992.
JANES — Journal of the Ancient Near Eastern Society of Columbia University, New York.
JAOS — Journal of the American Oriental Society, Baltimore, MD.
Jastrow — M. Jastrow, Dictionary of the Targumin, the Talmud Babli ..., I-II, New York, NY 1950.
JBL — Journal of Biblical Literature, Philadelphia, PA.
JCS — Journal of Cuneiform Studies, New Haven, CT.
JEOL — Jaarbericht van het Vooraziatisch-Egyptisch Genootschap Ex Oriente Lux, Leiden.
JESHO — Journal of the Economic and Social History of the Orient, Leiden.
JIVUF — Jahresbericht des Instituts für Vorgeschichte der Universität Frankfurt a. M.
JKF — Jahrbuch für Kleinasiatische Forschung. Internationale Orientalistische Zeitschrift, Heidelberg.
JNES — Journal of Near Eastern Studies, Chicago, IL.
JNSL — Journal of Northwest Semitic Languages, Stellenbosch.

JPOS	Journal of the Palestine Oriental Society, Jerusalem.
JSS	Journal of Semitic Studies, Manchester.
JSSEA	Journal of the Society for the Study of Egyptian Antiquities, Toronto.
KA	M. Dietrich - O. Loretz, Die Keilalphabete. Die phönizisch-kanaanäischen und altarabischen Alphabete in Ugarit, Münster 1988.
KAI	H. Donner - W. Röllig, Kanaanäische und aramäische Inschriften, I-III, Wiebaden 1969.
Kazimirski,	A. de Biberstein Kazimirski, Dictionnaire Arabe-Français, Paris 1860 (reprint Beyrouth, no date).
Kaškäer	E. von Schuler, Die Kaškäer. Ein Beitrag zur Ethnographie des alten Kleinasiens, Berlin 1965.
Kition 3	M.G. Guzzo Amadasi - V. Karageorgis, Fouilles de Kition, III. Inscriptions phéniciennes, Nicosia 1977.
KL	J. Pedersen, "Die KRT Legende", Berytus 61941 63-105.
KlPauly	Der Kleine Pauly. Lexikon der Antike in fünf Bänden, München 1975.
KME	A. Jirku, Kanaanäische Mythen und Epen aus Ras Schamra-Ugarit, Gütersloh 1962.
KTBš	Keilalphabetischer Text aus Bēt Šemeš (as in KA).
KTKL	Keilalphabetischer Text aus Kāmid el-Lōz (as in KA).
KTL	J. Gray, The KRT Text in the Literature of Ras Shamra. A Social Myth of Ancient Canaan, Leiden 1964.
KTS	Keilalphabetischer Text aus Sarafand (as in KA).
KTHST	Keilalphabetischer Text aus Hala Sultan Tekke (as in KA).
KTT	Keilalphabetischer Text aus Tabor (as in KA).
KTTNM	Keilalphabetischer Text aus Tell Nebī Mend (as in KA).
KTTT	Keilalphabetischer Text aus Tell Taanak (as in KA).
KTU$^{(1)}$	M. Dietrich - O. Loretz - J. Sanmartín, Die keilalphabetischen Texte aus Ugarit. Einschliesslich der keilalphabetischen Texte ausserhalb Ugarits, Kevelaer/Neukirchen-Vluyn 1976.
KTU$^{(2)}$	M. Dietrich - O. Loretz - J. Sanmartín, The Cuneiform Alphabetic Texts from Ugarit, Ras Ibn Hani and Other Places (KTU: second, enlarged edition), Münster 1995.
LÄ	W. Helck - E.Otto (- W. Westendorf), Lexikon der Ägyptologie, Iff., Wiesbaden 1975ff.

Lane	E.W. Lane, Arabic-English Lexicon, vols. 1-2, Cambridge 1984.
Landf.	A. Salonen, Die Landfahrzeuge des alten Mesopotamien nach sumerisch-akkadischen Quellen, Helsinki 1951.
LAPO	Litteratures anciennes du Proche-Orient, Paris.
LEA	W. Moran, Les Lettres d'El Amarna, Cf. AmL.
LEbla	L. Cagni, ed., La lingua di Ebla. Atti del convegno internazionale (Napoli, 21-23 aprile 1980), Naples 1981.
LEM	P. Marrassini, Formazione del lessico dell'edilizia militare nel semitico di Siria, Florence 1971.
Liddell-Scott	H.G. Liddell - R. Scott, A Greek-English Lexicon. With a Supplement, Oxford 1968.
LKK	H.L. Ginsberg, The Legend of King Keret. A Canaanite Epic of the Bronze Age, New Haven, CT 1946.
LLAetp	Ch. Fr. Dillmann, Lexicon Linguae Aethiopicae, Osnabrück 1970.
Loanwords	Y. Muchiki, Egyptian Proper Names and Loanwords in North-West Semitic, Atlanta GA 1999.
LPD	Ch. Virolleaud, La légende phénicienne de Danel, texte cunéiforme alphabétique ..., Paris 1936.
LS	C. Brockelmann, Lexicon Syriacum, Hildesheim 1966.
LSem	G. Garbini, Le Lingue Semitiche. Studi di Storia Linguistica, Naples 1972.
LVTL	L. Koehler - W. Baumgartner, Lexicon in Veteris Testamenti libros, Leiden 1958.
MAD	I.J. Gelb, Materials for the Assyrian Dictionary, 1, Chicago 1961; 2, Chicago ^{2}1961; 3, Chicago 1957.
MARI	Mari. Annales de Recherches Interdisciplinaires, Paris.
MEE	Materiali epigrafici di Ebla, Naples.
MFL	A. van Selms, Marriage and Family Life in Ugaritic Literature, London 1954.
MGD	P.L. Watson, Mot, the god of death, at Ugarit and in the Old Testament, (Yale Univ. Ph. D. Diss.), 1970.
MIO	Mitteilungen des Instituts für Orientforschung, Berlin.
MisEb	P. Fronzaroli, ed., Miscellanea eblaitica, 1, 2, 3, QuSe 15, 1988; 16, 1989; 17, 1990.
MLC	G. Del Olmo Lete, Mitos y leyendas de Canaán según la tradición de Ugarit, Valencia / Madrid 1981.
MLD	B. Margalit, A Matter of 'Life' and 'Death'. A Study of

	the Baal-Mot Epic (CTA 4-5-6), Kevelaer/ Neukirchen-Vluyn 1980.
MLE	Materiali lessicali ed epigrafici, I, Rome 1982.
MLMC	Fr. Briquel-Chatonnet, ed., Mosaïque de Langues Mosaïque culturelle. Le Bilinguisme dans le Proche-Orient Ancient, Paris 1996.
Modi	E. Verreet, Modi Ugaritici. Eine morpho-syntaktische Abhandlung über das Modalsystem in Ugaritischen, Leuven 1988.
Molek	G.C. Heider, The Cult of Molek: A Reassessment, Sheffield 1985.
Mondgott	G. Theuer, Der Mondgott in den Religionen Syrien-Palästinas: unter besonderer Berücksichtigung von KTU 1.24, Freiburg / Göttingen 2000.
MPDAI	F. Pecchioli Daddi, Mestieri, professioni e dignità nell'Anatolia Ittita, IncGr 79.
MROA	G. del Olmo Lete, ed., Mitología y religión del Oriente Antiguo, vols. I, II/1-2, Sabadell (Barcelona), 1993/95.
MSL	Materialien zum Sumerischen Lexikon, Rome.
MSS	P. Xella, Il mito di ŠḤR e ŠLM. Saggio sulla mitologia ugaritica, Rome 1973.
MU	M. Dietrich - O. Loretz, Mantik in Ugarit. Keilalphabetische Texte der Opferschau - Omensammlungen - Nekromantie. Mit Beiträgen von H.W. Duerbeck - J.-W. Meyer - W.C. Seitter, Münster 1990.
NA	R. Largement, La naissance de l'Aurore. Poème mythologique de Ras Shamra-Ugarit, Gembloux-Louvain 1949.
Naʕar	C. S. Leeb, Away from the Father's House. The Social Location of naʕar and naʕarah in Ancient Israel, Sheffield 2000.
NABU	Nouvelles assyriologiques breves et utilitaires, Paris.
NAT	S. Parpola, Neo-Assyrian Toponyms, Kevelaer/ Neukirchen-Vluyn 1970.
NE	R. Du Mesnil du Buisson, Nouvelles études sur les dieux et les mythes de Canaan, Leiden 1973.
NH	E. Laroche, Les noms des hittites, Paris 1966.
Nomades	J.-R. Kupper, Les nomades en Mésopotamie au temps des rois de Mari, Paris 1957.
NPN	I.J. Gelb - P.M. Purves - A.A. Mac Rae, Nuzi Personal Names, Chicago 1943.

NUS	Newsletter for Ugaritic Studies, Calgary.
NuzHur	Studies on the Civilization and Culture of Nuzi and the Hurrians, 1-5, Winona Lake 1982-95; 6ff., Bethesda 1994ff.
Nuzi	W. Mayer, Nuzi-Studien I. Die Archive des Palastes und die Prosopographie der Berufe, Kevelaer / Neukirchen-Vluyn 1975.
MVEOL	Mededelingen en Verhandelingen van het Voor-aziatisch-Egyptisch Genootschap, Leiden.
NYCI	J.C. de Moor, New Year with Canaanites and Israelites, 1-2, Kampen 1972.
OH	M. Heltzer, Die Organisation des Handwerks im "Dunklen Zeitalter" und im I. Jahrtausend v.u.Z. im östlichem [sic!] Mittelmeergebiet, Padua 1992.
Opfermaterie	F. Blome, Die Opfermaterie in Babylonien und Israel, I, Roma 1934.
OLP	Orientalia Lovaniensia Periodica, Leuven.
OLZ	Orientalische Literaturzeitung, Berlin.
Or	Orientalia. Nova Series, Rome.
OrAn	Oriens Antiquus, Rome.
Oriens	Oriens. Journal of the International Society for Oriental Research, Leiden.
PCD	N.J. Tromp, Primitive Conceptions of Death and the Nether World in the Old Testament, Rome 1969.
PEQ	Palestine Exploration Quarterly, London.
PeredSb	Peredneaziatskiy Sbornik, Moscow.
PET	M. Krebernik, Die Personennamen der Ebla-Texte, Berlin 1988.
PI	E. Zurro, Procedimientos iterativos en la poesía ugarítica y hebrea, Rome 1987.
PIBA	Proceedings of the Irish Biblical Association, Dublin.
PIH	S. Abbadi, Die Personennamen der Inschriften aus Hatra, Hildesheim 1983.
PLM	C.H. Gordon, Poetic Legends and Myths from Ugarit, Berytus 25, 1977, 1-133.
PNPPI	F.L. Benz, Personal Names in the Phoenician and Punic Inscriptions, Rome 1972.
PNT	S.B. Parker, The Pre-Biblical Narrative Tradition, Atlanta, GA 1989.
Poids	J.-C. Courtois, "Poids, prix, taxes et salaires, à Ougarit (Syrie) au IIe millénaire", in: R. Gyselen, ed., Prix,

salaires, poids et mesures, Paris 1990, pp. 119ff.

Proto-Akkadian
I.J. Gelb, Sequential Reconstruction of Proto-Akkadian, Chicago 1969.

PRU Le Palais Royal d'Ugarit, Paris.

Pss. P. C. Craigie, Word Biblical Commentary, Volume 19. Psalms 1-50, Waco, TX 1983.

PTU F. Grøndahl, Die Personennamen der Texte aus Ugarit, Rome 1967.

PU K. Aartun, Die Partikeln des Ugaritischen, 1. Teil, Kevelaer/Neukirchen-Vluyn 1974; 2. Teil, Kevelaer/Neukirchen-Vluyn 1978.

QuSe Quaderni di Semitistica, Florence.

RC G. del Olmo, La religión cananea según la liturgia de Ugarit, Sabadell (Barcelona) 1992.

RCAU M. Heltzer, The Rural Community in Ancient Ugarit, Wiesbaden 1976.

RCG C.E. L'Heureux, Rank among the Canaanite Gods. El, Baʕal, and the Rephaʔim, Missoula, MT 1979.

RDAC Report of the Department of Antiquities, Cyprus, Nicosia.

RGG Die Religion in Geschichte und Gegenwart (ed. K. Galling), Tübingen ³1957-62.

RGTC Repertoire Géographique des Textes Cunéiformes. Beihefte zum Tübinger Atlas des Vorderen Orients, Wiesbaden.

RHA Revue hittite et asianique, Paris.

Rituale G. Pettinato, Il rituale per la successione al trono di Ebla, Rome 1992.

RlA Reallexikon der Assyriologie und Vorderasiatischen Archäologie, Band Iff., Berlin etc. 1932ff.

RNDH E. Laroche, Recherches sur les noms des dieux hittites, Paris 1947.

RPLHA Revue de Philologie, de Littérature et d'Histoire anciennes, Paris.

RR The Review of Religions, New York.

RSF Rivista di Studi Fenici, Rome.

RSM D. Nielsen, Ras Šamra Mythologie und Biblische Theologie, Leipzig 1936.

RSOu Ras Shamra-Ougarit. Publications de la Mission Française Archéologique de Ras Shamra-Ougarit, Paris.

RSP L.R. Fisher etc., eds., Ras Shamra Parallels. The Texts from Ugarit and the Hebrew Bible, I-III, Rome 1972-81.

RTU N. Wyatt, Religious Texts from Ugarit. The Words of Ilimilku and his Colleagues, Sheffield 1998.

RY J.C. de Moor, The Rise of Yahwism. The Roots of Israelite Monotheism, Leuven 1990; ^{2}1997.

SAA State Archives of Assyria, Helsinki.

SAG A. Deimel, Sumerisches Lexikon, III/1. Sumerisch-akkadisches Glossar, Rome 1934.

SAIO E. Lipiński, Studies in Aramaic Inscriptions and Onomastics, 1, Leuven 1975.

Salmanticensis
Salmanticensis, Salamanca.

Sal29 J. L. Cunchillos, Estudio del Salmo 29. Canto al Dios de la fertilidad ... , Valencia 1976.

SAU W.H. van Soldt, Studies in the Akkadian of Ugarit, Kevelaer/Neukirchen-Vluyn 1991.

ScHier Scripta Hierosolymitana, Jerusalem.

SD A.F.L. Beeston - M.A. Ghul - W.W. Müller - J. Ryckmans, Sabaic Dictionary / Dictionnaire sabéen, Louvain-la-Neuve/Beyrouth 1982.

SDB Supplément au Dictionnaire de la Bible, Paris.

SEL Studi epigrafici e linguistici sul Vicino Oriente antico, Verona.

Semitica Semitica. Institut d'études sémitiques de l'Université de Paris, Paris.

SFPK B. Bandstra, The Syntactic Function of the Particle ky in Biblical Hebrew and Ugaritic (Yale Univ. Ph.D. Diss.), 1982.

SfM J. Hoftijzer, A Search for Method. A Study in the Syntactic Use of the h-locale in Classical Hebrew, Leiden 1981.

SG A.F.L. Beeston, Sabaic Grammar, Manchester 1984.

SHJP B. Oded et al. (eds.), Studies in the History of the Jewish People and the Land of Israel, Haifa 1974.

SGUPT S.B. Parker, Studies in the Grammar of Ugaritic Prose Texts (The Johns Hopkins Univ. Ph. D. Diss.), 1967.

Siedlungsgeographie
G.G.W. Müller, Studien zur Siedlungsgeographie und

	Bevölkerung des mittleren Osttigrisgebietes, Heidelberg 1994.
Šiqlu	S. Karwiese, Šiqlu, Kite und Stater. Der Weg zu einer neuen Metrologie des Altertums. I. Mesopotamien, Paris 1990.
SLE	P. Fronzaroli, ed., Studies on the Language of Ebla, 1984.
SLOBA	S. Lieberman, The Sumerian Loanwords in Old-Babylonian Accadian, Missoula 1977.
SMEA	Studi Micenei ed Egeo-Anatolici, Rome. Cf. IncGr.
SMS	Syro-Mesopotamian Studies, Malibu, California.
SN	G. Garbini, Il semitico di nord-ovest, Naples 1960.
Song	M.H. Pope, Song of Songs. A New Translation with Introducion and Commentary, Garden City, NY 1977.
SP	J.C. de Moor, The Seasonal Pattern in the Ugaritic Myth of Baʕlu, Kevelaer/Neukirchen-Vluyn 1971.
SPARI	M. Maraqten, Die semitischen Personennamen in den alt- und reichsaramäischen Inschriften aus Vorderasien, Hildesheim / Zürich / New York 1988.
SPGÄ	R. Stadelmann, Syrisch-palästinische Gottheiten in Ägypten, Leiden 1967.
SQF	G. Conti, Il sillabario de la quarta fonte della lista lessicale bilingue eblaita, Florence 1990.
SSS	A. Strobel, Der spätbronzezeitliche Seevölkersturm, Berlin/New York 1976.
StEb	Studi Eblaiti, Rome.
Stelen	E. Edel, "Die Stelen Amenophis' II", ZDPV 69, 1953, 97-176.
StMar	Studia Mariana publiées sous la direction de A. Parrot, Leiden 1950.
Storia	M. Liverani, Storia di Ugarit nell'età degli archivi politici, Rome 1962.
StPh	Studia Phoenicia, Leuven.
Studien	M. Dietrich - O. Loretz, Studien zu den ugaritischen Texten I. Mythos und Ritual in KTU 1.12, 1.24, 1.96, 1.100 und 1.114, Münster 2000.
StUL	K. Aartun, Studien zur ugaritischen Lexikographie, I, Wiesbaden 1991.
Subartu	A. Ungnad, Subartu. Beiträge zur Kulturgeschichte und Völkerkunde Vorderasiens, Berlin/Leipzig 1936.

SUL — M. Held, Studies in Ugaritic Lexicography and Poetic Style, Baltimore, Maryland 1957.

Šulmu — P. Vavroušek - V. Souček, eds., Šulmu. Papers on the Ancient Near East. Presented at International Conference of Socialist Countries (Prague 1986), Prague 1988.

SWET — J.E. Hoch, Semitic Words in Egyptian Texts of the New Kingdom and the Third Intermediate Period, Princeton 1994 [cited by paragraph].

Syria — Syria. Revue d'art oriental et d'archéologie, Paris.

Syria Handbook — H. Klengel, Syria 3000 to 300 B.C. A Handbook of Political History, Berlin 1992.

Tākultu — R. Frankena, Tākultu. De sacrale maaltijd in het Assyrische ritueel, med een overzicht over de in Assur vereerde goden, Leiden 1954.

Tel Aviv — Tel Aviv. Journal of the Tel Aviv University. Institute of Archaeology, Tel Aviv.

Tessili — S. Ribichini - P. Xella, La terminologia dei tessili nei testi di Ugarit, Rome 1985.

TH — D. Pardee, Les textes hippiatriques, Paris 1985.

Thespis(1) — T.H. Gaster, Thespis. Ritual, Myth, and Drama in the Ancient Near East, New York ^{1}1950.

ThLS — R. Payne-Smith, Thesaurus Linguae Syriacae, I, II, Oxford 1879, 1901 (repr. Hildesheim / New York 1981).

TI — I.J. Gelb, Thoughts about Ibla, SMS 1/1,1977, pp. 3-30.

TNT — F.O. Hvidberg-Hansen, Une étude sur la religion canaanéo-punique, I-II, Copenhagen 1979.

TopAn — M.C. Astour, Continuité et changement dans la toponymie de la Syrie du nord, in: La toponymie antique. Actes du Colloque de Strasbourg 1975, Leiden [no date], pp. 117-141.

TOu — Littératures anciennes du Proche-Orient. Textes Ougaritiques, I. Mythes et légendes, Paris 1974; II. Textes religieux. Rituels. Correspondance, Paris 1989.

TPM — D. Pardee, Les textes para-mythologiques de la 24e campagne (1961), Paris 1988.

TPNAH — J.D. Fowler, Theophoric Personal Names in Ancient Hebrew, Sheffield 1988.

Trade	W.F. Leemans, Foreign Trade in the Old Babylonian Period, Leiden 1960.
Trattato	G.F. del Monte, Il trattato fra Muršili II di Ḫattuša e Niqmepaʕ di Ugarit, Rome 1986.
TRU	P. Xella, I testi rituali di Ugarit, I. Testi, Rome 1981.
UA	I. Al-Yasin, The Lexical Relation between Ugaritic and Arabic (Princeton Univ. Ph. D. Diss.), 1950.
UBL	Ugaritisch-Biblische Literatur, Münster.
UBL 12	N. Wyatt - W.G.E. Watson - J.B. Lloyd, Ugarit, religion and culture. Proceedings of the International Colloquium on Ugarit, religion and culture, Edinburgh 1994, Münster 1996.
UDGG	D.T. Tsumura, The Ugaritic Drama of the Good Gods. A Philological Study (Brandeis Univ. Ph. D. Diss.), 1973.
UF	Ugarit-Forschungen, Kevelaer/Neukirchen-Vluyn.
Ug	Ugaritica, Paris.
UG	J. Tropper. Ugaritische Grammatik, Münster 2000.
UGU	J. Aistleitner, Untersuchungen zur Grammatik des Ugaritischen, Leipzig 1954.
UHP	M. Dahood, Ugaritic-Hebrew Philology, Rome 1965.
UHT	C. Cohen - D. Sivan, The Ugaritic Hippiatric Texts: a Critical Edition, New Haven, CT 1983.
ULe	J.C. de Moor, Ugaritic Lexicography, in: P. Fronzaroli, ed., Studies on Semitic Lexicography, Florence 1973, p. 61-102.
ULx	M. Dahood, Ugaritic Lexicography, in: Mélanges E. Tisserant, I. Écriture Sainte - Ancien Orient, Vatican City 1964, pp. 81-104.
UPA	B. Margalit, The Ugaritic Poem of Aqht, Berlin 1989.
UR	G.D. Young, ed., Ugarit in Retrospect. Fifty Years of Ugarit and Ugaritic, Winona Lake, IN 1981.
UT	C.H. Gordon, Ugaritic Textbook, Rome 1965 (vocabulary cited by number; grammar cited by §).
UVAT	J.L. Boyd III, A Collection and Examination of the Ugaritic Vocabulary Contained in the Accadian Texts from Ras Shamra (Univ. of Chicago Ph.D. Diss.), 1975.
UVST	J. Huehnergard, Ugaritic Vocabulary in Syllabic Transcription, Atlanta, GA 1987.
VDI	Vestnik drevney istorii. Journal of Ancient History, Moscow.

VE Vocabulary of Ebla, reconstructed in MEE 4. Cf. EV.
Vid J.-A. Zamora, La vid y el vino en Ugarit, Madrid 2000.
VO Vicino Oriente, Rome.
VT Vetus Testamentum, Leiden.
VTS Supplements to Vetus Testamentum, Leiden.
WäS A. Erman - H. Grapow, Wörterbuch der ägyptischen Sprache, vols. 1-7, Berlin 1926-63.
WbMyth Wörterbuch der Mythologie (ed. H.W. Haussig.) Erste Abteilung: Die Alten Kulturvölker, I. Götter und Mythen im vorderen Orient, Stuttgart 1965.
WCJS World Congress of Jewish Studies, Jerusalem.
Wehr (- Cowan) H. Wehr, A dictionary of Modern Written Arabic (ed. J. Milton Cowan), Wiesbaden ^{3}1971.
Weltfrieden H. Gross, Die Idee des ewigen und allgemeinen Weltfriedens im Alten Orient und im Alten Testament, Trier 1956.
WGE H. Waetzold - H. Hauptman, eds., Wirtschaft und Gesellschaft von Ebla. Akten der Internationalen Tagung Heidelberg 4.-7. November 1986, Heidelberg 1988.
WKAS M. Ullmann, Wörterbuch der klassischen arabischen Sprache, Wiesbaden 1970ff.
WL F.F. Hvidberg, Weeping and Laughter in the Old Testament. A Study of Canaanite-Israelite Religion, Leiden, etc., 1962.
WList M.Dietrich - O. Loretz, Word-List of the Cuneiform Alphabetic Texts from Ugarit, Ras Ibn Hani and Other Places (KTU: second, enlarged edition), Münster 1996.
WO Die Welt des Orients, Göttingen.
WSVES D. Sivan - Z. Cochavi-Rainey, West Semitic Vocabulary in Egyptian Script of the 14th to the 10th Centuries BCE, Beer-Sheva 1992.
WTM J. Levy, Neuhebräisches und Chaldäisches Wörterbuch über die Talmudim und Midraschim ..., Leipzig ^{2}1924.
WTS E. Littmann - M. Hoffner, Wörterbuch der Tigrē Sprache, Wiesbaden 1962.
WuS J. Aistleitner, Wörterbuch der ugaritischen Sprache (ed. O. Eissfeldt), Leipzig 1963.
YN W. Herrmann, Yariḫ und Nikkal und der Preis der

	Kuṯarāt-Göttinnen. Ein kultisch-magischer Text aus Ras Shamra, Berlin 1968.
YOS	Yale Oriental Series, New Haven.
ZA	Zeitschrift für Assyriologie und Vorderasiatische Archäologie, Berlin.
ZAW	Zeitschrift für die alttestamentliche Wissenschaft, Berlin.
ZDMG	Zeitschrift der Deutschen Morgenländischen Gesellschaft, Wiesbaden.
ZDPV	Zeitschrift des Deutschen Palästina-Vereins, Wiesbaden.

IV. Additional Abbreviations

Aeg	Aegyptus, Milan.
Fs. Dietrich	O. Loretz. - K. A. Metzler. - H. Schaudig, eds., Ex Mesopotamia et Syria Lux. Festschrift für Manfried Dietrich zu seinem 65. Geburtstag, Münster 2002.
MKNAWL	Mededelingen der Koninklijke Nederlandse Akademie van Wetenschappen afd. Letterkunde, Amsterdam.
StBT	Studien zu den Boğazköy-Texten, Wiesbaden.
StylSt	Y. Avishur, Stylistic Studies of Word-Pairs in Biblical and Ancient Semitic Languages, Kevelaer / Neukirchen -Vluyn 1984.
TMMANE	M.Stol, On Trees, Mountains, and Millstones in Ancient Near East, Leiden 1979.
UM	J. Obermann, Ugaritic Mythology: A Study of its Leading Motifs, New Haven CT, 1948.
UPN	S.B. Parker, Ugaritic Narrative Poetry, Atlanta GA, 1997.
Vocabulary	E.J. Pentiuc, West Semitic Vocabulary in the Akkadian Texts from Emar, Winona Lake IN 2001.

* * * * *

(ʔ)a/i/u

i (I) interr. adv. "where?" (Hb. *ʔy*, HALOT 37f.; Akk. *ai*, AHw 23; CAD A/1 220; Ebla cf. PN *a*-(DN), Fronzaroli ARES 1 12; cf. Krebernik PET 70. Cf. *iy*; cf. Gibson CML 142; Loewenstamm IEJ 15 1965 128 n. 28; Avishur UF 10 1978 34f.; Tropper UF 26 1994 475; diff.: Albright, BASOR 94 1944 31; Mustafa AcOrHun 29 1975 103; Badre etc. Syria 53 1976 103; De Moor - Spronk UF 14 1982 170; Fensham JNSL 14 1988 95ff.; Dietrich - Loretz UF 26 1994 70: particle introducing oath, 'truly!, verily!, woe!', Arab. *ʔiy*, Akk. *ī*; Driver CML 133; Rin AE 44, 198: neg. particle 'no(t)', Ph. *ʔy*, Akk. *ai*, *ē*). ¶ Forms: *i*.

Where?: *i iṯt* where is/are?, 1.14 IV 38; in bkn ctx. *i ap DN* [...]*i DN* where, then, is DN [...], where (is) DN, 1.5 IV 6-7.

i (II) interj. "oh!" (Hb. *ʔ(y)*, HALOT 38; Akk. *ai*, *ayi*, *aya*, AHw 23; CAD A/1 220; JAram. *ʔê(y)*, DJPA 47; Eg. *i*, CDME 7. Cf. De Moor - Spronk UF 14 1982 170; Watson UF 31 1999 786). ¶ Forms: *i*.

Oh!: *ap ab i k mtm tmtn* father, oh, like mortals you also die, 1.16 I 3 (cf. *ibid.* ln. 17). Cf. in bkn ctx. 1.5 IV 6, 7.

Cf. ik.

u disj. conj. "or, that is, also, as if; or (is it that)?" (Hb., Ph. *ʔw*, HALOT 20, DNWSI 21; Syr. *ʔaw*, LS 7; Arab. *ʔaw*, Lane 122f.; Eth. CDG 47; Akk. *ū*, AHw 1398f.; cf. Aartun PU 2 90f.; Dijkstra UF 21 1989 144. For a possible interrogative meaning of *u(n)* cf. Margalit UF 8 1976 148; for an exclamatory meaning "oh!" cf. Dietrich - Loretz - Sanmartín UF 7 1975 152). ¶ Forms: *u*, *uy*.

Disj. conj. or: ★a) *b urm u špnt* as a burnt offering or as a presentation offering, 1.119:13; ★b) derived use with explanatory meaning, that is (> and, also): *ḫt nqh u qrb ḫt* the wand is ready, and the wand approaches!, 1.169:5; *qra u nqmd mlk* invoke also king PN, 1.161:12 (cf. ln. 26); redundant explanatory use, *w u. mndʕ k igr w u igr ʕm špš* perhaps I shall stay (here), that is, (perhaps) I shall stay with the 'Sun', 2.34:12; cf. *dy l ydʕ yṣḥk u zb* (when) the unknown calls you and ..., RSOu 14 52 [KTU 9.435]:1 (cf. Bordreuil - Pardee RSOu 14 p. 390: '(Lorsque) l'inconnu t'appelle et se met à écumer'); *u + ap*: *u ap mḫ(!)rh ank l aḥwy* and I shall not leave his warrior strength alive, 1.18 IV 27; ★c) disj. use in a correlative *u (...) u (...)* or (...) or (...); both (...) and (...): *u mlk u bl mlk* someone, king or not, 1.4 VII 43; *u ymn u šmal* both on the right and on the left, 1.23:63-64; *u tḫṭin (...) u tḫṭin* whether you have sinned (...) or whether you have sinned (...), 1.40:19-22 and par.; *u l p (...) u l p* according to the custom of (...) and according to the custom of (...), 1.40:20ff. and par. (cf. *ulp*); ★d) introducing a disjunctive interrog. *u ilm tmtn* or do gods (also) die?, 1.16 I 22 and par.; *ap (...) u ṯn ndr[h]* is he going to (...) or change his vow?, 1.15 III 29; *u ḫštk lntn ʕtq* or is your portal a perpetual lament?, 1.16 I 4 and par.; ★e) *uy* or (Tropper UG 793, 835 = *u* + encl. *-y*: 'leitet einen neuen Abschnitt innerhalb eines Briefes'): *uy alp* [...] or the oxen [...], RSOu 14 51 [KTU 9.425]:21; cf. 2.3:13.

In unc. ctx.: *mlk rb bʕly u ...*, 2.23:2; *u qšt pn hdd* 1.9:13; *ʕmy u ky*, 2.23:5; *u bu al tbi*, 1.169:18 (De Moor UF 12 1980 430). Cf. *ušbtm*, 2.36:15 (cf. Dijkstra UF 21 1989 144; KTU: *u šbtm*); RSOu 14 46 [KTU 9.423]:8', 9'.

aupš/ṯ(n) PN (Hurr. Cf. Liverani, AANLR 8/19 1964 175; Grøndahl PTU 214, 251; Huehnergard UVST 235 n.100; AkkUg 379; Bordreuil - Caquot Syria 56 1979 310; Van Soldt SAU 36); ¶ syll.: *a-up-šu*, PRU 3 170 (RS 8.279):10'; 206 (RS 16.294):2; DUMU *a-up-še*[*-e*?], PRU 6 79:10. Var. *aupṯ*, 4.224:14; var. *aupṯn*, 4.649:3. Cf. *apṯ*.

PN: ★a) 4.85:8 (*qmnzy*); 4.102:12; 4.103:4; 4.224:14; 4.649:3; 4.769:59; ★b) *bn PN*: 1.87:58; 4.393:6; 4.617:12; 4.782:30. Cf. *au*[, 4.725:2.

ab (I) n. m. 1) "father"; 2) "ancestor" (Hb., Ph., Pun., Aram. *ʔb*, HALOT 1s.; DNWSI 1-3; Amor. /ʔabum/, Huffmon APNMT 154; Buccellati Amorites 205f.; Gelb CAAA 13, 41ff.; Ebla *a-bù* and var. in PNN, Krebernik PET 70; PUZUR$_4$*-ra-a-ba$_4$/bù*, *qá-na-ab*, Müller Biling. 171, 174; cf. ARET 8 51; cf. A-MU = *a-bì*, Pettinato Rituale 197; Fronzaroli ARET 11 137f.; cf. AB.ÁŠ, Arcari Biling. 326f.; Sanmartín AuOr 9 1991 170; Akk. *abu*, AHw 7f.; CAD A/1 67-75; ESA *ʔb*, DOSA 1; Arab., Eth. *ʔab*, Lane 10f.; CDG 2); ¶ syll. Ug.: cf. the element /ʔabu/ in PNN, Grøndahl PTU 86f.; Sivan GAGl 194f.; PRU 6 83 IV 5; Ug 5,97:4; ¶ RS Akk.: cf. NU = *a-bu* = *at-ta-ni* = *a-da-nu*, Ug 5 130 obv. II 9'; cf. Nel JNSL 5 1977 53-66; ¶ par.:

bny (+ bnwt), *ḥtk*. ¶ Forms: sg. abs. *ab*; cstr. *ab*; suff. *aby*, *abk*, *abh*, *abn*.

1) Father, ★a) *um tšmẖ*{.}*m ab* (my) mother pleased (my) father, 2.16:11 (cf. /*š-m-ẖ*/; cf. diff.: Cunchillos TOu 2 299 n. 18: 'que Mère se réjouisse (à cause) de Père', prep. *m*(*n*); KTU: rdg *mad*; *ap ab i k mtm tmtn* father, oh!, like mortals even you die, 1.16 I 3 and par.; *tbkyk ab ġr bʕl* for you, father, the mountain of DN weeps, 1.16 I 6 and par.; *lk l abk yṣb* go to your father, PN, 1.16 VI 27-28; *ʕl abh yʕrb* into the presence of his father he entered, 1.16 VI 40 and par.; *ab* (*dnil*), 1.19 IV 29 and par.; *bkm tšu abh* at once he helped his father up, 1.19 II 10; *abh* (*ḫrẖb*, father of *nkl*), 1.24:19-20, cf. ln. 9; *aqrbk abh bʕl* I shall introduce you to her father, DN, 1.24:27, cf. ln. 29-30; *nṯṯt um ʕlt b aby* one shocked mother launches herself on my father, 1.82:9 (// *bk*, unc. ctx.; cf. Del Olmo CR 375 n. 145); in unc. ctx.: *ht aby ṯṯ tl/d*[, 2.17:9; ★b) espec. of El: *il abn* DN, our father, 1.12 I 9; *šlm ab w il* hail, father and god!, 1.123:1; *ṯr abh/k il* and *ṯr il abh/k/y* the bull DN, his / your / my father, 1.2 I 36 and par.; *mlk ab šnm* king, father of years, 1.4 IV 24 and par. (cf. *šnt* for other explanations); *ab adm* father of mankind, 1.14 I 37 and par.; *ab bn il* father of the sons of DN, 1.40:33 and par.; father of individual gods: 1.3 V 35 and par. (*bʕl*); 1.3 V 10 and par. (*ʕnt*); 1.2 III 19 (*ʕṯtr*); 1.114:14 (*ṯġr bt il* guardian of the house of DN); *abh il m*[*lk* his father DN, the king (?), 1.117:3; ★c) said of the chief / father of a flock: *ab nšrm* father of the eagles (*hrgb*), 1.19 III 15.

2) Ancestor: *bt ab* paternal house, 1.19 I 32 (cf. Akk. *bīt abi*). In bkn ctx.: *ab* (PN?), 4.258:14; *ab* 7.45:3, 4; *ab*[, 4.55:25; 4.69 V 22; 4.332:21; 4.335:32; 4.382:24; 4.448:4; 4.635:8; 4.706:1; *abh*, 1.92:24; *aby*, 1.18 1 26; *ab*[*y*], 2.6:2.

Cf. abbl(y), abdg, abḏ/šr, abġl, ablḥ, a/ibm, abmlk, abmn, a/ibn, abrm, abrpu, abršn, abršp, abṣn, abšẖr, aby, a/iby, abyt, abyy, aẖtab, ayab, ib (III), ibyn, ilabn, ilib (I), ilib (II), ʕṯtrab, bnib, hyabn, mlkbn, rmib, ršpab, tnabn.

ab (II) n. m. "ghost, spirit (of dead)" (etym unc.; cf. Hb. *ʔwb* < /ʔāb/ HALOT 20, Arab. *ʔāba*, Lane 123f.: 'to return, come back (at night)', and Hitt *a-a-pi*, HW[2] 181ff.: 'Opfergrube'. For the diff. opinions cf. Margalit UF 7 1975 309 n. 29; UF 8 1976 149f.; UF 16 1984 159 n. 284; Ebach - Rüterswörden UF 12 1980 205ff.; Tropper Nekromantie 189). ¶ Forms: sg. *ab*.

Ghost, spirit (of dead): *aṯt ab ṣrry* necromancer of the heights, 1.16 I 5 (cf. Hb. *ʔšt ʔwb*).

ib (I) n. m. "enemy" (Hb. *ʔyb*, HALOT 38f.; Akk. *ay(y)ābu*, AHw 23f.; CAD A/1 222ff.; EA Akk.: *ʔibu*, Sivan GAGl 199); ¶ syll. Ug.: [EN(?) = *ná*]*k*(?)*-ru* = *tu-ur-bi* = *e-bu*, Ug 5 130 III 15'; cf. Van Soldt BiOr 47 1990 731 and cf. Huehnergard UVST 106; ¶ RS Akk.: *ki-i-m*[*a a-y*]*a-bi*, Ug 5 168:2; ¶ par.: *qm*, *ṣrt*, *šnu*. ¶ Forms: sg. *ib*; cstr. *ib*; suff. *ibk*, *ibh*, *ibn* (encl. *-n* in 1.103+, *passim*; cf. Tropper UF 26 1994 466ff.); pl. abs. *ibm*, cstr. *ib*; suff. *iby*.

Enemy: *mn ib ypʕ l bʕl* which enemy has gone out against DN?, 1.3 III 37 and par. (// *ṣrt*); *ib bʕl* the enemies of DN, 1.4 VII 35 (// *šnu*); cf. ln. 37; *ntʕn b arṣ iby* we shall attack, in the 'earth', my enemies, 1.10 II 24 (// *qm*); *ht ibk tmḫṣ* now your enemy you must crush, 1.2 IV 9 (// *ṣrt*); *tmḫṣ alpm ib* strike a thousand enemies, 1.19 IV 59; *hn ib d b TN* behold the enemy that is in TN, 2.33:10; *hn ibm šṣq* behold (the) enemies besiege me, *ibid.* ln. 27 (and cf. ln. 17); *l pn ib* in the face of the enemy, 2.33:29; *ibn yḫlq bhmt ḥwt* the enemy will destroy the cattle of the land, 1.103+:16; *ibn yspu ḥwt* the enemy will consume the land, 1.103+:51; *mlkn yšlm l ibh* the king will have to return (everything) to his enemy, 1.103+:54; *mlkn ybʕr ibh* the king will leave his enemy (aside), 1.103+:58; *ḥwt ib(h)* the land of the (/ of his) enemy, 1.103+:10, 37, 59; cf. *bhmt ib*]*h* the cattle of his enemy, *ibid.* ln. 15; *ḥwt ib tḫlq* the land of the enemy will be destroyed, 1.103+:59; 1.140:6; *ib mlk* foe(s) of the king, 1.103+:17 and *passim ibid.* In bkn ctx. *ib ʕltn* the enemy against us, 2.39:31; *ibk*, 2.72:44. In bkn ctx. 1.2 IV 39.

ib (II) n. m. 1) "fruit" / "bud, flower"; 2) "gem"; 3) second element in the DN *nkl w ib* (Hb. *ʔb*, HALOT 2; Aram. *ʔnbʔ*, Jastrow 80; Syr. *ʔebbō*, LS 1; Kaufman AIA 58; cf. Ebla PNN EN-*bù*-DN, Fronzaroli ARES 1 17f.; Akk. *inbu*, AHw 381f.; CAD I/J 144ff. Cf. Driver Fs. Bakoš 100); ¶ syll. Ug.: cf. the element /ʔinbu/ in PNN, Sivan GAGl 200; ¶ par.: *ṣp*. ¶ Forms: sg. *ib*; cstr. *ib*.

1) Fruit / bud, flower: *yḫsp ib* the fruit / bud has wilted, 1.19 I 31.

2) Gem: the pupils of her eyes *ib iqni* gems of lapis lazuli, 1.14 III 43 and par. (// *ṣp*; diff.: Blau IOS 2 1972 74ff.; Dijkstra - De Moor UF 7 1975 187: 'pure', 'the purest', Akk. *(uqnū) ebbu*).

3) Element of the DN *nkl w ib* (/nikkalu-ibbu/; cf. Del Olmo AuOr 9 1991 69 n. 18); *ašr nkl w ib* I am going to sing to DN, 1.24:1; *nkl w ib d ašr* DN to whom I sing, 1.24:37; *tn nkl yrḫ ytrḫ tʕrbm b bhth* allow DN to marry DN, may DN enter his house, 1.24:17; Unc.: *š lnh w l ib*, 1.111:21 (cf. Del Olmo CR 202; Dietrich - Mayer ALASP 7/1 21).

ib (III) (< *ab*; element of the DN *ilib*; Dietrich - Loretz - Sanmartín UF 6 1974 450; diff.: Hoffner JBL 86 1967 387f.: 'ritual pit', Hitt. *a-a-bi*; Wyatt UF 9 1977 289: 'ghost', Hb. *ʔôb*; cf. Margalit UF 7 1975 309 n. 29; 8 1976 149f., cf. *ab*); ¶ RS Akk.: DINGIR-*a-bi*, Ug 5 18:1. For the allomorphs *(-)ib(-)* in PNN cf. *ab*.

Cf. ilib (I), ilib (II).

ib (IV) PN (Sem.).

PN: *bn* PN *bn i*(?)*b* 4.261:23(?). Cf. *ibnkl* (Hurr.), 1.42:47, 48.

ibʕlt MN f. (cf. Xella TRU 27f.: Ph. *yrḫ pʕlt*; De Moor ARTU 171 n. 1: 'where-is-the-Mistress?'; diff.: Herdner Ug 7 31: theophoric).

MN: *b yrḫ ibʕlt* in the month (of) *i.*, 1.119:1, 11.

abbl(y) PN (Sem. Cf. Grøndahl PTU 20, 86; Benz PNPPI 257f.).

PN: ★a) 4.431:7; ★b) *bn PN*: 4.309:3; 4.368:1:17; 4.377:20.

abbt PN (Sem.(?) Cf. Watson AuOr 13 1995 218).

PN: 4.778:18 (*bn ġly*); 4.782:24 (*bn ġly*).

/ʔ-b-d/ vb G: 1) "be missing, lacking, weaken, feel lost,"; 2) "to be lost, spoilt"; 3) "to be ruined"; Gt: "to perish" (Hb. *ʔbd*, HALOT 2f.; Aram., Ph., *ʔbd*, DNWSI 4f.; cf. Arab. *ʔabada*, Lane 4ff.; Eth. *ʔabda*, CDG 2f.; Ebla cf. /ʔ-b-d/t/ G in A.ZÁḪ = *a-ba-tum*, *a-bu*$_x$(NI)*-du*, VE 610; *i-a-ba-at*, Pettinato Rituale 213 (diff.: Fronzaroli ARET 11 153: /l-p-t/); D in NÌ.GILIM.DI = *ù-bù-tu*, VE 124c; Š in NÌ.GILIM.A/E.DI = *sa/su-bù-tum*, VE 124a; Krebernik ZA 73 1983 41 n. 146; cf. Akk. *abātu*, AHw 5; CAD A/1 41ff.; cf. EA Akk. *ḫal-qa-at : a-ba-da-at*, EAT 288:52); ¶ syll. Ug.: N inf./ n. suff. LÚ.MEŠ *ú-ru-ba-nu ša* : *na-ba-di-šu-nu*, PRU 3 37 (RS 16.267):8; Sivan GAGl 138, 199; Huehnergard UVST 104; ¶ par.: /ʕ-r-w/. ¶ Forms: G suffc. *abd*; prefc. *yabd*, *tubd* (cf. Tropper UF 22 1990 367: /yôbVd/ < /yaʔbVd/); Gt suffc. *itbd* (metathesis > *itdb*, cf. Verreet UF 19 1987 319); prefc. *yitbd*.

G.1) To be missing, lacking, weaken, feel lost: *w b ym mnḫ l abd* and in DN calm was not lacking, 1.2 IV 3 (diff.: Gibson CML 141: 'destruction'; cf. De Moor CARTU 124); *bʕl yabd* DN weakened, 1.11:3.

2) To be lost, spoilt: (the merchandise to the value of *nn* shekels) *abd b anyt* was lost on board, 4.394:2 (diff.: Márquez AuOr 11 1993 106: rdg *k*(!)*bd*).

3) To be ruined: (know that) *špšn tubd* the 'Sun' is being ruined,

2.39:21 (Sanmartín UF 9 1977 259 n. 7; cf. Tropper UF 22 1990 367).

Gt. To perish: *bt mlk itbd* (incorrect spelling: *itdb*) the family of the king perished, 1.14 I 8 (// *ʕrwt*); *w b kl hn špḥ yitbd* and in their entirety, yes, the family perished, 1.14 I 24.

Cf. **abd (I), abdy**.

abd (I) n. m. "ruin, destruction" (< /ʔ-b-d/; see Moab. *'bd*, DNWSI 5; cf. De Moor ARTU 147: 'destructive venom'; diff.: Caquot TOu 2 84 n. 257: 'a peri'); ¶ **par.**: *ḥmt*, *ṯmdl*. ¶ **Forms**: sg. *abd*.

Ruin, destruction: *isp (...) l p nṯk abd* remove (...) from the mouth of the biter, ruin, 1.107:45 and par. (// *ḥmt*, *ṯmdl*); *lnh mlḫš abd (...) ydy* from which the conjuror destruction (...) does eject, 1.100:5 and par. (// *ḥmt*; diff. Del Olmo CR 361: 'destroy' /ʔ-b-d/).

Cf. **/ʔ-b-d/**, **abdy**.

abd (II) PN (Probl. allographs of *ʕbd (II)*).

PN: *bn abd*, 4.635:48; bkn. [*b*]*t abd*[, 4.727:24.

Cf. **ʕbd (II)**.

ubdit n. f. "share-cropping, leasing system, tenancy" (< *ubdy*; cf. Heltzer IOKU 34; JNSL 9 1982 71-74; BAfO 19 1982 112-120). ¶ Forms: sg./pl. *ubdit*.

Share-cropping, leasing system, tenancy: *ubdit* leases(s): PNN, 4.12:14.

Cf.: **ubdy, updt**.

abdʕn, cf. *ʕbdʕn*.

abdbʕl PN; cf. *ʕbdbʕl*.

abdg PN (etym. unc. Cf. Grøndahl PTU 86; cf. *dg*).

PN: *bn PN*, 4.232:2.

abdḥr, cf. *ʕbdḥr*.

abdḫmn, cf. *ʕbdḫmn*.

abdy n. f. "ruin, destruction" (abstr. for concrete: 'destructive (poison); < /ʔ-b-d/; cf. Hb. *ʔbdwn*, HALOT 3; Syr. *ʔabdonō*, LS 2; Akk. *abtūtu*, AHw 7; cf. CAD A/1 6f. Cf. De Moor ZAW 100 1988 109 n. 24; cf. Xella TRU 361; Caquot TOu 2 97 n. 299); ¶ **par.**: *ḥmt*. ¶ **Forms**: sg. abs. **abdy**.

Ruin, destruction (said of the action of poison): *tʕbtnh abdy* and drained the ruin from him, 1.107:7 (// *ḥmt*; diff.: Pardee TPM 241: 'la destructrice').

Cf. /ʔ-b-d/, abd (I).

ubdy n. m. "land, plot, farming" (in a taxed leasing system; < Luw. stem *ubadi(d)* (*ú-pa-ti-tì*), cf. Starke WO 24 1993 21: 'Territorium, > Grundbesitz, Domäne'; cf. Hitt. *up(p)ati-*, Kronasser EHS 1 165 'eine Fronleistung?', <(?) *up(pa)-* '(her)schicken'; > OAss. *ubadinnum*, Matouš ArOr 47 1979 38: 'Menschengruppe einheimischer Personen, die auf einem Gemeingut arbeiten'; cf. AHw 1423: *upatinnu*. Cf. Márquez Ilku 280 n. 717; cf. Güterbock Oriens 10 1957 360; Rainey JNES 24 1965 18 n. 24; Heltzer RCAU 67ff.; IOKU 23ff.; JNSL 9 1982 71ff.; BAfO 19 1982 112ff.; UF 19 1987 446 n. 1; diff.: Gray ZAW 64 1952 51-55: 'perpetual grant', Arab. *ʔabadī* ; cf. Renfroe AULS 77). ¶ Forms: sg. *ubdy*; pl. *ubdym*, cstr. *ubdy*.

Land in a taxed leasing system, ★a) *spr ubdym b TN* list/record of lands leased in TN, 4.309:1 (list of PNN); administration of estates: *ubdy mdm* lands leased to the *m.*, 4.103:1; cf. *mrynm*, ln. 7; *mrim*, ln. 20; *ʕšrm*, ln. 30; *mri ibrn*, ln. 37; *ṯġrm*, ln. 39; *šrm*, ln. 41; *nqdm*, ln. 44; *trrm*, ln. 48; *mḏrġlm*, ln. 54; *mḫṣm*, ln. 57; ★b) esp. fields *(šd)*: *spr ubdy TN* list/record of leased lands of TN, 4.631:1; *šd ubdy TN d bd skn* leased fields of TN that (revert(?)) to the hands of the prefect, 4.110:1; cf. *šd ubdy*[, 4.39:1; 4.389:3 and *passim*; vineyards: *krm ubdy* leased vineyard, 4.244:7; *ṯlṯ krm ubdym l mlkt b TN* three vineyards in a leasing system for the queen in TN, *ibid.* ln. 9; two vineyards (as fixed property) *w ṯlṯ ubd[ym* and three (more) in a lease system, *ibid.* ln. 10; others: *zt ubdym b TN* (revenues from the) olive-trees of the leased lands in TN, 4.164:3; *ubdy yṣḥm* lands leased to the sizers, 4.692:1.

Cf. ubdit, updt.

abḏl PN (etym. unc. Cf. Watson AuOr 8 1990 114, 243).

PN: *abḏl* 4.188:7 (KTU: *abġ*(?)*l*).

abḏ/šr PN (etym. unc. Cf. Grøndahl PTU 196f., 271: Sem.-Hurr.; Fensham JNSL 2 1972 48 n. 6); ¶ syll.: cf. *a-ba-šu-r*[*i*], Ug 5 4:12'.

PN: ★a) 1.81:19; 4.617:29; ★b) *bn PN*: 4.71 III 6; 4.422:38.

abg PN (Hurr. Cf. Grøndahl PTU 308; diff.: Dahood CBQ 44 1982 16: 'my father is the voice').

PN: *bn PN*, 4.309:12.

abġl PN (Sem.-Hurr.; Dietrich - Loretz UF 9 1977 341. Cf. Pardee AfO 36/37 1989/90 392); ¶ syll.: *a-bi-ḫe/ḫé-li*, PRU 3 p. 240; PRU 6 p. 137; cf. Van Soldt SAU 128, 352.

PN: 4.75 II 3; 4.86:3; 4.134:12; 4.188:7; 4.281:20; 4.370:12; 4.635:25 (*aḏ[ddy]*); 4.635:26 (*a[ḏddy]*). In bkn ctx.: 4.609:14; 4.75 IV 12 (*bn gdn*); 4.381:21.

abky PN (Hurr.(?); cf. Nuzi *a-pa-ak-ku-ia*, Cassin - Glassner AAN 24; diff.: Lipiński FoOr 21 1984 72).

PN: *bn PN*, 4.723:13.

abl PN (etym. unc.); ¶ syll.: cf. *a-bal-la-a*, PRU 4 189 (RS 17.314) 2 and *passim*; 172f. (RS 17.145) 2 and *passim*.

PN: *bn PN*, 4.371:10.

(i)blbl n. m. generic meaning "messenger, bearer" ((?); probl. the pattern qlql < */w-b-l/, Ug. /y-b-l/; cf. Akk. *babbilu*, AHw 94; CAD B 8f. Cf. Sanmartín SEL 5 1988 175). ¶ Forms: pl. *blblm*; suff. *iblblhm*.

Messenger, bearer(?): *spr blblm* list of messengers(?), 4.288:1; to the king have been sent *a/iġlhm w iblblhm* his *a/i.* and his bearers(?), 2.62:11.

ablḥ PN (etym. unc. Cf. Grøndahl PTU 86).

PN: *bn PN*, 4.412 I 30.

ablm TN in mythological texts (Belmonte RGTC 12/2 1: **ʔAbilūma*. Cf Astour RSP 2 254f.; Del Olmo MLC 509; Pardee AfO 36/37 1989/90 480; Margalit UF 8 1976 177-181; MacLaurin PEQ 110 1978 113).

TN: *TN qrt zbl yrḫ* TN, the town of Prince DN, 1.19 IV 1 and par.; *qrt ablm d ʕlk mḫṣ aqht ġzr* you, town of TN, upon whom weighs the death of noble PN, 1.19 IV 3 and par.

ibln PN (etym. unc. Cf. Grøndahl PTU 27, 87f., 301; Fronzaroli JSS 22 1977 154 n. 2; Pettinato Ebla(1) 19; Watson AuOr 8 1990 244; AuOr 13 1995 219); ¶ syll.: cf. *ia-ab-lu-nu*, RSOu 7 3 edge 4. Cf. *ubln*.

PN: *bn PN*, 4.35 I 18; 4.311:10; cf. in bkn ctx.: 4.93 IV 1; 4.545 II 7.

ubln PN (Hurr. Cf. Grøndahl PTU 210, 223, 229; Van Soldt SAU 354 n. 214). Cf. *ibln*.

PN: 4.223:1-2; bkn:]ubln 4.47:4.

a/ibm PN (Sem. Cf. Grøndahl PTU 17, 53, 86f.; Bordreuil SEL 5 1988 26); ¶ syll.: cf. *a-bu-ú-mu*, PRU 4 189 (RS 17.314): 27; *a-bi-ma*, PRU 6 79:13. Var. *ibm*, 4.350:12; 4.781:8.

PN: ★a) 4.63 II 2; 4.780:1; 4.781:8; ★b) *bn PN*: 4.75 III 1; 4.350:12; ★c) *bt PN:* 4.75 VI 2.

ibm PN; cf. *a/ibm*.

abmlk PN (Sem. Cf. Grøndahl PTU 45-47, 87, 157; Sivan GAGl 243; Van Soldt SAU 20); ¶ syll.: *a-bi-ma-al-ku*, PRU 6 79:17; *a-bi-ma-li-ki*, Ug 5 98:7 (Berger UF 1 1969 123); *a-bi*-LUGAL, Ug 5 8:2; cf. AD.LUGAL, PRU 6 50:27.

PN: 4.75 IV 10 (*bn ilrš*); 4.86:8 (*bn un*[).

abmn PN (Sem. Cf. Grøndahl PTU 53, 86; Dahood *apud* Pettinato Archives 290; Sivan GAGl 195; Pardee AfO 36/37 1989/90 391); ¶ syll.: *a-bi-ma-nu* and var., cf. PRU 3 p. 240; PRU 4 p. 244; RSOu 7 5:10.

PN: 4.33:40 (*bn qdmn*); 4.63 II 31; 4.115:6; 4.130:6; 4.134:11; 4.155:13 (*bn ʕbd*); 4.281:25 (*ilštmʕy*); 4.282:11; 4.307:3; 4.313:21; 4.350:9 (*bn qṣy*); 4.382:34 (*bn br*[); 4.782:13 (*bn św̃n*). Cf. in bkn ctx. 4.281:3. In 4.778:8, rdg *abm*(!)*n* (*bn śwn*) (KTU: *abqn*).

abn n. m. 1) "stone"; 2) "stone / flint knife"; 3) "unit of weight, weight" (Hb., Ph., Pun., Aram. *ʔbn*, HALOT 7f.; DNWSI 6f.; Akk. *abnu*, AHw 6f.; CAD A/1 54-61; cf. *abattu*, AHw 4f.; CAD A/1 39ff.; Amor. /ʔabnum/, cf. Gelb CAAA 13, 46. Cf. Van Zijl Baal 59ff.); ¶ RS Akk.: NA_4 *(passim)*; ¶ par.: *ʕn*, *ʕṣ*, *ḥẓ*, *mdbr*, *pslt (II)*, *šnt*, *yʕr*. ¶ Forms: sg. *abn*; pl. abs. *abnm*; cstr. *abn*.

1) Stone, ★a) *abnm l thggn* (the) stones (that) do not whisper, 1.82:43 (// *ʕṣm*; cf. /ʔ-g-g/; Caquot SEL 5 1988 42f.); *rgm ʕṣ w lḫšt abn* a matter of wood (shaft) and a chatter of stone (tip), 1.3 III 23 (cf. diff.: Caquot - Sznycer TOu 1 165; Zurro Salmanticensis 30 1983 397); *tm tgrgr l abnm w l ʕṣm* reside there next to stones and trees, 1.23:66 (// *mdbr*); *bt abn* the daughter of stone, 1.100:1 (// *ʕn*, *šmm w thm*); [*k t*]*ld at abn* [if it gives] birth as an omen (to a swelling in the shape of a) stone, 1.103+:1; cf. Pardee AfO 33 1986 118ff., 126ff.; *rḥqt abn l abn* she removes stone after stone, RSOu 14 53 [KTU 9.432]:32' (cf. 31') (// *pslt (II)*); in unc. ctx.: 1.1 V 23; 1.4 II 2; 1.18 IV 40 (cf. /b-n-y/; 1.133:18 (cf. Pardee TPM 156). ★b) types: *abn brq* the stone / head of the lightning, 1.3 III 26 and par. (cf. Akk. *aban birqi*; Hb. *ʔbny ʔš*; cf. Sasson RSP 1 387f.; diff. Dahood UF 1 1969 25: 'I understand', **byn*); *abn yd* stone projectiles, 1.14 III 13 and par. (// *ḥsk*; cf. Loewenstamm IEJ 15 1965 128 n. 21); for *abn ph* 1.19 I 8 cf. also *p (III)*; *abn srp* alum, 4.626:10 (cf. RS Akk.: NA_4 KA.BI, PRU 3 208 (RS 16.110):4',8'; 209 (RS 16.359C):3', 7'; NA_4 *ga-bi*, *passim*;

cf. AHw 1254; Sanmartín AfO 34 1987 54ff.; Van Soldt UF 22 1980 322ff., 350f.); cf. 4.182:10, 27; 4.206:6; 4.776:2; cf. in bkn ctx. 4.774:1. Cf. *abn* 5.22:13 (cf. *a/ibn*, PN; *ab*). Bkn ctx.: *abnm*, 1.1 V 11; *bn abnm*, 1.1 V 23.

2) Knife (made of) stone / flint: *ġr b abn ydy* (his) skin with the (knife made of) stone he ripped (// *yʕr*), 1.5 VI 17; 1.6 I 2.

3) Weight: *abn mznm* (stone) weights (// *mšrrm*), 1.24:36-37 (cf. Akk. *aban kīsi*; Hb. *ʔbn kys*, *ʔbn ṣdq*; cf. Dahood ULx 84). Bkn ctx.: *abn*[, 1.4 II 2; *ab*[*n*, 4.774:1.

a/ibn PN (Sem.(?). Cf. Grøndahl PTU 17, 30, 87f.; Dietrich - Loretz OLZ 62 1967 535; Sivan GAGl 195; Benz PNPPI 258; Watson AuOr 13 1995 219; cf. Xella UF 20 1988 387ff.: /ʔabn=/, cf. *abn*); ¶ syll.: *a-ba-ni*, PRU 6 83 III 13; *ab-ba/bá-na*, PRU 6 27 8 and *passim* (cf. Huehnergard UVST 222). Var. *ibn*, 4.658:13; cf. *abn*, 5.22:13 (Dietrich - Loretz KA 190: 'Stein' / PN).

PN: ★a) 4.370:3; ★b) *bn PN*: 4.33:24 (*uškny*); 4.335:25; 4.423:21; 4.658:13 (*ibn*); 4.715:2. In bkn ctx.: 4.367:5; 4.427:13.

ibn PN; cf. *a/ibn*.

ubn PN (Hurr.(?); cf. Grøndahl PTU 228f.; Van Soldt BiOr 46 1989 650; UF 21 1989 337 n. 17; SAU 31, 37, 39, 41; Watson AuOr 14 1996 96); ¶ syll.: cf. *ú-be-na*, PRU 6 140:4; *u-bi-nu*, Ug 5 88:17'.

PN: ★a) 4.7:6 (*bn ʕdn*); 4.115:4; 4.131:5; 4.141 II 8; 4.148:2; 4.165:15; 4.344:2; 4.609:9; 4.723:7; 6.18:3; ★b) *bn PN*: 4.71 III 3; 4.98:5; 4.704:4; bkn 4.494:2; ★c) *aḫ PN*: 4.103:5 (*ršpab aḫ PN*).

ubnyn PN (Hurr.(?); cf. Grøndahl PTU 229).

PN: ★a) 4.137:11; 4.348:19; ★b) *bt PN*: 1.80:2 (cf. *bt (II)* 5).

ibr (I) n. m. of a stocky male animal; 1) "bull"; 2) "horse" (Hb. *ʔbyr*, HALOT 6; cf. Akk. *ab(ā)ru*, AHw 7; CAD A/1 38; Eg. *íbr*, *ʔa-bí-ra*, WäS 1 63; Helck Bez. 507 (2). Cf. Sanmartín UF 10 1978 349f.; Sasson RSP 1 389); ¶ syll. Ug.: cf. the element /ʔa/ib(b)īru/ in PNN, Sivan GAGl 194, 199; Huehnergard UVST 269 n. 11; ¶ par.: *dkr*, *ḥmr*, *rum*, *ṯr*. ¶ Forms: sg. *ibr*, pl. *ibrm*; suff. *ibrh*.

1) Bull: they have horns (...) and humps *km ibrm* like bulls, 1.12 I 32 (// *ṯrm*); DN buckled *km ibr* like a bull, 1.12 II 55 (// *ṯr*); a cow (...) which *ibr tld* gave birth to a bull (// *rum*), 1.10 III 20; *k ibr l bʕl yld* for a bull has been born to DN, 1.10 III 35 (// *rum*); *ibr y bʕl nšqdš* a bull, DN, we shall consecrate to you, 1.119:29 (// [*d*]*kr*).

2) Horse: he will not be able to sleep (...) *l qr ṯigt ibrh* for the noise

of the neighing of his horses, 1.14 III 16 and par. (// *ḥmrh*).
Cf. in bkn ctx. *ibr klhm dlhẓ*, 1.9:11; *mlk nhr ibrx*[, 1.9:16.

ibr (II) n. m. "wing"(?) (Hb. *ʔbr*, *ibrh*, HALOT 9; Syr. *ʔebrō*, LS 3; Akk. *abru*, AHw 7; CAD A/1 64. Cf. De Moor SP 172; Dijkstra UF 15 1983 29f.). ¶ Forms: pl. cstr. *ibr*.
Wing(?): *ibr mnt* the wings(?) of destiny, 1.4 VII 56; 1.8:9 (cf. De Moor ARTU 65). Cf. in bkn ctx. 1.9:11, 16.

ubr PN (Akk. Cf. Watson AuOr8 1990 244).
PN: *bn PN*, 4.371:19; 4.617:16.

ubrʕ(y) TN (Belmonte RGTC 12/2 303: *ʔUburʕā*. Cf. Heltzer RCAU 15; Görg UF 6 1974 474f.; Astour RSP 2 266; UF 13 1981 7; JAOS 86 1966 281; Bordreuil Syria 61 1984 1, 7; Van Soldt UF 28 1996 656, UF 30 1998 723); ¶ syll.: URU *u-bur-a*, PRU 3 188 (RS 10.044):4'; 189 (RS 11.790):3'; 190 (RS 11.800);1'; PRU 6 118:6'; RSOu 7 4:38; cf. Huehnergard UVST 249, 251; Van Soldt SAU 338. ¶ Forms: *ubrʕy*, *ubrʕ*.
TN: ★a) *ubrʕy*, 2.26:12; 4.27:4, 15; 4.63 III 1; 4.68:28; 4.100:1; 4.124:8; 4.375:12; 4.380:20; 4.381:20; 4.610 (I) 14; 4.685:8; 4.777:2; RSOu 14 36 [KTU 9.417]:6; ★b) *ubrʕ*: *skn ubrʕ*, 4.288:4. Cf. 4.622:2. In bkn ctx. 4.693:2.

ubrʕn PN (< *ubrʕ*, TN. Cf. Grøndahl PTU 27, 88).
PN: *bn PN*, 4.110:3.

ubrʕy GN m. (< *ubrʕ(y)*, TN). ¶ Forms: sg. *ubrʕy*; pl./du. *ubrʕym*.
GN: 4.96:10; 4.616:7. Bkn ctx.: 4.33:18, 19; 4.50:2.

ibrd PN (Sem.(?); cf. Grøndahl PTU 88, 133; Berger WO 5 1969/70 279; Dahood *apud* Pettinato Archives 277; Ribichini - Xella RSF 15 1987 8); ¶ syll.: cf. *i-bar-dì*, PRU 3 83 (RS 16.157):5; *i-bar-di*, PRU 6 43 rev. 9'. Cf. *iwrd*.
PN: *bn PN*, 4.33:26 (*mʕrby*); 4.628:5; cf. in bkn ctx.: 4.217:3; 4.424:23.

ib/wrḏr PN (Hurr. Cf. Grøndahl PTU 224f., 249; Dietrich - Loretz OLZ 62 1967 535; Rainey UF 3 1971 168f.; Lipiński UF 13 1981 123ff.); ¶ syll.: cf. EN.LUGAL, cf. PRU 3 p. 246; PRU 6 86 I 13; Ug 5 10 obv. 4, rev. 8', 14'.
PN: 2.10:1; 2.14:1; 4.7:5; 4.343:6; 4.678:3.

abrḫṭ PN; cf. *iwrḫṭ*.
PN: RSOu 14 39 [KTU 4.790]:23'.

ibrkḏ PN.

PN: 2.21:7.

ibrkyṯ PN (Hurr. Cf. Grøndahl PTU 205, 224, 238; Laroche GLH 147; Dietrich - Mayer UF 28 1996 186).

PN: 4.264:10.

abrm PN (Sem. Cf. Grøndahl PTU 44ff., 86f., 182; Ribichini - Xella RSF 15 1987 8; Sivan GAGl 195, 263; Pardee AfO 36/37 1989/90 392); ¶ syll.: *a-bi-ra-mì*, PRU 3 20 (RS 15.63):1; PRU 6 143:2; *a-bi-ra-m*[*u*, PRU 6 85:10'; 107:8.

PN: 4.433:4; 4.352:2 (*alṯyy*), 4; *a*]*brm*, 4.433:4.

ibrm PN (Hurr.(?); cf. Dietrich - Loretz OLZ 62 1967 535; Grøndahl PTU 87, 182: /ʔab=rm/); ¶ syll.: EN-*ri-mu*, PRU 6 104:4.

PN: 4.607:20.

ib/wrmḏ PN (Hurr. Grøndahl PTU 210, 224, 241; Van Soldt SAU 20 and n. 180, 27, 36); ¶ syll.: *ib-ra-mu-zi*, EN-*mu-za* and var., cf. PRU 3 p. 246; PRU 6 138:16; Ug 5 59:1 (cf. Huehnergard UVST 224f.); cf. EN-*mu-šu*, RSOu 7 2:11', 24'.

PN: 4.7:12; 4.103:10, 51; 4.219:8 (Van Soldt SAU 126); 4.357:20; 4.417:14; 4.607:6; 4.675:5; RSOu 14 39 [KTU 4.790]:20'.

abr[PN.

PN: 4.647:7.

abrn PN (Sem.(?); cf. Grøndahl PTU 88). Cf. *ibrn*.

PN: *bn PN*, 4.617:21.

ibrn PN (Sem. Cf. Grøndahl PTU 224, 422; Rainey UF 3 1971 156; Dietrich - Loretz - Sanmartín UF 6 1974 20f.; Huehnergard UVST 269f. n. 11; Van Soldt SAU 3, 11f.); ¶ syll.: *i-bi-ra-na*, cf. PRU 3 p. 246; DUMU-*i-bi*[, PRU 3 196 (RS 15.42+) I 2; PRU 4 188 (RS 17.292):2; PRU 6 p. 139; cf. LÚ(.MEŠ) *mur-i* ^{m}*i-bi-ra-na*, PRU 3 162 (RS 16.348): 5; PRU 6 93:16. Cf. *abrn*, *iwrn*.

PN: *il PN*, 1.113:16 and *passim*; *mru/i PN*, 4.47:3; 4.68:64; 4.99:12; 4.103:37; 4.105:1; 4.126:24; 4.610:44; 4.752:7.

abrpu PN (Sem. Cf. Grøndahl PTU 86, 180; Sivan GAGl 264; Parker UF 4 1972 99; Watson AuOr 13 1995 218); syll: *a-bir*$_{y}$(BUR$_{5}$)*-pí-i*, PRU 3 167 (RS 15.139):5; *a-bir*$_{x}$(BAR)*-pa-a*, RS 22.02: *a-bir*$_{x}$(BAR)*-pu-u*, RS 22.02 rev. 12' (Van Soldt SAU 18 n. 162; 324 n. 145f.).

PN: 4.96:10 (*ubrʕy*); 4.214 III 5; 4.75 VI 4 (*bn kbd*).

ubrš PN (Hurr.(?); cf. Grøndahl PTU 228f.); ¶ syll.: cf. DUB(?)-*bir*$_{5}$-*ši*,

PRU 3 134 (15.137):4; DUB(?)-*bi-ir-ši*, RSOu 7 5:6; cf. Huehnergard AkkUg 368 n. 27; Van Soldt SAU 354 n. 214. Cf. *abršn*.

PN: *bn PN*, 4.41:12; 4.214 III 3; 4.290:7; in bkn ctx.: 4.769:34; cf. unc. rdg: 4.611 17.

abršn PN (Sem. Cf. Grøndahl PTU 16, 86, 101; Watson AuOr 8 1990 114); ¶ syll.: *a-bir*$_y$(BUR$_5$)-*ša-nu*, PRU 3 202 (RS 16.257+) III 44; PRU 6 82:1 (cf. Huehnergard AkkUg 361 n. 13; Van Soldt SAU 324 n. 146); cf. *a-bi-ir-ši*, PRU 3 58 (RS [Varia 8] = "15.Z"):7; *a-bir*$_y$(BUR$_5$)-*ši*, RS 16.114 rev. 11' (cf. Van Soldt SAU 324 n. 146; cf. PRU 3 p. 34). Cf. *ubrš*.

PN: 4.45:8; 4.225:15; 4.281:7; 4.645:3. In bkn ctx. cf. *abrš*[, 4.75 IV 6 (*bn*] *ḫrpn*; cf. Weippert ZDPV 82 1966 323f.).

abršp PN (Sem. Cf. Grøndahl PTU 45, 86, 181; Watson AuOr 13 1995 218).

PN: 4.63 I 35; *abrš*[, 4.75 IV 6 (*bn*] *ḫrpn*).

abrt[TN (Cf. Belmonte RGTC 12/2 2: **Abrātu*).

TN: 4.748:11.

ibrtlm PN (Hurr. Cf. Grøndahl PTU 207, 224, 260; Van Soldt SAU 20).

PN: 4.136:3.

ib/wryn PN (Hurr. Cf. Grøndahl PTU 225); ¶ syll.: cf. *ib-ri-ia*, PRU 6 78:24; cf. EN-*ia*, 72:11.

PN ★a) 4.307:14; 4.320:19; ★b) *bn PN*: 4.222:21.

ibsn n. m. "warehouse" (Akk. *abūsu*, AHw 9; CAD A/1 92f.; cf. Hb. *ʔbws*, HALOT 4); ¶ RS Akk.: cf. É*(-ti) a-bu-sí/*TI, PRU 3 181f. = PRU 4 47f. (RS 11.732) A 8, B 8; PRU 4 82 (RS 17.382 + 380):45; 231 (RS 17.244):3. ¶ Forms: sg. *ibsn*.

Warehouse: *št ibsn lkm* I leave the warehouse to you, 3.9:5.

ubs/ś TN (Belmonte RGTC 12/2 304: *ʔUbūśu*. Cf. Heltzer RCAU 15; Astour UF 13 1981 7; Segert UF 15 1983 206; Bordreuil Syria 66 1988 272; UF 20 1988 17f.;Van Soldt UF 28 1996 656; UF 30 1998 731); ¶ syll.: URU *u-bu-sú/sí*, PRU cf. 3 p. 268 (cf. Huehnergard UVST 251).

TN: *ubś*: 4.68:38; 4.302:8; 4.621:10; RSOu 14 35 [KTU 388] II 19; *ubs*: 4.693:49; 783:2, 4.

abṣdq PN (Sem. Cf.Grøndahl PTU 86, 187f.).

PN, in bkn ctx.: *a*]*bṣdq*, 4.151 I 11.

absṇ PN (Sem.(?). Grøndahl PTU 189; cf. Dahood Bib 46 1965 49: Hb. PN *ʔbṣn*).

PN: *absṇ*, 4.609:5.

abšḫr PN (Sem.).

PN: *bn PN*, 4.723:14.

abškn PN (Hurr.(?); cf. Grøndahl PTU 219, 289; Berger WO 5 1969/70 275); ¶ syll.: cf. *a-bu-uš-ga-*[*n*]*a*, Syria 18 246 (RS 8.145):31; *a-bu-uš-qa-*[*n*]*a*, PRU 3 18 (RS 15.24+):1; *a-bu-uš-ka-n*[*i*], PRU 6 128:6; cf. *a-bu-uš-qa-ma*(?), PRU 3 10 (RS 10.046):7.

PN: 4.141 I 14; 4.194:19; 4.285:7.

abšr, cf. *abd/šr*.

abšti PN (Hurr. Cf. Grøndahl PTU 218, 258; Watson AuOr 8 1990 114); ¶ syll.: *a-bi-iš-ta-e* and var., cf. PRU 3 p. 240.

PN: *bn PN*, 4.344:11; 4.720:5.

abštp PN (Hurr.(?); poss. mistake for *abšti*).

PN: 4.344:11.

/ʔ-b-ṯ/ vb Š: "?" (Cf. Tropper UG 588). ¶ Forms: Š(?): *tṯibṯn*.

Š(?): *w b yn tṯibṯn*, 1.175:8.

aby adj. m. "ancestral" ((?); <(?) *ab*; cf. Obermann HDBS 14). ¶ Forms: pl. *abym*.

Ancestral(?): unc. rdg: *rʕh abym*(?) his ancestral(?) companions, 1.22 I 27.

a/iby PN (Sem. Cf. Grøndahl PTU 17, 51, 86; Bordreuil SEL 5 1988 28; Schult ZDPV 85 1969 198f.); ¶ syll.: cf. (f)*a-ba/be/bi-ya*, cf. PRU 3 p. 240; cf. *a-bu-ia*[, PRU 6 85:11'; DUMU *ab-bi-ya*, RSOu 7 3 rev. 13'. Var. *iby* probl. in 6.37:1.

PN: ★a) 4.130:5; 6.37:1 (rdg *iby ḫ*[?); RSOu 14 49 [KTU 9.433]:24; ★b) *bn PN*: 4.7:12. Cf. in bkn ctx. 2.17:9; 4.332:1; 4.554:3; 4.593:8.

ibyḫ[PN.

PN: *ibyḫ*[, 6.37:1.

uby(n) PN (etym. unc. Cf. Grøndahl PTU 228f.; Bordreuil - Caquot Syria 56 1979 310; Watson AuOr 13 1995 220).

PN: ★a) 4.84:2; 4.399:12; 4.728:5; ★b) *bn uby*, 4.769:17; *bn ubyn*, 4.93 IV 11; 4.645:4.

abyn adj. m. "poor, wretch, insolvent" (Hb. *ʔbywn*, HALOT 5; Akk. *abiʔānum*, ARMT 10 296; Von Soden MIO 15 1969 322-326;

Dietrich - Loretz - Sanmartín UF 8 1976 433f.; Dijkstra - De Moor UF 7 1975 174; Muchiki Loanwords 280; Dietrich - Loretz UF 25 1993 119ff.; diff.: Margalit UF 15 1983 69f.: 'disdainful', AOrab. *ʔaba(y)*); ¶ syll. Ug.: cf.]*na-ak-di* = *i-b/pu-ú*, Ug 5 137 II 43', and cf. Huehnergard UVST 91; cf. RS Akk. *nayyālu*, AHw 717; CAD N/1 152; ¶ par.: *anḫ*. ¶ Forms: sg. *abyn*; pl. *abynm*.

Poor, wretch: *abyn at dnil* what a wretch you are, PN!, 1.17 I 16 (// *anḫ*; for other interpretations, cf. Del Olmo MLC 367; cf. Watts UF 21 1989 448: *aby nat dnil* 'my father! the seemly offering of Danil'); insolvent: *m abynm* GN, insolvent, 4.70:6. Cf. in bkn ctx. 1.22 I 27.

ibyn PN (Sem. Cf. Grøndahl PTU 17, 53, 87); ¶ syll.: *a-bi-ia-nu*, PRU 195 (RS 15.09) A 17.

PN: ★a) 4.607:21; cf. in bkn. ctx.: 4.496:2; ★b) *bn PN*, 4.377:4.

abyt PN (Sem. Cf. Grøndahl PTU 54; Weippert ZDPV 82 1966 330); ¶ syll.: DUMU *a-bu-ia-ti*, PRU 3 195 (RS 15.09) A 118.

PN: *bn PN*, 4.611:3.

abyy PN (Sem. Cf. diff.: Grøndahl PTU 53).

PN: 4.103:51.

/ʔ-d/ vb G: general commercial meaning "to overcharge, levy; to exact" (cf. Arab. *ʔāda*, Lane 124; Tigr. *ʔawwada*, WTS 380; cf. Eg. *ʕdd / ʕu-di-d<i>*, WäS 1 237; Helck Bez. 510 (47). Cf. Dietrich - Loretz - Sanmartín UF 6 1974 455; Cunchillos EEU 129; Renfroe AULS 77f.). ¶ Forms: G prefc. *tud*; inf. *ad*.

G. To overcharge someone, to levy expenses on him: *al tud* do not overcharge PN, 2.26:19; to exact an amount (*l*- for something): *ad at lhm* you exact (a price) for them, 2.26:20 (diff.: Cunchillos TOu 2 319 n. 14: 'rembourser / payer').

Cf. ud.

ad n. m. "father" (childish onomatopeia; cf. Sum. ad (-da), Deimel SAG 9; Amor. /ʔad/, Huffmon APNMT 156; Buccellati Amorites 206; cf. Grøndahl PTU 88f.; Ebla cf. A.DU-, Krebernik PET 71; Fales EDA 422; Sanmartín AuOr 9 1991 170. On its connection with *adn* cf. Virolleaud Syria 14 1933 144; Sanmartín UF 9 1977 269 n. 2; Bordreuil - Caquot Syria 57 1980 345); ¶ par.: *um*; syll. Ug. cf. PNN *a-du-ú*, PRU 6 85:7'; 91:4; cf. Sivan GAGl 195. ¶ Forms: sg. m. *ad*.

Father: *tṣḥ(n) (y) ad ad* she(they) cried: father, father!, 1.23:32, 43. Cf. in bkn ctx. *gb ad* the cup(?) of the father, 1.172:23.

Cf. adʕl, adbʕl, adnʕm, adt, ady.

-id temporal adv. morpheme used to form distributive numerals, "time" (cf. *id*; ESA *ʔd*, DOSA 5, 518: *šlṯtʔd* "three times". Cf. Borger VT 10 1960 71f.; Renfroe AULS 11ff.; diff.: Aartun PU 1 16: *yd* 'Hand'). ¶ Forms: *(-)d*, *(-)id*.

Time, adverbializing morpheme with numbers: *šbʕd w šbʕid mrḥqtm qlt* seven times and seven times from afar I prostrate myself, 2.12:8-9; cf. 2.64:14; *ṯnid* twice, 2.50:18; 2.64:14; *ṯlṯid* three times, 1.18 IV 23 and par.; 1.163:5; *ʕšrid* ten times, 2.42:12.

Cf. ʕšrid, šbʕ(i)d, ṯlṯid, ṯnid.

id temporal adv. functor "then"; conj. "when" (Hb. *ʔz*, HALOT 26f.; Aram. *ʔdyn*, DNWSI 13; Arab. *ʔiḏ*, Lane 38f.; ESA *ʔḏ*, DOSA 5; Eth. *yĕʔĕze*, CDG 625; cf. Aartun PU 2 97; Dietrich - Loretz - Sanmartín UF 7 1975 543). ¶ Forms: *id*.

When / then: *id ydbḥ mlk* when the king sacrifices, 1.115:1; cf. 1.41:50; 1.164:1,3; *id iph mlk* when the king visits, 1.90:1; cf. 1.168:1,8; *id likt TN* when you sent the message to TN, 2.82:3. In bkn ctx., 1.4 I 34, rdg*il*(!). Cf. idk, idy.

ud n. m. "pay, payment" ((?); Dijkstra UF 21 1989 143: (< /ʔ-d/). ¶ Forms: *ud* sg. suff. *udh*.

Pay, payment(?): *udh mġt* (the time of) his payment(?) has arrived, 2.36:8 (unc. ctx.); *sprn mnḥ ud* record of the delivery of payment(?), 3.10:1 (cf. Bordreuil ALASP 7 4).

adʕl PN (Sem. Cf. Grøndahl PTU 89, 108).

PN: 4.63 II 46.

adʕ(y) PN (Sem. Cf. Grøndahl PTU 50, 142; Van Soldt SAU 41); ¶ syll.: cf. *a-du-ú*, cf. PRU 6 p. 138; cf. diff.: Sivan GAGl 195; cf. *ady*, *ʕdy*, PNN.

PN: 4.86:14; 4.347:10.

adbʕl PN (Sem. Cf. Grøndahl PTU 46, 89, 117; cf. Benz PNPPI 260).

PN: 4.609:19; 4.727:3; 4.753:20.

udbr n. m.; an object ((?); etym. unc.). ¶ Forms: sg./pl. *udbr*[.

An object:]*x ʕšr udbr*[, 4.312:5; cf. *ibid.* ln. 9 (cultic ctx.?). In bkn ctx. 4.248:4.

add DN, 1.65:9, cf. *hd(d)*.

adḥ[Bkn PN, 4.635:62.

idk narrative adv. functor "then, and so, so then" (*id* + emphatic suff. *-k*, cf. Aartun PU 1 5f., 49, 'dann, fürwahr'; Van Zijl Baal 70).

¶ Forms: *idk*.

Then, and so, so then, only in the formula *idk al / l y/ttn pnm ʕm / tk (...)* so then, he / they set (his / their) face towards (...), 1.4 VIII 1 and *passim* in narrative texts. In bkn ctx.: *idk niṯ* 1.86:21.

adlḏn PN (Hurr.; cf. Grøndahl PTU 206, 221, 255; Van Soldt SAU 37); ¶ syll.: *a-dal*-ŠEŠ/*še-ni* and var. cf. PRU 3 p. 242; Huehnergard UVST 224; AkkUg 362.

PN: *bn PN*, 4.69 I 12; 4.340:19; 4.356:7; cf. in bkn ctx. 4.451:2; 4.604:2.

idly PN.

PN: *idly*, 4.383:7.

/ʔ-d-m/ vb G: "to become red, turn the colour red; to put on red make up (cf. Hb. *ʔdm*, HALOT 14; cf. Akk. *ada(m)mu*, AHw 10; CAD A/1 95; *adamatu*, AHw 10; CAD A/1 94f.; Arab. *ʔadama*, Lane 35ff.; cf. Eth. *ʔaddama*, CDG 7f. Cf. Pedersen Berytus 6 1941 101f.; De Moor Or 37 1968 213 n. 1; Ashley EAR 147 224f.; Dressler AT 538, 557; Kühne UF 6 1974 162f.); ¶ par.: /r-ḥ-ṣ/; syll. Ug. cf. /ʔadmāni/ in *i-na* A.ŠÀ : *ad-ma-ni*, PRU 3 123 (RS 15.145):8, 12; Sivan GAGl 195; Huehnergard UVST 104; Van Soldt SAU 302. ¶ Forms: G prefc. *tidm*, *yadm*, *tidm* (cf. Dijkstra - De Moor UF 7 1975 211f.).

G. To become red, turn the colour red: *ṯkm tidm* (incorrect spelling: *tium*) *b ġlp ym*ṯ up to her shoulders she rouged herself with sea snails, 1.19 IV 42; to put on make up: *trtḥṣ w tadm* wash yourself and put on make up, 1.14 II 9 and par. (diff.: De Moor - Spronk UF 14 1982 160: 'to glow').

Cf. adm (I).

adm (I) n. m. 1) "man"; 2) "man (coll.), mankind, people" (etym. relationship to /ʔ-d-m/ unc.; cf. Hb., Ph., Pun., *ʔdm*, HALOT 14; DNWSI 13f.; Amor. cf. DN /ʔadmu/, Buccellati Amorites 130; Gelb CAAA 13, 46f.; Ebla cf. *ad-mu*, Krebernik PET 75; ESA *ʔdm*, DOSA 5. Cf. Ginsberg JAOS 70 1950 158ff.; Pedersen Berytus 6 1941 72; Fensham JNSL 4 1975 12; Loretz - Xella MLE 1 1982 45); ¶ par.: *lim (I)*. ¶ Forms: sg. *adm*.

1) Man: *pit adm* the temples of the man, 1.107:3; *l adm // l bn adm* oh man!, 1.169:14-15 (Loretz - Xella MLE 1 1982 38, 45).

2) Man, mankind, people: *ab adm* the father of mankind, 1.14 I 37 and par.; *tṣmt adm* she destroyed the people, 1.3 II 8 (// *lim*).

Cf. /ʔ-d-m/.

adm (II) adj. m. "obtained, acquired" (< OAss. *adāmum*, AHw 10; CAD A/1 95f.). ¶ Forms: sg. *adm*.

Obtained, acquired: *sprn ṯhr w adm* our pure bronze has already been acquired, 2.39:33 (for other opinions cf. Watson AuOr 10 1992 228 n. 38).

idm "?" (cf. Kapelrud Ug 6 326: 'red flames', *ʔdm*; Gray JNES 10 1951 150 n. 42: 'potion', Arab. *idm*; De Moor ARTU 132: 'red drink').

? : in bkn ctx.: *idm adr (...)*[// *idm ʕrẓ tʕr*[, 1.12 II 29-30. Cf. *idmnn* 1.55:4.

udm TN; mythical city of king *pbl* (Belmonte RGTC 12/2 304f.; cf. EA Akk.: URU *ú-du-mu*, EAT 256:24; cf. OB/OAss. toponyms *Admu(m)*, NA *Udūmu*, *Uṣumai*, Astour RSP 2 267f. Cf. De Langhe ETL 16 1939 307f.; Albright BASOR 89 1943 14; Buccellati Cities 127; Fisher JSS 8 1963 35f.; Astour UF 5 1973 33f., 39; Caquot - Sznycer TOu 1 492f.; Ribichini MLE 1 1982 51f.; De Moor ARTU 196; De Moor - Spronk UF 14 1982 165; Margalit UR 158 n. 113; Pardee TPM 215). ¶ Forms: *udm*, du. *udmm*.

TN: *ymġy l udm rbt w udm ṯrrt* he reached TN, the great, and TN, the powerful, 1.14 IV 47-48 and par.; *arḫ tzġ l ʕglh (...) k tnḥn udmm* the cow lows for her calf (...) as the two TN lament (for her), 1.15 I 7.

Cf. udmy.

udmʕt, cf. *dmʕ*.

]idmt, 4.351:2.

udmy GN m. (< *udm*, TN; see Van Soldt UF 28 1996 657). ¶ Forms: pl. *udmym*.

GN: 4.337:15. Cf. *umdym*, 4.394:5 (scribal mistake?).

/ʔ-d-n/ vb G: "to give ear, to pay attention, listen"(?) ((?) denom. of *udn* 'ear'; Hb. *ʔzn* hi., HALOT 27; Akk. *wazzunu*, AHw 1494; Bordreuil - Pardee RSOu 14 p. 391, unless denom. from *adn* 'master', cf. *ibid.*; Tropper UG 643). ¶ Forms: G/D prefc. *tudn*.

G/D. To give ear, pay attention, listen(?): *km l tudn dbbm kšpm* (...) *yšpk kmm arṣ kšpm dbbm* just as the sorcerers do not listen(?) to the demons... so the sorcerers spill to the ground the demons, RSOu 14 52 [KTU 9.435]:8.

Cf. udn (I).

adn (I) n. m. 1) "lord, master"; 2) "noble father" (Hb. *ʔdwn*, HALOT 12f.; Ph., Pun. *ʔdn*, DNWSI 15-17; Amor. cf. /ʔ-d-n/, Huffmon

APNMT 159; /ʔadanum/, Gelb CAAA 13, 46; /ʔadun-/, /ʔadān-/, Garbini LSem 94f.; Grøndahl PTU 89f. Cf. Virolleaud Syria 17 1936 215; RA 38 1941 4; Ginsberg Or 5 1936 162; Cassuto GA 146; Herrmann YN 10; Weippert UF 6 1974 417; Dietrich - Loretz - Sanmartín 7 1975 551; Sanmartín UF 9 1977 269ff.; Bordreuil - Caquot Syria 57 1980 366; Loretz UF 12 1980 287-292; Adonis 25ff.; Smith BC 1 150 n. 58, 289 n. 122 = *ad* + *-n*); ¶ par.: *um*, *bʕl*; ¶ syll. Ug.: NU = *a-bu* = *at-ta-ni* = *a-da-nu*, Ug 5 130 II 9'; in PNN: /ʔadān-/, /ʔadōn-/, Sivan GAGl 195; Huehnergard UVST 104; cf. Van Soldt BiOr 46 1988 650. ¶ Forms: sg. *adn*; suff. *adny*, *adnk*, *adnkm*, *adnhm*.

1. ★a) Lord: *adnkm* your lord, 1.2 I 17 and par. (// *bʕlkm*); *at adn tpʕr* you have been proclaimed 'lord', 1.1 IV 17; cf. in bkn ctx. *adn* [*bn i*]*lm* divine 'lord', 1.3 V 9; royal title: at the approach of *adn ilm rbm* the 'lord of the great gods', 1.124:1 (cf. Del Olmo CR 313; Van der Toorn BiOr 48 1991 60; for other attributions cf. Pardee UF 15 1983 132f.; cf. Pope Fs. Finkelstein 179; Dietrich - Loretz MU 214f.); PN [*a*]*dny* PN my lord, RSOu 14 49 [KTU 9.433]:2; PN *adn(k)* (your) lord, 1.6 VI 58; 1.16 I 57; *adnkm* 1.15 VI 5; 1.16 I 60; and reply *l aḫk l adnk* to your brother, your lord, 2.14:19; ctx. inc. *adnk šqrb* to(?) your lord offer it, 1.16 I 44; cf. *adny*, 2.39:9; ★b) master: *ṯlṯ bʕlm w adnhm* three unskilled labourers and their master, 4.360:3; cf. in bkn ctx. 2.18:4; 7.218:2. Unc. ctx. *ksp ṯlṯt ʕml l adn* three shekels of silver he earned(?) for (his) master, 5.11:8.

2. Noble father: *adnh yšt mṣb mznm* your noble father arranged the beam of the scales, 1.24:33 (// *umh*); *l PN adny rgm tḥm PN bnk* to PN, my lord, say: message of PN, your son, 2.64:2. In bkn ctx.: 1.24:13.

Cf. adn (II), adnʕm, adnnʕm, adnṣdq, adt, iladn, mrạdn.

adn (II) PN (Sem. Cf. Grøndahl PTU 50, 89f.; Berger WO 5 1969/70 276; Rainey Or 56 1987 393). Cf. *ʕdn (IV)*.

PN: ★a) 4.609:33; ★b) *bn PN*: 4.90:3; 4.122:18; 6.16:2; RSOu 14 45 [KTU 9.418]:7.

idn n. m. "authorization, full powers" (?) (Arab. *ʔiḏn*, Lane 42f.; Dietrich - Loretz - Sanmartín UF 6 1974 472; cf. De Moor JNES 24 1965; Verreet UF 18 1986 378; diff.: Dietrich - Loretz UF 16 1984 354: 'Termin', Akk. *adānu*, *(ʕ)edānu*; cf. Renfroe AULS 78). ¶ Forms: sg. *idn*.

Authorization, full powers(?): *rʕ yšṣa idn ly* (so that) my friend may provide me with an authorization(?), 2.15:5.

udn (I) n. m. "ear" (Hb. *ʔzn*, HALOT 27f.; Aram. *ʔdn*, DNWSI 26; Akk. *uznu* AHw 1447f.; Arab. *ʔuḏn*, Lane 43; Eth. *ʔezen*, CDG 52); ¶ par.: *qdqd*. ¶ Forms: sg. *udn*; pl. suff. *udnk*, *udnh*.

Ear: *ištmʕ w tqġ udn* listen and let (your) ear be alert, 1.16 VI 42 and par.; *ql b udnk (...)* (may) my voice (penetrate(?)) your ears, 1.13:23; *hlmn (...) ṯlṯid ʕl udn* he struck him (...) three times above the ear, 1.18 IV 34 and par. (// *qdqd*); *w in udn ymn b[h] (...) w in udn šmal b[h]* and if its right ear is missing (...), and if its left ear is missing, 1.103:35, 37.

Cf. /ʔ-d-n/.

udn (II) n. m. "(place of) dominion" (cf. *adn (I)*; cf. Gray LC 47; Van Zijl Baal 62; Sanmartín UF 10 1978 449f.; Bordreuil - Pardee MARI 7 66; diff.: Gordon UL 20, 'nest': Akk. *adattu* [cf. De Moor ULe 100 n. 2; Dijkstra UF 2 1970 334]; Gordon PLM 80, 'ear', cf. *udn (I)*; Dietrich - Loretz UF 14 1982 77ff., 'Ruheplatz', Hb. *ʔdn*; cf. Del Olmo IMC 1755 for the various opinions); ¶ par.: *kḥṯ (+ drkt)*, *ksu (+ mlk)*, *mrym (+ ṣpn)*. ¶ Forms: sg. suff. *udnh*.

(Place of) dominion: *mšṣṣ k ʕṣr udnh* who drove (him) out like a bird (from the place) of his dominion, 1.3 IV 2 (// *mrym ṣpn*, *ksu mlk*, *kḥṯ drkt*).

adnʕm PN (Sem. Cf. Grøndahl PTU 15, 32f., 44,90, 163; Poulter - Davies VT 40 1990 237ff.; Kornfeld WZKM 71 1981 41); ¶ syll.: cf. *a-da-nu-um-mu*, PRU 3 67 (RS 16.262): 9, 10, 13.

PN: 4.141 I 1, II 26.

adnn PN (etym. unc.).

PN: *bn PN*, 4.54:8.

adnnʕm PN (Sem. Cf. Grøndahl PTU 32f., 44, 90, 163; Watson AuOr 8 1990 114).

PN: 4.171:5. Cf. 4.141 I 1.

adnṣdq PN (Sem. Cf. Grøndahl PTU 32f., 90, 187).

PN: 4.7:8; 4.129:8.

(adnty), 2.83:5; probl. incorrect spelling of *adtny*. Diff.: Bordreuil - Caquot Syria 57 1980 361: variant of *adty*. Cf. *adt*..

adr (I) adj./n. m. 1) "wonderful, magnificent, strong, of good quality"; 2) "noble, notable" (Hb. *ʔdyr*, HALOT 13f.; Ph. *ʔdr*. DNWSI 18f.; Ebla cf. *a*-BAN*(tar$_x$, tir$_5$)*, Krebernik PET 70; Sanmartín AuOr 9 1991 171; EA Akk. URU *a-du-ri*, EAT 256:24; cf. West AOAT 233 29:

PN *a-di-ri-yo*, Linear B. Cf. Virolleaud Syria 16 1933 261; Greenfield ZAW 73 1961 226ff.; Blau - Greenfield BASOR 200 1970 17; Sawyer - Strange IEJ 14 1964 98; UT 92; Dijkstra - De Moor UF 7 1975 181, 187; Sanmartín UF 9 1977 371-373; Watson SEL 12 1995 220; diff. [especially for 1.17 V 7], Herdner Syria 26 1949 152: 'clôture', Aram. *ʔdr*; Driver CML 135: 'corn-heap', Aram. *ʔdr*; Virolleaud LPD 139; Driver CML 135: 'giant tree', Aram. *ʔdrʔ*; Gaster Thespis(1) 452; UT 92; Ashley EAR 65: 'threshing floor', Aram. *ʔdrʔ*, Akk. *adru*, *bīt adri*, strictly 'granary'; cf. *adr (II)*; Virolleaud LPD 211: derived from *ndr* 'vouer'; Dahood Bib 38 1957 62ff.: verbal derivative from *dry* 'to cut'; cf. Merrill JNSL 3 1974 44; Dressler AT 244f.; Schoors RSP 1 59f.); ¶ par.: *ʕrẓ*, *qdš*, *rḫ̮b (+ mknpt)*; syll. Ug. *a-du-rù*, Ug 5 137 III 34'; Sivan GAGl 196; Huehnergard UVST 104; Van Soldt SAU 302. ¶ Forms: sg. *adr*, pl. *adrm*; cstr. *adr*, for f. *adrt* cf. *adrt*.

1) Wonderful, magnificent, strong: *adr ṯqbm* the most wonderful ash trees, 1.17 VI 20 (cf. 21-25); *adr <qnm> b ġl il {qnm}* the most wonderful <canes> of the divine hollows, 1.17 VI 23 (cf. Dijkstra - De Moor UF 7 1975 187: 'excellent are', prefc. G; diff.: Garbini OrAn 29 1990 57ff.: 'tagliare', impv., **ʔdr*); *ḥlm adr* magnificent fortress, 1.16 I 8 and par. (// *qdš*, *rḥb mknpt*); (your ship was met) *by gšm adr* by a heavy downpour, 2.38:14 (cf. diff.: Bordreuil Semitica 40 1991 30: 'ADR, nom de mois'); *ṯn kndwm adrm* two strong garments *k.* (or: pieces of *k.* fabric), 4.4:2 (cf. *dq*).

2) Noble, worthy: *yṯb b ap ṯġr tḥt adrm d b grn* he sat at the entrance of the gate among the worthies who (gather) in the threshing floor, 1.17 V 7; *yn (...) l adrm b TN* wine (...) for the worthies of TN, 4.246:7; *adr sr*[noble(s) of TN(?), 1.176:19 (cf. Caquot - Bordreuil Syria 57 1980 351). unc. ctx. *p adrm* and the nobles, 2.3:19 Cf. in bkn ctx. *idm adr (...)*[, 1.12 II 29; *adr*[, 2.83:10.

Cf. adrdn, adrt.

adr (II) n. m. "granary" (Akk. *adru*, AHw 13; CAD A/1 129f.; Aram. *ʔdr*, DNWSI 18). ¶ Forms: sg. *adr*.

Granary: door *l aḥd adr* for one granary, 4.195:5.

adr (III) n. m. a variety of tree ("poplar"(?); cf. Sum. $adar_x$, cf. Lieberman SLOBA 136; Akk. *adaru*, AHw 11; CAD A/1 102f.: *adāru*. Cf. De Moor JNES 24 1965 362). ¶ Forms: pl. *adrm*.

Poplar(?): *mit adrm b ʕšrt* one hundred *a.* (poles) for ten (shekels), 4.158:8.

adr (IV) n. m. "fibula"(?) (cf. Akk. *edēru*, AHw 186; CAD E 29f. Cf. Stieglitz JAOS 99 1979 20; Ribichini - Xella Tessili 27, 59 n. 93; Watson UF 28 1996 705f.; diff. Baldacci BiOr 46 1989 119: 'mighty', *adr (I)*; Cecchini SEL 1 1984 47: 'battente', Akk. *an-du-ru-ú*). ¶ Forms: pl. *adrm*.

Fibula(?): *pldm b adrm p.*-garments (provided) with(?) fibulae(?), 4.4:5 (diff.: *pldm d* (incorrect spelling: *b* ?) *adrm p.*-garments which are to be(?) strong; cf. *ibid.* ln. 2: *ṯn kndwm adrm*; cf. *adr (I)*).

udr n. m. "nobility, the most noble" (cf. *adr (I)*; Hb. *ʔdr*, HALOT 16; Ph. *ʔdr*, DNWSI 6. Cf. Oldenburg CEB 127 n. 4; Gibson CML 143; Rin AE 163; De Moor ARTU 55; diff.: Margalit MLD 216ff.: 'granary', Akk. *adru*, Aram. *ʔdrʔ*; De Moor - Spronk UF 14 1982 159 n. 55: 'slopes', root /n-d-r/; Caquot - Sznycer TOu 1 208: 'chameaux', Akk. *udru*; Gordon UT 19.94: 'quarry', Watson SEL 16 1999 39: root /d-r-y/; cf. also Sasson RSP 1 390); ¶ par.: *mḥmd*. ¶ Forms: sg. *udr*.

Nobility, the most noble: may they bring you *udr ilqṣm* the most noble gem(s), 1.4 V 17 and par. (// *mḥmd*).

adrdn PN (etym. unc. Cf. Grøndahl PTU 16, 43, 61, 90, 123; Huehnergard UVST 254, 262; AkkUg 368; Van Soldt SAU 38; Watson AuOr 14 1996 94); ¶ syll.: cf. *ad-da-ru*, PRU 4 183 (RS 17.319):22.

PN: 4.147:9; 4.148:3; 4.264:5. Cf. in bkn ctx. 4.141 I 10; 4.183 I 22.

idrm PN (etym. unc. Cf. Grøndahl PTU 53, 90; Dietrich - Loretz UF 13 1981 208).

PN: *bn PN*, 4.69 II 2; 4.377:8; 4.786:11; cf. 4.452:2; 4.511:2; 4.528:4.

idrn PN (Hurr.(?); cf. Laroche GLH 128; cf. Grøndahl PTU 61, 90; Lipiński SAIO 1 138); ¶ syll.: *id-da-ra(-na)*, PRU 3 86 (RS 15.119):7', 12'.

PN: *bn PN*, 4.65:9; 4.322:9. In bkn ctx.: 4.694:3.

idrp "?", an element in the titulary of the god *ršp* (cf. Xella TRU 99f.; Aartun UF 16 1984 14: 'Schutz', Arab. *darf*; cf. Renfroe UF 18 1986 51).

? : *ršp idrp š* DN (of) *i.*, a ram, 1.148:32.

adrt adj./n. f. 1) "of good quality"; 2) "noblewoman, worthy"; 3) "the best(?)" (f. of *adr (I)*; cf. Macdonald UF 10 1978 165ff.). ¶ Forms: sg. *adrt*; du. *adrtm*; pl. *adrt*.

1) Of good quality: *yryt adrt* corals(?) of good quality, 4.411:7 (cf. *dqt*).

2) Noble, worthy: *aṯt(m) adrt(m)* one / two / nn noble lady(/ ladies), 4.102:4 and *passim*.

3) The best(?): *mrḥh l adrt*[(she set) her nostrils(?) to the best ... (?), 1.92:7 (bkn ctx.; cf. Dijkstra UF 26 1994 117f. : 'largest one').

adt n. f. "lady" (< m. *adn*; Ph., Palm. *ʔdt*, DNWSI 16f.; Ebla cf. NÌ-LAK 384 = *a-da-na-du*, VE 75, and cf. Conti SQF 74: /ʔadāntu(m)/. Cf. Dressler AT 336; Dijkstra DDD[2] 6f.); syll. Ug. /ʔadatt-/ < /ʔadant-/, cf. PNN *a-da-ti-ya*, PRU 3 113 (RS 16.353):29; ÌR-*a-da-ti*, PRU 4 183 (RS 17.319):23; *a-da-ta-ya*, PRU 6 83 IV 11; *šùm-a-da-ti*, PRU 6 107:6; *um-mi-a-da-ti*$_7$, *ibid.* ln. 7; Grøndahl PTU 89f.; Sivan GAGl 195. ¶ Forms: sg. suff. *adty*, *adtny*.

Lady, in the royal titulary: *l mlkt adty* to the queen, my lady, 2.12:2; 2.24:2; 2.33:1, cf. ln. 4, 19; 2.68:1; 2.24:2; *l pʕn adty* at the feet of my lady, 2.12:7: 2.68:4; 2.24:5: 2.33:3; *qlt ʕm adty* I bow before my lady, 2.12:12 (cf. 2.68:8); *iršt adty* the request of my lady, 2.22:4; lady (and) mother: *l umy adtny* to my mother, our lady (du. suff.), 2.11:1, cf. ln. 5, 15; *l mlkt umy adty* to the queen, my mother and my lady, 2.82:2; *ʕm adty* with my lady, 2.68:15. Cf. *adnty*, 2.83:5, probl. mistake for *adtny*. Bkn ctx. 2.25:2;]*p adt*[, 7.56:3.

Cf. adty, ʕbdat, hyadt.

idt, n. f. "?" (cf. De Moor CARTU 127: 'obligation'). ¶ Forms: sg.(?) *idt*.

? : *idt*[, 1.15 III 30 (//(?) *ndr*[).

udt 4.152:3.

adty PN (Sem. Cf. Grøndahl PTU 51, 89f.; Van Soldt SAU 37); ¶ syll.: DUMU *a-da-ta-ya*, PRU 6 83 IV 11.

PN: *bn PN,* 4.13:36; 4.69 III 13; 4.344:7; 4.410:7; 4.422:3; 4.616:4; 4.769:7. Cf. in bkn ctx. 4.494:4.

idṯn PN (Hurr. Cf. Grøndahl PTU 251, 423); ¶ syll.: cf. *i-di-še-ni*, PRU 6 73:9 (cf. Huehnergard UVST 231 n. 91).

PN: 4.129:6; 4.277:12; 4.296:11; 4.649:5. In bkn ctx.: 4.21:2; 4.118:7.

ady PN (Sem. Cf. Grøndahl PTU 51, 89); ¶ syll.: cf. *a-du-ú*, PRU 6 85:7'; (DUMU.MEŠ) *a-da-a-a*, RSOu 7 40:20 and *passim ibid.*; *ad-di-ya*, RSOu 7 3:rev. 9', 11'. Cf. *adʕ(y)*, *ʕdy*.

PN: ★a) 4.63 I 41; 4.65:5; 4.93 I 6; ★b) *bn PN*: 4.93 I 3; 4.124:10; 4.225:13; 4.412 II 31; 4.753:17.

idy adv. of time "already" (cf. *id* + /y/; cf. Dietrich - Loretz - Sanmartín UF 6 1974 21; Caquot TOu 2 63 n. 163; diff.: Van Zijl

JNSL 2 1972 74f.: 'waterflood', Hb. *ʔēd*, Job 36:27; De Moor UF 11 1979 650: 'to fulfil', Arab. *ʔadā*). ¶ Forms: *idy*.

Already: *idy alt l aḥš idy alt in ly* already I do not feel the curse, already the curse does not affect me!, 1.82:2.

aḏdd TN (Belmonte RGTC 12/2 3: **ʔaḏdādu*. Cf. Astour RSP 2 255ff.; Pardee AfO 36/37 1989/90 482; Huehnergard UVST 225 n. 73, 231 n. 94); ¶ syll.: URU *áš-da-di*, PRU 6 156:3.

TN: *kkr aḏdd* talent of TN, 4.709:2 (cf. *kkr (I)*). Cf. *aḏddy*.

aḏddn PN (< *aḏdd*, TN. Cf. Grøndahl PTU 27, 422).

PN: 4.214 IV 7.

aḏddy (I) GN m. (< *aḏdd*, TN). ¶ Forms: sg. *aḏddy*; pl. *aḏddym*.

GN: 4.96:3; 4.635:16 and *passim ibid*; 4.721:3.

aḏddy (II) PN (< *aḏddy*, GN m. Cf. Grøndahl PTU 422; cf. Van Soldt SAU 18f.).

PN: 4.352:9.

aḏdt PN (etym. unc. Cf. Grøndahl PTU 26, 422).

PN: *bn PN*, 4.106:8.

aḏmln PN (Hurr. Cf. Grøndahl PTU 221).

PN: 4.417:12. Cf. bkn ctx. 4.83:1.

aḏmny PN (Hurr. Cf. Grøndahl PTU 221, 241).

PN: 4.15:2.

aḏmṯn PN (Hurr. Cf. Grøndahl PTU 212, 221, 251).

PN: *bn PN*, 4.70:4.

uḏn PN (etym. unc.); ¶ syll.: cf. *ú-za-nu*, PRU 3 196 (RS 15.42+) II 23'. Cf. *ʕzn*.

PN: *bn PN*, 4.90:9. Cf. *uḏn*, 1.149:1 (Hurr. ctx.).

uḏr (I) n. m. "express messenger, courier" (Hurr. *izuri*, GLH 130; cf. KAR = *la-sà-mu* = *i-zu-ri* = *ma-al-sà-mu*, Ug 5 137 II 18'; Laroche Ug 5 p. 461 31; GLH 130; Dietrich - Loretz - Sanmartín UF 6 1974 459; Cunchillos TOu 2 323f.; diff.: De Moor UF 17 1985 219: 'promised tribute', < */n-ḏ/d-r/). ¶ Forms: sg. suff. *uḏrh*.

Express messenger, courier: PN *uḏrh* is his messenger, 2.30:15. Cf. unc. rdg in 2.33:20 (cf. Dijkstra UF 19 1987 44 n. 33: *uḏ[n*(?)]; KTU: *uḏr*).

Cf. uḏr (II)

uḏr (II) PN (etym. unc. Cf. *uḏr (I)*). Cf. *i/uḏrn(n)*.

PN: *bn PN*, 4.769:18.

i/uḏrn(n) PN (etym. unc. Cf. Dietrich - Loretz - Sanmartín UF 6 1974 21, 459; Lipiński OLP 12 95f.); ¶ syll.: cf. *ú-šur-na-na*, RS 23.79 III 5'; *u-zu-ur-na-na*, RS 25.132 I 12'; cf. Van Soldt SAU 315 n. 120. Cf. var. *uḏrnn* in 3.9:19. Cf. *uḏr (II)*.

PN: *bn PN*, 3.9:19; 4.64 V 8; 4.86:13; 4.428:8.

igʕ,]*ʕlk igʕ ʕ*[, 7.163:6.

agb/pṯr PN (Hurro-Akk. Cf. Grøndahl PTU 205f., 215, 249, 318; Dietrich - Loretz Ug 6 pp.173f.; Ug 7 147; MU 9; Dietrich - Loretz - Sanmartín UF 6 1974 19; Xella TRU 185; Pardee AfO 36/37 1989/90 392; Van Soldt SAU 199f.); ¶ syll.: *a-gap*-LUGAL, PRU 3 202 (RS 16.257+) III 44 (cf. *a-k*[*a*]*p*(?)-LUGAL, *ibid.* II 36); PRU 6 86 I 9. Var. *agpṯr* in 1.141:1; 4.286:7.

PN: ★a) 1.141:1; 4.96:4; 4.278:2; 4.286:7; 4.374:4; 4.631:10; 4.644:7; 4.696:9; ★b) *bn PN*: 4.714:2; 6.62:1.

agd(y)n PN (Hurr. Cf. Grøndahl PTU 215, 262; Kienast UF 11 1979 450; Van Soldt SAU 40); ¶ syll.: cf. *ak-te-na*, Syria 15 1934 138 (RS [Varia 3]):19.

PN: ★a) 4.631:15; ★b) *bn PN*: 3.4:3.

ag/kd/ṯṯb PN (Hurr. Cf. Grøndahl PTU 205, 207, 210, 212, 215f., 264; Dietrich - Loretz OLZ 62 1967 535, 551; Van Soldt SAU 345); ¶ syll.: *a-ki*-[d]U/IM, PRU 3 p. 238; PRU 6 52:3, 11; *a-kid*-[d]IM, PRU 4 49 (RS 17.340):3; cf. Huehnergard AkkUg 401.

PN: ★a) *agdṯb*, 4.307:8, *ag*]*dṯb* 4.35 I 2; *akdṯb* 22; *agṯṯb*, 4.320:3; 4.632:2; ★b) *bn agdṯb*, 4.658:12; *bn akdṯb*, 4.713:1.

/ʔ-g-g/ vb G: general meaning “to moan, mutter” ((?); cf. Akk. *agāgu*, AHw 14; CAD A/1 139f.; cf. Hb. *hgh*, *hgyg*, HALOT 237, 238; De Moor - Spronk UF 16 1984 249); ¶ par.: /y-t-n/ *(+ ql)*. ¶ Forms: G prefc. *tiggn*.

G. To moan(?): *k abnm l tiggn* like stones that do not moan(?), 1.82:43 (*// l ttn <ql>*).

aglby PN (Hurr. Cf. Grøndahl PTU 205, 216, 245); ¶ syll.: cf. *a-ga-li-bi*, Ug 5 53:10.

PN: *bn PN*, 4.69 VI 3; 4.313:8; 4.344:13.

agmn PN (etym. unc. Cf. *agm*, TN. Cf. Grøndahl PTU 91, 215, 241); ¶ syll.: cf. *ag-mi-ni*, Ug 512:43.

PN: *bn PN*, 4.12:5; 4.93 IV 4; 4.313:8; 4.327:2; 4.783:3.

agm(y) TN (Belmonte RGTC 12/2 4: *ʔAgimu*. Cf. Astour UF 11 1979 17; Heltzer RCAU 8; Bordreuil UF 20 1988 15); ¶ syll.: URU *a-gi-mu*, cf. PRU 3 p. 265; PRU 6 131:10; Ug 5 102:16'; RSOu 7 4:29 (cf. Huehnergard UVST 218).

TN: *agm*, 1.91:31; 4.68:49; 4.365:28; 4.610 (II) 3; 4.686:2; RSOu 14 35 [KTU 388] I 31; *agmy*, 4.355:2, 11. For the rdg *]gmy* in 4.355:2 (KTU: *a]gmy*) see Belmonte AuOr 17/18 1999/2000 21; Belmonte RGTC 12/2 229 ('variante fonética de *Qmy*').

agmy PN (< GN < *agm(y)*, TN; cf. Grøndahl PTU 26, 91; Schneider APNÄQNR 226; Van Soldt SAU 26).

PN: 4.98:3; 4.183 II 16; 4.690:12.

agmz PN (Hurr. Cf. Grøndahl PTU 215, 241).

PN: ★a) 4.350:10; ★b) *bn PN:* 4.335:5.

ʔgn, 6.70:1; cf. agn.

agn n. m. "cauldron, earthenware bowl" (cf. Akk. *agannu*, AHw 41; CAD A/1 142f.; Hb., Aram., Ph. *ʔgn*, HALOT 11; DNWSI 9f.; Kaufman AIA 33; cf. EA *2 a-ga-nu ša* NA$_4$, EAT 14 III 65; cf. Eg. *íkn*, WäS 1 140; Hitt. *aganni-*, Laroche RA 47 1953 40; HW(2) 52f.; Tischler HEG 10; Puhvel HED 24. Cf. Greenstein JANES 8 1976 54; Dietrich - Loretz KA 235; Hoch SWET 36; Muchiki Loanwords 63; diff.: Pope EUT 80, UF 11 1979 701-705; Foley UF 19 1987 72: 'fire', // *išt*; Segert - Zgusta ArOr 21 1953 274f.: Arab. *ʔağğa*, Lat. *ignis*, Sans. *agni*; Xella MSS 67: 'braciere'; Du Mesnil NE 89, 93: 'tour' < **gnn*; Cunchillos AD 52: 'estanque'; cf. in general Trujillo UR 149ff.; Renfroe AULS 78); ¶ syll. Ug.: cf. TN URU *a-ga-na*, PRU 6 102:10; URU *a-ga-na-a*, AnOr 48 1971 29 (RS [Varia 11 = "1957.3"]):3 (cf. Belmonte RGTC 12/2 4). ¶ Forms: sg. *agn*. Cf. *ʔgn* in 6.70:1.

Cauldron, earthenware bowl: *w ʕl agn šbʕdm* and seven times over the cauldron, 1.23:15; *mšʕltm l riš agn* two consecrated women(?) on top of the cauldron, *ibid.* ln. 31, 36 (Del Olmo IMC 143-146). Cf. *ʔgn z pʕl PN* earthenware bowl which PN made, 6.70:1 (Dietrich - Loretz KA 234f.).

agny GN m. (Cf. Heltzer RCAU 8; Van Soldt UF 28 1996 657; Belmonte RGTC 12/2 4); ¶ syll.: cf. URU *a-ga-na*, PRU 6 102:10; URU *a*$^{!?}$*-ga-na*, PRU 6 102:2′; URU *a-ga-na-a*, AnOr 48 1971 29 (RS [Varia 11 = "1957.3"]):3. ¶ Forms: sg. *agny*.

GN: 4.379:9.

agpṯ(n) PN (Hurr. Cf. Grøndahl PTU 215, 251f.); ¶ syll.: cf. *a-gab-šu*, PRU 6 99:16.

PN: ★a) *agpṯn*, 4.97:4; 4.631:2; ★b) *bn agpṯ*: 4.382:25.

agpṯr cf. *agb/pṯr*.

agr PN (Sem.(?). Cf. Watson AuOr 8 1990 114).

PN: ★ a) 4.243:33; ★ b) *bn PN*, 4.753:22.

ugr (I) n. m. "field, soil" (Akk. *ugāru* AHw 1402f.); ¶ RS Akk.: A+GÀR, A.ŠÀ.A.GÀR.MEŠ, Huehnergard AkkUg 441; ¶ par.: *ʕpr*. ¶ Forms: sg. suff. *ugrm* (encl. *-m*).

Soil: *kry (...) ʕẓm yd ugrm* dig (...) (your) forearm in the soil, 1.12 I 25 (// *ʕpr*; diff.: Schloen JNES 52 1993 216: 'hireling', < /ʔ-g-r/).

ugr (II) DN; one of the two messenger-boys of Baal, *gpn w ugr* (cf. Pope WbMyth 284f.; Albright BASOR 83 1941 41 n. 19; Ginsberg BASOR 95 1944 25ff.; Segert - Zgusta ArOr 21 1953 272; Cassuto Anath 131; Fensham OrAn 5 1966 162f.; De Moor SP 53; Loewenstamm EI 14 1978 1 n. 1; Haas - Thiel UF 11 1979 339f.; Stolz Fs. Kraus 357f.).

DN *gpn w ugr*: 1.3 III 36; 1.4 VII 54; VIII 47; 1.5 I 12; 1.8:7.

ugr (III) PN (cf. *ugr (II)*, DN; cf. Van Soldt SAU 33); ¶ syll.: cf. DUMU *ug-ru-na*, PRU 3 48 (RS 16.248):10 (cf. Sivan GAGl 201; cf. Huehnergard AkkUg 367); DUMU *ú-ga/ga$_5$-a[r*, Ug 5 51:8 and *passim ibid.*

PN: *bn PN*, 4.52:8; 4.54:11. Cf. unc. rdg 4.244:17(?).

agršn PN (Hurro-Sem.(?). Cf. Watson AuOr 8 1990 114).

PN: *bn PN*, 4.760:2.

agrt n. f. "mistress" (< "she who hires"; act. ptc. f. sg. G of /ʔ-g-r/; cf. Akk. *agāru*, AHw 16; CAD A/1 146; Hb., Aram. *ʔgr*, HALOT 11, DNWSI 10f.; Arab. *ağara*, Lane 23. Cf. Kaufman AIA 33; Dijkstra - De Moor UF 7 1975 212; diff.: Yamashita RSP 2 43f.: 'hired woman'). ¶ Forms: sg. suff. *agrtn*.

Mistress: *agrtn bat b ḏdk* our mistress entered your caves, 1.19 IV 51.

Cf. agr, agršn.

ugrt TN; the city of Ugarit (Belmonte RGTC 12/2 305ff.: *Ugarit*. Cf. Van Soldt BiOr 46 1989 648: /ʔugarit-/; UF 28 1996 657; cf. Sivan GAGl 201: /ʔUgarītu/; Ebla: cf. *u$_9$-ga-ra-at^{ki}*, MEE 3 56:5; cf. Pettinato MEE 3 p. 229; Or 47 1978 55; Liverani SDB IX 1296; Van

Soldt BiOr 40 1983 693; Steinkeller VO 6 1986 37; Archi RA 82 1987 185f.; Astour WGE 144f.; OB/Mari Akk.: *ú-ga-ri-it/tim*^{ki}, Groneberg RGTC 3 245; cf. esp. ARMT 23 p. 594; ARMT 25 p. 247; Villard UF 18 1986 387ff.; Alalakh Akk.(VII/IV): *ú-ga-ri-it*, cf. AT p. 157; Wiseman JCS 8 1954 27; Klengel OLZ 57 1962 454; txt. Hitt./Bo. Akk.: *ú-ga-ri-it(=)*, Del Monte - Tischler RGTC 6 451; Del Monte RGTC 6/2 177; Eg. (RN) *ʔá-kú-ri-tá* (*y-k3-ry-ṯy*) and var.(?) *ʔ(a)-kú-*ta_2 (*y-k3-ṯt*), Edel ZDPV 69 1953 149; Helck Bez. 158 and *passim* (esp. 542, 559, 571; cf. Liverani SDB IX 1298; Giveon UgRetr 55f.); ¶ RS Akk.: URU.KI, *passim* (cf. *qrt*); ¶ syll.: KUR(.URU)/URU *u/ú-ga/*ga_5*-ri-it/ta/ti/te*$^{(ki)}$, cf. PRU 3 p. 267; PRU 4 p. 256; PRU 6 p. 147; Ug 5 p. 337; RSOu 7 p. 138; cf. var. URU *ugar*(A.GÀR)*-ít*(ÍD), PRU 3 126 (RS 16.162):23 (cf. URU *u-ga-ri-it*, *ibid.* ln. 3); KUR *ú-ga-rít*(RAD), PRU 4 105 (RS 18.03):30; Ug 5 23:3; 44:1, 7; 55:6; RSOu 7 7:2; 14:2; 30:6; 35:7; cf. KUR *ú-ga<-ri>-it*, RSOu 7 18:2, 8; cf. Huehnergard UVST 217, 251.

TN: *passim*. Cf. *ily ugrt* (*il (I)*); *bʕl ugrt* (*bʕl (II)*); *bn ugrt* (*bn (I)*); *bt ugrt* (*bt (I)*); *ḥmyt ugrt* (*ḥmt (I)*); *mlk ugrt* (*mlk (I)*); *mlkt ugrt*; *šr ugrt*. Bkn: *u*(!)*grt* 1.119:10.

ugrtn PN (< *ugrt*, TN).

PN: *bn PN*, 4.715:26.

ugrty GN m. (< *ugrt*, TN; Van Soldt SAU 33); ¶ syll.: cf. *PN* URU *u-ga-ar-ti(-ya)*, PRU 6 79:15f.; Huehnergard UVST 239; Van Soldt SAU 336. ¶ Forms: sg. *ugrty*, *ugrtym*.

GN: 2.81:27-28; 4.33:8-9; 4.750:3. In Hurr. ctx.: *ugrtw*, 1.125:7.

ugry PN (Cf. Grøndahl PTU 51, 91).

PN: 4.63:45.

agtṯp PN; cf. *ag/kd/ṯṯb*.

agy(n) PN (Hurr. Cf. Grøndahl PTU 215f.; Van Soldt SAU 34); ¶ syll.: cf. *a-ga-ia*, PRU 6 50:21; *a-gu-ya*, Ug 5 5:28; *a-gi-ia-na*, PRU 3 37 (RS 15.81):1.

PN: ★a) *agyn*, 4.75 IV 9; 4.80:22; 4.379:9 (*agny*); 4.609:36; 4.631:8; *agy*, 4.753:1; 4.761:3 (*bn* [); ★b) *bn PN*: 4.37:2; 4.50:16; 4.70:2,5; 4.123:10; 4.313:25; 4.761:3.

igy PN (Hurr.(?); cf. Grøndahl PTU 224; Watson AuOr 11 1993 214).

PN: ★a) 4.344:17; ★b) *bn PN*, 4.410:9 (cf. Van Soldt SAU 37).

agy(n)t PN (Hurr. Cf. Grøndahl PTU 215f., 262; Pardee AfO 36/37

1989/90 392; Van Soldt SAU 33); ¶ syll.: cf. *ak-ia-an-ti*, PRU 3 49 (RS 16.263):11.

PN: ★a) *agyt*, 4.55:12; ★b) *bn agynt*: 4.33:35.

agytn PN (Hurr. Cf. Grøndahl PTU 215, 262).

PN: *bn PN*, 3.2:6.

agzr cf. agzrt, agzry.

agzrt adj. f. "anxious, longing, eager" (?) (< m. **agzr*., var. of the ʔqtl(?) pattern of *agzry*; cf. De Moor NYCI 2 21 n. 84; Del Olmo UF 13 1981 60; diff.: Sanmartín UF 5 1973 269: 'Stück', **gzr*). ¶ Forms: sg. f. *agzrt* (mistake: *azrt*, 1.13:30).

Anxious(?): *agzrt ʕnt (...) a<g>zrt ʕnt wld* anxious(?) did DN become (...) anxious(?) (was) DN to give birth / for the son, 1.13:29-30.

Cf. agzry.

agzry adj. m. "ravenous, glutton" (probl. augmented denom. form (pattern: ʔqtly) of **gzr*, cf. Hb. *gzr*, HALOT 187. Cf. Albright BASOR 71 1938 37 n. 13; Gaster Thespis[1] 426, 432; De Moor NYCI 2 20 n. 84; Pope UF 11 1979 717; diff.: Montgomery JAOS 54 1934 63; Dahood Bib 56 1975 264; Gray JNES 8 1949 74: 'cruel', 'terrible', said of *ʕṯtr*, Hb. *ʔkzry*, Pr 17:11 and Is 13:9, Akk. *ezēzu*, Ug. *ʕrẓ*, Largement NA 38: 'insulaire', Arab. *ğazīrat* (cf. Gaster SMSR 10 1934 159 n. 1); Dietrich - Loretz UF 9 1977 53: 'Abbild', rdg *agzr ym*, **gzr*, Hb. *gzrh* and Akk. *karāṣu*; Virolleaud Syria 14 1933 143; Du Mesnil NE 94, 99, 106, 109; Caquot - Sznycer TOu 1 359; Watson UF 9 1977 280f.; Lipiński OLP 3 1974 117: 'qui fendent la mer', rdg *agzr ym*, **gzr* (diff.: Gray LC 98 n. 72: 'who delimit the day'). ¶ Forms: pl. *agzrym*.

Ravenous: *agzrym bn ym* the ravenous ones though only one day (old), 1.23:58, 61.

Cf. agzrt.

agzw PN (etym. unc. Cf. Grøndahl PTU 255).

PN: *bn PN*, 4.7:8.

a/iġl n. m. "emancipated (slave)" ((?); Hurro-Akk. *eḫ̮elena*, Laroche GLH 75; Giacumakis 72. Cf. Sanmartín SEL 5 1988 175; < Hurr. *eḫ̮(e)li*, cf. Alal. Akk. *šūzubu*(KAR), Laroche GLH 75f.; Dietrich - Loretz WO 5 1969/70 92; AHw 1295: *šūzubu*). ¶ Forms: pl. suff. *a/i*(?)*ġlhm*.

Emancipated (slave)(?): to the king have been sent [*a/i*]*ġlhm w iblblhm* his emancipated (slaves)(?) and his bearers(?), 2.62:11.

aġld PN (Hurr.); ¶ syll.: cf. *aḫ-la-ti*, PRU 3 204 (RS 16.257+) edge I 1, 4; II 6.

PN: *bn PN*, 4.71 IV 4. Cf. *gt PN*, 4.382:32 (Belmonte RGTC 12/2 82: **Gittu-Aġladi*).

aġlḏrm PN (Hurr.).

PN: 4.276:13.

aġl[, 4.506:1; 4.649:6.

aġli PN (Hurr. Cf. Grøndahl PTU 214; Dietrich - Loretz OLZ 62 1967 546; WO 4 1967/68 302, 304); ¶ syll.: DUMU *a-ḫa-la-e*, PRU 6 70:10.

PN: *bn PN*, 4.204:8; 4.260:7; 4.769:40.

a/iġlkḏ/z PN (Hurr. Cf. Grøndahl PTU 204f., 214f., 238; Dietrich - Loretz WO 4 1967/68 302; OLZ 62 1967 546; Van Soldt SAU 126). Cf. var. *ġlkz*.

PN: *aġlkz*, 4.103:52; *iglkḏ*, 4.607:23; 4.769:50.

aġlmn PN (Hurr. Cf. Grøndahl PTU 214, 241; Dietrich - Loretz OLZ 62 1967 546; WO 4 1967/68 302); ¶ syll.: [*e*]*ḫ-li-m*[*e*?]*-ni*, PRU 6 138:9; *a-ḫal-me-ni*, Ug 5 86:24. Cf. var. *ġlmn*.

PN: ★a) 4.296:12; 4.370:5, 17; ★b) *bn PN*: 4.290:5.

aġltn PN (Hurr. Cf. Grøndahl PTU 214f., 262; Dietrich - Loretz OLZ 62 1967 546; WO 1967/68 302; Van Soldt SAU 151); ¶ syll.: *a-ḫal-te-nu* and var., cf. PRU 3 p. 238; PRU 6 p. 137; Ug 5 4:8' (cf. Huehnergard UVST 240 n. 120); *eḫ-li-*[d]IM, PRU 6 45:34.

PN: ★a) 4.33:4 (*mid*[*ḫy*); 4.115:1; 4.285:12; 4.295:7 (]*y*); 4.307:9; 4.313:20; 4.320:8; 4.370:39; 4.417:17 (*ypry*); 4.753:7; bkn ctx.: 4.122:23; 4.643:16; 4.659:3; RSOu 14 39 [KTU 4.790]:21'; ★b) *bn PN*, 4.69 VI 13.

a/i]ġlṯr PN (Hurr. Cf. Grøndahl PTU 214f., 249f.).

PN: *a/iġ*]*lṯr*, 4.428:5.

a/iġlyn PN (Hurr. Cf. Grøndahl PTU 214; Dietrich - Loretz OLZ 62 1967 546; UF 9 1977 341; Watson AuOr 13 1995 218); ¶ syll.: cf. *a-ḫal-i*[*a-na*, PRU 3 162 (RS 16.286):8; *a-ḫal-ia-nu*, RS 22.399+:10 (Van Soldt SAU 441). Cf. var. *ġlyn*.

PN: ★a) 4.159:7; 4.631:17 (*bn kzbn*); 4.696:7; ★b) *bn PN* 4.63 III 19.

iġr (?; rdg unc.), 2.33:13.

uġr TN, residence of the goddess Anat (<(?) Arab. *ġār*, Lane 2307f.;

Hb. *mʕrh*, HALOT 615f.; cf. Rin AE 101); ¶ par.: *inbb*. TN: *an šnt uġr l rḥq ilm* I must leave TN for the farthest god, 1.3 IV 34 (// *inbb*).

aġt TN (Belmonte RGTC 12/2 5: *ʔAġatu* / *Aḫatu*. Cf. Heltzer RCAU 9; Xella MLE 1 1982 53ff.; Bordreuil UF 20 1988 13, 15; Pardee AfO 36/37 1989/90 483; Van Soldt UF 28 1996 659); ¶ syll.: URU *a-ḫa-tu*, cf. PRU 6 p. 146 (cf. Huehnergard UVST 241).

TN: 4.49:5; 4.68:14; 4.244:16; 4.382:19; 4.553:5; 4.610 II 40; 4.686:11 (Xella MLE 1 1982 53ff.); RSOu 14 35 [KTU 9.388] II 3; 40:9. Cf. 1.112:25 (diff. rdg Del Olmo CR 246).

aġty PN (unc.; cf. *aḫty*).

PN: 4.748:10 (*ʕmṯdy*); cf. *ʕmṯdy*.

aġyn PN; cf. *a/iḫyn*.

iġyn PN; cf. *a/iḫyn*.

aġzr(?) n. "?" (poss. title of nobility or courtier; ʔqtl <(?) */ġ-z-r/; diff.: Caquot Ug 7 p. 132: PN; Pardee AfO 29/30 1983/84 326; Cunchillos TOu 2 418 n. 219: PN or vb /ġ-z-r/). ¶ Forms: sg.(?) m.(?) *aġzr*[.

? : in bkn ctx.: *w rgmt l aġzr*[and did you/ she say to the *a*., 2.73:13.

Cf. ġzr.

aġzt n. f. "wedding, betrothal" (< Hurr.(?) < Akk. *aḫuzzatu*, AHw 23; CAD A/1 217; cf. De Moor ULe 92 n. 1.; ARTU 142 n. 7: 'protection-marriage'. Less likely < Arab. *ġazza* / *ġazā*, VIII: *ʔiġtizāz* / *iġtizā*, Kazimirski DAF 2 463, Lane 2257; cf. Del Olmo MLC 516; diff.: Herrmann YN 3: 'Herbst', season of raiding parties, Arab. *ġazā*); ¶ par.: *qẓ*. ¶ Forms: sg. *aġzt*.

Wedding, betrothal: DN *mlk aġzt* king of the wedding(-season), 1.24:3 (// *qẓ*).

/ʔ-h-b/ vb G: "to love" (Hb., Aram. *ʔhb*, HALOT 17f.; DNWSI 20; Ebla cf. /ʔ-(ʔ)-b/, Krebernik PET 35). ¶ Forms: G. prefc. *yuhb* (/yiʔhab/(?)); Sivan UF 21 1989 362; cf. diff.: Tropper UF 22 1990 367: /yôhVb/ < /yaʔhVb/); suffc. cf. *ihbt*(?).

G. To love: *yuhb ʕglt b <arṣ> dbr* he loved a heifer in the <Land of> Pestilence, 1.5 V 18. In bkn ctx.: *l ihbt* have you not / if(?) you have loved(?), 2.31:49 (cf. *ahbt*); *yu*[*h*]*b mn*[, 1.92:31-32.

Cf. ahbt.

ahbt n. f. "love" (< /ʔ-h-b/; Hb. *ʔhbh*, HALOT 18); ¶ par.: *dd*, *yd*. ¶ Forms: sg. cstr. *ahbt*; cf. *ihbt*, 2.31:48, G suffc. of /ʔ-h-b/ or var. of *ahbt*.

Love: *ahbt ṯr tʕrrk* perhaps the love of the Bull has moved you?, 1.4 IV 39 (// *yd*); *ahbt ṯly* the love of DN, 1.3 III 7; cf. 1.7:23; 1.101:18 (// *dd*; cf. Dietrich - Loretz UF 17 1985 143f.).

Cf. /ʔ-h-b/.

ihbt, in bkn ctx.: *l ihbt yb*[*x*] *rgmy* 2.31:49 (G suffc. of /ʔ-h-b/ or var. of *ahbt*; cf. ahbt).

ahl n. m. "tent, mansion" (Amor. /ʔahlum/, Gelb CAAA 13, 37; Ebla cstr. *a-ʔà-al*$_6$, suff. *a-ʔà-al*$_6$*-zu*, Krebernik QuSe 18 100; cf. *a-lu*, Krebernik PET 72; Hb. *ʔhl*, HALOT 19; cf. Arab. *ʔahl*, Lane 121; ESA *ʔhl*, CAME 101; DOSA 7; Akk. *ālu*, AHw 39; CAD A/1 375ff.; NA *aʔlu*, AHw 39; CAD A/1 374; Eg. *íhr / ʔa-hi-l*, WäS 1 119; Helck 508(11); diff. Sanmartín WZKM 86 1996 391ff.: 'Stadt'); ¶ syll. Ug.: cf. URU *ya*(PI)*-na-a-lum*, PRU 3 125 (RS 15.147) rev. 6' (cf. Gelb CAAA 37); ¶ par.: *ḏd*, *minš*, *mškn*,. ¶ Forms: sg. suff. *ahlh*; pl. *ahlm* (cf. the spelling *b* <*a*>*hlm*, 1.19 IV 52); suff. *ahlhm*.

Tent, mansion: *tity ilm l ahlhm* the gods went to their tents, 1.15 III 18 (// *mšknthm*); cf. *ahlh*, 1.17 V 32; *mġyt pġt l ahlm* DN reached the tents, 1.19 IV 50 (// *minš šdm*; cf. Delekat UF 4 1972 12); cf. *bat b* <*a*>*hlm* she entered the tents, *ibid.* ln. 52 (// *ḏdk*; diff.: Pope UF 19 1987 223: *bat b hlm* 'has come here'); *št ḥršm l ahlm* casting spells from the tents, *ibid.* ln. 60.

ahn, 1.17 V 5, cf. *aphn*.

iht n. f. pl.(?) "islands, coastal region" (Hb., Pun. *ʔy*, HALOT 38; DNWSI 43; cf. Eg. *íw*, WäS 1 47. Cf. Sanmartín UF 10 1978 352 n. 26; Dietrich - Loretz UF 22 1990 70ff.); ¶ par.: *gbl*, *qʕl*. ¶ Forms: pl. cstr. *iht*.

Islands, coastal region: *iht np šmm* the islands / regions of the heavenly heights, 1.3 VI 8 (// *gbl*, *qʕl*).

aḥd adj. num. 1) "one, only one, oneself"; 2) used as a noun "only one, solitary, single"; 3) adverbial use "in unison" (Hb. *ʔḥd*, HALOT 29f.; Pun. *ʔḥd*, NPun., Aram. *ḥd*, DNWSI 32ff.; Akk. *(w)ēdu*, AHw 1494f.; CAD E 36ff.; Arab. *ʔaḥad*, Lane 27; ESA *ʔḥd*, DOSA 10; Eth. *ʔaḥadu*, CDG 12) also Akk. *edēnu* CAD E 27; syll. Ug. [AŠ = *it-te-tù* = Hurr. (?) = *a*]*-ḫa-du*, Ug 5 138:1' (cf. AŠ = *e-de*$_4$*-nu* [, Ug 5 135 obv. 17'); Borger RA 63 1969 172; Huehnergard UVST 105; Van Soldt SAU 302; ¶ par.: *almnt*, *ʕwr*, *trḫ (+ ḥdṯ)*, *zbl*. ¶ Forms: m. sg. *aḥd*; suff. *aḥdy*; f. *aḥt*; du. *aḥdm*; cf. allomorph *yḥd* (1.14 II 43).

1) Number one: ★a) elliptical syntagms: *aḥt l DN*, 1.48:15ff.; *TN aḥd*, 4.380:28-31; 4.303:3; RSOu 14 36 [KTU 9.417]:3, 4, 5, 7, 8, 9, 10,

11, 13, 14, 16; *PN aḥd*, 4.129:2-13; 4.775:10,17; 4.169:6; 4.190:1ff.; *aḥd ʕl TN* one to TN's account, 2.26:15; *štn PN aḥd ly* may PN deliver one to me, 5.10:9; *aḥd b bnk / aḫk* one of your sons / brothers, 1.6 I 46; 1.6 V 19/22; in list of professions, 4.752:3, 7, 8; 4.141 III 3; team of oxen (*ṣmd*), 4.618:23ff.; ★b) genitive syntagms: *aḥd ḫbṯ* one free (labourer) 4.360:8; *aḥd nġr krm* a single guardian of the vineyard, 4.141 III 17; *aḥd adr* one granary, 4.195:5; ★c) appositional syntagms: *krm aḥd* one vineyard, 4.244:5; *aṯt aḥt* one woman, 4.102:10; *pġt aḥt* one girl 4.102: 7 and *passim*; *ġzr aḥd* one lad 4.102:19ff.; *ṣbr aḥd* one *ṣ.*, 4.375:3ff.; *bnš aḥd* one labourer, 4.420:5; *bt aḥt* one daughter, 4.360:5; *ptḥ aḥd* one door, 4.195:9; *unṯ aḥd lh*[PN(N) has(have) a loan pending, 4.86:4; *bt aḥd b TN* one house in TN, 4.750:9; cf. *bt b TN aḥd*, *ibid.* ln. 8 (cf. *yḥd*, *ibid.* ln. 5-7); same: *ym aḥd* (on) the same day, 1.115:14 (diff.: De Tarragon TOu 2 202 n. 180: 'premier jour'); *š aḥd* one sheep, 4.751:3; *ysr aḥd* one potter, 4.367:8; *krk aḥt* one pickaxe, 4.625:6; *ḥmr w izml aḥt* load and *i.*: one 5.3:6; *alp aḥd* one bull, 4.295:6; 4.296:11; cf. 4.231:7, 8; *aḥdm* (du.) two separate items (not a pair): 4.532:1-6; 4.89:4; 4.302:2ff.; 4.384:2, 3 in bkn ctx. (cf. *ṣmd*; Del Olmo UF 11 1979 181; diff. Gordon Or 67 1998 284); *trm aḥdm* two poles, 4.167:3; in bkn ctx.: *aḥdm*, 4.208:1, 5-7; *aḥdm* two separate (horses), 4.384:5; *l bš aḥd* one garment, 4.146:1; 4.156:3, 4; *dprn aḥd* one juniper (tree), 4.158:20; *lmd aḥd* one apprentice, 4.138:4, 5, 7; 4.154:6; *šrt aḥt* one *š.*, 4.410:6; ★d) composite numbers: [ʕ]*šrm aḥd* twenty-one, RSOu 14 39 [KTU 4.790]:10'; *tšʕm mrḥ aḥd kbd* ninety-one lances, 4.169:9; *ʕšrm l mit aḥd* one hundred and twenty-one, 4.775:2; ★e) special uses: *pat aḥt* one side, frontal border (south eastern side?) of an estate: *tšʕ ṣmdm ṯlṯm bd PN w pat aḥt in bhm* thirty-nine yokes in the hands of PN which lack one side (border to the south east?), 4.136:4 (cf. Hb. *pʔt ngb(h)* // *pʔt hʔḥt*, Ex 27:9; cf. *pat*).

2) Only one, solitary, single (used as a noun adj.): *aḥdy* I am the only one, 1.4 VII 49; *aḥd bth ysgr* the single (man) closed his house, 1.14 IV 21 (// *almnt*, *zbl*, *ʕwr*, *trḫ ḥdṯ*; cf. 1.14 II 43: *yḥd*).

3) In unison, as one man (adverbialized): in unison *aḥd* will the gods answer, 1.2 I 25 (cf. *ank*, *ibid.* ln. 28; Sanmartín UF 9 1977 262; diff.: Del Olmo MLC 171: 'veo', **ḥdy*; Dahood UF 11 1979 143: 'community', // *yḥd*; survey in Wyatt RTU 60 n. 109).

In bkn ctx. 4.5:1ff.; 4.73:5; 4.78:2; 4.205:9; 4.249:3; 4.239:2f.; 4.294:2; 4.542:2; 4.765:3, 25.

Cf. **aḥdh, yḥd**.

aḥdh adv. "together, at the same time" (< *aḥd*; cf. Hb. *yḥdw*, HALOT 405f.; Aram. *kḥdh*, DNWSI 33: *ʔḥd₄*; Ebla cf. /waḥadma/ *wa-ad-ma*, Fronzaroli MisEb 2 12f.; for the morphology cf. Akk. *ištēniš* [< *ištēn*], AHw 400; CAD I/J 275ff.). ¶ Forms: *aḥdh*.

Together, at the same time: grind (/d-k(-k)/) ingredients *aḥdh* together, 1.71:10 and par.; pour them out (/n-s-k/) together *aḥdh*, 1.71:25 and par.; *št aḥdh dm zt ḫrpnt* apply / drink at the same time the juice of early olives, 1.114:31; *ṣin aḥdh* the flock (all) together, 1.49:5.

aḥl interj. "if only!" (in the syntagm *aḥl an*; cf. Hb. *ʔḥly*, HALOT 38; NA *aḫūla*, *aḫūlamma* 'alas! woe!', CAD A/1, 213. Cf. Cassuto BOS 2 196f.; Dijkstra - De Moor UF 7 1975 204; Ashley EAR 167; diff. Sanmartín UF 9 1977 266 n. 34: 'wehe!'; Margalit UF 16 1984 140f.: 'I pray!', **ḥly*; Ajjan NU 388: 'verdir', Arab. *ʔaḥala*). ¶ Forms: *aḥl*.

If only!: *aḥl an bṣql ynpʕ (...) tispk yd aqht* if only, everywhere, oh shoot that sprouts (...), the hand of PN would gather you!, 1.19 II 15, 22.

Cf. an (I).

iḫmlk PN; cf. *a/iḫmlk*.

aḥrtp PN; cf. *a/iḫršp*.

aḥẓx[*whn aḥẓx[*, 1.6 V 23.

aḫ (I) n. m. 1) "brother (by blood)"; 2) "lover; companion, colleague, equal"; 3) "friend" (Hb., Ph., Pun., Aram. *ʔḥ*, HALOT 29; DNWSI 28ff.; Akk. *aḫu*, AHw 21; CAD A/1 195ff.; Ebla /ʔaḫum/ in ŠEŠ.MU = *a-ḫu-um*, VE 1043; Krebernik ZA 73 1983 37; Fronzaroli EL 135; StEb 7 1984 148; cf. *a-ḫu* and var. in Ebla PNN, Krebernik PET 72; Müller Biling. 170f.; Fales EDA 424; *ba-na-aḫ*, Müller Biling. 173; Sanmartín AuOr 9 1991 171f.; Amor. /ʔaḫum/, Huffmon APNMT 160f.; Buccellati Amorites 206; Gelb CAAA 13, 37f.; Arab. *ʔaḫ*, Lane 33; ESA *ʔḫ*, DOSA 12f.; Eth. *ʔĕḫĕw*, *ʔĕḫʷ*, CDG 13f.); ¶ syll. Ug.: cf. the element *a-ḫu-*, *a-ḫi-*, *a-ḫa-* in PNN; Grøndahl PTU 91f.; Sivan GAGl 196; cf. PNN *e-ḫé-ya-nu*, PRU 3 192 (RS 12.34):28; *i-ḫi-ma-nu*, PRU 3 137 (RS 15.190):4; *i-ḫi-ya-nu/na*, PRU 3 54 (RS 15.90):5, 10; Ug 5 5:25; ¶ RS Akk.: ŠEŠ(.MEŠ), *passim*; ŠEŠ DÙG.GA, PRU 6 15:3; 18:2, 17; ŠEŠ DAM, PRU 6 15:10; cf. Š]EŠ = *a-ḫu* = *še-e-n*[*i*, Ug 5 135 rev. 19'; [*a-n*]*a*(?) *a*(?)-*ḫ*[*i-š*]*u*(?, PRU 4 136 (RS 16.270):35; cf. PRU 3 232; PRU 4 259; Ug 5 340; ¶ par.: *ary (I)*, *atṯ*, *ʕl (III) (+ umt)*, *bn (I) (+ um)*, *yly*. ¶ Forms: sg. *aḫ*; suff. *aḫy*, *aḫk*, *aḫh*; pl. *aḫm*; suff. *aḫy*, *aḫym* (encl. *-m*; cf. UT 128; Dahood UHP 50), *aḫk*,*aḫh*, *aḫyh* (*mater lectionis*(?)); du. *aḫm* (cf. 1.22 I 5-10); graphic variants

(< allophones by vowel harmony): sg. suff. *iḫy*, *uḫy*, *iḫh*(?), *uḫh*, *iḫk*; pl. suff. *iḫh*.

1) Blood brother: PN *aḫ* PN, 4.103:5; *PN w PN aḫh w PN aḫh w PN+ bnh w PN bth w PN aṯth* PN and PN, his brother, and PN, his brother, and PN, his son, and PN, his daughter, and PN, his wife, 3.4:4-5; wine of PN and wine *d iḫh* of his brother(s), 4.123:23; *hlm aḫh tph (...) aḫh tbky* as soon as she saw brother (... upon the face of) her brother she wept, 1.16 I 53, 55; *tqrb aḫ* she approached her brother, 1.16 II 17; *imḫṣ mḫṣ aḫy* I am going to kill the one who killed my brother, 1.19 IV 34 and par. (// *ʕl umty*); *aḫym ytnt bʕl spuy* my brothers you made into my food, DN, 1.6 VI 14 and par. (// *bnm umy*); *šbʕ aḫm lh* she had seven brothers, 1.14 I 9 (// *bn um*); *ṯṯm ṯkm bm ṯkm aḫm* there, shoulder to shoulder, were the (two) brothers, 1.22 I 5 (cf. ln. 8-11); *tn aḫy* give me my brother!, 1.6 II 12; *iḫhyṯ ʕr mšrrm* her brothers arranged the pointer(?),1.24:35 (// *aḫt{ṯ}h*).

2) In a figurative sense, ★a) lover, in the Baal-Anat relationship: *qm aḫk* the adversaries of your lover, 1.10 II 25; ★b) neighbour, companion colleague, equal: *tp aḫh w nʕm aḫh* the beauty of its neighbour and the grace of its neighbour, 1.96:2; *at aḫ w an aḫtk* you are (my) companion and I, your companion, 1.18 I 24 (cf. Dressler AT 340ff.; UF 11 1979 211-217; Xella AuOr 2 1984 151-153); *in bn lh km aḫh* he has no son like his equals, 1.17 I 19 (// *aryh*); *yld bn ly km aḫy* a son will be born to me like my equals, 1.17 II 15 (// *aryy*); *bl iṯ bn lh k*(!)*m aḫh* may he have a son like his equals!, 1.17 I 20 (// *aryh*); *lbš km lpš dm aḫh* he put on like a cloak the blood of his equals, 1.12 II 46 (// *aryh*); *šbʕt l šbʕm aḫh ym*[his seventy-seven companions he [killed, 1.12 II 48; *šr aḫyh* the prince of his equals, 1.12 II 50 (// *ylyh*); *ṣḥ aḫh b bhth* he invited his colleagues into the palace, 1.4 VI 44 (// *aryh*); *ṣḥn bʕl ʕm aḫy (...) w lḥmm ʕm aḫy lḥm* invite me, DN, together with my ompanions (...) to eat food with my companions, 1.5 I 23-25 (// *aryy*); *ytn bt lk km aḫk* he will grant you a house like your equals, 1.4 V 28 (// *aryk*); *tn aḥd b aḫk* give me one of your companions, 1.6 V 20 and par. In bkn ctx.: *aḫh tbky*, 1.16 I 55; 1.4 VIII 38, 39; 1.16 II 11.

3) 'Brother' > 'friend' (formal usage in correspondence between equals): to the king of TN *aḫy* my brother, message of the king of TN *aḫk* your brother, 2.38:2-3; *w aḫy mhk b lbh al yšt* and may my brother not worry, *ibid.* ln. 26; *l mlk TN iḫy* to the king of TN, my brother, 2.44:3; *l aḫy l rʕy* to my brother and friend, 5.9 I 8, cf. ln. 10; to PN *bn*(!)*y aḫy* my son and brother, 2.14:3; *w ht/m yšal aḫy ṯryl* and

so, let my brother, my son, ask PN, 2.14:10, 15; cf. *l aḫk l adnk* to your brother and lord, *ibid.* ln. 18; *w ht yšmʕ uḫy l gy* now, my brother, listen to my voice, 2.4:18; *w ank aštn l iḫy* and I shall reply to my brother, 2.41:18; *w uḫy yʕmsn ṯmn* and my brother will compensate me there, *ibid.* ln. 20; *w [u/i]ḫy l ybʕrn* and may my brother not fail me, *ibid.* ln. 22. In bkn ctx.: *hlny aḫy*, 2.67:4.

Cf. iġyn, aḫrṭp, aḫdbn, a/iḫġl, a/iḫmlk, a/iḫmn, uḫn, a/iḫn(y), a/iḫqm, aḫrm, aḫršn, a/iḫršp, aḫt (I), aḫt (II), a/iḫy, a/iḫyn, awaḫ, ay(a/i)ḫ, gdaḫ.

aḫ (II) n. m. "shore" (?) (cf. Eg. *íyḥ, íḥy*, WäS 1 39, 122; Akk. *aḫu*, AHw 21f.; CAD A/1 205ff.; Hb. *ʔḥw*, HALOT 30f.; Rainey UF 3 1971 169; Muchiki Loanwords 250f.: 'meadow', Eg. *3ḫ(.y)*). ¶ Forms: sg. *aḫ*.

Shore(?): *aḫ šmk* the shore(?) of TN, 1.10 II 9, 12 (on its identification as the region of Lake Huleh, Aram. *ymʔ / ʔgmʔ d smk*, Gk *Semakhonitis*, cf. Virolleaud Syria 17 1936 156f.; Dussaud Syria 17 1936 283-295; Gray LC 81f.).

iḫ cf. *aḫ (I)*.

/ʔ-ḫ-d(/ḏ)/ vb G: 1) "to collect, to take (back), grasp, seize, hold"; 2) "to occupy space, cover"; 3) "to requisition, recruit, conquer, capture"; 4) "to take to (: take refuge in)"; 5) "to affect"; 6) "to start, begin to, undertake (inchoative meanings)"; N: "to be able, contain" (Hb. *ʔḥz*, HALOT 31f.; Aram. *ʔḥd/z*, DNWSI 35ff.; cf. Ebla Gt inf. /ʔaḫḫuḏum/ in RU = *a-ḫu-sum*, VE 1289'; Š inf. /šaʔḫuḏum/ in DIM = *sa-ḫu-sum*, EV 056; act. n. /tuštāḫiḏum/ in DILI.RU = *du-uš-da-ḫi-sum*, EV 055; Kienast Biling. 251; cf. Fronzaroli EL 135, 140, 149; Krebernik QuSe 18 135; Amor. /ʔ-ḫ-ḏ/, Gelb CAAA 14; Akk. *aḫāzu*, AHw 18ff.; CAD A/1 173ff.; ESA *ʔḫd*, DOSA 10ff.; Arab. *ʔaḫaḏa*, Lane 28ff.; Eth. *ʔaḫaza*, CDG 14); ¶ par.: /m-ḫ-ṣ/, /ṣ-m-t/, /ṣ-q/, /š-t/. ¶ Forms: G suffc. *aḫd, aḫḏ, aḫdt, aḫt*; prefc. *yaḫd, yiḫd, yuḫd, tiḫd, tuḫd, iḫd*; suff. *aḫdhm, iḫdn, tiḫdn, yuḫdm*; impv. *uḫd*; ptc. *uḫd*.

G. 1) To collect, to take (back), grasp, seize, hold: *iḫd hn[d]* I shall collect this, 2.33:21; oxen of PN *dt aḫd ḥrṯh* which his herdsman has collected, 4.296:8 (cf. ln. 15, 17); cf. ox(en) *d aḫd b TN* which (they) have gathered in TN, *ibid.* ln. 11, 13, 14, 16; *qšthn aḫd b ydh* his bow he took in his hand, 1.10 II 6; *aḫdt plkh* she took her spindle, 1.4 II 3; *ks yiḫd il b yd* a cup did DN take in (his) hand, 1.15 II 16, cf. 1.17 I 34; *tiḫd knrh b ydh* she took the lyre in her hand, 1.101:16 (// *št*); *yiḫd bʕl bn aṯrt* DN seized the sons of DN, 1.6 V 1; *aḫḏ aklm* the

'Voracious Ones' seized (him), 1.12 II 35 (// *ṣmt*); *bṯnm uḫd bʕlm* grasp the serpents, oh DN!, 1.82:6; *tiḫd bn ilm mt* she seized divine DN, 1.6 II 30; *tiḫd mt b sin lpš* she held DN by the hem of the cloak, 1.6 II 9 (// *qṣ*); *yiḫd b qrb (...) tiḫd b ušk* he grasped her vulva (...,) she grasped his penis, 1.11:1-2; [*m*]*rḥh yiḫd b yd* his lance grasped in (his) hand, 1.16 I 47, in bkn ctx. 1.92:12 (cf. *mrḥ (II)*); *šmalh tuḫd ʕṯtrt* his left (hand) DN grasped, 1.2 II 40; *al aḫdhm b y*[certainly I shall seize them with my rig[ht (hand), 1.3 V 22; *p ʕbd ank aḫd ulṯ* am I perhaps a slave who grasps the trowel? 1.4 IV 60; *tiḫd šnth* her teeth held (him), 1.19 I 9 (// *št*; diff.: Dijkstra - De Moor UF 7 1975 198: 'are affected', N prefc.); cf. *p (III)*; *lm aḫt* why did you take?, RSOu 14 51 [KTU 9.425]:4; *d aḫt d*[which you took..., *ibid.* ln. 23 (cf. *tiḫdn*, ln. 7).

Idiomatic use, ★a) (+ *yd*): 'to help' *aḫd ydh b škrn* may he take (him) by the hand in his intoxication, 1.17 I 30 / II 5, 19; ★b) (+ *akl* "grain"): 'fattening (horses)': *k yiḫd akl śśw* if the horse tends to be bloated with barley, 1.72:16, 21; 1.97: 2; cf. *k aḫd akl* if it has been bloated with barley, 1.85:12, 15 (Sanmartín AuOr 6 1988 233); fifteen bowls (...) *d yaḫd l PN* which are collected from PN, 4.44:28 (cf. Verreet UF 15 1983 233f.; Tropper UF 22 1990 367).

2) To cover: *alp šd aḫd bt* one thousand yokes of land will the palace cover, 1.4 V 56.

3) To requisition, recruit, conquer, capture: *l šmn iṯrhw p iḫdn PN* concerning the oil: follow it and I, PN, shall requisition it, 2.15:7 (cf. De Moor JNES 24 1965 359f.; Dietrich - Loretz - Sanmartín UF 6 1974 472; Sanmartín UF 9 1977 260; diff.: Verreet UF 15 1983 230; Dietrich - Loretz UF 16 1984 354 n. 25; Watts UF 21 1989 446 n. 25: *ḫdy* 'to be glad, rejoice'; for *-hw* cf. Tropper UG 54); cf. *aḫnnn w iḫd* I shall denature (cf. *ḫnn*) it (: the oil) and proceed to requisition it, *ibid.* ln. 10; *l yiḫd PN b unṯ* PN is not recruited for service, 2.19:1; *ṯṯ l ṯṯm aḫd ʕr* sixty six cities he conquered, 1.4 VII 9; *mlkn yiḫd ḥwt ibh* our king will conquer the land of his enemies, 1.103:7, cf. 1.163:7; *hm qrt tuḫd* if the city is captured, 1.127:29 (cf. Verreet UF 17 1985 327); *ṯnn ʕz yuḫd ib mlk* the powerful vizier will seize the enemy of the king, 1.103:17; *ḫrd ʕps aḫd kw sʕt* the border guard(?) has confiscated one *k.* of *s.*-(grain), 2.47:17.

4) To take to (: take refuge in): *ib bʕl tiḫd yʕrm* the enemies of DN took to the woods, 1.4 VII 35; *km aḫt ʕrš mdw* for you have taken to the bed of sickness, 1.16 VI 35, 51 (cf. Rainey IOS 3 1973 54 nn. 98f.; Dietrich - Loretz UF 9 1977 48; Renfroe UF 22 1990 280 n. 4;

diff.: Del Olmo MLC 322: 'como tu hermana es la cama de la dolencia', cf. *aḫt (I)*).

5) To affect: *ʕn bʕl aḫd*[[(fear(?)] affected the eyes of DN, 1.12 II 31; cf. 32-33.

6) To start, begin to, undertake (inchoative meanings): *tiḫd d iṯ b kbdk* undertake what you have in your mind, 1.18 I 17-18 (// *št*); *qdš yuḫdm šbʕr* DN began to illuminate, 1.4 IV 16 (cf. Cassuto BOS 2 186f.; Sanmartín UF 3 1971 178 n. 29; diff.: Watson UF 10 1978 399: 'to kindle'; cf. also AuOr 10 1992 227 n. 31). In bkn ctx.: *ʕṣ amr yuḫ*[*d*, 1.22 II 17; also 1.75:4; 4.306:7; 2.33:16; 1.18 I 9; RSOu 14 51 [KTU 9.425]:4, 7, 23.

Cf. aḫdy, aḫt (II), m(a/i)ḫdy, miḫd.

uḫd adj. m. "(re)captured" (< /ʔ-ḫ-d/ḏ/). ¶ Forms: sg. *uḫd*.

Captured: PN *uḫd* (re)captured, 4.635:4, 5, 9 (Dietrich - Loretz - Sanmartín UF 5 1973 85).

aḫdbn PN (Sem. Cf. Ribichini - Xella RSF 15 1987 9; cf. diff.: Huehnergard JAOS 107 1987 723).

PN: 4.90:6.

aḫdy PN (Sem. Cf. Grøndahl PTU 93).

PN: *bn PN*, 4.281:21.

a/iḫġl PN (Sem.-Hurr.(?); cf. Grøndahl PTU 92, 141; Dietrich - Loretz UF 9 1977 341; Watson AuOr 8 1990 114).

PN: *iḫġl*, 4.130:4; *aḫġl*, 4.297:5 (*ṯlrby*).

uḫl PN (etym. unc.).

PN: *bn PN*, 4.723:11.

a/iḫmlk PN (Sem. Cf. Grøndahl PTU 17, 91, 158; Benz PNPPI 264); ¶ syll.: *a-ḫi*-LUGAL, ŠEŠ.LUGAL, cf. PRU 3 p. 238; RSOu 7 25:2. Var. *iḫmlk* in 4.339:22.

PN: ★a) 4.261:15 (*bn nskn*); 4.339:22; 4.609:33; 4.727:7, 9; ★b) *bn PN*: bkn ctx. 4.711:7.

a/iḫmn PN (Sem. Cf. Grøndahl PTU 422; Sivan GAGl 20; Bordreuil SEL 5 25; Watson AuOr 11 1993 214; Muchiki Loanwords 14); ¶ syll.: *a/i-ḫi-ma-nu* and var. cf. PRU 3 p. 238; ŠEŠ-*mu-nu*, PRU 3 202 (RS 16.257+) III 54; ŠEŠ-*ma-nu*, Ug 5 12:43. Var. *aḫmn* in 4.31:10; *iḫmn* in 4.282:4.

PN: *(a)ḫmn* 4.31:10; 4.282:4; 4.296:6.

a/i/ḫn(y) PN (Sem. Cf. Aistleitner UGU 27; Grøndahl PTU 17, 91f.,

166; Stamm AS 16 1965 414, 422); ¶ syll.: *a-ḫu-nu*, PRU 6 72:14. Var. *iḫn(y)* in 4.65:13; 4.317:8. Cf. *uḫn*.

PN: 4.65:13; 4.103:55; 4.317:8; 4.356:6; cf. *aḫn*, *ibid.* ln. 11-12.

uḫn PN (Sem. Cf. Grøndahl PTU 92, 163). Cf. *a/iḫn(y)*.

PN: ★a) 4.244:13; 4.619:4; ★b) *bn PN:* 4.39:7; 4.393:10.

uḫnp TN (Belmonte RGTC 12/2 319: *ʔUḫnappu*. Cf. Heltzer RCAU 15; Astour UF 13 1981 7; Bordreuil Syria 61 1984 2, 7; UF 20 1988 10, 17; Van Soldt UF 27 1996 657f.; UF 30 1998 723, 727); ¶ syll.: URU *uḫ-na/nap-pí*, cf. PRU 3 p. 265; RSOu 7 4:33; Huehnergard AkkUg 394.

TN: 1.91:34; 4.27:2; 4.348:5; 4.355:14; 4.380:32; 4.414:5; 4.610 II 7; 4.629:4; 4.661:3; 4.693:22; 4.777:7; RSOu 14 35 [KTU 9.388] I 20.

Cf. Bordreuil UF 20 1988 10 for the rdg *u*[*ḫnp*], 4.73:6.

uḫnpy GN m. (< *uḫnp*; Belmonte RGTC 12/2 319). ¶ Forms: sg. *uḫnpy*. - GN: 4.658:10; cf. 4.629:4 (?).

a/iḫqm PN (Sem. Cf. Grøndahl PTU 17, 37, 40, 63, 91f., 178; Stamm AS 16 1965 417, 419; Pardee AfO 36/37 1989/90 392). Var. *iḫqm* in 2.4:22.

PN: 2.4:21; 4.86:23 (*birt*[*y*]); 4.297:1 (*uškny*).

/ʔ-ḫ-r/ vb generic meaning G: "to go behind" > D: "to retain"(?); Š: "to delay"(?) (cf. Hb., JAram. *ʔḥr*, HALOT 34f.; DJPA 47; Ebla cf. *aḫ-ra*, Krebernik PET 75; EA Akk. *aḫāru*, cf. CAD A/1 170 and cf. AHw 18; ESA *ʔḫr*, DOSA 13; Arab. *ʔḫr*, Lane 31). ¶ Forms: D ptc. *maḫr*, Š prefc. *yšiḫr*, suff. *tšiḫrhm*.

D. To retain(?): in bkn ctx., *maḫr*[which retains[(?), 1.166:7.

Š. To delay(?): in bkn ctx., *al tšiḫrhm* do not delay them(?), 2.79:4; cf. *yšiḫr* he will delay(?), 2.42:11 (cf. Pardee UF 19 1987 205).

Cf. aḫr, uḫry (I), uḫry (II), uḫryt.

aḫr adv., prep., conj. 1) "afterwards, then"; 2) "with"; 3) "after, when" (< /ʔ-ḫ-r/; cf. Aartun PU 1 13f.; Hb., Pun., Aram. *ʔḥr*, HALOT 35; DNWSI 38ff.; Akk. cf. *a-ḫa-ar-ru*-[, YOS 2 52:7 and cf. GAG 118e, AHw 18, CAD A/1 170; cf. EA Akk. EGIR-*šu* : *aḫ-ru-un-ú*, EAT 245:10 and Hb. *ʔḥrwn*, HALOT 35); ¶ par.: *ʕmn*. ¶ Forms: *aḫr*, *aḫrm* (encl. *-m*).

1) Afterwards, then (adv.): *aḫr al trgm l aḫtk* then you shall certainly say to your sister, 1.16 I 31 (diff.: De Moor ARTU 213, CARTU 124:

'backwards', 'come back!');]*ṯlṯ*{.}*id ynphy yrḫ b yrḫ aḫrm* [ ] three times the moon is cf.n(?) in the month(?), then [, 1.163:5.

2) With (prep.): *aḫr nkl yrḫ ytrḫ* DN gets married with DN, 1.24:32 (// *ʕmn*; UT 355; Dahood UL 84; Bib 51 1970 392; Del Olmo Claretianum 10 1970 341f.; for other solutions cf. Del Olmo MLC 460); *aḫr špšm* with the sun (at sunrise; cf. *infra:* 3: when), 1.14 IV 46 and par. (Dahood; diff.: Badre *et al.* Syria 53 1976 115; Dietrich - Loretz UF 22 1990 77 'am Abend', but cf. *hn špšm*, 1.14 III 14; *mk špšm*, 1.14 III 3; V 6).

3) After, when (conj.): *aḫr mġy / mġyt* when he / she had arrived, 1.4 III 23; cf. 1.4 V 44; 1.15 II 11; *aḫr ymġy* when he had arrived, 1.17 V 25; cf. 1.2 I 30. In bkn ctx. 1.15 V 5.

aḫrm PN (Sem. Cf. Grøndahl PTU 44, 46, 91, 182); ¶ syll.: *a-ḫi-ra-mu*, PRU 6 79:14.

PN: 4.617:30; 4.734:10, 11.

aḫršn PN (Sem.(?); cf. *ḫršn*).

PN: 4.760:2 (*b*[*n*).

a/iḫršp PN (Sem. Cf. Grøndahl PTU 20, 23, 91, 181; Astour CRRA 18 1972 22; Van Soldt SAU 20); ¶ syll.: ŠEŠ.dMAŠ.MAŠ, PRU 6 51 rev. 4'. Allograph: *aḥrṯp* in 4.277:5.

PN: ★a) 4.277:5; 4.370:7; ★b) *bn PN*, 3.9:18.

uḫry adj. m. 1) "last, final" (temporal sense); 2) used as a noun > "posterity, offspring, descendants" (< /ʔ-ḫ-r/; cf. Akk. *aḫrû*, AHw 21; CAD A/1 194; cf. Ph. *ʔḥry*, DNWSI 41; OAram. *ʔḥr*, DNWSI 38; Hb. *ʔḥr*, HALOT 34; Ebla cf. *a-ḫé-rí*, Fronzaroli ARET 11 138. Cf. Dietrich - Loretz - Sanmartín UF 7 1975 138; Del Olmo IMC 142 n. 326ff.); ¶ syll. Ug.: cf. /ʔuḫrāyu/ in É : *ḫi-ri-ti ù* A.ŠÀ.MEŠ *ša uḫ-ra-a-yi*, PRU 3 52f. (RS 15.85):18 'lands (destined for the burial of) posterity'; cf. diff.: Sivan GAGl 201; Huehnergard UVST 106: *uḫryt*. ¶ Forms: sg. abs. *uḫry*; f. sg. *uḫryt*, cf. *uḫryt*.

1) Last: *ʕdb uḫry mṯ ydh* (may) his stick be placed the last, 1.19 III 56 and par. (diff.: Ullendorff JSS 7 1962 344: 'thereupon'; Dijkstra - De Moor UF 7 1975 209: 'tip', cf. Hb. *ʔḥry hḥnyt*, for other interpretations cf. Del Olmo IMC 142 nn. 326-329)).

2) Used as a noun > posterity, offspring, descendants: *uḫry ykly ršp* DN will destroy the descendants (of the king), 1.103+:39-40. (cf. Del Olmo CR 356 n. 76; cf. Dietrich - Loretz MU 133f.; cf. *uḫryt*). In bkn ctx.: 1.12 II 27.

uḫryt adj. f. "final", used as a noun > "destiny, final destiny" (< *uḫry*; Hb. *ʔḥryt*, HALOT 36f.; Akk. *aḫrâtu*, CAD A/1 194f.; Ebla cf. /aḫirtum/ in *a-ḫé-tum*, *a-ḫir-tum*, Fronzaroli SEL 12 1995 63); ¶ par.: *aṯryt*. ¶ Forms: sg. abs. *uḫryt*.

Destiny, final destiny: *mt*(!) *uḫryt mh yqḥ* a man, as (his) final destiny, what can he attain?, 1.17 VI 35 (// *aṯryt*).

aḫt (I) n. f. 1) "sister (related by blood)"; 2) "lover; companion"; 3) "friend" (< *aḫ (I)*; Hb. *ʔḥwt* HALOT 31; Ebla /ʔaḫātum/ in NIN.NI = *a-ḫa-tum*, Krebernik ZA 73 1983 42; Fronzaroli EL 134; Sanmartín AuOr 9 1991 170f.; Amor. /ʔaḫātum/, Gelb CAAA 13, 38); ¶ RS Akk.: NIN, *passim*; PRU 3 232; PRU 4 259; Ug 5 340 (cf. NIN, Ug 5 55:2, and cf. Nougayrol *ibid.* n. 4); syll. cf. PN *a-ḫa-ti/tu$_4$*-LUGAL, PRU 3 53 (RS 15.89):8, 11; Grøndahl PTU 92; cf. Dietrich - Loretz UF 15 1983 303f.; cf. TN URU *a-ḫa-tu*, PRU 6 95:9; 105:6'; Sivan GAGl 196; Huehnergard UVST 105; ¶ par.: *aḫ (I)*, *anšt*, *bt (I)*, *ybnt*. ¶ Forms: sg. *aḫt*; suff. *aḫty*, *aḫtk*, *aḫth*; pl. *aḫt*; suff. *aḫt{t}h* (cf. Dietrich - Loretz - Sanmartín UF 9 1977 345).

1) Sister (related by blood): PN *w aḫth* PN and his sister, 4.658:46; PN *w aḫth b š<ʕ>rt* and his sister, (the one who is) in TN, 4.360:11 (see Van Soldt UF 28 1996 688); *ṣḥ aḫtk* call your sister, 1.16 I 28 (// *bt*); *rgm l aḫtk* say to your sister, 1.16 I 38; *aḫtt!h l abn mznm* her sisters (arranged) the stones of the balance, 1.24:36 (// *iḫh*); *aḫth šib yṣat* his sister had gone out to draw water, 1.16 I 51; *al trgm l aḫtk (...) dm aḫtk ydʕt k rḥmt* you will certainly speak to your sister (...,) since I know that your sister is compassionate, 1.16 I 31-32; *mṯbh aḫt ppšr* [in] her residence the sister of PN, 1.82:36.

2) In figurative meaning, ★a) lover, in the relationship Baal-Anat: *hlk aḫth bʕl yʕn* the coming of his sister DN saw, 1.3 IV 39 (// *ybnt abh*); *nʕmt bn aḫt bʕl* the most charming among the (female) companions of DN, 1.10 II 16; 1.10 III 10 (cf. *aḫt*, 1.10 II 20; cf. *aḫt* // *ybnt ab*, 1.3 IV 39); ★b) companion, equal: *at aḫ w an aḫtk* you are (my) companion and I am your companion, 1.18 I 24 (cf. *aḫ (I)*).

3) 'Sister' > 'friend' (formal usage in correspondence between equals): *l mlkt TN aḫty* to the queen of TN, my sister, 2.21:3; l PN *aḫty* to PN, my sister, RSOu 14 49 [KTU 9.433]:24. Cf. PN *l aḫth*, 5.10:1. Cf. 5.11:12.

Cf.: aġty, aḫ (I), aḫt (II), aḫtab, aḫtmlk, aḫty.

aḫt (II) PN (Sem. Cf. Grøndahl PTU 92; Benz PNPPI 265).

PN: *bn PN*, 4.617:33.

aḫtab PN (Sem. Cf. Grøndahl PTU 86, 92; Watson AuOr 8 1990 127).

PN: 4.147:13.

aḫtmlk PN (Sem. Cf. Grøndahl PTU 31, 55, 92, 158; Zadok BASOR 230 1978 58; Cunchillos EEU 85 n. 476; TOu 2 283 n. 5; Huehnergard UVST 105; Sivan UF 21 1989 360; Lipiński OLP 12 1981 85; Dietrich - Loretz UF 15 1983 303; Bordreuil *et al.* CRAIBL 1984 417 n. 25; Van Soldt JEOL 29 1985/86 70f.; SAU 14; Izre'el AmAk 1 20; Singer AmAk 2 181; Watson AuOr 8 1990 115); ¶ syll.: var. *a-ḫa-tu*$_4$*/ti*-LUGAL, NIN.LUGAL, NIN-*mi-i*[*l-ki*, cf. PRU 3 p. 238; PRU 4 p. 244.

PN: 2.11:4.

aḫty PN (Sem. Cf. Grøndahl PTU 51, 56, 92; Caquot Syria 46 1969 261).

PN: 4.75 VI 2 (*bt abm*).

a/iḫy PN (Sem. Cf. Grøndahl PTU 17, 21, 53, 92; cf. Benz PNPPI 263f.); ¶ syll.: cf. *a-ḫi-ia-a*, PRU 6 72:5'; bkn ctx. DUMU(?) ŠEŠ(?)-[, PRU 6 84:3. Var. *aḫy* in 4.739:9.

PN: ★a) 4.35 II 17 (*bn bʕln*); 4.170:4; 4.214 I 9; 4.739:9 (*bn adn*); ★b) *bn PN*: 4.366:7; 4.617:4. In bkn ctx. 4.427:15.

a/iḫyn PN (Sem. Cf. Grøndahl PTU 17, 21, 53, 92; Stamm AS 16 1965 414, 424); ¶ syll.: *e/i-ḫé/ḫi-ia-nu*, ŠEŠ-*ia-nu* and var., cf. PRU 3 p. 243, 245; PRU 6 p. 137; Ug 5 5:25; cf. Huehnergard UVST 263 n. 215. Var. *iġyn* in 4.69 II 16.

PN: ★a) 4.75 II 6; 4.75 IV 11 (*bn ḫyrn*); 4.86:10 (*bn nbk*[); 4.175:13; 4.204:1; 4.370:18; 4.635:41; 4.692:3; ★b) *bn PN* 4.45:5; 4.69:2:16; 4.75 III 7. In bkn ctx.: 4.114:11; 4.105:4. Cf. bkn]*aġyn*, 4.461:2.

ik interr. functor "how?, why?" (Hb. *ʔyk*, HALOT 39; Aram. *ʔyk*, DNWSI 45; De Moor SP 235; Aartun PU 1 7ff.). ¶ Forms: *ik*, *ikm* (encl. *-m*).

How?, why?: *ik mġyt rbt aṯrt ym ik atwt qnyt ilm* how is it that the Great Lady DN arrives, how is it that the progenitress of the gods comes?, 1.4 IV 31-32 and par.; *ik tmtḫṣ* how can you fight?, 1.6 VI 24 and par.; *ik tmgnn rbt aṯrt ym* how is it that the you welcome the Great Lady DN?, 1.4 III 28 and par.; *ik yṣḥn* how is it that he invited me?, 1.5 II 21; *ikm yrgm bn il krt* how can it be said that PN is the son of DN?, 1.16 I 20; *ik al yšmʕk* how, in fact, do you wish that he listens (: him to listen) to you?, 1.6 VI 26 and par.; cf. in unc. ctx. *ik al yḥdṯ yrḫ* how, of a truth, will DN be renewed?, *ik al yḥdṯ yrḫ* how will DN not renew himself? 1.18 IV 9 (cf. Dietrich - Loretz Fs. Cazelles 116). Cf. in bkn ctx. *ik mḫ[ṣt* how can you strike (...)?, 1.2 I 40; *ik ġb*[, 1.2 II 6; *ik l ilm*, 1.176:22; *w ikm kn*, 2.7:10.

Cf. ikmy, iky.

uk positive emphatic functor "yes, certainly, for certain" (Hb. *ʔk*, HALOT 45; Tigr. *ʔakē*, WTS 375; diff.: Aartun PU 2 91: *u* 'oder'). ¶ Forms: *uk*.

Yes, certainly, for certain: *ʕbdh uk škn* it is certain that your servant puts (it in his letter), 2.39:6; *b bʕly uk nġr* for certain I will take care of my lord, *ibid.* ln. 8.

akdṯb PN; cf. *ag/kd/ṯṯb*.

/ʔ-k-l/ vb G: 1) "to eat; to devour"; 2) "to consume"; 3) "to make use of, to use" (Hb., Ph., Aram. *ʔkl*, HALOT 46f.; DNWSI 51f.; Akk. *akālu*, AHw 26f.; CAD A/1 245ff.; EA Akk. inf. *a-ku-lí*, EAT 148:12; Ebla cf. G inf. /ʔakālum/ in KÚ = *a-ga-lu-um*, VE 156, EV 0191; Krebernik ZA 73 1983 6; QuSe 18 125; cf. Ì.KÚ = *a-gul-la*, VE 896; Krebernik ZA 73 1983 34; Civil Biling. 82; Hecker Biling. 209; cf. n. act. /tuštākilum/ in TEŠ.TEŠ.KU = *du-uš-da-gi-lum*, VE 164; EV 0422; Kienast Biling. 251; cf. diff.: Krebernik ZA 73 1983 6; cf. *i-gú-ul* <(?) /yiʔkul/, Krebernik QuSe 18 119; Arab. *ʔakala*, Lane 71ff.); ¶ par.: /k-l-y/, /q-r-ṣ/, /š-t-y/. ¶ Forms: G prefc. *yikl*, var. *yukl* (Tropper UF 22 1990 367: /yôkVl/), *tikl*; suff. *tikln*; inf. *ikl*; ptc. act. m. cf. *akl (I)*, f. cf. *aklt*. Cf. the spelling *yʔkl* in 4.767:2.

G. 1) To eat, devour; ★a) to eat: *bt ikl* dining room (gen. inf.: of eating), 1.22 I 24; cf. in bkn ctx. *l tikl w l tš*[*t*], you shall eat and drink(?), 1.88:3; *yikl*[, 1.12 II 13; cf. *yʔkl dw* the sick man has to eat it, 4.767:2 (Dietrich - Loretz KA 251); ★b) to devour, said of animals: *kbd k iš*<t> *tikln* our innards they devour like fire, 1.12 I 10 (// *tqrṣn*); *širh l tikl ʕṣrm* his flesh the birds will certainly devour, 1.6 II 35 (// *tkly*).

2) To consume (said of fire, + *b*): *tikl išt b bhtm* the fire continued to consume in the palace, 1.4 VI 24 and par.

3) To make use of, use: PN *yukl krm* will make use of the vineyard, 4.244:16 (cf. Akk. *kirâm ikkal*).

Cf. akl (I), akl (II), aklt (I), aklt (II).

akl (I) adj./n. m. "voracious, glutton" (< act. ptc. G /ʔ-k-l/; cf. Akk. *ākilu*, AHw 29; CAD A/1 266f.; cf. *akkilu*, CAD A/1 275; Arab. *ʔakū/īl*, *ʔākil*, Lane 72f.); ¶ par.: *ʕqq*, *ġll*, *nṯk*. ¶ Forms: sg. *akl*; pl. *aklm*.

Voracious (said of the snake): *p akl* mouth of the devourer, 1.107:35, 45 (// *nṯk*); the 'Voracious Ones, Gluttons', said of certain lesser deities: *ḫl ld aklm* writhe (and) give birth to the 'Voracious Ones', 1.12 I 26 (// *ʕqqm*); *wn ymġy aklm* and behold, he arrived next to the 'Voracious Ones', *ibid.* ln. 36 (// *ʕqqm*); *aḫḏ aklm* the 'Voracious Ones' seized (him), II 35 (// *ġllm*).

Cf. aklt (I).

akl (II) n. m. 1) "grain, fodder"; 2) "food, victuals" (< /ʔ-k-l/; Hb. *ʔkl*, HALOT 47; Akk. *ak(a)lu*, AHw 26; CAD A/1 238-245; Ebla /ʔaklu/ in NINDA.LAM = *a-ga-lu bù-da-ma-tim* "cake of terebinth nuts", NINDA.GÉME = *a-ga-lu* ᵈNISABA "bread (made) of cereal", Krebernik ZA 73 1983 2, 4; Fronzaroli EL 134; Fales QuSe 13 175; Civil Biling. 88; ESA *ʔkl*, CAME 103; DOSA 15; Arab. cf. *ʔakl*, *ʔuk(u)l*, *ʔakla*, Lane 72f.; Eth. *ʔĕkl*, CDG 15. Cf. Sanmartín UF 9 1977 263ff.); ¶ syll. Ug.: cf. 30 GÍN KÙ.BABBAR.MEŠ *a-ka-li*, PRU 6 155 6; Sanmartín AuOr 9 1991 172; ¶ par.: *ḥṭṭ*. ¶ Forms: sg. *akl*; suff. *akln*.

1) Grain, fodder (probl. 'barley'): measured in *dd*: 2.71:18; 4.284:4; 4.688:4; in accounting: *spr akl* book of accounts of grain, 4.636:1; *lḥt akl* tablet concerning grain, 2.39:17; 2.46:10; *akl ḥpr bt* grain of the temple rations, 4.688:2; *tgmr akl* total (outlay) of grain, 4.271:1 and *passim*; 4.636:2 and *passim*; *akl l qryt* grain (brought) from the cities, 1.14 II 28 and par. (// *ḥṭṭ*); *akln b grnt* our grain in the threshing floors has been set on fire, 2.61:8; cf. the syntagm *ʔḫd akl* to become bloated with barley, 1.72:16, 21 (*ak*(!)*l*); 1.85:12, 15; 1.97:2 (Sanmartín AuOr 6 1988 233; diff. Cohen - Sivan UHT 26f.; Cohen UF 28 1996 126: 'pain'); they did not give them *akl* grain (for the road), 2.70:22; *akl b ḥwtk inn* there is no grain in your land, 2.39:19; *b ṯmnt iynm akl* the eighth day, as a (sacrifice of) grief (?), (a measure of) grain, 1.112:12 (cf. Del Olmo AuOr 2 1984 202; cf. diff.: Dietrich - Loretz TUAT 2 316: '(es darf) auf keinen Fall Verzehr (stattfinden)').

2) Food, victuals: GNN *lqḥ akl* who have received victuals, 4.41:1 (cf. *šmn*, 2ff.); *alp l akl* a (head of) cattle for consumption, 6.13:3 (cf. *alp b mḥrṯt*, 6.14:3; cf. Bordreuil - Pardee Semitica 41/42 1993 24ff.); *akl b ʕ*(!)*mm tšt* they placed the food in the entrails(?), 1.19 I 9 (diff.: Cooper UF 20 1988 21: 'butcher-knife', Hb. *mʔklt*); *akly* [*bn nšm*] *akly hmʕ*[*t arṣ*] my food is the people, my food is the multitude[s of the land], 1.6 V 24-25. Bkn ctx.: 1.107:54; 2.1:7; 2.39:30; 2.46:15.

akl (III) n. m. "swallowing" 1.6 V 24-25: cf. *infra /k-l-y/*.

ikl n. m. "act of eating, meal, banquet" (noun < inf. /ʔ-k-l/; diff. Healey UF 10 1978 91 n. 21: 'mourning house', Akk. *ikkillu*). ¶ Forms: sg. *ikl*.

Act of eating, meal, banquet: *bt ikl* dining room (inf. gen.: of eating), 1.22 I 24.

aklt (I) adj./n. f. "devouring" (< m. *akl (I)*). ¶ Forms: sg. *aklt*.

Devouring (said of Anat): *aklt ʕgl ỉ(!)l* devouring the divine bullock, 1.108:9 (De Moor UF 1 1969 178; cf. diff.: rdg *⊕l*, KTU p. 125).

aklt (II) n. f. "waste land, stubble" (probl. pass. ptc. f. G /ʔ-k-l/; Sanmartín UF 9 1977 265f.; cf. Renfroe UF 18 1986 68f.; cf. also Akk. *kullatu* "clay, mud (pit)", AHw 1569; CAD K 506); ¶ par.: *ḥmdrt*. ¶ Forms: sg. *aklt*.

Waste land, stubble: *šblt tpʕ b aklt* shoot that sprouts in the stubble, 1.19 II 23 (// *ḥmdrt*); *ysb aklth* he went through his stubble, 1.19 II 19; cf. *ibid.* ln. 20: *ak<l>t*.

ikmy conj. "since" (*i* + *km* + *y* or *ik* + *my*; see Bordreuil - Caquot Syria 57 1980 360; cf Pardee AfO 31 1984 223: 'however that may be'; diff. Lipiński OLP 12 115 n. 174: Akk. *ayyikāma*). ¶ Forms: *ikmy*.

Since: *ikmy ḥy PN* since PN is alive, 2.82:17.

ikrn PN (etym. unc. Cf. Gelb - Purves - MacRae NPN 219; Grøndahl PTU 94).

PN: 4.84:6; 4.289:6.

aktmy PN (Anat.(?); cf. Grøndahl PTU 270); ¶ syll.: cf. *a-kut-mi-ni*, PRU 6 50:22.

PN: *bn PN*, 4.63 IV 10.

aktn PN (Hurr. Cf. Grøndahl PTU 216, 261; Watson AuOr 8 1990 115); ¶ syll.: *a-kut-te-nu*, PRU 6 50:3,9, cf. *ibid.* ln. 22; cf. *ak-te-na*, Syria 15 1934 138 (RS [Varia 3]):19.

PN: *bn PN*, 4.357:14.

akṯn "?", 1.107:48 (bkn ctx.; cf. Dietrich - Loretz - Sanmartín UF 7 1975 129: *kṯy* 'stark zunehmen', Akk. *kašû*; Pardee TPM 255: *nkṯ* 'rompre, détruire', Hb., Arab.).

aky PN (Hurr. Cf. Grøndahl PTU 216; Masson Cyprominoica 47; Dietrich - Loretz KA 209; cf. Dahood Fs. Cazelles AOAT 212 82 n. 10; Eg.: Muchiki Loanwords 66); ¶ syll.: cf. *ak-ku-ia*, RSOu 7 5:15; *a-ki-ia-nu*, RS 22.002 rev. 8' (Van Soldt UF 21 1989 372).

PN: ★a) 6.68:1 (*bn ypṯḥd*); ★b) *bn PN*: 4.170:13.

iky interr. functor "what of?, what about?, how?, why?" (*ik* + emph. *-y*; Aartun PU 1 7f.; Parker SGUPT 101ff.; Hoftijzer UF 3 1971 360; Tropper UF 26 1994 476f.; diff.: Cunchillos UF 12 1980 148f.; TOu 2 293f. n. 6: advers. part. 'pour ma part', Hb. *ʔak* / Akk. *ak(k)i* / Ug. *i* + *k* + *y*); ¶ RS Akk.: *am-mi-ni(-i)* and other variants, EAT 45:15, 23; 46:7; cf. PRU 4 41 (RS 17.227 and dupl.):9 // KTU 3.1:8; cf. Huehnergard AkkUg 194; Van Soldt SAU 408. ¶ Forms: *iky*.

What of?, what about?, how?, why?: *iky lḥt spr d likt ʕm PN* what about the letter that I sent to PN?, 2.14:6; why did you write to me saying: *iky aškn ʕṣm l bt DN* how shall I allocate the beams for the temple of DN?, 2.26:5; *iky* [, 3.1:8 (cf. *am-mi-ni(-i) (...)*, PRU 4 41 (RS 17.227 and dupl.):9; Knoppers BASOR 289 1993 84. In unc. ctx.: *iky l ilak* how am I not going to send?, 2.21:11.

uky "?"; in bkn ctx. 2.23:5.

akyn PN (Hurr. Cf. Grøndahl PTU 216); ¶ syll.: *a-ki-ia-nu*, RS 22.002 obv. 8' (Van Soldt UF 21 1989 372).

PN: *akyn*, 4.658:5.

Cf. aky.

al (I) neg. functor "no; not" (in volitive statements; Hb., Ph., Aram. *ʔl*, HALOT 48; DNWSI 55; ESA *ʔl*, DOSA 16; cf. Eth. *ʔal-*, CDG 17; Akk. *ul* < *ula*, AHw 1406f. Cf. Brockelmann GvG 1 499f.; UT 13.35f.; BGUL 65.21f.; Aartun PU 1 20ff.; Verreet UF 18 1986 372f.); ¶ RS Akk.: cf. *ul*, *ú-ul*, cf. Huehnergard AkkUg 239f.; Van Soldt SAU 510ff. ¶ Forms: *al*.

1) No, not + prefc. 2 p., in prohibitions: *ttn tn w l ttn w al ttn* you give, give, do not give, may you give, 5.9 14 (scribal exercise); *at umy al tdḥl w ap mhkm b lbk al tšt* you, my mother, do not be afraid and also do not worry, 2.30:21-23; *al tud* to not overcharge, 2.26:19; *ḥẓk al tšʕl* do not shoot your arrows, 1.14 III 12; *al tšt urbt* do not put (in) a skylight, 1.4 V 64 and par.; *al tqrb* do not approach, 1.4 VIII 15; *al tšrgn* do not delude me, 1.17 VI 34; *al tšmḫ* do not rejoice, 1.3 V 20-21 and par.; *al tṣr udm* do not besiege TN, 1.14 III 29 and par.; *bn al tbkn al tdm ly al tkl bn qr ʕnk* my son, do not weep for me, do not wail for me, do not drain, my son, the source of your eyes, 1.16 I 25-27; *bu al tbi* do not enter at all, 1.169:18; *(...) al tmk // al tʕlg (...) // al tapq apq* (...) do not be cast down // do not stammer (...) // do not make yourself scarce, 1.169:11-12 (cf. Loretz - Xella MLE 1 1982 38; cf. diff.: Dietrich - Loretz TUAT 2 335, interr. with a neg.

meaning, cf. *al (II)*); *al tdḫln* do not fear, 2.16:12; cf. in bkn ctx. *ibid.* ln. 19: *al ttbb riš.* In bkn ctx., in bkn ctx. *al td*[*d*(?) let her not disappear(?),1.4 VI 10; *al tṣu* do not(?) go out/they are not(?) to go out, 1.164:19; *špḥ al thbṭ* do not wipe out the family, 2.47:16; *al tšiḫrhm* do not(?) delay them, 2.79:4; cf. *al (II).*

2) not, + prefc. 3 p., in prohibitive statements: *al ydd mt mrzḥ* a member of the *m.* is not to start (saying), 3.9:12; *uḫy al ybʕrn* my brother, do not fail me, 2.41:22; *aḫy mhk b lbh al yšt* my brother, do not worry, 2.38:27 and par.; *al yʕdbkm k imr b ph* he is not to put you like a lamb in his mouth, 1.4 VIII 17; *šršk b arṣ al ypʕ* your root in the earth is not to establish itself, 1.19 III 53; *b*]*šrk al ttn ln*[*ġr*] do not waste [the ...] of your [fl]esh against the guard[ian], 1.92:34-35 (cf. Dijkstra UF 26 1994 118); *al ybʕr b ydh* may he not set fire to (the house) with his hand, RSOu 14 50 [KTU 9.434] 22 (or 'destroy': Bordreuil - Pardee RSOu 14 p. 378). In bkn ctx.: *al tġl*[, 1.3 I 1; *al yns*[, 1.4 III 5; *al ašt b*[, 1.5 III 11; *al ḫtl*[, 1.176:26; *al ytbʕ*[, 2.18:3; *al tšt*[, 2.31:14; 2.31:61; 4.62:2.

Cf. **l (I)**, **bl (I)**.

al (II) pos. functor "surely, yes" (in volitive statements; for etym. and morph. cf. *al (I)*; probl. elliptical syntagm or suprasegmental idiom: rhetorical question. Cf. De Moor SP 128f.; Aartun PU 1 31; Renfroe AULS 78). ¶ **Forms**: *al.*

1) Yes, + prefc. 1 p., cohortative statements: *dll al ilak* assuredly, I will send a messenger, 1.4 VII 45; *al aḫdhm* certainly I shall seize them, 1.3 V 22.

2) (Yes) do + prefc. 2/3 p., precative statements: *ik al yšmʕk* how, then, will he listen to you?, 1.6 VI 26; *al tšt b šdm mmh* may she pour out, yes, in the fields her waters 1.16 I 34; *al yḥdṯ yrḫ* renew himself, yes, may DN, 1.18 IV 9; *al trgm l aḫtk* tell, yes, your sister, 1.16 I 31; *pnm al ttn ʕm (...)* and thus, you will set face for (...), 1.2 I 14 and par.; cf. *al ttn pnm*, 1.4 VIII 1 and par.; *al tpl (...) al tštḥwy pḫr mʕd* fall down, yes, (...), prostrate yourselves, yes, before the plenary assembly, 1.2 I 15; *al tdy ʕz tġrn* do repel the strong one from our gate, 1.119: 28.

Cf. **bl** (II), **l** (II).

al (III) n. m. "ram (of superior quality)" (< */ʔ-l/; cf. Akk. *ālu*, Ahw 39; CAD A/1 374f.; De Moor - Spronk UF 16 1984 241; cf. *ayl*); ¶ **par.**: *imr, qmṣ, ṣin.* ¶ **Forms**: pl. *ilm*; du. *alm.*

Ram: *šql ṯrm w mri ilm* they slaughtered bulls and fat rams, 1.22 I 13

(// *ṣin*, *imr*, *qmṣ*); rdg *il<m>* in par. text 1.4 VI 42;]*ydbr ṯrmt alm*]he says: my victuals are two rams, 1.82:8 (cf. Del Olmo CR 375).
Cf. ayl.

al (IV), element of TN: *gt al* 4.382:27 (Belmonte RGTC 12/2 82: *Gittu-Allai*).

il (I) n. m. 1) “god”; 2) DN, epithet used as a noun (Hb., Ph., Pun., Aram. *ʔl*, HALOT 48-50; DNWSI 53ff.; Amor. /ʔi/elum/, Gelb CAAA 14; Ebla *ì-lu*, Krebernik QuSe 18 108; the element /ʔil(um)/ in PNN: cf. spellings in *i-lum-*, *-ì*(NI)*-lum/lu/la/li*; cf. *-il*, *-lì*(NI), *-lu/lum* (spelling with aphaeresis); *-ì*(NI)*-a*, *-/ʔi/-a* (spelling with syncope); cf. Von Soden EDA 85 n. 42; Krebernik PET 91, 99ff.; Akk. *ilu*, AHw 373f.; CAD I/J 91-104; ESA, *ʔl*, DOSA 15; Arab., *ʔilā(h)*, Lane 82f.); ¶ syll. Ug.: cf.]*e-ni* = *i-lu*, UF 11 1979 479:31; [AN = *ilu*] = *e-ni* = *i-lu-ma*, *ibid.* ln. 30; cf. Van Soldt UF 21 1989 365; BiOr 47 1990 731; IDIM [...] = DINGIR-lu_4, Ug 5 137 III 9;] = [*k*]*u*-[*m*]*ur-wi* = DINGIR-lu_4, *ibid.* ln. 35”; the element /ʔilu-/ in PNN and TNN; Sivan GAGl 199f.; Huehnergard UVST 107; cf. the syllabic value *ìl*, *èl*(?) (AN), Huehnergard AkkUg 354; ¶ RS Akk.: DINGIR(.MEŠ), *passim*; cf. DINGIR-lu_4, Ug 5 18 2; Ug 5 170 1'-3'; Huehnergard AkkUg 82f., 355; cf. AN = *i-lu* [, Ug 5 133 obv. 14'; ¶ par.: *ab*. ¶ Forms: sg. *il*; suff. *ilm* (encl. *-m*); *iln*(!) (1.19 IV 57; cf. *iln (I)*); pl. *ilm*; du. *ilmy* (encl. *-y*; cf. Tropper UF 26 1994 476); cstr. *il*, *ily* (*-y*, *mater lectionis*; Blau - Loewenstamm UF 2 1970 25; Tropper UF 26 1994 475; Izre’el RSOu 11 259; Smith BC 128 n. 22).
1) God, ★a) as a class: *ilm w ilht* gods and goddesses, 1.25:2; *nhr il rbm* DN, the great god, 1.3 III 39; *ilm w nšm* gods and men, 1.4 VII 51; *ʕdk ilm hn mtm* around you are the gods, and also men, 1.6 VI 48; *ilmy nʕmm* the two handsome gods, 1.23:60; ★b) activities of the gods: *u ilm tmtn* or do gods die?, 1.16 I 22; *il d yqny ḏdm* the god who created the caves, 1.19 IV 57; *il yṯb b ʕṯtrt* // *il ṯpẓ hdrʕy* the god who resides in TN // the god who judges in TN, 1.108:2-3; *b grnt ilm* in the threshing floor (are) the gods, 1.20 II 9; *tbrk ilm tity* the gods blessed (him and) left, 1.15 III 17; *ilm tġrk tšlmk tʕzzk* may the gods protect you, grant you well-being, strengthen you, 5:9:2-4 and par.; RSOu 14 49 [KTU 9.433]:7, 26; RSOu 14 50 [KTU 9.434]:4; [*my*] *b ilm ydy mrṣ (...) in b ilm ʕnyh* who among the gods will cast out the illness? (...) There was no one among the gods who answered him, 1.16 V 16-22 and par.; *tbʕ w l yṯb ilm* the gods left without lingering/staying, 1.5 I 9 and par.; *w tdʕ ilm* and the gods will know, 1.5 V 16; *tn ilm d tqh* deliver, gods, the one to whom you pay

homage, 1.2 I 18; *ilm lḥm yṯb (...)* the gods sat down to eat (...) *ilm tphhm (...)* the gods saw them (...); *ttly i*(!)*lm rišthm (...)* the gods lowered their heads (...); *aḥd ilm tʕny (...)* I cf., gods, that they humiliate you (...); *šu ilm raštkm* lift up, gods, your heads, 1.2 I 20-27; *ʕd lḥm šty ilm* while the gods were eating (and) drinking, 1.4 VI 55 and par.; *hw ybl argmnk k ilm* he will bring you a tribute like the (other) gods, 1.2 I 37; *in bt l bʕl km ilm* DN has no house like the gods, 1.4 IV 51 and par.; *b yn yšt iln*(!) by the wine that our god drinks!, 1.19 IV 57 (text: *ik*a); ★c) object or purpose of an action: *ʕnt tph ilm* DN espied the gods, 1.3 III 32; *tšlḥm tššqy ilm* he gave the gods food and drink, 1.17 V 29; *uzr ilm ylḥm* enrobed, he fed the gods, 1.17 I 2 and par.; *šbʕ pamt l ilm* seven times (as an offering) to the gods, 1.43:8; *w yqr*[*y*] *dbḥ ilm* and he offered a sacrifice to the gods, 1.19 IV 23 and par.; *iqra ilm* I am going to invoke the gods!, 1.23:1; *aḥdy d ymlk ʕl ilm* I am the only one who will reign over the gods, 1.4 VII 50; ★d) gods of a place or region: *il bldn* gods of the country, 1.162:1; *ily ugrt* the gods of TN, 2.16:4; *kl il alṯy* all the gods of TN, 2.42:8; *il mṣrm* the gods of TN, 2.23:22; *il d*]*dm il lb*[*n*]*n* gods of TN(?), gods of TN, 1.148:43 (cf. Akk. DINGIR.MEŠ *da-ad-me-ma* DINGIR.MEŠ *la-ab-a-na*, Ug 5 170:3'-4'); *il šd* the gods of the steppe, 1.108:12; *ilm arṣ* the gods of the underworld, 1.5 V 6 (cf. 1.106:30; KTU rdg *išm*); *il limm* the god of the peoples, 1.27:8 and par.; *il bt* the god of the house (: dynasty(?)), 1.102:1; 1.39:13; 115:3, 7, 9; 1.123:29; cf. 1.53:8; 1.81:7; *ḥqkpt il klh* TN, that is all (of one) god, 1.3 VI 14 and par.; ★e) classes and groups of gods: *il tʕḏr bʕl* the helper gods of DN, 1.47:26 and par.; *ilm krm, alpm, kḥṯt, rḥbt* the lamb-, bull-, throne-, jar-gods, 1.4 VI 47-54; divine ancestors: when *adn ilm rbm* arrived, the lord of the 'great gods' 1.124:2 (*ilm rbm*: deified ancestors of the dynasty; cf. Pardee UF 15 1983 132f.; cf. Pope Fs. Finkelstein 179; cf. Gordon Eblaitica 1 26f. with n. 43: *ilm (rbm)*, pl. *majestatis*); ★f) qualifying a deity or place: *il ḫš il add* the god of the divine TN, DN, 1.65:9 (cf. RS Akk.: [d]IM *be-el* ḪURSAG *ḫa-zi*, Ug 5 18:4; [d]U [d]ḪURSAG *ḫa-zi*, Ug 5 170; for the various interpretations cf. Xella TRU 213f.; Del Olmo - Sanmartín AuOr 13 1995 259ff.); *il mlk* the god DN, 1.111:18 (cf. Del Olmo CR 201 n. 111; Dietrich - Mayer ALASP 7 20); *il hd* the god DN, 1.12 I 41 and par.; *b tk ġry il ṣpn* in the midst of my mountain, the god TN, 1.3 III 29 and par.; *ngr il ilš* the herald, the god DN (/ the divine herald, DN), 1.16 IV 3, 6; dynastic gods: *il ibrn* (etc. RN), the god PN, 1.113:16 and par.; ★g) possessions or property of the gods: *passim* gen. in nominal syntagms (freq. as the adjective "divine"); cf. *um, inš,* *ʕbd, ʕdt, bn (I), bt (I), bt (II), dd, ġl, grnt, hnn, ḫš, klbt, ks, mdd, mru, mṯbt, nʕm, nʕmn, nr, nrt, pḫr, qnyt, šd, yd*; cf. *ybm l ilm* 'brother-in-law' of the gods, 1.6 I 31 (cf. Del Olmo IMC 75f.); *yd ilm (...) ʕz mid* the power of the gods... is very strong, 2.10:13 (diff.: Pardee Fs. Pope 1987 67f. and n. 11: 'catastrophic illness', DN, god of pestilence); ★h) metonymic usage, statues of gods: *mlk ylk lqḥ ilm aṯr ilm ylk pʕnm* the king shall go to welcome the gods, after the gods he shall walk on foot, 1.43:23; *tʕln ilm b ḫmn* the gods will go up to the 'chapel', 1.112:8; *lbš il yštk // ʕrm il yštk* may they put on you the vestment of a god // may they dress you in the cape of a god, 1.169:13 (Loretz - Xella MLE 1 1982 38); estates or fields (?) of gods: cf. in unc. ctx. *ytn ilm bdhm bd PN_1 gṯr w bd PN_2 bʕl* may the (fields of the?) gods be delivered into his hands: DN_1 in the hands of PN_1 and DN_2 in the hands of PN_2, 2.4:20 (cf. *šd gṯr, ibid.* ln. 16, 18; cf. RS Akk. *it-ta-din DN*, PRU 3 171 (RS 16.173):8'-10'; diff.: Cunchillos TOu 2 273f.: 'les dieux le livreront'; Dietrich - Loretz JA 72; Watson SEL 6 1989 47: 'statues, images').

2) DN: El (cf. syll. Ug.: *iluma*, UF 11 1979 478:30; Van Soldt UF 21 1989 366; cf. *rbt ilm* you are great, oh DN!, 1.4 V 3), epithet used as a noun, *passim* in god lists, cf. 1.118:2 and par.; cf. *il w aṯrt* DN and DN, 1.65:5; *passim* in cultic texts, cf. offerings *l il* to DN, 1.39:2; cf. 1.164:7; *passim* in narrative texts. Cf. ★a) activities of the god: *il aṯtm k ypt* DN really wished to seduce the two women, 1.23:39; *il dbḥ b bt* DN gave a feast in his house, 1.114:1; cf. *ibid.* ln. 17; *il yṯb b mrzḥh* DN sat in the house of his feast, 1.114:15 (cf. 1.1 IV 4; 1.108:2); *mrṯ yḥrṯ il* must that DN cultivated, 1.22 I 20; *ks yiḥd* [*il*] DN took a cup, 1.15 II 16 (cf. 1.17 I 34); *yʕny il bšbʕt ḥdrm* DN replied from the seven rooms, 1.3 V 26; *tgr il bnh* DN has opposed his son!, 1.1 IV 12; *il hlk l bth* DN went to his house, 1.114:17; *tḥmk il ḥkm* your mesage, DN, is wise, 1.3 V 30; *il ḫṭh nḥt il ymnn mṭ ydh* DN lowered his sceptre, DN placed the wand of his hand upright, 1.23:37; *w b ḥlmh il yrd* and in his dream DN came down, 1.14 I 36; *d b ḥlmy il ytn* the one that in my dream DN granted me, 1.14 III 46 and par.; *ql il k mt* DN fell like a dead person, 1.114:21; *hlm il k yphnh* as soon as DN saw her, 1.4 IV 27 and par.; *ybrk il krt* DN blessed PN, 1.15 II 19; *gm yṣḥ il l btlt ʕnt* aloud DN shouted to Virgin DN, 1.6 III 22 and par.; *šbʕ šnt il mla* during seven years DN had filled, 1.12 II 44; *yqḥ il mštʕltm* DN took two consecrated women (?), 1.23:35 and par.; *il yẓḥq bm lb* DN laughed in his heart, 1.12 I 12; *ilm ypʕr šmthm* whose names DN will proclaim, 1.12 I 28; [*bnt*] *bhth y ilm al tšmḫ* within your house, oh DN!, do not rejoice, 1.3 V

20; *i*[*l w*] *ḥrn yisp ḥmt* DN and DN remove the venom, 1.107:38; *ik al yšmʕk ṯr il* how of a truth do you wish Bull DN to hear you?, 1.6 VI 27; ★b) object or purpose of an action: *l pnʕn il l tpl* at the feet of DN they fell, 1.2 I 30 and par.; *l pʕn il thbr w tql* at the feet of DN he bowed and fell, 1.4 IV 25 and par. (formulae of the prostration sequence; cf. Del Olmo MLC 54f.); *bʕl qm ʕl il* DN stood next to DN, 1.2 I 21; *rgm l il ybl* word was brought to DN, 1.23:52; *ql bl l il* take (this) message to DN, 1.100:3; *idk l ytn pnm ʕm il* and so he set face for DN, 1.2 III 4; *šmtr uṯkl l il* cutting of a grape cluster for DN, 1.87:2 and par.; unc. ctx.: *tḥt il* under DN, RSOu 14 53 [KTU 9.432]:2'(?); ★c) titles: *ṯr il aby/k/h* the Bull, DN, my (/ your / his / her) father, 1.2 III 21 and par.; *ltpn il d pid* kindly DN, the benevolent, 1.6 III 4 and par.; *il abn* DN, our father, 1.12 I 9; *il ṣpn* DN of TN, 1.47:1 (cf. Del Olmo Fs. Díez Macho 294); *il mlk d yqnnh* DN, the king who established him, 1.4 IV 48; *il šr* DN, sovereign, 1.123:3 (cf. Foley UF 19 1987 71 n. 40); *rbt ilm* you are great, DN!, 1.4 V 3; ★d) El's possessions or property (often to be understood as in 1.g): *ab bn il* father of the sons of DN, 1.40:33 and par. (cf. 1.65:1-3); *bn(m) il* son(s) of DN, *passim*; *bt il* daughter(s) of DN, 1.23:42 (cf. 1.3 III 46); *aṯt il* women of DN, 1.23:42 (cf. ln. 60, *aṯty*); *mdd / ydd il* beloved of DN, 1.3 III 39 and par., title of the gods Yam and Mot); *yd il* the member of DN, 1.23:34 and par.; *yd il* the love of DN 1.4 IV 38; *dr il* the family of DN, 1.39:7 and par.; *ḏd il* the cave / tent of DN, 1.3 V 7 and par., denoting El's residence; *mṯb il* residence of DN, 1.4 IV 52 and par.; *ʕbd il* servant of DN, 1.14 III 51; *ġlm il* the servant of DN, 1.15 II 20; *šm il*, the name of DN, 1.22 I 6; *šnt il* the years of DN, 1.108:27; *qym il* the assistants of DN, 1.22 I 5; *bt il* the house (/ temple) of DN, 1.17 II 5; *ytnt il* the gift of DN, 1.14 III 31 and par.; *bšrt il* the good news of DN, 1.10 III 33; *ṯlḥnt il* the table of DN, 1.114:6; *w šd šd ilm* but the field if the field of DN, 1.23:13, 28 (cf. 1.6 IV 2, 13); *qdš il* the sanctuary of DN, 1.119:6; the meaning of the lexeme is uncertain in 1.65:6-18: *ḥnn / nṣbt / šlm / mrḥ / nit / ṣmd / dṯn / šrp / knt / ġdyn il* n. of DN / divine n. (cf. Del Olmo CR 341f. and n. 26; AuOr 10 1992 255).

Cf. in bkn ctx. *il yṣġd ḥ*[, 1.174:1; cf. 1.176:14, 16, 20, 22. For 1.4 VI 42 (*il*) and 1.22 I 13 (*ilm*) cf. *il (II)*.

Cf. ilabn, ilib (I), ilib (II), iladn, ilʕnt, ildgn, ildn, ilgdn, ilgn, ilgt, ilh, ilhd, ilḥu, ilḥbn, ilkšy, ilmd, ilmhr, ilmlk, iln (I), iln (II), ilnqsd, ilqṣm, ilrb, ilrm, ilrpi, ilrš, ilršp, ilṣdq, ilšḥr, ilšlm, ilšn, ilšpš, ilštmʕ, ilt (I), ilt (II), ilṯhm, iltm, ilṯr, ilṯtmr, ily, ilym, ilyn, ilyqn, ilyy, amril, ʕbdil(m), ʕnil, bdil, bnil, bnilh, bnilt, hwil, nil, ḥyil, ḥyl, mril, nẓril, piln, rbil, ṣdqil, ṯbil, yaršil, ybnil, ydbil, yknil, ymil, yrġmil, yšril, yṯil.

il (II) n. m. "ram"; pl. *ilm*, 1.4 VI 42; 1.22 I 13; cf. *al (III)*.

ul n. m. "(military) force" (< /ʔ-w-l/, Cohen DRS 12; Hb. *ʔwl*, *ʔylwt*, *ʔl*, HALOT 21, 41, 48; cf. Fensham JNSL 7 1979 24f.); ¶ syll. Ug.: cf. the element /ʔūl(l)u/ in PNN, Sivan GAGl 201; ¶ par.: *ʕẓm*. ¶ Forms: sg. *ul*, suff. *ulny* (du.; or lengthened form **uln* */ʔul-n/ > *ulny* /ʔul-n-y/?).

(Military) force: *ṣbu ul mad* your army (will be) an immense force, 1.14 II 35 and par. ; *l arṣ ypl ulny* our / my forces fell to the ground, 1.2 IV 5 (// *ʕẓm*; diff.: Caquot - Sznycer TOu I 135, n. k, 'corpulent'; Aartun PU I 45, n. 6, 'stark': lengthened form **uln* */ʔul-n/ > *ulny* /ʔul-n-y/).

Cf. uln (II), ulnhr.

ilib (I) DN 1) "father god" (deified ancestor; ancestral or family god); 2) "El-father", invocation of the DN El (for the element *ib* < *ab* cf. *ib (III)*. Cf. Hb. PN *ʔlyʔb*, HALOT 55; Akk. ^{d}*a-ba*$_{4}$, Gelb - Kienast AKDT 169; Kienast - Sommerfeld GlAKI 3f.; RS Hurr. : *in atn*, KTU 1.110:2; 1.111:3; cf. Laroche GLH 63f.; Ug 5 507, 523. Cf. Dietrich - Loretz - Sanmartín UF 6 1974 450f.; 8 1976 52; Rainey RSP 2 78f.; Sznycer Semitica 29 1979 50ff.; Lambert UF 13 1981 299ff.; Xella SSR 5 1981 85ff.; Polselli RSO 56 1982 21ff.; Healey SEL 2 1985 15ff.; Van der Toorn UF 25 1993 379ff.; Kennedy CBQ 61 1999 766); ¶ RS Akk.: DINGIR *a-bi*, Ug 5 18:1; ¶ par.: *ʕm*. ¶ Forms: sg. *ilib*, suff. *iliby*, *ilibh*.

1) Father god, family god: *nṣb skn ilibh* who erects the stele of the family god, 1.17 I 26 and par. (// *ʕm*).

2) Father El: *ilib* DN (in list of gods) 1.47:2; 1.118:1 (cf. RS Akk.: DINGIR *a-bi*, Ug 5 18:1; cf. Del Olmo Lete Fs. Díez Macho 295); *ilib š* (to) DN: one ram, 1.148:23 and par.; *ilib gdlt* (to) DN: one cow, 1.109:12 and par.; *ṯn šm lilib* two rams to DN, 1.162:6; *i*]*d ydbḥ mlk l ilib* when the king sacrifices to DN, 1.164:3; *alp w š šrp l ilib* one (head of) cattle and one ram in holocaust to DN, 1.164:6 and par.; *ilib il*, 1.74:1; *ilib* (the sacrifice of) DN, 1.91:5 (cf. Del Olmo CR 259).

ilib (II) PN (Sem. Cf. Grøndahl PTU 95).

PN: 4.727:13.

ilabn PN (Sem. Cf. Grøndahl PTU 46, 87, 94; cf. Xella UF 20 1988 387ff.; Watson AuOr 8 1990 116); ¶ syll.: cf. ^{m}DUMU-^{m}DINGIR. IGI.AD, PRU 3 194 (11.839):12; PN DUMU ^{m}DINGIR.IGI.AD, *ibid.* ln. 16; cf. Huehnergard AkkUg 400 n. 85. Cf. *bnʕnt*.

PN: 4.226:3.

iladn PN (Sem.).
PN: "UF 29, 826":4 (cf. Lemaire UF 30 1998 461).
Cf. **adn (I)**, **il (I)**.

alit DN f. ("the most powerful", elative ʔqtl-pattern f. of the root /l-ʔ-y/; cf. Ebla *a-li*-PI-*tum*, Krebernik QuSe 18 101. Cf. Dijkstra - De Moor UF 7 1975 213; De Tarragon TOu 2 173 n. 102; Watson SEL 10 1993 55).
DN: *š l alit* a ram for DN, 1.90:19; [*al*]*it š* for DN, a ram, 1.168:15.
Cf. **aliy**, **aliyn**.

aliy adj. m. "the most powerful" (elative pattern ʔqtl- of the root /l-ʔ-y/; cf. *aliyn*); ¶ **par.**: *aliyn bʕl*. ¶ **Forms**: sg. cstr. *aliy*.
The most powerful (cstr. elatative in gen. syntagm): *aliy qrdm* the most powerful of heroes, 1.3 III 14 and par. (// *aliyn bʕl*).
Cf. **alit**, **aliyn**.

aliyn adj. m. "the very / most powerful" (elative ʔqtl(ān-) pattern of the root /l-ʔ-y/. Cf. Van Zijl Baal 342f.; De Moor SP 68f.; Dijkstra - De Moor UF 7 1975 213; Grave UF 12 1980 226; Dietrich - Loretz UF 12 1980 391ff.; Verreet UF 16 1984 315; Wyatt UF 24 1992 405; Smith BC 153; cf. Deiana Forte 29: ptc. G /l-ʔ-y/ with prothetic /ʔa-/; cf. Ebla /lāʔi(y)/ in PNN; Krebernik PET 94; Fronzaroli ARES 1 22; Catagnoti MisEb 1 260); ¶ **syll. Ug.**: cf. the element /lāʔiy/ in PNN; Grøndahl PTU 154; Sivan GAGl 241; ¶ **par.**: *zbl*; cf. *aliyn bʕl* // *aliy qrdm*. ¶ **Forms**: sg. *aliyn*.
Very Powerful (apposition): *aliyn bʕl* the 'Very Powerful' DN, 1.5 VI 9 and par. (// *zbl bʕl arṣ*); cf. *mt aliyn bʕl* dead is the 'Very Powerful' DN, 1.5 VI 9; *mlkn aliyn bʕl* our king is the 'Very Powerful' DN, 1.3 V 32 and par.
Cf. **aliy**, **bʕl (II)** 3.b.

ilʕnt PN (Sem. Cf. Grøndahl PTU 46, 95, 111; De Moor UF 1 1969 171 n. 21; Loewenstamm UF 14 1982 123).
PN: ★**a)** 4.617:43; in bkn ctx.: 4.607:14; ★**b)** *bn PN*: 4.623:11.

alb PN (etym. unc. Cf. Laroche GLH 42, 44; Gelb - Purves - MacRae NPN 199f.).
PN: *bn PN*, 4.700:4.

ulb(y) PN (etym. unc.).
PN: *bn PN*, 4.281:13; 4.309:2; 4.628:2.

ilbʕl PN (Sem. Cf. Grøndahl PTU 95, 117; Masson Semitica 39 1990 42; Bordreuil - Caquot Syria 57 1980 364f.; Watson AuOr 11 1993 214); ¶ **syll.**: cf. DINGIR.EN, PRU 3169 (RS 16.145):4; DINGIR.[d]U,

Ug 5 95:9.
PN: ★a) 4.75 V 12; 4.141 I 4 (KTU: *ibʕl*); 4.261:21; 4.381:22; 4.609:3; 4.754:14; 4.775:17; ★b) *bn PN:* 4.340:6; 4.377:7; 4.410:10; 4.583:2.

ilbd PN (etym. unc. Cf. Grøndahl PTU 94ff., 118).
PN: *ilbd*, 4.783:7; cf. 4.593:9.
Cf. bdil.

ilbt DN, protector deity of palace and dynasty, identity unspecified (cf. *il (I)*, *bt (II)*; Pardee AfO 36/37 1989/90 436).
DN: in lists, 1.102:1; *k ydbḥ mlk (...) l bbt ilbt* when the king sacrifices (...) to DN (and) DN, 1.115:3; *b qdš ilbt* in the 'sanctuary' of DN, 1.115:7; *š l ilbt* a ram to DN, 1.115:9; *ilbt gdlt*, (to) DN a cow, 1.39:13 (cf. 1.53:8); *šlm ilbt*, hail, O DN!(?), 1.123:29.

ulbtyn PN (etym. unc.); ¶ syll.: cf. *ul-bu-ut-ia-nu*, Syria 15 1934 133 (RS 4.466+):7.
PN: *bn PN*, 4.280:4; cf. bkn ctx.: 4.383:3.

ildgn PN (Sem. Cf. Grøndahl PTU 95, 123, 423).
PN: 4.63 III 9; 4.607:17; 4.609:20.

ildn PN (Sem.; Bordreuil - Caquot Syria 57 1980 364f.).
PN: 4.775:6.

ildy PN (etym. unc. Cf. Cassin - Glassner AAN 1 67: *Iltaya*).
PN: 4.130:3; 4.617:20; 4.635:33 (*aḏddy*).

uldy PN (etym. unc.).
PN: *bn PN*, 4.309:18.

ilḏ PN (etym. unc. Cf. Dietrich - Loretz - Sanmartín UF 5 1973 81).
PN: 4.96:12.

alḏy GN m. ((> PN?); cf. Dietrich - Loretz - Sanmartín UF 5 1973 81; Pardee Syria 65 1988 189 n. 54). ¶ Forms: sg. *alḏy*.
GN (> PN?): *akly*, 4.609:21. cf. 1.125:6.
Cf. alṯy, alẓy.

ilg, 4.751:11, cf. *lg (I)*.

algbṯ n. of mineral or stone (cf. Sum. al-ga-mèš; Ebla cf. BUR AL-GU-PEŠ$_7$ = BUR *ur-gú-ba-su*, MEE 3 45+46 // MEE 61 ln. 71; Civil EDA 153; Akk. *algamišu*, AHw 35; CAD A/1 337f.; Hb. *ʔlgbyš*, HALOT 51; cf. Eg. *írqbś / ʔá-l-qa-bí-ś<á>*, WäS 1 116; Helck Bez. 508 (10); cf. Nougayrol Ug 5 101 n. 1; Sasson RSP 1 392; Heltzer GPOTU 62 n. 216); ¶ syll. Ug.: NA$_4$.MEŠ.GE$_6$: *al-ga$_{14}$-ba-šu*, Ug 5 30:4', 10'. ¶ Forms: sg. *algbṯ*.
Mineral or stone: *arbʕ kkr algbṯ arbʕt ksph* four talents of *a.* to the

value of four (shekels), 4.158:15.

ilgdn PN (Sem. Cf. Grøndahl PTU 95, 126f.).
PN: 4.277:13.

ilgn PN (Sem. Cf. Grøndahl PTU 95, 129; Dietrich - Loretz - Sanmartín UF 6 1974 21, 23f.).
PN: 4.63 I 34.

algp PN(?) (Hurr. Cf. Grøndahl PTU 206, 216, 239).
PN(?): 1.66:3.

ilgt PN (Sem. Cf. Grøndahl PTU 95, 131; Fowler TPNAH 185).
PN: 4.277:2.

ilh DN ("the 'Divine One'", referring to the deified dead (kings); cf. Emar pl. /ilaū/ Pentiuc Vocabulary 82f.; Arab. *ʔilāh*, Lane 82f.; Hb. *ʔl(w)h*, *ʔlhym*, HALOT 52f.; Aram. *ʔlh*, DNWSI 57-60; Amor. /ʔil(l)a/, Gelb CAAA 14; cf. Dietrich - Loretz - Sanmartín UF 7 1975 552f.; Dietrich - Loretz UF 12 1980 177; Del Olmo AuOr 5 1987 42 n. 13; Loretz UF 24 1992 159ff.; Levine - De Tarragon RB 100 1993 103ff.: 'god' or DN *il*); ¶ par.: *ṯʕ*. ¶ Forms: sg. *ilh*; du./pl. *ilhm* (or sg. + encl. *-m*).
DN, the 'Divine One': *dqtm ilh alp w š ilhm* two ewes (to) DN, one (head of) cattle and one ram (to) the DN, 1.39:5 and par. (// *ṯʕ*, *ṯʕm*; cf. 1.41:6, 12, 14, 18, 28, 30; 1.87:7, 13, 15, 19, 30, 32-33, where they occur as recipients of sacrificial offerings, distinct from El and the other gods).
Cf. bnilh.

ilhd PN (Sem. Cf. Grøndahl PTU 95, 133).
PN: 4.63 I 7; 4.63 III 33; 4.609:7; 5.18:1 (*bn kzn*), 3 (*bn ily*), 7 (*bn šmmn*).

ilhnm cf. *iln (I)*.

ilḥu PN of *krt*'s son (Sem. Cf. Grøndahl PTU 308; Astour UF 5 1973 38; De Moor - Spronk UF 14 1982 184; Watson AuOr 14 1996 95).
PN, son of *krt*: *ġzr ilḥu* the noble PN, 1.16 I 46 and par. (cf. Miller UF 2 1970 163).

ilḥbn PN (Sem. Cf. Grøndahl PTU 37, 39, 65, 134, 162).
PN: *bn PN*, 4.63 III 44.

alḫb, element of TN *gt alḫb*, 4.243:16 (Belmonte RGTC 12/2 82f.: *Gittu-Alli-ḫeba*).

alḫn (I) n. m. "quartermaster" (< "miller", Del Olmo UF 10 1978 51; IMC 193; Heltzer IOKU 80; cf. Akk. *alaḫḫinu*, AHw 31; CAD A/1 194ff.; Diakonoff ArOr 47 1979 40; Wilhelm AdS 2/1 158f.; Watson

UF 27 1995 534; Nuzi Akk.: É *a-la-aḫ-ḫe-en-ni*, Mayer Nuzi 1 177); syll. Ug: cf. PN DUMU *a-la-ḫi-ni*, PRU 6 70:11; Huehnergard UVST 107. ¶ Forms: pl. *alḫnm*.
Quartermaster: *bt alḫnm* storehouse of quartermasters, 4.392:4.

alḫn (II) PN (< Akk. Cf. Grøndahl PTU 270, 276, 363; Dietrich - Loretz - Sanmartín UF 6 1974 19); ¶ syll.: DUMU *a-la-ḫi-ni*, PRU 6 70:11.
PN: 4.102:25; 4.337:11.

ilk PN (etym. unc.); ¶ syll.: cf. *il-ku-ia/ya*, PRU 3 55 (RS 15.92): 5 and *passim ibid.*
PN: *PN rʕ[y*, 4.153:1 (cf. Márquez NABU 1993/7).

(ilk), 6.66:2; cf. *ilrm*.

alkbl PN (Hurr. Grøndahl PTU 216, 239).
PN: *bn PN*, 4.369:16 (*šb[ny*). Cf. 2.39:22.

ulkn PN / DN, name of an (Anat.?) ancestral king. Cf. Grøndahl PTU 274, 278; Lewis Cults 17; Wyatt RTU 432 n. 14).
PN / DN: *ulkn rpa*, 1.161:4.

ilkšy PN (Hurro.-Sem.(?); cf. Gelb - Purves - MacRae NPN 230f.; Grøndahl PTU 237f.).
PN: *bn PN*, 4.617:9.

all n. m.; outer garment (type of "cape, cloak"; Hurr. *alāli-*, Neu Das Hurritische 41: // Hitt. TÚG *kušiši-*; Fs. Thomas 512; StBo 32 314 n. 22; cf. Akk. *allānu*, CAD A/1 356, and cf. AHw 37. Cf. Sanmartín UF 10 1978 350; Waetzoldt ZA 77 1987 297; Ribichini - Xella Tessili 28f.; Dietrich - Loretz UF 22 1990 49f.; Watson SEL 6 1989 52 n. 33; AuOr 8 1990 139f.; UF 32 2000 567); ¶ par.: *kst*, *lpš*. ¶ Forms: sg. *all*; pl. *allm*.
Luxury garment: *šbʕ lbšm allm l DN* seven *a.*-garments for DN, 4.168:9 (Xella UF 11 1979 836 n. 10); *allm lbnm* [...] *all šmt* [...] *all iqni* white *a.*, [...] *a.* (of) carnelian red, [...] *a.* (of) violet purple, 4.182:4-6; cf. *lbš all*, *ibid.* ln. 21; outer garment: she grasped him *b qṣ all* by the hem of (his) *a.*, 1.6 II 11 (// *lpš*; cf. Ribichini - Xella Tessili 28f.); *tmzʕ (...) all* she tore (...) the *a.*, 1.19 I 37 (*a<l>*), 48 (// *kst*); he wore *km all dm aryh* like an *a.* the blood of his kin, 1.12 II 47 (// *lpš*).

ill PN (Anat. Cf. Grøndahl PTU 273; Tischler HEG 354).
PN: 4.214 II 8.

ull TN (Belmonte RGTC 12/2 321: **ʔU/Alullu*. Cf. Heltzer RCAU 15; Honeyman JKF 2 1953 81; Astour UF 13 1981 9; CRRA 18 20; NuzHur 1 19 no. 64; Van Soldt UF 28 1996 658; UF 29 1997 690f.;

UF 30 1998 734); ¶ **syll.**: cf. URU *a-lu-ul-la/li*, cf. PRU 4 p. 253; cf. Astour UF 5 1973 33 n. 47.
TN: 4.68:19; 4.244:12. For the allograph *a*[*ll*, 4.308:16, cf. Van Soldt UF 28 1996 658 n. 28; for the rdg *u/a*]*ll* cf. Belmonte RGTC 12/2 321.

illḏr(m) PN (Hurro-Anat.; cf. *ill*. Cf. Grøndahl PTU 250, 273).
PN: 2.24:3; 4.361:2; 4.362:1; 4.607:22.

illm PN (etym. unc. Cf. Watson AuOr 8 1990 116); ¶ **syll.**: cf. [f]*i-la-la-*[*a*]*m*(?), PRU 6 149 II 6.
PN: *bn PN*, 4.93 IV 24.

ully (I) GN m. (< *ull*, TN). ¶ **Forms**: pl. *ullym*.
GN: *ullym abynm*, insolvent GNN (pl.), 4.70:6.

ully (II) PN (etym. unc.; cf *ully*, GN; Grøndahl PTU 26, 274; Bordreuil - Caquot Syria 57 1980 357); ¶ **syll.**: cf. DUMU *ú-lu-li-ya*, PRU 3 196 (RS 15.42+) I 16; *ú*(?)*-li-li-ya*(?), 40 (RS 15.173):1.
PN: *bn PN*, 4.101:1:5; 4.245 II 5 (Van Soldt SAU 126); cf. in bkn ctx. 2.81:14.

ulm (I) TN (Belmonte RGTC 12/2 320: **ʔUllamu*. Cf. Heltzer RCAU 15; Astour RSP 2 269; UF 13 1971 5; NuzHur 1 19 no. 62; Van Soldt SAU 120; UF 28 1996 658; UF 30 1997 722); ¶ **syll.**: URU *ul-la-mi/mì*, cf. PRU 3 p. 267; Ug 5 99:4; RSOu 7 4:16; cf. Huehnergard UVST 251.
TN: 3.7:5, 6, 16; 4.27:9, 20; 4.63 I 1; 4.160:6, 10; 4.177:6; 4.213:10; 4.254:4; 4.307:2; 4.348:3; 4.365:7; 4.375:10; 4.380:7; 4.384:4; 4.414:8; 4.566:3, 4; 4.610 (I) 8; 4.618:9, 26; 4.625:4; 4.643:24; 4.693:7 (*ul*(!)*m*); 4.725:6; 4.784:8; 7.42:3, 5; RSOu 14 35 [KTU 9.388] I 22; 36 [KTU 9.417]:4; cf. *skn ulm*, 4.160:6; cf. in unc. ctx.: *ʕbd ulm*, 1.79:3 (rdg *i*(!)*lm*?).

ulm (II) PN (< *ulm (I)*, TN, used meton. as a PN; diff. Watson NABU 1998 17: Hurr.).
PN: *ulm*, 4.177:6.

ilmd PN (Sem. Cf. Grøndahl PTU 37, 40, 95, 133, 156).
PN: *bn PN*, 4.354:3; 4.350:15.

almg n. m. of a type of wood, probably "aloe" (Akk. *elammakk/ggu*, AHw 196; CAD E 75f.; Hb. *ʔlmgym*, HALOT 57f.; cf. Greenfield - Mayrhofer VTS 16 1967 83-89; Sasson RSP 1 392; Briquel-Chatonnet RCCPhRIJ 255ff.). ¶ **Forms**: sg. *almg*.
A type of wood: *ṯlṯm almg* thirty (talents / logs?) of *a*., 4.91:8.

ilmhr PN (Sem. Cf. Grøndahl PTU 95, 156; Rainey IOS 3 1973 39); ¶ **syll.**: cf. DINGIR.UR.SAG, PRU 3 169 (RS 16.145):5, 10; 194 (RS

11.839):21; PRU 6 53 rev. 9' (Huehnergard AkkUg 348, 410).
PN: 4.63 I 9; 4.631:18; 4.775:10. Cf. in bkn ctx. *ilh*[, 4.194:11.

ulmk PN (etym. unc. Cf. Grøndahl PTU 228, 234).
PN: 4.307:16. Cf. in bkn ctx. *ulm*[, 4.725:6.

ilmlk PN (Sem. Cf. Grøndahl PTU 95, 97, 157f.; Nougayrol Ug 5 p. 13 n. 2; De Moor BiOr 26 1969 106; Dietrich - Loretz UF 12 1980 387-389; cf. Woudhuizen UF 26 1994 529: *ilimaliki,* Linear C); ¶ syll.: DINGIR.LUGAL, PRU 3 p. 245; PRU 4 203 (RS 18.20+) rev. 15'; Ug 5 p. 328; cf. Van Soldt SAU 21, 27ff., 34; cf. DINGIR-*mil-ku*, PRU 4 294 (RS 19.70):8; DINGIR.LIM-*mu-lik*, PRU 4 215 (RS 17.288):27; DINGIR-*mu-lik*, PRU 6 82:16.
PN: *ilmlk* 1.6 VI 54 (*šbny*); 1.16 VI 59 (cf. 1.4 VIII 49; 1.17 VI 56); 4.115:9(?); 4.133:2; 4.165:13; 4.261:10; 4.382:28 ([*bn*] *ktṯ*[); 4.607:16; 4.616:2; 4.659:8; 5.18:9 (*b<n>*). Bkn ctx.: 1.17 left edge 1 (*šbny*); 4.98:24 (*bn x*[); 4.386:11.

ilmn PN (Sem. Cf. Grøndahl PTU 53, 96; cf. Liverani OrAn 7 1968 290); ¶ syll.: cf. DINGIR-*mu-na*, cf. PRU 3 p. 245.
PN: 4.141 I 13; cf. 4.658:26.

ulmn n. m. "widowhood" (cf. Hb. *ʔlmn*, HALOT 58; cf. *almnt*); ¶ par.: *ṯkl.* ¶ Forms: sg. *ulmn.*
Widowhood: *bdh ḫṭ ulmn* in his hand (he holds) the sceptre of widowhood, 1.23:9 (// *ṯkl*).

almnt n. f. "widow" (Hb. *ʔlmnh*, HALOT 58; Ph. *ʔlmnt*, DNWSI 63; Syr. *ʔarmaltō*, LS 735; Arab. *ʔarmala*, Lane 1060; Akk. *almattu*, AHw 38; CAD A/1 362ff.); ¶ par.: *ʕwr, qṣr (+ npš), yḥd (/ aḥd), ytm, zbl.* ¶ Forms: sg. *almnt.*
Widow: *almnt škr tškr* the widow hired/s out her services, 1.14 II 44; IV 22 (// *yḥd (aḥd), zbl, ʕwr*); *l tšlḥm (...) almnt* you did not feed (...) the widow, 1.16 VI 50 (// *ytm*); *l tdn dn almnt* you did not judge the widow's cause, 1.16 VI 33, 46 (// *qṣr npš*); *ydn dn almnt* he judged the widow's cause, 1.17 V 8 and par. (// *ytm*).
Cf. ulmn.

ulmy (I) GN m. (< *ulm*, TN). ¶ Forms: sg. *ulmy.*
GN: 4.339:5.

ulmy (II) PN (etym. unc. Cf. *ulmy*, GN; cf. Grøndahl PTU 26, 228; Cassin - Glassner AAN 1 155).
PN: *bn PN*, 4.63 I 19.

aln (I) n. m. "oak grove" (coll. < "oak"; cf. Sasson RSP 1 393; Astour RSP 2 258; Watson Or 45 1976 441; cf. Hb. *ʔlwn*, HALOT 54; Akk. *allānu*, AHw 37; CAD A/1 354f.; Ebla cf. *al*$_6$*-la-na*, Waetzoldt MEE

10 90; Sanmartín AuOr 9 1991 173; cf. Eg. *ínrn / ʔal-l_2-lú-na*, WäS 1 98; Helck Bez 507(4); cf. Syr. *ʔilānāʔ*, LS 15; diff.: Schloen JNES 52 1993 215 n. 41: 'household', reading *al-n*, Akk. *ālu* (but cf. *supra*: Ug. *ahl*); syll. Ug/ ¶ RS Akk.: cf. A.ŠÀ.MEŠ [(m)]*al-la-an(-)* PN, PRU 3 131 (RS 15.118):4; PRU 3 109 (RS 16.251):5; cf.]*al-la-ni*, PRU 3 131 (RS 15.122):9; Huehnergard UVST 107; ¶ par.: *mlbr*. ¶ Forms: sg. *aln*.

Oak grove: *ẓi b aln tkm* go to the oak grove (of) TN, 1.12 I 20 (// *mlbr*).

aln (II) DN; Hurro-Hitt. underworld goddess ('the Lady', Hurr. *allai*, Laroche GLH 42; DN Hurro-Hitt. *allani*, Laroche GLH 43; Neu Hurr. 41: 'Sonnengöttin der Erde'; Wilhelm Or 61 1992 128. Cf. Laroche Ug 5 p. 525); ¶ RS Akk.: cf. [d]*al-la-tu_4*, Ug 5 18:22 (// *arṣy*, 1.47:23; 1.118:22). ¶ Forms: *alnd* (1.132:19, 23; Hurr.: DN + direct. /DN=da/).

DN: 1.132:19, 23. In Hurr. ctx., cf. 1.60:13; 1.116:21; 1.135:10. Cf. 1.42:51.

iln (I) n. m. "deity, god" (cf. Ph. *ʔln,ʔlnm*, Pun. *alonim*, DNWSI 63f.; Syr. *ʔalohonō*, LS 21; < *il (I)*); ¶ par.: *il*. ¶ Forms: sg. *iln*; pl. *ilnm*; extended pl. *ilhnm*.

Deity, god: ★a) predicative use in the gen. *klb ilnm* divine puppy, 1.19 I 10 (cf. Pun. PN *klbʔlm*; cf. Virolleaud LPD 126; Benz PNPPI 131; Del Olmo IMC 129 n. 292; Huehnergard UVST 107; diff.: Margalit UF 16 1984 121); unc. ctx. 1.19 IV 57 (*ila*, rdg *iln*(!) "our god", *il (I)*; cf. Del Olmo MLC 400; diff.: Margalit UF 8 1976 186; 16 1984 176f.) and 1.112:30 (cf. Herdner Ug 7 23); ★b) referring to cult statues: (donations)]*t ilhnm b šnt* of / for the gods by year, 4.182:1. Cf. 1.91:17.

Cf. iln (II), ilny.

iln (II) PN (Sem. Cf. Grøndahl PTU 52, 96; Watson AuOr 14 1996 95); ¶ syll.: cf. *i-li-na*, PRU 6 83 IV 15 (for AN-*ni*, PRU 6 82:10, cf. *ʕn (III)*, PN).

PN: ★a) 4.382:21 (*bn* [-); 4.609:21; ★b) *bn PN*, 4.215:5; 4.350:11.

uln (I) cf. *ul*.

uln (II) PN (Sem. Cf. Grøndahl PTU 103); ¶ syll.: cf. *ú-lu-ni*, PRU 3 195 (RS 11.839):19; *ú-la-nu*, PRU 6 70:14; cf. 85:30'; cf. Huehnergard UVST 251.

PN: 4.7:16; 4.63 I 39, II 7-8, 17; 4.232:13; 4.778:2; 4.782:3.

ulnhr PN (Sem. Cf. Grøndahl PTU 43, 103, 165); ¶ syll.: DUMU *ú-lu-na-a-ri*, PRU 3 202 (RS 16.126+) B III 48; cf. Huehnergard UVST 244 n. 129, 248; Van Soldt SAU 34, 331 n. 160.

PN: *bn PN*, 4.112 II 4.

ilnḥm PN (Sem. Cf. Grøndahl PTU 94-97, 165).
PN: 4.785:16 (*bn ʕzn*).

ilnnn PN (etym. unc. Cf. Grøndahl PTU 426).
PN: 4.631:20 (*bn irpṯr*).

ilnqsd PN (etym. unc.; incorrect spelling?).
PN: 4.715:24.

alnr PN (Hurr. Cf. Weippert GGA 216 164 193; Grøndahl PTU 216, 243; Dietrich - Loretz OLZ 62 1967 536; KA 183f.; Watson AuOr 14 1996 95; cf. West AOAT 233 30: *a-ra-na-ro*, Linear B).
PN: 4.16:6; 5.7:1 (*r.n.l.a*, rdg *sinistrorsum*); 5.7:3.

alnṯr PN (Hurr. Cf. Grøndahl PTU 216, 248f.).
PN: *alnṯr*, 4.391:18 (in bkn ctx.)

ilny adj./n. "divine one", used basically of dead and deified heroes / kings (adjective derived from *iln*; cf. De Moor SP 241f.; Del Olmo AuOr 5 1987 63f.); ¶ par.: *il (I)*, *rpu*. ¶ Forms: pl. *ilnym*.
Divine one: [*aṯr*]*h ltdd ilnym* after him the 'divine ones' left, 1.21 II 4 and par.; *mġy (...) ilnym l mṭʕt* there arrived (...) the 'divine ones' at the plantations, 1.20 II 6 and par.; *iqra* [*ilnym h*]*kly* I call you, 'divine ones', to my palace, 1.21 II 3 and par.; *rḥq ilnym* the most distant 'divine one', 1.3 IV 35 and par.; *špš tḥtk ilnym* DN you subdue the 'divine ones', 1.6 VI 47 (cf. Del Olmo MLC 235).

ulny, cf. *ul*.

alp (I) n. m. 1) "(head of) cattle"; 2) "bullock"; 3) "yearling calf, young (head of) cattle" (Hb., Ph., Pun., Aram. *ʔlp*, HALOT 59; DNWSI 64; Amor. /ʔalpum/, Huffmon APNMT 166; Gelb CAAA 13, 48; Akk. *alpu*, AHw 38; CAD A/1 364ff.); syll. Ug: cf. PNN *il-pí-ya*, PRU 3 193 (RS 15.42+15.110) I 19; *i-li-pí-ya*, Ug 5 96:26; Grøndahl PTU 98; Sivan GAGl 21; ¶ RS Akk.: GU_4, PRU 3 217; PRU 6 155; KTU 4.768:1 and *passim ibid.*; ¶ par.: *ibr*, *arḫt*, *ayl*, *ḥmr*, *klb*, *rum*, *ṣin*, *ṯr*, *yʕl*, *ypt*. ¶ Forms: sg. *alp*, pl. abs. *alpm*, cstr. *alp*, suff. *alpy*, *alph*, *alphm*; du. *alpm*.
1) (Head of) cattle (cf. *infra:* 2 bullock), ★a) in general: *šbʕm arbʕ kbd alpm* seventy four (head of) cattle, 4.749:4; *ʕšrt ksp b alp* ten (shekels) of silver for one (head of) cattle, 4.337:21; five *alp bqr* (head of) cattle and thirteen *ṣin* (head of) sheep, 4.691:1; TN *alp* one (head of) cattle, 4.616:17; PN *wṯlṯ alph* and his three (head of) cattle, 4.417:5; PN, his won, his wife, *alp w ṯmn ṣin* one (head of) cattle and eight of sheep, 4.295:2; *bnšm dt iṯ alpm lhm* people who have cattle, 4.422:1; *ʕl alpm bnš* in charge of the (head of) cattle: an individual;

alp PN b TN (nn) ʕglm (head of) cattle of PN in TN: (nn) calves, 4.783:1 and *passim ibid.*; *mrrt alp* gall of (head of) cattle, 1.175:2, cf. ln. 13; *ṯn alpm* two (head of) cattle, 4.275:18; *(nn) dd(m) l alpm* nn 'cauldronfuls' for the (head of) cattle, RSOu 14 42 [KTU 9.420]:9', 11'; ★b) *bt alpm* stable of the (head of) cattle, 4.358:1 (cf. RS Akk.: É-*tu₄* GU₄.MEŠ, PRU 3 92 (RS 16.189):18); ★c) for slaughter (*ṭbḫ*): *ṭbḫ alpm ap ṣin* they slaughtered cattle and sheep, 1.22 I 12 and par. (// *ṯrrm*, *ʕglm*); *alp yṭbḫ l kṯrt* they sacrificed a (head of) cattle to the DNN, 1.17 II 29; for meat: *ṯmnym ṭbṯḫ alp* eighty *ṭ.*-pieces of (head of) cattle, 4.247:19; he set *alp* a (head of) cattle before her // *mria* a fatling directly before her face, 1.3 IV 41 and par; ★d) sacrificial material: *alp l akl* a (head of) cattle for consumption, 6.13:3; *alp b mḥrṯt* a (head of) cattle for work, 6.14:3 (cf. *infra:* 2.b); *ṯṭbḫ šbʕm alpm k gmn DN* he slaughtered seventy (head of) cattle as an offering to DN, 1.6 I 20 (// *rumm*, *ṣin*, *aylm*, *yʕlm*, *ḥmrm*); *passim* in ritual texts: *b ym mlat tqln alpm* on the day of the full moon are felled two (head of) cattle, 1.109:4; *ṯn alpm* two (head of) cattle, 1.111:15; *alp l mg*(?)*d*(!)*l bʕl ugrt* a (head of) cattle next to the tower (for) DN of TN, 1.119:12; *b ym* <*mlat*> *alpm* on the day <of the full moon>, two (head of) cattle, 1.130:16; for DN *alp šrp* one (head of) cattle as a holocaust, *ibid.* ln. 22; *alp w š* one (head of) cattle and one of sheep, 1.148:2, and *passim* in cultic texts (cf. 1.162:3; 1.170:3, 9; 1.173:3ff.); *alp š* one head (of cattle and) one of sheep, 1.43:6; *ṯn šm w alp* two sheep and one (head of) cattle, 1.436:2; *alp w š šrp alp šlmm* one (head of) cattle and one of sheep as a holocaust, one (head of) cattle as a peace offering, 1.105:23; 1.109:27; cf. 1.164:5; 1.168:10; 1.170:3; 1.171:2; *alp* [ ] *wuz* one (head of) cattle ... and one goose, 1.109:29; *šbʕ alpm* seven (head of) cattle, 1.105:5; *kbd alp* the liver of an ox, 1.39:2; 1.109:9; *ġṣb šmal alpm* the left *ġ.* of two bulls, 1.109:27. Cf. in bkn ctx. *šbʕ alpm ʕl* [seven (head of) cattle..., 1.111:17 (for the various readings and interpretations cf. Del Olmo CR 201 n. 112).

2) Bullock, ★a) *alpm w ṯmṯt* bullocks and personnel, 4.231:9 (cf. RS Akk.: LÚ.MEŠ.SIPA GU₄, PRU 3 11 (RS 15.18):10; cf. LÚ.Ù.DAB GU₄, Ug 5 96:11); cf. PN + *alp*(*m*): 4.261:14, 15, 17, 18, 20, 23; 4.295:6, 8, 13, 17; ★b) work bullock (+ *ḥrṯ*): the lowing *alp ḥrṯ* of work bullocks, 1.14 III 18 and par. (// *ibr*, *ḥmr*, *klb*; cf. *alp b mḥrṯt*, 6.14:3; *supra:* 1.d); *alp PN dt aḫd ḥrṯh* bullocks of PN who has collected his cowherd, 4.296:8; *lḥt alpm ḥrṯm* tablet concerning work bullocks, 2.45:22; *alpm aršt lk* the bullocks you requested for yourself, 2.45:24 (cf. l. 26); *(nn) drt l alpm* (nn *dd*) of bran for the bullocks,

4.636:9 and *passim ibid.*; *ṣmd alpm* yoke of bullocks, 4.367:10; 4.618:10; 4.691:8 (cf. RS Akk.: *ta-pal* GU_4, PRU 6 49:11'); ★c) 'tame' bullock: *alpm alpnm* two 'tame' bullocks, 4.247:25; ★d) fattened (animal) (+ *mru*): (fodder) *l alpm mrim* for the fatling bullock, 4.128:1; (cuts) *alp mri* of fattened (animal), 4.247:16-17.
3) Yearling calf, calf, bullock, young (head of) cattle, ★a): *alp šnt* yearling calf, 1.86:1; *alp dkr* calf, *ibid.* ln. 2; *alp pr* bullock, *ibid.* ln. 3; ★b) in mythological ctx.: *št alp qdmh* he set an ox in front of her, 1.4 V 45 (and par.); *arḫt tld*[ ] *alp* the heifers gave birth to [ ] a yearling calf, 1.10 III 2 (// *ypt*); cf. in bkn ctx. *ibid.* ln. 15-16, *alp* // *a<l>p*; *bʕl yabd l alp* DN perished for the calf, 1.11:4; a category of gods: *špq ilm alpm yn* he provided the calf-gods with wine, 1.4 VI 49 (// *ilht arḫt*). In bkn ctx. *ṯn alpm yrḫ* two bulls, one month old(?), 1.46:11 (cf. Del Olmo CR 280 n. 74; diff. Dijkstra UF 16 1984 72: 'two heads of cattle, it is the month of ...').
In bkn ctx.: 1.11:16; 1.56:4; *w ḥẓ alp*, 1.90:6;]*hn w alp*, 4.14:2; RSOu 14 51 [KTU 9.425]:10, 18, 21.

alp (II) num. "(one, a) thousand" (<(?) collective "herd"; Hb., Pun., Aram. *ʔlp*, HALOT 59; DNWSI 65f.; ESA *ʔlf*, DOSA 18f.; Arab. *ʔalf*, Lane 80; cf. Eth. *ʔĕlf*, CDG 19. Cf. Brockelmann GvG 1 487; Moscati ICGSL 118); ¶ RS Akk.: 2 *li-im* KÙ.BABBAR 1 *li-im* KÙ.GI, PRU 3 92 (RS 16.189):15; x *li-im*, PRU 3 185 (RS 16.146+161):23, 25; *passim* in econ. texts; cf. *li-im*, 4.435:22; 4.610 (I) 44; (II) 49, 51, 53; ¶ par.: *rbt*. ¶ Forms: sg. *alp*, pl. *alpm*; du. *alpm*. (One, a) thousand ★a) in cstr. gen.: *alp ymm* a thousand days, 5.9 I 4 (// *rbt*); *alp ksp* a thousand (shekels of) silver, 1.24:20; 3.8:11; cf. 4.212:1; *alp ṯlṯ* one thousand (shekels of) copper, 4.310:7 *alp ḥẓm* arrows, 4.169:2 (cf. *ibid.* ln. 2-3 and cf. *infra:* 2.a); ★b) adv., by the thousand: (+ *l-*): they walk *l alpm* by the thousand, 1.14 II 39 and par. (// *rbt*); he poured out silver *l alpm* by the thousand, 1.4 I 27 (// *rbbt*); may he smite *alpm ib* enemies by the thousand, 1.19 IV 59; ★c) in appos.: *alp ḥẓr* one thousand mansions, 1.1 II 14 (// *rbt*); *alp šd* one thousand yokes, 1.1 III 2 and par. (// *rbt*); *alp kd* one thousand jars, 1.3 I 15 (// *rbt*); *alp nṯq* one thousand darts/spears(?), 4.169:2 (cf. *supra:* 1.a); ★d) distributive: two ropes *alp alp*(sic.!) *amt* of one thousand cubits each, 4.247:30; ★e) elliptical use: *alp* one thousand 4.271:1; 4.261:23; *w hm alp l tšʕn* but if they do not pay one thousand (shekels of silver), 3.8:13; ★f) two thousand (du. in appos.): *alpm śśwm* two thousand horses, 2.33:24, 32, 38;*kkrm alpm* two thousand talents, 4.720:5; elliptical use: *PN alpm* PN two thousand,

4.261:14 and *passim*; *alpm arbʕt mat* two thousand four hundred, 4.407:1; *alpm ḫmš mat* two thousand five hundred, 4.132:1; 4.626:8; g) thousand(s), pl.: *ṯlṯ ḫmš alpm* copper for five thousand, 4.181:2; *arbʕ alpm mitm* four thousand two hundred, 4.626:2; *arbʕ alpm pḥm ḫmš mat* four thousand five hundred of scarlet purple, 4.203:3; *alpm ṯlṯ ktt* two thousand (shekels of) powdered copper, 4.203:14; *arbʕ alpm iqni ḫmš mat kbd* four thousand five hundred (shekels of) violet purple, 4.203:5.
In bkn ctx.]*nt qdm alpm mznh*, 2.81:25.

alp (III) PN ((?); RSOu 14 p. 358).
PN(?): RSOu 14 40 [KTU 9.419]:12.
Cf. alp (I), alpn, alpy.

ulp cf. *u*, *l (I)*, *p (II)*, only in 1.40; 1.84; 1.154 (cf. Xella TRU 262f.; Del Olmo CR 155f.; De Moor - Sanders UF 23 1991 291f.; diff.: De Tarragon TOu 2 142ff.: 'chef', cf. Hb. *ʔlwp* and in syll. Ug. the element /ʔullūpu/ in PNN, Sivan GAGl 201).
Cf. in bkn ctx.: *an slg ulp* I am PN, the 'chief', 1.66:11.

ulpm PN (etym. unc. Cf. Grøndahl PTU 17, 98; cf. AAN 1 155); ¶ syll.: cf.]*ul-lu-pí*, PRU 3 194 (RS 11.787):11; cf. Sivan GAGl 201; Huehnergard UVST 19, 251, 270.
PN: *bn PN*, 4.412 III 2.

alpn n. m. "domesticated, tame" (Hb. *ʔlwp*, HALOT 54; Arab. cf. *ʔulf*, *ʔalūf*, Lane 80; cf. Aram. *ʔlp*, DNWSI 64f. vb *ʔlp (I)*; Hb. *ʔwlpn*, DJPA 39; diff. Aartun StUL 11ff.: 'an (Dienst) geübter, (ein)geübter (Raub-/Greifvogel)'; De Moor UF 28 1996 157: 'sardines, anchovies'). ¶ Forms: pl. *alpnm*.
Domesticated, tame: *alpm alpnm* two domesticated (bullocks), 4.247:25.

alpy PN (Hurr.(?); cf. Laroche GLH 4; Watson AuOr 13 1995 218; cf. diff.: Grøndahl PTU 98); ¶ syll.: cf. *il-pí-ya*, PRU 3 196 (RS 15.42+) I 19; *i-li-pi-ya*, Ug 5 96:26.
PN: 4.214 I 18.

ilqṣm n. m. "gem", "divine/precious stone"(?) (etym. unc. Cf. Oldenburg CEB 127 n. 5: *ʔl* + *qṣm*, Arab. *qaṣim*; Sanmartín UF 10 1978 351f.: 'das Auserlesenste', ʔqtl pattern from **lqṭ*, Akk. *liqṭu*, AHw 555, CAD L 206ff.; Nougayrol Ug 5 101 n. 1: 'corindon'(?), Akk. *algamišu*, but cf. *algbṯ*); ¶ par.: *ḫrṣ*, *ksp*. ¶ Forms: sg. *ilqṣm*.
Gem, precious stone (?): *yblk udr ilqṣm* may they bring you the most noble gem(?), 1.4 V 17 and par. (// *mid ksp*, *mḫmd ḫrṣ*).

ilrb PN (Sem. Cf. Grøndahl PTU 44, 95, 179; Stamm Beitr. 195f.). Cf.

rbil.
PN: 3.3:11 (*bn ilyn*); 4.63 III 41; 4.63 IV 15.

ilrm PN (Sem. Cf. Grøndahl PTU 46, 95, 182; Bordreuil - Caquot Syria 56 1979 310; Van Soldt SAU 21, 29); ¶ syll.: DINGIR-*ra-mu*, PRU 6 30:20; Ug 5 58:1; 65:1; spelling *ilr*(!)*mh*, 6.66:2 (with *-h* as *mater lectionis*?).
PN: 4.607:19; 4.769:9; *mšmn ilr*(!)*mh* seal of PN, 6.66:2.

ulrm PN (rdg and etym. unc.).
PN: *bn ulrm*(?), 4.759:6.

ilrpi PN (Sem. Cf. Grøndahl PTU 47, 95, 180; Parker UF 4 1972 99).
PN: *bn PN*, 4.347:7.

ilrš PN (Sem. Cf. Weippert ZDPV 82 1966 322ff.; Grøndahl PTU 16, 95, 101; Bordreuil - Caquot Syria 57 1980 364f.). Cf. *ilršp*.
PN: ★a) 4.775:18; ★b) *bn PN:* 4.75 IV 10; 4.366:11; 4.371:2.

ilršp PN (Sem. Cf. Weippert ZDPV 82 1966 322ff.; Grøndahl PTU 95, 181; Bordreuil - Caquot Syria 57 1980 364f.); ¶ syll.: cf. DINGIR.[d]MAŠ.MAŠ, PRU 3 75 (RS 16.344):4, 12; DINGIR.[d]GìR.UNU.GAL, *ibid.* ln. 9.
PN: 4.313:5 (*bn* []); 5.18:5 (*bn ḥnn*).

ils PN (etym. unc. Cf. Grøndahl PTU 102, 224).
PN: *bn PN*, 4.309:6.

ilsk PN (etym. unc. Cf. Grøndahl PTU 224, 234).
PN: ★a) 4.102:8; ★b) *bn PN*, 4.723:1; cf. in bkn ctx.: 4.64 II 10.

ilṣdq PN (Sem. Cf. Grøndahl PTU 45, 47, 95, 187).
PN: ★a) 4.215:4; 4.628:1 (*bn zry*); ★b) *bn PN:* 4.226:9; 4.704:6.

ilṣy PN (Sem.(?); cf. Watson AuOr 8 1990 116); ¶ syll.: *il-ṣi-ya*, PRU 3 71f. (RS 16.356):4, 6.
PN: 4.103:47; 4.607:13.

ilš (I) DN, gatekeeper god / divine herald (cf. Pope WbMyth 289; De Moor ARTU 159 n. 13; Xella TRU 64 for the various interpretations).
DN: *yṣḥ ngr il ilš* he called the herald, the god, DN, 1.16 IV 6 and par.; *ilš ngr bt bʕl* DN, herald of the house of DN, 1.16 IV 7, 11; *š dd ilš* and one ram (and) one cruet (of oil to) DN, 1.87:7; 1.41:6.
Cf. ilš (II), ilšn, bnilš.

ilš (II) PN (Sem. Cf. Grøndahl PTU 98, 423; De Moor - Spronk UF 14 1982 188); ¶ syll.: *i-li-šu*, PRU 6 83 IV 18.
PN: ★a) *bn PN*, 4.232:17; ★b) *bt PN*, 4.781:2.

ilšḥr PN (Sem. Cf. Grøndahl PTU 95, 192; Stamm AS 16 1965 417 n. 48).

PN: *bn PN*, 4.110:15.

ilšlm PN (Sem. Cf. Grøndahl PTU 18, 95, 97, 193); ¶ syll.: DINGIR-*ša-li-ma*, PRU 3 53 (RS 15.89):6; DINGIR-*ša-lim* PRU 3 161 (RS 16.281):6; DINGIR-*šal-ma*, PRU 6 57:6'; DINGIR-*ša-al-mi*, PRU 6 49:9'.

PN: 3.8:19 (*bn prqdš*); 4.382:27 (*bn gsn*).

ilšmḥ PN (Sem. Cf. Grøndahl PTU 94ff.; Hb. *šmḥ*, HALOT 1557).

PN: 4.781:8.

ilšn PN (Sem. Cf. Thureau-Dangin RA 37 1940 104; Grøndahl PTU 95, 98; Dietrich - Loretz - Sanmartín UF 5 1973 81; Gelb - Purves - MacRae NPN 70; Cassin - Glassner AAN 1 67).

PN: 4.79:3; 4.609:36.

ilšpš PN (Sem. Cf. Grøndahl PTU 46, 95, 97 195; Brooke UF 11 1979 n. 58; Bordreuil - Caquot Syria 57 1980 364f.; Van Soldt SAU 21, 29, 126); ¶ syll.: DINGIR.dUTU*(-šu)*, Syria 18 1937 251ff.:30; Ug 5 7:17.

PN: ★a) 4.65:12; 4.131:11; 4.219:6; 4.384:14; 4.425:13; 4.775:21; in bkn ctx.: 4.680:4 (cf.]*ilšp*[*š* or]*i l šp*[*š*, 2.28:2); ★b) *bn PN*, 4.611:16.

ilštmʕ TN (Belmonte RGTC 12/2 141: **Ilištamʕu*. Cf. Grøndahl PTU 60; Heltzer RCAU 15; Astour RSP 2 264f.; UF 13 1981 7; Röllig RLA 5 52; Bordreuil UF 20 1988 12, 16f.; Pardee AfO 36/37 1989/90; Van Soldt UF 28 1996 659; UF 30 1998 723); ¶ syll.: URU DINGIR-*iš-tam-i*, cf. PRU 3 p. 266 (del. RS 16.15:16 with RSP 2 353 no. 152b); PRU 6 p. 146; Ug 5 p. 335; AnOr 48 1971 27 (RS [Varia 12] = "1957.4"):3; cf. Huehnergard UVST 250.

TN: ★a) 1.79:1(?; cf. *ilštmʕy*); 4.68:29; 4.110:1; 4.119:1; 4.365:21; 4.369:14; 4.380:21; 4.382:26, 33; 4.610 (I) 15; 4.629:10; 4.685:9; 4.693:19; 4.698:1; 4.750:9; RSOu 14 48:2; ★b) *gt ilštmʕ*, 1.79:7; 1.80:1 (Belmonte RGTC 12/2 87).

ilštmʕy GN m. (< *ilštmʕ*, TN. Cf. Van Soldt SAU 33; UF 28 1996 659; UF 30 1998 723; Belmonte RGTC 12/2 141). ¶ Forms: sg. *ilštmʕy*; pl. *ilštmʕym*.

GN: 1.79:1(?; cf. *ilštmʕ*); 4.33:29, 30, 31; 4.45:1; 4.51:8 (rdg *ilšt*<*m*>*ʕy*); 4.79:1; 4.86:25-26, 28; 4.124:3; 4.181:7; 4.281:25.

alt (I) n. f. "curse" (Hb. *ʔlh*, HALOT 51; Ph. *alt*, DNWSI 60f.; cf. Akk. *iʔlu*, AHw 373; CAD I/J 91; *i/eʔiltu*, AHw 191; CAD E 51f.; *uʔiltu*, AHw 1405; diff.: De Moor UF 11 1979 650; De Moor - Spronk UF 16 1984 239: 'sworn obligation'; Caquot SEL 5 1988 31ff.: 'appui' (?), cf. *alt (II)*). ¶ Forms: sg.(?) *alt*.

Curse: *idy alt l aḥš idy alt in ly* already I do not feel the curse, already the curse does not affect me!, 1.82:2. In bkn ctx.: 1.55:5.

alt (II) n. f. "support, pillar" (?) (Van Zijl Baal 235f.; De Moor SP 236f.; Renfroe AULS 78f.; cf. Hb. *ʔyl*, HALOT 40; also possible: "footstool, base", Akk. *littu* CAD L 219 (c); AHw 557); ¶ par.: *ḫṭ*, *ksu*. ¶ Forms: pl.(?). cstr. *alt*.
Support, pillar(?): *l ysʕ alt ṯbtk* I will certainly rip out the supports(?) of your seat, 1.6 VI 27 and par. (// *ksa*, *ḫṭ*).

ilt (I) n. f. 1) "goddess"; 2) "'the goddess'", epithet used as noun, said of *aṯrt* (cf. *il (I)*; Ph., Pun. *ʔlt*, DNWSI 53f.; ESA *ʔlt*, DOSA 15; Akk. *i/eltu* AHw 373; CAD I/J 89f.; Ebla cf. MUNUS.BE.AL$_6$ *il-tum*, Krebernik QuSe 18 122); ¶ par.: *aṯrt (II)*, *il (I)*, *ʕnt*. ¶ Forms: sg. *ilt*; du. *iltm*; pl. *ilht* (cf. *ilh*).
1) Goddess, ★a) as a category/class: *ilm w ilht* gods and goddesses, 1.25:2; *k in b ilht qlṣk* for among the goddesses there is no opposition (like) yours, 1.3 V 28; *tštql ilt l hklh* the goddess went down to her palace, 1.3 II 18 (// *ʕnt*); *w tqdmnn ilht* and the goddesses presented, RSOu 14 53 [KTU 9.432]:37'; ★b) classes and groups of goddesses: *iltm ḫnqtm* the two strangling goddesses, 1.39:18 and par.; *ilht ḫprt, arṯt, ksat, dkrt*, the ewe-lamb-, cow-, throne-, cup-goddesses, 1.4 VI 48-54; *š ilt mgdl š ilt asrm* one ram for the goddess of the tower // of the prisoners, 1.39:11 and par.; *aṯth ngrt ilht* his wife(wives), the herald goddess(es), 1.16 IV 4 and par.; ★c) qualifying a deity or place: *šmʕ ilht kṯrt* listen goddesss DN!, 1.24:11 (cf. ln. 40); cf. in bkn ctx. *l ilt*[(...) *l ilt bt*[(...) *l ilt* [x]*xpn*, 1.81: 5, 8, 21.
2) 'The goddess', epithet used as a noun, said of *aṯrt* (cf. *il (I)*): *ilt w ṣbrt ary*(!)*h* the goddess and the clan of her kin, 1.3 V 37 and par.; *ilt ṣdnym* the goddess of the Sidonians (?), 1.14 IV 35 (// *aṯrt ṣrm*); *w ṯḫss aṯrt ndrh w ilt*[and DN remembered his vow and the goddess [, 1.15 III 26; *mdbḥt bt ilt* the altar of the temple of 'the goddess', 1.41:24 and par. In bkn ctx.: 1.1 IV 14;]*w bnh ilt*, 1.117:4.
Cf. ʕbdilt, ʕzilt, bnilt.

ilt (II) PN (Sem.(?). Cf. Grøndahl PTU 98; Ribichini - Xella SEL 8 1991 159; Watson AuOr 13 1995 291; AuOr 14 1996 95).
PN: *bn PN*, 4.35 I 19. Cf. in bkn ctx. 4.512:3.

altġ PN (Hurr.(?) Cf. TN Allat, *Allatḫe*, *Alatḫama*, Van Soldt SAU 215 n. 292; Belmonte RGTC 12/2 14f.: **Allat*).
PN: *bn PN*, 4.214:8.

ilṭḥm PN (Sem. Cf. Grøndahl PTU 31, 96, 210; Astour CRAA 18 19 n. 107; Cifford CMC 57; Van Soldt SAU 21ff.); ¶ syll.: DINGIR-*taḫ*-

mu and var., cf. Syria 18 1937 246 (RS 8.145):27; PRU 3 p. 246; PRU 4 p. 246; PRU 6 p. 139; Ug 5 69:2; cf. DINGIR-*taḫ-ḫi-me*, PRU 3 194 (RS 11.839):6? (Van Soldt SAU 338 n. 179); cf. Huehnergard UVST 243 n. 127; AkkUg 343, 371.

PN: 2.49:9; 4.63 II 5; 4.180:6; 4.366:5 (*bn dnn*); 4.366:12 (*bn śrn*); 4.371:13; 4.690:8 (*biry*); in bkn ctx.: 4.674:1; 4.398:8. Cf. *ilṭ*[, 4.512:3.

Cf. ṯḥm, yṯḥm.

iltm PN (Sem. Cf. Grøndahl PTU 45, 96, 201, 423; Oldenburg CEB 28).

PN: 4.86:16 (Van Soldt SAU 41).

alty PN (etym. unc.).

PN: 4.343:3.

alṯ TN (Belmonte RGTC 12/2 16).

TN: 1.54:10; 1.131:7.

ulṯ n. m. of a tool for moulding or mixing clay ("trowel, float, mould"(?); cf. Hb., Aram. *lwš*, HALOT 525; DNWSI 570; Akk. *lâšu*, AHw 556; CAD L 110; Arab. *lāṯa* Lane 2677ff.; cf. De Moor UF 12 1980 432; CARTU 128: 'brick-mould'; Renfroe AULS 79); ¶ par.: *lbnt*. ¶ Forms: sg. *ulṯ*.

Bricklayer's tool for moulding clay (trowel, float, mould(?)): *ʕbd (...) aḫd ulṯ* slave (...) who takes hold of the *u.*, 1.4 VI 60 (// *lbnt*); of bronze: *ulṯ ṯlṯ* an *u.* of bronze, 4.390:7.

alṯn PN (< *alṯy*, TN. Cf. Grøndahl PTU 27, 98, 301; Dietrich - Loretz - Sanmartín UF 5 1973 81).

PN: *bn PN*, 4.93 II 9; 4.232:14; 4.681:2. Cf. in bkn ctx.: 4.526:1.

ilṯr PN (Sem. Cf. Ribichini - Xella RSF 15 1987 13 and n. 50).

PN: 4.607:32.

alṯt PN (< *alṯy*, TN. Cf. Grøndahl PTU 98; Astour JESHO 13 1970 122; Dietrich - Loretz - Sanmartín UF 5 1973 81).

PN: 4.175:12.

ilṯtmr PN (Sem. Cf. Grøndahl PTU 96, 197; Van Soldt SAU 317).

PN: *bn PN*, 4.103:11.

alṯy (I) TN (Belmonte RGTC 12/2 11f.: *Alašiya*. Cf. Astour RSP 2 259, 340; Wachsman BA 49 1986 37ff.; Pardee Syria 65 1988 189 n. 54; AfO 36/37 1989/90 481f.); ¶ syll.: KUR] URU *a-la-ši-ia*[ki], KTU

4.102:31; KUR *a-la-ši-ia*, RSOu 7 35:29; cf. KUR(.URU) *a-la-ši-a/ia/ya*(ki), PRU 4 p. 253; Ug 5 p. 335.

TN: *any TN* the ship of TN, 4.390:1; *kl il alṯy* all the gods of TN, 2.42:8.

alṯy (II) PN (< *alṯy*, TN. Cf. Grøndahl PTU 98; Laroche GLH 42; cf. West AOAT 233 30: PN *a-ra-si-yo*, Linear B).

PN: 4.705:9.

alṯy(y) GN m. (< *alṯy*, TN); syll.: PN KUR *a-lì*(ŠI)-*ši-yu*, PRU 6 54:15; [LÚ].MEŠ KUR *a-lì-ši*-PI, PRU 6 147:5. ¶ Forms: sg. *alṯyy*, var.: *alṯy*.

GN: *k yqny ġzr b alṯyy* when he was (about to) acquire a youth from a GN, 1.141:1 (Dietrich - Loretz MU 10); PN *alṯy(y)*, 4.343:3; 4.352:2; *l p alṯy* according to the custom (of the) GN, 1.40:29 and par.; cf. (wine) *l alṯy* for the (god) GN, 4.149:8 (Sanmartín UF 21 1989 341). In bkn ctx.: 4.155:3.

ilwn PN (Hurro-Anat.(?); cf. Gelb - Purves - MacRae NPN 44; Cassin - Glassner AAN 1 43; cf. Grøndahl PTU 273; Watson AuOr 13 1995 219); ¶ syll.: cf. *i-lu-wa*, PRU 4 234 (RS 17.112): 9 and *passim ibid.*; DINGIR-*a-?-ni*, PRU 6 135:3; *al-lu-wa-ma*, RS 25.138:3 (Lackenbacher Fs. Sjöberg 319).

PN: 4.83:4.

aly(y) PN (Hurr. Cf. Grøndahl PTU 216).

PN: *bn PN*, 2.72:13 (cf. copy RSOu 7 plate XIX); 4.366:6; 4.753:3. Cf. 1.42:45 (Hurr.).

ily PN (Sem. Cf. Grøndahl PTU 51, 96; Berger WO 5 1969/70 278; Bordreuil SEL 5 1988 28); ¶ syll.: *i-lu-ya*, RA 38 1941 4 (RS 11.856):6; DINGIR-*ya*, PRU 3 36 (RS 15.180):2; *i-li-ya*, Ug 5 84:3; 95:3; AN.LIM-*li-ia*, Ug 5 159:3 (cf. Nougayrol Ug 5 p. 35).

PN: ★a) 4.63 II 22; 4.347:5; 4.625:22 (*mrily*); 4.488:2; ★b) *bn PN* 3.10:22. Bkn: *ily*[, 4.227 II 11; 4.334:3; 4.432:21; 4.488:2; 4.583:1; RSOu 14 45 [KTU 9.418]:8.

ilym PN (Sem. Cf. Grøndahl PTU 95, 144). Cf. *ymil*.

PN: 4.116:13.

ilyn PN (Sem. Cf. Grøndahl PTU 53, 96; Astour AnOr 48 27; Bordreuil - Caquot Semitica 28 1978 9; Syria 56 1979 310; 57 1980 363; Van Soldt SAU 333); ¶ syll.: DINGIR-*ia-nu*, cf. PRU 3 p. 246; PRU 4 p. 246; PRU 6 p. 139; AnOr 48 29 (RS [Varia 12] "1957.4"):2; Ug 5 95:13; cf. Van Soldt SAU 151.

PN: ★a) 4.232:3, 37; 4.277:6; 4.607:18; Bkn: 4.772:4; 4.785:28; ★b) *bn PN*, 4.229:11; 4.340:1; 4.759:9; 4.769:6. Bkn: 3.3:11, 4.63 II 47.

ilyqn PN (Sem. Cf. Watson AuOr 8 1990 116).
PN: 4.607:24.

ilyy PN (Sem. Cf. Grøndahl PTU 53, 96f.); ¶ syll.: cf. [f]*e-li-ia-ya*, PRU 3 110 (RS 8.208):5.
PN: ★a) 4.244:24; ★b) *bn PN*, 4.791:18 (cf. Bordreuil SEL 5 1988 28).

alz PN (Hurr. Cf. Grøndahl PTU 22, 205, 216, 218; Dietrich - Loretz - Sanmartín UF 5 1973 81; Rainey IOS 3 1973 50; Van Soldt SAU 357); ¶ syll.: *al-la-zi* and var. *a-la-an-zu*, PRU 3 66 (RS 16.252): 2, 6, 10, 21; *a-la-zi*, Ug 7 pl. 2. rev. 15'; RSOu 7 3 obv. 15'; cf. Huehnergard AkkUg 115.
PN: *bn PN*, 4.77:12; 4.93 II 14; 4.348:15; 4.412:27; 4.422:4; 4.755:7. Cf. in bkn ctx. 4.498:7; 4.526:3.

alzy GN m. (cf. Dietrich - Loretz - Sanmartín UF 5 1973 81; Pardee Syria 65 1988 189 n. 54; cf. Astour UF 1 1969 7 on Hurr. *alṯ(d)* and the TN Alliše in Alalakh, Belmonte RGTC 12/2 15: **Alluzu*). ¶ Forms: sg. *alzy*.
GN: 4.272:1.
Cf. alḏy, alṯy.

im conj. 1) cond. "if" and 2) disj. "either... or..." (Hb. *ʔm*, HALOT 60f., Ph.-Pun. *ʔm*, DNWSI 68f.; Arab. *ʔin*, Lane 106f.; Aram. *ʔn*, DNWSI 68f.; DJPA 63f.; Eth. *ʔĕmma*, CDG 22f.; cf. *hm*. Cf. Aartun PU 2 95; De Moor ULe 95; Garbini SNO 57). ¶ Forms: *im*.
1) Cond. conj. if: *im aḥd b aḫk* if one of your brothers (slakes my thirst (?)), 1.6 V 21; *im mlkytn yrgm* if PN says (it), 2.15:8 (cf. *hn hm yrgm mlk* then, if the king says, 2.33:30); *im klt knyt* if the perfect brides 1.3 I 26.
2) Disj. conj. or: *im PN im PN im* either *PN* or PN, or PN, or PN, 2.72:12-13; *im ht l b mṣqt yṯbt* or if the city is in(?) a difficult situation, 2.72:20 (Bordreuil - Pardee RSOu 7 88:20f.). In bkn ctx.: 4.17:2.
Cf. hm (I).

um n. f. "mother" (Hb., Ph., Pun., Aram. *ʔm*, HALOT 61; DNWSI 66ff.; Emar /ʔimmu/ Pentiuc Vocabulary 89; Amor. /ʔi/ummum/, Gelb CAAA 14; Ebla /ʔummum/ in AMA.MU = *ù-mu-mu*, VE 1044; Krebernik ZA 73 1983 37; Fronzaroli EL 151; StEb 7 1984 152f.; cf. *um(-ma)*, Krebernik PET 109; Sanmartín AuOr 9 1991 173f.; Akk. *ummu*, AHw 1416f.; ESA *ʔm*, DOSA 19; Arab. *ʔummu*, Lane 89f.; Eth. *ʔĕmm*, CDG 22); syll. Ug: cf. the element /ʔummu/ in PNN, Sivan GAGL 201; ¶ RS Akk.: AMA, PRU 3 237; PRU 4 264; cf. Ug

5 169:9' and *passim*; cf. Huehnergard AkkUg 377; ¶ par.: *ad, adn (I), aḫ (I), aḫt (I), arḫ*. ¶ Forms: sg. *um*, suff. *umh, umy*; pl. suff. *umhthm*. Mother, ★a) of men and gods: *tṣḥ um um* she cried: mother, mother!, 1.23:33 (// ad); *umh kp mznm* her mother arranged the scales of the balance, 1.24:34 (// *adn, iḫh, aḫth*); *l umy adtny* to my mother, our lady (suff. du.), 2.11:1; *l mlkt umy* to the queen, my mother, 2.13:2; 2.30:1; cf. 2.16:2; 2.34:2; *l mlkt umy adty* to the queen, my mother and lady, 2.82:1; *l pʕn umy qlt* I fall at the feet of my mother, 2.13:5 and par.; *l umy yšlm* may it be well with my mother, *ibid.* ln. 6; 2.30:5; *[l]y umy <y>šlm* may it be well with my mother, 2.72:5; cf. 5.10:3; *ṯmny ʕm umy mnm šlm* there, with my mother may all go well, 2.34:8 and par.; *ky tdbr umy l pn qrt* already declared my mother before the city, 2.72:18; *w at umy al tdḥl* and you, mother mine, do not fear, 2.30:21; *umy tdʕ* know, my mother, 2.16:6; *lḥt šlm k likt umy ʕmy* the letter of greeting that my mother sent me, 2.34:6; *um tšmḫ{.}m ab* (my) mother pleased (my) father, 2.16:10. In bkn ctx.: *nṯṯt um ʕlt b aby* one shocked mother launches herself on my father, 1.82:9; *dmt um il[m* tower of the mother of (?) the god[s(?), 2.31:46; *um bnš* 4.351:1; *w l PN umy* and to PN, my mother, RSOu 14 49 [KTU 9.433]:3; ★b) of animals: *um pḥl (...) qrit l špš umh* the mother of the stallion (...) invokes the Sun, her mother, 1.100:1-2 and par.; *bn ḫpṯ l umhthm* the young of the loose (cattle low) for their mothers, 1.15 I 6 (// *arḫ*); *um nšrm* mother of the eagles, 1.19 III 29 (// *ab*); ★c) *bn um* sons of one mother, 1.14 I 9 (// *aḫm*); *bnm umy* sons of my mother, 1.6 VI 11 and par. (// *aḫym*); *ṯar um* maternal relatives, 1.14 I 15 (cf. Verreet UF 19 1987 324ff.).
Cf. umt, umy, ištrmy, ʕṯtrum.

amd adv. "always" (cf. Arab. *ʔamad*, Lane 95; Margalit UF 8 1976 177; 19 1984 155f.; diff.: Watson UF 8 1976 375 n. 30: Akk. *madādu*; Hillers Fs. Iwry 105ff.: vb *mdd, mdw/y*, 'to clothe' with diff. rdg; Renfroe AULS 79: mistake for *t*(!)*md*, Hb. *tmyd*); ¶ par.: *ʕlm, ʕnt, dr*. ¶ Forms: *amd*.
Always: *amd gr bt il* always be a guest of the sanctuary, 1.19 III 47 (// *ʕnt ... p ʕlmh*, // *ʕnt p dr dr*).

amdn PN (Hurr.(?); cf. Grøndahl PTU 217, 262; Van Soldt SAU 34); ¶ syll.: cf. *am-ma-da-na*, PRU 3 202 (RS 16.257+) III 38.
PN: *bn PN*, 4.69 VI 30; 4.233:8. In bkn ctx.: 4.413:2; 4.633:13; 4.761:7.

amdy PN (Hurr.(?); cf. Grøndahl PTU 217).
PN: *bn PN*, 4.335:22. In bkn ctx.: 4.413:2; 4.633:13; 4.761:7.

umdy GN; cf. *udmy.*

amḏy TN (Belmonte RGTC 12/2 19: **ʔAmmiḏā(yu).* Cf. Heltzer RCAU 8; Xella MLE 1 1982 53; Bordreuil UF 20 1988 10, 12f.; Pardee AfO 36/37 1989/90 482; Van Soldt UF 28 1996 659; UF 30 1998 725); ¶ syll.: URU *a/am-mi/mì-za/ša(-ú),* cf. PRU 3 p. 265; cf. Huehnergard UVST 224; Val Soldt SAU 337).
TN: 4.48:11; 4.68:43; 4.73:13; 4.346:6; 4.380:16; 4.610 (I) 29; 4.693:27; RSOu 14 35 [KTU 9.388] I 36.

amht, cf. *amt (I).*

umḫ(y) PN (etym. unc. Cf. Watson AuOr 14 1996 96).
PN: *bn PN,* 4.35 I 6; 4.692:11.

ummt PN (bkn?) (Sem. etym. unc. Cf. Grøndahl PTU 99, 162, 147; Watson AuOr 14 1996 96).
PN: *bn ummt*[, 4.64 V 4.

amn (I) DN (< Eg. *ymn,* Otto LdÄ 1 238ff.; Helck WbMyth 331; cf. Muchiki Loanwords 66; cf. Hb. *ʔmwn,* HALOT 62; Akk. *Amunu, Amāna,* Deimel Panth 49f.; the element /amān-/ in EA PNN, Hess AmPN 216); ¶ syll.: cf. PN *a-ma-an-ma(-aš)-šu,* PRU 4 109 (RS 17.28) 4 and *passim ibid.*
DN: *l pn amn w l pn il mṣrm* nefore DN and before the gods of TN, 2.23:21. For 5.11:21 cf. *amn (III).*

amn (II) TN (Belmonte RGTC 12/2 17: **ʔAmānu.* Cf. Astour RSP 2 260); cf. (ḪUR.SAG) *a/am-ma-(-a)-na,* Del Monte - Tischler RGTC 6 11f.; Hb. *ʔmnh,* Ct. 4:8.
TN: *ġr amn,* 2.33:16.

amn (III) adj. m. "faithful"(?) (Hb., Aram., Samal. /ʔ-m-n/, *ʔmn,* HALOT 63f.; DNWSI 72f.; Pun. *emanethi,* DNWSI 73: *ʔmnh*; Arab. *ʔamina,* Lane 100ff.; Eth. *ʔamna,* CDG 24. Cf. Caquot Ug 7 398).
¶ Forms: sg. *amn*[.
Faithful(?): in bkn ctx. *d lb amn* of a faithful(?) heart, 5.11:21 (cf. Hb. *lbb nʔmn*; alternatively, Pardee AfOB 19 1982 45: 'according to the heart (of Amon)', cf. *amn (I)*).

/ʔ-m-r/ vb Gt: "to look at"; N: "to be seen(?)" (Akk. *amāru,* Ahw 40ff.; CAD A/2 5-27; Eth. *ʔammara, ʔaʔmara,* CDG 25; Ebla cf. IGI.ŠÈ.DU = *a-me-lum,* Fronzaroli LE 135; StEb 7 1984 148; cf. /M-L/, Krebernik PET 54; *a/i/da/ne-mur*(ḪAR)-(DN), Müller Biling. 182; Fronzaroli ARES 1 16ff.; Amor. cf. /ʔ-m-r/, Gelb CAAA 14. On the existence of a Ug root */ʔ-m-r/ (II) 'to say' cf. *amr (I).* Cf. Sanmartín UF 5 1973 263ff.; De Moor SP 129ff.); syll. Ug: cf. PNN *a-mar-*[d]IM, PRU 4 108 (RS 18.114):6; 166 (RS 17.129):3, 5; *a-mur-*[d]IM, Ug 5

51:7; ¶ RS Akk.: *a-ma-ru*, Ug 5 133 obv. 7'; 134:1'; ¶ par.: /ʕ-n/. ¶ Forms:
Gt prefc. *yitmr*, *ytmr*; N prefc. *yamr*.
Gt. To look at: *ytmr bʕl bnth* DN looked at his daughters, 1.3 I 22 (// *yʕn*; cf. De Moor SP 81: 'to look for'); *išt ištm yitmr (...) lšnhm* like a great blaze they looked at (...) his tongue, 1.2 I 32 (cf. diff.: Dobrusin JANES 13 1981 8 n. 12: subj. *ištm* [du. f.] or 'messengers' [du. m.]).
N. To be seen(?): cf. in bkn ctx.: *w l yamr* and was / was not seen(?), 1.172:22.
Cf. amril, amrbʕl, amry.

amr (I) n. m. 1) "order, demand"; 2) "word(?)" (Hb. *ʔ(w)mr*, HALOT 67; Pun(?), Aram., Edom. *ʔmr*, DNWSI 77f.; ESA *ʔmr*, DOSA 21; Arab. *ʔamr*, Lane 96f. On the existence of a Ug root */ʔ-m-r/ (II) 'to say' cf. De Moor SP 81, 129 (1.2 I 15-16); UF 12 1980 432 (1.169:11); Sanmartín UF 5 1973 263-270 (1.13:26-30); cf. Amor /ʔ-m-r/, Huffmon APNMT 168; Gelb CAAA 14, and cf. Hb., Ph., Pun., Aram. *ʔmr*, HALOT 65ff.; DNWSI 73ff.; ESA *ʔmr*, DOSA 21; Arab. *ʔmr*, Lane 95f. Diff.: De Moor UF 12 1980 306; Del Olmo MLC 493); ¶ par.: *dʕt*. ¶ Forms: sg. *amr*.
1) Order, demand: *qmm aṯr amr* standing, they transmitted (their) demand, 1.2 I 31 and par. (// *dʕthm*).
2) Word(?), in bkn ctx.: *amrk* your word(?), 1.16 IV 1 (De Moor - Spronk UF 14 1982 187: // *pk*; diff.: Del Olmo MLC 316: 'vista'; cf. Segert UF 18 1986 290 n. 69); 1.95:3; 1.107:16, 17, 20.

amr (II), cf. *imr (I)*.

amr (III) TN (Belmonte RGTC 12/2 21ff.: *Amurru*. Cf. Astour RSP 2 260f.; Pardee AfO 36/37 1989/90 439); ¶ syll.: KUR(.MEŠ) *a-mur-ri* / MAR.TU[ki], cf. PRU 3 p. 265; PRU 4 p. 253; Ug 5 p. 335; RSOu 7 17:5, 25; Dietrich - Loretz IOSt 18 1998 335-363; Izre'el AmAk 2 64-100 *passim*; ¶ par.: *yman*.
TN: *ṣʕ il dqt k amr* a divine platter worked in the TN style, 1.4 I 41 (// *yman*); *mlk amr* the king of TN, 2.72:26, 29; *bt mlk amr* the daughter of the king of TN, 2.72:17, 24, 32. In bkn ctx.: *ʕṣ amr yuḫ*[*d*, 1.22 II 17; cf. 4.94:14. Cf. Hurr. *amrw*, 1.125:6.

amr[Bkn PN *bn amr*[, 4.93 I 20.

imr (I) n. m., "lamb" (Hb. *ʔmr*, HALOT 67; Ph., Pun., Aram. *ʔmr*, DNWSI 78; Akk. *immeru*, AHw 378; CAD I/J 129ff.; cf. Del Olmo BSA 7 1993 184ff.); ¶ RS Akk.: *i*]*m-me-er-tu*.MEŠ, PRU 6, 120:4; cf. Sanmartín BSA 7 1993 200f.; ¶ par.: *il (II)*, *ʕgl*, *ʕgṯ*, *llu*, *ṯr*.

¶ Forms: sg. *imr*; suff. *imrh*; broken pl.(?) *amr* (or allophone).
Lamb: *lqḥ imr dbḥ b ydh* he took a sacrificial lamb in his hand, 1.14 III 56 and par. (// *llu*); *ʕdbnn ank imr b py* I myself put him (like) a lamb in my mouth, 1.6 II 22 and par. (// *llu*); [*a*]*msḫnn k imr l arṣ* I can pull him like a lamb to the ground, 1.3 V 1; *tʕdb imr b pḫd* she prepared a lamb from among the yearlings, 1.17 V 22 and par. (diff.: 'a lamb from the flock', Akk. *puḫādu*, Arab. *faḫid*, cf. Margalit UF 15 1983 80); *k lb ṯat l imrh* like the heart of the ewe for her lamb, 1.6 II 29 and par. (// *ʕgl*); *ṭṭbḫ imr wlḥm* she slaughtered a lamb and ate (it), 1.16 VI 20 and par. (// *mgṯ*); *šql (...) imr qmṣ llim* they slaughtered (...) lamb, suckling lambs in heaps, 1.22 I 14 and par. (// *ṯrm, ilm, ʕglm*); *imr w ynt qrt l ṯʕ* a lamb and a domestic dove to the Hero, 1.119:10.
Bkn ctx.: *tdbḥ amr* they sacrificed lambs, 1.20 I 10 (cf. *ʕl*(!) *amr*, 1.22 II 17); *im*]*r špr* fine lambs (?), 1.108:10 (cf. Hb. *ʔmry špr* Gen 49:21; Akk. *immir supūri*, CAD S 396-398; cf. Gevirtz JBL 103 1984 516f.; Dietrich - Loretz UF 16 1984; Pardee TPM 99ff., 106ff.). Bkn: 1.86:16.
Cf. imrt.

imr (II) TN(?) (Belmonte RGTC 12/2 69ff.: *E/imar*. Cf. Astour UF 2 1970 3); ¶ syll.: cf. URU/KUR *e-mar*, PRU 3 16 (RS 12.05):7'; PRU 4 217 (RS 17.143):13, 21; Ug 5 57:11; RSOu 7 30:8, 19; cf. LÚ URU *e-mar*, RSOu 7 32:31.
TN(?): in Hurr. ctx., 1.131:5.

amril PN (Sem. Cf. Grøndahl PTU 37, 41, 96, 99).
PN: 4.643:15.

amrbʕl PN (Sem. Cf. Grøndahl PTU 37, 41, 61, 99, 117; Dietrich - Loretz Fs. Altheim 1969 23; Lipiński Or 40 1971 329; Weinfeld UF 4 1972 139; Coogan Or 44 1975 197); ¶ syll.: *a-mar-*[d]IM/U, cf. PRU 4 p. 244; PRU 6 36: 2 and *passim ibid.*; RSOu 7 15:5; *a-mur-*[d]IM, Ug 5 51:7 and *passim ibid.*
PN: 4.116:16; 4.261:8 (?); 4.644:6.

amrr DN, one of the two messenger-boys of the goddess *aṯrt*: *qdš (w) amrr* ('Blessed', elative ʔqll pattern of /m-r-r/; cf. Virolleaud Syria 13 1932 135; Mullen Council 214 n. 172; diff. Dietrich - Loretz UF 5 1973 74: 'Amurru', spelling of the long consonant /rr/).
DN: 1.3 VI 11 (// *dgy aṯrt*); 1.4 IV 3, 8, 13; *qdš yuḫdm šbʕr amrr k kbkb* DN se began to shine, DN like a star, 1.4 IV 17; *qdš w amrr* DN_1 and DN_2, 1.123:26.

imrt PN (Sem. Cf. Grøndahl PTU 99).

PN: *bn PN*, 4.75 III 10; 4.713:5; RSOu 14 44:1.

amry PN (Sem. Cf. Grøndahl PTU 51, 99).
PN: 4.41:8; 4.44:32; 4.723:5. Cf. in bkn ctx.: 1.77:1; 4.415:5.

amṣ n./adj. m. "strong" (cf. Hb. *ʔmyṣ*, HALOT 63; DNWSI 73; Miller UF 2 1970 161; Dahood RSP 3 73f.). ¶ Forms: sg. *amṣ*.
Strong:]*mlkn amṣ*]our king (is) strong, 2.33:5; *ydk amṣ yd*[(may) your hand (be) strong, your hand[, 1.82:14 (cf. Del Olmo, CR 376).

amšrt DN(?) (possibly a copyist or dictation mistake for **aṯrt*).
DN(?): in an offering list, *l amšrt š* to DN(?): a ewe, 1.162:15.

amt (I) n. f. 1) "(female) slave, maidservant"; 2) "servant", formula of politeness (Hb. *ʔmh*, HALOT 61; Ph., Pun., *ʔmt*; Aram. *ʔmh*, DNWSI 70f.; Amor. /ʔamtum/, Gelb CAAA 13, 49; Akk. *amtu*, AHw 45; CAD A/2 80-85; ESA *ʔmt*, DOSA 19; Arab. *ʔama*, Lane 103; Eth. *ʔamat*, CDG 26; cf. Ebla /ʔam(a)tum/ in MÍ = *ʔa*$_5$(NI)*-ma-tum*, VE 1160; Krebernik ZA 73 1983 41; ARET 5 49); ¶ RS Akk.: (MÍ.MEŠ.)GEMÉ(.MEŠ), *passim*, PRU 3 232; PRU 4 259; PRU 6 150; Ug 5 340; ¶ par.: *ʕbd*. ¶ Forms: sg. *amt*; suff. *amtk*; pl. *amht* (cf. UT 8.8).
1) Slave: *hm amt aṯrt* is DN a slave?, 1.4 IV 61 (// *ʕbd*); *tdmmt amht* lasciviousness with (female) slaves, 1.4 III 21-22 (diff.: cf. Dietrich - Loretz UF 18 1986 448: 'Tadeleien der Mägde'); *amt yrḫ* (female) slave of DN, 1.12 I 15-16 (Wyatt UF 8 1976 417; Watson UF 9 1977 282); maidservant: *bn amt* maidservants, 1.14 II 3 and par. (diff.: Wyatt UF 19 1987 383: royal title 'born of the sacred marriage'; Hendel EP 50: 'craftsmen'); *kd bn amht* a jar for the maidservants, 4.230:9; *bt amt* maid, 4.659:7.
2) 'Servant', a term for an inferior in letters: *amtk* your servant, 2.70:12, 19 (cf. RS Akk.: *um-ma PN* GÉME*-ki*, PRU 6 2:3). In bkn ctx.: RSOu 14 51 [KTU 9.425]:20.

amt (II) n. f. "elbow", "ell" (Hb., Aram. *ʔmh*, HALOT 61f.; DNWSI 69f.; Akk. *ammatu*, AHw 44; CAD A/2 70ff.; Ebla /ʔammatum/ in Á.KÙŠ = *a-ma-tum*, VE 541; Krebernik ZA 73 1983 20; Fronzaroli EL 135; StEb 7 1964 149; ESA *ʔmt*, DOSA 19f.; Eth. *ʔĕmat*, CDG 26); ¶ RS Akk.: cf. (PN to PN) *a-na* DUMU.MEŠ*-šu* DUMU.MEŠ *am-ma*-TI *ir-ku-uš-šu*, PRU 3 55 (RS 15.92):6; cf. Ug 5 2:4; 81:4; 82:5; according to Rainey Or 34 1965 15 n. 7s., RSP 2 91: 'sonship of a cubit' (DUMU.MEŠ *am-ma-ti*); but cf. CAD A/2 75: *ammatu* D; Sivan GAGl 190; Huehnergard UVST 189; very unlikely Hurr. *ammati* 'grand-père', Laroche GLH 47; cf. Sanmartín UF 21 1989 335ff.; ¶ par.: *uṯ*, *ṯkm*, *yd*. ¶ Forms: sg. *amt*; adv. suff. *amth*, *amtm*;

du.(?) *amtm*.

Elbow, ★a) anatom.: *yrḥṣ ydh amth* she washed her arms up to the elbow, 1.14 III 53 and par. (// *ṯkm*; cf. Aartun PU 1 41); *kry amt ʕpr* dig (your) elbow in the earth, 1.12 I 23 (// *yd*; cf. Dahood RSP 3 121); ★b) as a measure, ell: two ropes *alp alp amt* of a thousand ells each, 4.247:30; I am going to consume (you) *ḏrqm amtm* in lumps, ell by ell, 1.5 I 6 (// *uṭ*; cf. Dietrich - Loretz UF 12 1980 405; Sanmartín *ibid.* 438; diff.: cf. Del Olmo IMC 158f.: 'perecí', cf. /m-t/); twelve *ḫpnt śśwm amtm tkyġ yd llḫhm* sets of protective padding for horses, of two ells, of the *t.*(?) type, with their *l.*, 4.363:4.

imt n. f. "truth", adv. use "certainly, truly", "in truth, straight to the point" (Hb. *ʔmt*, HALOT 68f.; cf. Dahood ULx 84; De Moor SP 187; Tropper Or 61 1992 448-453; diff.: Margalit MLD 101; Abou Assaf AAAS 29/30 1979/80 261: 'herbe, paille', Arab. *ʔamat*; Gray LC 52, n. 4: 'to be thirsty', Arab. *ʔamma*; Cassuto BOS 2 142: 'to slay', ʔafʕel of **m(w)t*). ¶ Forms: sg. *imt*.

In truth > certainly, straight to the point: *hm imt imt* or (said) straight to the point, 1.5 I 18; *p imt b klat ydy ilḥm* and it is true that with both hands I swallow, 1.5 I 19.

Cf. mt (IV).

umt n. f. "family, clan" (Hb. *ʔmh*, HALOT 62; Akk. *ummatu*, Ahw 1414f.; Arab. *ʔummat*, Lane 90; cf. Malamat UF 11 1979 527ff., esp. 532f.; Renfroe AULS 79); syll. Ug: cf. /ʔummatu/ in A.ŠÀ *i-na* AN.ZA.GÀR *um-ma-ti*, PRU 3 79ff. (RS 16.239):22; Huehnergard UVST 107; ¶ par.: *bt (II)*. ¶ Forms: sg. *umt*, suff. *umty*, *umtk*, *umtn*(?).

Family, clan: *umt* [*krt*] the family of PN, 1.14 I 6 (// *bt*); *ʕl umty* my kin, 1.6 IV 19; 1.19 IV 35 and par. (// *aḫy*; cf. Caquot - Sznycer TOu I 264 n. m); bkn ctx. *umtn* our clan(?), 1.63:10. In Hurr. ctx.: 1.131:12.

amtm PN (etym. unc. Cf. Dietrich - Loretz - Sanmartín UF 5 1973 95; Watson AuOr 8 1990 115).

PN: ★a) 4.363:4 (*tkyġ*); ★b) *bn PN*: 4.617:49.

amtrn PN (etym. unc. Cf. Nougayrol PRU 3 p. 124ff.; Astour CRRA 18 12; Kienast UF 11 1979 448); ¶ syll.: *a-mu/ma-ta-ru-nu* and other allographs, PRU 3 p. 239; PRU 6 p. 137; cf. *a-mu-ta-ra/ri*, Ug 5 28: rev. 1' and *passim ibid.*

PN: ★a) 4.344:8; 4.357:19; ★b) *bn PN*: 3.2:10, 16; 4.410:8. Cf. in bkn ctx. 4.357:29.

umy PN (Sem. Cf. Grøndahl PTU 51, 99; Watson AuOr 14 1996 96).

PN: *bn PN*, 4.96:8.

an (I) pers. pn. "I" (Hb. *ʔny*, HALOT 71; DNWSI 81; Aram. *ʔnh/ʔ*, DNWSI 79f.; Ebla *an-na*, ARET 2 119; ARET 5 50; cf. *a-na-*, ARET 8 17; Gelb TI 19, EDA 69; Krebernik PET 72; Conti QuSe 13 1984 161; Amor. /ʔanā/, Gelb CAAA 13, 49f.; cf. Huffmon APNMT 168; OB *ana* (?), cf. GAG § 41 g*, cf. CAD A/2 110f.; Arab. *ʔana*, Lane 103ff.; Eth. *ʔana*, CDG 26; Brockelmann GvG 1 297ff.; Moscati ICGSL 102ff.); ¶ par.: *ank, at, atm*. ¶ Forms: *an*.
I, ★a) subject in NC: *p ʕbdk an* am I perhaps a slave? (// *ank*), 1.4 IV 59; *ʕbdk an* I am your slave, 1.5 II 12, 19; *at aḫ w an aḫtk* you are (my) companion and I am your companion, 1.18 I 24; ★b) emphatic subject in VC: *an rgmt l ym* I am going to reply to DN, 1.2 I 45; *an itlk w aṣd* I scoured and combed, 1.6 II 15; *an aqry b arṣ mlḥmt* I shall go meet war in the land, 1.3 IV 22; *aṯb an* I am going to stay put, 1.16 VI 38, 54; *w an mtm amt* dying, I must die, 1.17 VI 38; *an arnn* I am moaning 1.82:6; in antithesis: *atm bštm w an šnt* you can go slowly, but I am in a hurry(?), 1.3 IV 33 and par. (Watson UF 18 1986 416); *[k]t atn an*(!) *mṯbk* the podium which I gave (you) as a mansion, 1.13:11 (diff. rdg, KTU p. 35: *[a]n atn at*). In bkn ctx.: 2.31:22; 7.164:7.
Cf. ank.

an (II) adv. "wherever, anywhere" (Hb., Aram. *ʔn*, HALOT 69; DNWSI 79; ESA *ʔhn-*, DOSA 7; Arab. *ʔannā*, Lane 119f. Cf. Caquot - Sznycer TOu 1 264f.; Renfroe AULS 80; diff.: Dijkstra - De Moor UF 7 1977 204: 'anyhow', Akk. *anniam lā anniam*, etc.; Margalit MLD 171, 173f.: 'strength' [cf. *an (IV)*]). ¶ Forms: *an*.
Wherever anywhere,: *an l an y špš* wherever (you go), oh DN!, 1.6 IV 22-23 (cf. Hb. *ʔnh w ʔnh* I Kgs 2:36, 42; II Kgs 5:25); *ʕl arṣ l an [isp ḥ]mt* from the earth anywhere remove the venom, 1.107:33; *aḥl an bṣql ynpʕ (...) tispk yd aqht* if only, everywhere, oh shoot that sprouts (...), the hand of PN would gather you!, 1.19 II 15, 22 (diff.: Cassuto BOS 2 196: 'for pity's sake', Hb. *ʔnʔ*, Sanmartín UF 9 1977 266: 'Wehe mir!' [cf. *an (I)*]).

an (III) n. m. "strength" (Hb. *ʔwn* HALOT 22; Ebla cf. *ù-nu*, Krebernik PET 109. Cf. Gaster Thespis[1] 449; De Moor SP 203; Dahood UF 1 1969 24; Rin AE 215; Van Zijl Baal 161, 191; Rainey UF 3 1971 159; diff.: Caquot - Sznycer TOu 1 257: 'maintenant', Akk. *anumma*). ¶ Forms: pl. *anm*.
Strength: *dq anm* of feeble strength (lit. weak of strengths), 1.6 I 50 (plur. abstract?).

in n. m. ("lack of, absence") lexicalized as a verbal functor 1) "there is not, does not exist"; 2) + *l* / *b* "(he/she/it) does not have" (Hb. *ʔyn*, HALOT 41f.; DNWSI 46; Pun. cf. DNWSI 46; Akk. *yānu*, AHw 411f.; CAD I/J 323f. Cf. Tropper UG 820ff.); ¶ RS Akk.: *(i-)ia-(a)-nu*, etc., PRU 3 43 (RS 16.270):21 and *passim*; cf. Huehnergard AkkUg 41, 201; Van Soldt SAU 413, 472f.; ¶ par.: *bl (l)* + *iṯ*. ¶ Forms: sg. *in*, suff. *inn, inm, innm* (encl. *-n, -m*), cf. allomorph(?) *inmm*, 2.10:9.
1) There is/are not: *in b ilm ʕnyh* there was not among the gods one who answered him, 1.16 V 22 and par.; *k in b ilht ql[ṣ]k* for there is among the goddesses no opposition against you / like yours, 1.3 V 28 and par.; *ṯpṭn d in d ʕlnh* our judge, above whom there is no one, 1.3 V 33 (cf. Akk. *qarrad la šanan*, Erra I 8); *p d in b bty ttn* rather, what is not in my house shall you give me, 1.14 III 38; *in bʕl b bhth*(!) DN is not in his house, 1.10 II 4; *ht hm in mm nḫtu* now, if we are not destroyed (?), 2.10:9 (cf. Cunchillos TOu 2 278 n. 12: rdg *in mm* 'n'y a rien du tout'); *in šmt in ʕẓm* there was no fat, there was no bone, 1.19 III 11 and par.; *ky akl b ḥwtk inn* for there is no grain in your region, 2.39:20; *mdrǵlm dt inn bd tlmyn m.* who have not been entrusted to PN, 4.379:1; *in dbḥ* [there is no banquet, 1.176:9; *w hm inm ʕbdmlk nplṭ* but if PN had not been saved, 2.82:10. Cf. in bkn ctx. *w in ʕṣr* and (if(?)) there is/are no bird(s) (?), 1.50:8; *mly innm* [there is no engraver(?) [, 2.73:11 (cf. Cunchillos TOu 2 417).
2) He/she/it does not have, + *l* / *b*: *d in bn lh* who has no son, 1.17 I 18 and par. (// *bl iṯ*); *w in aṯt lk* since you have no wife, 1.2 III 22; *w unṯ in bh* and he is not subject to any loan, 3.5:21; [*w un*]*ṯ inn lhm* they are not subject to any loan, 3.4:16; *tšʕ ṣmdm ṯlṯm bd PN w pat aḥt in bhm* thirty nine yokes of land in the hands of PN whick lack one side (: without adjacent farms to the south), 4.136:5 (cf. *pat*); *w in bt l bʕl k ilm* but DN has no house like the gods, 1.3 V 38 and par.; *in ḥẓm lhm* they have no arrows, 4.180:1; *w l ṯt mrkbtm inn uṯpt* and two chariots have no quiver, 1.145:7; *idy alt in ly* already I do not have (: it does not affect me) the curse!, 1.82:2; *dt inn mhr lhm*(!) who have no guard, 4.214 I 4; *mdrǵlm d inn msgm lhm m.* who have no skins, 4.53:1; *w in šq ymn b*[*h* and (if) it has no right thigh, 1.103:26 and par. (cf. ln. 7-16, 26-36).

in ṯln DN or Hurr. divine epithet ('the deity *ṯln*'; cf. Laroche Ug 5 p. 523; GLH 212. Cf. Del Olmo CR 208 n. 127; Dietrich - Mayer ALASP 7 14, and cf. *il ṣpn*, 1.47:1; 1.118:1). ¶ Forms: *in ṯlnd* (Hurr.: direct. /eni *ṯln*=da/).
DN or divine epithet: 1.132:4, 18, 22. In Hurr. ctx., cf. 1.110:1;

1.111:8; 1.116:1. In bkn ctx.: 7.95:7.

un n. m. "grief, misfortune" (Hb. *ʔwn*, *ʔwny*, HALOT 23. Cf. Cazelles Semitica 29 1979 5ff.; Dietrich - Loretz UF 18 1986 106; diff. Watson UF 8 1976 377; 'season', Arab. *ʔān*, cf. Renfroe AULS 80; Margalit UF 16 1984 130: precative particle, Hb. *ʔannā(ʔ/h)*, Akk. *unni/ennu*); ¶ **par.**: *plṯt*. ¶ **Forms**: sg. *un*.

Grief, misfortune: *yṣq ʕmr un l rish* he poured out ash of grief upon his head, 1.5 VI 15 (// *plṯt*); specific use: *yṣly ʕrpt b ḫm* he implored the clouds in the terrible drought, 1.19 I 40 (cf. Del Olmo IMC 134, n. 306 for this and other meanings based on different homographs: Dietrich - Loretz UF 5 1973 274: 'Stärke', Hb. *ʔwn*; De Moor UF 6 1974 496 n. 5: 'spell', Hb. *ʔwn*). Unc. ctx.: 1.79:3.

anan TN (Belmonte RGTC 12/2 24: **ʔAnānu*. Heltzer RCAU 8; Van Soldt UF 28 1996 659); ¶ **syll.** Ug.: URU *a-na-ni-yi*, PRU 3 41:9.

TN: 4.643:8; 4.652:2.

inbb TN, residence of the goddess *ʕnt* (Belmonte RGTC 12/2 142f.: **ʔInibab*. Etym. unc.; cf. Hurr. **enibaba* < *en paba* "god (of the) mountain"(?); Arab. *ʔunbūb*, Lane 2752; Hb. *nbb*, *nbwb*, HALOT 659, 660; see Aistleitner ZAW 57 1939 203; *enbūbu*, AHw 180; CAD E 137ff.; cf. Ginsberg ANET 137 n. 14; Dietrich - Loretz- Sanmartín UF 7 1975 123; Dietrich - Mayer UF 26 1994 76. See Astour JNES 27 1968 20; Pardee AfO 36/37 1989/90 482); ¶ **par.**: *uġr*. ¶ **Forms**: *inbb*, suff. loc. *inbbh*.

TN: *w an šnt (...) inbb l rḥq ilm* but I have to leave (...) TN for the most distant god, 1.3 IV 34 (// *uġr*); *w rbṣ l ġrk inbb* and go to rest on your mount TN, 1.13:9; *ql bl ʕm*(!) *ʕnt w ʕṯtrt inbbh* take (this) request to DN and DN in TN, 1.100:20. See 1.44:4 (Hurr.).

ind neg. functor "not at all, no-one" (extended form : *in* + *-d*; Bordreuil - Pardee RSOu 14 p. 403).

Not at all, no-one: *w ind ylmdnn* and there is no-one who has taught him (it), RSOu 14 53 [KTU 9.432]:42'; also in (unpublished) RS 94.2284:9, 11.

ands PN (Kass.(?). Cf. Dietrich - Loretz OLZ 62 1967 536).

PN: *bn PN*, 4.222:15. Bkn: 4.83:12.

anġn PN (etym. unc. Cf. Watson AuOr 8 1990 249f.); ¶ **syll.**: cf. *a-ni-ḫu-ti*, PRU 6 43 rev. 12'.

PN: *bn PN*, 4.418:1.

anhb n. m. of sea snail (cf. Akk. *(a)yānibu*, AHw 411; CAD I/J 322; Oppenheim Or 32 1963 211; De Moor Or 37 1968 214f. n. 3; Renfroe AULS 80f.; not in Sasson RSP 1 III.). ¶ **Forms**: pl. *anhbm*.

A sea snail: *rḥ gdm w anhbm* (they perfumed her) with the perfume of coriander and sea snails, 1.3 II 3; *ttpp anhbm* she anointed herself with (essence of) sea snails, 1.3 III 1 and par.

anẖ adj. "complaining" (Hb. *ʔnḥ*, HALOT 70f.; Akk. *anāẖu*, AHw 49; CAD A/2 105f.; cf. Arab. *ʔnḥ* (sic!), Lane 112f.; Dijkstra - De Moor UF 7 1975 175; Dietrich - Loretz- Sanmartín UF 8 434 n. 2. Diff.: Dahood Bib 38 1957 69: Aphel of *nwẖ*); ¶ par.: *abyn.* ¶ Forms: sg. m. *anẖ*.

Complaining: *abyn at (...) // anẖ* how wretched you are (...), // how complaining!, 1.17 I 17.

anẖr n. m. of marine animal ("dolphin" *orcinus orca*(?); Akk. *nāẖiru*, AHw 714f.; CAD N/1 137; Dietrich - Loretz - Sanmartín UF 7 1975 538; missing from Sasson RSP 1 III. Cf. Astour RSP 2 305; cf. Margalit MLD 98: 'whale', root */n-ẖ-r/ 'to snort, spout' + prothetic /ʔ/; De Moor UF 11 1979 64: 'sperm whale'; Wyatt RTU 117 and n. 14: 'shark'); ¶ par.: *lbu.* ¶ Forms: sg. *anẖr.*

Marine animal (dolphin(?)): *brlt anẖr b ym* the longing of the *a.* in the sea (// *lbim*), 1.5 I 15; cf. var. *npš anẖr b ym* the appetite of the *a.* in the sea (// *lbim*), 1.133:5.

ank p. pn. "I" (Hb. *ʔnky*, HALOT 72; Ph., Pun., Moab., Yaud. *ʔnk(y)*, DNWSI 82; Amor. /ʔanāku/, Gelb CAAA 13, 50; EA *a-nu-ki*, 287:66, 69; cf. *a-na-ku*, *a-na-ku-ma*, Kn 1375; Rainey EAT 63; Akk. *anāku*, AHw 49; CAD A/2 106ff.; cf. Eg. *ínk*, WäS 1 101; Brockelmann GvG 1 298; Moscati ICGSL 102ff.; Aartun PU 1 48); ¶ syll. Ug.:]*a-na-ku* = *iš-te-en$_6$* = *a-na-ku*, Ug 5 130 III 12'; cf. Rainey UF 3 1971 159; Sivan GAGl 106; Huehnergard UVST esp. 108, 293; Van Soldt SAU 302). ¶ Forms: *ank*, *ankn* (encl. *-n*; Aartun PU 1 48, 62; Tropper UF 26 1994 468).

I, ★a) subject in NC: *ẖrd ank* I am already (a recruit of the) guard, 2.16:13; *p ʕbd ank* am I perhaps a slave?, 1.4 IV 60, cf. *ht ank ʕbdk* now, I am your slave, 2.76:5; *ank ʕm mlakth šmʕh* I was advocate/auditor in his embassy, 2.17:6 (Cunchillos TOu 2 307); *ank ʕny mlak ym* I myself am going to reply to the message of DN, 1.2 I 28; *ank mlkt mntn* I am the queen of TN, RSOu 14 53 [KTU 9.432]:34'; ★b) emphatic subject in NC + fin. ¶ Forms: *likt ank lḥt* I have sent a tablet, 2.72:23; *ankn rgmt* I myself have said, 2.42:6; *w ap ank nẖt* as for me, I also have rested, 2.11:13; *ank ḥrš lqḥt w ḥwt hbt* I, the craftsman, have accepted and completed the task(?), 2.70:14 (Dietrich - Loretz UF 16 1984 66ff.; Verreet UF 18 1986 384); *ank kl dṛʕhm kl npš klklhm bd rb tmtt lqḥt* I myself have collected their cargo, all the persons, all that is theirs from the hands of the chief of the (salvage) team, *ibid.* ln. 18; *w ank ṯṯ ymm kl lḥmt* for my part, I have fought against them all for six days, 2.82:8; *w ank kl ḏrʕ kl npš kl klhm* and I (then collected) all their seed grain, all the persons (and) all their gear, 2.38:18; *w ṯṯb ank lhm* and I returned them to them (the ships), 2.38:23; cf. *w ilḥmn ank* I myself will fight, *ibid.* ln. 21; *ank aḥš mġy* I am going to make haste to come, 2.34:10; *ank aštn l iḫy w ap ank mnm ḫsrt* (with what you lack) I shall provide my brother, and (there you shall load??) all that I lack also to me, 2.41:17ff.;*ank* [*a*]*št ašisp w ašt* I propose that I carry out the concentration (of troops (?)), 2.33:11; *w ap ank* [*a*]*ḫd* and I also shall begin, 2.33:15; *ap ank aḥwy* I also shall give life, 1.17 VI 32; *ank ispi uṭm* I was consumed piece by piece (?), 1.5 I 5 (cf. Del Olmo IMC 158f.); *ank atn ʕṣm lk* I am selling you logs, 2.26:7; *ank ašṣu* I will take out, 2.3:17; *kt ġrk ank ydʕt* the podium of your mountain, which I know, 1.13:10; *ank iḥtrš w aškn* I myself will perform an incantation and shall prepare, 1.16 V 25; *bn nšrm arḫp ank* among the eagles I myself shall fly about, 1.18 IV 21; *ank l aḥwy* I will revive him, 1.18 IV 26; *ank ibġyh* I will reveal it to you, 1.3 III 28 and par.; *aṯbn ank w anḫn* I shall sit down and rest, 1.6 III 18; *aqry ank* I shall go to meet him, 1.3 IV 28; *w ank aṣḥk* as for me, I shall call you, RSOu 14 52 [KTU 9.435]:2; ★c) + inf. abs.: *ṯṯb ank lhm* I gave them back to them, 2.38:23; cf. in bkn ctx. *rgm ank*, 2.31:41, 53; 2.42:25; *ngš ank aliyn bʕl // ʕdbnn ank k imr b py* I met DN, I placed him like a lamb in my mouth, 1.6 II 21-22 (UT 9.29, 13.57; Segert BGUL 93); ★d) with ellipsis of the vb: *lm ank* for what (would) I (want) ...?, 1.14 III 33 and par.; ★e) emphatic of suff. pn.: *ank in bt ly* as for me, I have no house, 1.2 III 19. In bkn ctx.:]*ank nši*, 2.31:17; 1.1 IV 18; 1.18 I 26; 1.18 IV 40; 2.3:10, 11, 16; 2.31:16, 23, 36, 39, 48, 57; 2.32:44; 2.48:6; 2.63:11; 2.50:21; RSOu 14 49 [KTU 9.433]:16, 21, 33.

Cf. an (I).

unk "?"; possibly a spelling mistake, not erased, rdg *hn* {*unk*} *bnk* here is your son, 5.11:3. Cf. diff.: Caquot Ug 7 392: allophone of *ank*; Aartun UF 16 1984 3f.: 'Leidender, Kränklicher', Arab. *ʔanaka*).

inm deictic functor "behold" (< Akk. *inūma*, AHw 383f.; CAD I/J 158f.; Márquez AuOr 10 1992 152f.); ¶ RS Akk.: *e/inūma*, Huehnergard AkkUg 196f.; Van Soldt SAU 462 and *passim*. ¶ Forms: *inm*.

Behold: *inm ʕbdk hwt yrš* behold your servant has a word (of complaint), 2.41:14.

ann (I) DN (origin unc.; cf. Astour JAOS 86 1966 283 n. 63; De Moor UF 2 1970 190, 198; Gödecke UF 5 1973 154; Dietrich - Loretz-Sanmartín UF 6 1974 19).
DN: *bt il ann* sanctuary of DN, 4.149:18-19.

ann (II) PN (Hurr.(?); cf. *ann (I)*, DN; Ribichini - Xella SEL 8 1991 158; cf. Grøndahl PTU 217f.; Watson AuOr 13 1995 218); ¶ syll.: cf. PNN *a-na-ni*, PRU 6 78:6; cf. *an-na-na*, PRU 6 69:11'; [f]*a-na-ni-*[d]NIN.GAL, PRU 6 2:3.
PN: ★a) 4.141 II 3. Cf. bkn 4.382:32 (*bn pyx*[); 4.658:40; ★b) *bn PN*, 4.222:16; 4.631:13, 19.

unn PN (Hurr. Cf. Grøndahl PTU 223, 229).
PN: ★a) 4.609:6, ★b) *bn PN*, 4.615:4.

anna, cf. *annu*.

annu PN (Hurr.(?)); ¶ syll.: cf. *a-na-na-e*, RSOu 7 9:6. Cf. accus. *anna*, 2.75:9.
PN: 2.75:9.

annd PN (Hurr. Cf. Grøndahl PTU 218, 260).
PN: *bn PN*, 4.412 III 10.

annd/tn PN (Hurr. Cf. Grøndahl PTU 207, 218, 262; Van Soldt SAU 38; Watson AuOr 13 1995 218); ¶ syll.: *a-na-ni-te-na*, PRU 6 50:23; *a-na-an-te-nu*, Ug 5 159:17; RSOu 7 3 edge 1; 20:4.
PN: ★a) 3.10:14 (*bn yrm*); 4.148:7; 4.339:24; 4.370:8; 4.378:3; 4.623:4 (*bn t*[); 4.791:7 (*bn yrm*); RSOu 14 50 [KTU 9.434]:3; ★b) *bn PN*, 4.93 IV 7. Cf. in bkn ctx. 4.84:3; 4.141 II 4; 4.417:15.

anndr PN (Hurr. Cf. Grøndahl PTU 206, 218, 249; Kienast UF 11 1979 448); ¶ syll.: *a-na-ni-za-ar-ru*, PRU 3 203 (RS 16.257+) IV 18; *a-na-ni*-LUGAL(*-ma*), PRU 6 138:8; RSOu 7 32:18 and *passim ibid.*; 34:1.
PN: 3.2:5 (*bn agytn*); 4.244:15; 4.295:15 (*yknʕmy*); 4.631:7. Cf. in bkn ctx. 4.84:9; 4.292:1.

anndy PN (Hurr. Cf. Grøndahl PTU 218, 252; Van Soldt SAU 126).
PN: 4.101:6; 4.245 II 2; 4.753:16.

annḫ n. m. "mint" ((?); cf. Akk. *ananiḫu*, AHw 50; CAD A/2 111; Syr. *nōnḥō*, LS 431. Cf. Driver CML 135; Caquot - Sznycer Tou 1 371; De Moor NYCI 2 19; Watson UF 17 1985 348 n. 13; Ratner - Zuckerman HUCA 27 1987 40ff. reject the Syr. isogloss; diff.: Virolleaud Syria 14 1933 140; Gaster SMRS 1934 158; Sidersky MelSyr 1939 635; Gray LC 97 n. 2; Xella PP 150 1973 198 n. 21: 'young, young animal', with other etym., esp. Arab. *nuḫḫat*, Hitt. *annanuḫḫa-* [cf. HEG 27; HW(2) 77f.]; cf. Renfroe AULS 81); ¶ par.:

gd. ¶ Forms: sg. *annḫ̮*.

Mint(?): (offer) *ʕl išt (...) annḫ̮ b ḫ̮mat* over the fire (...) mint(?) in butter, 1.23:14 (// *gd*).

annḫ̮b PN (Hurr. Cf. Grøndahl PTU 217f.; Watson AuOr 8 1990 115); ¶ syll.: ᶠ*a-na-ni-ḫé*-BI(*bat*ₓ), PRU 3 62 (RS 16.158):3; Huehnergard AkkUg 375 n. 36.

PN: 4.707:17.

annmn PN (Hurr. Cf. Grøndahl PTU 218, 240; Watson AuOr 14 1996 95); ¶ syll.: cf. *a-na-an-me-ni*, RSOu 7 3 obv. 4.'

PN: 4.339:25; 4.609:26; 4.631:11; 4.750:3 (*ugrty*).

annmt PN (Hurr.(?); cf. Grøndahl PTU 240; Van Soldt SAU 40).

PN: 4.155:12.

annpdgl PN (Hurr. Cf. Xella TRU 272; De Moor - Sanders UF 23 1991 290).

PN: 1.84:3.

annšn PN (Hurr. Cf. Grøndahl PTU 218; Dietrich - Loretz- Sanmartín UF 5 1973 105).

PN: 4.633:14; 4.761:6.

anntn PN; cf. *annd/tn*.

annṯb PN (etym. unc. Cf. Grøndahl PTU 218, 257); ¶ syll.: cf. *a-na-ša-bu*, Ug 7 pl. 50:7', rev. 7' (Huehnergard UVST 230 n. 87); cf. *a-na-an*-ᵈIM, Ug 5 69:1; Huehnergard AkkUg 348 ("161:21" [sic!]).

PN: 4.115:3; 4.219:7; 4.226:1; 4.386:3; RSOu 14 39 [KTU 4.790]:22'; RSOu 14 40 [KTU 9.419]:7.

anny PN (Hurr.(?). Cf. Grøndahl PTU 217f.); ¶ syll.: *a-na-ni-ya*, PRU 3 45 (RS 16.140):5; ᶠ*a-na-na-ya*, PRU 3 64f. (RS 16.200): 2 and *passim ibid.*; cf. *a-na-ni-ya*[, PRU 6 83 IV 1; *a-na-na-e*, RSOu 7 9:6.

PN: *bn PN*, 4.77:9; 4.93 I 10; 4.215:3; 4.760:4; 4.769:55. Cf. in bkn ctx.: 4.112 II 6.

annyn PN (Hurr.(?). Cf. Grøndahl PTU 217f.); ¶ syll.: *a-na-an-ia-nu*, PRU 3 36 (RS 11.718):2'; *a-na-ni-ya(-a)-nu*, PRU 6 50:28; 74:4'; 118:3'.

PN: ★a) 4.727:15; ★b) *bn PN*: 4.12:12; cf. 4.412 II 17.

anp, 1.12 II 37, cf. *ap (II)*.

unp PN (Hurr. Cf. Grøndahl PTU 206, 210, 229).

PN: *bn PN*, 4.281:10. Cf. Hurr. 1.149:1.

unpṯ PN (Hurr. Cf. Grøndahl PTU 229, 250f.; Watson AuOr 13 1995 220); ¶ syll.: cf. *u-na-bi-ši*, RS 22.399+:3, 11 (Van Soldt SAU 363 n. 243).

PN: 4.696:3.

inr n. m. "dog, cur" (metath. of *irn*, like Amh. *anär* "panther", AED 1211; Sirat Semitica 15 1965 23, n. 1; Aartun UF 15 1983 1ff.; Pardee TPM 53f.; cf. Dietrich - Loretz MU 129; diff.: Delekat UF 4 1972 20: *kinr* 'was für eine Leuchte!'; De Moor UF 1 1969 171: Hitt. *innara* 'on one's own account'; Ajjan NU 13: Arab. *nāra, tanawwara* 'beaten'); ¶ par.: *klb*. ¶ Forms: sg. *inr*.

Dog, cur: *k inr ap ḫštk* like a dog at the entrance to your mausoleum, 1.16 I 2 and par. (// *klb*); *l inr tʕdbn ktp* to a dog you extend a shoulder blade, 1.114:13 (// *k*(!)*lb*).

Cf. irn, bninr.

anrmy PN (Anat. Cf. Grøndahl PTU 270).

PN: 4.166:7; 4.337:18. Cf. in bkn ctx.: 4.364:10.

anry PN (Anat.; cf. Grøndahl PTU 270).

PN: 4.727:4.

ansny PN (Hurr.(?); cf. Haas - Thiel UF 11 1979 338; Watson AuOr 8 1990 249).

PN: 4.609:31.

/ʔ-n-š/ vb generic meaning G: 1) "to languish, fall ill"; 2) "to become livid, sick (with rage) > to get annoyed, suffer (from rage)" (cf. Hb. *ʔn(w)š*, HALOT 70; Akk. *enēšu*, AHw 217f.; CAD E 166f.; cf. Cassuto GA 149f.; Rin AE 59f., 96, 110. For the various meanings proposed ['pleasant, human, compassionate', 'courageous, valiant', etc.] cf. Del Olmo MLC 516; Ashley EAR 114; Dressler AT 326f.; De Moor SP 132, 137, 233; Van Zijl Baal 28f.; UF 7 1975 503ff.; Dietrich - Loretz UF 9 1977 47ff.; Margalit UF 15 1983 93f.; UF 16 1984 175f.; Renfroe AULS 81f.). ¶ Forms: G suffc. *anš*, *anšt*.

G. 1) To languish, fall ill: *anšt ʕrš zbln* you have languished in the bed of sickness, 1.16 VI 36, 51 (cf. Dietrich - Loretz UF 9 1977 48; Renfroe UF 22 1990 280; diff.: Del Olmo MLC 322: 'compañera (tuya) es la yacija de la enfermedad'; cf. Gray Keret 77: *anšt ʕrš* 'concubine').

2) To become livid, sick (with rage) > to get annoyed, suffer (from rage); with reference to *zbl bʕl* Prince DN became livid with rage *ṯb ap d anšt* may the anger I suffer depart *m k anšt* I already know, daughter, that you have become livid (with anger), 1.3 V 27 and par.

Cf. anšt.

anš n. m. "muscle, tendon" (Hb. *nšh*, HALOT 729; cf. Syr. *genešyō* < Aram. *gîd našyāʔ*, LS 126; Driver CML 135; De Moor SP 137; UF 12 1980 425f.; diff.: Caquot - Sznycer TOu 1 132 n. x, 167; Sznycer

Semitica 17 1967 24: 'trembler', Arab. *nāsa*, Akk. *nâšu*; Dahood RSP 1 241; II 33; Cassuto GA 131; Oldenburg CEB 197; Dietrich - Loretz UF 9 1977 48; Baldacci UF 10 1978 417 n. 4; Margalit UF 15 1983 93: 'to be ill, weak', Hb. *nwš*, Akk. *enēšu*, in connection with Ug. /ʔ-n-š/); ¶ par.: *pnt (+ ksl)*. ¶ Forms: pl. cstr. *anš*.

Muscle, tendon: they did contract (...) *anš dt ẓrh* the muscles of her back, 1.3 III 35 and par. (// *pnt kslh*).

inš n. m. "people" (cf. Arab. *ʔanisa*, *ʔu/ins*, *ʔanas*, Lane 113; cf. Dietrich - Loretz UF 9 1977 50; Del Olmo AuOr 2 1984 201 n. 20; 5 1987 66; Loretz UF 24 1992 164ff.). ¶ Forms: sg. *inš*.

People: *inš ilm* divine people, deified ancestors, recipients of offerings usually 'two birds (from the coop)', 1.39:22; cf. 1.41:5, 27, 40; 1.46:8; 1.105:26; 1.106:2, 7; 1.112:5; 1.132:14-15, 21, 24; 1.134:4; 1.171:5 (cf. Loretz UF 24 1992 164ff. with reference to Nuzi DINGIR(.MEŠ DINGIR).ERÍN.MEŠ; diff.: De Moor UF 2 1970 321; SP 132: 'the most gentle of the gods'; Herdner Ug 7 24, 28f.; De Tarragon CU 131f. 163: cult personnel; Xella TRU 41, 83; UF 13 1981 331: 'la malattia divina'); *yšlm (...) l inšk l ḥwtk* hail to (...) your people, your country!, 2.81:7 (cf. *a-na* M[Í.MEŠ-*k*]*a* DUMU.MEŠ-*ka (...)* ANŠE.KUR.RA-*ka* G[IŠ.GIGIR.MEŠ-*ka*] *ù ma-ti-ka ga-ab-bi-ša da-an-ni-iš lu šu-ul-mu*, EAT 2:4-5; Bordreuil - Caquot Syria 57 1980 356f.). In bkn ctx.: 1.90:7; 1.123:31; 1.173:7.

a/inšr(m) PN (Hurr. Cf. Grøndahl PTU 207, 223, 249).

PN: ★a) 4.204:2; ★b) *bn PN*, 4.110:10.

anšt n. f. "illness, weakness" (< /ʔ-n-š/; Akk. *e/anšutu*, AHw 220; CAD E 172; < *enēšu*, AHw 217f.; CAD E 166f.; cf. Hb. *ʔnš*, HALOT 73; cf. Dietrich - Loretz Fs. Delcor 115f.; diff.: Margalit UF 15 1983 93: 'to cf., perceive', * *ʔnš*). ¶ Forms: sg. *anšt*.

Illness: *b anšt npẓl* free yourself from the illness!, 1.169:15 (Loretz - Xella MLE 1 1982 45; Dietrich - Loretz TUAT 2 335; cf. diff.: De Moor UF 12 1980 432; ARTU 185: 'fury of the shade', rdg *anšt ap ẓl*). In bkn ctx.: *b anšt*, 1.18 IV 10; 1.15 V 27.

inšt n. f. "relatives" (coll. f.; cf. *inš*; royal officials(?); cf. Nuzi Akk.: *ni-šu-ut* É.GAL; cf. Akk. *nišūtu*, AHw 798; CAD N/2 297ff.; cf. Dietrich - Loretz UF 9 1977 50; diff. Aartun UF 16 1984 4f.: '(ortsansässige besitzlose) Bürger (Kollektiv-Begriff)', Syr. *(ʔ)anāšūṯā*, Arab. *ʔanūsat*). ¶ Forms: sg. *inšt*.

Relatives (social group, probl. class of royal officials): 4.38:5; 4.47:5; 4.99:3; 4.416:9; 4.610:48. Cf. in bkn ctx. 1.6 VI 41.

antn PN (Hurr. Cf. Grøndahl PTU 218, 422); ¶ syll.: cf. *a-na-te-nu* and

var., cf. PRU p. 240; PRU 6 p. 137; *a-na-*^{d}IM, PRU 6 24 rev. 1' and *passim ibid.*; cf. AN-*te-na*, PRU 6 73:2; 170:29; AN-*ti-na*, RSOu 7 25:4. Cf. *ʕntn*.
PN: 4.70:7 (*bn iwrtn*). In bkn ctx.: 4.658:3.

unṯ n. m. "obligation, servitude, tax" (cf. Alal. Akk. *unuššuḫuli*, Ahw 1422; Dietrich - Loretz WO 3 1966 194-197; Giacumakis AA 110; Hillers HTR 64 1971 257ff.; < Hurr.(?), cf. Diakonoff HU 142: Hurr. root /un=/ < Akk. *ilku*, < *alāku* + afform. /=šše/i/); ¶ RS Akk.: *ilku*, *pilku* (*il-ku*, BÍL-*ku*, BI-*il-ku*), PRU 3 226ff.; Boyer PRU 3 293-299; Huehnergard UVST 168; cf. Dietrich - Loretz UF 4 1972 165f.; CAD I/J 227; ¶ syll. Ug.: *unuššu*; cf. PNN *ú-nu-uš-ša ša* É *up-pa-lu*, PRU 3 53 (RS 15.89):20; PNN *ú-nu-uš-ša ú-pa-lu*, PRU 3 61 (RS 16.156):15;
PN *ú-nu-ša* *<ša>* É.MEŠ *up-pal*, PRU 3 63 (RS 16.167):17; Ahw 1422; Kienast UF 11 1979 443; Sivan GAGl 202; Márquez Ilku 184ff. ¶ Forms: sg. *unṯ*; pl. cstr. *unṯ*, suff. *unṯhm*; du.(?) *unṯm* (rdg unc.).
Obligation, servitude, corvée as tribute, ★a) personal: *unṯ aḥd lh*[PN(N) has(have) a loan pending, 4.86:4; cf. *unṯ*(?)*m aḥ*[*d* two(?) corvées: on[e ..., *ibid.* ln. 17; *unṯ aḥd* one corvée, 4.209:1-22; in bkn ctx.: 4.637:2; *GNN d ʕrb b unṯ* GNN who have entered service, 3.7:1; *l yiḫd PN b unṯ* PN is not recruited for service, 2.19:2; cf. *br PN b unṯ ʕd ʕlm* PN remains free of corvée in perpetuity, 2.19:5; *unṯ inn lhm* they (PNN) are not obliged to any corvée, 3.4:16; *ṯb l unṯhm* (until they pay the deposit) they go back to giving their services, 3.4:19; ★b) concerning real estate: *unṯ in mnm bh* (the house) has no corvée at all, 3.2:18; *unṯ in bh* (the field) has no corvée, 3.5:20.

/ʔ-n-y/ vb G: "to sigh, groan" (Hb. *ʔnh*, HALOT 70; cf. Arab. *ʔanna*, Lane 103ff.; ESA cf *ʔny*, DOSA 22. Cf. De Moor SP 107; Van Zijl Baal 160f.; diff.: Cassuto GA 140, Whitaker FAUL 63: 'alas!'; Al Yassin LRUA 27: 'a little while', Arab. *ʔana*, but cf. Renfroe AULS 82; Driver CML 136: 'happened'); ¶ par.: /b-k-y/. ¶ Forms: G inf. / ptc.(?) *any*.
G. To sigh, groan: *any l yṣḥ* sighing, he cried, 1.3 V 35 and par.
Cf. ta/unt.

any(t) n. f. "ship" (Hb. *ʔny*, *ʔnyh*, HALOT 71; cf. EA Akk. GIŠ.MÁ: *a-na-yi* (gen.), EAT 245:28; cf. Eg. *ʔi-na-ya*, Helck UF 2 1970 35; Akk. (< Can.) *inītu* AHw 382; cf. Dietrich - Loretz UF 22 1990 94 n. 32; Cunchillos TOu 2 351f.); ¶ RS Akk.: GIŠ.MÁ(.MEŠ), PRU 6 156 *passim*; Huehnergard AkkUg 366. ¶ Forms: sg. *any(t)*; suff. *anyk*, *anykn* (Dietrich - Loretz - Sanmartín UF 5 1973 81; Tropper UF 26

1994 467: pn. suff. *-k-* + encl.*- n*); pl. *anyt*, suff. *anyth*, *anythm*. Ship, ★a) *anyt TN* ship(s) of TN, 4.81:1; *mlkn ybqṯ anyt* the king himself has to look for a ship, 2.42:26; *l anyt tšknn ḫmšm l mit* as for the ships, you are going to equip one hundred and fifty, 2.47:3; the merchandise *abd b anyt* was lost on board ship, 4.394:3; *any TN d b TN* the ship of TN which is in TN, 4.390:1; *anykn dt likt mṣrm* (as for) your ship which you sent to Egypt, 2.38:10; *anyk ṯt by TN ʕryt* your other (: number two) ship is unrigged in TN, 2.38:24; *any tšknn* [you shall equip a ship [, 2.47:4; cf. in bkn ctx. *mlk yštal b hn* [...] *hmt w anyt* which the king claims for them [...] them and the ship(s), 2.42:24 (cf. Verreet UF 16 1984 321); *ḥṯb d anyt grgmšh* bill of the ship (bound) for TN, 4.779:13. ★b) *anyt ym* seagoing ship(s), 2.46:13 (Dahood RSP 1 87, 118); *anyt mlk* ships of the king, 4.421:2; *ḥṯb d anyt grgmšh* bill of the ship, (destination) TN, 4.779:13; ★c) *lbš anyth bʕrm* the singed sails of his ship, 4.338:16 (Márquez AuOr 11 1993 105); *ṣbu anyt* crew, 4.40:1 and *passim ibid.* (RS Akk.: ÉRIN.MEŠ GIŠ.MÁ, PRU 6 138:20); *ḥrš anyt* caulkers, 4.125:1 (Dahood RSP 2 49); *ksp anyt d ʕrb b anyt* naval security that has been left in deposit for the ships, 4.338:11-12 (Dietrich - Loretz - Sanmartín UF 6 1974 473; Pardee JAOS 95 1975 613; cf. diff.: Márquez AuOr 11 1993 103: rdg {*anyt*} <TN>); *PN bʕl any d bd PN* PN, worker in the fleet, in the hands of PN, 4.647:7; *spr npṣ any* list of naval equipment, 4.689:1; *ṣbu anyt* crew, 4.40:7, 10.

anẓ, cf. /n-ẓ(-y)/.

ap (I) adv. / conj. 1) "also, even, besides"; 2) "and also, and besides"; in negation "nor"; 3) "but / then, since, as" (Hb., Aram., Ph., Pun. *ʔp*, HALOT 76; DNWSI 92f.; Ebla *ap*, ARET 2 119; 3 340, 4 286; 7 206; 8 52; Fronzaroli StEb 4 1981 167ff.; ARET 11 140. Cf. Aartun PU 2 88ff.; Van Zijl, Baal 107f.). ¶ Forms: *ap*; lengthened by suff.: *aphn*, *apn*, *apnk*, cohesive functors of narrative (for their morphology cf. Whitaker FAUL 161; Aartun PU 1 40ff., 47ff., 61ff.).

1) Adv., also, even, besides: *ap yṣb yṯb b hkl* also DN sat in his palace, 1.16 VI 25; *ap ʕnt ttlk w tṣd* also DN scoured and combed, 1.5 VI 25; *ap mṯn rgmm argm* another thing I am also going to say to you, 1.3 IV 31; *ap ab (i) k mtm tmtn* father, (oh) like mortals do you also die, 1.16 I 3 and par.; *ap ilm lḥm yṯb* the gods also sat down to eat, 1.2 I 20; *ap ank aḥwy* I also will give life, 1.17 VI 32; *w ap ank nḫt* I, for my part, also I have rested, 2.11:13; *w ap ank mnm ḫsrt* and all that I also lack 2.41:19. In bkn ctx., *w ap ank* [and I also [, 2.33:15; *apnnk*, 1.21 II 5, probl. rdg *ap a*(!)*nk* also I ..., (cf. Del Olmo

MLC 419; diff.: Aartun PU 2 90: 'dann'); *w ap*, 2.81:18; *ap hw*, *ibid.* ln. 29; in unc. ctx., *hm ap amr*[although I shall even drive out[, 1.2 IV 2 (cf. /m-r(-r)/ (I)); *w hm ap l*[, 1.1 IV 26; *w ap mlk* and also the king, 2.33:20; *ap mṯn rgmm argmk* furthermore, I am also going to say to you, 1.4 I 19 and par.; *ap mh*(!)*rh ank l aḥwy* and I shall not leave his warrior strength alive, 1.18 IV 26.
2) Coordinating adverbial conj.: ★a) and also, and besides: *ap bnt ḥry kmhm* and also the daughters of PN were as many as they, 1.15 III 24 (// *bt*); *ṭbḫ alpm ap ṣin* they slaughtered (head of) cattle and also ewes, 1.22 I 12 and par.; *akln b grnt l bʕr ap krmm ḫlq* our grain in the threshing floors has been set on fire, and also the vineyards were lost, 2.61:10;]*ṯbtk ap l pḫrk ʕnt tqm* your mansion and also your family may DN help, 1.82:39; *l tštql (...) ap l tlḥm lḥm trmmt* come down, then, (...), and also eat the bread of offering, 1.6 VI 43; in bkn ctx., *ʕn mkṯr apq*[, 1.4 II 30; *ap ʕnt tm*[*ṯḫṣ* and also DN fought, 1.7:37; *u* + *ap*: *u ap mh*(!)*rh ank l aḥwy* and I shall not leave his warrior strength alive, 1.18 IV 27; ★b) neg., nor: (+ *l*), *l yblt ḫbṯm ap ksphm l yblt* you have not brought those who had to be set free, nor have you brought the money (of its deposit), 2.17:2; (+ *al*), *at umy al tdḥl w ap mhkm b lbk al tšt* you, my mother, neither fear nor worry, 2.30:22.
3) Consecutive conj., but / then, since, as: *ap krt bnm il* is PN, then, a son of DN?, 1.16 II 48 and par.; *ap qšth l ttn ly* but his bow was not given/delivered to me, 1.19 I 16; *i ap bʕ*[*l* where, then, is DN?, 1.5 IV 6; cf. in bkn ctx. 1.15 III 28; *wn ap ʕdn mṭrh bʕl* since thus DN will be able to store his rain, 1.4 V 6.
In unc. ctx.: *w ap ht k škn*, 2.3:20; 1.18 I 5; 1.104:6; 2.23:32; 2.49:13; 2.73:16; 7.2:2; RSOu 14 51 [KTU 9.425]:9.
Cf. aphm, aphn, apn (II), apnk.

ap (II) n. m. 1) "nose"; 2) "muzzle, beak"; 3) "anger"; 4) "front, entrance" (Hb. *ʔp*, HALOT 76f.; Aram. *ʔ(n)p*, DNWSI 83f.; Akk. *appu*, AHw 60; CAD A/2 184f.; ESA *ʔnf*, DOSA 23; Arab. *ʔanf*, Lane 116; Eth. *ʔanf*, CDG 28; Ebla /ʔappu(m)/ in KIRI$_4$.DÙ = *ša-gi-lum*(*/lu-um*) *a-bù*, VE 212; Krebernik ZA 73 1983 9f.; KA.TAR = *na-ša-núm wa bur-ra-zu-um a-pá-a*, VE 195; Pettinato Biling. 45; Sanmartín AuOr 9 1991 174; for the spelling *a*(?)-*ba*(?)-*tum* cf. Fronzaroli SEL 12 1995 60: /ʔappatum/. Cf. De Moor ULe 80); ¶ syll. Ug.: KAR = *ap-pu* = *pu-u*[*ḫ*]-*ḫi* = *ap-pu*, Ug 5 137 II 19'; Huehnergard UVST 108, 208; Van Soldt SAU 302; ¶ par.: *bmt*, (?) *brlt*, *ḥdr*, (?) *mtn*, (?) *qrn*, *qṣrt (+ npš)*. ¶ Forms: sg. *ap*; pl./du. *apm*; suff. *apk*, *aph*, *apkm*, *apkn*, *aphm* (Del Olmo MLC 169, 524); cf.

anpnm, 1.12 II 37: variant */ʔan(V)p(V)n/ + du. suff. *-m* (cf. Del Olmo MLC 484) or read *an pnm* (KTU; cf. *an (III)*, *pnm*).

1) Nose: *qḥ apk b yd* seize your nose with (your) hand, 1.16 I 41 (// *brlt*(?); Watson JANES 8 1976 106-111; De Moor UF 11 1979 644f.; diff.: Greenstein IOS 18 1998 112f. 'take your timbrel *tp* in your hand'); may his soul go out *km qṭr b aph* like smoke from his nostrils, 1.18 IV 26 and par.; pour the mixture *b aph* into its nostrils, 1.71:7 and par. (*passim* in hippiatric texts; not: 'in front of', cf. Dahood UHP 51); in bkn ctx.:]*ap w ḫr apm*]or nasal fossae, 1.103:6. On *aphm*, 1.2 I 13, cf. *aphm* (diff.: Caquot - Sznycer TOu 1 128; Del Olmo MLC 169, 640: *ṯbr aphm* 'their nasal fossae'). In bkn ctx.: 1.126:2.

2) Muzzle (of an animal), beak (of a bird): (offering of) *ap w npš* one muzzle and one (piece of) offal, 1.43:12 and par. (Del Olmo AuOr 7 1989 123; *passim* in rituals; cf. 1.164:4; 1.168:2, 9; 1.173:8); *w aph k ap ʕṣr* if its muzzle is like a bird's beak, 1.103+:41 (cf. Pardee AfO 33 1986 125, 138f.). Cf. *anpnm yḥr*[*r* their muzzles(?) became hot, 1.12 II 37 (reading unc.; cf. *supra:* forms; poss. // *mtnm*, *qrnh*; cf. *an (III)*, *pnm*).

3) Anger (by meton.): *u ṯḫṭin b apkn/m* or whether you have sinned by your anger, 1.40:22 and par. (// *b qṣrt npš*); *ap anš zbl bʕl* livid with anger became Prince DN, 1.2 I 35, 43; *ap d anšt* the anger that I suffer, 1.6 V 21.

4) Front, entrance (c.Sem.; in syntagms and prepositional use): *ap lb* chest, 1.5 VI 21 and par. (// *bmt*; cf. Akk. *appi libbi*, Gaster RR 9 1944/45 281); *ap ḫšt* entrance of the sepulchre(?), 1.16 I 3, 17 and par. (cf. *ḫšt*; cf. Akk. *(ina) apti qabri(m)*, CAD A/2 199; AHw 61f.); *ap sgrt* anteroom, 1.3 V 11, 27 (// *ḥdr*; cf. OAram. *ʔp bbʔ*, Herdner RES 1942/5 47; Caquot - Sznycer TOu 1 175; Dijkstra - De Moor UF 7 1975 181; Dahood UF 1 1969 28 suggests 'chamber, court', from the Hb. and Akk. root **ʔpp* 'to enclose'; cf. also Pope EUT 65; Ward JNES 20 1961 32: Eg. *ip(.t)*; Watson UF 31 1999 785f.; UF 32 2000 568); *ap z/ḏd* nipple, 1.23:24, 59, 61 (cf. Akk. *appi tulī*, CAD A/2 187); *ap ṯǵr* porch, 1.17 V 6). Cf. in bkn ctx. *ʕl ap*[before, in front of(?), 2.42:18 (KTU: *aḥ*[). Cf. ap (III).

ap (III) TN (Belmonte RGTC 12/2 27: **ʔAppu*; cf. *ap (II)*. Cf. Heltzer RCAU 8; Astour RSP 2 261; Astour UF 13 1981 5; Bordreuil UR 48; Syria 61 1984 5; Pardee AfO 36/37 1989/90 482; Van Soldt SAU 225; UBL 11 368 n. 20; UF 28 1996 660; UF 30 1998 718); ¶ syll.: URU *ap-pí*, RSOu 7 4:1.

TN: 4.365:1; 4.380:1; 4.683:2; 4.693:1; 4.784:2; RSOu 14 35 [KTU

9.388] I 23.

apʕ n. m. "viper" (Hb. *ʔpʕh*, HALOT 79; HAT 90; Ebla cf. AMA.MUŠ = *i-ba-ù-um*, MEE 96 VI 8f.; Civil Biling. 91; Arab. *ʔafʕā*, Lane 2421; cf. Dijkstra - De Moor UF 7 1975 199); ¶ par.: *klb*. ¶ Forms: sg. *apʕ*.

Viper: (I wounded him) *k apʕ il b gdrt* like a divine viper in a hedge, 1.19 I 13 (// *klb*).

ipd n. m.; type of garment (usually: 'tunic'; cf. Hb. *ʔp(w)d*, HALOT 77; Syr. *pedtō*, LS 557; Ebla /ʔipdum/ in ŠU.DAG = *ib-tum*, VE 513; Conti SQF 145; Akk. *epattu*, *epadātu*, AHw 222; CAD E 183. Cf. Dahood UF 11 1979 142f.; De Moor SP 187; Ribichini - Xella Tessili 31f.; Durand MARI 6 661; Watson UF 30 1998 751f.: Eg. *ifd* 'cloth'; Watson UF 31 1999 786: Hitt. *ipantu*). ¶ Forms: sg. *ipd*; suff.(?) *ipdk*; pl. *iptt* (regressive assimilation); du. *ipdm*.

Type of garment: *tšʕ iptt b ṯqlm w rbʕt* nine *i.* for two and a quarter shekels, 4.707:11; *ipd ʕšrm b ḫmšt* twenty *i.* for five (shekels), *ibid.* ln. 13; for PN *ipdm* two *i.*, *ibid.* ln. 22; *ipd ʕl PN* one *i.* on PN's account, 4.780:1, 3f., 7; cf. *ṯn ipdm*, *ibid* ln. 2; cf. in bkn ctx. 4.275:3; 4.594:5. Cf. in unc. ctx. *ipdk*: *ttrp šmm k r<k>s ipdk* the heavens were slackened like the belt of your *i.*, 1.5 I 5 (cf. ln. 31) (?); Del Olmo MLC 213: 'tu túnica'; Sanmartín UF 12 1980 439: 'ich werde dich aufzehren' (< /n-p-d/; cf. Dietrich - Loretz UF 12 1980 407); Margalit MLD 93: '(poisonous) prick'; cf. Renfroe UF 18 1986 72). Cf. in unc. ctx. *ip{.}d prk*, 1.5 V 2, and cf. in bkn ctx. 1.5 V 24 (cf. *ibid.* /l-b-š/, ln. 23, De Moor SP 183; Del Olmo IMC 71ff.). On *updt*, 4.264:1 (Ribichini - Xella Tessili 31: pl. of *ipd*) cf. *updt*. In bkn ctx.: 1.136:10.

updt n. f. "share-cropping (plot)" (< *ubdy*; Heltzer IOKU 34; JNSL 9 1982 71-74; BAfO 19 1982 112-120; UF 19 1987 446; cf. Akk. *upatinnu*, AHw 1423). ¶ Forms: pl. *updt*.

Share-cropping (plot): *spr updt d bd PN* list of share-cropping (plots) that pass to the hands of (/ are in the power of) PN, 4.264:1.

aphm illative adverbial functor in narrative "immediately afterwards, next" (< *ap (I)* + emphatic functor *-hm* ; cf. Aartun PU 2 89f.; cf. *ap (II)*). ¶ Forms: *aphm*.

Immediately afterwards, next: *aphm tbʕ ġlm*[*m*] immediately afterwards, depart, lads, 1.2 I 13 (diff.: *ṯbr aphm* 'their nasal fossae', Caquot - Sznycer TOu 1 128; Del Olmo MLC 169, 640); *aphm kšpm dbbm ygrš* immediately afterwards, may the wizards cast out the *d.*-demons, 1.169:8 (Loretz - Xella MLE 1 1982 43; diff.: De Moor UF

12 1980 431: 'his fury').

aphn illative functor in narrative "immediately afterwards, next" (< *ap (I)* + emphatic functor *-hn*; cf. Aartun PU 1 70). ¶ Forms: *aphn*.
Narrative correlation: *apnk (...) aphn (...)* then (...), next (...), 1.17 V 14, 34;1.19 I 20. Cf. *ap{.}hn*, 1.17 II 28; *aph*, 1.17 I 1; *ahn*, 1.17 V 5: mistakes for *aphn*. Cf. *ap.ht*, 2.3:20.
Cf. aphm.

apn (I) n. f. "wheel" (Hb. *ʔwpn*, HALOT 23). ¶ Forms: pl. *apnt*, suff. *apnthn*; du. *apnm*.
Wheel: *ṯmn mrkbt (...) yd apnthn* eight chariot bodies (...) with their wheels, 4.145:3; in pairs: *ṯlṯ ṣmdm w ḥrṣ apnt* three pairs of wheels as a lot, 4.145:9; cf. 4.169:7; *ṣmdm a[pnt* two pairs of wheels, 4.88:1; *apnm* one pair of wheels *ibid.* ln. 3-8; *ṯlṯ šmdm* three pairs, *ibid.* ln. 9. Cf. *apnm*, 5.22:26; cf. in bkn ctx. 4.67:5-10.

apn (II) adverbial functor "and in addition, and also" (< *ap (I)* + encl. *-n*; cf. Aartun PU 2 90); ¶ RS Akk.: *ap-pu-na* AnOr 48 11ff. (RS [Varia 9 = "1957.1"]):14; *ap-pu-na-ma*, PRU 3 52 (RS 15.85):11; 102 (RS 15.138 + 16.393b):12; PRU 4 52 (RS 17.369a):21'; 163 (RS 17.341):21'; 193 (RS 17.423):3; cf. AHw 60; CAD A/2 189f. ¶ Forms: *apn*.
An in addition, and also: *yʕn pdry bt ar apn ṭly bt rb* he saw DN, daughter of light, and also DN, daughter of drizzle, 1.3 I 24. Cf. in bkn ctx., *apn* [, 1.16 II 57.

apn (III) PN (Hurr.(?); cf. Gelb - Purves - MacRae NPN 200; Benz PNPPI 274; Muchiki Loanwords 16f.).
PN: ★a) 4.370:43; 4.424:22; ★b) *bn PN*, 4.371:17. Cf. in bkn ctx. 4.35 II 7.

apnk adverbial functor of illation "then", (< *ap (I)* + encl. *-n-* + *-k*; cf. Aartun PU 2 90; cf. Whitaker FAUL 161; Ashley EAR 9; Dressler AT 2). ¶ Forms: *apnk*.
Then, ★a) used alone: *apnk (...) yʕl b ṣrrt ṣpn* then (...) went up to the heights of TN, 1.6 I 56; *apnk (...) yrd l ksi* then (...) he came down from the throne, 1.5 VI 11; *apnk (...) mrḥh yiḫd b yd* then (...) his nose(?) he grasped with (his) hand, 1.16 I 46; *apnk (...) yṣly ʕrpt* then (...) he cast a spell on the clouds, 1.19 I 38; *apnk (...) tšlḥm tššqy ilm* then (...) she gave food and drink to the gods, 1.17 V 28; cf. in unc. ctx. *apnk PN (...) b bth yšt* then PN (...) in his house he prepared, 1.15 II 8; ★b) introducing the narrative correlation: *apnk (...) aphn (...)* then (...), next (...), 1.17 II 27; V 4, 13, 33; 1.19 I 19; in bkn ctx.: 1.15 II 8.

/ʔ-p-q/ vb D: "to escape, make onself scarce, leave" (denom. (?); cf. Arab. *ʔafāq*, *ʔaffaq*, denominative *ʔafaqa* "to go to remote lands", cf. Lane 68f. Diff.: Bordreuil - Caquot Syria 57 1980 349: Hb. *ʔpq* [cf. *ʔpq (II)*, HALOT 80]; De Moor UF 12 1980 432: 'to let flow freely', der. of *apq*; Loretz - Xella MLE 1 1982 44: 'davonlaufen', Hb. *ʔbq*; Arab. *ʔabaqa*; Watson NUS 30 1983 12: 'be massive, solid', Akk. *epēqu*). ¶ Forms: D prefc. *tapq*; inf. *apq*.
D. To move away, make onself scarce: *al tapq apq* do not make yourself scarce, 1.169:12.

apq n. m. "spring, source" (preferable to 'channel, conduit'; cf. Hb. *ʔpyq*, HALOT 78; cf. already Follet Bib 37 1956 224ff.; cf. Dahood RSP 1 10f.; Pope EUT 72-80; Dressler AT 299; Clifford CMC 49f.; Loretz UF 21 1989 260ff.; Renfroe AULS 82); ¶ syll. Ug.: cf. PN *ip-pí-qi*, PRU 4 226 (RS 17.393):4; cf. Sivan GAGl 21; ¶ par.: *mbk*. ¶ Forms: sg. *apq*.
Spring, source: (DN lives) *qrb apq thmtm* in the heart of the spring of the two oceans, 1.4 IV 22 and par. (// *mbk nhrm*; Aitken UF 21 1989 20); *ʕn mkṯr apq*[*ym*] cf., expert(?) of the source [of the sea], 1.4 II 30.

upqt n. f. "bed of a torrent"(?) (cf. *apq*; Hb. *ʔpyq*, *ʔpqh* TN, HALOT 78, 80; cf. Oldenburg CEB 185 n. 5; diff.: Caquot - Sznycer TOu I 312 n. f, 'ou bien tu as obtenu', *u* + /p-q/). ¶ Forms: sg. *upqt*.
Bed of a torrent: in bkn ctx., *abnm upqt* stones of the torrent(?), 1.1 V 11, 24.

aps n. m. "extremity, edge, end" (Hb. *ʔps*, HALOT 79); ¶ par.: *hdm*; ¶ syll. Ug.: cf. URU *ap-su/sú-na/ni*, cf. PRU 6 146; RSOu 7 6:9; PRU 6 77:4; 134:13; Ug 5 12:20; PN: *ap-su-na*, PRU 6 72:3; Astour RSP 2 261; cf. Grøndahl PTU 100; cf. EA *upsu*, Rainey EAT p. 85. ¶ Forms: sg. suff. *apsh*.
Extremity, edge, end: *rišh l ymġy apsh* his head did not reach its edge, 1.6 I 61 (// *hdm*).
Cf. apśny.

apsny GN m. (< *apśny*, TN); ¶ syll. Ug.: LÚ URU *ap-sú-na-yu*, PRU 3 37 (RS 15.81):10; *ap-su-ni-yi-ma*, PRU 6 77:10; cf. Huehnergard UVST 227; Van Soldt SAU 336; UF 28 1996 660. ¶ Forms: sg. *apnsy*.
GN: 4:80:11; 4.295:1; 4.417:9.

apśny TN (Belmonte RGTC 12/2 27f.: *ʔApsunā*. Cf. Heltzer RCAU 8; Astour RSP 2 261; NuzHur 1 14 no. 9; Pardee AfO 36/37 1989/90 239f. (RS 17.369+): 9', 10', rev. 7; PRU 6 p. 146; Ug 5 12:20; RSOu

7 6:9; PN: ^{m}*ap-su-na*, PRU 6 72:92923.
TN: PNN *apśny* (from) TN, 3.8:5,8.

apṯ PN (Hurr.(?); cf. Grøndahl PTU 219, 252; Watson NABU 1999 54 n. 15). Cf. *aupš/ṯ*.
PN: ★a) 4.141 II 17; ★b) *bn PN*, 4.377:11.

ipṯ(n) PN (Hurr.; cf. Grøndahl PTU 225).
PN: 4.84:4; 4.734:5.

ipṯl PN (Hurr.(?); cf. Grøndahl PTU 225; Bush GHL 307; PNN 220; Heltzer RCAU 15); ¶ syll.: *ip-ša-li*, PRU 3 131 (RS 15.118):8; 196 (RS 15.42+) II 3; in Hurr. ctx., ŠU $^{(m)}$*ip-ša-li*, Ug 5 468 (RS 19.147):6; (RS 19.164 D):3; bkn ctx. 471 (RS 19.149):10; cf. Van Soldt SAU 21.
PN: ★a) 4.215:2; in bkn ctx. cf. 4.182:25; ★b) *gt PN*, 4.125:11; 4.213:19, 4.397:5; 4.522:1; 4.618:7, 25; 4.625:13 (cf. Kühne UF 6 1974 161; RSOu 7 6:9; PN: ^{m}*ap-su-na*, PRU 6 72:3.
TN: PNN *apśny* (from) TN, 3.8:5,8.

/ʔ-p-y/ vb G: "to bake (in the oven); to make bread, to make into bread" (Hb. *ʔph*, HALOT 78; Aram. *ʔpy*, DNWSI 94f.; Akk. *epû*, AHw 231; CAD E 247f.; Ebla /ʔapāʔum/ in NIDNA.DU_8.DU_8 = *a-ba-lum*, VE 44; EV 0237; Krebernik QuSe 18 133; cf. n. NI-*bí-tum*, ARET 9 399). ¶ Forms: G suffc. *apy*; prefc. *yip*; ptc. *apy* (cf. *apy*).
G. To bake (in the oven): *yip lḥm* bake bread, 1.14 II 30 and par.; make bread: *nʕr d apy PN* rancid (?) flour which PN made into bread, 4.362:4; *d apy ʕbdh* which your servant made into bread, *ibid.* ln. 5. Cf. apy.

apy n. m. "baker" (< ptc. m. sg. G /ʔ-p-y/; Hb. *ʔph*, HALOT 78; Ph. cf. *ʔph* Zauzich - Röllig Or 59 1990 327ff. [PN?], *ʔpm*, Heltzer OH 70; cf. *ʔpy*, DNWSI 94f.; Ebla f. *a-bí-tum*, *a-bí-a-tum*, ARET 9 377; cf. ʔa_5(NI)-*bí-tum*, ARET 9 399; Bonechi NABU 1992 13; Sanmartín AuOr 9 1991 175; Akk. *epû*, AHw 231; CAD E 248. Cf. Heltzer IOKU 81; Yamashita RSP 2 44/2); ¶ syll. Ug.: [MU = *n*]*u-ḫa-ti-mu* = *is-ḫa-ri-ni* = : *a-pí-*[*ú/yu*], Ug 5 130 III 4'; Huehnergard UVST 52, 108, 312; Van Soldt BiOr 46 1989 648; SAU 302: cf. Sivan GAGl 17, 162; ¶ RS Akk.: LÚ.MU, PRU 3 199 (RS 16.257+) tr. I 1; PRU 6 93:25 (cf. Bottéro ARMT 7 p. 274 n. 1; Mayer Nuzi 179f.). ¶ Forms: pl. *apym*; cstr. *apy*.
Baker: *apym* (guild of) bakers, 4.125:10; (grain) *l apy TN* for the bakers of TN, 4.387:26; (money) *l apy* for the baker (collect.(?)), 4.212:5.

aqhr n. m. "?" (Cf. Sanmartín AuOr 8 1990 94: 'ice'(?), Hb. *qrr*,

HALOT 1149; Arab. *qarra*, Wehr 751f.; Akk. *qarḫu*, AHw 903; CAD Q 131; Hb. *qrḥ*, HALOT 1140; Abu Assaf AAAS 29/30 1979/80 262: '(viande) séchée', Arab. *ʔqhr (+ lḥm)*; cf. Renfroe AULS 82). ¶ Forms: sg. *aqhr*.

? : a commodity: *lth aqhr* a *l.* of *a.*, 4.14:3; *kṯ aqh*[*r* a *k.* of *a.*, 4.61:4.

aqht PN, epic hero (etym. unc., possibly an elative < */q-h-t/: cf. Margalit RB 95 1988 210ff.: 'Most Obedient'; cf. also Grøndahl PTU 75; De Moor BiOr 26 1969 106; Aartun Fs. Hospers 9ff.; Del Olmo MLC 517; Watson AuOr 8 1990 115; cf. West AOAT 233 29: PNN *a-ka-to*, *a-ka-ta-yo*, Linear B).

PN: 1.17 V 36 and *passim* in 1.17.-1.19.

iqnu n. m. 1) "gem of lapis lazuli"; 2) "violet blue"; 3) "violet purple or violet textile" (Sum. gìn, cf. Civil EDA 145; Akk. *uqnû*, AHw 1426; cf. Hitt. *ku(wa)nna-*, HW 122; Gk *kýanos* Liddell - Scott 1004; Linear B *ku-wa-no*, cf. Ribichini - Xella Tessili 32; diff. De Moor UF 8 1976 157: 'snails producing blue purple', and cf. Van Soldt UF 22 1990 346 n. 170); ¶ RS Akk.: *uqnû*; cf. NA_4.ZA.GÌN, PRU 4 224 (RS 17.422):11 and *passim*; ^{d}LÁMA NA_4.GIŠ.NU_{11}.GAL *ša i-na uq-ni-i i-za-az*, Ug 5 169:26'-27'; cf. SÍK.ZA.GÌN(.NA.MEŠ), PRU 6 p. 159; Huehnergard AkkUg 412; cf. SÍK.ZA.GÌN (/SÍK.SA_5 : *ta-ba*(?)*-ri*), Owen Tel Aviv 8 1981 7ff.:40; SÍK.ZA.GÌN *ta-kíl-tu*$_4$, PRU 3 187 (RS 15.43):5; PRU 6 149 II 8; SÍK.ZA.GÌN *ḫas-ma-na/ni*, PRU 3 187 (RS 15.43):6; 4 42 (RS 17.227 and dupl.):24 and *passim ibid.*; 50 TÚG.SIG_4.ZA.MEŠ *ša* GIŠ.GU.ZA *ša* SÍK.ZA.GÌN, PRU 3 184 (RS 16 146 + 161):13; cf. SÍK.ZA.GÌN *ḫaš-ma-na* SÍK.ZA.GÌN : *ḫa-an-da-la-ti ù* SÍK.ZA.GÌN : *du-pa-aš-ši*, Ug 5 48:9-10 (cf. Dietrich - Loretz WO 3/2 1966 227ff.; Landsberger JCS 21 1967 158f.; Huehnergard AkkUg 74f.; Van Soldt UF 22 1990 340-343); SÍG(!).ZA.GÌN *ù* TÚG.GAD.ME, RSOu 7 22:14 (cf. Huehnergard Syria 74 1997 247)); ¶ par.: *ḫrṣ*, *ksp*. ¶ Forms: sg. *iqnu*, gen. *iqni*; obl. pl. *iqnim* (Blau UF 11 1979 60).

1) Gem of lapis lazuli: PN (...) *d ʕqh ib iqni* whose pupils are gems of lapislazuli, 1.14 III 43 and par. (diff.: De Moor - Spronk UF 14 1972 168f.: 'the purest lapis-lazuli'); *bht ṯhrm iqnim* palace of the purest lapis lazuli (stones), 1.4 V 19 and par. (// *ksp*, *ḫrṣ*); *išlḥ ẓhrm iqnim* I shall give her purest lapis lazuli, 1.24:21-22 (// *ksp*, *ḫrṣ*).

2) Violet blue: *s*]*pśg iqni* (object in) violet blue enamel, 4.182:8.

3) Espec. violet purple: *iqnu*, 4.738:5; *šʕrt iqnim* wool in violet purple, 4.341:4; *all iqni* a cloak of violet purple, 4.182:6, 7; *iqn*]*i l DN qrt* (...) of violet purple for the DN of the town, *ibid.* ln. 15; *ḫpn*

d iqni w šmt a cloak of violet purple and reddish, 4.168:1; (the singers go dressed in)]*iqnu šmt*[of violet and red, 1.23:21; various quantities: 4.182:12 and *passim*; 4.203:5; 4.247:28; 4.779:6; cf. *mit iqni* one hundred (shekels) of purple, 4.778:14; 4.782:20; *mitm iqnu* two hundred (shekels) of purple, 4.778:17; 4.782:26; for payment of tribute: *ḫmš mat pḥm ḫmš mat iqnu*, five hundred (shekels) of ruby purple (and) five hundred (shekels) of violet purple, 3.1:23 (cf. RS Akk.: 5 *me-at* SÍK.ZA.GÌN.MEŠ 5 *me-at* SÍK.ZA.GÌN *ḫas-ma-na*, PRU 4 42 (RS 17.227 and dupl.):23-24); *ks ḫrṣ (/ ksp) ktn mit pḥm mit iqni l (...)* a cup of gold (/ silver), a tunic, one hundred (shekels) of red purple and one hundred (shekels) of violet purple for (...), 3.1:28 and *passim ibid.* (cf. RS Akk.: 1 GAL (/ *ka-sû*) KÙ.GI.MEŠ (/ KÙ.BABBAR.MEŠ) 1 TÚG.GADA 1 *me-at* SÍK.ZA.GÌN *(ḫaš-ma-ni)* 1 *me-at* SÍK.ZA.GÌN *(ḫaš-ma-ni / ta-kíl-tu$_4$) a-na (...)*, PRU 4 42f. (RS 17.227 and dupl.): 25-37; PRU 4 82 (RS 17.382+380): 40-47; cf. diff.: Knoppers BASOR 289 1993 88: 'lapislazuli gems'; cf. 1). In bkn ctx.: 1.1 II 5; 1.4 VII 1.

Cf. qnuy.

aqšr adj. m. "which sloughs its skin, sloughing", said of snakes (Arab. *ʔaqšar*, Lane 2525. Cf. Bowman - Coote UF 12 1980 135ff.; Bordreuil UF 15 1983 299f.; cf. De Moor UF 9 1977 367 n. 5: 'slippery'). ¶ Forms: *aqšr*, allophonic var.: *ʕqšr*.

Which sloughs its skin, sloughing: *nḥš ʕqšr* snake which sloughs its skin, 1.100:12 and par.; cf. in bkn ctx. *bdh aqšr*[through him the sloughing (serpent), 1.82:20.

/ʔ-r/ vb G: "to shine" (Hb. *ʔwr*, HALOT 24; Ebla cf. PNN *ar-ra*(-DN), *ar*-DN, DN-*ar*, Müller Biling. 169; cf. Krebernik PET 75f.; Amor. cf. /ʔ-w-r/, Gelb CAAA 14; cf. Caquot - Sznycer TOu 1 395; De Moor UF 11 1979 643, 653). ¶ Forms: G prefc. suff. *yark*.

G. To shine: *yrḫ yark* may DN shine for you, 1.24:39 (diff. Aartun StUL 16ff.: 'sexuell erregen, reizen; koitieren', **ʔrr (ʔw/yr)*; others: root *ʔrk*; cf. Herrmann NY 16).

Cf. a/ir.

a/ir n. m. "light" (< /ʔ-r/; Hb. *ʔwr*, HALOT 24f.; Ebla cf. /ʔūr/ (cstr.) in vocabularies: GI$_6$.SÁ = *ù-ru mu-si-im*, TM.75.G.5653+ rev. X 16-17; Fronzaroli MisEb 2 13; Sanmartín AuOr 9 1991 177f.; cf. Akk. *urru*, AHw 1433; *ur (I)*); ¶ syll. Ug.: cf. the element /ʔār/ in PN *a-ri-ya*, PRU 6 144:6; Ug 5 89:3, 7; Sivan GAGl 198. ¶ Forms: sg. *ar*, var. *ir*.

Light: *ar yrḫ* light of DN, 1.24:38; *bt ar* daughter of light, 1.3 III 6 and par. (diff.: 'mist, dew, honey', Arab. *ʔary*, Hb. *ʔry*, cf. Driver / Gibson CML 135 / 142; De Moor SP 82f., 104, 110; UF 7 1975 590f.; Sasson RSP 1 394; cf. Renfroe AULS 82f.). Cf. in unc. ctx. *krm ar*, 1.92:24 (Dijkstra UF 26 1994 119: *ar*, TN); *ir*, var. of *ar* in *lbšt b ir* clothed in light, 1.13:25 (cf. Caquot EI 14 1978 17; Del Olmo MLC 493; diff.: Widengren SK 93 n. 59: 'Glanz', Arab. *ʔiratu*. Diff. rdg: *bir* 'well', // *mrġt*, metaphor of the beloved woman: Dietrich - Loretz TUAT 2 342 n. 25a; cf. De Moor UF 12 1980 309: metaphor for female genitals).

Cf. ur (I), uryy.

ar TN (Belmonte RGTC 12/2 37f.: *ʔAru*. Cf. Dietrich - Loretz - Sanmartín UF 5 1973 83; Heltzer RCAU 8; Xella MLE 1 1982 53; Bordreuil Syria 61 1984 1, 5; Syria 66 1989 263ff.; Astour UF 11 1979 16; UF 13 1981 5f.; Pardee AfO 36/37 1989/90 482; Van Soldt UF 28 1996 660; UF 30 1998 718); ¶ syll.: cf. URU *a-ru/i*, cf. PRU 3 p. 265; PRU 4 p. 253; PRU 6 53 rev. 10'; Ug 5 99:3; RSOu 7 4:20; RS 22.233:1, 25.142:3 (Van Soldt UF 28 1966 660); RS 88.2013:9 (Lanckenbacher NABU 1989 36).

TN: 1.92:24; 2.26:10; 4.27:5, 16; 4.68:48; 4.139:5; 4.214 I 4; III 1; 4.365:4; 4.369:10; 4.375:4; 4.380:4; 4.382:23, 24; 4.384:3; 4.610:30; 4.683:6; 4.684:7; 4.693:4; 4.777:3; 4.784:6; RSOu 14 36 [KTU 9.417]:2.

ir n. m., 1.13:25, cf. *a/ir*.

ur n. m. 1) "warmth, heat"; 2) "fire, combustion", as a type of sacrifice (Hb. *ʔwr*, HALOT 24f.; cf. Arab. *ʔuwār/ʔūr*, Freitag LAL 1 69; cf. Herdner Ug 7 34; cf. Alalakh Akk.: the element /ʔūru/ in PNN, Sivan GAGl 202). ¶ Forms: sg. *ur*, pl./suff. encl. *-m urm*.

1) Warmth, heat: *yġlm ur* hot parched field, 1.19 II 17 and par. (diff.: Sanmartín UF 9 1977 267f.; Sasson RSP 1 395; Dijkstra - De Moor UF 7 1975 204; Margalit RB 91 1984 111ff.; ZAW 99 1987 393: a particular plant, Hb. *ʔwrh*). Bkn ctx. *mhr ur*, 1.10 I 11.

2) Type of sacrifice: *b urm u šnpt* as a burnt offering or a peace offering(?), 1.119:13 (cf. Del Olmo SEL 12 (1995) 46; diff.: De Moor ARTU 172); *w b urm lb rmṣt* and as a burnt sacrifice, a roasted heart, 1.39:8; 1.89:19 (diff.: Levine Fs. Freedman 472; De Tarragon TOu 2 137f., n. 14: 'in the morning' / 'clairté (du jour)', Hb. *ʔwr*, Akk. *urru*). Cf. in bkn ctx. 1.104:23 (De Moor - Spronk UF 14 1982 161 n. 65: 'greenery' // *gml* 'ripe fruit'); 1.176:12.

Cf. uryy.

irab TN (Belmonte RGTC 12/2 143: **ʔIrābu* land 2. Cf. Heltzer RCAU 15; for *ʔIrābu* 1 and 2 see Van Soldt UF 28 1996 661; UF 30 1998 725); ¶ syll.: *ʔIrābu* 2: [URU *ir*]-*a-bu*, Ug 5 102:5' (Berger UF 1 1969 123).
TN: 4.48:9 (: *ʔIrābu* 1); 4.553:2 (: *ʔIrābu* 2).

arbʕ n. num. "four" (< /r-b-ʕ/; Hb., Ph., Pun., Aram. *ʔrbʕ*, HALOT 83f.; DNWSI 101f.; Akk. *erbe*, AHw 232f.; CAD E 255; ESA *ʔrbʕ*, DOSA 477; Arab. *ʔarbaʕ*, Lane 1019; Eth. *ʔarbāʕ*, CDG 36); ¶ par.: *ṯlṯ*. ¶ Forms: sg. m. *arbʕ*, f. *arbʕt*; *arbʕtm* (encl. *-m* (?); pl. *arbʕm*, cf. *arbʕm*.
Numeral four, ★a) elliptical syntagms: *TN arbʕ* TN: four (traders), 4.27:14, 17, 22; 4.380:27, 34 (donkeys/workmen); *pld b arbʕt a p.* for four, 4.146:7; *arbʕt ksph* four is its price, 4.158:15; *nsk arbʕt* the smith: four, 4.98:17, 20 (shekels); in a numerical sequence, *arbʕ* four (times), 1.161:28; *arbʕ l ṯkṣ* four (skins) for PN (?), 4.52:120; *arbʕ b arbʕm* four (heifers) for forty (shekels), 4.142:2-3; *arbʕt ksph* its price is four (shekels), 4.158:15-16; *arbʕ l* (professional groups or persons) four (jars of wine) for x, 4.216:8; 4.274:4, 6; *arbʕ bd PN* four (jars of wine) delivered to/into the hands of PN, 4.219:4; *arbʕ ʕl PN* four (jars) of oil on PN's account, 4.313:22; *arbʕ* four (persons)(?), four PNN, 4.319:1; *arbʕ b TN* four (workmen/men) in TN, 4.358:6; *PN arbʕ* PN: four (jars of wine), 4.715:4-5; *TN arbʕ* TN: four (rations), RSOu 14 35 [KTU 9.388]:12. In bkn ctx.: *arbʕ ʕtkm* [...]there are four (barges?) tied up (?), 4.421:4; ★b) syntagms in the genitive: *arbʕ ʕṣrm* four birds, 1.48:8; TN *arbʕ yn* TN four ('jars') of wine, 1.91:24, cf. ln. 31; *arbʕ ḫpnt* four *ḫ.*, 1.148:19; *arbʕ ʕṣm* four logs, 2.26:9; *arbʕ ktnt* four tunics, 3.1:21; *arbʕ spm* four bowls, 4.34:7; 4.44:24, 30; *arbʕ bnšm* four individuals, 4.40:17; *arbʕ šurt* four *š.*, 4.44:4, 10, 14; *arbʕ dblt* four fig cakes, 4.60:5, 9; *arbʕ yn / š*[*mn*] four (jars) of wine / oil, 4.123:8, 9; 4.230:1; 4.285:2; 4.313:4; 4.717:3; *arbʕ ḥršm* four workmen, 4.141 III 5;*arbʕ prt* four heifers, 4.142:2; *arbʕ ḫpnt pṯt* four *ḫ.* of linen, 4.152:9; *arbʕ kkr(m)* four talents, 4.158:14; 4.123:2; 4.288:8; 4.626:2; *arbʕ ḫsnm* four 'dependents', 4.163:2; *arbʕ ṯrtnm* four magistrates, 4.163:9; *arbʕ qlʕm* four shields, 4.167:10, cf. 4.63 II 45; *arbʕ mdrnm* four broadswords(?), 4.167:11; *arbʕ ṣmdm apnt* four pairs of wheels, 4.169:7; *arbʕ ṯqlm* four shekels, 4.226:10; *arbʕ npš* four individuals, 4.228:3; *arbʕ uzm* four geese, 4.247:21; *arbʕ yn* four (jars) of wine, 4.246:6; 4.285:6; *arbʕ šd* four acres, 4.339:10; *arbʕ aṯt* four women, 4.349:2; 4,360:9; *arbʕ bnšm* four men, 4.355:5, 9, 11, 12, 16-18, 22, 33, 34, 37, 39; *arbʕ ġzlm* four spinners, 4.358:9; *arbʕ*

kdwtm four *k.*, 4.341:10; *arbʕ bnth* four of her daughters, 4.360:3; *arbʕ ḥ*[*mrm*] four donkeys, 4.377:25; 4.380:3, 20, 21; *arbʕ ddm* four cauldronfuls, 4.387:18; RSOu 14 40 [KTU 9.419]:6; RSOu 14 42 [KTU 9.420]:12; cf. 4.60:7; RSOu 14 39 [KTU 4.790]:12; *arbʕ š*[*rt*] four *š*, 4.410:11; *arbʕ nʕrm* four lads, 4.419:4; *arbʕ ṯqt* four *ṯ*, 4.595:4; *arbʕ qšt w arbʕ uṯpt* four bows and four quivers, 4.624:2, cf. 4.63 II 45; *arbʕ mrḥm* four lances, 4.624:8, 10; *arbʕ r*[*ʕym*] four shepherds, 4.729:11; *arbʕ bhtm* four houses, 4.750:2; *arbʕ ʕglm* four calves, 4.783:8; ★c) appositional syntagms: *qdšm arbʕ* four *q.*, 4.752:5; *TN arbʕ* TN four, 4.267:4; 4.73:9; *PN arbʕt* PN four, 4.281:10; *sʕrt arbʕ* of wool four (shekels), 4.630:11. In bkn ctx.: *b ar<b>ʕt*, 4.101:1-2; ★d) as a distributive: *arbʕ arbʕ mṯbt azmr* four huts (made) of branches on each side, 1.41:51; ★e) in a rhetorical progression: *ṯlṯ yrḫm (...) // arbʕ (...)* it is three months that (...), // it is four months that (...), 1.16 II 23; ★f) composite numbers: fourteen: *arbʕ ʕšr*, 4.48:3; 4.174:5; 4.349:1; 4.362:3; 4.618:5; bkn: 1.87:24; *arbʕ ʕšrh*, 1.106:19; 1.112:26-27; 4.282:1; 4.290:1; *arbʕt ʕšrt*, 1.87:4, cf. 1.41:4; 1.87:54-55; 1.105:17; 1.109:1; 1.112:17; 4.341:16; 4.658:13; *ʕšr arbʕ*, 4.244:18; *arbʕ l ʕš*[, 4.775:5; twenty-four: *arbʕ l* [[*š*]] *ʕšrm*, 4.173:8; 4.243:11; thirty-four: *ṯlṯm arbʕ*, 4.632:18; forty-four *arbʕm arbʕ*, 4.697:6, cf. *a*[*r*]*bʕ l arbʕ*[*m*], 4.417:7; sixty-four: *ṯṯm arbʕ*: 4.213:7; seventy-four cauldronfuls, *šbʕm dd arbʕ* 4.243:18; *šbʕm arbʕ kbd alpm* seventy-four oxen, 4.749:3; eighty-four *ṯmnym arbʕt*, 4.369:6, cf. 4.709:7; one hundred and four: *mit arbʕt*, 4.270:4; one hundred and thirty-four *ṯlṯm l mit arbʕ*, 4.411:4-5; *ḫmšm l mit arbʕ*, 4.174:14; *ṯlṯ* [*mat*] *arbʕ* three hundred and four, 4.387:14; four hundred: *arbʕ mat*, 4.91:2; 4.777:13; four hundred and twenty: *arbʕ mat ʕšrm*, 4.274:2; *arbʕ mat ʕšrm*, 4.274:2; four hundred and forty: *arbʕ mat arbʕm*, 4.296:6; four hundred and fifty-seven and a half: *arbʕ mat ḫmšm šbʕt w nsp*, 4.779:8; four thousand: *arbʕ alpm*, 4.203:3, 5; 4.626:2. In bkn ctx.:]*mšm arbʕ kbd*, RSOu 14 44:10'.

In unc. ctx.: *arbʕtm* four(?), RSOu 14 53 [KTU 9.432]:15 (cf. Bordreuil - Pardee RSOu 14 p. 397, 399: 'quatre', but Tropper UG 347: 'viermal' or 'vierfach'; cf. *ibid.* 377: or encl. *-m;* cf. *ṯlṯtm* (*ṯlṯ (I)*) and *ḥmštm* (*ḥmš (I)*).

In bkn ctx.: *arbʕ* 2.29:1; 4.73:14; 4.244:2; 4.302:6; 4.306:5; 4.396:13; 4.399:13; 4.466:3; 4.573:5; 4.575:2, 3; 4.627:3; *arb*[*ʕ* 1.41:22; 4.20:3; 4.355:42; 4.362:5; 4.388:11; 4.530:2; *a*]*rbʕ* 4.624:14; *arbʕt*: 1.57:2; *arbʕ*[*t*: 4.386:1; *arbʕ l*[, RSOu 14 39 [KTU 4.790]:8'.

Cf. **arbʕm, arbḫ, mrbʕt, /r-b-ʕ/, rbʕ, rbʕt.**

arbʕm n. "forty" (pl. of *arbʕ*). ¶ Forms: *arbʕm*.

The number forty, ★a) elliptical syntagms: *all iqni arbʕm* a violet purple *a.* for a total of forty, 4.182:6; *arbʕ b arbʕm* four (heifers) for forty (shekels), 4.142:3; TN *arbʕm* forty, 4.683:2; *b arbʕm* for forty, 4.341:15, 17, 18; *arbʕm d ktn* forty (shekels) of / for a tunic, 4.779:6; *ṣṣ PN arbʕm* salt of PN, forty, 4.340:7; 4.344:8; *PN w aḫth arbʕm* PN and his sister, forty, 4.658:46; ★b) appositional syntagms: *arbʕm ksp* forty in silver, 3.10:15, 17, 21; 4.290:6, 15; 4.369:11; 4.341:2; 4.778:1, 9; 4.782:1; 4.791:9, 12, 17; *arbʕm kkr* forty talents, 4.342:4; *arbʕm ṯqlm* forty shekels, 4.123:8; *arbʕm šmn mr* forty of myrrh (-scented) oil, 4.91:15;*arbʕm yn* forty (jars) of wine, 4.213:3; 4.230:11; 4.400:14; *arbʕm kdm kbd yn* a total of forty jars of wine, 4.213:16; *arbʕm qšt* forty bows, 4.169:1; *arbʕm šmn w krsim* forty *(kd)* and two *k.* of oil, RS 94.2392+:4 (Tropper UG 420); ★c) composite numbers: *aḥd kbd arbʕm* forty-one, 4.6302; *ṯn l arbʕm* forty-two, 4.777:9; *arbʕm ṯlṯ* forty-three, 4.213:22; 4.310:3; *arbʕm arbʕ* forty-four, 4.697:6; *arbʕm ḫmš(t)* forty-five, 4.174:9; 4.213:4; 4.782:15; *ḫmš kbd arbʕm* forty-five, 4.44:12; 4.284:3; *ṯmn l arbʕm* forty-eight, 4.144:5; *ṯmn kbd arbʕm* forty-eight, 4.212:4; one hundred and forty: *arbʕm l mit*, 4.158:3-4; 4.243:12; *arbʕm mit*, 4.213:25; *mit arbʕm*, 4.213:28; 4.280:11; 4.721:1; *arbʕm l mit ṯn* one hundred and forty-two, 4.179:16; *ḫmšm lmit arbʕ* one hundred and fifty-four (?), 4.143:5; [*mi*]*tm arbʕm ṯmn kbd* two hundred and forty-eight, 4.352:5; *arbʕ mat arbʕm* four hundred and forty, 4.296:7; *ḫmš mat arbʕm* five hundred and forty, 4.338:10.

In bkn ctx.: *arbʕm*: 1.76:2, 4, 7; 4.216:22; 4.257:4; 4.333:2; 4.396:2; 4.636:32; *arbʕ*[*m*] 4.243:32.

Cf. **arbʕ**.

arbdd n. m. "rest, tranquillity" ((?); cf. Hb. *rbd*, HALOT 1176; Arab. *rabada*, Lane 1009f.; ʔqtll- pattern, cf. Del Olmo IMC 153ff.; Janowski UF 12 1980 239ff.; cf. De Moor UF 17 1986 219f. [Arab. *barada*]; diff.: Dahood ULx 85: rdg *arb dd*, 'aphel imperative from **rbb*, to rain down'; Sanmartín UF 8 1976 461f.: 'gift, sacrifice of love', Hurr. *ar=b=dd (but cf. Wilhelm SMEA 29 1992 239 n. 4); Aartun StUL 19ff.: 'etwas sehr Nötiges', **ʔrb*; for other explanations cf. Del Olmo IMC 153ff.; Renfroe AULS 83; Smith BC 206f.); ¶ **par.**: *šlm*. ¶ **Forms**: sg. *arbdd*.

Rest, tranquillity(?): *sk (...) arbdd l kbd šdm* pour out (...) rest(?) in the heart of the field, 1.3 III 17 and par. (// *šlm*).

arbḫ adj./n. m. "four-year-old, four year old animal" (?); < *arbʕ-* + Hurr. suff. *-(u/o)-ḫḫe*; Sanmartín UF 9 1977 374f.; diff.: De Moor UF

17 1985 227: 'the Barker'(?), root *nbḫ/ḥ > *ʔabbāḫu > *ʔarbāḫu*;* Watson UF 28 1996 701: 'dog', Hurr. *erbi* + suff. *-ḫḫe*; Dijkstra UF 26 1994 118: 'locust', rdg *arby*(!), // *qrẓ*, survey in Wyatt RTU 371 n 14); ¶ par.:(?) *aylt.* ¶ Forms: sg. m. *arbḫ*.
Four-year-old(?): in bkn ctx., *l šmal*[...] *arbḫ* on his left[... he discerned(?)] a four-year-old(?), 1.92:10 (//(?) *aylt*).

irbl PN (?) (etym. unc. Cf. Grøndahl PTU 225f.; Watson AuOr 14 1996 95); ¶ syll.: cf. *i-ri-ib*-AN, Ug 5 9 (RS 17.61):3, 21; *i-ri-bi-li*, PRU 3 64 (RS 16.190): 5, 9, 11; *i-ri-bi-la*, PRU 3 70 (RS 16.279):4; Van Soldt SAU 27 n. 221; further *i-ri-ib*[, PRU 3 149-150 (RS 16.184): r4 (cf. Grøndahl PTU 327).
PN(?), as part of a toponym: *gt irbl*, 4.200:10; 4.788:6(?), 8(?) (Belmonte RGTC 12/2 94); cf. rdg *bn irbl*, 8.30:6 (RSOu 7 96:6'; KTU 4.778:6: *gt irbṣ*).
Cf. irbṣ.

arbn PN (Hurr. Cf. Grøndahl PTU 220, 223). Cf. *irbn*, *irpn*.
PN: 4.133:1.

irbn (I) TN (Belmonte RGTC 12/2 143. Cf. Heltzer RCAU 15; Van Soldt UF 28 1996 661).
TN: 4.355:34.

irbn (II) PN (etym. unc. Cf. Ribichini - Xella RSF 15 1987 10; Grøndahl PTU 28, 100, 223, 226; Bordreuil Semitica 32 1982 13). Cf. *arbn*, *irpn*.
PN: *bn PN*, 4.76:1.

irbṣ n. m. in the TN *gt irbṣ* ("repose"(?); cf. /r-b-ṣ/).
TN: *gt irbṣ* 'Farmstead of Repose(?)' (<(?) /r-b-ṣ/), 4.122:1 (Belmonte RGTC 12/2 94); 4.788:6(?), 8 ((?); cf. rdg *bn irbl*, 8.30:6 [RSOu 7 96:6']; see *irbl*).
Cf. irbl.

urbt n. f. 1) "skylight, window"; 2) a cult installation (Hb. *ʔrbh*, HALOT 83; Ebla cf. *ur-pù-um*, Archi Eblaitica 1 15. Cf. Loewenstamm VT 34 1984 193f.; Fronzaroli SEL 7 1990 153; Huehnergard UVST 275; diff. Watson UF 28 1996 702: 'place of slaughter', Hurr. *urb*-); ¶ par.: *ḥln*. ¶ Forms: sg. *urbt*; suff. *urbtm* (encl. *-m*).
1) Skylight, window: *al tšt urbt b* [*bhtm*] do not put a skylight in the house, 1.4 V 64 and par. (// *ḥln*); *w tṣu (...) k qṭr urbtm* and it will go out (...) like smoke through a skylight, 1.169:3 (diff.: Aartun UF 16 1984 5: 'Zufluchtsort', /ʔ-r-b/, Hb. *ʔereb*, ar. *ʔurbat*).
2) A cult installation: *w b urbt ilib š* and in the *u.*, (to) DN one ram,

1.109:19; in bkn ctx.: *w bu*[*rbt* ...] *ytk* and in the *u.* [(an offering)] he shall pour (out), 1.41:11 and par.; in bkn ctx. [*b*] *tdṯ yṯb mlk b ur*[*bt*] on the sixth day the king / DN will be installed in the *u.*, 1.171:6 (cf. Del Olmo CR 33: 'niche, alcove'; De Moor ARTU 160 n. 24: 'lattice').

irbtn PN (Hurr. Cf. Ribichini - Xella UF 15 1987 10f.). Cf. *iwrtn.*
PN: *bn PN*, 4.7:17.

irby n. m. "locust" (Hb. *ʔrbh*, HALOT 83; Aram. *ʔrbh*, DNWSI 101; *Akk. erbu*, AHw 234; CAD E 256ff.); ¶ par.: *ḥsn*, *qṣm.* ¶ Forms: sg. *irby*; pl. *irbym.*
Locust: *km irby tškn šd* like locusts they settled in the field, 1.14 IV 29 and par. (// *ḥsn*); *ʕlh k irbym kp* above her like locusts palms (of hands were flying), 1.3 II 10 (// *qṣm*).

ardn PN (etym. unc. Cf. Berger WO 5 1969/70 279); ¶ syll.: cf. *a-ra-ad-ni*[, PRU 3 36 (RS 11.718):3'. Cf. *artn.*
PN: *bn PN*, 4.723:8.

irdyn PN (Hurr. Cf. Grøndahl PTU 207, 226, 262; Watson AuOr 14 1996 95).
PN: 4.631:16 (*bn ḫrġdġ*).

ardl[**n** (?), 7.42:4 (Hurr. TN(?)).

argb PN (etym. unc. Cf. Gelb - Purves - MacRae NPN 203; Grøndahl PTU 179).
PN: *bn PN*, 4.617:41.

argd PN (etym. unc.).
PN: 4.749:1.

argdd PN (etym. unc.).
PN: 4.336:4; 4.753:19.

a/irgmn n. m. 1) "payment of tribute to the Hittite court"; 2) "tribute" in general; 3) "offering" (< Luw. *arkamma(n)-*, HW(2) 302ff.; cf. Tischler HEG 59f.; Puhvel HED 143-146; Starke WO 24 1993 20ff.; cf. Hurr. /arg=am=anne/, Diakonoff HU 79 n. 82: 'aus dunkelrotem Purpur'; Akk. *argamannu*, AHw 67; CAD A/2 253; Hb. *ʔrgmn*, HALOT 84; Palm. *ʔrgwn*, DNWSI 103; Aram. Kaufman AIA 35 > Arab. *ʔurguwān*, Lane 1505. Cf. Del Olmo CR 113 n. 92; Dietrich - Loretz WO 3/2 1964/6 218, Pardee UF 6 1974 277f.; Sanmartín UF 10 1978 455f; Ziderman BASOR 265 1987 25ff.; Van Soldt UF 22 1990 344 n. 164; cf. Dijkstra UF 21 1989 144: also 'purple dyed cloth'; Smith BC 308; diff. Heltzer RCAU 33 n. 74: 'tribute collectors, tribute-deliverers'); ¶ RS Akk.: *mandattu* (CAD M/1 13; Sanmartín UF 10 1978 455 n. 5; PRU 4 41 (RS 17.227 and dupl.):20

// KTU 3.1:18); ¶ par.: *mnḥ*. ¶ Forms: sg. *argmn*, *irgmn*; suff. *argmny*, *argmnk*: pl. *argmnm*, cstr. *argmn*.
1) Payment of tribute to the Hittite court: *spr argmn špš* register of contributions to the Sun, 4.610:1 (cf. [*ṭup-pu an-nu-ú*] *ša ma-an-da*[*-at* ᵈ]UTU*-ši*, PRU 4 47 (RS 11.732):1); *spr irgmn* register of tribute, 4.181:1; *spr argmnm* register of the contributions, 4.369:1; *spr argmn nskm* register of contributions to the smiths, 4.261:1; (copper) *l argmn l nskm* (intended) for tribute (and delivered)to the smiths, 4.43:3 (Sanmartín UF 10 1978 455f.); *argmn d ybl PN l špš arn* tribute which PN brings to the Sun of TN, 3.1:18 (Knoppers BASOR 289 1993 86f.); *argmn PN mlk* tribute of king PN, *ibid.* ln. 24 (Dietrich - Loretz WO 3/2 1964/6 218 n. 55); *ḫrṣ argmny* the gold of my tribute, 2.36:6.
2) Tribute: *hw ybl argmnk* he will bring you tribute, 1.2 I 37 (// *mnḥy*): in bkn ctx.: 4.390:12.
3) Ritual offering: on the fourteenth day *riš argmn* first-fruits of the offerings / tributes, 1.41:4; 1.87:5 (Del Olmo AuOr 5 1987 261 n. 16: 'first offering(s)' > 'offering of first-fruits'; diff. Dietrich - Loretz - Sanmartín UF 7 1975 145: 'Erste Qualität Purpur'; De Moor ARTU 159 n. 10: 'purple').

irgn PN (etym. unc. Cf. Grøndahl PTU 28, 100; Watson AuOr 13 1995 220); ¶ syll.: cf. *ir-ri-gi*(?)*-na*, PRU 4 183 (RS 17.319):18.
PN: 4.129:9.

argnd PN (Hurr.).
PN, *ilmlk* [*bn*(?)] *argnd*, 4.386:11. Cf. in bkn ctx.: *bn argn*[, 4.694:2.

irgy PN (etym. unc. Cf. Grøndahl PTU 28, 100, 205, 226); ¶ syll.: cf. *ir-ki-ia-nu*, Ug 5 12:47; cf. Huehnergard UVST 218; AkkUg 401; Van Soldt SAU 351.
PN: *bn PN*, 4.232:10.

urgy PN (probl. allomorph of *irgy*).
PN: 4.63 I 45.
Cf. irgy.

a/irġn n.of substance used in pharmacopea (?) ("unripe date, of one month(?)", cf. Akk. *arḫānu*, AHw 67, CAD A/2 255, Pardee TH 61f.; Watson NUS 35 1986 11; diff.: Cohen - Sivan UHT 31: 'fennel(?)', Akk. *urānu*; Cohen UF 28 1996 131f.). ¶ Forms: sg. *a/irġn*.
Substance used in pharmacopea: *št irġn ḥmr* a *š.* of reddish *i.*, 1.85:17, 28; 1.72:23, 34; *arġn ḥmr*, 1.97:4.

urġnr PN (Hurr. Cf. Grøndahl PTU 204, 211, 229, 243; Dietrich - Loretz WO 4 1967/68 302).

PN: 4.177:9.

urǵṯṯb PN (Hurr. Cf. Grøndahl PTU 204, 208, 211, 229, 264; Cunchillos TOu 2 360 n. 3; Van Soldt SAU 6, 45); ¶ **syll.**: *ur-ḫ̮i-*[d]U-*ub*, PRU 4 176 (RS 17.346):7, 10.

PN: 2.68:3; 4.410:30.

arḫ̮ n. f. "cow, heifer" (Amor. /ʔarḫ̮um/, Gelb CAAA 13; Akk. *arḫ̮u*, AHw 67; CAD A/2 263; Sasson RSP 1 397); ¶ **par.**: *alp (I)*, *bn (I)*, *ḫprt*, *kr*, *ṯat*. ¶ **Forms**: sg. *arḫ̮*; pl. *arḫ̮t*.

Cow: *arḫ̮ tzǵ l ʕglh* the cow lows for her calf, 1.15 I 5 (// *bn*); *k lb arḫ̮ l ʕglh* like the heart of a cow for her calf, 1.6 II 6, 28 (// *ṯat*); *arḫ̮ td rgm* the cow gave voice, 1.93:1; *špq ilht arḫ̮t yn* he provided the cow-goddesses with wine, 1.4 VI 50 (// *kr*, *ḫprt*, *alp*); heifer: *l arḫ̮* oh heifer!, 1.13:22; *ʕnt arḫ̮ bʕl* DN, the heifer of DN, 1.13:29; *tʕn arḫ̮* she saw a heifer, 1.10 II 28; *tḥbq arḫ̮*[she embraced the heifer[, 1.10 III 22s.; *arḫ̮t tld* the heifers gave birth, 1.10 III 1; in bkn ctx.: *arḫ̮ arḫ̮*[a heifer, a heifer[, 1.10 III 19.

urḫ̮, 4.131:2.

Cf. **urḫ̮ln**.

arḫ̮lb PN (Hurr. Cf. Dietrich - Loretz - Sanmartín UF 5 1973 82; Van Soldt SAU 4f., 354; Huehnergard AkkUg 370f.); ¶ **syll.**: *ar(i)*/SUM-*ḫ̮al-bá*, *passim*, cf. PRU 3 p. 242; *a-ri-ḫ̮al-bá*, PRU 3 193 (RS 12.34+):19 (cf. SUM-*hal-bá*, ln. 3).

PN: *il PN*, 1.113:20.

urḫ̮ln PN (Hurr. Cf. Grøndahl PTU 204, 210, 223, 229).

PN: 4.131:2 spelling: *urḫ̮.ln* (cf. Watson AuOr 8 1990 127).

/ʔ-r-k/ vb G: "to be long, grow long" (Hb., Ph., Aram. *ʔrk*, HALOT 88; DNWSI 108; Akk. *arāku*, AHw 63f.; CAD A/2 223-226; cf. ESA *ʔrk*, DOSA 27; Arab. *ʔaraka*, Lane 50f.). ¶ **Forms**: G suffc. *ark*; prefc. *tirkm* (encl. *-m*; Aartun PU 1 57); impv. *ark*.

G. To be long, grow long: *tirkm yd il km ym* the hand of DN grew as long as the sea, 1.23:33; *ark yd il k ym* the hand of DN was as long as the sea, *ibid.* ln. 34; (said of age): *ḥwt aḫ̮t wn ark* be revived, sister, and be long (in years)!, 1.10 II 20 (alternatively: impv. N: *w nark* and be lengthened; diff. De Moor UF 11 1979 463: /ʔ-r/).

Cf. **urk, arkd, arkt**.

ark PN (Hurr.(?). Cf. Grøndahl PTU 101, 205, 221, 234, 422; cf. West AOAT 233 30: PN *a-ri-ke-u*, Linear B).

PN: 4.63 II 42.

urk n. m. "length" (< /ʔ-r-k/; Hb. *ʔrk*, HALOT 88; Ph., Pun., Aram. *ʔrk*, DNWSI 108; Akk. *urku*, AHw 1431). ¶ **Forms**: sg. *urk*.

Length: *urk ym bˁly* (may) my lord (have) length of days, 2.23:20 and par. (cf. Hb. *ʔrk ymym*, Dt 30:20 and par.).

arkbt PN (Hurro-Akk. Cf. Grøndahl PTU 219).
PN: *bn PN*, 4.75 III 12.

arkd n. of a projectile ((?); cf. Akk. *ariktu* and Sum. giš.gíd.da, CAD A/2 267; AHw 68; Römer AfO 40/41 1993/94 24ff.; cf. Eg. *ʔá-r-q-ta*, Helck Bez. 508 (10a); cf. Dietrich - Loretz UF 10 1978 429). ¶ Forms: sg. *arkd*.
A type of projectile(?): PN *ḥrš arkd* maker of *a.*, 4.277:9 (cf. *kld*).
Cf. **arkt**.

arkd̲(n) PN (Hurr. Cf. Grøndahl PTU 219, 238).
PN: 4.141 I 12; 4.723:2.

arkšt PN (etym. unc.).
PN: *bn PN*, 4.631:4.

arkt n. f. "length (of arm, etc.) > "long arm, span" (abstr. in /-ût/; < /ʔ-r-k/; cf. Hb. *ʔr(w)kh*, HALOT 85; cf. Pun. *ʔrkt*, DNWSI 108: *ʔrk*$_4$; Akk. *ariktu*, AHw 68; CAD A/2 267. Cf. Dijkstra - De Moor UF 7 1975 193; Caquot - Sznycer TOu 1 175). ¶ Forms: sg. suff. *arkty*.
Length (of an arm) > (long) arm, span: (I can reach them) *b gdlt arkty* with the power of my long arm, 1.3 V 23 and par.
Cf. **arkd**.

arm PN (etym. unc. Cf. Gelb - Purves - MacRae NPN 28). Cf. *irm*, PN.
PN: *bn PN*, 4.232:5. For *arm* TN, 4.750:5, see *ˁrm (II)*.

irm PN (Hurr.(?); cf. AT p. 138; Gelb - Purves - MacRae NPN 210; cf. Watson AuOr 8 1990 396).
PN: 4.399:5.

urm PN (etym. unc. Cf. Grøndahl PTU 275); ¶ syll.: cf. *ú-ru-mì-ya*, Ug 5 5:8.
PN: *bn PN*, 4.263:4.

armgr PN (etym. unc.).
PN: *bn PN*, 4.214 II 4.

urmn PN (etym. unc. Cf. Grøndahl PTU 275).
PN, in bkn ctx.: *urmn*[, 7.42:6.
Cf. **urm**.

armsġ PN/GN ((?); cf. Grøndahl PTU 268, 292; Dietrich - Loretz OLZ 62 1967 536f.; WO 4 1967/68 305; Nougayrol Ug 5 p. 50.
PN: *kbsm armsġ* (two?) fullers GN (or: fullers: PN), 4.125:20.

armwl PN (Anat. Cf. Grøndahl PTU 272, 297; Van Soldt SAU 36).

PN: 4.7:4, 14; 4.102:9; 4.246:5; 4.364:6; 4.423:20, 22; 4.616:14.

army PN (etym. unc. Cf. Grøndahl PTU 26, 220, 272).
PN: ★a) 4.232:7, 9; 4.309:10. ★b) *bn PN*, 4.63 III 22.

urmy PN (etym. unc., cf. Grøndahl PTU 275); ¶ syll.: *ú-ru-mì-ya*, Ug 5 5:8.
PN: *bn PN*, 3.10:16; 4.791:10.
Cf. urm, army.

arn (I) n. m. "chest" (Hb. *ʔrwn*, HALOT 85f; Ph., Aram. *ʔrn*, DNWSI 109f.; Akk. *arānu*, AHw 65; CAD A/2 231). ¶ Forms: sg. *arn*.
Chest: *arn w mznm* a chest and scales, 4.385:5.

arn (II) TN of the Hitt. region (Belmonte RGTC 12/2 32: *Arinna* 1. Cf. URU *a-ri(-in)-na-*, URU TÚL*-na*, Del Monte - Tischler RGTC 6 33ff., Del Monte RGTC 6/2 10f.: Arina IV; Neu StBT 26 354).
TN: *špš arn* (the goddess) 'Sun of TN', 3.1:19 (// ^{d}UTU*-ši*, PRU 4 41. (17.227):20; cf. Hitt. ^{d}UTU of Arinna, epithet of the goddess Wurunšemu; cf. Goetze Kleinasien 136; Von Schuler WbMyth 197; Del Monte - Tischler RGTC 6 35).

irn (I) n. m. "puppy, puppy-dog" (cf. Arab. *ʔarana* Kazimirski DAF 27; *miʔrān* Hava 7; Akk. *mīrānu* AHw 658; CAD M/2 105; Watson NUS 21 1980 8; 36 1986 17; Aartun UF 15 1983 1ff.; Rendsburg JAOS 107 1987 623f.: 'goat', in modern South Arabian dialects; diff.: Caquot SDB 9 1412: 'lézard', Akk. *urnu*; cf. Dietrich - Loretz MU 129). ¶ Forms: sg. *irn*.
Puppy, puppy-dog: *pnh pn irn* (if) his/its face is (like) muzzle of a puppy-dog, 1.103+:33.
Cf. inr, bnirn.

irn (II) PN (Watson AuOr 8 1990 116; cf. *i-ru-na* PRU 6 55 10' 20').
PN: *bn PN*, 4.281:16.

urn PN (etym. unc.). Cf. *bninr*, *bnirn*.
PN: ★a) 1.42:43 (Hurr.) ★b) *bn PN*, 4.90:5.

arnbt PN (Sem. Cf. Grøndahl PTU 28, 101, 119; Fronzaroli OrAn 11 1972 260f.; Hurr. cf. Watson AuOr 13 1995 219); ¶ syll.: DUMU *ar-na-ba-ti*, PRU 6 82:23; Sivan GAGl 197; Watson AuOr 8 1990 115.
PN: *bn arnbt*, 4.412 II 7.

arny (I) TN (Belmonte RGTC 12/2 29: *ʔAraniya*. Cf. Heltzer RCAU 8; Astour RSP 2 263; Bordreuil UF 20 1988 11f.; Pardee AfO 36/37 1989/90 483; Van Soldt SAU 337; UF 28 1996 661); ¶ syll.: URU *a-ra-ni-ya*, PRU 3 188 (RS 10.44):3'; RSOu 7 4:39; URU *a-ra-ni-ia*, PRU 4 215 (RS 17.288):8 and *passim ibid.*
TN: 4.63 II 1; 4.68:27; 4.100:2; 4.365:10; 4.380:10; 4.610 (I) 11;

4.693:9; 4.750:18; RSOu 14 36 [KTU 9.417]:8.

arny (II) GN m. (< *arny*, TN). ¶ Forms: sg. *arny*.
GN: 4.80:6; 4.123:7.

arny (III) PN (< *arny*, GN).
PN: 4.285:11.

irp n. m.; a vessel or container (?) (of cedar wood?; cf. Hurro-Hitt. GIŠ *eripi-*, HW[2] 92; HEG 109; Eg. *irp*, but cf. Muchiki Loanwords 281; Watson AuOr UF 32 2000 568). ¶ Forms: du. *irpm*.
A vessel or container (?): *ṯn irpm* two *i.*, 4.123:20 (cf. *spl, mmsk, mqrt*, *ibid.* ln. 17-19).

irpbn PN (Hurr. Cf. Grøndahl PTU 221, 226, 244; Dietrich - Loretz - Sanmartín UF 5 1973 82; Bordreuil - Caquot Syria 56 1979 310); ¶ syll.: *ar(i)*(SUM)*-pa-ba-ni*, PRU 6 37:4'. Cf. *gṯpbn, pbn*.
PN: ★a) 4.187:2; ★b) *bn PN*, 4.769:12.

arpḫn PN (cf. Arrapḫa, TN; Belmonte RGTC 12/2 36. Cf. Grøndahl PTU 27, 301); ¶ syll.: *ar-rap-ḫa-na*, PRU 3 203 (RS 16.257+) IV 13.
PN: *bn PN*, 4.232:29.

irpn PN (Hurr.; cf. Gelb - Purves - MacRae NPN 28; Cassin - Glassner AAN 129). Cf. *arbn, irbn*.
PN: 4.399:2.

a/irpṯr PN (Hurr. Cf. Grøndahl PTU 211, 221, 249; Ribichini - Xella RSF 15 1987 13; Watson AuOr 13 1995 219).
PN: ★a) 4.33:7 (*yʕrty*); ★b) *bn PN*, 4.631:20.

arr TN 1) a mythological mountain, probl. an alternative name of mount *ṣpn* or the name of a 'district' of Mount *ṣpn* (Belmonte RGTC 12/2 35: *Arr* 2; cf. Clifford CMC 76; Dietrich - Loretz - Sanmartín UF 5 1973 84f.); 2) TN *Arruw/ya*, probl. on the border with Siyannu (Belmonte RGTC 12/2 35ff.: *Arr* 1, *?Arruwa*; cf. Bordreuil Syria 61 1984 4f.; Van Soldt UF 28 1996 666 n. 93. Cf. also Heltzer IOKU 109 n. 32; Syria 66 1989 263ff.; Van Soldt UBL 11 365 (2), 370; Görg Fs. Fecht 142ff.); ¶ syll.: for 2, cf. URU *ar-ru-wa*, PRU 7 71ff. (RS 17.335+):14'; 76ff. (RS 17.368):4'; URU *a-ar-ru-wa*, Ug 5 27:44.
1) A mythological mountain or the name of a 'district' of Mount *ṣpn*: she climbed *b arr bm arr w b ṣpn* to TN, to TN and(?) to 'Ṣapānu', 1.10 III 29-30; see also]*arr b ym*, RSOu 14 53 [KTU 9.432]:19.
2) Probl. TN *Arruw/ya* on the border with Siyannu: cf. *śśw PN arr* horses of PN from/of TN(?), 4.384:1; *spr ḫrd arr* list of the soldiers of TN(?), 4.683:1; *mʕr arr*, 4.355:32 (Bordreuil Syria 61 1984 5f.); *msmt ʕbs arr d qrht* treaty concerning the boundary stones (?) of TN of the cities, 6.27:2 (for the rdg cf. Van Soldt UF 21 1989 380 n. 30: '*a.*-

district of the towns'). Read *mʕr ḥr[r]* in 4.365:33 (Van Soldt UF 28 1996 677).
Cf. mʕr.

irrṯrm PN (Hurr. Cf. Grøndahl PTU 226, 250; Cunchillos TOu 2 327 n. 3; cf. KTU: rdg *iwrṯrm*?).
PN: 2.33:2.

arspy GN m. (Heltzer RCAU 9). ¶ Forms: sg. *arspy*.
GN: 4.52:11.

ars/św(n) PN (Anat. Cf. Grøndahl PTU 26, 272, 297, 301; Segert UF 15 1983 211f.; Tropper UF 27 1995 522; Watson AuOr 14 1996 95; cf. diff. Ward JNES 20 1961 32ff.); ¶ syll.: *ar-sú-wa*, PRU 3 155 (RS 16.242):17; Ug 5 10:3; *ar-sú-wa-nu* and var., PRU 3 52f. (RS 15.85):13, 22; 155 (RS 16.242):7, 9; PRU 6 82:5; Ug 5 9:15; 10 rev. 6'; cf. [f]*ar-sú-wa-tu*$_4$, PRU 6 149 II 4; cf. Huehnergard AkkUg 40.
PN: ★a) 4.33:6 (*bṣry*; Van Soldt SAU 33); 4.35 II 4, 12 (*bn qqln*); 4.54:2, 10 (*yʕr*[*ty*]); 4.153:9; 4.331:5; ★b) *bn PN*, 4.51:11 (*bṣ*]*ry*); 4.69 II 14; 4.281:5.

arṣ n. f. 1) "earth, ground"; 2) "the world, the inhabited earth, country"; 3) "the lower world, solid ground"; 4) "the underworld, the netherworld"; 5) DN (Hb., Ph., Pun., *ʔrṣ*, HALOT 90f.; DNWSI 110ff.; Aram. *ʔrʕ/q*, DNWSI 110ff.; Ebla *ar-ṣa-tù*, ARET 8 17; Sanmartín AuOr 9 1991 175; Akk. *erṣetu*, AHw 245; CAD E 308ff.; ESA *ʔrḍ*, DOSA 27; Arab. *ʔarḍ*, Lane 48. Cf. Tromp PCD 23ff.); ¶ syll. Ug.:]*ar-ṣu*, Ug 5 137 III 14'; Sivan GAGl 197; Huehnergard UVST 110; Van Soldt SAU 302; ¶ RS Akk.: KI(.MEŠ), *erṣetu(m)*, *passim*; cf. [d]IDIM *ù* [d]IDIM, Ug 5 18:11; [d]KI [, Ug 5 170 14'; [d]*sa-mu-ú ù* [d]*er-ṣe-tum*, PRU 4 137 (RS 18.06+):6'; DN [*ú*](?)-*šu-gal* AN-*e u* KI-*tim*, Ug 5 17:4; ¶ par.: *ʕpr (I)*, *ʕrpt*, *ʕṣ*, *hr (I)*, *ksu*, *mṯt*, *nšm*, *šd*, *šmm*, (?) *ym*. ¶ Forms: sg. *arṣ*, suff. *arṣh* (adv./emph. -*h* (?), cf. Aartun PU 1 41); *art*, 1.19 III 6, rdg *arṣ*(!).
1) Earth, ground: his tears fell *km ṯqlm arṣh* like shekels to the earth, 1.14 I 29 (// *mṯt*; cf. Aartun PU 1 41); I can drag him *k imr l arṣ* like a lamb to the ground, 1.3 V 1; cf. 1.6 V 4; *yql l arṣ* fall / he falls to the ground, 1.2 IV 23, 26; *l arṣ zrm* shall you remain transfixed to the ground?, 1.169:14 (cf. Del Olmo CR 386 n. 189; for other opinions cf. Caquot TOu 2 58 n. 151); *npl l arṣ* fallen to the earth, 1.5 VI 8-9; *l arṣ ypl ulny* our / my forces fell to the ground, 1.2 IV 5. *yṯb l arṣ* he sat on the ground, 1.5 VI 14 and par.; (her jar) *l arṣ ṯṯbr* shattered on the ground, 1.16 I 54; *tdʕṣ pnm w tr arṣ* she pressed (her) feet (down) and jumped to the ground, 1.4 V 21 and par.; a delight *l arṣ mṭr bʕl*

for the earth is the rain of DN, 1.16 III 5, 7 (// *šd*); striking *l arṣ brqm* to the earth his lightnings, 1.4 V 9 (// *ʕrpt*); *šršk b arṣ al ypʕ* may your root not take root in the earth, 1.19 III 53; [*tṣ*]*un b arṣ* [... they] come out of the earth, 1.83:3 (//(?) *ym*); *ybl arṣ* produce of the earth, 1.5 II 5 (// *ʕṣ*); *ʕl arṣ l an* [*isp ḥ*]*mt* from the earth everywhere remove the poison, 1.107:37 and par. (// *hrm*);]*tdrk brḥ arṣ* [if] you tread on a fleeing (serpent) on the ground, 1.82:38 (cf. Del Olmo CR 378); *yšpk kmm arṣ* may they spill it likewise on the ground, RSOu 14 52 [KTU 9.435]:12. Cf. in bkn ctx. *l arṣ pʕn*[, 1.174:2; 1.1 II 10; 1.1 V 28; 1.17 VI 15; 1.82:2.
2) The world, the inhabited earth, country: *hmlt arṣ* multitudes of the land, 1.3 III 28 and par.(// *nšm*); *tlm ġṣr arṣ* the hills that limit the world, 1.4 VIII 4; *qṣm arṣ* the ends of the earth, 1.16 III 3; *qryy b arṣ mlḥmt* go to meet war in the country, 1.3 III 14 and par. (// *ʕprm*); *ymlk b arṣ* he ruled in the land, 1.6 I 65; *arṣ drkt* the country of (my) rule, 1.4 VII 44; *arṣ nḥlth* the land of his inheritance, 1.3 VI 16 and par. (// *ksu*); *qlh q*[*dš y*(?)]*tr arṣ* his holy voice makes the earth tremble/shake, 1.4 VII 31.
3) Lower world, solid earth, ★a) // *šmm* "heaven/sky": *šmn arṣ* oil of the earth, 1.3 II 39 and par.; *tr arṣ w šmm* travelling through the earth and the heavens, 1.16 III 2; *špt l arṣ špt l šmm* a lip to the earth and the other to the sky, 1.23:62; *tant šmm ʕm arṣ* the whisper of the heavens with the earth, 1.3 III 24; ★b) elements: *kbd arṣ* the heart of the earth, 1.3 III 16 and par. (// *šd*); *msdt arṣ* foundations of the earth, 1.4 I 40; *ʕnt arṣ* springs of the earth, 1.3 IV 36 and par.; *bmt ar*[*ṣ*] *ṯṯn* the heights of the earth shook, 1.4 VII 34.
4) The underworld, hell: *zbl bʕl arṣ* the prince, master of the underworld, 1.5 VI 10 and par.; *aṯr bʕl ard b arṣ* after DN I shall go down to the underworld, 1.5 VI 25 and par.; *yrdm arṣ* those who go down to the underworld, 1.4 VIII 9; 1.5 V 16; *il k yrdm arṣ* DN was like those who go down to the underworld, 1.114:22; *aṯr bʕlk arṣ* follow your lord to the underworld, 1.161:21 (// *ks<i>h*); *rd arṣ rd* go down to the underworld, go down, *ibid.* ln. 22; *ḫrt ilm arṣ* cave of the chthonian deities, 1.5 V 6 and par. (1.19 III 6, rdg *arṣ*(!)); *rpi arṣ* the chthonian *r.*, 1.15 III 3, 14; 1.161:2, 4, 5, 9 and par.; may (someone) *l arṣ mšṣu qṭrh* from the underworld set free his sprit , 1.17 I 27 and par. (// *ʕpr*); *bt ḫpṯt arṣ* residence of infernal seclusion, 1.4 VIII 8 and par.; *ntʕn b arṣ iby* we shall pierce my enemies in the underworld, 1.10 II 24 (// *ʕpr*); cf. *arṣ dbr* the 'Land of Pestilence', 1.5 VI 6 and par. (// *šd šḥlmmt*); *mġt / mġny l nʕmy arṣ* I /we arrived at the

'delight' of the land, 1.6 II 19 / 1.5 VI 5.

5) DN: *arṣ w šmm* DN and DN, 1.118:11 (cf. dIDIM *ù* dIDIM, Ug 5 18:11; d*sa-mu-ú ù* d*er-ṣe-tum*, PRU 4 137 (RS 18.06 + 17.365):6'); cf. 1.47:12; *arṣ w šmm š* DN and DN: a ewe, 1.48:5, 24.

In bkn ctx., *ṯbt ḥš*[*n* ...]*y arṣ ḥšn*[, 1.5 III 4; 1.12 I 3.

arṣy DN of one of Baal's daughters (Pardee AfO 36/37 1989/90 439f.; Aartun StUL 22ff.; Watson SEL 10 1993 54).

DN: *arṣy bt yʕbdr* DN, daughter of *y.*, 1.3 III 7 and par.; in cultic context *dqtm w gdlt l arṣy* two ewes and a cow to DN, 1.106:32; *arṣy š* DN, a ram, 1.148:7. In god lists: 1.118:22 and par.

/ʔ-r-š/ vb G/D: "to request, wish, demand, negotiate(?)" (Hb., Pun. *ʔrš*, HALOT 91; DNWSI 114f.; Akk. *erēšu*, AHw 239f.; CAD E 281-285; cf. Amor. /ʔ(?)-r-ś/, Gelb CAAA 14. Cf. Dietrich - Loretz UF 12 1980 174); ¶ **par.**: /š-t/, /y-t-n/. ¶ **Forms**: G/D suffc. *aršt*; prefc. *yarš*, *yirš*, *taršn* (Verreet UF 17 1985 322f.; Sivan UF 22 1990 315; Tropper UF 22 1990 367f.; UF 23 1991 356ff.); impv. *irš*.

G/D. To request, wish, demand: *irš ksp ḥym w atnk* ask for silver, life and I will give you (them), 1.17 VI 17, 26, 27 (*ḥym*); *arš l aḫtk* he requested your sister, 5.11:12; *alpm aršt lk* the bullocks you requested for yourself, 2.45:24; cups *d*(!) *yarš PN* which PN requests, 4.44:26; in unc. ctx.,]*yirš snp ln* he requests us ..., 2.81:26; *mh taršn* what do you wish of me?, 1.3 V 28 and par.; *mlk ṯr abh yarš* does he wish the kingship of the Bull, his father?, 1.14 I 42; *iršt aršt l aḫy* the request that I made of my brother, 5.9 I 7; *spr bnš mlk d taršn ʕmsn* register of the personnel of the king who negotiate(?) cargo, 4.370:2. In bkn ctx.: *arš*[, 2.23:16, 18.

Cf. **ilrš, irš, aršm, iršt, iršy(n), yaršil.**

arš DN, name of a monster (Cf. Cassuto BOS 2 117 n. 13: 'the venomous one', MHb. *ʔrs*; Gray UF 11 1979 316 n. 5: 'many-headed', < *rʔaš*; Margalit MLD 159: 'whale' < *rš*, // *anḫr*; for the various etymologies cf. De Moor SP 242).

DN: *mdd ilm arš* the beloved of DN, DN, 1.3 III 43; *ym arš w tnn*, 1.6 VI 51.

irš n. m. "demand, scarcity" (*nomen actionis* < /ʔ-r-š/; Dietrich - Loretz MU 186). ¶ **Forms**: sg. *iršn* (+ determinative suff., cf. Dietrich - Loretz MU 104).

Demand, scarcity: *iršn ykn* there will be scarcity, 1.163:10.

urš[bkn PN (?) (Watson AuOr 14 1996 96: Hurr.(?)).

PN (?): 4.447:1; 4.639:5.

aršḫ TN (Belmonte RGTC 12/2 30: **Araššiḫ*. Cf. Pardee AfO 36/37

1989/90 483; TPM 215; Caquot TOu 2 91 n. 280; Del Olmo CR 367 n. 111; De Moor ARTU 153 n. 26; cf. GLH 53: *Aranzaḫ(i)*, RGTC 6/1 524f.).

TN: *aršḫ rbt w aršḫ ṯrrt* TN the great (city), TN the powerful (city), 1.100: 63-64; 4.629:6.

aršm PN (etym. unc. Cf. Grøndahl PTU 61, 101; Watson AuOr 8 1990 115).

PN: 4.153:2.

aršmg PN (Hurr. Cf. Grøndahl PTU 207, 220, 253; Nougayrol Ug 5 p. 50; Dietrich - Loretz- Sanmartín UF 5 1973 82f.; Huehnergard AkkUg 370f.); ¶ syll.: *ar(i)*(SUM)*-ša/ši-mi-ga*, PRU 4 169ff. (RS 17.158):10 and *passim ibid.*; *ar(i)*(SUM)-^{d}UTU*(-ga)*, PRU 4 171f. (RS 17.42):1 and *passim ibid.*

PN: 4.194:3; 4.332:9; 4.339:11. Cf. in bkn ctx.: 4.151 I 2; 4.332:2.

iršt n. f. "request, wish; commercial order; cultic consultation (?)" (< /ʔ-r-š/; Akk. *erištu*, AHw 241f.; CAD E 298ff.; Hb. *ʔršt*, HALOT 92; cf. Ebla /ʔiršatum/, /ʔirištum/ in ʔAL$_6$.DU$_{11}$.GA = *i-rí-sa-tum*, VE 234; Fronzaroli EL 143; StEb 7 1984 151sf.; Sanmartín AuOr 9 1991 175f.; cf. diff. Krebernik ZA 73 1983 10: /ʕirištum/. Cf. Dietrich - Loretz UF 12 1980 178; Van Soldt UF 22 1990 324); ¶ syll. Ug.: [KAM = *mēreltu* =]*x-še* = *i-*[*r*]*i*(?)*-iš*[*-tu*$_4$], UF 11 1979 479:28; Huehnergard UVST 110, 273; Van Soldt BiOr 46 1989 651; BiOr 47 1990 735; SAU 303; cf. element /ʔiršu-/ in PNN, Sivan GAGl 200. ¶ Forms: sg. *iršt*, suff. *irštk*.

Request, wish; commercial order; cultic consultation, ★a) request, wish: *iršt adty* the request of my lady, 2.22:4; *iršt aršt* the wish that I expressed, 5.9 I 7; *mnm irštk* any wish of yours, 2.41:16; *l iršt*[*k* according to [your] wish, 1.108:20-21; ★b) commercial order: *iršt yṣḥm* order of the metalworkers, 4.626:1; in bkn ctx.: 4.218:7; ★c) cultic consultation (?): in bkn ctx. 1.104:1 (cf. Del Olmo CR 308; De Tarragon TOu 2 178 n. 112).

iršy(n) PN (Sem. Cf. Grøndahl PTU 51, 101; Shehadeh Fs. Lambdin 243 n. 260; Watson AuOr 13 1995 220); ¶ syll.: DUMU *ir-še-ia-na*, Ug 5 161:22. Cf. *iršn*.

PN: ★a) *iršy*, 4.338:6; in bkn ctx.: 4.646:2; ★b) *bn iršyn*, 4.69 II 12; 4.93 IV 19; 4.340:5.

art (I) n. f. "shield, buckler(?)" (cf. EA Akk. KUŠ *a-ri-tum*, cf. Ahw 68f.; CAD A/2 269f. diff. De Moor UF 28 1996 157: 'roe, spawn', Bab. *erūtu*); ¶ RS Akk.: cf. LÚ *A.RIT*, PRU 3 68 (RS 16.269):6; cf. Huehnergard AkkUg 154 n. 161). ¶ Forms: pl. *art*.

Shield, buckler(?): three hundred *art ḥkpt* bucklers(?) of TN, 4.247:26.

art (II) TN (Belmonte RGTC 12/2 38f.: *?Arutu*. Cf. Heltzer RCAU 9; Astour UF 13 1971 8; Bordreuil UF 20 1988 11; Pardee AfO 36/37 1989/90 483; Van Soldt UF 28 1996 661f.); ¶ syll.: URU *a-ru-tu/tu$_4$/te/ti*, cf. PRU 6 p. 146; RS 25.132 III 2 (Van Soldt UF 28 1996 662); RS 25.455A I 8 (Arnaud SMEA 32 1993 128); [URU *a*]*r-ru-ti*, Ug 5 66:2'.

TN: 4.68:10; 4.95:3; 4.235:3; 4.244:2; 4.310:8; 4.610 (II) 8; 4.629:12; 4.631:1. Cf. in bkn ctx. 4. 113:7 (KTU:]*kt*); 4.308:1 (KTU:]*k*[; 4.686:5; 7.46:4. Cf. in unc. ctx. 6.44:1.

irt n. f. "breast; slope" (Akk. *irtu*, *iratu*, AHw 386, CAD I/J 183ff.; Syr. *ratō* LS 705. Cf. Dressler AT 96f.); ¶ RS Akk.: *i-na i-ir-ti TN*, Ug 5 20 obv. 19; ¶ syll. Ug.: G[AB?] = [...] = *a*(?)-*ḫé-er-ni* = *i-r*[*a*(?)-*tu*$_4$(?)], Ug 5 137 II 53'; Huehnergard UVST 109; ¶ par.: *yd (I)*. ¶ Forms: sg. cstr. *irt*; suff. *irty*, *irtk*, *irth*, *irtm* (encl. *-m* (?)).

Breast; slope; ★a) breast: *št rimt lirth* may she place the zither/harp on her breast, 1.3 III 5 and par. (// *yd*, 1.101:17); *w tnḫ b irty npš* and my soul will rest in my breast, 1.6 III 19 and par.; *tšt b*[...] *irtk* put it within [...] your breast, 1.18 I 19; *rḫn t*(!)*t dm*(!) (KTU: *rḫn*{*n*} *t dt*) *l irtk* the sweetness (?) that your breast harbours, 1.4 V 5; *b ym irtm mnm* on DN (his) chest was strengthened, 1.2 IV 3 (cf. Del Olmo IMC 56); ★b) slope, side (of a mountain): *prʕ bṣq b irt lbnn* first-fruits that sprouted from the slope of TN, 1.22 I 25 (cf. RS Akk.: *i-na i-ir-ti* ḪUR.SAG *li-ib-na-ni*, Ug 5 2' obv. 19).

In bkn ctx.: 1.5 V 25.

artn PN (Hurr. Cf. Grøndahl PTU 27, 220, 262); ¶ syll.: *ar-te-nu*, cf. PRU 3 p. 242; RSOu 7 2:8', 22'; cf. *ar-ta-na*, Ug 5 86:4. Cf. *ardn*.

PN: 4.129:3; 4.141 I 7; 4.609:30; 4.614:1; 4.753:12. Cf. in bkn ctx.: 4.504:1:3; 4.614:1; RSOu 14 39 [KTU 4.790]:19'.

urt(n) PN (Hurr. Cf. Grøndahl PTU 260f., 275, 286, 423, 425; Watson AuOr 14 1996 97); ¶ syll.: *ú-ri-te*, RSOu 7 31:22; *ur-te-nu*, Syria 18 1937 247 (RS 8.146 [= "8.213"]):28; cf. RSOu 7 p. 136; cf. *ur*-^{d}IM, RSOu 25:1; cf. Van Soldt SAU 221 n. 333s.; cf. *ur*-DA-*nu*, PRU 3 14f. (RS 12.33) rev. 2'. Var. *(bn) urt* in 4.617:44.

PN: ★a) 4.115:2; 4.219:5; 4.337:4; 4.341:15; RSOu 14 52 [KTU 9.435]:14; in bkn ctx.: 4.332:3; RSOu 14 49 [KTU 9.433]:1; ★b) *bn PN*, 4.617:44.

artṯb PN (Hurr. Cf. Grøndahl PTU 220, 264; Dietrich - Loretz - Sanmartín UF 5 1973 82); ¶ syll.: *ar(i)*(SUM)-^{d}U/IM, cf. PRU 3 p. 242; PRU 4 p. 245.

PN: 4.102:4; 4.204:12; 4.281:28.

arty GN m. (< *art*, TN; Dietrich - Loretz - Sanmartín UF 5 1973 85); ¶ syll.: cf. PN URU *a-ru-ti-yu*, PRU 6 138:1, 14; cf. Huehnergard UVST 239; Van Soldt SAU 336. ¶ Forms: sg. *arty*.

GN: 4.33:10, 11; 4.85:3; 4.244:8.

artyn PN (Hurr.(?); cf. Grøndahl PTU 27, 220, 258; Dietrich - Loretz-Sanmartín UF 5 1973 85; Watson AuOr 8 1990 116).

PN: 4.53:4 (*ary*); 4.715:23. Cf. *artsn*, 4.214:6 (rdg *arty*(?)*n*?).

Cf. arty.

arw n. m. "lion" (Hb. *ʔryh*, HALOT 87f.; Aram. *ʔry*, DNWSI 107; Ph. *ʔrw*, DNWSI 104; Guzzo Amadasi - Karageorgis Kition 3 A 2,3 pp. 14ff.; Dahood UF 1 1969 144; Eg. *rw* WäS 2 403; cf. *ír / ʔá-r-ya*, WäS 1 106; Helck Bez 508(8); see Amor. /ʔarwiyum/, Gelb CAAA 13; Akk. *arwium* AHw 73; CAD A/2 294: *armû*; cf. Emar /ʔaryu/ Pentiuc Vocabulary 32f.: 'gazelle'). ¶ Forms: sg. *arw*.

Lion: *pn arw* protome of a lion, 6.62:2 (Dietrich - Loretz UF 13 1981 98f.; UF 23 1991 83f.).

arwd(n) PN (etym. unc. Cf. Grøndahl PTU 27, 272; Astour RSP 2 262; cf. *Arwada*, TN, Belmonte RGTC 12/2 39; cf. Van Soldt SAU 358; cf. West AOAT 233 30: *a-ra-da-yo*, Linear ★b); ¶ syll.: cf. NP URU *a-ru-a-di-yu*, PRU 6 79:7, 8.

PN: ★a) 4.258:7; ★b) *bn PN*: 4.45:3; 4.51:8 (*ilšt*<*m*>*ʕy*, Van Soldt SAU 33); 4.55:4.

arwn PN (Anat.; cf. Grøndahl PTU 272); ¶ syll.: *ar-wa-nu*, PRU 3 206 (RS 16.294):4; PRU 6 79:16).

PN: *arwn*, 4.783:1.

arws/ṯ PN (Anat. Cf. Grøndahl PTU 268, 272f.); ¶ syll.: *ar-wa(-aš)-šu*, cf. PRU 3 p. 242.

PN: ★a) 4.129:11; ★b) 4.69 I 15; 4.222:20.

ary (I) n. m. "fellow, friend, kin" (cf. Hitt. (LÚ) *ara-*, HW(2) 221ff.; cf. Eg. *íry*, WäS 1 105; Ward JNES 20 1961 32; Akk. cf. *e/irâ*, *a/iria*, AHw 386; CAD E 254; Arab. *ʔarā*, Lane 51; but cf. Renfroe AULS 83sf: Akk. *ayyaru* 'jünger Mann'. Cf. Van Zijl Baal 228; cf. Gray UF 3 1971 66 n. 43: Akk. *arûtu*, Eg. *ʔryw*); ¶ par.: *aḫ (I)*, *bn (I)*. ¶ Forms: sg. suff. *aryy*, *aryk*, *aryh*.

Fellow, friend, kin: (he has no) *šrš km aryh* offspring like his kinsmen, 1.17 I 19 and par. (// *aḫh*); he invited *aryh b qrb hklh* his fellows to his palace, 1.4 VI 44 (// *aḫh*); *qran hd ʕm aryy* invite me, DN, together with my fellows, 1.5 I 23 (// *aḫy*); *ḥẓr km aryk* a mansion like (the one of) your fellows, 1.4 V 29 (// *aḫk*); he clothed himself *km all dm aryh* like an *a.* with the blood of his kinsmen, 1.12 II 47 (// *aḫh*); *ilt w ṣbrt aryh* the goddess and the clan of her kin (exclaimed), 1.4 IV 50 and par. (// *bnh*); *tšmḫ ht aṯrt w bnh ilt w ṣbrt aryh* may DN now rejoice, and the sons of the goddess and the clan of her kin, 1.6 I 41.

ary (II) TN (Belmonte RGTC 12/2 30: *?Arāyu.* Cf. Dietrich - Loretz - Sanmartín UF 5 1973 83; Heltzer RCAU 8; Astour UF 13 1981 4; Xella MLE 1 1982 513; Pardee AfO 36/37 1989/90 482; Van Soldt SAU 337; UF 28 1996 661); ¶ syll.: cf. URU *a-ra-yu,* Ug 5 103:4'; RSOu 7 4:40.
TN: 4.49:3; 4.68:8; 4.308:11 (Belmonte RGTC 12/2 30); 4.113:4; 4.224:18; 4.380:23; 4.610 (II) 31; 4.762:6; 4.553:9; 4.686:15; RSOu 14 35 [KTU 9.388] II 7.

ary (III) GN m. (< *ar,* TN. Cf. Dietrich - Loretz - Sanmartín UF 5 1973 83; Belmonte RGTC 12/2 38). ¶ Forms: sg. *ary,* pl. *arym.*
GN: 4.33:12-15; 4.51:1; 4.53:4, 10; 4.80:2-3(?), 5; 4.181:5; 4.244:16, 18; 4.379:3, 7; *nsk arym* caster(s) of the GNN, 4.310:6; 4.317:7; 4.781:3.

ary(n) PN (Hurr.(?); cf. Grøndahl PTU 27, 220; De Moor UF 2 1970 200; Dietrich - Loretz - Sanmartín UF 5 1973 83; Watson AuOr 13 1995 219); ¶ syll.: cf. *a-ri-ya,* PRU 6 144:6; *a-ri-ya*[, Ug. 5 89:3, 7. Cf. *iryn.*
PN: 4.53:10; 4.55:14; 4.80:16 (cf. Van Soldt SAU 33); 4.96:3 (*adddy*); 4.244:18.

iry PN (Hurr. Cf. Grøndahl PTU 226).
PN: 1.87:61.
Cf. iryn.

iryn PN (Hurr. Cf. Grøndahl PTU 226; Watson AuOr 13 1995 220). Cf. *aryn.*
PN: ★a) 4.512:1; ★b) *bn PN,* 4.35 I 21; 4.93 IV 16; 4.103:40; 4.229:6.

uryn n. m.; Hittite official (Hitt. *ura(/i)yanni-;* HW 235; Pecchioli Daddi MPDAI 266ff.); ¶ RS Akk.: LÚ *ú-ri-ia-an-nu,* PRU 4 77 (RS 17.368) rev. 5'. ¶ Forms: sg. *uryn.*
Hittite official: *spr ʕpsm dt št uryn l mlk ugrt* document concerning the landmarks(?) which the *u.* set up for the king of TN, 6.29:3.

uryy PN (Sem.(?); cf. Grøndahl PTU 53, 103; Watson AuOr 14 1996 96).
PN: *bn PN,* 4.12:8; 4.309:8.

arz (I) n. m. of a conifer 1) (traditionally:) "cedar"; 2) "staff of cedar"

(Hb., Aram. *ʔrz*, HALOT 86; DNWSI 105; Ebla /ʔarzatum/ in GIŠ.NUN.SAL = *ar-za-tum*, VE 471; Krebernik ZA 73 1983 17; QuSe 18 112; Fronzaroli EL 136; StEb 7 1984 150: *Abies cilicia*; Sanmartín AuOr 9 1991 176; Arab. *ʔarz*, Lane 47; Eth. *ʔarz*, CDG 41. Cf. De Moor SP 60 n. 60; Sasson RSP 1 396); ¶ syll. Ug.: *ar-zu*, PRU 6 114:3; *ar-zi-ma*[, Ug 5 153 obv. 1; Sivan GAGl 198; Huehnergard UVST 109; ¶ par.: *ʕṣ*, *lbnt*; cf. *nṭq*. ¶ Forms: sg. *arz*, pl. *arzm*, suff. *arzh*.

1) A conifer (trad.: "cedar"): *šryn mḥmd arzh* TN coveted for its cedars, 1.4 VI 19, 21 (// *ʕṣh*); *bt arzm yklInh* a palace of cedar they shall complete for him, 1.4 V 10 (// *lbnt*).

2) Staff of cedar: when *arz b ymnh* the (staff of) cedar is shot from his right, 1.4 VII 41 (Rin AE 175; Cathcart Nahum 89f.).

Cf. arz (II).

arz (II) PN (Sem. Cf. Grøndahl PTU 29, 101).

PN: *bn PN*, 4.33:25 (*šʕrty*); 4.63 II 45.

is PN (etym. unc.).

PN: ★a) 4.123:8; ★b) *bn PN*, 4.12:7; 4.412 II 16.

isg PN (etym. unc.).

PN: 4.83:3.

asm n. m. "granary" (Hb. *ʔsm*, HALOT 73f.; Akk. *išittu*, var. NA *e/isittu*, AHw 395; CAD I/J 243f.; cf. *sissimu*, CAD S 325 < **simsim*(?); Emar *masīmu*, Pentiuc JNES 58 1999 95; cf. Watson NABU 1986 83). ¶ Forms: sg. *asm*.

Granary: *tštk b qrbm asm* may (his hand) put you inside the granary!, 1.19 II 18, 25.

/ʔ-s-p/ vb G/D: "to gather, take away, remove, sweep away"; Gpass.(?): "to be gathered, to collect"(?); Gt: "to gather for oneself, carry off"; Š: "to regroup, concentrate"(?) (Hb., Ph.(?), *ʔsp*, HALOT 74f.; NPun. *ʕsp* (sic!), DNWSI 89; Akk. *esēpu*, AHw 248f.; CAD E 330f.); ¶ par.: /m-t/, /n-p-l/, /š-t/. ¶ Forms: G/D suffc. *aspt*(?); prefc. *tisp*, *tasp*, *yasp*, *yisp*, suff. *yisphm*; impv. *isp* (Verreet UF 17 1985 320f.); Gpass. prefc. *tusp*, Gt prefc. *yitsp*, Š prefc. *ašisp*. Cf. the spelling *ʔsp* (G suffc.) in 4.767:1.

G/D. To gather, take away, remove,sweep away: *tispk yd aqht* may the hand of PN gather you! (// *tštk*), 1.19 II 17, 24; *isp špš l hrm ġrpl // ʕl arṣ lan isp ḥmt* remove, DN, the storm clouds from the mountains, from the earth, everywhere, remove the venom!, 1.107:44 and par.; may DN(N) *t/yisp ḥmt* remove the venom!, 1.107:38 and par.; may the gods *yasp ḥmt* remove the venom, 1.107:36; cf. in bkn

ctx. *w tasp naṯt*, 1.175:3; *aspt qlh* I have gathered his news(?), 2.31:52; *yisphm bʕ[l* DN took them away(?) DN, 1.12 II 24. Cf. PN *ʔsp ʕs kprt* has collected henna plants, 4.767:1 (cf. Dietrich - Loretz KA 251).
Gpass.(?) To be gathered, to collect(?), in bkn ctx.: *k ḥṣ tusp[* like gravel, it collects(?)[, 1.1 IV 11.
Gt. Gather for oneself, carry off: *mḫmšt yitsp ršp* the fifth (wife) DN gathered to himself, 1.14 I 18 (// *tmt*, *ttpl*; Verreet UF 19 1987 330).
Š. To regroup, concentrate ((?), troops, etc.): *ank ašt ašisp* I propose that I carry out the concentration (of troops(?)), 2.33:12.
Cf. **mispt**.

usp "?"; in bkn ctx.: 7.51:3. Cf. **/ʔ-s-p/**.

/ʔ-s-r/ vb G: "to tie, yoke, hook up"; D: "to make prisoner"(?) (Hb., Aram., Ph. *ʔsr*, HALOT 75; DNWSI 90f.; Akk. *esēru*, AHw 249; CAD E 334ff.; ESA *ʔśr*, DOSA 28; Arab. *ʔasara*, Lane 57f.); ¶ **par.**: /ʕ-l-y/, /r-k-s/, /ṣ-m-d/. ¶ **Forms**: G suffc. *asr*, D prefc. suff. *tasrn*.
G. To tie, yoke, hook up: *asr sswm* they yoked the horses, 1.20 II 3 (// *tṣmd*); *asr mrkbt* they yoked the chariots, 1.22 II 22 (// *tʕln*); *l[a]sr pdm rišh[m] ʕl pd asr* the locks of their head(s) were not tied (: braided); on top of a lock they tied a ..., 1.19 II 31-32.
D. To make prisoner(?), in bkn ctx.: *tasrn* you will have to make him prisoner(?), 1.1 V 9, 22 (// *trks*; cf. Sanmartín UF 9 1977 261).
In bkn ctx.: 1.1 II 7.
Cf. **asr**, **/ʔ-z-r/**.

asr n. m. "prisoner, captive" (< /ʔ-s-r/; Hb. *ʔsyr*, HALOT 73; Akk. *asīru*, AHw 74; CAD A/2 331f.; Eg. *íṯr / ʔá-sí-ra*, WäS 1 151; Helck Bez 509(20); cf. Landsberger AfO 10 1935 144; Loretz UF 10 1978 121-160); RS Akk. LÚ *a-sí-ru/i*, PRU 3 8 (RS 8.333):24, 27; ¶ **par.**: *ʕbd (I)*. ¶ **Forms**: sg. *asr*, suff. *asrkm* (pn. suff. *-k-*, encl. *-m*); pl. *asrm*.
Prisoner, captive: *bn dgn asrkm* the son of DN is your prisoner, 1.2 I 37 (// *ʕbdk*); *ilt asrm* the goddess of captives, 1.39:11; cf.]*asrm*]of prisoners, 4.382:6; *asrm*, 2.31:24.
Cf. **asr(n)**.

asr(n) PN (Sem. Cf. Grøndahl PTU 61, 102; cf. West AOAT 233 30: PN *a-sa-ro*, Linear B).
PN: ★**a)** 4.204:9; 4.520:4; ★**b)** *bn PN*: 4.233:3; 4.617:47; 4.700:7.
Cf. in bkn ctx. 4.635:52.

ass PN (etym. unc.).
PN: *bn PN*, 4.75 III 8 (Tropper AuOr 13 1995 236: *n/ass*).

uss PN (etym. unc.).
PN: *bn PN*, 4.658:18.

usy PN (etym. unc. Cf. Grøndahl PTU 229f.).
PN: *usy*, 4.769:29.
Cf. usyy.

asyy PN (etym. unc. Cf. Grøndahl PTU 102, 422; Stamm ANG 216, 223).
PN: *bn PN*, 4.611:4.

usyy PN (etym. unc. Cf. Grøndahl PTU 229f.); ¶ syll.: cf. DUMU *ú-sí-ia-yu*, PRU 3 196 (RS 15.42+) II 6'; cf. Huehnergard AkkUg 44.
PN: *bn PN*, 4.280:8.

ʔs̱p, allograph of *asp*, 4.767:1; cf. /ʔ-s-p/.

uṣb PN (Akk.(?); cf. Gelb - Purves - MacRae NPN 169; Grøndahl PTU 309; Watson AuOr 8 1990 116); ¶ syll.: cf. *uz-zu-b*[*i*(?), PRU 3 198 (RS 16.359 ★b):3.
PN: *bn PN*, 4.93 IV 5.

uṣbʕ n. f. "finger; claw" (Hb. *ʔṣbʕ*, HALOT 81; Aram. *ṣbʕ*, DNWSI 241; Ebla /ʔisbaʕum/ in ŠU.TUR = *i-sa-ba-um* TUR, *iš-ba-um* TUR, VE 500; ŠU.GÍD = *iš/iš*$_{11}$*-ba-ḫum* VE 528; cf. Krebernik ZA 73 1983 18; Krecher Biling. 151; Arab. *iṣbaʕ*, *ʔušbūʕ*, Lane 1646; Eth. *ʔaṣbāʕt*, CDG 45; cf. Akk. NI-*es-bet-tú*, cf. AHw 782: *neṣbettu*, CAD N/2 190. Diff.: Hvidberg WL 43 n. 4: also 'hand'; Penar Biblica 50 1969 558: 'arm'); ¶ par.: *yd*. ¶ Forms: sg.suff. *ubʕh*, pl. *uṣbʕt*, sf. *ʔṣbʕth*.
Finger, claw: *trḥṣ (...) uṣbʕth* she washed (...) her fingers, 1.3 II 33 and par. (// *ydh*; cf. 1.14 III 54 and par.; 1.101:15); *yrtqṣ (...) km nšr b uṣbʕth* he leaped (...) like an eagle from her fingers, 1.2 IV 16 and par. (// *b(y)d*);*k šr knr uṣbʕ(t)h* like a musician (takes hold of) the harp, her fingers (took hold of the weapons), 1.19 I 8 (// *ydh*); *w ykrkr uṣbʕth* and he twidddled his fingers, 1.4 IV 30 (// *pʕn*). Cf. in bkn ctx. *tmt uṣbʕ(t)*, 1.15 V 16;]*pt uṣbʕ*[7.33:3.

/ʔ-ṣ-l/ vb G/Gpass.: general meaning "to meet, be gathered"(?) (cf. Arab. *waṣala*, Wehr 1072; Lane 3054f.; Hb. *ʔṣl (III)*, HALOT 82. Cf. Xella TRU 85; diff.: Herdner Ug 7 30: 'mettre en réserve', Hb. *ʔṣl (II)*). ¶ Forms: G/Gpass. prefc. *tuṣl* (cf. Verreet UF 17 1985 327: G juss.).
G/Gpass. To meet, be gathered: *tuṣl šlḥmt* the provisions are / will be gathered, 1.106:25 (or rdg *tṣu* they take out). Cf. (?) *muṣl*[, 7.41:5.

iṣr n. m. "bundle" (?) (Arab. *ʔaṣara*, *ʔayṣar*, Lane 2061ff. Cf. De Moor UF 1 1969 181; Caquot TOu 2 48 n. 102; Renfroe AULS 84; diff.: Pope - Tigay UF 3 1971 118, 123f.; Margalit ZAW 86 1974 4ff.: rdg

iṣrrt 'bundles, sacks' < *ṣr(r)*, or: 'heights, cliffs' < *ṣrrt*; Dietrich - Loretz, UF 17 1985 135f.: 'treasure-house, store-house', Hb. *ʔwṣr*); ¶ par.: *brqm*. ¶ Forms: pl. cstr. *iṣr*.
Bundle: *šbʕt brqm (...) // ṯmnt iṣr rʕt* seven rays (...) // eight bundles of thunder, 1.101:4.

iš, 1.12 I 10, rdg *iš<t>*; cf. *išt*.

ašʕt n. f. probably a measure of capacity (etym. unc.); ¶ RS Akk.: cf. *ša-i-tum* (for oil), Ug 5 99:10 (cf. Nougayrol Ug 5 p. 193 n. 2). ¶ Forms: sg. *ašʕt*.
Measure of capacity(?): *ṯlṯ pṯt ašʕt šmn uz* three cases of (one) *a.* (?), with goose fat, 4.247:22.

išbʕl PN (Sem. Cf. Grøndahl PTU 31, 102, 117; Dietrich - Loretz OLZ 62 1967 537; De Moor BiOr 26 1969 106; Blau IOS 2 1972 61; Schoors RSP 1 8f.; Van Zijl BibEssays 159ff.; Pardee UF 10 1978 313f. and n. 101; Tsevat HUCA 46 1975 75ff.; Lipiński OLP 5 1974 5ff.; Bordreuil Syria 52 1975 113ff.; Bordreuil - Lemaire Semitica 26 1976 50; cf. Woudhuizen UF 26 1994 259: *isi₁pali*, Linear c); ¶ syll.: cf. *i-ši-*[d]U, PRU 3 193 (RS 12.34+):25; cf. Weippert ZDPV 82 1966 313 n. 198; Lipiński VT 17 1967 72f.; Cross CMHE 64 n. 72; Sivan GAGl 202.
PN: *bn PN*, 4.617:35; 4.623:8; 4.785:18.

ašbḥ PN (Sem. Cf. Grøndahl PTU 75, 191; Watson AuOr 8 1990 115).
PN: *bn PN*, 4.232:21.

išd n. m. "leg", metonymy > "step" (Akk. *išdu*, AHw 393f., CAD I/J 235ff.; Ebla cf. DÚR = *iš-dum*, VE 13 75'; cf. Healey UF 18 1986 31 n. 29); ¶ syll. Ug.: for *iš*-TUM, Ug. 5 131 8', cf. Van Soldt BiOr 47 1990 732; SAU 303: rdg *iš-tu*$_4$ /iš(i)tu/ 'fire' (cf. Huehnergard UVST 111: *iš-du*$_4$ /ʔišdu/ 'leg'); cf. the onomastic element /ʔišdu/ in PNN; cf. Grøndahl PTU 146; Sivan GAGl 200: Akkadism?; ¶ par.: *bn (II) (+ ʕn(m)), pʕn, riš*. ¶ Forms: pl./du. suff. *išdk, išdh*.
Leg, step: *tmll išdh* she caresses his legs, 1.101:6 (// *rišh, bn ʕnh*; cf. Dietrich - Loretz UF 17 1985 141); *ʕmy twtḥ išdk* towards me your steps hasten, 1.3 III 20 and par. (// *pʕn*). Bkn ctx. *išdym* [, 1.45:9 (cf. Rendsburg JNSL 8 1980 81ff.).
Cf. išdn.

išdn PN (Sem.; vd. *išd*).
PN: *bn i*[*š*]*dn*, 4.769:58.

ušḫr DN, cf. *i/ušḫry* (probably apocopated form; < Akk. DN *išḫara*?; cf. alph. Hurr. *išḫr*, 1.116:21; *ušḫr*, 1.135:1, 10. Cf. Dietrich - Loretz UF 13 1981 86).

DN: only in the syntagm *ušḫr ḫlmẓ* DN, the 'Snake', 1.115:2, 12 (cf. Del Olmo CR 267).

i/ušḫry DN, Hurro-Mesop. deity (cf. Lambert RlA 5 176f.; Edzard WbMyth 90; etym. unc., cf. Zurro SBE 67: < *šḥr/šḫr*, Ebla ^{d}BARA$_{10}$-*ra* = *iš-ḫa-la*, VE 809; cf. Mander MROA 2/1 20, 34ff.; cf. Diakonoff Eblaitica 2 17; Stieglitz Eblaitica 2 82; Pardee AfO 36/37 1989/90 433f.; for Mari cf. Durand MROA 2/1 220f.); ¶ syll.: ^{d}*iš-ḫa-ra*, Ug 5 18 23; Nougayrol Ug 5 56). ¶ Forms: *ušḫry*, var. *išḫry*.
DN: *passim* in god lists, 1.118:23 and par. (cf. 1.102:2); *ušḫry š* (to) DN a ram, 1.148:8 and par.; *ušḫry gdlt* (to) DN one cow, 1.39:13. Cf. var. *išḫry*: *ġb išḫry* the sacrificial pit of DN, 4.149:13; *npš l iš*[*ḫ*]*ry* one (piece of) offal to DN, 1.119:14; *šbʕ lbšm allm l ušḫry* seven *a.*-garments for DN, 4.168:10.

ušk n. m. "testicle" (Hb. *ʔšk*, HALOT 95; Syr. *ʔeskotō*, LS 52; Akk. *išku*, AHw 396;, CAD I/J 250; Ebla /ʔiškum/ in ŠIR = *iš-gúm*(LUM), Fronzaroli StEb 7 1984 152; cf. VE 1279', 1280', Fales QuSe 185; Eth. *ʔeskit*, CDG 43. Cf. Astour SEL 5 1988 20 n. 54); ¶ par.: *qrb*. ¶ Forms: du. *uškm*, suff. *uškh*.
Testicle: *w tiḫd b ušk*[*h*] and she seized/grasped his testicles, 1.11:2 (// *qrb*; diff.: Caquot - Sznycer TOu 1 289 n. 1; Watson UF 9 1977 277: rdg *ušr*); [*w*] *in uškm bh* and if it has no testicles, 1.103+:14.

uškn TN (Belmonte RGTC 12/2 330f.: **ʔUškānu*. Cf. Heltzer RCAU 15; Honeyman JKF 2 1953 81; Bordreuil Syria 61 1984 6f.; Lemaire UF 29 1997 463; Van Soldt SAU 33, 318, 480 n. 9; UF 28 1996 662; UF 29 1997 463, UF 30 1998 723); ¶ syll.: URU *uš/úš*(BE)-*ka-ni*, cf. PRU 3 p. 267; PRU 6 70:6; Ug 5 12:9 and *passim ibid.*; 187:5; RSOu 7 4:10; RS 88.2013:11 (Lackenbacher NABU 1989/36; cf. Astour RSP 2 345; UF 13 1981 7f. n. 39; Van Soldt SAU 318 n. 129; cf. URU *úš-ka-*^{d}IŠTAR, PRU 3 68 (RS 16.269):10 (cf. Van Soldt SAU 480 n. 9).
TN: 4.27:3, 14; 4.68:32; 4.119:5; 4.309:1; 4.365:19; 4.375:2; 4.380:18; 4.384:6; 4.629:10; 4.685:6; 4.693:17; 4.715:1; 4.750:6; 4.772:5; 4.777:5; 4.781:6; "UF 29,826":4 (cf. Lemaire UF 30 1998 461); RS 94.2614:1 (Bordreuil AntSem 2 1997 60 n. 1); RSOu 14 36 [KTU 9.417]:12; 48:3; cf. *skn uškn*, 4.288:2; *grn uškn* threshing floor(s) of TN, 4.296:16 (cf. *grn (I)*).

uškny (I) GN (< *uškn*, TN). ¶ Forms: sg. *uškny*; pl. *ušknym*.
GN: 3.5:6; 3.10:5, 7; 4.33:21-24; 4.261:13; 4.297:1; 4.339:13, 14; 4.386:4, 12; 4.792:6; RSOu 14 51 [KTU 9.425]:8; *spr ušknym* list of GNN, 4.335:1 (cf. *ibid.* ln. 13, PN). Bkn ctx. 4.300:1.

uškny (II) PN (< *uškny*, GN. Cf. Grøndahl /PTU 192).
PN: *bn PN*, 4.335:13.

aškrr n. m. of a substance used in pharmacopea ("wax"(?), cf. Akk. *e/iškuru*, AHw 369; CAD I/J 251f., Sanmartín UF 10 1978 350; diff.: Cohen - Sivan UHT 27f.; Cohen UF 28 1996 128; De Moor UF 16 1984 355 n. 6: 'henbane'(?), Akk. *šakirû*; Pardee TH 59: 'nom de plante', Akk. *ašqulālu*). ¶ Forms: sg. *aškrr*.
Substance used in pharmacopea: *št aškrr* a *š.* of *a.*, 1.85:13; 1.71:11; 1.72:18. (De Moor UF 16 1984 355f. reads *aškrr* in 1.114:15, with the meaning 'henbane'; cf. Dietrich - Loretz TUAT 2 344: 'volltrunken', unc.: rdg *ašk*[*r* (?)).

ušn n. m. "present, gift" (< /ʔ-w-š/ + *-n*; Hb. *ʔwš*, HALOT 26; Ph. *mʔš*, DNWSI 589f., Arab. *ʔaws*, Hava 16; cf. Dahood UL 85; Renfroe AULS 14ff.); ¶ syll. Ug.: cf. the element /ʔušnu/ in TN, Sivan GAGl 202; ¶ par.: *ytnt*. ¶ Forms: sg. *ušn*.
Present, gift: *w ušn ab adm* and a present of the father of man(kind), 1.14 III 31 and par. (// *ytnt*).

ušpġt n. f.; a garment Nuzi Akk. TÚG *us/špaḫḫu*, AHw 1438; cf. Dietrich - Loretz UF 3 1971 372; Ribichini - Xella Tessili 33f.; Baldacci BiOr 46 1989 119; diff.: De Moor BiOr 23 1966 130f.; UF 17 1985 229: 'neck-guard', Hurr. *gurpiši*, but cf. Ug. *grbz*, Xella UF 22 1990 470). ¶ Forms: sg. *ušpġt*, pl. *ušpġtm*.
A garment: *trmt lbš w ktn ušpġt* as an offeringa garment and a tunic *u.*, 1.43:4; *ʕ*(!)*š*(!)*rm ušpġtm* twenty(!) *u.*, 1.148:21. Cf. in unc. ctx.: *ušpġt tišr*, 1.92:26 (cf. Dijkstra UF 26 1994 117, 120: 'a coat of cypress-wooden mail').

ušr n. m. "penis, male member" (Akk. *išaru*, *(m)ušāru*, AHw 392; CAD I/J 226f.). ¶ Forms: sg. suff. *ušrh* (cf. *ušk*).
Penis: [*w gd*]*l ušrh mrḥy mlk tnšan* if there is a swelling in its penis, the spears of the king will be raised, 1.103+:47 (cf. Dietrich - Loretz MU 101).

ušryn(?) PN (morph. and etym. unc. Cf. Grøndahl PTU 103; De Moor BiOr 26 1969 106). Cf. *uṯryn*.
PN: *ušry*[*n*(?), 4.75 II 9. Cf. *šd bd bn uṯryn*, 4.103:6 (cf. Grøndahl PTU 423).
Cf. uṯryn.

išryt n. f. "happiness" (Hb. *ʔšr*, HALOT 97. Cf. Ashley EAR 276; Pope Fs. Finkelstein 176; Margalit OLP 19 1988 87; diff.: Aartun UF 17 1985 35f.: 'prima Qualität', **s/šry*, Arab. *sariya*, *sarā*, *ʔasrā*, Syr. *sarwaya*). ¶ Forms: sg. *išryt*.

Happiness: *yn išryt*, wine of happiness, 1.22 I 19 (cf. 1.45:1). Cf. in bkn ctx. *mt išryt* (you will be) a happy man (lit. man of happiness) (?), 1.18 I 2, 28.

išt n. f. 1) "fire"; 2) "blaze"; 3) "cautery(?)"; 4) DN (Hb. *ʔš*, HALOT 92; Aram. *ʔš(h)*, DNWSI 121f.; Ebla /ʔišātu(m)/ in ^{d}IZI = *ì-sa-du*, VE 783; cf. Krebernik ZA 73 1983 30; QuSe 18 130; Fronzaroli EL 143; StEb 7 1984 152; cf. the element /ʔišātu(m)/ in PNN: *ì*(NI)*-sa-du/tum*, Fronzaroli StEb 7 1984 152; Mander MROA 2/1 16f.; Krebernik PET 269; cf. PN NI*-ša-du*, Krebernik PET 269; cf. DN ^{d}*ì*(NI)*-sa-du*, TM.75.G.1764 obv. VIII 4; Pettinato Culto 125 (209); cf. TN *ì*(NI)*-sa-du*^{ki}, TM.75.G.5188 rev. III 15; MEE 277; Pomponio UF 15 1983 156; Sanmartín AuOr 9 1991 176f.; Akk. *išātu*, AHw 392f.; CAD I/J 227ff.; Eth. *ʔĕsāt*, CDG 44); ¶ syll. Ug.: NE = *i-ša-*[*t*]u_4 = [(Hurr.: ?)] = *i-ši-t*[u_4], UF 11 1979 479 (RS 20.189):37; Huehnergard UVST 110; Van Soldt BiOr 46 1989 651; BiOr 47 1990 732; SAU 303; cf. (...)]*x* = : *iš-tu*$_4$, Ug 5 131:8'; cf. Van Soldt BiOr 47 1990 732; SAU 303 (cf. diff. Huehnergard UVST 111: /ʔišdu/ 'leg'); ¶ RS Akk.: NE (IZI) / *išātu*, *passim*; Huehnergard AkkUg 372; cf. IZI$^{i\text{-}ša\text{-}ti}$, PRU 3 14 (RS 16.111):12 and cf. Wilcke AuOr 10 1992 118 n. 17; cf. Izreʔel AmAkk 1 31); ¶ par.: *ḥrb*, *ḫtr*, *kbrt*, *mr*, *nblat*, *pḥm*, *rḥ*. ¶ Forms: sg. *išt*; du. *ištm*.

1) Fire: *tšt išt b bhtm* they lit a fire in the palace, 1.4 VI 22 (// *nblat*); *tikl išt b bhtm* the fire was consuming in the palace, 1.4 VI 25 and par. (// *nblat*); *kbd k iš*<*t*> *tikln* our innards they devour like fire, 1.12 I 10 (// *mr*; diff.: Dietrich - Loretz - Sanmartín UF 7 1975 165: rdg *iš* 'ein Tier', Akk. *ašû*; for other meanings cf. Gray UF 31971 62 n. 5; Wyatt UF 8 1976 416; Aartun WO 4 1967/68 287f. Dietrich - Loretz Studien 33f.); *td išt b bhtm* the fire was extinguished in the palace, 1.4 VI 32 (// *nblat*); *štt ḫptr l išt* she placed a cooking pot on the fire, 1.4 II 8 (// *pḥm*); *b išt tšrpnn* in the fire she burned him, 1.6 II 33 (// *ḥrb*, *ḫtr*, *rḥ*); *šrp b išt* combustion by fire, 1.6 V 14 (// *ḥrb*, *rḥ*, *kbrt*); *ʕsr thrr l išt* you have roasted a bird on the fire, 1.23:41 and par. (// *pḥm*); (they shall offer) *ʕl išt šbʕd* over the fire seven times, 1.23:14. In bkn ctx.: 1.2 III 3.

2) Flame, blaze: *išt ištm* fire of two flames (> blaze): *išt ištm yitmr (...)* [*lš*]*nhm* like a great blaze their tongue (...) was cf.n, 1.2 I 32 (// *ḥrb*; cf. diff. Watson AuOr 10 1992 240: 'yes, a fire', encl. *-m*).

3) Cautery(?): *št b npš išt* apply a cautery(?) to the throat, 1.88:2.

4) DN: *mḫšt k*{.}*lbt ilm išt* I crushed the Divine Bitch, DN, 1.3 III 45 (// *ḏbb*; cf. *supra* Ebla ^{d}IZI = *ì-sa-du*, VE 783; ^{d}*ì-sa-du*, TM.75.G.1764

obv. VIII 4; cf. Lebrun EC 39).

ištir, cf. /š-ʔ-r/.

ištnm DN (cf. the Hittite sun god. [d]*Ištanu-*, HW 91; HEG 428ff.; Von Schuler WbMyth 198; cf. Sanmartín UF 21 1989 341 n. 46).
DN: *kd l DN* a jar (of wine) for DN, 4.149:3.

ištrmy PN (Akk. Cf. Kienast UF 11 1979 450). Cf. *ʕṯtrum*.
PN: 3.4:8 (*bt ʕdbmlk*).

ištš "?"; in unc. ctx.: 2.3:22.

uštyn PN (Hurr. Cf. Watson AuOr 8 1990 116); ¶ syll.: cf. *uš-ta-a-nu*, PRU 6 75 rev. 4'; *uš-ta-ya*, 99:22.
PN: *bn PN*, 4.219:4.

ušy PN (etym. unc. Cf. Grøndahl PTU 229f.; Watson AuOr 8 1990 244; AuOr 13 1995 220); ¶ syll.: cf. DUMU.SAL *ú-ši-i*, PRU 3 167 (RS 15.139):19.
PN: 4.147:12 (*šbnt*; cf. *šbny*).

išyy PN (etym. unc.).
PN: *bn PN*, 4.7:20.

at (I) pers. pn m./f. sg. "you" (< m. /ʔanta/; f. /ʔanti/; Gordon UT § 6.1; Tropper UG 209; cf. Hb. m. *ʔth*, f. *ʔt*, HALOT 100, 102; OAram., Ph. m./f. *ʔt*, DNWSI 85f.; Aram. m. *ʔnt(h)*, f. *ʔnty*, DNWSI 85f.; Amor. m. /ʔatta/, Gelb CAAA 13; Akk. m. *attā*, f. *attī*, AHw 87; CAD A/2 502-505, 511f.; Ebla cf. m. *an-da*, ARET 2 119, 132; Gelb EDA 69; Sanmartín AuOr 9 1991 174f.; Arab., Eth. m. *ʔanta*, f. *ʔanti*, Lane 104; CDG 32. Cf. Moscati ICGSL 104); ¶ syll. Ug.: ZA = *at-ta* = *ši-ni*-AM = *at-ta*, Ug 5 130 II 4'; Huehnergard UVST 47, 280, 293; Sivan GAGl 198; Van Soldt BiOr 47 1990 731; ¶ RS Akk.: m. *at-ta*, *passim*; *at-tá*, PRU 4 54 (RS 17.334):6; *at-ta-mi*, PRU 3 113 (RS 16.353):20; *at-ta-a*, Ug 5 35:17; f. *at-ti-ma*, PRU 3 13 (RS 16.111):10; ¶ par.: *an*. ¶ Forms: m./f. *at*.
You, ★a) subject in NC: *sglth at* you are his property, 2.39:12; *hm at dbr* behold you say, 2.71:13; *at nġṯ* you (are in) TN, 2.45:20; *abyn at* how poor you are, PN!, 1.17 I 16; *at aḫ w an aḫtk* you are (my) companion and I am your companion (f.), 1.18 I 24; ★b) emphatic subject in VC: *at ʕmy l mġt* you did not come to me, 2.36:10; *at brt lbk* you are pure of heart(?), 2.8:4; *ad at lhm* you demand (a price) for them, 2.26:20; *ẓi at* you go, 1.12 I 14; *at qḥ ʕrptk* take your clouds, 1.5 V 6; *at adn tpʕr* you have been proclaimed lord, 1.1 IV 17; *w at umy al tdḥl* and you, my mother, have no fear, 2.30:20; *at ypʕt b*[you have risen against[, 1.2 I 3; *at ʕl qštk tmḫṣh* are you going to wound him for his bow?, 1.18 IV 12; *w hm at trgm* but if you say, 2.3:8, 18;

w k at trg[*m* and how is it that you sa[y...?, 2.45:28; *at ṯṯb ʕm ʕbdk* you send (word) back to your servant, RSOu 14 50 [KTU 9.434]:19. Cf. in bkn ctx. *at kx*[, 2.80:9; ★c) with ellipsis of the vb: *m at* what is the matter with you?, 1.14 I 38 (De Moor - Spronk UF 14 1982 158); in correspondence: *w at* and as for you, 2.73:12 (Pardee AfO 29/30 1983/84 326); ★d) emphatic of suff. pn.: *šmk at ygrš* your name is *y.*, 1.2 IV 11, cf. ln. 19; *p at mk tšk*[*ḥ*] and thus you will meet (?), 2.74:14. In 1.13:11 read *an*(!) (cf. *an (I)*).

In bkn ctx.: *at bl at*, 1.12 II 7, 23; 1.16 V 41; *qṣʕtk at l ḥ*[, 1.18 IV 41; 2.36:7; 2.42:26; *at ʕm*[, 2.63:14; *at mġ nšk*[, 2.73:19.

at (II) n. f. "omen, ominous sign, augury" (Hb. *ʔwt*, HALOT 26; DNWSI 130f.; Akk. *ittu*, AHw 406; CAD I/J 304-310; cf. Dietrich - Loretz MU 102 n. 95). ¶ Forms: sg. *at*; pl. cstr. *att*.

Omen, ominous sign, augury: *att ṣin* omens in small cattle, 1.103+:1; [*k t*]*ld at abn* if it gives birth as an omen to a (swelling in the shape of ★a) stone, 1.103+:1.

atdb, element in the unknown compound DN *atdb w* ⊕*r*.

DN: *atdb w* ⊕*r*, 1.123:25 (a frequent grapheme in this text).

atlg TN (Belmonte RGTC 12/2 45: *Atallig*. Cf. Heltzer RCAU 9; Xella MLE 1 1982 54; Bordreuil Syria 61 1984 5; Astour UF 13 1981 5; Pardee AfO 36/37 1989/90 483; Van Soldt UF 28 1996 662; UF 29 1997 699; UF 30 1998 718); ¶ syll. Ug.: URU *a-tal-lig*, cf. PRU 3 p. 265; PRU 4 291 (RS 19.81):12; Ug 5 12:15; RSOu 7 4:15; URU *a-tal-li-gi*$_5$, PRU 4 72 (RS 17.335):18.

TN: 2.26:16; 4.27:8, 19; 4.68:44; 4.348:2; 4.365:5; 4.369:12; 4.380:5; 4.390:2; 4.618:13, 27; 4.625:1; 4.683:7; 4.693:5; 4.784:5; RSOu 14 35 [KTU 9.388] I 25.

atlgn PN (< *atlg*, TN. Cf. Grøndahl PTU 422).

PN: 4.373:4. Cf. bkn. ctx.: 4.754:3.

atlgy GN m. (< *atlg*, TN); ¶ syll. Ug.: cf. URU *a-ta-li-gu-yu*, PRU 6 79:15; cf. Huehnergard UVST 239; Van Soldt SAU 336. ¶ Forms: sg. *atlgy*.

GN: 4.45:9.

utly PN (< GN?, etym. unc. Cf. Astour Or 38 1969 403 n. 5; Gelb - Purves - MacRae NPN 169; Cassin - Glassner AAN 1 163; Watson AuOr 8 1990 117).

PN: 4.348:14.

atm pn. p. m. "you (pl.)" (Hb. *ʔtm*, HALOT 102; Aram *ʔ(n)tm*, DNWSI 85ff.; Ebla *an-da-nu*, Fronzaroli StEb 5 1982 60; Gelb LEbla 25; Conti QuSe 13 1984 162; Akk. *attunu*, AHw 88; CAD A/2 515f.;

Arab. *ʔantum*, Lane 104; Eth. *ʔantĕmu*, CDG 33. Cf. Moscati ICGSL 105; Tropper UG 209f.); ¶ **par.**: *an*. ¶ **Forms**: *atm*.

You (pl.), emphatic subject in VC: *atm bštm w an šnt* you can go slowly, but I am in a hurry, 1.3 IV 33 and par. (Watson Or 53 1984 334; UF 18 1986 416); *šmʕ atm* you, listen, 1.22 II 13.

itml adv. "the previous day, yesterday" (Hb. *ʔtmwl*, HALOT 103; Aram. *ʔtml(y)*, Kaufman AIA 60; Akk. *(it)timāli/u*, AHw 1359; cf. GAG § 72 b; Eth. *tĕmālĕm*, CDG 575f.). ¶ **Forms**: *itml*.

The previous day, yesterday: *itml ykb*[*d* (...) the previous day will be honoured, 1.119:19.

atn (I) n. f. "donkey, she-ass" (cf. Hb. *ʔtwn*, HALOT 102; Aram. *ʔtn*, DNWSI 136; Akk. *atānu*, AHw 86; CAD A/2 481ff.); ¶ **par.**: *ʕr (II)*, *pḥl*. ¶ **Forms**: pl. suff. *atnty*, *atnth*.

Donkey, she-ass: *ʕdb gpn atnth* they prepared the harnesses of their donkeys, 1.4 IV 12 (// *ʕr*, *pḥl*); cf. *ibid*. ln. 7.

atn (II) PN (Hurr. Cf. Grøndahl PTU 26, 222; Caquot - Sznycer TOu 1 271; Van Soldt UF 21 1989 365ff.; SAU 20, 26 and n. 209; cf. West AOAT 233 31: PN *a-ta-no*, Linear B); ¶ **syll.**: *at-ta-nu* and var., PRU 3 161 (RS 16.281)4, 13; 171 (RS 16.173):12'; PRU 6 84:1; Ug 5 27:23; cf. PRU 6 22 rev. 4', 5', etc.; *at-te-nu*, PRU 4 183 (RS 17.319):16; *a-te-na*, Ug 5 12:40.

PN: ★**a)** 4.35 II 7 (*bn ap*[...]*n*); 4.70:5 (*bn agyn*); 4.261:18 (*bṣry*); 4.307:4; 4.348:13; 4.498:6; in colophons to lit. texts: *atn prln* PN, the diviner, 1.6 VI 55; 1.17 l. edge 2; RSOu 14 53 [KTU 9.432]:40'; ★**b)** *bn PN*, 4.93 II 2; 4.753:21. In bkn ctx.: 4.494:3.

itn PN (etym. unc.; cf. Watson AuOr 13 1995 220; AuOr 14 1996 96; Muchiki Loanwords 17) ¶ **syll.**: cf. in bkn ctx. *it-ta-na*[, PRU 3 36 (RS 11.718):7'.

PN: *bn PN*, 4.616:9.

atnb PN (Hurr. Cf. Grøndahl PTU 222, 245).

PN: ★**a)** 4.46:13; ★**b)** *bn PN*: 4.65:7; 4.93 IV 13; 4.106:9; 4.432:18; 4.692:4. In bkn ctx.: 4.422:5.

itnn n. m. "present" (etym. unc.; possibl. < MAss. *utnannu* < Hurr. *uatnannu*; cf. Von Soden UF 20 1988 309ff.; or else < W. Sem. /y-t-n/; cf. Hb. *ʔtnn*, HALOT 103); ¶ **par.**: *mhr*. ¶ **Forms**: sg. suff. *itnny*, *itnnk*.

Present: give me / I give you *bn bṯn itnny/k* the sons of the snake as my/your (wedding) present, 1.100:74, 76 (// *mhry/k*; cf. De Moor ZAW 100 1988 111).

atyn PN (Hurr. Cf. Grøndahl PTU 222); ¶ **syll.**: *at-tu-ia-nu*, Syria 18

1951 49 rev. 6; PRU 3 193 (RS 12.34+):23, 38; cf. *at-te-ya*, PRU 3 200ff. (RS 16.257+) II 7, III 53.
PN: ★a) 4.75 I 2; IV 4; ★b) *bn PN*, 4.69 III 2.

/ʔ-t-w/ vb G: "to come, go" (Hb. *ʔth/ʔ*, HALOT 102; Aram. *ʔty*, DNWSI 133ff.; Ebla cf. TÙR.DU_8 = *a-du-wu-um*, VE 1396'; Butz Biling. 124 n. 134; Amor. /ʔ-t-y(?)/, Gelb CAAA 14; ESA *ʔtw*, DOSA 28; Arab. *ʔatā*, Lane 15ff.; Eth. *ʔatawa*, CDG 46f.); ¶ par.: /m-ġ-y/. ¶ Forms: G suffc. *atwt*; prefc. *tity*, *tit*; impv. *at*, *atm* (encl. *-m*; Aartun PU 1 57; Verreet UF 17 1985 323).
G. To come, go: *ik atwt qnyt ilm* how is that the progenitress of the gods comes?, 1.4 IV 32 (// *mġyt*); *atm w ank ibġyh* come and I shall reveal it (to you), 1.3 III 28 (cf. *at*, 1.1 III 16); *ilm (...) d tit* the gods (...) who have come 1.20 II 10; *at mt tn aḫy* come, DN, give me my brother!, 1.6 II 12; *tbrk ilm tity tity ilm l ahlhm* the gods blessed (and) went, the gods went to their tents, 1.15 III 17-18; cf. 1.20 II 4, 1.22 II 23.

uṯ n. m. "span, half cubit" (Akk. *ūtu*, AHw 1447; Ebla cf. ŠU.LUL = *ù-du/dum(/du-um)*, VE 501; Civil Or 56 1987 240. Cf. Sanmartín UF 12 1980 439; Dietrich - Loretz 12 1980 407; cf. diff. Del Olmo IMC 159 n. 383: 'rotura, trituración', Arab. *ʔatta*, but cf. Renfroe AULS 84ff.; Smith BC 284: 'nose'); ¶ par.: *amt (II)*. ¶ Forms: sg. *uṯ*; pl./du. *uṯm* (encl. *-m*).
Span, half cubit: *ispi uṯm* I shall eat (you) by the span, 1.5 I 5 (// *amtm*; for the various explanations cf. Del Olmo IMC 159 n. 383); [*u*]*ṯ ṯbr aphm* their nasal fossae (open) a span, 1.2 I 13; cf. in bkn ctx.]*uṯm ḏr*[*qm*, 1.18 IV 3.

uṯb n. m.; a garment with passemanterie (cf. Akk. *adapu*, *eda/uppātu*, AHw 11, 185; *edapu*, CAD E 22; cf. Mari Akk.: TÚG *uṭ-ba* GAL, cf. Durand ARMT 21 395ff., 403ff.; MARI 6 662; Ribichini - Xella Tessili 33; Huehnergard UVST 274 n. 36). ¶ Forms: pl. *uṯbm*.
Garment with passemanterie: *ṯlṯ uṯbm bd PN b ʕšrt ksp* three *u.* delivered to PN for ten (shekels) of silver, 4.337:11.

aṯṯ PN (Sem.(?). Cf. Watson AuOr 8 1990 243; cf. Dietrich - Loretz-Sanmartín UF 5 1973 105).
PN: 4.635:43.

iṯ (I) n. m. ("presence, existence") lexicalized as a verbal functor 1) "to be, exist"; 2) + *l* "to have" (Aram. *ʔyty*, DNWSI 111; Syr. *ʔīt*, LS 16; Hb. *yš*, HALOT 443f.; Pun. *yš*, DNWSI 111; Ebla cf. /ʔiṯāwu/ in A.GÁL, AN.GÁL = *i-ša-wu*, VE 624, 789; Krebernik ZA 73 1983 24; Fronzaroli EL 143f.; Civil Biling. 83; Krecher Biling. 161; Müller

Biling. 191 [cf. AN.GÁL = *ba-ša-um*, VE 991]; Akk. *išû*, AHw 402f.; CAD I/J 289ff.; term. adv. *-iš*, Mayer Or 64 1995 166f.: /yiṯ(ay)/. Cf. Sasson RSP I 8f.; Dietrich - Loretz UF 26 1994 63ff.; Tropper UG 819f.); ¶ RS Akk.: (people) NU.TUK *la i-šu-ni₇*, PRU 3 102 (RS 15.138+):15, cf. *ibid.* ln. 19; Huehnergard AkkUg 410; ¶ par.: *ḥy*. ¶ Forms: sg. (with verbal inflection in the stative) 1 m. *iṯt*, 3 m. *iṯ*; 3 f. *iṯt* (cf. De Moor JNES 24 1965 357f.).

1) To be, exist: *k iṯ zbl bʕl arṣ* because the Prince, Lord of the earth does exist, 1.6 III 9 and par. (// *ḥy*); *aḥd hm iṯ šmt hm iṯ ʕẓm* I shall cf. whether there is fat, whether there is bone, 1.19 III 4 and par.; *w yḥd iṯ šmt iṯ ʕṣm* and he looked: there was fat, there was bone, 1.19 III 39; *ḫd d iṯ b kbdk* seize what is in your mind, 1.18 I 18; *iṯ yn d ʕrb* there is wine that entered, 1.23:74; *w km iṯ* and when he is (there), 1.41:55; *aṯr iṯ bqṯ* wherever he is, look for him, 2.39:34; *bnšm d iṯ bd rb ʕprm* personnel that is at the disposal of the chief of the *ʕp.*, 4.752:1; *i iṯt aṯrt* where is(are you) DN?, 1.14 IV 38 (diff. Parker UF 11 1979 694 n. 8); *iṯt ʕmn mlkt* I am with the queen, 2.13:15; *ʕmn mlk (...) iṯt* I am with the king, 2.30:14, cf. 2.13:15 (cf. Cunchillos TOu 2 322f. n. 9; diff. Pardee AfO 31 1984 224f.: 'a *ʔiṯt*'); in unc. ctx.: *iṯ ph kṯ*[[*ṯ*]] *ġbt*, 1.101:8 (for the various opinions cf. Caquot TOu 2 49 n. 112); in bkn ctx.: *sḥ*[*m*] *iṯ*, 2.73:18 (cf. Cunchillos TOu 2 420).

2) To have, + *l*: *dm rgm iṯ ly* for I have a matter, 1.3 III 21 and par.; *bl iṯ bn lh* may he have a son!, 1.17 I 20; *hm iṯ (yn...) iṯ yn d ʕrb* if there is (wine...), there is wine which entered, 1.23:72, 74; *bnšm dt iṯ alpm lhm* people who have (head of) cattle, 4.422:1 (cf. 4.296:1); *mnm iṯ l ʕbdk* whatever your servant has, 2.70:29; *kl d iṯ* [*l špš ml*]*k rb* all that the 'Sun', the Great King, has, 2.81:9.

In bkn ctx.:]*u iṯ*, RSOu 14 49 [KTU 9.433]:37.

iṯ (II) PN (etym. unc.).

PN: *bn PN*, 4.616:11.

iṯb MN; ¶ syll.: *i-na* ITI *i-ši*(?)-[*bi*(?)], PRU 6 152:4; Huehnergard UVST 111).

MN: [*yrḫ*] *iṯb*, [in the month of] *i.*, 4.219:15 (cf. 4.220:6).

iṯg PN (etym. unc.).

PN: 4.720:4.

iṯgh PN (?).

PN (?): *iṯgh dd*, RSOu 14 40 [KTU 9.419]:4.

aṯḫlm n. "(a type of ritual)" (Hurr. *ašḫ-ul-*, GLH, 60; Neu Das Hurritische 1988 15 n. 35; Wilhelm Or 61 1992 129; Dietrich - Mayer

ALASP 7 1995 12ff.; Dietrich - Mayer Fs Röllig 79ff.; Dietrich - Mayer UF 28 1996 169ff.; Dietrich - Mayer Subartu 4,2 1998 264; cf. Kammenhuber UF 2 1970, 302; Xella TRU 308; Del Olmo SEL 12 1995 43; CR 36, 200 n. 103, 211; Watson UF 27 1995 535; UF 28 1996 702 and n. 7). ¶ **Forms**: *aṯḫlm* (pl. / adv. *-m (I)* (?)).
(A type of ritual): in Hurr. texts: 1.110:1; 1.111:8; 1.116:3.9.10, 31; 1.125:1; 1.132:4.

uṯḫt DN < n. f. "incense burner" (cf. Akk. *šēḫtu*, Nougayrol Ug 5 58; AHw 1209; CAD Š/2 264ff.; cf. *ḫršḫ*); ¶ **RS Akk.**: ᵈDUG.BUR.ZI. NÍG.NA, Ug 5 18:30. ¶ **Forms**: sg. *uṯḫt*.
Incense burner: *uṯḫt* 'Incense Burner' (in lists of DNN), 1.47:31; 1.118:30 (cf. alph. Hurr. *aḫġrṯḫnd ḫbrṯḫnd* ('DNN', dat., direct.), 1.125:14; Laroche Ug 5 506; 526).
Cf. **ḫršḫ**.

uṯkl n. m. "bunch, cluster" (Hb. *ʔškwl*, HALOT 95; Arab. *ʔiṯkāl*, *ʔuṯkūl*, Lane 345; Ebla /ʔa/iṯkālum/ in ŠE.GEŠTIN = *iš₁₁-ga-um*, *áš-ga-lum*, VE 660; Krebernik ZA 73 1983 26; Krecher Biling. 160; Civil Or 56 1987 236; Eth. *ʔaskāl*, CDG 42f.; cf. Akk. *is/šḫunnatu*, AHw 387; CAD I/J 190. Cf. Virolleaud GLECS 7 1954/57 22; Astour WO 4 1967 279; Chiera AION 46 1986 291ff.). ¶ **Forms**: sg. *uṯkl*.
Cluster: [*šmṭ*]*r uṯkl l il* cutting of a cluster for DN, 1.87:2 and par.

iṯl n. m. "saliva, phlegm, spittle" (Akk. *ušultu*, AHw 1443; cf. Watson SEL 4 1987 57-65; UF 22 1990 422; De Moor JNES 24 1965 363f.; Dijkstra - De Moor UF 7 1975 196: Hitt. *iššalli*; Dressler AT 369f.; diff. cf. Del Olmo MLC 523: 'exhalación', Arab. meton. use *ʔaṯl*, Hb. *ʔšl*; Margalit UPA 156, 342f.: 'a plant'); ¶ **par.**: *qṭr*, *rḥ*. ¶ **Forms**: sg. *iṯl*.
Saliva, phlegm, spittle: *tṣi (...) km iṯl brlth* (...) like phlegm may his soul go out, 1.18 IV 25 and par. In bkn ctx. 1.1 II 9.

/ʔ-ṯ-m/ vb Gt: "to fall into debt, continue to owe" (Hb. *ʔšm*, HALOT 95f.; Arab. *ʔaṯama*, Lane 21f.; Sanmartín UF 10 1978 351). ¶ **Forms**: Gt prefc. *yiṯṯm*, *tiṯṯmn*.
Gt. to fall into debt ★**a)** + *ʕl* for something: *ʕl alpm (...) tiṯṯmn* they fell into debt (...) for two oxen(?), 4.398:2; cf. *ʕl (...) tiṯṯmn*, *ibid.* ln. 3; ★**b)** to continue to owe (+ accus.): PN *śś*[*wm*] *yiṯṯm* they continue to owe two horses, *ibid.* ln. 5.
In bkn ctx. 2.21:21, 24.

iṯm (I) n. m. "firm-fleshed cattle" (?) (ESA *ʔṯy(m)*, DOSA 31; Arab. *ʔāṯīṯ*, Lane 18. Cf. De Moor UF 1 1969 178; SP 181: Arab. *waṯīm*; diff.: Astour JAOS 86 1966 281; Virolleaud Ug 5 557: 'péché', Hb.

ʔšm, Arab. *ʔitm*); ¶ par.: *ṣin* (?). ¶ Forms: sg. *itm*, suff. *itmh*.
Firm-fleshed cattle(?): in bkn ctx. *itm muid* [, firm-fleshed cattle (?) in abundance [, 1.5 III 24 (cf. De Moor ARTU 75); *itmh*, 1.108:14.

itm (II) DN, second element of the divine name *šgr w itm* (etym. unc; cf. possib. *itm (I)*; cf. De Moor UF 1 1969 178; Wansbrough Akkadica 37 1984 47).
DN: *itm*, 1.148:31.

utpt n. f. "quiver" (Hb. *ʔšph*, HALOT 96; Akk. *išpatu*, AHw 397; CAD I/J 257f.; Hurr. *išpa(n)ti*, GLH 127; > Eg. *íśp.t*, WäS 1 132; Helck Bez. 505; Hoch SWET 40; cf. Watson UF 30 1998 752); ¶ RS Akk.: KUŠ *iš-pa-tu*, PRU 6 162:5; KUŠ.É.AMAR.RU, PRU 6 131 *passim*; cf. Huehnergard AkkUg 383. ¶ Forms: sg./pl. *utpt*.
Quiver, ★a) in military equipment: 4.53:15; 4.624:3, 4, 7, 9; ★b) in chariots: *l tt mrkbtm inn utpt* two chariot bodies lack quivers for, 4.145:7; ★c) types: *utpt ḥzm* quiver for arrows, 4.204:1, 2, 4; *utpt srdnnm* for *s.*, *ibid.* ln. 3, 5-12. Cf. in bkn ctx. 4.670:2.

/ʔ-t-r/ vb G: "to go, follow"; D: "force to follow, to transmit" (Hb. *ʔšr*, HALOT 97; Arab. *ʔatara*, Lane 18ff.; cf. Amor. /ʔ-š-r/, Gelb CAAA, 14; Akk. *ašāru*, AHw 79; CAD A/2 420ff.; Ebla cf. the element *a-šur$_x$-*, *a-šu-ur/ur$_x$-* in PNN, Krebernik PET 63. Cf. Dietrich - Loretz UF 16 1984 57ff.); ¶ par.: /h-l-k/, /t-n-y/. ¶ Forms: G suffc. *atr*, prefc. *yatr*; impv. *itr* (Verreet UF 17 1985 322f.); inf. abs.(?) *atr*, ptc. pl. *atrm* (cf. *atr (I)*); D suffc. *atr*, prefc. *yatr*.
G. To go, follow: *l rbt km yr atr* by the myriad like early rain they go, 1.14 II 41 and par. (// *hlk*); *atr tlt klhm* they go in threes all of them, 1.14 II 42 and par. (// *hlk*; diff.: De Moor ARTU 195: 'after two / three'); *l šmn itrhw* as for the oil: follow it, 2.15:6 (for *-hw* cf. Tropper UG 54; diff.: Watts UF 21 1989 446: var. of *atr* 'there'); *atr atrm* the following follow, 1.45:7-8; *ʕlh nḥ[š] yatr* (if), besides (there) follows a (swelling) in the form of a serpent (?), 1.103+:2. Cf. in bkn or unc. ctx. 1.107:28. Cf. *atr bʕlk l ks<i>h atr bʕlk arṣ* (go down) after(?) your lord, oh throne, after(?) your lord to the netherworld, 1.161:20 (inf. abs. used as an impv.(?), Dietrich - Loretz UF 15 1983 21, UF 16 1984 58f.; alternatively cf. *atr (II)* vb).
D. To force to follow, to transmit: *qmm atr amr* standing, they transmitted (their) demand, 1.2 I 31 and par. (// *tny*; Del Olmo MLC 171; Dietrich - Loretz UF 16 1984 57). In bkn ctx., *y atr*, 1.16 V 6 (Verreet UF 17 1985 322).
Cf. atr (I), atr (II), atr (III), atr (IV), atrt (I), atryt, matr.

atr (I) n./adj. m. "the following" (< ptc. G /ʔ-t-r/; Dietrich - Loretz UF

16 1984 58). ¶ Forms: m. pl. *atrm.*
Following: *atr atrm* the following follow, 1.45:7-8.

atr (II) adv./prep. 1) "then, afterwards; behind, immediately after"; 2) "behind, after; towards, for" (< n. m. "footstep"(?); cf. /ʔ-ṯ-r/; Hb. *ʔšwr*, HALOT 99; ESA *ʔṯr*, DOSA 31; cf. Arab. *ʔi/uṯra*, Lane 19; Eth. *ʔaśar*, CDG 45. Cf. Brockelmann GvG 1 499; Aartun PU 2 50f.; Dietrich - Loretz UF 16 1984 60ff.); ¶ par.: *l (I) (+ pnm).* ¶ Forms: *aṯr*, suff. *aṯrk*, *aṯrh*.

1) Adv. ★a) (of time) then, afterwards: *aṯr in mr* then, no pain(?), 1.124:16 (cf. *mr (II)*); ★b) (of place) behind, immediately after: *aṯr btlt ʕnt* behind (went) DN, 1.4 IV 18 (// *l pnm*; Dietrich - Loretz UF 16 1984 62). Cf. in bkn ctx. *aṯr*, 1.103:2 (Dietrich - Loretz TUAT 2 96: 'folgt', /ʔ-ṯ-r/; Pardee AfO 33 1986 124: 'in place of').

2) Prep. ★a) (local) behind, after: *aṯr ilm ylk pʕnm* after the gods (the king) shall walk on foot, 1.43:24 (diff. Xella TRU 24: 'luogo'; cf. *aṯr (III)*); *aṯrh (...) l tdd (...)* after him (...) they left (...), 1.20 II 2 and par.; *aṯr bʕl ard b arṣ* after DN I shall go down to the netherworld, 1.5 VI 24 and par.; cf. *aṯr bʕlk l ksi aṯr bʕlk arṣ rd* after(?) your lord, oh throne, after(?) your lord to the netherworld descend, 1.161:20 (cf. Aartun PU 2 51; Dijkstra UF 17 1985 151; diff. Dietrich - Loretz UF 16 1984 58f.: inf. abs. G of /ʔ-ṯ-r/); ★b) (directional suffix) towards, for: *km lb ʕnt aṯr bʕl* thus (did beat) the heart of DN for DN, 1.6 II 9, 30; ★c) (temporal) after: behold *bn bn aṯrk* your grandsons after you, 1.22 I 3; *aṯr ršp ʕṯtrt* after (the strophe of(?)) DN, (the one of(?)) DN, 1.100:77 (Dietrich - Loretz UF 16 1984 62).

aṯr (III) n. m. "remain(s), what is left" ((?); < /ʔ-ṯ-r/; cf. Arab. *ʔaṯr*, *ʔaṯar*, *ʔaṯārat*, Lane 18f. Cf. Del Olmo MLC 369, 519; diff.: Dijkstra - De Moor UF 7 1975 175f.; Healey UF 11 1979 356; Dietrich - Loretz UF 16 1984 59f.: 'holy places (of a deity)', Akk. *ašru*; Husser UF 27 1995 126: 'vers la terre'); ¶ par.: *qṭr.* ¶ Forms: sg./pl. suff. *aṯry*, *aṯrk*, *aṯrh*.

Remain(s), what is left(?): a son *l ʕpr ḏmr aṯrh/k/y* who from the dust may protect my / your / his remain(s)(?), 1.17 I 28, 46; II 2, 17 (// *qṭrh/k/y*).

aṯr (IV) interr. adv. "where?" (< n. m. "place"; cf. /ʔ-ṯ-r/; cf. Akk. *ašru*, AHw 82f.; CAD A/2 456ff.; Ph., Pun., Aram. *ʔšr*, DNWSI 27f.; EA Akk. cf. Rainey UF 3 1971 162; EAT 65. Diff.: Dahood UHP 53: Hb. rel. pn. *ʔšr*). ¶ Forms: *aṯr.*

Where? (adv.): *aṯr iṯ bqṯ* find out where it is, 2.39:34.

aṯrn PN (cf. *aṯry*, GN. Cf. Grøndahl PTU 27, 103, 301; Rin BZ 11

180); ¶ **syll.**: *aš-šu-ra-na*, PRU 3 198 (RS 16.359 B):4'.
PN: 4.692:2; cf. 4.75 V 3.

aṯrt (I) n. f. "back part (of the head), nape"(?) (< /ʔ-ṯ-r/; Dietrich - Loretz UF 16 1984 60; diff.: Pardee AfO 33 1986 125: 'in place of(?)'; cf. *aṯr (II)*). *aṯrt*.
Back part (of the head), nape(?): (if the foetus has) *l aṯrt ʕnh* one of its eyes in the nape of its neck, 1.103+:49 (cf. *b lṣbh*, *ibid.*).
Cf. **aṯryt**.

aṯrt (II) DN; El's wife (cf. *il (I)*; Hb. *ʔšrh*, HALOT 99; DNWSI 129; Amor. /ʔaš(i)ra(tum)/, Gelb CAAA 14; EA Akk. cf. PN ÌR-[(d)]*a-ši-ir-tV*, -[(d)]*aš-ra-tV*, EAT *passim*; Hess AmPN 235ff. Cf. Lipiński OLP 3 1972 101-109; Caquot - Sznycer TOu 1 69f.; Maier ʔAšerah 3ff.; Müller Biling. 196; Margalit VT 40 1990 291f.; Dietrich - Loretz UBL 9 125ff.; Wiggins UF 23 1991 383ff.; Watson SEL 10 1993 51f.; UF 25 1993 431); ¶ **syll.**: cf. PN ÌR-*a-šar-ti*, PRU 3 RS 205 16.155-3 5, Ug 5 9:20; Sivan GAGl 198; Huehnergard AkkUg 383; ¶ **par.**: *ilt*.
DN: ★**a)** *passim* in narrative ctx.; cf. 1.4 IV 53; *aṯrt // ilt*, 1.3 V 36 and par.; 1.15 III 25; *ḫlb aṯrt* the milk of DN, 1.15 II 26; *ap zd aṯrt* the nipples of DN, 1.23:24; ★**b)** epithets: *rbt aṯrt ym* the Great Lady, DN of the Sea, 1.4 I 21 and par. (Albright ARI 77f.; De Moor SP 145; Gordon Fs. Craigie 127ff.); *qnyt ilm* Progenitress of the gods, 1.4 III 26, 35 and par.; *aṯrt ṣrm // ilt ṣdynm* DN of TN // 'Goddess' of TN, 1.14 IV 35-36, 38-39 (cf. Betlyon JNES 44 1985 53ff.); cf. *aṯrt w rḥm(y)*, 1.23:13, 28; ★**c)** associates: *dgy rbt aṯrt ym* 'tritons' of the Great Lady, DN of the Sea, 1.4 II 31 and par.; *ʕnn aṯrt* manservant of DN, 1.4 IV 59; *amt aṯrt* maidservant of DN, 1.12 I 15; *bn aṯrt* sons of DN, 1.4 IV 51; *šbʕm bn aṯrt* the seventy sons of DN, 1.4 VI 46; *aṯrt w bnh* DN and her sons, 1.6 I 40; cf. *il w aṯrt*, 1.65:5; ★**d)** in god lists: 1.65:5; 1.118:19 (?); 1.148:25 (rdg prob. *a*(!)*ṯrt*); ★**e)** *passim* in offering lists; cf. 1.39:6; 1.41:15; 1.112:24; 1.148:7, 31; *alp l bʕl w aṯrt*, 1.46:8. Cf. in bkn ctx. 1.103:49.

aṯry (I) GN m. "Assyrian" (Astour RSP 2 263f.); ¶ **syll. Ug.**: cf. KUR *aš-šur*, PRU 4 151 (RS 17.59):6, 11, 12; cf. Ug 5 56:7'; RSOu 7 46:32 and *passim ibid.* ¶ **Forms**: pl. *aṯrym*.
GN: 4.230:3. Cf. in bkn ctx.]*aṯry*, 4.58:4.

aṯry (II) PN (< *aṯry*, GN: Cf. Grøndahl PTU 103, 301; Dietrich - Loretz - Sanmartín UF 5 1973 105).
PN: 4.332:15; cf. in bkn ctx. 4.58:4.

uṯryn "crown prince" in Hittite court (etym. unc. Cf. /ʔ-ṯ-r/; Dietrich - Loretz BO 23 1966 129; WO 3 1966 239; Huehnergard UVST 112; cf.

Goetze RHA 12 1954 4; Liverani RSO 38 1963 151 n. 6; Sivan UF 21 1989 361); ¶ syll. Ug.: LÚ.MEŠ *mur-ú uš-r*[*i-ia*]*-ni*, PRU 3 203 (RS 16.257+) IV 21; Huehnergard UVST 112; Sivan UF 21 1989 361; ¶ RS Akk.: LÚ *tar-te-ni*, PRU 4 42 (RS 17.227 and dupl.): 28; LÚ *tar-te-en-ni* DUMU LUGAL, PRU 4 44 (RS 17.347): 13'; cf. PRU 4 p. 264; Dietrich - Loretz WO 3 1964/66 239; Wilhelm UF 2 1970 277-282; Liverani SDB 53 1337; Pecchioli Daddi MPDAI 521; Van Soldt SAU 11f. ¶ Forms: sg. *uṯryn*.

Crown prince: (gifts) *l uṯryn* for the *u.*, 3.1:30 (cf. RS Akk.: *a-na* LÚ *tar-te-ni*, PRU 4 42 (RS 17.227 and dupl.): 28; var. LÚ *tar-te-en-ni* DUMU LUGAL, PRU 4 44 (RS 17.347): 13'; cf. Knoppers BASOR 289 1993 89). Cf. in bkn ctx. *ṯḥm uṯryn*[, 2.67:1. Cf. *šd bd bn uṯryn*, 4.103:6 (cf. *md (II)*); cf. Grøndahl PTU 423.

Cf. trd/tn.

aṯryt n. f. "final outcome, fate, destiny" (< /ʔ-ṯ-r/; Dijkstra - De Moor BO 34 1974 8; UF 7 1975 189; Dietrich - Loretz UF 16 1984 60; diff.: Margalit UF 8 1976 166: 'substitute', 'souvenir', Arab. *aṯr* (*sic*!)); ¶ par.: *uḫryt*. ¶ Forms: sg. *aṯryt*.

Final outcome, fate, destiny: *mh yqḥ mt aṯryt* what can a man attain as the final outcome? 1.17 VI 36 (// *uḫryt*).

Cf. aṯrt (I).

aṯt n. f. 1) "woman"; 2) "married woman, wife"; 3) "lady" (Hb. *ʔšh*, HALOT 93; Ph., Pun. *ʔšt*, Aram. *ʔnth*, DNWSI 115ff.; Akk. *aššatu*, AHw 83f.; CAD A/2 462ff.; Akk. < Can. *iššu*, AHw 399; CAD I/J 267; ESA *ʔnṯt*, DOSA 23; Arab. *ʔuntā*, Lane 112; Eth. *ʔaněst*, CDG 32; cf. Ebla /unuṯum/ in NAM.MÍ = *ù-nu-sum*, EV 0221; Krebernik ZA 73 1983 45f.; Fronzaroli EL 151; StEb 7 1984 153); ¶ RS Akk.: DAM, MUNUS/MÍ, PRU 3 232; PRU 4 260, 262; PRU 6 150f.; Ug 5 340; KTU 4.165:18; ¶ par.: *aṯrt (II)*, *bn (I)*, *ġzr*, *ġlmt*, *mddt*, *mtrḫt*. ¶ Forms: sg. *aṯt*; suff. *aṯty*, *aṯtk*, *aṯth*, *aṯtn* ((?) 1.82:29); pl. *aṯt*; du. abs. *aṯtm*, cstr. *aṯt*, *aṯty* (encl. *-y* (?), Aartun PU 1 44; *mater lectionis* for /-ê/(?)).

1) Woman: two labourers, a freedman *w arbʕ aṯt* and four women, 4.360:9; *k tld aṯt* if a woman gives birth 1.140:1 and par. in birth omens; *il aṯtm k ypt* DN he wanted in fact to seduce the two women, 1.23:39; *aṯtm tṣḥn and mt mt* both women shouted: oh man, man!, *ibid.* ln. 40; cf. ln. 46; *tlḥm aṯt* the women can eat (of the sacrifice), 1.115:8; *ks qdš l tphnhn aṯt* the holy cup which a woman cannot see, cf. 1.3 I 14 (// *aṯrt*); *šrḥq aṯt l pnnh* he dismissed the women from his presence, 1.3 IV 40 (diff.: Aartun StUL 26f.: 'Überfluss, Reichliches',

* *ʔ<u>t</u>t*); *nps a<u>t</u>t* woman's clothing, 1.19 IV 46 (// *ġzr*); *bd a<u>t</u>t* a woman's weeping, 1.16 I 19 and par. For *bʕl a<u>t</u>t* : cf. *infra*: 2.c. Cf. in bkn ctx. (if the family of)]*x a<u>t</u>t yqḥ ʕz* ...] a woman takes a goat, 1.127:26.
2) Married woman, wife, ★a) *npy a*[[*x*]]*<u>t</u>t* atonement of the (king's) wife, 1.40:36; + ge./pn. suff.: *a<u>t</u>tm a<u>t</u>t il a<u>t</u>t il w ʕlmh* the two women will be wives of DN, wives of DN for ever, 1.23:42; *a<u>t</u>ty il ylt* both women of DN have given birth, *ibid.* ln. 52, 60; *a<u>t</u>t PN* the wife of PN, 4.386:19; PN *yd a<u>t</u>th* with his wife, 4.644:4, 9; *ilš (...) w a<u>t</u>th* DN (...) and his wife, 1.16 IV 8 and par.; PN *w PN aḫth (...) w PN bnh w PN bth w PN a<u>t</u>th* and PN, his brother, (...), and PN, his son, and PN, his daughter, and PN, his wife, 3.4:9; PN *w PN a<u>t</u>th* and PN his wife, 4.339:3, 4, 6-9, 12, 15, 19, 23; 4.625:20; PN *w bnh w a<u>t</u>th w alp w <u>t</u>mn ṣin* and his sons and his wife and an ox and eight ewes, 4.295:2; cf. *ibid.* ln. 3-16; *ʕšrm ksp ʕl PN w ʕl PN a<u>t</u>th* twenty shekels of silver in the charge of PN and of PN his wife, 4.369:19; *l ašt a<u>t</u>ty nʕry <u>t</u>h l pn ib* I am not going to leave either my wife or my boy(s) there before the enemy, 2.33:28; *bm nšq a<u>t</u>th* [...] *b ḥbqh* on kissing his wife [...], on embracing her, 1.17 I 39; *trḫ ḥd<u>t</u> ybʕr l <u>t</u>n a<u>t</u>th* the newly wed leaves his wife to another, 1.14 II 49; 1.14 IV 27 (// *mdd<u>t</u>*); *gm a<u>t</u>th k yṣḥ* in a loud voice he shouted to his wife, 1.17 V 15; ★b) to have, take, acquire a wife, to marry her: *hn a<u>t</u>*[*t l ʕbd(y/k/h)*] behold a wife for my / your / his servant, 2.25:5; *in a<u>t</u>t lk km ilm* you have no wife like the gods, 1.2 III 22; *a<u>t</u>t tqḥ* the woman you have taken, 1.15 II 21-22 (// *ġlm<u>t</u>*); *a<u>t</u>t ṣdqh l ypq* I certainly acquired a lawful wife, 1.14 I 12 (// *mtrḫ<u>t</u>*); *y a<u>t</u>t itrḫ* oh women whom I married!, 1.23:64 (// *bn*); *a<u>t</u>t trḫ w tbʕr* he married a woman, but she went away, 1.14 I 14; ★c) *bʕl a<u>t</u>t* married man, 4.153:2-5 (for fiscal or admin. purposes., cf. *ššlmt*; diff.: Ribichini - Xella Tessili 30; Xella UF 22 1990 469f.; Watson SEL 6 1989 47; Tropper UG 111: a textile). Cf. in bkn ctx. *a<u>t</u>t ḥr*[, 1.174:7.
3) Lady: *a<u>t</u>t w bnh* a lady and her son, 4.102:1; *a<u>t</u>t w <u>t</u>n bnh* a lady and her two sons, 4.102:5; *a<u>t</u>t w <u>t</u>t bth* a lady and her two daughters, *ibid.* ln. 22; *a<u>t</u>t w pġt* a lady and the maid, *ibid.* ln. 6; *a<u>t</u>t w <u>t</u>n nʕrm* a lady and two servants, *ibid.* ln. 8; *a<u>t</u>tm w pġt aḥt* two ladies and one maid, 4.102:10; *<u>t</u>t a<u>t</u>tm w pġt aḥt* two ladies and one maid, 4.102:11; *a<u>t</u>t(m) adrt(m)* one / two / x noble lady/ladies, *ibid.* ln. 4 and *passim*; cf. *arbʕ a<u>t</u>t* four women, 4.349:2.
In bkn ctx. *ḫlm a<u>t</u>t i<u>t</u>t*, RSOu 14 53 [KTU 9.432]:35 (Bordreuil - Pardee RSOu 14 p. 399, 404: 'et la 'danse' de la femme (est son) don'); *a<u>t</u>tn* our women, 1.82:29; *<u>t</u>l<u>t</u> a<u>t</u>t* three women,4.419:3; cf. 1.94:29; in unc. ctx., *a<u>t</u>t l <u>t</u>lḥmy*, 5.11:6; 4.419:6; 1.15 V 23.

Cf. **a/iṯtl, aṯtš, aṯtyn, aṯtyy, tinṯt**.

iṯt "?" (bkn ctx.).

? : *ḫlm aṯt iṯt*, RSOu 14 53 [KTU 9.432]:35 (Bordreuil - Pardee RSOu 14 p. 397, 402: 'et la 'danse' de la femme (est son) don').

iṯtbnm MN (cf. *iṯb*; cf. Ebla ^d^*aš-da-bi*(NE)/*bi*₅(BÍL); ITI *aš-da-bi*₅; Von Soden EDA 82; ARET 9 353, 392; Mander MROA 2/1 35f.; Hurro-Hitt. DN *Aštabi*, Laroche GLH 61); ¶ **RS Akk.**: MN *i/iš(-ši)*-GI, RS 22.217A+, 22.229, 25.453+; cf. De Jong - Van Soldt JEOL 30 1987/88 71 n. 14: GI =(?) *tibnu(/ūma)*.

MN: *b yrḫ iṯtbnm* in the month of *i.*, 4.269:30 (cf. 4.387:13; 4.609:1).

a/iṯtl PN (Hurr.(?); cf. Grøndahl PTU 221, 223; Watson AuOr 11 1993 214); ¶ **syll.**: cf. *iš-te-lu*, AnOr 48 26 (RS [Varia 11 = 1957.3]):6; PRU 6 150:3.

PN: ★**a)** 5.9 I 1; IV 3 cf. in bkn ctx.: 4.358:3 (*i*{.}*ṯt*[); 4.556:2; 4.651:4; **b)** *bn PN*: 4.307:20.

iṯtqb TN (Dietrich - Loretz- Sanmartín UF 7 1975 157; Van Soldt UF 28 1996 663; Belmonte RGTC 12/2 148f. Cf. /ṯ-q-b/).

TN: 1.105:9.

iṯtr[Bkn PN, 4.754:18 (*b*<*n*>).

aṯtš PN (Hurr. Cf. Grøndahl PTU 208, 221; Ribichini - Xella RSF 15 1987 13).

PN: *bn PN*, 4.232:15.

aṯtyn PN (Hurr. Cf. Grøndahl PTU 221); ¶ **syll.**: cf. *aš-t*[*a*-, PRU 3 137 (RS 15.190):4.

PN: 4.696:4.

aṯtyy PN (Hurr. Cf. Grøndahl PTU 221); ¶ **syll.**: cf. *aš-t*[*a*-, PRU 3 137 (RS 15.190):4.

PN: *bn PN*, 4.611:10.

uwaḫ PN (etym. unc. Cf. Grøndahl PTU 298).

PN: 4.364:7.

uwil PN (etym. unc. Cf. Grøndahl PTU 273, 298; Kornfeld Fs. Cazelles 1981 213).

PN: 4.75 II 8.

awl n. m. "priority, supremacy" (?) (cf. Arab. *ʔawwal*, Lane 126; Kapelrud Ug 6 328 n. 33; survey: Dietrich - Loretz SUL 91; diff.: Gaster Thespis[1] 451; Gray JNES 10 1951 151 n. 50; LC 79 n. 3; UF 3 1971 67 n. 53: 'to obtain help', Arab. *waliya*, *ʔālu* 'family'; Aartun WO 4 1967/68 289: Hb. *ʔwyl* 'hilflos'; survey: Dietrich - Loretz Studien 91); ¶ **par.**: *ttkn*. ¶ Forms: sg. *awl*.

Priority, supremacy(?): *i<š>ttk l awl* he ceased to have supremacy(?), 1.12 II 56 (// *ttkn*).
Cf. awldn.

iwl[, in bkn ctx. *iwl[*, 4.46:2 (PN(?); cf. Huehnergard UVST 274; Tropper UG 175).
Cf. awl.

awldn PN (etym. unc. Cf. Grøndahl PTU 98, 123).
PN: 4.54:9; 4.129:5.

awpn PN (etym. unc.).
PN: 4.204:4.

awr, 4.332:11 awr; cf. *a/iwrṯġrn*.

iwrd PN, 4.619:3.

iwrḏn PN (Hurr. Cf. Grøndahl PTU 225, 231).
PN: 2.14:1; 4.243:30.

iwrḏr PN; cf. *ib/wrḏr*.

iwrġl PN (Hurr. Cf. Dietrich - Loretz WO 4 1967/68 301; UF 9 1977 341; Dijkstra UF 25 1993 159).
PN: 4.244:26; cf. *awrġl* 1.42:30.

iwrḫṭ PN (Hurr. Cf. Grøndahl PTU 207, 224, 233; for Hurr. cf. Laroche GLH 110; Wilhelm Or 61 1992 130; Van Soldt SAU 341); ¶ syll.: EN-*ḫu*(!)(RI)-*ṭu*, Ug 5 161:20 (cf. Huehnergard AkkUg 413 n. 112); EN-*ḫu-ṭV*, Ug 5 71:4'; RSOu 7 2:10', 25; 22:2. Var. *abrḫṭ*, 4.309:27.
PN: ★a) 4.103:13, 25; ★b) *bn PN*, 4.309:27.

iwrḫz PN (Hurr. Cf. Grøndahl PTU 204, 225, 231; Dietrich - Loretz-Sanmartín UF 5 1973 98f.; Van Soldt SAU 357); ¶ syll.: cf. EN-*ḫa-zi*, PRU 4 201 (RS 18.02):6.
PN: ★a) 4.635:37; ★b) *bn PN*, 4.367:7.

iwrkl PN (Hurr. Cf. Grøndahl PTU 205, 225, 234; Van Soldt SAU 37).
PN: 3.4:2, 13, 18; 4.282:2; 4.357:15.

iwrmḏ PN; cf. *ib/wrmḏ*.

iwrmḫ PN (Hurr. Cf. Grøndahl PTU 225; Van Soldt SAU 326).
PN: 4.194:9.

iwrn PN (Hurr. Cf. Grøndahl PTU 225). Cf. *ibrn*.
PN: *bn PN*, 4.545 II 8 (bkn).

iwrnr PN (Hurr. Cf. Grøndahl PTU 224f., 243); ¶ syll.: cf. EN.ḪI, RS 23.36 (cf. Van Soldt SAU 20 and n. 177).
PN: 4.16:5.

iwrpzn PN (Hurr. Cf. Grøndahl PTU 225, 245).
PN: 2.14:2; 4.102:5, 10; 4.226:2; 4.336:3; 4.547:3. Cf. in bkn ctx.

4.384:13; 4.607:5.

iwrtḏl PN (Hurr.; cf. Grøndahl PTU 225; Berger WO 5 1969/70 281); ¶ syll.: cf. EN-*ta-ša-lu* and var. EN-*ta-šal*, cf. PRU 3 p. 244.
PN: 4.424:21; 4.607:8.

iwrtn PN (Hurr. Cf. Grøndahl PTU 225, 262).
PN: ★a) 4.183 II 23; ★b) *bn PN*: 4.70:7.

a/iwrṯġrn PN (Hurr. Cf. Grøndahl PTU 225, 248; Dietrich - Loretz WO 4 1967/68 301; Watson AuOr 8 1990 114, 127); ¶ syll.: EN-*ri-šu-ḫur-na*, PRU 6 109 A 5.
PN: 4.332:11; 4.607:7.

iwrṯrm, cf. *irrṯrm*.

iwryn PN; cf. *ib/wryn*.

ay adj. m. "anyone, all, of any kind; each" (cf. *iy*; cf. Moscati ICGSL 114f.; cf. Brockelmann GvG 1 328f.; Arab. *ʔayy*, Lane 132f.; Akk. *ayyumma*, AHw 26; CAD A/1 236ff.; cf. *ayû*, CAD A/1: *ajû* 2b; Eth. *ʔay*, CDG 49; diff.: Cross CMHE 115 n. 12; Clifford VT 25 1975 300 n. 7; Driver CML 137; Gray LC n. 8: interj. *ʔay* 'oh!'; Largement NA 29f.; Caquot - Sznycer TOu 1 369: Hb. *ʔy* 'île, côte'; WuS 15: name of a deity [but cf. Lipiński Syria 44 1967 253-282]; Cutler-Macdonald UF 14 1982 36f: negative particle [but cf. Tsumura AJBI 4 1978 23-31]; Margalit UF 15 1983 113: 'indeed', Arab. *iy*; for various opinions cf. Xella MSS 45f.; Foley GG 29ff.); ¶ RS Akk.: cf. *a-i-ú-ti-me-e* NAM.RA.MEŠ, PRU 4 97f. (RS 17.79+): 13';]*a-i-ú-um-ma*, *ibid.* ln. 29'. ¶ Forms: sg. m. *ay*.
Anyone, all, of any kind: eat *b lḥm ay* food of any kind // drink *b ḫmr yn ay* intoxicating wines of any kind, 1.23: 6, cf. *y*]*n ay*, 1.17 VI 3; each: *yrdt (...) ll ay* who go down (...) each night, 1.24: 44. Cf. in bkn ctx. *ay abšrkm dnil*, 1.19 II 36 (Cooper UF 20 1088 25: 'oh!'; cf. Del Olmo MLC 512).

iy interr. adv. "where?" (cf. Hb. *ʔ(y)*, *ʔyh*, HALOT 37f.; Amor. /ʔayya(n)/, /iyya/, Gelb CAAA 13; cf. *ay*, *i*. Cf. Tropper UF 26 1994 475; UG 752); ¶ syll. Ug.: cf. the element /ʔiyya/ in PNN, Sivan GAGl 200. ¶ Forms: *iy*.
Where?: *iy aliyn bʕl iy zbl bʕl arṣ* where is Very Powerful DN, where is the patron prince of the underworld?, 1.6 IV 15-16 and par.
Cf. ayab, ay(a/i)ḫ, iybʕl, iydm, aym, iytlm, iyṯr, ayy.

uy, vd. *u*.

ayab PN (Sem. Cf. Grøndahl PTU 48, 86, 93; Lipiński Syria 44 1967 261ff.).
PN: 4.153:4; 4.214 III 10.

ay(a/i)ḫ PN (Sem. Cf. Grøndahl PTU 15, 48, 91, 93; Lipiński Syria 44 1967 264ff.); ¶ syll.: *a-ia-a-ḫi*, PRU 3 38 (RS 16.354):6; *a-ia-aḫ-ḫi*, PRU 4 219 (RS 17.424 C+):10; DUMU *a-ia-aḫ-ḫi*, Syria 15 1934 138 (RS [Varia 3]):25. Var. *ayiḫ* in 4.86:28; *ayḫ* in 4.214 II 6.
PN: ★a) 4.86:28 (*ilšt*[*mʕy*); 4.338:8; ★b) *bn PN*: 3.3:3; 4.79:6; 4.214 II 6.

ayiḫ PN; cf. *ay(a/i)ḫ*.

iybʕl (I) DN; name of an invocation and statue of the god Baal ('Where is DN?'; < *iy* + *bʕl (II)*).
Invocation and statue of the god Baal: (purple vestments) *l DN* for DN, 4.168:2 (cf. *ʕṯtrt*, *ṯrmnm*, *ušḫry*, *mgmr*, ln. 4, 5, 10, 12).

iybʕl (II) PN (Sem. Cf. Grøndahl PTU 48, 93, 117; Lipiński Syria 44 1967 271f.).
PN: *bn PN*, 4.334:4.

iydm PN (Sem. Cf. Grøndahl PTU 48).
PN: 4.16:2.

ayḫ PN; cf. *ay(a/i)ḫ*.

ayl (I) n. m. "deer" (Hb., Ph., Pun., Aram. *ʔyl*, HALOT 40; HAT 46; DNWSI 45; Akk. *ayyalu*, AHw 24; CAD A/1 225f.; Ebla cf. *a-a-lu-*[*um*(?)], ARET 8 15; Amor. /ʔayyalum/, Huffmon APNMT 161; Gelb CAAA 13, 41; Arab. *ʔiyyal*, Lane 128; cf. Eg. *íyr* / *ʔe-yu-l* "ram", WäS 1 38; Helck Bez. 507 (1)); ¶ RS Akk.: cf. PN DUMU *a-ia-li*, PRU 3 89 (RS 15.123+16.152):4; Grøndahl PTU 94; TN ḪUR.SAG.ḪI.A *ša a-ia-li* PRU 4 66 (RS 17.62):20'; Sivan GAGl 199; ¶ par.: *alp*, *ḥmr*, *rum*, *ṣin*, *yʕl*. ¶ Forms: sg. *ayl*; f. *aylt*; pl. *aylm*.
Deer: *ṭbḫ šbʕm aylm* she slaughtered seventy deer, 1.6 I 24 (// *alpm*, *ḥmrm*, *rumm*, *ṣin*, *yʕlm*). Cf. sg. in PN *bn ayl*, 4.617:14.
Cf. a/il, ayl (II), ayln, aylt (I).

ayl (II) PN (Sem. Cf. *ayly*, TN. Cf. Grøndahl PTU 27, 94); ¶ syll.: DUMU *a-ia-li*, PRU 3 89 (RS 15.123+):4.
PN: *bn PN*, 4.617:14.

ayln PN (Sem. Cf. *ayl (I)*, *(II)*; cf. Lipiński Syria 44 1967 278f.).
PN: *bn PN*, 4.309:22; 4.339:27. Cf. in bkn ctx. 4.658:42.

aylt (I) n. f. "hind" (< m. *ayl*); ¶ par.: *rum*. ¶ Forms: sg. *aylt*; pl. *aylt*.
Hind: *aylt tġpy ṯr* a hind was espying(?) a bull, 1.92:11 (cf. Dijkstra UF 26 1994 117, 119); *ʕn k ḏd aylt* the spring (for which yearn), in truth, the herd of hinds, 1.5 I 17, cf. 1.133:8 (// *rumm*). Cf. in bkn ctx. 1.1 V 19.
Cf. ayl (I), aylt (II).

aylt (II) PN (Sem. Cf. *ayl (II)*, PN).
PN: *bn PN*, 4.338:9. Cf. in bkn ctx. 4.658:42.

ayly TN (Belmonte RGTC 12/2 48: *ʔAyalā*. Cf. Astour Or 38 1969 401f.; RSP 2 258, 344; UF 13 1981 7; Heltzer RCAU 8; Van Soldt UF 27 1995 658; UF 30 1998 728); ¶ syll.: LÚ.MEŠ A.SÀ *a-ia-la*, RS 25.132 III 3 (Van Soldt UF 28 1996 658 n. 26); ḪUR.SAG.ḪI.A *ša a-ia-li*, PRU 4 66 (RS 17.62+):37; ḪUR.[SAG] *ú*(!)*-ga-ri* DÀR, PRU 4 51 (RS 17.340+) rev. 4'; cf. PRU 4 p. 51; Belmonte AuOr 17/19 1999/2000 14, 19.
TN: 4.643:17; 4.645:2.

aym PN (Sem. Cf. Ribichini - Xella RSF 15 1987 7).
PN: 4.595:3.

aymr DN; name of a magic mace (< *ay* + /m-r(-r)/ (I); cf. Del Olmo MLC 512; but cf. Smith BC 343 n. 214).
DN: 1.2 IV 19.

iyn n. m. of a type of sacrifice (probl. of mourning(?); base */ʔ-n/; cf. Hb. *ʔwn*, HALOT 22; Arab. *ʔayn*, Lane 139; Nab., Palm. *ʔwn*, DNWSI 22f.; Del Olmo AuOr 2 1984 198 n. 9; SEL 12 1995 45; Eg. *iw*, CDME 12 and *iyt* ,CDME 10; Watson UF 30 1998 751, cf. Del Olmo CR 234 n. 58; diff.: Cazelles Semitica 29 1979 58: 'apaisement'; Watson UF 30 1998 751: 'offering, provisions', Eg. *iyw*). ¶ Forms: sg. *iynm* (encl. *-m*(?)).
Type of sacrifice (probl. of mourning(?): *b ṯmnt iynm akl* on the eighth day, as a (sacrifice of) mourning(?), (a measure of) grain, 1.112:11 (cf. diff.: Dietrich - Loretz TUAT 2 316: '(es darf) auf keinen Fall Verzehr (stattfinden)').

iyrḏ PN (etym. unc. Cf. *ḫiari*, MN in Nuzi, Alalakh, AHw 342; Grøndahl PTU 223, 252; Lipiński Syria 44 1967 275).
PN: 4.147:18.

iyry PN (etym. unc. Cf. *ḫiari*, MN in Nuzi, Alalakh, AHw 342; Grøndahl PTU 223; Lipiński Syria 44 1967 269; Berger WO 5 1969/70 272).
PN: 4.222:18.

iytlm PN (Hurro-Sem. Cf. Grøndahl PTU 94, 260; Lipiński Syria 44 1967 268f.; Astour CRRA 18 13; Van Soldt SAU 32, 36; Watson AuOr 14 1996 95).
PN: ★a) 2.14:14; 4.165:2; 4.223:6-9; 4.344:9; 4.357:18; 4.367:9; 4.374:1; 4.379:6; 4.409:2; 4.410:28; 4.425:11; 4.680:2; in bkn ctx.: 4.357:9; ★b) *bn PN*, 4.309:21.

iyṯr PN (Hurro-Sem. Cf. Grøndahl PTU 48, 94, 249, 260).

PN: ★a) 4.153:5; 4.194:5; 4.615:1; in bkn ctx.: 4.50:17; 4.285:5; ★b) *bn PN:* 4.364:2; 4.547:2; 4.617:5.

ayy PN (Sem. Cf. Grøndahl PTU 93; cf. Lipiński Syria 44 1967 253ff.; OLP 12 1981 98; Bordreuil - Lemaire Semitica 29 1979 77f.); ¶ syll.: cf. *a-i-ú*, Ug 5 27:24. Cf. *ʕyy*.
PN: 4.611:6.

az n. m.; a textile, fabric (?) (cf. Ribichini - Xella Tessili 27: Hurr. *aššianni* 'sorte de broderie'; Heltzer UF 19 1987 447: Myc. *a-ze(-ti-ri-ya)* a fabric; cf. Xella UF 22 1980 468f.; Watson UF 31 1999 785). ¶ Forms: sg. *az*.
A textile(?): *ṯn mrdt az* two *m.* of *a.*, 4.205:6 (cf. *mrdt*).
Cf. azt, ʕz.

uz n. f. "goose, gander" (Arab. *(ʔi)wazz*, Lane 125; Akk. *ūsu*, Ahw 1438. Cf. Herdner Ug 7 30). ¶ Forms: sg. *uz*, pl. *uzm* (UT § 8.4), cstr. *uz*.
Goose, gander, ★a) *w uz il*(!) *arṣ* and a goose/gander to the gods of the underworld, 1.106:30 (diff. KTU rdg *ilm*); *tgmr uz PN* total value of the ganders of PN, 4.296:5-6; *alp* [ ] *wuz* one (head of) cattle ... and one goose, 1.106:30; fattened: *uz mrat mlḥt* a fattened goose in salt, 4.247:20; *arbʕ uzm mrat* four fattened geese, *ibid.* ln. 21; ★b) *šmn uz* goose fat, 4.247:21; *ṯn rʕy uzm* two gooseherds, 4.129:1.

uzʕrt adj. f. "the smallest, youngest" (Hb. *zʕyr*, HALOT 276; Aram. *zʕyr*, DNWSI 337f.; Arab. *zaʕīra*, Lane 1231. Cf. Lipiński UF 3 1971 84; diff.: De Moor UF 1 1969 181: 'thin-haired', Arab. *ʔazʕar*, Hb.-Aram *zʕr*, Pope - Tigay UF 3 1971 128: 'wicked', Arab. *ʔazʕar*, *zaʕārat*, Irwin UF 15 1983 55f.: 'she of the rain', Hb. *śʕyr*, Caquot TOu 2 48 n. 107: DN, the other daughter of *Baʕlu*, Pardee TPM 143: '(gouttes de pluie) rapides', Arab. *zʕr*, or determinative of *pdry*, cf. Avishur SSWP 717; Dietrich - Loretz UF 17 1985 140); ¶ par.: *ṭly*. ¶ Forms: sg. *uzʕrt*.
The smallest, youngest: *rišh tply ṭly bn ʕnh uzʕrt* DN adorns his head, the youngest, his forehead, 1.101:6.

izl PN (etym. unc. Cf. Watson AuOr 14 1996 95; cf. MN *Izali* in Alalakh, AHw 408).
PN: *bn PN*, 4.35 I 17.

izldn PN (Hurr.(?); cf. Grøndahl PTU 227, 423; Van Soldt SAU 29f., 162f.); ¶ syll.: *i-za-al-da(-na)*, Ug 5 1:5'; 3 rev. 19'; 6:24.
PN: 4.320:5.

izly PN (etym. unc. Cf. MN *Izali* in Alalakh, AHw 408).
PN: 4.348:4.

a/izml n. f.; kind of sack (Akk. *azamil(l)u*, AHw 92; CAD A/2 525; Ribichini - Xella Tessili 27f.; Huehnergard UVST 282 67); ¶ RS Akk.: 10 GÍN KÙ.BABBAR.MEŠ *a-za-mi-la-te*[, PRU 6 155:8. ¶ Forms: sg. *izml*; cf. var.(?) *az*[*ml*(?).
Kind of sack: *ḫmšm izml* fifty *i.*, 4.284:2; *ḥmr w izml aḥt* one 'load' and one *i.*, 5.3:7 (Cf. Veenhof AOATT 8); *ṯlṯ azml* three *a.*, 5.23:3. Cf. in bkn ctx.: *ṯṯ az*[*ml(?)*, 4.390:10 (Cf. Dietrich - Loretz - Sanmartín UF 5 1973 85; Caquot ACF 1976 462).
Cf. **izmly**.

izmly PN (etym. unc.; Cf. *izml*; Ribichini - Xella RSF 15 1987 11).
PN: *bn NP*, 4.7:3.1.

azmr n. m. "branches" (cf. Hb. *zmwrh*, HALOT 272f.; De Moor UF 1 1969 177 n. 68; Sasson RSP 1; Xella TRU 69; for the morphol. cf. the Akk. var. *azamru*, *zamru*, AHw 1509; CAD A/2 525, Z 41; Postgate BiOr 37 1980 68f.; Dalley OBTR no. 204:5; Powell BSA 3 131). ¶ Forms: sg. *azmr*.
Branches: *arbʕ arbʕ mṯbt azmr* four huts (made) of branches on each side, 1.41:51.

/ʔ-z-r/ vb G: "to gird, bind"(?) (cf. *uzr* and Hb. *ʔzr*, HALOT 28;Arab. *ʔzr*, Lane 52f.). ¶ Forms: G prefc. *yazr*, *tizr*.
G. To gird, bind (the statue (?) ritually with a cloth(?)): *tizr pnm* bind the face (with a cloth), 1.116:9 (cf. Xella TRU 320); in bkn ctx.: *yazr*, 1.82:13.
Cf. **/ʔ-s-r/**, **izr**, **uzr**, **mizrt**.

izr n. m. "investiture" (?) (cf. /ʔ-z-r/; *uzr*. Cf. Xella TRU 342; diff.: De Tarragon TOu 2 175 108: 'tissu'). ¶ **Forms**: sg. *izr*.
Investiture(?): *a*]*lp izr* (sacrifice of) the bull of the investiture(?), 1.91:8 (cf. Del Olmo UF 19 1987 13, 15f.; diff.: Dietrich - Loretz TUAT 2 322: 'ein Ochse, ein Schurz').

uzr adj. m. "clothed, enrobed" (cf. /ʔ-z-r/; cf. Hb. *ʔzwr*, *ʔzr*, HALOT 27, 28; Arab. *ʔazara*, *ʔizr*, *ʔizār*, Lane 52f. Cf. Del Olmo IMC 117, n. 257; Sanmartín UF 9 1977 369f.; Dietrich - Loretz 10 1978 66f.; Caquot Semitica 37 1987 6ff.; Huehnergard UVST 105, 275; Watson AuOr 10 1992 241; NABU 2002 4 n. 87 diff.: Cazelles, in DBS 5 1342: '(rite d')incubation', 'vision', *u* + < *zr*, *dr(t)*; but cf. AICSFP 673ff.: 'stimulant divin', Pun. *ʔzrm*; Caquot - Sznycer TOu 1 419 n. c: 'stimulant', Arab. *azr*, Obermann HDBS 8 n. 10; Dijkstra - De Moor UF 7 1975 172f.: 'sacrifice', a + < **nzr*, Ajjar NU 32: a type of offering, Arab. *ʔiḏar*, Tsevat UF 18 1986 345ff.: 'statues', Hitt. *eš-ri*). ¶ Forms: sg. *uzr*, suff. *uzrm* (encl. *-m*).

Enrobed: *uzr ilm ylḥm* enrobed, he fed the gods, 1.17 I 2 and par.; cf. *uzrm*, *ibid.* ln. 21.

azrt, cf. *agzrt*.

uzry PN (etym. unc. Cf. Cassin - Glassner AAN 1 163; Ribichini - Xella RSF 15 1987 12; Watson AuOr 14 1996 96).
PN: rdg unc. *b*]*n uzr*(?)*y*, 4.103:58.

azzlt DN (cf. ESA *ʕzzlt*, DN. Cf. WbMyth 502; De Moor UF 2 1970 198).
DN: *ḫpn l azzlt* a *ḫ*. for DN, 4.182:57.

aẓḥn DN, second element of the unknown compound DN *aẓḥn tlyn*.
DN in god list: *aẓḥn tlyn*, 1.123:24.

ʕ

ʕbb n. m. "greedy, glutton, guzzler" ((?); cf. Arab. *ʕabba*, Lane 1931. Cf. De Moor UF 17 1985 226f.; Dijkstra UF 26 1994 119). ¶ Forms: sg. *ʕbb*.

Greedy, glutton, guzzler (?): in bkn and unc. ctx., *tšpl bʕl ʕbb*[she knocked down the 'glutton'(?), 1.92:14.

/ʕ-b-d/ vb G: "to work (a field), to cultivate, to produce" (Emar /ʕabādu/ Pentiuc Vocabulary 21; Hb. *ʕbd*, HALOT 773f.; Ph., Pun., OAram., Palm., DNWSI 806ff.); ¶ par.: *ḥrṯ*. ¶ Forms: G ptc. act. m. pl. cstr. *ʕbd*.

G. To work (a field), to cultivate: *ʕbd dgn* those who cultivate the grain, 1.16 III 13 (// *ḥrṯm*; cf. De Moor UF 11 1979 646: Hb. *ʕbdy pštym*, Is 19:9; Schwab ZAW 99 1987 336 n. 47); to produce: *ʕbd ṭl* he has produced dew, RSOu 14 53 [KTU 9.432]:15'.

ʕbd (I) n. m. 1) "servant, slave"; 2) "servant (said of a special class of mercenaries or subordinate employees); person of a lower rank"; 3) "faithful, devout person" (Hb., Ph., Pun., Aram., Palm. *ʕbd*, HALOT 774f.; DNWSI 816ff.; Amor. /ʕabdum/, Gelb CAAA 15, 88ff.; Huffmon APNMT 189; Emar Akk. /ʕabd-/, Arnaud AuOrS 1 10; NB *abdu*, AHw 6; CAD A/1 51; ESA *ʕbd*; DOSA 349; SD 11; Arab. *ʕabd*, Lane 1935); ¶ syll. Ug.: ÌR = *ar-du* = *pu-ra-ne* = *ab-du*, Ug 5 137 III 4; cf. the element /ʕabdV-/ (ÌR) in PNN, Grøndahl PTU 104f.; Sivan GAGl 203; Huehnergard UVST 158; Van Soldt SAU 306; ¶ RS Akk.: (LÚ.MEŠ.)ÌR(.MEŠ), *passim*, cf. PRU 3 pp. 217, 232; PRU 4 p. 260; PRU 6 p. 150; Ug 5 p. 340; Huehnergard AkkUg 356; *ar-du*, Ug 5 137 III 4; *ar-dú*, RS 20.122 II 20, Van Soldt SAU 245 n. 11; cf. PN ÌR LUGAL, PRU 4 286 (RS 19.68):33; *passim*; ÌR LUGAL KUR *ú-ga-ri-it*, PRU 3 107 (RS 17.238):3; ÌR ÌR LUGAL KUR *ú-ga-ri-it*, *ibid.* ln. 5; *a-na-ku* ÌR-*du ša* [d]UTU-*ši* LUGAL GAL EN-*ia*, PRU 4 49 (RS 17.340):12; ¶ par.: /ʔ-ḫ-d(/ḏ)/ *(+ ult)*, *ʕnn*, *bn (I) (+ amt (I))*, *sid*.

¶ Forms: sg. abs./cstr. *ʕbd*; suff. *ʕbdk*, *ʕbdh* (cf. *ʕb*[*dm*], encl. *-m*(?), 2.39:12); pl. abs. *ʕbdm*; cstr. *ʕbd*; du. suff. *ʕbdk*.
1) Servant, slave: *ʕbd ḥrn* slave(s) of DN, 1.82:41 (of certain demon(s); cf. De Moor - Spronk UF 16 1985 249); *p ʕbd ank* am I perhaps a slave?, 1.4 IV 59-60 (// *ʕnn*, *aḫd ult*; cf. in bkn ctx.] *ʕbd ank*, 2.50:21); *ʕbdk an w d ʕlmk* your slave am I in perpetuity, 1.5 II 12 and par.; *ʕbdk bʕl y ymm* your slave is DN, oh DN!, 1.2 I 36; *akl (...) ḥpr ʕbdm* grain (... of the) rations of the slaves, 4.636:3 and *passim ibid.*; *ptḥ aḥd l bt ʕbdm* a door for the building of the slaves, 4.195:9; *nʕr d apy PN w (...) d apy ʕbdh w mrbʕt l ʕbdm* (nn of) rancid(?) flour that PN made into bread and (nn + four) that his slave made into bread, and fourfold for the slaves, 4.362:5-6; *ʕbd* slave, 5.9:19; *ʕbd ʕlm* slaves in perpetuity, 1.14 III 23 and par. (// *bn amt*; cf. Hb. *ʕbd ʕwlm*; cf. Yamashita RSP 2 66f.); cf. in bkn and unc. ctx. *tšpl bʕl ʕbb*[she knocked down the 'glutton'', 1.92:14 (cf. De Moor UF 17 1985 226f.; Dijkstra UF 26 1994 119; diff.: Margalit AuOr 7 1989 71: rdg *ʕbd*[*il*).
2) Servant (said of a special class of mercenaries or subordinate employees); person of lower rank: ★a) servant: *ʕbdm* servants, 4.87:2; 4.99:1; 4.126:13; [*spr*] *ʕbdm* list of servants, 4.320:1 (cf. *b TNN*, *ibid.* ln. 2, 8; *btwm*, *ibid.* ln. 13; *b šdm*, *ibid.* ln. 18); *ʕbdm PNN* servants: PNN, 4.71 III 10; 4.35 II 2; *PN ʕbd* PN, servant, 4.75 VI 3; 4.183 II 19; 4.332:10-11; (a farm of) *PN ʕbd l PN* PN, servant, for PN, 4.424:20; *PN ʕbd mlk* PN, servant of the king, 2.47:14 (cf. RS Akk.: ÌR LUGAL); ★b) in correspondence, a person of superior rank, *passim*: *tḥm PN ʕbdk* message of PN, your slave, 2.81:5; RSOu 14 50 [KTU 9.434]:4 and *passim*;; cf. *mlk (...) ʕbdh* the king (...) his servant, 2.19:11; *mlk bʕly (...) l ʕbdh* the king, my lord (...) to his slave, 2.33:24 and par.; *mlkt adty (...) ʕbdk* the queen my lady (...) your servant, 2.12:5; *(adty ...) rgm tṯtb l ʕbdh* (may my lady ...) send a reply to her servant, 2.12:15 and par.; *umy adtny (...) PN w PN ʕbdk* my mother, our lady (...) PN and PN, your two servants, 2.11:4; *at ṯtb ʕm bdk* you send (word) back to your servant, RSOu 14 50 [KTU 9.434]:20 (cf. ln. 10); *bt ʕbdh* the house of his servant, RSOu 14 50 [KTU 9.434] 22.
3) Faithful, devotee of a DN: *ʕbd il*, the slave of DN, 1.14 III 51 and par. (title of king *krt*; cf. 1.15 II 19); *ʕbd ilm* 2.7:10; *ʕbd aliyn bʕl* slave of DN, 1.3 I 2 (or verbal form "he served"(?); // *sid*); [*ks*] *yiḫd il ʕbdh* [a cup] did DN take for(?) his slave, 1.17 I 34 (// *dnil*, rdg *il ʕbdh*, Dietrich - Loretz UF 10 1978 70f.; or text corrupt and rdg *il* {ʕ} *bdh* ... DN in his hand (?); cf. Dijkstra - De Moor UF 7 1975 177;

Del Olmo MLC 370). Cf. in bkn ctx.]*ʕbd ilm*[, 4.26:2; in unc. ctx. *ʕbd i*(!)*lm*, 1.79:3.

Bkn: 1.15 IV 10; 2.57:2; 2.76:12; 4.318:2; 1.15 I 3: *ʕbdn*(?).

Cf. abdadt, abdʕn, abdbʕl, abdḥr, abdḫmn, ʕbd (II), ʕbdil(m), ʕbdilt, ʕbdʕn, ʕbd(ʕ)nt, ʕbdʕṯtrt, ʕbdbʕl, ʕbdgṯr, ʕbdḥgb, ʕbdḥr, ʕbdḥ(y), ʕbdḫmn, ʕbdkṯr, ʕbdlbit, ʕbdmhr, ʕbdmlk, ʕbdn, ʕbdnkl, ʕbdnt, ʕbdpdr, ʕbdpr, ʕbdrpu, ʕbdrš̄, ʕbdršp, ʕbdssm, ʕdbšḫr, ʕbdṯrm, ʕbdy, ʕbdym, ʕbdyrġ, ʕbdyrḫ, riʕbd, yʕbd.

ʕbd (II) PN (Sem. Cf. Grøndahl PTU 50, 423; Van Soldt SAU 7, 27, 38, 40, 83, 309); ¶ syll.: *ab-du*, PRU 6 36:4, 18; Ug 5 52:24; (DUMU) ÌR-*du/dì*, cf. PRU 3 p. 241; Ug 5 p. 327; PRU 4 219 (RS 17.424 C+):9; PRU 6 36:4 and *passim ibid.*; ÌR-du_4, Ug 5 4:10'; cf. Nougayrol PRU 3 pp. 78ff.; Huehnergard UVST 213f.; AkkUg 356; Van Soldt SAU 309.

PN: ★a) 4.35 II 5; 4.63 I 18; 4.281: 11 (*bn ytrš̄*); 4.286:8; 313:19; 4.609:5, 24; 4.617:27; 4.635:35; 4.754:18 (*bn iṯtr*[); in bkn ctx.: *ʕb*[*d* and *ʕbd*[, 4.77:4; 4.227 II 7; 4.529:3; 4.536:2; 4.554:5; 4.570:3; 4.746:2, 8; ★b) *bn PN:* 4.35 I 24; 4.98:19; 4.116:6; 4.155:13; 4.214 I 16; 4.311:2; 4.340:21; 4.424:20; in bkn ctx.: 4.432:18; 4.760:8. Cf. NP *bn abd*, 4.635:48; bkn. [*b*]*t abd*[, 4.727:24 (allographs(?)).

Cf. abd (II).

ʕbdadt PN (Sem. Cf. Grøndahl PTU 14, 90, 105); ¶ syll.: ÌR-*a-da-ti*, PRU 4 183 (RS 17.319):23; ÌR-*a-da-tu*, PRU 6 79:19; cf. 185:2'.

PN: 3.3:12 (*bn ʕbdkb*); 4.183 II 28; 4.281:24; 4.609:12; in bkn ctx.: 4.214 IV 14.

ʕbdil(m) PN (Sem. Cf. Grøndahl PTU 96, 105); ¶ syll.: ÌR. DINGIR*(-ma/mu)*, cf. PRU 3 p. 240; PRU 6 p. 138; Ug 5 p. 326; RSOu 7 3:8'; var. ÌR-*i-li*, Ug 5 7:8 and *passim ibid.*; ÌR.DINGIR-*lim*, Ug 5 56:9'; ÌR.DINGIR.MEŠ, RSOu 7 5:11.

PN: ★a) 4.35 I 3 (*bn k*[); 4.133:2; 4.147:11; 4.183 II 25; 4.188:10; 4.261:11; 4.283:5; 4.285:9; 4.314:3; 4.659:5 (*bn ṣdqn*); 4.730:7; in bkn ctx.: 1.9:20; 4.223:8; ★b) *bn PN:* 4.33:41 (Van Soldt SAU 33); 4.51:16 (*hzpy*; Van Soldt SAU 33); 4.720:3; 4.723:12; in bkn ctx.: 4.754:9 (*hzpy*).

ʕbdilt PN (Sem. Cf. Grøndahl PTU 97, 105; Van Soldt SAU 7, 19, 38); ¶ syll.: ÌR.DINGIR-*tù/ti*, Syria 28 1951 173ff. 6 (RS 14.16):6, 9; PRU 3 79 (RS 16.239):5; 148 (RS 16.178):21; PRU 6 82:2; RSOu 7 3:9; cf. Van Soldt BiOr 46 1989 647; SAU 309.

PN: 3.8:17 (*bn.m*); 4.35 II 14 (*bn qqln*); 4.609:25; in bkn ctx.: 4.151 I 8; 4.311:5; 4.730:4.

ʕbdʕn PN (Sem. Cf. Grøndahl PTU 19, 105, 110; Bordreuil SEL 5 1988 26; Zadok UF 17 1985 394 n. 123). Allographic var. *abdʕn*.
PN: ★a) 4.75 V 23; ★b) *bn abdʕn*: 4.12:9; 4.33:31 (*ilštmʕy*); 4.233:5.

ʕbd(ʕ)nt PN (Sem. Cf. Grøndahl PTU 18, 20, 105, 111); ¶ syll.: ÌR-*a-na-ti*,PRU 3 91 (RS 16.170): rev. 2'-3'; 33 (RS 16.129):19; 167 (RS 15.139):7; PRU 4 72ff. (RS 17.335+):5 and *passim ibid.*; 77 (RS 17.368):5'; 80 (RS 17.382+):6, 10; ÌR-*a-na-tu*$_4$, Ug 5 27:47; cf. ÌR-*a-*[*n*]*a*(?)[-T]E(?), 98:10; cf. Van Soldt SAU 19 n. 168 and cf. *ʕbdilt*. Var. *ʕbdnt* in 4.277:4, 8.
PN: 4.151:6; 4.277:4, 8; 4.609:7.

ʕbdʕṯtr PN (Sem. Cf. Grøndahl PTU 105, 114); ¶ syll.: cf. the title LÚ.SIPA LÚ.ÌR.[d]IŠTAR, Ug 5 84:18.
PN: 4.232:49; in bkn ctx.: 4.75 II 1.

ʕbdbʕl PN (Sem. Cf. Grøndahl PTU 105, 117; Jirku AnOr 37 1969 10; Benz PNPPI 371; Watson AuOr 8 1990 127; AuOr 11 1993 218; cf. Cypro-Minoan *a-pu-tu-pa-lo*, Masson Sem 39 1990 42); ¶ RS Akk.: ÌR.[d]IM, *passim*, Kinlaw SPNATU 8; Grøndahl PTU 316; PRU 6 p. 138; Ug 5 p. 326. Var. *abdbʕl*, 4.635:48; cf. Berger WO 5 1969/70 280.
PN: ★a) 4.75 III 3 (*bn kdn*); 4.110:21; 4.183 II 18; 4.222:18; 4.742:4; 4.766:5; ★b) *bn PN*: 4.635:48; 4.750:4.

ʕbdgṯr PN (Sem. Cf. Grøndahl PTU 105, 131; Dietrich - Loretz UF 12 1980 175).
PN: 4.151:4; 4.214 I 10.

ʕbdḥ(y) PN (Sem. Cf. Grøndahl PTU 19, 105, 137; Marcus JSS 17 1972 78); ¶ syll.: ÌR-*ḫa-ya*, Syria 28 1951 173ff. 6 (RS 14.16):25.
PN: *bn PN*, 4.93 IV 10; 4.687:3.

ʕbdḥgb PN (Sem. Cf. Grøndahl PTU 105, 135; Jirku ArOr 37 1969 8; ArOr 42 1973 102f.; Astour JESHO 13 1970 11f.; Bordreuil - Caquot Syria 56 1979 311; Van Soldt SAU 32; Watson AuOr 8 1990 123); ¶ syll.: ÌR-*ḫa-gáb*, cf. PRU 3 p. 240; PRU 6 30:6 and *passim ibid.*; 38:19; Ug 5 58:3.
PN: 4.69 I 23; 4.769:10, 12 (*bn irpbn*).

ʕbdḫr PN (Sem. Cf. Grøndahl PTU 19, 105, 136; Jirku ArOr 37 1969 10; Bordreuil SEL 5 1988 29 n. 16; Muchiki Loanwords 278). Var. *abdḫr*, 4.33:36; 4.40:11.
PN: ★a) 4.318:1:5 (*bn bddn*); ★b) *bn PN*: 4.33:36 (*snry*); 4.40:11; 4.611:7.

ʕbdḫmn PN (Sem. Cf. Grøndahl PTU 105, 230; Huehnergard UVST 212, 240; Benz PNPPI 313; Bordreuil Semitica 32 1982 13; SEL 5

1988 26, 29 n. 15; Van Soldt SAU 19; Watson AuOr 8 1990 127; AuOr 14 1996 102); ¶ syll.: *ab-di-ḫa-ma-ni*, PRU 3 64 (RS 16.200):3; ÌR-*ḫa-ma-nu*, cf. PRU 3 p. 240; RSOu 7 3 (RS 34.036) mg. 2. Allographic var. *abdḫmn*, 9.461:20.
PN: 4.75 I 3 ([*bn*] *ybdn*); 4.93 II 18; 4.170:14; 4.177:3; 4.332:12; 4.617:17; 4.787:2; 9.461:20.

ʕbdkb PN (Sem.; unc. theonymic element; possibly a defective spelling of **kbb* "Kubaba"). Cf. *kbby*.
PN: *bn PN*, 3.3:12.

ʕbdkṯr PN (Sem. Cf. Grøndahl PTU 34, 105, 152; Watson AuOr 14 1996 102f.); ¶ syll.: ÌR-*ku*(?)-*ša-ri*, Ug 5 98:9.
PN: 4.151 I 3; 4.175:6; 4.177:8; 4.183 II 19; 4.194:21.

ʕbdlbit PN (Sem. Cf. Milik - Cross BASOR 134 1954 6f.; Grøndahl PTU 105, 154).
PN: 4.63 III 38.

ʕbdmhr PN (Sem. Cf. Bordreuil - Caquot Syria 56 1979 311; cf. Grøndahl PTU 156; Rainey IOS 18 1998 442).
PN: *bn PN*, 4.769:14.

ʕbdmlk PN (Sem. Grøndahl PTU 34, 105, 158; Van Soldt SAU 16, 126); ¶ syll.: cf. ÌR.LUGAL, cf. PRU 3 p. 241; PRU 6 28: rev. 5', 9'; Ug 5 p. 326; RSOu 7 2:3'; 3:rev. 11'. Cf. *ʕbdṯrm*.
PN: ★**a)** 3.2:9 (*bn amtrn*), 15 (*bn amtrn*); 4.75 III 2 (*bn śrn*), IV 8 (*bn ʕmyn*); 4.103:2, 16; 4.141:20; 4.214 IV 5; 4.244:6; 4.609:15; in bkn ctx.: 4.69 I 27; 4.81:6; ★**b)** *bn PN:* 4.412 III 25; 4.644:3; 4.714:6; ★**c)** *bt PN:* 3.4:9.

ʕbdn PN (Sem. Cf. Grøndahl PTU 52, 105f.); ¶ syll.: cf. *ab-di-na*, PRU 194 (RS 11.839):7; cf. *a*[*b*(?)-]*du-ni*, PRU 6 144:2. Cf. *ʕbdʕn*.
PN: 3.9:20 (*bn sgld*); 4.313:4; 4.339:19.

ʕbdnkl PN (Sem. Cf. Grøndahl PTU 34, 104f., 166f.); ¶ syll.: ÌR-*ni-kál*, cf. PRU 3 p. 241; PRU 4 201 (RS 18.02):5; Ug 5 6:31; ÌR-*ni-kal*, PRU 4 201 (RS 18.02):9; cf. Huehnergard AkkUg 382, 386.
PN: *bn PN*, 4.63 II 43.

ʕbdnt PN; cf. *ʕbd(ʕ)nt*.

ʕbdpdr PN (Sem. Cf. Grøndahl PTU 105, 171f.; Watson AuOr 8 1990 127); ¶ syll.: ÌR-*pí-dar*$_6$(TAR), Ug 5 7:14; cf. Huehnergard AkkUg 354; Van Soldt SAU 29 n. 236. Probl. rdg *ʕbdp<d>r* in 4.222:17.
PN ★**a)** 4.269:7; ★**b)** *bn PN:* cf. *ʕbdp<d>r*, 4.222:17.

ʕbdpr PN; cf. *ʕbdpdr*.

ʕbdrpu PN (Sem. Cf. Grøndahl PTU 105, 180); ¶ syll.: ÌR-*rap-i*, PRU 3 146 (RS 16.139):8; cf. Huehnergard UVST 249.

PN: 4.269:15; 4.609:33.

ʕbdrš̄ PN (Cf. Dietrich - Loretz KA 155; cf. Grøndahl PTU 16, 101, 104; Lipiński UF 20 1988 140; Watson AuOr 13 1995 226; AuOr 14 1996 103); ¶ syll.: ÌR-*di-ir-ši*, PRU 3 203 (RS 16.257+) IV 8; cf. DUMU-ÌR-*ir*(?)-*šu-na*, 195 (RS 15.09) A 5.

PN: 4.31:1.

ʕbdršp PN (Sem. Cf. Grøndahl PTU 105, 181; Watson AuOr 8 1990 127; Van Soldt SAU 19, 26f., 40f.); ¶ syll.: ÌR-*ir-šap(-pa)*, PRU 3 169 (RS 16.145):12, 16; ÌR-*ra-ši-ip*, Ug 5 98:8; cf. ÌR.MAŠ.MAŠ, cf. PRU 3 p. 241; PRU 4 234 (RS 17.112):18; PRU 6 p. 138; Ug 5 9:17, 19; ÌR.[d]NIN.URTA, Syria 28 1951 173ff. (RS 14.16):31 (cf. Van Soldt SAU 26 n. 204); PRU 4 231 (RS 17.123):16 and *passim ibid.*

PN: 4.222:9; 4.258:5; 4.298:5; 4.635:35 (*a*ḏ*dy*); 4.754:16 (*bn ġtr*).

ʕbdssm PN (Sem.; for the theonym cf. Grøndahl PTU 187; Caquot - Masson Syria 45 1968 317ff.; Fauth ZDMG 120 1970 229ff.; Sznycer RDAC 1984 117f.; Ribichini - Xella SEL 8 1991 166).

PN: 1.75:12.

ʕbdšḫ̮r PN (Sem. Grøndahl PTU 16, 105, 192).

PN: *bn PN:* 4.98:19; RSOu 14 46 [KTU 9.423]:10; cf. in bkn ctx. *ʕbdš*[*ḫ̮r*, 4.383:8.

ʕbdṯrm PN (Sem. Cf. Grøndahl PTU 105, 250; Van Soldt SAU 3, 14, 40); ¶ syll.: ÌR.[(d)]LUGAL-*ma*, PRU 3 74 (RS 16.283):6 and *passim ibid.*; cf. PRU 4 p. 252. Cf. *ʕbdmlk*.

PN: *bn PN*, 4.283(= 4.314):4.

ʕbdy PN (Sem. Cf. Grøndahl PTU 51, 105; Bordreuil - Caquot Syria 56 1979 311 n. 12; Syria 57 1980 384f.); ¶ syll.: ÌR-*ya*, PRU 3 71 (RS 16.295): 4 and *passim ibid.*; ÌR-*de*$_4$-*ya*, RS 23.22+ VI 8'; Van Soldt SAU 40, 310 n. 116.

PN: ★a) 4.775:16; ★b) *bn PN:* 4.50:10; 4.232:48; 4.628:6; 4.754:15; 4.769:64; 4.785:10.

ʕbdym PN (Sem. Cf. Grøndahl PTU 105, 144; Watson AuOr 14 1996 102); ¶ syll.: cf. (DUMU) ÌR.A.AB.BA, PRU 3 199 (RS 16.257+) A I 7", 16"; Huehnergard AkkUg 441.

PN: ★a) 4.7:7; 4.103:18, 47; ★b) *bn PN:* 3.3:10. In bkn ctx.: 4.341:3.

ʕbdyrġ PN; cf. *ʕbdyrḫ̮*.

ʕbdyrḫ̮ PN (Sem. Cf. Grøndahl PTU 21. 105, 145; Dietrich - Loretz WO 4 1967/68 304; Bordreuil -Caquot Syria 57 1980 364f.); ¶ syll.: ÌR.[d]XXX, cf. PRU 3 p. 241; PRU 6 p. 138; Ug 5 p. 326; Huehnergard AkkUg 403: Van Soldt SAU 17 n. 151, 19, 29. Allographic var.

ʕbdyrġ in 4.277:2.
PN: ★a) 2.45:18; 4.35 II 18 (*bn gṯtn*); 4.46:10; 4.75 II 11; 4.98:12 (Van Soldt SAU 38); 4.141 I 5 (Van Soldt SAU 38); 4.148:1; 4.226:6; 4.277:2; 4.339:10, 18 (*bn ṯyl*); 4.364:3; 4.609:18 (Van Soldt SAU 38); 4.658:24; 4.727:19, 22; 4.775:7; in bkn ctx.: 4.357:31; 4.584:4; ★b) *bn PN:* 4.424:22, bkn ctx.

ʕbk n. m. of a plant (cf. Akk. *abukat(t)u*, AHw 8; CAD A/1 81f.; Dietrich - Loretz - Sanmartín UF 6 1974 44; Cohen (- Sivan) UHT 37f.; UF 28 1996 144; Sanmartín AfO 35 1988 228). ¶ Forms: sg. *ʕbk*.
A plant, in pharmacology: *pr ʕbk* fruits of the *ʕb.*, 1.85:26.

ʕbl PN (Sem.(?); cf. Grøndahl PTU 29, 106).
PN: *bn PN*, 4.63 III 15; 4.90:8; 4.93 IV 17; 4.311:12; 4.412 II 33.

/ʕ-b-r/ vb G: "to pass, go through" (Hb. *ʕbr* HALOT 778ff.; Ebla cf. *ʕabārum*, ARET 5 61 (*a-ba-rí-im*, ge.; cf. Krebernik QuSe 18 102); cf. *a-bar-rí-iš*, Fronzaroli EL 133; cf. QuSe 18 104; Akk. *ebēru* AHw 182f.; CAD E 10ff.; ARM 27 303; Arab. *ʕabara* Lane 1936ff. Cf. cf. De Moor SP 156; Dietrich - Loretz UF 22 1990 69, 72). ¶ Forms: G suffc. *ʕbr*, impv. *ʕbr*.
G. To pass: *ʕbr iht np šmm* pass the islands / zones of the celestial peaks, 1.3 VI 8 and par.; *ʕbr gbl ʕbr qʕl* pass summits, pass heights, 1.3 VI 7; *ʕb(!)r l [ʕr] ʕrm* he passed from [town] to town, 1.4 VII 7.
Cf. ʕbr (I), ʕbr (II).

ʕbr (I) n. m. "passer-by" < "guest" (probl. < /ʕ-b-r/, ptc. G; Dijkstra UF 20 1988 46 n. 63, 49; diff.: Ribichini -Xella UF 12 1980 434ff.; 'difunto' < Hb. *ʕwbrym*; cf. Gordon PLM 31 n. 18: 'merchant', Hb. *ʕbr*). ¶ Forms: pl. *ʕbrm*.
Guest: *k ksp l ʕbrm zt ḫrṣ l ʕbrm kš* like silver for the guests was/were the olive(s), the dates like gold for the guests, 1.22 I 15.

ʕbr (II) PN (Sem.(?); cf. Grøndahl PTU 423); ¶ syll.: cf. *a-bu-ri*, RSOu 7 5:7.
PN: *bn PN*, 4.69 III 12; 4.116:14.

ʕbs, cf. *ʕp/bs*.

ʕbṣ (I) n. m. "mace" (cf. Arab. *ʕaḫb*, Lane 2071, with metathesis. Cf. Cassuto GA 126; diff. De Moor SP 106: 'to hasten', Aram. *ʕbq*; cf. Grelot JSS 1 1956 202ff.; JSS 2 1957 195; Jongeling JSS 17 1972 195; Gray LC 46 n. 4: 'grudge', Arab. *ʕabaqa*); ¶ par.: *ʕṣ*. ¶ Forms: sg. suff. *ʕbṣk*.
Mace: *ḥšk ʕṣk ʕbṣk* grasp your staff (and) your mace, 1.3 III 18 and par.

ʕbṣ (II) PN (Sem.(?); cf. Grøndahl PTU 106; De Moor BiOr 26 1969 106).
PN: *bn PN*, 4.617:40.

/ʕ-b-š/ vb "?" (etym. unc. Cf. De Moor SP 117: rdg *ṯbš*; Dietrich - Loretz UF 10 1978 434f.: rdg *ṯbš*; De Moor - Spronk CARTU 175: 'give substance', rdg *ṯbš* D; Ashley EAR 260: PN; Dietrich - Loretz TUAT 3 1312: 'verbünden'; Korpel UBL 12 100 n.3: 'to create', Akk. *epēšu*): ¶ Forms: prefc. *yʕbš*.
? : *ṯm yʕbš šm il mtm yʕbš brkn šm il ġzrm* there (...) the name of DN the mortal (heroes), (...) blessing him, the name of DN, the nobles, 1.22 I 6-7 (rdg unc.; cf. Pitard JNES 51 1992 266; BASOR 285 1992 57).

/ʕ-b-ṯ/ vb G(?) "to drain" ((?) < /ʕ-b-d/? Cf. Caquot TOu 2 97 n. 300; Pardee TPM 245: *ʕbṯ*). ¶ Forms: G(?) prefc. *tʕbṯhn*.
G(?). To drain(?), in unc. ctx.: *w tʕbṯnh abdy* and drained(?) the ruin from him, 1.107:7.

ʕby PN (Sem. Cf. Grøndahl PTU 29, 106); ¶ syll.: cf. DUMU *ab-bi-ya*, RSOu 7 3:rev. 13'.
PN: 4.371:16; in bkn ctx.: 4.604:3.

ʕd (I) 1) prep. "up to, until; close to, around"; 2) conj. "until; while, when" (Hb., Ph., OAram. *ʕd*, HALOT 786f.; DNWSI 825f.; Ebla cf. *a-ti*, Krebernik ZA 73 1983 36; QuSe 18 102; *a-dè*(NE), Limet SLE 65; ARET 7 204; /ʕadi=ma/ *a-ti-ma*, Fronzaroli MisEb 1 17; *a-di-ma*, Pettinato Rituale 181; Fronzaroli ARET 11 140; Akk. *adi*, AHw 12f.; CAD A/1 112ff.; but cf. Sima AfO 46/47 1999/2000 213ff.; ESA *ʕd*, *ʕdw/y*, DOSA 353; SD 12. Cf. Aartun PU 2 52f., 97f.; diff.: Gray UF 3 1971 66 n. 41; Dijkstra - De Moor UF 7 1975 183f., in some texts: 'moreover', 'again', Hb. *ʕwd*). ¶ Forms: *ʕd*; suff. *ʕdk*, *ʕdm* (encl. *-m*.).
1) Prep. ★a) up to, until, temporal: *ʕd šbʕt šnt* up to the seventh year, 1.19 IV 14; *ʕd ʕlm* until eternity / for ever, 3.5:14 and par. (RS Akk.: *adi dārīti*, etc.; cf. Van Soldt SAU 459, 461); local: *uṣbʕth ʕd ṯkm* (he washed ...) his fingers / arms up to the shoulder, 1.14 III 54 and par.; *ʕd ksm mhyt* up to the borders of the meadows, 1.5 VI 4; modal: *ʕd šbʕ (...) ʕd škr*, until satiety (...) until intoxication, 1.114:3-4 and par.; in unc. ctx.: *ʕd mġyy b ʕrm* until I reach the city(?), 2.71:16; ★b) close to, around: *ʕdk ilm (...) ʕdk kṯrm* around you are the gods (...), around you, DN, 1.6 VI 48-49 (diff. Virolleaud Syria 15 1934 239: 'témoin, garant', Hb. *ʕd*; Pope Fs. Finkelstein 172: 'comrade', **ʕd*, *ʕwd*; Gray LC 187 n. 9: 'associates, allies', **wʕd*). Cf. in unc.

ctx. *ʕd ruš*, 2.63:9.

2) Conj. ★a) until: *ʕd tšbʕ tmtḫṣ* until she was sated she fought (or: until satiety), 1.3 II 29 and par. (cf. *infra* 1.4 VI 55; 1.6 I 9); *ʕdn yštal ʕmnk* when he requires a reply from me, 2.71:10 (cf. Sivan UF 22 1990 311f.); *al atn ks[p lhm ʕd] ilak [ʕm mlk]* I shall not give them money until the king commands (...), 2.42:20; *ʕd tṯṯbn ksp* until they give back the money (?), 3.4:17; ★b) while, when: *ʕd lḥḥm šty ilm* while the gods ate (and) drank, 1.4 VI 55 and par.; *ʕdm [t]lḥm tšty* while you eat and drink, 1.15 VI 2; *ʕd tšbʕ bk* when she was sated with weeping, 1.6 I 9. Cf. in bkn ctx. *ʕd l hklh* (?) 1.19 IV 26 (cf. De Moor ARTU 262: 'returned [to his] palace'); *ʕd mġy[* until he arrives (?), 2.1:8; *ʕdh* 1.62:8; RSOu 14 49 [KTU 9.433]:35.

ʕd (II) n. m. "time, period" (/ʕ-d/ "to repeat, last" > "time, cycle"; cf. Hb., *ʕwd*, HALOT 795f.; DNWSI 825; Arab. *ʕāda*, Lane 2188ff. Cf. De Moor SP 148f.; diff.: Largement NA 46, 55: 'sanctuaire, grenier à provisions'); ¶ par.: *šnt.* ¶ Forms: sg. *ʕd.*

Time, period: *ṯmn nqpt ʕd* eight revolutions of time, 1.23:67 and par. (// *šnt*; diff. Gray UF 3 1971 66 n. 41: 'to number', 'enmity', Arab. *ʕadda*, *ʕadiya*); *b ʕd ʕlm* in perpetuity, 5.9 I 6 (cf. *bʕd*).

Cf. ʕdt (II).

ʕd (III) n. m. 1) "throne, throne-room"; 2) the 'testimony', a term for a cultic installation (Hb. **ʕd*, *ʕdwt*, HALOT 787f., 790f. Cf. Largement NA 46; Del Olmo AuOr 7 1989 28 n. 8; Renfroe AULS 17ff.; diff.: De Moor SP 161: 'platform'; Gulde UF 30 1998 308; Dussaud Syria 17 1936 61; Du Mesnil NE 93 n. 3: 'sanctuaire, édicule', Arab. *ʕawāḏ*, *maʕāḏ*); ¶ par.: *kḫṯ*, *ksu.* ¶ Forms: sg. *ʕd*; suff. *ʕdh.*

1) Throne, throne-room: *šbʕm yrgm ʕl ʕd* seven times it is recited in front of the throne, 1.23:12 (cf. *mt yṯb (...)* DN is seated (...) *ibid.* ln. 8; diff. Driver CML 141: 'lute', Arab. *ʕūd*; Tsumura UDGG 38: 'custom', Arab. *ʕādat*; Foley GG 40f.: 'assembly', Hb. *ʕdh*; Renfroe AULS 19: 'cycle', cf. *ʕd (II)*); *yṯb krt l ʕdh* PN sat on his throne, 1.16 VI 22 (// *ksi mlk*, *kḫṯ drkt*; cf. Renfroe AULS 17ff.).

2) The 'testimony', a cultic installation: *w tnrr b ʕd bt bʕl ugrt* and they shall be burnt in the 'testimony' of DN of TN, 1.119:9 (cf. Cunchillos EPHEA 93 1984 236).

In bkn ctx.: *b ʕd bʕlkm*, 4.17:16 (cf. *bʕd*).

ʕd (IV) element of the composite DN *ʕd w šr* (an attribute or a deified object; cf. *ʕd (II)* and *ʕd (III)*; cf. Del Olmo CR 182 n. 47 with ref. to Is 9:5-6; diff. Tsumura UF 6 1974 409ff.: 'Enemy (and Evil)' said of

Mot, cf. *mt w šr.*

Element of the DN: *ʕd w šr*, 1.123:13.

/ʕ-d-b/ vb G: 1) "to put, place, leave, set"; 2) "to prepare, arrange"; Š: "to order to be set up/make arrangements for" (cf. esp. "to leave" > "to place" / "to abandon"; cf. ESA *ʕḏb*, DOSA 354; SD 12; Hb. *ʕzb*, HALOT 806f.: *ʕzb (II)*. Cf. Hb. *ʕzb*, HALOT 807f.: *ʕdb (I)*; Akk. *ezēbu*, AHw 267ff.; CAD E 416ff. Cf. Ullendorff BHL 123f.; Van Zijl Baal 134f.; Dahood ULx 96f.; cf. diff. Dietrich - Loretz UF 17 1985 105f.; UF 25 1993 125ff.; Williamson ZAW 97 1985 74ff.; Renfroe AULS 20f.); ¶ par.: /y-t-n/. ¶ Forms: G suffc. *ʕdb*, *ʕdbt*; prefc. *tʕdb*, *yʕdb*; with suff. *ʕdbk* (for **aʕdbk*, cf. UT § 5.38), *tʕdbn*, *tʕdbnh*; impv. *ʕdb*; inf. *ʕdb*; with suff. *ʕdbk*, *ʕdbnn*; act. ptc. cstr. pl. *ʕdb*; pass. ptc. sg. *ʕdb*; Š prefc. with suff. *tšʕdbn*(?). G. 1) To put, place, leave, set: *l brkh yʕdb qṣʕt* on his knees he placed / left the arrows, 1.17 V 27 (// *ytnn*); *ʕm bʕl l yʕdb mrḥ* with DN he will not be able to set (> measure) (his) lance, 1.6 I 51 (diff.: Margalit ZAW 99 1987 395: 'to raise', Hb. *ʕzb (II)*); *šu ʕdb l špš rbt* take (and) place (them) next to the Great Lady, DN, 1.23:54 (cf. *šu ʕdb tk mdbr* take (and) place (them) in the holy desert, 1.23:65; diff. Dietrich - Loretz UF 17 1985 112: 'Gabe'); *arḫp (...) ʕl aqht ʕdbk* I shall fly about (...) above PN shall I place you, 1.18 IV 22 and par. (cf. Forms *supra*); *yʕdb u ymn u šmal bphm* they put (food) left and right into their mouths, 1.23:63; *ʕdbnn ank imr bpy* I myself put him (like) a lamb in my mouth, 1.6 II 22; *bʕdh ʕdbt tl̠t* behind her she shot (lit. placed) the bolt, 1.100:71 (// *sgr*, for other interpretations cf. Dietrich - Loretz UF 17 1985 113; cf. *ʕdbt*); *ʕdb uḫry mṭ ydh* (may) his cane be placed last, 1.19 III 56 and par. (?); for other interpretations cf. Del Olmo IMC 141f.; cf. *uḫry*, and Margalit UF 16 1984 156ff.: 'to raise', Hb. *ʕzb (II)*); *al yʕdbkm k imr b ph* he is not to place you like a lamb in his mouth, 1.4 VIII 17.

2) To prepare, arrange, place, grow, ★a) in gen.: *ʕdb gpn atnth* he / they prepared the harness of her she-ass, 1.4 IV 12 and par.; *yʕdb ksa w yṯb* he places a chair, and sits down (or: it is repeated), 1.100:7 and par.; *w yrd (...) ʕdb akl* and PN should down (...) to prepare food / grain, 1.14 II 27 and par.; *ʕdb imr b pḫd* prepare a lamb from among the yearlings, 1.17 V 16 and par.; *ʕdb dgn* those who grow grain, 1.16 III 13 (// *ḥrṯm*); *ʕdbt bhth bʕl yʕdb hd ʕdb (...)* the layout of his house did DN arrange, did DN arrange (...) 1.4 VI 39; *ʕṯtrt tʕdb nšb lh* DN prepared a slice(?) for him, 1.114:10; *yʕdb yrḫ gbh* DN prepares (his piece of) loin, 1.114:4; *yʕdb lḥm lh* he provides him with (a piece) of

meat, 1.114:7; *tʕdb ksu w yṯṯb* they prepared a throne and he sat down (on it), 1.4 V 46; *w yʕdb d b tkh* and he prepares what is within it, RSOu 14 53 [KTU 9.432]:28', 37'; ★b) in ritual terminology (with the meaning of an impersonal jussive): *w ynt qrt yʕdb l ʕnt* and one 'domestic' dove will be prepared for DN, 1.41:10 and par.; cf. in bkn ctx. *w ksp yʕdb* and silver is placed (for the offering), 1.50:11. Ctx. unc. 1.1 II 10, 11; III 9; 1.14 V 19; 1.176:10.
Š. To order to be set up: *w tšʕ[d]bn npṣh* and ordered his equipment to be set up, 2.31:50 (cf. Dietrich - Loretz UF 17 1985 109).
Cf. ʕdb, ʕdbt, mʕdb.

ʕdb adj. m. "available, ready, prepared" (< ptc. m. G /ʕ-d-b/; cf. Dietrich - Loretz - Sanmartín UF 5 1973 94f.; Dietrich - Loretz UF 17 1985 111). ¶ Forms: sg. *ʕdb*.
Available, ready, prepared, said of an estate: *šd PN ʕdb* the field of PN: available, 4.631:13, 19 (cf. *l / bd qrt*, *passim ibid.*).

ʕdbʕl PN (Sem. Cf. Grøndahl PTU 106f.).
PN: *bn PN*, 4.723:4.

ʕdbt n. f. "layout, arrangement" (< /ʕ-d-b/; cf. Gibson CML 154; diff. cf. Dietrich - Loretz UF 17 1985 112f.; UF 25 1993 128ff.: 'Werk; Bau, Haus'). ¶ Forms: sg. *ʕdbt*.
Layout, arrangement: *ʕdbt bhth bʕl yʕdb hd ʕdb ʕdbt hklh* the layout of his house did DN arrange, DN did arrange the layout of his palace, 1.4 VI 38.

/ʕ-d(-d)/ vb tD/tL: "to declare, respond" (Arab. *ʕadda / ʕāda*, Lane 1969ff., 2188ff. Cf. Van Zijl Baal 87; Caquot - Sznycer TOu 1 200 n. b; De Moor - Spronk CARTU 158; diff. Ginsberg ErIs 5 1958 62*; Held ErIs 9 1969 72* n. 15: 'to send (a message)'; Sanmartín UF 12 1980 345ff.: 'beteuern', Hb. *hʕyd*; Margalit MLD 39: 'to rise up', Hb. *ʕdd*); ¶ par.: /ṯ-b/. ¶ Forms: tD/tL prefc. *ytʕdd*.
tD/tL. To declare: *ytʕdd rkb ʕrpt* the Charioteer of the clouds declared, 1.4 III 11 (// *yṯb*). Bkn ctx. 1.5 IV 25.
Cf. ʕdd (I), ʕdd (II), yʕdd.

ʕdd (I) n. m. "herald" (< /ʕ-d-d/; cf. OAram. *ʕdd*, DNWSI 827f. Cf. De Moor SP 168; Gray LC 53 n. 3; Cody ZAW 93 1981 305; Renfroe AULS 87; Leslau JSS 11 1966 226f.; diff. Margalit MLD 69: 'custom', pl. 'taxes, duties', Arab. *ʕādat*; Sanmartín UF 12 1980 347: 'der für Verträge Zuständige', Sem. **ʕd*); ¶ par.: *dll*. ¶ Forms: sg. *ʕdd*.
Herald: *ilak (...) ʕdd l ydd il* I am going to send (...) a herald to the beloved of DN, 1.4 VII 46 (// *dll*).

ʕdd (II) PN (Sem. Cf. Grøndahl PTU 107; Sivan GAGl 205); ¶ syll.:

cf. *a-da-da*, Ug 5 13:3; *a-da-da-a*, PRU 3 145 (RS 16.139):4.
PN: 4.734:6.

]ʕdḫin, 4.608:23.

ʕdm, 1.15 VI 2, cf. *ʕd (I)*.

ʕdmlk PN (Sem. Cf. Grøndahl PTU 106, 158).
PN: 4.148:5; 4.214:7.

ʕdmn PN (Sem. Cf. Grøndahl PTU 53, 106f.); ¶ syll.: cf. *ad-du-mi-nu*, Syria 18 1937 247 (8.146 [= "8.213"]):33.
PN: 4.645:8 ([*bn*] *ynḥm*).

ʕdmt n. f. "desolation" (Arab. *ʕadima*, Lane 1975f. Cf. Bordreuil - Pardee Syria 59 1982 126; diff.: Pope Fs. Finkelstein 180: 'violent', Arab. *ʕadama*, but cf. Renfroe AULS 87f.; Gaster Fs. Rose 104 n. j: 'how long', Akk. *adi mati*, *admati*, Hb. *ʕd mty*; Caquot ACF 75 1975 429: 'cesser, faire défaut', Arab. *ʕadima*; also Xella TRU 286; De Moor ZAW 88 1986 344). ¶ Forms: sg./pl.(?) abs./cstr. *ʕdmt*.
Desolation: *ʕdmt w ʕdmt ʕdmt* desolation, yes, desolation of desolations!, 1.161:17.

/ʕ-d-n/ vb G/D: "to assemble, stock up, store" (denominative (?) of *ʕdn (I)*. Cf. Sauren - Kestemont UF 3 1971 197 n. 22; diff. De Moor SP 149: 'to appoint the time', **yʕd*, Aram. *ʕdn*, Arab. *ʕiddān*, Akk. *adānu*; Loretz SEL 12 1995 118: 'die Zeit festlegen', cf. *ʕdn (I)*). ¶ Forms: G/D prefc. *yʕdn*; inf. *ʕdn*.
G/D. To stock up, store: *wn ap ʕdn mṭrh bʕl yʕdn ʕdn ṯkt b glṯ* since thus DN will be able to store his rain, the abundance(?) of the *ṯ.*-boat in the snow, 1.4 V 6-7 (diff.: Margalit ZAW 86 1974 11 n. 35: 'trident', Arab. *ʕadana*; Dietrich - Loretz - Sanmartín UF 6 1974 33: 'Saison- oder Terminarbeiter'; Fensham JNSL 7 1979 22f.: 'seasonal labourer' **ʕdy*; Weinfeld SEL 1 1984 127 n. 4; Margalit RB 91 1984 108 n. 26; Smith UF 18 1986 314 n. 5: 'irrigating / watering / abundance', Aram. of Fekhireh *mʕdn*).
Cf. ʕdn (I), ʕdn (II).

ʕdn (I) n. m. 1) "store, silo"; 2) "abundance" (?) (Arab. *ʕaddana*, *ʕaddīnat*, *maʕdin*, Lane 1976f., preferable to **ʕdy* "réunir"; cf. Badre *et al.* Syria 53 1976 122; Fensham JNSL 7 1979 22 n. 53; 15 1989 87ff.: 'abundance'; for other opinions cf. /ʕ-d-n/); ¶ par.: *ḥḥmt*. ¶ Forms: pl. suff. *ʕdnhm*.
1. Store, silo: *kly lḥm b ʕdnhm* the grain in their stores was finished, 1.16 III 14 (// *ḥmthm*).
2. Abundance (?): *ʕdn ṯkt b glṯ* the abundance(?) of the *ṯ.*-boat in the snow, 1.4 V 7.

ʕdn (II) n. m. 1) "troop"; 2) "gang" (Arab. *ʕadānat*, Lane 1976. Cf. Badre et al. Syria 53 1979 108; Watson Or 48 1979 113; Bib 63 1982 256f.; diff. etym. in Renfroe UF 19 1987 233: 'expeditionary force' < */ʕ-d-w/y/ + *-n*; Wesselius UF 15 1983 313: 'north', from ctx.); ¶ par.: *skn*. ¶ Forms: sg. cstr. *ʕdn*; pl. *ʕdnm*.
1) Troop: *b ʕdn ʕdnm kn npl bʕl* against the crack troops thus DN fell, 1.12 II 52 (// *skn*); *ʕdn ngb w yṣi (...) w yṣi ʕdn mʕ* let the troops of victualling march off (...) and let the troops march off together, 1.14 II 32, 34 and par.
2) Gang: *ʕšt ʕšr b TN yd ʕdnm* eleven (*bnšm* workmen) in TN with (their) gangs, 4.358:8. In unc. ctx.: *ḥpr ʕdn dd akl* the ration of the gang is a 'cauldronful' of grain, 2.71:18.
In bkn ctx.: *ʕdn*[, 4.40:2; 7.61:14.

ʕdn (III) PN (Sem. Cf. Grøndahl PTU 52, 106f.; Astour CRRA 18 17; Lemaire Syria 58 1981 316; Van Soldt BiOr 46 1988 650; SAU 31, 441); ¶ syll.: *ad-du-nu*, RA 38 1941 4 (RS 11.856):16; PRU 3 150 (RS 16.188):6; PRU 4 184 (RS 17.319):25; Ug 5 52:25; 88:17'; RSOu 7 25:39; cf. RS 22.223 (Van Soldt SAU 441 n. 107); cf. *a-du-nu* and var., cf. PRU 6 p. 138; cf. *a-du-ni-*[d]U, PRU 3 196 (RS 15.42) II 20' (Van Soldt BiOr 46 1988 650). Cf. *adn*.
PN: ★**a)** 4.46:6; 4.63 I 8; 4.86:22 (*b*[*n*); 4.129:4 (Van Soldt SAU 35); 4.141 II 5 (Van Soldt SAU 38); 4.227 I 9; 4.261:7, 22; 4.343:9 (Van Soldt SAU 35); 4.378:4 (Van Soldt SAU 35); 4.398:12; 4.609:3 (Van Soldt SAU 38), 20, 27; 4.635:36 (*bn knn*); 4.658:19 (*bn šš*); 4.690:6 (*biry*); 4.729:8 (Van Soldt SAU 35); in bkn ctx.: 4.40:2; 4.332:4; 4.347:8; ★**b)** *bn PN*, 4.7:6 (Van Soldt BiOr 46 1988 650; SAU 31, 37, 41); 4.617:7, 34; 4.739:8.

ʕdr[4.227 II 9; 4.381:17; 4.388:9.

ʕdrš/ḏ 4.106:9.

ʕdršp PN (Sem. Cf. Grøndahl PTU 106f., 181).
PN: ★**a)** 4.134:8; 4.153:7; 4.269:17; 4.286:5; 4.307:17; 4.609:13; 4.690:4 (*bn šḫyn*); 4.783:5; in bkn ctx.: 4.147:1; ★**b)** *bn PN:* 4.52:3.

ʕdš/ṯ PN (etym. unc.; Arnaud AuOr 17/18 1999/200 153: 'lentille', Hb., Arab.); ¶ syll.: cf. DUMU(?)-*a-da-šu-na*, PRU 3 196 (RS 15.42+) I 20. PN: *bn PN*: 4.170:15; 4.261:12.

ʕdt (I) n. f. 1) "assembly"; 2) "confluence"; 3) "flowing current"(?) (< "meeting"; < */w/y-ʕ-d/; cf. Hb. *mwʕd*, *ʕdh*, HALOT 557f., 789f.; Aram. *ʕdh*, DNWSI 828; cf. Eg. *ʕá-du-tá*, Helck Bez. 510 (46). Cf. Macdonald UF 11 1979 523); ¶ par.: *mbk (+ nhrm), yblt*. ¶ Forms: sg. *ʕdt*, suff. *ʕdtm* (encl. *-m*).

1) Assembly: *ʕdt ilm* the assembly of the gods, 1.15 II 7, 11.
2) Confluence; *b ʕdt thmtm* at the confluence of the two oceans, 1.100:3 (// *mbk nhrm*; diff. Tsevat UF 11 1979 761: 'Thronraum', cf. *ʕd* (III).
3) Flowing current(?): *ʕdtm yʕdynh* with a flowing current(?) he made it disappear, 1.100:66 (// *ybltm*; diff.: Belmonte AuOr 10 1993 115: 'junco', Akk. *udittu*; Dietrich - Loretz Studien 364: *ʕdy* 'beschreiten, überschreiten'; for other opinions cf. Caquot TOu 2 292 n. 286).

ʕdt (II) n. f. "date, moment" (< *ʕd (II)*; cf. De Moor SP 160f.; diff.: Gray LC 51 n. 7: 'tools', Arab. *ʕuddat*; Margalit MLD 60: 'confluence', *ʕdt (I)*; Sanmartín UF 11 1979 725: 'besondere Konstellation', Akk. *ittu*, *idatu*; Mullen JBL 102 1983 212 n. 21: 'assembly', *ʕdt* (I)); ¶ par.: *ym*. ¶ Forms: sg. *ʕdt*.
Date, moment: *bnm ʕdt* on (this very) date, 1.4 VII 16 (// *bn ym*). In bkn ctx.: 1.16 V 5.

/**ʕ-d-y**/ vb D: "to make disappear / remove" (Hb. *ʕdh*, HALOT 789f.: *ʕdh I*; Aram. *ʕdy*, DNWSI 829: $ʕdy_1$; ESA *ʕdw/y*, DOSA 352ff.; Arab. *ʕadā*, Lane 1977ff.; Eth. *ʕadawa*, CDG 56f. Cf. Caquot TOu 2 92 n. 286); ¶ par.: /y-b-l/. ¶ Forms: D prefc. with suff. *yʕdynh*.
D. To remove / make disappear: *ʕdtm yʕdynh* with a flowing current(?) he made it disappear, 1.100:66 (// *yblnh*).

ʕdy PN (Sem. Cf. Grøndahl PTU 51, 106f.); ¶ syll.: cf. (DUMU.MEŠ) *ad-di-ya*, RSOu 7 3:rev. 9', 11'; *a-da-a-a*, 40:20 and *passim ibid.* Cf. *ady*.
PN: ★a) 4.124:15; 4.188:6; 4.273:8; 4.321:2 (*bn slʕy gbly*); 4.352:8; 4.364:5; 4.609:26; 4.617:28; 4.706:12; ★b) *bn PN:* 4.55:27; 4.93 II 16; 4.229:10; 4.366:9; 4.617:48.

ʕdyn PN (Sem. Cf. Grøndahl PTU 52, 107; Bordreuil - Caquot Syria 57 1980 364); ¶ syll.: *a-du-ia-nu*, PRU 3 195 (RS 15.09) A 20; Van Soldt BiOr 46 1988 650.
PN: 4.63 II 14; 4.86:13 (*bn uḏrn*[; cf. Van Soldt SAU 41); 4.159:6; 4.183 II 17; 4.417:12; 4.748:4; 4.775:4.

ʕḏbm, in bkn ctx.: 1.12 II 26.

ʕḏbt n. f. "squad, caravan" (cf. Arab. *ʕazab*, Lane 2033f.; cf. Hb. *ʕzbwn*, HALOT 808; cf. Del Olmo MLC 599; Dietrich - Loretz UF 17 1985 114f.; diff.: Gaster Thespis[1] 447, 450: 'band, company'; Driver CML 140: 'convoy', Arab. *ʕṣb*; Gray JNES 10 1951 149: 'vegetation', Hb. *ʕṣb*, Arab. *ʕušb*; Caquot - Sznycer TOu 1 208 n. y: 'marchandises importées', Hb. *ʕzbwn*; Gordon PLM 95f.; Gibson CML 154: '(building) wares'; Van Zijl Baal 122ff.: 'trading goods': Hb. *ʕzbwn*;

Dietrich - Loretz UF 25 1993 128ff.: 'Vorbereitungen', cf. *ʕdbt*; Margalit ZAW 99 1987 395 n. 23: 'ladders, scaffolding'); ¶ par.: *ḫrn*. ¶ Forms: sg. *ʕdbt*.

Squad, caravan: *ṣḥ (...) ʕḏbt b qrb hklk* summon (...) a squad within your palace, 1.4 V 14 and par. (// *ḫrn*).

/ʕ-ḏ-r/ vb G: "to help, rescue" (Hb., Ph., Pun., Aram. *ʕzr* HALOT 810f.; DNWSI 836; Palm., Aram. *ʕdr*, DNWSI 830f.; Amor. /ʕ-ḏ-r/, Gelb CAAA 15; Arab. *ʕaḏara*, Lane 1983ff.; ESA *ʕḏr*, DOSA 355; cf. Mari Akk. *ḫāziru*, AHw 339; CAD Ḫ 166. Cf. Baisas UF 7 1973 41ff.; diff.: Aartun UF 17 1985 7f.: 'Verteidigen', Arab. *ʕaḏara*); syll. Ug. cf. the element /ʕāzir-/ in PNN, cf. Sivan GAGl 206; ¶ par.: *plṭ*. ¶ Forms: G prefc. with suff. *yʕḏrk*.

G. To rescue: *w yʕḏrk* and may he help / rescue you, 1.18 I 14 (// *ypltk*).

Cf. ʕdr, ʕḏrt, bʕlmʕḏr, tʕḏr, y(ʕ)ḏrd, yʕḏrn.

ʕḏr, in bkn ctx., 4.86:18 (element of PN?).

ʕḏrt n. f. "help" (Hb. *ʕzr(h)*, HALOT 812; Syr. *ʕedrō*, LS 513; Amor. *ʕaḏrum*, Gelb CAAA 15; EA Akk. *izirtu*, AHw 408; CAD I/J 319; ESA *ʕḏr*, DOSA 355; Eg. cf. *ʕu-ḏá-r*, Helck Bez. 510 (49). Cf. Aartun UF 17 1985 7; Dietrich - Loretz MU 163); ¶ syll. Ug.: [DAḪ = *re*]-*e*(?)-[*ṣ*]*ú*(?) = *ma-zi-ri* = *i-zi-ir*[-*tu*$_4$], Ug 5 130 III 7'; Huehnergard UVST 53f., 158f.; Van Soldt BiOr 46 1989 648; SAU 306 (cf. Sivan UF 21 1989 360). ¶ Forms: sg. *ʕḏrt*.

Help: *ʕḏrt tk*[*n*? there will be(?) help[, 1.140:8.

/ʕ-g-d/(?) bkn ctx.: *tʕgd dqr*, 4.275:17. PN(?); cf. *dqr*.

ʕgl (I) n. m. "calf, bullock" (Hb., Pun., OAram. *ʕgl*, HALOT 784f.; DNWSI 824; Ebla ALIM = *ù-gi-lum*, VE 1192; Civil Biling. 90; Arab. *ʕigl*, Lane 1964. Cf. Sasson RSP 1 430f.; diff. Couroyer RB 94 1987 214ff. 'buffalo'); ¶ par.: *imr*, *bn (I) (+ ḫpṯ)*. ¶ Forms: sg. *ʕgl*, suff. *ʕglh*; fem. *ʕglt* (cf. *ʕglt*); pl. *ʕglm*.

Calf, bullock: *k lb arḫ l ʕglh* as the cow's heart (beats) for her calf, 1.6 II 28 and par. (// *imrh*); *arḫ tġġ l ʕglh* the cow lows for her calf, 1.15 I 5 (// *bn ḫpṯ*); *ʕgl il* Divine bullock, 1.3 III 44 (epithet of the monster *ʕtk*); *ʕglm dt šnt* one year old bullocks, 1.22 I 13 and par. (// *imr*); *aklt ʕgl* who consumes the Bullock, 1.108:9; *npš ʕgl* the soul of a bullock, 1.5 V 4 (cf. Del Olmo IMC 71ff.); *alp PN b TN (nn) ʕglm* head (of cattle) of PN in TN: (nn) calves, 4.783:2 and *passim ibid.* In bkn ctx.: 7.184:9.

ʕgl (II) PN (Sem. Cf. Grøndahl PTU 424).

PN: 4.658:8.

ʕglt n. f. "heifer" (< *ʕgl (I))*. ¶ Forms: sg. *ʕglt*.
Heifer: *yuhb ʕglt* he loved a heifer, 1.5 V 18.

ʕglt(n) PN (Sem. Cf. Grøndahl PTU 28f., 424; Van Soldt SAU 37). Var.(?) *ʕglt* in 4.340:20.
PN: *bn PN*, 4.131:12; 4.340:20; 4.410:36-39; cf. in bkn ctx.: 4.410:23.

ʕgm n. m. "groan, moan" (Hb. *ʕgm*, HALOT 785; Arab. *ʕağama*, Lane 1966; cf. Akk. *agāmu*, AHw 15; CAD A/1 142 and cf. Watson AuOr 7 1989 131. Cf. Dietrich - Loretz Fs. Elliger 34f.; Margalit UF 11 1979 543; for the various readings [: *r/p/agmm*] cf. Del Olmo MLC 291). ¶ Forms: pl. *ʕgmm*.
Groan: (he entered his room to weep) *b ṯn ʕgmm w ydmʕ* repeating his groans, (and) shed tears, 1.14 I 27.

ʕgml n. m. of a cultic installation of the palace ((?); perhaps related to the root *ʕgm*: 'room for lamentation'; Del Olmo AuOr 5 1987 262 n. 24; CR 108 n. 83 Xella TRU 65, cit. Job 30:25. Diff.: De Moor NYCI 2 15 n. 40; Dietrich - Loretz - Sanmartín UF 7 1975 145: mythical animal; Xella TRU 65: 'vitelli', metath. of *ʕglm*; Levine - De Tarragon RB 100 1993 95: rdg *tgml*, Hb. *tgmwl* 'present, gift'). ¶ Forms: sg. *ʕgml*.
Cultic installation(?): *yʕrb (...) tk ʕgml* (the king) shall enter (...) within the *ʕgml*, 1.41:9 and par.

ʕgrn(?) PN (rdg and etym. unc.; cf. Grøndahl PTU 108: *ʕgrt*).
PN: *bn PN*, 4.106:22(?).

ʕgw(n) PN (etym. unc.); ; ¶ syll.: cf. *a-ga*-Aʔ, PRU 6 86 II 3 (cf. 92:9'); DUMU *a-gu-wa*, Ug 5 5:28; *a-gu-a-nu*, PRU 6 78:1; *a-gu-wa-nu*, 29.100:3, 11 (cf. Van Soldt SAU 333 n. 161).
PN: ★a) 4.670:3; ★b) *bn ʕgw*, 4.90:4; 4.63 III 20; 4.63 IV 7; *bn ʕgwn*, 4.69 VI 15.

ʕgy PN (etym. unc.); ¶ syll.: cf. DUMU *a-gu-ya*, U 5 5:28.
PN: *bn PN*, 4.611:19; in bkn ctx.: 4.769:65.

ʕky (I) TN (Belmonte RGTC 12/2 6f.: *ʕAkkā*. Cf. Astour RSP 2 308; Lipiński OLP 12 1981 110f.); ¶ syll.: cf. URU *a-ki-yu*, PRU 6 79:18; cf. 81:6'(?); cf. Van Soldt SAU 336.
TN: 2.38:25; 2.82:4.

ʕky (II) PN (cf. *ʕky (I)*, TN. Cf. Grøndahl PTU 26, 108; Dietrich - Loretz - Sanmartín UF 5 1973 95; Watson AuOr 11 1993 218; Belmonte AuOr 17/18 1999/2000 15); ¶ syll.: cf. *ak-ku-ya*, RSOu 7 5:15.
PN: 4.63 III 37.

/ʕ-l/ vb Gp/N "to be suckled" > "to nurse, suck" (Hb. *ʕwl*, HALOT

797; Arab. *ʕāla*, Lane 2200ff. Cf. De Moor - Spronk, CARTU 159: N). ¶ Forms: Gp/N prefc. *yʕl*.
Gp/N. To be suckled > to nurse, suck: *yʕl šrh* he sucked his navel, 1.10 III 25 (cf. De Moor ARTU 115 n. 37).
Cf. ʕl (III).

ʕl (I) prep. of 1) spatial situation: "upon, on top of"; "next to, in the presence of"; "from"; 2) causal relationship: "for, because of"; 3) relationship of exchange or benefit: "against, on the account (of), charged to"; 4) sequential relationship: "on, after" (< n. m. "height, high part"; Hb., Ph., Pun., Aram., *ʕl*, HALOT 825ff.; DNWSI 844ff.; Arab. *ʕalā*, Lane 2144f.; Eth., *laʕla*, *laʕal*, CDG 304; OAkk. *al*, Akk. *el(i)*, AHw 200f.; CAD E 73, 89; Ebla cf. $al_{(6)}$ (MAḪ), Krebernik ZA 72 1982 181f.; QuSe 18 103; Limet EDA 66; ARET 2 119; 3 338; 4 285; 5 61; 7 204; 8 51; 9 377; MEE 10 206; Pettinato Rituale 181, 215; Fronzaroli ARET 11 138f.; cf. al_6-*a*, Fronzaroli ARET 11 139. Cf. Pardee UF 7 1975 328ff.; UF 8 1976 215ff. [279]; UF 9 1977 205ff.; Moscati ICGSL 121; Aartun PU 2 53ff.; Dahood RSP 1 292f.; Gordon UT § 10.13; Segert BGUL 78f.); ¶ par.: *bm tḥt (I)*. ¶ Forms: *ʕl*; suff. pn. *ʕlk*, *ʕlh*, *ʕln*, *ʕlnh*; extended ¶ Forms: *ʕln* (encl. -*n* prep.; cf. *ʕl (II)*); *ʕlt* (+ encl. -*t*); *ʕltn* (+ encl. -*t* + -*n*).
1) Situation or preeminence, ★a) upon, above, on top of, over: *w ʕl agn* and on top of the cauldron, 1.23:15; *ʕlh nšr*[*m*] *trḫpn* above him the eagles flew about, 1.18 IV 30 and par.; cf. 1.19 I 32; *ʕl* [*aqht*] *tʕdbnh*, above [PN] placed him, 1.18 IV 32; *hm tʕpn ʕl qbr bny* if they fly over my son's grave, 1.19 III 44; *ʕl išt šbʕd* seven times over the fire, 1.23:14; *ʕl pd asr* on top of a lock (of hair) they tied a ..., 1.19 II 32; *hlmn (...) ṯlṯid ʕl udn* he struck him (...) three times above the ear, 1.18 IV 34; *ʕlh k irbym kp* above her like locusts palms (of hands were flying), 1.3 II 10 and par. (// *ṯṯh*); *ʕl kbkbm* above the stars, 1.13:17; *ʕl tl k ʕṯrṯrt* over/above the hillock is like a diadem (?), 1.16 III 11 (// *bm*); *išḫn (...) nyr rbt ʕln* heat (up?) (...), Great Lantern, above him!, 1.161:19, cf. 1.6 VI 22 (diff.: Caquot - Sznycer TOu 2 108 n. 333: 'qu'en haut'; De Moor ZAW 88 1976 344: 'from above'; cf. *ʕl (II)*); *aḥdy d ymlk ʕl ilm* I am the only one who will rule over the gods, 1.4 VII 50 and par.; cf. [[t]]*qšm ʕl dl* the oppressors of the poor, 1.16 VI 48 ; *ymlk PN ʕln* PN will reign over us, 1.15 V 20, cf. *ibid.* ln. 23; with extended form *ʕln yblhm ḫrṣ* upon their rods of gold, 1.4 I 37; *ʕlk l tʕl bṯn* (so that) upon you the serpent does not climb, RSOu 14 52 [KTU 9.435]:3 (cf. ln 6.); *mth l tšlm ʕln* may his death bring well-being upon us!, 1.111:24 (Dietrich - Loretz ALASP 7 19); ★b) in, with (instrumental): *qḥ (...) rṯt ʕl ydm* take (...) a net in both

hands, 1.4 II 33; *ša ġr ʕl ydm* lift the mountain with / upon (your) hands, 1.5 V 13 and par.; ★c) in front, in command, in charge: *ʕbd mlk d št ʕl ḫrdh* official of the king placed in command of his guard, 2.47:15; ★d) next to, before, in front of, in the presence of: *bʕl qm ʕl il* DN was standing next to DN, 1.2 I 21; *yšr (...) ʕl bʕl* he sang (...) before DN, 1.3 I 21, cf. 1.17 VI 31; *ʕl abh yʕrb* he entered into the presence of his father, 1.16 VI 39 and par.; cf. 1.15 VI 6; *ʕlh ṯrh tšʕrb* into his presence she made his 'bulls' enter, 1.15 IV 17 and par.; *šbʕd yrgm ʕl ʕd* seven times it is recited in front of the throne, 1.23:12; cf. in bkn ctx. *ib ʕltn* the enemy before us, 2.39:31; *TN ʕlt* TN, next to, 4.271:9; ★e) from, from upon: *ʕl arṣ lan* [*isp ḥ*]*mt* from the earth everywhere remove the venom, 1.107:12 and par.; *km zbln ʕl rišh* as if it were the illness from his head, 1.16 VI 9; he hit *km zbln ʕl rišh* his head as if it were the illness, 1.16 VI 9. Unc. ctx.: 1.16 I 43.
2) Relationship of cause, ★a) according to: *ʕl hwt kṯr w ḫss* according to the words of DN, 1.4 VII 20; in unc. ctx.: *qšt yqb* [*yb*]*rk ʕl aqht k yq*[*bh*] he named the bow (?), blessed (it), for PN, yes, he named it (?), 1.17 V 35-36; *ʕlk*; ★b) because of: *bʕlm pht qlt* because of you DN I have seen prostration, 1.6 V 11 ff.; ★c) for: *ʕl qšth imḫṣh ʕl qṣʕth hwt l aḥw* for his bow I wounded him, for his arrows I did not leave him alive, 1.19 I 14-15 and par.; *ʕl alpm (...) tiṯṭmn w ʕl (...)* for two oxen (...) they went into debt and for (...), 4.398:2; ★d) responsibility: *d ʕlk mḫṣ aqht* upon whom weighs the death of PN, 1.19 III 52 and par.
3) Relationship of exchange or profit, on account, charged to (RS Akk.: UGU, *passim*; Van Soldt SAU 459f.), against: *kd šmn ʕl PN* a jar of oil on PN's account, 4.313:1 and par.; cf. 4.225:11ff.; 4.780:5ff.; 4.782:9, 13, 17, 21, 24, 28 (// *kd šmn PN*); *(nn) ksp ʕl PN*, (nn shekels) of silver on PN's account, 4.369:17 and par.; 4.632:2, 6, 10, 15, 20, 21; 4.381:18-22; 4.386:1, 10, 19; 4.135:2; 4.290:7; 4.781:6, 7; 4.782:3-4, 9-10, 17, 21-22, 24-25, 28-30; *mit ṯlṯ mḫsrn ʕl nsk TN* one hundred (shekels) of copper in deficit of the smiths of TN, 4.310:2; *arbʕ ʕṣm ʕl ar*, four trunks / logs on the account of TN, 2.26:10 and par.; various amounts and products *ʕl PN* on the account of PN, 4.123:2, 4-10; cf. 4.258:4, 8, 10, 14, 15; *w mnm šalm dt tknn ʕl ʕrbnm hnhmt tknn* and any claims they bring up, against these guarantors they bring them up, 3.3:7; expenses *ʕl hwt* on the account of the country, 4.779:11; *ipd ʕl PN* one *i.* on PN's account, 4.780:1, 3, 4, 7; *ʕl gtt* on the account of the farmsteads, RSOu 14 35 [KTU 9.388]:II 35; *ṯtb ʕl bṯnt trtḥ*[*ṣ*] you turned / shall turn against the female serpents (and) you shall wash yourself, 1.82:35.

4) Relationship of sequence, on, after: *(ym...) w ʕl y(!)m(!)* (on the day...) and on the (following) day, 4.279:2; *krpn ʕl krpn* cup after cup, 1.17 VI 6.
In bkn and unc. ctx.: *ʕl ydm prʕ*[, 1.1 IV 19;]*ʕln*, 1.4 III 52; *ʕl ḥbš x*[, 1.5 IV 22;]*k aṯtk ʕl*[, 1.15 V 23; *ʕl*[*n*, 1.19 II 45;1.19 IV 26; *dt ʕl lty*, 1.20 I 9; w *ʕl aḫ*[, 2.42:18;]*ʕln*, 4.154:2; *ʕl ṯnyx*[, 4.258:2;]*ʕl ʕb*[, ln. 14; cf. RSOu 14 49 [KTU 9.433]:22; RSOu 14 53 [KTU 9.432]:4.

ʕl (II) adv. 1) "above, on top"; 2) "next, in addition" (< n. m. "height, high part"; cf. Aram. *ʕl*, DNWSI 843f.): ¶ par.: *tḥt*. ¶ Forms: *ʕl*; suff. *ʕlm* (encl. *-m*), *ʕln* (encl. *-n*)., suff. *ʕlnh*.
1) Above, on top: *w ʕl tlbš npṣ aṯt* and on top she put on woman's clothing, 1.19 IV 46 (// *tḥt*); *w ʕl yṣhl pit* and above he made (his) temple(s) shine, 1.17 II 9; in the lengthened form: *ʕln pnh tdʕ* above her face sweated, 1.3 III 34 and par.; *bʕl ṯpṭn d in d ʕlnh* DN is our judge, above whom there is no one, 1.3 V 33 and par.; *tmll išdh qrn*[*m*] *d*(!)*t ʕlh* she caresses his legs, the horns that he has above, 1.101:7 (cf. Dietrich - Loretz UF 17 1985 129ff. (cf. Caquot TOu 2 49 n. 109). In bkn ctx.: 1.3 V 14.
2) Next, in addition (in the lengthened form *ʕlm*; diff.: Tropper UG 332: 'the following day'): *ʕlm tʕrbn gṯrm* next, the (two) DN enter, 1.43:9; *ʕlm tġz b ġb* in addition, a *t*.-offering in the *ġ*., 1.105:21, cf. ln. 3, 7, 11f.; *ʕlm ʕlm gdlt* next: two offspring of a cow, 1.109:32 (cf. *ʕl (II)*); *ʕlm yʕ*[*rb* next (the king) shall [enter, 1.41:8; 1.87:9; *ʕlm tṣul / tṣu šlḥm*[*t*] next, they gather / take out the provisions, 1.106:28; *w ʕlm ylk ġzr* and next, the lad will go, 1.175:14; *w ʕlm b qr*[and next in the pond (?), 1.164:10; *ʕlm š š*[*qr*]*b l* next, one ram will be offered to, 1.87:56; *ʕlm ṯn šm* next, two rams, 1.132:13 (in Hurr. ctx., cf. Dietrich - Mayer UF 28 1996 168); *ʕlm mḫṣm ḫsr* next, the beaters(?) are missing!, 6.48:4 (cf. Dietrich - Loretz ESTU 7). In bkn ctx.: *ʕlm*1.111:14; 1.136:13; *ʕlm kmm* next(?), ditto, 1.49:7; 1.50:6.

ʕl (III) n. m. "offspring" (Hb. *ʕwl*, HALOT 797; OAram. *ʕl*, DNWSI 843; Syr. *ʕûlō*, LS 516; Arab. *ʕayyil*, Lane 2201; Eth. *ʕewāl*, CDG 78. Cf. De Moor SP 224; Del Olmo BSA 7 1993 189; Huehnergard UVST 159); for RS Akk. ÙZ.MÁŠ.MEŠ Ú.LU, Ú.LU.ME, PRU 6 120:3,5, cf. Sanmartín BSA 7 1993 202; ¶ par.: *aḫ (I)*. ¶ Forms: sg. abs.(?)/cstr. *ʕl*; du. cstr. *ʕlm*(?).
1) Offspring, young (of animals (?)), calf(?): *ʕlm ʕlm gdlt l bʕl* next: two offspring of a cow to DN, 1.109:32 (diff. Herdner Ug 7 21: rdg *ʕlm* {*ʕlm*} *gdlt*).
2) Infant, said of members of a clan: *ʕl umty* my kin, 1.19 IV 35 and

par. (// *a<u>h</u>y*; diff. Margalit UF 16 1984 168ff.: 'suckling', taking *umt* as an allomorph of *um*). In unc. ctx.: *ʕlh yd d*[*nil* (...)]*xx ʕlh yd*, 1.19 IV 26 (cf. De Moor ARTU 262).
For 1.105:12, 21 cf. *ʕl (I)*.
Cf. ʕlln.

ʕl (IV) n. m. "yoke" ((?); Hb. *ʕl*, HALOT 827f.; Arab. *ġull*, Lane 2278; Akk. EA *ḫullu*, CAD Ḫ 230; DNWSI 843; Sivan GAGl 221 Cf. Dietrich - Loretz - Sanmartín UF 7 1975 168). ¶ Forms: sg. *ʕl*.
Yoke (?): *(nn) ʕl bd PN* (nn) yokes(?) in the hands of PN, 4.749:1-2 (cf. *alpm*, *ibid.* ln. 4; alternatively: calves, cf. *ʕl (II)*).

ʕlby PN (Sem.(?); cf. Grøndahl PTU 309; Watson AuOr 8 1990 123).
PN: 4.277:6.

/ʕ-l-g/ vb G: "to stutter" (Hb. *ʕlg*, HALOT 828; cf. Arab. *ʕalağa*, Lane 2128f. Cf. Caquot UF 11 1979 102 n. 3; Avishur UF 13 1981 23; diff. Zevit UF 13 1981 194f.; 15 1983 319: 'heavy'). ¶ Forms: G prefc. *tʕlg*.
G. To stutter: *al tʕlg lšnk* may your tongue not stutter, 1.169:11.
Cf. tʕlgt.

ʕllmn, cf. *ʕllmy/n*.

ʕllmy/n adj./n. m. "eternal", attribute of the *rpum* (< *ʕlm*; cf. Del Olmo IMC 42; Dietrich - Loretz - Sanmartín UF 8 1976 50; Healey UF 10 1978 86; Good UF 13 1981 118f.; Sapin UF 15 1983 177 n. 86; cf. Caquot - Sznycer TOu 1 307 n. c; diff. De Moor SP 117: 'child-of-whom?' > 'usurper', *ʕll + my/n* [cf. Virolleaud DA 97]; Sapin UF 15 1983 177 n. 86: 'pays des morts, enfers', Hb. *ʕlm*; Pope Fs. Finkelstein 170, 178f.: 'wise, savant', Arab. *ʕalāmiyy*). ¶ Forms: sg. *ʕllmy*, *ʕllmn*.
Eternal, ★a) adjective: *zbl mlk ʕllmy* the royal prince, eternal, 1.22 I 10; *<u>t</u>r ʕllmn* 'Bull- / Eternal King' (PN), 1.161:7 (cf. Del Olmo CR 194 n. 81); ★b) subst.: *b<u>t</u>t ʕllmn* the ignominy of the 'Eternal', 1.1 IV 5.

ʕlln PN (Sem.(?); cf. De Moor BiOr 26 1969 106).
PN: *bn PN*, 4.309:24.

/ʕ-l-m/ vb G/N: "to be hidden, be unknown, go unnoticed" (Hb. *ʕlm*, HALOT 834f.; cf. Eth. *ʕlm*, *taʕalma*, CDG 61). ¶ Forms: G/N prefc. *yʕlm*.
G/N. To be hidden, be unknown, go unnoticed: *rgm l mlk šmy w lh yʕlm* mention my name to the king, otherwise it will go unnoticed, 2.14:14.

ʕlm (I) n. m. "eternity, perpetuity" (often used adv.: "for ever", or in

a gen. syntagm: "eternal"; ESA *ʕlm*, Beeston SD 15; Arab. *ʕālam*, Lane 2140f.; Hb. *ʕ(w)lm*, HALOT 798f.; Ph., Pun., OAram., Nab., Palm. *ʕlm*, DNWSI 859ff.; cf. Thompson Fs. Vööbus 159ff.; Niehr Fs. Röllig 295ff.; Ebla cf. [d]*ì-lam*, Xella WGE 354); ¶ par.: *dr dr*. ¶ Forms: sg. abs. *ʕlm*; suff. *ʕlmk*, *ʕlmh* (adv. *-h*); pl. *ʕlmt* (?).
Eternity, perpetuity, ★a) (in adv. syntagms: "in perpetuity, for ever", etc.; cf. RS Akk.: *ana dāriti*, Kienast UF 11 1979 442f.): *ʕbdk an w d ʕlmk* your slave am I in perpetuity, 1.5 II 12 and par.; *att il w ʕlmh* wives of DN and this in perpetuity, 1.23:42 and par.; *l ht w ʕlmh* from now and for ever, 1.19 IV 6 (// *dr dr*); *ʕnt brḥ p ʕlmh* from now and for ever be a fugitive, 1.19 III 48 and par. (// *dr dr*); *ʕd ʕlm* for ever, in perpetuity 2.19:5, 15; 3.2:17; 3.5:14 (cf. 5.9 I 6, *b ʕd ʕlm*; Hb. *ʕd ʕlm*); 3.5:20; *ʕm ʕlm* for eternity, 1.3 V 31 and par.; ★b) in gen. syntagms > adj. "eternal": *ʕbd ʕlm* slaves in perpetuity > eternal, 1.14 III 23 and par. (cf. Hb. *ʕbd ʕlm*); *mlk ʕlm* eternal king, 1.108:1 and par., title of the divinized king (Pope UF 19 1987 458; Pardee TPM 89f.); cf. *nmry mlk ʕlm* Nimmureya (Amenophis III), eternal king, 2.42:9 (cf. Eg. *ḥq3 ḏt*, Gaál Fs. Wessetzky 97ff., title of Osiris); *tqḥ mlk ʕlmk* you shall take possession of your eternal kingdom, 1.2 IV 10; *šḥr ʕlmt* (until) the dawn of eternities / for ever, 3.5:15 (cf. Akk. *urra(m) šēra(m)*; AHw 1432); *rʕ ʕ lm* eternal friend, 5.9 I 11; *l špš ʕlm* to the eternal 'Sun', a royal and divine title, 2:42:7.
In bkn ctx.:]*ptr ʕlm*, 4.190:3;]*šd ʕlm*, 4.637:4.

ʕlm (II), cf. *ʕl (I)*, *ʕl (II)*.

ʕln, cf. *ʕl (I)*, *ʕl (II)*.

ʕlpy PN (Sem.(?); cf. Grøndahl PTU 309); ¶ syll.: cf. *il-pí-ya*, PRU 3 196 (RS 15.42+) I 19; cf. Huehnergard UVST 250.
PN: 4.205:20; 4.225:12; 4.617:22.

ʕlr PN (etym. unc.).
PN: ★a) 4.15:5; ★b) *bn PN:* 4.635:19.

ʕlṣ n. m. "rejoicing" (less probl. a verbal n.: "to rejoice"; cf. Hb., Pun. *ʕlṣ*, HALOT 836f.; DNWSI 863; Akk. *elēṣu*, *elṣu*, *ulṣu*, AHw 200f., 1410f.; CAD E 88, 110. Cf. Loewenstamm UF 3 1971 93; Caquot TOu 1 128 n. h); ¶ syll. Ug.: cf. the elements /ʕilṣ-/, /ʕulṣ-/ in PNN; Sivan GAGl 206f. ¶ Forms: sg. cstr. *ʕlṣ*; pl. *ʕlṣm*.
Rejoicing: *bʕlṣ ʕlṣm npr* with great rejoicing they left, 1.2 I 12.
Cf. ilṣy.

ʕlt cf. *ʕl (I)* 1.d.

/ʕ-l-y/ vb G: 1) "to go up, rise"; 2) "to attack, assail, launch oneself (upon)"; Š: 1) "(to cause / allow to) rise, raise"; 2) "to fire, shoot"; 3) "to offer"; Špass.: "to be mounted" (Hb. *ʕlh*, HALOT 828ff.; Ph., Pun. *ʕly*, DNWSI 852f.; Ebla cf. *li*$_9$-*ʔà-la-a*, Pettinato Rituale 205; Akk. *elû*, AHw 206ff.; CAD E 114ff.; ESA *ʕly*, DOSA 365; SD 15; Arab. *ʕalā*, Lane 2142ff.); ¶ par.: /h-l-k/, /r-k-b/, /y-ṯ-b/. ¶ Forms: G suffc. *ʕly*, *ʕl*, *ʕlt*, *ʕly*; prefc. *tʕl*, *yʕl*, *tʕln*, *nʕl*; impv. *ʕl*; Š suffc. *šʕly*, *šʕlyt*; prefc. *tšʕl*, *tšʕlyn*, *yšʕly*; Špass. prefc. *tšʕly*. Št ptc. pass. du. *mštʕltm* (1.23:35-36), cf. *mštʕlt*.

G. 1) To go up, rise, ★a) absol.: *yʕl w yškb* he went up and lay down, 1.17 I 14 and par.; *hm yrḫ b ʕl[yh] w pḥm nʕmn yk[n]* if the moon, when it rises, is reddish, it will be favourable, 1.163:12; cf. *ibid.* ln. 14, 16 (Dietrich - Loretz MU 187f.). ★b) + accus.: *qdš bʕ[l] nʕl* to the sanctuary of DN we shall go up, 1.119:33 (// *ntlk*); ★c) (+ *l*): *hyn ʕly l mpḫm* DN went up to the bellows (of the forge), 1.4 I 23; *w ʕl / ʕly l ẓr mgdl* and go up / he went up above the tower, 1.14 II 21 / IV 2 (// *rkb*); *l aršh yʕl* and let him go up to his bed, 1.17 I 38; *tʕln l mrkbthm* they went up to their chariots, 1.20 II 4 and par.; *ʕl l ṯkm bnwn* go up on top of the building, 1.16 IV 13; ★d) (+ *ʕm*): *w tʕl ʕm il* and she went up towards DN, 1.13:20; ★e) (+ b): *yʕl bʕl b ġr* DN went up onto the mountain, 1.10 III 11 (// *yṯb*; cf. ln. 27); *w tʕl bkm b arr* and next he went up onto (Mount) TN, 1.10 III 29; *yʕl b ṣrrt ṣpn* he went up to the heights of TN, 1.6 I 57 (// *yṯb*); ★f) (+ *lʕ*): *ʕlk l tʕl bṯn* (so that) upon you the serpent does not climb, RSOu 14 52 [KTU 9.435]:3 (cf. ln. 6).

2) To attack, assail, launch oneself (upon): ★a) absol.: *w hm ḫt ʕl* and if Ḫatti attacks, 2.30:17 and par.; ★b) (+ accus.): *hm mt yʕl bnš* if Death / DN attacks someone, 1.127:30 (diff. Dietrich - Loretz MU 36: 'verderben', * *ʕ(w)l*; cf. Del Olmo CR 95 n. 38); *w tʕl ṯh* and they will attack in the direction of TN(?), 2.33:37 (cf. *ʕly ṯh*, *ibid.* ln. 25); ★c) (+ ★b): *um ʕlt b ab* one (shocked) mother launches herself upon my father, 1.82:9 (cf. *ʕlt bk*, she launches herself upon you, *ibid.* ln. 10). In bkn ctx.: *w tʕl trṯ*, 1.17 VI 7 (cf. 1.5 IV 20).

Š. 1) To (cause / allow to) rise, raise: *tšʕlynh b ṣrrt ṣpn* she raised him up to the peaks of TN, 1.6 I 15; *tšʕly hwt* (that) she (DN) did not allow him to rise, 1.19 II 38.

2) To fire, shoot: *ḥẓk al tšʕl qrth* do not fire your arrows against the city, 1.14 III 12 (diff. Loewenstamm IEJ 15 1965 120 n. 20: Aram. *ʕll* (Š)).

3) To offer (cultic term.; cf. Akk. *šūlû*, AHw 209: *elû* (Š.2.h.); CAD E 130: *elû* (9.c.); Hb. *hʕly*, HALOT 830: *ʕlh* (Hif.4.c.); Pun. *hʕlʔ*, DNWSI 853: *ʕly*$_1$ (Yiph / Hiph 2): *šʕly dġṯt b šmym* he offered his ... offering to the heavens, 1.19 IV 30 and par.; *skn d šʕlyt ṯryl l dgn*

stele that PN offered to DN, 6.13:1 and par. (Dijkstra - De Moor UF 7 1975 175; Dietrich - Loretz - Mayer UF 21 1989 135); *pgr d šʕly ʕzn l dgn p.* (-sacrifice) which PN offered to DN, 6.14:1.
Špass. To be mounted (in a sexual sense): *tš[ʕ]ly tmn l tmnym* she was mounted eighty eight times, 1.5 V 21 (// *škb*); cf. De Moor SP 187; Watson NUS 35 1986 12.
Št. cf. *mštʕlt.*
In bkn ctx.: 2.22:8.
Cf. ʕly (I), ʕly (II), mʕlt, mštʕlt, nʕl, tʕlt.

ʕly (I) adj. m. "most high, exalted" (divine epithet; < /ʕ-l-y/; Hb. *ʕly, ʕlywn,* HALOT 832f.; Arab. *ʕaliyy,* Lane 2146f.; Ebla cf. AN.ŠÈ = *a-i-lum,* VE 782 and cf. Mander MEE 10 92; cf. *a/ʔà-lum* in Xella WGE 354; cf. Dahood ThSt 14 1953 452ff.; ULx 97; Richardson JBL 90 1971 260 n. 16); ¶ syll. Ug.: cf. A.Š[À.ḪI.A] ^d*a*(?)*-li-yi,* PRU 6 55:4'; Huehnergard UVST 160; ¶ par.: *bʕl.* ¶ Forms: sg. *ʕly*; pl. *ʕly*[*m*(?)].
Most High, exalted: *nʕm (...) w l šd mṭr ʕly* a delight (...) and for the field the rain of the Most High!, 1.16 III 8 and par. (// *bʕl*); *ytnm qrt l ʕly*[*m*(?)] glory (?) be given to the exalted ones (?)!, 1.23:3 (diff. cf. Gibson CML 154: 'on high'; cf. *qrt* for other interpretations).
Cf. adʕl, yrmʕl.

ʕly (II) n. m. "place of sacrifice, propitiatory" ((?) < a 'raised' cultic structure; < /ʕ-l-y/; Xella TRU I 68; Del Olmo AuOr 5 1987 260 n. 11; diff. Ward JNES 44 1985 329ff.; Del Olmo SEL 3 1986 56 n. 11: 'recámara superior', Hb. *ʕlyh,* Eg. *ʕr.t* (?), cf. Xella SEL 13 1996 19ff.; De Moor NYCI II 17 n. 54: prep. + *-y*; Dietrich - Loretz TUAT 2 325: 'Podest'); ¶ syll. Ug.: cf. A.ŠÀ.MEŠ(??) *e*(?)*-la-yi,* PRU 6 29:5; Huehnergard UVST 160. ¶ Forms: sg. *ʕly,* suff. *ʕlyh* (adv. *-h*).
Place of sacrifice, propitiatory(?): *w bt bʕlt bt*[*m*] *rmm w ʕly* [*md*]*bḥt* and (this in) the temple of the 'Lady of the Lofty Mansions', i.e., (in) the 'place of sacrifice' of the altar, 1.87:41 and par.; *b tdṯ tn* [*d*]*d šmn ʕlyh* and on the sixth (day): two cruets of oil in the 'place of sacrifice', 1.41:46 and par. (cf. 1.126:20); *š qdšh ʕly* [*ḫm*]*nh* one ram in the 'sacristy' in the 'place of sacrifice', in the *ḫ.*, 1.106:14.

ʕlyqm "?", 1.172:19 (bkn ctx.; rdg *ʕl yqm*?).
Cf. /q-m/.

ʕlyt "?", 1.176:6 (bkn ctx.: *ʕlyt dk/w*[).

ʕm (I) prep. 1) of direction: "to, towards, up to"; 2) of accompaniment: "with, together with, next to, before"; 3) in a commercial sense, "on the account of, to the credit of" (Hb. *ʕm,* HALOT 839f.; OAram., Nab. Pal. *ʕm,* DNWSI 867ff.; ESA *ʕm,* DOSA 370; SD 16f.; Arab. *maʕa,*

Lane 3022; Moscati ICGSL 121. Cf. Pardee UF 7 1975 329ff.; UF 8 1976 215ff.; UF 9 1977 205ff.; Aartun PU 2 56ff.; Gordon UT § 10.14 10; Segert BGUL 78). ¶ Forms: *ʕm*; suff. pn. *ʕmy*, *ʕmh*, *ʕmn*; Extended forms *ʕmm* (cf. 1.14 VI 37, encl. *-m*), *ʕmn* (encl. *-n*), *ʕmy* (encl. *-y*: 2.39:15); suff. pn. *ʕmny*, *ʕmnh* (+ *-y/h*).
1) Relationship of direction: to, toward, for, up to: *tḥm ydn ʕm mlk* message of PN to the king, 2.47:1; *w tʕl ʕm il* and she went up towards DN, 1.13:20; *ql bl ʕm il* take (this) request to DN, 1.100:2 and par.; *idk l ttn pnm ʕm il* thus, he set face for DN, 1.4 IV 21 and par., 1.2 I 14, 20; 1.4 VIII 2, 3, 4, 1.5 II 14; 1.6 IV 8; in the extended form *ʕmm*, 1.14 VI 37; *yṯb ʕm bʕl* he turned towards DN, 1.6 VI 12; *k ymġy* (...) *ʕm dtn* when he comes near (...) to DN, 1.124:2, 11; *at ʕmy l mġt* [... *w*] *mla*[*k*]*tk ʕmy l likt* you did not come to me nor did you send me your message, 2.36:10-11; *passim* with /l-ʔ-k/: DN *ylak PN* (...) *ʕm PN* sent PN (...) to say to PN, 1.24:16; cf. 2.26:4 (diff. Cunchillos TOu 2 316 n. 3: 'tu m'as fait une commande'); 2.33:36; 2.34:6 (cf. 2.14:8); 2.46:10; 2.42:11, 21; 2.39:18; 2.32:2; 2.30:18; 2.17:4; 2.45:25; 2.50:7; 2.14:8; 2.10:11; *ybnn hlk ʕm mlk amr* PN left for the king of TN, 2.72:26 (cf. *ʕmy špš (...) lm l tlk*, 2.39:15); *tlkn ṯn ṯnm ʕmy* repeat it to me, yes (do), 2.72:16; (he proceeded (?)) *ʕm aliyn bʕl* towards DN, the Victor, 1.6 V 10; *ʕmy pʕnk tlsmn ʕmy twtḥ išdk* towards me your feet hurry, towards me your feet hasten, 1.3 III 19 and par.; *ʕmy tṯṯb rgm* may you send me a reply, 2.16:19; *at ttb ʕm ʕbdk* you send (word) back to your servant, RSOu 14 50 [KTU 9.434]:20; *št b spr ʕmy* put it writing for me, 2.10:19; *yrdt (...) ʕm lẓpn il* she descends (...) towards the Benevolent, DN, 1.24:44; *ṣḥ hm ʕm nġr mdrʕ* they shouted to the guardian of the sown, 1.23:69; in a temporal sense: *ḥkmt ʕm ʕlm* your wisdom is for eternity (: eternal), 1.4 IV 42 (cf. 1.3 V 30: *ḥkm*<*t*>*k*).
2) Relationship of accompaniment: with, together with, next to, before: *hlny ʕmny kll šlm ṯmny ʕm umy mnm šlm* here with with me all is well, may all be well with my mother!, 2.13:9-12, *passim* in letters (cf. Cunchillos TOu 2 257ff.); cf. e.g. *ʕmny šlm kll* with me all is at peace, 2.16:15 (cf. 2.13:10 and par.); *hnny ʕmny kll mid šlm* behold here with me everything is very well, 2.11:11 (cf. 2.34:7 2.36:3; 2.39:3; 2.73:3); 2.29:17; 2.12:12; 2.72:7-8; 2.39:3; RSOu 14 49 [KTU 9.433]:9, 13, 29, 37; RSOu 14 50 [KTU 9.434]:10; *ṯ*]*mn ʕmk* [*m*]*nm šlm* there with you, whatever the situation, 2.65:3; *ṣḥn bʕl ʕm aḫy (...) ʕm aryy w lḥmm ʕm aḫy* invite me, DN, together with my brothers (...), together with my kin, to eat with my brothers, 1.5 I 22-24 and par.; *ik tmḫṣ ʕm aliyn bʕl* how can you fight with DN, the Victor?, 1.6

VI 25; *ʕm bʕl l yʕdb mrḥ ʕm bn dgn* with DN he will not be able to measure (his) lance, with the son of DN, 1.6 I 51-52 (diff. Dietrich - Loretz Fs. Craigie 113: 'vor'); *tant šmm ʕm arṣ thmt ʕmn kbkbm* the whispering of the heavens with the earth, of the abysses with the stars, 1.3 III 21 and par.; *ašsprk ʕm bʕl šnt ʕm bn il tspr yrḫm* I will make you count years with (: like) DN, with the son of DN you shall count months, 1.17 VI 28-29; *ṯlḫhw ʕmh bqʕt* PN (and) with her PN, 1.24:48; take *ʕmk šbʕt ġlmk (...) ʕmk pdry (...) ʕmk ṭly* with you your seven lads (...), with you DN, (...) with you DN, 1.5 V 8-11; *ʕmh trd nrt ilm* with her down went the Luminary of the gods, 1.6 I 8; *škb ʕmnh šbʕ l šbʕm* he lay with her seventy-seven times, 1.5 V 20; *iṯt ʕmn mlkt* I am with the queen, 2.13:15; *ʕmn nkl ḫtny* with DN is my wedding, 1.24:32; *pat ʕm mk<k>t grgrmš* the frontiers with the kingdom of TN, 2.75:8; (may the king, my lord) *bnš bǹny ʕmn mlakty hnd ylak ʕmy*, send me an intermediary with this my messsage, 2.33:34; cf. 2.17:7; *igr ʕm špš* I shall lodge with the 'Sun', 2.34:12; *mdy ʕmk* my cape with you, RSOu 14 51 [KTU 9.425]:16.
3) Commercial meaning, on the account of, to the credit of: *ʕmy mnm irštk...*, on my account (will go) any wish of yours, 2.41:15; *w kd ištir ʕm qrt*, and a jar remains on the credit of the city (: is owing to it), 4.290:3 (for other possible cases with this meaning cf. Bordreuil CRAIBL 1987 295).
In bkn and unc. ctx.: 2.76:4; 1.176:21; 2.81:19; 2.34:29; 1.15 I 4; 2.62:10; 2.77:17; 2.79:1.

ʕm (II) n. m. "lineage, ancestors" (Hb., Ph., OAram., Nab. *ʕm*, HALOT 837ff.; DNWSI 864ff.; Ebla cf. *a-mu*, Krebernik PET 72; cf. /ʕummānum/ in ÉRIN.KI.GAR = *ù-ma-núm*, VE 140; Krebernik ZA 73 1983 6; Sanmartín AuOr 9 1991 178; Amor. /ʕamm-/, Huffmon APNMT 196f.; Gelb CAAA 15; ESA *ʕmm*, DOSA 371; SD 16; Arab. *ʕmm*, Lane 2149. Cf. Dietrich - Loretz UF 10 1978 67f. n. 331; UF 19 1987 25; Good ShP 1983); ¶ **syll. Ug.**: cf. the element /ʕamm-/ in PNN; Sivan GAGl 202f.; ¶ **par.**: *ilib*. ¶ Forms: sg. suff. *ʕmy*, [*ʕmk*], *ʕmh*.
Lineage, ancestors (coll. use): *nṣb (...) bqdš ztr ʕmh* who erects (...) in the sanctuary the votive cippus of his ancestors, 1.17 I 27 and par. (// *ilibh*). Cf. *kdm ʕm mlkt* two jars for the lineage(?) of the queen, 4.230:4.
Cf. **ʕmlbu, ʕmn, ʕmnr, ʕmrpi, ʕmtdl, ʕmṯtmr, ʕmy, ʕmyd, ʕmyn, knʕn, mrʕm, nbʕm, šršʕm, ṯbʕm, yrbʕm, ytrʕm**.

/ʕ-m-d/ vb G/D(?) "?" (cf. Hb. *ʕmd*, HALOT 840ff.; Ebla /ʕamādum/ in AN.ÚŠ = *a-ma-du-um*, VE 787; cf. /ʕam(ā?)dum/ in AD.ÚŠ = *a-*

ma-tum, VE 1415; /maʕmadum/ in GIŠ.AD.ÚŠ = *má-ma-tum*?/*du*, VE 483; Krebernik ZA 73 1983 30; Fronzaroli EL 135, 145; cf. /ʕamidum/ in GIŠ.À = *a-me-tum*, Fronzaroli EL 136; cf. PN *a-mi-du* /ʔaʕmid(u)/, Müller Biling. 182; Akk. *emēdu*, AHw 211f.; CAD E 138ff.; Arab. *ʕamada*, Lane 2151ff.). ¶ Forms: G/D(?) prefc. (with suff.?) *yʕmdn*.
G/D(?). In bkn ctx.: *yʕmdn*, 1.7:34; in unc. ctx., *yʕm*[*d*]*n pn ʕṯtr*, 1.2 III 12.

ʕmd n. m. "support or foot of a wall" ((?); cf. Akk. *imdu*, AHw 375; CAD I/J 109f.; element /ʕimdu-/ in PN Alalakh Akk., Sivan GAGl 206. Cf. Caquot TOu 2 55. Cf. diff. Loretz - Xella MLE 1 1982 41: 'Bleibestätte', Hb. *ʕmd*; De Moor UF 12 1980 429: 'column', Hb. *ʕmwd*; ARTU 184: 'approaching person', Syrian Arab. *ʕmd*; Avishur UF 13 1981 18: 'ceiling beam', Arab. *ʕamada*); ¶ par.: *urbt*. ¶ Forms: sg. suff. *ʕmdm* (encl. adv. *-m*).
Support or foot of a wall(?): *w tṣu (...) k bṯn ʕmdm* and out you go (...) like a snake through the foot of the wall(?), 1.169:3 (// *urbtm*).

ʕmḏtmr, cf. *ʕmṯtmr*.

ʕmḏl PN.
PN: 4.165:8.

/ʕ-m-l/ vb G: "to earn" ((?) < "to exert oneself"; cf. Hb. *ʕml*, HALOT 845; Arab. *ʕamila*, Lane 2158ff.; cf. Akk. *nēme/alu*, AHw 776; CAD N/2 157ff. Cf. rdg and interpretation in Pardee BAfO 17 1982 48; diff. Caquot Ug 7 396: 'ouvrage'). ¶ Forms: G suffc. *ʕml*.
G. To earn(?): unc. ctx. *ksp ṯlṯt ʕml l adn* three shekels of silver he earned(?) for (his) master, 5.11:8.

ʕmlbu PN (Sem. Cf. Grøndahl PTU 109, 154).
PN: ★a) 4.165:7 (Van Soldt SAU 37); 4.260:10; 4.344:6 (Van Soldt SAU 37); 4.498:8; ★b) *bn PN:* 4.356:8 (Van Soldt SAU 37); 4.432:6.

/ʕ-m-m/ vb Gpass.: "to be covered, dark" ((?); Hb. *ʕmm*, HALOT 846; Arab. *ġamma*, Lane 2289ff. Cf. De Moor SP 172; Emerton Fs. Williams 41; diff.: Margalit MLD 71: 'turban'(?), Arab. *ʕimmat*). ¶ Forms: Gpass. suffc. *ʕmm*.
Gpass. To be covered, dark(?): *b ġlmt ʕmm ym* the sea is covered(?) in darkness, 1.8 II 8 and par. (cf. diff. De Moor SP 164: '[they] veil Yāmu'; Dijkstra UF 15 1983 29: 'kinsman of Yom', rdg *ʕm-m*, de *ʕm (II)*).

ʕmm, cf. *ʕm (I)* 1.

ʕmn (I) PN (Sem. Cf. Grøndahl PTU 52, 109); ¶ syll.: cf. *am-mi-na*, PRU 3 194 (RS 11.839):20.
PN: ★a) 4.317:6; cf. in bkn ctx. 4.178:4; ★b) *bn PN:* cf. in bkn ctx.

4.445:2.

ʕmn (II), cf. *ʕm (I)* 2.

ʕmnr PN (Sem. Cf. Grøndahl PTU 109, 165f.; Rainey UF 3 1971 171; Astour JNES 48 1989 37).
PN: *bn PN*, 4.222:21 (Van Soldt SAU 37); 4.356:3, 4 (Van Soldt SAU 37); 4.377:2; 4.432:10.

ʕmq (I) n. m. "valley" (Hb., Ph., Pun. *ʕmq*, HALOT 847f.; DISO 217; Emar Akk. *am-qu*, Arnaud AuOrS 1 11; EA Akk. cf. TN KUR(.KUR.MEŠ) *am-qí*, Sivan GAGl 206: *ʕimqu* / *ʕamqu*; Emar /ʕamqu/, Pentiuc Vocabulary 31f.; Helck Bez. 128, 272: Eg. *ʕá-m-qu*; Arab. *ʕa/umq*, Lane 2157); ¶ syll. Ug.: dḪUR.SAG.MEŠ *u a-mu-<qa->ṭ[u₄ / a-mu-q[u*, Ug 5 18:18; Huehnergard UVST 160f.; Van Soldt SAU 306; cf. AN.ZA.GÀR : *am-qa*, PRU 3 118 (RS 15.155):12; Van Soldt SAU 306 (cf. *ʕmq (II)*); cf. diff. Sivan GAGl 204; Huehnergard UVST 160; ¶ par.: *gn*, *qryt*. ¶ Forms: sg. *ʕmq*; pl. *ʕmqt*.
Valley, ★a) *w hln tmtḫṣ b ʕmq* and then DN fought in the valley, 1.3 II 6 and par. (// *bn qrytm*); *k ʕmq ytlṯ bmt* like a valley he ploughed (his) back, 1.5 VI 21 and par. (// *k gn*); ★b) element in DN: *ġrm w ʕmqt*, 1.148:6 and par. (cf. *supra*:syll. Ug.); ★c) element in TN: *gt ʕmq*, 4.625:9 (cf. *ʕmq (II)*; Belmonte RGTC 12/2 83: *Gittu-ʕAmqa*).
In bkn. ctx.: 1.151:14; 2.36:18.

ʕmq (II) adj. m. "tough, strong" (cf. Akk. *emūqu*, AHw 216f.; CAD E 157ff. and cf. *emqu*, AHw 215; CAD E 151f. Cf. Margalit UF 15 1983 86f.); syll. Ug. cf. AN.ZA.GÀR : *am-qa*, PRU 3 118 (RS 15.155):12 and cf. *ʕmq (I)*; Sivan GAGl 204; Huehnergard UVST 160; cf. diff. Van Soldt SAU 306. ¶ Forms: sg. *ʕmq*.
Tough, strong: *ʕmq nšm* the toughest of men, 1.17 VI 45. Cf. TN *gt ʕmq*, 4.625:9 (cf. *ʕmq (I)*).

ʕmqt DN; cf. *ʕmq (I)* b.

ʕmr n. m. "ash(es), dust" (etym. unc., cf. *ʕpr (I)*. Cf. Fenton UF 1 1969 69; Grabbe UF 8 1976 63; Emerton Fs. Williams 43; diff. De Moor, SP 191f.; Dijkstra - De Moor UF 7 1975 200 n. 241: 'ears of grain', 'sheaf', Hb. *ʕmr* HALOT 844f.; Caquot - Sznycer TOu 1 250: 'ordure', Arab. *ġamar*, Dietrich - Loretz UF 18 1986 105: 'Gras, Heu', Arab. *ġamīr*, Hb. *ʕmyr*); ¶ par.: *ʕpr*. ¶ Forms: sg. *ʕmr*.
Ash(es): *ʕmr un* ashes of grief, 1.5 VI 14 (// *ʕpr*).

ʕmrbi PN; cf. *ʕmrpi*.

ʕmrpi PN (Sem. Cf. Grøndahl PTU 17, 47, 109, 180; Stol SEL 8 1991 210; Van Soldt SAU 20, 784 and *passim*); ¶ syll.: *a-mu-ra-pí*(BI), PRU 4 208 (RS 17.226):4, 8, 10; RSOu 7 14:2; *am-mu-ra-pí*(BI), PRU

3 6 (RS 13.7 ★b):2; PRU 4 209 (RS 17.355):12, 16; Ug 5 23:2; cf. Van Soldt SAU 316f. n. 125. Var. *ʕmrbi* in 5.22:21.
PN: ★a) 1.161:31; 2.39:2; 2.76:2 11; 2.78:2; 4.707:22; 4.775:19; 5.22:21 (cf. Dietrich - Loretz KA 193) 9.530:2; ★b) *il PN:* 1.113:20; cf. *il ʕmph*, *ibid.* ln. 15.

/ʕ-m-s/ vb G: 1) "to load (with)"; 2) "to erect, build" (Hb., Ph., Pun. *ʕms*, HALOT 846f.; DNWSI 872; Amor. / *ʕms*/, Huffmon APNMT 198; Gelb CAAA 15. Cf. Heltzer StPh 4 239ff.; Emerton Fs. Williams 41f.); ¶ par.: /ʔ-ḫ-d(/ḏ)/, /k-l-l/. ¶ Forms: G prefc. with suff. *yʕmsnh*, *yʕmsn*{.}*nn*; impv. *ʕms*; ptc. pass. cf. *mʕms*.
G. 1) To load (someone with someone): *yʕmsn*{.}*nn ṯkmn w šnm* they loaded DNN with him, 1.114:18 (cf. Voigt UF 22 1990 412: *yʕmsnnn* 'die ihn trugen' (du) /yaʕmusāninnūni/); *ʕms mʕ ly aliyn bʕl* load me, please, with DN, the Victorious One, 1.6 I 12; *mnm ḫsrt w uḫy yʕmsn* with all that I lack, may my brother load me, 2.41:21 (cf. *ʕmsn*). Cf. *mʕms* (// *aḫd*).
2) To erect, build: *bt lbnt yʕmsnh* they shall erect a palace of brick, 1.4 V 11 (// *ykllnh*).
Cf. ʕms, ʕmsn.

ʕms PN (Sem. Cf. Grøndahl PTU 109; Heltzer StPh 4 1986 239ff.).
PN: *bn PN*, 4.335:3.

ʕmsn n. m. "load, cargo" (< /ʕ-m-s/). ¶ Forms: sg. *ʕmsn*.
Load, cargo: *spr bnš mlk d taršn ʕmsn b ṣr* register of the personnel of the king who negotiate(?) cargo in TN, 4.370:2 (cf. diff. Sivan UF 22 1990 315 and n. 28: PN).

/ʕ-m-t/ vb G: "to hit" (Arab. *ʕamata*, Lane 2150; Del Olmo MLC 601f.; Aartun UF 17 1985 10; diff. Delekat UF 4 1972 21: 'Blindheit', Arab. *ʕmy*; De Moor UF 11 1979 647 n. 48: 'to roll', Arab. *ʕmt*; Saliba JAOS 92 1972 109f.: 'squeeze', Arab. *ʕmt*; Badre *et al.* Syria 53 1976 124: 'entourer', Arab. *ʕmt*; Margalit UF 8 1976 157: 'to attach', *ʕmm*). ¶ Forms: G cprf. *tʕmt*.
G. To hit: *ḫṭm tʕmt pṭr* w with a rod he hit him (making) an aperture (for it), 1.16 VI 8.

ʕmtr ritual PN of the Ugaritic king (cf. *ʕm (II)*, /t-r/; Del Olmo CR 172: Niqmepaʕ or ʕAmmiṯtamru).
PN ritual: 1.102:20,23; 1.106:5.

ʕmṯdy PN/GN (unc.).
PN/GN: *aġty ʕmṯdy*[, 4.748:10.

ʕmṯtmr PN (Sem. Cf. Huehnergard JAOS 107 1987 714 n. 5; Dietrich - Loretz UF 19 1987 24f.; Watson AuOr 8 1990 123; Stol SEL 8 1991

210; Van Soldt SAU 784 *passim*); ¶ syll.: *a*-MIŠ(ŠID)*-tam-ru*, *am-mi*-IŠ*-tam-ru*, *passim*, cf. PRU 3 p. 239; PRU 6 p. 137; Ug. 5 p. 326; cf. *a(m)-mi*-IZ*-tam-ru*, PRU 3 62f. (RS 16.167):2; 64f. (RS 16.200):6; *a*[*m*-M]EŠ(?)*-ta-a*[*m-r*]*i*, o: *a*[*m*-ME-E]Š*-ta-a*[*m-r*]*i*, PRU 3 146f. (RS 16.153):2; *a*[*m*-M]EŠ(?)*-tam-ru*, o: *a*[*m*-ME-E]Š*-tam-ru*, PRU 3 165 (RS 16.384):2; cf. Huehnergard JAOS 107 1987 718 and n. 23; Huehnergard AkkUg 380f. n. 51; Van Soldt SAU 315ff. and n. 125. Var. *ʕmyḏtmr* in 6.23:2; 6.75:2.
PN: ★a) 1.161:11 (*mlk*), 25 (*mlk*); 3.2:2 (*bn nqmpʕ*); 3.5:2 (*bn nqmpʕ*); 6.23:2; 6.75:2 (*mlk ugrt*; cf. Bordreuil - Pardee Syria 61 1984 11-14; Van Soldt SAU 317 n. 125); ★b) *il PN*, in bkn ctx., 1.113:13, 22. In Hurr. ctx.: *ʕmṯtmrw*, 1.125:7.

ʕmtḏl PN (Sem. Cf. Grøndahl PTU 109, 309).
PN: ★a) 4.344:5; cf. *ʕm*[[*t*]]*ḏl*, 4.165:8 (cf. Van Soldt SAU 37); ★b) *bn PN*: 4.77:10.

ʕmy PN (Sem. Cf. Grøndahl PTU 51, 109); ¶ syll.: *am-ma-ya*, PRU 6 2:22.
PN: ★a) 4.16:4; 4.197:26; 4.399:8 (*bn mrzḥ*); 4.592:4; ★b) *bn PN*, 4.98:14; 4.117:6; 4.357:25 (cf. Van Soldt SAU 37).

ʕmyd PN (Sem. Cf. Grøndahl PTU 109, 133, 142; Dietrich - Loretz OLZ 62 1967 545).
PN: 4.344:3.

ʕmyḏtmr, cf. *ʕmṯtmr*.

ʕmyn PN (Sem. Cf. Grøndahl PTU 53, 109); ¶ syll.: cf. *am-mu-ia-nu*, PRU 3 192 (RS 12.34):36; *am-mi-ia-nu*, PRU 3 169 (RS 16.145):19; PRU 4 201 (18.02):15; PRU 6 38:18.
PN: ★a) 4.75 V 20 (*bn* [); 4.76:4 (*bn ġḥpn*); 4.232:36; 4.315:10; 4.727:5; 4.728:7; ★b) *bn PN*: 4.69 III 5; 4.75 IV 8; 4.77:11; 4.280:12 (cf. Van Soldt SAU 17, 139); 4.290:11 (cf. Van Soldt SAU 37); 4.356:5 (cf. Van Soldt SAU 37); 4.677:5; 4.755:9(?); 4.785:19.

/ʕ-n/ vb G/D(?): "to see, look (at), watch, spy" (denominative < *ʕn (I)*; cf. Arab. *ʕayyana*, *ʕāyana*, Lane 2214; Hb. cf. HALOT 817: *ʕyn*; Ph. cf. DNWSI 840f.: *ʕyn*$_3$. Cf. De Moor SP 234); ¶ par.: /ḥ-d-y/, /p-h-y/.
¶ Forms: G/D(?) prefc. *tʕn*, *yʕn*; impv. *ʕn*; with suff. *ʕnhn*(!).
G/D(?). To see, look (at), watch, spy: *w yšu ʕnh w yʕn w yʕn btlt ʕnt* he lifted his eyes and saw, and saw the virgin DN, 1.10 II 14-15; *hlk aḫth bʕl yʕn* the walk of his sister DN he saw, 1.3 IV 39 and par.; *ʕn gpn w ugr* look, DNN, 1.4 VII 53; 1.8 II 6 ; *yʕn pdry bt ar* he looked at DN, daughter of light, 1.3 I 23; *k tʕn zl ksp* when she saw the reflection of the silver, 1.4 II 27; *krpn l tʕn atrt* a cup that not even

DN looked at, 1.3 I 15 (// *l tphnh*); *mid tmtḫṣn w tʕn* she fought very much and watched (it), 1.3 II 23 (// *tḥdy*); *ʕnhn*(!) look after him!, 1.24:8 (diff. De Moor ARTU 143: 'her 'well'', cf. *ʕn (I)* ; *lksm mhyt ʕn* look towards the edge of the meadows!, 1.16 III 4; *yʕn krt ḥtkn rš* PN watched his lineage left ruined, 1.14 I 21 and par.
In bkn ctx.: 1.6 VI 9; *ʕn il*, 1.98:2. For {*wnʕn*}, 1.24:31, cf. *wn*.
Cf. ʕyn.

ʕn (I) n. f. 1) "eye"; 2) "spring" (Hb., Ph., OAram., Nab., Pal. *ʕ(y)n* HALOT 817ff.; DNWSI 839f.; Ebla /ʔaynay(a)/ < /ʕaynayn/ in *a-na-a*, ARET 4 286; IGI.DU$_8$.DU$_8$ = *ḫu-ma-zu a-na-a*, *ḫu-mu-zu* 2.IGI, VE 712; IGI.DAR = *dal-da*-NI 2.IGI, *dal-da*-NI*-um a-na-a*, VE 715; IGI.ÍL = *na-si-ì*(NI) *a-na-a*, VE 723; IGI.KÙ.DUB.IGI.GAR = *šà-a-du ma-ḫa-rí a-na-a*, VE 728; Krebernik ZA 73 1983 27f.; Fronzaroli EL 136, 143; Krecher Biling. 152; Castellino Biling. 367; Sanmartín AuOr 9 1991 180; Akk. *īnu*, AHw 383; CAD I/J 153ff.; Mari Akk. KÁ ḪI*-ni-im*, cf. Durand MARI 7 51 n. 38; EA Akk. *ḫe-na-ia*, EAT 144:17 and the element /ʕēn-/ *passim* in TNN, Sivan GAGl 206; Arab. *ʕayn*, Lane 2214ff.; Eth. *ʕayn*, CDG 79f.); ¶ syll. Ug.: cf. element /ʕēn-/ in PNN, Sivan GAGl 206; cf. Emar PN *ḫé-ni-e*, Wiseman - Hess UF 26 1994 506; for the spelling *e-nu*, Ug 5 153:3 cf. Huehnergard UVST 159: Ug.?; ¶ par.: 1) *qdqd*, *riš*, *yd*; 2) *brky*, *ġyr*. ¶ Forms: sg. *ʕn*; with suff. *ʕnn* (*-n* of determination); cstr. sg./du.(?) *ʕn*; du. abs. *ʕnm*, with suff. *ʕnk*, *ʕnh*, *ʕnkm*, *ʕnn*; pl. *ʕnt*.
1) Eye, ★a): *ʕn bʕl qdm ydh* the eye(/s) of DN precede(s) his hands, 1.4 VII 40; *ʕn bʕl aḫd*[[(fear(?)] affected the eyes of DN, 1.12 II 31 *qr ʕnk* the spring of your eyes, 1.16 I 27 (// *my*(!) *rišk*); *ašlw b ṣp ʕnh* I shall find rest in the glance of her eyes, 1.14 III 45; *w yšu ʕnh bʕl* and DN the Victorious raised his eyes, 1.10 II 13 and par.; *ʕnkm l bʕl tšun* raise your eyes to DN, 1.119:27; *b nši ʕnh w tphn* on lifting his eyes, then he saw her, 1.4 II 12 and par.; ★b) in incantations: *ʕnn hlkt* the evil eye, 1.96:1 (cf. Akk. *īnu lemuttu muttalliktu*, CT 17 33:5; CAD M/2 306); *ʕn bty ʕn btt (...) ʕn mḫr ʕn pḫr ʕn ṯġr* the eye of the evil-doing man, the eye of the evil-doing woman, (...) the eye of the potter, the eye of the tax-collector, the eye of the gatekeeper, 1.96:5-8 and par. (cf. Del Olmo CR 380 n.166); ★c) syntagms: *yn ʕn* wine of the eye(s), sparkling, 1.6 IV 18; *bn ʕnm* between the eyes / on the forehead, 1.2 IV 22 and par. (// *bn ydm*, cf. ln. 14 and par.); RSOu 14 53 [KTU 9.432]:35'; cf. *tply ṯly bn ʕnh* DN adorns his forehead, 1.101:5; *ylm bn* [*ʕ*]*nk ṣmdm* hit on your forehead with a mace (?), 1.82:16. In bkn ctx.: *d ʕnn* (...) what our eyes (...), 1.10 II 33; *nšb b ʕn*, 1.1 V 6 (cf. /ʕ-n-y/); *bn ʕnkm*, 1.3 VI 3; *bn ʕnh*, 1.2 IV 40; *w ʕnh*

b lṣbh (if it has...) and the other eye in the space between its eyebrows, 1.103+: 49, 57.

2) Spring: *šibt ʕn* the women drawing water from the spring, 1.12 II 59; *tḥt ʕnt arṣ* beneath the springs of the earth, 1.3 IV 36 (diff. De Moor ARTU 13: 'furrow', cf. *ʕn* (II)); *ʕn k ḏd aylt* the spring (for which yearn), in truth, the herd of hinds, 1.5 I 17 (// *brky*), 1.133:8 (// *brkt*); *bt ʕn bt abn bt šmm w thm* the 'daughter of spring, daughter of stone, daughter of sky and abyss', 1.100:1. In unc. ctx.: *aġwyn ʕnk (...)*, 1.82:42 (cf. Del Olmo CR 378 n. 157).

Cf. **ʕnmk, ʕnqpat**.

ʕn (II) n. m. "furrow" (Hb. *mʕnh*, HALOT 615; cf. Arab. *ʕinw*, Lane 2179. Cf. Gray LC 71 n. 3; De Moor SP 99f. n. 15; Dietrich - Loretz UF 10 1978 425); ¶ **par.**: *nrt*. ¶ **Forms**: sg. *ʕn*; pl. *ʕnt*.

Furrow: *pl ʕnt šdm* parched were the furrows of the fields, 1.6 IV 1-2 and par.; *bʕl ʕnt mḥrṯ* 'lord' of the furrows of the ploughed land, 1.6 IV 3 and par.; *nʕm l ḥtt b ʕn* it is a delight for the wheat in the furrow!, 1.16 III 9 (// *bm nrt*). In unc. ctx. *yṣq šmn* [...] *ʕn*, 1.16 III 2 (cf. Del Olmo MLC 315); in bkn ctx.: 1.3 V 137; 1.167:7.

ʕn (III) PN (< DN. Cf. Grøndahl PTU 110); ¶ **syll.**: cf. PN DUMU AN-*ni*, PRU 6 82:10-13; cf. Van Soldt SAU 38. Cf. *bn ʕn*, PN.

PN: ★**a)** cf. *ʕn*, 5.22:8 (Dietrich - Loretz KA 190 n. 146); ★**b)** *bn PN*: 4.33:32; 4.35 II 19 (cf. Van Soldt BiOr 46 1988 647; SAU 38); 4.232:47; 4.753:14; RSOu 14 46 [KTU 9.423]:8.

ʕnil PN (Sem. Cf. Grøndahl PTU 96, 110; Muchiki Loanw. 32, 219).

PN: 4.159:3.

ʕnbr PN (etym. unc.; cf. Grøndahl PTU 110).

PN: 4.617:29.

ʕnmk(y) TN (Belmonte RGTC 12/2 73f.: **ʕŽnu-makāy(yu)*. Cf. Heltzer RCAU 13; Virolleaud Syria 21 1940 126, 146; Dietrich - Loretz - Sanmartín UF 5 1973 113ff.; Astour UF 13 1981 7f.; RSP 2 309, 353; Van Soldt UBL 11 376f.); ¶ **syll.**: URU IGI-*ma-ka*, PRU 3 190 (RS 11.800):9'; RSOu 7 4:46; URU IGI-*ma-ka-ya*, Ug 5 102 6'; RS 25.455A (Arnaud SMEA 32 1993 128; cf. Van Soldt SAU 338f. n. 177.

TN: 4.68:52; 4.95:9; 4.113:6; 4.243:28; 4.244:3,9; 4.303:5; 4.365:38; 4.380:26; 4. 610 (II) 26 (Van Soldt UBL 11 376; Bordreuil UF 20 1988 12: *ʕnq[pat*); 4.693:54; 4.770:6; RS 94.2463:9 (*ʕn.mky*; Bordreuil Aniquités Sémitiques 2 61; in bkn ctx.: 4.94:14; 4.308:7; 4.621:17; 4.686:18. Bkn ctx.: *ʕn[mky*, RSOu 14 35 [KTU 9.388] II 12 (Bordreuil - Pardee RSOu 14 p. 352).

ʕnn n. m. 1) "manservant, servant"; 2) "herald, messenger" (etym. unc.; cf. /ʕ-n-y/ (I) > "the one who answers, speaks"(?); /ʕ-n-w/ > one "humiliated, made subject" > "slave, vassal"(?); Arab. *ʕanna*, Lane 2162ff. "to present oneself, intervene" > "representative"(?); Arab. *ʕawn* "help", Lane 2203f.; *ʕawwana* "to help", Hava 511, + *-n* > "assistant, helper"(?). Cf. Hb. *ʕnn*, 'cloud' > 'messenger, escort'; Hb. *ʕwnn*, > 'conjuror'; for the various opinions cf. De Moor SP 129f.; Van Zijl Baal 22, 102ff.; Good UF 10 1978 436f.; Gray UF 11 1979 322 n. 42; Wyatt UF 24 1992 422; Renfroe AULS 22ff.); ¶ par.: *ʕbd*. ¶ Forms: sg. *ʕnn*; pl.(?) *ʕnnm*; cstr. *ʕnn*, suff. *ʕnnh*.
1) Manservant, servant: *p ʕbd ank ʕnn aṯrt* but am I perhaps a slave, a manservant of DN?, 1.4 IV 59 (// *ʕbd*); *tn bʕl w ʕnnh* hand over DN and his servants, 1.2 I 35 and par. (// *ʕbdk*; cf. in unc. ctx. 2.8:4).
2) Herald, messenger: *w nġr ʕnn ilm* and pay attention, divine heralds, 1.4 VIII 15; *lk lk ʕnn ilm* go, go, divine heralds, 1.3 IV 32 and par. In bkn ctx.: *ʕnnm*, 7.135:3.
Cf. ʕnnn.

ʕnnn PN (Sem.(?)).
PN: 4.405:6.

ʕnq n. m. "necklace" ((?); Hb. *ʕnq*, HALOT 859; Akk. *unqu*, AHw 1422; Arab. *ʕunq*, *ʕanaq*, Lane 2175f. Cf. De Moor NYCI 2 12 n. 29; diff. Driver CML 141: 'ring-shaped loaf'; Aartun UF 17 1985 10f.: 'aufragende lange Gegend', Arab. *ʕunuq*, *miʕnāq*; Watson UF 31 1999 780: 'gem, bead', Eth. *ʕenqʷe*). ¶ Forms: sg. *ʕnq*.
Necklace(?): *yn* (...) *ʕnq smd lbnn* wine (...) necklace(?) of the flowery vines of TN, 1.22 I 19.
Cf. ʕnqt.

ʕnqpat TN (Belmonte RGTC 12/2 74: **ʕēnu-qapʔat*. Cf. Heltzer RCAU 13; Virolleaud Syria 21 1940 146; Dietrich - Loretz OLZ 63 1967 545; Astour RSP 2 309, 353; UF 13 1981 7; Van Soldt UF 28 1996 826; UF 29 1997 464; UF 30 1998 723, 737); ¶ syll.: URU IGI-*qáp-at*, cf. PRU 3 p. 266; RSOu 7 4:35; cf. Huehnergard UVST 248.
TN: 4.68:53; 4.296:11; 4.348:26; 4.365:20; 4.380:19; 4.610 (I) 12 (*ʕnqp<a>t*); 4.683:20; 4.685:7; 4.693:18; 4.698:4; "UF 29 826" (Lemaire UF 30 1998 461):9; RSOu 14 36 [KTU 9.417]:11; bkn ctx.: *ʕn*[*qpat*, RSOu 14 35 [KTU 9.388] II 12 (Bordreuil - Pardee RSOu 14 p. 352). Bordreuil UF 20 1988 12 reads *ʕnq*[*pat* in 4.610 (II) 26; Van Soldt UBL 11 376: *ʕnm*[*k(y)*).

ʕnqpaty GN m. (< *ʕnqpat*, TN). ¶ Forms: sg. *ʕnqpaty*.
GN: 4.86:27, 30.

ʕnqt PN (Sem. Cf. Grøndahl PTU 110).
PN: 4.175:11.

ʕnt (I) DN, name of the goddess, Baal's 'sister' (Amor. /ʕanat/, Huffmon APNMT 201; Gelb CAAA 15; Hb. *ʕnt*, HALOT 860; Akk. EA cf. PN *a-na-ti*, EAT 170:43; Hess AmPN 34; Eg. *ʕnty*, cf. Lüddeckens LÄ 245ff.; Stadelmann SPGÄ 91ff. Cf. Pope WbMyth. 235ff.; Dijkstra - De Moor UF 7 1975 193; Hvidberg-Hansen TNT 104ff.; Gray UF 11 1979 321f. n. 42; Van Zijl Baal 65; Caquot - Sznycer TOu 1 87 n. 1; Lambert VTS 40 132; Wyatt AuOr 5 1987 188ff.; Watson SEL 10 1993 48ff.); ¶ syll.: ^{d}*a-na-tu*$_4$, Ug 5 18:20 (// 1.118:20; 1.47:21); cf. ^{d}*a-an-t*[*u*$_4$, PRU IV 86 (RS 17.338) rev. 3'; 93 (RS 17.357) rev. 4'; cf. ^{m}DINGIR.IGI.AD, PRU 3 194 (RS 11.839):12, 16 and cf. Huehnergard AkkUg 400 n. 85.; cf. the element /ʕanat-/ in PNN; Sivan GAGl 204 (for ÌR.AN-*tù/ti*, cf. *ʕbdilt*). ¶ Forms: du. *ʕntm* (1.43:17, 20); suff. *ʕnth* (1.43:13).
DN: ★a) *passim* in narrative ctxs; cf. 1.3 II 3-30; ★b) epithets: cf. *bʕlt (+ ṣpn), btlt, ḫlš, ḫbly, slḫ (II), ybmt (+ limm),*; *bʕlt mlk bʕlt drkt bʕlt šmm rmm bʕlt kpt (...) di dit rḫpt (...) aklt (...) št (...)* Lady of royalty, Lady of power, Lady of the high heavens, Lady of the firmament, who flies winged, who hovers (...), who devours (...), who drinks (...), 1.108:6-9; ★c) *passim* in offering lists; cf. *dqtm w ynt qrt yʕdb l ʕnt* two ewes and one domestic dove shall he prepare for DN, 1.41:10; 1.87:12; *alp w š šrp l ʕnt* one head of cattle and one ram to DN as a burnt offering, 1.168:11; see *l ʕnth* to his DN, 1.43:13; *l ʕntm* to the (two) ND, 1.43:17, 20; in Hurr. ctx.: *ʕntd*, 1.110:7; 1.116:17; ★d) special syntagms: *ʕnt w ʕṯtrt*, 1.107:39; 1.114:22 (cf. the sequence *ʕṯtrt w ʕnt*, *ibid.* ln. 9); *ʕnt w ʕṯtrt inbb(h)*, 1.100:20.
Cf. ilʕnt, ʕbdʕnt, ʕntn, bnʕnt, šmʕnt.

ʕnt (II) adv. "now" (Hb. *ʕth*, HALOT 901f,; Aram. *ʕnh*, *ʕntʔ/h*, DJPA 412; cf. Knutson RSP 2 415ff.); ¶ syll. Ug.: unattested; for the spelling *at-ta* in PRU 3 (RS 15.11): 11 cf. Van Soldt BiOr 46 1989 648 (diff. Sivan GAGl 205); ¶ par.: *ht. ʕnt.* ¶ Forms: *ʕnt*; allomorph, with assim. suff. *ʕtn* (< /ʕvntv-n-/).
Now: *ʕnt (...) w ʕlmh ʕnt p dr dr* now (...) and for ever, now and for (all) generations, 1.19 III 48; *l ht w ʕlmh l ʕnt p dr dr* from now and for ever, from now and for all generations, 1.19 IV 6; *ʕnt akly* [*nšm*] now [men] are my food, 1.6 V 24 (Margalit MLD 185); *ʕtn ank ḫrd* I am already a soldier of the guard, 2.16:13 (cf. Stieglitz JAOS 101 1981 371 n. 7; Dietrich - Loretz UF 18 1986 113: 'zur Zeit', *ʕt + n*; diff.: Cunchillos TOu 2 301 n. 20: 'gardien', Arab. *ʕatin*; Márquez

AfO 45 1997/98 373: scribal error).

ʕntn PN (< *ʕnt*, DN. Cf. Grøndahl PTU 52, 111). Cf. *antn*, *bnʕnt*.
PN: ★a) 4.610:26; ★b) *bn PN*, 4.37:1.

/ʕ-n-w/ vb G: "to be / remain depressed, humbled"; D: "to humiliate, knock down" (Hb. *ʕnh*, HALOT 852ff.; Ph., JAram. *ʕny*, DNWSI 876f.; ESA *ʕnw*, DOSA 373; Arab. *ʕana*, Lane 2178ff.). ¶ Forms: G prefc. *tʕn*, *yʕn*; D prefc. *tʕny*.
G. To be / remain depressed, humbled: *w tʕn* yes, remain humbled!, 1.16 VI 58; cf. /ʕ-n-y/ (I)).
D. To humiliate, knock down: *aḥd ilm tʕny* I see, gods, that they humiliate you, 1.2 I 26 (diff. De Moor ARTU 32: 'to answer', rdg *a*(!)*ʕny*; cf. De Moor - Spronk CARTU 13; (his two opponents) *aqht yʕn* PN was knocked down, 1.19 I 12 (diff. De Moor ARTU 248: 'to say', cf. /ʕ-n-y/ (I)).

/ʕ-n-y/ (I) vb G: "to answer, say" (Hb., Pun., OAram., Nab. *ʕny*, HALOT 851f.; DNWSI 875; Arab. *ʕanā*, Lane 2180f.; cf. Akk. *enû*, AHw 220f.; CAD E 173ff.; Eg. *ʕá-ni-n<i>*, Helck Bez. 509 (34)); ¶ par.: /n-š-ʔ/ *(+ gh)*, /ṣ-ḥ/, /ṯ-b/ (Verreet MU 99ff.; Meier UF 21 1989 280ff.). ¶ Forms: G suffc. / inf. *ʕn*, with suff. *ʕnhm*; prefc. *yʕn*, *yʕny*, *tʕny*, *tʕn*, with suff. *tʕnyn*, *tʕnynn*, *yʕnyn*, *yʕnynn*; act. ptc. *ʕny*, with suff. *ʕnyh*.
G. To answer, say: *w ʕn aliyn bʕl* and DN, the Victorious, answered 1.4 VI 7 and par.; *w yʕn yrḫ nyr šmm* {*wn ʕn*} and DN, the luminary of the heavens, answered {answered as follows}, 1.24:30; *w ʕnhm nġr* and the guard answered them, 1.23:73; *w yʕn(y) aliyn bʕl* and DN, the Victorious, answered, 1.4 V 63 and par. with different subjects; *w yʕny bn ilm* and the son of DN answered, 1.133:1 and par. with different subjects; *w tʕn btlt ʕnt* and the Virgin DN answered, 1.6 IV 21 and par., with different subjects; *yʕn ġlmm yʕnyn* the lads answered, they answered as follows, 1.3 IV 5; *w tʕnyn ġlm bʕl* and the (two) pages of DN answered, 1.10 II 3; *bkm yʕny* weeping he answers(shall answer), 1.107:12 (cf. 1.1 V 7, 20); *tʕny* you must answer, 1.124:5; *w yʕny*{.}*nn dtn* and DN shall answer him, 1.124:13 and par.; *w ank ʕny* I myself am going to answer, 1.2 I 28; *in b ilm ʕnyh* there was no one among the gods who answered him, 1.16 V 16 and par.; *w tʕn (...)* [*tšu*] *gh w tṣḥ* and she answered (...,) // [she raised] her voice and shouted, 1.17 VI 52; *w ʕrbm tʕnyn* and the officiants answer him, 1.23:12 (// *yrgm*; or: "they chorus it"(?), cf. /ʕ-n-y/ (II)); *tʕny ank mlkt mntn* she answers: I am the queen of TN, RSOu 14 53 [KTU 9.432]:34'. Cf. bkn ctx. *aġwy ʕnk* I am going to

twist your 'responsible ones', 1.82:42 (cf. Del Olmo CR 378 n. 157); In unc. ctx.: *w yʕny* and he said, 1.16 III 1-2; [*w yʕ*]*nyh pdr* and DN answered him, 1.92:33.
Cf. mʕn, mʕnt.

/ʕ-n-y/ (II) vb G/D: "to sing, praise" ((?); Arab. *ġanā*, Lane 2302f. Cf. Hb. *ʕny*, HALOT 854. Cf. De Moor SP 93f.; UF 1 1969 224 n. 2); ¶ par.: /b-d/, /š-r/. ¶ Forms: G/D prefc. suff. *yʕnynn*.
G/D. To sing, praise(?): *nʕmn* [*y*]*ʕnynn* the handsome bard who praises him(?), 1.17 VI 32 (// *ybd*, *yšr*; diff. Dijkstra - De Moor UF 7 1975 189: 'to answer (the wishes)', *ʕny (I)*); *w ʕrbm tʕnyn* and the officiants chorus it/him, 1.23:12 (// *yrgm*; or: "answer him"(?), cf. /ʕ-n-y/ (I)).

/ʕ-p/ vb G: "to fly"; L: "to fly (around someone)" > "to attempt to seduce, bewitch" (Hb. *ʕwp*, HALOT 800f.; Arab. *ʕāfa*, Lane 2198; cf. *ʕawf*, *ibid.*; cf. eg. *ʕpy*, WäS 1 179. Cf. De Moor UF 1 1969 202 n. 6; ARTU 47; Aartun StUL 98f.); ¶ par.: /ġ-ẓ-y/. ¶ Forms: G prefc. *tʕpn*; inf. *ʕp*; L prefc. *tʕpp*.
G. To fly: *hm tʕpn ʕl qbr bny* if they fly over my son's tomb, 1.19 III 44; *w tr b ʕp* and she flew away, 1.10 II 11; *bʕl ymšḥ b ʕp* DN will anoint (them) with (the power to) fly, 1.10 II 23; *l mhrk w ʕp* yes, your wariors, fly!, 1.13:8.
L. To fly (around someone) > to attempt to seduce, bewitch: *tʕpp ṯr il d pid* she attempted to bewitch the Bull DN, the Bountiful, 1.4 II 10 (// *tġẓy*).
Cf. ʕpṣpn.

ʕp n. m. "bird" (< ptc. act. /ʕ-p/; Hb. *ʕwp*, HALOT 801; Syr. *ʕaupō*, LS 517; Eth. *ʕof*, CDG 78; cf. Ph. *ʕpt*, DNWSI 878: *ʕph*$_1$; Arab. *ʕawf*, Lane 2198). ¶ Forms: pl. m. suff. *ʕpmm* (with encl. *-m*); f. *ʕpt*.
Bird: *w ḫlq ʕpmm*[and may the birds perish[...!, 1.18 IV 42; *ʕpt šmm* the birds of the sky, 1.22 I 11 (cf. 1.23:62: *ʕṣr šmm*).

ʕpʕp n. m. "pupil (of eye)" (Hb. *ʕpʕpym*, Ginsberg LKK 17, 39, and cf. HALOT 861; Ebla cf. SIG$_7$.GI.ZI = *íb-íb-ba-tum*, VE 1204, MEE 3 68 III 6; cf. Civil EDA 151. Cf. Dahood ULx 97; RSP 1 301; diff. Dietrich - Loretz BiOr 23 1966 131: 'Wimpern'); ¶ par.: *ʕq*. ¶ Forms: pl. cstr. with suff. *ʕpʕpk*, *ʕpʕph*.
Pupil (of eye): *ʕpʕph sp trml* her pupils (are) alabaster bowls, 1.14 VI 30 and par. (// *ʕq*); *ʕpʕpk* your pupils, RSOu 14 53 [KTU 9.432]:5'.

/ʕ-p(-p)/ cf. /ʕ-p/, L (Pardee CS I 257 n. 135: Arab. 'to prepare drink').

/ʕ-p-r/ vb G. "to supply (something), to provide" (cf. Akk. *epēru*, cf. AHw 223: *epērum(I)*, correcting the etymology; diff.: Tropper UG

139, to *ʕbr*). ¶ Forms: G prefc. *tʕpr*.
G. To supply (something), to provide: *tʕpr* you will supply (it to the troops), 2.71:12.

ʕpr (I) n. m. 1) "dust"; 2) "earth, ground"; 3) "steppe" (Hb., Aram. *ʕpr*, HALOT 861f.; DNWSI 879; Syr. *ʕafrō*, LS 539; Akk. *eperu*, AHw 22f.; CAD E 184ff.; EA Akk. *(ḫ)aparu*, CAD A/2 166; Ḫ 84; Sivan GAGl 204; Gianto SEL 12 1995 68; Arab. *ʕaf(a)r*, Lane 2090; Eth. *ʔafar*, CDG 10; cf. Hb. *ʔpr*, HALOT 80. Cf. Dietrich - Loretz UF 18 1986 106); ¶ par.: *ugr*, *arṣ*, *ʕmr*. ¶ Forms: sg. *ʕpr*, pl. *ʕprm*.
1) Dust, ★a) in the physical sense, earth: *ʕpr plṯt* dust of humiliation, 1.5 VI 15 (// *ʕmr un*); ★b) meton. for 'tomb, underworld', etc.): *l ʕpr ḏmr aṯrh* who protects his remains from the dust, 1.17 I 28 and par. (// *arṣ*); *w b ʕpr qm aḫk* and in the dust (we shall pin) your brother's enemies, 1.10 II 25 (// *arṣ*); *d l ylkn ḥš (...) b ʕpr* who cannot go quickly (...) for the dust, 1.1 IV 8 (// *arṣ*; bkn ctx.); *špl ʕpr* plunge yourself, do, into the dust, 1.161:22.
2) Earth, ground: *w l ʕpr ʕẓmny* and to the ground (fell) my / our power, 1.2 IV 5 (// *arṣ*); *kry amt ʕpr* dig (...) (your) forearm in the soil, 1.12 I 24 (// *ugrm*; diff. Schloen JNES 52 1993 216: cf. *ʕpr (II)*); *ʕpr btk ygršk* may the dust of your house evict you, 1.82:12 (cf. *qr btk*, *ibid.* ln. 40, and De Moor - Spronk UF 16 1984 238).
3) Steppe: *št b ʕprm ddym* put harmony in the steppes, 1.3 III 15 and par. (// *arṣ*).
Bkn: 1.7:27; 1.167:6.

ʕpr (II) n. of a social group ("stranger, foreigner, refugee"; <(?) /ʕ-b-r/; cf. Bottéro Ḫabiru; RlA 4 14-27; DHA 6 1980 211f.; Kupper Nomades 249-259; Loretz Habiru; Von Soden UF 16 1984 364-368; Astour UF 31 1999 31-50; Akk. *ḫab/piru* (*ḫa*-BI/BIR/BI$_4$-*ru*), cf. AHw 322: *ḫapiru*; CAD Ḫ 84f.: *ḫapiru* (cf. AHw 304: *ḫabbātu(m)* I, II and Von Soden UF 16 1984 366); Akk. Mari cf. Durand Fs. Garelli 24 n. 27s.; Eg. *ʕpr(w)* WäS 1 181; Helck Bez. 486ff.; Hitt. (LÚ) *ḫa-(a/ab-)bi-ri-* (/ SA.GAZ)(*-ia-aš*, etc.), Bottéro Ḫabiru 71 and n. 2; Hb. cf. *ʕbry*, HALOT 782f.; Weippert Landnahme 66ff.; Loretz Habiru 89ff.; Moran AmL 392f.; Astour UF 31 1999 31ff.); Woudhuizen UF 26 1994 529: *kapari-*, Linear ★c); ¶ syll. Ug.: (oil) MIN (= UGU) PN DUMU PN *ḫa-pí-ri*, PRU 6 112:5; cf. Sivan GAGl 205, Huehnergard 161; Akk. RS: LÚ(.MEŠ) SA.GAZ, LÚ(.MEŠ) SAG.GAZ, LÚ.MEŠ SA.GAZ.ZA; cf. PRU 3 p. 219, 233; PRU 4 p. 260; PRU 6 p. 150; Huehnergard AkkUg 364, 366; cf. A.ŠÀ LÚ SA.GAZ [d]UTU-*ši*, PRU 4 108 (RS17.238)7; DINGIR.MEŠ *ḫa-pí-r*[*i*, PRU 4 88 (RS 17.349):9' (Del Monte Trattato 30); LÚ.MEŠ SA.GAZ *ša* AN.ZA.GÀR *im-ḫa-ṣu*,

PRU 4 162 (RS 17.341):2'; LÚ.MEŠ SA.GAZ.ZA *a-na* É*-ti-šu la-a i-ru-ub*, PRU 3 105 (RS 15.109 + 16.296):54; LÚ.MEŠ SA.GAZ.ZA *it-ti-ia ú-ul aš-bu*, PRU 3 3 (RS 16.03):6. ¶ Forms: pl. *ʕprm*.

A social group (stranger, foreigner, refugee): ★a) *bnšm d iṯ bd rb ʕprm* personnel that is at the disposal of the chief of the *ʕp*., 4.752:1; *ʕprm arbʕ mat* four hundred *ʕp*., 2.47:7; ★b) element in TN *ḫlb ʕprm*, TN.

Cf. ḫlb ʕprm.

ʕprt n. f. of an object or material (etym. unc., cf. *ʕpr (I)* or "lead"(?), Hb., Pun *ʕprt*, HALOT 863; DNSWI 879; cf. Akk. *abāru*, AHw 4: *abāru I, II*; CAD A/1 36ff.; cf. Bordreuil CRAIBL 1987 290: 'vêtements *eparattu*'). ¶ Forms: pl. *ʕprt*.

An object or material: *ṯṯ mat ʕprt* six hundred (pieces / shekels(?) of) *ʕprt*, 4.780:9.

ʕp/bs n. m. "landmark, boundary(?)" (cf. Van Soldt UF 21 1989 385: Akk. *kudurru*; etym. unc., NABU 1997 90: EA 366:34; Tropper UF 29 1997 666f.; cf. Hitt. NA_4 *ḫuwaši* "stele" Darga RHA 27 1969 17; Güterbock Fs. Bittel 215f.; Tischler HEG 333f., also used as a boundary stone: Imparati RHA 32 1974 125-135); ¶ RS Akk.: cf. NA_4.MEŠ, PRU 4 p. 77 (RS 17.368) rev. 7'. ¶ Forms: sg. *ʕb/ps*; pl. *ʕpsm*.

Landmark, boundary(?), ★a): *spr ʕpsm dt št uryn l mlk ugrt* document about the landmarks(?) which the *u.* set up for the king of TN, 6.29:1 (cf. LÚ *ú-ri-ia-an-nu (...)* NA_4.MEŠ *i-na* ZAG.MEŠ *(...) il-ta-ka-an*, PRU 4 p. 77 (RS 17.368) rev. 7'); *mṣmt ʕbs arr* treaty concerning the boundaries(?) of TN(?), 6.27:1 (cf. Van Soldt UF 21 1989 380, 384); ★b) syntagms: *ḫrd ʕps* frontier guard(?): *ḫrd ʕps aḫd kw sʕt* the border guard(?) has confiscated one *k.* of *s.*-(grain), 2.47:17; cf. in bkn ctx. *ḫrdk ʕps* [, *ibid.* ln. 19 (cf. diff. Dietrich - Loretz UF 19 1987 29: *ḫrd ʕps* 'der rebellische Wachsoldat').

In bkn ctx.: *mn ʕps* [, RSOu 14 51 [KTU 9.425]:14 (for discussion cf. Bordreuil - Pardee RSOu 14 pp. 384f.: 'retenir(?)').

Cf. ʕpsn.

ʕpsn PN (etym. unc.).

PN: 4.170:6.

ʕpṣpn PN (Sem. Cf. Grøndahl PTU 37f., 111, 189).

PN: 4.366:9 (*bn ʕdy*).

ʕpt, cf. *ʕp*.

ʕpṯb PN (etym. unc.).

PN: *bn PN*, 4.617:17.

ʕpṯn PN (etym. unc.; cf. Grøndahl PTU 309; Berger WO 5 1969/70 281).
PN: 4.35 I 4 (*bn ṯsq*[); 4.46:9; 4.98:9; 4.366:11 (*bn ilrš*); 4.370:44.

ʕpṯrm PN (etym. unc.; cf. Grøndahl PTU 309; Berger WO 5 1969/70 281; Dietrich - Loretz - Sanmartín UF 5 1973 95; UF 6 1974 34; Dietrich - Loretz UF 10 1978 423).
PN: 4.116:5; 4.350:10 (*bn agmz*); 4.609:10; 4.628:6 (*bn ʕbdy*).

ʕq n. m.(?) "pupil" (etym. unc.; cf. Arab. *ʕaqq* "a deep excavation" / *ʕaqīq*, various kinds of precious stones, Lane 2096. Cf. Herdner TOu 1 525 n. c; diff. Tsumura UF 6 1974 411 n. 38: 'eyebrow'; Pedersen KL 101: 'diadem', Akk. *agû*; in general cf. Renfroe AULS 88f.); ¶ par.: *ʕpʕp*. ¶ Forms: sg. suff. *ʕq*.
Pupil: *d ʕqh ib iqni* whose pupils are gems of lapis lazuli, 1.14 III 43 and par. (// *ʕpʕph*).
Cf. ʕqy.

/ʕ-q-b/ vb G: "to accept or perform a property transfer, to succeed, to effect an exchange of goods"; D: "to place obstacles, traps, to oppose" (ESA, Arab. *ʕqb*, CAME 211f.; DOSA 379; Lane 2097; denom. < *ʕqb*; cf. Hb. *ʕqb*, HALOT 872f.; JAram., Syr. *ʕqb*, Jastrow 1104; LS 541f.; Eth. *ʕaqaba*, CDG 66; Amor. cf. /ʕ-q-b/, Huffmon APNMT 203f.; Gelb CAAA 15); ¶ syll. Ug.: *vacat* (rdg *ia/na-du-* in the spellings *ia/na*-DU- of PNN; cf. Rainey IOS 5 1975 29; Huehnergard AkkUg 374; JAOS 107 1987 722; diff. Sivan GAGl 207: *ia-qub-*). ¶ Forms: G suffc. *ʕqb*; D ptc. suff. *mʕqbk*.
G. To accept or perform a property transfer, to succeed, to effect an exchange of goods: *šd snrym dt ʕqb b ayly* farms of the GNN who have accepted / performed a (property) transfer in TN, 4.645:1 (diff.: Dietrich - Loretz BiOr 23 1966 131: 'direkt folgen auf' > 'benachbart, nahe sein' > 'sich anschliessen'; Pardee UF 7 1975 364; UF 8 1976 261: 'to be rough, hilly in (??)').
D. To place obstacles, traps, to oppose; cf. *mʕqb (I)*.
Cf. mʕqb (I), (II).

ʕqb n. m./f.(?), "hock, heel" (Hb., Aram. *ʕqb*, HALOT 872f.; DNSWI 881; JAram. *ʕqbh*, Jastrow 1104; Akk. *eqbu*, AHw 231; CAD E 248f.; Arab. *ʕaqib* / *ʕaqb*, Lane 2100f. Cf. Aartun StUL 99ff.); ¶ par.: *gd*, *qrn*. ¶ Forms: pl. *ʕqbt*.
Hock, heel: *mtnm b ʕqbt ṯr* tendons from the hocks of a bull, 1.17 VI 23 (// *gd*, *qrn*).

ʕq[l] "?" (Dietrich - Loretz MU 154 n. 470: 'verkrüppelt ist', or rdg *ʕq*[*r*] 'Bereich des Untauglichsein').

? : unc. rdg *w ʕq[l*(?)], 1.103+:56.

ʕqltn adj. m. “winding” (Hb. *ʕqltwn*, HALOT 874; Syr. *ʕūqolō*, LS 542; cf. Arab. *ʕaqala*, Lane 2113ss); ¶ par.: *brḥ* (cf. Renfroe UF 20 1988 227 n. 29). ¶ Forms: sg. *ʕqltn*.

Winding: *tkly btn ʕqltn* you finished off the winding serpent, 1.5 I 2 and par. (// *brḥ*; cf. Hb. *nḥš ʕqltwn*, Is 27:1).

ʕqq n. m. “destructive (one)”, divine epithet (< ptc. m. G /ʕ-q-q/, cf. Arab. *ʕaqqa*, Lane 2095ff. Cf. Oldenburg CEB 200 n. 6; Renfroe AULS 24ff.; diff. Watson NUS 30 1983 12: ‘deformed’, Akk. *eqēqu, uqququ*); ¶ par.: *akl (I)*. ¶ Forms: pl. *ʕqqm*.

Destructive (one): *w ld ʕqqm* yand give birth to the ‘Destructive (Ones)’, 1.12 I 27 (// *aklm*); *w ymẓa ʕqqm* and he came upon the ‘Destructive (Ones)’, 1.12 I 37 (// *aklm*).

ʕqr “ ?”

? : *šbʕ ʕqr/r/w*[seven *ʕ*.[, RSOu 14 33 [KTU 9.422]:3.

ʕqrb n. m. “scorpion” (Hb. OAram *ʕqrb*, HALOT 875; DNWSI 883; Akk. *aqrabu*, AHw 62; CAD A/2 207; Arab., Eth. *ʕaqrab*, Lane 2111; CDG 68).

Scorpion: *tḥtk qn l tqnn ʕqrb* beneath you may the scorpion not rise up, RSOu 14 52 [KTU 9.435]:5 (cf. ln 7).

ʕqrbn n. m. of a medicinal plant (*salsola tragus*(?); cf. Hb. *ʕqrbn*, Syr. *ʕaqrabanyā*, Arab. *ʕuqruban*, Löw Flora 1 7; 4 73, 141, 193; cf. Akk. (*zuqi/aqīpu* >) *zuqi/aqīpānu*, AHw 1538; CAD Z 166; cf. Dietrich - Loretz - Sanmartín UF 6 1974 45; Cohen - Sivan UHT 13; Pardee TH 47f.). ¶ Forms: sg. *ʕqrbn*.

Plant in hippiatric pharmacopea: *št ʕqrbn* a *š*. of *ʕq*., 1.85:2.

Cf. ʕqrb

ʕqšr, 1.100:12 and par.; cf. *aqšr* (diff. Dietrich - Loretz UF 12 1980 159: ‘schuppig’, Arab. *qašara*; Tsumura UF 6 1974 411: ‘evil eyebrow’, rdg *ʕq šr*; Levine - De Tarragon RB 95 1988 495: ‘coily’, /q-š-r/; for the various opinions cf. Bordreuil UF 15 1983 299f.; Renfroe AULS 89).

ʕqy PN (Sem.(?)); ¶ syll.: DUMU *a-qa-ya*, PRU 3 195 (RS 15.09) B I 10; cf. Grøndahl PTU 216.

PN: *bn PN*, 4.124:5; 4.711:5.

/ʕ-r/ vb G: “to become agitated, irritated”; N: “to wake up”; L: “to move”, “to be(come) exacerbated” (Hb. *ʕwr*, HALOT 802f.; Arab. *ʕāra, ʕayyara*, Lane 2207ff.; Akk. *êru*, AHw 247; CAD E 326f. Cf. De Moor SP 237; UF 16 1984 356; Emerton Fs. Williams 40f.; Tropper AuOr 19 1996 138); ¶ par.: /ḫ-s-s/, /ṯ-t-ʕ/, /y-r-ʔ/. ¶ Forms: G prefc.

yʕr; ptc. *ʕr*; L prefc. *yʕrr*; with suff. *tʕrrk*.

G. To become agitated: *yʕr mt b qlh* DN became agitated in his fall, 1.6 VI 31 (// *yru*, *ṯtʕ*); in unc. ctx.: *kḥṣ km ʕr* he did leave like one agitated, 1.16 IV 5 (diff. Aistleitner MKT 102: 'wie ein Wildesel'; cf. *ʕr (II)*).

N. To wake up: *km trpa hn nʕr* on applying the remedy, see, he woke up, 1.114:28.

L. ★a) To move: *ahbt ṯr tʕrrk* perhaps the love of the Bull has moved you?, 1.4 IV 39 (// *yḫssk*); ★b) to be(come) exacerbated: *yʕrr w yʕn* he became exacerbated and answered, 1.24:30 (cf. Del Olmo MLC 459f., Theuer Mondgott 178f. for other versions).

ʕr (I) n. m. "city" (Hb., Ph. *ʕ(y)r*, HALOT 821f.; DNWSI 883f.; Ebla cf. /ʕīrīyatum/ in URU.BAR = *ì-rí-a-tum*, Fronzaroli EL 143; *ìr-a*-LUM, Archi WGE 131; cf. *er-me* [= URU.BAR], Pettinato AfO 25 1974/77 27; Arcari Biling. 326; cf. Watson UF 31 1999 788); ¶ par.: *pdr*. ¶ Forms: sg. *ʕr*, suff. *ʕrm* (encl. *-m*), *ʕrhm*; du./pl. *ʕrm*.

City: *ʕb*(!)*r l*[*ʕr*] *ʕrm* he passed from city to city (// *pdrm*), 1.4 VII 7; *ṯṯ lṯṯm aḫd ʕr* sixty six cities he conquered (// *pdr*), 1.4 VII 9; *ʕrm tdu mt*(!) from the city she scared away DN, 1.16 VI 6 and par. (// *pdrm*; diff. rdg KTU: *m*<*nt*>*h* (?)); [*tity l*] *ʕrhm* they came to / from their city, 1.22 II 24 and par. (diff. De Moor - Spronk UF 7 1975 215: 'stallions', // *mrkbt*; cf. *ʕr (II)*); *gr*{.}*nn ʕrm* attack the cities! 1.14 III 6 (// *pdrm*; /g-r(-y)/ inf. used as an impv.; cf. used as narr. *grnn*, *ibid.* IV 49; cf. De Moor-Spronk 14 1982 166: 'twin-city'); *b qrb ʕr* within the city (?), 1.62:5; *ʕr d qdm* the city of the east / primordial city, 1.100:62 (cf. diff. Young UF 9 1977 310; UF 11 1979 846: 'nakedness', 'the desert', Arab. *ʕarāʔ*, Tsevat UF 11 1979 763: 'ein Baum, Osttamariske', short form of *ʕrʕr*, Arab. /ʕarā/, Syr. *ʕara*, Akk. *eʔru*). In unc. ctx.: *ʕd mġyy b ʕrm* until I reach the city(cities(?)), 2.71:17;]*kmn ʕrhm*[, 1.18 I 32 (cf. Margalit OLP 19 1988 88). In bkn ctx.: 1.14 V 24.

ʕr (II) n. m. "donkey, ass" (Hb. *ʕyr*, HALOT 822; Arab. *ʕayr*, Lane 2208s; Akk. Mari *ḫâru*, *(ḫ)aʔ/yaru*, AHw 328; CAD H 118; cf. Sasson RSP 1 433); ¶ par.: *pḥl*. ¶ Forms: sg. *ʕr*.

Donkey, ass: *mdl ʕr smd pḥl* they harnessed the donkey, saddled the ass, 1.4 IV 9 and par.; *yštn aṯrt lbmt ʕr* they set DN on the back of the donkey, 1.4 IV 14 and par. (// *pḥl*); *w šqrb ʕr mšr* offer, yes, a donkey of justification, 1.40:26; *hn ʕr* behold the ass, 1.40:34 and par. (cf. Del Olmo CR 150ff.). In bkn ctx.: *w ʕr l*... and a donkey to ..., 1.119:16.

ʕrʕr n. m. "tamarisk" (*tamarix gallica*; Hb. *ʕrʕr*, HALOT 887; Syr. *ʕarō*, *ʕarûrō*, LS 544; cf. Arab. *ʕarʕar*, Lane 1990f. Cf. Astour, JNES 27 1968 24f.; De Moor UF 2 1970 326 n. 131; Sasson RSP 1 434; Dietrich - Loretz - Sanmartín UF 7 1975 124; Young UF 9 1977 292f.; Tsevat UF 11 1979 765; diff. Belmonte AuOr 11 1993 114f.: 'enebro', Arab. *ʕarʕar*); ¶ par.: *ʕdt*, *ʕṣ (+ mt)*, *ssn*, *yblt*. ¶ Forms: sg. *ʕrʕr*; suff. *ʕrʕrm* (encl. *-m*).

Tamarisk: *l bʕl ṣpn b ʕrʕr pamt ṯlṯm* to DN, with tamarisk, thirty times, 1.109:29; *ydy b ʕṣm ʕrʕr*, he ripped out a tamarisk from among the trees, 1.100:64 (// *ʕṣ mt*; Pardee TPM 216; diff. Watson AuOr 19 1992 237: 'with tamarisk wood'); *ʕrʕrm ynʕrn*(!)*h* with the tamarisk he shook it, 1.100:65 (// *ssn*, *ʕdt*, *yblt*).

/ʕ-r-b/ (I) vb G: 1) "to enter"; 2) "to enter to work, to start in service, to register; to be assigned, delivered"; 3) "to enter", "to set", in the astronomical sense; 4) "to enter, die"; N: "to be annexed"; Š: "to cause to enter, introduce" (Akk. *erēbu*, AHw 234ff.; CAD E 259-273; cf. Hb. *ʕrb*, HALOT 877; Arab. *ġrb*, Lane 2240ff.; Eth. *ʕar(a)ba*, CDG 69; cf. ESA *ġ/ʕrb*, DOSA 382f., 397. Cf. Van der Weiden VD 44 1966 102; Greenfield EI 9 1969 64; Xella MSS 149ff.; Avigad - Greenfield IEJ 32 1982 118ff.; Van Zijl Baal 165f.; Emerton Fs. Williams 43; Tropper UF 29 1997 666); ¶ syll. Ug.: cf. *iḫ-ra-bu* /(y)iʕrabu/, G: prefc. sg., RS 25.423:13 (unpubl.); Van Soldt BiOr 46 1989 650; SAU 330 n. 157; ¶ RS Akk.: *erēbu* (cf. *infra* 2.a); ¶ par.: /l-q-ḥ/, /t-r-ḫ/, /y-r-d/. ¶ Forms: G suffc. *ʕrb*, *ʕrbt*; prefc. *tʕrb*, *yʕrb*, *tʕrbm* (encl. *-m*); impv. *ʕrbn*; N prefc. *nʕrb* ; Š prefc. *ašʕrb*, *tšʕrb*.

G. 1) To enter, ★a) abs.: *km ġlmm w ʕrbn* like young servants you will have to enter, 1.3 III 9; (he opened) *w ʕrb hm* and they entered, 1.23:71; ★b) a place (+ *b*; Pardee UF 7 1975 364; UF 8 1976 261): *ʕrb b bth kṯrt* the DN entered her house, 1.17 II 26; *hy bth tʕrb* she entered her house, 1.7:3; *ʕrb ḥrn bth* DN entered his house, RSOu 14 53 [KTU 9.432]:33'; [*ʕ*]*rb bʕl b qrb bt* DN entered within (his) house, 1.4 VII 13 (cf. RS Akk.: *erēbu ina (libbi)*, Van Soldt SAU 448f.); *ʕrb b ẓl ḫmt* he entered the shade of the tent, 1.14 III 55 and par.; *yʕrb b ḥdrh ybky* he entered his room to weep, 1.14 I 26; *w yʕrb b phm ʕṣr šmm w dg b ym* and into their mouth(s) enter the birds of the sky and the fish of the sea, 1.23:62; *ʕrb bkyt b hklh* (female) mourners entered his palace, 1.19 IV 9; *yʕrb bʕl b kbdh* DN will enter his innards, 1.5 II 3 (// *yrd*); *ʕr*[*bt*] *pġt minš šdm* PN entered the encampment, 1.19 IV 48; in a cultic sense: *k tʕrb ʕṯtrt ḫr gb bt mlk* when DN enters the *g*. of the palace, 1.43:1 (cf. l. 9) and par. (cf. Akk. *erubbatum*, AHw 248, 1554; CAD E 327; Hilgert JCS 46 1994 29ff.); cf. *ʕlm yʕ*[*rb* next (the king) shall [enter, 1.41:8; 1.87:9; with a matrimonial meaning: *ib*

tʕrbm b bhth may DN enter his house, 1.24:18 (// *ytrḫ*); ★c) to come into someone's presence, present oneself before someone (+ *ʕl*, *l pn*; Pardee UF 7 1975 364): *ʕl abh yʕrb*(!) he came into the presence of his father, 1.16 I 12 and par.; *tdʕ ky ʕrbt l pn špš* you must know that I have come into the presence of the 'Sun', 2.16:7.
2) To enter, in connection with work or commerce: ★a) to enter to work, begin in service, to register: *spr npš d ʕrb bt mlk* list of the people who have entered to work in the royal palace, 4.338:2 (cf. Akk. RS: *i-na* ÌR.MEŠ*-ut-ti ša šàr* KUR *u-ga-ri-it i-te-er-bu-ni*, PRU 4 52 (RS 17.369 ★a):14'); *GNN d ʕrb b unṯ* GNN who have entered service, 3.7:1 (Akk. *ana ilki erēbu*, Márquez AuOr 11 1993 251); ★b) to be assigned, delivered (merchandise, etc.): *ṯmn mrkbt dt ʕrb bt mlk* eight chariot bodies that have been assigned to the royal palace, 4.145:2; *šbʕm lbš d ʕrb bt mlk* seventy garments that were delivered to the palace, 4.337:16; *iṯ yn d ʕrb b ṯk*[*ṯ*] there is wine that entered in ..., 1.23:74. Cf. in bkn ctx.: GN (pl.) *ʕrb*, 4.634:1-5 (and cf. /ʕ-r-b/ (II)).
3) To enter, set, in an astronomical sense: *ʕrbt špš ṯġrh ršp* the sun set(s), her gatekeeper being DN, 1.78:2 (cf. Dietrich - Loretz MU 57f.; cf. *ʕrb (I)*).
4) To enter (in a funerary sense), die: during *ṯlṯ ymm llm yʕrb mlk* three days (and three) nights the king 'enters' (the funeral of the king is celebrated), 1.111:2 (in connection with 3; cf. Del Olmo CR 203). Unc. ctx.]*upqt ʕrb*, 1.1 V 24;]*tʕrb b ši*, 1.1 V 26;]*km tʕrb*[, 1.94; *PN ʕrbt*[, 4.18:4.
N. To be annexed: *šdm d nʕrb gt npk* fields that were annexed to TN, 4.103:45 (Tropper UG 534).
Š. To make (someone/something) enter, introduce: *ʕlh ṯrh tšʕrb* into his presence she made his 'bulls' enter, 1.15 IV 18 and par. (cf. RS Akk.: IGI.DU$_8$.A*-šu a-na* LUGAL*-ri ú-še-ra-ab*, PRU 3 107 (RS 16.238):13); in a matrimonial sense: *ġlmt tšʕrb ḥẓrk* the damsel that you have introduced into your mansion, 1.15 II 22, cf. 1.14 IV 41 (// *tqḥ*).
In bkn ctx.: 1.126:23; 4.634:1-5(?).
Cf. ʕrb (I), ʕrb (II).

/ʕ-r-b/ (II) vb G: "to give a guarantee or pledge, stand surety for, leave a deposit" (ESA *ʕrb*, CAME 212; DOSA 381; Arab. *ʕrb*, Lane 1991f.; Hb., Ph., Aram. *ʕrb*, HALOT 876; cf. DISO 221; Alal. Akk. cf. *ana qātāti* (/ ŠU.DU$_8$.A) *erēbum*, AHw 235: *erēbu(m)* G.4.d.γ; Giacumakis 96); ¶ RS Akk.: A.ŠÀ.MEŠ *PN (...) e-ru-ub a-na PN*, PRU 3 13 (RS 16.131):17; cf. Huehnergard UVST 162; *PN qa-ta-at-ti iṣ-ṣa-bat ša PN*, PRU 3 37 (RS 15.81):4, 11; cf. Kienast UF 11 1979 435; Hoftijzer -

Van Soldt UF 23 1991 206ff. ¶ Forms: G suffc. *ʕrb*; prefc. cf. *tʕr[b*.
G. To give a guarantee or pledge, stand surety for something or someone leave a deposit for something or someone (+ *b*; cf. Pardee UF 7 1975 364; 8 1976 261f.): *rišym dt ʕrb b bnšhm* GN who have stood surety for their personnel, 4.347:1; *PN (w PN) ʕrb b PN* PN (and PN) have given a guarantee for PN so and so, *ibid.* ln. 3 and *passim. ibid.*; *spr ʕrbnm dt ʕrb b PN* list of guarantors who have given a guarantee for PN, 3.3:2; *PNN ʕrb b PNN* PNN have stood surety for PNN, 3.8:6; *ksp anyt d ʕrb b anyt* ship's pledge that has been deposited for the ships, 4.338:12 (Dietrich - Loretz - Sanmartín UF 6 1974 473; Pardee JAOS 95 1975 613; diff. Dietrich - Loretz UF 22 1990 93f.: 'Silber für die Schiffe, die zu den Schiffen hinzugekommen sind'; Márquez AUOR 11 1993 101ff.: rdg {*anyt*} <TN> 'ships that entered TN'; cf. /ʕ-r-b/ (I)). Cf. in bkn ctx. *hm tʕr[b*(?) *b*(?)] *mkr hn*(!)*d* if [gurantees(?)] are given for this trader, 4.42:24. Cf. in bkn ctx.: 1.16 V 1-3; GN (pl.) *ʕrb*, 4.634:1-5 (y cf. /ʕ-r-b/ (II)).
Cf. nʕrb, ʕrbn.

ʕrb (I) n. m. 1) "entry"; 2) "setting of the sun, sunset" (< /ʕ-r-b/ (I); cf. Hb. *ʕrb*, HALOT 877f.; Akk. *er(e)bu*, AHw 233f.; CAD E 258f.; Arab. *ġarb*, Lane 2241f. Cf. Xella UF 16 1984 339ff.; Dietrich - Loretz UF 22 1990 75ff.); ¶ par.: *yṣu (I)*. ¶ Forms: sg. *ʕrb*.
1) Entry: *ʕrb [b]th ytn w yṣu l ytn* entry to his house was permitted but exit was not permitted, 1.15 II 10 (// *yṣu*).
2) Sunset: *ʕrb špš w ḥl mlk* at sunset the king (remains) desacralized, 1.46:9 and par.; *ʕrb špš l ymġ krt* at sunset PN will certainly arrive, 1.15 V 18; (cf. Akk. *ereb šamši*; cf. *ṣbu špš*).
Cf. mʕrb.

ʕrb (II) n. m. "officiant" (< ptc. G /ʕ-r-b/ (I); cf. Akk. *ērib bīti*, AHw 240; CAD E 290ff., class of priests; cf. Eth. *ʕrb*, DOSA 381f. Cf. Gaster Thespis 419; Herrmann YN 12; Xella MSS 149ff.). ¶ Forms: pl. *ʕrbm*.
Officiant: *w ʕrbm tʕnyn* and the officiants chorus it / reply, 1.23:12; *šm ʕrbm* the names of the officiants, 1.23:18; *šlm ʕrbm* to the health of the officiants!, 1.23:26 (cf. *ibid.* ln. 7).

ʕrbn n. m. "guarantor, surety" (< /ʕ-r-b/ (II); abstr. for concr.; cf. ESA *ʕrbn*, DOSA 382; Arab. *ʕurbān*, Lane 1994; Hb. *ʕrbwn*, HALOT 881; Aram. *ʕrbʔ*, *ʕrbn*, DNWSI 886; > Gk *arrabōn*, Liddell - Scott 246; > Arab. *ʕarabūn*, Lane 1994; Eth. *ʔ/ʕarabon*, CDG 69; cf. Akk. *erubbātum*, AHw 248; CAD E 327; ESA *tʕrbm*, DOSA 382); ¶ syll. Ug.: (PN and PN) [LÚ].MEŠ *ú-ru-ba-nu*, PRU 3 37 (RS 16.287):7; Sivan GAGl 207; Huehnergard UVST 162; Hoftijzer - Van Soldt UF

23 1991 196f.; ¶ RS Akk.: LÚ.MEŠ ŠU.DU$_8$.A, PRU 6 69: 1', 8'. ¶ Forms: pl. *ʕrbnm*.

Guarantor, surety: *spr ʕrbnm dt ʕrb b PN* list of the guarantors who stand surety for PN, 3.3:1; *mnm šalm dt tknn ʕl ʕrbnm hnhmt tknn* any claims they bring up, against these guarantors they bring them up, 3.3:7 (three PNN follow; cf. *hnhmt*). In bkn ctx.: 4.699:3.

ʕrgz (I) n. m.; an aromatic and medicinal substance ("juniper berries(?)"; cf. *dprn*, 4.158:22; etym. unc.; Sanmartín AuOr 6 1988 232; Gulde UF 30 1998 185ff. Cf. Del Olmo MLC 604: Arab. *ʕarǧūdu* 'aromatic and medicinal plant'; Cohen - Sivan UHT 19f., 35f.: 'a tree or plant'; cf. Pope Song 574ff. 'walnut'; Pardee TH 53f.: 'noix'(?); Dietrich - Loretz UF 18 1986 118ff.: 'Nuss', Hb. *ʔgwz*); ¶ par.: *zt (+ dm)*, 1.24:43. ¶ Forms: sg. *ʕrgz*, pl. *ʕrgzm*.

An aromatic substance ("juniper berries(?)"): *yrdt b ʕrgzm* they go down with *ʕ.* (// *zt dm*), 1.24:43; hippiatric use: *št ʕrgz* a *š.* of *ʕr.*, 1.85:10; 1.71:10; 1.72:14; *bṣql ʕrgz* a branch of *ʕr.*, 1.85:5; 1.71:5; 1.72:7; as a market commodity: *ḫmšm ʕrgz b ḫmšt* fifty *ʕr.* for five (shekels; + *dprn*, + *mqd*), 4.158:22. Bkn ctx. *d ʕrgzm*, 1.20 I 8.

ʕrgz (II) TN (Belmonte RGTC 12/2 29: **ʕAragizu*. Cf. Heltzer RCAU 13; Virolleaud Syria 21 1940 146; Astour UF 13 1981 7; Dietrich - Loretz UF 18 1986 120; Bordreuil UF 20 1988 17f.; Van Soldt UF 30 1998 732); ¶ syll.: URU *a-ra-gi-zi*, RSOu 7 4:22.

TN: 4.365:36; 4.610 (II) 25; 4.621:16; 4.693:45; 4.750:2; in bkn ctx.: 4.68:41; 4.94:15; 4.302:4; 4.676:3 (Belmonte RGTC 12/2 29; KTU:]*rsg*). Cf. 4.684:4.

ʕrgzy PN (Sem. Cf. *ʕrgz*, TN). - PN: 4.55:27.

/ʕ-r-k/ vb G: "to prepare" (Hb. *ʕrk*, HALOT 884f. (?)Aram. *ʕrk*, DNWSI 887; Syr. *ʕrak*, LS 548; Arab. *ʕaraka*, Lane 2023. Cf. Herdner Ug 7 30). ¶ Forms: G prefc. *tʕr*[*k*].

G. To prepare: *w l ll tʕr*[*k*] *ksu* and at night they prepare the throne, 1.106:27.

ʕrk (I) n. m. "bookkeeping account, list, fiscal valuation" (< /ʕ-r-k/; cf. Hb. *ʕrk*, HALOT 885; Ph., Pun. *ʕrk(t)*, DNWSI 887f.; diff.: Tropper - Vita AoF 26 1999 310ff.: '(Opfer-)Zurüster'). ¶ Forms: sg. *ʕrk*.

Bookkeeping account, list, fiscal valuation: *ʕrk bʕl ḫlb d l ytn šmn* valuation of the owners of TN who have not supplied oil, 4.728:1.

ʕrk (II) n. m.; a type of offering (?); < /ʕ-r-k/. Cf. De Moor UF 2 1970 319: 'loaves of bread', Hb. *mʕrkt*; De Tarragon CU 47: '(pains) disposés', Hb. *ʕrk*; Herdner Ug 7 13: 'gâteaux'(?), Hb., Arab. *ʕrk*,; Del

Olmo CR 249 n. 96; cf. diff. Xella TRU 28: 'edificio'; Virolleaud Ug 5 590; Fisher HTR 63 1976 488s n. 18: 'hommes de guerre', Hb. *ʕrkym*; Gianto Bib 68 1987 400: 'valuation', Hb., Ph. *ʕrk*). ¶ Forms: du. *ʕrkm*.

A type of offering(?): *bʕl ʕrkm* to DN: two *ʕr.*-(offerings(?)), 1.105:18. In 1.119:2 rdg(?) *bʕl u*(!)*g*(!)*rt*, cf. Del Olmo CR 296 n. 10.

ʕrm (I) n. m.; a cloak or blanket (Ribichini - Xella Tessili 56f.; Durand MARI 6 661; cf. Akk. *(ḫ)arāmu*, AHw 323; CAD A/2 228ff.; cf. Akk. *ermu*, AHw 242; CAD E 302); ¶ par.: *lbš*. ¶ Forms: sg. cstr. *ʕrm*.

Cloak or blanket: *ʕrm il yštk* may they put on you in the divine *ʕr.* / of DN (// *lbš*), 1.169:13.

ʕrm (II) TN (Belmonte RGTC 12/2 34f.: *ʕArmu*. Cf. Heltzer RCAU 13; Virolleaud Syria 21 1940 146; Astour RSP 2 311, 341; UF 11 1979 23; UF 13 1981 7; Bordreuil UF 20 1988 12f.; Van Soldt UF 30 1998 728); ¶ syll.: URU *ar*$_x$(SUM)-*me/u*, PRU 3 189 (RS 11.790):28'; 190 (RS 11.800):25'; 191 (RS 11.841):29'; RSOu 7 4:7; RS 22.233:8, 25.132 III 9 (Van Soldt UF 28 1996 682); cf. Nougayrol PRU 3 p. 269; Dietrich - Loretz - Sanmartín UF 5 1973 82ff.; Huehnergard AkkUg 370. Cf. A.ŠÀ.MEŠ *a-ra-mi-ma*, PRU 3 148 (RS 16.178):10.

TN: 4.68:22; 4.348:28; 4.610 (II) 17; 4.621:3; 4.684:4; 4.686:20; 4.693:40; 4.770:13; RSOu 14 35 [KTU 9.388] II 28. Allograph *arm*, 4.750:5.

ʕrmn PN (etym. unc.; cf. *ʕrm*, TN; Grøndahl PTU 112); ¶ syll.: cf. DUMU *ar-mu-na*, PRU 3 203 (RS 16.257+) IV 10, 20.

PN: *bn PN*, 4.93 II 13.

ʕrmt TN (Belmonte RGTC 12/2 34. Cf. Heltzer RCAU 13; Dietrich - Loretz - Sanmartín UF 7 1975 152; Astour RSP 2 311; UF 11 1979 23; 13 1981 6).

TN: 4.355:36; cf. *npy ʕrmt* atonement of TN, 1.40:27; 1.84:13.

ʕrmy (I) GN m. (< *ʕrm (II)*, TN; Van Soldt SAU 33). ¶ Forms: sg. *ʕrmy*.

GN: 4.33:5; 4.51:13; cf. PN, 4.55:22.

ʕrmy (II) PN (< *ʕrmy*, GN; cf. Grøndahl PTU 112).; ¶ syll.: cf. (DUMU) *ar-mi-ya*, PRU 3 35 (RS 15.37):13; Ug 5 86:25.

PN: 4.55:22, bkn ctx.

/ʕ(?)-r-p/ vb G/D "to cover", "to darken", "to make it pour down" (?) (etym. and rdg unc.; possibly denom. < *ʕrp (II)*; cf. Hb. *ʕrp*, HALOT 887; Akk. *erēpu*, AHw 238; CAD E 279f.; for the rdg /ṯ-r-p/ cf. Tropper UG 165: 'peitschen'(?). Arab. *ṯfr*; survey: Wyatt RTU 368 n. 4.). ¶ Forms: G/D prefc. *tʕrp*.

G/D. To cover, darken, make it pour down (?): *tʕrp ym ḏnbtm* it covered(?) the sea with (its) tail, 1.83:6 (Cf. Del Olmo AuOr 14 1996 131; Tropper UG 165: 'es peitschte(?) das Meer mit dem Schwanz'). Cf. ʕrp (II).

ʕrp (I) n. m., a type of garment (with a hood(?); Del Olmo Transeuphratène 14 1998 167ff.; Watson NABU 1998 83; UF 31 1999 790: Eg. *ʕrp*. Cf. Sanmartín AuOr 10 1992 101; diff.: Dietrich - Loretz - Sanmartín UF 7 1975 165; Ribichini - Xella Tessili 45: 'oscuro, negro', Akk. *erēpu* and der.). ¶ Forms: pl. *ʕrpm*.
A garment (with a hood(?)): *lbšm ʕrpm* garments of the *ʕr.* type, 4.721:2, 13.

ʕ(?)rp (II) n. m. "storm cloud" (rdg unc. Cf. Akk. *urpu*, AHw 1432; etym. connection with /ʕ-r-p/ unc. Cf. Del Olmo AuOr 14 1996 131; for the rdg *ṯrp* see Tropper UG 165). Formas: pl. cstr. *ʕrp*.
Storm cloud: *mnḫm ʕrp ym* the storm clouds of the sea / DN, 1.83:4. Cf. ʕrpt, ġrpl.

ʕrpt n. f. "cloud(s)" (Akk. *erpetu*, *urpatu*, AHw 243, 1432; CAD E 302ff. Cf. De Moor SP 98; Emerton Fs. Williams 44; Watson NABU 1998 83); ¶ par.: *arṣ*. ¶ Forms: sg./pl. *ʕrpt*.
Cloud(s): *rkb ʕrpt* Charioteer of the clouds, epithet of the god Baal (cf. *rkb (I)*; Hb. *rkb b ʕrbwt*, Ps. 68:5 nd cf. *ibid.* 34; cf. Loretz UF 19 1987 101ff.); *yṣly ʕrpt* he implored the clouds, 1.19 I 39; *yr ʕrpt tmṭr* may the clouds bring rain!, 1.19 I 40; *w at qḥ ʕrptk* and you, take your clouds, 1.5 V 7 (cf. *rḥ*, *mdl*, *mṭr*, *ibid.* ln. 7-8; cf. 1.13:34); [*yḥd*] *b ʕrpt* [*nšrm*] [he saw the eagles] in the clouds, 1.19 II 57; *ypth bdqt ʕrpt* may he open a loophole in the clouds, 1.4 VII 19 and par.; *w <y>tn qlh b ʕrpt* and may he give his voice from the clouds, 1.4 V 8 (// *l arṣ*). Unc. ctx. *ʕrpt tḥt*, 1.8 II 11 (cf. 1.4 VII 57).

ʕrq n. m. "cart, wagon" (Akk. *ereqqu*, AHw 238; CAD E 296f.; Dietrich - Loretz - Sanmartín UF 5 1973 107). ¶ Forms: sg. *ʕrq*.
Cart, wagon: *ḥrš ʕrq* cartwright, 4.46:13-14; 4.243:2. Cf. in unc. ctx. *ʕrq dm*, *ʕrq špš*, 1.107:46-47. (cf. Dietrich - Loretz - Sanmartín UF 7 1975 129; Xella TRU 248; Pardee TPM 254). In bkn ctx. cf. *PN*(?) *ʕrq*, 4.186:1-3.

/ʕ-r-s/ vb G: "to rejoice" (Arab. *ʕarasa*, Hava 463. Diff. Hoftijzer UF 3 1971 363: 'to make a short pause during the night', Arab. *ʕarrasa*; Dijkstra - De Moor UF 7 1975 195: 'to give a marriage-feast', Arab. *ʔaʕrasa*; Driver CML 141: 'tilth', Akk. *erēšu*). ¶ Forms: G prefc. *nʕrs*.
G. To rejoice: *ištir b ḏdm w nʕrs* stay in the grottoes and we will rejoice, 1.18 IV 15.

ʕrš n. m. "bed, makeshift bed, stretcher" (Hb. *ʕrś*, HALOT 889; Akk. *eršu*, AHw 246; CAD E 315ff.; Arab. *ʕaršu*, *ʕarīš*, Lane 2000f.; cf. Eth. *ʕarat*, CDG 71. Cf. Saracino UF 14 1982 192f.). ¶ Forms: sg. *ʕrš*; suff. *ʕršh*, *ʕršm* (encl. *-m*; diff. Margalit VT 36 1986 487: 'double-couch', rdg *ʕ*(!)*ršm* in 1.19 IV 60; cf. *ḥrš (II)*).
Bed, makeshift bed, stretcher: *km aḫt ʕrš mdw anšt ʕrš zbln* for the bed of sickness has taken you, you have languished in the bed of illness, 1.16 VI 35-36, 51-52; *zbl ʕršm yšu* let the sick person carry his own stretcher, 1.14 II 45 and par.; *l ʕršh yʕl* let him go up to his bed, 1.17 I 38; *mddt nʕmy ʕrš (...) ysmsmt ʕrš* dispensers of the delight of the bed (...), of the beauty of the bed, 1.17 II 41-42; *trbd ʕrš pdry* the bed of DN is prepared, DN, 1.132:2; *tnʕr ʕrš* the bed is unmade, 1.132:26. In bkn ctx.: 2.22:2; 4.248:5.

/ʕ-r-w/ vb G: "to be consumed" (Arab. *ʕarā*, *ʕuriya*, Lane 2027ff. Cf. Del Olmo MLC 605; diff.: Dietrich - Loretz Fs. Elliger 33; Verreet UF 19 1987 318f.: 'vernichtet sein', cf. /ʕ-r-y/); ¶ par.: /ʔ-b-d/. ¶ Forms: Gpass. suffc. *ʕrwt*.
G. To be consumed: *umt* [*krt*] *ʕrwt* the family of PN was consumed, 1.14 I 7 (// *itdb* [rdg *itbd*]).
Cf. /ʕ-r-y/.

/ʕ-r-y/ vb G: "to be naked, unrigged" (cf. Hb., Aram. *ʕrh*, HALOT 881f.; DNWSI 887; Ph. *ʕry*, DNWSI 887; Arab. *ʕariya*, Lane 2029f.; Akk. *erû*, AHw 247f.; cf. CAD E 320f.). ¶ Forms: G suffc. *ʕryt*.
G. To be be naked; said of ships, to be unrigged *anyk ṯt by TN ʕryt* the other (: number two) ship of yours is unrigged in TN, 2.38:24.
Cf. /ʕ-r-w/, ʕry.

ʕry adj. m. "naked, uncovered" ((?)< /ʕ-r-y/; cf. Hb. *ʕryh*, HALOT 883; Syr. *ʕaryat*, LS 548; Akk. *erium*, *erû*, AHw 242, CAD E 302, 320). ¶ Forms: sg. with adv. suff. *ʕrym* (encl. *-m*(?)).
Uncovered(?): in bkn ctx.: *ʕrym l bl* [*sk*] in the open(?), without [covering], 1.16 II 29 (cf. ln. 31);]*tb ʕrym*, 2.8:3.

ʕrẓ adj. m. "terrible", epithet of the god *ʕṯtr* (Hb. *ʕryṣ*, HALOT 884; Arab. *ʕāraḍa*, Lane 2004f.; cf. Syr. *ʕrōṣō*, LS 550. Cf. Oldenburg CEB 41; De Moor SP 204; *id.* Xella UBL 12 389; diff. 'rich man', Arab. *ʕarīḍ*, ARTU 85; Watson UF 12 1980 443f.: 'broad (of intellect)', Arab. *ʕaruḍa*; Margalit MLD 149f.: 'narrow passage, canal', Hb. *ʕrwṣ*; Gray LC 66 n. 4; Craigie ZAW 85 1973 223: 'to flash', Arab. *ʕaraṣa*; Greenfield Fs. Delcor 194f.: 'hero', Hb. *ʕryṣ* // *gbwr*). ¶ par.:(?) *adr*. ¶ Forms: sg. *ʕrẓ*.
Terrible: *ʕṯtr ʕrẓ* DN, the terrible, 1.6 I 54 and par.; cf. in bkn ctx.: *idm*

ʕrẓ tʕr[, 1.12 II 30 (//(?) *adr*).

ʕs̲, allograph of *ʕṣ*, 4.767:1; cf. *ʕṣ*.

ʕsb "?"; unc. ctx. 1.94:26.

ʕsl PN (Sem.(?); cf. Grøndahl PTU 28, 112).
PN: *bn PN*, 4.658:6.

ʕsn PN (etym. unc.).
PN: 4.141 II 13.

ʕšr, 4.31:2, 4, 5, 11, cf. *ʕšr (I)*.

/ʕ-s-y/s(?)/ vb "?" in bkn ctx. (for the various options cf. Rin AE 160; Del Olmo MLC 603: 'beber un trago', Hb. *ʕss*; MHb. *ʕsh*; Oldenburg CEB 118 n. 3: 'to be pressed'; Hvidberg WL 43 n. 3: 'wander about in the night', Arab. *ʕasā*, cf. Driver CML 140: *id.*; De Moor ARTU 53: 'to do'); ¶ par.: /(t-)ġ-t[(-?). ¶ Forms: *ʕs*[.
? : *ʕs*[, 1.4 IV 34 (KTU: *ʕs*[*t*]).

ʕṣ n. m. 1) "tree, plant, (vine-)stock"; 2) "beam, log; wood(?)"; 3) "staff" (Hb., Pun. *ʕṣ*, HALOT 863f.; DNWSI 879f.; Aram. *ʕq*, DNWSI 879f.; Ebla /ʕiḍu/ in GIŠ.ŠINIG = *i-zu ba-ne(-um)*, VE 395; GIŠ.URUDU.URUDU = *i-zu gu*-PI, VE 411; Krebernik ZA 73 1983 15f.; Fronzaroli EL 144; Sanmartín AuOr 9 1991 178; Akk. *iṣ(ṣ)u*, AHw 390f.; CAD I/J 214-219; ESA *ʕḍ*, DOSA 378; Arab. *ʕīḍ*, *ʕayḍa*, Lane 2317; Eth. *ʕĕḍ*, CDG 57); ¶ syll. Ug.: [GIŠ = *iṣṣū*(?)] = *ta-li* = *iṣ-ṣú*-[*ma*(?)], Ug 5 130 III 8'; Huehnergard UVST 54, 161; cf. Sivan UF 21 1989 360; cf. *i-ṣú*, UF 11 1979 479:13; Van Soldt BiOr 46 1989 651; SAU 306; ¶ RS Akk.: GIŠ.(MEŠ), cf. PRU 6 p. 156; Huehnergard AkkUg 378; ¶ par.: *arẓ*, *abn*. ¶ Forms: sg. abs. *ʕṣ*, cstr. *ʕṣ*; suff. *ʕṣk*; pl. *ʕṣm*, cstr. *ʕs̲* (cf. Dietrich - Loretz KA 250f.); suff. *ʕṣh*.

1) Tree, plant, (vine-)stock; ★a) tree: *pr ʕṣm* the fruit of trees, 1.5 II 6; *lbnn w ʕṣh* TN and its trees / woods, 1.4 VI 18 and par. (// *arẓ*); *ydy b ʕṣm ʕrʕr* he ripped out a tamarisk from among the trees, 1.100:64 (cf. Pardee TPM 215f.); *rgm ʕṣ w lḫšt abn* it is a matter of wood and a chatter of stone, 1.3 III 23 and par.; *ʕṣ mt* tree of death, *ibid.* ln. 65; *t̠m tgrgr l abnm w l ʕṣm* (settle) there next to stones and trees, 1.23:66; ★b) plant: *ʕs̲ kprt* henna plants, 4.767:1 (cf. Dietrich - Loretz KA 250ff.); ★c) vine: *dm ʕṣm* juice of vines, 1.4 IV 38 and par. (// *yn*). In unc. ctx. *ʕṣm l ttn* trees that do not emit (a sound(?)), 1.82:43.

2) Beam, log; wood(?); ★a) beam, log: *ʕṣm l bt dml*, the beams for the temple of DN, 2.26:6; *ank atn ʕṣm lk* I am going to distribute the beams to you, *ibid.* ln. 8; *arbʕ ʕṣm ʕl TN* four beams to the account of TN, *ibid.* ln. 9; *l ʕṣm tspr* you shall write regarding the tree-trunks,

ibid. ln. 17; ★b) wood(?): *rgm ʕṣ*, a matter of wood / word of the tree, 1.3 III 23 and par. (// *abn*); *amrmrn ʕṣ qdš* I shall shake holy wood, RSOu 14 52 [KTU 9.435]:3.
3) Staff: *ḥšk ʕṣk ʕbṣk* grasp your staff (and) your mace, 1.3 III 18 and par.; *ʕṣ brq*, staff of lightning (?), 1.101:4. Dijkstra UF 20 1988 42 reads *ʕṣ amr* 'the sceptre of Amurru' in 1.22 II 17.
Cf. ʕṣy.

ʕṣp "?", bkn ctx. 1.93:7 (cf. Caquot UF 11 1979 104; Aartun UF 17 1985 11).

ʕṣr (I) n. m. 1) "bird"; 2) esp. "domestic fowl, poultry" (Akk. *iṣṣūru*, AHw 390; CAD I/J 210-214; cf. Arab. *ʕuṣfūr*, Lane 2064f.; etym. connection with Aram. *ṣnpr* unc., DNWSI 973; Hb. *ṣip(w)r*, Pun. *ṣpr*, HALOT 1047; DNWSI 973; cf. Landsberger MSL 8/2 145f.; cf. CAD Ṣ 155: *ṣibāru*; diff. Von Soden AHw 390: *iṣṣūru*); syll. Ug.(?): cf. LL ÍD.MUŠEN = *u-ṣú-ru*, MSL 11 43ff. A III 42; NA_4.NÍR.PA.MUŠEN. NA = [*ša*] *kap-pa u-ṣú-ri*, MSL 10 37ff. A 110; cf. Huehnergard UVST 162; ¶ par.: *lḥm*. ¶ Forms: sg. *ʕṣr*, du./pl. *ʕṣrm*, suff. *ʕṣrmm* (encl. *-m*).
1) Bird: *yr b šmm ʕṣr* he shot a bird in the sky, 1.23:38; *ʕṣr tḫrr l išt* you have roasted a bird on the fire, 1.23:41 and par.; *w yʕrb b phm ʕṣr šmm* and into their mouth enter the birds of the sky, 1.23:62; *širh l tikl ʕṣrm* his flesh the birds certainly did eat, 1.6 II 36; cf. espec. *ʕṣr dbḥ* sacrificial bird, 1.14 III 59 and par. (// *lḥm*; diff. Aartun UF 17 1985 11: 'must', Arab. *ʕaṣīr*, JAram. *ʕṣrʔ*). Cf. *tqdm ʕṣr* they offer a bird, 1.161:30 (diff.: Kuyt - Wesselius VT 35 1985 109ff.: *ʕṣr* 'fiesta, festival'; Dijkstra UF 20 1988 46: 1.20 II 11 rdg *tpḥ ʕṣr* 'the appels of the feast(?)', with *ʕṣr (II)*); *mšṣṣ k ʕṣr udnh* who drove (him) out like a bird (from the place) of his dominion, 1.3 IV 1; *w aph k ap ʕṣr* if its muzzle is like a bird's beak, 1.103+:41.
2) Espec. domestic fowl, poultry (Sanmartín AuOr 8 1990 96f.; cf. Akk. *iṣṣūru 2*, AHw 390; CAD I/J 212, ★a) as food: *ṯlṯ ʕṣrm* three birds, 4.751:5; *mat nṣ ṯlṯm ʕṣr* six hundred birds and thirty domestic fowl, 4.14:5; ★b) as sacrificial victim, *passim*: *ʕṣr l ṣpn* one domestic fowl to DN, 1.105:24 and par.; *ʕṣrm l inš ilm* two domestic fowl to the 'divine people', 1.39:21 and par.; 1.171:5; *nkld šrpm ʕṣrm* to DN, as a holocaust, one domestic fowl, 1.111:6; *ʕṣrm l šmn* two domestic fowl for DN, 1.164:8; [*ṯ*]*lṯ ʕṣrm* three domestic fowl, 1.48:3; *arbʕ ʕṣrm* four domestic fowl, 1.48:18; *w in ʕṣr*[ ] and (if) there are no domestic fowl, 1.50:7; *alpm ʕṣrm gdlt* two bulls, two domestic fowl, a cow, 1.148:9; *w l ll ʕṣrm* and at nightfall: two domestic fowl, 1.50:7; *ʕṣrm l inš ilm* two birds to the divine people, 1.106:1 (cf. ln 7); *kmm l pn*

ll ʕṣrmm ditto before nightfall: two domestic fowl, 1.132:17; *b rbʕ ʕṣrmm* on the fourth (day): two domestic fowl, 1.119:20; *tqdm ʕṣr* they offer a bird, 1.161:30.
In bkn ctx.: 1.8:12; 1.27:5; 1.48:1; *w in ʕṣr* and there is no bird, 1.50:8; 1.136:12.
Cf. ʕṣr (II).

ʕṣr (II) PN (Sem. Cf. Grøndahl PTU 28, 113).
PN: *bn PN*, 4.112 II 2; cf. in bkn ctx.: 4.635:56.

ʕṣy PN (Sem.(?). Cf. Watson AuOr 11 1993 218).
PN: 4.367:6; cf. in bkn ctx.: 4.98:25.

ʕšd n. m. of a substance (either edible or a perfume; etym. unc.). ¶ Forms: pl. *ʕšdm*.
A substance: *kd yn l PN w kd ḥmṣ w lth ʕšdm* a jar of wine for PN and one of vinegar and a *l.* of *ʕš.*, 4.269:27; *prs ʕšdm* a *p.* of *ʕš.*, 4.786:11.

/ʕ-š-n/ vb "?"; cf. in bkn ctx.]*yʕšn*, 7.61:7.

ʕšq PN (Sem. Cf. Grøndahl PTU 29, 113).
PN: 4.124:4.

/ʕ-š-r/ vb D: "1) "to invite"; 2) "to give a banquet" (etym. unc.; Ebla cf. *ašārum*, ARET 8 12; cf. the element /(ʔ)-S-L/ in PNN, Krebernik PET 63; *a-šur*(/*šu-ur/úr*)(-DN), Müller Biling. 179; Arab. *ʕaššara / ʕāšara*, Lane 2050f.; Eth. *ʕaššara / ʕašur*, CDG 73; for Hb. cf. *ʕšr* hi., HALOT 898. Cf. De Moor SP 71f.; Dijkstra - De Moor UF 7 1975 189f.; Airoldi Bib 55 1974 181f.; Dietrich - Loretz Fs. Leslau 309ff.); ¶ par.: /d-b-ḥ/, /m-l-ʔ/, /q-d-š/. ¶ Forms: D suffc. *ʕšr*, prefc. *yʕšr*, *nʕšr*, ptc. act. *ʕšr*, inf. *ʕšr*.
D. 1) To invite: *ndd yʕšr w yšqynh* he rushed to invite him and offer him drink, 1.3 I 9; *k bʕl k yḥwy yʕšr* {*ḥwy yʕšr*} *w yšqynh* like DN when he gives life to the(?) one he invites {...} and offers him drink, 1.17 VI 30 (diff.: Van der Toorn BiOr 48 1991 46: 'one serves him'; De Moor ARTU 238: 'he is served').
2) To give a banquet: *mlk ʕšr ʕšrt* the king gives a banquet, 1.16 I 40, 62(?) (// *dbḥ*); *ʕšrt bʕl* [*nʕ*]*šr* a banquet, DN, (to you) we shall give, 1.119: 32-33 (// *nšqdš*, *nmlu*); *ʕšr ʕšr b bt ilm* a banquet is held in the temple of the gods, 1.43:2.

ʕšr (I) n. num. 1) card. "ten"; 2) as an ord. > "tenth" (Sem. c., cf. Moscati ICGSL 116; Gordon UT p. 45ff.; Segert BGUL 87; cf. Blau - Loewenstamm UF 2 1970 31; Dietrich - Loretz UF 5 1973 73; Ebla cf. ŠÚ+ŠA = NI-*sa/si-lu* (/ʔišlū/ < /ʕišrū/) "20", VE 750; Brugnatelli SLE 91; Krecher Biling. 149; cf. *ù-su-rí*, ARET 2 143). ¶ Forms: sg. m. *ʕšr*

(cf. the allomorph *ʕšr*, 4.31:2 and *passim ibid.*); f. *ʕšrt*; pl. *ʕšrm*, "twenty"; *ʕšr* / *ʕšrh* / *ʕšrt* in the compound numbers 11-19.
1) Cardinal ten, *passim*. Cf. *t̠lt̠ ʕšrh* twenty three, RSOu 14 40 [KTU 4.419]:1.
2) As an ordinal, > tenth: *b ym ʕšr* on the tenth day, 1.104:15 (cf. Xella TRU 1 128).
Cf. ʕšrid, ʕšrm, ʕšrt, mʕšr.

ʕšr (II) n. m. of an office, group or class (etym. unc.; "marshal, headwaiter"(?), cf. */ʕ-š-r/*; with no obvious connection with *rb ʕšrt* (*ʕšrt (II)*, *rb (I)*); cf. Ebla *a-śi-ra-tum*, [Fronzaroli] ARET 9 379; Sanmartín AuOr 9 1991 179; W. Akk. *aširūma*, CAD A/2 440; Rainey EAT 66; Moran AmL no. 268 n. 5; cf. AHw 80 and CAD A/2 440: *āširu(m)*. Cf. Rainey JNES 26 1967 296-301; Astour ABAW NF 75 1972 15ff.; Cutler - Macdonald UF 9 1977 23f.; Thiel UF 12 1980 352 n. 26; Heltzer IOKU 152ff.; Aartun UF 17 1985 12f.; Huehnergard UVST 163); ¶ syll. Ug.: LÚ.MEŠ *a-ši-ri-ma*, PRU 3 134 (RS 15.137):9; LÚ(.MEŠ) *a-ši-ru-ma*, PRU 3 201 (RS 16.257+) III 1; PRU 6 93:4; 116:4; 131:3; cf. [LÚ.MEŠ *muš-ke-nu*]-tu_4 LÚ.MEŠ *a-ši-ru-ma*, PRU 3 201 (RS 16.257+) III 30; cf. Sivan GAGl 205; Huehnergard UVST 163. ¶ Forms: pl. *ʕšrm*.
An office, group or class ("marshal, headwaiter"(?)): *ʕšrm*, 4.68:68; 4.99:2; 4.103:30; 4.126:3; 4.412 III 15; 4.416:3; 4.745:2; 4.752:4. The rdg *bt ʕšrm* 'house of the *ʕš.*' in 4.392:3 is unlikely; rd *l šant t̠t̠ lbt ʕšrm* for six rims(?), hoops(?) twenty (in number), (cf. Del Olmo UF 10 1978 47-51; IMC 190, 206; cf. Dietrich - Loretz UF 11 1979 191: *l bt ʕšrm bt alḫnm* 'für das Haus zwanzig, (nämlich das Haus der Verwalter)'; diff.: Astour ABAW NF 75 1972 22f.: 'corporate office of the *aširuma*'; Heltzer IOKU 154: 'house of the *ašīru*' (*sic*!), cf. *ʕšr (III)*; Vita UF 28 1996 694ff.: 'veinte (raciones-*prs*)'). Cf. in unc. ctx. *šbʕ* [*ʕ*]*šrm*, 4.712:1 (cf. Van Soldt UF 21 1989 381: 'seven supervisors-of-ten').

ʕšrid adv. "ten times" (< *ʕšr (I)* + *-(i)d* iterative afform.; Dietrich - Loretz UF 5 1973 77; cf. UT p. 51; BGUL 54).
Ten times: *ʕšrid likt*[ten times he/she has (you have) sent[, 2.42:12.

ʕšrm n. num. "twenty" (pl. of *ʕšr (I)*). ¶ Forms: *ʕšrm*.
Numeral twenty: ★a) elliptical syntagms, *passim*, e.g.: *PN ʕšrm* PN twenty, 4.165:11; ★b) appositional syntagms, *passim*, e.g. *ʕšrm ddm* twenty cauldronsful, 4.128:1; *ʕšrm dd* twenty *d.*, RSOu 14 42 [KTU 9.420]:10; ★c) composite numbers, *passim*, e.g. *ʕšrm arbʕ* twenty four, 4.142:2; cf. *ʕšrm aḥd* twenty one, RSOu 14 39 [KTU 4.790]:10';

bkn ctx.: RSOu 14 44:9.

ʕšrt (I) n. f. 1) "banquet"; 2) a type of offering, "banquet offering" (< /ʕ-š-r/; cf. Eth. *ʕašur*, CDG 73; diff.: Dijkstra UF 16 1984 74: 'the tithe', cf. De Moor ARTU 174; Dietrich - Loretz TUAT 819: 'Libation'); ¶ par.: *dkr*, *ḥtp*. ¶ Forms: sg. *ʕšrt*.

1) Banquet: *mlk ʕšr ʕšrt* the king gives a banquet, 1.16 I 41, 62(?); *ʕšrt bʕl* [*nʕ*]*šr* a banquet, DN, (to you) we shall give, 1.119:32 (// *dkr*, *ḥtp*).
2) Banquet offering: *tqln alpm yrḫ ʕšrt l bʕ*[*l spn*] two month-old head of cattle are felled as a banquet offering to DN, 1.109:5 and par. In 1.15 II 8-9 rdg: *ṯġr* (Greenstein IOS 18 1998 109).

ʕšrt (II) n. f. "group of ten, ten" (< *ʕšr (I)*; Hb. *ʕśrh*, HALOT 895; Akk. *ešertu*, AHw 254; CAD E 365; *šurtum*, AHw 1443: cf. *wakil ušurti*, CAD A/1 279: *aklu A* c.3'; cf. Salonen BiOr 25 1968 160; cf. Hurro-Akk. *emantu*, AHw 211; CAD E 137). ¶ Forms: sg. *ʕšrt*.

Group of ten, ten: *PN rb ʕšrt* PN: chief of ten, decurion, 4.609:2, 5, 7, 8; *spr rb ʕšrt*, list of decurions, 4.714:1 (cf. Akk. *rab ešerti*, AHw 254: *ešertu II*, 938: *rabû* D.2.a; CAD E 365; *wakil ušurti*, AHw 1443: *ušurtum*; CAD A/1 279: *aklu A* c.3'; cf. Salonen BiOr 25 1968 160; Kinnier Wilson Wine Lists 90; cf. Hurro-Akk. *emantuḫlu*, AHw 211; CAD E 137).

ʕšrt (III), cf. *ʕšr (I)*.

ʕšt(y) n. of card. num. "one" (Akk. *ištēn*, AHw 400, CAD I/J 275-278; Gelb Proto-Akkadian 37; Hb. *ʕšty*, HALOT 898f.; Aram. (?) cf. DNWSI 895f.: *ʕšt?*. Cf. Gordon UT p. 46; Cecchini Or 50 1981 106ff.; Tropper UF 29 1997 666f.). ¶ Forms: sg. *ʕšt*, *ʕšty* (*-y* = *mater lectionis*(?)).

One, ★a) first number in a numerical scale: *ʕšty w ṯʕ*[*y*] *(...) tqdm* one (time: it is recited) and an offerer (...) offer(s), 1.161:27 (cf. *ibid.* ln. 30); ★b) in a syntagm with *ʕšr*: "eleven", cf. *ʕšt ʕšr*, 1.112:13; 4.141 III 7; 4.358:7; *ʕšt ʕšrh*, 4.290:4; 4.609:52. Bkn.: 2.27:1; 4.323:4; 4.390:11; 4.552:2, 7.

/ʕ-š-y/ vb G: 1) "to make, process, work", in farming; 2) to do something (bad)", "to annoy" (Hb. *ʕśh*, HALOT 899ff.; Moab. *ʕšy*, DNWSI 890f.; Arab. *ʕašiya*, Lane 2055 [preferable to Arab. *ġašiya*]; ESA *ʕšy*, CAME 210). ¶ Forms: G ptc. act. *ʕšy*; pass. ptc. *ʕšy*.

G. 1) To make, process, work, ★a) said of fields: *šd ʕšy*, worked field, arable, ready (cultivated and sown(?)), 4.282: 7, 10, 14 (cf. *krm*, ln. 8, 12, *ibid.*; cf. Dijkstra - De Moor UF 7 1975 177: Akk. *eqlu eršu*); ★b) referring to a type of wine: *yn ʕšy* wine (that is) made, processed, ready(?), in bkn and unc. ctx. 1.17 VI 8 (cf. Dijkstra - De Moor UF 7

1975 184; diff. Caquot TOu 1 430 n. i: 'exprimé', Hb. *ʕiśśā*).
2) To do something (bad) + *l* to someone (Hb. *ʕšh l*, HALOT 891f.; Arab. *ʕašiya ʕalā*, Lane 2055; cf. Akk. *epēšu ana*, AHw 225: *epēšu (II)* 5.h.; CAD E 228f.: *epēšu* 2.f.): *grš d ʕšy lnh* who ejects one who does something, 1.17 I 29 and par. (cf. Driver CML 140; Ug 6 184: 'to turn away, to rebel', Hb. *ʕśh*, Arab. *ʕašâ*; Avishur UF 17 1985 54: 'to oppress > oppressor', Hb. *ʕiśśā*).

ʕt TN (Belmonte RGTC 12/2 44).
TN: 4.68:24.

/ʕ-t-d/ vb "?".
In unc. ctx.: *tʕtd tkl* [, 1.5 III 5.

ʕtgr adj. m. "excluded, expropriated, held"(?) (< /ʕ-g-r/; cf. ESA *ḥgr* and *ʕgr*, DOSA 166, 352; Arab. *ḥğr* and *ʕğr*, Lane 516f., 1958f.; cf. Akk. *egēru*, AHw 190; CAD E 41f.). ¶ Forms: pl. *ʕtgrm*.
Excluded, expropriated, held(?): (PNN and family:) *ʕtgrm*, 4.420:7, 12 (bkn ctx.).

/ʕ-t-k/ vb D: "to tie, fasten, bind" (cf. Arab. *ʕataka*, Lane 1948. Cf. Gray JSS 11 1966 236; De Moor SP 91; Pope UF 3 1971 376; Renfroe AULS 26ff.); ¶ par.: /b-ṣ-r/, /š-n-s/. ¶ Forms: D suffc. *ʕtkt*; impv. *ʕtk*.
D. To tie, fasten, bind: *ʕtkt rišt l bmth* she fastened heads to (her) back, 1.3 II 11 and par. (// *šnst*); *l ḥbšk ʕtk iš* to your waist tie heads, 1.13:7 (// *bṣr*).
Cf. ʕtk (II).

ʕtk (I) n. m. of a monster (cf. Gray UF 11 1979 316 n. 6: 'the Savage One', Arab. *ʕataka*. Cf. Day GCD 80ff. 181).
A monster: *ʕgl il ʕtk* the divine Bullock, *ʕt.*, 1.3 III 44.

ʕtk (II) adj. m. " anchored, moored" ((?); said of ships; cf. ESA *ʕtk*, DOSA 388; cf. /ʕ-t-k/ and cf. Dietrich - Loretz - Sanmartín UF 6 1974 34). ¶ Forms: sg. *ʕtk*; pl. *ʕtkm*.
Anchored, moored((?); said of ships): *anyt mlk*[...] *w tlṯ brm d*[...] *arbʕ ʕtkm* [...] *ʕtk (...)* the ships of the king [...] and three barges [...] four are moored(?) [...] moored(?) (...), 4.421:4-5.

ʕtn, 2.16:13, cf. *ʕnt*.

/ʕ-t-q/ vb G: "to pass"; N: "to become old, to age" (Hb. *ʕtq*, HALOT 904f.; Syr. *ʕteq*, LS 553; Ebla cf. *-ti-ik/ig/gV*, Krebernik PET 42; Catagnoti MisEb 1 264; cf. *i-ti-ga-am*$_6$, (?) /yiʕtiqam/, Krebernik QuSe 18 120; Akk. *etēqu*, AHw 260ff.; CAD E 384ff.; Arab. *ʕatuqa*, Lane 1947. Cf. Pardee UF 5 1973 229ff.; Sanmartín UF 10 1978 453f.); ¶ par.: /m-t/. ¶ Forms: G prefc. *tʕtq*, emph. *yʕtqn*, *tʕtqn*; N: suffc. *nʕtq*.
G. To pass: 1) of time: *ym ymm yʕtqn* one day and two passed, 1.6 II

26 and par.
2) of space: *b ḥwt ngṯ tʕtqn* they pass through the land TN, 2.36+:26 (Tropper UG 52); see *tʕtq by ḥwt* they pass through the land, 2.73:4.
N. To become old, to age: *k klb b btk nʕtq* like a dog (that) has become old in your house, 1.16 I 16 and par (// *tmtn*).
Bkn: 7.136:3.
Cf. **ʕtq, šʕtqt**.

ʕtq adj. m. "perennial, durable" (< /ʕ-t-q/; Hb. *ʕtyq*, HALOT 903; Aram. *ʕtq*, DNWSI 898; Arab. *ʕatīq*, Lane 1947). ¶ **Forms**: sg. *ʕtq*.
Perennial, durable: *ḫštk l ntn ʕtq* your grave has become a perennial lament, 1.16 I 18 and par.

ʕṭ n. m. of a kind of fish ((?). Cf. Van Soldt UF 22 1990 337 n. 113; diff. Aartun StUL 96f.: 'Raub-Greifelvogel', Hb. *ʕayiṭ*; for other proposals cf. Ribichini - Xella Tessili 56; Baldacci BiOr 46 1989 120; Xella UF 22 1990 473; De Moor UF 28 1996 155: Syrian Arab. *ʕaḍāḍi* 'the biter'); ¶ syll. Ug.: KU$_6$.MEŠ : *ú-ṭu*, RS 23.368, cit. Nougayrol PRU 6 p. 119 n. 1. ¶ **Forms**: sg. *ʕṭ*.
A kind of fish(?): *a*[*lp*] *ʕṭ* a thousand (shekels / pieces of) *ʕṭ*, 4.247:24.
In bkn ctx.; *šbʕ ʕṭ*[seven *ʕṭ*, RSOu 14 33 [KTU 9.422]:2 (Bordreuil - Pardee RSOu 14 p. 349: 'sept oiseaux'); 4.765:8.

/ʕ-ṭ-p/ vb G: "to be weak" (Hb. *ʕṭp*, HALOT 814f.: *ʕṭp II*; Arab. *ʕaṭafa*, Lane 2079ff. Cf. Dietrich - Loretz MU 107). ¶ **Forms**: prefc. energic or suffixed *tʕṭpn*.
G. To be weak: *yld bhmth tʕṭpn* the young of his small cattle will be weak, 1.103+:2.

ʕṭrṭrt n. f. "diadem, crown" ((?); cf. Hb. *ʕṭrh*, HALOT 815; Ph, Pun. *ʕṭrt*, DNWSI 838. Diff.: Dietrich - Loretz UF 10 1978 424f.: 'e. wohlriechende Pflanze'; De Moor UF 11 1979 646: 'fragrant herbs'; Izreel IOS 18 1998 426: 'type of grain', EA (gloss) *ḫu-ṭá-ri-ma*). ¶ **Forms**: sg. *ʕṭrṭrt*.
Diadem(?): *ʕl tl k ʕṭrṭrt* (the rain) upon the hillock is like a diadem(?), 1.16 III 11 (cf. Lipiński Syria 44 1967 284ff.; Sasson RSP 1 431; Badre *et al.* Syria 53 1976 122, 124, rdg *ʕṭrṭrm*).
Cf. in bkn ctx.: *ʕṭr*[, 1.16 V 44, VI 8; and cf. De Moor UF 11 1979 646f. n. 44; ARTU 221: 'primrose' (cf. *pṭr*).

ʕṯb "?"; 1.166:14.

ʕṯlṯ PN (bkn?; etym. unc.).
PN: *bn ʕṯlṯ*[, 4.37:3.

ʕṯqb n. m. a kind of tree (etym. unc.; cf. De Moor UF 3 1971 349f.: *Fraxinus ornus* L., 'the punctured', < * *ṯqb* ; diff.: Cazelles Syria 33

1956 53: 'bossu', Akk. *asqubītu*; Caquot EI 14 1978 16: 'les Forts', Arab. *ṯaqafa*, Aram. *tqyp*). ¶ Forms: pl. *ʕṯqbm*.
A kind of tree: *ṯm tpl (...) k yrkt ʕṯqbm* there they have fallen (...), like logs, 1.13:14.
Cf. ʕṯqbt.

ʕṯqbt PN (Sem. Cf. Grøndahl PTU 113; De Moor UF 3 1971 350 n. 6; Watson NUS 35 1986 11).
PN: 4.63 II 27.

ʕṯrb n. m.(?) of an ingredient or medicine in the hippiatric texts (etym. unc.; cf. Pardee TH 65: Arab. *ʕuṯrubun* 'arbrisseau semblable au grenadier' [< Biberstein - Kazimirski 2 170]; Cohen UF 28 1996 140f.: Akk. *azupīru*). ¶ Forms: sg. *ʕṯrb*.
Ingredient in the hippiatric texts: *pr ʕṯrb* fruit of the *ʕṯ.*, 1.97:12 and par. Bkn.: 1.85:24.

ʕṯt "?"; 2.23:3.

ʕṯtpl/r DN in combination with *ʕṯtr* (cf. De Moor UF 2 1970 315; Dietrich - Loretz - Sanmartín UF 7 1975 165; Xella TRU 57f.; Pardee TPM 252f.; cf. Ebla *áš-da-píl*, Stieglitz Eblaitica 2 81).
DN: variants *ʕṯtr w ʕṯtpl*, 1.46:4; *ʕṯtr ʕṯtpr*, 1.123:10; *ʕṯtr w ʕṯtpr*, 1.107:41.

ʕṯtr DN m. (ESA *ʕṯtr*, *ʕśtrm*, *ʕtr*, Höfner WbMyth 497ff.; Moab. *ʕštrkmš*, KAI 181:17; cf. pre-Sarg. Mari DN dMÙŠ.UŠ, Gelb - Kienast AKDT 5 n. 4: dINANNA.NITA 'Aštar'; Kienast - Sommerfeld GlAKI 17; cf. Ebla DN f. d*aš(/áš-)dar*, dMÙŠ, *passim*, cf. dMÙŠ = *aš-dar*, VE 805; Krebernik ZA 72 1982 31; Sanmartín AuOr 9 1991 179f.; Pettinato Rituale 243; pre-Sarg. Mari *aš-dar*, Charpin MARI 5 6 I 2 and *passim*; OB Mari, Alalah, EA, Ugarit, Emar: d"UŠ"*(iš$_8$)*.DAR, dINANNA(MÙŠ), *passim*, Oliva Ishtar 108ff.; Emar *aš-tar*, Arnaud Emar 6/3 43:12 and *passim*; in PNN from Emar d*Aš-tar-* (Ninurta(?)), cf. Arnaud AuOrS 1 15. Cf. Roberts ESP 39, 100f.; Caquot Syria 35 1958 45ff.; Pope WbMyth. 249f.; Huffmon APNMT 171ff.; Waterston UF 20 1988 357ff.; Blažek, Fs. Petraček 133ff.); syll. Ug. cf. dL[UGAL.MÁR(?).DA(?)] = *aš-ta-bi-*[*ni*(?)] = *aš-ta-ru*, Ug 5 137 IV b 16(?); Huehnergard UVST 164; Van Soldt SAU 306; cf. the element /ʕaštar-/ in PNN, Sivan GAGl 205; ¶ RS Akk.: cf. d*aš-ta-bi*, Ug 5 18:17 (// *ʕṯtr* KTU 1.47:18; 1.118:17).
DN: 1.2 III 12, 18, 24 and *passim*; 1.24:28; 1.118:17; 1.148:30; *ʕṯtr ʕrẓ* DN the terrible, 1.6 I 55 and par. Bkn ctx.: 1.142:2; 1.159:4; 4.216:10. In Hurr. ctx.: 1.111:19.
Cf. TN *gt ʕṯtr*, 4.696:6 (Belmonte RGTC 12/2 83: *Gittu-ʕaṯtari*); NP

bnʕṯtr.

Cf. ʕbdʕṯtr, ʕṯtrab, ʕṯtrum, ʕṯtrn, ʕṯtr (II), ʕṯtry, bnʕṯtr.

ʕṯtrab PN (Sem. Cf. Grøndahl PTU 86, 113); ¶ syll.: *aš-tar-a-bi*, PRU 3 141 (RS 16.134):3, 8; Ug 5 86:26; cf. Huehnergard UVST 232.

PN; ★a) 4.260:4; 4.432:17; ★b) *bn PN*: 4.232:12.

ʕṯtrum PN (Sem. Cf. Grøndahl PTU 45f., 113; Watson AuOr 14 1996 103). Cf. *ištrmy*.

PN: 4.410:31; 4.426:1; 4.504:2; cf. in bkn ctx.: 4.485:4.

ʕṯtrn PN (Sem. Cf. Grøndahl PTU 52, 114).

PN: 4.75 II 4; 4.86:31; cf. in bkn ctx.: 4.769:41. Cf. 1.142:2.

ʕṯtrt (I) DN (Hb. *ʕštrt*, HALOT 899; Ph. *ʕštrt* cf. Harris GPL 135f.; Ebla ^{d}INANNA = *aš-dar*, VE 805; Krebernik QuSe 18 96; for ^{d}*aš-dar* and ^{d}EN.TE = *áš/iš-*^{tá}*tár*, VE 804, cf. Mander MROA 2/1 19f., 42; pre-Sarg Mari. cf. ^{d}"DIŠ".DAR*-ra-at* and ^{d}NIN$^{tá\text{-}ra\text{-}at}$, Gelb - Kienast AKDT 5 n. 4; GlAKI 14, 23; Ebla (Ur III) ^{d}*eš*$_4$*-tár*, Gelb - Kienast AKDT 370; Kienast GlAK 14f.; Emar Akk. ^{d}*aš-tar-ti*, Arnaud Emar VI/3 153:2, 413:3', *passim* in PNN, cf. Arnaud AuOrS 1 164; Alalah Akk. PN *aš-tar-ti*, AT 130; Akk. EA TN URU *aš-tar-ti*$_7$*/ti*, EAT 197:10; 256:21; PN ÌR.^{d}INANNA(MÙŠ) / *ab-di-aš-ta-<ar->ti*, Hess AmPN 10; Eg. *ʕa-ś-tá-r-tá/tu* and var. *ʕá-śi-tá*, Stadelmann SPGÄ 101; Lüddeckens LÄ 499ff.; Helck Bez. 456ff.; NA ^{d}*aš-tar-tu*, Borger Asarhaddon 69 IV 18. Cf. Roberts ESP 39; Pope WbMyth 250ff.; Herrmann MIO 15 1969 51; Wilcke RlA 5 74ff.; Ribichini - Xella RSF 7 1979 145ff.); ¶ RS Akk.: ^{d}INANNA(MÙŠ), ^{d}"U"*(iš*$_8$*)*+DAR, *passim*, Huehnergard AkkUg 363, 397; cf. ^{d}"U"*(iš*$_8$*)*+DAR$^{iš\text{-}tar}$, Ug 5 18:24 (// *ʕṯtrt*, KTU 1.47:25; 1.118:24; cf. Nougayrol Ug 5 p. 56).

DN: ★a) *passim* in narrative ctx.: 1.2 I 40; 1.2 IV 28; 1.14 III 42 and par. (// *ʕnt*); RSOu 14 53 [KTU 9.432]:18′; ★b) *ʕṯtrt w ʕnt* / *ʕnt w ʕṯtrt*: 1.100:20; 1.107:39 and par.; 1.114:9, 10 and par.; cf. the sequence *lʕṯtrt l ʕnt*, 2.42:7-8; ★c) *passim* in offering lists: cf. *šʕrt l šr DN* wool for the singer of DN, 4.168:4; ★d) special syntagms: *ʕṯtrt ḫr* DN of the tombs, 1.43:1; 1.112:13 (cf. Eg. *ʕa-s-tá-ra ḫá-rú*, *ʕa-śi-tá-ya ḫá-rú*, Helck Bez. 459; Baniyas: ^{d}INANNA(MÙŠ) *ḫur-ri*, Lackenbacher Fs. Birot 159; RS: ^{d}"U"+DAR *ḫur-ri*, PRU 3 171 (RS 16.173):9'; 4 230 (RS 18.01), 3, 6; 6 35; cf. Del Olmo AuOr 2 1984 202 n. 27; A2CISFP 1 367ff.; cf. diff. Herrmann WO 7 1973 135ff.; Dietrich - Loretz JA 45ff.: 'von Ḫurri'; cf. *ḫr*); *ʕṯtrt mr(h)* DN of Mari, 1.100:78 (cf. Bordreuil MARI 4 1985 545ff.); *ʕṯtrt šd* of the steppe, 1.148:18 and par.; cf. RS: ^{d}INANNA(MÙŠ) EDIN, PRU 4 121 (RS 17.352):12; 124 (17.367):2'; *ʕṯtrt šm bʕl* DN, name of DN, 1.16 VI 56 and par.; cf. RS: dINANNA(MÙŠ) EDIN, PRU 4 121 (RS 17.352):12; 124 (17.367):2'; *ʕṯtrt šm bʕl* DN, name of DN, 1.16 VI 56 and par.; *md ʕṯtrt* expert of DN, 4.245 I 1, 11; ★e) in Hurr. ctx.: *ʕṯtrt ndrg / abḏr*, 1.81:18-19; ★d) espec., initiates of a cult or DN: *md ʕṯtrt* list of the *m.* of DN, 4.245 I 1, 11; cf. in bkn ctx.: 4.188:19; ★f) *bt ʕṯtrt* shrine of DN, 4.219:2; ★g) TN *gt ʕṯtrt*, 4.125:6 (Belmonte RGTC 12/2 83: *Gittu-ʕaṯtarti*). - Cf. ʕṯtrt (II).

ʕṯtrt (II) TN (Belmonte RGTC 12/2 43: **ʕAštartu* / **ʕAṯtartu*, name of a city, the destination of the dead and deified kings, probably located in Bashan; Eg. *ʕ-s-[ta-]r-tum*, execr. texts, Helck Bez. 55 no. 25; *ʕa-s-tá-r-tu*, Helck Bez. 129 no. 28; EA *aš-tar-te*, EAT 197:10; *aš-tar-ti*, EAT 256:21; cf. Astour JNES 27 1969 21; RSP 2 313f.; Margulis JBL 89 1970 292ff.; Dietrich - Loretz UF 12 1980 172ff.; Pardee TPM 96ff.); ¶ par.: *hdrʕy*. ¶ Forms: *ʕṯtrt*; suff. *ʕṯtrth* (*-h* adv.).
TN: *ql bl ʕm mlk ʕṯtrth* take the cry to DN, in TN, 1.100:41; *mlk b ʕṯtrt yisp ḥmt* DN of TN remove the poison, 1.107:42; *il yṯb b ʕṯtrt* the god who sits in TN, 1.108:2 (// *hdrʕy*); *śśw ršp* / *mlkʕṯtrt* the horses of DN, RSOu 14 39 [KTU 4.790]:16', 17' (cf. Dietrich - Loretz UF 21 1989 129; cf. Ph. *mlkʕštrt*, KAI 3 58; Benz PNPPI 345; Bordreuil - Pardee RSOu 14 p. 356 n. 12f.) .

ʕṯtry PN (< *ʕṯtr*, DN. Cf. Grøndahl PTU 51; Bordreuil SEL 5 1988 28f.).
PN: *bn PN*, 4.7:13; 4.93 I 4; 4.782:10; RSOu 14 46 [KTU 9.432]:7; cf. in bkn ctx. 4.225:2. For *bn ʕṯtr*, 4.778:6, cf. Bordreuil SEL 5 1988 28. In 5.10:1 (scribal exercise?) written *ʕṯty*.

ʕwr n. m. "blind man" (Hb. *ʕwr*, HALOT 803; Syr. *ʕwīrō*, LS 518; Eth. *ʕĕwwĕr*, CDG 79; Arab. *ʔaʕwar*, Lane 2195; cf. *ʕawira*, Lane 2193ff.); ¶ par.: *zbl*. ¶ Forms: sg. *ʕwr*; f. cf. *ʕwrt*.
Blind: *ʕwr mzl ymzl* the blind man gropes his way, 1.14 II 46 and par. (// *zbl*; cf. Del Olmo IMC 167ff.).

ʕwrt n. f. "blind" (< *ʕwr*). ¶ Forms: sg. *ʕwrt*.
Blind: *ʕwrt yštk bʕl* may DN leave you blind, 1.19 IV 5.

ʕyn PN (Sem.(?); cf. Grøndahl PTU 309).
PN: ★a) 4.273:5; ★b) *bn PN*, 2.70:11, 17; 4.348:18; 4.357:26; 4.366:10; 4.371:7; 4.422:52; 4.617:6; 4.692:15.

ʕyy PN (etym. unc.); ¶ syll.: cf. *a-i-ú*, Ug 5 27:20. Cf. *ayy*.
PN: 4.356:12.

ʕz (I) n. m. "strength" (< /ʕ-z-z/; cf. Hb. *ʕ(w)z*, HALOT 805f.; Ph. *ʕz*, DNWSI 835); syll. Ug. cf. the element /ʕuzz-/ (< *ú-zv-*, *uz-zv-*, *ḫu-zv-*) in PNN, cf. Sivan GAGl 208; Huehnergard UVST 252 and n. 165; ¶ par.: *ḏmr*. ¶ Forms: sg. *ʕz*, suff. *ʕzk*.

Strength: ... *b ʕz [rpi] mlk ʕlm* (he will endow you (?)) with the strength of DN, eternal king, 1:108:21; *l r[p]i arṣ ʕzk* from DN of the earth (is / be) your strength, 1.108:24.

ʕz (II) n. m. 1) "caprine animal, kid, goat" (cf. Hb., Pun. *ʕz*, HALOT 804f.; DNWSI 875; OAram. *ʕnz*, DNWSI 875; Amor. cf. /ḫazzum/, AHw 339; Akk. *enzu*, *ezzu*, AHw 221f.; CAD E 180ff.; Arab. *ʕanz*, Lane 2173. Cf. Del Olmo BSA 7 191); ¶ RS Akk.: (UDU.)ÙZ, PRU 6 117:2; 119:1; 120:1; cf. 42 ÙZ.MÁŠ.MEŠ Ú.LU, PRU 6 120:3; cf. Sanmartín BSA 7 1993 200, 203). ¶ Forms: sg. *ʕz*, pl. *ʕzm*.
Caprine animal, kid, goat, in rituals: (if the family of) *aṯt yqḥ ʕz* a woman takes a goat, 1.127:26; (if) *bt bn bnš yqḥ ʕz* the family of someone takes a goat, 1.127:31; (a kid) *b bz ʕzm* from the udder of goats (is sacrificed), 1.80:4.

ʕz (III) adj./s. m. "strong, powerful" (< /ʕ-z-z/; Hb. *ʕz*, HALOT 805f.; Akk. *ezzu*, AHw 270; CAD E 432 ff.; cf. the element /ʕazz-/ in PNN from Alalah and EA; Sivan GAGl 205); ¶ par.: *qrd*. ¶ Forms: sg. *ʕz*.
1) Strong, powerful: *ṯnn ʕz yuḫd ib mlk* the powerful Vizier will seize the enemy of the king, 1.103+:17; *yd ilm p k mtm ʕz mid* here the power of the gods is very strong, very much so, like death / DN, 2.10:13.
2) The strong one (used as a noun): *k gr ʕz ṯġrkm* when a strong one attacks your gates, 1.119:26 (// *qrd*); *ydy ʕz l ṯġrkm* he will repel the strong one from your gates, 1.119:35 and par. (// *qrd*).

ʕzilt PN (Sem. Cf. Watson AuOr 14 1996 103); syl.: *a-zi-il-tù*, RSOu 7 31:18.
NP: RSOu 14 49 [KTU 9.433]:4, 23.

ʕzbʕl ritual PN of the Ugaritic king (cf. */ʕ-z(-z)/*, *bʕl (II)*; Del Olmo CR 175: ʕAmmiṯtamru).
Ritual PN: *ʕzbʕl*, 1.102:27.

ʕzl PN (etym. unc.; cf. Dietrich - Loretz KA 157: allograph of *ġzl*; cf. Watson AuOr 8 1990 123). Cf. *ġzl*.
PN: *bn PN*, 4.31:8 (rdg unc.).

ʕzn PN (Sem. Cf. Grøndahl PTU 112; Dietrich - Loretz OLZ 62 1967 545; Van Soldt SAU 27, 63, 177f.); ¶ syll.: *ú/uz-ze-nu/ni/na*, cf. PRU 3 p. 260; PRU 4 236 (RS 17.251):7; PRU 6 p. 144; Ug 5 p. 333 (cf. Huehnergard UVST 252 n. 165); *uz-ze-e-na*, RSOu 7 15:2 (Van Soldt SAU 286 n. 80); *uz-zé-ni*, RSOu 7 24:6 (Van Soldt SAU 223, 286 n. 80); cf. RS 34.158 (Van Soldt SAU 221 n. 329). Cf. *uḏn*.
PN: ★a) 4.35 I 9 (*bn mll*); 4.76:1 (*bn irbn*); 4.93 II 8 (*bn mlk*; Healey SEL 5 1988 107); 4.148:6 (Van Soldt SAU 39); 4.214 IV 3; 4.232:34;

4.281:26 (*bn brn*), 31; 4.609:7 (Van Soldt SAU 39), 22, 28, 31; 4.562:3; 4.773:3; 4.780:11; 5.11:1 *(bn byy*); 6.14:2 (Healey SEL 5 1988 106f.); in bkn ctx.: 4.319:4; ★b) *bn PN:* 4.69 II 13; 4.320:11; 4.785:16.

/ʕ-z(-z)/ vb G: "to be strong, have power"; D: "strengthen" (Hb., OAram. *ʕzz*, HALOT 808fs.; DNWSI 835; Ebla cf. *a-zu*, Krebernik PET 73; Akk. *ezēzu*, AHw 269f.; CAD E 427ff.; ESA *ʕzz*, DOSA 360f.; Arab. *ʕazza*, Lane 2030ff.; Eth. *ʕazzaza*, CDG 81. Cf. Stamm UF 11 1979 757); ¶ syll. Ug.: cf. PNN *ia-aʔ-za-na*, Ug 5 12:6; *ta-a-zi*, PRU 6 8:2; cf. Sivan GAGl 208. ¶ Forms: G suffc. *ʕz*, prefc. *yʕzz*, D prefc. with suff. *tʕzzk*.

G. To be strong, have power: *ʕz ym l ymk* DN was strong and did not fall, 1.2 IV 17; *mt ʕz bʕl ʕz* DN was strong, DN was strong, 1.6 VI 17 and par.; *yd ilm p k mtm ʕz mid* here the power of the gods is very strong, very much so, like death / DN, 2.10:13 (cf. Song 8:6; diff. Cunchillos TOu 2 279: 'pouvoir'; cf. Pardee Fs. Pope 66f.); *mlkn yʕzz ʕl ḫpṯh* the king will have power over his mercenaries, 1.103+:57.

D. To strengthen: *ilm tġrk tšlmk tʕzzk* may the gods guard you, keep you, strengthen you, 5.9:4.

Cf. in bkn ctx.]*tʕzzn*, 1.103:20; *yʕzz ʕl*[, 1.140:4 (cf. Tropper UF 26 1994 463, 465).

Cf. ʕz (I), ʕz (III), ʕzilt, ʕzbʕl, ʕzn.

ʕẓm (I) n. f. "bone" (Hb., Ph. *ʕṣm*, HALOT 869; DNWSI 880; Syr. *ʕaṭmō*, LS 520; Ebla cf. GIŠ.GI.NA = *a-za-mu-um*, Krebernik ZA 73 1983 16; cf. *ga-ba-bu ʔa*$_x$(NI)*-za-da*, Fronzaroli EL 137, 140; Akk. *eṣemtu*, AHw 251; CAD E 341ff.; Arab. *ʕaẓam* Lane 2087; Eth. *ʕaḍm*, CDG 58); ¶ par.: *šmt.* ¶ Forms: sg. *ʕẓm.*

Bone, ★a): *aḥd hm (...) iṯ ʕẓm* I shall see whether (...) there is bone, 1.19 III 5 and par. (// *šmt*); *in ʕẓm* there was no bone, 1.19 III 11 and par.; ★b) *ʕẓm yd* forearm, 1.12 I 24 (diff. Schloen JNES 52 1993 216: 'mighty', cf. *ʕẓm (II)*; Wyatt RTU 163 n. 8: 'nails', lit. 'bones of the hand').

ʕẓm (II) adj. m. "imposing, powerful" (Hb. *ʕṣwm*, HALOT 867; Arab. *ʕaẓīm*, *ʕuẓām*, Lane 2087f.). ¶ Forms: sg. *ʕẓm.*

Imposing: *ʕẓm ri* imposing in appearance, 1.3 I 12.

Cf. ridn.

ʕẓm (III) n. m. "power, excellence" (Hb. *ʕṭm*, HALOT 869; Arab. *ʕuẓm*, Lane 2087. Diff. Caquot - Sznycer TOu 1 135f. n. k: 'corpulent'); ¶ par.: *ul.* ¶ Forms: sg. suff. *ʕẓmny.*

Power, excellence: *w l ʕpr ʕẓmny* and our power (fell) to the ground,

1.2 IV 5 (// *ul*).
Cf. ʕẓmt.

ʕẓmt PN (Sem. Cf. Grøndahl PTU 77, 112f.; cf. 1.6 VI 18).
PN: *bn PN*, 4.352:7 (*rišy*).

ʕẓrn "(?) "
In bkn ctx.: 1.166:11, 15; 1.167:10.

b

b (I) prep. of 1) spatial situation: "in; through, on; by, at; within, inside, in, to, against, between, upon; from; with, in; of, from among" and 2) temporal situation: "dating from, in, during, to; for"; 3) relationship of cause or reason, exchange or benefit: "for, of/from, in"; 4) relationship of accompaniment and instrument: "with, among, to"; 5) modal relationship: "as /in the manner of" (Hb. *b*, HALOT 103ff.; Ph., Pun., Aram. *b*, DNWSI 137ff.; ESA *b*, DOSA 33f.; Arab. *bi*, Lane 141-144; Eth. *ba*, CDG 82; Moscati ICGSL 121; cf. Akk. */ba/ [cf. *bašû*, AHw 112]; Ebla cf. BA [*bi*$_6$/*ba*], /bi/a/, ARET 2 120; ARET 5 61; Sanmartín AuOr 9 1991 180f. Cf. Pardee UF 7 1975 329-378; UF 8 1976 215-322; UF 9 1977 205-231; Aartun PU 2 1-26; Dahood RSP 1 133-141; Gordon UT § 10.1-2, 10.4s.); ¶ syll. Ug.: [MU] = *i*(?)-*na* = *i-gi-da* = *bi-i*[, Ug 5 130 III 6'; cf. /bi-/ in UR = *mi-it-ḫa-ri-iš* = [(Hurr.)] = *bi*-RU[, UF 11 1979 479:36; Van Soldt SAU 303; cf. Sivan GAGl 132; UF 18 1986 308f.; UF 21 1989 360: phonetic complement *bí*; cf. Huehnergard UVST 53 n. 8; ¶ RS Akk.: cf. Ug 5 130 III 6'; *ištu, ina, passim*, cf. Van Soldt SAU 447ff., 451f., 456, 461; ¶ par.: *ʕl (I), b, bʕd, bm, bn (II), bnm, l (I), tḥt*; prep. syntagms ¶ par.: *b + qrb*, *b + tk* (cf. Dahood RSP 1 133-141; RSP 3 40). ¶ Forms: *b*, *by* (with the spelling phonetic / complement -*y*; Blau - Loewenstamm UF 2 1970 25 n. 35: < /bī/; diff.: Dietrich - Loretz - Sanmartín UF 5 1973 86; Pardee UF 8 1976 268; Hoftijzer UF 11 1979 388 n. 23; Tropper UF 26 1994 460 n. 13, 474 n. 10: < /bi/; Aartun PU 1 47, 2 24: + emph. ext. -*y*; cf. Huehnergard UVST 53 n. 8 and Sivan GAGl 132 on the syll. spelling *bi-i*[); suff. pn. *by, bk, bh, bhm, b{.}hn*; emph. ext. *bm, bn, bnm* (De Moor SP 160f.; cf. Aartun PU 1 47, 59, 64f.; 2 24f., 25f.). Extended adv. *bkm*; cf. *bd*.

1) Spatial situation, ★a) place in which something occurs, in, through, on: they work *b ugrt* in TN, 4.141 III 8; (the fleet is) *by ʕky* (actually) in TN, 2.38:25; *tʕtq by ḥwt* they should pass through the land, 2.36:26; *ntbt mṣrm b ḥwt ugrt* the (right of (?)) passage through the country (of) TN, 2.36:16; *b ṯy(n)dr* in TN, 2.13:14; 2.30;13; 6.21:2;

they are not *b spr* in the book, 4.338:3; RSOu 14 53 [KTU 9.432]:43'; a son *b bt* in the house, 1.17 I 25 (// *b qrb hklh*); *bn ġlmt* in thick fog, 1.4 VII 55 (// *b ġlmt*); *b py (...)* // *b špty* in my mouth (...), // on my lips (...), 1.24:45-46; he laughed *bm lb* in (his) heart, 1.12 I 12 (// *bm kbd*); I cannot rule *b ṣrrt ṣpn* on the heights of TN, 1.6 I 62; she fought *b ʕmq* in the valley, 1.3 II 6 (// *bn (II) qrytm*); he sat down *b ap ṯġr* in the porch, 1.17 V 6 (// *tḥt adrm*); eat *b ṯlḥnt lḥm* food on the tables, 1.4 IV 36 (// *b krpnm, b k<s>*; cf. Artun PU 2 3); *yn b ḥmthm* thewine in their wineskins (was finished), 1.16 III 15; *tikl išt b bhtm* the fire continued to consume in the palace, 1.4 VI 24 and par.; *bh pʕnm* on her (her) feet shook, 1.3 III 32 (// *bʕdn, ʕln*); be exalted *b pḫr qbṣ* in the assembly of the clan, 1.15 III 15 (// *b tk*); *aḫth b TN* his sister, (the one who is) in TN, 4.360:12; *ḥmm b bšrk* heat(?) in your flesh, RSOu 14 53 [KTU 9.432]:7'; *bʕl qdšm b nhr* DNN (/ DN and the saints) are in the river, RSOu 14 53 [KTU 9.432]:17'; *b rḥbn* in (the river) *r.*, RSOu 14 53 [KTU 9.432]:18'; *b ym* in the sea, RSOu 14 53 [KTU 9.432]:19'; *w yʕdb d b tkh* and he prepares what is within it, RSOu 14 53 [KTU 9.432]:28', 37'; *hwt b špth* the word on her lips, RSOu 14 53 [KTU 9.432]:32'; ★b) existence ("there is (not) in" > "to have"): *bhm qrnm* they shall have horns, 1.12 I 30; *bhm pn bʕl, ibid.* ln. 33; *in bʕl b bhth*(!) DN is not in his palace, 1.10 II 4 (// *b qrb hklh*); *unṯ in bh* (the field) has no corvée, 3.5:20; *pat aḥt in bhm* yokes (of an estate) which lack one side (border to the south east?), 4.136:5 (cf. *pat*); ★c) situation of proximity, by, at: she held DN *b sin lpš* by the hem of the cloak, 1.6 II 10 (// *b qṣ all*); she girded palms *b ḥbšh* at her waist, 1.3 II 13 (// *l bmth*); ★d) goal of movement or action, within, inside, in, into, to, against, beween, upon : may (his hand) *bm qrbm asm* put you inside the granary, 1.19 II 25; 'virgin oil' was poured *b ṣʕ* into a plate, 1.3 II 32; pour *yn ʕn b qbʕt* sparkling wine into a goblet, 1.6 IV 18; pour wine *b gl* in a cup, 1.14 II 19 (// *b gl*); he took a sacrificial lamb *b ydh* in his hand, 1.14 III 56; she entered *b ḏdk* (into) your grottoes, 1.19 IV 51 (// *b <a>hlm*); DN will enter *b kbdh* (into) his innards, 1.5 II 4 (// *b ph*); it is poured *b aph* into its nostrils, 1.71:7 and par.; she plunged her knees *b dm ḏmr* in the blood of the wariors, 1.3 II 14 (// *b mmʕ mhrm*); he went up *b arr* to (Mount) TN, 1.10 III 29 (// *bm arr w b ṣpn*); I am going down *b arṣ* to the underworld, 1.5 VI 25; *um ʕlt b aby* a mother throws herself onto my father, 1.82:9; he invited his brothers *b bhth* to his house, 1.4 VI 44 (// *b qrb hklh*); *ʕlt bk ʕlt bk*, she launches herself upon you, 1.82:10; he reproached (lit.: made reproaches against) *b il abh* DN, his father, 1.114:14; he put a cup *b klat ydh* in both his hands, 1.3 I 11 (// *bdh*); may the king's countenance shine *by/n* upon me / us, 2.16:10; 2.13:18; in unc. ctx.: *ʕd mġyy b ʕrm* until I arrive at the city(?), 2.71:16; *b lḥmy* in my food, RSOu 14,53 [KTU 9.432]:13' (in unc. ctx.); ★e) origin of a quality or process, from: *PN b TN* PN, from TN, 4.31:1 and *passim ibid.*; *rb tmtt lqḥ kl ḏrʕ b dntm* captain of the (salvage) crew has collected all the seed-grain from their containers(?), 2.38:18; in the event of evicting them *b bty* from my household, 3.9:8; they went *b bth* from his house, 1.17 II 39; let his soul go out *km qṭr b aph* like smoke from his nostrils, 1.18 IV 26; ou went *b špth hwth* his word from his lips, 1.2 IV 6 (// *b ph*); they cleaned *b bt dm ḏmr* from (her) house the blood of the warriors, 1.3 II 31; she washed *b dʕt* sweat from him, 1.16 VI 10; she washed her hands *b dm ḏmr* of the blood of the warriors, 1.3 II 34 (// *b mmʕ mhrm*); *br PN b unṯ* PN remains free of corvée, 2.19:5; *w yqḥ bhm aqht* and she collected PN from amon gthem, 1.19 III 39; *w b bt mlk mlbš ytn lhm* and from the palace clothes are given to them, 4.168:8; *alp b mḥrṯt* work ox, 6.14:3; and (he will be able to give) his 'voice' *b ʕrpt* from the clouds 1.4 V 8 (// *l arṣ*; cf. 1.d); ★f) material, with, in: chariots *ṣpyt b ḫrṣ* plated with gold, 4.167:2; divine platform *nbt b ksp* moulded in silver, 1.4 I 31 (// *b dm ḫrṣ*); *prsa b br* covered with tin, *ibid.* ln. 35; ★g) partitive use, of, from among: give me *aḥd b bnk* one of your sons, 1.6 I 46; (a ram.....) (a ewe is sacrificed and) *kll ylḥm bh* of which all shall eat, 1.115:10; prepare *imr b pḫd* a lamb from among the yearlings, 1.17 V 17; he took a thousand jars *b ḫmr* of wine, 1.3 I 16 (// *b mskh*); *my b ilm* who from among the gods?, 1.16 V 20; *in b ilm ʕnyh* there was no one among the gods who answered him, 1.16 V 22. 2) Temporal situation, ★a) time when something happens, dating from, on, during, in: *bn ym* // *bnm ʕdt* today // on this very day (cf. De Moor SP 160f.; diff.: Margalit MLD 58: 'son-of-sea / confluence'; Lipiński UF 20 1988 138: 'fils de la mer'), 1.4 VII 15-16; *b ym ḥdṯ b yrḫ pgrm* the new moon of the month MN, 4.172:1-2; 4.336:1-2; (wine consumed) *b dbḥ mlkt* during the queen's sacrifice, 4.149:14; and he approached *b šal* asking, 1.14 I 38; he takes him by the hand *b škrn* in intoxication, 1.17 I 30 (// *k šbʕ yn*); he remained asleep *bm bkyh* in his weeping, // he fainted *b dmʕh* in his tears, 1.14 I 31-32; DN came down *b ḥlmh* in his dream, 1.14 I 35-36 (// *b ḏhrth*); there was conception *bm nšq* on kissing (them), // there was pregnancy *b ḥbq* on embracing (them), 1.23:56; *b šbʕ ymm* on the seventh day, 1.17 I 15; *špšm b šbʕ* at dawn on the seventh (day), 1.14 III 15 and par.; *by šnt mlit* in years of plenty, 2.2:7 (or: in a full year, cf. Tropper

UG 52); ★b) time foreseen for something, for: *b šnt* for a year, 4.182:1; *b tlṯ šnt* for three years, 4.168:12.
3) Relationship of cause or reason, exchange or benefit, ★a) relationship of cause or reason, due to, by, in, regarding, with, as: (ships wrecked) *b gšm adr* due to a heavy downpour, 2.38:13; we rejoiced *b ḥyk* in your life, 1.16 I 14; you have sinned *b apkn/m* by your anger, 1.40:22 and par. (// *b qṣrt npš*); *w mlk yštal b*{.}*hn* may the king make a claim regarding them (the ships), 2.42:23; her liver swelled *b ṣḥq* with laughter, 1.3 II 25 (// *b šmḫt*); PN *ṯlṯm ksp b nṯk* thirty shekels of silver as interest, 4.682:12; cf. in bkn ctx. PN *b nṯk*, *ibid.* ln. 3; *yqḥ bk* he will get (the omen) by means of you, 2.71:12; ★b) oath, by: *b yn yšt iln*(!) by the wine that our god drinks!, 1.19 IV 57; ★c) of exchange and profit, for, in (*b pretii*; Pardee UF 8 1976 299f.; cf. ¶ RS Akk.: *ina*, Van Soldt SAU 456): a garment *b ʕšrt* for ten (shekels), 4.146:2; cf. *ibid.* ln. 3-8; cf. 4.31:2 and *passim ibid.*; talents *b kkr aḏdd w b kkr ugrt* in talents of TN or in talents of TN, 4.709:2-3; *ʕrb b mtn* stand surety for PN, 3.3:3; cf. in bkn ctx. *k*]*śmm b krsi* spelt in exchange for(?) *k.*, 4.225:17.
4) Relation of accompaniment and instrumental, ★a) company, (together) with, among, to: *šbʕ b ḥrṯm ṯlṯ b ṯġrm* seven (unskilled labourers go) with the ploughmen, three with the gatekeepers, 4.141 III 1-2; (they were) *ṯkm b ṯkm* shoulder to (lit. with) shoulder, 1.22 I 5; barley (sent) *b ṯydr* with PN, 6.21:2; I send you PN *b kd šmn* with a 'jar' of oil, 4.710:3; they come *b dbḥ nʕmt* with sacrifices of thanksgiving, 1.23:27; be numbered *b yrdm arṣ* among those who go down to the underworld, 1.4 VIII 8; ★b) instrumental, with: I gulp down *b klat ydy* with both hands, 1.5 I 19; *al ybʕr b ydh* may he not set fire to (the house) with his hand, RSOu 14 50 [KTU 9.434] 23 (or 'destroy': Bordreuil - Pardee RSOu 14 p. 380); (his) skin he ripped *b abn* with (the knife made of) stone, 1.5 VI 17 (// *b yʕr*); she split him *b ḥrb* with a knife, 1.6 II 31 (// *b ḫṯr*, // *b išt*, // *b rḥm*); he struck (them) *b ktp* with a scimitar, 1.6 V 2 (// *b ṣmd*); sings and plays *b knr w ṯlb b tp w mṣltm* with lyre and flute, with tambourine and cymbals, 1.108:4; sings and plays *b mrqdm d šn* ivory castanets, 1.108:4-5 (// *b ḥbr*); honour DN *b dbḥk* with your sacrifice, 1.14 II 25 (// *b mṣdk*).
5) Modal relation: *b mgnk* as your present, 1.16 I 45 (cf. RS Akk. *ana maga(n)ni*, cf. *mgn (I)*).
In bkn ctx.:]*qḥ by*, 1.2 III 19; 1.57:7; 2.2:7; 2.60:4; 7.137:8. For KTU *b dmr* in *ddm l ybr*[*k*] {*b dmr*} *prs l uxmxx*, 4.377:32 (corrupt text) see Sanmartín UF 20 1988 274f.: rdg *bd mr*<*ynm*> (see under *prś/s).*
Cf. bd (IV), bkm.

b (II), scribal mistake or assimilated form of *bn*, 6.1:1; cf. 5.18:9; cf. *bn (I)*.

/b-ʔ/ vb G: "to enter, come, reach" (Hb. *bwʔ*, HALOT 112ff.; Ph., Pun. *bʔ*, DNWSI 146; Ebla /B-ʔ/, cf. Krebernik PET 35; Akk. Māri *bâʔum*, AHw 117; Arab. *bāʔa*, Lane 270ff.; Eth. *boʔa*, CDG 114f.; cf. Akk. *bâʔu*, AHw 116; CAD B 178ff.: *bâʔu(m)* ★i); ¶ par.: /g-l-y/, /q-l/ (Št), /t-b-ʕ/. ¶ Forms: G suffc. *bat*, *bu*; cpref. *uba*, *tbu*, *tba*, *tbi*, *tbun*, *ybu*; inf. *bu*.
G. To enter, come, reach: *agrtn bat b ḏdk // (ʕnt) bat b <a>hlm* our mistress entered your caves // (DN) entered (your) tents, 1.19 IV 51-52; *tgly ḏd il w tbu* she made her way to the cave of DN and entered, 1.6 I 35 and par.; *bt krt bu // tbu bkt tgly w tbu // nṣrt tbu pnm* into the house PN she made her entry, // weeping she made her way (to the house of PN) and entered, sobbing she penetrated within, 1.16 VI 3-4 (// *tbʕ*, *gly*); *ʕl krt tbun* into the presence of PN they entered, 1.15 VI 6; *bt krt tbun* they entered the house of PN, 1.15 IV 21; *ptḥ bt w uba* open the house so that I may enter, 1.100:72 (// *ištql*); *bu al tbi* do not enter at all, 1.169:18 (De Moor UF 12 1980 430).

buly PN (etym. unc.; cf. Watson AuOr 8 1990 117).
PN: *bn PN*, 4.366:8.

bir TN < n. f. "well" (Belmonte RGTC 12/2 55f.: *Biʔru*. Cf. Hb., Aram. *bʔr*, HALOT 106, DNWSI 141f.; OAram. *byr*, DNWSI 155; Pun. *bʕr*, *bʕʔr* DNWSI 141f.; ESA *bʔr*, CAME 111; DOSA 35; Arab. *bīr*, Lane 145; Akk. *bē/ūru*, AHw 122; CAD B 342f.; cf. Ebla /buʔratum/ in AB.A = *bù-la-tum*, VE 1343; Krebernik ZA 73 1983 43; StEb 7 1984 158; *bur-ti*, Pettinato Rituale 182 [diff.: Fronzaroli ARET 11 141: 'esterno']); cf. Eg. *b-ʕ-r*, Helck Bez. 511 (55); Sivan - Cochavi WSVES 15. Cf. Heltzer RCAU 9; Virolleaud Syria 21 1940 142; Rainey UF 3 1971 170; Astour RSP 2 269f., 346; UF 13 1981 7; Van Soldt UF 28 1996 663; UF 29 1997 463; UF 30 1998 727); ¶ syll. Ug.: cf. TN URU *bi-i-ri*, PRU 3 93 (RS 16.244):7; 99 (RS 16.284):5'; cf. URU TÚL, cf. PRU 3 p. 267; Ug 5 102:17'; RSOu 7 4:34; cf. Huehnergard UVST 254; AkkUg 404; cf. PN DUMU BUR$_5$-*a-na*, PRU 6 82:1; cf. Sivan GAGl 211; Huehnergard AkkUg 361 n. 13.
TN: ★a) 1.91:29; 4.27:13; 4.68:30; 4.355:13; 4.365:29; 4.380:31; 4.683:19; RSOu 14 35 [KTU 9.388] I 29; ★b) *gt TN*, 4.397:13; 4.625:30; 4.636:2; "UF 29, 826":5 (Lemaire UF 30 1998 461). For 1.13:25 cf. *a/ir*. Bkn: 4.629:5; 4.661:2; *bnš bir*[, 2.77:9.

birt (I) TN (> PN?); <(?) EA *Bīrūta*, TN; cf. Dietrich - Loretz UF 12 1980 402; Astour RSP 2 270, 346); ¶ syll.: cf. KUR *bi-ru-ú/ut-ti*,

PRU 4 161 (RS 17.341) rev. 14', 17'; KUR PÚ.MEŠ-*ti*, PRU 3 12 (RS 11.730):1; RSOu 7 37:1; KUR PÚ.MEŠ, Ug 5 41:25.
TN (> PN?): 4.771:10.

birt (II) PN (Sem. Cf. *birt (I)*, TN; cf. Grøndahl PTU 27, 114; Bordreuil - Caquot Syria 57 1980 361; Watson AuOr 8 1990 244; cf. West AOAT 233 35: PN *pe-ri-ta*, Linear B).
PN: 4.771:10.

birtn PN (Sem. Cf. *birt (I)*, TN; cf. Grøndahl PTU 27, 114); ¶ **syll.**: DUMU PÚ-*ta-na*, PRU 3 201 (RS 16.257+) II 49; cf. Huehnergard AkUg 404.
PN: *bn PN*, 4.77:13; 4.93 I 7; 4.422:5; 4.692:13.

birty GN m. (cf. *birt*); ¶ syll.: DUMU.MEŠ KUR *bi-ru-ú/ut-ti*, PRU 4 161 (RS 17.341) rev. 14', 17'; LÚ.MEŠ KUR PÚ.MEŠ, Ug 5 41:25.
¶ Forms: pl. *birtym*.
GN: *pdyhm PN mit ksp b yd birtym* PN redeemed them for one hundred (shekels of) silver from the hands of GN, 3.4:15; *nskm birtym* casters GN, 4.337:3. Bkn ctx.: *aḫqm birt[y*, 4.86:23. For the rdg *bir[y]* in 4.86:23 cf. RGTC 12/2 56 (KTU: *birt[y]*).

biry GN m. (< *bir*, TN). ¶ Forms: sg. *biry*.
GN: 4.360:1; 4.690:6, 8. For the rdg *bir[y]* in 4.86:23 cf. Belmonte RGTC 12/2 56 (KTU: *birt[y]*).
Cf. **bir**.

buš[PN (Cf. Watson AuOr 13 1995 220; AuOr 14 1996 97); ¶ **syll.**: cf. *bi-ʔ-ši*, RSO 7 33:18'.
PN, bkn:]*bn buš*[, 4.223:1.

bišt adj. f., "bad, foul-smelling" (Akk. *bīšu*, *biʔšu*, AHw 131; CAD B 270f.; Aram. *bʔš*, DNWSI 142; ESA *hbʔs*, DOSA 34; Arab. *bāʾis* Lane 147; Eth. *baʔāsi*, *bĕʔus*, CDG 82; cf. Hb. *bʔš*, HALOT 107; cf. Del Olmo CR 89 n. 11). ¶ Forms: sg. *bišt*.
Bad, foul-smelling: *ṯr bist* a bad / foul-smelling *ṯr*, 1.48:8 (diff.: De Tarragon TOu 2 168: 'un *taureau* dans le *fe[u*' (?); rdg *b išt* with KTU).

bʕd adv., prep., 1) "behind"; 2) "behind; to, for" (Hb., HALOT 141; Ebla cf. /B-ʔ-D/, Krebernik PET 36; Fronzaroli StEb 7 1984 158f.; ESA *bʕd*, *bʕdn*, DOSA 49; Arab. *baʕdu*, Lane 225; Eth. *bāʕd*, CDG 83. Cf. Aartun PU 2 52). ¶ Forms: *bʕd*; suff. *bʕdy*, *bʕdh*, *bʕdhm*, *bʕdn*, *bʕdm* (encl. *-n, -m*).
1) Adv., behind: *bʕdn ksl tṯbr* behind (her) loins collapsed, 1.3 III 33; *l tšlḥm (...) bʕd kslk almnt* you did not feed (...) the widow behind your back, 1.16 VI 49.

2) Prep., ★a) behind: *bʕdh bhtm mnt bʕdh bhtm sgrt* behind her, the house of incantation, behind her the house she closed, 1.100:70-71. Bkn ctx.: *špš bʕdh* DN behind him, 1.45:6; *bʕd bʕlkm* behind(?) your 'lord(s)'; ★b) for: *w ptḥ hw prṣ bʕdhm* and he opened a breach for them, 1.23:70. Cf. in bkn ctx.]*ddyn bʕd ddyn*, 2.31:47; 4.373:3. For 5.9:6 cf. *ʕd (II)*.

Cf. **bʕdy**.

bʕdy PN (Sem.).

PN: 6.4:2(?).

/b-ʕ-l/ vb G: "to make, manufacture; to work" Š: "to have (something) made" (Hb., Ph., Pun. *pʕl*, HALOT 950f.; DNWSI 924ff.; Arab. *faʕala*, Lane 2420f.; ESA cf. *fʕl*, DOSA 407; Amor. cf. /bʔ(?)l/, /šbʕl/, Gelb CAAA 16, 33; cf. OAkk. *šupaʔʔulum*, AHw 1279f.: *šupêlu(m)*; CAD Š/3 320ff.: *šupêlu*. Cf. Grabbe UF 11 1979 307ff.; Tropper UG 589, unless Špass.). ¶ Forms: G cpref. *ybʕl*, suff. *ybʕlnn*, *ybʕlhm*; act. ptc. m. *bʕl* (cf. *bʕl (I)*). Cf. the spelling *pʕl* (suffc.) in 6.70:1 (cf. Dietrich - Loretz KA 239).

G. 1) To make, manufacture (tr.): *ybʕl qšt (...) qṣʕt* so that (DN) may make a bow (..., and) arrows, 1.17 VI 24; (clothes:) PN *mḫṣ bnš mlk ybʕlhm* weaver, man of the king, will make them, 4.182:56; cf. *ibid.* ln. 58: *ybʕlnn* he will make them. Cf. *ʔgn z pʕl PN* earthenware bowl which PN made, 6.70:1 (Dietrich - Loretz KA 234).

2) To work (intr.): (labourers) *dt tbʕln b TN* who work in TN, 4.141 III 6, 8, 10.

Š. To have (something) made: *yšbʕl ymġy (...) p l yšbʕl ḫpn* they have arrived (...) and, see!, they have had a *ḫ.* made, 2.70:27.

Cf. **bʕl (I)**.

bʕl (I) n. m. 1) "labourer, unskilled labourer"; 2) "craftsman, artesan, maker" (< /b-ʕ-l/; cf. Hb. *pwʕl*, HALOT 950f.; ESA *fʕl*, DOSA 407; Dietrich - Loretz - Sanmartín UF 5 1972 115; 6 1974 20, 22). ¶ Forms: sg. *bʕl*; pl. *bʕlm*, cstr. *bʕl*; du.(?) *bʕlm*.

1) Labourer, unskilled labourer: *ṯlṯ bʕlm w adnhm* three unskilled labourers and their master, 4.360:2; cf. *ṯlṯtm bʕlm w aḥd ḫbṯ* two triads of unskilled labourers and one alone, *ibid.* ln. 7, cf. ln. 6; (for the temple of DN:) *bʕl bt PN* an unskilled labourer of the house of PN, 4.15:2-9, cf. 11; PNN *bʕl any d bd PN* labourers of the fleet, at PN's disposal, 4.647:7; also an occasional unskilled labourer in public service: (PNN of professional guilds) *bʕl šd* farm labourers, 4.183 I 1; 4.609:53; PN *(yd) ṯn bnh bʕlm* with his two sons, unskilled labourers, 4.360:5, 11 (diff.: Dietrich - Loretz UF 14 1982 308: du. *bʕlm* 'two

unskilled labourers'); *ṯṯ ḥmrm bʕlm ṣmdm alpm* six donkeys (and two(?)) unskilled labourers (and) two pairs of oxen, 4.691:7.
2) Craftsman, artesan, maker (cf. Bo. *ēpiš* ..., CAD E 200; AHw 226; cf. Heltzer IOKU 83f.): *bʕl tdṯt* makers of pectorals, 4.609:35; *bʕl tġpṯ(m)* makers of felt, 4.183 II 10; 4.370:13; 4.609:36. Cf. *bʕl ḫr*[, 4,224:6.

bʕl (II) n. m. 1) "lord; owner of (or resident in) a place, owner of thing, boss of a place or thing; person of superior rank"; 2) >specifying an attribute; 3) DN (Hb., Ph., Pun., Aram., Nab., Palm. *bʕl*, HALOT 142ff.; DNWSI 182ff.; Amor. /baʕlum/, /beʕlum/, Gelb CAAA 16; Ebla /baʕ(a)lu/ in UMUM(?) = *ba-lu da-a-tim*, VE 1245; Krebernik ZA 73 1983 42; cf. ^{d}<BE.>KALAM.TIM = *ba₇*(BE)*-lu ma-tim*, VE 795b; cf. Krebernik ZA 73 1983 31; QuSe 18 96; Butz Biling. 122 n. 126; Lambert Biling. 398, 401; MARI 4 1985 529 n. 4; Mander MROA 2/1 18, 38f.; cf. BE(AL_6), Krebernik QuSe 18 106, 108f.; cf. *ba-al*$_6$, Krebernik PET 76f.; BE(BAD), Krebernik PET 78; Von Soden EDA 83 n. 30; cf. PN *i-da-ba-ḫal*, Milano ARET 4 117; Fronzaroli ARES 1 19; cf. Sanmartín AuOr 9 1991 182f.; Akk. *bēlu*, AHw 118ff.; CAD B 191-198; ESA *bʕl*, CAME 116; Arab. *baʕl*, Lane 228); ¶ syll. Ug.: [EN = *be*]*-lu* = *e-wi-ri* = *ba-a-lu-ma*, Ug 5 130 III 14'; [LÚ = *bēlu* = *e*(?)*-wi-ri* = *ba-a-lu-ma*, Ug 5 137 rev. II 30'; [LUGAL = *bēlu* = *ewiri* = *b*]*a-a-lu-ma*, *ibid.* ln. 33'; cf. [AN(?) = *šarru*(?) = *ta-ni* = *ba*(!?)*-a-*[*lu*(?)](?), UF 11, 1979, 479 (RS 20.189):31; [AN(?) = *šarrānu*(?)] = *zi-ia-ni* = [*b*]*a*(?)*-a-*[*lu-ma*(?), UF 11, 1979, 479 (RS 20.189):32; [UD(?) = *bēlu*(?) = (Hurr.: ?) = [*b*]*a*(?)*-a-lu*, Ug 5 138:6'; cf. Huehnergard UVST 114; Van Soldt BiOr 46 1989 651; SAU 303; cf. [EN = *ša*]*r-rum i-wi-ir-ni ma-al-ku*, Ug 5 130 III 13'; cf. the theophoric element /baʕlu/ in PNN; Grøndahl PTU 114; Sivan GAGl 208; cf. theophoric PNN ^{d}U/IM*-la/li-*; Grøndahl PTU 114-117; Sivan GAGl 208; syll. Ug. of 3: DN, cf. *infra*: 3: DN; ¶ RS Akk.: *bēlu*, (LÚ.MEŠ.)EN(.MEŠ), PRU 3 233; PRU 4 260; PRU 6 150; Ug 5 340; cf. LU *be-el ar-ni*, PRU 3 169 (RS 16.145):4; LÚ.EN É*(-ti) a-bu-sí/ti*, PRU 3 181f. = PRU 4 47f. (RS 11.732) A 8, B 8; PRU 4 82 (RS 17.382+):45; 231 (RS 17.244):3; EN *di-ni(-šu)*, PRU 3 4 (RS 16.112):11; PRU 4 164 (RS 17.68):11; LÚ.MEŠ.EN.MEŠ/ḪI.A DI.ḪI.A/MEŠ*(-ti)*, PRU 3 5 (15.14):20, 22; PRU 4 216 (RS 17.83):14; 226 (RS 17.391):6, 10; EN KASKAL, Ug 5 57 rev. 5'; *be-el* / EN *ḫi-ṭì-ka*, PRU 4 140 (RS 17.372 A+) rev.10; 142 (RS 17.228):8-9; 145 (RS 17.318+):4', 15'; DINGIR.MEŠ EN.MEŠ *ma-mi-ti*, PRU 4 100 (RS 17.04) rev. 1'; 288 (RS 19.101) rev. 6'; LÚ *be-li pa-qid-ia*, Ug 5

43:7; PN AN.EN, PRU 3 169 (RS 16.145):4; DUMU *ba-liq-bá*, PRU 3 103 (RS 15.109+):13; RS Akk. of 3: DN, cf. *infra*: 3; ¶ par.: *adn*; for the par. of 3: DN, cf. *infra*: 3. ¶ Forms: sg. *bʕl*, *bʕlm* (encl. *-m*; cf. *infra*: 3: DN), suff. *bʕly*, *bʕlk*, *bʕlh*, *bʕlny* (suff. pn. *-n-* + emph. encl. *-y*; Aartun PU 1 45f.), *bʕlkm*, *bʕlhn*; sg. *bʕln* (afform. *-n*: Dietrich - Loretz MU 104; Tropper UF 26 1994 466ff.); cstr. pl. *bʕl*.

1) Lord ★a) esp. of kings: *bʕl kl ḫwt mṣrm* Lord of the whole land of Egypt, 2.81:3; *špš bʕlk* the 'Sun', your lord, 2.39:19; *špš mlk rb bʕlh/y* the 'Sun', the great king, his / my lord, 2.23:2 and par.; 3.1:12 and par.; *mlk bʕly* the king, my lord, 2.33:22 and par. (rdg *<b>ʕly* in 2.33:26); *bʕln yǵtr* the lord (him) the guard will attack(?), 1.103:39; *tqṣrn* [...] *ymy bʕlhn* shortened shall be the days of their/his lord, 1.103:34; *krt bʕlkm* PN, your lord, 1.15 IV 28; *l ymǵ krt (...) bʕlny* certainly PN will go (...), our lord, 1.15 V 20; ★b) said of certain gods: *tḥm ym bʕlkm* message of DN, your lord, 1.2 I 17 and par. (// *adnkm*); *bt bʕlk* the house of your lord, 1.1 IV 6; *rgm bʕlh* the words of your lord, 1.2 I 42; *ilhm bʕlm* 'the Divine Lords' (divine invocation), 1.39:9 and par. (diff.: 'the (7) Divine Baals', Dietrich - Loretz TUAT 2 310; cf. *infra:* 3, DN: *bʕlm*, 1.47:6-11; 1.118:5-10); cf. in bkn ctx. *bʕd bʕlkm* behind(?) your 'lord(s)', 4.17:16; ★c) owner of (or resident in) a place, owner of thing, boss of a place or thing: *bʕl ḫlb* owners of TN, 4.728:1; *aṯr bʕlk l ksi aṯr bʕlk arṣ rd* after your owner, oh throne, after your owner go down to the underworld, 1.161:20-21; boss: *zbl bʕl arṣ* the prince, boss of the underworld, 1.5 VI 10 and *passim* of the DN *bʕl* (cf. *infra:* 3, DN; Dietrich - Loretz UF 12 1980 391ff.; Toombs Fs. Freedman 613ff.; cf. Ebla ᵈ<BE.>KALAM.TIM = *baʔ*(BE)*-lu ma-tim*, VE 795b; cf. Krebernik ZA 73 1983 31; Butz Biling. 122 n. 126; Lambert Biling. 398, 401; cf. Gordon Eblaitica 1 20: Sum. ᵈen.ki); *yštk bʕl ʕnt mḥrṯt* did they make you 'Lord' of the furrows of the ploughed land?, 1.6 IV 3; *bʕl ḥkpt* 'Patrons/Bosses' of TN (title of the DN *kṯr-ḫss*), 1.17 V 20 and par. For *bʕl šd* cf. *bʕl (I)* 1; ★d) in letters, a person of higher rank, *passim*: *l PN bʕly rgm* to PN, my lord, say:, 2.61:2 and par.; *l pʕn bʕly (...) qlt* at the feet of my lord (...) I fall, 2.64:13 and par.; (to wife and mother:) *šlm bʕlkm* greetings from your lord, 5.10:3; RSOu 14 50 [KTU 9.434]:2, 6, 12, 21. In bkn ctx.: RSOu 14 49 [KTU 9.433]:17.

2) Specifying an attribute (+ n.): *bʕl aṯt* (newly) wed (for fiscal purposes), 4.153:2-5; *bʕl ššlmt* subject to the *š.* (loan), 4.153:6-11 (Sanmartín UF 20 1988 270 n. 270); *bʕl gml* 'he of the First Quarter' (title of the DN *hll*), 1.24:42; cf. *miḫd*; *bʕl knp* 'the winged one' (or 'the winged Baal (DN)'?), 1.46:6; *bʕl qrnm w ḏnb* 'the one with horns

and a tail' (title of a demon), 1.114:20; *bʕl ṣdq* legitimate lord (title of the crown prince), 7.63:4; cf. in unc. ctx. *bʕl ʕbb* 'the gobbler', 1.92:14 (cf. De Moor UF 17 1985 226f.; Dijkstra UF 26 1994 119). For *bʕl*{.}*šlm*, cf. *bʕlšlm*, PN.
3) DN < Baal 'the Lord'; Pope WbMyth 1 253ff.; Del Olmo MLC 64ff., 81ff.; De Moor TWAT 1 706ff.; Wyatt UF 24 199 2 408ff.; ¶ par.: *bn il*, *bn dgn*, *hd*, *ʕly*; RS Akk.: ᵈIM, ᵈU, PRU 4 257; PRU 6 149; Ug 5 338; cf. ᵈIM II-VII, Ug 5 18:5-10; ᵈU, Ug 5 170:7'-10', 12'; cf. ᵈIM/ᵈU(*-li/la*) in Ug. PNN (Grøndahl PTU 114-117); syll. Hurr., ¶ syll. Ug.: ᵈIM.ZU.AN.NA = *te-eš-ša-a*[*b*] = *ba-a-lu*, Ug 5 137 IV b 17; syll. Hurr. cf. the element *-te-šub*, ᵈIM/ᵈU(*-ub*) in Hurr. PNN (Grøndahl PTU 263f.); alph. Hurr. *ṯṯb*, Ug 5 539; (cf. Laroche Ug 5 p. 454); cf. *ṯṯb ḫlbġ*, 1.42:10; Laroche Ug 5 p. 523. Cf. Ph., Pun., Aram. DNN *bʕl*, Eissfeldt RGG(3) 805f.; Emar Akk. cf. the element *ba-aḫ-la-* and *ba-ʔ-la-* in PNN; Fleming UF 26 1994 128 n. 6; Akk. ᵈ*bēlu*, Edzard WbMyth 1 46; OAss. ᵈ*bēlum*, cf. Hirsch BAfO 13/14 1961 22ff.; cf. *be-el*-ŠUL-*ba*-BÀN-*da*, Ug 5 123 (RS 24.309):210 // [ᵈ*be-e*]*l*-ŠUL-*ba-at*, Ug 5 126 (RS 20.175):210; > Gk *Bēlos*, Edzard WbMyth 1 123. ¶ Forms: *bʕl*, *bʕlm* (encl. *-m*: 1.2 IV 9 and par.; 1.6 V 11; 1.47:6-11; 1.118:5-10; 1.119:28); ★a) DN Baal, *passim* in 1.1-1.6; 1.10-1.13; ritual and magical texts; cf. esp.: *ib bʕl* enemies of DN, 1.4 VII 35 (*passim bʕl* // *hd*; in 1.4 VII 38 rdg *bʕl* // *hd*{*t*}); *bt bʕl*(?) temple of DN, 1.63:12; 1.104:13; 1.17 I 31 and par.; *mṭr bʕl* the rain of DN, 1.16 III 7 and par. (// *ʕly*); *mhr bʕl* the warrior of DN (title of a celestial person), 1.22 I 8 and par.; *ġr bʕl* the mountain of DN, 1.16 I 6; *pḫr bʕl* assembly of DN, 1.39:8; 1.41:16; 1.87:18; *ql bʕl* the voice of DN, 1.19 I 46; *rpu bʕl* the *r.* of DN (title of a celestial person), 1.22 I 8; *mt ʕz bʕl ʕz* DN was strong, DN was strong, 1.6 VI 17 and par.; *mt ql bʕl ql* DN fell down, DN fell down, 1.6 VI 21; *bʕl mt* DN is dead, 1.5 VI 23 and par.; *mt aliyn bʕl* dead is the 'Most Powerful' DN, 1.5 VI 9 and par.; *l pnh yrd* [?] *aliyn bʕl* before her DN descended, 1.92:31 (bkn ctx., cf. Dijkstra UF 26 1994 117; cf. De Moor UF 17 1985 228); *npš*] *bʕl thwyn* [the appetite] of DN wants (...), 1.92:36 (bkn ctx.; cf. Dijkstra UF 26 1994 118, 122); *b hm pn bʕl* and (they will have) the face of DN, 1.12 I 33; *bʕlm* (another manifestation of the same) DN, 1.47:6-11; 1.118:5-10 (cf. RS Akk.: ᵈIM II-VII, Ug 5 18:5-10; ᵈU, Ug 5 170:7'-10', 12'; Dietrich - Loretz TUAT 2 302; cf. *ilhm bʕlm*, *supra*: 1.a); *dgn w bʕl* (the only combination of these two gods), 1.123:4 (cf. ★b) immediately following; ★b) titles: *aliyn bʕl* DN, the 'Very Powerful', *passim*; rdg *aliyn* {*bn*} *bʕl* in 1.5 II 18; *bʕl* // *bn dgn* DN // son of DN, 1.2 I 19

and par.; *bʕl* // *bn il* DN // divine person(s), 1,17 VI 29 (cf. *bn (I)*: 5.a); ★c) DN + n.: cf. *bʕl knp* the winged DN (or simply 'the winged one'?, cf. *supra:* 2), 1.46:6; bkn cf. *]kbkb bʕl w pdry kbkb*, RSOu 14 53 [KTU 9.432]:10; ★d) DN of TN: *bʕl ṣpn* DN of TN, 1.47:5; 1.118:4 (*passim* in rituals and cultic lists; ¶ RS Akk.: ^{d}IM *be-el* ḪUR.SAG *ḫa-zi*, Ug 5 18:4; ^{d}U ^{d}ḪUR.SAG *ḫa-zi*, Ug 5 170:19'; cf. ^{d}IM ḪUR.SAG *ḫa-zi*, PRU 4 257, *passim*; PRU 6 58:3'; ^{d}IM *be-el* ḪUR.SAG *ḫa-zi*, PRU 3 76 (RS 16.144):12; 84 (RS 16.157):27; 108 (RS 16.238):18); *bʕl ugrt* DN of TN, 1.109:16 and *passim* in cultic lists (rdg *bʕl <ug>rt* in 1.119:2, Del Olmo AuOr 7 1989 29 n. 10 [cf KTU p. 134 n. 2]); *bʕl ḫlp* DN of TN, 1.109:16 and par. in cultic lists (cf. ¶ RS Akk.: ^{d}U *ḫal-pí*, Ug 5 170:18; RS Hurr.: *ṯṯb ḫlbġ*, 1.42:10, and Laroche Ug 5 p. 520; diff.: Nougayrol Ug 5 p. 322); *zbl bʕl arṣ* cf. *supra*: 1.c. Cf. *yrgbbʕl*, *yrġmbʕl*, 1.102:16, 26 (cf. *ibid.* ln. 15, 22), in the titulary of the Ugaritic king; cf. Dietrich - Loretz - Sanmartín UF 7 1975 545; Del Olmo UF 18 1986 85 n. 12; RC 118. Cf. in unc. ctx. *]bt bʕl ḥẓ ršp*, 1.82:3 (De Moor - Spronk UF 16 1984 239: rdg *ḥẓ ršp* '([may] Baʕlu [st]op) the arrows of Rashpu!'; altern. Gordon UT 854: rdg *bʕl ḥẓ* 'Lord of the Arrow' [*ršp*]; cf. Renfroe AULS 56: 'Lord of Fate'; cf. *supra:* 2).

Cf.: ibʕlt, abdbʕl, adbʕl, ilbʕl, amrbʕl, išbʕl, iybʕl, ʕbdbʕl, ʕdbʕl, ʕzbʕl, bʕl (III), bʕldʕ, bʕldn, bʕlmʕḏr, bʕlmṯpṭ, bʕln, bʕlrm, bʕlsip, bʕlskn, bʕlṣdq, bʕlṣn, bʕlšlm, bʕlt, bʕltn, bʕly, bʕlyskn, bʕlytn, bʕlz, bl (IV), blšpš, ḏmrbʕl, mddbʕl, mtbʕl, mtnbʕl, plśbʕl, šbʕl, šmbʕl, ṯpṭbʕl, ybʕbʕl, ydbʕl, ypʕbʕl, yrgbbʕl, yrġmbʕl, yrmbʕl.

bʕl (III) PN (Sem. Cf. Grøndahl PTU 116); ¶ syll.: cf. *ba-ʔa-lu-ú*, PRU 6 72:10; ^{d}IM, PN in RSOu 7 34:2. Cf. *bʕly*, *bl*.

PN: 4.63 IV 17, cf. in bkn ctx. *bʕl*[, 4.725:3.

bʕldʕ PN (Sem. Cf. Grøndahl PTU 37, 39, 62, 116, 142); ¶ syll.: ^{d}IM-*i-da-ʔa*, PRU 6 79:1 (Huehnergard UVST 246).

PN: 4.376:1.

bʕldn PN (Sem. Cf. Grøndahl PTU 20, 116, 123; Dietrich - Loretz - Sanmartín UF 5 1973 110); ¶ syll.: *ba-aʔ-la-da/dá-ni*, PRU 6 p. 141 (Huehnergard UVST 246; AkkUg 109; Van Soldt SAU 310, 331). Cf. *bʕltn*.

PN: ★a) 4.134:13; 4.307:13; ★b) *bn PN:* 4.86:11 (*bn bʕld*[).

bʕlmʕḏr PN (Sem. Cf. Grøndahl PTU 32f., 113, 116; Van Soldt UF 21 1989 376 n. 15); ¶ syll.: cf. ^{d}IM-*ma-zi-ri*, PRU 3 142 (RS 16.136):8; ^{d}IM-*ma-a-ši-ir*, RSOu 7 17:10, 14; cf. Huehnergard Syria 34 1997 217.

PN: 4.172:3; 4.266:3; 6.16:1.

bʕlmṯpṭ PN (Sem. Cf. Grøndahl PTU 32f., 116, 200).
PN: 4.214 II 5.

bʕln PN (Sem. Cf. Grøndahl PTU 52, 117; Van Soldt SAU 40); ¶ syll.: *ba-a-la-nu*, Ug 5 86:18 (cf. Huehnergard UVST 254; Van Soldt SAU 331 n. 159); cf. dIM-*la-na*, PRU 4 227 (RS 17.393):23; cf. in bkn ctx.: PRU 3 193 (RS 12.34+):15; 199ff. (RS 16.257) II 49; PRU 6 85:16'.
PN: ★a) 3.5:12 (*bn kltn*); 4.133:3; 4.141 II 22 (Van Soldt SAU 39); 4.159:1; 4.188:17; 4.281:8; 4.332:16; 4.496:3 4.609:12 (Van Soldt SAU 39), 21 (*alṣy*), 23, 28; 4.729:2; 4.787:5; cf. 4.320:17; ★b) *bn PN:* 4.7:17; 4.35 II 17; 4.98:11; 4.360:1 (*biry*); 4.617:2; 4.753:10 (Van Soldt SAU 17); ★c) *gt PN*, 4.358:6; 4.636:5 (Belmonte RGTC 12/2 83).

bʕlrm PN (Sem. Cf. Grøndahl PTU 44, 116, 182).
PN: 4.370:9.

bʕlsip PN (Sem. Cf. Grøndahl PTU 37, 40, 116, 184).
PN: 4.80:3 (*ar*[).

bʕlskn PN (Sem.(?); cf. =š/zk= Gelb - Purves - MacRae NPN 258, 278; cf. Grøndahl PTU 37, 40, 116, 185; Dietrich - Loretz - Sanmartín UF 6 1974 42); ¶ syll.: cf. *ba-la-as-ki*, MSL 10 153 (RS 20.32) colophon: 1 (Van Soldt SAU 331 n. 159); (DUMU) dIM*(-la)-as-ki*, PRU 3 121 (RS 15.136):7; PRU 3 123 (RS 15.145):14; PRU 3 169 (RS 16.145):23; (DUMU) dU*(-la)-as-ki*, PRU 3 124 (RS 15.167+):4; PRU 6 49:19'. Cf. *bʕlyskn*.
PN: 4.214 I 15; 4.377:28.

bʕlṣdq PN (Sem. Cf. Grøndahl PTU 45, 47, 116, 187).
PN: ★a) 4.180:7; ★b) *bn PN:* 4.232:6.

bʕlṣn PN (Sem. Cf. Grøndahl PTU 116, 189); ¶ syll.: cf. *ba-a-la*-ZI, PRU 3 135 (RS 15.140):4 (cf. Van Soldt SAU 331 n. 159: *ba-a-la-sí*). Cf. *bʕlz*.
PN: 4.22:3; 4.183 II 21.

bʕlšlm PN (Sem. Cf. Grøndahl PTU 116, 193; Rainey IOS 5 1975 22; Watson AuOr 8 1990 127); ¶ syll.: cf. EN-*šu-la-mu*, Ug 5 14:2.
PN: 4.293:2; 4.332:10, 19; 4.679:5.

bʕlt n. f. "lady" (f. < *bʕl (II)*; hb *bʕlh*, HALOT 145; Ph., Pun., *bʕlt*, DNWSI 182ff.; Eissfeldt RGG(3) 806; Ebla d*ba-al-tum*, dBAD.MÍ, Von Soden EDA 84; cf. MUNUS.BE.AL$_6$ *il-tum*, Krebernik QuSe 18 106; Amor. /baʕlatum/, /baʕla/, /beʕlatum/, /beʕltum/, /beʕla/, Gelb CAAA 16; Akk. *bēltu*, AHw 118: CAD B 187-191; ESA *bʕlt*, CAME 116; DOSA 50; Arab. *baʕlat*, Lane 228; > Gk *Baaltís*, Pope WbMyth

1 285); ¶ RS Akk.: NIN, GAŠAN, PRU 3 232; PRU 4 258, 260; PRU 6 150; Ug 5 340; cf. GAŠAN KUR *ú-ga-r*[*i-it*, PRU 3 14 (RS 12.33):2; he will deposit a certain amount *i-na* ŠU MÍ.LUGAL-*ti* NIN-*šu*, PRU 3 162 (RS 16.348):8; DNN: dNIN *ku-ba-ba* GAŠAN KUR.URU *kar-ga-miš* dNIN.GAL [GA]ŠAN URU *nu-ba-an-ni* dNIN.GAL [GA]ŠAN URU *gur-a-ti*, PRU 4 157 (RS 17.146):50-52 cf. PN Ì.dNIN, Grøndahl PTU 316; cf. NIN = *aḫātu*, Nougayrol Ug 5 p. 157 n. 4; Huehnergard AkUg 408. ¶ Forms: sg. *bʕlt*, suff. *bʕlth*. Lady, in the divine titulary: ★a) *bʕlt bhtm* 'Lady of the Palace', 1.105:16 and *passim* in rituals and cultic lists (cf. Akk. *dbēlet*(NIN) *ekalli*(*m*)(É.GAL), *passim* in Alalakh, Mari, Qatna, Emar (cf. Durand MROA 2/1 178ff.); in Ugarit, epithet of the DN *pdry*(?); cf. *pdry bt mlk* 'DN of the Royal Palace', 1.91:7 and 1.139:14; Saracino UF 14 1982 196 n. 29; Dietrich - Loretz TUAT 2 322; diff.: epithet of *ʕnt*: Virolleaud CRAIBL 1962 97; De Moor SP 86 n. 4); cf. esp.: *k tdd bʕlt bhtm* when the 'Lady of the Palace' comes in procession, 1.91:14; *bt bʕlt bhtm* temple of the 'Lady of the Palace', 1.41:37 and par.; *ṯlḥn bʕlt bhtm* table of the 'Lady of the Palace', 1.109:31 (cf. 1.31+:3, Dijkstra UF 16 1984 73); *bʕlt btm* in 1.48:4; in bkn ctx., 2.31:48; ★b) in the titulary of the goddess *ʕnt*: *bʕlt mlk bʕlt drkt bʕlt šmm rmm bʕlt kpṯ* 'Lady of Royalty, Lady of Power, Lady of the High Heavens, Lady of the Firmament', 1.108:6-8 (cf. Olyan UF 19 1987 161-174); cf. *mdrġlm d bt bʕlt mlk* (service) watchmen in the temple of the 'Lady of Royalty', 4.54:1. Bkn: *l bʕlt* [, 1.81:6.

bʕltn PN (Hurro-Sem.(?); cf. Grøndahl PTU 40, 62, 116, 147, 260ff.). Cf. *iwrtn*, *bʕldn*.
PN: *bn PN*, 4.611:2.

bʕly PN (Sem. Cf. Grøndahl PTU 20, 51, 117; Watson NUS 27 1982 5); ¶ syll.: *ba*[*-ʔa*(?)]*-li-ya*, PRU 6 83 rev. III 15; dIM*-li-ya*, PRU 3 203 (RS 16.257+) IV 12; dIM*-ya*, PRU 4 284 (RS 19.68):8; dU*-li-ya*, Ug 5 42:7; cf. *ba-ʔa-lu-ú* PRU 6 72:10; EN*-l*[*a*, RSOu 7 16:27. Cf. *bʕl*, PN.
PN: ★a) 4.80:14 (*mlx*[]); 4.116:3; 4.389:6; 4.710:1; ★b) *bn PN*: 4.360:7; in bkn ctx.: 4.69 VI 4.

bʕlyskn PN (Sem. Cf. Grøndahl PTU 42, 116, 185; Dietrich - Loretz - Sanmartín UF 6 1974 42; Segert UF 15 1983 208). Cf. *bʕlskn*.
PN: 4.75 III 9 (*bn ss*).

bʕlytn PN (Sem. Cf. Grøndahl PTU 37, 40, 116, 147).
PN: 4.628:2 (*bn ulb*).

bʕlz PN (Sem. Cf. Grøndahl PTU 20, 102, 112, 116); ¶ syll.: cf. *ba-a-*

la-ZI, PRU 3 135 (RS 15.140):4 (cf. Van Soldt SAU 331 n. 159: *ba-a-la-si*). Cf. *bʕlṣn*.
PN: 4.356:3 (cf. Watson AuOr 8 1990 127: rdg *gl*{.}*bʕlz*, but cf. Márquez UF 27 1995 319 n. 4; cf. *gl (III)*).

/b-ʕ-r/ (I) vb D: "to ignite; to burn; scorch the earth"; Š: "to illuminate" (Hb. *bʕr*, HALOT 145f.; cf. De Moor SP 109; Cazelles Semitica 23 1973 5ff.: Dietrich - Loretz - Sanmartín UF 7 1975 554ff.; Dion RB 84 1980 321ff.; Emerton Fs. Williams 39; Dietrich - Loretz UF 22 1990 51f.). ¶ **Forms**: D cpref. *ybʕr*, suff. *ibʕr.nn* (?); Š inf. *šbʕr*. **D**. To ignite, set on fire, scorch the earth:*ybʕr* [*rkb ʕr*]*pt* [*q*]*rnh* let [the Charioteer of the clo]uds ignite his lightning flashes, 1.3 IV 26; *akln b grnt l bʕr* our grain on the threshing floors has been set on fire, 2.61:9 (// *ḫlq*); *mlkn ybʕr ibh* the king will scorch the earth of the enemy, 1.103:58 (//(?) *ḫlq*; cf. Dion RB 87 1980 321ff.: 'faire disparaître'; Pardee Fs. Fitzmyer 81ff.; AfO 33 1986 132: 'to destroy'); *al ybʕr b ydh* may he not set fire to (the house) with his hand, RSOu 14 50 [KTU 9.434] 23 (or 'destroy': Bordreuil - Pardee RSOu 14 p. 378). Bkn ctx.: *ibʕr.nn*, 2.37:9 (Pardee AfO 29/30 1983/84 326: 'I will destroy (?) it/him/her'); *ibʕr an*[*k*] *(...) an*[*k*] *bʕr*, 2.31:55, 57 (see also /b-ʕ-r/ (II)).
Š. To illuminate: *qdš yuḫdm šbʕr* DN began to illuminate, 1.4 IV 16 (// *k kbkb*; diff.: Rendsburg JAOS 107 1987 625f.: 'the context suggests a forward movement', MSA 'to go (out) at night'; Dietrich - Loretz UF 22 1990 54: 'wegführen', /b-ʕ-r/ (II)).

/b-ʕ-r/ (II) vb D: "to abandon, forsake; to leave" (Hb. *bʕr*, HALOT 146; cf. /b-ʕ-r/ (I); Fensham JNSL 9 1981 67ff.); ¶ par.: /y-ṣ-ʔ/. ¶ Forms: D cpref. *ybʕr*, suff. *tbʕrn*, *ybʕrn*, *ibʕr.nn* (?).
D. To abandon, forsake, leave: *ybʕr l ṯn aṯth* he left his wife for another, 1.14 II 48 and par. (// *yṣa*; cf. Dietrich - Loretz - Sanmartín UF 7 1975 554f. for this and other versions in connection with *bʕr (I)*); *lm tbʕrn* why have you abandoned me?, 1.16 II 18 (cf. Wyatt RTU 228 n.235 - survey, diff.: 'lied to me'; Margalit UF 27 1995 220: 'to enter, penetrate'); *w* [*u*]*ḫy al ybʕrn* and may my brother not abandon me, 2.41:22; *ilm tbʕrn ḥwt hyt* the gods will forsake that land, 1.103:56 and par. Bkn ctx. *ibʕr an*[*k*] *(...) an*[*k*] *bʕr*, 2.31:55, 57 (see also /b-ʕ-r/ (I)); cf. *ibʕr.nn*, 2.37:9 (or: /b-ʕ-r/ (I)).

bʕr adj. m. "burnt, singed" ((?) < /b-ʕ-r/ (I); cf. Márquez AuOr 11 1993 105). ¶ Forms: pl. *bʕrm*.
Burnt, singed ((?) said of textiles treated to become durable): *lbš anyth bʕrm* the sails of his ship were singed (?), 4.338:11.

bʕyn PN (Sem.(?); cf. Gaster Syria 16 1935 226; Grøndahl PTU 114; Lipiński BiOr 37 1980 12; Van Soldt SAU 33). Cf. /b-ġ-y/, *byn*.
PN: *bn PN*, 4.33:3 (*šx*[); 4.51:14 (*šk<m>y*); 4.53:8; 4.55:12.

bb PN (etym. unc. Cf. Grøndahl PTU 117; Dahood JBL 100 1981 608; Watson AuOr 11 1993 214; AuOr 13 1995 220); ¶ syll.: *ba-ba*, PRU 4 182 (RS 17.299):1.
PN: *bn PN*, 4.63 IV 9; cf. *bb*, 2.31:27.

bbru PN (etym. unc.); ¶ syll.: cf. BA(!?)-*bi-ri*, PRU 3 33 (RS 16.114):2' (cf. Berger WO 5 1969/70 272; cf. Nougayrol: *sú*(?)-*bi-ri*).
PN: 4.393:11.

bbt (I) TN, residence of the god *ršp* (Belmonte RGTC 12/2 54f.: *Bibita*. Hurro-Hitt. ᵈ*Nubadig bibitẖi* / *bibitā*, Sem. *b-bt*, GLH 187: *Nubadig*. Cf. Barré JAOS 98 1978 465ff.; diff.: Astour JNES 27 1968 20, Akk. *bābu*; Margalit UF 8 1976 172 n. 86, Akk. *bābtu*). ¶ Forms: *bbt*, suff. *bbth*.
TN: *ql b<l> ʕm ršp bbth* take (this) request to DN in TN, 1.100:31; *ršp bbt* DN of TN, 1.105:25; 1.171:3.

bbt (II) DN, protective deity of the palace / dynasty (cf. *bbt (I)*; < Sem. *b bt (II)*, cf. Ug. *b bt mlk*, 4.137:14; 4.163:16; *b bt bʕl*, 1.46:16; 1.109:11; Hb. *ʕl byt*, "superintendente"; cf. GLH 187. Cf. Conrad ZAW 83 1971 179 n. 184; Dietrich - Loretz - Sanmartín UF 7 1975 544; Janowski UF 12 1980 247; diff.: Fisher Ug 6 197 n. 6: Akk. *bābtu*, 'a goddess of the gate' [cf. De Tarragon TOu 2 201 n. 175]; Freilich JSS 31 1986 119ff.: *l b bt* 'within the house'; Levine PL 10 n. 19: *l b bt* 'in the inner sanctum' [but cf. Xella TRU 107]; Aartun UF 16 1982 6ff.: Arab. *babat*, 'Schnecke mit Haus' [but cf. Renfroe UF 18 1986 49f.]; altern. Sem. /binu/ + /bēti/ > */bibbēti/; cf. Ug. *btbt*; cf. Del Olmo Fs. Díez Macho 281 n. 35; Akk. *mār bīti*, DINGIR.DUMU.É, DINGIR.A.É, cf. Krebernik RlA 7 355f.). ¶ Forms: *bbt*; du. *bbtm*.
DN: *l bbt il bt* to DN, god of the palace, 1.115:3, 11; *l bbtm gdlt* to the two DN, a cow, 1.46:9.

bbt (III) PN (etym. unc.; cf. *bbt (I)*, *bbt (II)*).
PN: *bn PN*, 4.382:33.

/b-d/ vb G: "to intone a song; to improvise" (Hb. *bdʔ/h*, HALOT 109; Arab. *badaʔa / badā*, Lane 163ff., 172; cf. *badaha*, Lane 169f.; cf. De Moor SP 75; diff.: Lipiński UF 2 1970 86: 'raconter', Hb. *bdym*; cf. Müller UF 1 1969 81ff. 'Orakelpriester'). ¶ Forms: G prefc. *ybd*.
G. To intone a song: *qm ydb w yšr* rising, he intoned and sang, 1.3 I 18; *ybd w yšr ʕlh* (who) inones and sings in his presence, 1.17 VI 31.

Cf. bd (I).

bd (I) n. m. "song" (< /b-d/; cf. Loretz Psalmen 2 421; diff.: Margalit UF 8 1976 147: '(in)to the hands of', cf. *bd (IV)*; survey Wyatt RTU 220 n. 198); ¶ par.: *bky, ntn* (+ <*ql*>). ¶ Forms: sg. m. *bd*.
Song: *bd aṯt* a woman's song, 1.16 I 5, 19; 1.16 II 42.

bd (II) n. m. "separation, isolation" (Hb. *bd*, HALOT 108f.; Arab. *budd*, Lane 161ff.; cf. Akk. *badādu*, AHw 95, CAD B 303: *buddudu*; cf. Gibson CML 143; Del Olmo IMC 526; cf. *bddy*). Used as an adv. *l bdm* (cf. Hb. *l bd*).
Separation, isolation > used as an adv. "alone": *l bdm ard* alone I shall go down, 1.2 III 20.
Cf. bddy.

bd (III) DN, part of the composite divine name *ṯḫr w bd* (cf. *bd (I)* 'deified song / singer'; cf. Xella TRU 222).
DN: *ṯḫr w bd* (1.123:27).
Cf. bddn.

bd (IV) prep. 1) "into the hands of, (intended) for"; 2) "from the hands of"; 3) "at the hands of, for" (< *b (y)d*; Ph. *bd*, DNWSI 433f.; Akk. EA *ba-di-ú*, EAT 245:35; DNWSI 433; Sivan GAGl 209. Cf. Van Zijl Baal 36f.; Blau - Loewenstamm UF 2 1970 30 n. 68-72; Garbini LSem 95: *b* + *ʔd*); ¶ syll. Ug.: cf. the element /bādu/ in PNN, Sivan GAGl 209; ¶ RS Akk.: *ana qāti, ina qāti, ištu / ultu qāti*, ŠU(*-ti/ti*), *passim*; Huehnergard AkUg 192f.; Van Soldt SAU 446 n. 128, 457 n. 181, 461; ¶ par.: *b, bd*. ¶ Forms: suff. *bdy, bdk, bdh, bdhm*; *bdm* (encl. *-m*, 4.132:2; (cf. *yd*).
1) Into the hands of, (intended) for, ★a) *ytn ks bdh* he placed a cup into his hand, 1.3 I 10; *bd dnil ytnn qšt* into the hands of PN he put the bow, 1.17 V 26; *bd ḫss msbṭm* into his hands DN (took) the handles, 1.4 I 24; *bdh ḫṭ tkl* with the sceptre of sterility in his hand, 1.23:8; *qḥ rṯt bdk* take a net in your hand, 1.4 II 32; ★b) *passim* in admin. texts of delivering or selling objects, goods or personnel "in the hands of" someone: (document) *bd PN* intended for PN, 4.710:1 (Dietrich - Loretz KA 163); *apnt bd rb ḥršm* wheels (delivered) into the hands of the chief of the workshop, 4.145:9; *npṣm bd mri skn* equipment intended for the *m.* of the prefect, 4.92:1; *(nn) ṣ(!)md bd marynm* (nn) pairs (of draught animals delivered) into the hands of the *m.*, 4.377:34; *yn d ykl bd r*[...] *b dbḥ mlk* wine they deliver (for consumption) into the hands of the *r.*[...] in the royal sacrifice, 1.91:1; oil *bd PN* (delivered) into the hands of PN, 4.171:5; *(nn) ksp ʕl PNN w mit zt bdhm* (nn shekels) of silver to the account of PNN and one

hundred (jars) of olives (delivered) into their hands, 4.386:13; *ṯlṯ uṯbm bd PN b ʕšrt ksp* three *u.* (delivered) to PN for ten (shekels) of silver, 4.337:11; *ṯlṯ d yṣa bd PN l argmn l nskm* copper transferred to PN for the tribute (and delivered) to the smiths, 4.43:4 (Sanmartín UF 10 1978 455f.; cf. Pardee UF 12 1980 433); *ktn d TN pḥm bh w ṯqlm ksph mitm pḥm bd skn* a tunic from TN with red purple for a value of two shekels (and) two hundred (shekels) of red purple into the hands of the prefect, 4.132:5; *alpm pḥm ḫmš mat kbd bd PN* two thousand five hundred (shekels) of ruby purple (delivered) into the hands of PN, 4.132:1; *ktnt bdm PN* tunic delivered likewise into the hands of PN, *ibid.* ln. 2 (cf. *bd*, 4.337:18); *kdwṯ ḥdṯ bd PN* a new *k.* garment into the hands of PN, 4.205:19; *ʕšr kkr šʕrt bd PN b arbʕm* ten talents of wool into the hands of PN for forty (shekels), 4.341:15; *spr npṣm d yṣ{.}a b miḫ(!)d(!)* (spelling mistake: *milḫ*) *(...) bd PN* list of garments that have been delivered by means of payment of customs duties (...) into the hands of PN, 4.166:7; royal personnel *bd PN* (ceded) into the hands of PN, 4.141 II 26; *bnšm d iṯ bd rb ʕprm* personnel that is at the disposal of the chief of the *ʕp.*, 4.752:1; PN *bṯr bd mlkt* emancipated: at the queen's disposal, 4.382:1-2; *PNN bd skn* PNN in the hands of the prefect, 4.635:8, 11, 12, 15, 37, 75; *mdrġlm dt inn bd tlmyn m.* who have not been entrusted to PN, 4.379:1; PN *bʕl any d bd PN* worker of the fleet, at PN's disposal, 4.647:7; *(nn) lmdm bd PN* (nn) apprentices handed over to PN, 4.138:3 and *passim ibid.*; 4.154:1 and *passim ibid*; *lmd aḥd bd PN* an apprentice handed over to PN, 4.138:4 and *passim ibid.*; *PN₁ w PN₂* (...) *bd PN₃* into the hands of PN_3, 4.609:31; *rʕym dt bd PN* shepherds into the hands of PN, 4.374:1; cf. 4.729:1; *yṣḥm bd PN* metal-casters entrusted to PN, 4.609:9; ★c) *passim* in admin. txt. for the transfer of rural estates; cf. *šd bd PN* a field, into the hands of PN, 4.103:2-6; *ṯn šdm bd PN*, two fields, into the hands of PN, 4.357:19 and *passim*; *ṯlṯ šdm bd PN*, three fields, into the hands of PN, 4.357:29; *šd PN₁ bd PN₂* the field of PN_1, into the hands of PN_2, 4.103:8 and *passim*; *šd PN l / bd qrt* the field of PN, for / into the hands of the city, 4.631:6, 9; *passim*; *šd PN₁ bd PN₂ w šd nḥlh bd PN₃* the field of PN_1, into the hands of PN_2, and the field of his heir into the hands of PN_3, 4.103:11-12 and *passim*; *šd PN₁ bd PN₂ nḥlh* the field of PN_1, into the hands of PN_2, his heir, 4.631:2; *passim*; *šd ubdy TN d bd skn* leased fields of TN that (revert(?)) to the hands ofthe prefect, 4.110:1; *spr updt d bd PN* list of share-cropping (plots) that pass to the hands of (/ are in the power of) PN, 4.264:2; *krm ubdy bd PN* vineyard leased to PN, 4.244:7; *šmn škrm bd ʕ*[...]

oil for the hired (personnel) in the hands of NP[...] , RSOu 14 38 [KTU 9.424]:2'; *l ḥmrm d bd* [...] for the donkeys in the hand of [...], RSOu 14 39 [KTU 4.790]:9', 11', 13'. Cf. in unc. ctx. *ytn ilm bdhm bd* PN_1 *gṯr w bd* PN_2 *bʕl* may the (fields of the?) gods be delivered into their hands: DN_1 into the hands of PN_1 and DN_2 into the hands of PN_2, 2.4:20 (cf. *šd gṯr, ibid.* ln. 16, 18; diff.: Cunchillos TOu 2 273f.: 'les dieux le livreront').

2) From the hands of: *trtqṣ bd bʕl* it leapt from the hands of DN, 1.2 IV 13 and par.; *bd aliyn bʕl* from the hands of DN the Victorious, 1.1 IV 22; *qḥ ks bdy* take the cup from my hand, 1.19 IV 54 and par.; *ank kl ḏrʕhm kl npš klklhm bd rb tmtt lqḥt* I (then) collected all their seed grain, all the people (and) all their gear, from the hands of the captain of the (salvage) crew, 2.38:21; *lqḥ ṯqlm ksp bd amtk* he received two silver shekels from the hands of your servant, 2.70:19; *mnk mnkm l yqḥ bt hnd bd PNN* may nobody snatch this house from the hands of PNN, 3.2:14; *bnš bnšm l yqḥnn bn PN w bd PN bnh ʕd ʕlm* may nobody snatch it from the hands of PN or from the hands of his son, in perpetuity, 3.5:17-19; *mnḥ bd PN* delivery entrusted to / from the hands of PN, 4.91:1 (cf. Liverani UF 11 1979 502).

3) At the hands of, through, through the mediation of: *riš ġly bd nsʕk* may your branches fall at the hands of those who uproot you, 1.19 III 54; *qmḥ d kly k ṣḥ* PN_1 *bd* PN_2 flour that they delivered when PN_1 claimed it through the mediation of PN_2, 4.362:2; in bkn ctx.: *bdh aqšr*[through him the sloughing (serpent), 1.82:20.

Unc. ctx.: *bdm*, 1.4 I 31, rdg *b dm*; *bd*, 1.2 IV 3, rdg *a*(!)*bd*; *bdk b*[, 1.16 V 7; *bdh ydrm pit adm*, 1.107:3; *bdh*, RSOu 14 49 [KTU 9.433]:37. For KTU *b dmr* in *ddm l ybr*[*k*] {*bd mr*} *prs l uxmxx*, 4.377:32 (corrupt text) see Sanmartín UF 20 1988 274f.: rdg *bd mr*<*ynm*> (see under *prś/s*).

Cf. bdil, bddn, bdy(n), bdn, yd.

bdil PN (Sem. Cf. Grøndahl PTU 47, 96, 118; Teixidor Syria 45 1968 367; Dahood Or 46 1977 475; Dahood *apud* Pettinato Archives 314; cf. Dietrich - Loretz OLZ 62 1967 537; UF 1 1969 212; De Moor BiOr 26 1969 106); ¶ syll.: cf. BI.DI-*ʔi-lu*, BI.DI.DINGIR, Ug 5 39:7, 23. Cf. *btl*.

PN: bkn ctx. *bdil*[, 4.75 II 2.

bdd "?" (Bkn ctx; cf. Tsumura UF 22 1990 398; Richardson UBL 11 279: *b dd* 'in the pot', or a nominal form of *bddy*).

? : *b*] *ʕl bdd*, 7.222:5.

bddn PN (Sem.(?); cf. Grøndahl PTU 47, 118, 123; De Moor UF 2

1970 315; Bordreuil - Caquot Syria 56 1979 310; Van Soldt SAU 12 n. 108; cf. Dietrich - Loretz OLZ 62 1967 546; UF 1 1969 212; De Moor BiOr 26 1969 106); ¶ syll.: [DUMU] *ba-di-da-na*, PRU 3 203 (RS 16.257+) IV 25; DUMU *ba-dì-da-na*, PRU 3 142 (RS 16.134):5; Ug 5 7:16 (cf. Van Soldt SAU 309); cf. DUMU *pa-at-ti-ta-na*, PRU 6 55:7'.

PN: ★a) 4.425:11; ★b) *bn PN:* 4.69 V 7 (Van Soldt SAU 29); 4.93 I 9; 4.318:5; 4.769:37; RSOu 14 45 [KTU 9.418]:3.

bddy adj. m. "alone, disconnected" (Hb. *bdd*, HALOT 110f.; Arab. *badād*, Lane 162; cf. Dijkstra - De Moor UF 7 1975 206; Del Olmo IMC 137 n. 313); ¶ syll.: cf. the element /bādidu/ in PNN, Sivan GAGl 209. ¶ Forms: sg. m. *bddy*.

Alone, disconnected: *bddy yṣa* [*x*] disconnected did (the message) try to emerge, 1.19 II 28 (bkn ctx.).

Cf. bd (II).

bdl n. m. "substitute, reserve personnel" (cf. Arab. *badal*, Lane 168; Ebla *ba-da-lu(m)*, cf. ARET, MEE, *passim*; cf. Archi UF 20 1988 2f.; Lipiński WGE 257-260; cf. Fronzaroli EL 137; StEb 7 1984 156f.; Sanmartín AuOr 9 1991 183f.); ¶ syll. Ug.: cf. LÚ.MEŠ.DAM.GÀR.MEŠ : *bi-da-lu-ma*, PRU 3 200 (RS 16.257) A II 12; LÚ.MEŠ *bi-da-lu-na*, PRU 3 205 (RS 15.172):14; Sanmartín SEL 5 1988 171ff.; Renfroe UF 20 1988 221ff.; Lipiński WGE 258; Huehnergard UVST 112; cf. PN DUMU-*bi*-DA-*la-ya*, PRU 3 195 (RS 15.09) B I 22. ¶ Forms: pl. *bdlm*, cstr. *bdl*.

Substitute, reserve personnel, ★a) *spr bdlm* list of reserve personnel, 4.134:1; ★b) in particular classes and groups: *bdl mrynm* substitutes of the titulars of the chariot, 4.69 III 6; *bdl mdrġlm* substitutes of the guards, *ibid.* VI 17; cf. *bdlm*, 4.232:42, and cf. *ibid. mrynm*, ln. 33; cf. ¶ RS Akk.: *supra*; ★c) of particular TNN: *bd*(!)*l TN* reserve personnel of TN, 4.214 III 1; 4.96:1; cf. *bdl qrṭy PN* GN substitute: PN, 4.85:6 (cf. *qrṭym* GN, *ibid.* ln. 1); *bdlm dt yṯb b*[reserve personnel detailed(?) in[, 4.86:29; *bdl TN dt inn mhr lhm*(!) reserve personnel with no troop assigned to them, 4.214 I 4. In unc. ctx.: *bdlm*, 4.116:20 (PN?).

Cf. in bkn ctx. *bdlm dt*[, 4.86:21;]*bhtm bdlm*[, 4.312:4, 7.

Cf. bdlm.

bdlm PN (etym. unc.; cf. Grøndahl PTU 118; Dietrich - Loretz UF 1 1969 212); ¶ syll.: cf. DUMU *bi*-DA-*la-ya*, PRU 3 195 (RS 15.09) B I 22. Cf. *btl*, *btlyn*.

PN: ★a) 4.116:20 (unc. ctx., PN?; cf. *bdl*); ★b) *bn PN:* 4.724:5.

bdm, cf. *bd (IV)* 1.

bdn PN (Sem.(?); cf. Grøndahl PTU 118; Dietrich - Loretz OLZ 62 1967 546; UF 1 1969 212; De Moor BiOr 26 1969 106; ZAW 88 1976 342; Watson AuOr 11 1993 214); ¶ **syll.**: cf. *ba-du-ni*, PRU 4 22 9 (RS 18.54 ★a):11'. Cf. *btn*.
PN: ★**a)** 4.46:8; 4.63 IV 12; 4.609:30, 34; 4.631:7; 4.728:6 (*bn ṯ*[); ★**b)** *bn PN:* 4.247:33; 4.343:1; 4.617:30.

bdqt n. f. "fissure, opening, loophole" (Hb. *bdq*, HALOT 111; JAram. *bdqʔ*, Jastrow 141; Akk. *butuqtu*, AHw 144; CAD B 358. Cf. De Moor SP 161f.); ¶ **par.**: *ḥln*, *urbt*. ¶ **Forms**: sg. *bdqt*.
Fissure, opening, loophole: *w ypth̩ bdqt ʕrpt* may he open a loophole in the clouds, 1.4 VII 19 and par.

bdy(n) PN (Sem.(?); cf. Grøndahl PTU 118; Dietrich - Loretz OLZ 62 1967 546; UF 1 1969 212; De Moor BiOr 26 1969 106); ¶ **syll.**: cf. *bi-da-ya*, Syria 18 1937 245f. (RS 8.145): 6 and *passim ibid.* (cf. Berger WO 5 1969/70 274; cf. Grøndahl PTU 118f., 330). Cf. *btw/y*, *pdy(n)*.
PN: ★**a)** 4.191:14; 4.277:9; ★**b)** *bn PN:* 4.561:3.

bgrt PN (etym. unc.).
PN: *bn PN*, 4.93 IV 22.
Cf. **brqt**.

bġr n. m. "shout" (Hb. *pʕr*, HALOT 953; Syr. *pʕar*, LS 598; Arab. *faġara*, Lane 2421f. Cf. Caquot UF 11 1979 102; TOu 2 38 n. 81; diff.: Dahood Bib 49 1968 366: 'to moo', Hb. *nʕr*); ¶ **par.**: *tʕlgt*. ¶ **Forms**: sg. *bġr*. Shout: *bġr b py* there is a shout in my mouth, 1.93:1 (// *tʕlgt*; diff.: De Moor UF 11 1979 649: rdg *b ġr*, 'in negligence', Arab. *ġirrat*). Bkn ctx. *ʕdb bġrt*, 1.1 III 9 (rdg *b ġrt*?).
Cf. **/p-ʕ-r/**.

/b-ġ-y/ vb G/D: "to reveal, show" (< "to look for, desire", Hb. *bʕh*, HALOT 141; OAram. *bʕy*, DNWSI 180ff.; Akk. *buʔʔū*, AHw 145; CAD B 360ff.; Arab. *baġā*, Lane 231ff. Cf. Ginsberg ANET 136; Smith BC 181; diff.: Loewenstamm UF 14 1982 127f.: 'nachspüren', **bġy*; Caquot - Sznycer TOu 1 166 n. 1, 'devoiler', Arab. *faġā*). ¶ **Forms**: G/D prefc. with suff. *ibġyh*.
G/D. To reveal: *atm w ank ibġyh* come and I will reveal it to you, 1.3 III 29 and par. Bkn ctx. *ybġ dd*, 1.172:20 (cf. Bordreuil - Caquot Syria 57 1980 345: 'désirer'). Cf. **bʕyn**.

bhl PN (etym. unc.; cf. Watson AuOr 11 1993 214).
PN: *bn PN*, 4.240:4 (Cf. Bordreuil etc. CRAIBL 1984 425 for the PN *bil* in RIH 83).

bhmt n. f. "cattle" (Hb. *bhmh,* HALOT 111f.; Arab. *bahīmat,* Lane 200). ¶ Forms: sg. *bhmt*; suff. *bhmth*; *bhmtn* (determinative *-n*). Cattle: *ibn yḫlq bhmt ḥwt* the enemy will destroy the cattle of the land, 1.103+:16 (cf. in bkn ctx. *ibid.* ln. 2, 8, 15); *bhmtn tḫlq* the cattle will perish, 1.163:1, 15 (cf. Dietrich - Loretz MU 171).

bht, cf. *bt (II).*

bhṯ n. m. "shame" (cf. JAram. *bhtʔ,* Jastrow 143; Syr. *behtotō,* LS 62; cf. Akk. *bâšu,* AHw 112 and cf. CAD B 5ff.: *baʔašu* B. Cf. Sanmartín UF 10 1978 445; diff.: Caquot - Sznycer TOu 1 244: 'salut à toi!', ESA *bhṯ*; De Moor SP 180: 'to hasten to meet a guest', ESA *bhṯ,* Arab. *bahaṯa*). ¶ Forms: sg. *bhṯ.*
Shame, used as an interj. "for (my) shame!": *bhṯ bn ilm mt* for shame, oh divine DN!, 1.5 II 11 and par. - Cf. /b-ṯ/.

bḥl, cj. in 4.377:24, allophone of *pḥl*; cf. Del Olmo UF 11 1979 184; Dietrich - Loretz UF 17 1985 103.

bḫr n. m. "lad" (Hb. *bḥwr,* HALOT 118. Cf. Jirku KME 102; Aartun UF 16 1984 8; diff.: Gray KTL 21 63: 'incense', Arab. *baḫūr*; cf. Mari Akk. *biḫrum / biʔrum,* AHw 122: *bē/īru(m) II, be/iʔru(m)*; CAD B 211f.: *bēru* B; Gelb CAAA 16); ¶ RS Akk.: cf. [LÚ.]MEŠ *b*[*i*]*-ḫi-ru TN,* PRU 6 71:5'; Sivan GAGl 211; Huehnergard UVST 112f.; ¶ syll. Ug.: cf. ŠUL = *eṭ-lu* = *uš-ta-ni* = *ba* (Nougayrol: *ma*)*-aḫ-ḫu-rù,* Ug 5 137 II 24'; Huehnergard UVST 84, 113; Van Soldt SAU 303; cf. Sivan UF 21 1989 359. ¶ Forms: sg. *bḫr.*
Lad: *ʕln bḫr* [*yml*]*k* over us a lad will reign, 1.15 V 22 (bkn ctx.).

bk n. m. "beaker, large cup" (cf. Aram. *bq,* DNWSI 186; Gk *bîkos,* Liddell - Scott 311; cf. Lipiński UF 2 1970 81; De Moor SP 72f.); ¶ par.: *dn (II), krpn, ks (II).* ¶ Forms: sg. *bk.*
Beaker, large cup: *bk rb* a large beaker, 1.3 I 12; *bk mla* he filled a large cup 1.45:10.

bkm 1) adv. "next, straight away"; 2) temp. conj. "after, immediately after" (< *b* + *k(n)* + *m*; Hb. *bkn,* HALOT 130, 483. Cf. Aartun BiOr 24 1967 288f.; PU 1 6f.; Margalit UPA 360 and n. 13). ¶ Forms: *bkm.*
1) Adv., next, straight away: *bkm tmdln ʕr bkm tṣmd pḥl bkm tšu abh,* straight away he harnessed the ass, straight away he yoked the donkey, straight away he helped his father up, 1.19 II 8-9 (diff.: Gordon PLM 22: 'weeping', *bky*; Margalit UF 16 1984 135ff.: 'to be silent', **bkm*); *w tʕl bkm b arr* and next she went up (mount) TN, 1.10 III 29 (diff. Aartun WO 4 1968 291; Caquot - Sznycer TOu 1 218, 288, 'sur la hauteur', *b-km,* Arab. *kīm*; see Renfroe AULS 57ff.);

bkm ša straight away, get up, 6.48:3.

2) Conj., after, immediately after: *bkm yṯb bʕl l bhth* after DN was seated in his house, 1.4 VII 42.

/b-k-r/ vb D: "to grant primogeniture; to name as heir" (denom. of *bkr*; cf. *infra*). ¶ Forms: D cpref. *abrkn*.

D. To grant primogeniture: *ṣġrthn abrkn* to the youngest of them I shall grant primogeniture, 1.15 III 16.

bkr n. m. "first-born, eldest" (Hb. *bk(w)r*, HALOT 131; Ebla /bakkārum/ in NE:SAG = *ba-ga-lu-um*, NE.SAG = *ba-ga-lu*, VE 243; Krecher Biling. 148; Mander MEE 10 108; /bukrum/ in DUMU.SAG = *bù-ga/gú-lu/ru*$_{12}$, VE 270; Krebernik ZA 73 1983 13; QuSe 18 111; Fronzaroli EL 148; StEb 7 1985 159; Krecher Biling. 160; PN *bu*$_x$(KA)*-ga-lum*, Mander MEE 10 89; Akk. *bukru*, AHw 137; CAD B 309f.; Arab. *bikr*, Lane 241; Eth. *bak*^{w}*r*, CDG 94); ¶ par.:(?) *alm*. ¶ Forms: sg. *bkr*, suff. *bkrk*, du. *bkrm*.

First-born, eldest: ★a) of a human: *nʕmt špḥ bkrk*the most graceful of the clan of your firstborn, 1.14 III 40 and par.; *k bk*[*r*] *zbl amrkm* like the firstborn of a prince I shall bless / strengthen you, 1.13:28; ★b) of an animal: *šir bkrm*, meat of two firstborn, 1.82:9 (//(?) *alm*). Cf. /b-k-r/.

/b-k-y/ vb G: "to weep" (Hb. *bkh*, HALOT 131; Aram. *bky*, DNWSI 163; Ebla cf. G inf. /bakā'um/ in ÉR = *ba-ga-um*, VE 717; Krebernik ZA 73 1983 27; cf. PNN *ib-gi/ki-*(DN), Dahood Ebla 184; Fronzaroli ARES 1 18; cf. Krebernik PTE 37f.: /B-G-ʔ/ (< /p-q-ḥ/, /p-q-d/?); Akk. *bakû*, AHw 97; CAD B 35ff.; Arab. *bakā*, Lane 242; Eth. *bakaya*, CDG 94); ¶ RS Akk.: cf. *bakû*, Ug 5 17 rev. 13'; ¶ syll. Ug.: cf. TN URU BE-*ka-ni*, Sivan GAGl 211: the element /bikyu/; cf. diff. Astour RSP 2 344f.; Van Soldt SAU 318 n. 129: rdg URU *úš-ka-ni*; ¶ par.: /d-m-ʕ/, /d-m-m/, /n-ṣ-r/. ¶ Forms: G cpref. *abky*, *ibky*, *tbky*, *tpky*, *tbk*, *tbkn*, *ybky*, *ybk*; suff. *tbkyk*, *tbkn*, *tbkynh*; act. ptc. m. *bky*; f. *bkyt* (cf. *bkyt*), *bkt*; impv. *bky*; inf. *bky*, *bk* (*bk*; cf. cf. Huehnergard UVST 288 n. 93), suff. *bkym*, *bkm* (encl. *-m*), *bkyh*.

G. To weep: *bn al tbkn* my son, do not weep for me, 1.16 I 25 (// *al tdm*); *ybky w yšnn ytn gh bky* he wept and ground (his) teeth, raised his voice weeping, 1.16 I 12-14 and par.; *tbkyk ab ġr bʕl* for you, father, the mountain of DN weeps, 1.16 I 6 and par.; *u ḫštk l bky ʕtq* and is your mausoleum a perennial lament?, 1.16 II 41 (// *bd*; cf. 1.16 I 4: *ntn*); *yʕrb b ḥdrh ybky* he went into his room to weep, 1.14 I 26 (// *ydmʕ*); *bm bkyh w yšn* in his weeping he fell asleep, 1.14 I 31 (// *ydmʕ*); *mat krt k ybky* what's the matter (with) PN that he weeps?,

1.14 I 39 (// *ydmʕ*); *d[y]k bbk krt*, enough weeping, PN!, 1.14 II 7 (// *b dmʕ*); [*ʕl*] *krt tbkn* for PN they wept, 1.15 V 12; *tbkn w tdm ly* she will weep and moan for me, 1.16 I 30; *bkm tʕrb* weeping she entered, 1.16 II 50; *bkm yʕny DN* weeping DN answers, 1.107:12; [*lpn*] *aḫh tbky* before her brother she wept, 1.16 I 55; *bkt tgly w tbu* weeping she made her way (to the house of PN) and entered, 1.16 VI 4 (// *nṣrt*; diff.: Aartun PU 1 6: < *b* + *kn* + *t*); [...] *aqht w tbk* [watched (?)...] PN and wept, 1.18 IV 39; *tbky pġt bm lb* PN wept in her heart, 1.19 I 34; *abky w aqbrn* I shall weep and bury him, 1.19 III 20 and par.; *tbkynh w tqbrnh* she wept for him and buried him, 1.6 I 16; *ʕd tšbʕ bk* when she was sated with weeping, 1.6 I 9 (// *tšt udmʕt*); *pẓgm ġr ybk* those lacerating (their) skin wept, 1.19 IV 11 and par. (// *ydmʕ*); *ybky km nʕr* he weeps like a boy, 1.107:8; cf. ln. 40 *tpky*); *ksi nqmd ibky (...) lpnh ybky ṯlḥn mlk* Oh throne of PN, weep (...), may the royal table weep in front of him!, 1.161:13-15 (// *ydmʕ*, *yblʕ udmʕth*; cf. Bordreuil - Pardee Syria 59 1982 126).

Bkn ctx.: *bkym*, 1.16 II 54; *ybky*, 1.129:2.

Cf. **bky**, **bkyt**.

bky n. m. "weeping, lament" (verbal n. < /b-k-y/); ¶ **par.**: *bd (I)*. ¶ Forms: sg. *bky*.

Weeping, lament: *ḫštk l bky ʕtq* your sepulchre has become a perpetual lament(?), 1.16 II 41 (// *bd*, cf. *ntn*, 1.16 I 4, 18).

bkyt n. f. "mourners" (< act. ptc. G /b-k-y/); ¶ **par.**: *mšspdt*. ¶ Forms: pl. f. *bkyt*.

Mourner: *ʕrb bkyt b hklh* (female) mourners entered his palace, 1.19 IV 9-10 (// *mšspdt*); *t[bʕ b] bty bkyt* go from my house mourners, 1.19 IV 20.

bl (I) adv. / emph. functor: 1) negative-indicative, "no, not"; 2) affirmative-volitive, "yes" (Hb., Pun. *(?)bl*, HALOT 7, 131; DNWSI 165; Ebla cf. *ba-lu(-ma)*, ARET 7 207. Cf. Aartun PU 1 26f.; Whitley ZAW 84 1972 213ff.; Van Zijl Baal 129). ¶ Forms: *bl*, *blt* (encl. *-t*).

1) Adv. negative functor: *bl ṭl bl rbb šrʕ thmt bl ṭbn ql bʕl* here was neither dew nor drizzle, nor flow (?) of the two oceans, nor sweetness of DN's voice, 1.19 I 44-45 (cf. Del Olmo MLC 389; diff.: Gordon UMC 132: 'let there be no...'; De Moor ARTU 251, 'without...', cf. *bl (II)*); *u mlk u bl mlk* anyone, king or not, 1.4 VII 43. Cf. in unc. ctx. *bl ym* 2.45:23 (cf. Hoftijzer Fs. Kraus 125: rdg *bl ym*: 'kein Tag, niemals').

Bkn ctx.: *at bl at*, 1.12 II 7, 23; *bl tbḥ*, 1.107:46.

2) Emph. affirmative functor: *bl iṯ bn lh* may he have a son!, 1.17 I

20; *bl / blt nmlk* come, we will enthrone (DN)!, 1.6 I 48 and par.; *bl ašt urbt* I am going to put a skylight, 1.4 V 61 and par. Bkn ctx.: *bl išlḥ* I am going to send, 1.14 V 21.

bl (II) prep. "without" (Hb. *bly*, HALOT 133; Akk. *balu*, AHw 100f.; CAD B 70ff.; Arab. *bal*, Lane 243f.; Eth. *ʔenbala*, CDG 27; cf. Aartun PU 1 26). ¶ Forms: *bl*.
Without: *ḫ̮pṯ d bl spr // ṯnn d bl hg* mercenaries without number, archers without counting, 1.14 II 37-38; *tspi širh bl ḥrb // tšt dmh bl ks* consumes its flesh without a knife, drinks its blood without a cup, 1.96:4-5; *bl bnš* there is nobody, no-one, 2.45:27 (cf. *bnš*, 1.c.); *bl bnh* without his sons, 4.243:11. In bkn ctx.: *l bl sk* without covering, yes, 1.16 II 31.

bl (III) n. m.; a kind of beer (MA *billu*, AHw 126; CAD B 228f.; cf. Loretz - Xella MLE 1 43; diff.: various scholars, e.g. Watson UF 24 1992 369f.: 'without', *bl II*); ¶ par.: *lḥm*. ¶ Forms: sg. *bl*.
A kind of beer: *tšt b ḫ̮lṣ bl ṣml* drink, squeezing (it) out, the beer of abstinence, 1.169:7.

bl (IV) PN (etym. unc.; cf. Grøndahl PTU 20, 116, 288; Watson AuOr 13 1995 220). Cf. *bʕl*, PN.
PN: *bn PN*, 4.309:4; cf. in bkn ctx.: 4.662:2.

/b-l-ʕ/ vb G: "to swallow" (Hb. *blʕ*, HALOT 134f.; JAram. *blʕ*, DJPA 104f.; Arab. *blʕ*, Lane 249; Eth. *balʕa*, CDG 94f.); ¶ par.: /b-k-y/. ¶ Forms: G cpref. *yblʕ* (Verreet UF 17 1985 326).
G. To swallow: *yblʕ udmʕth* may it swallow its (own) tears, 1.161:16 (// *ybky*; cf. Dietrich - Loretz UF 15 1983 20; diff.: cf. Wesselius UF 15 1983 314; Taylor UF 17 1985 317: 'swallows its tears').

blbl, 4.288:1, cf. (i)blbl.

bld cf. *ld*.

bldn n. m. "land" (Arab. *balad*, Lane 247; Cf. Bordreuil - Pardee Semitica 41-42 1993 47; diff.: De Moor NYCI 2 27: 'God of the injustice', < *bl dn*; De Tarragon CU 168: TN < *b ldn*; Dietrich - Loretz TUAT 2 322: 'Bēl-dīni'). ¶ Forms: sg. *bldn*.
Land: *il bldn* gods of the land, 1.91:6; 1.162:1 (diff.: Caquot SDB 9 1979 1405: "notre pays", cf. *bld*). Cf. in bkn ctx. [...]*bldn* PN (?), 4.307:11; 4.320:15 (Watson AuOr 13 1995 220).

blḫ̮dr n. m.; piece of cloth or garment (Hurr. > **pilaḫ̮(a)=t=are-*; Sanmartín UF 12 1980 335; cf. Akk. Nuzi: *pilaḫ̮āʔu*, AHw 863; Mayer Nuzi 36 n. 1; Ribichini - Xella Tessili 34; cf. *plk*). ¶ Forms: du. *blḫ̮drm*.
Piece of cloth or garment: *blḫ̮drm* (two) *b.*, 4.4:6.

Cf. **pġndr, plk**.

blkn PN (etym. unc.; Watson AuOr 13 1995 221).
PN: 4.638:5.

blmt n. m. "immortality" (compound noun *bl (II)* + *mt (II)*; UT § 8.74; Spronk BA 154; Pope UF 19 1987 457); ¶ **par.**: *ḥym*. ¶ **Forms**: sg. *blmt*, suff. *blmtk*.
Immortality: (ask for) *blmt w ašlḥk* immortality and I will grant it to you, 1.17 VI 27 (// *ḥym*); *blmtk ngln* in your immortality we rejoiced, 1.16 I 15; II 37 (// *b ḥyk*).
Cf. **bl (II), mt (II)**.

bln n. m. "mixed fodder" (Akk. *ballu*, AHw 99f.; CAD B 63f.; Hb. *blyl*, HALOT 133; cf. Arab. *balīla* "porridge", Lane 245; Pun. *bll*, DNWSI 167. Cf. Sanmartín AuOr 6 1988 234; AfO 35 1988 228; diff. Dietrich - Loretz - Sanmartín UF 6 1974 39, Cohen - Sivan UHT 33f., Cohen UF 28 1996 133f.; Pardee TH 63f.: 'mandrake', Akk. *pillû*, *billu*; De Moor JEOL 27 1981/82 113 n. 37: 'fern'). ¶ **Forms**: sg. *bln*.
Mixed fodder: *št bln qṭ* a *š*. of mixed fodder from flax seed, 1.85:18; 1.72:26.

blšpš PN (Sem.(?); cf. Grøndahl PTU 20; Dietrich - Loretz - Sanmartín UF 5 1973 106; Stamm ANG 150, 182; Gelb - Purves - MacRae NPN 242; Cassin - Glassner ANN 1 105f.).
PN: 4.44:32 (*amry*).

blšš PN (etym. unc.).
PN: 4.277:10.

blt cf. *bl (I)*; cf. Hb. *blty*; Ph. *blt*, HALOT 136; DNWSI 167; Amor. /baltē, baltī/, Gelb CAAA 16.

/b-l-y/ vb G: "to devour, consume" (Hb. *blh*, HALOT 132; Aram. *blʕ*, DNWSI 165; Akk. *belû*, AHw 121; CAD B 72ff.; Arab. *baliya*, Lane 255; Eth. *balya* CDG 198; cf. De Moor UF 1 1969 187 n. 148; Dietrich - Loretz - Sanmartín 7 1975 538); ¶ **par.**: /l-ḥ-m/. ¶ **Forms**: G suffc. *blt*.
G. To devour, consume: *npš blt ḥmr* my appetite devours in heaps, 1.5 I 18 (// *ilḥm*; cf. Del Olmo IMC 69f.; diff.: Jirku KME 57: 'mein Leben ist vernichtet'; Caquot-Sznycer TOu 1 242: 'ma gorge (ne) s'humecte(?) (que) de fange', Hb. *bll*).

bly PN (etym. unc.; cf. Grøndahl PTU 20, 117, 288); ¶ **syll.**: cf. DUMU *bu-lu-ya*, PRU 3 169 (RS 16.145):20. Cf. *bʕly*, *blym*, *ply*.
PN: ★**a)** 4.116:9; ★**b)** *bn PN*: 4.65:10; 4.69 I 2; 4.76:6; 4.93 II 3; 4.356:13; 4.377:10; 4.386:2 (*gbʕly*); 4.681:3; 4.785:20.

blym PN (etym. unc.; cf. Hoftijzer Fs. Kraus 124f.: 'niemals'). Cf. *bly*.

PN: 4.272:7.

blẓn PN (etym. unc. Cf. Grøndahl PTU 268, 288, 299).
PN: *bn PN*, 4.63 II 9.
Cf. plzn.

bmmt PN (etym. unc.).
PN: *bn PN*, 4.412 III 14.

bmt n. f. 1) "back, rump, loin"; 2) "height, hill" (Hb. *bmh*, HALOT 136f.; Moab. *bmt*, DNWSI 167f.; Akk. *bāmtu*, AHw 101; CAD B 78. Cf. De Moor SP 91; Dietrich - Loretz UF 18 1986 109); ¶ par.: *ap (II) (Ib)*, *ḥbš*. ¶ Forms: sg. *bmt*; cstr. *bmt*; suff. *bmth*; pl. cstr. *bmt*.
1) Back, rump, loin: ★a) *k ʕmq yṯlṯ bmt* like a valley he ploughed (his) back, 1.5 VI 22 and par. (// *ap (Ib)*); *yštn aṯrt l bmt ʕr l ysmsmt bmt pḥl* they placed DN on the back of the ass, on the best of the donkey's back, 1.4 IV 14s. and par.; *ʕtkt rišt l bmth* she fastened heads to (her) back, 1.3 II 12 and par. (// *b ḥbšh*); ★b) as meat: *ʕšr bmt alp mri* ten loins of fattened ox, 4.247:17 (cf. ln. 16: *ṣlʕt alp mri*).
2) Height, hill: *bmt ar*[*ṣ*] *tṯṯn* the heights of the earth shook, 1.4 VII 34.

/b-n/ vb G: 1) "to understand"; 2) "to take note"(?); tL.: "to observe intently, scrutinize" (Hb. *byn*, HALOT 122f.; Arab. *bāna*, *tabayyana*, Lane 285ff.; Eth. *bayyana*, CDG 115f.); ¶ syll. Ug.: cf. the element /byn/ in PNN, Sivan GAGl 211); ¶ par.: /š-m-ʕ/, /y-d-ʕ/. ¶ Forms: G suffc. *bn*; prefc. *tbn*; impv. *bn* (for the supposed form *abn* in 1.3 III 26 and par. cf. *abn*); tL prefc. with suff. *itbnnk*.
G. 1) To understand: *rgm (...) l tbn hmlt arṣ* a matter (...) that the multitudes of the earth do not understand, 1.3 III 27 (// *tdʕ*); *bn l rkb ʕrpt* understand, oh Charioteer of the clouds!, 1.4 V 60 (// *šmʕ*); *šmʕk l arḫ w bn* what you hear, O heifer!, understand, 1.13:22. In bkn ctx.: *l ydʕ l bn* not knowing, not understanding, 1.107:6 (cf. De Moor ZAW 100 1988 109); *y*]*bn rgm w ydʕ* understand the matter and know, 2.8:6.
2) To take note (?): *bn km yr* take note(?) how he fires, 1.82:3 (unc. ctx.; cf. De Moor (- Spronk) UF 16 1984 239; ARTU 176).
tL. To observe intently, scrutinize(?): *itbnnk* I am going to observe you intently, 1.169:17 (cf. De Moor UF 12 1980 430).

bn (I) n. m. 1) "son"; 2) 'Son of DN'; 3) "young (of an animal)"; 4) > "person of inferior rank, subject; (pl.) family, clan; heirs"; 5) > stating a quality; 6) > member of a group; 7) "son of" in onomastics (Hb., Ph., Pun., *bn*, HALOT 137f.; DNWSI 168ff.; Amor. /bi/unum/, Huffmon APNMT 175f.; Gelb CAAA 16; Akk. *bi/ūnu*, AHw 127,

138; CAD B 242f., 322; ESA *bn(w)*, CAME 115; DOSA 46f.; Arab. *ibn*, Lane 262f.); ¶ RS Akk.: DUMU(*-ru/i/a*.MEŠ), *passim*; cf. PRU 3 233; PRU 4 261; PRU 6 151; Ug 5 340; cf. espec.: DUMU MUN, PRU 4 196 (RS 17.78):3 and *passim*; DUMU.MEŠ DUMU.MEŠ, PRU 3 43 (RS 16.270):32 and *passim*; DUMU(.MEŠ) LUGAL(*-ri*), PRU 4 86 (RS 17.338):7 and *passim*; DUMU.MEŠ MÍ.LUGAL-*ti*, PRU 3 120 (RS 16.204) rev. 11'; 145 (RS 16.138):35; DUMU.MEŠ KUR-*ti*, PRU 3 11 (RS 15.18):4'; LÚ(.MEŠ).DUMU(.MEŠ) KIN(-*ri*/*ra*), PRU 3 13 (RS 11.730):7; 14 (RS 16.111):28; PRU 4 36 (RS 17.132):33; 83 (RS 17.382+):54; 106 (RS 17.137):10'; 225 (RS 17.422):29; 229 (RS 18.54A): 21'; 294 (RS 19.70):9; PRU 6 7 B 15; 8:15, 19; 179:23; Ug 5 21:25'; 38:28; 41:7; 56:13'; 100:2; DUMU.MEŠ *ši-ip-ru*, PRU 3 105 (RS 15.109+):54; cf. 43 (RS 16.270):27; DUMU.MEŠ *šip-ri-ka*, PRU 4 191 (RS 17.247):10, 16; ¶ par.: *aḫ (I)*, *il*, *ary (I)*, *att (I)*, *ʕgl*, *bkr*, *bn (I)*, *bt (I)*, *hmlt*, *klt (I)*, *pḫr*, *ṣbrt*, *špḥ*, *šr*, *šrš*, *ydd*. ¶ Forms: sg. *bn*, *bnm* (encl. *-m*); suff. *bny*, *bnk*, *bnh*, *bnkm*; pl. *bnm*; cstr. *bn*; suff. *bny*, *bnh*. Cf. the spelling *b* (*b<n>*?) in *PN b PN*, 6.1:1 and cf. Dietrich - Loretz KA 242f. and n. 288.

1) Son ★a) of men and gods: PN *(...) w* PN *aḫh (...) w* PN *bnh w* PN *bth w PN aṯth* and PN, his brother, (...), and PN, his son, and PN, his daughter, and PN, his wife, 3.4:6; PN *w bnh* and his son(s), 4.16:12; *ṯn bn* PN two sons of PN, 4.364:1; PN *w ṯn bnh* and his two sons, 4.339:26s.; PN *yd ṯn bnh* with his two sons, 4.360:4; PN *bl bnh* without his son(s), 4.243:11; *bnm w bnt* sons and daughters, 2.2:9 (cf. *bnm*, *ibid.* ln. 8); *ʕmṯtmr bn nqmpʕ mlk ugrt* PN, son of PN, king of TN, 3.2:3 and par.; *bn mlk w bt mlk tʕln pamt šbʕ* the son and the daughter of the king go up seven times, 1.112:6 (cf. *supra* ¶ RS Akk.: DUMU LUGAL); *l mlkt umy rgm tḥm mlk bnk* to the queen, my mother, say: message of the king, your son, 2.13:4; 2.30:3 (cf. *supra* RS Akk.: DUMU MÍ.LUGAL); *hn* {*unk*} *bnk* behold your son, 5.11:3; *tḥm ʕzilt bnkm* message of PN your (pl.) son, RSOu 14 49 [KTU 9.433]:5; ★b) esp. in the royal legends: *ykn bnh b bt* may there be son of his in the palace, 1.17 I 25 (// *šrš*); *tqrb w ld bn lh* // *(...) bnm lh* she conceived and gave birth to a son, // (...) several sons, 1.15 III 20-21; *in bn lh km aḫh* he has no son like his equals, 1.17 I 18 (// *šrš*); *yld bn ly km aḫy* a son is going to be born to me like my equals, 1.17 II 14 (// *šrš*); *tld šbʕ bnm lk* she will bear you seven sons, 1.15 II 23; *bn krt kmhm tdr* the sons of PN were as many as were promised, 1.15 III 23 (// *bnt*); behold *bn bn aṯrk* your grandchildren

after you, 1.22 I 3 (// *bnk*); *qbr bny* the grave of my son, 1.19 III 44; ★c) in mythological texts: *šbʕm bn aṯrt* the seventy sons of DN, 1.4 VI 46 (// *aḫ*, *ary*); *yiḫd bʕl bn aṯrt* DN he seized the sons of DN, 1.6 V 1; *tn aḥd b bnk am{.}lkn* give me one of your sons to make him king, 1.6 I 46; *tgr il bnh* DN has opposed(?) his son, 1.1 IV 12; *šm bny yw* the name of my son is DN, 1.1 IV 14; cf. in bkn ctx.: *bn bʕl*[, 1.86:17; ★d) in incantations and magical texts: *hl ġlmt tld bn*[behold the damsel will give birth to a son, 1.24:7; *y bn ašld* oh sons whom I have sired!, 1.23:65 (// *aṯt*); *amr bnkm* I shall strengthen your son, 1.13:28 (// *bk*[*r*]).
2) 'Son of DN', ★a) in the royal titulary: *ap krt bnm il* is PN then 'son of DN'?, 1.16 I 10; II 48 (// *šp*ḥ); *ikm yrgm bn il krt* how can it be said that 'PN is the son of DN'?, 1.16 I 20 and par. (// *špḥ*); ★b) in the divine titulary: *bʕl* // *bn dgn* DN // son of DN, 1.2 I 19 and par., *passim* of the DN Baal; rdg *aliyn* {*bn*} *bʕl* in 1.5 II 18.
3) Young of an animal: *bn bṯn* young of a viper, 1.100:74-75; *bn ḫpṯ l umhthm* the young of the loose (cattle low) for their mothers, 1.15 I 6 (// *ʕgl*).
4) Special uses: ★a) *bny* 'my son' > a person of lower rank, a subject (diplom. form.): *ṯmny ʕm bny mnm šlm* how are things there with 'my son'?, 2.46:7; cf. *ibid.* ln. 9, 12; *l PN bn*(!)*y aḫy rgm* to PN, 'my son (and) brother', say:, 2.14:3; cf. *ibid.* ln. 11, 16; ★b) pl. cstr./suff. *bn* 'sons of' > family, clan: *šlm PN šlm bn*(!)*h* peace to PN, peace to his family, 1.161:32; esp. of the main deities: *aṯrt w bnh* DN and her fmily, 1.3 V 37 and par. (// *ṣbrt aryh*); *mḫṣ bny* the assassins of my family, 1.4 II 25 (// *ṣbrt aryy*); *bn il dr bn il mpḫrt bn il* the family of DN, the family circle of DN, the family assembly of DN, 1.65:1-3 and par.; (does not have, etc.) DN (...) *ḥẓr k bn aṯrt* a mansion like the family of DN, 1.3 IV 48 and par. (// *ilm*); *mẓll bnh* the shelter of his family, 1.4 I 13 (// *klt*); cf. redundantly: *bt bn bnš yqḥ ʕz* if the family of someone takes a kid, 127:30; ★c) pl. *bn(m)* 'sons (of)' > heirs, offspring: (donation) *l PN w l bnh ʕd ʕlm* to PN and his heirs, in perpetuity, 3.2:11; 3.5:14; no-one can snatch it *bd PN w bd bnh ʕd ʕlm* from the hands of PN or from the hands of his heirs, in perpetuity, 3.5:19;3.2:17;]*b*(?)*nm aqny*]may I procreate offspring, 1.14 II 4 (//]*šrm*); ★d) dependent person: *bn mrynm* dependents of titularies of the war chariot, 4.137:4; 163:8; 4.173:5; *bn mṣrym* Egyptian dependents, 4.230:10.
5) Stating a quality (sg. / pl. + n. sg.): ★a) *bn adm* man, 1.169:15 (// *adm*); ★b) *bn il(m)* divine being: *ʕm bn il tspr yrḫm* you shall count

the months like divine being(s), 1.17 VI 29 (// *ʕm bʕl*); *passim* of the DN Mot: *bn ilm mt* the divine DN, 1.5 I 12 and par. (// *ydd{.bn} il*); *pḫr bn il* divine assembly, 1 4 III 14 (cf. *pḫr ilm*, 1.47:29 and par.; ¶ RS Akk.: ᵈ*pu-ḫur* DINGIR.MEŠ, Ug 5 18:28); in bkn ctx.: *bn il* // (?) *pḫr kkbm*, 1.10 I 3; ★c) *bn um* blood brother, 1.14 I 9 (// *aḫm*); cf. *bnm umy*, 1.6 VI 11, 15 (// *aḫym*); cf. *ṯar um*, 1.14 I 9 (Verreet UF 19 1987 325); ★d) *bn ḫrn* messenger, 2.61:3 (cf. *supra* ¶ RS Akk.: DUMU.MEŠ *šipru* / KIN); *bn amt* servants, 1.14 II 3 and par. (cf. Fensham VT 19 1969 312ff.; Rainey RSP 2 82, 91); ★e) *bn ym*, ('sons of one day' >) newborn, 1.23: 23, 59, 61 (diff.: Lipiński OLP 3 1972 117: 'sons of Yam'; Nielsen RSM 72: 'sons of the day / sun'; Albright BASOR 71 1938 37: 'my two sons'; cf. for the various opinions Caquot - Sznycer TOu 1 359; Trujillo UR 136); ★f) *bn mrzḥ* member of cult association, 4.399:8; ★g) *bn qdš* holy one, 1.2 I 21 and par. (// *ilm*; on the various interpretations of 'sons of the Holy One / of the sanctuary / of holiness / of Qudšu'; cf. De Moor SP 130; Cross CMHE 37, 177 n. 133; Cunchillos AD 47ff.; Dietrich - Loretz UF 22 1990 62; Wyatt UF 24 1992 406f.); ★h) cf. in unc. ctx. *bn ḥtt* 'the scabby ones', 1.82:23 (cf. De Moor - Spronk UF 16 1984 244f.: 'sons of disease'; cf. *ḥtt*).

6) Member (sg. / pl.) of a group (+ n. pl. / TN): *bn nšm* men, 1.6 II 18 (// *hmlt arṣ*); *hwt bn nšm* a man's word, RSOu 14 52 [KTU 9.435]:10; *bn ilm*, cf. *supra*: 5.b: *bn il(m)*; *bn mṣrym* Egyptians, 4.230:10; *bn ugrt* Ugaritian, 1.40:26 and par. (cf. Block SR 13/3 1984 301ff.); *bn am(h)t* servants, 1.14 II 3 and par.; 4.230:9; cf. *bn bʕl tġpṯ* member(s) of the professional group of maker(s) of packsaddles / felt, 4.370:13 (cf. *ḥrš btm*, *ibid.* ln. 14).

7) In personal names, ★a) inner element of a PN: "*bn* + DN" (cf. *supra*: 2.a); "*bn* + TN" (cf. *supra*: 6); "*bn* + GN" (cf. *supra*: 6); "*bn* + n." (cf. *supra*: 5); *passim* (Grøndahl PTU 118f.); cf. RSOu 14,46 [KTU 9.423]:1'-18'; ★b) special use in patronymics: "*bn* + PN", *passim* (Grøndahl PTU 118; also with non-Semitic PNN). On the spelling *b* (*b<n>*?) in PN *b* PN, 6.1:1 cf. Dietrich - Loretz KA 242f. and n. 288).

Cf. bnib, bnil, bnilh, bnilt, bninr, bnirn, bnʕn, bnʕnt, bnkṯrt, bnlbnm, bnn (II), bnqdšt, bnrpš, bnš, bnšpš, bt (I).

bn (II) prep. "between, among" (Hb. *byn, bynwt*, HALOT 123; Ph. *bn*, DNWSI 152; OAram. *bny*, DNWSI 152ff.; Aram., Nab. *byn*, DNWSI 152ff.; Syr. *bayna, baynot*, LS 68; Ebla cf. /bayna(y?)/ in MI.SÁ = *ba-na me-si-im*, VE 817; Krebernik ZA 73 1983 32; Hecker Biling. 210

n. 30; Conti SQF 196; Arab. *bayna*, Lane 287ff.; ESA *byn*, DOSA 41; Eth. *bayna*, CDG 116. Cf. De Moor SP 90; Aartun PU 2 51f.); ¶ par.: *b*. ¶ Forms: *bn*.

Between, among: *nʕmt bn aḫt bʕl* the most graceful among the sisters of DN, 1.10 II 16; *bn ydm* on the chest, 1.2 IV 14 and par. (// *ktp*; cf. Hb. *byn ydym*; Avishur UF 12 1980 125ff.; diff.: Marcus Fs. Loewenstamm 111ff., 'back'); *bn ktpm* on the shoulder, 1.2 I 42 (cf. Hb. *byn ktpym*; Avishur *ibid.* 131f.); *bn ʕnm* on the forehead, 1.2 IV 22 (// *qdqd*; cf. Hb. *byn ʕynym*; Avishur *ibid.* 126ff.; cf. 1.2 IV 40; 1.3 VI 3; 1.82:16; 1.101:5; RSOu 14 53 [KTU 9.432]:35'); *bn qrytm* between the (two) cities, 1.3 II 6 and par. (// ★b); *bn ṯlḥnm* between the tables, 1.3 II 30 (// ★b); *bn nšrm* among the eagles, 1.18 IV 21 and par.; *bn abnm* among the stones, 1.1 V 23 and par.

Cf. bnny.

bn (III) cf. *b (I)* (ESA *bn*, DOSA 45f.).

bnib PN (Sem. Cf. Grøndahl PTU 87, 100; De Moor BiOr 26 1969 105).

PN: rdg unc. *bni*(?)*b* : 4.261:23.

bnil PN (Sem. Cf. Grøndahl PTU 94, 118f.; Dietrich - Loretz - Sanmartín UF 6 1974 22; Van Soldt SAU 32 n. 259, 163); ¶ syll.: cf. DUMU.DINGIR, cf. PRU 3 p. 253; PRU 4 201 (RS 18.02):18 (Van Soldt SAU 11); Ug 5 2 rev. 22'; 3 rev. 6'.

PN: 3.10:17; 4.86:12 (*bn yṣr*[]); 4.297:3 (*gt PN*, (Belmonte RGTC 12/2 83: **Gittu-Bin-ʔili*); 4.377:19; 4.609:8, 19; 4.616:10; 4.623:6 (*bn tlm*[*yn*]); 4.732:2; 4.791:13.

bnilh PN (Sem. Cf. Grøndahl PTU 95).

PN: 3.7:4 (*mḏrġl*).

bnilt PN (Sem. Cf. Grøndahl PTU 98).

PN: 4.35:19.

bninr PN (Sem. Cf. Ribichini - Xella RSF 15 1987 11f.). Cf. *bnirn*.

PN: 4.715:4; 4.723:16; cf. bkn ctx. 4.229:4.

bnirn PN (etym. unc.; Ribichini - Xella RSF 15 1987 12; Watson AuOr 8 1990 116); ¶ syll.: cf. DUMU-*i-ru-na*, PRU 55:10', 20'). Cf. *bninr*.

PN: 4.281:16.

bnʕn PN (Sem. Cf. Grøndahl PTU 110; Zadok UF 17 1985 394 n. 123); ¶ syll.: ᵐDUMU-*a-nu*, Ug 5 8 rev. 3'; cf. PN DUMU DUMU-ᵐ*a-ni*, Ug 5 159:17 (Nougayrol Ug 5 p. 263 n. 3: rdg PN DUMU ᵐDUMU-*a-ni*). Cf. *ʕn (III)*.

PN: 4.33:32 (*rqdy*); 4.232:47.

bnʕnt PN (Sem. Cf. Grøndahl PTU 111); ¶ syll.: cf. mDUMU-mDINGIR.IGI.AD, PRU 3 194 (11.839):12; PN DUMU-mDINGIR.IGI.AD, *ibid.* ln. 16; cf. Huehnergard AkkUg 400 n. 85.
Cf. *ilabn.*
PN: 4.307:6; 4.320:4.

bnʕṯtr NP (Sem.).
NP: 4.778:6.

bnkṯrt PN (Sem. Cf. Grøndahl PTU 152); ¶ syll.: cf. [DUMU-]*ku-ša-ri*[, PRU 6 82:20.
PN: 4.412 II 5.

bnlbnn PN (Sem. Cf. Grøndahl PTU 154).
PN: 4.65:4.

bnn (I) n. m.; a luxury item (etym. unc.; cf. in periph. Akk. *pinnu* AHw 864: gold or bronze appliqué or decoration in the form of a button; diff. De Moor 28 1996 157: 'carp' Arab. *bunnīy*, Syr. Arab. *benni*; Watson UF 32 2000 568: 'bead' Eg. *bnn*). ¶ Forms: sg. *bnn.*
A luxury item: *mit bnn* one hundred *b.*, 4.247:27 (between *art ḥkpt* and *iqnu*).

bnn (II) PN (etym. unc.; cf. Grøndahl PTU 119; Watson AuOr 13 1995 221); ¶ syll.: *bu-na-ni*, PRU 6 148:5'.
PN: 4.377:16; cf. in bkn ctx.: 4.258:10.

bnnbdg DN Hurr. (< *nbdg*, Hurr. DN. Cf. Grøndahl PTU 206, 243; Laroche GLH 186f.; Wilhelm RlA 7 173f.: 'Nupatik / Nupadak').
PN: 4.69 I 18. Cf. the DN *nbdg*, *passim* in Hurr. ctxs. Rdg]*nbdgn* in 7.43 5.

bnnkl PN (Sem. Cf. Grøndahl PTU 166).
PN: 4.63 I 40.
Cf. nkl.

bnnklb PN (etym. unc. Cf. Grøndahl PTU 16, 100, 166, 244).
PN: 4.93 IV 20; in bkn ctx., 4.260:9; 4.432 (I) 16; 4.708:4.
Cf. ib (II), nkl.

bnny n. m. "intermediary, neutral person" (MHb. *bynwny*, Jastrow 163; < *bn (II)*; Albright BASOR 150 1958 38; Cunchillos TOu 2 339; diff. Heltzer OLA 6 1979 479: 'created me'; Lipiński OLP 12 1981 107f.: 'de ma taille', Akk. *bunnannû, biniannu*, etc.). ¶ Forms: sg. bnny.
Intermediary, neutral person: (may the king send me) *bnš bnny ʕmn mlakty hnd* some intermediary with this my embassy, 2.33:34.

bnpdr PN ((?) < *pdr (II)*, DN. Cf. Dietrich - Loretz UF 1 1969 213; Ribichini - Xella UF 16 1984 271; SEL 8 1991 167).

PN: : 4.655:8. Cf. in bkn ctx. *pdr*[, 2.1:4 (cf. Cunchillos TOu 2 270 n. 5).

bnqdšt PN (Sem. Cf. Grøndahl PTU 176); ¶ syll.: <DUMU->*qa-diš-ti*, Ug 5 7:14 (Sivan GAGl 260; cf. Nougayrol Ug 5 p. 11 n. 1; Van Soldt SAU 29 n. 236).
PN: 4.69 V 11; 4.412 I 12.

bnr, element of the mythical TN *mrrt-tġll-bnr*, scene of *Aqht*'s violent death (Belmonte RGTC 12/2 191: *Mirartu-Taġullalu-Banīri*(?). Cf. Dietrich - Loretz - Sanmartín UF 5 1973 119ff.; Dijkstra - De Moor UF 7 1975 209; Margalit UF 11 1979 522; Watson UF 8 1976 374 n. 20; UF 30 1998 752: 'date-palm which produces dates'; Astour RSP 2 303. Cf. De Moor ARTU 260 n. 230: *mrrt-tġll-bnr* 260 'the gallbladder that brings into the fire', cf. *bnr*).
TN: 1.19 III 50, 51f.
Cf. mrrt (III), tġll.

bnršp PN (Sem. Cf. Grøndahl PTU 181f.; Watson AuOr 8 1990 127).
PN: 4.33:12 (ary); 4.155:15; 4.170:9.

bnssm PN (Sem. For the theonym cf. Grøndahl PTU 187; Caquot - Masson Syria 45 1968 317ff.; Fauth ZDMG 120 1970 229f.; Sznycer RDAC 1984 117f.; Ribichini - Xella SEL 8 1991 166).
PN: 4.170:18.

bnš n. m. 1) "man, an individual, someone, person; people, personnel"; 2) "service personnel"; 3) "farmhand, labourer" (<(?) *bn (I)* + **(?)nš*, cf. Sem. /ʔ-n-š/ and *bn nšm*, RSOu 14 52 [KTU 9.435]:10; Aistleitner UGU 47; Albright BASOR 150 1958 38; Akk. *mār nišī*, cf. AHw 797; CAD N/2 283ff.; cf. Yamashita RSP 2 46; cf. Ebla /našī/ in *na-se*$_{11}$ / NA.SE$_{11}$(SIG), Krebernik ZA 72 1982 218; Fronzaroli EL 147f.; Archi WGE 133; Grégoire - Renger WGE 22ff.; ARET 7 228; 8 63; 9 398; *na-sa-a*, Fronzaroli NABU 1989 2; Akk. *nišū*, AHw 796f.; CAD N/2 283-289; Arab. *nās*, Lane 2866f.; cf. Hb. *nšym*, HALOT 729; Syr. *neššē*, LS 450); ¶ RS Akk.: cf. LÚ(.MEŠ), ÉRIN(.MEŠ), *passim*; cf. *amīlu*, *ṣabû*, PRU 3 232, 235; PRU 4 259, 262; PRU 6 150f.; Ug 5 340; Huehnergard AkUg 383, 393; ¶ syll. Ug.: ZA = *a-mi-lu* = *tar-šu-wa-an-ni* = : *bu-nu-šu*, Ug 5 130 II 5'; NU = *a-mi-lu* = *tar-šu-wa-an-ni* = *bu-nu-šu*, *ibid.* ln. 8'; [LÚ = *amīlu* = *tar-š*]*u-wa-ni* = *bu-nu-šu*, Ug 5 137 II 31'; [UR (= *amīlu)* = *tar-š*]*u-wa-an-ni* = : *bu-nu-šu*, Ug 5 131:7'; cf. Huehnergard UVST 114; Van Soldt BiOr 47 1990 732. ¶ Forms: sg. *bnš*, pl. *bnšm*, cstr. *bnš*, suff. *bnšhm*.
1) Man, an individual, someone, person of m. sex, ★a) in general: *(nn) bnšm b TN* (nn) men in TN, 4.355:2 and *passim*; *hm mt yʕl bnš*

if death threatens someone, 1.127:30; *bt bn bnš yqḥ ʕz* if the family of someone takes a goat, *ibid.* ln. 31 (cf.]*bnš*, ln. 15); *yhbṯ bn*(!)*š* may he/they remove this individual, 2.4:19; *bt l bnš trgm*[the daughter(?) will say to the man[, 2.2:5 (in unc. ctx.; cf. *ibid.* ln. 2); cf. in bkn ctx. 1.86:8, 26, 30; ★b) used collectively, people, personnel: *bn*]*š d bt mlk* people (busy / working) in the palace, 4.766:12; *bnšm d iṯ bd rb ʕprm* personnel at the disposal of the chief of the *ʕp.*, 4.752:1; *tgmr bnš l b bt mlk* total of the people currently in service in the palace, 4.137:13; *bnš {l} d yškb {l} b bt mlk* people who currently reside/lodge in the palace, 4.163:15; *ʕl alpm bnš tiṯṯmn* for two oxen(?) people fell into debt, 4.398:1; *bnšm dt iṯ alpm lhm* people who have cattle, 4.422:1; *bnšm dt l TN ṯb* people who have returned to TN, 4.339:1, cf. *l mlk*, ln. 17; cf. in bkn ctx. [*bn*]*šm dt iš*[, 4.617:1; 4.655:1; *bnš TN* people of TN, 4.125:18; *bnš gt nn*, *ibid.* ln. 2 and *passim* (cf. Heltzer IOKU 63ff.; Dietrich - Loretz UF 9 1977 344); ★c) special syntagms: *ṯryn aḥd d bnš* a suit of armour for a man, 4.169:6; cf. (...) *d bnšm*, 4.363:2; *bnš bnny* intermediary, 2.33:33; *bnš kld* archers, 4.277:1; cf. *bnš*[*m m<n>dym* the '*Ummān-manda*', 2.62:4 (cf. ÉRIN.MEŠ MAN.DÁ.ME, PRU 4 180 (RS 17.286):6; Sanmartín SEL 5 1988 174f.; cf. *mndy*); the syntagm *bnš bnšm* + *l* (+ vb) 'no-one': *bnš bnšm l yqḥnn* no-one shall snatch it, 3.5:16; *mn bnš* whoever it may be, 2.45:25; *bl bnš* there is nobody, no-one, *ibid.* ln. 27; *bnšm* [...] *w thbzn* the people [...] will be slaughtered, 1.163:2. 2) Personnel in service, ★a) in the service of individuals: *bnš PN*, 4.44:24 and *passim*; cf. 4.46:2; 4.103:52 (or rdg *bn*{*š*}?; cf. *bn (I)* 7); 4.243:32; 4.343:6-7; 4.358:3; 4.367:9; *bnš tpnr* personnel of the *t.*, 4.44:23, 28; *rišym dt ʕrb b bnšhm* GN who have stood surety for his personnel, 4.347:2; *bnšm h*[[*x*]]*mt ypḥm* members of his personnel are the witnesses, 4.659:6; *PN ṯlṯ bnšm* PN: three members of personnel, RSOu 14 48:1; ★b) esp. *bnš (mlk)* 'man/men (of the king)', personnel directly connected with the royal service (cf. *infra*: 3): PN *bnš mlk* 'man of the king', 3.2:6; PN *bnš mlkt* 'man of the queen', 4.22:3; *mḫṣ bnš mlk* weaver, 'man of the king', 4.182:56; *spr bnš mlk* list of the 'men of the king', 4.370:1; 4.141 I 1; 4.144:1; *spr ḥpr bnš mlk* list of rations of the 'men of the king', 4.609:1; *ḥpr bnšm* rations of the 'men (of the king)', 4.243:2ff.; *tgmr bnš mlk* sum total of 'men of the king', 4.141 II 25; cf. *tgmr yṣḥm (nn) bnš mlk* total of the bronzesmiths: (nn: all of them) 'men of the king', 4.151 II 6; *spr bnš mlk d b riš* list of the 'men of the king' in TN, 4.367:1; *PN bnš mlk d b riš* PN: 'man of the king' who is among the 'majordomos', 3.2:6;

cf. *bnš b TN*, "UF 29 1997 826 1": 7,8; *bnšm d b*[, 4.393:13; 4.395:1. 3) Farmhand, labourer (cf. *supra*: 2), ★a) *(nn) bnšm w ḥmr* (nn) farmhands and a donkey, 4.29:2, 4; *(nn) ḥmr(m) w (nn) bnšm* (nn) donkeys and (nn) farmhands, 4.380:3-26; cf. in bkn ctx.: *d bnš ḥmr*[, 1.86:12; *bt alpm ʕšr bnšm* cattle shed: ten farmhands, 4.358:2; unspecified: *ḫmš bnšm* five farmhands, 4.138:1 (cf. *lmd(m)*, ln. 3 and *passim*); [*ḫ*]*mš bnš* five labourers, 4.301:1; ★b) in squads: *(nn) ṣmdm (nn) bnš yd ytm yd rʕy ḥmrm* (nn) pairs (of bullocks), (nn) farmhands with two foremen and the muleteer, 4.618:2, cf. *ibid.* ln. 5, 8, 14, 15-16, 18, 20, 22; in various places: *(nn) bnšm b TN* (nn) farmhands in TN, 4.355:2 and *passim*; ★c) on board ship: *ṣbu anyt (nn) bnš(m)* crew: (so many) farmhands, 4.40:5, 9, 13, 15, 17 (¶ RS Akk.: ÉRIN.MEŠ GIŠ.MÁ, PRU 6 138:20).

Bkn ctx. *bnš bir*[2.77:9; cf. 2.9:6; 2.17:16; 2.35:18; *um bnš*, 4.351:1; *bnš aḥd*, 4.420:5; 4.762:6; *tʕr bnš*, 7.55:6.

Cf. /ʔ-n-š/, bn (I).

bnšpš PN (Sem. Cf. Grøndahl PTU 34, 195); ¶ syll.: DUMU-[d]UTU*(-ši)*, PRU 3 195 (RS 15.09) B I 17; PRU 6 79:5; RSOu 7 3:7. PN: 4.63 IV 6; 4.194:18; 4.227 I 11; 4.628:5; 4.666:4; cf. in bkn ctx.: 4.422:43. For *bt špš*, RSOu 14 44:6, cf. Bordreuil - Pardee RSOu 14 p. 361: rdg *bn*(!)*špš* ?; cf. *špš (I)* 3.a).

bnt (I) n. f. "masonry, building, construction" (< /b-n-y/; cf. Akk. *binītu*, AHw 126f.; CAD B 238; Sanmartín UF 10 1978 445f.).

Masonry, building, construction: *bnt bhtk y ilm* // *bnt bhtk al tšmḫ* (in the) masonry of your palace, oh DN, (in the) building of your palace do not rejoice, 1.3 V 20 and par. (// *b rm hklk*; diff.: Gordon PLM 83: 'thou hast built'; Dijkstra - De Moor UF 7 1975 193: 'the sons'; Del Olmo: MLC 190: 'dentro de tu casa no te regocijes, ... no te alegres en lo alto de tu palacio'); *<b>hty bnt dt ksp* my palace is a building of silver, 1.4 VI 36 and par. (diff.: Del Olmo MLC: mi casa he construido, la de plata, Del Olmo MLC 206; [cf. /b-n-y/]); *tṣb qšt bnt DN* she loads/loaded the bow, the construction of DN, 1.17 VI 13.

bnt (II) n. f. 1) "produce"; 2) "creature" (< /b-n-y/; Akk. *binûtu*, AHw 127; CAD B 243f.). ¶ Forms: sg. cstr. *bnt*.

1) Produce: *bnt šdm* the produce of the field, 1.12 II 44 (Dijkstra - De Moor UF 7 1975 185; Du Mesnil Berytus 26 1978 64 n. 55; cf. diff.: Del Olmo MLC 484: 'vaguadas de los campos', Arab. *banātu l-arḍ*, Virolleaud Syria 16 1935 262 n. 1).

2) Creature: *bnt ṣʕṣ* // *bnt ḫrp* 'agitated(?) creature(s)' // 'crazy(?) creature(s)', 1.82:18; // *bnt mʕmʕ* creature(s) of colic(?), *ibid.* ln. 41

(titles of demons; cf. De Moor - Spronk UF 16 1984 244).
Cf. bnwt.

bnt (III) n. m. "tamarisk" (cf. Akk. *bīnu*, AHw 127; CAD B 239ff.; Ebla cf. /baynim/, /baynu(m)/ in GIŠ.ŠINIG = *i-zu ba-ne(-um)*, *ba-nu*, VE 395; Krebernik ZA 73 1983 15; QuSe 18 139. Cf. Dietrich - Loretz MU 218; diff.: Sanmartín UF 10 1978 445f.: 'Modell, Figurine', Akk. *binītu*; Pardee UF 15 1983 136: 'berries(?), odor(?)', Arab. *bnn*). ¶ Forms: sg. *bnt*.
Tamarisk: *bnt qḥ* take (a bunch of) tamarisk, 1.124:8.

bnt (IV), cf. *bt (I)*.

bnṯmq PN (< *ṯmq*, DN. Cf. Ribichini - Xella SEL 8 1991 169).
PN: 4.65:2; 4.93 III 3; 4.106:20; 4.1227; 4.226:10. Rdg *b* <*bn*> *ṯmq*, 4.658:7.

bnwn n. m. "building" (< /b-n-y/; Hb. *bnyn*, HALOT 140; Aram. *bnwy*, DNWSI 173; ESA *bnw*, DOSA 47; Syr. *benyonō*, LS 78; Arab. *bunyān*, Lane 261). ¶ Forms: sg. *bnwn*.
Building: *ʕl l ṯkm bnwn* go up on top of the building, 1.16 IV 13.

bnwt n. f. "creature" (< /b-n-y/; Sivan UF 14 1982 216 n. 137: pass. ptc. G; cf. Huehnergard UVST 287 n. 92; cf. Akk. *binûtu*, AHw 127; CAD B 243f.). ¶ Forms: pl. f. *bnwt*, suff. *bnwth* (poss. pl. of *bnt (III)*).
Creature: *bny bnwt* creator of creatures, 1.4 II 11 and par., title of the god El (cf. Akk. *bān binûti*, Tallqvist AGE 129; diff.: De Moor SP 144 n. 2: 'the Progenitor of the generations'); *w ṯṯkl bnwth* for his offspring were left without sons, 1.100:62 (diff.: Dietrich - Loretz - Sanmartín UF 7 1975 124: 'Zeugungskraft'; but cf. Dietrich - Loretz TUAT 2 349: 'Geschöpfe').

/b-n-y/ vb G: 1) "to build"; 2) "to recompose, rebuild"; N: "to be built" (?) (Hb. *bnh*, HALOT 139; Ph., Pun., Aram. *bny*, DNWSI 175; Amor. /bny/, Gelb CAAA 16; Ebla cf. the element /B-N(?)-ʔ/ in PNN, Krebernik PET 40; *ib-na-*, *ba-na*(-ND), Müller Biling. 173, 184; *ba-ne-ti*, cf. Krebernik BFE 152, 156; Müller EDA 105; Sanmartín AuOr 9 1991 184; Akk. *banû*, AHw 103; CAD B 83ff.; ESA *bny*, CAME 115; DOSA 48; Arab. *bny*, Lane 260f.); cf. ¶ RS Akk.:]*a-bi ba-an*, Ug 5 168:18'; DN *ib-nu-šu-nu-ti*, Ug 5 17:20; in the sky *ib-ba-ni* ŠUB, *ibid.* rev. 12'; I, PN, *u-bá-an-ni-šu* (D), PRU 4 99 (RS 17.79+):50'; ¶ syll. Ug.: cf. the element /yabn(ī)-/ in PNN; Sivan GAGl 142, 157, 212; cf. ideogr. DÙ in PN DÙ.[d]UTU (/Yabni-Šapšu/, PRU 6 18:3; Van Soldt UF 21 1989 372 n. 22); ¶ par.: /r-m/. ¶ Forms: G cpref. *ybn*, *tbn*, *tbnn*, *abn*; impv. *bn*; inf. cstr. *bn*; act. ptc.

m. sg. *bny* (cf. *bny*); N cpref. *ybn* (?) (Verreet UF 17 1985 328).
G. 1) To build: *tbʕ bn bht ym* go, build the palace of DN, 1.2 III 7 (// *rmm*); *bn bht ksp w ḫrṣ* build a palace of silver and gold, 1.4 V 18, 33; ([quickly] *bhth tbnn* they built his palace, 1.4 VI 16 (// *trmm*). For *bnt*, 1.4 VI 36, cf. *bnt (I)*.
2) To recompose, rebuild: *knp nšrm <bʕl> ybn // bʕl ybn diy hmt* may <DN> rebuild the wings of the eagles, // may DN rebuild their pinions, 1.19 III 12-13 and par. Cf. in bkn ctx., *abn ank* I shall rebuild you(?), 1.18 IV 40 (diff. Margalit JNSL 9 1981 105: 'culpable am I', Arab. *'bn*; Caquot SEL 2 1985 94 'discerner, comprendre', /b-n/).
N. To be built (?): *ybn bt l bʕl km ilm* let a house be built for DN like (that of) the gods, 1.4 IV 62 (possibly also impersonal G 'they build' or G pass. 'let it be built').
Cf. bnt (I), bnt (II), bnwn, bnwt, bny.

bny n. m. "architect, builder; maker, creator" (< act. ptc. G /b-n-y/; Ph., Pun. *bnʔ*, Heltzer HO 70; Akk. *bānû*, AHw 103; CAD B 94f.; Arab. *bannāʔ*, *bānin*, Lane 261; Wehr - Cowan DMWA 95); ¶ RS Akk.: *a-bi* DIŠ-*en ba-ni* LÚ.MEŠ, Ug 5 17:33. ¶ Forms: sg. *bny*.
'Architect, Builder', in the titulature of the prince: *nqmpʕ bn nqmd mlk ugrt (...) bny k*(?) *lb mlk* PN, son of PN, king of TN, (...) 'architect', by royal wish, 7.63:7 (Del Olmo UF 18 1986 87); 'Maker, Creator', in the divine title *bny bnwt* 'creator of creatures', 1.4 II 11; III 32 (// *ṯr il*); 1.6 III 5, 11 (// *lṭpn il*); 1.17 I 24. (// *ṯr il ab*); cf. Pope UF 19 1987 222; cf. Akk. *bān binûti*, Tallqvist AGE 129.

/b-q-ʕ/ vb G: "to split, open" (Hb. *bqʕ*, HALOT 149f.; cf. Aartun UF 16 1984 8f.). ¶ Forms: G cpref. *ibqʕ*, ybqʕ; suff. *tbqʕnn*.
G. To split, open: *ybqʕ kbdthm* he opened their entrails, 1.19 III 10 and par.; *ibqʕ kbdh*, I shall open her entrails, 1.19 III 32 and par.; *b ḥrb tbqʕnn* with a knife she split him, 1.6 II 32.
Cf. bqʕ (I), bqʕ (II), bqʕt (I), bqʕt (II), bqʕty.

bqʕ n. m. "valley" / TN "The Valley" (Hb. *bqʕh* HALOT 150; MHb. *bqʕh*, Jastrow 186f.; cf. Arab. *baqʕat*, *biqāʕ*, Lane 235). ¶ Forms: sg. *bqʕ*.
Valley / TN: *arbʕ uzm mrat bqʕ* four fattened geese of the valley / TN, 4.247:21; *mit ygb bqʕ* one hundred *y.* of the valley / TN, *ibid.* ln. 23 (cf. Aartun UF 16 1984 9: TN).
Cf. bqʕ (II), bqʕt.

bqʕt (I) DN; one of the *kṯrt* goddesses (/Bāqiʕatu/ "Midwife", ptc. f. G < /b-q-ʕ/; cf. Watson UF 9 1977 283; Herrmann YN 24, 47).
DN of one of the *kṯrt* goddesses, 1.24:48.

bqʕt (II) TN (Belmonte RGTC 12/2 51f.: *Baqʕatu*. Cf. Heltzer RCAU 9; Rainey IOS 2 1972 402; Helck Bez. 54: *b-q-ʕ-tum*; Virolleaud Syria 21 1940 142; Astour RSP 2 271, 344; UF 13 1981 6; Bordreuil Syria 61 1984 1, 4f.; UF 28 1996 663f.; UF 30 1998 725, 734); ¶ syll.: URU *ba-aq-at*, PRU 3 189 (RS 11.790):12'; PRU 4 48ff. (RS 17.340+):22'; 63ff. (RS 17.237+):34; cf. Huehnergard UVST 249.
TN: 4.48:8; 4.63 II 21; 4.100:6; 4.235:8 (Van Soldt UF 28 1996 664); 4.355:9; 4.380:12; 4.643:9; 4.683:16; 4.693:13 (*bqʕ*[t]); 4.777:4; RSOu 14 36 [KTU 9.417]:10.

bqʕty GN m. (< *bqʕt (II)*). ¶ Forms: sg. *bqʕty*. - GN: 4.25:6.

bql n. m. "malt" (Akk. *buqlu*, AHw 139; CAD B 323ff.; Stol RlA 7 322-329; Ebla /buqlum/ in DIM$_4$ = *bù-gu-lum*, *bù-gu-lu-um* VE 856; Archi StEb 2 1980 88; Krebernik ZA 73 1983 33; Krecher Biling. 151; Syr. *buqlō*, SL 87; Arab. *baql*, Lane 236; Wehr (- Cowan) 68; Eth. *baqʷl*, CDG 100f.). ¶ Forms: sg. *bql*.
Malt: *qmḥ bql* malt flour, 1.71:25; 1.85:32.

/b-q-r/ vb G/D: "to examine, scrutinise" (Hb., Nab., JAram. *bqr*, HALOT 151; DNWSI 187; Ebla cf. *ba-qá-ru*$_{12}$ *a-ba-qá-ra* / *a-ba-qá-ru*$_{12}$ *a-ba-qá-ru*$_{12}$, Pettinato Rituale 218 [diff.: Fronzaroli ARET 11 140: /p-k-r/ 'legare']; Arab. *baqara*, Lane 133f.; cf. Dietrich - Loretz - Sanmartín UF 6 1974 465; Dietrich - Loretz MU 61; Dombradi WO 28 1997 31ff.). ¶ Forms: G/D cpref. *tbqrn*.
G/D. To examine: *kbdm tbqrn* two livers shall be examined, 1.78:5.

bqr (I) n. m. "cattle, herd of cattle" (Hb., Ph. *bqr*, HALOT 151; DNWSI 187; Ebla /baqarum/ in ÁB.LU = *ba-ga-lum*, VE 1101; Krebernik ZA 73 1983 39; Mari Akk.: cf. *bu-qá-ru*, ARM 2 131:39; AHw 129; CAD B 323; Emar /ba/uqaru/, Pentiuc Vocabulary 36f.; cf. Akk. PN *bu*-GA-*ar*, MAD 3 100; ESA *bqr*, CAME 117; DOSA 53; Arab. *baqar*, Lane 234). ¶ Forms: sg. *bqr*.
Cattle, herd of cattle: *ḫmš alp bqr* five oxen from the herd of cattle, 4.691:1 (Sanmartín UF 20 1988 272 n. 29). Bkn ctx.]*bqr*, 1.92:12 (cf. Dijkstra UF 26 1994 117, 119).

bqr (II), 1.14 III 9; cf. *mqr*.

bqš PN (etym. unc.; cf. Grøndahl PTU 29, 120; Watson AuOr 11 1993 214).
PN: *bn PN*, 4.75 IV 13.

/b-q-ṯ/ vb D: "to search for, look for; to investigate, find out" (Hb., Ph. *bqš*, HALOT 152; DNWSI 188). ¶ Forms: D cpref. *w abqṯ*; impr. *bqṯ*.
D. To search for, look for, investigate, find out: *w abqṯ aliyn bʕl* and I shall search for DN, the Powerful / Victorious, 1.6 IV 20; *aṯr iṯ bqṯ*

wherever he is look for him, 2.39:34; *mlkn ybqṯ anyt* our king must look for ships, 2.42:26.

br (I) n. m. type of barge (cf. Eg. *bʔ(y)ʔr*, *bí-r*, WäS 1 465; Helck Bez. 511 (56); Gk *bâris*, Liddell - Scott 307; Hb. (cj.) *br*, HALOT 153; cf. Alt AfO 15 1945/51 70). ¶ **Forms**: sg. *br*, pl. *brm*.
A type of barge: *ṯlṯ brm* three *b.*, 4.421:3 (cf. *anyt mlk*, *ibid.* ln. 2); *br PN*, 4.81:2-19 (cf. *anyt*, *ibid.* ln. 1; *ṯkt*, *ibid.* 4-5, 8). Cf. in bkn ctx. *br*, 4.647:1, 4, 6.

br (II), 1.4 I 35; 4.608:3; 4.769:18; cf. *br(r)*.

bri PN (etym. unc.; cf. Grøndahl PTU 28, 120; Bonnet SEL 7 1990 118).
PN: *bn PN*, 4.103:38.

/b-r-d/ vb G/D: "to divide, separate" (Hb. *prd*, HALOT 962f.; Syr. *prad*, LS 593; JAram. *prd*, Jastrow 1215; Akk. *parādu*, AHw 827; Arab., Eth. *farada*, Lane 2363f.; CDG 165. Cf. Cassuto GA 108; Lipiński UF 2 1970 78f.; Van Zijl Baal 47; diff.: Rin AE 74: 'to cool', Arab. *barada*; De Moor SP 70: 'to cut', rdg *br d* < **bry*, but cf. CARTU 131). ¶ **Forms**: G/D cpref. *ybrd*.
G/D. To divide, separate: *ybrd ṯd lpnwh* he divided the breast in his presence, 1.3 I 6. Cf. **brdd, brdn**.

brdd PN (Sem. Cf. Virolleaud Syria 21 1940 110; Grøndahl PTU 32, 37f., 120, 133; Xella UF 18 1986 444; Ribichini - Xella RSF 15 1987 8).
PN: 4.7:3; 4.103:31 (Van Soldt SAU 36); 4.763:9.

brdn PN (etym. unc.; cf. Grøndahl PTU 51, 120; Ribichini - Xella RSF 15 1987 8); ¶ **syll.**: cf. *bur-ru-dì-na*, PRU 3 194 (RS 11.787):8 (cf. Huehnergard AkUg 386).
PN: ★**a)** 4.356:13; ★**b)** *bn PN*, 4.255:4 (rdg unc.); 4.713:3 (rdg unc.).

brḏl n. m. "iron" (Hb., Ph. *brzl*, HALOT 155f.; DNWSI 196; Aram. *przl*, DNWSI 936; Amor. /barzillu/, Artzi JNES 28 1969 268ff.; Akk. *parzillu*, AHw 837; ESA *frzn*, CAME 220; DOSA 409); ¶ **RS Akk.**: cf. GÍR AN.BAR, PRU 6:6. ¶ **Forms**: sg. *brḏl*.
Iron: *kkrm brḏl* two talents of iron, 4.91:6.

brḥ adj. m. 1) "fleeing, "slippery"; 2) "fugitive" (Hb. *br(y)ḥ*, HALOT 156; cf. Ebla ŠÀ.ḪUL.GIG = *ba-rí-ù/um da-du*, VE 591; INIM.ḪUL = *sa-ga-lu/ru*$_{12}$ *ba-rí-ù-tum*, EV 0154; Krebernik QuSe 18 138; cf. Akk. *barḫu*, AHw 107; cf. CAD B 110; cf. Eth. *barrĕḥa*, CDG 104. Cf. Aartun WO 4 1967/68 282ff.; Van Zijl Baal 158; Wakeman GBM 57 n. 3; Van der Lugt - De Moor BiOr 31 1974 5; Renfroe UF 20

1988 226-232); ¶ **syll.** Ug.: cf. lex. list PA.GÁ = *nu-ʔu-ú* LÚ *ba-ar-ḫu*, Nougayrol RA 63 1969 83ff. (RS 29.103) IV 8'; PA.PA.GÁ = *nu-ʔu-ú* MÍ *ba-ri-iḫ-tu*$_4$, *ibid.* IV 9'; Huehnergard UVST 114f.; ¶ **par.**: *ʕqltn*, *gr.* ¶ **Forms**: sg. *brḥ*; pl.(?) *brḥm*.

1) Fleeing, said of the serpent: *bṯn brḥ* the fleeing serpent, 1.5 I 1 (// *ʕqltn*; diff.: Albright BASOR 83, 1941, 39 n. 5; Gray LC 31 n. 3: 'primaeval', **brḥ*; Gordon Or 22 1953 243f.: 'evil', Arab. *barḥ*; Zurro Bib 61 1980 412ff.: 'malo', Ebla *ba-ri-um*). Bkn ctx.: *tdrk brḥ arṣ* (if) you tread on a fleeing (serpent) on the ground, 1.82:38 (cf. De Moor - Spronk UF 16 1984 248; diff.: Gordon UT n. 516: 'shaft, bar', Hb. *bryḥ*).

2) Fugitive, said of a man: *ʕnt brḥ p ʕlmh* from now and for ever be a fugitive, 1.19 III 48 (diff.: Margalit UF 8 1976 177; UR 133 n. 17: 'the flow of time' / 'now, yesterday and unto eternity', **brḥ*, Arab. *al-bariḥa(ta)*).

In bkn ctx.: *brḥm*, 7.219:1.

/b-r-k/ (I) tD: "to kneel (down), bend one's knees (to give birth)" (denom. < *brk*; Hb. *brk*, HALOT 159; Arab., Eth. *baraka*, Lane 193ff.; CDG 105); ¶ **par.**: *ḫl.* ¶ **Forms**: tD impv. suff. *tbrk*{*k*}.

tD. To kneel (down), bend one's knees: *tbrk*{*k*?} *w ld* bend your knees and give birth, 1.12 I 26 (// *ḫl ld*).

Cf. **brk**.

/b-r-k/ (II) Gpass: "to be blessed"; D: "to bless" (Hb., Ph., Pun., Aram., Nab., Pal. *brk*, HALOT 159f.; DNWSI 198ff.; Arab., Eth. *barraka*, *bāraka*, Lane 193; CDG 105; cf. Akk. *kārabu*, AHw 445f.; CAD K 192ff.; > cf. Eg. *bí-rĕ-ka*, Helck Bez. 511 (60). Cf. Toll ZAW 94 1982 111ff.); ¶ **par.**: /m-r(-r)/ (II). ¶ **Forms**: Gpass. ptc. f. *brktm* (encl. *-m*); D cpref. *tbrk*, *ybrk*; suff. *tbrkn*, *tbrknn*; inf. suff. *brkn*; *brkm* (encl. *-m*).

Gpass. To be blessed: *l tbrkn alk brktm* bless me so that I may go blessed, 1.19 IV 32 (// *nmrrt*).

D. To bless: *l tbrk* [*krt*] will you not bless PN?, 1.15 II 14 (// *l tmr*); *brkm ybrk* [*ʕbdh*] *ybrk il krt* truly he blessed [his servant], DN blessed PN, 1.15 II 18-19 (cf. 1.77:2-3); *tbrk ilm* the gods blessed (him), 1.15 III 17; *ybrk dnil* he blessed PN, 1.17 I 34; *l tbrkn alk brktm* bless me so that I may go blessed, 1.19 IV 32 (// *tmrn*); *l tbrknn l ṯr il* do bless him, oh Bull DN!, 1.17 I 23 (// *tmrnn*); *yʕbš brkn šm il* ...... blessing him, the name of DN, 1.22 I 7.

brk n. f. "knee" (Hb., *brk*, HALOT 160f.; Akk. *bi/urku*, AHw 129, 140 CAD B 255ff.; Arab. *rukbat*, Lane 1143; Eth. *bĕrk*, CDG 105); ¶ **syll.**

Ug.: cf. [*bi*(?)]-*ir*(?)-*ku*, Ug 5 137 III 30"; cf. Huehnergard 115, 102, 305; ¶ **par.**: *ḫlq*, *kḫṯ*, *yd*. ¶ **Forms**: sg. *brk* (1.7:9); du. *brkm*; suff. *brkh*; pl. suff. *brktkm*, *brkthm*.
Knee: *špk (...) dm km šḥt l brkh* shed (...) (his) blood, like an assassin over his knees, 1.18 IV 24; *l brkh yʕdb qṣʕt* on his knees he left the arrows, 1.17 V 27 (// *bd*); *tšu (...) l ẓr brkthm* they lifted (...) from upon their knees, 1.2 I 29 and par. (// *ln kḫṯ*); *brkm tġll b dm* (her) knees she plunged in the blood, 1.3 II 13 and par., cf. 1.7:9 (// *ḫlqm*). Bkn ctx. *brkh*, 1.172:25.

brkt, cf. *brky*.

brky n. f. "pool, swamp" (Hb. *brkh*, HALOT 161; DNWSI 202; Emar /birrīka/ātu/, Pentiuc Vocabulary 40f.; ESA *brkt*, DOSA 58; Arab. *birkat*, Lane 194; > Eg. *brkt*, *bí-r-qa-tá*, WäS 1 466; Helck Bez. 511 (62)); ¶ **par.**: *ʕn*. ¶ **Forms**: sg. *brty*; pl. *brtk* (diff.: De Moor UF 1 1969 186: morphol. var. *brky/t*; Dietrich - Loretz - Sanmartín UF 7 1975 538: *brky*, mistake for *brkt*; Dietrich - Loretz UF 10 1978 435: du. suff. *brky*, pl. *brkt*, 'Knie').
Pool, swamp: *brky tkšd rumm* the pool that the wild bulls seek, 1.5 I 16; cf. pl. swamps: *brkt šbšt k rumm* the swamps that attract, yes, the wild bulls, 1.133:6.

brlt n. f. 1) "hunger, appetite, relis+h"; 2) "spirit, life force" (etym. unc.; cf. Hurr. /wurr=/, Laroche GLH 298; cf. Cutler - Macdonald UF 5 1973 67ff.: Akk. *meriltu*, *mereštu*, but cf. Dijkstra - De Moor UF 7 1975 196 n. 218; cf. Pope UF 13 1981 305f.: Arab. *buraʔil*, *burʔulat*; Rendsburg JAOS 107 1987 626f.: MSA *ʕāberét* / *ʔabrét*); ¶ **par.**: *npš*. ¶ **Forms**: sg. *brlt*, suff. *brlth*.
1) Hunger, appetite, relish: *brlt anḫr b ym* the hunger of the shark (that lives) in the sea, 1.5 I 15 (// *npš*); *tptḥ brlth l ṯrm* she opened his relish to feed himself, 1.16 VI 12 (// *npš*); *yḥ (...) brlt ġzr* may the Noble revive (...) his appetite, 1.17 I 37 (// *npš*); *ʕdb imr (...) l brlt hyn* prepare a lamb (...) for the hunger of DN, 1.17 V 18 and par. (// *npš*).
2) Spirit, life force: *tṣi (...) km iṯl brlth* (...) like phlegm may his spirit go out, 1.18 IV 25 and par. (// *npšh*).

brn PN (etym. unc.; cf. Grøndahl PTU 309); ¶ **syll.**: cf. BUR-*ra-na*, PRU 3 199 (RS 16.257+) A I 4"; PRU 4 201 (RS 18.02):15; cf. PRU 6 p. 142; BU-*ra-na*, Syria 18 1937 247 (RS 8.146 [= "8.213"]):13, 16; PRU 3 74 (RS 16.385);12. Cf. *prn*.
PN: *bn PN*, 4.281:26; 4.410:6. Cf. in bkn ctx. *br*[, 4.488:4.

brq (I) n. m. "ray, lightning" (Hb., Aram. *brq*, HALOT 162; DNWSI

203; Akk. *be/irqu*, AHw 122; CAD B 258f.; Arab. *barq*, Lane 190; Eth. *mabra/ĕq*, CDG 106); ¶ syll. Ug.: cf. the element /bur(a)qu-/ in PNN, Sivan GAGl 213; ¶ par.: *ql (I)*, *rʕt*. ¶ Forms: sg. *brq*; pl. *brqm*.
Ray, lightning: *abn brq* the 'stone / head' of the lightning, 1.3 III 26 and par. (cf. *abn*); (he will be able) *šrh l arṣ brqm* to release his lightnings to the earth, 1.4 V 9 (// *qlh*). Bkn ctx.: *šbʕt brqm* seven rays, 1.101:3; *ʕṣ brq* the staff of a ray, 1.101:4 (// *rʕt*); [...] *ksl k brq* [...] *thmt brq* (the bow's) sinew [shone?] like a ray, [...] the abyss a ray, 1.17 VI 11. In bkn. ctx.:]*k yġḏ thmt brq* as lightning moves the abyss, 1.17 VI 12.
In unc. ctx. *hm tġrm l mt brq*(!)*k* or(?) and/or unite your rays (against) DN, 1.82:5 (cf. Caquot TOu 2 65 n. 174; diff. rdg in KTU: *brtk*; cf. De Moor (- Spronk) CARTU 72; ARTU 176: 'your covenant').

brq (II) PN (Sem. Cf. Grøndahl PTU 50, 120f.; Watson AuOr 13 1995 221); ¶ syll.: cf. *bu-ra-qu*, Ug 5 97:7.
PN: ★a) 4.181:3 (*maḫdy*); 4.300:2; 4.313:9; in bkn ctx.: 4.262:9; ★b) *bn PN*: 4.98:15; 4.350:5; 4.724:4; in bkn ctx.: 4.64 IV 4.

brqd PN (Sem. Cf. Grøndahl PTU 32, 37f., 121, 133).
PN: 4.377:15.

brqn PN (Sem. Cf. Grøndahl PTU 52, 121); ¶ syll.: cf. *bur-qa-nu/na*, Syria 18 1937 246 (RS 8.145)32; RA 38 1941 (RS 11.856):17 (cf. Berger WO 5 1969/70 275); PRU 3 37 (RS 15.81):4, 6; PRU 4 237 (RS 17.251):27; PRU 6 141:1 Ug 5 12:6 (cf. Van Soldt SAU 20, 26f., 508); *bu-ra-qu-nu*, PRU 3 195 (RS 15.09) B I 9; cf. BU-*ra*-KA-*nu*, PRU 6 50:5, 11, 21 (cf. Huehnergard UVST 220; cf. Van Soldt SAU 320 n. 136).
PN: ★a) 3.8:23 (*spr*, Van Soldt UF 20 1988 313 n. 4; SAU 20, 26f.); 4.53:5 (*ṯlḫḫ*), 11; 4.141 I 9; 4.278:8; 4.410:32; 4.753:11; ★b) *bn PN*: 4.232:46.
Cf. prgn.

brqt PN (Sem. Cf. Grøndahl PTU 120f.).
PN: *bn PN*, 4.787:7. - Cf. brq (II), bgrt.

/b-r(-r)/ vb G: "to be or remain pure, clean, free" (Hb., Nab., Pal. *brr*, HALOT 162f.; DNWSI 203; JAram. *brr*, Jastrow 198; ESA *brr*, CAME 119; DOSA 59; Arab. cf. *barra*, Lane 175f.; ¶ RS Akk.: *zakû ištu / ina*, *passim*; cf. PRU 3 230f.; PRU 6 154; Van Soldt SAU 449, 452. ¶ Forms: G suffc. *br*, *brt*.
G. To be or remain pure, clean, free of legal obligations: *km špš d brt kmt br PN b unṯ ʕd ʕlm* like the sun, which is free, similarly PN remains free of debt in perpetuity, 2.19:3-4; in bkn ctx., *at brt lbk* you

are pure of heart(?), 2.8:4; cf. 2.3:5.

Cf. **br (II)**, **br(r)**, **brr**, **brrn (I)**, **brrn (II)**, **tbrrt**.

br(r) n. m. "tin" (cf. *brr* < /b-r(-r)/; cf. Eth. *bĕrur*, CDG 106; Aram. *brrʔ*, Jastrow 198; Akk. cf. *barru*, AHw 107; CAD B 113. Cf. Zaccagnini OA 9 1970 317ff.; Heltzer GPOTU 29f.; Van Selms UF 7 1975 472; Dietrich - Loretz UF 10 1978 61); ¶ **par.**: *bẓr*; ¶ **RS Akk.**: AN.NA(.MEŠ), Ug 5 12:6 and *passim ibid.*; cf. AN.NA *ša* EN-*ia ú-še-bi-la ki-i* KI.LÁ.BI 8 GÚ.UN AN.NA *ù* 7 *me-at šu-ut*, Ug 5 38:22ff. (Zaccagnini OA 9 1979 322 n. 59); AN.NA.BABBAR.MEŠ, PRU 6 155:7; ¶ **syll. Ug.**: cf. 1 GÚN *bu-ri* GAL, PRU 6 158:14; Huehnergard UVST 115. ¶ **Forms**: sg. *brr*, var. *br*.

Tin, ★**a)** in commerce: *ʕšrm kkr brr* twenty talents of tin, 4.91:12; *kkr br* a talent of tin, 4.608:3; ★**b)** often mentioned together with *ṯlṯ* copper: *ḫmš kkrm alp kbd ṯlṯ l nskm birtym (...) w ṯṯ mat brr b ṯmnym ksp ṯlṯt kbd* five talents one thousand shekels of copper for the smiths GNN (...) and six hundred (shekels) of tin for eighty three of silver, 4.337:4; *ḫmš kkr brr kkr ḫmš mat kbd ṯlṯ šmn* five talents of tin and one talent five hundred (shekels) of copper (in exchange for) oil, 4.272:3; *ṯmn kkr ṯlṯ ṯmn kkr brr* eight talents of copper, eight talents of tin, 4.203:2; *alpm ṯlṯ ktt alp brr* two thousand (shekels) of powdered copper (and) one thousand of tin, 4.203:15; ★**c)** transport: *ṯn ḥmr[m...] l brr* two donkeys for the tin, 4.268:3; ★**d)** for luxury items: *hdm il*(!) *d pršа b br* a divine footstool covered in tin, 1.4 I 35 (// *bẓr*; cf. Van Selms UF 7 1975 472; Dietrich - Loretz UF 10 1978 61).

Cf. **brr**.

brr adj. m. "pure, purified, clean" (< /b-r(-r)/; cf. Hb. *br*, *brwr*, HALOT 153, 155; Akk. cf. *barru*, AHw 107; Ebla cf. *bu-ru*$_{12}$ / *ba-ra-ru*$_{12}$, ARET 5 5 III 6f., 10f.; Vattioni EDA 218). ¶ **Forms**: sg. m. *brr*.

Pure, purified, clean (cultic lang.): *yrtḥṣ mlk brr* the king shall wash himself (remaining) purified, 1.119:5 and *passim* in rituals; *yṯb mlk brr* the king sits down, already purified, 1.87:7-8 and par.; *mlk brr* the king is purified, 1.87:49 and par.

Cf. **br(r)**.

brrn (I), first element of the composite DN *brrn aryn* "The Brillant One(?)-DN", a demon(?) (cf. the Akk. demon *barīrītu*, AHw 107; CAD B 111; cf. Xella TRU 221f.).

Element of the composite DN: *brrn aryn*, 1.123:23.

brrn (II) PN (Sem. Cf. Grøndahl PTU 121).

PN: *bn PN*, 4.200:9; 4.631:21.

brs/ś(m) PN (etym. unc.; cf. Grøndahl PTU 289, 299; Segert UF 15

1983 212); ¶ **syll.**: cf. *bur*-ZU-*mi*, Syria 18 1937 246 (RS 8.145):28. Var. *brś* in 4.759:8; *b*(?)*rsm*, 4.785:17.
PN: *bn PN*, 4.69 II 19; 4.106:11; 4.759:8; 4.785:17.

brz/sn PN (etym. unc.; cf. Grøndahl PTU 268, 289, 298; Van Soldt SAU 11); ¶ **syll.**: cf. BUR-ZA-*nu*, PRU 3 193 (RS 12.34+):27 (cf. Huehnergard AkUg 386). Var. *brsn* in 4.69 I 10. Cf. *prsn*.
PN: *bn PN*, 4.66:6; 4.69 I 10 (Van Soldt SAU 11); 4.103:17; 4.436:2; 4.623:5, 7 (Van Soldt SAU 11); 4.631:22; 4.785:22.

brzt PN (etym. unc.; cf. Grøndahl PTU 114, 183, 288, 291).
PN: *bn PN*, 4.617:13.

bsbn PN (etym. unc. Cf. Xella TRU 75).
PN: 1.87:58 (*hzpḫ*).

bsn PN (etym. unc.; cf. Watson AuOr 8 1990 244).
PN: ★**a)** 4.15:11; 4.300:3; ★**b)** *bn PN*: 4.229:3.

/b-ṣ-ʕ/; in bkn ctx.:]*lm tbṣʕ*, 1.147:13.

b(?)ṣmm, rdg unc. in 4.4:4, see *rṣm*.

bṣmn PN (etym. unc.).
PN: 4.183 II 29 (*spr*, Van Soldt UF 20 1988 313 n. 4; SAU 20, 26; Xella UF 22 1990 470); 4.364:13; 4.658:21 (*bn ḥrtn*).

bṣmy TN (Belmonte RGTC 12/2 60). TN: 4.408:4.

/b-ṣ-q/ vb G: "to sprout" (?) (Hb. *bṣq*, HALOT 148: 'to swell' > *bṣql* in Ug. and Hb.). **Forms**: G act./pass. ptc *bṣq* (?).
G. To sprout (?): *prʕ bṣq b irt lbnn* first fruits that sprouts/sprouted from the slope of TN, 1.22 I 25 (diff.: rdg *b ṣq*, KTU 65: 'auf dem Gipfel der Flanke des Lebanon!: TUAT 3 1314 n. 40).

bṣql n. m. "sprout, shoot; branch" (Hb. *bṣql(wn)*, HALOT 148, 2 Kgs 4:42; cf. Cassuto BOS 197; Sanmartín UF 9 1977 266; Margalit RB 91 1984 109ff.; ZAW 99 1987 394; Dietrich - Loretz UF 18 1986 115ff.); ¶ **par.**: *šṭ*. ¶ **Forms**: sg. *bṣql*.
Sprout, shoot; branch: *bṣql yph b palt* he saw a shoot in the waste land, 1.19 II 13 and par.; as a collect., branch: *bṣql ʕrgz* a branch of the ʕrgz-plant., 1.85:5 (// *šṭ*; diff.: Dijkstra - De Moor UF 7 1975 203f.; Cohen - Sivan UHT 19: 'a measure', // *šṭ*).

/b-ṣ-r/ (I) vb G: "to watch"; N: "to appear, allow oneself to be seen"(?) (Arab. *baṣira*, Lane 210ff. Cf. Watson JNSL 5 1977 73; Loretz UF 12 1980 279ff.); ¶ **par.**: /r-ḫ-p/. ¶ **Forms**: G cpref. *ybṣr*, N cpref. *tbṣrn*.
G. To watch: *ybṣr ḥbl diym* a flock of vultures watched (him), 1.18 IV 31 (*trḫp*).

N. To appear, allow oneself to be seen(?): bkn ctx. *mlkm tbṣrn* the kings allow themselves to be seen (?), 1.163:4 (cf. Bordreuil - Caquot Syria 57 1980 353; cf. diff.: Dietrich - Loretz MU 169, 176f.: 'werden entfernt bleiben'; Tropper UF 26 1994 461 n. 21: G 'lauern').
Cf. bṣr, tbṣr.

/b-ṣ-r (II) vb G: "to sever" (Hb. *bṣr*, HALOT 148; Aram. *bṣr*, Jastrow 185; Akk. *baṣāru*, AHw 110; CAD B 134; cf. Caquot EI 14 1978 15; Del Olmo IMC 92); ¶ syll. Ug.: cf. [... *i*]*a-ab-ṣi-ru ar-zi-ma*[, Ug 5 153:1; cf. Huehnergard UVST 12, 114; cf. the element /b-ṣ-r/ and /baṣīru/ in PNN and TNN, Sivan GAGl 209, 212; ¶ par.: /h-r-g/. ¶ Forms: G impr. *bṣr*.
G. To sever: *bṣr kp* sever palms, 1.13:5 (// *hrg*).
Cf. bṣr, tbṣr.

bṣr TN (Belmonte RGTC 12/2 53: **Baṣīru*. Cf. Heltzer RCAU 9; Virolleaud Syria 21 1940 142; Astour RSP 2 270f., 344; UF 13 1981 7; Bordreuil Syria 61 1984 2f.; Van Soldt UF 28 1996 663; UF 30 1998 728); ¶ syll.: URU *ba-ṣi/ṣí-ri*, PRU 3 33 (RS 16.114):2, 189 (RS 11.790):29'; PRU 6 80:4; RS 25.455+ I 10 (Arnaud SMEA 32 1993 128); RSOu 7 4:3; AnOr 48 1971 23 (RS [Varia 10] = "1957.2") rev. 7.
TN: 1.91:23; 4.68:45; 4.355:39; 4.370:3 (Dietrich - Loretz - Sanmartín UF 6 1974 23); 4.610 (II) 18; 4.621:4; 4.684:2; 4.693:41; 4.750:16; 4.777:11; RSOu 14 35 [KTU 9.388] II 29. For the rdg *b*[*ṣr*] in 4.686:21 cf. Belmonte RGTC 12/2 53.

bṣry GN m. (< *bṣr*, TN). ¶ Forms: sg. *bṣry*.
GN: 4.33:6; 4.51:11; 4.261:18.

bṣy PN (etym. unc.; cf. Zadok UF 17 1985 389; Xella UF 22 1990 470; Watson AuOr 8 1990 244; AuOr 11 1993 214).
PN: *bn PN*, 4.754:17.

/b-š/ vb G: "to go slowly, be late" (Hb. *bwš*, HALOT 117. Cf. Sanmartín UF 10 1978 354 n. 44; Cathcart JNSL 12 1984 38; diff.: De Moor UF 11 1979 647 n. 54: 'to go away, depart, Akk. *bêšu*; Aartun StUL 33f.: 'den Gang beschleunigen', **bšt*, Arab. *bast-*); ¶ par.: /š-n-w/. ¶ Forms: G suffc. *bštm*.
G. To go slowly: *atm bštm* you can go slowly, 1.1 III 18 and par. (// *šnt*).

/b-š-l/ vb G/D: "to cook" (Hb., Aram. *bšl*, HALOT 164; DNWSI 203; Syr. *bšel*, LS 99; Akk. *bašālu*, Ahw 111; CAD B 135ff.; cf. ESA *bsl*, DOSA 48f.). ¶ Forms: G/D cpref. *ybšl*; inf. abs. *bšl*.
G/D. To cook: *bšl ybšl* he will certainly cook, 1.147:7.

Cf. šbšlt.

/b-š-r/ (I) vb D: "to impart (good) news; to be happy to hear good news"; Dpass: "to hear, receive (good) news" (Hb. *bśr*, HALOT 163f.; Akk. *b/pa/ussuru*, AHw 142; CAD B 347; ESA *bšr*, DOSA 61; Arab. *bašara*, Lane 207f.; Eth. *bsr*, CDG 110; cf. Dietrich - Loretz UF 14 1982 303ff.). ¶ Forms: D cpref. with suff. *nbšrkm* (encl. *-m*); Dpass. cpref. *tbšr*, impv. *bšr*.

D. To impart (good) news; to be happy to hear good news: *n*(!)*bšrkm dnil* we are going to impart news to you, PN, 1.19 II 37 (diff.: Cooper UF 20 1988 25: 'let me convey your report', suj. sg.: *pġt*).

Dpass. To be happy about, receive (good) news: *bšrt il bšr*{*t*} *bʕl w bšr ḥtk dgn* receive the good news of DN, do receive the good news, offspring of DN, 1.10 III 34; *tbšr bʕl bšrtk yblt* take note, DN, of the news that I bring you, 1.4. V 26.

Cf. bšrt.

/b-š-r/ (II) vb D: "to kill(?)" (denom. < *bšr*, cf. Hb. *bśr qdš*, Jer 11:15; Hg 2:12; cf. HALOT 164: *bśr* 4.). ¶ Forms: D cpref. *ybšr*.

D. To kill (?): in bkn ctx. *ybšr qdš* is killed as a holy victim(?), 1.94:1, 23.

Cf. bšr.

bšr n. m. "flesh, meat" (Hb., *bśr*, HALOT 164, Pun., Aram., Pal. *bšr*, DNWSI 204; Syr. *besrō*, LS 82; ESA *bšr* DOSA 61f.; cf. Arab. *bašar*, *bašarat*, Lane 208); ¶ par.: *ṣʕ*, *yd*(?). ¶ Forms: sg. *bšr*, suff. *bšrh*.

Meat: ★a) *ḥrb b bšr tštn* they put the knife in the meat, 1.15 IV 25 and par. (*b ṣʕ*); ★b) body: *mks bšrh* which covered his flesh, 1.4 II 5; *ḥmm b bšrk* heat(?) in your flesh, RSOu 14 53 [KTU 9.432]:7'; ★c) possibly in a sexual sense cf. in unc. ctx. *l bšrh* to his 'flesh', 1.24:9 (// *yd*; cf. Herrmann YN 7ff.; cf. Rendtorff - Stolz UF 11 1979 712; De Moor ARTU 143).

In bkn ctx.:]*bšry*, 1.63:7; 7.163:5; *b*]*šrk al ttn ln*[*ġr*] do not waste [the ...] of your [fl]esh against the guard[ian], 1.92:34 (cf. Dijkstra UF 26 1994 118).

Cf. /b-š-r/ (II).

bšrt n. f. "news, good news" (cf. /b-š-r/ (I); Hb. *bśrh*, HALOT 164; Akk. *bussurtu*, AHw 142; CAD B 346f.; Arab. *bišārat*, Lane 208; Eth. *bĕsrāt*, CDG 110). ¶ Forms: sg. *bšrt*, suff. *bšrtk*.

News, good news: *bšrt il bšr*{*t*} *bʕl w bšr ḥtk dgn* receive the good news of DN, do receive the good news, offspring of DN, 1.10 III 34; *tbšr bʕl bšrtk yblt* take note, DN, of the news that I bring you, 1.4. V 27.

/b-t/ vb G: "to stay the night" (Aram. *byt*, *bt*, cf. HALOT 124; Akk. *biātu*, *bâtu*, AHw 124; CAD B 169ff.; Arab. *bāta*, Lane 279ff.; Eth. *beta*, CDG 116f.; cf. Pardee AfO 31 1984 216; Dijkstra UF 19 1987 44). ¶ Forms: G cpref. *ybt*.

G. To stay the night: ***k ybt mlk*** when the king stayed the night, 2.33:14.

bt (I) n. f. 1) "daughter"; 2) "damsel" 3) > stating a quality; 4) > member of a group; 5) "daughter of" in onomastics (< *bn (I)*; cf. Hb., Ph., Pun. *bt*, HALOT 165f.; DNWSI 170ff.; Amor. /bin/ttum/, Gelb CAAA 16; Akk. *bintu*, AHw 127; CAD B 238f.; *bun(a)tu*, AHw 138; CAD B 317; mas. *biʔtu*, AHw 127; ESA *b(n)t*, CAME 115; DOSA 46f.; Arab. *ibna*, *bint*, Lane 262); ¶ par.: *bn (I)* (1.15 III 24), *klbt* (1.3 III 46), *pġt*; ¶ RS Akk.: DUMU.MÍ(.MEŠ), *passim*, cf. PRU 3 233; PRU 4 261; PRU 6 151; Ug 5 340; cf. esp.: DUMU.MÍ ^{d}UTU-*ši*, PRU 4 208 (RS 17.226):3; 209 (RS 17.355):2; 227 (RS 17.429):7'; DUMU.MÍ ^{mí}*ra-bi-ti*, PRU 4 141 (RS 17.228):5 and *passim* in RS (cf. PN ^{mí}*bi-it-ta/i-ra-bi-ti*, AnOr 48 11f. (RS [Varia 9] "1957.1"):6, 10, 18); cf. PRU 4 128 (RS 17.348) rev. 4'); DUMU.MÍ LUGAL-*ri*, PRU 3 69 (RS 16.276):7. ¶ Forms: sg. *bt*, suff. *bty*, *bth*; pl. abs./cstr. *bnt*, suff. *bnth*; du. abs. *btm*, suff. *bth*.

1) Daughter ★a) of men and gods: PN...]*aṯth w bth* his wife and his daughter, 4.519:4; PN (...) *w PN aḫh (...) w PN bnh w PN bth w PN aṯth* and PN, his brother, (...), and PN, his son, and PN, his daughter, and PN, his wife, 3.4:7; *aṯt w ṯt bth* a lady and her two daughters, 4.102:22; PN *w arbʕ bnth* and his four daughters, 4.360:3; PN (...) *w bt aḥt* and one daughter, *ibid.* ln. 5; PN (...) *yd bth* with his daughter, 4.80:15; 4.659:2; *bnm w bnt* sons and daughters, 2.2:9; PN *klt bt špš* PN, the bride, daughter of the Sun (: Hitt. king), 6.24:2 (cf. Van Soldt UF 21 1989 389ff.); *t*]*qrb w ld bn*{.}*t lk* she is on the point of bearing him daughters, 1.15 III 6 (// *pġt*); *ap bnt ḥry kmhm* and also the daughters of PN were as many as they, 1.15 III 24 (// *bn PN*); *gm l bth* (PN shouted) aloud to his daughter, 1.19 I 49; *bt ḥmḥ*<*m*>*h dn*(!)*n* the daughter whose conception(?) (proves) our strength, 1.16 I 29 (// *aḫtk*); *ytmr bʕl bnth* DN looked at his daughters, 1.3 I 23; *ydʕtk bt* I know you, oh, daughter, 1.18 I 16 and par.; *tbʕ bt* depart, oh daughter, 1.18 I 17 and par.; *btm bt il bt il w ʕlmh* the two daughters will be daughters of DN, daughters of DN for ever, 1.23: 45; *bn mlk w bt mlk tʕln pamt šbʕ* the sons and the daughters of the king shall go up seven times, 1.112:6, cf. 1.106:10; 1.171:1; *bt mlk amr* the daughter of the king of TN, 2.72:16 and *passim* (cf. *supra* ¶ RS Akk.:

DUMU.MÍ LUGAL); cf. in bkn ctx.: *hm l atn bty lh* if I do not give him my daughter, 2.31:64; cf. in unc. ctx.: *bt l bnš trgm*[the daughter(?) shall say to the man[, 2.2:5; ★b) esp., daughter of natural and cosmic beings; cf.: *bt ar* 'daughter of light' (epithet of the DN *pdry*), *bt rb* 'daughter of the drizzle' (epithet of the DN *ṭly*), *bt yʕbdr* 'daughter of *y.* (epithet of the DN *arṣy*), 1.3 III 6-8 and par.; *bt ʕn bt abn bt šmm w thm qrit l špš umh* the 'daughter of spring, daughter of stone, daughter of sky and abyss', invokes the Sun, her mother, 1.100:1 (epithets of an anonymous deity with the title *um pḥl pḥlt* 'mother of he stallion, of the Mare' [Ištar?, Dietrich - Loretz TUAT 2 345]); *bnt hll* 'daughters of DN', 1.17 II 26 and par. (epithet of the *kṯrt* goddesses; cf. *bnt (II)*).
2) Damsel: *kpr šbʕ bnt* henna of seven damsels, 1.3 II 2 and par. (cf. diff.: Aartun StUL 30ff.: 'Geruch, Duft', **bnn*).
3) Stating quality (+ n. sg): *bt il* 'the divine one', 1.3 III 46 (epithet of the f. demon *ḏbb*; // *k*{.}*lbt ilm*); *bt amt* handmaid, 4.659:7. Cf. *bt ḫbr* 'Daughter-of-TN', 1.14 II 29 and par. (cf. Hb. *bt ṣywn* and Badre Syria 53 1976 107; Del Olmo MLC 550; De Moor - Spronk UF 14 1982 163).
4) Member of a group (+ TN): *bt ugrt* Ugaritian woman, 1.40:35 and par.; PN *bt ugrt*, 3.4:11.
5) Patronymic: "PN *bt* + PN", *passim*; cf. 3.4:9; 4.75 III 5, 6, 13; VI 2.
Unc. *ḥr ḥr bnt*, 1.82:13; *bnt yš*[, 1.107:13 (?). For *bnt šdm*, 1.12 II 42 cf. *bnt (II)*.
Cf. bn (I).

bt (II) n. m. 1) "house, building; residence, home"; 2) "palace"; 3) "temple"; 4) "room"; 5) "family"; 6) "storehouse"; 7) "workshop" (Hb., OAram., Nab., Pal., *byt*, HALOT 124ff.; DNWSI 156ff.; Ph., Pun., Moab. *bt*, DNWSI 156ff.; Amor. /bītum/, Gelb CAAA 16; Ebla /baytu(m)/ in É.RA = *ba-du* LAMxKUR.KI, VE 336; Krebernik ZA 73 1983 14; Conti SQF 120; cf. KI.GUL = *ba-du-um*, VE 835; Fronzaroli EL 137 and cf. diff. Conti SQF 200; cf. *ba-da-a* (/baydā(y)?/), Fronzaroli StEb 7 1984 158; Gelb EDA 67; cf. BA.AD, Krebernik PET 76; cf. Sanmartín AuOr 9 1991 184s.; Akk. *bītu*, AHw 132ff.; CAD B 282ff.; ESA *b(y)t*, CAME 113; DOSA 41f.; Arab. *bayt*, Lane 280f.; Eth. *bet*, CDG 116f.; ¶ RS Akk.: É = [*b*]*i-tu* = *še*(?)-*?-?* [, Ug 5 135 rev. 13'; É = *bi-tu*$_4$ [, Ug 5 137 I 6; É(.MEŠ/ḪI.A), *passim*, cf. PRU 3 25 n. 4, 216f.; PRU 6 158; *bītu*(É) + *eqlu*(A.ŠÀ), *passim*, cf. PRU 3 216; cf. esp.: É *a-bi-šu*, PRU 3 33 (RS 16.129):15;

57 (RS 15.120):15; 6 40:5; 53 rev. 4'; É(-*ti*) *a-bu-sí*/TI, PRU 3 181f. = PRU 4 47f. (RS 11.732) A 8, B 8; PRU 4 82 (RS 17.382+):45; 231 (RS 17.244):3; É.ḪI.A ANŠE.KUR.RA, PRU 3 80 (RS 16.239):21; É DINGIR.MEŠ-*ni*, PRU 3 19 (RS 15.11):12; É-*ti* ᵈN[IN(?), PRU 6 23:18; É *du-me-te*, PRU 6 122:2; É *du-up-pa-aš-ši*[, PRU 4 151 (RS 17.59) rev. 3; É (:) *eššu*(/GIBIL), PRU 3 52 (RS 15.85):3; 96 (RS 16.249):4; 119 (RS 16.204):4; É-tu_4 GU_4.MEŠ, PRU 3 92 (RS 16.189):18; É : *ḫe-re-ti*, PRU 3 52 (RS 15.85):17; É.ḪI.A KISLAḪ.MEŠ : *ḫé-ya-ma*, PRU 3 103 (RS 15.109+):15; É *ḫe-e-ia*, PRU 3 87 (RS 15.119) rev. 7'; É KISLAḪ : *ta-am-qì*, PRU 3 (RS 16.145):3; É *ki-li*, Ug 5 35:7; É : *ku-na-ḫi*, Ug 5 5:10, 20; É MÍ.LUGAL-*ti*, PRU 3 110 (RS 8.208):3; É-tu_4 : *ta-ar-bá-ṣí*, PRU 3 92 (RS 16.189):17; É *ur-ši ša* PN, PRU 4 109 (RS 17.28):5; ¶ syll. Ug.: cf. PNN *bé-ta-ya*, Syria 18 1937 246 (RS 8.145):6; *be-ta-na*, PRU 3 106 (RS 16.206):7; *bé-ti*$_4$-(DINGIR)/ *ʔi-lu*, Ug 5 39:7, 23; cf. É-tu_4 : *qú-bu-ri*, PRU 3 51f. (RS 15.86):8, 18; cf. Grøndahl PTU 118; Sivan GAGl 14, 210; cf. É(?)] *qi-*[*id-š*]*u*, Ug 5 137 III 29'); ¶ par.: *umt*, *hkl*, *ḥẓr*, *ḫšt*, *ṯlḥn*. ¶ Forms: sg. *bt*; suff. *bty*, *btk*, *bth*; du. *btm*; pl. (1) *bht*; (2) *bhtm* (*/bêhātūma/) > *btm* (*/bôtūma), *plene*: *bwtm*, *btwm* (cf. UT 463; Ginsberg Tarbiz 5 1933/34 86; De Moor SP 89; Dietrich - Loretz - Sanmartín UF 7 1975 559); cstr. pl. *bht*; cf. *bt*, 4.16:1 (*infra:* 5); suff. *bhty*, *bhtk*, *bhth*.

1) House, building; residence, home, ★a) house, building: *bt* PN house of PN, 4.727:1-24; *passim* in admin. texts; RSOu 14 40 [KTU 9.419]:11; cf. *bt PN (...) d b TN* the house of PN (...) located in TN, 3.2:5; *bt trtn* house of PN, 5.11:5 (Grøndahl PTU 460; diff. Aartun UF 17 1985 28); *bt aḥd b mʕr* a house in TN, "UF 29, 826":6 (Lemaire UF 30 1998 461); *ṯn btm b TN* two houses (du.) in TN, 4.750:13, 16, 17, 18 (cf. *arbʕ / ṯlṯ bhtm*, *ibid.* ln. 2, 12; *bt yḥd / aḥd*, *ibid.* ln. 5-11); *ḫrš b(h)tm* bricklayer(s) (cf. RS Akk.: LÚ.(MEŠ.)DÍM É(.MEŠ), PRU 6 93:11; 131:1), 4.35 I 16; 4.38:6; 4.47:10; 4.183 I 1; 4.370:14; 4.545:6; 4.609:18; 4.630:9; *mnk mnkm l yqḥ bt hnd bd PN w bd bnh ʕd ʕlm* may no-one at all snatch this house from the hands of PN or from the hands of his heirs in perpetuity, 3.2:14; *ṯlṯ ʕšr pṯḥ b tk bt* thirteen door in the interior of the building, 4.195:8; *ʕpr btk ygršk* may the dust of your house evict you, // *qr btk* the walls of your house, 1.82:12 (cf. *qr btk*, *ibid.* ln. 40, and De Moor - Spronk UF 16 1984 238); *aḥd bth ysgr* the one living alone closed his house, 1.14 IV 21 (cf. *ibid.* II 43); grown old *k klb b btk* like a dog in your house, 1.16 I 2 and par. (// *ap ḫštk*); *bhtm sgrt* she shut the house, 1.100:70;

to satiety *tmtḫṣ b bt* (DN) fought in (her) house, 1.3 II 29 (// *bn ṯlḥnm*); *b b*(!)*t dm ḏmr* from the house (of DN they cleaned) the blood of the warriors, 1.3 II 31; *bt ʕbdh* the house of his servant, RSOu 14 50 [KTU 9.434] 21; *w šlm bth* and the wellbeing of his house, RSOu 14 50 [KTU 9.434]:17; *bt ʕbdh* the house of his servant, *ibid.* ln. 21; ★b) residence, home: *aṯt(m) (...) b bt PN* (two) lady(ladies) in PN's home, 4.102:1-30; *mrzḥ d qny PN b bt<h>* cult association that PN founded in his home, 3.9:4; (I will pay a fine) *km agrškm b bty* if I evict you from my home, *ibid.* ln. 8; *b qrb bt* within (his) residence, 1.4 VII 14; *bt krt bu tbu* in the residence of PN entered, 1.16 VI 3; *ng mlk l bty* depart, king, from my residence, 1.14 III 28 and par. (// *l ḥẓry*); *d in b bty ttn* what is not in my residence you shall give me, 1.14 III 38 and par.; *hm ḥry bty iqḥ* if I take PN to my home ..., 1.14 IV 40 (// *ḥẓry*); of gods: *bt l bʕl k(m) ilm* a residence for DN as (for) the (other) gods, 1.3 V 3 and par. (// *ḥẓr*); *ank in bt ly km ilm* as for me, I do not have a residence like the gods, 1.2 III 19 (// *ḥẓr*); *bt bʕlk* the residence of your lord, 1.1 IV 6; *il (...) yqḥ yš<t> b bth* DN (...) tok them and placed them in his residence, 1.23:36; *mġy hrn l bth* DN arrived at his residence, 1.100:67 (// *l ḥẓrh*); *il hlk l bth DN* went to his residence, 1.114:17 (// *l ḥẓrh*; cf. *ibid.* ln. 1); *w ysb bt mḫrh* he turns to the house of his *m.*, RSOu 14 53 [KTU 9.432]:30'; ★c) special uses: *bt ab* paternal house: (eagles were flying about) *ʕl bt abh* over his paternal house, 1.19 I 32 (cf. ¶ RS Akk.: *bīt abišu, supra*; cf. Ebla É*-a-bí* // É.A.MU, Pettinato Rituale 254); cf. in unc. ctx. *bt qbṣ* house of the clan, 1.79:7 (cf. Heltzer RCAU 73); *bt ḫpṯt* reserve or quarters for 'escapees' (cf. Alalakh Akk.: É *ḫu-up-še-na*, AT 186:4ff..; *passim*): (descent) *bt ḫpṯt arṣ* to the underworld reserve of 'escapees'', 1.4 VIII 7 and par.; *bt mlk* royal palace, cf. *infra*: 2; *bt ʕbdm* building of the servants, 4.195:9; *bt skn* house of the superintendent, 4.361:1 (diff. Grøndahl PTU 410: PN; cf. 4.102:17; 4.592:3); cf. *bt ṯʕy* the house of the officiant, 1.119:8; *bt* family unit in economy: *k tšal bt ʕbdk* when you order a reply in the house of your servants, 2.70:24; *bt, bt il(m), bt DN* temple, cf. *infra*: 3.

2) Palace, mansion, ★a) *bt mlk* royal palace, 1.41:20 and par.; 4.168:6; 4.274:7; 4.341:21; 4.337:16; 4.338:2; 4.721:7; *maṯr bt* inspector of the palace, 6.66:9; *bnš d bt mlk* people (lodged) in the royal palace, 4.766 upper edge (cf. *l d bt* that are not resident, 4.137:14; 4.163:16); *npš d ʕrb bt mlk* people who have entered the royal palace, 4.388:2; *k tʕrb ʕṯtrt šd bt mlk* when DN enters the royal

palace, 1.91:10 (cf. *ibid.* ln. 11); 1.148:18; cf. 1.43:10; *dlt bt* door of the palace, 6.66:10; *gb bt mlk* fosa(?) of the royal palace, 1.43:2 (cf. Dietrich - Loretz JA 48f.); (sacrifice to DN in) *bt mlk*, 1.39:12; [*p*]*dry bt mlk* 'DN of the Royal palace', 1.91:7 and par.; *ykn bnh b bt* may there be a son of his in the palace, 1.17 I 25 and par. (// *b qrb hklh*); *dn*{.}*il bth ymġyn PN* arrived at his palace, 1.17 II 24 and par. (// *hklh*); (the goddesses) *ʕrb / tbʕ b bth* entered / left his palace, 1.17 II 26, 39; *il dbḥ b bth* DN gave a feast in his palace, 1.114:1 (// *b qrb hklh*; cf. *ibid.* ln. 17); *ṯġr bt il* gatekeeper of the palace of DN, *ibid.* ln. 12; ★b) palace, centre of administration: *ḥpr bt* ration(s) of the palace, 4.269:1; 4.288:3; *ksp d šlm PN ʕl bt* capital that PN paid on the palace account, 4.755:2; ★c) often pl. *bh/wt(m)* urban complex of the palace and of religion, palace, royal residence: *ʕbdm (...) btwm* servants (...) in the palace, 4.320:13 (cf. b *TNN*, *ibid.* ln. 2, 8; *b šdm*, *ibid.* ln. 18); *bʕlt bhtm* 'Lady of the Palace', 1.105:16 and *passim* in rituals and cultic lists (cf. Akk. ^{d}*bēlet*(NIN) *ekalli(m)*(É.GAL), *passim* in Alalah, Mari, Qatna, Emar; in Ugarit: epithet of the DN *pdry*(?); cf. [*p*]*dry bt mlk* 'DN of the Royal palace', 1.91:7 and par.; Saracino UF 14 1982 196 n. 29; Dietrich - Loretz TUAT 2 322; diff.: epithet of *ʕnt*, Virolleaud CRAIBL 1962 97; De Moor SP 86 n. 4); cf. *bʕlt btm* in 1.41:37 and par.; 1.48:4; 1.94:24; *bnt bhtk y ilm bnt bhtk al tšmḫ* (in) the construction of your palace, oh DN, (in) the construction of your palace do not rejoice, 1.3 V 19-20 (// *b rm hklh*); *klat ṯġrt bht ʕnt* DN closed the gates of her palace, 1.3 II 4 and par.; *bht zbl ym* the palace of prince DN, 1.2 III 8 and par. (// *hkl*); *in bʕl b bhth*(!) DN is not in his palace, 1.10 II 4 (// *b qrb hklh*); *ib tʕrbm b bhth* may DN enter his house, 1.24:18-19 and par.; *bhtm mnt* the house of incantation, 1.100:70 (cf. *bt mnt*, *ibid.* ln. 71, // *hkl*, *ibid.* ln. 72); ★d) esp. in 1.3.-1.4., myth of the "Palace of Baal": *alp šd aḫd bt* one thousand yokes of land will the palace cover, 1.4 V 56 (// *hkl*); *bt arzm ykllnh* // *bt lbnt yʕmsnh* a palace of cedar they shall complete for him, a palace of brick they shall erect for him, 1.4 V 10-11; often pl. *bht*: *ḥš bhtm tbnn* quickly let a palace be built, 1.4 V 53 and par. (// *hklm*); *bn bht ksp w ḫrṣ* // *bht thrm iqnim* build a palace of silver and gold, // a palace of the purest lapislazuli, 1.4 V 18-19 and par.; *<b>hty bnt dt ksp* my house is a construction of silver, 1.4 VI 36 and par. (// *hkly*; cf. *bnt (I)*); *bl ašt urbt b bhtm* I am going to put a skylight in the palace, 1.4 V 61 and par. (// *b qrb hklm*); *ypth ḥln b bhtm* he opens a window in the palace, 1.4 VII 17 and par. (// *b qrb hklm*); *tšt išt b bhtm* they lit a fire in the palace 1.4 VI 22 and par. (// *b hklm*); *tikl išt* *b bhtm* the fire was consuming in the palace, 1.4 VI 25 and par. (// *b hklm*); *ʕdbt bhth bʕl yʕdb* layout of his house did DN arrange, 1.4 VI 38 (// *hklh*); *ṣḥ ḫrn b bht*(!)*k* call a squad into your palace, 1.4 V 13 and par. (// *hklk*); *ṣḥ aḫh b bhth* he invited his fellows to his palace, 1.4 VI 44 (// *hklh*); *tṯṯbn b bt* they shall enthrone him in the palace, 1.41:55.

3) Temple, sanctuary, chapel: *bt* the temple (often not further specified), cf. 4.128:4; 4.269:29; 4.274:5; 4.644:7; *b bt* in the temple, 1.116:10; 1.119:22; *bnt qḥ w št b bt* take (a bunch of) tamarisk and place (it) in the temple, 1.124:9; *bt il* temple (cf. RS Akk.: É DINGIR.MEŠ-*ni*, PRU 3 19 (RS 15.11):12), 1.12 II 60 (// *bt ḫrš*); 4.15:1; *amd gr bt il* always be a protected one of the sanctuary, 1.19 III 47; cf. esp.: *bt il* temple of DN, 4.341:5; *bt il ann* temple of DN in TN, 4.149:17, 19; *l ydbḥ mlk bt il* the king must sacrifice in the temple of DN, 1.119:14; // *bt bʕl* temple of DN, 1.17 II 5 and par.; *bt il bt* temple of the god (/ of the gods) of the dynasty, 1.115:3 (cf. *qdš il bt*, *ibid.* ln. 7); *bt ilm rbm* temple of the 'great gods', 4.149:1 (*ilm rbm*: deified ancestors of the dynasty; cf. Pardee UF 15 1983 132f.; cf. Pope Fs. Finkelstein 179); *bt ilm* temple of the gods, 1.43:2; *bt ilt* temple of the goddess, 1.41:24 and par.; *bt bʕl*(?) temple of DN, 1.63:12; 1.104:13; 1.124:8; // *bt il* temple of DN, 1.17 I 31 and par.; *ntbt bt bʕl ntlk* the path of the temple of DN we shall tread, 1.119:33; *bt bʕl ugrt* temple of DN of TN, 1.105:6; 1.109:11; 1.119:3, 9; *bt bʕlt btm* temple of the 'Lady of the Palace', 1.41:37 and par.; *bt bʕlt mlk* temple of the 'Lady of Royalty', 4.54:1; *bt dgn* temple of DN, 1.104:13; *bt dml* sanctuary of DN, 2.26:6; *bt ʕṯtrt* temple of DN, 4.219:2; *bt ršp gn* sanctuary of DN of the 'Cemetery', 4.219:3; *bt šr* sanctuary of DN, 1.104:14. In 1.104:21, rdg *w m<ṯ>bt ilm* (De Moor - Spronk UF 14 1982 161 n. 65; cf. KTU: *wm.bt*); *bt špš* temple(?) of DN(?), RSOu 14 44:6; *ʕrb ḥrn bth* DN enters his house, RSOu 14,53 [KTU 9.432]:33'; *m*[*y*] *b bt* who is in the house?, ibid. ln. 33'.

4) Room: they ate and drank in *bt ikl* the dining room, 1.22 I 24 (cf. *ikl*); cf. *bt tu* guardroom, 4.195:10.

5) Immediate social circle, family, court, dynasty: *bt bn bnš yqḥ ʕz* if the family of someone takes a goat, 1.127:31; *bt mlk itdb (itbd*(!)) the family of the king perished, 1.14 I 7 (// *umt*); *bt gbl* the court of TN, 2.44:8; *ngr bt bʕl* herald of the court of DN, 1.16 IV 7; *ky likt bt mlk tḥmk* I have already transmitted your messsage to the royal court, 2.36:5, 14; *šlm PN (...) šlm bth* peace to PN, (...) peace to his court, 1.161:33; *skn bt mlk* prefect of the royal house, 7.63:5 (title of the

royal prince; cf. Del Olmo AuOr 5 1987 47; cf. LÚ.GAR-*kín* É MÍ.LUGAL, Ug 5 161:21; LÚ.MÁŠKIM É.GAL (PRU 3 112 (RS 15.114):7; MÁŠKIM É MÍ.LUGAL-*ti*, Thureau-Dangin Syria 18 1937 248 (RS 8.208):3); *il bt* god of the dynasty, 1.102:1; 1.39:13; 115:3, 7, 9; 1.123:29; cf. 1.53:8; 1.81:7; 1.109:33; *ilt bt* goddess of the dynasty, 1.81:8. Cf. *bt šbn* houses(?) of TN, 4.16:1 (followed by PNN); cf. in unc. ctx. *bt PN* the house(?) of PN, 1.80:2 (cf. *bt (I)*).

6) Storehouse, workshop: *bt alḫnm* storehouse of quartermasters, 4.392:4; *bt ḥrš* forge, 1.12 II 61 (// *bt il*); *bt mrkbt* chariot workshop, 4.392:2 (Del Olmo IMC 192).

7) Stable, shed: *bt alpm* cattle shed, 4.358:1 (cf. ¶ RS Akk.: É-*tu*$_4$ GU$_4$.MEŠ, PRU 3 92 (RS 16.189):18).

In bkn ctx.: *bhtm*, 4.182:33; *bhtm bdlm*[, 4.312:4, 7; house: *b bt ytn* in the house give, RSOu 14 53 [KTU 9.432]:1' (also *ibid.* in bkn ctx. ln. 29').

Cf. **bbt (II)**, **btbt**.

bt (III) n. m. "length, piece"(?) (of cloth(?); < /b-t(-t)/, Ribichini - Xella Tessili 34f.; cf. Hb. *bt*, HALOT 168; Arab. *batt*, Lane 148). ¶ **Forms**: pl. cstr. *bt*.

A length or piece (of cloth(?)): *npṣ bt ṯn ṯlṯ mat* a set of pieces of crimson (cloth), three hundred (shekels), 4.123:16.

btbt DN, tutelary god of the palace (< /bit(t)-bêti/; cf. Akk. *mārat bīti*, DINGIR.DUMU.MÍ.É, Frankena Tākultu 124:96; Lambert RlA 7 355 Lipiński BO 41 1984 438; cf. *bbt*).

DN.: *ṯn šm l btbt* two rams for DN, 1.112:24 and par. (cf. 1.105:22); *(nn) iqn*]*i l sk btbt* (nn) of purp]le for the cloak of DN, 4.182:18.

Cf. **bbt (II)**.

btl PN (etym. unc.; cf. Watson AuOr 8 1990 117); ¶ **syll.**: cf. BU-*ta-lu*, Ug 5 7:15. Cf. *bdil*.

PN: 4.609:25.

btlt n. f. "virgin", title of the goddess Anat in myth and epic (Hb. *btwlh*, HALOT 166f.; JAram. *btwltʔ*, Jastrow 200; Akk. *batūltu*, Ahw 115; CAD B 173s; Arab. *batūl*, Lane 150); ¶ **par.**: *ybmt limm*. ¶ **Forms**: sg. *btlt*; suff. *btltm* (encl. *-m*).

Virgin: *btlt ʕnt* Virgin DN, *passim* (// *ybmt limm*); *al tšgrn y btltm* do not entangle me, oh Virgin!, 1.17 VI 34; *btlt p ʕn*[*t*] *w p nʕmt aḫt b*[*ʕl* deflowered was the vulva of DN, of the most graceful of DN's sisters, 1.10 III 9-10. In unc. ctx.: [*b*]*tlt bʕl yḥmdnh* the virgin(?) - DN desired her, 1.92:29 (cf. Dijkstra UF 26 1994 117); poss. dittog. *{b<t>lt}* in 1.10 III 9 or rdg *blt* (cf. KTU 32 n. 3; cf. /b-l-y/).

btlyn, PN(?), in bkn ctx.: 4.72:3.

btn (I) n. m. “inside of the house” (Hb. *bytn*, HALOT 129; Akk. *bītānu*, AHw 131f.; CAD B 274ff.; diff. Dietrich - Loretz MU 218: ‘Palast’, *bt (II)* + *-n*). ¶ Forms: sg. *btn*.
Inside of the house: *btn mḥy* clean the inside of the house!, 1.124:14.

btn (II) PN (etym. unc.; cf. Grøndahl PTU 52, 118; Dietrich - Loretz UF 1 1969 212; Bordreuil - Caquot Syria 56 1979 310; Van Soldt SAU 40; Watson AuOr 13 1995 221); ¶ syll.: *be-ta-na*, PRU 3 106 (RS 16.206):7; PRU 6 38:18; 83 III 4.
PN: *bn PN*, 4.769:47; cf. in bkn ctx.: 4.315:2; 4.708:5.

btr(y) PN (etym. unc.; cf. Grøndahl PTU 121; Dietrich - Loretz OLZ 62 1967 546; UF 1 1969 212; Watson AuOr 11 1993 214). Var. *btr* in 4.335:2.
PN: *bn PN*, 4.122:20; 4.335:2; 4.681:4.

btšy PN (etym. unc.; cf. Grøndahl PTU 55f., 119, 244, 309; Dietrich - Loretz OLZ 62 1967 546; UF 1 1969 213; Kienast UF 11 1979 450).
PN: 3.4:7 (cf. Van Soldt SAU 40).

/b-t(-t)/ vb G: “to cut” ((?); Ribichini - Xella Tessili 34f.; cf. Caquot ACF 76 1976/7 460; Hb. *bt(t)*, cf. HALOT 168; HAT 187; Arab. *batta*, Lane 147f.). ¶ Forms: G impv. *bt*.
G. To cut(?): *bt ly ṯn ḫpnm* cut(?) two *ḫ*. for me, 5.11:16.
Cf. bt (III).

btw/y PN (etym. unc.; cf. Grøndahl PTU 119; Dietrich - Loretz OLZ 62 1967 546; UF 1 1969 212); ¶ syll.: cf. É-TE-PI, Syria 18 1937 248 (RS 8.208):6 (cf. Grøndahl PTU 118, 331: *bît*^{e}*-ya*). Var. *btw* in 4.700:10. Cf. *bdy(n)*.
PN: ★a) 3.9:4; ★b) *bn PN*, 4.371:15; 4.700:10; in bkn ctx.: 4.682:7.

bṭr n. m. “emancipated, free” (pseudocorrection of spelling, cf. < /p-ẓ-r/, **pṭr*, Ph., pal.(?) *pṭrt*, DNWSI 909; cf. Dietrich - Loretz - Sanmartín UF 5 1973 105; diff.: Mack-Fisher Maarav 5/6 1990 207ff: ‘veterinary surgeon’). ¶ Forms: sg. *bṭr*.
Emancipated, free: PN *bṭr bd mlkt* emancipated: at the queen’s disposal, 4.382:1-2.
Cf. /p-ẓ-r/.

/b-ṯ/ vb G: “to be ashamed” (Hb. *bwš*, HAOT 116f.; Aram. *bht*, Jastrow 143; Syr. *bhet*, LS 61f.; Akk. *bâšu*, AHw 112; CAD B 5ff.; cf. ARM 27 303: *bêšum*. Cf. De Moor SP 117, 139, 179; Van Zijl Baal 44; Sawyer (- Stephenson) BSOAS 33 1970 469f.; Dietrich - Loretz - Sanmartín UF 6 1974 464f.; Wyatt RTU 68 n. 150: ‘dry up’, Hb. *ybš*). ¶ Forms: G cpref. with suff.(?) *ybṯ{.}nn*; impv. *bṯ* (on the

supposed form *bṯṯ* in 1.78:1 cf. *ṯṯ*).
G. To be ashamed: *bṯ l aliyn bʕl* be ashamed, oh most powerful DN!, 1.2 IV 28 and par.; *ybṯnn aliyn bʕl* he was ashamed (of it(?)), was the most powerful DN, 1.2 IV 31.
Cf. bhṯ.

bṯn n. m. "serpent, dragon" (Hb. *ptn*, HALOT 990; Aram. *ptn*, *ptnʔ*, Jastrow 1255; Syr. *patnō*, LS 618; Ebla cf. /baṯmum/ in MAḪ.MUŠ = *ba-ša-mu-um*, Fronzaroli EL 138; *ba-ša-nu-um*, EV 0031; Akk. *bašmu*, AHw 112; CAD B 351f.; cf. Sasson RSP 1 401f.: Hb. *bšn*?; cf. Day GCD 113ff.); ¶ par.: *lsm*, *nḥš*, *rum*, *šlyṭ*. ¶ Forms: sg. *bṯn*; pl. *bṯnm*, f. *bṯnt*.
Serpent, dragon: *bṯn brḥ (...) bṯn ʕqltn* the fleeing serpent (...), the winding serpent, 1.5 I 1-2 and par. (// *šlyṭ*); *ynṯkn k bṯnm* they bit like serpents, 1.6 VI 19 (// *rumm*, *lsmm*); *km bṯn yqr* like a serpent he hissed, 1.17 VI 14; *lbh km bṯn* her heart like (that) of a serpent, 1.19 VI 61; *bṯnm uḫd bʕlm* grasp the serpents, oh DN!, 1.82:6; [...] *bṯnm w ṯṯb ʕl bṯnt trtḥ*[*ṣ*] [you shall cast a spell (?) against] the male serpents and you/they shall repeat/sit, against the female serpent (, and) you/they shall wash, 1.82:35; *tn (...) w bn bṯn itnny* give (me) (....) and the offspring of the serpent as a wedding gift, 1.100:74 and par. (// *nḥšm*); *tṣu (...) k bṯn ʕmdm* out you go (...) like a snake through the foot of the wall(?), 1.169:3; *ʕlk l tʕl bṯn* (so that) upon you the serpent does not climb, RSOu 14 52 [KTU 9.435]:4 (cf. ln. 6); *riš bṯn* the head of the snake, 1.175:11.
Cf. in bkn ctx. *mm b bṯn*[, 1.166:28.

bṯṯ (I) n. f. "shame; shamelessness" (cf. *bṯ*; Hb. *bšt*, HALOT 165; Akk. *bā/ūštu*, AHw 112, 143; CAD B 142ff., 351f.); ¶ par.: *tdmmt*. ¶ Forms: sg. *bṯṯ*.
Shame, shamelessness: *dbḥ bṯṯ* shameful sacrifice, 1.4 III 19 (// *tdmmt*); *k bh bṯṯ l tbṯ* for in it the shame(lessness) is truly obvious, 1.4 III 21. Bkn ctx. *bṯṯ ʕllmn* disgrace of the 'eternal', 1.1 IV 5 (cf. Del Olmo IMC 42); unc. ctx. *ʕn bṯṯ tpnn*, 1.96:2.

bṯṯ (II) n. f. "evildoing woman, witch" (< *bṯy*); ¶ par.: *bṯy*. ¶ Forms: sg. *bṯṯ*.
Evildoing woman, witch: *tpnn (...) ʕn bṯṯ* the eye of the evildoing woman does distort (...), 1.96:6 (// *bṯy*); *ʕn bṯṯ l bṯṯ ṯṯb* may the eye of the evildoing woman revert to the evildoing woman, *ibid.* ln. 12-13 (// *bṯy*).

bṯy n. m. "evildoer, wizard" (cf. Aram. *byš*, DJPA 102; Akk. *bīšu*, AHw 131; CAD B 270f. Cf. Del Olmo CR 382 n. 168 and cf. Arab.

bṭy, DAFA 1 376; diff. De Moor UF 11 1979 647f.: 'flatterer', Arab. *bṭy*; Ford UF 30 1998 243f. and 243 n. 138; Caquot TOu 2 43: PN); ¶ par.: *bṯt*. ¶ Forms: sg. *bṭy*.
Evildoer, wizard: *tpnn ʕn bṭy* the eye of the evildoer does distort, 1.96:6 (// *bṯt*); *ʕn bṭy l bṭy ṯṯb* may the eye of the evildoer revert to the evildoer, *ibid.* ln. 11-12 (// *bṯt*).
Cf. bṯt (II).

by PN (etym. unc.; cf. Van Soldt SAU 45f.); ¶ syll.: cf. *be*-PI, Syria 15 1934 137 (RS [Varia 3]):6.
PN: *bn PN*, 4.181:5 (*ary*); cf. in bkn ctx.: 4.681:8. Cf. *bn bw*[, 4.106:14.

byn PN (etym. unc.; Watson AuOr 8 1990 117); ¶ syll.: cf. *be-ia-nu*[, PRU 3 35 (RS 15.37):15. Cf. *bʕyn*.
PN: 1.175:8; 4.86:30 (*ʕnqp*[*aty*).

byy PN (etym. unc.).
PN: ★a) 1.142:1 (*bn try*); 4.334:2; 4.396:20; in bkn ctx.: 4.488:3; ★b) *bn PN*: 4.170:25; 5.10:1; 5.11:1; RSOu 14 40 [KTU 9.419]:10. In bkn ctx.: 4.334:2; 4.617:11; cf. 5.11:17 (text *bby*).

bz n. m. "udder" (cf. Aram. *bz/t*, DNWSI 149f.; JAram. *bî/ûzzāʔ*, Jastrow 205; Syr. *buzzāʔ*, LS 64; Arab. *buzz*, DAFA 1 601; Wehr - Cowan 70; Dozy 1 80; Sanmartín UF 11 1979 723. Diff. Pardee UF 7 1975 347; UF 8 1976 234: 'booty'). ¶ Forms: sg. *bz*.
Udder: (a kid) *b bz ʕzm* from the udder of goats (is sacrificed), 1.80:4.

bẓr n. m. of a precious metal (trad. "refined gold"; Hb. *bṣr*, HALOT 149; Arab. *baṣrat*, Lane 211; cf. Van Selms UF 7 1975 472; Loretz UF 12 1980 279ff.); ¶ par.: *br(r)*. ¶ Forms: sg. *bẓr*.
A precious metal, trad. 'refined gold': *nḫt bẓr* a divan of fine gold, 1.4 I 34 (// *br*, diff. Gibson CML 56, 147 and KTU: rdg *b ẓr*).

d

-d, cf. *-id.*

d determinative / relative functor: 1) genitival, functor introduces nominal expansions : "the one(s) of", etc.; 2) relative functor, introduces expansions of verbal or nominal clauses: "who, whom, he who", etc.; 3) abs. use, without explicit antecedent: "the (one) who / which / that /"; 4) in compound conjunctions, "since, as" (Emar /zu/, Pentiuc Vocabulary 196; Hb. *zh, zw,* f. *zʔt,* HALOT 263ff.; DNWSI 299ff.; Ph., Pun. *z,* DNWSI 299ff.; (O)Aram., Palm., Nab., JAram. *zy, d(y),* f. *zʔt,* DNWSI 399ff.; OSA *ḏ,* DOSA 89f.; Arab. *ḏū, ḏī, ḏā,* Lane 984ff.; Eth. *za, zĕ,* CDG 629f.; cf. Ebla /ḏū-/ *šu-* in PNN, Fronzaroli MARI 5 267; Catagnoti MisEb 1 254; Akk. *šu,* AHw 1254. Cf. Gordon UT § 6.23-24.; Segert 49, 84); ¶ **syll. Ug.**: [LÚ = *ša*?] = *a-wi* (PI) = *du-ú,* Ug 5 137 II 29'; Sivan GAGl 215; Huehnergard UVST 117; Van Soldt SAU 303; Neu SBoT 337 n. 66. ¶ **Forms:** m. sg. *d, dy* (*d* + encl. *-y;* see Bordreuil - Pardee RSOu 14 p. 388); f. *d, dt;* pl. *d, dt, dtm* (*dt* + encl. *-m*); see allomorph *ḏ.*

1) The one(s) of: ★**a)** determinative of quality, type: *il d pid* DN he of / benevolence (> 'the Benevolent One'), epithet of the god El, 1.5 VI 12 and *passim*; *hyn d ḥrš yd* DN the ambidextrous craftsman, 1.17 V 18 and par.; *klt lḥmh d nzl* a measure of his bread of offering, 1.14 III 58 and par.; *ʕbdk an w d ʕlmk* I am your servant in perpetuity, 1.5 II 12; *mrqdm d šn* castanets of ivory, 1.108:5, cf. 1.19 IV 27; *ẖpn d iqni w šmt* a cape of violet and reddish purple, 4.168:1; *ṯryn aḥd d bnš* one suit of armour for a man, 4.169:6; *yip lḥm d ẖmš* bake bread of the fifth (month), 1.14 II 30 and par.; *(qmḥ) d nšlm* (flour) of (: as) guarantee, 4.328:1-10; *msg d tbk* leather of (type) *t.*, 4.167:15; *nʕl il d qblbl* a divine palanquin with carrying poles, 1.4 I 36; *ʕr d qdm* the city of ancient times, 1.100:62; *šlty d šbʕt rašm* the tyrant with seven heads, 1.3 III 42 and par.; *lpš d sgr bh* a cloak with (appliqués of) gold, 4.166:6; *d ʕqh ib iqni* whose eyeballs/pupils are (gems of) lapis lazuli, 1.14 III 45 and par.; *drkt dt drdrk* your perpetual dominion, 1.2 IV 10 and par.; *<b>hty (...) dt ksp hkly (...) dtm ẖrṣ* my house of

silver, my palace (...) of gold, 1.4 VI 37; *gnpm dt ksp dt yrq nqbnm* the harness of silver, the caparisons of gold, 1.4 IV 10-11 and par.; *(dbḥm) dt nat* (sacrifices) of sorrow, 1.127:4 and par.; *ʕglm dt šnt* bullocks of one year, 1.22 I 13 and par.; *pldm dt šʕrt* cloaks of wool, 4.270:8; *ḥṯb d anyt* bill of the ship, 4.779:13; *kl d iṯ [l špš]* all that the 'Sun' has, 2.81:9; *dbḥ d* sacrifice of, RSOu 14 33 [KTU 9.422]:1; ★b) determinative of property, belonging, place: *d PN* belonging to PN, 4.333:12; *šir(m) šd (...) d PN* (2) *š.*-measures(s) of land (...) belonging to PN, 4.282:2, 3, 6, 9, 11, 13, 15; *yn (...) d PN w (...) yn d iḫh* wine (...) of PN and (...) wine of his brothers, 4.123:22-23; *ġṣb šmal d alpm* the left *ġ.* of two head of cattle, 1.109:27; *tgmr šmn d PN* total of the oil of PN, 4.313:27; *ksp d mkr TN / TN / nqdm* silver (tribute) of the traders of TN / of TN / of the 'chief shepherds', 4.369:2-8; *PN (...) mru mlki d škn* PN (...) *m.* of the king (and) of the prefect(!), 6.66:6; *arr d qrht*, TN of TN, 6.27:2 (for the rdg. cf. Van Soldt UF 21 1989 380 n. 30: '*a.*-district of the towns': 'translation highly dubious'); *šlm d ḥwtk* the well-being of your land, 2.36:4; *dbbm d msdt arṣ* beasts of the foundations of the earth, 1.4 I 40; *dbbm d ġzr* demons of the (adolescent) youth 1.169:1; (crew and weaponry) *d mrkbt mlk* of the royal chariot(s), 4.167:12; *k]d ztm d PN* a jar of olives of PN, 4.429:3 and par.; (a door) *d sgrm* of the courtyards(?), 4.195:4; *ktn d TN* a tunic from TN, 4.132:4; *anš dt ẓrh* the muscles of her back, 1.3 III 35 and par. With a metalinguistic antecedent, cf. *d rb* the ('jar') of the chief, 6.2:1, Dietrich - Loretz KA 223f. (but UF 30 1998 887: rdg *l* (?)); *d ṯbil* (document) of PN, 1.92:1 (cf. *infra*: 3); *l ḥmrm dt tblm* the donkeys of PN 4.790:15'; ★c) specifying value: *ḫmš ṯnt d ḫmš mat* five *ṯ.* for five hundred shekels, 4.203:9; cf. *ḫmš ṯnt d mit* five *ṯ.* for one hundred, *ibid.* ln. 10; *ḫmš ṯnt d ṯlṯ mat* five *ṯ.* for three hundred, *ibid.* ln. 11; *ṯt ṯnt d alp* two *ṯ.* for one thousand, *ibid.* ln. 13; *kt il dt rbtm* a twenty thousand (shekel) divine podium, 1.4 I 30.

2) Which, who, the one(s) who/that: ★a) as subject: (chariot crew) *bd rb ḥršm d šṣa ḥwyh* in the hands of the chief cartwright, who consigned (it) to the storehouse, 4.145:10; *qrht d tššlmn* cities which make loans (in favour of) TN, 4.95:1; *il d yqny ḏdm* the god who created the caves, 1.19 IV 58; *ṯlṯ d yṣa bd PN l argmn l nskm* copper which was transferred to PN for the tribute (and delivered) to the smiths, 4.43:1; cf. 4.166:1; neg.: *d l yṣa* which did not come out, 4.341:21; *sp (...) d yaḫd lg ynm* bowls (...) which (each) contain a 'quart' of wine, 4.44:28; *yn (...) d*(!) *ntn b*(!) *ksp* wine that was sold for cash, 4.274:3; *ilnym d tit* the divine ones who came, 1.20 II 10;

mdrġlm d inn msgm lhm guardsmen who have no (animal) skins, 4.53:1 (cf. *infra: dt inn bd (...)*, 4.379:1); *any TN d b TN* ship of TN which is in TN, 4.390:2; *mdrġlm d bt bʕlt mlk* guardsmen (on duty) in the temple of DN, 4.54:1; *adrm d b grn* the nobles (who meet) in the threshing floor, 1.17 V 7; *ḥln d dmt* the window which is in the fortress, 2.31:46; PN (f.) *d b ḥlmy il ytn* what DN granted me in my dream, 1.14 III 46 and par.; *PNN bʕl any d bd PN* workers of the fleet who are at the disposal of PN, 4.647:7; *bnš mlk d bd adnʕm* people of the king who have been entrusted to PN, 4.141 II 26; *updt d bd PN* list of share-cropping (plots) that pass to the hands of PN, 4.264:1; cf. 4.248:2 (bkn); *ib d b TN* the enemy who is in TN, 2.33:10; *bnš mlk d b TN* people of the king who are in TN, 3.2:7; *l ḥmrm d bd* for the donkeys in the hand of, RSOu 14 39 [KTU 4.790]:9', 11', 13'; *ḫpṯ d bl spr ṯnn d bl hg* mercenaries without number, archers without count, 1.14 II 37-38 and par.; *km špš d brt* like the sun, which is free, 2.19:3; *rpš d (l) ydyt* latifundia which are (not) untilled land, 4.348:1, 20; *il d ydʕnn* the god who knew him, 1.114:6; *mlk d yknnh* the king who established him, 1.3 V 36 and par. (cf. bkn ctx. 1.10 III 6); *yn d ntn b ksp* wine sold for cash, 4.219:1 (cf. 4.274:3); *yṣr d yṯb b* the potter who lives in TN, 2.382:26 and par.; *yn d ykl* wine that is consumed, 1.91:1; *klhm d lh* all of theirs, 1.9:11; *yn d l ṭb* wine which is not of good quality (table wine), 4.213:2, 5, 7, 10, 12, 13, 15, 17, 19, 23; *il d (l) ydʕnn* the god who does (not) know him, 1.114:76-77; *mrkbt mlk d l ṣpy* chariots of the king which were not plated, 4.167:6; *spr npš d ʕrb bt mlk* list of people who have entered the royal palace, 4.338:1; *ksp anyt d ʕrb b anyt* surety for the ship which has been deposited for the ships, 4.338:12; *GNN d ʕrb b unṯ* GNN who have gone into service, 3.7:1; *iṯ yn d ʕrb* there is wine that entered (in plenty(?)), 1.23:74; *šdm dt nʕrb gt npk* fields that comprise the guarantee of TN, 4.103:45; *hdm il*(!) *d prša b br* a divine footstool that is covered with tin, 1.4 I 35; *trm d ṣpy* rods / poles which have been plated, 4.167:2 (cf. l. 6); *mlk (...) d šbʕ [a]ḫ̮m lh* the king (...) who had seven brothers, 1.14 I 8; *aḥdy (...) d yšb*[*ʕ*] *hmlt arṣ* I am the only one (...) who will satisfy the multitudes of the earth, 1.4 VII 51; DN *d ašr* DN whom I sing, 1.24:38; *il (...) d yšr* the god (...) who is sung, 1.108:3; PN *ʕbd mlk d št ʕl ḫ̮rdh* official of the king who was placed in command of his guard, 2.47:15; *bnš {l} d yškb {l} b bt mlk* people who lodge in the palace, 4.163:15; *spr bnš mlk d taršn ʕmsn b ṣr* list/record of personnel of the king who negotiate(?) loading in TN, 4.370:2; *ql d tbʕ mṣr*(?)*m* the courier who left for Egypt, 4.213:27; *ql d ybl prd* the messenger who leads the mule, 4.337:12;

d ṯṯ [mr]kbt w ḥrṣ [yd tr]hm (equipment) which (corresponds to) a lot of six chariot bodies with their (steering) poles, 4.363:9; *ġzr (...) d in bn lh* the nobleman (...) who has no son, 1.17 I 18; *bdlm dt yṯb b*[reserve personnel detailed(?) in[, 4.86:29; *bdl TN dt inn mhr lhm*(!) reserve personnel with no troops assigned, 4.214 I 4; *bnšm dt it alpm lh* people who have no oxen, 4.422:1; *rʕym dt bd PN* shepherds who depend on PN, 4.374:1; *mḏrġlm dt inn bd PN*, guards who do not depend on PN, 4.379:1; *šd ubdy TN dt bd skn* leased fields of TN which depend on the governor, 4.110:2; *šd snrym dt ʕqb b ayly* estates of the GNN who have accepted / made a transfer in TN, 4.645:1; *ḥršm dt tbʕln b TN* craftsmen who work in TN, 4.141 III 6 (cf. *ibid.* ln. 8 *ḥrš* ★d); *spr mḏr*[*ġlm*] *d*(!)*t hlk b*[list of guards who went to, 4.33:2; *mnm šalm dt tknn* any claims they bring up, 3.3:6; *bnšm dt l TN ṯb* people who return to TN 4.339:1 (cf. *bnšm dt l TN* people who return) to TN, *ibid.* ln. 17); *d ttbʕn ṯbq* those who go to TN, RSOu 14 43 [KTU 9.421]:1; *il mṣrm dt tġrn npš špš* the gods of TN who protect the life of the Sun, 2.23:22; *qrn*[*h*] *d*(!)*t ʕlh* his horns which are above him, 1.101:7; *rišym dt ʕrb b bnšhm* GNN who offer guarantees for their personnel, 4.347:1; *spr ʕrbnm dt ʕrb b PN* list of the guarantors who offer guarantees for PN, 3.3:2; *mrkbt dt ʕrb bt mlk* chariots that came into the palace, 4.145:1; *tšʕ dt tqḥ*[*n*] *šʕrt* none who opt for (paying in) wool, 4.395:2 and par.; *ṯlḥn il d mla mnm* a divine table was full of species (of animals), 1.4 I 38; *aḥdy d ymlk* I am the only one who will rule, 1.4 VII 49; *mlk d mlk* the king who rules, 2.47:12; *tgmr yn d nkly* total of wine which was consumed, 4.231:15 and par; *ksp d nkly* money that was spent, 4.280:6; (money) *d škn l ks ilm* that was intended for the cup of the gods, 4.280:14; *šmn d nšdd mzy* oil that was placed at the disposal (on the occasion of a rite(?)) *m.*, 4.272:1; ★b) functioning as object: *nʕr d apy PN* rancid flour(?) which PN made into bread, 4.362:4; *d apy ʕbdh* which your servant made into bread, *ibid.* ln. 5; *d tqh d tqyn hmlt* the one you protect, the one you protect, multitude(s), 1.2 I 18 and par.; *aḥd alp PN d aḫd b TN* one ox which PN has collected in TN, 4.296:11 and par.; *šh d ytn ṣtqn* his ram, that PN delivered, 1.80:2; *qmḥ d kly b bt skn l PN* flour which was delivered to PN in (/ for) the house of the prefect, 4.361:1; *qmḥ d kly k ṣḥ* PN_1 *bd* PN_2 flour that was liquidated when PN claimed (it), PN_1 through the mediation of PN_2, 4.362:1; *bnš d likt* the man whom I sent, 2.45:24; *rgm d l tdʕ nšm* a matter that men do not understand, 1.3 III 27 and par., cf. 1.10 I 3; *(nn) šmn d lqḥt PNF* (nn jars of) oil which PNF takes, 4.290:2; *lḥt spr d likt* the tablet that you sent, 2.14:7; *mʕrb d yqḥ bt mlk* tribute offering which the palace will take, 1.41:20 (cf. 2.45:5); *mnm rgm d tšmʕ ṯmt* anything that you find out about there, 2.10:17; *mrṯ d štt* and the must that you drank, 2.34:32; *ṯlṯ d ybl PN* copper that PN brings, 4.272:7; *argmn d ybl PN l špš arn* tribute that PN brings to the 'Sun' of TN, 3.1:18; *ʔgn z pʕl PN* earthenware bowl that PN made, 6.70:1 (Dietrich - Loretz KA 234); *anykn dt likt mṣrm* this ship of yours which you sent to Egypt, 2.38:10; *alp PN dt aḫd ḥrṯh* oxen of PN which their ox-driver collected, 4.296:8; *spr ʕpsm dt št uryn l mlk ugrt* document about the boundary-stones(?) which the *u.* placed for the king in TN, 6.29:1; ★c) genitival function: *anhbm d alp šd ẓuh b ym* sea-snail(s) whose exhalation is (noticeable) at a thousand acres in the sea, 1.3 IV 45 and par.; *(PN) d k nʕm ʕnt nʕmh* whose charm is like that of DN, 1.14 III 41 and par.; *nqdm dt kn npṣhm* 'head shepherds' whose military equipment has been delivered, 4.624:1; ★d) circumstantial: *ṯpṭn in d ʕln* our judge, whom no-one is above, 1.3 V 33; *ṣʕ (...) d bh rumm l rbbt* platter (...) in which there were wild bulls by the myriad, 1.4 I 43; TN *d ʕlk mḫṣ aqht* TN upon which hangs the death of PN, 1.19 III 52 and par.; *ap d anšt* the anger which makes me livid, 1.6 V 21; *ʔgn (...) z l PN* earthenware bowl (...) of PN, 6.70:2 (Dietrich - Loretz KA 234).; *w yʕdb d b tkh* and he prepares what is within it, RSOu 14 53 [KTU 9.432]:28', 37'.

3) The one (who /that), without explicit ant.: *p d in b bty ttn* rather the one who is not in my house shall you give me, 1.14 III 38 and par.; *d iph* the one whom I saw, 1.10 II 32; *d iṯ b kbdk* the one you have in your mind, 1.18 I 18; *d ḫsrt* the one you are lacking, 2.41:17; *d yšt l lṣbh* the one (he /one) shall place on his space betwen the eyebrows / forehead, 1.114:29; *grš d ʕšy lnh* who ejects one who does something (to his father), 1.17 I 29 and par.; *d ʕnn* the one that (my eyes(?)) saw, 1.10 II 33; *dy l ydʕ yṣḥ* the one whom he does not know calls, RSOu 14 52 [KTU 9.435]:1 (see Bordreuil - Pardee RSOu 14 p. 388); unc.: *dt b u*[those of TN/PN(?), RSOu 14 51 [KTU 9.425]:22.

4) In compound conjunctions, since, as: *k d lbšt b ir* as you have been clothed in light (?), 1.13:25; *k d ʕl qšth imḫṣh* since, for his bow I wounded him, 1.19 I 14.

Unc. ctx. *d mṣd*, 1.114:7. In bkn ctx. *dt l bn*[, 1.3 III 7; 1.4 II 45; *ilm d mlk*, 1.4 III 9;]*dr dt šmm*, 1.10 I 5; *d ʕrgzm*, 1.20 I 8; *dt ʕl lty*, 1.20 I 9; *dt ymtm*, 1.25:4; *d ymġy bnš*, 1.86:8; *w d l mdl*, *ibid.* ln. 13; *dt* [, 1.127:17; *qrt dt*, 2.33:7; *d štt*, 2.36:7; *d l nʕm*, 2.50:19; *dt nšu*, 4.11:7; *bdlm dt*, 4.86:21; *ṯlṯ dt* xx [...]*dt ṯgml*, 4.192:3-4; *ḥrš d*, 4.207:3;]*dt iṯ*[, 4.296:1; *mḫsm d*, 4.300:1; *ušknym dt b*[*d*], 4.335:1;

[*bn*]*šm dt iš*[, 4.617:1 (cf. 4.655:1); *ṯlṯm d nlqḥt*, 4.659:1; *d aḫ̮t d*[, RSOu 14 51 [KTU 9.425]:23; cf. 1.7:30; 1.12 I 3; 1.18 I 31; 2.45:13; 4.127:10; 4.300:1; 4.398:13; 4.415:1-5; 4.424:17(?).

/d-ʔ-y/ vb G: "to fly" (Hb. *dʔh*, HALOT 207); ¶ par.: /r-ḫ̮-p/. ¶ Forms: G inf. *du*, *di*; part. act. f. *dit* (for the forms *tdu*, 1.16 VI 6-7, and *ydu*, 1.103:42, cf. /n-d-ʔ/).
G. To fly: *nšrm tpr w du* may the eagles begin to fly!, 1.19 III 14 and par.; *w ʕnt di dit* may DN fly off (< DN of flying, may she fly), 1.108:8 (// *rḫ̮pt*; cf. Tuttle UF 8 1976 465f.; diff. De Moor ARTU 188, 'of the Kite, the She-Kite', cf. *diy (I)*; Pardee TPM 103ff.: 'DN de(s) aile(s)'). In bkn ctx.: *di š*[, 1.16 V 48.
Cf. diy (I), diy (II).

di, 1.108:8, cf. /d-ʔ-y/.

diy (I) n. m. raptor, conventionally "hawk" (Hb. *dʔh*, HALOT 207; cf. *dyh*, HALOT 220; cf. De Moor SEL 5 1988 66 n. 34: 'black kite', Arab. Syr. *hedâye*); ¶ par.: *nšr*. ¶ Forms: sg. *diy*; pl. *diym*.
Bird, conventionally hawk: *aštk (...) km diy b tʕrty* I shall place you (...) like a hawk in my quiver, 1.18 IV 18 and par. (// *nšr*); in flocks: *ybṣr ḥbl diym* a flock of hawks was watching, 1.19 I 33 and par. (// *nšrm*).

diy (II) n. m. "wing" (Arab. *daʔy*, Lane 840; cf. Van Zijl Baal 277; Tuttle UF 8 1976 465); ¶ par.: *knp*. ¶ Forms: pl.(?) cstr. *diy*.
Wing: *bʕl ṯbr diy hmt* DN broke his wings, 1.19 III 9 and par. (// *knp*); *bʕ ybn diy hmt* may DN rebuild his wings, 1.19 III 13 and par. (// *knp*).

dʕm PN (etym. unc.; cf Watson AuOr 14 1996 98).
PN: *bn NP*, 3.7:8.

dʕmm, 1.13:15; cf. *dʕt (II)*.

/d-ʕ-ṣ/ vb G: "to fix, lean, press" ((?); cf. Syr. *dʕaṣ*, LS 161; Akk. *dâṣu*, AHw 165; CAD 118f.; Arab. *dāġiṣat*, Lane 886. Cf. Margalit UF 8 1976 168; UF 15 1983 87; diff.: Ajjan NU 35: 'se préparer à s'élancer', Arab. *daʕsa*). ¶ Forms: G prefc. *tdʕṣ*.
G. To fix, lean, press(?): *tdʕṣ pʕnm w tr arṣ* she pressed(?) (her) feet (down) and jumped to the ground, 1.4 V 20 and par.

dʕt (I) n. f. 1) "knowledge, information, communiqué"; 2) "friendship", abstr. for concr. > "acqauintance, mate" (< /y-d-ʕ/; cf. *dʕt*, HALOT 228f.; Pun. *dʕt*, DNWSI 440: *ydʕ*$_1$; Ebla cf. /daʕ(a)tim/ in UMUN(?) = *ba-lu da-a-tim*, VE 1191; Krebernik ZA 73 1983 42; Akk. *di/aʔ(a)tu*, AHw 168; CAD D 130f. Cf. Pope Fs. Finkelstein 172; diff. Loretz - Xella MLE 1 43; Avishur UF 13 1981 22f.; Smith BC 289; Husser UF

27 1995 239: 'enchanteur'); ¶ **par.**: *amr (I)*, *ḥbr*. ¶ **Forms**: sg. suff. *dʕtk*, *dʕtkm*, *dʕthm*; pl. suff. *dʕtm* (encl. *-m*.).
1) Knowledge, information, communiqué: *ṯny dʕtkm* repeat your communiqué, 1.2 I 16 and par. (// *amr*).
2) Friendship, acquaintance, friend, mate: *DN ḥbrk w DN dʕtk* DN your companion and DN your acquaintance, 1.6 VI 50 (cf. Hb. *mwdʕ* and *md (II)*); *ġlm dʕtm* (may) the lad (cast out his) mates, 1.169:10 (// *ḥbrm*).
Cf. /y-d-ʕ/ (I).

dʕt (II) n. f. "sweat" (< /w-ḏ-ʕ/; cf. Hb. *zʕh*, HALOT 276, cf. *ibid.* 229: *dʕt III*; Aram. *dyʕtʔ*, Jastrow 303; Ebla /ḏuʕtum/ in IR = *šu-du-um*, VE 1041; Krebernik ZA 73 1983 37; Akk. *zūtu*, *zūʔtu*, AHw 1539; CAD Z 168). ¶ **Forms**: sg. *dʕt* (possibly m. sg. *dʕ* in 1.13:15).
Sweat: *trḥṣ*{.}*nn b dʕt* she washed him of sweat, 1.16 VI 10.
Cf. *k* [*dʕ*]*mm*, 1.13:15 (cf. De Moor (- Spronk) ARTU 139; CARTU 134: *dʕ* 'bead of sweat'); in unc. ctx.: *dʕt* (my drink) is sweat, RSOu 14 53 [KTU 9.432]:14' (metaph. for 'wine': Bordreuil - Pardee RSOu 14 p. 400).
Cf. /y-d-ʕ/ (II).

db (I) n. m. "threshold"(?) (cf. Akk. *dippu*, AHw 172; *dappu*, *dibbu*, CAD D 106, 134; cf. Xella UF 13 1981 309ff.). ¶ **Forms**: sg. *db*.
Threshold(?): [*i*]*d ydbḥ mlk (...) b db* when the king sacrifices (...) in the 'threshold'(?), 1.164:4 (perhaps a mistake for *g*(!)*b* or *db*<*r*>?).

db (II) n. m. "bear" (Hb. *db*, HALOT 207f.; Syr. *debbō*, LS 138; Ebla /dabbum/ in AZ = *da-bù(-um)*, *dab₆-bù*, VE 870a; Krebernik ZA 73 1983 33; Conti SQF 205; Akk. *dabbu*, *dabû*, AHw 148; CAD D 17; Arab. *dubb*, Lane 841; Eth. *dĕbb*, CDG 119; cf. Dietrich - Loretz UF 17 1985 132; Loretz ZAW 99 1987 417); ¶ **par.**: *ṯbt ġr*(?). ¶ **Forms**: sg. *db*.
Bear: *hd r*[*bṣ*] *km db* DN lay [down] like a bear, 1.101:2 (// *ṯbt ġr*(?); cf. KTU: rdg *k mdb*; Pardee TPM 299: 'flot').

dbat n. f. "strength" (Hb. *dbʔ*, HALOT 208. Cf. Cross VT 2 1952 163; Van Zijl Baal 249; Driver Ug. 6 185f.; diff. Sanmartín UF 12 1980 341ff.: 'Haartracht', Akk. *zappu* / *zabbu*, Arab. *ḏuʔaba*, Syr. *zeftō*; Caquot - Sznycer TOu 1 284 n. o: 'frapper', Arab. *dabaʔa*, Akk. *daʔāp/bu*; Kapelrud VG 95, rdg *d bat k*). ¶ **Forms**: sg. suff. *dbatk*.
Strength: *qrn dbatk* your strong horns, 1.10 II 21-22.

dbb (I) n. m. 1) "beast, mythical animal"; 2) "demon" (Arab. *dabbab*, *dubb*, *dābbat*, Lane 841f.; Hb. *db*, HALOT 207f.; cf. Dietrich - Loretz UF 10 1978 62; Loretz - Xella MLE 1 38f.; Van Soldt UF 21 1989

369ff.; cf. De Moor UF 12 1980 430; ARTU 46: 'flying demon' / 'winged monster', Ug. *ḏbb*; survey: Wyatt RTU 442 n. 2). ¶ Forms: pl. *dbbm*.

1) Mythical beast: *db bm d msdt arṣ* beasts of the foundations of the earth, 1.4 I 39 (cf. Caquot - Sznycer TOu 2 196 n. q, 'rampant', Arab. *dabba*; diff.: Margalit MLD 22, 'effusion', Arab. *ḏwb*).

2) Demon: *ydy dbbm d ġzr* expulsion of the demons of the young (adolescent), 1.169:1 (diff.: Del Olmo CR 385 n. 177: 'strength', Arab. *ġazr*; Avishur UF 13 1981 17: 'enemy' / 'evil words', Akk. *dabābu*; Aartun UF 16 1984 10f.: 'hinterhältige Unternehmung', Arab. *dabūb*; Caquot TOu 2 54 n. 122: 'parole', Akk. *dabābu*; cf. Dietrich - Loretz TUAT 2 335); *aphm kšpm dbbm ygrš* and then may the wizards cast out the demons, 1.169:9 (diff.: Caquot TOu 2 57 n. 141: 'qui parlent'; Dietrich - Loretz TUAT 2 335: '(Beschwörungs)worte', cf. previous text for these and other translations); in unc. ctx.: *km l tudn dbbm kšpm* (...) *yšpk kmm arṣ kšpm dbbm* just as the sorcerers do not listen to the demons... so the sorcerers spill to the ground the demons, RSOu 14 52 [KTU 9.435]:9, 13 (diff. Bordreuil - Pardee RSOu 14 52 p. 389f., 391f.: 'tourmenteurs', *dabābu*).

dbb (II) PN (Sem. Cf. Van Soldt UF 21 1989 372; Watson AuOr 11 1993 215; cf. Grøndahl PTU 122; Sivan GAGl 214); ¶ syll.: DUMU *da-bu-bi*, PRU 6 70:2; RS 22.02 rev. 8' (cf. Van Soldt UF 21 1989 372).

PN: ★a) 4.727:17 (cf. *bt (II)*); ★b) *bn PN*: 4.611:7. Cf. in bkn ctx. 4.69 VI 34; 4.633:12 (Van Soldt SAU 34).

/d-b-ḥ/ vb G: "to sacrifice", "to offer a sacrifice, give a banquet" (Hb., Pun., Aram. *zbḥ*, HALOT 261f.; DNWSI 301; Arab. *ḏabaḥa*, Lane 953ff.; Eth. *zabḥa*, CDG 631; cf. Van Zijl Baal 89f.; Xella TRU 344f.); ¶ par.: /ʕ-š-r/, /n-k-t/, /n-š-ʔ/ *(+ yd)*, /y-r-d/, /ṯ-ʕ-y/. ¶ Forms: G suffc. *dbḥ*; prefc. *tdbḥ*, *ydbḥ*, *ndbḥ*; suff. *tdbḥn*; impv. *dbḥ*; act. part.(?) *dbḥ* (cf. Emar /ḏābiḥu/, Pentiuc Vocabulary 193f.).

G. To sacrifice, offer a sacrifice, give a banquet: *dbḥ l ṯr abk* sacrifice to the Bull, your father, 1.14 II 23 and par. (// *ša ydk*, *šrd*); *krtn dbḥ dbḥ* behold PN offers a sacrifice / gives a banquet, 1.16 I 39 and par. (// *ʕšr*); *tdbḥ amr* they sacrificed lambs, 1.20 I 10; *dbḥn ndbḥ* behold the sacrifice that we offer, 1.40:32 and par. (// *nṯʕy*, *nkt*); *bt ṯʕy ydbḥ* the house of the officiant shall sacrifice, 1.119:8; *l ydbḥ mlk* the king must sacrifice, 1.119:13; *id ydbḥ mlk* when the king offers a sacrifice, 1.115:1; 1.164:1, 3; *il dbḥ b bth* DN gives a banquet in his house,

1.114:1 (// *ṣd*; cf. 1.1 IV 28); cf. unc. ctx. *w ṯmn ydbḥ mlġt*, 2.40:16; *dbḥ ṣṭqn l ršp* PN sacrificed to DN, 1.79:7.
Cf. **dbḥ, dbḥt, mdbḥ**.

dbḥ n. m. 1) "sacrifice, (sacrificial) banquet"; 2) "offering"; 3) month name(?) (Hb. Ph., Pun. *zbḥ*, HALOT 262f.; DNWSI 301f.; Ebla cf. /dubḫu/ in PNN *du-bù(-ḫu)*(-DN), *du-bí-ḫu*(-DN), *du-bù-ḫi*(-DN), Krebernik PET 167; Müller Biling. 195; Fronzaroli ARES 1 17; Sanmartín AuOr 9 1991 186; Aram. *dbḥ*, DNWSI 301f.; Akk. *zību*, AHw 1525; CAD Z 105f.; Arab. *ḏa/ibḥ*, Lane 953f.; Eth. *zĕbḥ*, CDG 631. Cf. Del Olmo SEL 12 1995 38ff.; Watson UF 31 1999 787); ¶ **syll. Ug.**: EZEN = *i-sí-nu* = *e-li*(?) = *da-ab-ḫu*, Ug 137 III 6; Sivan GAGl 213; Huehnergard UVST 117; Van Soldt SAU 303); ¶ **par.**: *dġt*, *ʕšrt*, *mṣd*. ¶ **Forms**: sg. *dbḥ*, suff. *dbḥk*, *dbḥn*; du. *dbḥm*; pl. *dbḥm*; cstr. *dbḥ*.

1) Sacrifice, (sacrificial) banquet: *w yqr*[*y*] *dbḥ ilm* and he offered a sacrifice to the gods, 1.19 IV 23 and par. (// *dġṯhm*); *lqḥ imr dbḥ b ydh* he took a sacrificial lamb in his hand, 1.14 III 56 and par.; *msrr ʕṣr db*[*ḥ*] the entrails of a sacrificial bird, 1.14 III 59 and par.; *dbḥ mlk* royal sacrifices, 1.91:2; *dbḥ ṣpn* sacrifice of DN, 1.91:3; cf. 1.148:1; *spr dbḥ ẓlm* book of instructions for the sacrifice of the spirits, 1.161:1; *dbḥ il bldn* sacrifice of the gods of the land, 1.162:1; *dbḥ mlkt* sacrifices of the queen, 4.149:14-15; *dm ṯn dbḥm šna bʕl* for DN hates two sacrifices, 1.4 III 17; *dbḥ bṯt w dbḥ dnt w dbḥ tdmm* the sacrifice of impudence and the sacrifice of lechery and the sacrifice of lasciviousness, 1.4 III 18-20; *šrd bʕl b dbḥk* honour DN with your sacrifice, 1.14 II 25 (// *mṣd*); *dbḥ kl yrḫ ndr dbḥ* monthly sacrifice, vow, sacrifice (in general), 1.127:1-3; *dbḥ kl kl ykly dbḥ k sprt* sacrifice of which everyone eats (/ that is completely consumed), sacrifice according to prescript, 1.127:7-9; *l k dbḥ* in sacrifice, 1.127:12; *u ṯḫṭin l dbḥm* or whether you have sinned in connection with the sacrifices, 1.40:23 and par. (// *ṯʕ*); *db*[*ḥ*] *l krt adnkm* a sacrifice / banquet PN, your lord, celebrates, 1.15 VI 5 and par.; *krtn dbḥ dbḥ* behold PN offers a sacrifice / gives a banquet, 1.16 I 40 (// *ʕšrt*); *hlkm b dbḥ nʕmt* coming with sacrifices of thanksgiving, 1.23:27; *b ym dbḥ ṯpḥ* on the day of the sacrifice of the stock, 1.48:13; *mitm yn ḥsp d nkly b dbḥ* two hundred (jars) of wine which have been consumed in the (royal) sacrifices, 4.213:24 (cf. 1.91:1-2; 4.149:14-15); *dbḥ DN* sacrifice of DN, 1.91:14; 1.116:1 (in Hurr. ctx.). In bkn ctx.: *dbḥ d* sacrifice of, RSOu 14 33 [KTU 9.422]:1.

2) Offering: *dbḥ šmn mr* an offering of myrhh-scented oil, 1.87:22 and par. (cf. Pun. *zbḥ šmn*, KAI 69:12; 74:9); *[rš]p ʕnt ḫbly dbḥm* DN (and) DN, two offerings, 1.39:17; *w dbḥ* and (as an) offering, 1.41:39 and par.
3) Month name: in bkn ctx.: *[y]rḫ dbḥ* the month of *d.* (sacrifice), 4.316:5 (cf. ln. 3: *[y]rḫ mgmr* and cf. Ph. *yrḥ zbḥ šmš*, Kition A 27:1; cf. DNWSI 470: *yrḥ*$_2$).
In bkn ctx.: *]ṯn dbḥm*, 1.75:11; *w dbḥ k*[, 1.87:43; *w l dbḥ*[, 1.127:24; *w dbḥ x*[, 1.136:4, 5; *in dbḥ*, 1.176:9; *]dbḥn*, 2.31:25.

dbḥt n. f. a type of sacrifice, sacrificial act (cf. *dbḥ*; cf. Arab. *ḏibḥat*, Lane 954; Eth. *zĕbḥat*, CDG 631. Cf. Del Olmo SEL 12 1995 39f.; Watson UF 31 1999 787; diff.: Dietrich - Loretz MU 12: pl. of *dbḥ*). ¶ Forms: sg. cstr. *dbḥt*.
A type of sacrifice, sacrificial act: *dbḥt PN d.* of PN, 1.142:1.

dbl, in unc. ctx.: *dbl ttnt yṯ*, 5.11:13 (?).

dblt n. f. "dried fig"; "fig cake" (Hb. *dblt*, HALOT 209; cf. Arab. *dublat*, Lane 850). ¶ Forms: sg. / pl. *dblt*.
Dried figs, ★a) *lth dblt lth ṣmqm* a *l.* of dried figs (and) a *l.* of raisins, 4.14:17; *mrbʕ qšḥm mrbʕ dblt mrbʕ ṣmqm* a quarter of cumin, a quarter of dried figs, a quarter of raisins, 4.751:10; use in pharmacy: *dblt yṯnt w ṣmqm yṯnm w qmḥ bql* rancid dried figs and rancid raisins and groat flour (should be mixed together), 1.71:27; 1.72:37; 1.85:31 (Cohen - Sivan UHT 40f.; Cohen UF 28 1996 149.); ★b) in fig cake: *arbʕ dblt* four fig cakes, 4.60:5, 9 (cf. Hb. and Arab., *supra*).

/d-b-r/ (I) vb G/D: "to guide, force to walk (Hb., Aram., Palm., JAram. *dbr*, HALOT 209f.; DNWSI 239; Jastrow 278; Arab. *dbr*, Lane 844f.; Wehr 312; cf. Badre etc. Syria 53 1976 125. There are quite a number of alternative interpretations, e.g. Dahood ULx 87: 'to follow'; De Moor ULe 91: 'to drive away'; Driver CML 154: 'to be carried off'; Gibson CML 144: 'to turn the back'; Margalit UF 8 1976 158: 'to speak' (cf. /d-b-r/ (II); Dietrich - Loretz UF 17 1985 126: 'ungerecht handeln'; Verreet UF 18 1985 371: 'fliehen'); ¶ par.: /ṯ-w-y/. ¶ Forms: G/D prefc. *tdbr*, *ydbr*.
G/D. To guide, force to walk: *k ġz ġzm tdbr* can you guide(?) warriors like a warrior?, 1.16 VI 43 and par. (// *ṯṯwy*; diff.: Renfroe UF 22 1990 282f.: 'to talk', cf. /d-b-r/ (II)): *k ġz ġzm tdbr // w ġrm ṯṯwy* 'when raiders raid, you talk // or invaders, you're idle'. On 1.82:8 cf. /d-b-r/ (II).

/d-b-r/ (II) vb D: "to say, declare" (Hb., Ph., Pun. *dbr*, HALOT 210f.; DNWSI 238f.; Ebla cf. INIM.DI = *ti-da-bir*$_5$*-lum*, VE 186; Krebernik

QuSe 18 123. Cf. Renfroe UF 22 1990 284). ¶ Forms: D prefc. *ydbr*, *tdbr*.

D. To say, declare: *ht at t*(!)*dbr* now you say, 2.71:14; *ky tdbr umy l pn qrt* so my mother has declared before the city, 2.72:18 (Pardee BiOr 34 1977 9; cf. Brooke UF 11 1979 70, 74); [*w*]*ydbr ṯrmt alm* and he declares: my victuals are two rams, 1.82:8.

Cf. dbr (I).

dbr (I) n. m. "matter, thing"(?) (< /d-b-r/ (II); Hb., Ph., Pun., Aram. *dbr*, HALOT 211f.; DNWSI 239f.; OSA *dbr*, CAME 125). ¶ Forms: pl. *dbrm*.

Matter, thing(?), in bkn. ctx.:]*xy kl dbrm hmt*] (...) all the matters (...), 2.32:8.

Cf. dbr (II).

dbr (II) n. m. "plague, pestilence" (Hb. *dbr*, HALOT 212; Ebla cf. ^{d}*da-bi-ir* DINGIR *eb-la*^{ki}, Mander MROA 2/1 47; Emar /dibīru/, Pentiuc Vocabulary 44. Diff.: 'further on', 'pasture', 'steppe', cf. Hb. *dbr*, Syr. *dabrō*, Van Zijl Baal 172f., 175 n. 3; De Moor SP 186; Astour Ug 6 14; Margalit MLD 123f.; Aartun UF 16 1984 11f.); ¶ par.: *šḥlmmt*. ¶ Forms: sg. *dbr*.

Plague, pestilence (in the poetic toponym 'Land of Pestilence', denoting the underworld): *mġny l nʕmy arṣ dbr* we reach the 'delight' (of) the 'Land of Pestilence', 1.5 VI 6 and par. (// *šḥlmmt*); *yuhb ʕglt b <arṣ> dbr* he loved a heifer in the <Land of> Pestilence, 1.5 V 18.

dbr (III) n. m. "chapel"(?) (cf. Hb. *dbyr*, HALOT 208; Pun. cf. DNWSI 240: *dbr*$_4$; Eth. cf. CDG 121: *dābe/ir*). ¶ Forms: sg. *dbrh* (+ adv -*h* (?)).

Chapel(?), in bkn ctx.:]*dbrh l špš*]in / to the chapel(?) for DN, 1.76:9f.

dby PN (etym. unc.).

PN: *bn PN*, 4.64 IV 10.

dd (I) adj./n. m. 1) "loved one"; 2) "love" (Hb., Aram. *dwd*, HALOT 215; DNWSI 243; Nab., Palm., *dd*, DNWSI 241; /dādum/, /dawdum/, etc., CAAA 17; Akk. *dādu*, AHw 149; CAD D 20; Mari-Akk. cf. Durand MARI 2 215ff.: 'oncle'; Eth. *dud*, CDG 123; Arab. *dādat*, Wehr 269; Ebla cf. /dūdu(m)/ in ŠÀ.KI.ÁG = *du-du*, *da-du-du*, VE 584; Krebernik QuSe 18 138; in PNN *du-du-*, Krebernik PET 82; Catagnoti MisEb 1 187 n. 10; Ebla cf. /dādu(m)/ in PAP.MU = *da-tum*, VE 1161; cf. Krebernik ZA 73 1983 22; cf. ŠÀ.ḪUL.GIG = *ba-rí-ù da-du*, VE 591; Fales QuSe 13 180; Catagnoti MisEb 1 187 n. 10; cf. in PNN *da-du*, *da-a-du*, *da-a-tum*, *da-tV*, Krebernik PET 82; Xella

WGE 354; Catagnoti MisEb 226ff.; Sanmartín AuOr 9 1991 185. Cf. Aartun StUL 39ff.: concrete 'reizende/liebliche Teile, d. h. Genitalien'); ¶ syll. Ug.: the element /dādu/ in PNN; Sivan GAGl 213; ¶ par.: *ahbt*, *yd*. ¶ Forms: sg. *dd*, suff. *ddh*.

1) Loved one: *šd ddh* the field of her loved one, 1.24:23.

2) Love: *t*(!)*šr dd DN (...) dd DN* who sings the love of DN (...) the love of DN, 1.3 III 5, 7 and par. (// *yd*, *ahbt*).

Cf. in bkn ctx.: *ybġ dd*, 1.172:20 (cf. Bordreuil - Caquot Syria 57 1980 345).

dd (II) n. m. 1) measure of capacity "cauldronful"; 2) container "cruet" (cf. Hb., Palm. *dwd*, HALOT 215; DNWSI 242; Aram. *dwdʔ*, Jastrow 283; Akk. *dūdu*, AHw 174; CAD D 170; cf. Hitt. *duddu-*, Van den Hout RlA 7 525; cf. Eg. *ddt*, WäS 5 501 [but see Muchiki Loanwords 281]. ¶ Forms: sg. *dd*, pl. *ddm* (spelling mistake *ddt* in 6.19:1; rdg *ddm*(!)); du. *ddm*.

1) Measure of capacity, 'cauldronful', ★a) *PN dd* PN: a 'cauldronful' (of grain), 4.55:4 and *passim ibid.*; *passim* in econ. txt.; *dd(m) l PN* one / two 'cauldronfuls' for PN, 4.175:3 and *passim ibid.*; *passim* in econ. txt.; *ḫmš ddm l PN* five 'cauldronfuls' for PN, RSOu 14 39 [KTU 4.790]: 18'-24, 26'; *ʕšr ddm l PN* ten 'cauldronfuls' for PN, *ibid.*, ln. 25'; *dd ilš* one 'cauldronful' (of grain) for DN, 1.41:6; 1.87:7 (cf. 2.); distributive use: *ṯṯm / ṯmnym dd dd kbd l mdrġlm* a total of sixty / eighty 'cauldronfuls', from 'cauldronful' to 'cauldronful' (i.e. by the cauldronful), for the watchmen, 4.387:9, 19; cf. 4.14:1, 7, 13; 1.41:6; 1.87:7, *supra*: 1; *(nn) dd(m) l alpm* nn 'cauldronfuls' for the head (of cattle), RSOu 14 42 [KTU 9.420]:9', 11' (cf. ln. 10', 12', 13'); ★b) for dry measure: *akl* grain, 4.284:4; *ddm akl* two 'cauldronfuls' of grain, 4.688:4; *drt* chaff, 4.243:10; *ḥṭm* wheat, 4.225:11; 4.269:32; 4.400:4, 9, 12, 17; 4.608:4; 6.61:2; *kśmn/m* spelt, 4.691:4; cf. *dd kśmm* one 'cauldronful' of spelt, 4.608 (II) 2; *nʕr* roasted flour(?), 4.402:1; 4.426:3; 4.788:4,7; *qmḥ* flour, 4.608:1; RSOu 14 40 [KTU 9.419]:3-12; cf. *lth ḫsr b šbʕ ddm* a missing *l.* in seven 'cauldronfuls', 4.361:3; *šʕrm* barley, *passim*; cf. 4.14:1, 7, 13; 4.608:3; 6.19:1 (rdg *dmm*(!)); 6.21:1; RSOu 14 39 [KTU 4.790]:3', 12', 14'; *ṯlṯ ddm šʕrm l ḥmrm dt tblm* three 'cauldronfuls' of barley for the donkeys of the smiths, 4.790:14; [*ʕ*]*šrm aḥd kbd dd* [*šʕ*]*rm l ḥmrm* twenty one 'cauldronfuls' of barley for the donkeys, RSOu 14 39 [KTU 4.790]:10'; *ḫmš ʕšr dd l śśw DN*, fifteen 'cauldronfuls' for the horses of DN, RSOu 14 39 [KTU 4.790]16' (cf. ln. 17'); unc. *dd gdl*

'cauldronful(s)' of *g.*, 4.14:1, 7, 13 (cf. *gdl*); cf. in bkn ctx. *dd gdl*, 4.426:4.

2) Cruet for oil: *dd šmn* a cruet for oil, 1.41:44; 1.87:48.

ddl PN (etym. unc.; cf. Grøndahl PTU 296, 424; Watson AuOr 13 1995 222); ¶ syll.: cf. *da-dì-lu*, RS 28.52:7 (cf. Van Soldt SAU 310 n. 117).

PN: 4.423:24.

ddm TN ((?); cf. Belmonte RGTC 12/2 63: *Didima*); ¶ syll.: cf. DINGIR.MEŠ *da-ad-me-ma*, Ug 5 170:3'; cf. Xella TRU 100; Del Olmo CR 137; Van Soldt UBL 11 373 n. 60.

TN(?): *il ddm š* the gods of TN(?), 1 ram, 1.148:43.

Cf. ddmy.

ddmš Hurro-Anat. DN (cf. Xella TRU 53; Nougayrol Ug 5 57ff.; 248f.; Laroche GLH 70); ¶ RS Akk.: ᵈ*Dá-ad-mi-iš*, Ug 5 18:27; cf. syll. Hurr. DINGIR.ŠU.ZI.AN.NA = *ta-at-mi-i*[*š*, Ug 5 137 IV b 18(?).

DN: in god lists: 1.47:28; 1.118:27 (cf. ᵈ*Dá-ad-mi-iš*, Ug 5 18:27); in cultic texts: 1.109:18; 1.120:3; 1.130:29; 1.148:8.

ddmy GN m. (localisation and identity unc.; cf. Xella TRU 1 265: Didima?; cf. De Moor - Sanders UF 23 1991 293; Belmonte RGTC 12/2 63: TN *Didima*). ¶ Forms: sg. *ddmy*.

GN: 1.40:20 and par.

Cf. ddm.

ddn (I) PN deified; var. of *dtn*; cf. *dt/dn (I)*.

ddn (II) PN; cf. *dt/dn (II)*.

ddy PN (Sem. Cf. Grøndahl PTU 424); ¶ syll.: cf. DUMU *da-de$_4$-ya* PRU 3 196 (RS 15.42+) II 17'; 199 (RS 16.257+) A I:9 (cf. Huehnergard UVST 213; Van Soldt SAU 10 n. 116); DUMU *du-da-a-ya*, 149 (RS 16.182+):6; *da-dá-a*, PRU 3 203 (RS 16.257+) IV 27; *ta-di-e*, RSOu 7 22:19.

PN: ★a) 4.16:3; 4.635:44 (*aḏddy*); ★b) *bn PN:* 4.659:4.

ddym n. m. *pl. tantum*, " harmony" (< "amours", abstr. pl. in /īy/ < *dd (I)*; cf. Brockelmann GvG 1 400. Cf. Nielsen RSM 76f.; Cassuto GA 125f.; Caquot - Sznycer TOu 1 164 n. f; Smith BC 202ff.; Fensham AION 15 1965 31ff.; diff.: Virolleaud DA 33: 'mandrakes', Hb. *dwdy / dwdʔym*, Eg. *ddyt*; cf. Van Zijl Baal 57f.; Sasson RSP 1 407; See Smith BC 202ff.); ¶ par.: *mlḥmt*. ¶ Forms: pl. t. *ddym*.

Harmony: *št b ʕprm ddym* place harmony in the steppes, 1.3 III 15 and par. (// *mlḥmt*).

ddy PN (Hurr.(?); cf. Grøndahl PTU 263; Laroche GLH 266f.; Watson AuOr 13 1995 222); ¶ syll.: cf. *ti-še-ia*, PRU 3 112 (RS 16.114):2'; *te-še-ia*, PRU 4 201 (RS 18.02):6. Cf. *ttyn*.
PN: 4.769:18 (*bn udr*).

dg n. m. "fish" (Hb., JAram. *dg*, HALOT 213; DNWSI 240); ¶ par.: *ʕṣr*. ¶ Forms: sg. *dg*; pl. *dgm*.
Fish: *ʕṣr šmm w dg b ym* the birds (collect.) of the sky and the fish of the sea, 1.23:63; *w kl šbšlt dg* and all types of fish stews, 1.106:22; *l dg w l kl*[*l*] no fish, none at all, 1.124:15 (cf. Del Olmo CR 314 n. 70); *ḫlu dg* (the sacrifice of) the fish-cake, 1.91:12 (cf. Del Olmo CR 262). In bkn ctx. *mnu dg* portions(?) of fish, 1.92:38 (cf. Dijkstra UF 26 1994 118). Cf. *dgm*, 5.23:14.
Cf. dgy.

/d-g-l/
Cf. mdgl, mgdl.

dgn (I) n. m. "grain, wheat" (cf. Hb., Ph., Aram. *dgn*, HALOT 214; DNWSI 241; cf. Arab. *dağana*, Lane 853f.; Eth. *degana*, CDG 126; cf. Emar /dagna/ātu/, Pentiuc Vocabulary 43). ¶ Forms: sg. *dgn*.
Grain: *ʕdb dgn* those who grow grain, 1.16 III 13 (cf. *lḥm*, *ibid.* ln. 14).

dgn (II) DN (etym. unc.; cf. Hb. *dgwn*, HALOT 213; Ph. cf. *ʔrṣt dgn*, KAI 14:19, cf. DNWSI 112: *ʔrṣ*$_1$ 3; Amor. /dagān/, Huffmon APNMT 180f.; Gelb CAAA 17; Ebla cf. $^{(d)}$*da-gan(/-ga-an)*, Krebernik PET 80; cf. ^{d}BE(BAD), Pettinato - Waetzoldt Or 54 1985 234ff.; Von Soden EDA 83; Lambert MARI 4 1985 529; Sanmartín AuOr 9 1991 185f.; OAkk. *(-)*$^{(d)}$*da-(ga-) an/gan(-)*, Roberts ESP 18f.; EA cf. the element $^{(d)}$*da-ga-an(-)* in PNN, Hess AmPN 237; Emar Akk. cf. spellings *(-)*$^{(d)}$*da-gan(-)* / ^{d}KUR; Arnaud RA 68 1974 190; Wilcke AuOr 10 1992 119 n. 24. Cf. Edzard WbMyth 1 49f.; Pope WbMyth 1 276ff.; Ringgren TWAT 2 148ff.; Von Soden RGG 2 18f.; Healey JNSL 5 1977 43ff.; Wyatt UF 12 1980 375ff.; Cooper - Pope RSP 3 361ff.; Pardee AfO 36/37 1989/90 446ff.; Renfroe AULS 91ff.); ¶ RS Akk.: ^{d}*da-gan*, Ug 5 18:3 (// *dgn*, 1.47:4; 1.118:3); 5 170:17'; Huehnergard UVST 118; cf. Sivan GAGl 213; ¶ par.: *bʕl (II)* 3.
DN, ★a) connected with Baal: *šlm (...) dgn w bʕl* hail (...) DN and DN! 1.123:4; *bʕl w dgn yisp ḥmt* may DN and DN remove the venom, 1.107:39; *bn dgn* son of DN, 1.2 I 35 and *passim* as an attribute of // *bʕl*; *ḥtk dgn* progeny of DN, 1.10 III 34 (// *bʕl*); in god lists: *dgn*, 1.47:4; 1.118:3 (between *il* and *bʕl ṣpn*); ★b) Dagan of Tuttul: *dgn ttl* the DN of TN, 1.24:14; take (this) request *ʕm dgn ttlh*

to DN in TN, 1.100:15; ★c) cultic references: *skn d šʕlyt ṯril l dgn pgr* stele which PN offered to DN: funerary sacrifice *p.*, 6.13:2; *pgr d šʕly ʕzn l dgn bʕlh* funerary sacrifice *p.* which PN offered to DN, his lord, 6.14:2 (cf. Dijkstra - De Moor UF 7 1975 175; Dietrich - Loretz - Mayer UF 21 1989 135; Bordreuil - Pardee Semitica 41/42 1993 24ff.); *passim* in lists of sacrifices, cf. 1.46:3; 1.109:21; 1.148:2, 10, 26; 1.162:9; 1.173:4; *passim*; *ṯr dgn* the bull of DN, 1.127:22.
Cf. in bkn ctx. *ṯlṯ šxn l dgn*, 1.48:5;]*š dgn*, 1.160:2; *dgn bʕl*[, 1.166:9;]*dgn*, 7.168:4.

dgt (?), 1.19 III 41, see *mdgt*.

dgy n. m.; name of a fish-shaped being, "triton" (< *dg (I)*. Diff.: Yamashita RSP 2 47f.: 'fisherman', 'a soldier'). ¶ Forms: du. cstr. *dgy*.
Fish-shaped being, "triton", title of the divine pair *qdš w amrr*. *dgy aṯrt* tritons of DN, 1.3 VI 10 and par.

dġ n. m. "residue = refuse of grapes/olives after pressing" (< Sum.-Akk. duḫ / *tuḫḫu*, AHw 1366; Stol BiOr 28 1971 170f.); ¶ RS Akk.: DUḪ = *tu-uḫ-ḫu* = *šu-ḫu-li* = *šu-ḫu-ut-t*[, Ug 5 137 III 3 (and cf. *ṯʕt*). ¶ Forms: pl. *dġm*.
Residue (of sesame or olives): *kdm dġm* two jars of marc, 4.284:7 (cf. Sum.-Akk. *supra*, and *šmm*, *ztm*, ln. 6, 8; diff.: Aartun StUL 43: 'Molke', Arab. *dūġ*, *dawġ*). In bkn ctx.: 7.99:3 (?).
Cf. ṯʕt.

dġṯ n. m. "offering of perfumes"(?) (cf. Hitt. *tuḫḫui-* / *tuḫḫuwai*; Tischler HEG 417ff.; for discussion cf. Hoffner JNES 23 1964 66ff.; De Moor JNES 24 1965 355; UF 2 1970 200; Dijkstra - De Moor UF 7 1975 210; Kümmel StBoT 3 1967 23 n. 72; Dietrich - Loretz UF 10 1978 1978 69f.; Alp Or 52 1983 14ff.; Margalit UF 16 1984 164ff.; Foley UF 19 1987 72; Del Olmo AuOr 16 1998 129ff.). ¶ Forms: sg. *dġṯ*; suff. *dġṯh*.
Offering of perfumes(?): *yšʕly dġṯh b šmym dġṯ hrnmy b kbkbm* he made his offering of perfumes(?) go up to the heavens, an offering of perfumes worthy of a GN to the stars, 1.19 IV 23-24 and par. (for the rdg cf. Dietrich - Loretz UF 10 1978 1978 69f.).
Cf. dġṯt.

dġṯt n. f. "offering of perfumes" (cf. *dġṯ*; fem. var. or abstr. of *dġṯ*; cf. Del Olmo MLC 538). ¶ Forms: sg./pl. *dġṯt*.
Offering of perfumes: in bkn ctx. *w ʕl agn šbʕdm dġṯt* [*dġ*]*ṯt* and seven times over the cauldron offerings of perfumes (should burn) two by two (?), 1.23:15.

/d-ḫ-l/ vb G: "to fear" (Hb., OAram., Aram., Palm. *zḥl*, HALOT 267f.; DNWSI 309f.; Syr. *dḥel*, LS 148f.; cf. Cunchillos TOu 2 324 n. 18; Ebla cf. ŠU.DU$_7$ = *da-ḫa-lu*, VE 522; cf. Vattioni Biling. 265). ¶ Forms: G prefc. *tdḥl*.
G. To fear: *w al tdḥln* and do not fear, 2.16:12 (diff.: Aartun UF 17 1985 26: rdg *trḥln*; Pardee AfO 31 1984 220: rdg. *twḥln*); cf. 2.30:21 (diff.: Pardee AfO 31 1984 225f., rdg *tdḥṣ*, 'do not be agitated', but cf. Renfroe AULS 94f.).

/d-k(-k)/ vb G: "to pound, grind, pulverize" (Hb. *dwk*, *dkk/h*, HALOT 216, 221; Akk. *dāku*, *dukk/qquk/qu*, AHw 151f., 162; CAD D 34ff., 190; Arab. *dakka*, *dāka*, Lane 898f., 933f. Cf. Fronzaroli AGI 60 1975 39f., 45; Cohen - Sivan UHT 13f.; Pardee TH 48f.). ¶ Forms: G prefc. *ydk*, suff. *tdkn*.
G. To pound, grind, pulverize: *št ʕqrbn ydk w ymss̀* a *š.* of *ʕq.* shall be pulverized and dissolved / pulverize and dissolve, 1.85:3; *ydk aḥdh w yṣq* grind together and pour /shall be ground together and poured, 1.85:6 and par.; *tdkn aḥdh* grind together / shall be ground together and poured, 1.72:39. In bkn ctx. *dk k kbkb*[*m*, 1.5 III 8. For the rdg *d k ym* in 1.6 V 3 cf. Del Olmo IMC 79ff. (diff. Dijkstra JNES 6 1974 64ff.: rdg *dk ym* 'crushers of Yammu'; Caquot - Sznycer TOu 1 265 n. c: 'fracas de la mer'; Watson, *apud* Wyatt RTU 140 n. 103: 'those mobilised', Akk *dekû*).

dkr n. m. "male animal" (Hb. *zkr*, HALOT 270f.; Aram. *d/zkr*, DNWSI 329f.; Nab., Palm. *dkr*, DNWSI 329f.; Ebla cf. NITA(.DIŠ *tenû* ("RUM")) = *ša-ḫa-lum* (/d̠ak̠arum/), VE 1112a, b; Krebernik ZA 73 1983 39; Sanmartín AuOr 9 1991 187; Ass. *zakkāru*, AHw 1505; Parpola WGE 296; Akk. *zakru*, *zikaru* AHw 1526; CAD Z 23, 110ff.; OSA *d̠kr*, DOSA 95; Arab. *d̠akar*, Lane 969f.); ¶ syll. Ug.: NÍTA = *zi-ka-rù* = *tu-ru-ḫi* = *da-ka-rù*, Ug 5 137 III 5; Sivan GAGl 214; Huehnergard UVST 118; Van Soldt SAU 303. ¶ Forms: sg. *dkr*, du. *dkrm*.
Male animal, ★a) unspecified: (as an offering) *dkrm* a pair of male animals, 1.43:19; [*d*]*kr DN nšqdš* a male animal, DN, (to you) we shall consecrate, 1.119:31; ★b) *alp dkr* male bovine (calf), 1.86:2. For the rdg *dk*(!)*r*(!) *š* in 1.43:6 cf. Dietrich - Loretz JA 52: 'ein männliches Jungtier von ein(em)[*sic*!] Schaf'; cf. *drk*.

dkrt n. f. "bowl", as a deity (Arab. *zukrat*, Lane 1239; cf. Akk. *diqāru*, AHw 172f.; CAD D 157ff.; Ph. cf. DNWSI 258: *dqrh*); ¶ syll. Ug.: cf. [KAM = *diqāru* = Hurr.: ? =] *di*-[Q]A-*ru*, UF 11 1979 79:27;

Huehnergard UVST 118; Van Soldt SAU 303; ¶ par.: *rḥbt.* ¶ Forms: pl. *dkrt.*

Bowl: *špq ilht dkrt* he supplied the bowl-goddesses (with wine), 1.4 VI 54 (// *rḥbt*).

dl adj. m. "poor" (Hb. *dl*, HALOT 221f.; Pun. *dl*, DNWSI 248; Akk. *dallu* AHw 154; CAD D 52; Arab. *ḏull*, *ḏalīl*, Lane 973); ¶ syll. Ug.: [SIG = *enšu* = *z*]*i/*[*m*]*u-na-ar-ḫi* = *da-al-lu*, Ug 5 137 II 14'; cf. Huehnergard UVST 118; Van Soldt SAU 303 and cf. Ug 5 137 II 13'; ¶ par.: *qṣr npš.* ¶ Forms: sg. *dl*; f. *dlt* (cf. *dlt (II)*).

Poor (adj. used as a noun): *l tdy* [[ṯ]]*qšm ʕl dl* you have not expelled the oppressors of the poor, 1.16 VI 48 (// *qṣr npš*).

Cf. dlt (II).

dlḫt adj. f. "thick, cloudy" (< **dlḫ*; Akk. *dalḫu*, AHw 154; CAD D 49; cf. Hb., Aram. *dlḥ*, HALOT 222; DNWSI 249; Akk. *dalāḫu*, AHw 132f.; CAD D 43ff. Cf. Sanmartín AuOr 6 1988 232; diff. Cohen - Sivan UHT 15f.: '*dalīqātu*-groats'; Pardee TH 49f.: 'jus nature', rdg *d lḥt*). ¶ Forms: sg. *dlḫt.*

Thick, cloudy (of mixtures, etc.): *št ʕqrbn ydk w ymsś*{.}*hm b mskt dlḫt hm b mndġ* he shall pulverize a *š.* of *ʕq.* (plants) and shall dilute it, either in a thick emulsion or in (flour of type) *m.*, 1.85:3.

/d-l-l/ vb D: "to oppress, subdue, subjugate" (Hb. *dll*, HALOT 223; Akk. *dalālu* D, AHw 153; CAD D 178; Arab. *ḏalla*, Lane 972ff. Cf. Dietrich - Loretz - Sanmartín UF 7 1975 113; Pardee Fs. Fitzmyer 82f.); ¶ par.: /ḫ-b-t/. ¶ Forms: D prefc. *tdlln*, *yd*{*d*}*ll.*; ptc. act. pl. suff. *mdllkm/n.*

D. To oppress, subdue, subjugate: *u šn ypkn (...) u l p mdllkm/n* or whether your (m./f.) dignity has been sullied (...) according to the custom of your oppressors, 1.40:30 and par. (// *ḫbtkm*); *mrḥy mlk tdlln* the spears of the king will subdue it, 1.103+:7; *mlkn yd ḫrdh yd*{*d*}*ll* (as for) the king, the hand of his guard will subjugate (him), 1.103+:46 (for other options cf. Dietrich - Loretz MU 141f.; cf. Tropper UF 26 1994 464f.: 'schwach sein', G); *ptm ydll* PN oppresses(?), 5.11:22.

Cf. dl, dlt (II), dlt (III).

dll (I) n. m. "courier, messenger, mediator" (Arab. *dalīl*, *dallāl*, Lane 901f.; cf. Akk. *dayyālu*, AHw 150; CAD D 27f. Cf. Driver CML 154; De Moor SP 168; diff.: Margalit MLD, 'tribute, homage', Akk. *dalālu*, *dalīlu*); ¶ syll. Ug.: element /dalīl/ in PNN; ¶ par.: *ʕdd (I).* ¶ Forms: sg. *dll.*

Courier, messenger, mediator: *dll al ilak* I shall send a courier, 1.4 VII 45 (// *ʕdd*).
Cf. dll (II).

dll (II) PN (Sem. Cf. Grøndahl PTU 65, 124); ¶ syll.: *da-li-li*, PRU 3 pg. 258; PRU 6 pg. 143; *dá-li-li*, PRU 3 153 (RS 16.205+):7; cf. Berger WO 5 1969/70 272; Huehnergard UVST 212; Van Soldt SAU 309.
PN: ★a) 4.617:37; ★b) *bn PN:* 4.63 III 28; 4.232:31; 4.374:13.

dlm "?"; in bkn ctx.: *bd r*[*x*]*m dlm*, 4.618:9.
Cf. dl.

/d-l-p/ vb G: "to soften, be consumed, break up" (Hb. cf. *dlp*, HALOT 223: *dlp I*; Akk. cf. *dalāpu*, AHw 153; CAD D 47ff.; Arab. *dalafa*, Lane 904f. Cf. Driver AO 17 1949 55f.; Van der Westhuizen UF 17 1985 357ff.; Aartun StUL 45ff.; Smith BC 350 and n. 229); ¶ syll. Ug.: cf. the element /dalpu/, Sivan GAGI 214; ¶ par.: /m-k(-k)/, /n-ġ-ṣ/. ¶ Forms: G prefc. *ydlp*.
G. To soften, break up: *l ydlp tmnh* his form did not break up, 1.2 IV 17 and par. (// *mk*, *ngṣ*).

dlt (I) n. m. "door" (Hb., Ph., Pun., JAram. *dlt*, HALOT 223f.; DNWSI 250; Akk. *daltu*, AHw 154; CAD D 52ff.; for Aram. *dš* cf. Kaufman AIA 45). ¶ Forms: sg. *dlt*.
Door: bkn ctx. *dlt tḥtn (...) dlt*, lower door (?) (...), door, 4.351:3, 4; *dlt bt* door of the palace, 6.66:10. Cf. in unc. ctx. *dlt*, 5.7:5 (> "solution"(?); (?)// *mʕn)*.

dlt (II) adj. f. "poor"(?) (< *dl*). ¶ Forms: sg. *dlt*.
Poor (?): in bkn and unc. ctx. *ytmt dlt tlk* the poor orphan went / will go, 1.82:22 (adj. used as a noun); *km dlt tlk* like a poor woman you shall walk / she went / will go, 1.82:24 (diff. De Moor - Spronk UF 16 1984 245: 'door').
Cf. dl.

dlt (III) n. f. "weakness, poverty" (cf. *dl*; diff.: Gibson CML 144: 'to guide', Arab. *dalla*; cf. Lipiński OLP 3 1972 117 n. 99; De Moor NYCI 2 20 n. 86; ARTU 122: 'tendril' / 'door', Hb. *dlyt/dlt*). ¶ Forms: sg. *dlt*.
Weakness, poverty: *špš mṣprt dlthm* may DN take care of their weakness, 1.23:25.

dly PN (etym. unc.; cf. Grøndahl PTU 65, 124); ¶ syll.: cf. TA-*la-ya*, PRU 3 61 (RS 16.156):8, 17; cf. Berger WO 5 1969/70 273; cf. Huehnergard UVST 214.

PN: ★a) 4.75 V 15 (*bn* []); ★b) *bn PN:* 4.389:11; 4.724:2. Cf.]*dly*, 4.396:9.

/d-m/ vb G: "to remain still" (Hb. *dwm*, *dmm*, HALOT 216, 226: *dmm I*; cf. Arab. *dāma*, Lane 935ff. Cf. Rainey RSP 2 227f.); ¶ syll. Ug.: cf. the element /dūmatu/ in TNN; Sivan GAGl 215. ¶ Forms: G impv. *dm*.

G. To remain still: *dm ym w ṯn* remain still one day and another, 1.14 III 10 and par.

dm (I) functor 1) illative "since" and 2) asseverative "so, then, for certain" (Syr. *dam*, LS 155f.; (?)< *d* + encl. *-m* ; cf. De Moor SP 107; Aartun PU 1 58). ¶ Forms: *dm*.

1) Since: *dm rgm iṯ ly w argmk* since I have a matter that I am going to tell you, 1.3 III 20 and par.; *dm l ġzr šrgk ḫḫm* for to a hero your tangle(s) (is)are a quagmire, 1.17 VI 34; *dm aḫtk ydʕt k rḥmt* since I know that your sister is compassionate, 1.16 I 32.

2) So then, for certain: *dm ṯn dbḥm šna DN* so then two sacrifices DN loathes, 1.4 III 17; *mt dm ḫt šʕqt dm lat*(!) for certain DN was defeated, for certain DN overcame 1.16 VI 13-14 and par. Cf. in unc. ctx.: *dm mt asḥ*[, 1.5 III 9 and par.

Bkn.: *dm k*[, 2.8:2; *dm ṯnid*, 2.50:18; 2.78:6.

dm (II) n. m. 1) "blood"; 2) "juice"; 3) "gush, bath" (Hb., Aram. *dm*, HALOT 224f.; DNWSI 251; Akk. *dāmu*, AHw 158; CAD D 75ff.; Arab. *dam*, Lane 917; Eth. *dam*. CDG 133; Ebla cf. DN *da-mu*, Krebernik PET 80; LAK 672 = *da-mu*, VE 970; Civil Biling. 96; diff. Lipiński EDA 93: OSA *dʕm* "soutenir"); ¶ syll. Ug.: cf. *da-mu* in Ug 5 153 rev. 1' and cf. Huehnergard UVST 119; Van Soldt BiOr 47 1990 734: Akkadian; ¶ RS Akk.: cf. $UŠ_2$.MEŠ : *da-mi*, PRU 4 146 (RS 17.318+) 23'; UŠ = *da-m*[*u*, Ug 5 137 I 24"; cf. 133 rev. 12'; cf. Izre'el AmAkk 1 31; ¶ par.: *mmʕ*, *šir*, *yn*. ¶ Forms: sg. *dm*; suff. *dmh*; pl. *dmm*.

1) Blood: *dm ḏmr* blood of the warriors, 1.3 II 31 and par. (// *mmʕ*); *k lbš km lpš dm aḫh // km all dm aryh* he wore like a garment the blood of his brothers // like a cloak the blood of his kin, 1.12 II 46-47; *tšt dmh l bl ks* it drinks its blood without a cup, 1.96:4 (// *šir*); *špk km šiy dm* spill his blood like an assassin, 1.18 IV 24 and par.; I shall make *šbth dmm* his greybeard run with blood, 1.3 V 2 and par. (// *mmʕ*).

2) Juice: *dm ʕṣm* juice of vines, 1.4 IV 38 and par. (// *yn*); *dm zt ḫrpnt* juice of an autumnal (> early(?)) olive, 1.114:31 (cf. *ḫrpnt*); cf.

zt dm(!) olive of juice (> juicy), 1.24:43 (Del Olmo IMC 148; for a different interpretation cf. De Moor ARTU 145).
3) Gush, bath (said of metals): *dm ḫrṣ* gush of gold, 1.4 I 32 (diff. Gaster BASOR 93 1944 20ff.; Sanmartín UF 12 1980 336: 'Anstrich, Lack', Arab. *damma*).
Bkn.: *tzd ʕrq dm*, 1.107:46 (cf. Pardee TPM 242, 253f.: 'elle / tu ne fera(s) pas croître le suintement de sang'; cf. /z-d/); *dm lšn x*[, 1.176:4; in bkn and unc. ctx., 1.24:9 (cf. De Moor ARTU 143: conj. 'for').

/d-m-ʕ/ vb G: "to shed tears, weep, sob" (Hb. *dmʕ*, HALOT 227; Arab. *damaʕa*, Lane 913f.); ¶ par.: *bky*. ¶ Forms: G prefc. *ydmʕ*, *tdmʕ*; inf. *dmʕ*; suff. *dmʕh*.
G. To shed tears, weep, sob: *ydmʕ nʕmn* (that) the handsome one sheds tears, 1.14 I 40 (// *ybky*); (enough) *b dmʕ nʕmn* of the handsome one shedding tears, 1.14 II 8 (// *bk*); *ybky (...) w ydmʕ* he wept (...) and shed tears, 1.14 I 27; *tdmʕ bm kbd* she shed tears within herself, 1.19 I 35 (// *tbky*); *ydmʕ kdd PN* they shed tears for the son of PN, 1.19 IV 12 and par. (// *ybk*); *tdmʕ km ṡġr* you weep like a baby, 1.107:11 and par. (// *tpky*); *ydmʕ hdm pʕnh* may the footstool of his feet shed tears, 1.161:14 (// *ybky*); *b dmʕh nhmmt* in his sobbing he fainted, 1.14 I 32 (// *bky*).
Cf. dmʕt.

dmʕt n. f. "tear" (< /d-m-ʕ/; cf. Hb. *dmʕh*, HALOT 227; Ebla /ʔid(i)maʕātum/ in ÉR.ÉR = *i-ti-ma-a-tum*, VE 716; Krebernik ZA 73 1983 27; Krecher Biling. 148; Akk. *dimtu*, AHw 171; CAD D 147f.; Arab. *damʕat*, Lane 913). ¶ Forms: sg. *dmʕt*; pl. *udmʕt*, suff. *udmʕth*.
Tear: *w l ytk dmʕt km rbʕt ṯqlm* and truly tear(s) fell like quarter shekels, 1.19 II 33; *tntkn udmʕth km ṯqlm arṣh* his tears ran like shekels to the earth, 1.14 I 28; *tšt k yn udmʕt* like wine she drank tears, 1.6 I 10; do not exhaust (...) *mḫ rišk udmʕt* the grey matter of your head in tears, 1.16 I 28; *yblʕ udmʕth* may it swallow its (own) tears, 1.161:16; in bkn ctx. *udmʕt*, tears, 1.45:11.

dmgy DN; slave of *aṯrt* (etym. unc.; cf. Grøndahl PTU 124; Gaster Thespis[1] 450; Du Mesnil Berytus 26 1978 59; Gray JNES 10 1951 149; UF 3 1971 61 n. 3; Wyatt UF 8 1976 417).
DN: *dmgy amt aṯrt* DN, the slave of DN, 1.12 I 16.

dml DN (< Sum. DN da-ma-al(?), Deimel PantBab 686; cf. Virolleaud PRU 2 p. 14; Nougayrol Ug. 5 58; Xella TRU 124).
DN: (offerings(?)) *l dml*, 1.81:20; *bt dml* temple of DN, 2.26:6. Cf. in bkn ctx. *(...) l dml*[, 4.182:34 (cultic ctx.).

Cf. dmlt, dmrn.

dmlt DN (f. of *dml*).
DN: Offerings for]*dmlt šlmm*]DN as a peace offering, 1.170:4.

/d-m-m/ (I) vb G: "to wail, moan, lament" (Hb. *dmm*, HALOT 226: *dmm II*; Akk. *damāmu*, AHw 155; CAD D 59ff. Cf. Van der Westhuizen UF 17 1985 365ff., 370); ¶ par.: /b-k-y/. ¶ Forms: G prefc. *tdm*.
G. To wail: *al tdm ly* do not wail for me, 1.16 I 26 and par.

***/d-m-m/ (II)**, cf. *tdmm*, *tdmmt* (See Wyatt RTU 46 n. 113).

dmqt DN; one of the *kṯrt* -goddesses (cf. Akk. *damiqtu*, AHw 157; CAD D 68ff. Cf. Herrmann YN 25; De Moor UF 2 1970 200; Van Lerberghe, Fs. Kraus 253; diff.: Watson Or 45 1976 439, 'skilled', Akk. *damqu*; cf. Xella UF 15 1983 281ff.: Ebla *da-mi-gu*).
DN: *dmqt ṣġrt kṯrt* DN, the youngest of the DNN, 1.24:50.

dmr, in KTU *ddm l ybr*[*k*] {*b dmr*} *prs l uxmxx*, 4.377:32 (corrupt text), cf. Sanmartín UF 20 1988 274: rdg *bd mr<ynm>* (see under *prś/s*).

dmrn DN, title of Baal ('the Powerful One, Valiant One'(?); cf. Pope WbMyth 255f.; UF 22 1990 500f.: Sem. */ḏ-m-r/ 'strong, brave'; cf. Gk *dēmaroûs*, CPHPB 44; Dossin Fs. Abel 3 59ff.; Cassuto Anath 59f.; Pope UF 3 1971 375f.; Wyatt UF 24 1992 410ff.); ¶ par.: *hd(d)*.
The 'Powerful One, Valiant One'(?): *nṯq dmrn* darts(?) of the 'Powerful One'(?), 1.4 VII 39 (// *hd*{*t*}); *yrṯy* [*n*]*ʕmh dmrn* the 'Powerful One'(?) wanted to possess(?) her beauty, 1.92:30 (cf. Dijkstra UF 26 1994 117, 121). Cf. 1.81:23.
Cf. dml.

dmt (I) n. f. "tower" (Akk. *dimtu*, AHw 170f.; CAD D 144ff.); ¶ RS Akk.: cf. (É.) AN.ZA.GÀR(.KI), *passim*; cf. Dosch Arrapḫe 17 and *passim*; Müller Siedlungsgeographie 163ff.; cf. *dimtu* in PRU 3 pp. 217f.; PRU 6 p. 158 (cf.: *gt*). ¶ Forms: sg. *dmt*.
Tower: *ḥln d b dmt um il*[*m* the window which is in the tower of the mother of(?) the god[s(?), 2.31:46.
Cf. dmt (II), dmtn, dmtqdš, dmty, gt.

dmt (II) TN (Belmonte RGTC 12/2 65f.: *Dumātu*. Cf. Heltzer RCAU 10; Astour RSP 2 277f., 346f.; UF 13 1981 9, 11; Bordreuil UF 20 1988 13, 15; Van Soldt UF 28 1996 666; UF 29 1997 702); ¶ syll.: URU *du-ma-tu*, PRU 6 p. 146; cf. GN *du-mati*(KUR)*-yu*, PRU 6 73:19; 132:5; *du-mati*(KUR)*-yu*((!)KI), PRU 6 73:19 (cf. Van Soldt SAU 336 n. 166).

TN: 4.49:6; 4.68:13; 4.113:1; 4.244:15; 4.308:14; 4.610 (II) 41; 4.686:12 (cf. Xella MLE 1 1982 54); 4.762:9; RSOu 14 35 II 9.
Cf. dmt (I).

dmtn PN (cf. *dmt (II)*, TN; Sem. Cf. Grøndahl PTU 26, 124; Astour RSP 2 277).
PN: *bn PN*, 4.50:11.

dmtqdš NT ('Tower > Royal Farm (cf. *gt*, (É.)AN.ZA.GÀR(.KI)) of the Sanctuary' (Belmonte RGTC 12/2 65: *Dumat-qidši*; see Van Soldt UF 28 1996 666; UF 29 1997 699; cf. also Heltzer RCAU 10; Astour RSP 2 278f., 346; UF 11 1979 17, 19); ¶ syll.: URU *du-ma-at/te qi-id-ši*, PRU 4 72 (RS 17.335+):21; PRU 6 78:6.
TN: *dmtqdš*, 4.643:4-7; 4.652:3.
Cf. dmt (I), qdš (II).

dmty PN (cf. *dmt (II)*, TN; Sem. Cf. Grøndahl PTU 26, 124; Astour RSP 2 277).
PN: 4.81:3.

dmyn PN (etym unc.; cf. */d-m/*, *dm (II)*).
PN: 7.61:15.
Cf. tmyn.

/d-n/ vb G: 1) "to judge"; 2) "to decree, proclaim, promulgate with authority" (Hb., BAram. *dyn*, HALOT 220; BDB 1088; Akk. *diānu*, *dânu*, AHw 167f.; CAD D 100ff.; Eth. *dayyana*, CDG 146; Watson UF 31 1999 787; UF 32 2000 568; cf. Arab. *dāna* (*dyn*), Lane 942ff.; Ebla cf. the element /D-N/ in PNN, Krebernik PET 42f. (80 > /d-n-n/)); ¶ par.: /ṯ-p-ṭ/. ¶ Forms: G prefc. *ydn*, *tdn*.
G.1) To judge: *l tdn dn almnt* you have not judged the case of the widow, 1.16 VI 33 and par.; cf. 1.17 V 7 and par. (// *ṯpṭ*).
2) To decree, declare (legitimate), promulgate with authority: *tdn mḥllm* the desacralizers shall proclaim (the sacred formula), 1.119:22 (Del Olmo RC 302 n. 30 ; diff.: Xella TRU 32: 'giungere', /d-n-y/); *ḥdṯh tdn hmt* on the day of the new moon they shall declare them (legitimate), 1.104:19 (or /d-n-y/?); in bkn ctx. 1.126:23 (cf. /d-n-y/).
Cf. bʕldn, bddn, dnil, dn (I), dnt (III), dnty, mdnt.

dn (I) n. m. "judgment, case, sentence" (< /d-n/; Hb., Aram. *dyn*, HALOT 210; DNWSI 254; Ebla /daynim/ in DI.KU$_5$ = *ba-ga-du da-ne-u*[*m*?], VE 1327; Krebernik ZA 73 1983 43; Fronzaroli EL 137; Akk. *dīnu*, AHw 171f.; CAD D 150ff.; Eth. *dayn*, CDG 146; cf. Arab. *dīn*, Lane 944); ¶ syll. Ug.: element /dīnu/ in PNN; Sivan GAGl 214; ¶ RS Akk.: *di-n*V, *passim*; DI(.MEŠ-*ti*), *passsim*; cf. Huehnergard AkkUg 401; ¶ par.: *ṯpṭ (II)*. ¶ Forms: sg. cstr. *dn*.

Judgment, case, sentence: *dn almnt* the widow's case, 1.16 VI 33 and par. (// *ṯpṭ*); *štk mlk dn* the king has ceased judgment, 1.12 II 58 (or inf. /d-n/?; diff. Dietrich - Loretz Studien 95: 'o mächtiger König'). Cf. Hurro.-Ug. *il.dn*, 1.128:26. In bkn ctx. 1.123:15 ((?)// *ṣdq mšr*); *b dnh lqḥt* because of his sentence I have detained (him), 2.62:8; cf. *lqḥ (...) b dnh*, 2.45:16.

dn (II) n. m. "vessel, vat" (Akk. *dannu*, AHw 161; CAD D 98; Arab. *dann*, Lane 918; for Aram. *dnʔ* cf. Kaufman AIA 46. Cf. Kapelrud Ug 6 328 n. 34, 331); ¶ par.: *bk*. ¶ Forms: sg. *dn*; suff. pl. *dnhm*.
Vessel, vat: *dn mt šmm* a vessel for people of heaven, 1.3 I 12 (// *bk*; diff.: KTU: rdg *ridn*, cf. Dietrich - Loretz UF 19 1987 27ff.); *rb tmtt lqḥ kl ḏrʕ b dnhm* the captain of the (salvage) crew has collected all the seed-grain from their containers(?), 2.38:18. (diff. Parker SGUPT 64: 'danger' Akk. *dannatu*).

dn (III) n. m. "strength, potency" (< /d-n-n/; cf. Akk. *dunnu*, Ahw 177; CAD D 184; Ebla cf. /dannum/ in DI.MA = *da-nu-um*, *da-núm*, VE 825; Fronzaroli EL 139; StEb 7 1984 160; cf. *da-na*, *du*-LUM*(núm?)*, Krebernik PET 80, 82). ¶ Forms: sg. suff. *dnn*.
Strength, potency: *bt ḥmḥ<mt>h dnn* the daughter whose conception (proves) our potency, 1.16 I 30 (diff.: De Moor ARTU 213: adj. 'strongest').
Cf. bʕldn, bddn, dnil, dnn, dnt (II), dnty.

dnil PN of an ancestral hero, the father of *aqht* (etym. unc., probl. hybrid of /d-n/ and */d-n-n/; cf. /d-n/, 1.17 V 4-8 and cf. the element /dānu-/ in PNN, Grøndahl PTU 123; Sivan GAGl 214; Akk. /d-n-n/ > cf. *dnn* and cf. Akk. PNN /dannʔilī/, Gelb MAD 3 113; Ebla cf. the element *da-na(-)* and PNN *da-na-il*, *da-na*-NI, *da*-NE-*lu*, *da*-NI-*lum*, Krebernik PET 80ff. (<(?) /d-n-n-/); Amor. Ur III *dan*-DINGIR /dannʔil-/, Gelb CAAA 294; cf. Buccellati Amorites 140; cf. Hb. *dnyʔl*, *dnʔl*, HALOT 228; Day VT 30 1980 174ff.; Zadok OLA 28 29.
PN of an ancestral hero, cf. 1.17 I 6 and *passim* in 1.17-19; in titles: *mt rpi* // *ġzr mt hrnmy* the 'Rapaite'// the Harnamite hero, 1.17 I 17 and *passim*.

dnn PN (Sem. Cf. Grøndahl PTU 52, 123; Rendsburg ArOr 49 1981 151f.); ¶ syll.: *da-na-nu* and var., Syria 18 1937 247 (RS 8.146 [= "8.213"]):27; Ug 5 86:3, 7; cf. PRU 6 p. 143; Van Soldt SAU 151.
PN: ★a) 4.86:5 (*bn ysr*[); 4.124:14; 4.377:1; 4.595:4; 4.623:10 (*bn dx*[); 4.759:4; ★b) *bn PN:* 4.366:4-5; 4.617:35.

dnt (I) "lechery, fornication" (Hb. *znwt*, HALOT 276; Arab. *za/inyat*, Lane 1260; Eth. *zĕnyat*, *zĕnet*, CDG 642; Ebla cf. GÉME.KAR.AK

= *za*-NE-*tum*, VE 1412; cf. Viganò *apud* Civil Biling. 89 n. 18); ¶ par.: *bṯt*, *tdmmt*. ¶ Forms: sg. *dnt*.
Lechery, fornication: *dbḥ dnt* sacrifice of lechery, 1.4 III 20 (// *bṯt*, *tdmmt*).

dnt (II) PN (Sem. Cf. Grøndahl PTU 123).
PN: *bn PN*, 4.214:2.

dnty PN, wife of *dnil* (cf. *dnil*).
PN: *mṯt dnty* 'Lady PN', 1.17 V 16, 22, 28.

/d-n-y/ vb G: "to approach, reach" ((?); OSA *dny*, DOSA 83f.; Arab. *danā* (/d-n-w/), Lane 920ff.). ¶ Forms: G prefc. *tdn*.
G. To approach, reach (?): *tdn ʕrb*[*m* the offic[iants approached(?), 1.126:23 (or: proclaimed(?), cf. /d-n/).

/d-p-r/ vb G: "to exhude a strong smell" (Arab. *dafira*, Lane 890. Diff.: De Moor, ARTU 272; ZAW 88 1976 332: rdg *b*(!) *pr* 'among the fruit'; cf. Gordon UL 103; cf. Ribichini - Xella RSF 7 1979 153 n. 42, 'ginepro', Akk. *daprānu*; survey: Wyatt RTU 322 n. 43). ¶ Forms: G suffc. *dpr*.
G. To exhude a strong smell: *dpr ṯlḥn* the table exhuded a strong smell, 1.22 I 16.

dprn n. m. "juniper" (Akk. *da/uprānu*, AHw 162; CAD D 189f.; Syr. *dafrānō*, LS 162); ¶ syll. Ug.: A.ŠÀ.ḪI.A : *di-ip-ra-ni-ma*, PRU 3 64 (RS 16.190):4; GIŠ *da-ap-ra-ni*, PRU 4 194 (RS 17.385):10; Kühne UF 6 1974 163; Huehnergard UVST 119; Sivan UF 21 1989 361; Van Soldt SAU 303. ¶ Forms: sg. *dprn*; pl. *dprnm*.
Juniper, ★a) commodity: *dprn aḥd b ṯql* juniper: one juniper of one shekel, 4.158:20; in hippiatric texts: *dprn*[juniper[, 1.72:28 (Cohen - Sivan UHT 35f.; Cohen UF 28 1996 139f.; Dietrich - Loretz UF 18 1986 118f.); ★b) in toponymy: *gt dprn* 'Farmstead of the Juniper', 4.175:9 (Kühne UF 6 1974 163; Belmonte RGTC 12/2 84, 401: *Gittu-diprānīma*; cf. *gt*); *ẓl dprn* 'Shade(s) of Juniper', 4.244:13 (Belmonte RGTC 12/2 358).

dq (I) adj. m. 1) "tiny, fine"; 2) "weak" (< /d-q-q/; Hb., Pun., *dq*, HALOT 229; DNWSI 257f.; Aram. *dqq*, DNWSI 258; Ebla cf. *du-gu/gúm*, Bonechi NABU 1992 13; Akk. *daqqu*, AHw 163; CAD D 107; Arab. *diqq*, Lane 806. Cf. Aartun WO 4 1967/8 279f.; Dijkstra JANES 6 1974 65); ¶ syll. Ug.: cf. [SIG = *ṣeḫru*] = *ga-al-gi* = *d*[*a*]-*aq*(!?)-*qú*, Ug 5 137 II 13'; Huehnergard UVST 119; cf. diff. Van Soldt SAU 303: *da-al-lu* (with Nougayrol Ug 5 p. 243). ¶ Forms: sg. m. *dq*.

1) Tiny, fine: *kndpnṯ dq* a fine *k.*(-garment), 4.4:3; *ḫpnt dqt* fine cloaks, 4.765:4; *yryt dqt* tiny corals(?), 4.411:3.
2) Weak: *dq anm* weak of strength, 1.6 I 50.
In unc. ctx.: *ṯn dqm*, 5.23:17; bkn. 2.57:5.
Cf. **dqt (I)**.

dq (II) PN.
PN: *bn PN*, 4.63 III 13.

dqn (I) n. m. 1) "beard"; 2) "chin" (Hb., Ph. *zqn*, HALOT 278; DNWSI 339; JAram. *dqn*, DJPA 154; *ziqnu*, AHw 1530f.; CAD Z 125f.; Ebla cf. /ḏaqa/ūnum/ in SU_6.DÙ = *ša-ga-núm*, *ša-gu-nu-um*, VE 199; Krebernik ZA 73 1983 8 (cf. /tuztaqqinum/ in KAxKID.SAR = *tù-uš-tá-gi-nu/núm*, VE 200; Pettinato Biling. 45; Kienast Biling. 251, 255); Arab. *ḏaqan*, Lane 967f.). ¶ **Forms**: sg. *dqn*; suff. *dqnk*, *dqnh*.
1) Beard: *šbt dqnh* the greyness of his beard, 1.3 V 2 and par. 1.4 V 4.
2) Chin: *yhdy lḥm w dqn* he lacerated (his) cheeks and chin, 1.5 VI 19.
Cf. **dqn (II)**, **ḏqnt**.

dqn (II) PN (Sem. Cf. Grøndahl PTU 29, 125). Cf. *ḏqnt.*
PN: **★a)** 4.33:37 (Van Soldt SAU 33); 4.54:3 (Van Soldt SAU 33); 4.98:17; 4.141 II 9 (Van Soldt SAU 39); 4.183 II 26 (Van Soldt SAU 26); 4.370:4; 4.424:7, 18; 4.609:6 (Van Soldt SAU 39), 23, 26; **★b)** *bn PN*, 4.787:10; cf. in bkn ctx.: 4.609:29.

dqr n. m.; a kind of pot or pan (Akk. *diqāru*, AHw 172; CAD D 157ff.; for Aram. *dqwrʔ* cf. Kaufman AIA 46f.; Watson UF 32 2000 568); ¶ **RS Akk.**: ÚTUL = *di-qa-ru*, Ug 5 133 obv. 10'. ¶ **Forms**: sg. *dqr.*
A kind of pot or pan:]*tʕgd dqr PN*(?): a pan, 4.275:17; cf. *dqr* pan(?), 5.22:2 (diff. Dijkstra UF 18 121 n. 4: 'chisel', JAram. *dqr*). Cf. in bkn ctx. *b ṯlṯ dqr ḥ*[the third day: a pan of ...[, 1.111:16 (cf. Del Olmo CR 201 n. 109).
Cf. **dqry**, **kdr**.

dqry PN (Sem. Cf. Grøndahl PTU 125; Watson AuOr 8 1990 118).
PN: 4.63 II 33; 4.108:4; 4.116:17.

dqt (I) adj./n. f. 1) adj. f. "small, tiny, fine" (< *dq*); 2) used as a n. f. "sacrificial ewe, sheep"; diff. Tropper UF 33 2001 545ff.: 'Flachbrot'; 3) DN (lexicalization of the f. adj. *dqt*; cf. *dq* and f. *dqt.* Cf. Levine JCS 17 1963 107f.; Astour JAOS 86 1966 283; Loewenstamm Bib 56 1975 118f.). ¶ **Forms**: sg. *dqt*; pl. *dqt*; du. *dqtm.*
1) Small, tiny, fine: *ḫpnt dqt* fine cloaks, 4.765:4; *yryt dqt* tiny corals(?), 4.411:3.

2) Sheep, ewe, for sacrificial use, *passim* in cultic texts (cf. esp. the dedic. formulae *dqt l DN* or *(l) DN dqt* in 1.39; 1.41; 1.46; 1.53; 1.87; 1.102; 1.105; 1.106; 1.109; 1.112; 1.119; 1.126; 1.130; 1.136; 1.138; cf. in Hurr. ctx. 1.132:8-12 (rdg *dqt{t}* in 8)): *npš w arbʕ ʕšrh dqt w šbʕ gdlt w kl šbšlt dg gnh* (they shall offer) one (piece of) offal and fourteen ewes and seven cows and all types of fish stews in the 'garden', 1.106:20; *dqtm b nbk šrp w šlmm* two ewes in the source as a holocaust and as a peace offering, 1.41:23; rdg *d*(!)*ktm* in 1.87:35; *dqt ṯʕ* a ewe in sacrificial offering, 1.39:1.

3) DN < 'the Little One', Syro-Anat. goddess *Daru Dakitu* in the circle of Hebat; Hurro.(-Akk.) [d]*da/ta-(a-)-ki-tum/tu/du(-)*; Hitt. [d]*Takiti-*; Laroche Ug 5 503; GLH 70f. 1.102:8; Astour RHA 36 1978 16; *dqt dqt* DN: a ewe, 1.39:15; cf. in Hurr. ctx.: *dqtd gdlt* for DN: a cow, 1.132:7; cf. 1.116:19.

Bkn 1.56:7; 4.189:1.

dqt (II) n. f. "manufacture, moulding" (< /d-q-q/; Dietrich - Loretz UF 4 1972 31; Kottsieper UF 18 1986 220; diff. Emerton JTS 16 1965 439f.: *d qt* 'of which the handle'; Caquot - Sznycer TOu 1 196: 'dont l'anse'; Dietrich - Loretz UF 10 1978 58, 62f.: *dqt (I)* 'Kleintier'; Margalit MLD 23 'thin, delicate'; Emerton JTS 16 1965 439f.; Caquot-Sznycer TOu 1 196: 'anse'); ¶ par.: *sknt.* ¶ Forms: sg. *dqt.*

Manufacture, moulding: *sʕ il dqt k amr* a divine platter of manufacture in the TN style, 1.4 I 41 (// *sknt*).

/d-r/ vb G "to surround" (?) (Hb. *dwr*, HALOT 217; Arab. *dāra*, Lane 930ff. Cf. Dijkstra UF 19 1987 44). ¶ Forms: G prefc. *ydr.*

G. To surround (?), in bkn ctx.: *x*]*ydr* he surrounded (?). 2.33:15;]*ydr*[, 7.64:5.

dr n. m. 1) "circle; association, chapter"; 2) "cycle, generation" (Hb. *dwr*, HALOT 217f.; Ph., Pun. *dr*, DNWSI 258f.; Amor. /dārum/, /dūrum/, Gelb CAAA 17; Ebla cf. *da-ar*, *dar*, Krebernik PET 79; ŠU.MU.NÍGIN = *da-lum*, VE 509; Hecker Biling. 211 n. 39; A.NÍGIN = *da- wa-lum*, *du-lum*, VE 629; Krebernik ZA 73 1983 23 n. 78; Akk. *dāru*, AHw 164; CAD D 107ff.; cf. *dūru*, AHw 178; CAD D 197f.; cf. Arab. *dār*, *daura*, Lane 931f.); ¶ RS Akk.: cf. *infra*: 2; ¶ par.: *ʕlm (I)*, *mpḫrt*, *pḫr*, ¶ Forms: sg. *dr*, pl.(?) cstr. *dr*, suff. *drk*, *drh*; du.(?) *drm* (or encl. *-m*?).

1) Circle of relatives and friends; association, chapter; ★a) circle of relatives and friends, esp. *dr (bn) il* circle (of friends and relatives) of DN: *dr il l mšknthm* the circle of DN (went) to their tents, 1.15 III 19 and par.; *passim* in lists and rituals; cf. *dbḥn ndbḥ (...) ytši l dr bn il*

l mpḫrt bn il may our sacrifice which we offer (...) rise to the family circle of DN, to the family assembly of DN, 1.40:25 and par.; *bn il dr bn il mpḫrt bn il* the family of DN, the family circle of DN, the family assembly of DN, 1.65:2 and par.; recipient of offerings: *dr il w pḫr bʕl gdlt* circle of DN and assembly of DN: a cow, 1.39:7; cf. 1.41:16; 1.87:17; cf. in bkn ctx.: *k dr{d} d yknn*[like the (family) circle from whom I was established[..., 1.10 III 6; cf. *drm ilm* the two families(?) of the gods, 1.123:32; cf.]*dr dt šmm*, 1.10 I 5 (cf. *ibid.* ln. 3, 4: *bn il*, *pḫr kkbm*); ★b) association, chapter: *dr khnm* chapter of priests, 4.357:24.

2) Cycle, generation, ★a) esp. in the gen. syntagm *dr dr-* (+ pn. suff.) "all (your / their) generations" > "perpetuity" (cf. RS Akk.: *a-di da-ri da-ri-ti-šu*, PRU 3 100 (RS 16 368):10) *tqḥ (...) drkt dt dr drk* you shall take possession (...) of your perpetual dominion, 1.2 IV 10 (// *ʕlmk*); ★b) adv. use *dr dr* "for all generations" > "in perpetuity" (adv. lexicalization of the nominal gen. syntagm *dr dr* (// *ʕlmh*; cf. RS Akk.: *ana / adi dāri dūri*, PRU 3 49 (RS 16.248):14; Ug 5 6:15; PRU 3 134 (RS 15.137): 7; *passim*; cf. Huehnergard UVST 202; Van Soldt SAU 454, 458; cf. AHw 164; CAD D 107f.): *ʕnt p dr dr* from now and for all generations, 1.19 III 48 and par. (spelling: *dr.dr*; // *ʕlmh*). In bkn ctx.: 1.6 IV 26; 4.120:3 (PN?).

/d-r-ʕ/ vb G: "to sow, scatter" (Hb., Aram. *zrʕ*, HALOT 282; DNWSI 340f.; OSA *ḏrʔ*, DOSA 99; Arab. *zaraʕa*, Lane 1225f.; Eth. *zarʔa*, CDG 642; Akk. cf. *drʕ*. Cf. Sanmartín UF 20 1988 273f.; Dietrich - Loretz UF 23 199 1 79ff.; UF 25 1993 124ff.); ¶ par.: /ṭ-ḥ-n/. ¶ Forms: G prefc. with suff. *tdrʕnn*; inf. *drʕ*.

G. To sow, scatter: (because of you I have seen) *drʕ b ym* sowing in the sea, 1.6 V 19; *b šd tdrʕ{.}nn* in the field she scattered him, 1.6 II 35 (// *ṯṯḥnn*).

Cf. drʕ, ḏrʕ (II), mdrʕ.

d/ḏrʕ n. m. 1) "seed, seed-grain, sowing"; 2) "(grain of) seed"; 3) "offspring" (< /d-r-ʕ/; Hb., Ph., Aram. *zrʕ*, HALOT 282f.; DNWSI 341f.; Amor. cf. /ḏarʕum/, Gelb CAAA 18; Ebla /ḏar(ā)ʕum/ in ŠE.MAR = *ša-la-um*, VE 659, Krebernik ZA 73 1983 26; Fronzaroli EL 150; StEb 7 1984 160s; cf. ŠE.AD$_6$ = *ša-la-ù ʔa$_5$-dar-tum*, *šar-ù ʔa$_5$-dar-tim*, *še$_6$(sar$_x$)-ù a-dar-du*, VE 684; Krebernik ZA 73 1983 26; Emar /ḏarʕu/, Pentiuc Vocabulary 192; Akk. *zēru*, AHw 1521f.; CAD Z 89ff.; Arab. *zarʕ*, Lane 1226; Eth. *zarʔ*, CDG 642. Cf. Pardee Fs. Fitzmyer 87); ¶ RS Akk.: NUMUN, *passim*; cf. ŠE *a-na numun*, PRU 6 103:1. ¶ Forms: sg. *drʕ*; var. *ḏrʕ*; suff. *ḏrʕhm*.

1) Seed, seed-grain, sowing: *b TN (...) drʕ w (...) drt* in TN: (so many *dd*) of seed and (so many) of bran, 4.243:12 and *passim ibid.* (cf. ŠE.NUMUN.MEŠ, PRU 6 104:9); *rb tmtt lqḥ kl ḏrʕ b dntm w ank kl ḏrʕhm kl npš kl klhm bd rb tmtt lqḥt* the captain of the (salvage) crew has collected all the seed-grain from the actual containers(?), and I (then) collected all the seed-grain from all the people (and) all their equipment/tools from the hands of the captain of the crew, 2.38:17-22; *drʕ ḥwt hyt yḫsl* the seed of that land will be destroyed, 1.103:55 (cf. *ibid.* ln. 14, 43); *mitm drʕ* two hundred (cauldronfuls) of seed-grain, 4.636:4 (cf. ibid. ln. 8, 13, 17, 22, 28).

2) (Grain of) seed: *drʕ*[seeds of[, 1.72:29 (in pharmacopea).

3) Offspring: *d*[*rʕ l*] *adny l yḫsr* my lord will not lack offspring, 2.39:9. Cf. in bkn ctx. *l drʕ hn*[, 2.81:15; *tḥm hy klm drʕ*, ln. 17; *drʕ ly*, ln. 23; *drʕ hnh*, 4.721:16.

Cf. /d-r-ʕ/.

drb "?", 4.385:8 (perhaps uncorrected scribal mistake?; cf. *mrbd*, *ibid.* ln. 9; cf. also *trb*, TN. Diff.: Stieglitz JCS 33 1981 52ff.: 'tine', MHb *dorbān*).

drdr, cf. *dr*, 2.

drḫ n. m. "chamois, mountain goat" ((?); cf. Akk. *turāḫu*, AHw 1372); ¶ RS Akk.: cf. DÀRA, PRU 3 206 (RS 16.274):1-5. ¶ Forms: pl./du. *drḫm*.

Chamois / mountain goat (?): in bkn ctx.]*lk drḫm* ... (of two) chamois(?), 1.82:37 (rdg. unc.; diff. rdg. and interpretation in De Moor (- Spronk) UF 16 1984 247f.; ARTU 180; CARTU 169: *h*]*lk d rḫm* ('be]haviour) of a carrion-vulture', Arab. *raḫam*, Hb. *rḫm*).

/d-r-k/ vb G: "to tread on, trample"(?) (Hb. *drk*, HALOT 231; Ph., Aram. *drk*, DNWSI 261). ¶ Forms: G prefc. *tdrk* (?).

G. To tread on, trample(?):] *tdrk brḥ arṣ* (if) you tread(?) on a fleeing (serpent) on the ground, 1.82:38, bkn ctx.

drk n. m. of a profession or social group, possibly "trader" (Del Olmo CR 286 n. 97; cf. Dietrich - Loretz - Sanmartín UF 6 1974 24f.; Hb. cf. *drk*, HALOT 231 *qal* 3; Aram. cf. DNWSI 261: *drk*$_1$; Akk. cf. AHw 1550: *darāku III*); RS Akk. / ¶ syll. Ug.: cf. KI.UŠ = TAR.KUM, Thureau-Dangin Syria 12 1931 231ff. (Ḫḫ II; MLS 5 p. 71:281); rdg *dar*$_6$-*ku*$_{13}$ unlikely, cf. Huehnergard UVST 119f. ¶ Forms: pl. *drkm*.

A profession or social group: *ddm akl l drkm* two 'cauldronfuls', of grain for the *d.*, 4.688:5 (ctx. unc.). Cf. in bkn ctx. *drk*, 4.765:7. Cf.

mzn drk trader's weight (: standard weight), 1.43:6 (cf. Del Olmo CR 286 n. 97; diff.: De Moor ARTU 169: '(food for a three day) journey').

drkt n. f. "rule, power" (Hb. *drk*, HALOT 232; Arab. *darak*, Lane 874f.; cf. Dahood UHP 55; Dietrich - Loretz - Sanmartín UF 6 1974 24f.; Dietrich - Loretz UF 12 1980 176); ¶ par.: *mlk (II)*. ¶ Forms: sg. *drkt*, suff. *drktk*, *drkth*.

Rule, power: *grš (...) l kḥṯ drkth* drive (...) from the seat of his power, 1.2 IV 13 and par.; *arṣ drkt yštkn* will he establish himself in the land of (my) rule?, 1.4 VII 44; *rd (...) l drktk* come down (...) from your power, 1.16 VI 38 and par. (// *mlk*); *mlk (...) yarš hm drk*[*t*] does he desire the kingship (...), or a power?, 1.14 I 42 (// *mlk*); *tqḥ (...) drkt dt drdrk* you shall take possession (...) of your rule for centuries of centuries, 1.2 IV 10 (// *mlk*); *bʕlt drkt* Lady of power, 1.108:7.

/d-r-q/, cf. *tdrq*.

/d-r(-r)/ vb G: "to flow copiously"(?) (Arab. *darra*, Lane 862ff.; Akk. *darāru*, AHw 163; CAD D 109; Hb. cf. HALOT 233: **drr*. Cf. De Moor ZAW 100 1988 108 n. 21; diff. Astour JNES 27 1968 33: 'to fall out (said of teeth)', Arab. *darama*; Dietrich - Loretz - Sanmartín UF 7 1975 130: 'geloben'(?), **ndr*; Wyatt RTU 391 and n. 2: 'sweated profusely'). ¶ Forms: G prefc. *ydrm*.

G. To flow copiously(?): in bkn and unc. ctx.: *ydrm pit adm* the man's temples flowed copiously(?), 1.107:3.

drṣy PN (etym. unc.).

PN: *bn PN*, 4.350:6; 4.700:6.

drt (I) n. f. "bran, chaff" (< /d-r-y/; cf. Arab. *du/arāwa*, Lane 965. Cf. Sanmartin UF 20 1988 273f.; diff. Dietrich - Loretz UF 23 1991 81: 'Abmessung, Ration', Arab. *drt*, Hb. *zrt*). ¶ Forms: sg. *drt*.

Bran, chaff: *b TN (...) drʕ w (...) drt* in TN: (nn *dd*) of seed and (nn) of bran, 4.243:12 and *passim ibid.*; cf. [[*drt b kkr*]] [[bran for one talent]], 4.131:4 (text erased); *(...) drt (...) drt l alpm* (nn *dd*) of bran, (nn *dd*) of bran for the oxen, 4.636:8 and *passim ibid.*

drt (II) PN (etym. unc. Cf. Grøndahl PTU 310).

PN: *bn PN*, 3.10:7 (*uškny*); 4.792:8 (*uškny*).

/d-r-y/ vb G: "to winnow" (Hb. *zrh*, HALOT 280; Emar /uḏarrû/, Pentiuc Vocabulary 189: D; Arab. *ḏarā*, Lane 964f. Cf. De Moor SP 209; Dietrich - Loretz UF 23 1991 79ff.); ¶ par.: /b-q-ʕ/, /d-r-ʕ/, /š-r-p/, /ṭ-ḥ-n/. ¶ Forms: G prefc. *tdry*; inf. *dry*.

G. To winnow: *b ḫṯr tdrynn* with a winnowing fork she winnowed him, 1.6 II 32 (// *tbqʕnn, tšrpnn, tṯḥnn, tdrʕnn*); *ʕlk pht dry* because of you I have seen winnowing, 1.6 V 13 (cf. ln. 16).

dšn, 1.19 IV 27; 1.108:5; rdg *d šn*; cf. *d, šn*.

dt, cf. *d*.

dt/dn (I) PN mythical ancestor, founder of the dynasty of Ugarit and leader of its deified clan (cf. Amor /Ditan(um)/, /Ditnum/, cf. /ditanum/ 'bison', Huffmon APNMT 184; Gelb CAAA 17; JNES 13 1954 209ff.; Kraus MKNAWL 28/2 1965 123ff.; Finkelstein JCS 20 1966 95ff., 101; Röllig AOAT 1 1969 265ff.; Grayson ARI 1 1. Cf. Astour UF 5 1973 36ff.; RSP 2 279ff.; Healey UF 10 1978 86; Caquot Fs. Loewenstamm 1ff.; Lipiński *ibid.* 111ff.; Annus UF 31 1999 13ff.). ¶ Forms: *dt/dn*.

PN: *dtn*, mythical ancestor: 1.15 III 4, 15; 1.124:2, 4, 11, 14. Var. *ddn*: cf. *qbṣ ddn* the clan of PN, 1.161:10; 1.163:3, 10. Cf. in bkn ctx. 1.170:2.

dt/dn (II) PN (etym. unc.; cf. Grøndahl PTU 122; Watson AuOr 13 1995 222); ¶ syll.: cf. DUMU *da*-TI-*ni*, PRU 3 202 (RS16.257+) III 40 (Van Soldt SAU 34); cf. *du-du-nu*, Ug 5 86:9; 97:1. Var. *ddn* in 4.760:5.

PN: *bn PN*, 4.69 VI 29; 4.422:53; 4.760:5. In bkn ctx. cf. 4.633:6.

Cf. dt/dn (I), ttn.

/d-ṯ/ vb G: "to soften, become soft" (Arab. *dayyaṯa* (*dyṯ*), Lane 941; Rainey UF 3 1971 159: probl. not connected with Akk. *diāšu, dāšu*, AHw 168; CAD D 121; Hb. *dwš*, HALOT 218; Arab. *dāsa* (*dws*), Lane 932ff.; Eth. *dasaya*, CDG 145). ¶ Forms: G prefc. *ydṯ*; inf. *dṯ*.

G. To soften, become soft: *dṯ ydṯ mʕqbk* your rival will certainly become soft, 1.18 I 19.

Cf. mʕqb.

dṯn n. m. "fat offering" (Hb. *dšn*, HALOT 234; Aram. cf. DNWSI 262f.: *dšn*; diff.: Healey UF 15 1983 51: 'thresher', cf. *dṯ/dwṯ*); ¶ par.: *šrp*. ¶ Forms: sg. *dṯn*.

Fat offering: *b dṯn il* in the fat offering of DN (we trust), 1.65:15.

dṯt n. f. "fodder or spring grass"(?) (Akk. *dīšu*, AHw 173; CAD D 163; cf. *dēšûtu*, AHw 167; Hb. *dšʔ*, HALOT 233f.; OSA *dṯʔ*, CAME 127; DOSA 86f. Diff. Dietrich - Loretz TUAT 2 310 n. 9/b: 'Fettasche', unc.). ¶ Forms: sg. *dṯt*.

Fodder or spring grass (?): *dṯt w kśm* (an offering of) spring grain(?) and spelt, 1.39:9; cf. 1.41:18; 1.87:20.

dw n. m. "sick person" (< /d-w-y/; cf. Hb. *dwh*, HALOT 216; DNWSI 243; Arab. *daw*, Lane 940; Eth. *duy*, *dawāyi*, *dĕwwuy*, CDG 145. Cf. Dietrich - Loretz KA 251, 254). ¶ Forms: sg. *dw*.
Sick person: *yʔkl dw* the sick person shall eat it, 4.767:3.

dwn PN (etym. unc.; cf. Gröndahl PTU 296; Watson AuOr 13 1995 222); ¶ syll.: cf. DUMU](?) *tu-a-ni*, PRU 6 90 rev. 7'.
PN: *bn PN*, 4.309:5; 4.354:7.

/d-w-y/ vb G: "to fall ill, become sick" (Hb. *dwh*, HALOT 216; JAram. *dwy*, DJPA 140; Akk. *dawû*, AHw 166; CAD D 80; Arab. *dawiya*, Lane 928, 940; Eth. *dawaya*, CDG 145f.); ¶ par.: /m-r-ṣ/. ¶ Forms: G inf. abs. *dw* (cf. UT § 9.52).
G. To fall ill, become sick: *mn k dw krt* how many (months since) PN became sick?, 1.16 II 20 (// *k mrṣ*; cf. UT § 9.29); *arbʕ k dw krt* four (months since) PN became sick, *ibid.* ln. 23. On 1.16 I 57, 60, cf. De Moor - Spronk UF 14 1982 184.
Cf. dw, mdw.

ḏ

ḏ (Emar /zu/, Pentiuc Vocabulary 196) allomorph of *d*: *il ḏ pid*, 1.24:45. Cf. *d*.

ḏbb DN, mythical female being defeated by Anat (Hb. *zbwb*, HALOT 261; Arab. *ḏubab*, Lane 952; cf. Amor. /ḏubābum/, CAAA 18. Cf. Dietrich - Loretz UF 12 1980 392; Van Soldt UF 21 1989 369ff.; diff.:Albright BASOR 84 1941 17 n. 26; Dahood UF 1 1969 36: 'flame', Hb. *šbyb*, cf. Watson UF 10 1978 397 n. 7; cf. Cooper - Pope RSP 3 363ff.); ¶ par.: *išt* (cf. *išt* 4).
DN: *bt il ḏbb* the daughter of El, DN, 1.3 III 46 (// *išt*).

ḏd (I) n. m. "breast, bosom" (Hb. *dd*, HALOT 214). ¶ Forms: sg. m. *ḏd*.
Breast, bosom: those who suck *b ap ḏd* from the nipple, 1.23:59 and par (cf. *ap (II)*).
Cf. ṯd, zd.

ḏd (II) n. m. "grotto, cave"(?) (Hb. cf. DNWSI 306: *zdh*; cf. Del Olmo IMC 156ff.; Sasson PEQ 1982, 112; Lawson UF 26 1994 549f. Diff.: Cassuto GA 145: 'tent-curtains', Akk. *šiddu*, cf. Watson SEL 12 1995 221f.; Clifford CMC 48ff., 125: 'tent', Arab. *ḏāda*, *ḏawd*; Dijkstra - De Moor UF 7 1975 192: 'encampment', *id.*; Pope UF 19 1987 223: 'abode'; Loretz UF 27 1995 727: 'anteroom, forecourt'; for other meanings proposed, 'field', 'mountain', 'territory', cf. Del Olmo *loc. cit.*; for the Arab. etym.. cf. Renfroe AULS 97ff.: Akk. *ś/šadādu*); ¶ par.: *ahl*, *qrš*. ¶ Forms: sg. m. *ḏd*; suff. *ḏdk*, pl. *ḏdm*.
Grotto, cave: *tgly ḏd il* she made her way to the grotto of DN, 1.6 I 34 and par. (// *qrš*); *ištir b ḏdm* stay(?) in the grottoes, 1.18 IV 15; *agrtn bat b ḏdk* our mistress entered your grotto, 1.19 IV 51 (// *ahlm*); *msr* [*t*]*bu ḏdm* sobbing she entered the grotto, 1.3 V 9; *il d yqny ḏdm* the god who created the grottoes, 1.19 IV 58.

ḏd (III) n. m. "flock, herd" (cf. Arab. *ḏawd*, Lane 987f. Cf. De Moor UF 1 1969 187; Del Olmo IMC 68f.; diff.: Dietrich - Loretz UF 23

1991 92ff.: rdg *kḏd* (< **kšd*) 'hetzen'; for a critique of the Arab. etym. cf. Renfroe AULS 100f.). ¶ **Forms**: sg. cstr. *ḏd*.
Flock, herd: *ʕn k ḏd aylt* the spring (which yearns for), in truth, the herd of hinds, 1.5 I 17; 1.133:8.

ḏdyn PN (etym. unc.; cf. Van Soldt SAU 357 n. 224); ¶ **syll**.: cf. ZA-ZI*-ia-na*, cf. PRU 3 255 (cf. Van Soldt SAU 7 n. 63, 357 n. 224). Cf. *ḏdyy*.
PN:]*PN bʕd PN*]of / from PN for(?) PN, 2.31:47 (unc. ctx.).

ḏdyy PN (bkn?; etym. unc.; cf. *ḏd (I)*).
PN, in bkn ctx.:]*ḏdyy*, 4.668:4.

ḏdyy PN (etym. unc.; cf. Van Soldt SAU 357 n. 224; Watson AuOr 11 1993 215; AuOr 14 1996 98). Cf. *ḏdyn*.
PN: *bn PN*, 4.245 II 3; cf. 4.668:9 *ḏdyy*.

ḏhrt n. f. "vision" (Hb. *zhr*, HALOT 265; Arab. *zuhrat*, Lane 1262; cf. De Moor SP 217; Dietrich - Loretz SEL 1 1984 85ff.; Greenfield BSOAS 57 1994 89; Tropper UBL 12 305ff.); ¶ **par**.: *ḥlm*. ¶ **Forms**: sg. suff. *ḏhrth*.
Vision: down came *b ḏhrth ab adm* in his vision the father of mankind, 1.14 I 36 (// *ḥlmh*).
Cf. **ḏrt**.

/ḏ-k-r/ v. G: "remember, mention, name", only in PNN (cf. Grøndahl PTU 196; Sivan GAGl 215f.; Ebla /zikir-/ in PNN: spellings *zi-kir-* (ZI.KIR), *zi-ki-rV* (ZI.KIR.RA); Krebernik PET 110; Catagnoti MisEb 1 253f. (Sem. /ḏakaru/ "male" would be represented by the gloss NITA(.DIŠ*tenû*("RUM")) = *ša-ḫa-lum* (/ḏakarum/), VE 1112a,b; cf. Krebernik ZA 73 1983 39.); cf. INIM.DI = *dal-da-gi-lum*, VE 186; Krebernik QuSe 181 123; *iš*$_{11}$*-gur-ma* < /yiḏkur-/; Krebernik QuSe 18 123); ¶ **syll**.: cf. PN *ia-aš-ku-ra-na*, PRU 3 198 (RS 16.359):9', van Soldt BiOr 46 1989 648 (corecting Sivan GAGl 274: < /š-k-r/).
Cf. **ḏkr**, **ḏkry**.

ḏkr PN (Sem. Cf. Grøndahl PTU 196; Sivan GAGl 215; Huehnergard UVST 96 n. 63; Van Soldt BiOr 46 1989 648); ¶ **syll**.: *za-ki-ru*, PRU 38 (RS 16.354):2.
PN: 4.484:3; 4.609:37; in bkn ctx.: 4.748:13.

ḏkry PN (Sem. Cf. Grøndahl PTU 196; Sivan GAGl 216; Van Soldt BiOr 46 1989 648; Van Soldt SAU 348 n. 205); ¶ **syll**.: cf. *zu-ku-ri-ia*, PRU 6 50:25; *zu-uk-ri-ia*, Ug 5 27:9; *zu-ku-ra-ya*, Ug 5 43:6; *zu-uk-ri-ia-nu*, PRU 3 199 (RS 16.257+) I 8" (Huehnergard UVST 225).
PN: 4.261:5; 4.383:4.

ḏld TN (cf. Belmonte RGTC 12/2 359: *Zulutu*). TN: 1.131 (Hurr.).

ḏmn PN (etym. unc.); ¶ **syll.**: cf. ZI-*me-ni*, PRU 6 147:2; ZÍ-*me-nu*, RS 34.169:2' (cf. Huehnergard UVST 226). Cf. *ẓmn*.
PN: 4.51:7 (*šʕrty*). Cf. 5.9 IV 2.

/ḏ-m-r/ (I) v. G: "to protect, guard" (CS. with various allophones: Amor. /ḏ-m-r/ > /D/S/Š/Z-m-r/, Gelb CAAA 18, 32; cf. (a) the series /ḏ-m-r/ in Ebla /(y)iḏtamar/, the element in PN *iš*$_{11}$ *da-mar-*, Krebernik PET 64, 232; ESA. *mḏmr*, CAME 129: *ḏmr* (cf. DOSA 96: *ḏmr II*); Arab. *ḏimr*, *ḏamīr*, Lane 978; (b) the series /š-m-r/ in Hb., Ph., Pun., Aram. (with Gt *ʔštmr*), DNWSI 1166f.; HALOT 1581ff.; Arab. *samara*, Lane 1424ff.; (c) the series /z-m-r/ in Hb. */z-m-r/ and deriv., HALOT 273ff. Cf. Loewenstamm 5 WCJS 229; VT 19 1969 464ff.; Sanmartín AuOr 9 1991 187f.); ¶ **syll. Ug.**: the element /yiḏtamar/ in PN *ʕammiḏtamru* (cf. *ʕmṯtmr* with var. *ʕmyḏtmr*, *ilḏtmr*, Grøndahl PTU 197; Van Soldt SAU 317). ¶ **Forms**: G act. ptc. *ḏmr*.
G. To protect: *l ʕpr ḏmr aṯrh* the one who from the 'dust' protects his remains, 1.17 I 28 and par. (diff.: Pope Fs. Finkelstein 164; Dietrich - Loretz UF 10 1978 68 n. 34: 'to sing', 'Gesang', cf. /ḏ-m-r/ (II); cf. UF 19 1987 25). Bkn: *ibʕr an*[*k x*]*ḏmr*, 2.31:55.
Cf. **ilṯtmr, ʕmṯtmr, ḏmr (III), ḏmrbʕl, ḏmrd, ḏmrn, ḏmry**.

/ḏ-m-r/ (II) v. G/D: "to sing, praise" (Hb. *zmr*, HALOT 274; Arab. *zamara*, Lane 1250f.; Akk. *zamāru* AHw 1508; CAD Z 36ff.; cf. Blau - Greenfield BASOR 200 1970 11f.; Clemens UF 25 1993 163ff.); ¶ **RS Akk.**: cf. EZEN = *za-am-ma-rum* = *ḫal-mi* = *ši-i-ru*, Ug 5 137 III 7. ¶ **Forms**: G/D (pass. or impers.) prefc. *yḏmr*.
G/D. To sing, praise: *il (...) yšr w yḏmr b knr* the god (...) who sing and praise (is sung and praised) to the sound of the harp, 1.108:3.

ḏmr (I) n. m. "guardian, warrior" (cf. /ḏ-m-r/ (I); cf. Hb. *zmry*, HALOT 274; Amor. /ḏāmirum/, CAAA 18; Arab. *ḏimr*, *ḏamir*, *ḏamīr*, Lane 978; cf. Rin AE 82); ¶ syll. Ug.: cf. the element /ḏamīru/, /zamīru/ in PNN, Sivan GAGl 215; ¶ **par.**: *mhr*. ¶ **Forms**: sg. m. *ḏmr* (in a collect. sense).
Guardian, warrior: (her) knees she plunged *b dm ḏmr* in the blood of the warriors, 1.3 II 14 and par.; they cleaned from (her) house *dm ḏmr* the blood of the warriors, 1.3 II 31 and par.

ḏmr (II) n. m. "fortress" < "protection" (cf. /ḏ-m-r/ (I); Amor. /ḏimrum/, CAAA 18; cf. Borger UF 1 1969 3f.; Dietrich - Loretz UF 12 1980 178); ¶ **syll. Ug.**: cf. the element /ḏimru/ in PNN, Sivan GAGl 215. ¶ **Forms**: sg. m. with suff. *ḏmrk*, *ḏmrh*.
Fortress: *l rpi arṣ ʕzk ḏmrk lank* of DN of the 'land' be your strength, your fortress, your power, 1.108:23 and par.

ḏmr (III) PN (Sem. Cf. Grøndahl PTU 197; Watson AuOr 14 1996 98).
PN: ★**a)** 4.647:1; ★**b)** *bn PN:* 4.348:17.

ḏmrbʕl PN (Sem. Cf. Grøndahl PTU 197).
PN: 4.75 II 5; 4.261:8; cf. in bkn ctx. 4.731:1.

ḏmrd PN (Sem. Cf. Grøndahl PTU 20, 133, 197; Huehnergard UVST 248 n. 154); ¶ **syll.**: *zi-im-rad-du*, PRU 3 193 (RS 12.34+):33; *ši-im-rad-du*, PRU 4 234 (RS 17.112):16; *ši-im-rad-dú*, RS 25.423:5, Van Soldt BiOr 46 1989 648; SAU 309 n. 115, 315 n. 120 (cf. Berger WO 5 1969/70 279; Rainey UF 3 1971 157; Van Soldt BiOr 46 1989 648).
PN: 4.682:10 (*bn ḥġmn*); 4.775:3. Rdg *gmrd* in 4.75 VI 7.

ḏmrn PN (Sem. Cf. Grøndahl PTU 51, 197).
PN: 4.423:1.

ḏmry PN (Sem. Cf. Grøndahl PTU 51, 197); ¶ **syll.**: *zi-im-ri-ya*, PRU 6 72:13' (cf. Huehnergard UVST 224f.).
PN: 4.347:3, 5, 9 (*bn yrm*; cf. Astour CRRA 18 17); 4.617:31; 4.655:7; 6.46:1.

ḏnb(t) n. m./f. "tail" (Hb. *znb*, HALOT 274f.; Arab. *ḏanab*, Lane 980f.; Ebla /ḏin(a/e)bu(m)/ in KUN = *šè-na-bù*, *šè-ne-bu$_x$*(rdg NI fot IR), VE 1371, 1372; Krebernik ZA 73 1983 44; Fronzaroli EL 150; StEb 7 1984 160; Sanmartín AuOr 9 1991 188; Akk. *zibbatu*, AHw 1523f.; CAD Z 100ff.); ¶ **syll. Ug.**: cf. the element /ḏani/ību/ in PNN, Sivan GAGl 215; ¶ **par.**: *lšn*. ¶ **Forms**: sg. m. *ḏnb*; du. f. *ḏnbtm*.
Tail: *bʕl qrnm w ḏnb* 'he of two horns and a tail', 1.114:20; unc. ctx. *ym lšnm (...) ym ḏnbtm*, 1.83:7.

ḏqnt PN (Sem. Cf. Grøndahl PTU 197). Cf. *dqn*.
PN: *bn PN*, 4.422:40.

ḏrʕ (I) n. f. "arm" (Hb. *zr(w)ʕ*, HALOT 280f.; DNWSI 342; EA Akk. cstr. *zu-ru-uḫ*, EAT 287:27; 288:34; DNWSI 342; Sivan GAGl 216: /ḏorōʕ(u)/; Aram. *drʕ*, DNWSI 342; Arab. *ḏirāʕ*, Lane 961f. Cf. Caquot EI 14 1978 15; Bordreuil - Caquot Syria 57 1980 357; Segert UF 20 1988 295); ¶ **par.**: *ap (II) (+ lb)*, *bmt*. ¶ **Forms**: sg. suff. *ḏrʕh*.
Arm: *yṯlṯ qn ḏrʕh* he ploughed the bone of arm, 1.5 VI 20 and par. (// *ap lb*, *bmt*); bkn ctx. *w ʕp l ḏr*[*ʕk*] *nšrk* your eagles fly from your arm, 1.13:8.

ḏrʕ (II), cf. *drʕ*.

ḏrdn PN (Hurr.; cf. Grøndahl PTU 252); ¶ **syll.**: cf. *sè-er-da-na*, Syria 18 1937 246 (RS 8.145):27 (Huehnergard AkkUg 370); *še-er-da-an-ni*, PRU 3 124 (RS 15.167+):13; *še-er-dá-an-ni*, PRU 3 131 (RS 15.118):5. Cf. *ṯrdnt*.

PRU 3 124 (RS 15.167+):13; *še-er-dá-an-ni*, PRU 3 131 (RS 15.118):5. Cf. *ṯrdnt*.
PN: 4.657:3 (bkn ctx.).

d/ṯrm PN (Hurr.; cf. Grøndahl PTU 250). Var. *ṯrm* in 4.391:6.
PN: ★a) 2.3:19; 4.391:6; 4.69 IV 2; ★b) *bn PN*: 4.64 V 12; 4.635:53.

ḏrq n. m. "fragment, lump" (?) (< /ḏ-r-q/; cf. Hb. *zrq*, HALOT 283; Akk. *zarāqu*, AHw 1515; CAD Z 65f.; Ebla BUR *za-lu-ga-am*, MEE 3 61 rev. III 11; KA.MUNU$_4$.MUNU$_4$ = *za-a-lú-gú-um*, EV 0157; Civil EDA 154f. Diff.: 'reddish, bloody', **šrq*; 'raw', **d/zrq*; 'enervated, exhausted', Arab. *šariqa*; 'idol', Arab. *šariq*; 'excrement', Arab. *ḏarq*, *ḏaraqa*; 'foot, Ug. *drq*; 'viscera', Akk. *šarqatu*; for these alternatives cf. Del Olmo IMC 158 n. 380; also Merlis AUL 55ff.: Akk. [d]*Zāriqum* DN; Watson SEL 12 1995 222f.: Akk. *šarāqu*, 'to cook meat'). ¶ Forms: pl. *ḏrqm*.
Fragment, lump (?): *ḏrqm amtm* (I am going to consume you) in lumps ell by ell, 1.5 I 6; cf. 1.18 IV 3.

ḏrr PN (etym. unc.; cf. Watson AuOr 8 1990 118).
PN: *bn PN*, 4.354:8.

ḏrt n. f. "vision" (syncope of *ḏhrt*; Greenfield BSOAS 57 1994 89; Tropper UBL 12 305ff.); ¶ **par.**: *ḥlm*. ¶ Forms: sg. *ḏrt*; suff. *ḏrty*.
Vision: he granted me *b ḏrty ab adm* in my vision the father of mankind, 1.14 III 47 and par. (// *ḥlmy*); *b ḏrt bny bnwt* in a vision of the creator of creatures, 1.6 III 5 and par. (// *ḥlm*); *b ḏrt*[*hm m*]*t krt* and in [their] vision PN was already [dead] (?), 1.15 VI 8.
Cf. **ḏhrt**.

ḏyn PN; cf. *š/ḏyn*.

g

g n. m. "(loud) voice, shout" (etym. unc.; cf. Albright JBL 60 1941 207f.; Cunchillos ES 29 204ff.: Sum. gù; Dahood CBQ 22 1960 402; ULx 86 100: possibly related to Hb. *gm* ; cf. Watson UF 28 1996 708). ¶ Forms: sg. suff. *gy*, *gh*, *ghm*, *gm* (encl. *-m*) in adv. use.
(Loud) voice, shout: *ytn gh bky* he raised his voice, weeping, 1.16 I 13 and par.; *yšu gh w yṣḥ* he raised his voice and exclaimed, 1.5 VI 22 and par., message formula (cf. Del Olmo MLC 55f.); *yšmʕ uḫy l gy* listen, my brother, to my voice > take notice of me, 2.4:19 (cf. Hb. *šmʕ l ql*); *gm l aṯth k yṣḥ* in a loud voice he thus shouted, 1.17 V 15 and par., *gm l ġ[l]mh bʕl k yṣḥ* in a loud voice DN shouted to his lads, 1.4 VII 52, formula of direct speech (cf. Del Olmo MLC 56; Watson AuOr 1 1983 253ff.); DN *ytn gh w yṣḥ* raised his voice and shouted, RSOu 14 53 [KTU 9.432]:33'; *ġzrm g ṭb* lads of dulcet voice, 1.23:14. In bkn ctx.: *gy*, 2.82:14.

gan n. m. "arrogance" (*/g-ʔ-y/; Hb. *gʔwn*, HALOT 169; Pun. cf. Poen. 1027 *gune*, DNWSI 207: *gʔn*); ¶ par.: *pšʕ*. ¶ Forms: sg. *gan*.
Arrogance: *ntbt gan* the path of arrogance, 1.17 VI 44.

gʕl "?"; in bkn ctx.: 1.98:7.

/g-ʕ-r/ (I) vb G: "to reproach" (Hb. *gʕr*, HALOT 199f.; on its relationship to /g-ʕ-r/ (II) cf. HALOT 199f. Cf. Kennedy JBL 106 1987 47sff.; Pardee TH 43); ¶ syll. Ug.: cf. PN DUMU *ga-ri*, PRU 3 196 (RS 15.42) II 16'; Sivan GAGl 217. ¶ Forms: G suffc. *gʕr*, prefc. *ygʕr*, suff. *tgʕrm* (encl. *-m*).
G. To reproach: *b šm tgʕrm ʕṯtrt* by (his) name he reproached DN, 1.2 IV 28 (cf. De Moor SP 139; Van Zijl Baal 43); *bhm ygʕr bʕl* DN reproached them, 1.2 I 24; *b il abh gʕr* DN, his father, he reproached, 1.114:14.
Cf. gʕr.

/g-ʕ-r/ (II) vb G: "to puff and blow, to gasp, breathe with stertors, roar" (Arab. cf. the series of allophones *ǧaʕara*, *ǧaʔara*, Hava 91; Lane 369f.; Dozy 1 198; on its relationship to /g-ʕ-r/ (I) cf. HALOT 199f.;

Pardee TH 43; Cohen UF 28 1996 114; diff.: Renfroe Or 57 1988 184: 'to void (dry) dung', Arab. **ǧˁr* I and VIII; but cf. Pardee AuOr 10 1992 154f.). ¶ Forms: G prefc. *ygˁr*.
G. To puff and blow, to gasp, breathe with stertors, roar: *k ygˁr śśw* if the horse puffs and blows, 1.85:2 (cf. 1.72:27; Pardee TH 42ff.; Cohen - Sivan UHT 12).

gˁr PN (Sem. Cf. Grøndahl PTU 13, 29, 34, 125); ¶ syll.: cf. DUMU *ga-ri*, PRU 3 196 (RS 15.42+) II 6; cf. Sivan GAGl 217, 221.
PN: ★a) 4.653:3 (bkn ctx.); ★b) *bn PN*: 4.103:21; 4.611:16. In bkn ctx.: 4.653:3 (?).

gˁt n. f. "bellowing" (Hb. *gˁh*, HALOT 199; Syr. *gˁō*, LS 127. Cf. Fensham JNSL 11 1983 74); ¶ par.: *nhqt*, *ṯigt*, *zġt*. ¶ Forms: sg. *gˁt*.
Bellowing: *l gˁt alp ḥrṯ* for the bellowing of his working oxen, 1.14 III 18 and par (// *zġt*, *ṯigt*, *nhqt*).
Cf. gˁyn.

gˁyn PN (Sem. Cf. Grøndahl PTU 125).
PN: *bn PN*, 4.33:33; 4.50:12 (*ḫrx*[]); 4.55:31 (cf. Van Soldt SAU 33); 4.214 II 2.

gb (I) n. m.; a cult installation (a kind of 'pit'?; Hb. *gb*, HALOT 170; Nab., Palm. *gb*, DNWSI 207; Akk. *gubbu*, AHw 295; CAD G 117; Arab. *ǧubb*, Lane 371; Eth. *gĕbb*, CDG 176. Cf. Del Olmo CR 283 n. 85; Caquot - Sznycer TOu 1 313; De Moor UF 17 1985 408 n. 10; Watson UF 30 1998 753; cf. *ġb*; diff.: Lipiński OLP 15 1984 115f.; Dietrich - Loretz TUAT 2 327: 'Lupanar', Hb. *gb*, HALOT 170: *gab I*; JA 47f.: 'Podest, Podium'; De Moor ARTU 169 n. 6: 'cistern'; Van der Toorn BiOr 48 1991 49ff.: 'internal part'). ¶ Forms: sg. *gb*.
A cult installation: *gb bt mlk* of the palace, 1.43:1; *gb bt ilm* of the temple, 1.43:2. In bkn ctx (*gb (II)*?):]*rq gb*, 1.1 V 13; *w yšt b gbh* and it will be placed in its cult installation, 1.175:13, cf. ln. 17; *gb ad*, 1.172:23 (cf. Bordreuil - Caquot Syria 56 1979 297; Syria 57 1980 345: 'vase'(?), 'coupe'). In unc. ctx.: *gb*[[*z*]]*gb*, 1.24:43 (cf. *gb (II)*).

gb (II) n. m. "spine, back; loin; body" (Hb. *gb*, HALOT 170; Syr. *gbībō*, LS 100; JAram. *gbʔ*, Jastrow 203; cf. Aram. *gb*, DNWSI 207: gb_3); ¶ par.: *tmnt*. ¶ Forms: sg. suff. *gbk*, *gbh*.
Spine, back, body ★a) *ṯḫta l gbk* do/they do evil to your back(s)!, 1.169:5 (// *l tmnth*); *l urtn l gbh l tmnth* for (the benefit of) PN, of his body, of his form, RSOu 14 52 [KTU 9.435]:14; ★b) as meat: *yˁdb yrḫ gbh* DN prepares (his piece of) loin, 1.114:5 (diff. Aartun StUL 34ff.: 'Grube', *gb (I)*). Cf. in bkn ctxs: *gbh l arṣ*, 1.1 V 28; *w yšt b gbh*, 1.175:13, cf. ln. 17; *gb ad*, 1.172:23 (cf. Bordreuil - Caquot Syria

56 1979 297; 57 1980 345: 'vase'(?), 'coupe'). In unc. ctx.: *gb*[[*z*]]*gb*, 1.24:43 (cf. *gb (I)*; cf. De Moor ARTU 145 n. 35: 'on top').

gbʕ n. m. "hill, height, peak" (Hb. *gbʕ*, *gbʕh*, HALOT 174; Emar Akk. /gabʕu/, Pentiuc Vocabulary 49f.; Akk. *gabʔu*, AHw 272, 1555; CAD G 6f.); ¶ syll. Ug.: the element /gabʕu/ in PN *gáb-a-na*, PRU 3 68 (RS 16.269):6, 8; cf. Sivan GAGl 217; ¶ par.: *ġr*. ¶ Forms: sg. *gbʕ*; pl. *gbʕm*.

Hill, height, peak: *kl gbʕ l kbd šdm* every height in the heart of the fields, 1.6 II 16 and par.; *b gbʕ tliyt* on the peak of victory, 1.3 III 31; *tblk (...) gbʕm mḥmd ḫrṣ* may (...) bring you (...) the hills, the most precious gold, 1.4 V 32 and par. Bkn ctx.: *mlk gbʕ hd*[, 1.9:10.

Cf. gbʕ(n).

gbʕl(y) TN (Belmonte RGTC 12/2 80: *Gibaʕlā*. Cf. Heltzer RCAU 9; Virolleaud Syria 21 1940 142f.; Astour JESHO 13 1970 114f.; UF 11 1979 15f.; UF 13 1981 5f., 11; Van Soldt SAU 337f. n. 177; UF 28 1996 664f.; UF 29 1997 699; UF 30 1998 718); ¶ syll.: URU gi_5(KI)-^{d}U*(-la)*, PRU 3 194 (RS 11.839):10, 15; PRU 6 131:11; Ug 5 95:16; RSOu 7 4:6; URU gi_5(KI)-^{d}IM, PRU 3 74 (RS 16.283):4'; URU gi_5(KI)*-bá-la*, PRU 4 72 (RS 17.335+):19; cf. URU gi_5(KI)*-ba-ʔ-li-yi*, PRU 6 79:4; cf. Lipiński OLP 12 1981 110; Van Soldt SAU 53, 337f. n. 177; cf. Nougayrol PRU 3 p. 265; PRU 6 p. 146; Huehnergard AkkUg 401f.: *^{al}ašar-baʕala/i*.

TN: 4.68:6; 4.365:6; 4.380:6; 4.610 (I) 7; 4.618:28 (Belmonte RGTC 12/2 80: rdg *gb<ʕ>l*, KTU:]*gbl*); 4.693:6; 4.750:11 (allograph *gbʕl*; cf. Van Soldt UF 28 1996 11; Belmonte AuOr 17/18 1999/2000 17 with n. 13); 4.784:7; 94.2614:5 (Bordreuil AntSem 2 1997 60 n. 5); "UF 29, 826":2; RSOu 14 35 [KTU 9.388] I 26; RSOu 14 36 [KTU 9.417]:3.

gbʕly (I) GN m. (< *gbʕl(y)*, TN); ¶ syll.: URU gi_5(KI)*-ba-ʔ-li-yi*, PRU 6 79:4; cf. LÚ URU gi_5(KI)-^{d}U*(-la)*, PRU 3 194 (RS 11.839)10, 15 (cf. Van Soldt SAU 53, 331 n. 159; cf. Nougayrol PRU 3, p. 194; PRU 6 p. 77; Huehnergard AkkUg 402: *^{al}ašar-ba-aʔ-li-yi*). ¶ Forms: sg. *gbʕly*; pl. *gbʕlym*.

GN: 4.33:27, 28 (Van Soldt SAU 33, 53); 4.40:16; 4.51:5; 4.386:2.

gbʕly (II) PN (< *gbʕly (II)*; cf. Grøndahl PTU 126; Zurro AuOr 1 1983 266).

PN: 4.177:2; 4.317:5;

gbʕ(n) PN (Sem. Cf. Grøndahl PTU 125f.; Caquot - Bordreuil Syria 56 1979 310; Watson AuOr 13 1995 221); ¶ syll.: cf. *gáb-a-nu*, PRU 3 68f. (RS 16.269):6 and *passim ibid.* Var. *gbʕ* in 4.63 II 10.

PN: ★a) 4.63 II 10; ★b) *bn PN:* 4.769:16.

gbl (I) n. m. "limit, frontier, end" (Hb. *gbwl* HALOT 171f.; Ph., Pun., Aram. *gbl*, DNWSI 209f.). ¶ Forms: sg. *gbl*.
Limit, frontier, end: *tqln b gbl šntk* if only you would run swiftly / fall at the end of your years!, 1.16 VI 57 and par. (diff. Margalit UF 8 1976 166f.; ZAW 99 1987 398ff.: 'all together', 'in a bunch', Palm. *gbl*, Arab. *ǧibl*, nHb. **gbl*; cf. Del Olmo IMC 111ff. for other explanations which propose *gbl (II)*).

gbl (II) n. m. "summit, mount" (Arab. *ǧabal*, Lane 379; cf. Del Olmo IMC 111; possibly related etym. to *gbl (I)*; cf. Renfroe AULS 103f.); ¶ par.: *PN* (?). ¶ Forms: sg. *gbl*.
Summit, mountain: *ʕbr gbl ʕbr qʕl* pass summits, pass heights, 1.3 VI 7 (diff. De Moor SP 51, n. 52; Sanmartín UF 10 1978 352 n. 26: TN, *gbl (III)*).

gbl (III) TN "Byblos" (Belmonte RGTC 12/2 95ff.: *Gublu*. Cf. Heltzer RCAU 9; Astour JAOS 92 1972 451f.; RSP 2 272, 348; Sivan GAGl 220; Dijkstra UF 23 1991 128ff.; cf. Hb., Ph. *gbl*, HALOT 173f.; Ur III cf. ÉNSI.GU$_5$.UB.LA.KI, Owen BibMes 25 1992 122; EA Akk. URU *gub/gu-ub-la/li*, EAT 1574; Rainey EAT 105; MA KUR *gu-bal*, Nashef RGTC 5 110; NA also URU *gu-ub-la-a-a*, KUR *gu-bal-a-a*, cf. Hrouda - Röllig RlA 3 673ff.; Eg. *kap-n-i$_2$*, Helck Bez. 60; *k(u?)p-ni*, Helck Bez. 263, 301; Gk *Byblos*); ¶ syll.: URU *gu-ub-li*, PRU 6 126:10 (cf. PRU 6 81 obv. 2'-3', 5'; Huehnergard UVST 218); KUR *gu$_5$-ub-li*, RSOu 7 9:10.
TN: *mlk gbl* the king of TN, 2.44:3; 4.338:13, 15; *bʕl gbl* the Baal of TN, 2.44:8. Cf. in bkn ctx. 4.618:28 (Belmonte RGTC 12/2 80: rdg *gb<ʕ>l*, cf. *gbʕl(y)*); 7.137:5.
Cf. gbln.

gbln PN (etym. unc. Cf. *gbl (III)*; Grøndahl PTU 126; Watson AuOr 11 1993 215). Cf. *kb/pl(n)*, PN.
PN: 4.63 III 94.

gbly GN m. (< *gbl*, TN); ¶ syll.: URU *gu-ub-li-yu*, PRU 6 81:rev. 2', 3', 5' (Belmonte RGTC 12/2 97). ¶ Forms: sg. *gbly*.
GN: 4.321:2.

gbrn PN (Sem. Cf. Grøndahl PTU 29, 126); ¶ syll.: DUMU *gu-ub-ru-na*, PRU 6 118:6'; cf. *ga-bi-ru*, PRU 3 196 (RS 15.42+) II 24'.
PN: ★a) 4.141 II 19; 4.730:6; ★b) *bn PN:* 4.309:17.

gbṯt n. f. "fleshy part of the back, hump" (cf. Aram. *gbš*, Jastrow 209; Akk. *gapšūtu, gipšu, gipšutu*, AHw 281, 290f.; CAD G 84f.; Caquot-Sznycer TOu 1 341 n. n.; Gibson CML 144; cf. Sanmartín UF 10

1978 349 n. 2); ¶ **par.**: *qrn*. ¶ **Forms**: sg. *gbṯ*.
Fleshy part of the back, hump: *bhm (...) gbṯt km ibrm* they will have (...) a hump like bulls, 1.12 I 31 (// *qrnm*).

gby PN (Sem.(?). Cf. Grøndahl PTU 126). PN: *bn PN*, 4.110:4.

gd (I) n. m. "coriander" (cf. Hb. *gd*, HALOT 176; cf. Arab. *ǧādiyy*, Lane 394. Cf. De Moor Or 37 1968 214; SP 85; De Moor - Spronk CARTU 132; Sasson RSP 1 403; Dahood RSP 3 92f.; Renfroe AULS 104; Cohen UF 28 1996 136); ¶ **par.**: *annḫ*. ¶ **Forms**: sg. *gdy*; pl. *gdm*.
Coriander: *kpr (...) rḥ gdm w anhbm* (they perfumed her) ... with the perfume of coriander and sea snails, 1.3 II 2 (diff. Aartun StUL 36f.: 'brünstige Ziegenböcke', **gdd*, but cf. *gd(y)*); (offering of) *gd b ḥlb* coriander(?) in milk, 1.23:14 (// *annḫ*; Caquot - Sznycer TOu 1 371; cf. Del Olmo MLC 441: *gd (III)*); *gd ḫlb* coriander from the massif, 1.85:20; 1.89:4; (cf. 1.97:13). Cf. **gd(y)**.

gd (II) n. m. "sinew, tendon" (Hb. *gyd*, HALOT 189; Syr. *gyodō*, LS 114; Akk. *gīdu*, AHw 287; CAD G 66f.); ¶ **par.**: *mtn*, *qn*, *qrn*, *ṯqb*. ¶ **Forms**: pl. *gdm*.
Sinew, tendon: *adr gdm b rumm* the toughest sinews of wild bulls, 1.17 VI 21 (// *ṯqbm*, *qrnt*, *mtnm*, *qnm*).

gdaḫ PN (Sem. Cf. Grøndahl PTU 126f.; Xella TRU 75).
PN: *bn PN*, 1.87:59.

gdl (I) adj. m. 1) "broad, wide"; 2) "fully grown, large"(?) (Hb. *gdl*, HALOT 179f.; Syr. *gdīl*, LS 105; cf. Sanmartín AuOr 8 1990 91; Watson UF 31 1999 787; cf. Ebla *ga-da*-LUM, an alimentary product, ARET 9 385); ¶ **RS Akk.**: cf. TÚG.GAD GAL-*tu*$_4$, Ug 5 28 l. e. 18' (cf. *rb (I)*). ¶ **Forms**: pl. *gdlm*.
1) Broad, wide, of garments: *ṯlṯ kdwṯm gdlm* three wide *k.*, 4.152:6.
2) Fully grown, large(?), of a type of grain or cereal(?): *ṯṯ dd gdl* six 'cauldronfuls' of *g.*, 4.14:1, 7, 13; cf. in bkn ctx. *dd gdl*, 4.426:4 and cf. *d*]*d nʕr*[, *ibid.* ln. 3 (cf. *nʕr (II)*).
Cf. **gdl (II)**, **gdlt (I)**, **gdlt (II)**, **mgdl**.

gdl (II) PN (Sem. Cf. Watson AuOr 8 1990 117; AuOr 11 1993 215).
PN: ★**a)** 4.788:3; 7.46:8; 7.140:1. ★**b)** *bn PN*: 4.240:2.

gdlt (I) n. f. "cattle, cow for sacrifice" (< "cattle"; lexicalization of the f. adj. *gdlt*; cf. *gdl (I)*; cf. *dq*); diff. Tropper UF 33 2001 545ff.: 'Dickbrot'. ¶ **Forms**: sg. / pl. *gdlt*.
Cattle, cow for sacrifice, *passim* in cultic literature (cf. esp. dedicatory formulae): *gdlt (l) DN* or *(l) DN gdlt* in 1.39; 1.41; 1.46; 1.53; 1.87; 1.106; 1.112; 1.119; 1.126; 1.132; 1.138; 1.162:18, 19.; cf. in Hurr.

ctx 1.132:5, 6, 7, 18, 19): *gdlt qdš il* one cow (is offered) in the sanctuary of DN, 1.119:6; *npš w arbʕ ʕšrh dqt w šbʕ gdlt w kl šbšlt dg gnh* one (piece of) offal and fourteen ewes and seven cows and all types of fish stew (are taken) to the 'garden', 1.106:21, cf. 1.112:26; *š dd šmn gdlt* one ewe, one jar of oil, one cow, 1.41:44 and par.; *alpm ʕṣrm gdlt* two oxen, two birds, one cow, 1.148:9.
Cf. gdl (I).

gdlt (II) n. f. "power, reach" (cf. *gdl (I)*; Hb. *gdwlh*, HALOT 178). ¶ Forms: sg. f. *gdlt*.
Power, reach: *b gdlt arkty*, with the power of my long arm, 1.3 V 23 and par.
Cf. gdl (I), mgdl, mgdly.

gdn PN (Sem. Cf. Grøndahl PTU 126; Watson AuOr 8 1990 117; AuOr 11 1993 215); ¶ syll.: cf. DUMU *gu-ud-da-na*(?), Ug 5 6:29. Cf. *gtn*, *kdn*, *ktn (II)*, *qtn (II)*.
PN: ★a) 4.96:98 (*bn urny*); 4.244:17; 4.658:18 (*bn uss*); 4.710:2; ★b) *bn PN*: 4.75 IV 12; 4.63 III 12.

gdrn PN (Sem. Cf. Grøndahl PTU 127; Watson AuOr 11 1993 215); ¶ syll.: DUMU *gu-da-ra-na*, PRU 3 202 (RS 16.257+) III 31, 35 (cf. Berger UF 1 1969 122: rdg *Gudda/ir*[*a*(*na*)] in Ug 5 6:29).
PN: *bn PN*: 3.7:7; 4.63 I 43; cf. in bkn ctx.: 4.617:19.

gdrt n. f. "hedge, fence" (Hb. *gdr*, *gdrh*, HALOT 180f.; Pun., Nab. *gdr*, DNWSI 215; Arab. *ǧadr*, Lane 389f.); ¶ par.: *ḫt*. ¶ Forms: sg. f. *gdrt*.
Hedge, fence: *k apʕ il b gdrt* like a 'divine' viper in a hedge, 1.19 I 13 (// *ḫth*; cf. Del Olmo IMC 127; cf. Cooper UF 20 1988 22: 'sheepfold').
Cf. gdrn.

gdš PN (etym. unc.; cf. Watson AuOr 8 1990 117).
PN: *bn PN*: 4.7:9.

gd(y) n. m. "kid" (Hb. *gdy*, HALOT 178; DNWSI 214; Pun. *gdʔ*, *gade*, DNWSI 213; Arab. *ǧady*, Lane 393; cf. NB *gadû*, AHw 273; CAD G 9. Cf. Del Olmo BSA 7 1993 186f.). ¶ Forms: sg. *gdy*, *gd*(?); du. *gdm*.
Kid, in cultic offering: *gdy lqḥ PN* PN took a kid, 1.79:4; *gdm klhn*(!) two kids for each, 1.111:7 (!) cf. Milik Ug 7 141); cf. in bkn ctx. [.]*gd*.*l r*[, 1.89:4; as merchandise: *ʕšrm gdy*{*x*} twenty kid (skins (?)) (for five units of oil and five of dregs), 4.150:3 (cf. *štp*; cf. Heltzer GPOTU 21; UF 12 1980 414 n. 4). For 1.3 II 2; 1.23:14; cf. *gd (I)*.

gdy PN (etym. unc. Cf. Grøndahl PTU 126; Sivan GAGl 217); ¶ syll.: cf. *ga-ad*-PI, PRU 3 133 (RS 15.132):19; cf. Huehnergard UVST 217.

PN: ★a) PN 4.150:3; ★b) *bn PN*: 4.423:23.

gg (I) n. m. "roof, flat roof, roof terrace, roofing" (Hb. *gg*, HAL; EA Akk. cf. /gaggu/ in *ga-ag-gi-m*[*i*], EAT 287:37; CAD G 9; Sivan GAGl 217. Cf. Fensham JNSL 7 1979 18). ¶ **Forms**: sg. *gg*; suff. *ggy*, *ggk*, *ggh*; pl. *ggt*.
Roof, flat roof, roof, terrace, roofing: *id* [*yd*] *bḥ mlk (...) b gg* then the king shall sacrifice (...) on the roof terrace, 1.41:50; *ṯḫ ggy b ym ṯiṯ* who plasters my roof when mud forms, 1.17 II 22 and par.; *w yrd krt l ggt* and may PN come down from the roof terraces, 1.14 II 27; *gg šmm* the roofing of the heavens, 1.13:11 (cf. De Moor ARTU: *mṯbk b gg* '[your] dwelling on the roof(?!)').

gg (II) PN (etym. unc. Cf. Grøndahl PTU 127; Huehnergard JAOS 107 1987 714 n. 2; ; Watson AuOr 8 1990 117; AuOr 11 1993 215; AuOr 13 1995 221).
PN: 4.102:2; cf. in bkn ctx.: 4.17:19; 4.678:5.

ggʕt PN (etym. unc.).
PN: *bn PN*, 4.364:4; cf. in bkn ctx.: 4.337:9.

ggn n. m. "insides", said of a person ((*g(n)gn*) < *gngn*; diff. Delekat UF 4 1972 22: 'Garde'; Margalit UF 8 1976 158; MLD 70: 'genie, soul', Arab. *ǧanan*, but cf. Renfroe AULS 105 n. 10; Dijkstra UF 26 1994 119: 'famulus'). ¶ **Forms**: sg. m. suff. *ggnh*.
Insides: *w ywsrnn ggnh* and his insides instructed him, 1.16 VI 26.
Bkn ctx.: *tšlḥm yrḫ ggn*, 1.92:16.

ggy PN (etym. unc. Cf. Grøndahl PTU 127; Dietrich - Loretz - Sanmartín UF 6 1974 23; Watson AuOr 8 1990 117; AuOr 14 1996 97); ¶ **syll.**: DUMU *ga-ga-ya*, Ug 5 12:1.
PN: *bn PN*, 4.429:3.

***/g-h(-h/y)/**
Cf. **tgh**.

ghl, 1.45:3, cf. *gl (I)*.

ghrt "?" (Bordreuil - Pardee RSOu 14 p. 390: /g-h-r/ vb 'résonner', Aram. Syr. 'weakness (of eyes, spirit)', Arab. 'power and clarity').
? : *ghrt phm w šptḥm* ... in their mouth and on their lips, RSOu 14 52 [KTU 9.435]:11 (Bordreuil - Pardee RSOu 14 p. 387: '(dès) qu'elle résonne dans leur bouche et sur leurs lèvres').

gḫt, in bkn and unc. ctx.: *ʕ*]*št ʕšr rmṯt gḫt*, 4.127:5.

/g-ḫ-ṭ/ vb G: "to cast out" (cf. Syr. *gʕaṭ*, LS 127; JAram. *gh/ḥṭ*, Jastrow 215; cf. De Moor UF 18 1986 255ff.; Dietrich - Loretz TUAT 2 335). ¶ **Forms**: G prefc. with suff. *tgḫṭk*.
G. To cast out: *tgḫṭk r*[*gm*] *bʕl tgḫṭk w tṣu* may the word of DN cast

you out, cast you out and out you go, 1.169:1-2.

/g-l/ vb G: "to rejoice"; D: "to make (teeth?) chatter / grind" (Hb. *gyl*, HALOT 189f.; cf. Arab. *ǧāla*, Lane 488ff. Cf. Van Zijl JNSL 2 1972 77ff.); ¶ **syll. Ug.**: cf. PN *ia-gi-li*, PRU 3 194 (RS 11.787):9; Sivan GAGl 221; ¶ **par.**: /n-š-y/, /š-m-ḫ/. ¶ **Forms**: G prefc. *ygl*, *ngln*, *tgwln*.

G. To rejoice: *b lmtk ngln* in your immortality we rejoice, 1.16 I 15 and par. (// *nšmḫ*).

D. To make (teeth?) chatter / grind": *k tgwln šntk* make your teeth chatter / grind, 1.82:4 (// *l tššy*; cf. De Moor ARTU 176: 'they make your teeth cry out'; Caquot TOu 2 64 n. 172: 'quand tes années accomplissent leur circuit', Arab. *ǧawwala*).

gl (I) n. m. "stentorian shout, cry of jubilation" (< /g-l/; Sanmartín UF 12 1980 339 n. 54: cf. Hb. *gyl(h)*, HALOT 190); ¶ **par.**: *nblu*. ¶ **Forms**: pl. *ghl*.

Stentorian shout, cry of jubilation (said of thunder): *šbʕt ghl ph* seven are the cries of his mouth, 1.45:3 (// *nbluh*).

gl (II) n. m. "cup" (Hb. *glh*, HALOT 192; Akk. *gullu*, AHw 297; CAD G 129; Arab. *ǧullat*, Lane 437; Ebla cf. *gú/ku*$_{17}$(TIK)*-li-lum*, Archi Eblaitica 1 67 n. 21: /gul(i)lum/ or /kulīlum/. Cf. Fensham JNSL 4 1975 18; Márquez UF 25 1993 319 n.4.); **par.**(?): *glgl*. ¶ **Forms**: sg. m. *gl*.

Cup: *yṣq b gl ḥtṯ yn b gl ḫrṣ nbt* he poured wine into a silver cup, honey into a golden cup, 1.14 IV 1-2 and par. Bkn ctx. *gl* [...] *yhpk* a cup [...] was overturned, 1.13:35 (cf. *glgl*, ln. 33).

gl (III) n. m. which qualifies a farm or field (etym. unc.); ¶ **RS Akk.**: cf. A.ŠÀ.MEŠ GA*-al-lu ša PN*, PRU 3 112 (RS 15.126):5 (unlikely Huehnergard UVST 174: EA Akk. *qallu* 'small', or else *qallu* 'forest', EAT 359 rev. 5, 18; AHw 894; CAD Q 66). ¶ **Forms**: sg. *gl*.

Qualifying a farm of field: *šd gl PN g.-field of* PN, 4.356:3 (for the altern. rdg. *šd ṣṣ*(!) *PN* "saline (/ salt marsh(?)) of PN" cf. RS Akk.: A.ŠÀ. MUN(.ḪI.A) : *ṣí-ṣú(-ú)-ma*, PRU 3 124 (RS 15.167+):12; PRU 6 28 rev. 2'. Cf. *ṣṣ*).

glʕd PN (Sem.. Cf. Grøndahl PTU 107, 128); ¶ **syll.**: DUMU *ga-la-a-da*, PRU 6 70:9. PN: ★**a)** 4.93 I 14; 4.412 III 11; ★**b)** *gt PN*, 4.125:2 (Belmonte RGTC 12/2 85: *Gittu-Galʕada*).

glb (I) n. m.; a type of barley (*Hordeum spontaneum* (?); cf. Akk. *gulbūtu*, AHw 296; CAD G 127; Dietrich - Loretz - Sanmartín UF 5 1973 106). ¶ **Forms**: pl. *glbm*.

A type of barley: *prś glbm* a *p.* of *g.*, 4.269:29; 4.275:16.

glb (II) TN (?) (Belmonte RGTC 12/2 77: *Galbā*. Cf. Dietrich - Loretz - Sanmartín UF 5 1973 106; Van Soldt UF 28 1996 665; UF 29 1997 701f.); ¶ syll.: cf. URU *gal-ba*, PRU 3 91 (RS 16.170 [: PRU 4 78]):10', 11'.
TN (?), in unc. ctx.: 2.62:5. For 4.610 (II) 28 cf. *ḫlb (II)* 2.e: *ḫlb ṣpn*.

glbt(y) TN (Belmonte RGTC 12/2 98: *Gulbatā*. Cf. Heltzer RCAU 9; Dietrich - Loretz - Sanmartín UF 5 1973 106f.; Astour UF 13 1981 7; Van Soldt SAU 338 n. 177; UF 28 1996 665; UF 29 1997 694; UF 30 1998 732); ¶ syll.: URU *gul-ba-ta*, PRU 3 190 (RS 11.830):12; 191 (RS 15.20):2; PRU 4 51 (RS 17.340):26'; RSOu 7 4:13; cf. LÚ URU *gu-la-bat*, RSOu 7 25:21.
TN: 4.267:4; 4.610 (II) 27; 4.621:11; RSOu 14 35 [KTU 9.388] II 14; cf. in bkn ctx.: 4.308:15; 4.643:21 (Van Soldt UF 30 1998 713); 4.676:2; 4.693:47 (cf. Bordreuil Syria 61 1984 9; UF 20 1988 17f.); allograph *glbt*, 4.94:13; 4.303:2 (cf. Van Soldt UF 28 1996 665; Belmonte RGTC 12/2 98).

gld(y) PN (etym. unc. Cf. Dietrich - Loretz OLZ 62 1976 537f.; Grøndahl PTU 127, 204, 238f.; Zadok JQR 71 1980/81 108; Sivan GAGl 218); ¶ syll.: cf. *gal-di*, PRU 6 83 II 9'; Huehnergard AkkUg 386. Var. *gldy* in 4.110:17.
PN: ★a) 4.75 III 5 (*bt klb*); 4.110:17; ★b) *bn PN*: 4.617:3 (bkn ctx.).

glgl (I) n. m. "cup" (?) (cf. *gl*; Hb. *glgl*, HALOT 190; Akk. *gulgullu*, AHw 296; CAD G 127. Diff. De Moor UF 12 1980 310: 'to roll', Hb. *gll*); ¶ par.: *gl*. ¶ Forms: sg. m. *glgl*.
Cup ((?), in bkn ctx.): *glgl a*[...]*m rḥ ḫd ʿrpt* a cup he [took in his hand wi]th(?) the wind, the downpour (and) the clouds, 1.13:33 (// *gl*).

glgl (II) PN (etym. unc. Cf. Grøndahl PTU 127; Watson AuOr 13 1995 221).
PN: *bn PN*: 4.339:13 (*uškny*).

gl[ḥ]t "?", 1.19 II 32.

gll, 4.683:31, see *glltky*.

glln PN (etym. unc. Cf. Grøndahl PTU 128; Watson AuOr 8 1990 117; AuOr 13 1995 221). Cf. *gllr*.
PN: 4.110:19.

gllr PN (rdg and etym. unc.). Cf. *glln*.
PN: *bn g*[[x?]]*llr*, 4.787:1 (Bordreuil Semitica 32 1982 13: *glln*).

glltky TN (Belmonte RGTC 12/2 77: **Galīlu-tūkiya*. Cf. Heltzer RCAU 9; Astour RSP 2 273, 347; UF 11 1979 20; Van Soldt UBL 11 366 n. 15; UF 28 1996 665); ¶ syll.: URU *ga-li-li-tu-ki-ia*, PRU 6 78:9; cf. Huehnergard UVST 185, 217; Van Soldt SAU 337 n. 177.

in 4.683:31.
TN: 4.408:5; 4.643:11, 12; 4.683:31 (var. spelling *gll.tky*).

gln PN (etym. unc. Cf. Grøndahl PTU 205, 234, 236; Dietrich - Loretz OLZ 62 1967 537f.; Sivan GAGl 218); ¶ syll.: cf. DUMU *gal-la-na*, PRU 6 47:4; 83 IV 10; RSOu 7 3 rev. 12'; cf. Huehnergard AkkUg 386; cf. Van Soldt SAU 40 for Syria 15 1934 137ff. (Lattaquié [RS Varia 3]):4, 29; DUMU *gi-la-na*, PRU 6 57:2. Cf. *kln*.
PN: ★a) 4.63 I 27; 4.635:43; 4.759:9 (*bn ilyn*); cf. 4.86:6 (*bn ʕṯt*[; rdg unc. *s/gln*); ★b) *bn PN*: 4.12:6; 4.309:11; 4.327:3; 4.379:1:3 (*ary*).

/g-l-ṯ/ vb G: "to jump, seethe"(?) (cf. Hb. *glš*, HALOT 195; JAram. *glš*, Jastrow 251. Cf. Van Zijl Baal 110; Lipiński UF 3 1971 86ff.; diff. Dijkstra UF 26 1994 118: 'engulfed'; Tuell JBL 112 1993 99ff.: 'flow in waves'; Wakemann GBM 102 n. 3: 'to go down', Hb. *glš*). ¶ Forms: G prefc. *tglṯ*.
G. To jump, seethe(?): in bkn ctx.: *w tglṯ thmt* and the abyss seethed (?), 1.92:5.

glṯ n. m. "snow" (metathesis < **ṯlg*; cf. Hb. *šlg*, HALOT 1503; Aram. *tlg*, Jastrow 1670; Akk. *šalgu*, AHw 1147; CAD Š 241f.; Arab. *ṯalǧ*, Lane 350; Eg. *śrg*, *śá-l-qu*, WäS 4 204; Helck Bez. 520 (199). Cf. Aartun WO 4 1968 280f.; De Moor UF 1 1969 181f.; diff. Lipiński UF 3 1971 86f.: 'tempête', *glṯ/glš*, cf. /g-l-ṯ/, cf. Caquot - Sznycer TOu 1 207f. n. u; Caquot TOu 2 49 n. 110: 'flot'; Loretz SEL 12 1995 118: 'Sturm'; Margalit MLD 214f. n. 1: 'bald', Syr. *glš*); ¶ par.: *mṭr*. ¶ Forms: sg. *glṯ*.
Snow: *ʕdn ṯkt b glṯ* the abundance(?) of the *ṯ*-boat in the snow, 1.4 V 7 (// *mṭr*). In bkn ctx.: *rišh b glṯ b šm*[*m*] his head in the snow of the heavens (?), 1.101:7; *glṯ isr*[, 1.8:13.

/g-l-y/ vb G/N: "to present oneself, make one's way, go" (Hb. *glh*, HALOT 191f.; Ph., Aram., *gly*, DNWSI 223f.; Syr. *glō*, LS 115; *ǧalā*, Lane 446ff.; Akk. *galû*, AHw 275. Cf. Mulder UF 2 1970 365; Aartun UF 16 1984 9f.; on the likely semantic development cf. Oldenburg CEB 129 n. 5, 189; Clifford CBQ 33 1970 231 n. 4; Sanmartín UF 10 1978 451 n. 6 (N?; cf. esp. 'to present oneself'); ¶ par.: /b-ʔ/, /y-t-n/ *(+ pnm)*. ¶ Forms: G/N: prefc. *tgly*, *tgl*, *ygly*, *ygl*.
G/N. To present oneself, make one's way, go: *w ygl w ynsk (...)* may he present himself and shed (...), 1. 82:1 (in bkn ctx.); *tgly ḏd il w tbu* she made her way to the cave of DN and entered, 1.4 IV 23 and par. (// *ttn pnm*; travel formula; cf. Del Olmo MLC 39; Watson AuOr 17/18 1999/2000 125ff.); *bkt tgly w tbu* weeping she made her way

(to the house of PN) and entered, 1.16 VI 4 (cf. Sanmartín UF 10 1978 451 n. 6: 'sich zeigen').

glyn(?) PN (etym. and rdg unc. Cf. Grøndahl PTU 204f., 236; Weippert ZDPV 82 1966 329f.; Watson AuOr 8 1990 244; AuOr 13 1995 221; Israel SEL 8 1991 139 n. 233); ¶ syll.: cf. *g*[*u-l*]*i-ya*, PRU 6 83 IV 17. Cf. *klyn*.

PN: *bn PN*: 4.106:18 (rdg unc.; KTU: *glyt/n*).

gm (I), cf. *g*.

gm (II) adv. "also, even" (Hb. *gm*, HALOT 195f. Cf. Dietrich - Loretz MU 107f.). ¶ Forms: *gm*.

Also, even: in bkn and unc. ctx. *gm šš*[(if) also (...), 1.103+:3 (diff. Pardee AfO 33 1986 129: rdg *gmš š*['smooth (without) h[air?]', Arab. *gamaša*, *gamîšun* (sic!)).

/g-m-ḏ/ vb G: "to rejoice" (Arab. *ǧamaza*, Lane 454; diff. Gray LC 76 n. 3: 'to convulse', Eth. *ǧamasa* (?)); ¶ par.: /ẓ-ḥ-q/. ¶ Forms: G prefc. *ygmḏ*.

G. To rejoice: *w ygmḏ bm kbd* and he rejoiced in (his heart, 1.12 I 13 (// *yẓḥq*).

gmḥ(n) PN (etym. unc. Cf. Grøndahl PTU 29, 128; Watson AuOu 8 1990 118). Var. *gmḥ* in 4.51:3.

PN: *bn PN*: 4.51:3; 4.55:28 (cf. Van Soldt SAU 33); 4.214 III 8.

gml (I) n. m. "first quarter (of the moon)" (Akk. *gamlu*, AHw 279; CAD G 34f. Cf. Driver CML 127 n. 6; Healey UF 15 1983 50; cf. Farber ZA 69 1980 303; Gallagher UF 26 1994 136; diff. Rin AE 293; Watson NUS 24 1981 9: 'sickle', metathesis of Hb. *mgl*, Syr. *maggĕlō̆*). ¶ Forms: sg. *gml*.

First quarter: *bnt hll bʕl gml* the daughters of DN, he of the first quarter, 1.24:42 (cf. Herrmann YN 21; Goetze JBL 60 1941 360).

gml (II) n. m. "?" (cf. Del Olmo AuOr 6 1988 100: 'totalidad', MHb. *gml*; Sanmartín UF 12 1980 335: 'Reserverind', Akk. *gimlu*; De Moor - Spronk UF 14 1982 161 n. 65: 'branches with ripe fruit', Hb. *gml*, // *ur (II)* 'greenery'; cf. *ur*). ¶ Forms: sg. m. *gml*.

? : in bkn ctx. *ṯmn ṯmn gml*[*h*] eight eight ..., 1.104:22.

gmm PN (etym. unc. Cf. Grøndahl PTU 128).

PN: 4.55:10.

gmn (I) n. m. "funeral offering" ((?), etym. unc.; cf. by metonymy Akk. *kamānu*, AHw 430; CAD K 110f.; Hb. *kwn*, HALOT 466. Diff.: Dietrich - Loretz - Sanmartín UF 8 1976 432: rdg *kgmn*, Hurro-Akk. *kukumnu*, AHw 501; CAD K 501; De Moor SP 199; ARTU 83 n. 405: 'to be defiled', Eth. *gammana*; Watson AuOr 7 1989 129ff.:

'mourning', root /(ʔ-)g-m/ + *n*; UF 28 1996 709; cf. also Sasson RSP 1 403f.; Rin AE 210f.; Caquot - Sznycer TOu 1 254f. n. e; Margalit MLD 141f.). ¶ **Forms**: sg. *gmn*.

Funeral offering(?): *ṯṭbḫ (....) k gmn* she slaughtered (....) as a funeral offering(?), 1.6 I 19-29.

gmn (II) PN (etym. unc. Cf. Grøndahl PTU 128; Watson AuOr 7 1989 129f.). Cf. *kmn*.

PN: 4.280:8 (*bn usyy*); *gm*[[*ḏn*]]*n*, 4.410:29.

gmnpk PN (etym. unc. Cf. Grøndahl PTU 128, 167).

PN: 4.638:3.

gmr n. m. "champion, fighter" (Hb. *gmr*, HALOT 197f.; Akk. *gāmiru*, AHw 278f., CAD G 34; Arab. *ǧammara*, Lane 452sf; Eth. *gamara*, CDG 194f. Cf. Dahood ThS 14 1953 595ff.; Dijkstra - De Moor UF 7 1975 214; Watson UF 9 1977 275; Dietrich - Loretz UF 19 1987 21; diff. Good UF 26 1994 150f.: rdg *km grm* 'like lion whelps'); **syll. Ug. / ¶ RS Akk.**: cf. the elements /gamir-/, /igmar-/ in PNN; Sivan GAGl 220; ¶ **RS Akk.**: ideogr. BE (/gamir, gimr, igmar/(?); Van Soldt UF 20 1988 314 n. 15; UF 21 1989 372 n. 22. ¶ **Forms**: sg. *gmr*.

Champion, fighter: ★**a)** *ytʕn k gmrm* they attacked (each other) like champions, 1.6 VI 16; for other opinions relating to names of objects and animals cf. Sasson RSP 1 404; Van Zijl Baal 267f., 346f. (for the rdg *ả*(!)*mrm* 'ibex, mountain goat(?)' cf. Del Olmo BSA 7 1993 187); ★**b)** 'the Champion', title of the god Baal: *hwt gmr hd* the word of the 'Champion' DN, 1.2 I 46 (Cooper RSP 3 444f.; cf. PNN *ig-mar/ma-ra-*ᵈIM, PRU 3 48 (RS 16.248):4, 7; *gmrd*, *gmr(h)d*).

Cf. **gmrd, gmr(h)d, gmrn, gmrš, gmrt, mgmr, tgmr, ygmr**.

gmrd PN; cf. *gmr(h)d*.

gmr(h)d PN (Sem. Cf. Virolleaud Syria 21 1940 110; Weippert ZDPV 82 1966 325; Grøndahl PTU 128, 133; Huehnergard UVST 248 n. 154; Van Soldt SAU 22, 27, 209); ¶ **syll.**: *ga-mi-rad-du/di* PRU 3 116 (RS 16.148+) rev. 8', 11' (cf. Huehnergard AkkUg 359); *gi-im-ra-du* PRU 3 203 (RS 16.257+) IV 10; cf. BE.ᵈIM, RS 20.181B; BE-ᵈU/IM, RS 22.346+; BE.U, RS 25.453+; cf. Van Soldt UF 20 1988 314ff. (c, h, m) con n. 15; SAU 20 n. 179. Var. *gmrhd* in 4.75 VI 7; 4.753:6.

PN: 4.7:10-11., 15 (cf. Van Soldt SAU 36); 4.75 VI 7 (*bn srṯ*); 4.103:14, 23-24., 49-50. (cf. Van Soldt SAU 36); 4.165:10 (cf. Van Soldt SAU 36); 4.425:15 (cf. Van Soldt SAU 36); 4.692:6-7. (cf. Van Soldt SAU 36, 177); 4.753:6 (cf. Van Soldt SAU 36).

gmrn PN (Sem. Cf. Grøndahl PTU 128). Cf. *kmrn*.

PN: ★a) 4.127:11; ★b) *bn PN*: 4.335:27.

gmrš PN (Hurro-Sem.(?). Cf. Weippert ZDPV 82 1966 322f.; Grøndahl PTU 128, 239, 250ff.; Sivan GAGl 220); ¶ syll.: *ga-mi-ir-šu*, PRU 3 203 (RS 16.257+) IV 11; *ga-me-er-šu/ši*, PRU 6 54:17; 83 III 9. Cf. *kmrṯn*.

PN: ★a) 4.75 IV 7 (*bn mrnn*); 4.313:18; ★b) *bn PN*: 422:41.

gmrt PN (Sem. Cf. Grøndahl PTU 77, 128).

PN: ★a) 4.277:7; ★b) *bn PN*: 4.63 I 10; 4.368:19; 4.377:18.

gmš PN ((?) < DN *kmṯ*; cf. Ribichini - Xella SEL 8 1991 160; Israel Semitica 41/42 1991/92 59 n. 1; Watson AuOr 8 1990 118; AuOr 13 1995 221); ¶ syll.: DUMU *ga-mi-ši*, PRU 3 167 (RS 15.139):7 (cf. Van Soldt BiOr 46 1988 649; Nougayrol PRU 3 p. 167: *ga-mi-lim*).

PN: *bn PN*, 4.611:18; 4.713:2 (rdg unc.).

gmz PN (etym. unc.; cf. Watson AuOr 8 1990 117).

PN: *bn PN*: 4.350:14.

gn (I) n. m. 1) "garden, orchard"; 2) "cemetery, (royal) pantheon"; 3) month name (Hb., Aram., Nab., Palm. *gn*, HALOT 198; DNWSI 227; Akk. *gannu*, *gannatu*, AHw 280; CAD G 41; Ebla cf. *gú-nu(gú-nu)*[ki], Mander MROA 2/1 30; Arab. *ǧannat*, Lane 463. Cf. Dietrich - Loretz - Sanmartín UF 6 1974 23f.; Del Olmo SEL 3 1986 62f.); ¶ syll. Ug.: cf. the elem. /gannu-/ in TN URU *ar-zi-ga-na*, Ug 5 27:42s., 52; Sivan GAGl 218; ¶ RS Akk.: $KIRI_6$(GIŠ.ŠAR)(.MEŠ), (A.ŠÀ.)$KIRI_6$ (.MEŠ); cf. Huehnergard AkkUg 384; cf. $KIRI_6$: *kì-ru-ú*, PRU 3 47 (RS 16.150):15; ¶ par.: *ʕmq*. ¶ Forms: sg. *gn*; suff. *gnh* (adv. *-h*).

1) Garden, orchard: *ṯḥrṯ km gn ap lb* he ploughed (his) chest like an orchard, 1.6 I 4 and par. (// *ʕmq*); *PN (...) ytn šd PN (...) yd gth yd gnh yd krmh yd klklh w ytn{.}nn l PN (...) ʕd ʕlm* PN (...) PN (...) has gifted the estate of PN (...) together with its farmstead, its olive-grove(s), its vineyard(s) and everything else and has ceded it to PN (...) in perpetuity, 3.5:8. Cf. 4.75 V 17.

2) 'Garden', cemetery, royal pantheon, ★a): *w kl šbšlt dg gnh* and all types of fish stews in the 'garden', 1.106:22; *ṯb rgm b gn* (there shall be) a giving of the reply in the 'garden', 1.106:23 (cf. Tsukimoto Kispum 61f.); ★b) In divine titles: *ršp gn* DN of the 'garden' (cf. Del Olmo SEL 1983 69 n. 38; Xella WGE 356; Xella NABU 1995 89; diff. Dietrich - Loretz - Sanmartín UF 6 1974 23f.: 'Schutz', **gnn* (?); Dahood - Pettinato Or 46 1977 230ff.: 'DN of TN', Ebla [d]*ra-sa-ap gú-nu(m)*[ki]; cf. Bonechi MARI 8 489ff.); cf. 6.62:2; thirteen measures (of wine) [*l b*]*t ršp gn* for the temple of DN of the 'garden', 4.219:3; in bkn ctx.: 1.165:3.

3) MN, probably corresponding to June-July (Watson Fs. Dietrich 549): *b ṯmn gn* on (day) eight of *g.*, 1.106:18 (cf. De Tarragon CU 24); *yrḫ gn* the month of *g.*, 4.220:5 (cf. 4.219:14).
Cf. gt.

gn (II) PN (Sem.(?). Cf. Grøndahl PTU 30, 129; Dietrich - Loretz - Sanmartín UF 6 1974 24).
PN: *bn PN*, 4.75 V 17.

gnb PN (Sem.(?). Cf. Grøndahl PTU 28, 129).
PN: *bn PN*, 4.50:7; 4.52:1 (cf. Van Soldt SAU 33).

gnʕ(y) TN (Belmonte RGTC 12/2 77f.: *Ganʕā*. Cf. Heltzer RCAU 9; Virolleaud Syria 21 1940 142; Astour RSP 2 274, 347; UF 13 1981 7; Bordreuil UF 20 1988 10, 12, 17; Xella MLE 1 1982 54; Van Soldt SAU 331 n. 159, 338 n. 177; UBL 11 377f.); ¶ syll.: URU *ga-an-a*, PRU 3 189 (RS 11.790):18'; PRU 3 190 (11.800):21'; 191 (RS 11.841):17'; PRU 6 53:9' (Van Soldt UF 28 1996 665); RSOu 7 4:27; URU *gán-na-a*, PRU 3 190 (RS 11.830):1 (cf. Van Soldt SAU 331 159); URU *ga-ni-a*, PRU 6 70 (RS 17.50):17 (cf. Van Soldt SAU 338 n. 177). Var. *gnʕ* in 4.382:14.
TN: 4.48:12 (Xella MLE 1 1982 54); 4.68:56; 4.73:11 (Belmonte AuOr 17/18 1999/2000 17); 4.213:23; 4.297:4; 4.365:26; 4.380:17; 4.382:4 (allograph *gnʕ*); RSOu 14 35 [KTU 9.388]: I 34. Bkn.: 4.610 (I) 30 (Xella MLE 1 1982 54; Belmonte AuOr 17/18 1999/2000 17 n. 15); 4.693:25 (Bordreuil UF 20 1988 17).

gnʕy GN m. (< *gnʕ(y)*, TN). ¶ Forms: pl. *gnʕym*.
GN: 3.3:13; 4.297:4.

gngn n. m. "insides, heart" (cf. Arab. *ǧanan*, Lane 403. Cf. Caquot - Sznycer TOu 1 218 n. u; Hoftijzer UF 4 1972 157 n. 17; Tropper UF 26 1994 461 n. 19; Watson UF 32 2000 568; but cf. Renfroe AULS 105; diff. De Moor SP 170f.: 'tunnel, libation pipe', = *knkn*, *kkn*, Arab. *ǧanan*; cf. Pope Maarav 1 1978 26); ¶ par.: *npš*. ¶ Forms: sg. suff. *gngnh*.
Insides, heart: *ystrn ydd b gngnh* may the 'beloved' instruct himself in his insides (: inmost being), 1.4 VII 49 (// *npšh*; cf. Del Olmo MLC 210 for other versions).
Cf. ggn.

gngnt part of the composite toponym *ḫlb gngnt*; cf. *ḫlb gngnt*, *ḫlb(y)*.

gntn PN (Sem. Cf. Grøndahl PTU 129, 424; Sivan GAGl 220); ¶ syll.: DUMU *gi-na-ta*(?)*-na*, PRU 3 113 (RS 15.114):4.
PN: *bn PN*, 4.422:47.
Cf. gt.

gny PN (Sem.(?). Cf. Grøndahl PTU 30, 129; Dietrich - Loretz - Sanmartín UF 6 1974 24; Astour RSP 2 273).
PN: 4.54:12.
Cf. **gnʕ(y)** TN, **gnʕy** GN, **kny** PN.

gnym PN (Sem.(?). Cf. Grøndahl PTU 129, 144; Astour RSP 2 273; Dietrich - Loretz - Sanmartín UF 6 1974 24).
PN: *bn PN*: 4.55:13.

gp n. m.(?) 1) "shore, bank"; 2) "boundary, slope, hillside" (MHb., Aram. *gyp*, Jastrow 241; cf. De Moor SP 166; Van Zijl Baal 148ff.; Schloen JNES 52 1993 217); ¶ **par.**: *yʕr*. ¶ **Forms**: sg. *gp*; pl. *gpt*.
1) Shore: *gp ym* the shore of the sea, 1.23:30; *gp thm* shore of the ocean, 1.23:30.
2) slope: *tiḫd (...) šnu bʕl gpt ġr* take refuge (...) did the adversaries of DN in the slopes of the hill, 1.4 VII 36 (// *yʕrm*; diff. Margalit MLD 64: 'slope', Arab.**ǧnf*; Gray LC 52 n. 6: 'the inmost recesses', Arab. *ǧanf*; Lipiński RY 205 n. 3: 'repaires', Arab. *ǧawf*; Caquot - Sznycer TOu 1 217 n. k: 'interieur', Arab. *ǧawf*; Dahood PNSP 18: 'ridge', Hb. *gwph*).

gpn (I) n. m. "(vine-)stock, vine, vineyard" (Hb. *gpn*, HALOT 200; Syr. *gupnō*, LS 128; Arab. *ǧafn*, Lane 434; OSA *gpnt*, DOSA 74; Akk. *gapnu*, AHw 281; CAD G 44ff.; Ebla cf. /gapnānu(m)/ in Ú.TIR = *ga-ba-na-na-um$_x$*, *kab-na-ne-um$_x$*, VE 1431'; ŠE.NINNI$_5$ = *kà-ba-na-na-ù*, EV 0392; Arcari Biling. 324); ¶ **syll. Ug.**: cf. A.ŠÀ.]ḪI.A : *ga*-BI-*ni* (TN), PRU 3 119 (RS 16.204):12; cf. Kühne UF 6 1974 164: < /gapinu/ (*/gapnu/); Sivan GAGl 218; cf. Huehnergard UVST 115f.: < /gabīnu/ 'hillock'(?)). ¶ **Forms**: sg. *gpn*.
(Vine-)stock, vine, vineyard: *yzbrnn zbrm gpn yṣmdnn ṣmdm gpn yšql šdmt km gpn* the pruners pruned him (like) a vine, the binders bound him (like) a vine, threw him out to the untilled land like a vine-stock, 1.23:9-11. Cf. *gpn lk*, 2.13:35; *gpn*, 5.23:11.
Cf. **gpn (IV)**, **gpn(y)**.

gpn (II) n. m. "harness" (Arab. *ǧafn*, *ǧaffafa*, *tiǧfāf*, Lane 434, 431f.; cf. Hb. *gpn*, Gn 49:11, HALOT 200; Sasson RSP 1 405; diff. Margalit UF 15 1983 105 n. 2; Margalit UF 16 1984 134f.: **gwp* + *n*, 'saddle-seat', cf. Greenfield Bib 45 1964 527ff.; but cf. Renfroe UF 18 1986 65ff.; Van der Lugt - De Moor BiOr 31 1974 25: 'reins', *gpn (I)*); ¶ **par.**: *nqbn*. ¶ **Forms**: sg. *gpn*; du./pl. *gpnm*; suff. *gpny*.
Harness: *ʕdb gpn atn[y]* prepare the harness of my she-ass, 1.4 IV 7; *št gpnm dt ksp* they put on the harnesses of silver, 1.4 IV 10 and par. (¶ **par.**: *nqbnm*; cf. 1.19 II 4).

gpn (III) DN; one of Baal's messenger-boys (*gpn w ugr*, cf. *gpn (I)*; cf. Segert - Zgusta ArOr 21 1953 273; Best UF 5 1973 58 n. 32; Haas - Thiel UF 11 1979 339f. Cf. Pope WbMyth 284f.; Albright BASOR 83 1941 41 n. 19; Ginsberg BASOR 95 1944 25ff.; Cassuto GA 131; Pope WbMyth 284f.; Fensham OrAn 5 1966 162f.; De Moor SP 53; Loewenstamm EI 14 1978 1 n. 1).
DN *gpn w ugr*: 1.3 III 36; 1.4 VII 54; VIII 47; 1.5 I 12; 1.8 II 6.

gpn (IV) TN (Belmonte RGTC 12/2 98: *Gupnā*. Cf. Kühne UF 6 1974 164f.; Van Soldt UF 28 1996 665; cf. Astour JNES 22 1963 232); ¶ syll.: cf. URU *gup-na*, RSOu 7 4:5; cf. *gpn (I)*.
TN: 4.358:7.
Cf. gpny.

gpn(y) PN (Sem.(?). Cf. Grøndahl PTU 30, 73, 129; Kühne UF 6 1974 164f.; Watson AuOr 8 1990 118, 245); ¶ syll.: cf. PN *gu-pa-na*, PRU 3 195 (RS 11.839):18 (cf. Sivan GAGl 221). Var. *gpny* in 4.125:17.
PN: ★a) 2.6:3; 4.339:20 (*bn tly*); ★b) *bn PN*: 4.261:24; cf. in bkn ctx.: 4.245:13.
Cf. gpny.

gpny GN (< *gpn (IV)*).
GN: 4.125:17.

gpp PN (etym. unc.).
PN: 4.706:4.

***/g-p-r/**
Cf. gpr.

gpr n. m. "opponent" (?) (act. ptc. G */g-p-r/; cf. Akk. *guppuru*, Ahw 281; CAD G *gubburu* 118. Cf. Del Olmo IMC 292; Caquot SEL 2 1985 102: 'vaincre'; diff. Virolleaud LPD 136: 'espèce d'arbre', Hb. *gpr*, Dijkstra - De Moor UF 7 1975 199: 'hero', Akk. *gab/pru*, Hb. *gbr*, *gbwr*, Margalit UF 16 1984 122f.: 'those-who-inhabit-the-pits', Arab. *ǧufrat*, but cf. Renfroe UF 18 1986 64; Ajjan NU 37: 'esclave', Arab. *ǧabr*, Cooper UF 20 1988 21: 'carcass', Arab. *ǧafīr*, survey: Wyatt RTU 291 n. 184). ¶ Forms: G/D suffc. *gprh*, *gprm* (encl. *-m*).
Opponent (?): *w ṯn gprm mn* and the two opponents(?) decided (their) fate (?), 1.19 I 11 (ctx. unc.).

/g-r/ vb N: "to lodge, take refuge, be protected"; R: "to settle" (OSA *gwr*, CAME 122; DOSA 68: cf. *gr*). ¶ Forms: N prefc. *igr* (/iggār/); R prefc. *tgrgr*.
N. To lodge, take refuge, be protected: *mndʕ k ank aḥš mġy mndʕ k igr w u igr ʕm špš* perhaps I shall hurry to come, perhaps I shall lodge (here) or else (perhaps) I shall lodge with the 'Sun', 2.34:12 (diff.

Lipiński OLP 12 1981 97: 'rester, se prolonger', Aram. *ngr*; Cunchillos TOu 2 343f. n. 17: 'faire un détour').
R. To settle, take up residence: *ṯm tgrgr l abnm w l ʕṣm* you settle there among the stones and tree-trunks, 1.23:66.
Cf. gr (I).

gr (I) n. m. "protected; guest, foreigner" (Hb., Ph., Aram., Nab., Palm. *gr*, HALOT 201; DNWSI 232; OSA *gwr*, CAME 122; DOSA 68; Arab. *ǧār*, Lane 483. Cf. Dietrich - Loretz - Sanmartín UF 7 1975 151; Margalit UF 16 1984 155f.); ¶ par.: *brḥ*. ¶ Forms: sg. *gr*; pl. cstr. *gr*.
Protected: *amd gr bt il* always be a protected one of the sanctuary, 1.19 III 47 (// *brḥ*; diff. Hillers Fs. Iwry 105f.: 'leprosy of El', rdg *grbt il*, Akk. *garbu*, *garbānu*; Renfroe UF 18 1986 457: 'as a leper', rdg *grb til*, Hb. *gārāb*, Akk. *garābu*, Aram. *garbā*, Arab. *jarab*; cf. Watson SEL 6 1989 47f.); guest, foreigner: *gr ḥmyt ugrt* guests of the walls of TN, 1.40:35 and par.; *gr yšb* (< *yṯb*) resident foreigner (!), 5.22:28. In bkn ctx.: *l ḫm g*(!)*r tqdm* to the pavilion of the guests(?) they proceeded, 1.15 IV 23 (diff. KTU: *mr*; De Moor (-Spronk) ARTU 209; CARTU 152: 'bitterness');]*x b grm*, 4.658:1.
Cf. /g-r/, gr (II).

gr (II) PN (Sem.); ¶ syll.: cf. DUMU *ga-ri*, PRU 3 195 (RS 15.42+) II 16' and /g-r/; cf. Sivan GAGl 221; diff. Grøndahl PTU 125, cf. /g-ʕ-r/ (I), /g-ʕ-r/ (II).
PN: *bn PN*, 4.655:6.

grʕ PN (Sem. Cf. Grøndahl PTU 29, 129; Watson AuOr 8 1990 245).
PN: 4.635:34 (*aḏddy*).

grb PN (etym. unc. Cf. Grøndahl PTU 129f., 279; Watson SEL 6 1989 48; AuOr 11 1993 215); ¶ syll.: cf. DUMU *ga-ra-bu*[(?)], PRU 6 41:1; *ga-ri-bu* and var., Ug 5 51:6 and *passim ibid.* Cf. *grp*, *krb*.
PN: *bn PN*: 4.366:13.

grbn PN (etym. unc. Cf. Grøndahl PTU 130, 279; Huehnergard JAOS 107 1987 723; Watson AuOr 11 1993 215; SEL 6 1989 48); ¶ syll.: cf. DUMU *gur-pa-na*, Syria 28 1951 173ff. no. 6 (RS 14.16):27; DUMU *gu-ur-ba-na*, PRU 3 204 (RS 16.257+) mg. II 5 (cf. Van Soldt SAU 26); *gu-ur-ba-nu*, PRU 6 150:1 (cf. Huehnergard AkkUg 218; AkkUg 409); *gur*$_{16}$(KUR)*-ba-na*, PRU 3 136 (RS 15.141):4; *ga-ar-pa-ni*, RSOu 7 15:12; cf. Sanmartín NABU 1994 45. Cf. *grp*, *krwn*.
PN : ★a) 4.75 VI 3 (*ʕbd nryn*); ★b) *bn PN*: 4.101:3; 4.245 II 4; 4.263:6; 4.371:8; 4.412 I 13; 4.775:5.

grbz n. m. "helmet", or, by extension, "cap, hood" (cf. Akk.

g/qurpis(s)u, AHw 929; CAD G 139; ARMT 23 205; ARMT 24 115f., Hitt. *GUR-ZI/ŠI-IP*, *KUR-PÍ-S/ŠI*, etc.; cf. *gurzipant-*, Tischler HEG 653f.; Hurr. *gurbiši*, GLH 155; cf. Zaccagnini JIVUF 1977 13f.; Kendall NuzHur 1 201ff.; Börker - Klähn HH 231 n. 36); ¶ **RS Akk.**: *gur*-BI-ZU.MEŠ, PRU 6 132 rev. 5'; cf. 21 URUDU.MEŠ *gu-ur*-BI-*su*, PRU 6 140:1; cf. Kühne UF 5 1973 189; cf. Huehnergard UVST 117; Sivan GAGl 221. ¶ **Forms**: pl. suff. *grbzhm*.
Helmet, or, by extension, cap, hood: (garments) *d bnšm yd grbzhm* for a man, with their hoods(?), 4.363:2.

grbzt PN (etym. unc.; cf. Bordreuil-Pardee RSOu 14 p. 356). Cf. *grbz*. PN: RSOu 14 39 [KTU 4.790]:24'.

grdn/y PN (Sem.(?). Cf. Grøndahl PTU 29, 130; Watson AuOr 8 1990 245). Var. *grdy* in 4.309:28;. PN: *bn PN*, 4.93 IV 18; 4.422:3.

/g-r-d-š/ vb G: "to be undermined, ruined" (Syr. *gardeš*, LS 132; cf. Dietrich - Loretz Fs. Elliger 33; Badre et al. Syria 53 1976 103; Verreet UF 19 1987 321f.; diff. De Moor - Spronk UF 14 1982 154f.: 'ruin', Hb. *gdš*; cf. Margalit UF 11 1979 542 n. 19: m. n. < 'to cut'; diff. Greenfield EI 9 1969 61); ¶ **par.**: /r-š(-š)/. ¶ **Forms**: G suffc. *grdš*.
G. To be undermined, ruined: *krt grdš mknt* PN was left ruined in his family seat, 1.14 I 11 (// *rš*).

grdy PN; cf. *grdn/y*.

grgmš TN (Belmonte RGTC 12/2 153ff.: *Kargamiš*. Cf. Astour RSP 2 295, 354; cf. Hawkins RlA 5 426ff.; Klengel GS 1 51ff., 71ff.; Syria 120ff.; Helck Bez. 289f.; cf. Hitt. KAR-*ga/qa-maš*, KAR-*ka-mi-is*, Del Monte - Tischler RGTC 6 p. 181f.; Rüster-Neu HZ 145 no. 112; MA/MB KAR-*ga-miš*, Nashef RGTC 5 155; cf. KUR ḪAR-*ga-muš*, Nashef RGTC 5 119; Eg. *qa-ri-qa-mi-š*ᵉ, *qa-r-qa-mᵉ-š*ᵉ, *k(a)-r-ka-mi-š*ᵉ, Helck Bez. 543, 550, 570); ¶ **syll.**: cf. LUGAL *ga-ar-ga-mi-iš*, RSOu 7 40:32; KUR(.URU) *kar/gar*$_{14}$(KAR)-*ga-miš*(MES), Ug 5 27:1; cf. PRU 3 p. 266; PRU 4 p. 254; PRU 6 p. 147; RSOu 7 p. 137 (cf. Sanmartín NABU 1994 50). ¶ **Forms**: *grgmš*; suff. *grgmšh* (*-h* adv.).
TN: *ṯtb d anyt grgmšh* bill of the ship (bound) for TN, 4.779:13; *m<k>t grgmš*, 2.75:8; cf. in bkn ctx.: 2.20:1; 2.36:21.

grgr (I) n. m. "throat"(?) (cf. Hb. *grgrt*, HALOT 201f.: **grgrwt*; cf. Arab. *ǧarǧara*, Lane 400f. Cf. Del Olmo IMC 172 n. 439; cf. diff. Gray KTL 69: 'javelin', Arab. *ǧarra*, *ǧārūr*, Sanmartín UF 12 1980 336: 'eine Art Wurfwaffe', Aram. *gyr?*, Margalit MLD 146 n. 2: < 'drag', Hb. *grr*); ¶ **par.**: *mrḥ*. ¶ **Forms**: sg. suff. *grgrh*.
Throat(?): *yiḫd (...) grgrh bm ymn* he grasped (...) his throat(?) with

his right, 1.16 I 48 (// *mrḫh*).

grgr (II) n. m. "javelin" (?) (Aram. *gērō*, Brockelmann LS 100; cf. *gry*, DJPA 136; Arab. *ǧurrat*, Lane 400. Cf. Gray KTL 69; Sanmartín UF 12 1980 336; Margalit MLD 146 n. 2: < 'drag', Hb. *grr*); ¶ par.: *mrḥ*. ¶ Forms: sg. suff. *grgrh*.

Javelin (?): *yiḫd (...) grgrh bm ymn* he seized (...) his javelin (?) in his right, 1.16 I 48 (// *mrḫh*).

grgš/s PN (etym. unc. Cf. Grøndahl PTU 23, 31, 129ff.; De Moor BiOr 26 1969 105; Priebatsch UF 12 1980 328); ¶ syll.: DUMU *gir-gi*$_5$(KI)-*ši*, PRU 3 124 (RS 15.163+):19 (cf. Van Soldt SAU 319 n. 130; cf. Nougayrol PRU 3 p. 124: *ia-ḫi*(?)-*ki-ya*(??)); DUMU *gir-gi-ši* and var., PRU 3 202 (RS 16.257+) III 33; *gir-gi-šu*, PRU 4 201 (RS 18.02):14; 203 (RS 18.20+) rev. 12'; cf. *gi-i*[*r*(?)]-*g*[*i*(?)-*s*]*ú*, PRU 6 85 rev. 18' (cf. Huehnergard AkkUg 386). Var. *grgs* in 4.33:29; 4.51:9; 4.52:13.

PN: ★a) 2.67:2; 4.50:14; 4.187:3; 4.194:1; 4.214 III 21 (*bn tlš*); ★b) *bn PN*: 4.33:29 (*ilštmʕy*; cf. Van Soldt SAU 33); 4.51:9 (Van Soldt SAU 33); 4.52:13 (Van Soldt SAU 33); 4.123:15; 4.377:9; 4.695:2; 4.787:4; ★c) *gt grgš*, "UF 29, 829":3 (Belmonte RGTC 12/2 85).

grgyn PN (Hurr. Cf. Watson AuOr 8 1990 245; AuOr 14 1996 98).
PN: 4.244:27; 4.337:24; 4.763:8.

grn (I) n. m./f. "threshing floor" (Emar /gurnu/, Pentiuc Vocabulary 53; Hb. *grn*, HALOT 203; cf. Arab. *ǧurn*, *ǧarīn*, Lane 414; Eth. *gʷĕren*, *go/urn*, CDG 203; Luw. *ga-ru-na-i*, Swiggers BiOr 37 1980 338; relationship to *grn (II)* unc.; cf. Akk. *magrānu*, espec. Nuzi *magrattu*, Wilhelm AdS 3 108; Richter NuzHur 7 70f. Cf. Dijkstra - De Moor UF 7 1975 181; Heltzer RCAU 76 n. 7;); ¶ par.: *mṭʕt*, *šd*, *ṯġr (I)*. ¶ Forms: sg. *grn*; pl. f. *grnt*, m. *grnm* (probl. morphol. var., cf. De Moor - Spronk UF 14 1982 171).

Threshing floor, ★a) *b grn yḫrb* on the threshing floor (the harvest) had withered, 1.19 I 30; *sʕt (...) b grnt ḥpšt* swept (...) from the threshing floors those gathering (straw), 1.14 III 8 (// *b šdm*), with m. morphol. var. *grnm* in 1.14 IV 52 (// *šdm*); *akln b grnt* our grain on the threshing floors (has been set on fire) 2.61:8; cf.]*ṯn d aḫd b grn uškn* (ox(en) of P)N which (they) have gathered in the threshing floor(s) of TN, 4.296:16 (or TN: *grn-uškn*?); ★b) place for social activities: *yṯb (...) tḥt adrm d b grn* he sat down (...) among the nobles who (gather) in the threshing floor, 1.17 V 7 and par. (// *b ap ṯġr*); *mġy rpum l grnt* the *r.* reached the threshing floors, 1.20 II 6 and par. (// *mṭʕt*);]*b grnt ilm* the gods (are already) in the threshing floors,

1.20 II 9 (// *b qrb mṭʕt*).

grn (II) adj. m. "current, of average quality"(?) (Akk. *gurnu*, Ahw 299; CAD G 139; Cohen - Sivan UHT 27; Cohen UF 28 1996 126f.; connection with *grn (I)* unc.; cf. Nuzi Akk.ŠE.MEŠ *ša ma-ag-ra-at-ti*, Wilhelm AdS 3 108; Richter NuzHur 7 78f.). ¶ **Forms**: sg. *grn*. Current, of average quality(?): *št mkšr grn* a *š.* of current(?) partly ground wheat (semolina)(?), 1.85:13, 16; 1.71:11; 1.72:17, 22; 1.91:3.

grp PN (etym. unc. Cf. Grøndahl PTU 130, 279; Watson AuOr 13 1995 222; West AOAT 233 32: PN *ka-ra-pi*, Linear B). Cf. *grb*, *krp*. PN: 4.63 I 23.

/g-r-š/ vb G: "to eject, drive out, evict, cast out" (Hb., JAram., Moab. *grš*, HALOT 204; Jastrow 273; DNWSI 236; cf. Ebla SAG.DU_8 = *gú-ra-zu-um*, Fronzaroli EL 141; var. *gu-rí-šu*, Krebernik ZA 73 1983 22 n. 72; cf. /G-L-S/, Krebernik PET 45; the element *ig-rí-iš*-(DN) in Ebla PNN, Van Huijssteen WGE 226; Fronzaroli ARES 1 19; Arab. *ǧšr*, Lane 426f.); ¶ **par.**: /ṭ-r-d/. ¶ **Forms**: G prefc. *ygrš* (cf. *ygrš*), *tgrš*; suff. *ygršk*, *agrškm*; impv. *grš*, suff. *gršnn* (suff. pn. *-nn*, UT § 6.17); ptc. m. sg. *grš*, suff. *gršh*, m. pl. *gršm* (cf. *grš*), f. sg. *gršt* (cf. *gršt*). G. To eject, drive out, evict, cast out: a son *grš d ʕšy lnh* who ejects one who does something (to his father), 1.17 I 29 and par.; *mṭm tgrš šbm* with (her) whip drove out the old men, 1.3 II 15; *tgrš (...) b ksl qšth* she drove out (...) with the sinew of her bow, 1.3 II 16; *ʕpr btk ygršk* may the dust of your house evict you, // *qr btk ygršk* may the walls of your house evict you, 1.82:12 (cf. *ibid.* ln. 40, and De Moor - Spronk UF 16 1984 238); *ygrš grš ym grš ym l ksih* DN_1 the one who drives (away) DN_2. Drive DN_2 from his throne! 1.2 IV 12; from a place, + *l*: *gršh l ksi mlkh* the one who drove him from his royal throne, 1.3 IV 2 (// *ṭrd*); *gršnn l ksi mlkh* drive him from his royal throne, 1.1 IV 24; + *b*: (I shall pay a fine) *km agrškm b bty* in the event of evicting them from my household, 3.9:6-7; *aphm kšpm dbbm ygrš* and then may the wizards also cast out the demons, 1.169:9. In bkn ctx.: 1.6 VI 2.
Cf. grš, gršt, ygrš.

grš n. m. "expeller, caster out, one in charge of driving out" (< ptc. act.(?) G or theme qittil /g-r-š/; see Emar /girrīšu/, Pentiuc Vocabulary 53; Ginsberg JANES 5 1973 133); ¶ **par.**: *ydy*. ¶ **Forms**: sg. *gršm* (encl. *-m*, Aartun PU 1 53).
Expeller, caster out, one in charge of driving out: *my b ilm (...) gršm zbln* who among the gods (will be able) to drive out the sickness?, 1.16 V 12 and par. (// *ydy*).

Cf. **gršt**.

gršt n. f. "expeller, caster out, one in charge of driving out" (< act. ptc. G /g-r-š/; cf. *grš*); ¶ **par.**: *ydt*. ¶ **Forms**: sg. *gršt*.
Expeller, caster out, one in charge of driving out: *aškn (...) gršt zbln* I shall nominate (...) a (woman) who drives out the sickness, 1.16 V 27 (// *ydt*).
Cf. **grš**.

/g-r(-y)/ vb G: "to attack"; (?)tD: "to oppose" (Hb. *grh*, HALOT 202; Aram. *gry*, DNWSI 234f.; Ebla cf. PNN *gú/gu$_4$-ra*(-DN), *gú-ra-u$_9$*, and cf. *gi-ra*(-DN), Müller Biling. 179f.; Akk. *gerû*, AHw 286; CAD G 61f. Cf. Greenfield EI 9 1969 62; De Moor - Spronk UF 14 1982 166 n. 109; Del Olmo IMC 43); ¶ **par.**: /š-r/ (II), Watson UF 17 1985 347. ¶ **Forms**: G suffc. *gr*, inf. suff. *grnn* (suff. pn *-nn*, UT § 6.17; cf. De Moor - Spronk UF 14 1982 166; diff. Aartun PU 1 62 n. 4, 76: energ. mood with *-n* + pn. suff. *-n* / emph. *-n*); (?)tD suffc. *tgr*.
G. To attack: *k gr ʕz tġrkm* when a strong one attacks your gates, 1.119:26; *gr*{.}*nn ʕrm* attack the cities!, 1.14 III 6 (// *šrn*; inf. functioning as impv.; with narrative functor cf. *grnn* // *šrnn*(!), *ibid.* IV 49; De Moor - Spronk 14 1982 166).
(?)**tD**. To oppose: *tgr il bnh* DN has opposed(?) his son, 1.1 IV 12 (Diff. De Moor SP 118 "appoint a deputy"; for the various opinions cf. Del Olmo IMC 43).

gsn PN (etym. unc.). Cf. *ksn*, *kzn*.
PN: ★**a)** 4.616:13; ★**b)** *bn PN*: 4.382:27.

gssn PN (etym. unc.).
PN: 6:63:1.

gšl(?) PN (rdg and etym. unc.).
PN: *bn gšl*(?), 4.309:16.

gšm n. m. "rain, downpour" (Hb. *gšm*, HALOT 205; Ebla cf. A.KI = *ga-sa-nu*, *gi-si-nu-um*, VE 613; Krebernik QuSe 18 134; É.SAG.BA = *gú-ša-mu*, VE 332; Vattioni EDA 209. See Watson Fs. Dietrich 547). ¶ **Forms**: sg. *gšm*.
Rain, downpour: (your ships were met) *by gšm adr* by a heavy downpour, 2.38:14.

gt n. f. 1) "wine or olive press," and, by extension, "farmstead, estate"; 2) element in TNN (cf. Hb. *gt*, HALOT 206; EA Akk. /gittu-/, /gintu-/, in TNN; Rainey EAT 105; Sivan GAGl 220; cf. Kienast UF 11 1979 451f.; Heltzer IOKU 49ff.; UF 31 1999 193ff.; Michaux-Colombot UF 29 1997 579ff.; Hoch SWET § 425; on Ebla *gi-tum*, *gú-tum* cf. Butz Biling. 115 n. 81, 83; EDA 348); ¶ **RS Akk.**:

(É.)AN.ZA.GÀR(.KI.MEŠ), *passim* (Huehnergard AkkUg 345; Van Soldt UF 21 1989 376 n. 12; cf. Dosch Arrapḫe 17 and *passim*; Müller Siedlungsgeographie 163ff.); cf. *dimtu* in PRU 3 216ff.; PRU 6 158 (cf. *dmt (I)*). ¶ Forms: sg. *gt*, suff. *gth*; pl. *gtt*.
1) Wine or olive press, and, by extension, farmstead, estate: *PN (...) ytn šd PN (...) yd gth yd zth yd krmh yd klklh w ytn{.}nn l PN (...) ʕd ʕlm* PN (...) PN (...) has gifted the estate of PN (...) together with its farmstead, its olive-grove(s), its vineyard(s) and everything else and has ceded it to PN (...) in perpetuity, 3.5:7 (rdg unc.; cf. diff. Kienast UF 11 1979 452: [*y*]*d z*(!)*th yd gnh*; KTU[2]: *yd gth yd zth*; cf. *zt*); *ʕl gtt* on the account of the farmsteads, RSOu 14 35 [KTU 9.388]:II 35; in unc. ctx.: 1.79:6; in bkn ctx.: 2.58:4.
2) Element in the TNN 'Farmstead (press) of' (cf. Astour RSP 2 274f.); qualified further ★a) by a n. of a social class or group, e.g.: *gt ḥrṯm* 'Farmstead of the Labourers', 4.141 III 11; 4.618:21; 4.625:17 (cf. Astour RSP 2 276f.; Belmonte RGTC 12/2 86: **Gittu-ḥarrāṯīma*); *gt mlk* 'Royal Farmstead', 1.105:11 (*mlk (I)*; cf. also TN *mlk (III)*, and d., *infra*; cf. RS Akk.: A.ŠÀ.ḪI.A LUGAL-*ri*, PRU 3 47 (RS 16.150):8); *gt mlkt* 'Farmstead of the Queen', 2.21:7f. (*skn gt mlkt ugrt* prefect of the 'Farmstead of the Queen of TN', 2.21:8; cf. Cunchillos UF 13 1981 46; Belmonte RGTC 12/2 88: **Gittu-malkati*; cf. diff. Dijkstra UF 19 1987 40 n. 14: rdg *skn b*(!)*t* prefect of the palace(!)); 4.143:1; *gt ngr* 'Farmstead of the Carpenter(?)', 4.125:3 (Belmonte RGTC 12/2 89f.: **Gittu-naggāri*(?)); ★b) by a DN: *gt al* 'Farmstead of Allai', 4.382:27 (cf. GLH 42f.; Belmonte RGTC 12/2 82: *Gittu-Allai*); *gt ʕṯtr*, 4.696:6 (Belmonte RGTC 12/2 83: **Gittu-ʕaṯtari*); *gt ʕṯtrt*, 4.125:6 (cf. Astour RSP 2 277; Belmonte RGTC 12/2 83: *Gittu-ʕaṯtarti*); *gt ṯrmn*, 1.48:19; 4.139:6; 4.243:20; 4.296:10 (Belmonte RGTC 12/2 95); ★c) by a PN (cf. Kühne UF 6 1974 161): *gt aǵld*, 4.382:32 (Belmonte RGTC 12/2 82: **Gittu-Aǵladi*); *gt alḫb*, 4.243:16 (Belmonte RGTC 12/2 82f.: *Gittu-Alli-ḫeba*); *gt ipṯl*, 4.125:11; 4.213:19, 4.397:5; 4.522:1; 4.618:7, 25; 4.625:13 (cf. Kühne UF 6 1974 161; Belmonte RGTC 12/2 87: **Gittu-Ipṯali*); *gt irbl*, 4.200:10 (Belmonte RGTC 12/2 94); 4.788:6(?), 8(?) (KTU: rdg *irbṣ*; see *irbl*, *irbṣ*); *gt bnil*, 4.297:3 (Belmonte RGTC 12/2 83: **Gittu-Bin-ʔili*); *gt bn ksd*(?)[, 4.297:7 (Belmonte RGTC 12/2 93); *gt bn ndk*, 1.79:4 (or rdg *bn ndr*(!) ?; Belmonte RGTC 12/2 84: **Gittu-Bin-nadri*(?)); *gt bn pri*, 4.297:2 (Belmonte RGTC 12/2 84: **Gittu-Bin-pirʔi*); *gt bn tbšn*, 4.96:1 (Belmonte RGTC 12/2 84: *Gittu-Bin-tubbi-šenni*(?)); *gt bn ṯlṯ*, 4.96:11; *gt bʕln*, 4.358:6; 4.636:5 (Belmonte

RGTC 12/2 83: **Gittu-Baʕalani*); *gt gbry*, 4. 296:13; *gt glʕd*, 4.125:2 (Astour RSP 2 275f.; Belmonte RGTC 12/2 85: **Gittu-Galʕada*); *gt grgš*, "UF 29, 826": 3 (Belmonte RGTC 12/2 85: **Gittu-Girgiši*); *gt yśd*, 4.139:7 (Belmonte RGTC 12/2 95); *gt krr*, 4.139:9 (Belmonte RGTC 12/2 88: **Gittu-Kiriri*); *gt mzln*, 4.110:16-22; 4.307:1 (cf. Kühne UF 6 1974 161; Belmonte RGTC 12/2 89: **Gittu-Muzalenni*); *gt mnḥm*, 4.139:4 (Belmonte RGTC 12/2 89: **Gittu-Muna ḫḫimi*); *gt psḥn*, 4.96:12 (Belmonte RGTC 12/2 94); *gt prn*, 4.110:3-14 (Belmonte RGTC 12/2 90: *Gittu-Purrani*); *gt špšyn*, 4.297:4 (Belmonte RGTC 12/2 91: **Gittu-Šapšiyani*); *gt tgbry*, 4.271:7, 9 (cf. 4.296:13 and cf. É.AN.ZA.GÀR *ta-ga-bi-ra(-ya)*, Ug 5 96:4, 15, 22; cf. Huehnergard UVST 116; Belmonte RGTC 12/2 92: **Gitti-Tagabirā(yi)*); *gt tgyn*, 4.97:6; 4.643:9 (Belmonte RGTC 12/2 92: **Gittu-Tagiyana*); *gt trǵnds*, 4.400:15 (Belmonte RGTC 12/2 95); *gt ṯryn*, 4.636:1; ★d) by a TN / GN: *gt ilštmʕ*, 1.79:7; 1.80:1 (Belmonte RGTC 12/2 87: **Gittu-Ilištamʕi*); *gt bir*, 4.397:13; 4.625:15; 4.636:1; "UF 29, 826":5 (Lemaire UF 30 1998 461; cf. Belmonte RGTC 12/2 84: **Gittu-Biʔri*); *gt gwl*, 4.213:18; 4.397:7; 4.618:4, 24 (cf. A.ŠÀ.MEŠ *gu-wa-li*(?), PRU 3 152 (RS 16.201):12; cf. Huehnergard UVST 116; Belmonte RGTC 12/2 86: **Gittu-Guwāli*); *gt ḫldy*, 4.636:10 (cf. URU *ḫu-ul-da*, PRU 3 133 (RS 15.132):7, 11; 144 (RS 16.138):19; cf. Huehnergard UVST 243; Belmonte RGTC 12/2 87: **Gittu-Ḫulda*); *gt ṭbq*, 4.213:5 (Belmonte RGTC 12/2 92: **Gittu-ṭibaqi*); *gt yknʕm*, 4.307:21 (Belmonte RGTC 12/2 93: **Gittu-Yakunaʕmi*); *gt yny*, 4.320:2 (4.696:9 ?; cf. Belmonte RGTC 12/2 93: **Gittu-Yēnā*); *gt knpy*, 4.243:18; 4.296:10 (cf. A.ŠÀ : *ka(-an)-na-pí*(BI)*-yu*(PI), PRU 3 79 (RS 16.239):7; 85 (RS 16.250):11; cf. Kühne UF 7 1975 255f.; Huehnergard UVST 138; Belmonte RGTC 12/2 87f., 402: **Gittu-Kannāpiyi*); *gt mʕrb*, 4.307:3 (Belmonte RGTC 12/2 88: **Gittu-Maʕbari*); *gt mʕrby*, 4.231:8; 4.307:3; *gt ṯpn*, 4.213:21; 4.618:1, 23 (cf. AN.Z[A(!).G]ÀR *ša-pu-ni*, RS 8.43:2; Van Soldt UF 21 1989 376, 5; Belmonte RGTC 12/2 93: **Gittu-ṯapuni*); *gt mlk*, 4.105:5; 4.750:13 (< *mlk (III)*; Belmonte RGTC 12/2 89: **Gittu-Mulukki*; cf. *supra*: a.); *gt ṣbr*[, 4.400:2 (cf. cf. A.ŠÀ(.MEŠ) : ZI-*ib-bi-ri*, PRU 3 79 (RS 16.239):6 (// A.ŠÀ PN, A.ŠÀ : *kan-na-pí-ya*); 83 (RS 16.157):7 (*i-na* ÌD *ra-aḫ-ba-ni)*; A.ŠÀ.ḪI.A PN (...) *ša i-na* A.ŠÀ.ḪI.A ZI*(-ib)-bi-ri*, PRU 6 55:19' and *passim ibid.*; cf. Huehnergard UVST 169f.); *gt ṯm*[*k*(?), 4.424:3 (Belmonte RGTC 12/2 93: **Gittu-ṯamuki*(?)); ★e) by a common noun: *gt irbṣ* 'Farmstead of Repose(?)' (<(?) /r-b-ṣ/), 4.122:1 (Belmonte RGTC 12/2 94; cf. *gt* *irbl*, 4.788:6(?), 8(?); see *irbl*, *irbṣ*); *gt dprnm* 'Farmstead of the Junipers', 4.175:9 (cf. A.ŠÀ.ḪI.A : *di-ip-ra-ni-ma*, PRU 3 64 (RS 16.190):4; cf. Kühne UF 6 1974 163; Huehnergard UVST 119; Belmonte RGTC 12/2 84, 401: **Gittu-diprānīma*); *gt ḥṣb* 'Farmstead of the Stonecutter(?)' (<(?) */ḥ-ṣ-b/), 4.409:7, 4.409:7 (Belmonte RGTC 12/2 86f: **Gittu-ḥaṣṣabi*).; *gt ḥdṯt* 'New Estate ', 4.213:12; 4.243:22; 4.707:21 (cf. Astour RSP 2 276; Belmonte RGTC 12/2 86: **Gittu-ḥadaṯatu*); *gt ʕmq* 'Farmstead of the Strong', 4.625:9 (cf. AN.ZA. GÀR : *am-qa*, PRU 3 118 (RS 15.155):12 and *ʕmq (II)*; cf. Huehnergard UVST 160; Belmonte RGTC 12/2 83: **Gittu-ʕamqa*); *gt mʕbr* 'Farmstead of the Pass', 4.243:12 (cf. É.AN.ZA.GÀR *ma-ba-ri TN*, Ug 5 96:6-7, 19-20; cf. Astour UF 13 1981 7; Huehnergard UVST 158; Belmonte RGTC 12/2 88: **Gittu-maʕbari*); *gt nb/pk*, 4.103:45; 4.269:19 (cf. A.ŠÀ(.MEŠ) : NAB/*na*-AB-*ki-ma*, PRU 3 49 (RS 16-263):5; PRU 6 56 rev. 5' and *passim ibid.*; (A.ŠÀ.)KIRI$_6$(.KI) *i-na* (:) *na-ba*/AB-*ki-ma/mi*, PRU 3 80 (RS 16.239):8; 83 (RS 16.157):9; KIRI$_6$: *kí-ru i-na* : *na-bá-ki-ma*, PRU 3 47 (RS 16.150):16; cf. Kühne UF 7 1975 260; Huehnergard UVST 151; Belmonte RGTC 12/2 89: **Gittu-nab/paki*); *gt nḫl*, 4.296:9 (cf. A.ŠÀ.MEŠ *na-ḫa-li*, PRU 3 109 (RS 16.251):7; cf. Huehnergard UVST 152; Belmonte RGTC 12/2 90, 403: **Gittu-naḫali*); *gt sġy*, 4.213:15 (Belmonte RGTC 12/2 94); *gt ġl*, 4.141 III 15; 4.200:8; 4.243:14; 4.636:15 (cf. A.ŠÀ.ḪI.A : *ḫu-li*, PRU 3 143 (RS 16.138):3; cf. Huehnergard UVST 164; Belmonte RGTC 12/2 86, 401: **Gittu-ġūli*); *gt sknm* 'Estate of the Stelae', 4.213:3; 4.243:7 (cf. É.AN.ZA.GÀR ZI-GA/QA-*ni-ma*, Ug 5 96:0, 17; cf. Huehnergard UVST 157; Belmonte RGTC 12/2 91: **Gittu-sikānīma*); *gt rbṯ*, 'Great Farmstead / Farmstead of the Lady Mayor', 4.125:16 (cf. A.ŠÀ *ra-ba-ti*, Ug 5 7:4; cf. Huehnergard UVST 176; Belmonte RGTC 12/2 91: **Gittu Rabbati*; AN.ZA.GÀR-GAL Ì.DUB, Ug 5 95:13); ★f) cf. esp.: *bnš gt NN* people of NN-Gt, 4.125:2 and *passim*; *bdl gt PN* the reserve personnel of Gt-PN, 4.96:1; *š gt mlk* a ram of NN-Gt, 1.105:11. Cf. *gt nṯṯ*, 1.79:1, 5; 4.409:8 (<(?) Hurr. *nešše*, GLH 181; Belmonte RGTC 12/2 90: **Gittu-neṯṯe*).

Cf. **ilgt, gn, gntn, gt.mlky, gtn.**

gt.mlky GN m. "inhabitant of *gt.mlk* 'the Royal Farmstead'" (cf. *gt* (a., d.); *mlk (I)*; cf. *mlk (IV)*). ¶ Forms: pl. *gt.mlkym*.

Inhabitant of 'Royal Farmstead': *gt.mlkym* inhabitants of 'the Royal Farmstead', 4.99:5; 4.126:19.

Cf. **gt, mlk (I), mlk (IV), mlkym.**

gtn PN (Sem.(?). Cf. Grøndahl PTU 131). Cf. PNN *gdn*, *kdn*, *ktn*, *qṭn*.

PN: 4.63 I 28.

gṯpbn PN (Hurr. Cf. Gelb - Purves - MacRae NPN 230f., 243; Laroche GLH 190f.). Cf. *irpbn, pbn.*
PN: 4.106:13.

gṯprg PN (Hurr. Cf. Gelb - Purves - MacRae NPN 230f., 245). Cf. *prgn, prkl.*
PN: *bn PN*, 4.106:12.

gṯr DN, eponym of the dead and deified king (Akk. *gašru*, AHw 283; CAD G 56ff.; Ebla cf. Ú.A = *ga*-SI-*lu*, VE 297; Arcari Biling. 321f.; Milano MARI 5 1987 546; diff. Pomponio-Xella AfO 31 1984 31; Conti SQF 114f.; Emar [d]*ga-aš-ru*, 274:19'; 373:119'; 379:5. Cf. Del Olmo AuOr 2 1984 203 n.30; 5 1987 62f.; Dietrich - Loretz JA 65ff.); ¶ syll. Ug.: [d]TIŠPAK = *mi-il-ku-un-ni* = *ga-š*[*a-ru*], Ug 5 137 IV a 15; cf.] *mi-il-ku-un-ni* = *g*[*a*]-*ša-ru*, *ibid.* IV b 13; Roberts ESP 53f.; Moran JCS 31 1979 72 n. 23; Huehnergard UVST 117; cf. the element /gaṯ(a)ru/ in PNN, Sivan GAGl 219); ¶ par.: *bʕl.* ¶ Forms: sg. *gṯr*; suff. *gṯrn* (determinative -*n* ?); du./pl. *gṯrm.*
Eponym of the dead and deified king: *l gṯrm ġṣb šmal d alpm* for the *g.* the left *ġ.* of two head of cattle, 1.109:26; *yrdn gṯrm mṣdh ṯn šm l gṯrm w rgm gṯrm yṯṯb* the two *g.* shall go down to the tower, two rams to the *g.* (shall they offer) and the *g.* shall communicate a word, 1.112:18-20; *ʕlm tʕrbn gṯrm* next the *g.* enter, 1.43:9; *l gṯr ṯql ksp ṭb* to *g.* one shekel of sterling silver, 1.43:11, cf. ln. 14, 17, 19; [DN] *w tšt ʕnt gṯr yqr* has established (him), *g.* PN, 1.108:6; cf. ln. 2: *gṯr w yqr.*; *šd gṯr* the field of DN, 2.4:15, 17; *w ytn ilm bdhm bd iḫqm gṯr* may he / they deliver (the statues of) the gods into their hands, DN into the hands of PN, *ibid.* ln. 21. In bkn ctx.: *gṯrn ylk*[, 1.166:25 (cf. Del Olmo AuOr 5 1987 63); 7.38:9.
Cf. ʕbdgṯr, gṯrn.

gṯrn PN (Sem. Cf. Grøndahl PTU 131; Sivan GAGl 219; Dietrich - Loretz UF 12 1980 173 n. 26; Watson AuOr 14 1996 98); ¶ syll.: DUMU *ga-aš-ra-na*, PRU 6 55:26'. Cf. *kṯrn.*
PN: *bn PN*, 4.7:5; 4.25:5 (*bqʕty*); 4.63 III 7; 4.103:52; 4.232:28 (cf. Van Soldt SAU 120).

gṯtn PN (etym. unc.).
PN: *bn PN*, 4.35 II 18 (*ʕbdyrḫ*); 4.41:9 (*mnn*).

gṯy PN (etym. unc.).
PN: 4.764:6.

gwl TN (Belmonte RGTC 12/2 99: **Guwālu.* Cf. Heltzer RCAU 9); ¶ syll.: cf. A.ŠÀ.MEŠ *gu-wa-li*(?), PRU 3 151 (RS 16.201):12 (cf.

Huehnergard UVST 116; Van Soldt UF 28 1996 665).
TN: ★**a)** 4.124:9; 4.348:23; 4.625:11; ★**b)** *gt TN:* 4.213:18; 4.397:7; 4.618:4, 24 (Belmonte RGTC 12/2 86: **Gittu-Guwāli*).

gyn(m) PN (etym. unc. Cf. Grøndahl PTU 310). Var. *gynm* in 4.44:28.
PN: ★**a)** 4.44:28 (Pardee UF 7 1975 377f.; Verreet UF 15 1983 233); 4.334:7; ★**b)** *bn PN:* 4.340:8.

gzl PN (Akk.(?). Cf. Dietrich - Loretz OLZ 62 1967 537; Grøndahl PTU 130); ¶ **syll.**: cf. ^{m}*gu-ú-za-li*, PRU 4 134 (RS 17.116):35' (cf. Nougayrol PRU 4 p. 247: profession).
PN: ★**a)** 4.75 III 4 (*bn qldn*); 4.356:14; ★**b)** *bn PN:* 2.22:3; 4.63 I 5; 4.389:2.

gzr n. m. "piece" (Hb. *gzr*, HALOT 187; Arab. *ǧazar*, Lane 418f.; cf. Dietrich - Loretz UF 9 1977 51ff.; diff. Pope UF 11 1979 707, 'glutton'; Gibson CML 144, 'cutter'); ¶ **syll.** Ug.: cf. PN DUMU *ga-za-ri-ya*, Ug 5 88:18'; Sivan GAGl 221. ¶ **Forms**: sg. m. *gzr*.
Piece: *gzr l <g>zr* piece after piece, 1.23:63.
Cf. **gzry**.

gzry PN (etym. unc. Cf. TNN EA *Gazru* and Alalakh *Gazurû*, Belmonte RGTC 12/2 79. Cf. Grøndahl PTU 130; Astour RSP 2 272); ¶ **syll.**: DUMU *ga-za-ri-ya*, Ug 5 88:18'.
PN: *bn PN:* 4.69 III 1.

/g-z-z/ vb G: "to shear" (Hb., Aram., Palm. *gzz*, HALOT 186; DNWSI 219; Amor. /gzz/, Gelb CAAA 19; Akk. *gazāzu*, AHw 284; CAD G 59f.; Arab. *ǧaḏḏa*, *ǧazza*, Lane 394, 416). ¶ **Forms**: G prefc. *ygz*, act. ptc. *gzz* (cf. *gzz*).
G. To shear: *b kl ygz ṯ<b>ḫ šh* the sacrificer will shear his ewe completely, 1.80:5. Cf. **gzz**.

gzz n. m. "shearer" (act. ptc. m. G < /g-z-z/; Amor. /gaziz(ān)um/, Gelb CAAA 19; Akk. *gāzizu*, AHw 284; CAD G 60; Arab. *ǧazzāz*, Wehr 122; cf. Ebla GÍR *ma-ga-zu*, Fronzaroli StEb 7 1984 169). ¶ **Forms**: pl. *gzzm*.
Shearer: (spelt and wheat) *l gzzm* for the shearers, 4.269:4, 26; *yn mṣb (...) l gzzm* ordinary wine (...) for the shearers, 4.213:30.
Cf. /g-z-z/.

ġ

ġb (I) n. m. "(sacrificial) pit" ((?); etym. unc.; cf. Arab. *ġabġab*, Lane 2222; Akk. *ḫabbu*, *ḫuppu*, AHw 304f., 356; cf. CAD Ḫ 239: *ḫuppu B*. Cf. De Moor UF 2 1970 320; De Tarragon CU 21ff.; TOu 2 176 n. 110; Xella UF 13 1981 328; diff.: Herdner Ug 7 14; Van der Toorn BiOr 45 1991 48f: 'porche'(?), 'canopy', Hb. *ʕb*, ESA *mġbb*; Polselli RSO 56 1982 21ff.: '(sacred) wood', Hb.-Ph. *ʕb*.); ¶ syll. Ug.: cf. *ḫa*-AB-BU, PRU 3 161 (RS 16.281):8; A.ŠÀ.ḪI.A PN *ša i-na* : *ḫa*-A[B-B]I, PRU 3 148 (RS 16.182+):6; cf. Huehnergard UVST 190. ¶ Forms: sg. cstr. *ġb*.
Sacrificial pit(?): *ġb ṣpn* / *ḫyr* / *ršp* / *išḫry* the pit(?) of DN / MN / DN, 1.105:3, 14, 16, 21; 1.91:15; 4.149:13.
Cf. ġb (III).

ġb (II) "?" (Cf. Driver CML 143; Gray UF 3 1971 65 n. 34: 'sick with (tertiary) fever', Arab. *ġabba*, *ġibb*; Wyatt RTU 166: 'malaria'; Dietrich - Loretz Studien 67: 'Laubwerk'(?)). ¶ Forms: *ġb*[.
? : in bkn ctx., *qrnh km ġb*[, 1.12 II 39 (// *ḥrr*).

ġb (III) PN (etym. unc.; cf. Dietrich - Loretz WO 4 1967/68 302).
PN: *bn PN*, 4.63 III 24.

ġbl (I) TN (Belmonte RGTC 12/2 102: *Ġubelu*. Cf. Dietrich - Loretz - Sanmartín UF 5 1973 95; Heltzer RCAU 14, 16 n. 24; Astour RSP 2 314 no. 85; UF 13 1981 5; Huehnergard JAOS 107 1987 723; UVST 243; Van Soldt UF 30 1998 718); ¶ syll.: URU *ḫu-be-li*, PRU 3 48 (RS 16.248):7; 76 (RS 16.160):7; PRU 6 80:13; Ug 5 49:4,9.
TN: 4.27:7,18; 4.348:21; 4.355:31; 4.683:4; RSOu 14 35 [KTU 9.388] III 3.

ġbl (II) PN (< *ġbl (I)*, TN, used meton. as a PN).
PN:4.177:7.

ġbn n. m. "well-being, opulence" (cf. Hb. *ʕbh*, HALOT 777; Akk. *ebû*, AHw 183; CAD E 16; Aram. cf. *ʕby*, DNWSI 820; Arab. *ʕabī*, Lane 1942; Eth. *ʕabya*, CDG 55. Cf. Dietrich - Loretz - Sanmartín UF 5 1973 96; Wansbrough CRRA 30 1986 207ff., rdg *ṭbny* [*ẓ* = *ṭ* for *ġ*]).

¶ Forms: sg. suff. *ġbny*.
Well-being, opulence: *ʕmy midy w ġbny* I enjoy my plenty and my well-being, 2.46:11.

ġbr TN ((?); see Belmonte RGTC 12/2 101. Only in cultic ctx.; identification unc.; Van Selms UF 3 1971 238 (Ṣumur); Sapin UF 15 1983 182 (*ḫabiru*) are both unlikely; cf. Xella TRU 265; Caquot TOu 2 145 n. 30; Del Olmo CR 157 n. 227).
TN(?): 1.40:4 and par.

ġbt "?" (Cf. De Moor UF 1 1969 182: 'milk' / 'fatling', Arab. *ġabībat*; NYCI 2 8: 'thickness of fatlings', rdg *ġbm*; Dietrich - Loretz UF 17 1985 142; Pardee TPM 147: 'Wolke', 'nuage', Hb. *ʕāb*; Caquot TOu 2 49 n. 112).
? : in unc. ctx., *kṯ*[[*ṯ*]] *ġbt*, 1.101:8.

ġdʕ PN (etym. unc. Cf. Watson AuOr 13 1995 227).
PN: *bn PN*, 4.371:6.

/ġ-d-d/ vb D: "to swell" (Arab. *ġadda*, *ġuddida*, Lane 2231. Cf. Cassuto GA 119; De Moor SP 94; Gray UF 11 1979 379 n. 24; Held Fs. Iwry 98 n. 10; Renfroe AULS 30f.; Watson JNSL 22 1996 76f.; diff.: Aartun WO 4 1967/68 297: 'Fliessen, Fluten', Arab. **ġḏḏ*, Hb. *ʕzz*, De Moor UF 17 1985 221: 'to shake', *ʕ/ġd/dd/ḏ*); ¶ par.: /m-l-ʔ/.
¶ Forms: D prefc. *tġdd*.
D. To swell: *tġdd kbdh b ṣḥq* her liver swelled with laughter, 1.3 II 25 and par. (// *ymlu*). In bkn ctx.: 4.646:6 (?).

ġdġd PN (etym. unc.).
PN: 4.635:31 (*aḏddy*).

ġdm "?" (Cf. Bordreuil - Caquot Syria 57 1980 354).
? : in bkn ctx., *ġdmh*[, 1.173:1; cf. *l bʕl ġdm*[, *ibid.* ln. 2.

ġdrg PN (etym. unc.).
PN: 4.42:1.

/ġ-ḏ-y/ vb G: "to move"(?); tD: "to shoot, leap" (Arab. *ġaḏā*, cf. *ġaḏḏa*, *taġaḏġaḏa*, *ʔistaġaḏġā*, Lane 2235f. Cf. Oldenburg CEB 74 n. 4; De Moor SP 167; UF 17 1985 221; diff.: Van Zijl Baal 153, 310: 'to be strong, prevail', Hb. *ʕzz*, Akk. *ezēzu* [but cf. De Moor UF 7 1975 185 n. 126]; Caquot - Sznycer TOu 1 218 n. p: 's'abattre'; Cassuto BOS 2 191: 'to approach', Arab. *ġašā*; Sanmartín UF 11 1979 725f.: 'füttern, ernähren'; Margalit MLD 66: 'resin' < 'fester, suppurate', Arab. *ġadda*; Puech RB 93 1986 192: 'briser'). ¶ Forms: G prefc. *yġḏ*; tD suffc. *tġḏ*.
G. To move(?): in unc. ctx.]*k yġḏ thmt brq* as lightning moves the

ocean, 1.17 VI 12 (cf. De Moor (- Spronk) CARTU 106; ARTU 237; cf. Renfroe AULS 106f.).

tD. To shoot, leap: *k tġḏ arz b ymnh* when the cedar (stave) shoots from his right, 1.4 VII 41.

ġdyn (II) PN (< *gdyn (I)*; cf. Dietrich - Loretz WO 4 1967/68 302, 307).

PN: 4.63 I 4.

ġḥpn PN (etym. unc.; cf. Dietrich - Loretz WO 4 1967/68 302).

PN: *bn PN*, 4.76:4.

ġl (I) n. m. term for a type of terrain ("depression" or "reedbed, swamp, hollow"; cf. Arab. *ġawl*, Lane 2311; cf. *ġīl*, Lane 2319. Cf. Sukenik BASOR 107 1947 14; Kühne UF 6 1974 166f.; Margalit AuOr 7 1989 77; Renfroe AULS 334ff.; Aartun StUL 103ff. ['Wald, Dickicht']; diff. Albright - Mendenhall JNES 1 1942 228 n. 14: 'suckling', Arab. *ġāla*, *ġayl*); ¶ syll. Ug.: A.ŠÀ.ḪI.A : *ḫu-li*, PRU 3 143ff. (RS 16.138):3; cf. Kühne UF 6 1974 166f.; Huehnergard UVST 164; Van Soldt BiOr 46 1989 647 (cf. Sivan GAGl 230). ¶ Forms: sg./pl. cstr. *ġl*, suff. *ġlh*.

Type of terrain (depression or reedbed, swamp): *adr* <*qnm*> *b ġl il* {*qnm*} the most splendid reeds from the divine reedbeds, 1.17 VI 23; *yṣi ġlh tṯmd* she desired the produce of her hollow (// her desert), 1.92:6 (cf. Dijkstra UF 26 1994 118); *ṯtb ʕṯtrt b ġl* DN settled in the hollow, 1.92:8. Cf. TN *gt ġl*, 4.141 III 15; 4.200:8; 4.243:14; 4.636:15 (cf. A.ŠÀ.ḪI.A : *ḫu-li*, PRU 3 143 (RS 16.138):3; cf. Huehnergard UVST 164; Belmonte RGTC 12/2 86, 401: **Gittu-ġūli*). Bkn ctx.:]*ġlhm*, 2.62:11.

Cf. ḥl (II).

ġl (II) PN (Hurr. Cf. Laroche GLH 75f.; Grøndahl PTU 204, 215; Dietrich - Loretz OLZ 62 1967 546; UF 9 1977 341; cf. Grøndahl PTU 141; Lipiński JSS 26 1981 279: Sem.).

PN: *bn PN*, 4.356:9.

ġl (III) n. m. / PN (cf. *ġl (I)*, *ġl (II)*).

Element in the composite topnym *gt ġl*: 4.141 III 15; 4.200:8; 4.243:14; 4.636:15.

Cf. ġl (I), ġl (II).

ġlb(x)[PN (bkn.).

PN: *bn ġlbx*[, 4.760:7; cf. 4.590:3.

ġlkz PN (Hurr.; var. of *a/iġlkḍ/z*. Cf. Grøndahl PTU 215, 238; Dietrich - Loretz OLZ 62 1967 546; WO 4 1967/68 302; Van Soldt SAU 126).

DNWSI 855ff.; Arab. *ġalla*, Lane 2277ff.; cf. Akk. *ḫalālu*, AHw 309; CAD Ḫ 34. Cf. De Moor SP 68; diff. Good JJS 33 1982 55ff. 'to glean'). ¶ Forms: D prefc. *tġll*.

D. To insert, plunge: *k brkm tġll b dm ḏmr* for she plunged (her) knees in the blood of warriors, 1.3 II 27 and par.

Cf. tġll.

ġll (I) n. m. "thirsty one", epithet of certain minor deities (Arab. *ġalīl*, Lane 2279. Cf. Virolleaud Syria 16 1935 261; Caquot Ac1CILSChS 204; surveys Wyatt RTU 165 n. 18; Renfroe AULS 107; diff. Ginsberg JPOS 16 1936 146 n. 30: 'fetter', Arab. *ġull*, Hb. *ʕwl*); ¶ par.: *akl (I)*. ¶ Forms: pl. *ġllm*.

Thirsty one: *w ṣmt ġllm* and they destroyed the 'Thirsty Ones', 1.12 II 34 (// *aklm*).

ġll (II) n. m. "intoxication (?)" (Arab. *ġawl* Lane 2310; Driver CML 143; Al-Yasin LRUA 115; De Moor ARTU 272; alt. Watson UF 31 1999 780: MSA *ġll* 'be carefree'; diff. Good JJS 33 1982 55ff.; Dijkstra UF 20 1988 49 n. 79: 'gleanings', Hb.-Aram. *ʕll*; TN).

Intoxication (?): he pours... *yn b ld ġll* wine into the goblet (?) of intoxication (?), 1.22 I 19 (Belmonte RGTC 12/2 101: TN).

ġlm n. m. 1) "boy, youth"; 2) "prince"; 3) the 'Noble', divine title (Hb. *ʕlm*, cf. HALOT 835: *ʕlm III*, *ʕlmh*; Aram. *ʕlym*, DNWSI 854f.; Ph. cf. DNWSI 862: $ʕlm_5$; Ebla cf. /ġalmim/ *ḫa-la-mi-im*, Fronzaroli EL 142; cf. *ḫa-lam*, Krebernik PET 88; Amor. cf. /ʔ(?)alm(ān)um/, Gelb CAAA 13, 48; Arab. *ġulām*, Lane 2286f. Diff. Dohmen TWAT 6 172f.: 'Stellvertreter', Akk. *ṣalmu*; cf. Dietrich - Loretz UF 19 1987 407f.); ¶ par.: *ḫnzr*, *šph*. ¶ Forms: sg. *ġlm*, suff. *ġlmh*; du./pl. *ġlmm*; cstr. *ġlm*, suff. *ġlmk*, *ġlmh*; fem. *ġlmt* cf. *ġlmt (I)*.

1) Boy, youth, ★a) lad: *mġyh w ġlm* he reached did the lad, 1 16 I 50; *gm l ġlmh k [tṣḥ]* aloud to her lad thus [she shouted], 1.4 II 29 and par.; *gm l ġ[l]mh bʕl k yṣḥ* in a loud voice DN shouted to his lads, 1.4 VII 52; *gm l ġlmh k [tṣḥw tqry ġlmm b št ġr* and met the lads at the foot of the mountain, 1.3 II 4 and par.; *tbʕ ġlmm l yṯb* the lads left without staying, 1.2 I 19 and par.; *šbʕt ġlmh* his seven lads, 1.6 VI 8 (cf. 1.5 V 9); ★b) page, servant: *w tʕnyn ġlm bʕl* and the (two) pages of DN replied, 1.10 II 3 and par.; *km ġlmm w ʕrbn* like servants you must enter, 1.3 III 8; *nʕmn ġlm il* the handsome servant of DN, 1.14 I 40 and par., title of king *krt* (cf. also 1.14 III 51 and par.); ★c) messenger: (go back to the narrative: repeat) *k tlakn ġlmm* when the messenger-boys were sent, 1.4 V 43; *hlk ġlmm* the gait of (the / two) messengers, 1.19 II 28.

2) Prince: *wld (...) ġlm l ʕbd il* giving birth to ... a prince to the servant of DN, 1.14 III 49 and par.; *tld yṣb ġlm* she shall give birth to prince PN, 1.15 II 25 (cf. 1.16 VI 39).
3) Noble, title ★a) of the god *ym*: *yitsp (...) mṯdṯt ġlm ym* (...) a sixth did Noble DN gather to himself, 1.14 I 19 (diff.: 'the servants of DN'; for the various opinions cf. Dietrich - Loretz UF 12 1980 204 n. 66; cf. Verreet UF 19 1987 330: 'Finsternis des Tages' [bad omen, = *ẓlm*]); ★b) of the god Horon: *ġlm dʕtm* (may) the Noble (cast out) his mates, 1.169:10 (// *ḥrn*); ★c) attribution unc.: *gdlt l ġlm* one cow to the Noble / Prince, 1.119:7 (cf. Del Olmo CR 297 n. 14).
Unc. ctx.: *ġlm l šdt ymm*: 1.2 III 11; *zbl bʕl ġlm*: 1.9:17; in bkn ctx. *bm ymn mḫṣ ġlmm yš*[, 1.2 I 39; *b ġlmk*, 1.176:18; 7.137:4.

ġlm(y) PN (Sem.(?). Cf. Grøndahl PTU 141; Layton ZAW 102 1990 80ff., 86; cf. Dietrich - Loretz OLZ 62 1967 546: Hurr.).
PN: *bn PN*, 4.55:6; 4.617:33.

ġlmn PN (Hurr., var. of *aġlmn* (?). Cf. Dietrich - Loretz OLZ 62 1967 546; Grøndahl PTU 215; Van Soldt SAU 33; cf. Grøndahl PTU 141; Layton ZAW 102 1990 80ff.; Watson AuOr 11 1993 218); ¶ syll.: cf. *ḫal-la-ma-na*, PRU 3 55 (RS 15.92):4 and p. 244.
PN: ★a) 4.214 II 9; 4.609:13; cf. bkn ctx.: 4.625:19; ★b) *bn PN*: 4.33:13 (*ary*); 4.51:1 (*ary*); 4.55:24; 4.232:22; 4.309:2.

ġlmt (I) n. f. 1) "damsel"; 2) "Damsel, Princess", divine title (< *ġlm*; cf. Hb., Aram. *ʕlmh*, HALOT 835f.; DNWSI 854f., 862; Ph. *ʕlmt*, DNWSI 862; Palm., *ʕl(y)mt*, DNWSI 855; pre-Sarg. Mari , Ebla: cf. *Al-ma*, Gelb MR 128; Amor. cf. /ʔ(?)almatum/, Gelb CAAA 48 and cf. *ibid.* 13; Arab. *ġulāma*, Lane 2287); ¶ par.: *aṯt*. ¶ Forms: sg. *ġlmt*; du. *ġlmtm*.
1) Damsel: *ašʕrb ġlmt ḥẓry* (if) I make a damsel enter my mansion, 1.14 IV 41 (cf. 1.15 II 22; // *aṯt*).
2) 'The Damsel', ★a) divine title, used for *nkl*: *hl ġlmt tld bn* behold, the Damsel will give birth to a son, 1.24:7; ★b) of unc. attribution.: *dqtm w g<d>lt l ġlmtm* two ewes and one cow to the two Damsels / Princesses, 1.119:8 (Del Olmo CR 297 n. 14); *š l ġlmt* one ram to the Damsel, 1.41:25/87:27; *w l ġlmt š* and to the Damsel, one ram, 1.39:19 and par. In bkn ctx.: [*ġ*]*lmt mrd*[, 1.123:19; 1.139:10.

ġlmt (II) n. f. "concealment, darkness, thick fog" (Hb. cf. *nʕlm*, HALOT 834f.: *ʕlm I* ni. ptc.; cf. De Moor SP 172; Caquot - Sznycer TOu 1 219 n. w; Segert UF 20 1988 296f.; diff. Van Selms MFL 75 n. 6, 109 n. 30; Wyatt StTh 39 1985 n. 29: DN, wife of Baal, mother of the divine couple *gpn (w) ugr*, cf. De Moor UF 2 1970 203); ¶ par.: *ẓlmt*; ¶ syll. Ug.: cf. *]ḫu-ul-ma-tu*$_4$, Ug 5 137 III 16'; Huehnergard UVST 43, 98ff., 164; cf. Sivan UF 21 1989 360. ¶ Forms: sg. *ġlmt*. Concealment, darkness, thick fog: *bn ġlmt ʕmm ym* the sea is covered in darkness, 1.8 II 7 and par. (// *ẓlmt*); *bn ġlmt* in thick fog, 1.4 VII 55 (// *b ġlmt*).

ġlp n. m. 1) "husk", lit. "sheath"; 2) "sea snail (shell), murex", used as a cosmetic (Arab. *ġalfa*, *ġilāf*, Lane 2283f.; cf. De Moor Or 37 1968 213f.; Dijkstra - De Moor UF 7 1975 211f.; Ribichini - Xella Tessili 57; Aartun StUL 105ff.). ¶ Forms: pl. cstr. *ġlp*, suff. *ġlph*.
1) Husk: *šblt b ġlph* the ears in their husk(s), 1.19 I 19.
2) Sea snail: *tid(!)m b ġlp ym* she rouged herself with sea snails, 1.19 IV 42.

ġlptr PN (Hurr. Cf. Dietrich - Loretz OLZ 62 1967 546; WO 4 1967/68 302; Grøndahl PTU 204f., 215, 249).
PN: 4.244:10.

ġlṣ PN (Sem.(?). Cf. Grøndahl PTU 29, 141).
PN: *bn PN*, 4.52:9.

ġlt n. f. "prostration, inactivity" (< /ġ-l-y/. Cf. Rabin ScHier 8 1961 396; De Moor - Spronk UF 14 1982 190; diff.: Dahood Bib 57 1976 196; RSP 2 26f.: 'mischief', Hb. *ʕwl*; Rendsburg JAOS 107 1987 627: 'to exceed, overdo, exaggerate', Arab. *ġlw*; Badre *et al.* Syria 53 1976 125: 'impôt, butin', Arab. [*ġlw*]). ¶ Forms: sg. *ġlt*.
Prostration, inactivity: *šqlt b ġlt ydk* you have made your hands fall in prostration, 1.16 VI 32 and par.

ġltn PN (Hurr.; var. of *aġltn*. Cf. Grøndahl PTU 214, 262; Dietrich - Loretz OLZ 62 1967 546; WO 4 1967/68 302).
PN: 4.609:24.

ġlwš PN (etym. unc.; cf. Watson AuOr 8 1990 247).
PN: 4.391:4.

/ġ-l-y/ vb G: "to fall (down) > to wither"; D: "to lower, bow" (cf. Arab. *ġalā*, Lane 2287f. Cf. De Moor SP 68, 232; Rendsburg JAOS 107 1987 627); ¶ par.: /ḫ-r-b/, /y-p-ʕ/, /ḫ-s-p/. ¶ Forms: G suffc. *ġly*; prefc. *yġly*; inf. *ġly*. D suffc. *ġltm*; prefc. *tġly*, *tġl*(?).
G. To fall (down) > to wither: *riš ġly bd nsʕk* may your crown fall / wither in the hands of those who uproot you, 1.19 III 54; *yġly yḫsp ib* the bud has withered and wilted, 1.19 I 31; *ʕlk pht ġly b šdm* on your account I have seen withering in the fields, 1.6 V 18.
D. To lower, bow: *tġly ilm rišthm (...) lm ġltm ilm rištkm* the gods

lowered their heads (...) why, gods, did you lower your heads?, 1.2 I 23-24.
Unc. ctx.: *al tġl*, 1.3 I 1.
Cf. **ġlt**.

ġly PN (Hurr. Cf. Laroche GLH 75f.; Grøndahl PTU 204, 215; Dietrich - Loretz WO 4 1967/68 302; cf. Grøndahl PTU 141; Lipiński JSS 26 1981 279: Sem.).
PN: ★a) 4.16:8; 4.617:34; ★b) *bn PN*, 4.778:18; 4.782:25.

ġlyn PN (Hurr.; var. of *a/iġlyn*. Cf. Dietrich - Loretz OLZ 62 1967 546; Grøndahl PTU 204, 215; cf. Grøndahl PTU 53, 141; Lipiński JSS 26 1981 279: Sem.). Cf. *ḫlyn*, PN.
PN: *bn PN*, 4.214 II 19. Cf. bkn ctx. 4.649:2.

/ġ-m-ʔ/ vb G: "to be thirsty" (var. of /ẓ-m-ʔ/; cf. Hb. *ṣmʔ*, HALOT 1032; Akk. *ṣamû*, AHw 1081; CAD Ṣ 95f.; ESA *ẓmʔ*, DOSA 227; Arab. *ẓamiʔa*, Lane 1923f.; Eth. *ṣamʔa*, CDG 557. Cf. De Moor ULe 96); ¶ **par.**: /r-ġ-b/. ¶ **Forms**: G suffc. *ġmit*; inf. abs. *ġmu*.
G. To be thirsty: *hm ġmu ġmit* or else you are thirsty, 1.4 IV 34 (// *rġb rġbt*).

ġmr n. m. of a class or of a supplementary or subordinate social duty (etym. unc.; cf. Bravmann JCS 7 1953 27ff.: 'inexperienced, tyro', Arab. *ġumr*, Alt VT 2 1952 153ff.: 'Rekruten', cf. Hb. *htʕmr*, HALOT 849: *ʕmr*); ¶ **syll.** Ug.: *PN*LÚ *ḫa-ma-ru-ú*[, PRU 6 79:11; PN LÚ *ḫa-*[*a*]*m-*[*r*]*u-ú*, *ibid.* ln. 13; *PNN (...) PN*LÚ *ḫa-am-ru*<*-šu*>*-nu*, *ibid.* ln. 9; LÚ.MEŠ *ḫa-am-ru-ma*, PRU 6 p. 150 n. 3 (RS 25.428):6-7; cf. *ḫ*]*a-ma-ru-m*[*a*(meš); cf. PRU 6 p. 150; Sivan GAGl 221; Huehnergard UVST 165; AkkUg 153; Van Soldt SAU 306. ¶ **Forms**: pl. abs. *ġmrm*; cstr. *ġmr*.
Members of a class or of a supplementary or subordinate social duty, ★**a)** referring to a TN: *ġmrm*, 4.63 I 11 (TN: *Ulm*), 33 (TN: *Mʕrby*); III 32 (TN: *Ubrʕy*); ★**b)** referring to a class or guild: *ġmr mkrm ġ.* of the traders, 4.214 IV 1; in bkn ctx.:]*n ġmrm*, 4.111:11.

ġmšd PN (etym. unc. Cf. Dietrich - Loretz WO 4 1967/68 302: Sem.; Van Soldt UF 30 1998 725).
PN: 4.93 IV 9.

ġn TN (Belmonte RGTC 12/2 101: *Ǵanu*. Cf. Heltzer RCAU 14; Van Soldt UBL 11 377); ¶ **syll.**: cf. URU *Ḫa-*[*n*]*i*, Ug 5 95:11; cf. URU *Ḫa-*[*n V*, PRU 3 190 (RS 11.800):16'.
TN: 4.346:3; cf.]*n*, 4.610 I 25 (Van Soldt UF 28 1996 636; Belmonte RGTC 12/2 101: [*ġ*]*n*(?)).

ġnb n. m. "grape(s)" (Hb., Aram. *ʕnb*, HALOT 851; DNWSI 874; Akk. *i/enbu* AHw 381f.; CAD I/J 144ff.; ESA *ʕnb*, DOSA 373; Arab. *ʕinab*, Lane 2167; cf. Akk. *ḫanābu*, AHw 319; CAD Ḫ 75; Kaufman AIA 59 n. 183. Cf. Emerton Fs. Williams 46); ¶ par.: *qẓ*. ¶ Forms: pl. *ġnbm*.

Grape(s): *ṭl yṯll l ġnbm* the dew that is distilled upon the grapes, 1.19 I 42 (// *qẓ*); *w ġnbm* and grapes, 1.23:26 (unc. ctx.).

Cf. ġnbn.

ġnbn PN (Sem.(?)).

PN: 4.393:2 (bkn ctx.; the rdg *ġn bn*[does not seem likely in this text).

/ġ-n-ṯ/ vb G: "to gulp down" (Arab. *ġaniṯa*, Hava 537. Cf. Virolleaud Ug 5 555; L'Heureux RACG 181; Del Olmo AuOr 5 1987 51 n. 51; diff.: cf. De Moor UF 1 1969 178: 'to subdue', Akk. *ḫanāšu*, *kanšu*; Dietrich - Loretz UF 12 1980 177: 'Unterwerfen', *id.*; Pardee TPM 109: DN Ḫaniš). ¶ Forms: G ptc. act. *ġnṯ*.

G. To gulp down: *il ġnṯ ʕgl il* the god who gulps down the divine bullock, 1.108:11.

ġprt n. f. of a garment (etym. unc.; cf. Akk. *epartu*, AHw 222; CAD E 183. Cf. Greenfield JCS 21 1967 90f.: Hb. *ʕpr*, *mʕprt*, etc.; Dietrich - Loretz WO 4 1967/68 309: Akk. *(ḫ)apparrû*; UF 17 1985 401; Heltzer GPOTU 46; Ribichini - Xella Tessili 57: Arab. *ġuffāra*, *ġifāra*; cf. Hitt. *ḫup(a)ar(a)-*, HW Erg. 1 7; HEG 293f.). ¶ Forms: pl. *ġprt*.

Garment (for effigies of the gods): *ʕšrm ġprt* twenty *ġ.*, 4.182:7; cf.]*ġprt*, *ibid.* ln. 24.

/ġ-p-y/ vb G: "to espy, observe" (?); allomorph of /ṣ-p-y/ (?) (cf. *ṣp*); cf. Hb. *ṣph*, HALOT 1045; Akk. *ṣubbû*, AHw 1107f.; CAD Ṣ 226. Cf.Dietrich - Loretz WO 4 1967/68 309; De Moor UF 17 1985 227; Dijkstra UF 26 1994 117; cf. diff.: Margalit AuOr 7 1979 79: Arab. 'sleep lightly'). ¶ Forms: G. prefc. *tġpy*.

G. To espy, observe: in unc. ctx., *aylt tġpy ṯr* a hind was espying(?) a bull, 1.92:11.

/ġ-r/ vb G: "to tumble, fall, hurry" (Arab. *ġāra*, Lane 2306ff. Cf. Rainey UF 3 1971 172; De Moor SP 134; diff.: Caquot - Sznycer TOu 1 136 n. l: 'grogner', < Arab. n. *waġr*, Gaster Thespis[1] 447: 'to watch for, lie in wait', Hb. *nṣr*, cf. Renfroe AULS 110f.). ¶ Forms: G prefc. *yġr*.

G. To fall, hurry: *w ṯtn gh yġr* and (Baal) shouting aloud/uttering a cry, fell, 1.2 IV 6.

ġr (I) n. m. 1) "mountain"; 2) DN 'Mountain' (Hb. *ṣwr*, HALOT 1016f.; DNWSI 974; Aram. *ṭwr*, DNWSI 420, 974; cf. Arab. *ẓirr*, Lane 1909. Cf. Segert UF 20 1988 295; Renfroe AULS 108f.; cf. De Moor JNES 24 1965 362f.: 'rock', 'woodland', Arab. *ġār*, Syr. *ʕarō*, Akk. *ēru*); ¶ **RS Akk.**: ^{d}ḪUR.SAG.MEŠ, Ug 518:18; ¶ **par.**: *arṣ*, *db (II)*, *gbʕ*, *ḥl (I)*, *ḫlb*, *ṣpn*, *tl (I)*, *yʕr*. ¶ **Forms**: sg. *ġr*, suff. *ġry*, *ġrk*, *ġrh*; pl. *ġrm*.

1) Mountain: *ġr amn* the mountain TN, 2.33:16; *ġr ks* the mountain TN, 1.1 III 12 (Dietrich - Loretz - Sanmartín UF 5 1973 99 n. 21); *ġr bʕl ṣpn* la mountain of DN, TN, 1.16 I 6 and par. (// *ḥlm*); *b tk ġry il ṣpn* on my divine mountain, TN, 1.3 III 29 and par.; *w rbṣ l ġrk inbb kt ġrk* and go and rest on your mountain TN, at the base of your mountain, 1.13:9-10; *idk pnk al ttn tk ġr knkny ša ġr ʕl ydm* then set your face, do, towards the mountain TN, lift up the mountain upon your hands, 1.5 V 12-13 (// *ḫlb*; cf. 1.2 I 20 and par.); *idk al ttn pnm ʕm ġr trġzz ʕm ġr ṯrmg* then set your faces towards mount TN, towards mount TN, 1.4 VIII 2-3 (// *tlm*; Belmonte RGTC 12/2 290, 301); *b št ġr* at the foot of the mountain, 1.3 II 5 and par.; *gpt ġr* the mountain slopes, 1.4 VII 37 (// *yʕrm*); *l ġr gm ṣḥ* from the mountain shout in a loud voice, 1.16 IV 16; *pk b ġr ṯn* make your voice echo in the mountain, 1.82:4 (// *ḫlb*; cf. Caquot SEL 5 1988 34f.); *bʕl yṯb k ṯbt ġr* DN sit down with the aplomb of a mountain, 1.101:1 (// *km db*; cf. *ṯbt*; for the various interpretations cf. Dietrich - Loretz UF 17 1985 129ff.; Caquot TOu 2 47 n. 98; Pardee TPM 130f; Wyatt RTU 388 n. 1; *ġrm t*(!)*ḫšn* the mountains were afraid, 1.4 VII 32 (// *arṣ*); [*km y*]*ṣḥ b ġr* while the gods were rejoicing on the mountain, 1.4 VII 5 (// *ṣpn*); *kl ġr l kbd arṣ* (scour) every mountain to the innards of the earth, 1.5 VI 26 and par. (// *gbʕ*); *b ġr nḥlty* on the mountain of my possession, 1.3 III 30 and par. (// *b gbʕ tliyt*); *b tk ġrh* in the midst of his mountain, 1.101:2; *tblk ġrm mid ksp* may the mountains bring you plenty of silver, 1.4 V 31 and par. (// *gbʕm*); *tʕl b ġr (...) b ġr tliyt* she climbed up the mountain (...) the mountain of victory, 1.10 III 27-28 (cf. ln. 11). In unc. ctx.: *ġr ṯyb b pšy* 1.93:3 (cf. Margalit SEL 1 1984 90: 'ridge'; Caquot TOu 2 38: 'montagne'; Dijkstra UF 18 1986 126: 'another', Arab. *ġayr*).

2) DN 'Mountain(s)': *ġrm w ʕm*[*q*]*t š* 'Mountains and Valleys', a ram, 1.148:6 (cf. 1.118:18; // ^{d}ḪUR.SAG.MEŠ *u a-mu-<qa->t*[*u*$_4$ / *a-mu-q*[*u*, Ug 5 18:18; Huehnergard UVST 160f.; Van Soldt SAU 306; cf. *ʕmq (I)*).

Unc. ctx.: *ġr mtny*, 1.1 V 12, 14, 25 (cf. Caquot - Sznycer TOu 1 313

n. h); *ġr ṯlm*, 1.117:9; *ġr*, RSOu 14 51 [KTU 9.425]:11 (or *ġr (II)* (?)). Cf. *ġr (IV)*.

Cf. ġr (IV), ġrn, ġrt (I).

ġr (II) n. m. "skin" (Hb. *ʕwr*, HALOT 803; Pun. *ʕrt*, DNWSI 887: *ʕrh*$_1$. Cf. Aartun WO 4 1967/68 286; De Moor JNES 24 1965 363; diff. Driver Ug 6 185: 'pit of [the] chin', Arab. *ġawr*, Hb. *ʕwr*); ¶ syll. Ug.: cf. SU = *ma-aš-ku* = *aš-ḫé* = *ú*(?)-*ru*, Ug 5 130 II 6'; Sivan GAGl 207; cf. Huehnergard UVST 48 n. 1; Van Soldt BiOr 47 1990 731. ¶ Forms: sg. *ġr*.

Skin: *pẓġm ġr* those who gash the(ir) skin, 1.19 IV 11 and par.; *ġr b abn ydy* (his) skin with a (stone) knife he ripped, 1.5 VI 17 and par.

ġr (III) n. m. "total, sum" (< Hurr. *ḫeyari*, Laroche GLH 101; cf. Akk. *ḫēru*, AHw 341; CAD Ḫ 176; Dietrich - Loretz UF 9 1977 332f.). ¶ Forms: sg. *ġr*.

Total, sum: *ġr mk*(!)*r*(!)*m* total of traders, 4.27:12; *ṣbu anyt (...) ġr (nn) bnš* crew of the ship (...) in total: (nn) individuals, 4.40:9 (cf. *ibid.* ln. 6). Cf. *tgmr ḫrd ġr (...)* final total of the troops: in total (...), 4.777:12 (or TN *ġr (IV)*?; cf. Bordreuil CRAIBL 1984 426).

ġr (IV) TN (< *ġr (I)*, name of a region of the kingdom of Ugarit. Belmonte RGTC 12/2 102: *Ġūru*; cf. Bordreuil Syria 61 1984 2f.); RS 7 4:9.

PN: 4.365:39; 4.380:22; 4.693:57; cf. *ḫrd ġr* troops of TN(?), 4.777:12 (cf. *ġr (III)*).

Cf. ġrn.

ġr (V) n. m.; an installation for the funerary cult (eytm. unc.; cf. /ġ-r/; *ġr (I)*. Cf. Xella TRU 67; De Tarragon TOu 2 155 n. 55; Del Olmo CR 33, 117 n. 117). ¶ Forms: sg. *ġr*.

An installation for the funerary cult: (sacrifices are offered) *b ġr* in the *ġ.*, 1.41:22; 1.87:24 (diff.: Dietrich - Loretz TUAT 2 312: 'beim Niederfallen').

Cf. /ġ-r/.

ġrbtym, GN pl., bkn (?); cf. in bkn ctx.:]*ġrbtym*, 4.55:15.

ġrdn PN (Hurr. etym. unc.; cf. Grøndahl PTU 262).

PN: 2.61:1.

ġrgn PN (Hurr.(?). Cf. Dietrich - Loretz WO 4 1967/68 302; Grøndahl PTU 204f., 235, 424; Huehnergard UVST 218, 241; AkkUg 381, 395; Van Soldt BiOr 46 1989 646f.; SAU 12; cf. Sivan GAGl 224); ¶ syll.: cf. (DUMU) *ḫar*-GA-*na*, PRU 3 92 (RS 16.189):6; 203 (RS 16.257+) IV 29, 30; PRU 6 27:4,16; DUMU *ḫa-ra*-GA-*na*, PRU 6 83 IV 6;

DUMU *ḫa-ra*-QA-*na*, PRU 3 200 (RS 16.257+) II 5. Cf. *bn ḥrk*[, 4.315:3.

PN: *bn PN*, 4.69 V 8; VI 9; 4.93 I 16; bkn ctx.: 4.413:5; 4.422:36; 4.564:4.

/ġ-r-m/ vb D: "to unite, heap up" (denom. < *ġrm*. Cf. Caquot TOu 2 64f. n. 73; diff. De Moor UF 16 1984 240: 'to take on an obligation, to pledge', but cf. Renfroe AULS 109). ¶ Forms: D prefc. *tġrm*.

D. To unite, heap up: *hm tġrm l mt brq*(!)*k* or(?) unite your rays (against) DN, 1.82:5 (ctx. unc.; cf. Caquot TOu 2 65 n. 174; Del Olmo CR 374 n. 140 diff. rdg KTU: *brtk*).

ġrm n. m. 1) "heap" > "swarm"; 2) "heap" > "men at arms" (Hb. *ʕrmh*, HALOT 887; Syr. *ʕrmtō*, LS 548; Arab. *ʕaramat*, Lane 2025; Emerton Fs. Williams 46f.). ¶ Forms: sg. *ġrm*, suff. *ġrmn* (adv. *-n*).

1) Swarm: *k qṣm ġrmn* like grasshoppers in a swarm, 1.3 II 11 (cf. Dietrich - Loretz UF 4 1972 30; diff. Cassuto GA 117: 'without number', metath. < Arab. *ġamura*; Oldenburg CEB 87 nn. 6s.: 'without number', Arab. *ġayr* + Sem. *mny*; Aartun WO 4 1967/68 295f.: 'Platane', Hb. *ʕrmwn*; De Moor SP 91: 'destruction, calamity', Arab. *ġarām* / *ġarīm*, but cf. in ARTU 5: 'plane-tree'; Gibson CML 155: 'vengeance, punishment', Arab. *ġarima*.

2) Men at arms: *w ġrm ṯṯwy* and will you give orders to troops?, 1.16 VI 44 (// *ġzm*; diff.: De Moor QuSe 2 1973 92 n. 2: 'usurer', Arab. *ġarīm*; Dietrich - Loretz UF 17 1985 126 n. 30: 'Unterdrücker', Arab. *aġrama*; Gibson CML 155: 'rival', *ġyr*; Mustafa AcOrHung 29 1975 103: 'Angreifer', Arab. *ġwr* '(IV. Stamm)'; Izre'el UF 8 1976 46f.: 'croak', Akk. *ḫarāru*; Renfroe UF 22 1990 283f.; AULS 37ff.: 'invader', Arab. *ġwr* 'IVth conjugation'; Wyatt RTU 240 n. 293).

ġrn PN (etym. unc. Cf. Dietrich - Loretz WO 4 1967/68 302; Grøndahl PTU 27, 141; Van Soldt SAU 33). Cf. *ḫrn(y)*, PN.

PN: ★a) 4.296:5; 4.609:14; ★b) *bn PN*, 4.33:34; 4.50:15.

ġrp(?)d PN (etym. unc.).

PN: *bn PN*, 4.214 I 13.

ġrpl n. m. "cloud, large storm cloud" (Hb. *ʕrpl*, HALOT 888; Syr. *ʕarpelō*, LS 549; Emerton Fs. Williams 43f.); ¶ par.: *ḥmt (III)*. ¶ Forms: sg. *ġrpl*.

Cloud, large storm cloud: [*isp š*]*pš l hr*[*m*] *ġrpl* remove, DN, from the mountains the storm cloud!, 1.107:34 and par. (// *ḥmt*).

ġrplt n. f. "cloudy (sky)" (fem. < *ġrpl*. Cf. Dietrich - Loretz MU 182 n. 584). ¶ Forms: sg. *ġrplt*.

Cloudy (sky): *ġrp*]*lt mẓrm ylk* cloudy (sky): rain will fall, 1.163:6.

ġrt (I) n. f. "rock"(?) (cf. *ġr (I)*; De Moor ARTU 22). ¶ Forms: sg./pl. *ġrt*.

Rock(?): in bkn ctx. *ʕdb b ġrt ṯ*[*bt* upon rock(?) he placed (the) seats, 1.1 III 9.

ġrt (II) PN (etym. unc.).

PN: 4.278:5.

ġs PN (etym. unc. Cf. Dietrich - Loretz WO 4 1967/68 302; Watson AuOr 8 1990 123).

PN: *bn PN*, 4.321:1.

ġṣb n. m.; fold of a bull's body (Arab. *ġaḍf*, *aġḍaf*, Lane 2267f. Cf. Del Olmo AuOr 7 1989 124f.; diff.: De Moor UF 2 1970 325: 'swelling, protuberance', Arab. *ġaḍbat*, Akk. *ḫabāṣu*; Blome Opfermaterie 162: 'Viertel', cf. Hb. *šwq ymyn*; Caquot ACF 76 1976/77 462: 'sévir', Hb. *ʕṣb*). ¶ Forms: sg. *ġṣb*.

Fold of a bull's body: *l gṯrm ġṣb šmal alpm* to the DN: the left *ġ*. of two bulls, 1.109:26. Unc. ctx.: *ġṣb ġṣb*, 1.167:3.

ġṣmn PN (Sem. Cf. Watson AuOr 8 1990 123).

PN: 4.75 I 4 ([*bn*]*xln*).

ġṣr n. m. "limit, border, edge" (cf. Hb. *ʕṣr*, HALOT 870f.; cf. Arab. *ġaḍara*, Lane 2266; cf. EA Akk. ptc. m. *ḫa-ṣí-ri*, EAT 138:80,130; CAD Ḫ 166; Sivan GAGl 207; DNWSI 881: *ʕṣr*. Cf. Emerton Fs. Williams 46; Margalit MLD 75f.; diff.: Driver CML 142: 'confined', Hb. *ʕṣr*, Dahood ULx 98: 'to be fertile, ample', Arab. *ġaḍira*). ¶ Forms: sg. cstr. *ġṣr*.

Limit, border, edge: *tlm ġṣr arṣ* the (two) hills (at the) edge of the earth, 1.4 VIII 4.

/ġ-t-r/ (I) vb G: "to implore, intercede, ask " (Hb. *ʕtr*, HALOT 905f.; cf. PN *ia-a*[*ḫ*]*-ti-ri*, EAT 296:4; Sivan GAGl 207; Hess AmPN 79). ¶ Forms: G prefc., *yġtr*. *tġt*[*r*].

G. To implore, intercede, ask: *yġtr ʕṯtr* DN will (also) intercede, 1.24:28. In bkn ctx.: *rġb rġbt w tġt*[*r*] if you are hungry ask (for anything), 1.4 IV 33 (cf. De Moor ARTU 53; diff.: Del Olmo MLC 608: 'tomar un bocado', rdg. *tġt*[, Arab. *tāʕa* / *ġatta*; Rin AE 160: 'to drink', Arab. *ġatta*; Oldenburg CEB 118 n. 2: 'to weary', Arab. *ġatta*; Driver CML 142: 'to roam, voyage', Hb. *t/ṭʕh*).

Cf. ġtr.

/ġ-t-r/ (II) vb G: "to kill"(?) (cf. Arab. *ʕatara*, Lane 1946. Cf. Dietrich - Loretz - Sanmartín UF 7 1975 138; cf. Renfroe AULS 109f.; diff.:

Pardee AfO 23 1986 138: 'to confront', Arab. *ġāra*, 'reflexive form'). ¶ Forms: G prefc. *yġtr*.
G. To kill(?): *bʕln yġtr* [*ḫ*]*rd* the lord (*casus pendens*), (him) the guard will attack(?), 1.103+:39.

ġtr PN (etym. unc.).
PN: *bn PN*, 4.754:16.

ġw PN (etym. unc.).
PN: ★a) 4.695:6; ★b) *bn PN*, 4.700:5.

/ġ-w-y/ vb D(?): "to twist" (cf. Aram. *ʕwy*, Jastrow 1049. Cf. Del Olmo CR 378 n. 156; diff.: De Moor - Spronk UF 16 1984 249: 'to pervert > turn into', Arab. *ġwy*, Hb. *ʕwh*; Tropper UG 662: 'sich vergehen, sich versündigen'). ¶ Forms: D(?) prefc. *aġwyn*.
D(?). To twist: *aġwyn ʕnk* I am going to twist your responsible ones (/ those who should reply to you), 1.82:42.

ġyr n. m. "hollow, pit, depth" (Arab. *ġawr*, Lane 2308. Cf. De Moor SP 134; Renfroe AULS 110ff. ['cave']; diff. Caquot - Sznycer TOu 1 171 n. z: 'rapide', Arab. *ġāra*); ¶ par.: *ʕn (I)*. ¶ Forms: pl. *ġyrm*.
Hollow, pit, depth: *ṯlṯ mtḥ ġyrm* a three measures (beneath) the depths, 1.3 IV 36 and par. (// *ʕnt*).

ġyrn PN (4.277:3), allograph of *ḫyrn*, PN.

ġz n. m. "warrior, raider" ((?); cf. Arab. *ġazā*, Lane 2257. Cf. Driver CML 142; Mustafa AcOrHung 29 1976 103; Renfroe UF 22 1990 282, 284; AULS 39ff. *ġzy* to invade; diff. Dietrich - Loretz UF 17 1985 123ff.: 'Gewalttäter', Arab. *ġazā*; Bernhardt Anmerkungen 115: 'wütend machen', Arab. *ġāẓa*; Izre'el UF 8 1974 446: 'to gargle', Akk. *azû*; De Moor - Spronk UF 14 1982 190: 'philanthropist, munificent', Arab. *ġuzzāẓ*); ¶ par.: *ġr*. ¶ Forms: sg. *ġz*, pl. *ġzm*.
Warrior, raider: *k ġz ġzm tdbr* can you guide(?) warriors like a warrior?, 1.16 VI 43 and par (// *ġrm*).

ġzl n. m. "spinner" (Arab. *ġazzal*, Lane 2256; Aram. cf. *ʕzl*, DNWSI 385; DJPA 401. Cf. Dietrich - Loretz WO 4 1967/68 308; Heltzer IOKU 95f.; Ribichini - Xella Tessili 19f.; Renfroe AULS 113); ¶ syll. Ug.: cf. PN *ḫa-zi-lu*, PRU 6 86 I 10 (cf. *ġzl(y)*). ¶ Forms: pl. *ġzlm*.
Spinner: *arbʕ ġzlm* four spinners, 4.358:9.
Cf. ẓzl, ġzl(y).

ġzl(y) PN (Sem. cf. *ġzl*. Cf. Grøndahl PTU 28, 141; Huehnergard UVST 241; cf. Dietrich - Loretz WO 4 1967/68 308); ¶ syll. Ug.: cf. PN *ḫa-zi-lu*, PRU 6 86 I 10. *ʕz*(?)*l* is possibly an allograph in 4.31:8.
PN: *bn PN*, 4.617:7; 4.769:54.

ġzr n. m. "1) "lad, youth"; 2) "Noble, hero"; 3) "champion, warrior", epithet of gods and heroes and of cult officials (Hb. *ʕzr*, HALOT 811; cf. Arab. *ġazīr*, Lane 2255. Cf. Miller UF 1 1979 90f.; UF 2 1970 162ff.; Van Selms MFL 95f.; De Moor SP 21, 31, 76; Xella MSS 138ff.; PP 150 1973 194ff.; Lipiński UF 2 1970 77; Sasson UF 14 1982 204ff.; Barr JSS 26 1981 279; Emerton Fs. Williams 46); ¶ par.: *aṯt*, *mt (III)*, *ṣbu (I)*. ¶ Forms: sg. *ġzr*, du. / pl. *ġzrm*.
1) Lad, youth, ★a) in general: *w pġt w ġzr aḥd* and a lass and a lad, 4.102:20 and par.; *aṯt w ṯn ġzrm* a woman and two youths, 4.102:23 and par.; [*ṯ*]*lṯ aṯt adrt w ṯlṯ ġzr*[*m*] three noble women and three lads, 4.102:16; *arbʕ ʕšr ġzrm* fourteen lads, 4.349:1; *ydy dbbm d ġzr* (may) the conjuror (expel) the 'demons' from the lad (adolescent youth), 1.169:1 (diff.: Del Olmo CR 385: 'banishment of the demons of strength'); *w ʕlm ylk ġzr* and next the lad will go, 1.175:14; *k yqny ġzr* when (he was about to) acquire a youth, 1.141:1; ★b) in musical ctx.: *ġzrm g ṭb* sweet-voiced lads, 1.23:14; *ġzr nʕm* a handsome lad [should sing], 1.23:17; *yšr ġzr ṭb ql* the sweet-voiced lad sang, 1.3 I 20.
2) Noble, hero, title ★a) of heroes (in the *dnil - aqht* Cycle): *dnil* (...) *ġzr* PN (...) the Noble, 1.17 II 28 and par.; *w yʕn aqht ġzr* and Noble PN replied, 1.17 VI 20 and par.; *nʕmn ġzr šṭ ṯrm* the handsome Noble has prepared bulls, 1.18 IV 14; *dm l ġzr šrgk ḫ̮ḫm* since for a Noble your lies are a quagmire, 1.17 VI 34; [*y*]*brkn šm il ġzrm* the Heroes blessed the name of DN, 1.22 I 7 (// *mtm*); *yḥ (...) brlt ġzr* may the Noble revive (...) his appetite, 1.17 I 37; *apnk ġzr ilḥu* then the Noble PN, 1.16 I 46 and par. (cf. ln. 58); ★b) of gods: *<m>t (...) ṯtʕ ydd il ġzr* DN (...) take fright did the beloved of DN, the Noble, 1.6 VI 31 and par.
3) Champion, warrior: *ṯṯʕr* (...) *hdmm lġzrm* she arranged (...) footstools like / for champions, 1.3 II 22 and par. (// *ṣbim*); *tlbš npṣ ġzr* she put on the clothes of a warrior, 1.19 IV 44. In unc. ctx.: 1.73:11.
Cf. aġzr.

/ġ-ẓ-y/ vb G/D: 1) "to give presents to"; 2) "to win over" (Arab. *ġaḍā*, Lane 2268f.; Hb. *ʕšh*, HALOT 866. Cf. De Moor Or 37 1968 213 n. 3; UF 1 1969 202 n. 6;); ¶ par.: /ʕ-p/, /m-g-n/. ¶ Forms: G/D suffc. *ġẓtm*; prefc. *tġẓy*, *tġẓyn*, [*n*]*ġẓ*.
G/D. 1) To give presents to: *tġẓyn qnyt ilm* they gave presents to the progenitrix of the gods, 1.4 III 26 and par. (// *tmgnn*; cf. ln. 35); *hm ġẓtm bny bnwt* have you given presents to the creator of creatures?,

1.4 III 31 (// *mgntm*).
2) To win over: *tġẓy bny bnwt* she won over the creator of creatures, 1.4 II 11 (// *tʕpp*).
Cf. mġẓ, tġẓyt.

h

-h (I) suffixed pronominal morpheme: 1) used with a noun, "his /her (hers) / its"; 2) used with a verb, "him / her / it"; 3) used with a preposition, *atr*, *ʕl*, *ʕm*, *b*, *bd*, *l*, *qdm*, *tḥt* (c.Sem. except Akk.; cf. Moscati ICGSL 106f.; Gordon UT § 6.7; Segert BGUL 47; Tropper UG 221ff.); syll. Ug.: /-hu/ū/, Huehnergard UVST 120. ¶ Forms: sg. *-h*; suff. *-hn* (< *-h (I)* + encl. *-n*; cf. Ginsberg / Gordon UT 36 n. 5; Tropper UG 228); *-hw* in 2.15:6 (*mater lectionis*, cf. Tropper UG 54); cf. also *-nh*.

1) Used with a noun: *passim*; cf. lengthened Forms: *qšthn aḫd b ydh* his bow he took in his hand, 1.10 II 6 (or dittography of *n/a*?); *yqṣrn ymy bʕhn* shortened shall be the days of his / their (!) lord, 1.103:34 (cf. ln. 33: *pnh*); in bkn and unc. ctx.: *lhn lg ynh*[to him a pitcher of wine ...[, 1.23:75 (cf. diff. De Moor ARTU 128 n. 69: a liquid measure, // *lg*, Hb. *hyn*, HALOT 245; Gibson CML 127, 145: 'here, hither', Arab. *huna*).

2) Used with a verb: *atm w ank ibġyh* and I shall reveal it (to you), 1.3 III 29; *tn ilm d tqh* deliver, gods, the one you pay homage to, 1.2 I 34 and par.; *tšthwy w tkbdh* she prostrated herself and honoured him, 1.4 IV 26 and par.; *ank ʕm mlakth šmʕh* I, next to his embassy, am his listener (act. part.), 2.17:7 (Cunchillos TOu 2 307 n. 14; diff.: Dietrich - Loretz UF 14 1982 87: 'höre (nun) ihn an!'); *in b ilm ʕnyh* there was no one among the gods who answered him,, 1.16 V 22; *kd ʕl qšth imḫṣh*, thus, for his bow I wounded him, 1.19 I 14; *rḥm ʕnt tngṯh* the damsel DN sought him, 1.6 II 27 and par.; *gršh l ksi mlkh* the one who threw him off his royal throne, 1.3 IV 2; *l ktp ʕnt k tšth* on the shoulders of DN, she did place him, 1.6 I 15; *ṭl šm tskh* (with) dew that the skies poured down for her, 1.3 II 40 and par.; *šr aḫyh mẓah* the prince that his brothers found, 1.12 II 50; *mʕmsh* [*k*] *šbʕ yn* who bears the burden (part. act.) of him [when] he is sated with wine, 1.17 I 30; *šmn itrhw* as for the oil: follow it, 2.15:6 (cf. Tropper UG 54).

3) Used with a preposition: *lpš d sgr bh* a cloak with (appliqués of) gold, 4.166:6; *ʕmh bqʕt* with her (is) DN, 1.24:48; *bʕdh bhtm (...) sgrt*

bʕdh ʕdbt tlt behind her the house (...) she closed, behind her she shot the bolt, 1.100:70-71; *k bh btt l tbt w bh tdmmt* for in it shamelessness is truly and in it there is lewd behaviour, 1.4 III 21-22; *yʕdb lhm (...) lh* he provided it with bread (...), 1.114:7; *ʕttrt tʕdb nšb lh*, DN provided him with a piece of meat, 1.114:10; *kll ylḥm bh* of which all shall eat, 1.115:10; *bdh ḫt tkl* in his hand (he had) the sceptre of sterility, 1.23:8; *tq(!)ḥ [ks] bdh* he took [the cup] from his hand, 1.19 IV 55, cf. ln. 54; *ʕmh trd nrt ilm* with her went down the luminary of the gods, 1.6 I 8; *tḥth k kdrt (...) ʕlh k irbym* at her feet like balls (...), above her like locusts, 1.3 II 9-10 and par.; *d in bn lh* who has no son, 1.17 I 18 and par.; *ytn ks bdh* he put a cup in his hand, 1.3 I 10; *atrh tdd iln[ym]* after him the divine ones left, 1.20 II 2 and par.; *w ttb mlakm lh* and you shall make the (two) messengers return to him, 1.14 III 33; *w tqrb w ld bn lh* she conceived and bore him a son, 1.15 III 20 and par.; *št alp qdmh* he placed an ox before her, 1.3 IV 41 and par.; *yšr ʕlh* he shall sing in his presence, 1.17 VI 31; *ʕlh nšr[m] trḫpn* over him the eagles flew about, 1.18 IV 30 and par.; *w lh yʕlm* otherwise it will go unnoticed, 2.14:14; *ʕlh trh tšʕrb* she made his 'bulls' enter his presence, 1.15 IV 17-18 and par.; *bh pʕnm ttt* her very feet (lit. on her, the feet) trembled, 1.3 III 32 and par.; *d bh rumm l rbbt* in which there were wild bulls by the myriad, 1.4 I 43; *ar[b]ʕ arbʕ mtbt azmr bh* in which there will be four plus four huts (made) of branches, 1.41:51; *tar um tkn lh* he had maternal relatives, 1.14 I 15; *d šbʕ [a]ḫm lh* he who had seven brothers, 1.14 I 9; *unt aḥd lh[* PN(N) has(have) a loan pending, 4.86:4; *unt in mnm bh* (the house) has no corvée at all, 3.2:18 and par.; *ytb ly il [...] w lh* DN will attend to me[...] and (it will go well) with him, 1.3 IV 54-55 *]mlk ytn lbš lh* the king will give the garment to him, 4.182:64. Cf. in unc. and bkn ctx. *bt* (rdg: *d(?)t*) *ʕlh*, 1.101:7.

-h (II) adverbial functor: 1) directional, local: "to, towards"; "against"; "in, on"; 2) temporal, "for, during"; 3) modal, "to, according to" or gerund (Hb. *-h*, Joüon GHB 222ff.; Hoftijzer SfM; Eth. *-hā*, Lambdin ICE 33. Cf. Gordon UT § 11.1; Segert BGUL 76; Aartun PU 1 41ff.; Tropper UG 320ff.). ¶ Forms: *-h*.

1) Directional, local: *nša [y]dh šmmh* he lifted up his hands to heaven, 1.14 IV 5; *yšu yr šmmh* he raised (it and) shot skywards, 1.23:38; his tears flowed *km tqlm arsh km ḫmšt mtth* like shekels to the ground, like five-shekel weights onto the bed, 1.14 I 29-30; *yrḥṣ ydh amth* he washed his hands to the elbow, 1.14 III 53 (// *ʕd*); *ḥẓk al tšʕl qrth* do not shoot your arrows against the city, 1.14 II 13; *ql bl ʕm dgn ttlh*

take (this) request to DN to (/ in) TN, 1.100:15 and par.; *ḥṭb d anyt grgmšh* bill for / of a ship (with destination / bound for) TN, 4.779:13; *kd l ḫty maḫdh* a jar for PN in TN, 4.149:5; *bḫbṯh ḥwt ṯth* in case he runs away to another country, 3.3:4 (cf. Hoftijzer - Van Soldt UF 23 1991 190); *w riš p qq w šrh yšt* and on (his) head, [mouth,] throat and navel one shall place /shall be placed... (?), 1.114:30 (cf. Watson AuOr 8 1990 266); *ṯn šmn ʕlyh* two cruets of oil in the place of sacrifice, 1.41:46 // 1.87:50; *d šṣa ḥwyh* who delivered (it) to the storehouse, 4.145:10. Cf. *qrht d tššlmn ṯlrbh* cities that compensate TN(?) by means of loans, 4.95:2.

2) Temporal: *lht w ʕlmh* from now and for ever (= eternity), 1.19 IV 6; *ʕnt brḥ pʕlmh* from now and for ever may you be a fugitive, 1.19 III 55 and par.; *aṯt il w ʕlmh* (they shall be) wives of DN and (this) in perpetuity, 1.23: 42 and par. *w ḥdṯh tdn hmt* and on the day of the new moon, they shall declare them (legitimate), 1.104:18-19 (diff. Del Olmo CR 309: 'and until the day of the new moon').

3) Modal(?): [*w*] *yqrb trẓẓh* (and) he approached at a run ((?) : at full speed), 1.16 I 49 (for this and other examples cf. Dahood ULx 88). The function of *-h* in composite numerals with *ʕšrh* (Gordon UT § 7.20; Tropper UG 350) is uncertain. Cf. *hlh.*

hayn PN (etym. unc.).

PN: *hayn*[, 4.118:3 (bkn ctx.).

hbm PN (etym. unc.).

PN: 4.313:1 (*šlmy*).

hbn n. m. "ebony" (Eg. *hbny*, WäS 2 487; Hb. *hbn*, HALOT 237; Syr. *ʔabnūsō*, LS 3; Arab. *ʔabnūs*, Lane 10; Eth. *ʔabnus*, CDG 4; Gk *ébenos*, Liddell - Scott 466f. Cf. Lambdin JAOS 73 1953 149; Dahood UHP 56; Helck Bez. 378; Muchiki Loanwords 281f.; diff.: Rendsburg JAOS 1982 626: 'sack, bag', MSA *hebbān*). ¶ Forms: sg. *hbn*.

Ebony: *ʕšrm hbn* twenty (logs(?)) of ebony, 4.402:6.

/h-b-r/ vb. G: "to bow" (cf. Arab. *habr*, *habīr*, "depressed land" Hava 812; cf. Ullendorff JSS 7 1962 339f., South Semitic **kbr*, Renfroe AULS 42ff.). ¶ Forms: G prefc. *thbr*, *yhbr*, impv. *hbr* (Tropper UF 22 1990 376; cf. diff.: Tropper - Verreet UF 20 1988 344 n. 21: G/D(?)).

G. To bow: (at the feet of DN) *hbr w ql* bow and fall down, 1.3 III 10 and par., prostration formula (cf. Del Olmo MLC 54f.); *l pʕn il thbr* at the feet of DN he bowed, 1.6 I 36 and par.; *yhbr špthm yšq* he bent down, he kissed their lips, 1.23:49 and par.

hbt, 2.70:16, cf. *hwt (I).*

/h-b-ṯ/ẓ/ vb. G/D(?): "to knock down, hit"; "to remove; to wipe out" (ESA *hbṯ*, DOSA 104; Arab. *habaṭa*, Lane 2876. Cf. Dijkstra UF 7 1975 564f.; Tropper UF 22 1990 376; 26 1994 4568f.; Renfroe AULS 114f.; Bordreuil - Pardee RSOu 14 p. 384). ¶ Forms: G/D(?): suffc./inf. *hbṯ*, prefc. *yhbṯ*, *thbṯ*, ar. *thbṯn*.
G/D(?). 1) To knock down, hit: *bn ḫrnk mġy hbṯ hw ḫrd w šl hw qrt* your messenger arrived, knocked down the guard (and) plundered the city, 2.61:5. In unc. ctx.: *lm l hbṯ* why has one not knocked down(?), RSOu 14 51 [KTU 9.425]:17 (cf. ln. 19, 24).
2) To remove, wipe out: *yhbṯ bn*(!)*š* may he/they remove this individual, 2.4:19; *špḥ al thbṯ* do not wipe out the family, 2.47:16; in bkn ctx.] *w thbẓn* and they will wipe (him) out(?), 1.163:3 (cf. Tropper UF 22 1990 376; UF 26 1994 461 n. 21: 'Gp-PK' /tuhbaṣūna/; Del Olmo CR 352: 'the people .... will be slaughtered'; Dietrich - Loretz MU 172f.: 'werden beseitigt', ni.).
Cf. **hbṯn**.

hbṯn n. m.; social group or class (cf. Akk. *ebēṭu* "to bind", AHw 183; CAD E 13ff.; *ubbuṭu*, AHw 1400; apparently not connected with /h-b-ṯ/; diff. Liverani RSO 44 1969 195; Dietrich - Loretz TUAT 1 214: 'Schläger'; cf. Sanmartín UF 21 1989 346 n. 91). ¶ Forms: sg. *hbṯn*; pl. *hbṯnm*.
Social group or class: PN *hbṯn*, 4.635:10; in the service of the royal palace: 4.137:6; 4.163:10; cf. 4.173:9; 4.174:6; 4.179:11.

hd(d) DN, alternative name of Baal (Hb. *hdd*, HALOT 238; Aram. [*h*]*dd*, KAI 222 A 25-26; cf. Ebla $^{(d)}$*ʔà-da*, Krebernik PET 74; Bonechi SEL 8 1991 67; Sanmartín AuOr 9 1991 188; Mander MROA 2/1 28ff.; Mari Akk., Amor. /had/(d)u/ and var., Huffmon APNMT 156f., Gelb CAAA 19; Durand MROA 2/1 177f. Cf. Roberts ESP 13ff.; Edzard WbMyth 1 135f.; Pope - Röllig WbMyth 1 253ff.; Van Zijl Baal 324ff.; De Vaux RB 78 1971 124f.; De Moor UF 20 1988 173ff.; Pardee AfO36/37 1989/90 448ff.; Smith BC 129 n. 25); ¶ RS **Akk.**: ^{d}U, ^{d}IM, *passim* < Ug. DNN *bʕl* or *hd(d)*, cf. Huehnergard AkkUg 394, 397; **syll. Ug.**: the element /(h)addu, (h)adadu/ in PNN; cf. Sivan GAGl 222; for the element /-(h)and/ in PN Niqmandu cf. Roberts ESP 13: already OAkk.; Van Soldt BiOr 46 1989 650: contamination < Hitt. */-anda/; cf. Emar *a-du-ut-ta*, Wiseman - Hess UF 26 1994 506 n. 26); ¶ **par.**: *bʕl*. ¶ Forms: *add*, *hd*, *hdd*.
DN: *il hd* the god DN, 1.10 II 5 and par.; *gmr hd* the avenger, DN, 1.2 I 46; *pn hdd* the face of DN, 1.9:13; *šnu hd* the foes of DN, 1.4 VII 36; *ib hd*{*ṯ*}, enemies of DN,1.4 VII 38 (cf. KTU *ad loc.*). Cf. 1.4

VI 39; 1.5 I 23 and par.; 1.12 II 54 (// *bʕl*). In bkn ctx. *šġr hd*, 1.9:18; *hd tngṯnh*, 1.1 V 17 and par.; *hd r*[, 1.101:1; *hdd*, 2.31:41. Cf. var. *il add*, 1.65:9. In bkn ctx., *yqr.un hd* may DN invite (me), 1.5 I 22; *i hd d*[, 1.5 IV 7.

Cf. ydbhd, yrgbhd.

hdm n. m. "footstool", "stool" (Hb. *hdm*, HALOT 239; Eg. *hdmw*, WäS 2 205; Helck Bez.: 517 [164], *h(a)-d-mú*; Hoch SWET 304; cf. Hurr. *atmi*, Nuzi Akk. GIŠ *atmu* [AHw 87], Haas AoF 20 1993 264; Watson NABU 1996 19); ¶ par.: *arṣ*, *kḥṯ*, *ksu*, *nẖt*, *ṯlḥn*. ¶ Forms: sg. *hdm*; pl. *hdmm*.

Footstool, stool: *hdm il*(!) a divine footstool, 1.4 I 34 (// *kḥṯ*, *nẖt*); his feet *l hdm yṯpd* he rested on the footstool, 1.4 IV 29 and par.; she arranged (...) *hdmm l ġzrm* the stools like champions, 1.3 II 22 (// *ksat*, *ṯlḥnt*); cf. *hdmm ṯṯr lhdmm* the stools she arranged like stools (*ibid.* ln. 37); he came down from the throne, *yṯb l hdm w l hdm yṯb l arṣ* and sat on the footstool and (coming down) from the footstool he sat on the ground, 1.5 VI 13 (// *ksu*, *arṣ*); his feet *l tmġyn hdm* did not reach the footstool, 1.6 I 60; *ydmʕ hdm pʕnh* may the footstool of his feet shed tears, 1.161:14.

hdrʕy TN (Belmonte RGTC 12/2 103: **Hadraʕā*), a mythical place, the residence of *rpu mlk* (Hb. *ʔdrʕy*, HALOT 17; Akk. Emar cf. dNE.IRI$_{11}$.GAL *be-el id-ri*, Emar 158:6, cf. Smith Early History of God 140 n. 14; Dietrich - Loretz UF 22 1990 55f. n. 11. Cf. Margulis JBL 89 1970 293f.; Astour RSP 2 282f. no. 36; Dietrich - Loretz UF 12 1980 171ff.; UF 21 1989 123ff.; UF 22 1990 55f.; TUAT 2 822; Pardee TPM 95ff.; Margalit BZAW 182 473; Görg UF 6 1974 474f.; De Moor ARTU 187 n. 3; Van Soldt UBL 11 371; diff. Bordreuil Maarav 5/6 1990 13: rdg *hd rʕy* 'Haddou le berger' [cf. Dietrich - Loretz - Sanmartín UF 7 1975 117; De Moor ZAW 88 1976 326f., 338f.; Levine - De Tarragon JAOS 104 1984 656]); ¶ par.: *ʕṯtrt (II)*.

TN, a mythical place: *il ṯpṭ b hdrʕy* the god who judges in TN, 1.108:3 (// *b ʕṯtrt*).

hdrt n. f. "revelation, vision (Hb. *hdr*, *hdrt*, HALOT 240; Syr. *hedrō*, LS 172. Cf. Cunchillos Sal29 54f., 61; Tropper UBL 12 305ff.; diff.: Sanmartín UF 12 1980 337f.: 'Trübsal', Akk. *i/edirtu*; Moore RB 93 1986 402ff.: 'royal visitation', Ahiqar xii 207 (?); Dietrich - Loretz SEL 1 1984 85ff.: mistake for *d/d(h)rt*); ¶ par.: *ḥlm*. ¶ Forms: sg. *hdrt*.

Revelation, vision: he came to himself (...) *w hdrt* and it was a revelation, 1.14 III 51 (// *ḥlm*).

/h-d-y/ G: "to lacerate (oneself)" (Arab. *hadda*, *hadaʔa*, Lane 2886f.,

hadā, Hava 822. Cf. Loewenstamm IOS 4 1974 1; De Moor SP 193; Tropper - Verreet UF 20 1988 343f., 349; Tropper UF 22 1990 376f.; Renfroe AULS 45ff.); ¶ par.: /ṯ-l-ṯ/. ¶ Forms: G prefc. *thdy*, *yhdy*.
G. To lacerate (onself): *yhdy lḥm w dqn* he lacerated (his) cheeks and chin, 1.5 VI 19 and par (// *yṯlṯ*).

hg n. m. "enumeration, count" (< /h-g-h/, HALOT 237; cf. Arab. *higā*, **hagā*, Hava 818); ¶ par.: *spr*. ¶ Forms: sg. *hg*.
Enumeration, count: *ṯnn d bl hg* the archers without count, 1.14 II 38 (// *spr*).

/h-g-g/ vb. G: "to murmur, whisper" (cf. Hb. *hgh*, *hgyg*, HALOT 237, 238; cf. Akk. *agāgu*, AHw 14; CAD A/1 139f. Cf. De Moor - Spronk UF 16 1984 249; Caquot TOu 2 70 n. 220); /y-t-n/ (+ *ql*). ¶ Forms: G: prefc. *thggn* (correcting scribal mistake *tiggn*).
G. To murmur, whisper: *abnm l th(!)ggn* stones that do not murmur, 1.82:43 (// *l ttn* <*ql*>).

hkl n. m. "palace" (Akk. *ekallum*, AHw 191f., CAD E 52ff.; Hurr. /ḫaikalli/ Neu StBoT 32 229; Hb. *hykl*, HALOT 244f.; Syr., *hayklō*, LS 174; Arab. *haykal*, Hava 831. Cf. Falkenstein Das Sumerische 24; Gelb MAD 2 25; Kaufman AIA 27f.; Lieberman SLOBA 216f.). ¶ Forms: sg. *hkl*, suff. *hkly*, *hklk*, *hklh*; pl./du. *hklm*.
Palace: *ṯġr hk[l]* doorkeeper of the palace, 4.224:8, 9; *trmm hklh* they erected his palace, 1.4 VI 17 and par.; *tštql ilt l hklh* the goddess went down to her palace, 1.3 II 18 and par.; I am going to place *(...) ḥln b qrb hklm* a window in the palace, 1.4 V 62 and par.; and he may have *(...) šrš b qrb hklh* offpsring in his palace, 1.17 I 26 and par.; *ʕrb bkyt b hklh* mourners entered his palace, 1.19 IV 10, cf. ln. 21; open *(...) hkl w ištql* the palace so that I can come in, 1.100:72; *rbt kmn hkl* ten thousand acres the palace (will cover), 1.4 V 57; *iqra [b h]kly* I call you [... to] my [pa]lace, 1.21 II 3 and par.; *hkly dtm ḫrṣ* my palace of gold, 1.4 VI 37; do not be glad *b rm [h]kl[k]* about the height of your palace, 1.3 V 21 and par.; they lit *(...) nblat b hklm* flames in the palace, 1.4 VI 23 and par., cf. ln. 33.

hkm "?" (Cf. De Moor (- Spronk) CARTU 136; ARTU 110: 'powder'). ¶ Forms: *hkm*.
? : in bkn ctx., *]pp hkm*, 1.10 I 2.

hl deictic functor 1) "behold, look!"; 2) as a conj. ★a) consecutive "and so, and then"; ★b) temporal "as soon as, no sooner ... than" (cf. Brown Maarav 4 1987 202ff.; cf. EA Akk. /allū(mi)/, Sivan GAGl 190; cf. AHw 37; CAD A/1 358; cf. Hb. *hlwʔ*, *hlm*, HALOT 249, 512; Arab. *hal*, Lane 3044. Cf. Aartun PU 1 40ff., 72; Brown Maarav

4 1987 202ff.; Tropper UG 750ff.); syll. Ug.: cf. [...] *al-li-ni-yu*, Ug 5 138:5'; Huehnergard UVST 121; cf. Sivan GAGl 190; ¶ par.: *ṯmny*. ¶ Forms: *hl*, suff. *hlk*, *hlh*, *hlm* (encl. *-m* ?), *hln*, *hlny* (encl. *-y* ; cf. Tropper UF 26 1994 477).

1) Behold, look!: *hl ġlmt tld bn* behold the damsel will give birth to a son, 1.24:7; *hlk qšt ybln hl yšrbʕ qṣʕt* behold he brought a bow, he had made the arrows fourfold, 1.17 V 12: *hlh tšpl hlh trm* look, one stooped, look, the other went up, 1.23:32 and par.; *hl ʕṣr ṯḥrr l išt* look, you have roasted a bird on the fire, 1.23:44 and par.; *hlny argmn d ybl PN*, behold the tribute that PN will pay, 3.1:18; *hlny ʕmny kll šlm* look, with us everything is well, 2.13:9 (// *ṯmny*); *passim* in letters: 2.1:3; 2.21:7; 2.24:8; 2.30:8, 12; *hlny bn ʕyn yštal* here PN urges, 2.70:11; *hlny ḫrṣ argmny ʕm špš* look, (here I deliver) the gold of my tribute, 2.36:5; *hlny lm mt bʕl*[look, why do the men of (my) lord[?, 2.73:8; redundant: *hln hn ʕmn šlm* behold, with me (all) is well, RSOu 14 49 [KTU 9.433]:9 (diff. Bordreuil - Pardee RSOu 14 p. 375: 'ici').

2) as a conjunction ★a) consecutive, and so, and then: *hlm yṯq nḥš* and so he will be able to immobilize the snake, 1.100:6 and par.; *w hln ʕnt tmtḫṣ* and then DN fought, 1.3 II 5 and par.; ★b) temporal, as soon as, no sooner ... than: *hlm ilm tphhm* as soon as the gods saw them, 1.2 I 21; *hlm il k yphnh* as soon as DN saw her, 1.4 IV 27 and par.; *hlm aḫh tph* as soon as she saw her brother, 1.16 I 53.

Bkn. *hlny*, 2.78:4; 2.79:2; 2.83:2; *hlh*, 4.666:3. Cf.]*hlk*, 1.107:13 (?). Cf. hnny.

hlh, cf. *hl*.

/h-l-k/ vb. G: "to go, go away; to run, flow; to roam" Gt: "to scour"; Š: "to cause to run, flow" (Hb., Ph., Pun., Moab., Aram. Nab., Palm. *hlk*, HALOT 246ff.; DNWSI 280f.; Ebla cf. /L-G/, Krebernik PET 50; AL_6.DU = *ʔà-a-gú-um* (/haʔākum/), VE 984; U.DU = *ʔà-la-gúm* (/halākum/), VE 1000; Krebernik ZA 73 1983 35f.; Fronzaroli EL 135; StEb 7 1984 164; Akk. *alāku*, AHw 31ff., CAD A/1 300ff.; ESA *hlk*, DOSA 111; Arab. *halaka*, Lane 3044); ¶ par.: /ʕ-l-y/, /ṣ-d/; cf. /m-ġ-y/. ¶ Forms: G suffc. *hlk*; prefc. *alk*, *tlk*, *ylk*, *ylkn*, *tlkn*; suff. *tlkm* (encl. *-m*); impv. *lk*; inf. *lkt*; act. ptc. f. *hlkt*; pl. *hlkm*; Gt prefc. *itlk*, *ttlk*, *ytlk*; Š prefc. *ašhlk*; cf. Tropper UF 22 1990 375.

G. ★a) To go, go away, roam: *hlk l alpm (...) ṯn ṯn hlk* they go by the thousand (...), two abreast they go, 1.14 II 39-41 and par.; *spr mdrġlm d*(!)*t hlk b*[list of watchmen who have gone (as a detail) to ..., 4.33:2; bless me *alk brktm (...) alk nmrrt* so that I may go blessed, (...) so that

I can go strengthened, 1.19 IV 32; *tlk w tr* she went and escaped, 1.10 III 17; *tlkm DN* DN set off, 1.23:16 (// *tṣd*); *tr b lkt*, she escaped running, 1.10 II 29; *lm l tlk* why do you not go?, 2.39:16; *d l ylkn ḥš* who cannot go quickly, 1.1 IV 7; *tlkn ym w ṯn* they went, one day and a second, 1.14 IV 31 and par. (cf. *mġy* ln. 34; cf. Aitken UF 19 1987 7); *km dlt tlk* like a poor woman you shall walk, 1.82:24, cf. ln. 22; *il hlk l bth* DN went to his house, 1.114:17; *mlk ylk lqḥ ilm aṯr ilm ylk pʕnm mlk pʕnm yl[k]* the king shall walk to welcome the gods; after the gods after the gods he shall walk on foot, 1.43:23-25; *rʕy ht alk* my companions, now I am going away, 1.21 II 6; *lk bty* go to my house, 1.22 II 8 and par.; *lk lk ʕnn ilm* go, go, divine heralds, 1.3 IV 32 and par.; *lk hrg* go, kill, 1.13:4; *lk l abk yṣb lk [l a]bk* go to your father, PN, go to your father, 1.16 VI 27; *lk l pny/h* walk in front of me / her, 1.82:10/38; *hlkm b dbḥ nʕmt* may they go with sacrifices of thanksgiving, 1.23:27; *ʕnn hlkt* the evil eye (/ that roams), 1.96:1 (cf. Akk. *īnu muttalliktu*, cf. Del Olmo CR 380 n. 166); *w ʕlm ylk ġzr* and next the lad will go, 1.175:14; *ytlk l lbnn* they went to TN, 1.4 VI 18; in bkn ctx.: *gṯrn ylk*[, 1.166:25 (cf. Del Olmo AuOr 5 1987 63); ★b) to run, flow: *nḫlm tlk nbtm* the torrents flow with honey, 1.6 III 7 and par.; *mẓrn ylk* the rain will fall (lit. flow), 1.163:6; *im PN im PN im mšmʕt mlk w tlkn* if PN or PN or the royal guard happen to go away, 2.72:15 (pleonastic *w*; cf. Brooke UF 11 1979 73; Bordreuil - Pardee RSOu 7 146); *ybnn hlk ʕm mlk amr*, PN has gone to the king of TN, *ibid.* ln. 25; *spr mḏrġlm dt hlk b*[list of watchmen who have gone into[, 4.33:2.

Gt. To scour, walk along: DN also *ttlk w tṣd* scoured and and combed, 1.5 VI 26 and par.; *bʕl ytlk wyṣd* DN scoured and combed, 1.12 I 34; the gracious gods *ttlkn šd tṣdn* scoured the field, combed the fringes of the desert, 1.23:67; *ntbt bt [bʕl] ntlk* the paths of the temple of [DN] we shall walk along, 1.119:34 (// *nʕl*).

Š. To cause to run, flow: *ašhlk šbtk [dmm]* I can make [blood] run through your greybeard, 1.3 V 24 and par.

In bkn ctx.: *hlkt tdrq*, 1.45:5; *hlkt*, 1.62:4; *w hlk hn*, 1.166:27; *alk*[, 2.39:22.

hlk (I) n. m. "walk, course" (< /h-l-k/); ¶ par.: *tdrq*. ¶ Forms: sg. *hlk*. Walk, course: *hlk bʕl at{t}rt k tʕn hlk btlt ʕnt* the walk of DN did DN contemplate, the walk of virgin DN, 1.4 II 13 and par. (// *tdrq*); *hlk kṯr k yʕn* the walk of DN he did contemplate, 1.17 V 10; cf. 1.19 I 27; *hlk ġlmm* the walk of the (two) pages, 1.19 II 28; astron.: *ydʕ[t] hlk kbkbm* she knows the course of the stars, 1.19 II 3.

hlk (II), cf. *hl.*

hll DN, astral deity (Hb. *hyll*, HALot 245; cf. Arab. *hilāl*, Hava 832; Eth. *helāl*, CCG 217; Du Mesnil EDP 2 6; diff.: Gordon UL 65: 'shouting', Sem. *hll*; Gallagher UF 26 1994 131ff.: 'Illil', DN; for these and other opinions cf. Herrmann YN 6 21; Margulis JANES 4 1972 55; Yamashita RSP I 55; Loretz UF 8 1976 133f.; Spronk Afterlife 224; Renfroe AULS 116; Gallagher UF 26 1994 135ff.; Theuer Mondgott 191).
DN: *bnt hll bʕl gml* the daughters of DN, lord of the first quarter, 1.24:41-42 and par. *ktrt bnt hll snnt* DN, the daughters of DN, the Swallows,1.17 II 27 and par.

/h-l-m/ vb. G: "to hit" (Hb. *hlm*, HALOT 249; cf. Collini SEL 4 1987 18); syll. Ug.: cf. Huehnergard UVST 121: /h-l-m/; Sivan GAGl 222: /hulmu/. ¶ Forms: G suffc. *hlm*; with suff. *hlmn*; prefc. *ylm*; with suff. *ylmn*, impv. *hlm*, suff. *hlmn*; cf. Tropper UF 22 1990 375f.
G. To hit: *hlm / ylm ktp zbl ym* hit / he hit prince DN on the shoulders, 1.2 IV 14/16 and par.; *hlmn ṯnm qdqd* hit / he hit him twice (on) the crown, 1.18 IV 22/33; vid. *hlm ṯ*[*nm q*]*dqd* they hit (him) twi[ce (on) the crown, 1.19 II 29; *ylm bn* [*ʕ*]*nk ṣmdm* hit on your forehead with a mace (?), 1.82:16; *ylmn ḫṭm* he struck with a rod, 1.114:8.

hlm, cf. *hl.*

hln(y), cf. *hl.*

-hm suffixed pronominal morpheme: 1) used with a noun, "their, theirs" (of them [both]); 2) used with a verb, "them"; 3) used with a preposition, *b*, *bd*, *bʕd*, *km*, *l*, (C.Sem.. except Akk.; Ebla cf. du. *-ʔa-u-ma-a*, in *a-bi-ʔa-u-ma-a*, Pettinato Rituale 185. Cf. Moscati ICGSL 106ff.; Gordon UT § 6.10, 13; Segert BGUL 47; Tropper UG 226). ¶ Forms: pl./du. *-hm.*
1) Used with a noun: *passim.*
2) Used with a verb: *al aḫdhm* I can certainly seize them, 1.3 V 22 and par.; *bʕl ymšḫhm* DN will anoint them, 1.10 II 23; *bʕl ngṯhm* DN approached them; *yisphm bʕ*[*l* DN gathered them, 1.12 II 24; *w ytn hm lk* and he will give them to you (?), 2.45:21; *lm l ytn hm mlk* why did the king not give them to (me)?, 2.33:26; *w ʕnhm nġr* and the guard answered them, 1.23:73; *hlm ilm tphhm* as soon as the gods saw them, 1.2 I 22; *k išalhm* how do I ask for them(?), 2.32:4; *bnš mlk ybʕlhm* the man of the king will make them, 4.182:56; *w pdyh*[*m*] *PN mit ksp* and PN redeemed them for one hundred silver (shekels), 3.4:12.

3) Used with a preposition: *w yqḥ bhm aqht* and from among them he took PN, 1.19 III 39; *w ytn ilm bdhm* and they shall deliver the gods into their hands, 2.4:21; *w b bt mlk mlbš ytn lhm* and from the palace, clothing will be given to them, 4.168:8 (cf. 1.9:12); *dt iṯ alpm lhm* who have oxen, 4.422:1; *d inn msgm lhm* who do not have *m.*, 4.53:2; *d in ḥẓm lhm* do not have arrows, 4.180:1; *pat aḫt in bhm* (farms) which lack 'one side', 4.136:5 (cf. *pat*); *unṯ inn lhm* they (PNN) are not obliged to any corvée, 3.4:17; *bhm ygʕr bʕl* DN reproached them, 1.2 I 24 (cf. 1.114:11); *w ṯṯb ank lhm* and I gave (it) back to them, 2.38:23; *bn krt kmhm tdr ap bnt ḥry kmhm* the sons of PN were as many as were promised and the daughters, as many as they, 1.15 III 25; *ptḥ prṣ bʕdhm* and he opened a breach for them, 1.23:70; [*al* (...)] *atn ks*[*p lhm*] I shall [not] give mone[y to them], 2.42:20; *bhm qrnm km ṯrm* they will have horns like bulls, 1.12 I 30; *w bhm pn bʕl* and they will have the appearance of DN, 1.12 I 32; *mit zt bdhm* one hundred (shekels) of olives in their hands(?), 4.386:13; *al tud ad at lhm ṯṯm ksp* do not overcharge PN(?): you exact sixty shekels for them, 2.26:20; *klt tn akl lhm* give them a *k.* in grain, 2.70:22.

hm (I) 1) "if", conditional conj.; 2) "perhaps", interr. functor in ★a) simple and ★b) compound questions (Hb. *ʔm*, HALOT 60f.; ESA *hm*, DOSA 111. Cf. Aartun PU 2 95f.; Van Zijl Baal 105f.; UT § 12.3, 5; BGUL 104; Tropper UG 793ff.; diff.: Aartun PU 1 70f.; Dietrich - Loretz UF 23 1991 95: 'siehe, wahrlich!'; cf. De Moor ULe 89, 93 n. 1. ¶ Forms: *hm* (cf. *im*).

1) If (conj.): *hm tʕpn ʕl qbr* if they fly over the grave, 1.19 III 44; *hm ḥry bty iqḥ* if I take PN to my home, 1.14 IV 40; *hm l aqryk b ntb pšʕ* if I meet you on the path of rebellion, 1.17 VI 43; *hm nliym* if we prevail, 1.19 II 35; *hm aṯtm tṣḥn* if both women shouted, 1.23:39 and par.; *w hm alp l tšʕn* but if they do not pay (shekels of silver), 3.8:13; *w hm at trgm* [and / but if you say [..., 2.3:8 and par.; *ht hm in mm nḫtu* now, if they have not been wiped out..., 2.10:9; *hm nṯkp* if he has already thrown them out (...), 2.10:14; *w hm ḥy... w hm iṯ* and / but if he is alive..., and if he exists..., 1.6 III 2-3; *hm* [*iṯ ln l*]*ḥm w tn* (...) *hm iṯ*[*ln yn*] [*w*] *tn* (...) if [there is] bread [for us], give us (...), if there is [wine for us], give us (...), 1.23:71-72; *hm l atn bty lh* if I do not give him my daughter (?), 2.31:66; *w hm ḫt ʕl* (...) *w hm l ʕl* (...) if Hatti attacks (...), but if it does not attack (...), 2.30:16-18; *hn hm yrgm mlk* (...) behold if the king says (...), 2.33:30; *hm qrt tuḫd* if the city is about to be seized, 1.127:29; *hm mt yʕl bnš* if DN goes up

against someone, 1.127:30; *hm škb ʕl thm* if he is lying over the abyss, RSOu 14 53 [KTU 9.432]:4'.
2) Perhaps...? (interrogative functor), ★a) in simple question: *hm yd il mlk yḫssk* perhaps the love of DN, the king, has aroused you?, 1.4 IV 38; ★b) in compound question, with a disjunctive, copulative or adversative meaning (often in a correlation *hm ... hm, ap ... hm, p ... hm,* "perhaps... or ... ?", "if... or if...", "either ... or ..."): he shall dilute it *hm b mskt dlḫt hm b mndġ* either in a thick emulsion or in*m.* (flour), 1.85:4 (Akk. *lu... lu...*; cf. Cohen - Sivan UHT 15); *p ʕdb ank (...) hm amt atrt* am I perhaps a slave (...), or is DN a slave?, 1.4 IV 61; *p np{.}š npš lbim (...) hm brlt (...) hm brky (...) hm imt imt (...)* (perhaps) I (do) have the appetite of a lion (...), or the longing (...), or (the thirst of) the pool (...), or (said) straight to the point (...)(?), 1.5 I 15-18; *p imt (...) ilḫm hm šbʕ (...) hm ks...* (perhaps) it is true that (...) I swallow and they are seven (...) and that my cup (...) (?), 1.5 I 20-21; *aḥd hm iṯ šmt hm i[ṯ] ʕzm* I shall look (to see) if there is fat or (: and) if there is bone, 1.19 III 4; *bt arzm (...) hm bt lbnt* a house of cedar (...) or (: and) a house of brick (...), 1.4 V 11; *mlk (...) yarš hm drk[t] k ab adm* kingship (...) does he desire or power like the father of mankind?, 1.14 I 42; *rġb rġbt (...) hm ġmu ġmit w (...)* no doubt you will be hungry (...), or else you will be thirsty, then (...), 1.4 IV 34; *lḥm hm štym* eat or (: and) drink, 1.4 IV 35; *mgntm (...) hm ġẓtm (...)* have you welcomed... or (: and) regaled (...)?, 1.4 III 31. Cf. the fixed syntagm *hm ap* in bkn ctx. *hm ap amr[* although(?) I threw ..., 1.2 IV 3; *w hm ap l[* then / but although [you do not throw it], 1.1 IV 26 (cf. 1; cf. Hb. *ʔp ʔm*). Cf. in unc. ctx. *hm tġrm l mt brq*(!)*k* or(?) unite your rays (against) DN, 1.82:5.
In bkn ctx.: *hm tʕr[b*, 2.42:24.

hm (II) p. pn. 3rd p. pl./du. m., "they, them, their, (both of them / their)" (c.Sem. except Akk.; cf. Hb. *hm(h)*, HALOT 250; Ph. *hmt*, DNWSI 264; Aram. *hm(w)*, DNWSI 265; Arab. *hum(ā)*, Hava 834f.; ESA *hmt*, DOSA 111, 113; Palm. *hn(w)n*, DNWSI 265. Cf. Moscati ICGSL 102; Gordon UT § 6.1; Segert BGUL 47f.; Tropper UG 210ff.). ¶ Forms: nom. *hm*; obl. *hmt.*
They, them ★a) nom.: *mḫsy hm (...) hm [mkly s]brt aryy* they are my assassins (...), they are (the destroyers) of the clan of my kin, 1.4 II 24; *w ngš hm (...) w ṣḥ hm* and they met (...) and they shouted, 1.23:68-69; *bnšm h[[x]]mt ypḥm* members of his personnel are the witnesses, 4.659:6; ★b) them, their (obl.): *kbd hmt* welcome them, 1.17 V 20 and par.; *bʕl yṯbr diy hmt* may DN break the (/ their)

wings, 1.19 III 44 and par.; *tdn hmt* they shall be proclaiming them (?), 1.104:19.

In unc. ctx.: *bʕlm hmt*, 1.2 IV 36; *hm tġrm l mt b rpk*, 1.82:5 (cf. *hm (I)*); *hmt*, 1.146:7; *kl dbrm hmt*, 2.32:8; *hmt w anyt*, 2.42:24; 2.44:10 (!). Cf. *hnhmt*.

hmlt n. f. "multitude" (Hb. *hmlh*, HALOT 251; cf. De Moor SP 107f.; Smith BC 290; diff.: Wyatt UF 24 1992 412ff.: 'tempest', Hb. *hmlt*); ¶ par.: *lim*, *nšm*. ¶ Forms: sg./pl. *hmlt*.

Multitude: *hmlt arṣ* the multitudes of the land, 1.3 III 28 and par. (// *nšm*); *my hmlt* what will happen to the multitude?, 1.6 I 7 and par. (// *lim*); *d tqyn hmlt* the one you protect, multitude(s), 1.2 I 18. Bkn ctx. *hmlt ḫt p*(?)*t*, 1.83:12.

hmry TN, name of the mythical city / residence of the god Mot (Del Olmo MLC 534: 'Fangosa', cf. Arab. *hamara*; De Moor ARTU 66 n. 306: 'deep pit, tunnel'; cf. Hoftijzer UF 4 1972 157 n. 17; Watson UF 28 1996 702 n. 9: Akk. *amirānu*).

TN, mythical residence of Mot: *qrth hmry* his city TN, 1.4 VIII 12 and par.

Cf. mhmrt.

hmt pn. p., obl. cf. *hm (II)*.

-hn (I) suffixed pronominal morpheme: used with a noun, "their, theirs" (c.Sem. except Akk.; cf. Moscati ICGSL 106ff.; Gordon UT § 6.13; Segert BGUL 47; Tropper UG 226f.). ¶ Forms: pl. *-hn*.

Their, theirs: *sprhn (...) mnthn* their counting (...) their list, 1.23:45-47; *ṣġrthn* the youngest of them, 1.15 III 16; *mšbʕthn b šlḥ ttpl* their seventh part was struck down by DN (?), 1.14 I 20; *w b klhn špḥ yitbd* and in their entirety, yes, the family perished, 1.14 I 24 (?)(cf. // *-h*); *w ṯmnt ksphn* and their (: *ktnt*) price is eight shekels, 4.132:3 (cf. ln. 6 referring to *ktnm*); *mḫrhn* their (: *anyt*) price, 4.338:18; *apnthn / ḥẓhn / trhn*, their (: *mrkbt*) wheels / arrows / steering poles, 4.145:3-5.

Bkn cxt.: *mġ hw lhn*, 1.23:75 (?); *km trpa hn nʕr*, 1.114:28;]*hn pbl hn*, 1.107:4; *tšṣḥq hn aṯ*[*t* , 2.25:5; *hn mlk / hn l ḥwth / hn ib d b mgṣḫ*, 2.33:8-10.

-hn (II), cf. *-h (I)*.

hn functor 1) deictic functor, "behold; look!; thus"; 2) adv. "here" (Hb. *hn(h)*, HALOT 251f.; Ph., Pun., Aram., Palm. *hn*, DNWSI 285ff.; EA Akk. *annû*, EAT *passim*, cf. AHw 53; CAD A/2 136ff.; Ebla cf. *an-ne*, Fronzaroli ARET 11 139; Arab. *ʔinna*, Hava 14. Eg. *in*, Ward JNES 20 1961 34. Cf. Aartun PU I 68ff.; Gordon UT § 12.7; BGUL

81; Tropper UG 749ff. For the possibility that it is a pronoun or 'article' cf. Liverani RANL 8/19 1964 181f.; Cunchillos AuOr 1 1983 155f.; Pardee AfO 31 1984 218 n. 23; Tropper UG 232; JSS 46 2001 24ff.). ¶ Forms: *hn*; cf. *hnm*, *hnn*, *hnny* (for *wn* cf. *w*).

1) Behold, look!, thus: *w hn aṯtm tṣḥn* and behold the two will shout, 1.23:46; *w hn špšm b šbʕ* and, look!, at dawn of the seventh (day), 1.14 III 14; *w hn šb*[*ʕ*] *b ymm* and behold seven days (had passed), 1.17 V 3; *hn b py sprhn* look!, in my mouth I have their count, 1.24:45; *hn ym w ṯn* thus, one day and another, 1.4 VI 24 and par.; *hn* [*l*]*bnn w ʕṣh* look!, the Lebanon and its trees, 1.4 VI 20; *phn aḫym ytn bʕl spuy* and look, DN made my brothers my food, 1.6 VI 10; *ʕdk ilm hn mtm* around you are the gods, and/so (also) men (/ the dead(?)), 1.6 VI 48; *hn š / ʕr* behold the ram / donkey, 1.40:17/34 and par. (diff.: Tropper JSS 24 2001 24f.: 'der Widder da / der Eselhengst da'); *hn šmn šlm* behold the pure oil!, 1.119:24; *hn b npš aṯrt* look, by the life of DN, 1.169:16; *hn špthm mtqtm* behold their lips were sweet, 1.23:50 and par.; *w hn ibm šṣq ly* and behold the enemies are besieging me, 2.33:27; *hn mrṯ d štt ašṣu b ldtk* thus /similarly the must that you noted (in your letter) I will deliver (to you) when you give birth, 2.34:32; *hln hn ʕmn šlm* here, behold, with me (all) is well, RSOu 14 49 [KTU 9.433]:9 (cf. 29); *w hnn ʕm ʕbdk mid šlm* behold, here with your servant (all) is very well, RSOu 14 50 [KTU 9.434]:9; *hn ym yṣq yn ṯmk* behold on (this) day wine of TN was served, 1.22 I 17; *hn ksp d šsʕn* look, the money that you told me to pay, 2.81:24; *hn l ḥwth* behold to his land (?), 2.33:9; *hn ib d b TN* behold the enemy that is in TN, *ibid.* ln. 10 (cf. ln. 17 and cf. Pardee AfO 31 1984 218).

2) As an adv., (to) here: *tmġyy hn alpm śśwm hnd* these two thousand horses must arrive here, 2.33:31 (cf. Tropper UF 26 1994 476; Renfroe AULS 116; diff.: Dietrich - Loretz - Sanmartín UF 6 1974 457; Cunchillos TOu 2 338 n. 39; Tropper JSS 24 2001 25: 'die(se)' / 'ces'); *hn ks mḥṯ l mlkt mntn* here is a *m.*-cup for the queen of TN, RSOu 14 53 [KTU 9.432]:39'; *mlk yštal b hn* the king requires a reply on this/here, 2.42:23; cf. in unc. or bkn ctx. *km trpa hn nʕr*, 1.114:28; *hn/a unk bnk*, 5.11:3; *hn p*[*rʕ*, 1.17 V 38; *hn* [*a*]*lpm śśwm*, 2.33:37 (cf. Tropper JSS 24 2001 25: 'die 2000 Pferde'); *hn q*[*xxxx*]*xd ydk*, 1.22 I 4; *tšṣḥq hn aṯ*[*t*, 2.25:5.

Bkn. 1.6 V 23; 1.22 I 2; 1.107:4, 22; 1.166:27; 1.176:24; 2.33:8; 2.49:4; 4.373:7.

Cf. hnd, hnhmt, hnk, hnm, hnny.

hnd demonstr. 1) adj. "this, these"; 2) pn. "this" (composite morpheme *hn* + *d*; Hb. *(h)zh*, HALOT 263ff. Cf. De Moor ULe 95; Cunchillos AuOr 1 1983 155ff.; Israel RSOu 11 257f.; Tropper UG 229f., cf. 738; JSS 24 2001 25: 'hier'). ¶ Forms: *hnd* with sg., pl., du. m. referent; *hnd(t)* with f. or unspecified referent.
1) Adj. this, these: *l ym hnd* from this day, 3.2:1 and par. (Akk. *ištu umi anni*); *l yqḥ bt hnd* he will not seize this house, 3.2:14; *ktb spr hnd (...) ʕbdh hnd (...) spr mlk hnd (...)* wrote this certificate (...) this his slave (...) this royal certificate, 2.19:9-13; *ydʕ k iḫd hn*[*d*] know that I shall collect this (?), 2.33:21; *alpm śśwm hnd* these two thousand horses, 2.33:32; (may the king send me) *bnš bnny ʕmn mlakty hnd* some intermediary with this delegation of mine, 2.33:35; *mkr hn*(!)*d* this trader, 2.42:25.
2) Pn. this: *anykn dt likt mṣrm hndt b TN mtt* (as for) your ship which you sent to Egypt, this has been wrecked in TN, 2.38:12; *w hndt yṯb l mspr* and this is what goes back to (: is repeated of) the narrative, 1.19 l. e. (IV 62); *w mspr hnd hwm* and the one who recited this is he himself, RSOu 14 53 [KTU 9.432]:41'. Bkn 2.79:1.

hndn adj. demonstr. "this" (allomorph of *hnd*; encl. suff. *-n*; Tropper UG 230). ¶ Forms: sg. m. *hndn*.
This: *lm tlikn ḫpṯ hndn* why are you sending this legionary?, 2.72:10. Cf. hnd.

hnh "?"; cf. in bkn ctx.: 4.721:16.

hnhmt adj. demonstr. "these" (composite morpheme *hn* + *-hmt*; Tropper UG 230, cf. 836).
These: *w mnm šalm dt tknn ʕl ʕrbnm hnhmt tknn* and any claims they bring up, against these guarantors they bring them up, 3.3:8 (Hoftijzer - Van Soldt UF 23 1991 190f.). For 2.42:23 (KTU: *hn.*[) and 4.659:6 (KTU: *h*[[x]]*mt*) cf. Tropper UG 231.

hnk demonstr. pn. "that, this" (composite morpheme: *hn* + *k*; cf. Arab. *hunaka*, Hava 839; cf. Pun. *hnkt*, DNWSI 289f. Cf. Rainey UF 3 1971 160; Cunchillos AuOr 1 1983 155ff.; cf. diff.: Aartun PU 1 70: 'siehe!'; Tropper UG 231, cf. 740: 'da, dort'). ¶ Forms: sg. m. *hnk*, f. *hnkt*.
That: *lm škn hnk l ʕbdh* why did he impose that on his servant?, 2.33:23; *bny hnkt yškn* may my son arrange that, 2.46:12. Unc.: *mlkt ugrt hnkt rgmt* the queen of TN has said this (?), 2.21:10; *hnk tšmʕm* what(?) you hear, 2.71:9 (cf. Tropper UG 740: both 'dort').

hnkt cf. *hnk*.

hnm deictic functor "behold" / "now (then)", introductory formula in

letters (Ug.-Akk. hybrid; cf. *hn* and Akk. *inūma*, AHw 383f.; CAD I/J 159ff.; Emar /anenna/ Pentiuc Vocabulary 26. See Márquez AuOr 10 1992 153; cf. Tropper UG 750); ¶ **RS Akk.**: *e/inūma*, Huehnergard AkkUg 196f.; Van Soldt SAU 462, 465 and *passim*. ¶ **Forms**: *hnm*.
Behold / now (then): *hnm ʕbdk hwt yrš* behold / now then, your servant has a cause for complaint, 2.41:14.
Cf. **hn**.

hnn "?" (> *hn (I)* + *-n* (?)).
? : bkn ctx.,]*y hnn (...)*, 2.65:1.

hnny adv. "here" (composite form: *hn* + *-n* + *y*; cf. Aartun PU 1 3; Tropper UF 26 1994 477; UG 738); ¶ **par.**: *ṯmny*. ¶ **Forms**: *hnny*.
Here: *hnny ʕmy kll mid šlm* here with me everything is very well, 2.11:10 and par. (letter formula; cf. Cunchillos TOu 2 257ff.).

/h-p-k/ vb. G 1)"to overturn, alter"; 2) "to return"; N "to roll over, rebel" (Hb., Ph., Aram., Palm. *hpk*, HALOT 253f.; DNWSI 291; cf. Akk. *abāku*, AHw 2; CAD A/1 855; Arab. *ʔafaka*, Lane 69. Cf. Dietrich - Loretz MU 149); **syll. Ug.**: cf. BAL = *na-bal-ku-tu*$_4$ = *tap-šu-ḫu-um-me* = *tu-a-pí-*[*ku*(?)], Ug 5 137 II 23'; cf. Huehnergard UVST 121; Van Soldt SAU 303; ¶ **par.**: /n-s-ʕ/, /ṯ-b-r/. ¶ **Forms**: G prefc. *yhpk*, *ahpk*, suff. *ahpkk*, energ. -n: *ahpkn*; inf. (+ encl. *-m*) *hpkm*, N prefc. *yhpk* (cf. Tropper UF 22 1990 377: N/G intr. (?)).
G. 1) To overturn, alter: *l yhpk ksa mlkk* yes, he will overturn your royal throne, 1.6 VI 28 and par. (// *ysʕ*, *yṯbr*); *hm yhpk śśw rgm* when the horse alters (its) whinny, 1.86:7 (cf. Del Olmo - Márquez AuOr 13 1995 258).
2) To return: *hpkm ahpk lbš w ahpkn ḫlpn* I shall certainly return the *l.* and I shall return the *ḫ.* RSOu 14 53 [KTU 9.432]:36'.
N. To roll over, rebel: *ḫrdn yhpk l mlk* the guard will rebel against the king, 1.103+:52.
In bkn ctx.: *ahpkk l*, 1.5 III 12; *yhpk*, 1.13:35.

hr (I) n. m. "mountain" (Hb., Ph., Pun. *hr*, HALOT 254f.; DNWSI 293; EA Akk. ḪUR.SAG : *ḫa-ar-ri*, EA 74:20; Sivan GAGl 222; DNWSI 293; Gianto SEL 12 1995 67f.; Emar /harru/, Pentiuc Vocabulary 57f.; Eg. *hr*, WÄS 2 498; Helck Bez. 517 [156]: *ha-rú*). ¶ **Forms**: pl. *hrm*.
Mountain: *isp* [*šp*]*š l hrm ǵrpl* remove, DN, the storm clouds from the mountains, 1.107:44 and par. (diff.: Caquot TOu 2 98 n. 309: 'sans relache'(?), Arab. *harima*). Cf. in bkn ctx.]*hr il*, 1.4 II 36 and cf. Hb. *hrry ʔl* (but cf. KTU *a. l.*: *n*]*hr il*). Bkn 7.53:3.

hr (II) n. m. "conception" (verbal noun < */h-r-y/*; cf. Akk. *mērû*, AHw

646ff.; CAD M/2 27); ¶ par.: *hmhmt.* ¶ Forms: sg. *hr*, suff. *hrh*; f. *hrt* cf. *hrt (I).*

Conception: *bm nšq w hr* on kissing (the) there was conception, 1.23:51 and par. (// *hmhmt*; diff. Aartun StUL 52ff.: 'Reizen, Erhitzung', Arab. *harr-*); *kbdh l ydʕ hrh* whose womb has not known his conception, 1.13:31. Bkn: *hry*, 1.11:5.

/h-r-g/ vb. G. "to kill" (Hb., OAram, Moab. *hrg*, HALOT 255; DNWSI 293; cf. Arab. *haraǧa*, Lane 2890); ¶ par.: /b-ṣ-r/. ¶ Forms: G impv. *hrg.*

G. To kill: *hrg ar[bʕt] ymm* kill during fo[ur] days, 1.13:5 (// *bṣr*). Cf. hrgb.

hrgb DN; mythical animal, male eagle (etym. unc.; cf. /h-r-g/, *ab* (?); cf. Hb, *ʔrgb*, HALOT 84; Akk. *argabu*, AHw 67; CAD A/2 253; Eth. *rěgeb*, CDG 464; Arab. *harǧaba*, *hirǧāb*, Lane 2890f.; *haǧaba*, Lane 2879. Cf. Cooper UF 20 1988 23 n. 16; cf. Geller VT 26 1976 374ff.; Caquot - Sznycer TOu 1 451 n. v; Aartun UF 16 1984 16; Margalit UF 16 1984 144f.; Watson JNSL 22 1996 74: Hurr. *argaba*).

DN, mythical animal: *hrgb ab nšrm* DN, father of the eagles, 1.19 III 15 and par.; *knp hrgb* the wings of DN, 1.19 III 22 and par.

hrnmy GN "native of the TN **hrnm*", epithet of *dnil* (cf. Belmonte RGTC 12/2 103: *Harnamu*, mod. TN *Hermil*, Eg. *ʔá-ra-na-ma*, *ha-r-nam*, Albright BASOR 130 1953 26f.; Helck Bez. 200, 317; Parker UF 4 1973 100f.; Dijkstra UF 11 1979 200; Sapin UF 15 1983 167 n. 48; De Moor ARTU 225 n. 6; Margalit UPA 258ff.; cf. Astour RSP 2 283ff. for the various interpretations; cf. diff. Dietrich - Loretz UF 21 1989 128: 'eine Gottheit'); ¶ par.: *rpu.* ¶ Forms: sg. *hrnmy.*

The Harnamite: *mt hrnmy* the Harnamite, 1.17 I 18 and par. (// *mt rpi*); *dǵṯ hrnmy b kbkbm* an offering of perfumes worthy of a Harnamite to the stars, 1.19 IV 24 and par.

/h-r-r/ vb. G: "to become inflamed about, crave" (< "to become heated")"; Akk. *(ḫ)arāru*, AHw 65f.; CAD A/2 236f.; Syr. *harhar*, LS 183; Tigr. *harär* 'wish ardently', Leslau EDH 86b; cf. Arab. *harra*, Lane 2888f.; Hb. *hrwn*, HALOT 256. Cf. Gray UF 3 1971 64 n. 24; Dahood UHP 57); ¶ par.: /ḥ-m-d/. ¶ Forms: G prefc. suff. *yhrrm* (encl. *-m*); cf. Tropper UF 22 1990 377.

G. To become inflamed about, crave: *bn dgn yhrrm* the son of DN became inflamed, 1.12 I 39 (// *yḥmdm*). Bkn ctx.: *il hrr[*, 1.12 II 9. Cf. /h-r-y/.

hrsn PN (etym. unc.).

PN: *bn PN*, 4.711:6.

hrt (I) n. f. "conception" (cf. *hr (II)*, /h-r-y/; cf. Ebla /harītum/ in ŠÀxMUNUS = *ʔà-rí-tum*, VE 594; Krebernik ZA 73 1983 23; QuSe 11 142); ¶ par.: *ḫllt*. ¶ Forms: sg. *hrt*.
Conception: *ʕrš hrt* fertile bed (< of conception), 1.17 II 41 (// *ḫllt*).
Cf. hrtn.

hrt (II) n. f. "shield" ((?); cf. Akk. *arītu*, AHw 68f.; CAD A/2 269f.; Dietrich - Loretz - Sanmartín UF 5 1973 87; cf. diff. Sanmartín AuOr 5 1987 151 n. 14: 'piedra de moler', Akk. *erû*, AHw 247; CAD E 322f.; *ḫarāru*, CAD H 92; *ḫarūru*, AHw 329; cf. Hitt. *ḫarra-*, *ḫararazi*, HEG 169, 171); syll. Ug. / Akk. RS: cf. DUMU LÚ A.RIT, PRU 3 68 (RS 16.269):6; cf. A.PA = *a-ri-tu₄*, AS 16 33ff.; Huehnergard UVST 122. ¶ Forms: du. *hrtm*.
Shield(?): *ṯt hrtm* two shields(?), 4.390:5.

/h-r-y/ vb. G "to conceive" (Hb. *hrh*, HALOT 255f.; Aram. *hrh*, DNWSI 293; Akk. *a/erû*, AHw 72; CAD E 325ff.); ¶ par.: /y-l-d/. ¶ Forms: G prefc. *thrn*; inf.(?) *hry*; cf. Tropper UF 22 1990 377.
G. To conceive: *hry w yld* there was conception and birth, 1.11:5; *w [th]rn w tldn mṯ* and [she co]nceived and gave birth to a boy, 1.5 V 22.
Cf. hr (II), /h-r-r/, hrt (I), hrtn.

hry (I) TN (Belmonte RGTC 12/2 103: **Harruya*(?); see Heltzer, RCAU 10; Van Soldt UF 30 1998 725).
TN: 4.365:13 (Bordreuil UF 20 1988 15: rdg *iry*); 4.546:1 (cf. Van Soldt UF 28 1996 666).

hry (II) GN (< *hry (I)*). ¶ Forms: m. pl. *hrym*.
GN: *hrym tiṯṯmn* the *h.* fell into debt, 4.398:3.

ht 1) adv.: ★a) "here"; ★b) "now"; 2) conj., "now" (cf. Hb. *hnh*, HALOT 251f.; Arab. *hunā*, Hava 839. Cf. Aartun PU 1 5, 71; Margalit ZAW 99 1987 391; Tropper UG 742f.); ¶ par.: *ṯmny*, *ʕnt*. ¶ Forms: *ht*.
1) Adv. ★a) of place, here: *ht ʕmny kll šlm* here with me all is well, 2.34:6 (// *ṯmny*; cf. *hnny*; diff.: Pardee AfO 31 1984 228: 'apodosis-marker'); cf. in unc. ctx. *w ht mlk syr* and here the king of TN..., 2.40:13 (cf. ln. 15: *ṯmn*); ★b) of time, now: *l ht w ʕlmh* from now and for ever, 1.19 IV 5 (// *ʕnt*); *ht tṣdn tinṯt* do women now hunt?, 1.17 VI 40; *ht ibk tmḫṣ* now you must crush your enemy, 1.2 IV 8-9; *ht tṣmt ṣrtk* now you must destroy your adversary, 1.2 IV 9; *tšmḫ ht aṯrt w bnh* now may DN and her sons rejoice!, 1.6 I 39; *rʕy ht alk* my companions, now I am going, 1.21 II 6; *w ht aḫy bny yšal* and now may my brother, my son ask, 2.14:10 and par.; *w ht luk (...) PN* and

now (...) PN has been sent, 2.17:4; [*w*] *ht yšmʕ uḫy l gy* [and] now may my brother listen to my voice, 2.4:18; *ht at ṯ*(!)*dbr* now you say, 2.71:13; *w ht ysny udrh* and now, PN is his messenger, 2.30:14; *w ht ank* [*a*]*št* and now I propose, 2.33:11. In bkn ctx.: *ht alpy* now my ox(en), RSOu 14 51 [KTU 9.425]:18 (diff. Bordreuil - Pardee RSOu 14 p. 380: 'voici').
2) Conj., now: *ht hm inmm nḫtu* now, if they have not been destroyed..., 2.10:8; *ht hm yrgm mlk* now, if the king says, 2.33:30; *im ht l*{.} *b mṣqt yṯbt qrt* if, now, the city is in(?) a difficult situation, 2.72:20; *ht ank ʕbdk* now, I am your slave, 2.76:5.
Unc. ctx.: *w ap ht k škn*, 2.3:20; bkn ctx.: *ht lik* [, 2.42:22; *w ht PN ṯt ṯl/d*[, 2.17:9; *ht* [...], 2.39:11, 13; bkn: 2.3:7; *w ht*, 2.35:10; *ht hln ḫrṣ*, 2.36:12; 2.73:3, 10; 2.81:21.

htm adv. "now" (allomorph of *ht*; encl. suff. *-m*; Tropper UG 743). ¶ Forms: *htm*.
Now: *htm iph* [*adty*] now I shall go to visit my lady, 2.25:4.
Cf. **ht**.

hw pn. m. 1) personal "he, it"; 2) demonstr. "this" (c.Sem. except Akk. and Qatab.; cf. Hb., Nab., Palm., JAram. *hwʔ(h)*, HALOT 240f.; DNWSI 264ff.; Ph., Pun., OAram. *hʔ*, DNWSI 264ff.; ESA *hw(ʔ/t)*, DOSA 105ff.; Arab. *huwa*, Hava 839; Moscati ICGSL 102ff.; Gordon UT § 6.1, 3; Segert BGUL 47f.; Tropper UG 211); **syll. Ug.**: [LÚ = (*šu-ú*?) = *ma-an-ni* = *ú-wa*, Ug 5 130 II 28'; Huehnergard UVST 86, 120; Van Soldt SAU 303; cf. Sivan UF 21 1989 360. ¶ **Forms**: sg. nom. *hw*; obl. *hwt*, *hwm* (encl. *-m*); for *-hw* in 2.15:6 see *-h (I)*.
1) He, it, pn. p. ★**a**) nom.: *hw ybl argmnk* he will bring you tribute, 1.2 I 37; in the opening of my oesophagus <*n*>*ḫtu hw* he was crushed/ground, 1.6 II 23; *hw km ḥrr* he (remained) like one who burns (with fever), 1.12 II 40; [*b r*]*ḥ*(?) *hw mḫ* in (his) spirit(?) he (feels) exuberant, 1.17 I 38; *w ptḥ hw prṣ* and he opened a breach, 1.23:70; *ʕ*[*bdm*] *sglth hw* he is a servant, his private property, 2.39:7; *hbṭ hw ḫrd w šl hw qrt* he knocked down the guard (and) plundered the city, 2.61:5-6; *ybl hw mit ḫrṣ* he personally took one hundred (shekels) of gold, 2.72:27; *w lqḥ hw šmn b qrnh* and he took oil in his horn, 2.72:29 (RSO 7 148); *w yṣq hw l riš bt mlk* and he will pour it (: oil) upon the head of the king's 2.72:31; *w mspr hnd hwm* and the one who recited this is he himself, RSOu 14 53 [KTU 9.432]:41'; in bkn ctx.: 2.31:41, 52, 54; ★**b**) obl.: of him, it, him, it (*hwt*): DN *ṯbr diy hwt* DN broke his wings, 1.19 III 23 and par.; prostrate yourselves *w kbd hwt* and pay him homage,1.3 VI 20 and par.; *ʕl qṣʕth hwt l aḥw*

for his arrows she did not leave him alive, 1.19 I 15 and par; twice *tšqy msk hwt* she gave him mixed wine to drink, 1.19 IV mg. (KTU: ln. 61); *nmgn hwt* we shall regale him, 1.4 III 36; *l tšʕly hwt* (that) she (DN) did not allow him to rise, 1.19 II 38. Bkn ctx. *šd hwt* his field, (the field of him), 2.4:16; *ḏrʕ mlk hwt* the seed of that king, 1.103:43.

2) This, demonstr. pn.: *hw ṯʕ nṯʕy hw nkt nkt* this is the offering we offer, this the victim we immolate, 1.40:32-33 and par.

Bkn: *mġ hw lhn*, 1.23:75;]*yirš snp ln d ym hw*, 2.81:26 (cf. ln. 27, 28, 29); *w kl hw*[, 2.3:4; *w bl bnš hw*, 2.45:27; [*am*]*r hw*[, 2.72:35. Cf. hwil.

hwil PN (Sem. Cf. Grøndahl PTU 45, 96, 134; Cross CMHE 64). PN: 4.110:7; RSOu 14 44:7.

hwt (I) n. f. 1) "word, statement"; 2) "matter, assignment(?)" (Akk. *awātu*, AHw 89f., CAD A/2 29ff.: *amatu*; cf. var. Ass. *abātu*; cf. Arab. *hawwata*, Lane 2905; Akk. Mari *ʔà*(É)-*wa-tum* /hawatum/, cf. Gelb LEbla 20f.; Eg. *hwt*, Ward JNES 28 1969 265ff.; Smith BC 160 n. 79; diff. Margalit RB 91 1984 113ff.; ZAW 99 1987 394: 'exhaled breath', Hb. **hwy*, *hwh*); syll. Ug.: cf. [MU = *zikru* = Hurr.: (?) =] *ú*-[P]I(!?)-[*t*]u_4, UF 11 1979 478:12; Huehnergard UVST 120f.; ¶ par.: *rgm*, *thm*. ¶ Forms: sg.(/pl.) *hwt*, suff. *hwty*, *hwth*. Var. *hbt* in 2.70:16(?).

1) Word, statement: *hwt aliy qrdm* word of the most powerful of heroes, 1.3 III 13 and par.; *hwt ydd* word of the 'loved one', 1.5 I 13; *hwt nʕmn* word of the handsome (servant of DN), 1.14 VI 41 (// *thm*, cf. Watson JNSL 25 1999 1ff.); as soon as (...) *b špth hwt* the word (issued) from his lips, 1.19 III 36 and par. (// *rgm*; formula of immediacy, cf. Del Olmo MLC 57); I have (...) *hwt w aṯnyk* a word that I wish to repeat to you, 1.3 III 22 and par. (// *rgm*); *ṯṯb bʕl l hwty* surely, DN, you shall to pay attention to my word(s), 1.4 VI 15 and par.; *hnm ʕbdk hwt yrš* behold your servant has a cause (of complaint), 2.41:14 (cf. Márquez AuOr 10 1992 153: < Akk. *aw/mātam rašû(m)*); *hwt bn nšm* a man's word, RSOu 14 52 [KTU 9.435]:10; *hwt ršʕ* the word of a bad person, *ibid.* ln. 9; *hwt špth* the word of his lips, RSOu 14 53 [KTU 9.432]:32'; *hwt ltpn* word of DN, 1.1 III 6; 1.6 IV 11; *hwt gmr hd* the word of the 'Champion' DN, 1.2 I 46; *ʕl hwt ktr w ḫss* according to the word of DN, 1.4 VII 20; *hwt bʕl* the word of DN, 1.93:4.

2) Matter, assignment(?): *ank ḥrš lqḥt w hwt hbt* I, the craftsman, have accepted and completed the assignment(?), 2.70:16 (Dietrich - Loretz

UF 16 1984 66ff.; Verreet UF 18 1986 384).
In bkn ctx.: 1.7:26; *hwt*[,1.17 VI 53;]*amr hwt*, 1.107:17; *w kl hwt*, 2.3:4; *hnm ʕbdk hwt*, 2.41:14.

hwt (II), cf. *hw*.

/h-w-y/ vb. G: "to want" (cf. Arab. *hawiya*, Lane 2904; Hb. cf. HALOT 242: *hwh (I)*. Cf. Greenstein JANES 5 1973 158f.; Del Olmo MLC 541; Dijkstra UF 26 1994 122). ¶ Forms: G prefc. energ. *thwyn*.
G. To want: *npš*] *bʕl thwyn* the appetite of DN wants (...), 1.92:36 (bkn ctx.; cf. Dijkstra UF 26 1994 118, 122). For *thw*, 1.5 I 14 and 1.133:4 cf. *thw*.

hy pn. f. 1) personal "she, it"; 2) demonstr. "that" (c.Sem. except Akk. and Qatab.; cf. Hb. *hyʔ(h)*, HALOT 240f.; Ph., Pun., Aram., Nab., Palm. *hʔ*, DNWSI 264ff.; ESA *hy(ʔ/t)*, DOSA 108ff.; Arab. *hiya*, Hava 842; Moscati ICGSL 102ff.; Gordon UT § 6.1, 3; Segert BGUL 47f.; Tropper UG 209, 211). ¶ Forms: sg. nom. *hy*; obl. *hyt*.
1) She, it, pn. personal ★a) nom.: *w prʕ hy ḫlh* and it will remove his sickness , 1.124:10; *npš hy mḫ* (in) her soul she (feels) exuberant, 1.19 IV 39; in bkn and unc. ctx.:]*hy bth tʕrb*, 1.7:3;]*rgm hy (...) yritn mġy hy*, 2.31:44-45; *hy bh*, 1.111:22; ★b) obl. her, of her, (*hyt*): prostrate yourselves (and) *kbd hyt* honour her, 1.3 III 10; DN *ṯbr diy hyt* DN broke her wings, 1.19 III 37.
2) That, demonstr. pn.: *trʕ ḥwt hyt* the seed of that land, 1.103:55 and par.
In bkn ctx.: *ṯḥm hy*, 2.81:17.
Cf. hyabn, hyadt.

hyabn PN (Sem. Cf. Virolleaud GLECS 8 1957/60 9; Grøndahl PTU 45, 87, 133, 163; Cross CMHE 64 n. 73; De Moor UF 2 1970 198; Watson AuOr 8 1990 118; cf. Xella UF 20 1988 387ff.).
PN: 4.110:20.

hyadt PN (Sem. Cf. Virolleaud GLECS 8 1957/60 9; Grøndahl PTU 45, 90, 133; Cross CMHE 64 n. 73).
PN: *bn PN*, 4.170:22 (bkn ctx.).

hyn DN, alternative name of the god *kṯr* (etym. unc., cf. syll. RS Hurr. ᵈA.A = *e-ia-an* = *ku-šar-ru*, Ug 5 137 IVa 19; Huehnergard UVST 141; Lipiński UF 20 1988 137ff.; cf. Arab. *hayn*, *hayyīn*, **hawwana*, Lane 3046; Hb. *hwn*, HALOT 242; Aram. *hwn*, DJPA 161; Syr. *hawwinō*, LS 173. Cf. Dietrich - Loretz UF 10 1978 59; UF 31 1999 168ff.; Cooper RSP 3 445; Smith BC 171).
DN, title of the god *kṯr*. *hyn d ḥrš ydm* DN the ambidextrous craftsman, 1.3 VI 23 and par.

hyrm "?"; in bkn ctx.: 1.9:8.

hyt, obl. of *hy*; cf. *hy*.

hzp TN (Belmonte RGTC 12/2 104: *Hizpu*. Cf. Heltzer RCAU 10; Astour UF 13 1981 7; Huehnergard UVST 250; Van Soldt UF 28 1996 666; UF 30 1998 727; Tropper - Vita UF 29 1997 679 n.3); ¶ syll.: URU *iz-pí*, PRU 3 189 (RS 11.790):24'; PRU 3 190 (RS 11.800):5'; PRU 6 131:7; Ug 5 104:3'; RSOu 7 4:23; 79:5; URU *iz-pu*, PRU 6 70:11; Ug 5 102:13' (in PRU 3 191 [RS 15.20]:4 rdg URU *ḫa*[*l*](!)*-bi*; Nougayrol: URU *aš*(?)*-pi*, cf. PRU 3 p. 265; Heltzer RCAU 16f. n. 26; cf. Astour RSP 2 349 no. 144).
TN: 1.91:28; 1.105:14 *hz<p>* (Dietrich - Loretz - Sanmartín UF 7 1975 158); 4.68:55 (Bordreuil UF 20 1988 10f.: rdg *izp*); 4.73:7 (Bordreuil UF 20 1988 10: rdg *izp*); 4.355:16; 4.365:31; 4.380:33; RSOu 14 35 [KTU 9.388] I 27.
Bkn 4.73:7; 4.629:2; 4.661:5; 4.770:4.

hzpḫ GN (Hurr.; < *hzp*, TN; Hurr. suff. /=ḫe/i/. Cf. Richardson JSS 23 1978 301; Xella TRU 75: possibly a mistake for *ḫzpy*). ¶ Forms: sg. *hzpḫ*.
GN: 1.87:58.

hzpy (I) GN m. (< *hzp*, TN. Cf. Richardson JSS 23 1978 301). ¶ Forms: sg. *hzpy*; pl. *hzpym*. Cf. *hzpḫ*.
GN: 4.50:8; 4.51:16; 4.754:9.

hzpy (II) PN (< *hzpy (I)*).
PN: *bn PN*, 4.753:18.

ḥ

ḥbl (I) n. m. 1) "cord, rope, mooring rope"; 2) "band, flock" (Hb., Aram. *ḥbl*, HALOT 286; DNWSI 345; Akk. *eblu*, AHw 183; CAD E 15; Ebla /ḥablum/ in GÁNA:ÉŠ = *ʔà-ba-lu*, VE 1174; Krebernik ZA 73 1983 41; Fronzaroli EL 133; StEb 7 1984 164f.; Krecher Biling. 148; Arab. *ḥabl*, Lane 504; Eth. *ḥabl*, CDG 223); ¶ RS Akk.: cf. 2 *ab-ša-nu*, PRU 6 141:6. ¶ Forms: sg. *ḥbl* (var. *ḫbl*, 4.689:5), suff. *ḥblh*; pl. *ḥblm*; du. *ḥblm*.

1) Cord, rope, mooring rope: *ṯn ḥblm alp alp amt* two ropes each a thousand ells, 4.247:30; *ṯmn ḥblm šbʕ šbʕ mat* eight ropes each seven hundred (ells), *ibid.* ln. 31; *spr nps any* (...) *w ḫbl* list of naval equipment: (...) and mooring rope(s), 4.689:5.

2) Band, flock (of birds): *ybṣr ḥbl diym* a flock of vultures watched (him), 1.18 IV 31 and par.; in bkn ctx.: *ḥbl kṯrt* the band (flock) of the DN, 1.10 II 30, 40; 1.11:6; *ḥblx ʕrpt tḥt*, 1.8:10, cf. 1.4 VII 57 (cf. Dijkstra UF 15 1983 30; De Moor SP 164, 173; Margalit MLD 73; OLP 19 1988 70f.).

ḥbl (II) n. m. "deposit, guarantee, pledge" (Akk. *ḫa/ubullu*, AHw 351; CAD Ḫ 216; for Aram. *h/ḥ(w)blʔ* cf. Kaufman AIA 56); ¶ syll. Ug.: cf. A.ŠÀ.MEŠ *ḫa-ba-li-ma* "distrained fields", PRU 3 45 (RS 16.140):8; cf. diff.: Huehnergard UVST 123; ¶ RS Akk.: KÙ. BABBAR UR$_5$.RA.MEŠ, PRU 3 60 (RS 16.141):16. ¶ Forms: sg. cstr. *ḥbl*.

Deposit, guarantee, pledge: *ksp ḥbl rišym* money as guarantee of the GN, 4.779:3 (cf. *supra* RS Akk.: *kasap ḫubulli*).

/ḥ-b-q/ vb G: "to embrace, take in one's arms, cover" (Hb. *ḥbq*, HALOT 287; Ebla /ḥabāqum/ in LÁ.LA = *ʔà-ba-gú-um*, VE 1184; Krebernik ZA 73 1983 42; Akk. *epēqu*, AHw 222; cf. CAD E 183: *epēqu A*; Syr. *ḥbaq*, LS 212; Eth. *ḥaqafa*, CDG 239); ¶ par.: /n-š-q/. ¶ Forms: G prefc. *yḥbq*, *tḥbq*; inf. *ḥbq*; suff. *ḥbqh*.

G. To embrace, take in one's arms, cover: *yḥbq qdš w amrr* DN-DN took (her) in (their) arms, 1.4 IV 13; *bsql yḥbq w ynšq* he embraced and kissed the shoot, 1.19 II 14 and par.; *tḥbq a[rḫ* she embraced the c[ow, 1.10 III 23; *b ḥbq ḥmḥmt* on embracing (them) there was pregnancy, 1.23:51 and par.; *b ḥbqh ḥmḥmt* on his embracing (them) there was pregnancy, 1.17 I 40 (// *nšq*).

In bkn ctx.: *DN yṯkḥ yḥ[bq* DN undresses (and) em[braces, 1.24:4; *mlak mṯḫr yḥb[q ...]* *mlak bn ktpm* a messenger with wounds(?) [he has covered(?) ...], 1.2 I 41. Bkn: *ḥbq l ḥršm*, 4.201:6.

ḥbr (I) n. m. "companion, associate" (Hb., Pun., Aram., Nab., Palm. *ḥbr*, HALOT 288; DNWSI 346f.; Syr. *ḥabrō* LS 212; Akk. *i/ebru*, AHw 363f.; CAD I/J 5ff.; Emar /ḫibbīru/ Pentiuc 65; Arab. *ḥabr/ḥibr*, Lane 498f. Cf. Caquot TOu 2 115 n. 353; diff.: Pardee, JNES 47 1988 63: Dijkstra UF 17 1985 149ff.: 'magic' / 'charmer, enchanter', Akk. *ubburu*; Hb. *ḥbr*); ¶ **par.**: *dʕt*. ¶ **Forms**: sg. m. suff. *ḥbrk*, *ḥbrm* (encl. *-m* ?); pl. cst. *ḥbr*.

Companion, associate: *ʕdk kṯr ḥbrk* around you, DN, your companion, 1.6 VI 49 (// *dʕt*); *bḥbr kṯr ṭbm* with / among the good companions of DN, 1.108:5 (// *mrqdm*; diff.: Del Olmo CR 187, n. 60, 'clappers', Arab. *ḥabara*, Akk. *ḫabāru*; but cf. Clemens UF 25 1993 73ff.; Loretz UF 32 2000 279: 'Beschwörer, Zauberer'); *ygrš ḥrn ḥbrm* may DN cast out the associates, 1.169:10 (// *dʕtm*; diff.: Loretz - Xella MLE 1 1982 38: 'Zauberer', Hb. *ḥbr II*, // *kšpm* also Husser UF 29 1997 239; cf. *ḥbr III*).

ḥbr (II) n. m. "pot" ((?); cf. Akk. *ḫubūru*, AHw 352; CAD Ḫ 220; cf. Virolleaud Syria 14 1933 151; Del Olmo MLC 448; diff.: De Moor ARTU 128: 'companion', cf. *ḥbr (I)*); ¶ **par.**: rdg ¶ **Forms**: sg. suff. *ḥbrh*.

Pot(?): *w ḥbrh mla yn[* and his pot(?) is full / fills with wine (?), 1.23:76 (// *lg*).

ḥbr (III) "?" (Bordreuil - Pardee RSOu 14 p. 398: Hb., Aram. 'charme').

? : in bkn ctx. *w ḥbr b[...]*, RSOu 14 53 [KTU 9.432]:3'.

ḥbš (I) n. m. 1) "cinch, belt"; 2) "waist" (etym. unc.; cf. Hb. *ḥbš*, HALOT 289; Syr. *ḥbaš*, LS 213; Arab. *ḥabasa*, Lane 500f.; Akk. *abšu*, AHw 7; CAD A/1 66: *abšu A*. Cf. De Moor SP 91f.; for a possible connection with OAss *e/ib/pišum*, AHw 230, CAD E 14f., cf. Watson NUS 36 1986 18: 'blankets'); ¶ **par.**: *bmt*, *tʕrt*. ¶ **Forms**: sg. *ḥbš*, suff. *ḥbš[y]*, *ḥbšk*, *ḥbšh*.

1) Cinch, belt: *tštn k nšr b ḥbšh* she put him like an eagle in her belt, 1.18 IV 28 and par. (// *tʕrth*; diff.: Watson JNSL 5 1977 71f.: 'arm, wristlet', EA *ḫa-ab-ši*; cf. Margalit UF 15 1983 100f.: '(game)bag, pouch', Arab. *ḥabasa, ḥabs*).

2) Waist: *šnst kpt b ḥbšh* she girded palms / hands, at her waist, 1.3 II 13 and par. (// *bmth*; diff.: Dietrich - Loretz UF 4 1972 30: 'Arm', EA *ḫapšu*; Caquot - Sznycer TOu 1 159 n. o: 'carnier', Arab. *ḥibs*); *l ḥbšk ʕtk riš*[*t* to your waist tie heads, 1.13:6 (par. 1.7:2; cf. 1.3 II 12: *ʕtkt rišt l bmth*).

Bkn ctx. *ʕl ḥbš x*[, 1.5 IV 22; *yn ʕšy l ḥbš*, 1.17 VI 8 (Gibson CML 146: 'governor', Hb. *ḥwbš*; Dijsktra - De Moor UF 7 1975 184: 'jar', Akk. *ḫabšu*).

ḥbš (II) TN (Belmonte RGTC 12/2 105: a town. Cf. Heltzer RCAU 11; Van Soldt UBL 11 377f. Not related with the country KUR *ḫa-bi-iš-še*, PRU 4 209 (RS 17.355):8; cf. Edzard RlA 4 27; Astour UF 12 1980 106ff.; 13 1981 6; Van Soldt UF 28 1996 667; UF 30 1998 725).

TN: 4.48:10. In bkn ctx.: [*ḥ*]*bš*, 4.610 (I) 28 (Bordreuil UF 20 1988 12: [*q*]*dš*).

/ḥ-b-ṭ/ vb N(?): "to beat oneself / be beaten" ((?); etym. unc.; cf. Hb. *ḥbṭ*, HALOT 285; Syr. *ḥbaṭ*, LS 209; Eth. *ḥanfaṭa*, CDG 236. Cf. De Moor - Spronk UF 16 1984 245; De Moor ARTU 179; Caquot TOu 2 62 n. 201); ¶ syll. Ug.: cf. Huehnergard UVST 190: *ḫa-ba-ṭu*[. ¶ Forms: N(?) prefc. *tḥbṭ*.

N(?). To beat oneself / be beaten(?): in bkn and unc. ctx., *tḥbṭ km ṣq* may they beat themselves / be beaten(?) like someone distressed, 1.82:25.

ḥby (I) DN; a demon (etym. unc.; for the various interpretations cf. Pardee TPM 60ff.; cf. also Liverani OrAn 8 1969 339: Eg. DN *ḥpy* 'Apis'; Gordon UF 18 1986 129ff.: Hb. *ḥby*, Is 26:20; *ḥbywn*, Hab 3:4; Ebla *ḫa-ba-ḫa-bi* (sic!), but cf. Xella SEL 3 1986 17-21; Aartun StUL 55f.: act. part. 'sich nähern', Arab. *ḥabā*).

DN: *ḥby bʕl qrnm w ḏnb* DN, the one with two horns and a tail, 1.114:19.

Cf. ḥby (II).

ḥby (II) PN (etym. unc. Cf. Bordreuil - Caquot Syria 57 1980 364f.; Watson AuOr 13 1995 222).

PN: 4.775:20.

Cf. ḥby (I).

ḥdg n. m. "chair (for birthing?)" (Arab. *ḥidǧ*, *ḥidāǧat*, Lane 530; cf. Gray JNES 10 1951 148 n. 24; Renfroe AULS 117f.). ¶ Forms: sg. suff. *ḥdgk*.

Chair (for birthing?): *qḥ ksank ḥdgk ḥtlk* take your stool, your chair (for birthing?), your nappies, 1.12 I 18.

ḥdn PN (etym. unc.; cf. Watson AuOr 13 1995 222); ¶ syll.: cf. *ḫu-ud-da-na*, RS 23.22+ VI 14' (Van Soldt SAU 341 n. 185). Cf. *ḫd/ty(n)*, PN.
PN: *bn PN*, 4.322:10; 4.720:2; 4.785:21; in bkn ctx.: 4.498:9.

ḥdr n. m. "room, chamber" (Hb., Ph., Pun. *ḥdr*, HALOT 293; DNWSI 350; Ebla /ḥadrum/ in É.TUR = *ʔà-da-ru*$_{12}$, VE 337; ŠÀ = *ʔà-da-ru*$_{12}$*/lu-um*, VE 595; Krebernik ZA 73 1983 14; Fronzaroli EL 134; StEb 7 1984 165; Conti SQF 121; Sanmartín AuOr 9 1991 189; Emar /ḥidru/, Pentiuc Vocabulary 67; OSA *ḫdrn*, *mḫdr*, CAME 154; DOSA 197; Arab. *ḫidr*, Lane 708; Eth. *ḫidr*, *māḫdar*, CDG 258f. Cf. Dahood UF 11 1979 146; Sznycer EtSem 70ff.); ¶ syll. Ug.: cf. G[Ú (Nougayrol: DUR) = *šubtu*? =]*-a-ri* = *ḫu-du-rù*, Ug 5 137 II 11'; Huehnergard UVST 78, 123; Sivan UF 21 1989 360; Van Soldt SAU 303; ¶ par.: *ap (II)* (+ *sgrt*); ¶ Forms: sg. *ḥdr*, suff. *ḥdrh*; pl. *ḥdrm*.
Room, chamber: ★a) *yʕn il b šbʕt ḥdrm* DN replied from the seven chambers (// *ap sgrt*), 1.3 V 11, 26; cf. *ḥdrm* rooms, 4.195:3, and cf. *d sgrm*, *ibid.* ln. 4; *yʕrb b ḥdrh ybky* he went into his room to weep, 1.14 I 26; cf. in bkn ctx.]*ḥdr*, 7.176; *tʕrb ḥ*[, 1.16 II 51 (cf. De Moor - Spronk UF 14 1982 186); ★b) *ḥdr mškb* bedroom, 4.195:6; *ḥdr ṯġr* hall, vestibule, 4.195:14. In bkn ctx.: *ḥdr*, RSOu 14 53[KTU 9.432]:34'.

/ḥ-d-ṯ/ vb G: "to be new, renew oneself" Š: "to renew" (Hb., Ph., Pun. *ḥdš*, HALOT 293f.; DNWSI 350; Aram. *ḥdt*, DNWSI 350; Akk. *edēšu*, AHw 186f.; CAD E 30ff.; OSA *ḥdṯ*, DOSA 167; Arab. *ḥadaṯa*, Lane 527ff.; Eth. *ḥaddasa*, CDG 225f.). ¶ Forms: G prefc. *yḥdṯ*; Š prefc. with suff. *-n tḥdṯn*.
G. To be new, renew oneself: *ik al yḥdṯ yrḫ* is it not certain that (now) DN renews himself?, 1.18 IV 9. In bkn ctx.: [...] *tḥdṯn (...)*, were renewing themselves, 1.92:4 (cf. Dijsktra UF 26 1994 116).
Š. To renew (assim. form?): *w tṯḥdṯn ṯnm w ḥdṯh tdn hmt* and they shall renew both and on the day of the new moon, they shall declare them (legitimate), 1.104:17-19 (diff. Del Olmo CR 309 and n. 49); cf. *ḥdṯ (II)*.
Cf. ḥdṯ (I), ḥdṯ (II), ḥdṯ (III), ḥdṯn.

ḥdṯ (I) adj. "new, recent" (Hb., Pun. *ḥdš*, HALOT 294; DNWSI 351; Aram. *ḥds/t*, DNWSI 351; Palm. *ḥdt*, DNWSI 351; Akk. *eššu*, AHw 258f.; CAD E 374ff.; Arab. *ḥadīṯ*, Lane 529; Eth. *ḥaddis*, CDG 225). ¶ Forms: sg. m. *ḥdṯ*; *ḥdṯh*, *ḥdṯn* (used adverbially, with encl. *-h* and *-n*); f. *ḥdṯt*.
New, recent: *w yṣi trḫ ḥdṯ* may the newly-wed also go out, 1.14 II 48

and par.; *kdwṯ ḥdṯ bd PN* a new *k*. in the hands of PN, 4.205:19; *trḥ ḥdṯ m*[*r*] a new little flask of myrrh, 1.124:7; *mšlḥ ḥdṯ* a new battering ram, 4.689:3; in place names: *gt ḥdṯt* 'New Farmstead', 4.213:12; 4.243:22; 4.707:21; cf. *ḥdṯ (II)*). Bkn: 4.182:50; 1.146:2.

ḥdṯ (II) n. m. "new moon" (Hb., Ph., Pun. *ḥdš*, HALOT 294f.; DNWSI 350f.); ¶ syll. Ug.: cf. the element /ḫud(a)ṯ-/ in PNN, Sivan GAGl 225. ¶ Forms: sg. *ḥdṯ*; pl./du. *ḥdṯm*; suff. *-h ḥdṯh*; allograph *ḫdś* in 1.171:7 (cf. Tropper UF 22 1995 521f.).
New moon: *ym ḥdṯ* day of the new moon (: first day of the month), 1.112:10 and par.; *b ṯṯ ym ḥdṯ ḫyr* on the sixth of the new moon of MN, 1.78:1 (for this and other opinions cf. Del Olmo CR 351 nn. 68-69); *(dbḥ mlk) ḥdṯm* the (royal sacrifice) of the new moons, 1.91:13; *w ḥdṯh tdn hmt* and on the day of the new moon, they shall declare them (legitimate), 1.104:18-19 (diff. Del Olmo CR 309: 'and until the day of the new moon'). In bkn ctx.: *b šbʕ ḫdś* on the seventh (day) of the new moon, 1.171:7; *b ḥdṯ yrḫ* on the new moon,1.163:2.
Cf. ḥdṯ (III), ḥdṯn.

ḥdṯ (III) PN (Sem. Cf. Stamm VTS 16 1967 322; Grøndahl PTU 30, 134; cf. Dietrich - Loretz WO 4 1967/68 304; Watson AuOr 14 1996 98); ¶ syll.: *ḫu-da-ši*, Syria 28 1951 173f. (RS 14.016):23; Ug 5 95:4; *ḫu-dá-ši*, PRU 3 133 (RS 15.132):5; Syria 28 1951 173f. (RS 14.016):23; cf. Sivan GAGl 225; Huehnergard UVST 212, 231, 242; Huehnergard AkkUg 368; Van Soldt SAU 309 n. 115.
PN: *bn PN*, 4.281:17.

ḥdṯn PN (Sem. Cf. Grøndahl PTU 30, 134); ¶ syll.: *ḫu-ud*(!)*-ša-nu*, PRU 3 199 (RS 16.257+) I 17"; cf. Sivan GAGl 225; Huehnergard UVST 230, 242. Cf. *ḥṯṯn* PN.
PN: 4.63 II 3; 4.116:11; 4.153:10; 4.243:34; 4.609:18, 19; 7.221:2, 3. Bkn 4.63 IV 8; 4.243:34.

/ḥ-d-y/ vb G: "to see, look, observe" (Hb. *ḥd/zh*, HALOT 292, 301; Ph., Aram., Palm. *ḥzy* DNWSI 357ff.; Ebla /ʔizāʔum/ in IGI.BAR.DA = NI*-ša-um*, EV 0126; Krecher Biling. 165; cf. Arab. *ḥazā*, Lane 562f. Cf. Dahood UF 1 1969 27; De Moor SP 93f.); ¶ par.: /ʕ-n/. ¶ Forms: G prefc. *aḥd*, *tḥdy*, *yḥdy*, *yḥd*; impv. *ḥd*.
G. To see, observe: *ibqʕ kbdh w aḥd* I shall open its entrails to see, 1.19 III 33 and par.; *yḥd hrgb* he saw DN, 1.19 III 15 (cf. ln 29); *tḫtṣb w tḥdy ʕnt* DN fought and was observing them, 1.3 II 24 and par. (// *tʕn*; diff.: Watson VT 31 1981 92ff.: */ḥ-d-y/ 'to be happy'; cf. De Moor SP 93f.); *w yḥdy mrḥqm* and will look into the distance, 1.127:32 (diff.: Dietrich - Loretz Mantik 37: '(weg)treiben', Arab.

hadā). Cf. in bkn ctx.: *ḥd hlny (...)* look!, here (...), 2.77:8; cf. *ibid.* ln. 15, 17 (cf. Márquez NABU 1993 36 [45]: Akk. *amur* and Eg. *ptr*, also: *tḥmk ḥdy*, 2.83:4; cf. diff.: Bordreuil - Caquot Syria 57 1980 361: 'ton message a réjoui(?)').

ḥḏm, 4.609:25, cf. *ḥẓ*.

ḥḏrt n. m.; an ingredient in hippiatric pharmacopaea (etym. unc. Cf. Pardee TH 60: 'pommier', Aram. *ḥazzûr* [with reservations]; Cohen (- Sivan) UHT 28f.; UF 28 1996 129f.: 'lettuce-plant', MHb. *ḥzrt*, Akk. *ḫassū*, Sanmartín AuOr 6 1988 234: 'albaricoque', Sum.-Akk. ḫašḫur/*ḫašuru*). ¶ Forms: sg. *ḥḏrt*.
An ingredient in hippiatric pharmacopaea: *pr ḥḏrt* fruit(s) of *ḥ.*, 1.85:14; also 1.71:12; 1.85:27; 1.72:19.

ḥgb n. m. "locust", as an attribute of DN *ršp* (Hb. *ḥgb*, HALOT 290; JAram. *ḥgb?*, Jastrow 424. Cf. Virolleaud PRU 5 11f.; Fulco Reshep 44; Dietrich - Loretz TUAT 2 324; diff.: Herdner Ug 7 28: 'portier', Arab. *ḥāǧib*; Ribichini - Xella RSF 15 1987 10: 'portiere'; Del Olmo AuOr 10 1990 151f.: 'víscera sacrificial', Arab. **ḥgb*, *ḥiǧāb*); ¶ syll. Ug.: cf. the element /ḥag(a)bu-/ in PNN; Sivan GAGl 222. ¶ Forms: sg. *ḥgb*.
Locust, as an attribute of *ršp ḥgb* 'DN (of the) locust', 1.90:2; 1.106:1; 1.134:3; 1.168:2.
Cf. ʕbdḥgb, ḥgbḏr, ḥgbn, ḥgbt, ḥgby, ḫgbt.

ḥgbḏr PN (Sem. Cf. Ribichini - Xella RSF 15 1987 10 n. 27).
PN: *bn PN*, 4.724:3.

ḥgbn PN (Sem. Cf. Grøndahl PTU 28, 52, 135; Jirku ArOr 41 1973 102f.; Ribichini - Xella RSF 15 1987; Sivan GAGl 222); ¶ syll.: cf. (DUMU) *ḫa-ag-ba-nu*, PRU 3 86 (RS 15.119) 5; 195 (RS 15.09) B II 5; 202 (RS 16.257+) B III 34; 203 (RS 16.257+) B IV 15; Ug 5 6:28; 12:8; (DUMU) *ḫa-ga-ba-na*, PRU 167 (RS 15.139):6, 10; PRU 6 45:29.
PN: ★a) 4.141 I 18 (Van Soldt SAU 38); 4.183 I 26; 4.263:9; 4.319:3; 4.609:11, 27; ★b) *bn PN*, 4.69 I 19; 4.77:28; 4.343:10; 4.383:2; 4.769:8, 16, 69; RSOu 14 40 [KTU 9.419]:8. Cf.]*ḥg bn kbs*, 4.682:9; in bkn ctx.. :]*gbn*, 4.151:10 (Kühne UF 6 1974 164 n. 43).

ḥgbt PN (Sem. Cf. Grøndahl PTU 21, 28, 135; Ribichini - Xella RSF 15 1987 10 n. 27). Cf. *ḫgbt*.
PN: 4.55:28; in bkn ctx.: 4.408:2.

ḥgby PN (Sem. Cf. Grøndahl PTU 28, 51, 135; Jirku ArOr 41 1973 102f.; Ribichini - Xella RSF 15 1987 10).
PN: *bn PN*, 4.93 II 5; 4.226:8; 4.348:29; in bkn ctx.: 4.498:10.

ḥgln PN (etym. unc. Cf. Watson AuOr 8 1990 118); ¶ syll.: cf. *ḫé*(?)-*gi-lu*, PRU 6 79:8.
PN: *bn PN*, 4.7:6.

/ḥ-g-r/ vb G: "to gird" (Hb. *ḥgr*, HALOT 291; cf. Syr. *ḥgar*, LS 214; Arab. *ḥaǧara*, Lane 516ff.; cf Akk. *egēru*, AHw 190; CAD E 41f.; Eth. *ḫagala*, CDG 228; Pun. cf. DNWSI 348: *ḥgr*$_2$). ¶ Forms: G prefc. *tḥgrn* (*-n*, 1st and 3rd p. sg. suff.).
G. To gird: bkn. ctx., *tḥgrn* [...] I shall gird myself [...], 1.14 III 44; *tḥgrn* she girds /they gird, 1.23:17.

ḥġmn PN (etym. unc.).
PN: *bn PN*, 4.682:10.

/ḥ-k-m/ vb G: "to be wise" (Hb., Aram. *ḥkm*, HALOT 314; DNWSI 371; Arab. *ḥakama*, Lane 616ff.; Eth. *ḥakama*, CDG 228f.; Akk. *ḫakāmu*, AHw 309; CAD Ḫ 32f. Cf. Müller, UF 1 1969 89 n. 81); ¶ par.: /r-b(-b)/. ¶ Forms: G suffc. *ḥkmt*.
G. To be wise: *rbt ilm l ḥkmt* you are great, DN, truly you are wise!, 1.4 V 3; *ḥkmt k ṯr lṭp*[*n*] you are wise like DN the Benevolent, 1.16 IV 2 (altern.: '(your) wisdom is like...', cf. *ḥkmt*). Cf. *ḥkmt*.

ḥkm adj. m. "wise" (cf. /ḥ-k-m/; cf. Hb. *ḥkm*, HALOT 314; Aram. *ḥkym*, DNWSI 371; Arab. *ḥakīm*, Lane 618). ¶ Forms: sg. *ḥkm*.
Wise: *tḥmk il ḥkm* your message, DN, is wise 1.3 V 30.

ḥkmt n. f. "wisdom" (cf. /ḥ-k-m/; Hb., Aram. *ḥkmh*, HALOT 314; DNWSI 371; Ph., *ḥkmt*, DNWSI 371; Arab. *ḥikmat*, Lane 617). ¶ Forms: sg. *ḥkmt*.
Wisdom: *ḥkmt ʕm ʕlm* (your) wisdom is eternal, 1.4 IV 41 (variant *ḥkmk* in 1.3 V 30; altern.: 'you are wise', cf. /ḥ-k-m/); *ḥkmt k ṯr lṭp*[*n*] (your) wisdom is like (that of) DN, the Benevolent One, 1.16 IV 2 (alternatively: 'you are wise', cf. /ḥ-k-m/).
Bkn ctx.:]*ḥkmt yx*[. 1.129:4.

ḥkpt TN; residence / territory of the god *kṯr* (Belmonte RGTC 12/2 105: *Ḥikuptaḥ*, Eg. of New Empire *ḥwt.k3.ptḥ*: Memphis; cf. WäS 3 5; Faulkner CDME 166; Zivie LÄ 25f.; Albright BASOR 70 1938 22; 77 1940 31; YGC 119, n. 69; Dijkstra - De Moor UF 7 1975 182; Margalit UF 15 1983 81; EA Akk.: URU *ḫi-ku-up-ta-aḫ*, EA 84:37; 139:8. Cf. Gk *Aigyptos*; cf. Watson JNSL 22 1996 74); ¶ par.: *kptr*. ¶ Forms: *ḥkpt*; *ḥ*{*q*}*kpt*, 1.3 VI 13, scribal mistake.
TN ★a) mythical: *ḥkpt il* the divine TN, 1.3 VI 13 and par.; *bʕl ḥkpt* the lord(s) of TN, 1.17 V 21, 31; *ḥkpt arṣ nḥlth* TN, the land of his property, 1.3 VI 15 and par.; I have to leave *ḥkp*[*t l rḥq ilnym*] TN for the most distant deity, 1.1 III 19 and par.; ★b) as a real TN: *ṯlṯ mat*

art ḥkpt three hundred bucklers(?) from (/ in the style of) TN, 4.247:26.

/ḥ-k-r/ vb G: "to knock down" (?) (cf. Akk. *ḫakāru*, AHw 309, 1558. Cf. Dietrich - Loretz BiOr 23 1966 129; diff.: Aartun UF 16 1984 17f.: "Becher, Pokal", Arab. *ḥu/akr*). ¶ Forms: G unc. form *ḥkr*[. To knock down (?): bkn ctx.: *ḥkr*, 1.93:6.

ḥl (I) n. m. 1) "strength, vigour"; 2) "fortress, stronghold"; 3) "tower, farm, estate", in onomastics (Hb. *ḥwl*, *ḥyl*, HALOT 311f.; OSA *ḥwl*, CAME 146; DOSA 169; Arab. *ḥayl*, *ḥaul*, Lane 675f., 688; cf. Hitt. *ḫali-*, *ḫila-*, HW(2) 3 30ff.; HEG 128f., 241ff. Cf. Sawyer - Strange IEJ 14 1964 98; Dietrich - Loretz - Sanmartín UF 7 1975 159ff.; diff.: Driver CML 138: 'circuit, region'; Ajjan NU 34: 'demeure', Arab. *ḥalla*; Albright Fs. Bertholet 3ff.: 'phoenix', Hb. *ḥwl*; for Ebla *ḫu-la-tum* cf. Dahood ArchEbl 306); ¶ syll. Ug.: cf. TN *ḥīlu*, see: *ḥl (III)*; ¶ par.: *ġr*. ¶ Forms: sg. *ḥl*, suff. *ḥlm* (encl. *-m*).

1) Strength, vigour: *ḥl amr bnkm* with vigour I shall strengthen your son, 1.13:27, cf. ln. 28-29.

2) Fortress, stronghold: *ṣpn ḥlm qdš (...) ḥlm adr ḥl rḥb mknpt* TN, the holy fortress, (...) the powerful fortress, the stronghold broad of span, 1.16 I 7-9 (// *ġr*).

3) Tower, farm, estate: *ḥl PN bd PN* the 'tower' of PN, in the hands of PN, 4.424:22.

Cf. ḥl (III).

ḥl (II) adj. "desacralized, 'free'" (cf. Hb. *ḥl*, HALOT 315; Arab. *ḥalāl*, *ḥill*, Lane 619ff.; Akk. *ellu*, AHw 204f.; CAD E 102ff.; Ebla cf. NISABA:A = *ʔà-a-um* (/ḥalālum/), VE 1227'; Krecher Biling. 141; cf. DI.DI = *ʔà-la-lum*, VE 635; cf. *à-lum* 'shiny', Mander MEE 10 88; *ʔà-li-um*, *ʔà-li-ù* (A:NAGA) 'purificatore', Bonechi MisEb 2 142; cf. ITU *ḫa-li*-NI and cf. Pettinato Rituale 190: *ḫa-li-ì* (Fronzaroli ARET 11 155: *ḫa-li*-NI); cf. *e-am*, Fronzaroli ARET 145: /ḥell-am/. Cf. Cazelles MUSJ 49 1975-1976 443ff.; Xella SSR 2 1978 381ff.; Aartun UF 16 1984 18f.). ¶ Forms: sg. m. *ḥl* (cf. *ḥlt (II)*).

Desacralized, 'free': *ʕrb špš w ḥl mlk* the sun sets / at sunset the king (shall remain) desacralized, 1.112:9 and par., cultic formula (cf. Del Olmo CR 24); *ṣbu špš w ḥl ym* the sun sets / at sunset and the day (remains) desacralized, 1.41:47 (diff.: De Moor ARTU 164: 'the host of the day'); *ṯṯb rgm b gn w ḥl mlk* there will be a reply in the garden and the king remains desacralized, 1.106:23, cf. 1.173:17.

Cf. ḥlbt, ḥll, ḥlt (II), mḥll.

ḥl (III) TN (<(?) *ḥl (I)*; see Belmonte RGTC 12/2 106: *ḥīlu-Aġalteni*

'Turm-Gehöft des Aġalteni', *ḫīlu(-yāmi)* 'Meersburg'; cf. Dietrich - Loretz - Sanmartín UF 7 1975 159; Van Soldt UF 28 1996 667; UF 30 1998 732); ¶ syll.: cf. URU *ḫi-li*, PRU 3 144 (RS 16.138):21; PRU 6 94:1', 2'; Ug 5 12:12; RSOu 7 4:21; cf. Berger UF 2 1970 340 ff.; Kühne UF 6 1974 166.

TN: ★a) *ḥl aġltn*, 4.320:8; ★b) *ḥl (ym)*, 4.68:40: *ḥl y*[*m*(?)]; 4.186:6; RSOu 14 35 [KTU 9.388] II 24; in bkn ctx. cf. *ḥl*[, 4.610 (II) 23 (cf. Bordreuil UF 20 1988 12). Bkn: 4.618:32.

Cf. ġl (I).

ḥlb n. m. 1) "milk"; 2) "cheese, butter" (Hb., Pun., Aram. *ḥlb*, HALOT 315f.; DNWSI 372; Jastrow 464; Arab. *ḥalab*, Lane 624; Eth. *ḥalib*, CDG 229; cf. NA *ḫilpu*, AHw 345; CAD Ḫ 187; Del Olmo BSA 7 1993 193f.); ¶ par.: *ḫmat*, *ṯd*; ¶ RS Akk.: GA; cf. GA.MEŠ, PRU 6 156:1; cf. GA.KIN.AG, PRU 6 4:8; Sanmartín BSA 7 1993 206. ¶ Forms: sg. *ḥlb*.

1) Milk: (offering of) *gd b ḥlb* coriander in milk, 1.23:14 (// *ḫmat*); *ġlm ynq ḥlb aṯrt* the prince who will feed on the milk of DN, 1.15 II 26 (// *ṯd*).

2) Cheese, butter (weighed in talents; cf. RS Akk.: 3 GUN GA.MEŠ, PRU 6 156:1): *kkr ḥlb* a talent of cheese, 4.707:20; *ḫmš kkr ḥlb* five talents of cheese, 4.272:2; in barter: *alp mitm kbd ṯlṯ ḥlb* one thousand two hundred (shekels) of copper (in exchange) for cheese, *ibid.* ln. 5 (cf. *ṯlṯ šmn* copper (in exchange) for oil, *ibid.* ln. 4; cf. Sanmartín SEL 5 1988 176f.).

Cf. ḥlbt.

ḥlbt PN (etym. unc. Cf. Grøndahl PTU 20, 135).

PN: *bn PN*, 4.617:12.

ḥll n. m. "desacralization, purification" (verbal noun < */ḥ-l-l/, cf. *ḥl (I)*; cf. Mari Akk. *ḫalīlum*, (Charpin -) Durand MARI 2 76; MARI 3 135 n. 36; cf. Akk. *tēliltu*, AHw 1344f.; Luw. *ḫalal-*, Laroche DLL 38; Hitt. *ḫalali-*, HW(2) 3 18. Cf. Dietrich - Loretz - Sanmartín UF 7 1975 160, 544; Janowski UF 12 1980 247 n. 102; Freilich JSS 31 1986 128 n. 36). ¶ Forms: sg. *ḥll*.

Desacralization, purification: *w š ḥll ydm* and a ram (as a sacrifice of) desacralization / purification of hands, 1.115:6 (cf. Del Olmo CR 266).

ḥlm (I) n. m. "dream" (Hb. *ḥlwm*, HALOT 317f., cf. *ḥlm* HALOT 320f.; Aram. *ḥlm*, DNWSI 375f.; Arab. *ḥulm*, Lane 632, cf. *ḥalama*, 631ff.); ¶ par.: *ḏ(h)rt*, *hdrt*. ¶ Forms: sg. *ḥlm*, suff. *ḥlmy*, *ḥlmh*.

Dream: *b ḥlm lṭpn il d pid* in a dream of the Benevolent One, DN the

Bountiful, 1.6 III 10 and par. (// *ḏrt*); *krt yḫṯ w ḥlm* PN came to himself and it was a dream, 1.14 III 50 (// *hdrt*); *w b ḥlmh il yrd* and in his dream DN came down, 1.14 I 35 (// *ḏhrth*); *d b ḥlmy il ytn* whom DN granted me in my dream DN, 1.14 III 46 and par. (// *ḏrty*).

ḥlm (II) n. m. "fully grown, mature animal," (cf. Hb. *ḥlm*, HALOT 320 [Job 39:4]; Syr. *ḥalīmō*, LS 235; Arab. *ḥālim*, Lane 633. Cf. Dietrich - Loretz - Sanmartín UF 7 1975 161); ¶ syll. Ug.: cf. [*ḫ*]*u-ul-ma-tu*$_4$, Ug 5 137 III 16'; cf. Huehnergard UVST 125; AkkUg 352. ¶ Forms: pl. *ḥlmm*.
Fully grown, mature animal: *s*[*p*]*r ḥlmm* list of fully grown animals, 1.86:1; in bkn ctx.: *b ḥlm (...)*, 1.86:28.

ḥln n. m. "window, opening" (Hb. *ḥlwn*, HALOT 318; cf. De Moor UF 2 1970 325); ¶ par.: *urbt*. ¶ Forms: sg. *ḥln*; pl. *ḥlnm* (cf. *ḫln*); cf. the spelling *ẖln*, 5.22:27.
Window, opening: *ypth ḥln b bhtm* he opened a window in the house, 1.4 VII 25-26 and par.; *ḥln d b dmt um il*[*m* the window that there is in the tower of the mother of the g[od(s)(?), 2.31:46; *ṯmn ḥlnm* eight windows, 4.195:15. Cf. the spelling *ẖln*, 5.22:27 (Dietrich - Loretz KA 191: 'Fenster').

ḥlq n. m. "part, limb" (Hb., Aram., Nab., Palm. *ḥlq*, HALOT 323f.; DNWSI 378f.; cf. Arab. *ḥalāq*, Lane 802. Cf. Rin AE 83: *ʔṣwʔr* [neck, throat]', Arab. *ḥalq*; Rendsburg JAOS 107 1987 628: 'throat, neck', MSA *ḥelqān*; Gray LC 42 n. 1: 'loin', Hb. *ḥlṣ*; Gray UF 11 1979 318 n. 19: 'thigh', Hb. **ḥlq*; Dussaud RHR 1938 137: 'poitrine', Arab. *ḥāliq*; Aartun UF 16 1984 20: 'vulva', Arab. *ḥalqat(ā)*, cf. Dietrich - Loretz UF 4 1972 30; De Moor SP 92: 'hips, buttocks', Akk. *ilku*; Caquot - Sznycer TOu 1 159 n. p: 'pans de jupe', MHb. *ḥālûq*; Collini SEL 6 1989 35: 'anello per caviglie, parte del corpo'); ¶ par.: *brk*. ¶ Forms: pl./du. *ḥlqm*.
Part, limb: *tġll (...) ḥlqm b mmʕ mhrm* she plunged (...) (her) limbs in the innards of the combatants, 1.3 II 28 and par. (// *brkm*).

ḥlš adj./n. epithet of the goddess *ʕnt* (etym. unc.; cf. De Moor UF 2 1970 325: 'appellative or place name'(?); Xella TRU p. 54: 'ʕAnat della devastazione', Hb. *ḥlš*). ¶ Forms: sg. m.(!) *ḥlš*.
Epithet of *ʕnt*: *ʕnt ḥlš*, 1.109:25.

ḥlt (I) MN (etym. unc., 'phoenix' (?); cf. Dahood in ArchEbl 306: Ebla *ḫa-li-tù*, cf. *ḥl*); ¶ syll. Ug.: ITI *ḫal-la-t*[*e*(?)], PRU 6 101:5'; ITI *ḫal-la-ti*, MSL 10 37, colophon: 5; cf. RS 25.455A+B III 6' (unpub.); Šivan GAGl 222; Huehnergard UVST 125; Van Soldt BiOr 46 1989 651; SAU 303. ¶ Forms: sg. *ḥlt*.

Month name: *yrḫ ḥlt* the month of *ḥ*., 4.219:13: 4.220:4.

ḥlt (II) n. f. "desacralization" (cf. *ḥl*; cf. Akk. *ellūtu*, AHw 205; CAD E 106; cf. diff.: Bordreuil - Caquot Syria 56 1979 299: verb, 'tu es désacralisé'). ¶ Forms: sg. *ḥlt*.

Desacralization: *w al tṣu y*(!)*ṣu w ḥlt* and shall not go out; (and if) he goes out there will be desacralization (?), 1.164:20.

ḥm n. m. "heat; drought" (cf. /ḥ-m-m/; Hb. *ḥm*, HALOT 325; Syr. *ḥumō*, LS 238; Arab. *ḥamm*, Lane 636; Ebla cf. /ḥammūtum/ in UD.GÁNA = *a(-wa)-mu ʔà-mu-tum*, VE 777; Krebernik ZA 73 1983 30; A.UD = *ma-wu ʔà-mu-tum*, VE 637; Krebernik ZA 73 1983 25; Fronzaroli EL 136; Akk. *ummu*, AHw 1417). ¶ Forms: sg. *ḥm*.

Heat, drought: *yṣly ʕrpt b ḥm un yr* he implored the clouds, in the terrible drought, the (early) rain, 1.19 I 40 (diff.: Margalit UF 16 1984 130f.: 'anxiety', Arab. *ʔaḥimma*). In bkn ctx.: *ḥm l šrr*, 1.2 IV 33.

Cf. **ḥmm**.

/ḥ-m-d/ vb G: "to desire" (Hb., Ph. *ḥmd*, HALOT 325; DNWSI 380; cf. Akk. EA [*ı*]*a-pu* : *ḫa-mu-du*, EAT 138:26; Sivan GAGl 223; DNWSI 380; Gianto SEL 12 1995 68; OSA *ḥmd*, DOSA 178f.; Arab. *ḥamida*, Lane 638ff.); ¶ **par.**: /h-r-r/. ¶ Forms: G prefc. with suff. *yḥmdnh*, *yḥmdm* (encl. *-m*); cf. *tḥmd*[(Dijkstra UF 26 1994 117: *tḥmd*[*nh*).

G. To desire: *bʕl ḥmdm yḥmdm* DN ardently desired (them), 1.12 I 38 (// *yhrrm*). In bkn ctxs.: *yṣi ǵlh tḥmd*[she desired the produce of her hollow (// of her desert), 1.92:6; *btlt bʕl yḥmdnh* the virgin - DN desired her, 1.92:29 (for both passages, cf. Dijkstra UF 26 1994 117). Bkn: *ḥmdm*, 1.12 II 8.

Cf. **mḥmd**.

ḥmdrt n. f. "parched field" (Akk. *ḫamadī/āru*, *ḫamadīrūtu*, AHw 315; CAD Ḫ 57f.; cf. Sanmartín UF 9 1977 265); ¶ **par.**: *aklt*. ¶ Forms: sg. *ḥmdrt*.

Parched field: *šblt ypḫ*(!) *b ḥmdrt* he spied an ear in the parched field, 1.19 II 21 (// *aklt*); *šblt tpʕ* [*b ḥ*]*mdrt ur* an ear which grows in the hot parched field, 1.19 II 23 (// *aklt*).

ḥmḥmt n. f. "pregnancy, conception" (< /ḥ-m-m/; cf. Tsumura UF 10 1978 388 n. 5; De Moor - Spronk UF 14 1982 182: 'heat, orgasm', cf. Aartun StUL 57f.; ; diff.: Margalit UF 27 1995 265f.: 'sanctuary, shelter, circumvallation', cf. Ug. *ḥmt*)); ¶ **par.**: *hr*. ¶ Forms: sg. *ḥmḥmt*, suff. *ḥmḥ<mt>h*.

Pregnancy, conception: *b ḥbq ḥmḥmt* on embracing (them) here was pregnancy, 1.23:51 and par. (// *hr*); in bkn ctx.: *ylt ḥmḥmt* (her) pregnancy bore (him) (?), 1.17 I 40-41; *bt ḥmḥ<mt>h dnn* the daughter whose conception(?) (proves) our strength, 1.16 I 29.

/ḥ-m-m/ vb Š: "to heat up" (Hb. *ḥmm, yḥm*, HALOT 328f., 407; Palm. *ḥmm*, DNWSI 382f.; Syr. *ḥam, ḥammem*, LS 238; Akk. *emēmu*, AHw 213; CAD E 147f.; Arab. *ḥamma, waḥima*, Lane 635ff., 3050; Hava 857; cf. Aartun UF 16 1984 20). ¶ Forms: Š prefc. *yšḥmm*.
Š. To heat up: in bkn ctx.: *y]ḥrkn w yšḥmm*, 1.175:7.
Cf. ḥm, ḥmḥmt, ḥmm, ḥmny.

ḥmm n. m. "heat" ((?) Cf. Bordreuil - Pardee RSOu 14 p. 401: Arab. *ḥumām* 'fever',). ¶ Forms: sg. *ḥmm*.
Heat(?): *ḥmm b bšrk* heat(?) in your flesh, RSOu 14 53 [KTU 9.432]:7'.
Cf. ḥm.

ḥmny PN (Sem. Cf. Grøndahl PTU 51, 135); ¶ syll.: cf. ᶠ*ḫa-mé-en-na-ya*, PRU 6 55:5'; cf. DUM]U(?) *ḫa-m[u-](?)ni[*, PRU 3 36 (RS 11.718):4'. Cf. *ḫmn*.
PN: *bn PN*, 4.108:3.

ḥmr (I) n. m. (and f.(?)) 1) "donkey"; 2) "load (measure of capacity); heap" (Hb., Aram., Palm. *ḥmr*, HALOT 327, 330; DNWSI 383f.; Akk. *imēru*, AHw 375f.; CAD I/J 110ff.; Arab. *ḥimār*, Lane 641. Cf. Sanmartín UF 20 1988 271f.; AuOr 8 1990 97f.); ¶ RS Akk.: ANŠE(.MEŠ), PRU 3 217; PRU 6 8:17, 17; ¶ par.: *ibr*. ¶ Forms: sg. *ḥmr*; pl. *ḥmrm*; sg./pl. suff. *ḥmrh*; du. *ḥmrm*.
1) Donkey: ★a) *arbʕ ḥmr[m...] l ṯlṯ* four donkeys for the [(transport of the)] copper, 4.268:1; *ṯn ḥmr[m...] l brr* two donkeys for the tin, *ibid.* ln. 4; 4.377:25, 30; *TN ḥmr* TN one donkey, 4.698:1; *TNN ḥmrm* TNN two donkeys, 4.698:3, 5; (...) *bnšm w ḥmr* (so many) unskilled labourers and a donkey, 4.29:2, 4; (...) *ḥmr(m) w* (...) *bnšm* (so many) donkeys and (so many) unskilled labourers, 4.380:3-26; *ṯṯ ḥmrm bʕlm ṣmdm alpm* six donkeys (and two(?)) unskilled labourers (and) two pairs of oxen, 4.691:7; *šʕrm l ḥmrm* barley for the donkeys, 6.19:1; *dd šʕrm l ḥmr ḥṭb* a *d.* of barley for the woodcutter's donkey, 4.269:24; *ṯlṯ ddm šʕrm l ḥmrm dt tblm* three 'cauldronfuls' of barley for the donkeys of the smiths, 4.790:14; *ʕšr dd kśmm w ḫmšm {ḥmr} kśmm <ḥmr>* ten 'cauldronfuls' of spelt (for human consumption(?)) and fifty {} of spelt <for a donkey>, 4.691:5 (cf. Sanmartín UF 20 1988 270ff.); cf. in bkn ctx. *]ḥmrm*, 3.6:3; *l ḥmrm d bd* for the donkeys in the hand of, RSOu 14 39 [KTU 4.790]:9', 11', 12', 14'; ★b) hearing *nqht ḥmrh* the braying of his donkey, 1.14 III 17 and par.

(// *ibrh*); cf. bkn ctx.: cf. *d bnš ḥmr*[, 1.86:12; ★c) *ḥmr škm* 'braying donkey, ass' (a special breed or age?), 4.14:6, 12, 18 (< Akk.; cf. AHw 1127: *šāgimu*; Sanmartín, AuOr 8 1990 97f.); ★d) *rʕy ḥmrm* donkey driver: (*nn*) *ṣmdm* (*nn*) *bnš yd ytm yd rʕy ḥmrm* (nn) pairs (of oxen), (nn) unskilled labourers with two foremen and the donkey driver, 4.618:3.

2) '(Donkey-)Load', measure of capacity; heap: ★a) 'load' (OAss measure of capacity; 1 anše = 10 bán = 100 sìla, *ca* 100 litres; cf. Akk. and Hb. *supra*; cf. Powell RlA 7 487f.), rarely in RS: *ḥmr* a 'load', 5.3:1-6 (cf. *izml*); ★b) as adv. accus. 'in heaps': *npš blt ḥmr* my appetite devours in heaps, 1.5 I 19 (Cassuto BOS 2 142; Dietrich - Loretz - Sanmartín UF 7 1975 538; Del Olmo MLC 548).

Bkn: 1.86:9; 4.426:2.

ḥmr (II) adj. m. "red, reddish" (cf. Hb. *ḥmr*, HAOT 330; Arab. *ḥmr*, Lane 640ff., *ʔaḥmaru* "sort of dates so called because of their colour", Lane 642; Pardee TH 61; Cohen-Sivan UHT 32; cf. Eth. *ḥamr*, CDG 234; cf. Akk. *emēru*, AHw 214; cf. *a/irġn*). ¶ Forms: sg. m. *ḥmr*.

Red, reddish (qualifying *a/irġn*): *št irġn ḥmr* a *š*. of reddish *i*., 1.85:17, 28; 1.72:23; cf. 1.71:15; *arġn ḥmr*, 1.97:4.

/ḥ-m-ṣ/ vb G: "to be(come) sour" > "to (be) spoil(t), to wither"(?) (cf. Hb. *ḥmṣ*, HALOT 329; Akk. *emēṣu*, AHw 214; CAD E 148f.; Arab. *ḥamuḍa*, Lane 644f.; Gk *ḥamḍa*, WTS 64. Cf. De Moor ARTU 248 n. 166; De Moor - Spronk CARTU 138; diff.: Margalit UF 16 1984 127f.: 'to rise up, be high, lofty', **ḥmṣ*). ¶ Forms: suffc. *ḥmṣ*.

G. To be(come) sour, wither: *b mth ḥmṣ ṣrr* for his death the young ear of corn withered, 1.19 I 17.

ḥmṣ n. m. "vinegar" (Hb. *ḥmṣ*, HALOT 329f.; DNWSI 382; cf. Aram. *ḥmʕ*, Jastrow 478; Ebla NINDA.AD$_6$ = *ʔà-me/i-zu(-um)*, Krebernik ZA 73 1983 42f.; Fronzaroli EL 136; StEb 7 1984 165f.; Akk. *emēṣu*, AHw 214; Arab. *ḥamuḍa*, Lane 644; cf. Eg. *ḥà-m-ṣa*, Helck Bez. 518 [169]; Sivan - Cochavi WSVES 83; Dijkstra - De Moor UF 7 1975 99). ¶ Forms: sg. *ḥmṣ*.

Vinegar: *kd yn l PN w kd ḥmṣ* a jar of wine for PN and one of vinegar, 4.269:27-28; *kdm ḥ*(!)*mṣ* two jars of vinegar, *ibid.* ln. 35; *w ḥmṣ w mlḥt* and vinegar and salt, 1.175:6.

ḥmt (I) n. f. "wall" (Hb. *ḥwmh*, HALOT 298; DNWSI 381; Ph., Moab. *ḥmt*, DNWSI 381; EA Akk.: *ḫu*(!)*-mi-tu*, EA 141:44; Sivan GAGl 223; DNWSI 381. Cf. Ginsberg JANES 5 1973 133f.); ¶ syll. Ug.:]*x : ḫa-mì-ti*, PRU 3 137f. (RS 16.86):4; Sivan GAGl 223; Huehnergard UVST 125; Van Soldt SAU 303; ¶ par.: *mgdl*, *ṯġr*.

¶ Forms: sg. *ḥmt*, pl. *ḥmyt* (cf. Ph. *ḥmyt*, DNWSI 381), suff. *ḥmytny*, *ḥmythm*.
Wall: *rkb ṯkmm ḥmt* mount the shoulders of the wall, 1.14 II 22 and par. (// *mgdl*); *gr ḥmyt ugrt* the guests of the walls of TN, 1.40:36 (*ḥmyt*) and par.; *k gr (...) qrd ḥmytkm* when (...) a powerful one (attacks) your walls, 1.119:27 and par. (// *ṯġrkm*); *ydy (...) qrd [l] ḥmytkm* he will repel (...) the powerful one from your walls, 1.119:36 and par.

ḥmt (II) n. f. “wineskin” (Hb. *ḥmt*, HALOT 331; Arab. *ḥamīt*, Hava 141; Akk. *ḫimtu*, AHw 346; CAD Ḫ 192; cf. Eth. *ḥmḥm* CDG 232). ¶ Forms: sg. suff. *ḥmthm*.
Wineskin: *kly yn b ḥmthm* the wine in their wineskins was finished, 1.16 III 15.

ḥmt (III) n. f. “venom” (Hb. *ḥmh*, HALOT 326; Akk. *imtu*, AHw 379; CAD I/J 192f.; Syr. *ḥemtō*, LS 242; Arab. *ḥum(m)a*, Hava 141; Eth. *ḥamot* CDG 235); ¶ **par.**: *abd*. ¶ Forms: sg. *ḥmt*.
Venom: *lnh ydy ḥmt* from it (: snake) expel venom, 1.100:6 and par. (// *abd*): *i*[*l w ḥ*]*rn yisp ḥmt* DNN remove the venom, 1.107:38 and par.; *isp (...) ḥmt l p nṯk* remove (...) venom from the mouth of the biter, 1.107:35 and par. Bkn ctx.: *l bn l pq ḥmt* [...]*xnh ḥmt*, 1.107:6-7; *tlu ḥ<m>t km nḫl* the venom remained drained like a torrent, 1.100:68 (cf. Del Olmo CR 368; diff.: Caquot TOu 2 92 n. 288: ‘la vie (re)devient forte’, rdg *ḥ<y>t*, and other interpretations).

ḥmṯ n. m. “belly” (Hb. *ḥmš*, HALOT 331; Akk. *emšu*, AHw 215; CAD E 153ff.; Syr. *ḥūmšō*, LS 242; Eth. *ḥĕmś*, CDG 234f. Cf. De Moor - Spronk UF 16 1984 240f.). ¶ Forms: sg. *ḥmṯ*.
Belly: *ḥmṯ ṯmṯ* belly that bleeds, 1.82:7. In bkn ctx.1.172:28.

ḥmyt, cf. *ḥmt (I)*.

ḥn, 1.123:15, cf. *ḥnbn*.

ḥnil PN (Sem. Cf. Grøndahl PTU 37f., 65, 96, 136; Watson AuOr 14 1996 98).
PN: 4.332:8.

ḥnbn DN (etym. unc.; cf. Astour JAOS 86 1966 283: ‘the Compassionate’, Arab. *ḥaniba*; cf. Xella TRU 221; Del Olmo RC 230 n. 34).
DN: *ḥnbn il dn*[DN, the god ..., 1.123:15 (possible alternative rdg: *ḥn bn il dn*[favour, divine...[!, and cf. /ḥ-n-n/; Hb. *ḥn*, HALOT 332; Ph., Aram. *ḥn*, DNWSI 386f.; Arab. *ḥanān*, Lane 653; Amor. /ḫinnum/, Huffmon APNMT 284, Gelb CAAA 20; Akk. *ennum*, AHw 219; CAD E 170; Eth. *ḥannā*, CDG 236. Cf. De Moor UF 2 1978 315;

Anbar NABU 1990/115).

/ḥ-n-n/ vb G/D(?): "to be / appear kind" (Hb. *ḥnn*, HALOT 334f.; Amor. */ḥ-n-n/*, Gelb CAAA 20; Akk. EA: *yi-iḫ-na-nu-ni*, EAT 137:81; *yi-in$_4$-né-nu-nu-mi*, EAT 253:24; cf. Sivan GAGl 224; Ph., Pun. *ḥnn*, DNWSI 389; Ebla cf. *ʔà-nu, en-na, in-na, in-* in PNN, Krebernik PET 74, 83f.; Müller Biling. 169; Catagnoti MisEb 1 258; Akk. *enēnu*, AHw 217; CAD E 162f.; cf. *utnēn(n)u*, AHw 1444; Arab. *ḥanna*, *tḥannana*, Lane 652ff. Cf. Watts UF 21 1989 444ff.). ¶ Forms: G/D prefc. with suff. *yḥnnn;* impv. *ḥnn*; suff. *ḥnny*.

G/D(?). To be / appear kind: *ḥnny l pn mlk* be kind to me before the king, 2.15:3. In unc. ctx. *ḥnn il* be kind(?), oh DN!, 1.65:6; in bkn ctx. *yḥnnn*, 1.10 I 12.

Cf. ḥn, ḥnil, ḥnbn, ḥnn, ḥnt, yḥnn.

ḥnn PN (Sem. Cf. Grøndahl PTU 21, 135f.; Sivan GAGl 223); ¶ syll.: (DUMU) *ḫa-na-(an-)nu*, PRU 3 144 (RS 16.138):7; 206 (RS 16.294):1; PRU 6 115:2. Cf. *ḫnn* PN.

PN: ★a) 4.75 IV 5 ([*bn*] *pls*); 4.214 III 9; 4.298:2; 4.729:3; ★b) *bn PN*, 3.8:22; 4.356:7; 4.422:46; 5.18:6.

ḥnt n. f. "kindness, favour" (cf. /ḥ-n-n/; cf. pl. tantum OAss *ennanātum* AHw 219; CAD E 169. Cf. Dijsktra - De Moor UF 7 1975 174; Dietrich - Loretz - Sanmartín UF 8 1976 433f.; Watts UF 21 1989 443s). ¶ Forms: sg. suff. *ḥnth*.

Kindness, favour: *yqrb bʕl b ḥnth* DN approached in his kindness, 1.17 I 16; *ḥnt il* the grace of DN, RSOu 14 53 [KTU 9.432]:39'.

ḥpn n. m. "greed, hoarding, rage" (cf. Arab. *ḥafana*, *iḥtafana* (*linapšihi*), Lane 604; diff.: Driver CML 139: 'impiety", Hb. *ḥwnp*, Arab., *ḥanafa*; Margalit UF 8 1986 161: 'cup-of-the-hand', Hb. *ḥpn*, etc.; but cf. Ug. *kp*; Renfroe AULS 49ff.: 'limit, term'(?), Arab. **ḥff*). ¶ Forms: sg. with suff. *ḥpnk*.

Greed: *b ḥpnk w tʕn* for your greed, be really humiliated!, 1.16 VI 58.

Cf. yḥpn.

ḥpr n. m. "ration, supply" (Akk. *ipru*, AHw 385; CAD I/J 166ff.). ¶ Forms: sg./pl. cstr. *ḥpr*, du. *ḥprm*.

Ration, supply: *spr ḥpr bt* record of the rations of the temple, 4.269:1; cf. *akl ḥpr bt* grain of the temple rations, 4.688:3; *spr ḥpr bnš mlk* record of rations of the 'king's men', 4.609:1; *ḥpr bnšm* rations of the '(king's) men', 4.243:2ff.; *akl (...) ḥpr ʕbdm* grain (... of the) rations of the servants, 4.636:3 and *passim ibid.*; *ḥpr bnšm* rations of the personnel, 4.242:23; *ḫzr lqḥ ḥpr* auxiliary personnel who have received the supply, 4.609:51; *mlk ṯn ḥprm* TN two rations, RSOu 14

36 [KTU 9.417]:1. In unc. ctx.: *ḥpr ʕdn dd akl* the ration of the gang is a 'cauldronful' of grain, 2.71:17.

ḥpšt n. f. "woman gathering (straw)" (part. act. G < /ḥ-p-š/; cf. Hb. *ḥpš*, HALOT 341; Arab. *ḥafaša*, Hava 132; diff.: Merlis AUL 70ff.: 'threshing woman', Akk. *ḫabāšu*); ¶ par.: *ḥṭbt*. ¶ Forms: pl. *ḥpšt*.
Woman gathering (straw): *sʕt (...) b grnt ḥpšt* swept (...) from the threshing floors those gathering (straw), 1.14 III 8 and par. (// *ṯṯbt*).

ḥqkpt (1.3 VI 13), cf. *ḥkpt*.

ḥqr TN (?) (Cf. Tropper - Vita UF 30 1998 691; Belmonte RGTC 12/2 106).
TN(?): in bkn ctx., ... *d*]*t yṯb b TN*(?) resident in TN(?), 4.557:1.

ḥr (I) n. m. "intestine(s)" (Akk. *erru, errū*, AHw 244; CAD I/J 181f.: *irrū*. Cf. Dietrich - Loretz MU 150f.; diff.: Pardee AfO 33 1986 143f.: 'vulva' (?), Arab. *ḥirr*). ¶ Forms: sg. *ḥr*, suff. *ḥrh*.
Intestine(s): *ḥrh b pith* (if) its intestines are in its temple, 1.103+:54; *ḥr w šr bh* (if) it has intestines and a navel (: in the space between its eyebrows), 1.103+:58. In bkn ctx.: *ḥr ḥr bnt*, 1.82:13; cf. ctx.*aṯt ḥr*[, 1.174:7.

ḥr (II) PN (etym. unc. Cf. Grøndahl PTU 65, 136). Cf. *ḫr (II)*, PN.
PN: ★a) 4.110:8; 4.139:5; 4.781:5; ★b) [*bn*] *PN*, 4.41:5.

ḥrb n. f. "knife; sword" (Hb., Aram. *ḥrb*, HALOT 349f.; DNWSI 403; Syr. *ḥarbō*, LS 254; cf. Arab. *ḥarb, ḥarbat*, Lane 540f.; Akk. *ḫarbu*, AHw 325; CAD Ḫ 97f.; cf. Eg. *ḥà-r-pu*, Helck Bez. 518 [172]. Cf. Couroyer RB 84 1977 71ff.; Healey UF 15 1983 49); ¶ par.: *ks, yd*. ¶ Forms: sg. *ḥrb*, suff. *ḥrbm* (encl. *-m*).
Knife, sword: ★a) *ḥrb b bšr tštn* they put the knife in the meat, 1.15 IV 25 and par. (// *yd*); *b ḥrb tbqʕnn* with a knife she split him, 1.6 II 31, cf. 1.6 V 13, haplography (cf. Del Olmo MLC 231); *tspi širh l bl ḥrb* it devours its flesh certainly without a knife, 1.96:4 (// *ks*); *ḥrb mlḥt* 'salted' knife, 1.3 I 7 and par. (cf. De Moor SP 70); ★b) *ḥrb lṭšt* sharpened sword, 1.2 I 32; *ḥrb tšt b tʕr*[*th*] the sword she put in its scabbard, 1.19 IV 45; *ṯm ḥrbm its* then with a sword I shall try (to attack him), 1.2 IV 4.

ḥrḥrt n. f. of a colour or dye "crimson red", by meton. probl. "flare-up"(?) (reduplicated form of /ḥ-r-r/, cf. Hb. *ḥrḥr*, HALOT 352, 357; Akk. *ḫurḫurātu*, AHw 359; CAD Ḫ 250f. Cf. Rin AE 43; diff.: Caquot TOu 1 123 n. j: 'brandons'(?), Hb. *ḥārā*); ¶ syll. Ug.: cf. NUMUN *ḫur-ḫu-ra-ti*, PRU 6 8:7(!?), 9; Sivan GAGl 225; Huehnergard UVST 126; cf. Van Soldt BiOr 47 1990 733; UF 22 1990 346f.; ¶ par.: *išt*. ¶ Forms: sg. suff. (encl. *-m* [?]) / du. *ḥrḥrtm*.

Flare-up(?): in bkn ctx., *ḥrḥrtm w dx*[*x*]*n* (a pair of(?)) flare-up(s)(?) ..., 1.2 III 13 (// *išt*).

/ḥ-r-k/ vb G: "to burn, grill" (Hb. *ḥrk*, HALOT 353; cf. Arab. *ḥaraqa*, *ʔaḥraqa*, Lane 551f. Cf. Aartun UF 16 1984 21). ¶ Forms: G prefc. with suffix *yḥrkn*.

G. To burn, grill: bkn ctx., *y*]*ḥrkn w yšḥmm* he shall burn and roast it, 1.175:7.

ḥrkn PN (Sem. Cf. Sivan GAGl 224); ¶ syll.: cf. DUMU *ḫa-ra-ka₄-na*, PRU 3 200 (RS 16.257) II 5.

PN: cf. in bkn ctx., *b*[*n*] *ḥrk*[*n*, 4.315:3.

ḥrm PN (Sem. Cf. Grøndahl PTU 136; Astour CRRA 18 14; Van Soldt SAU 32 n. 259); ¶ syll.: cf. DUMU *ḫa-ra-mì*, PRU 3 187 (RS 15.43):4; Sivan GAGl 224.

PN: ★a) 4.75:1 (*bn ngxn*); 4.775:14; ★b) *bn PN*, 4.69 I 9.

ḥrn DN, chthonian deity (Hb. *ḥwrwn*, HALOT 126f., 299f. Cf. Pope - Röllig WbMyth 1 288f.; Stadelmann Gottheiten 76ff.; Cooper RSP 3 365ff.; Caquot AAAS 29/30 1979/80 173ff.; Tsevat UF 11 1979 770f.; Bordreuil - Caquot Syria 57 1980 348; Xella WO 19 1988 55ff.; Kottsieper UF 16 1984 108f.; Pardee TPM 213ff.; Del Olmo RC 248f.).

DN: 1.16 VI 55; 1.100:61, 67; *ʕrb ḥrn bth* DN entered his house, RSOu 14 53 [KTU 9.432]:33'; cf. *ʕbd ḥrn* servants of DN, 1.82:41; *bt ḥrn* temple of DN, 1.124:6 *il w ḥrn* DN and DN, 1.107:38;take (this) request *ʕm ḥrn mṣdh* to DN, to TN, 1.100:58; *ḥrn ḥbrm* (may) DN cast out (his) associates, 1.169:9 (// *ġlm*). Cf. in bkn ctx.: 1.82:27; 1.107:29, 31; 1.176:20.

ḥrnq n. m. "orchard" (?) (cf. Akk. *urnuqqu*, AHw 1432. Cf. Herrman YN 14; Astour Fs Gordon 1980 2; diff.: Aartun StUL 58f.: 'Zisterne', Arab. *ḫirniq*); ¶ par.: *krm*. ¶ Forms: pl.(?) *ḥrnqm*.

Orchard(?): *atn (...) šd ddh ḥrnq*[*m*] I shall give her (...) as a field of his beloved an orchard (or: I shall turn ...the field of her love into an orchard), 1.24:23 (// *krm*).

/ḥ-r-r/ vb G: "to dry up, shrivel, burn up, catch fire"; D/(G?) "to burn, roast" (Hb. *ḥrr*, HALOT 357; Ebla /ḥal/ʔālum/ en ŠÀ.ḪUL = *ʔà-la/a-lum*, VE 590; Krebernik ZA 73 1983 23; Akk. *erēru*, AHw 238; CAD Ḫ 280; Arab. *ḥarra*, Lane 538ff. Cf. De Moor SP 179; SEL 5 1988 67 n. 39; Collini SEL 4 1987 39); ¶ par.: /ṣ-ḥ-r-r/, /š-ḫ-n/. ¶ Forms: G suffc. *ḥrr* (?); prefc. *yḥrr*, ptc. *ḥrr* (?); D/(G?) prefc. *tḥrr*.

G. To dry up, shrivel, burn up, catch fire: *b ph yrd k ḥrr zt* it will fall into his mouth when the olive tree shrivels, 1.5 II 5. In bkn ctx.,

anpnm yḥr[*r* their muzzles(?) became hot, 1.12 II 37 (// *yšḫn*); *hw km ḥrr* he (remained) like who burns (with fever), 1.12 II 40.
D/(G?). To burn, roast: *h*[*l*] *ʕṣr tḥrr l išt* look, you have roasted a bird on the fire, 1.23:41 (// *ṣḥrrt*).
Cf. ḥry, ḥrr, ḥrt(n).

ḥrr (I) PN (Sem. Cf. Grøndahl PTU 136).
PN: 4.214:11.

ḥrr (II) element in composite TN *mʕr ḥrr* ('the Northern *m.*'; cf. Van Soldt UBL 11 365 n. 9 (2), 381; UF 28 1996 677; UF 31 1999 771; Belmonte RGTC 12/2 195); ¶ syll.: URU *mu-a-ri* ḪU-*ra-ri*, RS 25.132 III 16 (Van Soldt UF 21 1989 380 n. 30).
Element in composite TN: *mʕr ḥr*(!)[*r*], 4.365:33.
Cf. mʕr.

/ḥ-r-ṣ/ vb G: "to cut, bite" ((?); cf. Arab. *ḥaraṣa*, Lane 547f.; Akk. *ḫarāṣu*, AHw 323f.; CAD Ḫ 92ff.; cf. Taanak Akk. /ḥarīṣ-/ in PNN, Sivan GAGl 223f.; for this and other interpretations cf. Del Olmo IMC 129, 159, 209); ¶ syll. Ug.: cf. A.ŠÀ.MEŠ : *ḫa-ar-ṣa-ti*, PRU 3 95f. (RS 16.246):11, 20, Kühne UF 6 1974 165f., Sivan GAGl 223, Huehnergard UVST 190, and cf. *ḥrṣ (I)*. ¶ Forms: G suffc. *ḥrṣ*; inf.(?) *ḥrṣ*.
G. To cut, bite(?): *k ḥrṣ abn ph* biting(?), yes, with her teeth (?), 1.19 I 8; *ḥrṣ klb ilnm* the divine puppy bit(?), *ibid.* ln. 10.
Cf. ḥrṣ (I).

ḥrṣ (I) n. m. "item, exact portion" (< /ḥ-r-ṣ/; cf. Akk. *ḫarṣu*, AHw 328; *ḫariṣ*, *ḫarīṣu*, CAD Ḫ 102f. Cf. for the various interpretations Del Olmo IMC 195 n. 517, 208f.; also Merlis AUL 77ff.: 'mace, club', Akk. *ḫilṣu*; Good UF 16 1984 77ff.: 'threshing sledge', Hb. *ḥārûṣ*). ¶ Forms: sg. *ḥrṣ*.
Item, exact portion (in the adv. construction *w ḥrṣ* as a single item, in one lot, in contrast to *aḥd(m)* separate items): ★a) together with *ṣmd* par: *ṣmdm w ḥrṣ* two pairs (of horses(?)) as one item, 4.384:11 (cf. *aḥd(m)* separate item(s), ln. 12ff.); *ṣmd w ḥrṣ* one pair as one item. 4.368:2 and *passim. ibid.*; 4.377:5, 6; *ḫmš ṣmdm w ḥrṣ* five pairs (of horses) in one lot, 4.169:4; *arbʕ ṣmdm apnt w ḥrṣ* four pairs of wheels as one lot, *ibid.* ln. 8; cf. *ṯlṯ ṣmdm w ḥrṣ apnt* three pairs of wheels as one lot, 4.145:8; ★b) in other constructions: *ṯṯ mrkbt w ḥrṣ yd trhm* a lot of six chariot bodies with their steering poles, 4.363:9. In bkn ctx.: 4.323:2; 4.577:2, 3.

ḥrṣ (II) n. m. "milk of lime" (Arab. *ḥurḍu*, Lane 548; Ginsberg BASOR 98 1941 23; Renfroe AULS 118ff.; diff.: Goetze JCS 1 1947

314f.: 'fine oil', Akk. *ḫarṣu*; Merlis AUL 7ff.: 'whiteness', Arab. *ḥurḍu*, Akk. *ḫarṣu*; Dietrich - Loretz UF 11 1979 194ff.: 'Beigaben', /ḥ-r-ṣ/; Caquot - Sznycer TOu 1 433: 'corruption', Arab. *ḥaraḍu*; Dijkstra - De Moor UF 7 1975 190: 'gold', *ḫrṣ*; Watson UF 22 1990 423: 'a mineral', Akk. *(ḫ)urīzu*; for the various interpretations cf. Sasson RSP 1 414; Del Olmo IMC 195, 209); ¶ par.: *spsg*. ¶ Forms: sg. *ḥrṣ*.

Milk of lime: *ysk (...) ḥrṣ l qdqdy* one shall pour (...) milk of lime upon my skull, 1.17 VI 37 (// *spsg*).

/ḥ-r-š/ vb Gt: "to make spells or incantations" (cf. *ḥrš (II)*; Eth. *ḥarasa*, CDG 243). ¶ Forms: Gt *iḥtrš*.

Gt. To make spells or incantations: *ank iḥtrš w aškn* I myself shall make an incantation and shall prepare, 1.16 V 26.

Cf. ḥrš (II).

ḥrš (I) n. m. 1) "craftsman, manual worker"; 2) "artisan, builder, armourer, fitter" (< /ḥ-r-š/; Hb., Ph., Pun. *ḥrš*, HALOT 358; DNWSI 408; cf. Akk. *eršu* "wise", AHw 246; CAD E 313ff. Cf. Loewenstamm AOAT 204 1980 78ff.; Dietrich - Loretz UF 31 1999 165ff.); ¶ syll. Ug.: ...] = *i-ṯ[i]n-ni* = *ḫa-ra-šu*, UF 11 1979 479 (RS 20.189):7; Huehnergard UVST 126; Van Soldt BiOr 47 1990 734; SAU 303; cf. *ḫ]a-ra-š[u*, Ug 5 137 III 18' and cf. Sivan GAGl 225: < /ḥ-r-ṯ/; Huehnergard JAOS 107 1987 723: /ḫar(r)ašu/ 'deaf'; cf. Van Soldt SAU 303 (RS 20.123 II 18?); ¶ RS Akk.: cf. LÚ(.MEŠ).DÍM É(.MEŠ), PRU 6 93:11; 131:1; LÚ.TIBIRA.GÍD, PRU 6 93:12; LÚ.NAGAR GIŠ.GIGIR, PRU 6 93:13. ¶ Forms: sg. *ḥrš*; pl. *ḥršm*, cstr. *ḥrš*, with suff. *ḥršy*; du. *ḥršm*.

1) Craftsman, manual worker: ★a) PN *ḥrš* craftsman, 4.103:3, 58; 4.321:1; *ṯlṯ l ḥr[šm* three (of wine) for the wor[kers ..., 4.216:2; *ṯlṯ šʕrt l ḥršm* three of wool for the workers, 4.705:2; *ṯn ḥršm* two workers, 4.141 III 12, 14; cf. in bkn ctx.4.207:3; 4.618:11, 12; *ḥrš dt tbʕln b TN* workers who are working in TN, 4.141 III 5, 7; *ank ḥrš lqḥt w ḥwt hbt* I, the craftsman, have accepted and carried out the task(?), 2.70:14 (Dietrich - Loretz UF 16 1984 66ff.; Verreet UF 18 1986 384); *ḥrš b TN* a craftsman in TN, "UF 29, 826":3 (cf. Lemaire UF 30 1998 461ff.); ★b) *rb ḥršm* head of the workshop, 4.145:9 (cf. *infra*: *ḥrš mrkbt*); *spr ḥršm* list of workmen, 4.155:1; 4.207:1. 4.215:1, cf. *infra*: *ḥrš qšt*; *bt ḥrš* workshop, forge, 1.12 II 61 (// *bt il*; diff.: Gray UF 3 1971 67 n. 54: 'house of confinement', Akk. *ḫarištu*, Arab. *ḫurš*; De Moor ARTU 134: 'the house of magic', cf. *ḫrš (II)*); ★c) in divine titles: *hyn d ḥrš yd(m) DN*, the ambidextrous craftsman, 1.3 VI 23 and

par. (Lipiński UF 20 1988 138); *kṯr ḥrš* DN the craftsman, 1.92:17. 2) Artisan, builder, armourer; ★a) artisan: *ḥrš* artisan, 4.610:19; *bn ḥrš* artisan, 4.545 II 6; *ḥrš qṭn* of trinkets, hardware((?); (cf. *qṭn*; cf. RS Akk.: LÚ.TIBIRA.GÍD, PRU 6 93:12; cf. Rainey IOS 3 1973 44f.), 4.47:9 (see *infra*); 4.98:9; 4.183 II 6; 4.370:35; 4.609:23; 4.630:12; 4.742:12; 4.745:8; ★b) boat-builder, shipwright: *ḥrš anyt* caulkers, 4.125:1; of buildings (cf. RS Akk.: LÚ(.MEŠ).DÍM É(.MEŠ), PRU 6 93:11; 131:1): *ḥrš b(h)tm* bricklayer(s) (cf. RS Akk.: LÚ(.MEŠ).DÍM É(.MEŠ), PRU 6 93:11): 4.35 I 16; 4.38:6; 4.47:10; 4.183 I 1; 4.370:14; 4.609:18; 4.630:8; of vehicles: *ḥrš mrkbt* cartwright(s) (cf. RS Akk.: LÚ.NAGAR GIŠ.GIGIR, PRU 6 93:13): 4.47:9 (see *supra*) 4.547:1; 4.98:6, 8; 4.141 III 20; 4.183 II 12; 4. 339:16; 5.547:1; 4.609:28; 4. 745:9; *ḥrš ʕrq* cartwright, 4.46:13-14; 4.243:2 (Dietrich - Loretz - Sanmartín UF 5 1973 107); ★c) master armourer, assembler: *ḥrš arkd* assembler of *a.*, 4.277:9; *ḥrš qšt* bow assemblers, 4.215:1 (Sanmartín UF 20 1988 266f. n. 7). Bkn: *ḥbq l ḥršm*, 4.201:6; *w ḥršy* and my craftsmen, RSOu 14 49 [KTU 9.433]:20.

Cf. ḥrš (III).

ḥrš (II) n. m. "magic spell" (cf. /ḥ-r-š/; Hb. *ḥrš*, HALOT 358; JAram. *ḥrš*, DJPA 216; Syr. *ḥe/aršē*, LS 259; Eth. *ḥaras* CDG 243). ¶ Forms: pl. *ḥršm*.

Spell: *št ḥršm l ahlm* she put spells in the tents, 1.19 IV 60.

ḥrš (III) PN (Sem. Cf. Grøndahl PTU 28, 136).

PN: *bn PN*, 4.214 II 15.

ḥrt(n) PN (etym. unc.).

PN: ★a) 4.371:14; ★b) *bn PN*, 4.658:21 (*ḥrtn*); 4.711:4.

/ḥ-r-ṯ/ vb G: "to plough, till, farm the land" (Hb. *ḥrš*, HALOT 357; Aram., Palm. *ḥrt*, DNWSI 407; Syr. *ḥrat*, LS 260; Arab. *ḥaraṯa*, Lane 541f.; Akk. *erēšu*, AHw 238f.; CAD E 285ff.; Eth. *ḥarasa*, CDG 243; cf. Akk. EA /ḫarāšu/, *aḫ-ri-šu*, EAT 365:11; Rainey UF 3 1971 165; Sivan GAGl 225; DNWSI 407; Ebla cf. AN.EDIN.AKA = *ti-ir-iš-du-um*, *da-ir-iš-du-um*, *te-rí-iš-du*, VE 790; Lambert Biling. 397; /L-S/, Krebernik PET 52. Cf. Loewenstamm JJS 10 1959 63ff.; Dietrich - Loretz UF 18 1986 109); ¶ syll. Ug.: *ḫ*]*a-ra-š*[*u*, Ug 5 137 III 18'; cf. Sivan GAGl 225: /ḥ-r-ṯ/, but cf. Huehnergard JAOS 107 1987 723; UVST 126: *ḫar(r)ašu* 'deaf'; Van Soldt SAU 303: RS 20.123 II 18?; ¶ par.: /ṯ-l-ṯ/. ¶ Forms: G prefc. *tḥrṯ*, *yḥrṯ*; ptc. act. sg. m. *ḥrṯ*; pl. m. *ḥrṯm*.

G. To plough, till, farm the land: *yḥrṯ k gn ap lb* he ploughed his chest like an orchard, 1.5 VI 20 and par. (// *yṯlṯ*); *ṯl*(!) *mrṯ yḥrṯ il* dew of must that DN had grown, 1.22 I 20 (diff.: Aartun 16 1984 21f.: 'Ackerland'); *alp ḥrṯ* work ox, 1.14 III 18 and par.; *alpm ḥrṯm* work oxen, 2.45:22.

Cf. ḥrṯ, mḥrṯt.

ḥrṯ n. m. "ploughman, farmhand, cowherd" (< /ḥ-r-ṯ/; Hb. cf. *ḥrš*, HALOT 358; Akk. *errēšu*, AHw 243; CAD E 304ff.; Arab. *ḥarrāṯ*, *ḥāriṯ*, Lane 542; Eth. *ḥarāsi*, CDG 243); ¶ par.: /ʕ-d-b/ (+ *dgn*). ¶ Forms: sg. *ḥrṯ*, suff. *ḥrṯh*; pl. *ḥrṯm*.

Ploughman, farmhand, cowherd: 4.65:1; 4.609:27; *šbʕ b ḥrṯm* seven (farmhands go) with the ploughmen, 4.141 III 1; (rations) *l ḥrṯm* for the ploughmen, 4.175:10; *ṯṯ ḥrṯm lqḥ šʕrt* six ploughmen receive (rations of) wool, 4.630:6; *nšu riš ḥrṯm* the farmhands raised their heads (// *ʕdb dgn*), 1.16 III 12; cowherd, who ploughs with oxen: *alp PN dt aḫd ḥrṯh* oxen of PN which his cowherd has collected, 4.296:9; cf. (...) *d aḫd ḥrṯ* (...) which his cowherd has collected, ln. 15, 17. In toponyms: *gt ḥrṯm* 'Farmstead of the Labourers', 4.141 III 11; 4.618:21; 4.625:17 (cf. Astour RSP 2 276f.; Belmonte RGTC 12/2 86: **Gittu-ḥarrāṯīma*).

ḥry PN (etym. unc.; cf. Arab. *ḥurrat*, *ḥurriyyat*, Lane 538f. Cf. Grøndahl PTU 56, 136; Sasson UF 6 1974 361; De Moor - Spronk UF 14 1982 168; Watson AuOr 13 1995 222).

PN: ★a) name of king *krt*'s wife, *passim* in 1.14.-1.16.; ★b) *bn PN*: 4.281:14.

ḥryt TN, residence of the god(s) *ẓẓ w kmṯ* (etym. unc.; cf. Astour JNES 28 1967; Caquot Syria 46 1969 246; Dietrich -Loretz UF 12 1980 161; Pardee TPM 212 n. 64; diff.: De Moor ARTU 150: rdg *qryth*). ¶ Forms: sg. suff. *ḥryth* (adv. *-h*).

Mythical TN: *ql bl ʕm ẓẓ w kmṯ ḥryth* take (this) request to DN, at TN, 1.100:36.

ḥrẓn PN (etym. unc. Cf. Ginsberg JAOS 70 1950 160; Grøndahl PTU 20, 23, 136, 140; Lipiński OLA 23 1988 129 n. 26; Watson AuOr 8 1990 119, 245); ¶ syll.: cf. DUMU *ḫa-ra-*ZI*-na*, Syria 18 1937 246 (RS 8.145):11; *ḫa-ru-*ZI*-en-ni*, Syria 15 1934 137 (RS [Varia 3]):11, 22; cf. *ḫu-ra-ṣa-na*, PRU 3 102 (RS 15.109):13; 118 (RS 15.155):13; PRU 6 83 III 5; cf. Sivan GAGl 224, 228. Cf. *ḫrṣn* PN.

PN: *bn PN*, 4.63 II 23; 4.69 V 10; 4.93 I 5, 8; 4.422:39; 4.711:3; 4.759:1. Bkn 4.260:3.

ḥsk adj. m. "awarded, assigned" (cf. Akk. *esēku*, AHw 248; cf. CAD E 327ff.: *esēḫu*). ¶ Forms: sg. *ḥsk*.

Awarded, assigned (of wine): *yn l mrynm ḥsk klh* wine for the *m.*: assigned in its entirely, 4.230:1.

/ḥ-s-l/ vb G: "to wipe out, destroy"; N: "to be destroyed" (Hb. *ḥsl*, HALOT 338; EA Akk.: *ḫa-sí-lu*, EA 263:13; cf. Sivan GAGl 225. Cf. Held AS 16 398ff.; Dietrich - Loretz - Sanmartín UF 7 1975 138; Pardee AfO 33 1986 137f.; Fs. Fitzmyer 87ff.; diff. Rainey UF 27 1995 706:D). ¶ **Forms**: G prefc. suff. *yḥslnn*; N prefc. *yḥsl*.

G. To wipe out, destroy: *mlkn yšdd ḥwt ibh w yḥslnn* the king will devastate the land of his enemy and destroy it, 1.103+:38 and par.

N. To be destroyed: *drʕ ḥwt hyt yḥsl* the seed of that land will be destroyed, 1.103+:55 and par. ln. 14.

ḥsm "?" (Cf. Bordreuil - Caquot Syria 57 1980 351).

? : in bkn ctx.: *ḥsm*, 1.176:15.

ḥsn n. m. "grasshoppers, locusts" (Hb. *ḥsyl*, HALOT 337f.); ¶ **syll.**: cf. the element /ḥasīlu/ in PNN; Sivan GAGl 223; ¶ **par.**: *irby*. ¶ **Forms**: sg. *ḥsn*.

Grasshoppers, locusts: *km ḥsn pat mdbr* like grasshoppers on the desert fringes, 1.14 I 1 and par. (// *irby*).

/ḥ-s-p/ vb G: "to draw, collect water" (Hb. *ḥśp*, HALOT 359f.; Arab. *saḥafa*, Lane 1318. Cf. De Moor SP 97; Gray UF 11 1979 320). ¶ **Forms**: G prefc. with suffix *tḥspn*; act. part. f. cf. *ḥspt*.

G. To draw, collect water: *tḥspn mh w trḥṣ* they drew water for her and washed (her), 1.3 II 38 and par.

Cf. **ḥsp, ḥspt**.

ḥsp adj. m. "decanted, drained, without sediment" (< pass. ptc. /ḥ-s-p/; cf. Emar /ḫaspu/ Pentiuc Vocabulary 58; see Xella TRU 343f.; Aartun UF 16 1984 21; De Moor NYCI 2 28 n. 117). ¶ **Forms**: sg. *ḥsp*.

Decanted, drained, without sediment (said of quality wine; often differentiated from *yn mṣb*): *yn ḥsp d nkly b dbḥ* decanted wine that has been used up during the sacrifice, 4.213:24; cf. *yn ḥsp l m*[*lk*(?) decanted wine for the k[ing(?), *ibid.* ln. 25; cf. *l yb*(?)[, ln. 26; *yn ḥsp l ql d tbʕ mṣr*(?)*m* decanted wine for the courier who left for Egypt, *ibid.* ln. 27; *tgmr yn mṣb (nn) w ḥsp (nn)* total of the cellar wine: (nn), and of decanted (wine): (nn), 1.91:36; with ellipsis of *yn*: *bir ʕšr mṣ*[*b w k*]*dm ḥsp* TN ten of cellar (wine) and two jars of decanted (wine), 1.91:29.

Cf. **/ḥ-s-p/**.

ḥspt n. f. "she who collects" (act. part. G < /ḥ-s-p/; cf. Dietrich - Loretz UF 17 1985 95ff.); ¶ **par.**: *ṯkmt*. ¶ **Forms**: sg. *ḥspt*.

She who collects: *ḥspt l šʕr ṭl* she who collects dew from the fleece,

1.19 II 2 and par. (// *ṯkmt*).
Cf. /ḫ-s-p/.

/ḥ-ṣ/(?) "?" vb (Bordreuil - Pardee RSOu 14 p. 400).
? : *b lḥmy yḥṣ* in my food he ..., RSOu 14 53 [KTU 9.432]:13'.

ḥṣ n. m. "gravel" (Hb. *ḥṣṣ*, HALOT 345; Akk. *ḫiṣṣu*, AHw 349; CAD Ḫ 204; Syr. *ḥṣoṣō*, LS 250f.; Arab. *ḥaṣān*, Lane 587; Eth. *ḥoṣā*, CDG 266f. Cf. De Moor SP 118); ¶ **par.**: *mll*. ¶ **Forms**: sg. *ḥṣ*.
Gravel: bkn ctx., *k ḥṣ tusp*[like gravel [that (?)] collects [in it], 1.1 IV 11 (// *mll*; cf. Del Olmo IMC 43; diff.: Caquot - Sznycer TOu 1 308 n. k: 'javelle', **ḥṣṣ/y*); *k ḥṣ k mʕk (...)* like gravel, like crumbs (...), 1.16 IV 5 (De Moor ARTU 218).

***/ḥ-ṣ-b/**
Cf. **ḥṣb**, **ḥṣbn**.

ḥṣb PN (etym. unc. Cf. Grøndahl PTU 137).
PN: in the composite toponym *gt ḥṣb*, 4.409:7 (<(?) */ḥ-ṣ-b/; Belmonte RGTC 12/2 86f.: **Gittu-ḥaṣṣabi*).
Cf. **ḥṣbn**.

ḥṣbn PN (etym. unc. Cf. Grøndahl PTU 21, 137; Watson AuOr 14 1996 98).
PN: *bn PN*, 4.33:14 (*ary*).

ḥṣn PN (Sem. Cf. Grøndahl PTU 137; Sivan GAGl 225; Huehnergard UVST 242); ¶ **syll.**: (DUMU) *ḫu-ṣa-nu*, PRU 3 79 (RS 16.239):4; 102 (RS 15.138+):25; cf. Sivan GAGl 225; Huehnergard UVST 242, 252 n. 165. Cf. *ḫsn (II)*, *ḫzn*, PNN.
PN: *bn PN*, 4.63 III 11; 4.232:19.

ḥṣqt(n) PN (Sem. Cf. Grøndahl PTU 23, 137); ¶ **syll.**: cf. *ḫa-ṣí-qá/qa-ta-nu*, PRU 3 142 (RS 16.134):5, 9; cf. Sivan GAGl 225; Huehnergard UVST 220, 240. In 4.692:9 probl. a var. with *-n*.
PN: *bn PN*, 4.428:7; 4.692:9.

/ḥ-š/ (I) vb G: "to hurry, make haste" (Hb. *ḥwš*, HALOT 300; Akk. *ḫâšu*, *ḫiāšu*, AHw 343; CAD Ḫ 146; Arab. *ḥaṯṯa*, Lane 511f.; Eth. *ḥosa*, CDG 250. Cf. De Moor SP 128; Grelot JSS 1 1956 202ff.); ¶ **syll.** Ug.: cf. PN *ia*-TAR-*ši*, PRU 3 160 (RS 16.282):6ff.; cf. Sivan GAGl 225: *ia-ḫuš$_x$-ši*, but cf. Huehnergard AkkUg 354 n. 4. ¶ **Forms**: G prefc. *aḥš*; impr. / inf. *ḥš* (adv. "quickly"; cf. Hb. *ḥw/yšh*).
G. To hurry, make haste: *d l ylkn ḥš* who cannot go quickly, 1.1 IV 7 (cf. 1.1 III 27); *ḥš rmm hk*[*lm*] quickly erect the palace, 1.4 V 52 and par.; *mndʕ ank aḥš mġy* perhaps I will hurry to come, 2.34:11.

/ḥ-š/ (II) vb G: "to feel" (cf. Hb. *ḥwš* 288; Akk. *ḫâšu*, AHw 334f.; CAD Ḫ 146f.; Arab. *ḥassa*, Lane 563f. Cf. Caquot SEL 5 1988 33;

Del Olmo CR 374). ¶ Forms: G prefc. *aḥš*.
G. To feel: [*i*]*dy alt l aḥš* already I do feel the curse!, 1.82:2 (diff.: De Moor UF 11 1979 650: 'to hasten', cf. *ḥwš I*).
Cf. /ḫ-š/.

ḥšbn PN (Sem. Cf. Grøndahl PTU 137; Sivan GAGl 225).
PN: *bn PN*, 4.309:7.

/ḥ-š-k/ vb G: "to seize, grasp" (cf. Hb. *ḥśk*, HALOT 359; Arab. *ḥašaka*, Lane 576; diff.: Cassuto GA 126: 'to spare', Hb. *ḥšk*, Pr 13:24; De Moor SP 106; ARTU 9: 'hurry up!', rdg *ḥš-k*; cf. Watson UF 9 1977 274). ¶ Forms: G imper. *ḥšk*.
G. To seize, grasp: *ḥšk ʕṣk ʕbṣk* grasp your staff (and) your mace, 1.3 III 18 and par.

ḥšn n. m. "?" (Cf. De Moor ARTU 74 n. 345: 'bliss', Arab. *ḥasanah*).
? : in bkn ctx., *ṭbt ḥš*[*n* ...]*y arṣ ḥšn*[, 1.5 III 3-4.

ḥt "?"
? : *ḥt l PN* ... for PN, 4.396:17. Cf. bkn.: 4.247:11 (?); 7.222:6 (?).

/ḥ-t-k/ vb G: "to subdue, control; exercise power" (cf. Hb. *ḥtk*, HALOT 364. Cf. De Moor SP 241; for the semantic development and differentiation cf. Rin AE 235; Falk JSS 14 1969 39ff.; Van Zijl Baal 252; Cross CMHE 14 n. 19; De Moor UF 1 1969 179; Healey UF 12 1980 408f.: 'care for', Akk. *etēku*; Dietrich - Loretz UF 12 1980 178); ¶ syll. Ug.: cf. Sivan GAGl 225: /ḥ-t-k/. ¶ Forms: G prefc. *tḥtk*.
G. To subdue: *špš rpim tḥtk špš tḥtk ilnym* DN (: *špš*) you subdue DN (: *rpim*), DN you subdue the divine beings, 1.6 VI 46-47 (diff.: De Moor SP 241: 'you are ruling'; Caquot - Sznycer TOu 1 270 n. i: 'en-dessous de toi', rdg *tḥt + k*; Husser UF 29 1997 235: 'fait descendre vers toi', Ug. /n-ḥ-t/).

ḥtk (I) n. m. "progenitor, father" (< (?) act. ptc. /ḥ-t-k/; cf. Ginsberg LKK 33); ¶ par.: *ab*. ¶ Forms: sg. suff. *ḥtkk*.
Progenitor: *hwt ltpn ḥtkk* word of the benevolent one, your progenitor, 1.6 IV 11 and par. (// *abk*). In bkn ctx.: *ḥt*[*kk*, 1.16 II 15.

ḥtk (II) n. m. "lineage, offspring" (< (?) pass. ptc. /ḥ-t-k/; cf. Van Selms MFL 94 n. 10); ¶ par.: *mknt, ṭbt*. ¶ Forms: sg. *ḥtk*, suff. *ḥtkh, ḥtkn*.
Lineage, offspring: *w bšr ḥtk dgn* do receive the good news, offspring of DN, 1.10 III 34 (// [*b*]*ʕl*; for the par. cf. ln. 11, 14; diff.: Wyatt UF 24 1992 415f.: 'Ruler of the Rain'); *krt ḥtkn rš* PN was left with his lineage ruined, 1.14 I 10 and par. (// *mknt*; diff.: De Moor SP 241: 'exerted the *patria potestas*', cf. /ḥ-t-k/; Dietrich - Loretz Fs. Elliger 32f.: 'Herrschaftsbereich', cf. *ḥtk (III)*; Verreet UF 19 1991 320, 335:

lexema *ḥtkn* 'Ahnenschaft'). Bkn ctx.: *l ḥtk*[, 1.81:9 (in a god list).

ḥtk (III) n. m. "sovereignty, power" (< /ḥ-t-k/; cf. Dietrich - Loretz UF 12 1980 178f.). ¶ Forms: sg. suff. *ḥtkk, ḥtkh*.
Sovereignty, power: *l rpi arṣ (...) ḥtkk*, of 'r. of the earth' (...) be your power, 1.108:23 and par. (in the series *ʕz, ḏmr, lan, nmrt*).

ḥtl n. m. "nappy" (Hb. *ḥtwl*, HALOT 364; cf. OAss. *ḫatlunum*, AHw 336; CAD Ḫ 150. Cf. Kapelrud Ug 6 322; Ribichini - Xella Tessili 37). ¶ Forms: pl. suff. *ḥtlk*.
Nappy: *qḥ ksank ḥdgk ḥtlk* take your stool, your birthing chair(?), your nappies, 1.12 I 19.

ḥtn "?" (*ḥt + n*?).
? : in bkn ctx.:]*ḥtn qn yṣbt*, 1.17 VI 9.

ḥtp n. m.; a type of sacrifice (cf. Akk. *ḫitpu*, AHw 349; CAD Ḫ 207; cf. Eg. *ḥtp*, WÄS 3 184ff.; Aram. *ḥtpy*, DNWSI 414f.; Arab. *ḥatf*, Lane 510. Cf. Spaliger JSSEA 8 1978 55, 59; Xella RSF 6 1978 135f.; Boyd UF 17 1985 64 n. 24; Hallo FS Levine 43-50; diff.: Rinaldi BiOr 22 1980 62: 'Räuber' > 'Beute, Opfer'); ¶ par.: *ʕšrt*, *mḏr*. ¶ Forms: sg. *ḥtp*.
A type of sacrifice: *ḥtp bʕ*[*l n*]*mlu* a *ḥ*.(-sacrifice), DN, shall we fulfil, 1.119:32 (// *mḏr*, *ʕšrt*).

ḥtt n. m.; a type of illness ("ringworm"(?) < Arab. *ḥatat*, *ḥutāt*, Lane 509; cf. De Moor - Spronk UF 16 1984 244f.; Del Olmo CR 377; diff.: Caquot TOu 2 68 n. 199: 'terreur', Hb. *ḥat(t)*, Akk. *ḫattu*, but cf. *ḫtt*). ¶ Forms: sg. *ḥtt*.
An illness (ringworm(?)): *bn ḥtt* the 'one with ringworm'(?), 1.82:23.

ḥtṯ n. m. "silver" (cf. Hattic */ḫat=/; cf. (KUR.)URU KÙ.BABBAR-*ti(-)* / (KUR.)URU *Ḫa-at-ti(-)*, URU KÙ.BABBAR-*ša(-)* / URU *Ḫa-at-tu-ša(-)*, cf. HW 67; Friedrich ZDMG 221 1942 490ff.; Tischler HEG 211ff.; cf. Watson UF 28 1996 704); ¶ par.: *ḫrṣ*. ¶ Forms: sg. *ḥtṯ*.
Silver: *yṣq b gl ḥtṯ yn* he poured wine into a silver cup, 1.14 IV 1 and par. (// *ḫrṣ*).
Cf. ḥtṯn.

ḥtṯn PN (etym. unc. Cf. Dietrich - Loretz WO 4 1967/68 304; Grøndahl PTU 30, 137; cf. Kienast UF 11 1979 450). Cf. *ḥdṯn*.
PN: 3.4:6 (Van Soldt SAU 40); 4.141 I 19, II 10; 4.277:11.

ḥṭb (I) n. m. "wood-cutter" (act. ptc. G < */ḥ-ṭ-b/; cf. Hb. *ḥṭb*, HALOT 306; Arab. *ḥāṭib*, Lane 594; Eth. *ḥaṭāb(i)*, CDG 248. Cf. Görg BN 5 1978 7ff.). ¶ Forms: sg. *ḥṭb*; pl. *ḥṭbm*.
Wood-cutter: PNN *ḥṭ*(!)*bm* wood-cutters, 4.609:20; *dd šʕrm l ḥmr ḥṭb* a *d.* of barley for the wood-cutter's donkey, 4.269:24.

Cf. ḥṭb (II), ḥṭbt.

ḥṭb (II) PN (Sem. Cf. Grøndahl PTU 28, 137).
PN: *bn PN*, 4.611:2.

ḥṭbt n. f. "/female) wood-cutter" (< *ḥṭb (I)*); ¶ par.: *ḥpšt*. ¶ Forms: pl. *ḥṭbt* (rdg *ḥṭb<t>* en 1.14 IV 51).
(Female) wood-cutter: *sʕt b šdm ḥṭbt*[[*h*]] the female wood-cutters swept from the fields, 1.14 III 8 (// *ḥpšt*); rdg *ḥṭb<t>* (// *ḫpšt*) en 1.14 IV 51 (diff.: De Moor-Spronk UF 14 1982 166: rdg *ḥṭbh*, coll. sg. 'its (i.e. the town's) wood-gatherers'; cf. *ḥṭb*: see also Greenstein IOS 18 1998 108).
Cf. ḥṭb.

ḥṭt n. f. "wheat" (Hb. *ḥṭh*, HALOT 307; Aram. *ḥ(n)ṭ(t)ʔ*, DNWSI 363; Arab. *ḥinṭa*, Lane 657; cf. Akk. *uṭṭatu* "grain", AHw 1446; Emar /ḥittu/, Pentiuc Vocabulary 70); ¶ par.: *akl*; ¶ RS Akk.: cf. GIG(.MEŠ), passim, PRU 6 158. ¶ Forms: sg./pl. *ḥṭt*, pl. *ḥṭm* (Gordon UT § 8.9); cf. the spellings *ḫṭm* in 4.710:4, 7; *ḫṭm*, 5.22:24.
Wheat: ★a) prepare *ḥṭt l bt ḫbr* wheat of TN, 1.14 II 29 and par. (// *akl*; cf. *bt (I)* 3.); *nʕm l ḥṭt b ʕn* a delight is (the rain) for the wheat in the furrow, 1.16 III 9; ★b) coll. pl. (*ḥṭm*) in econ. texts, measured in *dd*: 4.225:11; 4.269:25, 32; 4.400:4, 9, 13, 17; 4.608:4; 6.61:2 (Van Soldt UF 21 1989 382); measured in *prś/s*: 4.225:9; cf. *(...) prsm ḫṭm* (so many) *p.* of wheat, 4.710:4, 7 (cf. RS Akk.: GUR GIG(.MEŠ), PRU 6 107:10; 108 rev. 1; 152:1); *kbd ḥṭm* 4.211:5; used elliptically in 4.345:5. Cf. *ḫṭm*, 5.22:24 (cf. Dietrich - Loretz KA 191: 'Weizen').

ḥṯ n. m. "unleavened bread" (cf. Arab. *ḥuṯṯ*, Lane 521; Akk. *ḫaššu* AHw 334; CAD Ḫ 142f. Cf. De Moor NYCI 2 15; for discussion cf. Watson SEL 12 1995 223f.; Pardee TPM 106 n. 154). ¶ Forms: du. *ḥṯm*.
Unleavened bread: *w ṯn ḥṯm* and two unleavened loaves, 1.41:22 and par.

ḥṯb n. m. "bill, account" (< /ḥ-ṯ-b/; cf. Arab. *ḥisāb*, Lane 567; cf. Eg. *ḥsbw*, WäS 3 167. Cf. Rainey UF 3 1971 159; JAOS 94 1974 185 and n. 10; Bordreuil etc. CRAIBL 1984 433). ¶ Forms: sg. *ḥṯb*.
Bill, account: *ʕl ḥwt l ḥṯb d anyt grgmšh* on the country's account regarding the bill of the ship (bound) for TN, 4.779:12.
Cf. ḥṯbn.

ḥṯbn n. m. "balance, account(s)" (< /ḥ-ṯ-b/; Hb., Aram., Palm. *ḥšbn*, HALOT 360; DNWSI 441; Arab. *ḥusbān*, *ḥisāb*, Lane 566f. Cf. Liverani UF 11 1979 501ff.; Dietrich - Loretz UF 12 1980 274ff.). ¶ Forms: sg./pl. cstr. *ḥṯbn*.

Balance, account(s): *ḥṯbn PN* to PN's account, 4.158:2; *spr ḥṯbn sbrdnm* book of accounts of the bronzesmiths, 4.337:1. Cf. *ṯmn ʕšrh šmn ḥṯbn w ṯʕt* eighteen (jars) and one *ṯ* of oil on account, 4.771:7 (De Moor UF 17 1985 222f.; cf. Del Olmo UF 20 1988 32).
Cf. **ḥṯb**.

ḥwt n. f. "country, land, territory" (Hb. *ḥwh*, HALOT 296; Pun. *ḥwt*, DNWSI 353: *ḥwh₂*. Cf. De Moor SP 30 n. 47; Dietrich - Loretz - Sanmartín UF 6 1974 25f.; Herdner Ug 7 52f.; Wesselius AION 39 1979 105f.; ¶ syll. Ug.: U[N = *mātu* = *u*]*-mi-in₄-n*[*i*] = [*ḫ*]*u-wa-tu₄*, Ug 5 137 II 10'; A.ŠÀ.MEŠ *ḫu-wa-ti*, Syria 18 1937 251ff. (RS 8.146):5; Huehnergard UVST 123; Van Soldt SAU 303. ¶ Forms: sg. *ḥwt*; suff. *ḥwtk*; du.(?) *ḥwtm*.
Country, land, territory, ★**a)** in general: *bʕl kl ḥwt* lord of the whole country, 2.81:3; 2.76:10; *l adn ḥwt* to the lord of the country, 2.18:4; *ky akl b ḥwtk inn* for there is no grain in your land, 2.39:20; *yšlm (...) l ḥwtk* may it go well (...) with your country, 2.81:7; *šlm d ḥwtk* the well-being of your country, 2.36:4; *nġr ḥwtk* guard your territory (?), 2.47:2; *w mlk d mlk b ḥwt* and the king who rules in the country, 2.47:13; *b ḫbṯh ḥwt ṯth* in the event that he flees to another country, 3.3:4; *b yṣih*[*m*] *ḥwt* [*ṯth*]in the event that they go (?) to [another] country, 3.8:10; *ʕl ḥwt l ḥṯb d anyt grgmšh* on the country's account is the bill of the ship (bound) for TN, 4.779:12; *sb*[*rdnm(?) dt*] *yqḥ mit b ḥwt* bronzesmiths(?) who take one hundred from the country, 6.26:3 (Van Soldt UF 21 1989 379 n. 27); *mdtn tqln b ḥwt* many people will fall in the land, 1.103+:1; *rġbn ykn b ḥwt* there will be hunger in the land, 1.103+:5 and par.; *ibn yḫlq bhmt ḥwt* the enemy will destroy the small cattle of the land, 1.103+:16 and par.; *mlkn* [*y*]*šdd ḥwt ib* the king will destroy the land of the enemy, 1.103+:37 and par.; *ilm tbʕrn ḥwt* the gods will forsake the land, 1.103+:41, cf. ln. 56; *špšn tpšlt ḥwth hyt* the 'Sun' will (cause) the oppression of that land, 1.103+:45 (cf. Dietrich - Loretz MU 139f.); [*ibn y*]*rps ḥwt* [the enemy] will grind up the land, 1.103+:50; *ibn yspu ḥwt* the enemy will consume the land, 1.103+:51; *ḥwtn tprš* the land will be scattered, 1.103+:53;]*ḥwtn tḫlq* the land will be destroyed, 1.103+:4; *ḥwt ib tḫlq* the land of the enemy will be destroyed, 1.103+:59; 1.140:6; ★**b)** referring to a TN: *sknt k ḥwt yman* (its) form in the style of the country / land of TN, 1.4 I 42 (diff.: Aartun UF 16 1984 17: 'Tier', Aram. *ḥewĕṯā*, etc.); *ntbt mṣrm b ḥwt ugrt* Egypt's (right (?) of) way through the country of TN, 2.36:16; cf. *ḥwt qṭ w ḥwt nġṯ*, *ibid.* ln. 17; *ḥwt ugrt*, 2.81:18.

Bkn ctx.: *mlkn bʕly ḥwt*[, 2.42:10; *hn l ḥwth*, 2.33:9; *b ḥw*[*t*, 2.47:9; *šmʕt ḥwt*, 2.49:10; *ḥwtm*, 2.36:18, 19; *w l tḫlq ḥwt*[and the land will not be destroyed[, 2.73:6 (cf. ln. 2, 4, 5).

/ḥ-w/y-y/ (I) vb G: "to live, be alive"; D: 1) "to give (back) life / revive, leave alive, resuscitate"; 2) "to carry out, fulfil"; Dpass. "to be revived" (Hb., Aram. *ḥyh*, HALOT 309f.; DNWSI 354ff.; Ph. *ḥwy*, Pun. *ḥwʔ*, DNWSI 354ff.; Ebla /ḥw/yy(?)/, /ʔ(-ʔ)/, cf. Krebernik PET 34; cf. unc. *ʔa$_x$-i* (/ʔa(ḥ)yī/(?)), *a-ʔà-a* (/ʔaḥḥya/(?)), cf. Edzard StEb 4 1981 43f., 53f.; Müller Biling. 185, 188; cf. PN *a-wa*(-DN), Müller Biling. 185; Arab. *ḥayyā*, Lane 679ff.; OSA *ḥyw/ḥwy/ḥyy*, DOSA 168f., 173f.; Eth. *ḥaywa*, CDG 252. Cf. De Moor JNES 24 1965 360; Marcus JSS 17 1972 76ff.; Dijkstra - De Moor UF 7 1975 187ff.); ¶ **syll.** Ug.: KA[R] = Akk. ? = *eḫ-lu-um-me* = *ḫu-(wu)*PI*-ú*, Ug 5 137 obv. II 17', inf. abs. D: Verreet UF 19 1989 339f.; cf. Huehnergard UVST 123; Van Soldt SAU 303; cf. /ḫayā/, an element in PNN, Sivan GAGl 225; ¶ **par.**: /m-ḫ-ṣ/, /m-t/. ¶ **Forms**: G suffc. suff. *ḥytn* (as a stative and a precative); prefc. *tḥ*, *yḥ*; D prefc. *aḥwy*, *aḥw*, *tḥwy* (?), *yḥwy*, suff. *yḥwh*; suffc. *ḥwt*; impv. *ḥw*; Dpass. suffc. *ḥwt*. Cf. *ḥwy* in damaged text 1.17 VI 30 (cf. *infra*).

G. To live, be alive: *špḥ ltpn l yḥ* will the offspring of the Benevolent cease to live?, 1.16 I 23 and par. (// *tmtn*); *npš yḥ dnil* in (his) strength may PN (re)vive, 1.17 I 36 (cf. 1.19 IV 36; 2.23:18, bkn ctx.); *w yḥ mlk* and (long) live the king!, 2.7:9; *ḥytn w šlmtn* may you live and enjoy good health! 5.10:2; *ḥytn l* {*p*} *špš* may you live, oh Sun! (?), 5.11:4; may he live and not die, *yḥ l ymt* 6.30:1. Cf. in unc. ctx. *w tḥ ṭbt* (?), 1.82:34.

D. 1) To give (back) life / revive, leave alive, resuscitate: *k bʕl k yḥwy yʕšr* {*ḥwy yʕšr*} like DN certainly he gives life to(?) the one he invites, 1.17 VI 30 (diff.: Van der Toorn BiOr 48 1991 46: 'when he comes to life (again): one serves him', G + dittography; diff.: De Moor ARTU 238: '(...) he is served - (when) he has brought to life'); *ap ank aḥwy* I also shall give life, 1.17 VI 32; *ʕl qṣʕth ḥwt l aḥw* for his arrows you did not leave him alive, 1.19 I 16 (// *imḫṣh*); *(ʕl...) qṣʕth ḥwt l tḥ*[*wy*] (for...) his arrows you took away his (= did not leave him with) life?, 1.18 IV 13); *u ap mh*(!)*rh ank l aḥwy* and I shall not leave his warrior strength alive, 1.18 IV 27; *ql špš ḥw* voice of DN: give back life!, 1.82:6. Cf. in unc. ctx. *aḥw tm*, 1.82:19; 1.24:9-10.

2) To carry out, complete: *ank ḥrš lqḥt w ḥwt hbt* I, the craftsman, have accepted and completed the task, 2.70:15 (Dietrich - Loretz UF 16 1984 66ff.; Verreet UF 18 1986 384).

Dpass. To be revived: *ḥwt aḫt* may you be revived, sister!, 1.10 II 20 (optative prefc.; cf. De Moor UF 11 1979 643). Bkn: *tm ḥwy*, 1.176:17.

Cf. ʕbdhy, ḥy (I), ḥy (II), ḥy (III), ḥyil, ḥyl, ḥyn, ḥyt, yḥn, yḥṣdq, yḥšr.

/ḥ-w-y/ (II) vb Št: "to prostrate oneself" (Hb. *hšt̮ḥwh*, HALOT 295f.; Arab. *ḥawwā*, *taḥawwā*, Lane 678f. Cf. Emerton OTS 20 1977 41ff.; Davies VT 29 1979 493ff.; Kreutzer, VT 35 1985 39ff.); ¶ par.: /h-b-r/, /q-l(-l)/. ¶ Forms: Št prefc. *tšt̮ḥwy*, *yšt̮ḥwy*, suff. *yšt̮ḥwyn* (?).

Št. To prostrate oneself: *tšt̮ḥwy kbd hyt* prostrate yourselves (and) pay him homage, 1.3 III 10 and par. (// *hbr w ql*), prostration formula (cf. Del Olmo MLC 54).

ḥwy n. m. "storehouse, depot" (Hb. *ḥwh*, HALOT 296: *ḥwh I*; Arab. *ḥiwāʔ*, Lane 679); ¶ syll. Ug.: cf. /ḫāyu/, /ḫīyu/ in : *ḫi-i-yi-šu*, PRU 3 123 (RS 15.145):6, 11; É.AN.ZA.GÀR-*šu* : *ḫa-a-yi*, PRU 3 95 (RS 16.246):6; É *ḫe-e-ia/yu*, PRU 3 87 (RS 15.119) rev. 7', 9'; É.ḪI.A KISLAḪ.MEŠ *ḫé-yi-ma*, PRU 3 103 (RS 15.109+):15; Nougayrol PRU 3 p. 220; cf. diff.: Dietrich - Loretz - Sanmartín UF 5 1973 88: PN, Hurr. *ḫú-ú-ia*; Huehnergard UVST 127: 'vacant(?)'; Sivan GAGl 223: 'watchtower', cf. AHw 339: *ḫēja*; CAD Ḫ 168f.: *ḫeja*; Vita EU 46: 'lugar de reunión, campamento'). ¶ Forms: sg. *ḥwyh* (adv. *-h*).

Storehouse, depot: (equipment for chariots) *bd rb ḥršm d šṣa ḥwyh* by the hands of the chief of the assemblers, who delivered (it) to the storehouse, 4.145:10.

ḥy (I) adj. m. "alive" (cf. /ḥ-w-y/ (I); cf. Hb., Ph., Pun., Aram. *ḥy*, DNWSI 367ff.; EA Akk. *ḫa-ia-ma*, EAT 245:6; Sivan GAGl 223; DNWSI 367ff.). ¶ Forms: sg. *ḥy*.

Alive: *k ḥy aliyn bʕl* because alive is DN, the victorious, 1.6 III 20 and par. (// *iṯ*); *ikmy ḥy PN* since PN is alive, 2.82:17.

ḥy (II) n. m. "life" (adj. used as a noun cf. *ḥy (I)*; Hb., Ph., Pun., Aram., Nab., Palm. *ḥy(m/n)*, HALOT 308; DNWSI 365ff.; Ebla /ḥayy=u(m)/ in ᵈEN.KI = *ʔà-u₉*, VE 803; Krebernik ZA 73 1983 31; Kienast EDA 37ff.; Conti SQF 193 (for the DN Ea in Mari cf. Durand MROA 2/1 189ff.: /aya/); OSA *ḥyn*, *ḥyw(m)*, DOSA 173; Arab. *ḥayāh*, Lane 682; Eth. *ḥĕywat*, *ḥiwat*, CDG 252; Akk. cf. DN OAkk. *é-a*, Roberts ESP 20; OAss. *e-a-*, *i-a-*, Hecker GKT 28; Kienast EDA 37f.: /ḥayyā/); ¶ syll. Ug.: /ḥeyy=ūma/: [ḪI = *balaṭu* = Hurr.: ?] = *ḫe-yu-ma*, UF 11 1979 479 (RS 20.189):25; Ú[R(?) = Akk. (?) = *š*]*u-ḫu-ur-ni* = *ḫé-yu-ma*, Ug 5 131 6'; TIL = TIL-*la-tu* = *šu-ḫ*[*u-ur-ni* = *ḫ*]*é-yu-*[*m*]*a*, Ug 5 137 I 20; Huehnergard USVT 124; Van Soldt BiOr 46

1989 651; BiOr 47 1990 732; SAU 303, 337 n. 174; ¶ par.: *blmt*. ¶ Forms: sg. *ḥy*; pl. *ḥym*, suff. *ḥyk*.
Life: *ḥy tn* give life, 5.11:4, cf. *ḥy tn šlm tn* give life (and) give well-being, 5.10:2 (cf. Dietrich - Loretz KA 186 n. 124); *irš ḥym (...) irš ḥym w atnk* ask for life (...), ask for life and I shall give it to you, 1.17 VI 26-27 (// *blmt*); *b ḥyk abn nšmḫ* in your life, our father, we rejoiced, 1.16 I 14 and par. (// *blmt*); *p l ḥy np*[*š a*]*rš* and for the life of (his) soul I beg, 2.23:17.

ḥy (III) PN (Sem. Cf. Grøndahl PTU 50, 137); ¶ syll.: cf. [f]*ḫé-ia*-PI, PRU 3 86 (RS 16.250):21.
PN: *bn PN*, 4.366:4.

ḥyil PN (Sem. Cf. Grøndahl PTU 16, 43, 66, 96, 137; Marcus JSS 17 1972 78; Cross CMHE 64; Lipiński Syria 44 1967 273 n. 3; 50 1973 44; Dietrich - Loretz - Sanmartín UF 6 1974 454; De Moor - Spronk UF 14 1982 184); ¶ syll.: *ḫa-ya*-DINGIR, Syria 18 1937 (RS 8.146 ["8.213"]):32. Cf. *ḫyl*.
PN: 2.26:3; in bkn ctx.: 4.427:14; 4.497:2; 4.554:4.

ḥyl PN (etym. unc.; possbly allographic var. of *ḥyil*; cf. *ḥyly*. Cf. Grøndahl PTU 16, 96, 137; Dietrich - Loretz BiOr 23 1966 130). Cf. *ḥyil*.
PN: *bn PN*, 4.200:8; 4.214 II 1.

ḥyly adj. "fighter, powerful, strong" (cf. Hb., Aram. *ḥyl*, HALOT 311f.; DNWSI 369f.; Arab. *ḥayl*, Lane 688. Cf. Pope Fs. Finkelstein 170; diff.: Gray LC 128: 'my power'; De Moor SP 117; UF 1 1969 174 n. 54; Ribichini - Xella RSF 7 1979 152f.: 'the host of the filth', rdg *ḥyl ḫḫ*); ¶ par.: *ʕllmy*. ¶ Forms: sg. m. *ḥyly*.
Fighter, powerful: *ṯm yḥpn ḥyly* there (was) PN, the fighter, 1.22 I 9 (// *ʕllmy*).

ḥym, cf. *ḥy (II)*.

ḥyn PN (etym. unc. Cf. Grøndahl PTU 137; Watson AuOr 8 1990 118).
PN: ★a) 4.214 II 3; 4.232:35; 4.746:4; 4.763:2; ★b) *bn PN*, 4.51:6; 4.55:24 (Van Soldt SAU 33); 4.64 II 4.

ḥyt n. f. "life" (allomorph of *ḥy (II)*; cf. Margalit MLD 212 n.1; Marcus JSS 17 1972 72ff.). ¶ Forms: sg. *ḥyt*.
Life: *ḥyt ḥẓt ṯḥmk* (may) the lucky life (of) your message (be...) 1.3 V 31 and par. (diff.: De Moor UF 11 1979 643 n. 23: 'long live!', precative suffc. of /ḥ-y-y/; Renfroe AULS 54ff.: 'declaration, revelation', **ḥwy*; cf. Dietrich - Loretz UF 24 1992 34: 'Bekundung').
In unc. ctx. *ḥytn l p špš* may our life (pass (?)) according to the orders

of the ‘Sun’, 5.11:4.

ḥẓ n. m. “arrow” (Hb., Ph. *ḥṣ*, HALOT 342.; DNWSI 397; Aram. *ḥṭ/ṣ*, DNWSI 397; Akk. *uṣ(ṣ)u*, AHw 1439; Arab. *ḥaẓwat*, Lane 596; Eth. *ḥaṣṣ*, CDG 247); ¶ **RS Akk.**: GI.GAG.GUM.TAG.GA, PRU 6 133:4'-10'; ¶ **syll. Ug.**: cf. PN DUMU *ḫa-aṣ-ṣi*, PRU 6 10:17'; ¶ **par.**: *abn*. ¶ **Forms**: sg. *ḥẓ*, possibly allograph sg. cstr. *ḫẓ* in 1.172:21; pl. *ḥẓm*, var. *ḥḏm*: 4.609:25 (cf. *ḫḏġl*; diff.: Dohmen UF 15 1983 41: ‘Kleinschmied’), cstr. *ḥẓ*, suff. *ḥẓk*, *ḥẓhn*.
Arrow: ★**a)** *arbʕm qšt alp ḥẓm* forty bows, a thousand arrows, 4.169:2; *uṯpt ḥẓm* quiver for arrows, 4.204:1, 2, 4; *mrkbt* (...) *yd apnthn yd ḥẓhn yd trhn* chariot bodies (...) with their wheels, their arrows, their steering-poles, 4.145:4; cf. (chariots(?))]*d in ḥẓm lhm* which have no arrows, 4.180:1; ★**b)** *ḥẓk al tšʕl qrth* do not shoot your arrows against the city, 1.14 III 12 (// *abn ydk*); ★**c)** fletchers: *nsk ḥẓm* forgers of (metal tips for) arrows, 4.630:14 (var. *ḥḏm*, 4.609:25); *psl ḥẓm* carvers of (stone tips for) arrows, 4.141 III 19. Cf. in unc. ctx.]*bt bʕl ḥẓ ršp*, 1.82:3 (De Moor - Spronk UF 16 1984 239: rdg *ḥẓ ršp* ‘([may] Baʕlu [st]op) the arrows of Rashpu!’; altern. Gordon UT 854: rdg *bʕl ḥẓ* ‘Lord of the Arrow’ [Reshef]; cf. Renfroe AULS 56: ‘Lord of Fate’).
Cf. in bkn ctx., *ḫẓ* (for *ḥẓ* ?) *ksp b ydh* a silver arrow(?) in his hand, 1.172:21 (cf. Bordreuil - Caquot Syria 57 1980 345); *w ḥẓ alp*, 1.90:5.
Cf. **ḫḏġl**.

ḥẓr n. m. 1) “mansion”; 2) “quarter”, measure of length (Hb. *ḥṣr*, HALOT 345; Akk. *ḫa/iṣāru/ḫaṣīru*, AHw 331; CAD Ḫ 130, 202; Emar Akk. cf. *ḫi-za-ri*, Arnaud AuOrS 1 11; Syr. *ḥērtō̄*, LS 230; Arab. *ḥaḍar*, *ḥaẓīrat*, Lane 589, 596. Cf. De Moor UF 1 1969 172); ¶ **par.**: *bt (II)*, *hkl*, *kmn*. ¶ **Forms**: sg. *ḥẓr*, suff. *ḥẓry*, *ḥẓrk*, *ḥẓrh*.
1) Mansion: *in (...) w ḥẓr k bn aṯrt* he has neither (...) nor a mansion like the sons of DN, 1.4 IV 51 and par. (// *bt*); *rḥq krt l ḥẓry* move away, PN, from my mansion, 1.14 III 29 (// *bty*); *ʕrb (...) mšspdt b ḥẓrh* there entered (...) wailing women into his mansion, 1.19 IV 10 and par. (// *hklh*); *hm (...) ašʕrb ġlmt ḥẓry* if (...) I bring the damsel into mansion, 1.14 IV 42 (// *bty*); [*ġ*]*lmt tšʕrb ḥẓrk* the damsel you brought into your mansion, 1.15 II 23 (// *btk*); *ytn (...) w ḥẓr km aryk* they are going to build for you (...) and a mansion like (that of) your kin, 1.4 V 28 and par. (// *bt*); *yštql l ḥẓrh* he proceeded / went down to his mansion, 1.100:68, cf. 1.114:18 (// *bth*); *ḥẓr pʕlk yṭb* (in) the mansion, your work, may goodness reign, 1.13:21.

2) Quarter (measure of length): *b alp ḥẓr* through a thousand 'quarters', 1.1 II 14 and par. (// *kmn*; alternative of *šd* in the travel formula; cf. Del Olmo MLC 54f.).
Bkn: *ḥẓrh bbx*[, 7.35:1.

ḥẓt adj. f. "happy, lucky" (Arab. *ḥaẓẓ*, *ḥaẓẓiyy*, *ḥaẓīẓ*, Lane 595; diff.: Margalit MLD 212 n. 1: 'good-fortune, lottery', Arab. *ḥaẓẓ*, *ḥuẓwat*; Renfroe AULS 54ff.: 'lot, portion, fate', Arab. *ḥẓ*, cf. Dietrich - Loretz UF 24 1992 34: 'Schicksal'; De Moor UF 11 1979 643 n. 23: 'excellence, high rank', Arab. *ḥa/i/uẓwat*). ¶ Forms: sg. f. *ḥẓt*.
Happy: *ḥyt ḥẓt ṯḥmk* (may) the happy life of your message (be), 1.3 V 31 and par.

ḫ

ḫbb PN ((?); cf. Grøndahl PTU 310); ¶ **syll.**: cf. *ḫi-bi-bu/i*, Ug 5 85:4, 12.
PN(?): cf.]*rb spr ḫbb*, 1.75:10 (bkn ctx.).

ḫbdṯr PN (Hurr. Cf. Grøndahl PTU 206, 233, 249).
PN: *ḫbd*{.}*ṯr*, 4.46:11. Bkn 4.31:2.

ḫbl (I) n. m. "rubbish, waste, refuse" (Hb. *ḥbl*, HALOT 285; Arab. *ḫabl*, Lane 669f.; De Moor SP 118; Del Olmo IMC 42f.; diff. Caquot - Sznycer Tou 1 307: 'destruction', Arab. *ḫabāl*); ¶ **par.**: *rtn*. ¶ **Forms**: pl.(?) cstr. *ḫbl*.
Rubbish, waste, refuse: *ḫbl ṭtm* [on muddy refuse [he feeds(?)], 1.1 IV 8 (// *rtn*).

ḫbl (II), 4.689:5, cf. *ḥbl*.

ḫbly adj./n. f. epithet of the goddess *ʕnt* (etym. unc.; cf. Xella TRU 80: 'distruttrice', cf. *ḫbl (I)*; De Tarragon CU 171: TN). ¶ **Forms**: sg. *ḫbly*.
Epithet of Anat: *ʕnt ḫbly* DN *ḫ*., 1.39:17; 1.102:11; 1.162:14.

ḫbr TN, name of the city-state of king *krt* (Belmonte RGTC 12/2 107: *Ḫabūra*. Cf. Astour RSP 2 284f. no. 40; UF 5 1973 29ff.; Sauren - Kestemont UF 3 1971 196 n. 21; De Moor BiOr 31 1974 21; De Moor - Spronk UF 14 1982 163; Van Soldt UBL 11 372).
TN.: *ḫbr rbt ḫbr ṯrrt*, TN the great, TN the powerful, 1.15 V 19-20 and par.; *bt ḫbr* 'Daughter-of-TN', name of the capital, 1.14 II 29 and par. (cf. Badre *et al.* Syria 53 1976 107).

ḫbrtnr n. m.; a high Hittite dignitary (etym. unc.; not Hitt., HEG 298; cf. Knoppers BASOR 289 1993 89: 'chief steward', /ḫuburt=an=uri/, Hitt. *ḫuppar-*, Akk. *ḫuburtu*, *ḫūburu*; cf. Goetze RHA 12 1952 4ff.; not in GLH or MPDAI; Akk. cf. Akk. RS: *ḫuburtanuru*, AHw 352; CAD Ḫ 220); **Akk. RS**: *ḫuburtanuru*, cf. *a-na* LÚ *ḫu-bur-ta-nu-ri*, PRU 4 47f. (RS 11.732) A 5, 6; B 6, 7 (= PRU 3 181f.); PRU 4 82 (RS 17.382+):41, 43); PRU 4 42 (RS 17.227 and dupl.):32; cf. var. *a-na* LÚ *ḫu-bur-ta-nu-ra ù a-na* LÚ *ḫu-bur-ta-nu-ra ša-ni-i*, PRU 4 44 (RS 17.347):18's.; *PN* LÚ *ḫu-bur-ta-nu-ru ša šàr* KUR *kar-ga-mis*, PRU 3 41 (RS 16.180):3; cf. Sivan GAGl 229. ¶ **Forms**: sg. *ḫbrtnr*.

A high Hittite dignitary: (gifts) *l ḫbrṯnr* for the *ḫ*., 3.1:34, 36 (cf. Akk. RS: *a-na* LÚ *ḫu-bur-ta-nu-ri*, PRU 4 47f. (RS 11.732) A 5, 6; B 6, 7 (= PRU 3 181f.); PRU 4 82 (RS 17.382 + 380):41, 43); PRU 4 42 (RS 17.227 and dupl.):32); *l ḫbrṯnr ṯn* for the vice-*ḫ*., *ibid.* ln. 36 (cf. var. ¶ **RS Akk.**: *a-na* LÚ *ḫu-bur-ta-nu-ra ù a-na* LÚ *ḫu-bur-ta-nu-ra ša-ni-i*, PRU 4 44 (RS 17.347):18'-19').
Cf. **tpnr**.

ḫbrṯ n. f. "stewpot" (Hurr. *ḫubrušḫi* GLH 109; Hitt. *ḫuprušḫi-*, Tischler HEG 296f.; Nuzi Akk. *ḫurpušḫu*, Alalakh Akk. *ḫuprušḫu*, AHw 357; CAD Ḫ 241. Cf. Friedrich ZDMG 21 1942 489; De Moor ULe 67); ¶ **par.**: *ḫptr*. ¶ **Forms**: sg. *ḫbrṯ*.
Stewpot: *štt (...) ḫbrṯ l ẓr pḥmm* she placed (...) a stewpot on top of the embers, 1.4 II 9 (*// ḫptr*).

ḫbsn PN (etym. unc.).
PN: 4.307:15.

ḫbt (I) n. m. "pillager, destroyer" (< ptc. G /ḫ-b-t/; cf. Akk. *ḫabātu*, AHw 303f.; CAD Ḫ 9ff. Cf. Dhorme RB 40 1931 39: Dietrich - Loretz - Sanmartín UF 7 1975 153); ¶ **par.**: *mdll*, cf. /d-l-l/. ¶ **Forms**: pl. suff. *ḫbtkm*, *ḫbtkn*.
Pillager, destroyer: *u tḫṭin (...) u l p ḫbtkn* whether you have sinned (...) according to the custom of those who pillage you, 1.40:21 and par. (// *mdllkn*).

ḫbt (II) DN, Syro-Hurr. goddess (Cf. Nougayrol Ug 5 pp. 51f.; Laroche GLH 100f.; NH 348; Von Schuler WbMyth 1 172; Danmanville RlA 4 326ff.; Haas HBHS 30ff.; Wilhelm Hurrians 55f.; for Ebla cf. [d]*ḫa-a-pá-tu* and cf. Pomponio UF 15 1983 144f. n. 17f.; Trémouille SMEA 34 1994 87ff.; Durand MROA 2/1 258f.: 'Bien-amada'); ¶ **syll.**: [d]*ḫé-bat*, Ug 5 18:16 (// *pdry*, 1.47:17; 1.118:16; Laroche Ug 5 pg. 503, 525); cf. the element /ḫebV(t)/ in PNN, Grøndahl PTU 229f. ¶ **Forms**: *ḫbt*, *ḫbtd* (DN + Hurr, direct. =da).
DN: *ḫbtd*, 1.132:5, 14, 20; Hurr. ctx.: *ḫbt(d)*, *passim*; cf. 1.32:3, 9, 11, 12; 1.42:60, 62; 1.52:9, 13; 1.60:11; 1.64:32; 1.116:19

ḫb/pt(y) TN (Belmonte RGTC 12/2 132: *Ḫupatā(yu)*, *Ḫubatā*, *Ḫapatā(yu)*, **Ḫuppatu*. Cf. Virolleaud Syria 21 1940 144; GLECS 3 1940 98; Heltzer RCAU 9, 16 n. 19; Astour UF 13 1981 6; NuzHur 1 16 no. 23; Van Soldt SAU 337f. n. 177; UF 28 1996 670; UF 30 1998 727); ¶ **syll.**: cf. URU *ḫu-ba-ta*, PRU 3 189 (RS 11.790):21'; URU *ḫu-pa-ta*, Ug 5 102:15'; RSOu 7 4:47; URU *ḫu-pa-ta-ú*, PRU 3 191 (RS 11.841):14'; URU *ḫa-pa-ta-yu*, PRU 3 190 (RS 11.800

bis):15'; URU *ḫu-pa*$_{12}$*-ti*, RS 8.146 (RS 8213(!) Syria 18 1937 247):5; *ḫu-up-pa-ti*, PRU 3 148 (RS 16.178):11.
TN, ★a) *ḫbṯ*: 4.119:6; 4.382:15; ★b) *ḫpty*: 1.91:30; 4.68:49; 4.346:8; 4.355:12; 4.610 (I) 4; 4.686:3 (cf. Bordreuil UF 20 1988 15f.); RSOu 14 35 [KTU 9.388] I 30.

ḫbty GN m. (< *ḫb/pt(y)*, TN). ¶ **Forms**: sg. *ḫbty*.
GN: 3.10:3; 4.33:39; 4.53:3; 4.792:4.

/ḫ-b-ṯ/ v. G: "to flee, escape, be emancipated (from legal bonds), break one's links" (cf. Hb. *ḥpš* [pi., Qpass. / pu.], HALOT 341; cf. *ḫpṯ*; Dietrich - Loretz - Sanmartín UF 6 1974 27; Dietrich - Loretz UF 14 1982 85f.; Hoftijzer - Van Soldt UF 23 1991 189f.). ¶ **Forms**: G suffc. *ḫbṯ*; inf. cstr. suf. *ḫbṯh*; ptc. Gpass. sg. m. *ḫbṯ* and pl. m. *ḫbṯm*: cf. *ḫbṯ*.
G. To flee, escape, be emancipated (from legal bonds): *b ḫbṯh b ḥwt ṯth* on his escaping to another country, 3.3:4; to break one's links (with a place): PN *d ḫbṯ TN* who has broken his links with TN, 4.430:3 (cf. *d yṯb*, *ibid.* ln. 2).
Cf. **ḫbṯ**, **ḫpṯ**, **ḫpṯt**.

ḫbṯ adj./n. m. "emancipated; unattached" (< ptc. Gpass. /ḫ-b-ṯ/; diff.: Dietrich - Loretz - Sanmartín UF 6 1974 26f.; Milano VO 3 1980 187ff.; Hoftijzer - Van Soldt UF 23 1991 189f.: variant of *ḫpṯ*; Aartun UF 16 1984 22f.: Arab. *ḫabuṯa*: 'ruchloser Mensch'). ¶ **Forms**: sg. *ḫbṯ*, pl. *ḫbṯm*.
Emancipated: *l yblt ḫbṯm* you have not brought the emancipated (men), 2.17:1; unattached: *ṯlṯm bʕlm w aḥd ḫbṯ w arbʕ aṯt* two triads of labourers, plus one unattached, and four women, 4.360:8.
Cf. **/ḫ-b-ṯ/**, **ḫpṯ**.

ḫby PN (etym. unc.; cf. Grøndahl PTU 310; Watson AuOr 13 1995 222).
PN: ★a) 4.103:22; ★b) *bn PN*, 4.339:4.

ḫdi PN (Sem.(?). Cf. Grøndahl PTU 17, 138, 233).
PN: *bn PN*, 4.63 III 8.

ḫdbṯ PN (etym. unc. Cf. Grøndahl PTU 206, 233).
PN: 4.320:7.

ḫdd PN (Sem.(?)); ¶ **syll.**: cf. *ḫa*-DA-*ad-di*, Ug 5 28 obv. 12; Rainey IOS 5 1975 25; Huehnergard AkkUg 384; Watson AuOr 11 1993 215.
PN 4.80:2 (*ar*[).

ḫdlr, cf. *ḫdn ḫdlr*.

ḫdmn PN (Hurr. Cf. Grøndahl PTU 233; Van Soldt SAU 35); ¶ **syll.**: cf. *ḫ*[*u-u*]*t-mu-nu*, PRU 3 204 (RS 16.257+) mg. II 8.

PN: *bn PN*, 4.103:43; 4.624:9; 4.681:5.

ḫdn ḫdlr DN(N); two Hurro-Hitt. goddesses (Bo. ^{d}*ḫu-(u-)-te-na* ^{d}*ḫu-(u-)-te-el-lu-ur/úr-ra*, Laroche GLH 111. Cf. Laroche Ug 5 pp. 526, 530; Von Schuler WbMyth 1 176f.; Haas RlA 4 526); ¶ **syll.**: ^{d}*ḫu*(?)-*ti*(?)-*i*]*l*(?)-*lu-u*[*r-ra*(?) = ^{d}*ku*(?)-*ša*(?)]-*ra-tu*$_4$, Ug 5 137 IVb 8(?); cf. Laroche Ug 5 p. 526 n. 2; GLH 111; Dietrich - Loretz TUAT 2 305.
DN: 1.132:8. In Hurr. ctx., cf. 1.42:32, 33; 1.60:14; 1.64:29; 1.135:11.

ḫdpṯr PN (Hurr. Cf. Grøndahl PTU 233, 424; Huehnergard UVST 230 n. 87); ¶ **syll.**: DUMU *ḫu-du-up-ša-ri* PRU 3 200 (RS 16.257+) II 10.
PN: *bn PN*, 4.63 III 18; 4.64 II 7.

ḫdš$_2$bʕl PN (Sem. Cf. Grøndahl PTU 116f., 134).
PN: *ḫdš$_2$bʕl*[, 6.70:2.

ḫdś, 1.171:7, cf. *ḥdṯ (II)*.

ḫd/ty(n) PN (Hurr. Cf. Grøndahl PTU 21, 233; Van Soldt SAU 33; Watson AuOr 13 1995 222f.); ¶ **syll.**: cf. *ḫu-ti-ia*, Ug 5 27:41, 54; (DUMU) *ḫu-di/ti-ia/ya-na*, PRU 3 194 (RS 11.787):3 (Van Soldt SAU 345 n. 195); 149 (RS 16.182+):8, 11, 18; 201 (RS 16.257+) II 42; cf. *ḫu-da*, RSOu 7 3:13'; *ḫu-ud-da-na*, RS 23.22+ VI 14' (Van Soldt SAU 341 n. 185). Cf. *ḫtn*, PN.
PN: ★**a)** *ḫdyn*, 4.214 III 20; in bkn ctx., *ḫ*]*tyn*, 4.659:2; ★**b)** *bn ḫdy*, 4.635:55; *bn ḫty*, 4.343:5; *bn ḫdyn*, 4.33:8 (*ugrty*); 4.69 VI 11; 4.98:18; 4.724:6; RSOu 14 46 [KTU 9.423]:11; *bn ḫtyn*, 4.57:10; 4.281:18; 4.611:26; 4.643:11.

ḫḏ(ḏ) n. m. "downpour, squall" (Hb. *ḥzyz*, HALOT 302; cf. Arab. *ḫinḏīḏ*, Hava 187; *ḫazīz*, Hava 826; cf. Ginsberg LKK 37f.; diff.: Watson Or 45 1976 440f.; De Moor UF 14 1982 164; De Moor - De Vries UF 20 1988 176 n. 18: 'thunder', 'thunderstorm'); ¶ **par.**: *yr*.
¶ **Forms**: sg. *ḫḏḏ*; contracted form *ḫḏ*.
Downpour, squall: *hlk l alpm ḫḏḏ* they march by the thousand (like) a downpour, 1.14 II 39 and par. (// *yr*; diff.: Aartun StUL 59ff.: 'tüchtiger, heldenhafter', Arab. *hinḏīḏ*). In bkn ctx.: *rḥ ḫḏ ʕrpt* the wind, the squall (and) the clouds, 1.13:34.

ḫdġb PN (Hurr. Cf. Grøndahl PTU 204, 211, 232, 234; cf. Dietrich - Loretz WO 4 1967/68 302).
PN: ★**a)** 4.269:25, 28; ★**b)** *bn PN*, 4.690:2.

ḫḏġl n. m. "fletcher" (Hurro-Ug. **ḫḏ-* [< Ug. *ḥẓ* "arrow"] + Hurr. suff. **-ġl*; cf. Ug. var. *ḥḏm*: 4.609:25 [cf. *ḥẓ*]. Cf. Dietrich - Loretz WO 3 1966 199; Helzter IOKU 84 n. 15; cf. Laroche GLH 97 unexplained; cf. *nsk ḥẓm, psl ḥẓm*). ¶ **Forms**: pl. *ḫḏġlm*.

Fletcher: 4.609:16; master fletcher contrasted with *lmd*: 4.138:2; 4.154:5; 4.188:1.

ḫdl PN (Hurr.(?) Cf. Grøndahl PTU 234); ¶ syll.: cf. *ḫa-zi-lu*, PRU 6 86 I 10; cf. DUMU *ḫu-zi-la-a*, PRU 3 201 (RS 16.257+) A II 48. Cf. *ḫzli*.
PN: *bn PN*, 4.611:4.

ḫdm, in bkn ctx., 7.53:7.

ḫdmdr PN (Hurr. Cf. Grøndahl PTU 232f., 249; Dietrich - Loretz WO 4 1967/68 302; Huehnergard UVST 224; Van Soldt SAU 3, 14; Watson AuOr 11 1993 215); ¶ syll.: *iš-mi*-SAR-*ri*, PRU 3 138 (RS 16.131):8, 10; *iš-mi*-LUGAL-*ma*, PRU 4 123 (RS 17.35):6, 11; *ḫi-iš-mi*-LUGAL-*ma*, PRU 4 121 (RS 17.352):4 and *passim ibid.*; cf. PU.LUGAL-*ma*, RSOu 7 11:3.
PN: 4.643:25; in bkn ctx.: 4.190:2; 4.748:15; cf. 4. 178:6; 4.556:3.

ḫdmrd/t PN (Hurro-Sem. Cf. Virolleaud Syria 21 1940 110; Grøndahl PTU 233, 247; Dietrich - Loretz OLZ 62 1967 546; Bordreuil - Pardee RSOu 14 p. 379); ¶ syll.: cf. *ḫi/e-i/eš-mi*-[d]IM, Ug 5 27:6; 28:1.
PN: 4.102:22; *ḫdmrt*, RSOu 14 50 [KTU 9.434]:1.

ḫdmtn PN (Hurr. Cf. Grøndahl PTU 232f., 262); ¶ syll.: *ḫi*-IŠ-*mi-te-nu*, PRU 3 37 (RS 15.81):9.
PN: 4.417:4 (*tr*[*zy*).

ḫd/zmyn PN (Hurr. Cf. Grøndahl PTU 232; Berger WO 5 1968/69 273; Van Soldt SAU 35); ¶ syll.: *ḫi*-IZ-*mi-ia-na*, PRU 3 160 (RS 16.261+):8.
PN: 4.356:15; 4.374:12; 4.748:14.

ḫdnr PN (Hurr. Cf. Grøndahl PTU 212, 234, 243; Dietrich - Loretz WO 4 1967/68 302).
PN: *bn PN*, 4.56:5 (ctx. frg.).

ḫdpršp PN (Hitt.-Sem. Cf. Ribichini - Xella RSF 15 1987 9f.).
PN: 4.760:3 (*ḫdprš*(?)[*p*, bkn ctx.).

ḫdrġl n. m.; a type of server in the cult ('assistant, acolyte'; cf. Laroche GLH 96; cf. Alalakh Akk.: LÚ.MEŠ *ḫa-še-ru-ḫu-li*, AT 269:22; cf. AHw 333; CAD Ḫ 139. Cf. Dietrich - Loretz WO 3 1966 189ff.: Hurro-Ug. **ḫdr-* [< /ʕ-d/z-r/, Akk. *ḫaziru*, AHw 339] + Hurr. suff. /=(u)ḫli/. Cf. Laroche GLH 96 unexpl.; Del Olmo CR 234 n. 58: 'service'). ¶ Forms: pl. *ḫdrġlm* (*sic*; KTU: *ḫdrġl.x*[).
A type of server in the cult ('assistant, acolyte'): *b yrḫ ḫyr b ym ḥdṯ ḫdrġlm*[in the month MN, on the new moon, the 'assistants'[shall offer(?) ..., 1.112:2.
Cf. ḫzr.

ḫgbt PN (etym. unc. Cf. Grøndahl PTU 21; Ribichini - Xella RSF 15 1987 10). Possibly an allograph of *ḥgbt*, PN.
PN: *bn PN*, 4.214 II 11.

ḫḫ n. m. "mire, rubbish dump" (Akk. *ḫaḫḫu*, AHw 308; CAD Ḫ 28f. Cf. Gray LC 55 n. 8, 113; Dijkstra - De Moor UF 7 1975 189; Watson SEL 4 1987 61; diff.: Caquot - Sznycer TOu 1 220 n. g; Margalit MLD 80f.: 'gueule', 'Pit' < 'underworld', Hb. **ḥwḥ*, Arab. *ḫawḫat*; for the various opinions cf. Sasson RSP 1 415f.; Margalit MLD 80f.); ¶ par.: *hmry*, *mk*. ¶ Forms: sg. *ḫḫ*, suff. *ḫḫm* (encl. *-m*?; cf. Watson AuOr 10 1992 237).
Mire, rubbish dump: *ḫḫ arṣ nḥlth* a mire (is) the land of his possession, 1.4 VIII 13 and par. (// *hmry*, *mk*); *dm l ġzr šrgk ḫḫm* for to a hero your tangles are a quagmire, 1.17 VI 35.

/ḫ-l/ v. G: 1) "to writhe (with birth pangs)"; 2) "to skip, jump" (Akk. *ḫ(i)ālu*, *ḫâlu*, AHw 342; CAD Ḫ 55; Hb. *ḥyl*, HALOT 310f. Cf. Avishur UF 7 1975 34; Foley UF 19 1987 64 n. 14); ¶ par.: /b-r-k/, /h-l-k/. ¶ Forms: G inf., impv. *ḫl*.
G. 1) To writhe (with birth pangs): *ḫl ld aklm* writhe (and) give birth to the 'Voracious Ones', 1.12 I 25 (// *tbrk*).
2) To skip, jump: *tr b lkt wtr b ḫl*, she escaped running and she escaped skipping, 1.10 II 29 (// *b lkt*; diff.: Aartun UF 16 1984 23ff.: 'stolze Haltung', Arab. *ḫāl*).
Cf. ḫl, ḫlln, ḫllt.

ḫl n. m. "sickness, anxiety, pain" (< /ḫ-l/; cf. Hb. *ḥyl*, HALOT 312; Dietrich-Loretz MU 218; Del Omo MLR 290). ¶ Forms: sg. *ḫl*.
Sickness, anxiety, pain: *w prʕ[(t)] hy ḫlh* and this will wash (: remove) his sickness, 1.124:10.
Cf. ḫlm.

ḫli PN (etym. unc. Cf. Grøndahl PTU 29, 138, 230; Sivan GAGl 224).
PN: 4.282:6.

ḫlu n. m. "cake" ((?); etym. unc.; cf. Hitt. *ḫali-*, HW(2) 3 32: (NINDA) *ḫali-*; Hb. *ḥlh*, HALOT 317; Arab. *tiḫliʔ*, Hava 179. For this and other etymologies cf. Del Olmo CR 262; diff.: Dietrich - Loretz - Sanmartín UF 5 1973 108; Waetzoldt ZA 77 1987 298: 'Wollkleid', Akk. *ḫalûm*). ¶ Forms: sg. *ḫlu*.
Cake (?): (*dbḥ* ...) *ḫlu dg* (the sacrifice of ...) fish-cake, 1.91:12 (diff.: Baldacci BiOr 46 1989 119: 'fish-shaped jewel', Hb. **ḥlʔ/h*).

ḫlan PN (etym. unc. Cf. Grøndahl PTU 29, 138, 230; Sivan GAGl 224; Watson AuOr 11 1993 215); ¶ syll.: cf. DUMU *ḫal-a*(?)*-na*, PRU 3 199 (RS 16.257+) B III 15. Cf. *ḫlyn*, PN.

PN: ★a) 4.391:17; ★b) *bn PN*, 4.222:20; 4.350:2; 4.413:4; 4.715:5; in bkn ctx.: 4.526:2. Cf. *ḫluy*[4.75 V 13 (*bn* [).

ḫluy PN (Cf. Grøndahl PTU 138; Baldacci BiOr 46 1989 119).
PN: 4.75 V 13 (*bn* [).

ḫlb (I) n. m. "massif, promontory" (cf. Akk. *ḫalbu*, AHw 311; CAD Ḫ 40f.. Cf. De Moor SP 185); ¶ syll. Ug.: cf. the element /ḫalb-/ in TNN; cf. Sivan GAGl 226); ¶ par.: *ġr*. ¶ Forms: sg. *ḫlb*.
Massif, promontory: *ša (...) ḫlb lẓr rḥtm* lift (...) the massif on top of the palms (of your hands), 1.4 VIII 6 and par. (// *ġr*); *gd ḫlb* coriander from the massif, 1.82:4; 1.85:20.
Cf. ḫlb (II), ḫlby, ḫlbn.

ḫlb (II) TN (Belmonte RGTC 12/2 108f.: *Ḫalab* / *Ḫal(a)ba* 'Aleppo', not: *Ḫalba* 2, *ibid.* 110, or **Ḫalbu*, *ibid.* 111. Cf. Heltzer RCAU 9, 16 n. 20; Rainey UF 3 1971 137, 142; Dietrich - Loretz - Sanmartín UF 5 1973 108; Astour RSP 2 285f. no. 41; NuzHur 1 15 no. 21; Bonechi SEL 7 1990 15ff.; Van Soldt UF 28 1996 668); ¶ syll.: [KUR.UR]U *ḫal-bá*, RS 17.338+ (Del Monte Trattato 14ff.):18; [^{d}IŠKUR URU *ḫa-la-ab*], *ibid.* ln. 88; ^{d}U *ḫal-bi*, Ug 5 170:18'.
TN: ★a) 1.85:20; ★b) *bʕl ḫlb*, 1.109:16; 1.130:11; 1.134:8; 1.148:26; 4.728:2 (cf. Hurr. *(ṯb) ḫlbġ*, 1.42:10; 1.148:13).

ḫlb (III) TN (Belmonte RGTC 12/2 111: **Ḫalbu*, 'abgekürzter ON der Ḫalbu-Art'; not *ḫlb (II)* 'Aleppo' Van Soldt UF 28 1996 668); ¶ syll.: URU *ḫal-bi*, RSOu 7 4:32.
TN: 4.382:18.
Cf. ḫlb ʕprm, ḫlb gngnt, ḫlb krd, ḫlb rpš, ḫlb ṣpn.

ḫlb ʕprm composite TN (Belmonte RGTC 12/2 111: **Ḫalbu-ʕapurīma*. Cf. Virolleaud Syria 21 1940 143; RÉS 1940 74ff.; Heltzer RCAU 9; Astour RSP 2 286f. no. 42; 349 no. 143; Van Soldt UF 28 1996 669; 30 1998 725); ¶ syll.: URU *ḫal-bi* LÚ.MEŠ.SAG.GAZ, PRU 3 189 (RS 11.790):7'; [URU *ḫal-bi a*]*-pu-ri-ma*, 191f. (RS 11.841):6' (collation Van Soldt UBL 11 365 n. 9 (5)).
Composite TN: 4.48:1; 4.73:12; 4. 346:7; 4.380:16; 4.610 (I) 27; 4.693:28; 4.784:21; RSOu 14 35 [KTU 9.388] I 35.
Cf. ʕpr (II).

ḫlb gngnt composite TN (Belmonte RGTC 12/2 110f.: **Ḫalbā(yu)* / *ḫlb(y)*; cf. diff Van Soldt UF 28 1996 668; 30 1998 728. See also Dijkstra UF 23 1991 135; Bordreuil AntSem 2 1997 64f.).
Composite TN: 1.91:22; RSOu 14 35 [KTU 9.388] II 25 (cf. Bordreuil AntSem 2 1997 64f.).
Cf. ḫlb(y).

ḫlb krd composite TN (Belmonte RGTC 12/2 112: **Ḫalbu-karradi*. Cf. Van Soldt UBL 11 377f.; UF 28 1996 668; UF 30 1998 720, 725; cf. Virolleaud Syria 21 1940 143; GLECS 3 1940 98; Heltzer RCAU 9; Astour UF 13 1981 6; Huehnergard UVST 212); ¶ syll.: URU *ḫal-bu/bi kàr-ra-di*, PRU 3 189 (RS 11.790):6'; 190 (RS 11.800):11'; [URU *ḫal-bu/bi*] *kar-ra-di*, PRU 3 191 (RS 11.841):7'.
Composite TN: 3.7:14; 4.6:2; 4.48:2; 4.68:3; 4.119:7; 4.365:17; 4.380:13; 4.610 (I) 26; 4.685:5; 4.693:29; RSOu 14 35 [KTU 9.388] I 37. For 4.693:14, 46 (KTU *ḫlb k*[*rd*]) see *ḫlb rpš*, *ḫlb ṣpn* (Belmonte RGTC 12/2 112f.).

ḫlb rpš composite TN (Belmonte RGTC 12/2 112: **Ḫalbu-rapši*. Cf. Van Soldt UBL 377f.; UF 28 1996 669; UF 30 1998 725; Bordreuil AntSem 2 1997 66; cf. Virolleaud Syria 21 1940 144; GLECS 3 1940 98; Heltzer RCAU 10; Dietrich - Loretz UF 10 1978 430; Astour UF 13 1981 9; Van Soldt SAU 499 n. 65); ¶ syll.: URU *ḫal-bi rap-ši*, PRU 3 189 (RS 11.790):5'; PRU 4 182 (RS 17.299):2.
Composite TN: 4.48:7; 4.63 II 30; 4.100:5; 4.108:1; 4.235:9 (cf. Van Soldt UF 28 1996 669 n. 117); 4.365:12; 4.693:14 (KTU: *ḫlb k*[*rd*]; cf. Belmonte RGTC 12/2 112); 4.784:19; cf. in bkn ctx.: 4.683:13 (cf. Bordreuil UF 20 1988 11f.).
Cf. rpš (I).

ḫlb ṣpn composite TN (Belmonte RGTC 12/2 113: **Ḫalbu-ṣapuni*, *Ḫalbu Ḫazzi*, **Ḫalbu Nanā*. Cf. Van Soldt UBL 11 377f.; UF 28 1996 669; UF 29 1997 693f.; UF 30 1998 732; cf. Heltzer RCAU 10; Dietrich - Loretz - Sanmartín UF 5 1973 97f.; Astour RSP 2 287f. no. 43; 349 no. 144; UF 13 1981 2f., 8; Bordreuil Syria 61 1984 8f.); ¶ syll.: URU *ḫal-bu/bi* ḪUR.SAG *ḫa-zi*, PRU 3 190 (RS 11.830):13'; RSOu 7 4:19; cf. URU *ḫal*(!)-*bi*, PRU 3 191 (RS 15.20):4; cf. URU *ḫal-bi* ḪUR.SAG *na-na-a*, PRU 4 48ff. (RS 17.340) 26'; URU *ḫal-bi*, PRU 4 63-67 (RS 17.237):40'; PRU 6 118:4' (cf. Van Soldt UF 28 1996 668; Belmonte RGTC 12/2 113).
Composite TN: 4.68:50; 4.94:16; 4.303:4; 4.610 (II) 28 (KTU: *glb špn*); 4.676:4; RSOu 14 35 [KTU 9.388] I 15. For the rdg *ḫlb* <*ṣpn*> in 4.267:2 and 4.621:14 cf. Van Soldt UF 28 1996 688; for *ḫlb ṣpn* in 4.693:46 cf. Bordreuil UF 20 1988 18.
Cf. ḫš, ks, nny, ṣpn.

ḫlb(y) TN (Belmonte RGTC 12/2 110f.: *Ḫalbā(yu)* / *ḫlb gngnt*; cf. diff. Van Soldt UF 28 1996 667; UF 30 1998 728; see also Dijkstra UF 23 1991 135; Bordreuil AntSem 2 1997 64f.; Heltzer RCAU 9, 16 n. 20; Dietrich - Loretz - Sanmartín UF 5 1973 108; Astour RSP

2 285f. no. 41; NuzHur 1 15 no. 21); ¶ **syll.**: URU *ḫal-ba*, PRU 3 125 (RS 15.147):5; URU *ḫal-ba-yi*, Ug 5 95:19.

TN *ḫlby*: 4.274:4; 4.348:25; 4.610 (II) 24; 4.621:6; 4.770:8; 4.784:23. Cf. **ḫlb gngnt**.

ḫlby PN (< *ḫlb (II)* / *ḫlb (y)*; cf. *ḫlbym*).

PN: 4.337:6.

ḫlbym PN (Sem. Cf. Grøndahl PTU 138; Dietrich - Loretz - Sanmartín UF 5 1973 108).

PN: *bn PN*, 4.7:7; 4.93 I 2.

ḫldy GN / TN (Belmonte RGTC 12/2 131: *Ḫuldā*. Cf. Lipiński OLP 12 1981 110 n. 148; Huehnergard UVST 243, 290 n. 109; Van Soldt UF 28 1996 669); ¶ **syll.**: cf. URU *ḫu-ul-da*, PRU 3 133 (RS 15.132):7, 11; 144 (RS 16.138):19.

GN / TN, element in the compound toponym *gt ḫldy*: 4.636:10 (Belmonte RGTC 12/2 87: **Gittu-Ḫuldā*).

ḫlln PN (etym. unc. Cf. Grøndahl PTU 139; Watson AuOr 14 1996 99).

PN: *bn PN*, 4.53:12; 4.335:23.

ḫllt n. m. "procreation, childbirth" (< /ḫ-l/; cf. Dijkstra - De Moor UF 7 1975 180); ¶ **par.**: *hrt*. ¶ **Forms**: sg. *ḫllt*.

Procreation, childbirth: *ysmsmt ʕrš ḫllt* the beauty of the bed of procreation, 1.17 II 42 (// *hrt*).

Cf. **ḫlln**.

ḫlly PN (Sem.; etym. unc. Cf. Grøndahl PTU 139; Watson AuOr 8 1990 245).

PN: 4.391:12.

ḫlm "?" (bkn ctx.)

? : *ḫlm aṯt iṯt*, RSOu 14 53 [KTU 9.432]:35 (Bordreuil - Pardee RSOu 14 p. 397, 401: 'et la 'danse' de la femme (est son) don').

Cf. **ḫl**.

ḫlm (II) PN (etym. unc. Cf. Sivan GAGl 222; Watson AuOr 8 1990 245; AuOr 14 1996 99; Dahood *apud* Pettinato Archives 307); ¶ **syll.**: cf. DUMU *ḫal-la-ma-na*, PRU 3 55 (RS 15.92): 4; 67 (RS 16.255 A+E):5.

PN: 4.348:16.

ḫlmẓ n. m. "snake", epithet / emblem of the goddess *ušḫr* (Akk. *ḫulmiṭṭu*, AHw 354; CAD Ḫ 230; Hb. *ḥmṭ*, HALOT 327f.; Syr. *ḥūlmoṭō*, LS 235. Cf. De Moor UF 2 1970 316 n. 73; Young UF 9 1977 309; Dietrich - Loretz UF 13 1981 86; Schwemer NuzHur 7

104ff., 115; cf. diff.: Aartun UF 16 1984 24f. who connects it with */ḫ-l-m/ > 'Chamäleon'); ¶ par.: *qlḥ*. ¶ Forms: sg. *ḫlmẓ*.

Snake: *id ydbḥ mlk l ušḫr ḫlmẓ* when the king sacrifices to DN, the 'snake', 1.115:2; *š l ḫlmẓ* a ram to the 'snake', 1.115:4, cf. ln. 12.

h̲ln, allograph of *ḥln*, 5.22:27; cf. *ḥln*.

ḫlp PN (Sem. Cf. Grøndahl PTU 139; Watson AuOr 8 1990 246).

PN: *bn PN*, 4.172:4; 4.266:4; 4.611:11.

ḫlpn (I) n. m./f.; type of cloak or cape (cf. Akk. *naḫlaptu*, AHw 715; CAD N/1 138ff. Cf. Dietrich - Loretz BiOr 23 1966 129f.; Heltzer GPOTU 39, 65 n. 306; Ribichini - Xella Tessili 38; Van Soldt UF 22 1990 328; cf. Akk. *ḫulāpu*, Durand MARI 6 662); ¶ RS Akk.: TÚG.GÚ.È, Syria 18 1937 246 (RS 8.145):21; PRU 3 206 (RS 15.135):2-3; PRU 6 p. 159; cf. Ug 5 83:8 (Berger UF 2 1970 339f.); cf. TÚG.GÚ.È GADA, PRU 3 184 (RS 16.146+):12. ¶ Forms: sg. *ḫlpn*; pl. *ḫlpnt*; du. *ḫlpnm*.

Type of cloak or cape: ★a) *arbʕm ksp w ḫlpn ʕl PN* forty of silver and a *ḫ*. on the account of PN, 4.782:2; (personnel) *lqḥ ḫlpnt* have received *ḫ*., 4.630:5; *b yrḫ mgm*[*r*...] *yṣu ḫlpn*[*t* in the month MN[...] *ḫ*. have been distributed, 4.192:2; *tn ḫlpnm* two *ḫ*., 4.117:1; *spr npṣ PN* (...) *tn ḫlpnm* list of belongings of PN: (...) two *ḫ*., 4.385:6; *w ahpkn ḫlpn* and I shall return the *ḫ*., RSOu 14 53 [KTU 9.432]:36'; ★b) *ḫlpn pṯtm ḫ*. of linen, 5.10:5 (cf. RS Akk.: TÚG.GÚ.È GADA, PRU 3 184 (RS 16.146+):12).

Cf. ḫpn (I).

ḫlpn (II) PN (Cf. Grøndahl PTU 139; Van Soldt UF 29 1997 681).

PN: *bn PN*, 4.77:27.

Cf. ḫlp.

/ḫ-l-q/ v. G: "to perish, be destroyed"; D: "to destroy"; Dpass.: "to be destroyed, devastated" (Akk. *ḫalāqu*, AHw 310f.; CAD Ḫ 36ff.; Eth. *ḫalqa*, CDG 261. Cf. Dietrich - Loretz MU 120); ¶ par.: /m-t/. ¶ Forms: G suffc. *ḫlq*, *ḫlqt*; D prefc. *yḫlq*; Dpass. *yḫlq*, *tḫlq*.

G. To perish, be lost: *ḫlq zbl bʕl arṣ* perish did the prince, master of the underworld, 1.5 VI 10 and par. (// *mt*); *k mt aliyn bʕl k ḫlq* for DN, the victorious, is dead (...) has perished, 1.6 I 42 and par.; *akln b grnt l bʕr ap krmm ḫlq qrtn ḫlqt* our grain on the threshing floors has been set on fire, and also the vines have been destroyed, (and also) our city has been destroyed, 2.61:11-12. In bkn ctx. cf.: *w ḫlq ʕpmm*[and may the birds perish[...!, 1.18 IV 42.

D. To destroy: *ibn yḫlq bhmt ḥwt* the enemy will destroy the cattle of the land, 1.103+:16; cf.]*yḫlq bhmt*[...]will destroy the cattle[..., *ibid.* ln. 15.

Dpass. To be destroyed, devastated:]*ḥwtn tḫlq* the land will be devastated, 1.103+:4; *ḥwt ib tḫlq* the land of the enemy will be destroyed, *ibid.* ln. 59; 1.140:6. Cf. in bkn ctx.: *y*]*ḫlq mṯn rgm* wi]ll be destroyed, ditto, 1.103+:18; *w l tḫlq ḥwt*[and the land will not be devastated[, 2.73:6.

Cf. ḫlq.

ḫlq adj./n. m. 1) "ruined, spoilt"; 2) "missing" (< /ḫ-l-q/; cf. Akk. *ḫalqu*, AHw 313; CAD Ḫ 50). ¶ Forms: sg. *ḫlq*.

1) Ruined, spoilt, said of wine turned sour with time: *yn ḫlq* spoilt wine, 4.213:3 (Aartun UF 16 1984 26; cf. *yn mṣb* and Mari Akk.: GEŠTIN SUMUN, cf. ARMT 21 104f.; cf. *yn ṭb* generous wine, 4.213: 1 and *passim ibid.* [cf. Mari Akk.: GEŠTIN DÙG.GA, Finet AfO 25 1974/77 127; Durand ARMT 21 107ff.], contrasted with *yn d l ṭb* ordinary wine, of mediocre quality, 4.213:2 and *passim ibid.*).

2) Missing, of persons: PN *ḫlq* missing, 4.611:2 and par.; *kprm ḫlq 10* villages: missing: 10, *ibid.* ln. 8. Cf. in bkn ctx. 4.613:5, 6, 9.

Cf. /ḫ-l-q/.

/ḫ-l-ṣ/ G: "to squeeze" ((?); cf. Akk. *ḫalāṣu*, AHw 311; CAD Ḫ 40; cf. Arab. *ḫalaṣa*, Lane 785f.; cf. Del Olmo CR 385; Watson UF 24 1992 368; diff.: Bordreuil - Caquot Syria 57 1980 348, 'jus'; Loretz - Xella MLE 1 43: 'Festung', Akk. *ḫalṣu, ḫilṣu*; Margalit ZAW 99 1987 400f.: 'to be round' / '(rounded) drinking bowl', /ḫ-l-ṣ/; Aartun UF 16 1984 25: 'geklärter (Wein)', Arab. *ḫalaṣa*). ¶ Forms: G inf. *ḫlṣ*.

G. To squeeze: *tšt b ḫlṣ bl ṣml* drink, squeezing (it) out, the beer of abstinence, 1.169:7.

ḫlt "?"; in bkn ctx.: 1.172:11.

ḫ(?)ly TN(?) (unc. classification and rdg; see Van Soldt UF 28 1996 669; cf. Astour UF 13 1981 9; cf. Heltzer RCAU 14, 18 n. 55: *ġl*).

TN(?): 4.244:12((?); Belmonte AuOr 17/18 1999/2000 22; RGTC 12/2: rdg *zly*<*y*> / *Zilayā*).

Cf. ġl, ḥl (I), ḥl (III), zlyy (I).

ḫlyn PN (etym. unc. Cf. Grøndahl PTU 138, 215; Sivan GAGl 224); ¶ syll.: DUMU *ḫa-li-ia-na*, PRU 139 (RS 16.131):20. Cf. *ġlyn*, PN.

PN: *bn PN*, 4.64 II 9; 4.692:10.

ḫm n. m. "pavilion, tent" ((?); cf. *ḫym, ḫmt*; cf. Dietrich - Loretz UF 10 1978 60; Xella BH 186f.); ¶ par.: *mṯb*. ¶ Forms: sg. *ḫm*.

Pavilion, tent: unc. ctx., *l ḫm g(!)r tqdm* to the guest(?) pavilion they approached, 1.15 IV 23 (diff. KTU: *gr mr*; De Moor ARTU 209: 'tent of bitterness').
Cf. ḫmn, ḫmt, ḫym.

ḫmat n. f. "butter / curd" (Hb. *ḥmʔh*, HALOT 325; Aram. *ḥmʔtʔ*, Jastrow 475; Akk. *ḫimā/ētu*, AHw 346; CAD Ḫ 189ff.); ¶ par.: *ḥlb*. ¶ Forms: sg. *ḫmat*.
Butter / curd: *annḫ b ḫmat* (they sacrifice) a kid in butter / curd, 1.23:14 (// *ḥlb*).

ḫmn (I) n. m. "chapel, small temple" (< /ḫ-y-m/ + *n*; cf. Nab., Palm. *ḥmn*, DNWSI 382. Cf. Dijkstra - De Moor UF 14 1982 160f. n. 65; Xella MLE 1 12; BH 169ff., 187ff.; Del Olmo AuOr 2 1984 277ff.). ¶ Forms: sg. *ḫmn*, directional suff. *ḫmnh* (cf. *h (II)*).
Chapel, small temple: *tn šm ḫmnh* (they shall offer) two rams in the 'chapel', 1.112:3; *tʕln ilm b ḫmn* the gods shall go up to the 'chapel', 1.112:8; *[š]bʕ ṣin ḫmnh* seven ewes in the 'chapel', 1.106:13, cf. 1.48:13; 1.53:5; 1.104:16); *š (...) ḫmnh nkl* one ram ... in the 'chapel' of DN, 1.106:14; *id ydbḥ mlk b ḫmn* when the king sacrifices in the 'chapel', 1.164:1.
Cf. ḫm, ḫmt, ḫym.

ḫmn (II) DN, Hurr. name or divine epithet (Cf. Laroche JAOS 88 1968 148; Ug 5 519, 525; Del Olmo AuOr 2 1984 279 n. 16); ¶ syll.: cf. PN *ab-di-ḫa-ma-ni*, ÌR-*ḫa-ma-nu*, cf. Grøndahl PTU 230; cf. diff. Sivan GAGl 223: /ḥ-m-m/). ¶ Forms: *ḫmn(n)d* (Hurr.: dir. /DN=(ne=)da/).
DN: in Hurr. ctx., *in ḫmn(n)d*, 1.60:6; 1.116:6, 16).
Cf. ʕbdḫmn, ḫmn (III).

ḫmn (III) PN (Hurr. Cf. Grøndahl PTU 230; Bordreuil Semitica 32 1982 13). Cf. *ḥmny*.
PN: 4.54:5.

ḫmr n. m. "(sparkling(?)) wine" (Hb., Ph., Aram., Palm. *ḥmr*, HALOT 330; DNWSI 383f.; Arab. *ḫamru*, Lane 808f.; Akk. *ḫamru*, AHw 1559; Emar /ḫamru/, Pentiuc Vocabulary 55; Dietrich UF 21 1989 78 n. 63. Cf. De Moor SP 75; Dijkstra UF 17 1985 149; diff.: Dahood Bib 45 1964 408f.; UHP 39, 59, 64; RSP 1 186: 'wine-bowl, vat'; Lloyd UF 22 1990 180f. 'some sort of container for wine', Hb. *ḥmr*, but cf. De Moor SP 75, 78; Lipiński UF 2 1970 84f.; Dietrich - Loretz UF 4 1972 28; Loretz UF 21 1989 474; UF 25 1993 254); ¶ par.: *lḥm*, *msk*. ¶ Forms: sg. *ḫmr*.

(Sparkling(?)) wine: *al kd yqḥ b ḫmr* they / it took one thousand quarts of *ḫ*-wine, 1.3 I 16 (// *msk*); *w yšt b ḫmr yn ay* drink every kind of *ḥ*-wine, 1.23:6 (// *lḥm*). In bkn ctx.: 4.564:3.
Cf. **ḫmrm, ḫmrn**.

ḫmrm TN or cult installation (cf. Hurr. *ḫamri*, Laroche GLH 91; Hitt. *ḫamri-*, HW² 3 132f.; Akk. *ḫamru*, AHw 318; CAD Ḫ 70: *ḫamru A*; cf. Belmonte RGTC 12/2 130: TN; diff.: De Moor SP 75: PN).
TN or cult installation: *ḫmrm ṯṯ krm*[*m* TN/*ḫ*., six vineya[rds, 4.244:22.

ḫmrn TN (Van Soldt UF 28 1996 670: possibly an allomorph of *ḫmrm*; Belmonte RGTC 12/2 130: TN; diff. Aartun UF 11 1979 24f., rdg *zmrn*).
TN: 4.683:30.

/ḫ-m-s/ v. G: "to force(?)" (cf. Hb. *ḥms*, HALOT 329. Cf. Dahood BiOr 34 1970 362). ¶ **Forms**: prefc. *yḫms*.
G. To force(?): in bkn ctx. 6.48:2.

ḫ̱ms̄, 4.31:4-6, 11; cf. *ḫmš (I)*.

/ḫ-m-š/ v. D: "to repeat five times" (denom. < *ḫmš (I)*; cf. Eth. *ḫammasa*, CDG 262); ¶ **par.**: /ṯ-d-ṯ/. ¶ **Forms**: D prefc. *yḫmš*.
D. To repeat five times: *yḫmš rgm* he repeated the question five times, 1.16 V 17 (// *yṯdṯ*).
Cf. **ḫmš** (I).

ḫmš (I) n. num. "five" (Hb., Ph., Pun., Aram., Nab., Palm. *ḥmš*, HALOT 331; DNWSI 385; Akk. *ḫamiš*, AHw 317; CAD Ḫ 66f.; OSA *ḫms*, CAME 156f.; DOSA 205; Arab. *ḫamsa*, Lane 810; Eth. *ḫa/ĕms*, CDG 262). ¶ **Forms**: sg. *ḫmš* (allomorph *ḫ̱ms̄* in 4.31:4, 5, 6, 11); f. *ḫmšt* (cf. also *ḫmšt*); encl. *-m* (?) *ḫmštm*; pl. *ḫmšm* (cf. *ḫmšm*).
1) Numeral five, ★**a)** elliptical syntagms: *ḫmš šmn* five of oil, 4.150:2; *ḫmš šmn w ḫmš ṯʕdt* five (jars) of oil and five *ṯ*., 4.150:4-5; *ḫmš yn* five of wine, 4.149:14; *ḫmš ʕl PN* five to PN's account, 4.381:20; PN *ḫmš* five, 4.775:4; PN *ḫmšt* five, 4.281:4; *yṯbn yspr l ḫmš l ṣlmm* one will go back to recite five times in front of the statues, 1.23:57; *ḫmšt d pwt* five of madder, 4.771:3; *ḫmšt ḫndlt* five (pieces(?)) of *ḫ*., 4.182:17; ★**b)** genitive syntagms: *ḫmš ymm* five days, 4.95:10; *ḫmš kkrm* five talents, 4.709:4; *ḫmš ktnt* five tunics, 4.402:4; *ḫmš ḫrmṯt* five sickles, 4.625:7; *ḫmš ddm* five 'cauldronfuls', 4.790:17; RSOu 14 39 [KTU 4.790]:17', 18', 19', 20', 21', 22', 23', 24', 26; RSOu 14 40 [KTU 9.419]:11.
2) Compound numerals, ★**a)** fifteen: *ḫmš ʕšr*, 4.247:29; 4.786:6; RSOu 14 39 [KTU 4.790]:16'; allograph *ḫ̱ms̄ ʕs̄r*, 4.31:4, 5, 6, 11;

ḫmš ʕšrt, 4.341:6; *ḫmš ʕšrh*, 4.344:2; *ḫmš l ʕšrt*, 4.658:7; *ḫmš l ʕšrh*, 4.777:8; *ʕšrt ḫmš*, 4.226:8; twenty-five: *ḫmš l ʕšrm*, 4.786:3; *ḫmšt l ʕšrm*, 4.779:5; forty-five: *arbʕm (...) ḫmšt kbd*, 4.778:10; ★b) four hundred and fifty: *arbʕ mat ḫmšm šbʕt w nṣp kbd* four hundred and fifty-seven and a half, 4.779:8; five hundred: *ḫmš mat*, 4.261:7; 2.80:4; ★c) five thousand: *ḫmš alp*, 4.337:6; *ḫmš alpm*, 4.181:2. With encl. -m (?): *ḫmštm* five(?), RS 94.2184+ (unpub., Bordreuil - Pardee RSOu 14 p. 400: 'cinq'; cf. *arbʕtm* (*arbʕ*) and *ṯlṯtm (ṯlṯ (I)*; but see also Tropper UG 347 and cf. *ibid.* 377).
Cf. **/ḫ-m-š/, ḫmš (II), ḫmšm, ḫmšt, mḫmšt**.

ḫmš (II) adj. m. ord. "a fifth" (< *ḫmš (I)*; cf. Hb., Aram. *ḥmyšy*, HALOT 328; DNWSI 386; pun. *ḥmšy*, DNWSI 386); ¶ **par.**: *ṯdṯ*. ¶ **Forms**: sg. *ḫmš*.
A fifth (ordinal): *b ḫmš* the fifth (day), 1.41:38; 4.279:5; (he rested) *ḫmš ṯdṯ ym* a fifth (and) sixth day, 1.14 V 5 and par.; *yip lḥm d ḫmš* bake bread (to last till) the fifth (month), 1.14 II 30 and par. (// *ṯdṯ yrḫm*).

ḫmšm n. num. "fifty" (pl. of *ḫmš (I)*; cf. Hb. *ḥmšym*, HALOT 331; Ph., Pun. *ḥmšm*, Aram., Moab. *ḥmšn*, Nab., Palm., JAram. *ḥmšyn*, DNWSI 386). ¶ **Forms**: *ḫmšm*.
Numeral fifty, ★a) ellliptical syntagms: *ḫmšm yn* fifty of wine, 4.123:23; *ḫmšm ksp* fifty of silver, 4.338:14; 4.782:28; *ḫmšm ṯlṯ* fifty of copper, 1.148:20; ★b) appositional syntagms: *ḫmšm izml* fifty *i.*, 4.284:2; *ḫmšm ḥmr* fifty 'loads', 4.14:18; ★c) compound numbers: *ḫmšm ḫmš* fifty-five, 4.230:13; *ḫmšm ṯmn* fifty eight, 4.141 II 24; *ṯmn l [ḫ]mšm dd* fifty-eight cauldronfuls, RSOu 14 42 [KTU 9.420]:9; *tšʕ ma[t] ḫmšm* ... nine hundred and fifty..., RSOu 14 37:2.
Bkn: RSOu 14 39 [KTU 4.790]:3'.

ḫmšt n. f. "five-shekel weight" (f. < *ḫmš (I)*; cf. Del Olmo IMC 160ff.; Gibson CML 147; diff.: De Moor - Spronk UF 14 1982 157: '1/5 shekel'; Verreet UF 19 1987 328; Tropper UG 347, 374; KTU rdg *k mḫmšt*); ¶ **par.**: *ṯql*. ¶ **Forms**: pl. *ḫmšt*.
Five-shekel weight: his tears ran *km ḫmšt mṭth* like five-shekel weights onto the bed, 1.14 I 30 (// *km ṯqlm*). Cf. **ḫmš (I), mḫmšt**.

ḫmt n. f. "tent" (cf. *ḫym, ḫm, ḫmn*; cf. Arab. *ḫaymat*, Lane 837; Eth. *ḫaymat*, CDG 269. Cf. Dijkstra - De Moor UF 14 1982 160f.; diff.: Caquot - Sznycer TOu 1 513 n. l: 'bergerie', Arab. *ḫumm*; Xella BH 184ff.: 'chapelle, baldaquin'). ¶ **Forms**: sg. *ḫmt*.
Tent: *ʕrb b ẓl ḫmt* he entered the shade of the tent, 1.14 III 55and par.

Cf. ḫm, ḫmn, ḫym.

ḫndlt n. f.; type or colour of cloth (cf. Hitt. SÍG *ḫa-an-ta-la-*, Neu GAHT 50; Tischler HEG 154. Cf. Laroche Ug 5 p. 136 n. 1; Heltzer GPOTU 26, 58 nn. 127f.; Ribichini - Xella Tessili 38f.); ¶ syll. Ug.: cf. SÍG.ZA.GÌN : *ḫa-an-da-la-ti*, Ug 5 48:9; Van Soldt UF 22 1990 340f. ¶ Forms: pl. *ḫndlt*.

Type or colour of cloth: *ḫmšt ḫndlt* five (pieces(?)) of *ḫ*., 4.182:17.

ḫndrṯ n. m. of a fruit tree ("apricot tree, apple tree"(?); cf. Akk. *(ḫ)i/enzūru*, AHw 347; CAD Ḫ 170; Gelb Fs. Kraus 67ff.; < Hurr.(?), cf. Sanmartín AuOr 6 1988 232; cf. Mari Hurr.*ḫi-in-zu-ru-uš*, Thureau-Dangin Syria 36 1939 20 no. 6:7, cf. Laroche GLH 106f.; for other opinions cf. Renfroe AULS 123; diff. Haas - Thiel UF 11 1979 351; Van Soldt UF 29 1997 688: Hurr.(?); Cohen-Sivan UHT 22f., 49, 51; Cohen UF 28 1996 122f.: Indo-European). ¶ Forms: sg. *ḫndrṯ*; du. *ḫndrṯm*.

A fruit tree: ★a) its seedling(?): *1 PN/TN*(?) *ḫndrṯ(m)* for PN/TN(?): one (/ two) *ḫ*., 4.34:5, 6 (unc. ctx.; cf. *ibid.* ln. 8); ★b) ingredient (seeds / almonds of) in hippiatric pharmacopoeia: mash together *ḫndrṯ w ṯqd mr* (seeds / almonds of) *ḫ*. and bitter almond(s), 1.85:7; 1.71:7. Cf. bkn 4.34:5, 6; Cohen UF 28 1996 122f.

/ḫ-n-n/ v. D: "to denature, make rancid, unsuitable for use" ((?); cf. Hb. *ḥnn*, HALOT 335; Arab. *ištaḫanna*, Hava 186; Syr. *ḥannīnō*, LS 243. Cf. De Moor JNES 24 1965 359f.; diff.: Dietrich - Loretz UF 16 1984 353: 'begünstigen', < /ḥ-n-n/). ¶ Forms: D prefc. with suff. *aḫnnn*.

D. To denature, make rancid, unsuitable for use(?): *aḫnnn w iḫd* I will denature(?) it (: oil) and proceed to requisition it, 2.15:9 (cf. Syr. *ḥūnotō*, LS 243: 'oleum rancidum').

ḫnn PN (etym. unc. Cf. Grøndahl PTU 231; Watson AuOr 14 1996 99). Cf. *ḥnn*.

PN: *bn PN*, 4.170:19; 4.611:18.

ḫnnġ DN; a group of deities (etym. unc.). ¶ Forms: *ḫnnġd* (Hurr.: direct. /DN=da/).

DN: *ḫnnġd ṯt dqt* to the DN: two ewes, 1.132:9.

/ḫ-n-p/ v. G: "to act perversely" (Hb. *ḥnp*, HALOT 335f.; Arab. *ḥanafa*, Lane 658; Aram. *ḥnp*, DJPA 209; EA Akk. *ḫanāpu*, AHw 320; CAD Ḫ 76: *ḫanpa ša iḫnupu ana muḫḫiya*, EAT 288:8; cf. De Moor ARTU 177: D 'to treat viciously'). ¶ Forms: G prefc. with suff. *yḫnpk*.

G. To act perversely: bkn ctx., *w yḫpnk*[, 1.82:15.

Cf. **ḫnp**.

ḫnp n. m. "impiety, sin" (< /ḫ-n-p/; Hb. *ḥnp*, *ḥnph*, HALOT 336; cf. Arab. *ḥanafa*, Lane 658; Aram. *ḥnp*, DJPA 209; EA Akk. *ḫannipu*, AHw 321; CAD Ḫ 80: *ša ḫannipa īdeʔu*, EAT 162:74 [cf. Moran AmL 150]; cf. *ḫanpa ša iḫnupu*, EAT 288:8. Diff., Gray LC 115 n. 4: 'haughty', Hb. *ḥnp (lb)*, Job 36:13; Caquot - Sznycer TOu 1 435 n. e: 'colère', Arab. *ḫanafa*; Margalit UF 15 1983 94f.: 'pollution', Hb. *ḥnp*). ¶ Forms: sg. *ḫnp*; pl. *ḫnpm* (?).
Impiety, sin: bkn ctx., *ḫnp lb*[*k* the sin of [your] heart, 1.18 I 17. Cf. in bkn ctx. *rmm ḫnpm*, 1.9:15.

ḫnpt n. f. "?" (etym and rdg unc. Cf. Herdner TOu 1 563 n. y; Del Olmo MLC 589: 'back' > 'summit', rdg *nḫnpt*, Arab. *ḫanafa*, *ʔahnaf*; De Moor - Spronk CARTU 140: 'be defiled', rdg *nḫnpt*, N **ḫnp*; KTU 45: rdg *l n*{.}*ḫ npt*, but cf. Tropper AuOr 13 1965 233: rdg *ln ḫnpt*); ¶ par.: *ṯkm*. ¶ Forms: sg. *ḫnpt*.
? : *ʕl (...) ln ḫnpt mšpy*, 1.16 IV 14 (// *l ṯkm*).

ḫnq(n) PN (etym. unc.; cf. Grøndahl PTU 276); ¶ syll.: cf. (DUMU) *ḫi-na-qa-na*, Syria 15 1934 137ff. (RS [Varia 3]):1; PRU 4 183 (RS 17.319):16.
PN: *bn ḫnq*, 4.232:25; *bn ḫnqn*, 4.98:20; 4.233:6.

ḫnqt n. f. "strangler" (f. ptc. act. of /ḫ-n-q/; cf. Hb., Ph. *ḥnq*, HALOT 336; DNWSI 389f.; Syr. *ḥnaq* LS 244; Arab. *ḫanaqa*, Lane 818; Eth. *ḫanaqa*, CDG 263; Akk. *ḫanāqu*, AHw 320; CAD Ḫ 77ff. Cf. Xella TRU 80). ¶ Forms: du. *ḫnqtm*.
Strangler (as a divine epithet): *iltm ḫqntm dqtm* (to) the strangler-goddesses, two ewes, 1.39:18 (cf. 1.102:13).
Cf. **ḫnq(n)**.

ḫny(n) PN (etym. unc. Cf. Grøndahl PTU 231; Sivan GAGl 204; Hess AmPN 71ff.): ¶ syll.: cf. *ḫa-an-ya*, PRU 3 93 (RS 16.208) rev. 4'.
PN: *bn ḫny*, 4.170:17; *bn ḫnyn*, 4.69 VI 19; 4.93 III 2.

ḫnzr (I) n. m.; an official ((?); cf. (Hurro?)-Akk. *ḫanizarru*, AHw 321; cf. *ḫzr*. Cf. Caquot - Sznycer TOu 1 247f. n. g; diff.: De Moor SP 185ff.: 'boar', c.Sem. *ḫ(n)zr*, cf. syll. Ug. *ḫu-zi-rù*, Ug 5 137 II 25'); ¶ par.: *ġlm*. ¶ Forms: sg. suf. *ḫnzrk*.
An official(?): *ʕmk (...) ṯmn ḫnzrk* with you [go] (...) your eight *ḫ*., 1.5 V 9 (// *ġlm*). In bkn ctx. *ḫnzr*[, 7.218:3.
Cf. **ḫnzr** (II).

ḫnzr (II) PN (etym. unc. Cf. Ward JNES 20 1961 34f.; Grøndahl PTU 22, 28, 140; De Moor SP 185; Watson AuOr 8 1990 119; cf. Sivan GAGl 231). Cf. *ḫzrn*, *ḫzry*, PNN.

PN: *bn PN*, 4.64 II 2; 4.69 I 14; 4.98:16.

ḫp n. m. "shore" (Hb. *ḥwp*, HALOT 298; Arab. *ḫayf*, Lane 832f., cf. *ḥāffat*, Lane 672; Eg. *ḫá-pu*, Helck Bez. 518 [179]; Sivan - Cochavi WSVES 10. Cf. De Moor SP 90); ¶ syll. Ug.: cf. A.ŠÀ.MEŠ [...] *ša ḫu-up-pa-ti*, PRU 3 148f. (RS 16.178):11; cf. Huehnergard UVST 129; ¶ par.: /y-ṣ-ʔ/ (+ *špš*). ¶ Forms: sg. *ḫp*, suf. *ḫph* (?).
Shore: *lim ḫp y*[*m*] the people of the seashore, 1.3 II 7 and par. (// *ṣat špš*; Xella UF 16 1984 344 n. 48; Dietrich - Loretz UF 22 1990 77: 'westliche und östliche Himmelsrichtung'). In bkn ctx.: *ḫph*, 1.107:32.

/ḫ-p-n/(?) v. G/D: "to cover, protect, wrap up" ((?); cf. Ribichini - Xella Tessili 39 n. 32; cf. *ḫpn*; cf. Durand MARI 6 662). ¶ Forms: G/D prefc. *yḫpn*.
G/D(?). To cover, protect, wrap up(?), in bkn ctx.: *k yḫpn* may he protect(?), 2.23:4.
Cf. ḫpn (I).

ḫpn (I) n. m./f.; a garment or accessory (etym. unc., Durand MARI 6 662; cf. De Moor JNES 24 1965 361; UF 2 1970 311; Ribichini - Xella Tessili 36: < /ḫ-p-n/(?), and cf. Akk. *ḫubb/pputtu*, AHw 351; CAD Ḫ 215; cf. Aram., MHb. *ḥpny*, ANH 148; diff. Rendsburg JAOS 107 1987 628 Soq. *haf* vêtement); ¶ RS Akk.: cf. TÚG.GÚ.È (cf. *ḫlpn*; cf. Van Soldt UF 22 1990 328, 335). ¶ Forms: sg. *ḫpn*; pl. *ḫpnt*; du. *ḫpnm*.
1) For personal use: ★a) *ḫpn aḥd b ṯqlm* a *ḫ*. for two shekels, 4.156:3; *ṯn ḫpnm* two *ḫ*., 4.4:4; *yrḫ nql ṯn ḫpn*[*m* in the month of MN: two *ḫ*., 4.182:35; *bt ly ṯn ḫpnm* cut(?) two *ḫ*. for me, 5.11:16; *ṯlṯ ḫpnt* three *ḫ*., 4.152:5; *spr npṣm d yṣ*{.}*a b mid*(!)*ḫ ʕšrm ḫpn ḫmš* list of garments that have been delivered through payment of customs duty: twenty five *ḫ*., 4.166:2; in bkn ctx.: 4.609 II 17; ★b) *l PN ḫpn* for PN: a *ḫ*., 4.188:2 and *passim*; *ṯṯ lmd PN l*{.}*qḥ ḫpnt* six apprentices of PN have received *ḫ*., 4.188:18, 20; *ḫpn l azzlt* a *ḫ*. for DN, 4.182:57 (De Moor UF 2 1970 198); ★c) *ḫpn d iqni w šmt* a *ḫ*. of violet and reddish purple, 4.168:1; *ḫpn(t) pṯt(m) ḫ*. of linen, 4.156:5; 4.152:9; 4.190:4; 4.270:7; *ḫpnt šʕrt ḫ*. of wool, 4.152:10; *ḫpnt dqt* fine *ḫ*., 4.765:4.
2) For horses: protective padding (?): *ḫpnt śśwm* (sets of) protective padding for horses(?), 4.363:3, 7; *arbʕ ḫpnt* four (sets of) protective padding, 1.148:19.

ḫpn (II) PN (etym. unc.; cf. Grøndahl PTU 139; Ribichini - Xella Tessili 11; Muchiki Loanwords 211).
PN: 4.609:17.

ḫprt n. f. "ewe lamb, ewe" (metathesis of the pattern **ḫur(a)p-*, cf. Syr. *ḥurpō*, LS 258; Akk. *ḫurāpu*, AHw 357f.; CAD Ḫ 245; cf. Arab. *ḫarūf*, Lane 726. Cf. Del Olmo BSA 7 1993 185f.); ¶ **RS Akk.**: cf. UDU.NIM. MA, AnOr 48 27 ("RS 1957.4"):1; cf. Huehnergard AkkUg 74; Sanmartín BSA 7 1993 200; ¶ **par.**: *kr*. ¶ **Forms**: sg./pl. *ḫprt*.
Ewe lamb, ewe: *ilht ḫprt*, ewe lamb goddesses, 1.4 VI 48 (// *ilm krm*).

ḫps/śry PN (etym. unc.; cf. Segert UF 15 1983 212; Watson AuOr 8 1990 119; AuOr 14 1996 99).
PN: ★**a)** *ḫpsry*, 4.129:2; ★**b)** *bn ḫpśry*, 4.124:2.

ḫpśry PN; cf. *ḫps/śry*, PN.

ḫpš(?)[, 1.149:3.

ḫptr n. m. "cooking pot" (Hurro-Akk. *ḫuppat(a)ru*, AHw 356; CAD Ḫ 238; cf. Salonen HAM 88); ¶ **par.**: *ḫbrt*. ¶ **Forms**: sg. *ḫptr*.
Cooking pot: *štt ḫprt l išt* she placed a cooking pot on the fire, 1.4 II 8 (// *ḫbrt*).

ḫpty, cf. *ḫb/pt(y)*.

ḫpṯ n. m. 1) "fugitive, runaway"; 2) a 'legionary' or 'mercenary' of some kind; 3) "loose cattle, on the loose from the herd" (cf. /ḫ-b-ṯ/; Akk. *ḫupšu*, AHw 357; CAD Ḫ 214f.; Emar /ḥupṯu/, Pentiuc Vocabulary 78; Hb. *ḥpšy*, HALOT 341f.; Ph. *ḥpš*, DNWSI 397. Cf. Dietrich - Loretz - Sanmartín UF 6 1974 26f.; Dietrich - Loretz UF 14 1982 83f.; Yamashita RSP 2 51f.; Rainey RSP 2 92, 103f.; Ward UF 12 1980 441f.; Lipiński FO 21 1981 65ff.; diff.: Aartun UF 16 1984 28: 'kraftlos'); cf. **RS Hurr.**: cf. *ḫpṯml*, 1.149:4; GLH 114; ¶ **par.**: *ṯnn*. ¶ **Forms**: sg. *ḫpṯ*, suf. *ḫpṯh*.
1) Fugitive, runaway (member of a social group comprising fugitives, runaways, homeless persons): PN *ḫpṯ d yṯb b TN* 'fugitive' who lives in TN, 4.382:25; (oracle) *l ḫpṯ* concerning the 'fugitive', 1.144:3.
2) A 'legionary' or 'mercenary' of some kind' recruited from the 'fugitives': *ḫpṯ d bl spr* 'legionaries/legionary' (walk/s) without number, 1.14 II 37 and par. (// *ṯnn*); of a lower category: *lm tlikn ḫpṯ hndn p mšmʕt mlk inn* why are you sending me this 'legionary'? Isn't there a royal guard?, 2.72:10; *mlkn yʕzz ʕl ḫpṯh* the king will have power over his 'mercenaries', 1.103:57 (cf. Alalakh Akk.: ÉRIN.MEŠ *ḫu-up-še-na*, AT 129:1; *passim*).
3) Extended to cattle on the loose from the herd: *bn ḫpṯ l umhthm* the young of the loose (cattle low) for their mothers, 1.15 I 6 (cf. Nuzi Akk.: cattle *ša ḫu-up-ši*, HSS 9 143 rev. 10). In bkn ctx.: 4.351:6.
Cf. **/ḫ-b-ṯ/**, **ḫpṯt**.

ḫpṯt n. f.; state or group of *ḫpṯ* (abstr. or collect.; cf. Hb. *ḥpšyt*, HALOT 342. Diff., Dietrich - Loretz UF 14 1982 84: pl. of *ḫpṯ* in /-ūt(u)/. For other opinions cf. Tromp PCD 158f.; De Moor SP 185; Dahood Fs. Prado 164; Caquot - Sznycer TOu 1 220; Loretz UF 9 1977 165; Del Olmo MLC 553; Loretz Habiru 262f.). ¶ **Forms**: sg. *ḫpṯt*.
Status or group of *ḫpṯ*, 'escaped people, on the loose'; cf. espec. *bt ḫpṯt* reserve or quarters for 'escapees' (cf. Alalakh Akk.: É *ḫu-up-še-na*, AT 186:4ff.; *passim*): (descent) *bt ḫpṯt arṣ* to the netherworld house of 'escapees', 1.4 VIII 7 and par.

ḫqn PN (etym. unc.; cf. Watson AuOr 8 1990 246).
PN: *bn PN*, 4.658:41.

ḫqrn, bkn ctx.: 1.48:10.

ḫr (I) n. m. "cave, fossa, tomb" (Hb. *ḥr*, HALOT 348; Syr. *ḥurō*, LS 253; Arab. *ḫurr*, Lane 715; Akk. *ḫurru*, AHw 359; CAD Ḫ 252f.; Ebla cf. GIŠ.ḪUR = *ḫu-rí bù-bù-tim*, *ḫu-ru₁₂ bu*ₓ(NI)*-bu*ₓ*-tim*, VE 468; Fales QuSe 13 178; Conti SQF 136; ḪABRUD = *ḫu-ru₁₂-um*, *ḫur-rúm*, VE 839; Krebernik ZA 73 1983 33; Eg. cf. *ḫá-ru*, Helck Bez. 519 [184]; Watson NUS 26 1981 10f.; UF 32 2000 569); ¶ **RS Akk.**: cf. the element /ḫur(r-)/ in TNN, cf. Sivan GAGl 230: /ḫurru/. ¶ Forms: sg. *ḫr*.
Cave, fossa, tomb: *ʕṯtrt ḫr*, DN of the tomb(s), 1.43:1 and par. (Del Olmo A2CISFP 1 367ff.; Puech UF 25 1993 327ff.; cf. *ʕa-s-tá-ra ḫá-rú*, *ʕa-śi-tá-ya ḫá-rú*, Helck Bez. 459; Baniyas: ᵈINANNA(MÙŠ) *ḫur-ri*, Lackenbacher Fs. Birot 159; RS: ᵈ"U"+DAR *ḫur-ri*, PRU 3 171 (RS 16.173):9'; 4 230 (RS 18.01), 3, 6; 6 35. Cf. diff.: Herrmann WO 7 1973 135ff.; Dietrich - Loretz JA 45ff.: 'von Ḫurri'; Teixidor HTR 68 1975 151ff.; Lackenbacher Fs. Birot 153ff.: 'Hurrian' (> 'Syrian / Phoenician'); *w in ḫr apm* if it has no nasal fossae, 1.103+:6, 30. Cf. the spelling *ẖr*, 5.22:1 (cf. Dietrich - Loretz KA 189). Cf. in bkn ctx. *ḫr* [, 1.13:17 (cf. Del Olmo MLC 492; diff.: Merlis AUL 88ff.: 'vessel', Akk. *ḫarû*).
Cf. ḫrṣbʕ, ḫrt.

ḫr (II) PN (etym. unc.; cf. Watson AuOr 8 1990 246). Cf. *ḥr (II)*, PN.
PN: 4.278:6. Cf. in bkn ctx. 4.11:6; 4.244:33; *bn ḫr*[, 4.441:6. Cf. the spelling *ẖr*, 5.22:1 (cf. Dietrich - Loretz KA 189).

/ḫ-r-ʔ/ v. G: "to defaecate" (cf. Syr. *ḥrō*, LS 253; Arab. *ḫariʔa*, Lane 715). ¶ Forms: G prefc. *yḫru*, suffc. *ḫr*[*a*(?)] (1.72:12; rdg *(y)ḫr*[*u*?).

G. To defaecate: *w k l yḫru w l yṯtn śśw* and if the horse neither defaecates nor urinates, 1.85:9 and par.; cf. *k l ḫr*[*a*(?), 1.72:12 (rdg *(y)ḫr*[*u*?).

Cf. **ḫru, ḫra/i(n)**.

ḫri PN; cf. *ḫra/i(n)*.

ḫru n. m. "faeces, excrement" (cf. /ḫ-r-ʔ/; Hb. *ḥrʔ(ym)*, HALOT 348f.; Syr. *ḥeryō* LS 253; Arab. *ḫurʔ*, Lane 715). ¶ Forms: sg. suf. *ḫrih*.

Faeces, excrement: *ylšn b ḫrih w ṯnth* he soils him with his excrement and his urine, 1.114:21.

ḫra/i(n) PN (Sem. Cf. Grøndahl PTU 139; Van Soldt SAU 33; Watson AuOr 13 1995 222).

PN: *bn ḫri*, 4.125:5; *bn ḫran*, 4.33:30 (*ilštmʕy*); 4.51:10; 4.55:8; 4.90:1.

/ḫ-r-b/ v. G: "to wither, dry up" (Hb., Nab., JAram. *ḥrb*, HALOT 349; DNWSI 402f.: *ḥrb*$_1$; Syr. *ḥreb*, LS 254; Akk. *ḫarābu*, AHw 322; CAD Ḫ 87f.; Arab. *ḫariba*, Lane 715ff.); ¶ **par.**: /ġ-l-y/, /ḫ-s-p/. ¶ **Forms**: G prefc. *yḫrb*.

G. To wither, dry up: *b grn yḫrb* on the threshing floor (the harvest) had withered, 1.19 I 30 (// *yġly*, *yḫsp*).

ḫrbġlm TN (Belmonte RGTC 12/2 130. Cf. Dietrich - Loretz - Sanmartín UF 5 1973 110; Astour UF 13 1981 8f.; NuzHur 1 14 no. 9 n. 16; TopAn 129; Heltzer RCAU 10; cf. Kühne UF 6 1974 167 n. 73; Heltzer IOKU 89 n. 34; OLA 6 487f. n. 224; Sanmartín SEL 12 1995 180 n. 18; Van Soldt UF 28 1996 664 n. 79, 670; UF 29 1997 691; UF 30 1998 734); ¶ **syll.**: cf. possibly URU *ḫar-ba-ḫu-li-bé*, PRU 4 66 (RS 17.62+):15'; URU *ḫa-ar-bu*[-*ḫu-li*(?), PRU 6 148:3'; cf. Dietrich - Loretz - Sanmartín UF 5 1973 110 n. 1; Nougayrol PRU 6 p. 146; Astour UF 13 1981 9 n. 53; Belmonte RGTC 12/2 117: *Ḫarbuġūli*.

TN: 4.625:19; 4.644:8.

Cf. **kṯtġlm**.

ḫrd n. m. 1) "(royal) guard, militia, troop(s)"; 2) "soldier of the guard, militiaman" (< Hurr. *ḫuradi-*, Diakonoff HU 66, 78 n. 78; cf. Laroche GLH 114; > Akk. *ḫurādu*, AHw 357, 1562; CAD Ḫ 244f.; Hitt. *ḫuradi-*, Tischler HEG 300. Cf. Freydank AOF 4 1976 111ff.; Heltzer OrAn 18 1979 245ff.; IOKU 105ff.; Stieglitz JAOS 101 1981 371f.; Dietrich - Loretz UF 18 1986 113; Márquez AfO 45 1997/98 373ff.; Van Soldt UF 27 1995 484f.; Arnaud AuOr 17/18 1999/2000 152); **Akk. RS**: cf. rdg ÉRIN.MEŠ in 4.784:2, Van Soldt UF 27 1995 485f. ¶ **Forms**: sg. *ḫrd*, suf. *ḫrdk*, *ḫrdh*, *ḫrdn*; pl.(?) cstr. *ḫrd*.

1) (Royal) guard, militia, troops, ★a) (royal) guard: PN *ʕbd mlk d št ʕl ḫrdh* royal official placed in command of his guard, 2.47:15; *bʕln yġtr ḫrd* the lord, the guard will attack (him), 1.103+:39 (Del Olmo CR 356; diff.: Dietrich - Loretz TUAT 98; MU 133f.); *mlkn yd ḫrdh yd{d}ll* the king, the hand of his guard will humiliate (him), 1.103+:46; *ḫrdn yhpk l mlk* the guard will rebel against the king, 1.103:52; *bn ḫrnk mġy hbṭ hw ḫrd w šl hw qrt* your messenger arrived, knocked down the guard (and) plundered the city, 2.61:6; ★b) militia, troop(s): *spr ḫrd* list of the militia, 4.683:1; 4.777:1; 4.784:1; *tgmr ḫrd* total of the troops, 4.179:15; 4.777:12; *arbʕm yn l ḫrd* forty (jars) of wine for the troops, 4.230:12 (diff. Watson AuOr 8 1990 119: PN); ★c) *ḫrd ʕps* frontier(?) guard: *ḫrd ʕps aḫd kw sʕt* the frontier(?) guard has confiscated one *k.* of (grain) *s.*, 2.47:17; cf. in bkn ctx. *ḫrdk ʕps* [, *ibid.* ln. 19 (cf. *ʕp/bs*; cf. diff. Dietrich - Loretz UF 19 1987 29: *ḫrd ʕps* 'der rebellische Wachsoldat').
2) Soldier of the guard, militiaman: *ʕnt ḫrd ank* I am already a soldier of the guard, 2.16:13.
In bkn ctx.: 4.627:11.

]ḫrg, 4.682:5.

ḫrġḏġ PN (etym. unc.; for the segment *ḫrġ-* cf. Laroche NH 61 no. 303; for the segment *-ḏġ* cf. Gelb - Purves - MacRae NPN 257).
PN: *bn PN*, 4.631:16.

ḫrḫb DN; god of the summer and father of the goddess *nkl* (etym. unc.; Astour NuziHurr 2 50; for the various opinions cf. Herrmann YN 3; Wyatt UF 9 1977 289ff.; Dietrich - Loretz Studien 165ff.).
DN: *ḫrḫb mlk qẓ ḫrḫb mlk aġzt* DN, king of the summer(-fruit), DN, king (of the season) of weddings, 1.24:2-3.

ḫrk n. m. "latticework" (Hb., Aram., MHb. *ḥrk*, HALOT 353; WTM 2 111; ANH 155). ¶ Forms: sg. *ḫrk*.
Latticework: *spr npṣ any (...) mṣpt ḫrk* list of naval equipment: (...) a latticework crow's nest, 4.689:4.

/ḫ-r-m/ v. G: "to pierce" (Arab. *ḫarama*, Lane 730f. Cf. Del Olmo IMC 90; diff.: De Moor UF 12 1980 306: 'to destroy under the ban', Hb. *ḥrm*, syll. *ḫa-ri-mu*, but. cf. Arab. *ḥarama*); ¶ par.: /h-r-g/. ¶ Forms: G impv. *ḫrm*.
G. To pierce: bkn ctx.]*ḫrm ṯn ymm* pierce during two days, 1.13:3 (// *hrg*).

ḫrmln PN (etym. unc.; cf. Benz PNPPI 318).
PN: *bn PN*, 4.35 I 12; 4.103:42-43 (cf. Van Soldt SAU 38).

ḫrmṯt n. f. "sickle" (Hb. *ḥrmš*, HALOT 355. Cf. Healey UF 15 1983 50); ¶ syll. Ug.: cf. 2 URUDU *ḫa-ar-me-ša-tu* GIŠ.MÁ.MEŠ, PRU 6 141:3; Huehnergard UVST 130; Sivan GAGl 227; Van Soldt SAU 304; cf. Sanmartín AuOr 5 1987 150). ¶ Forms: sg./pl. *ḫrmṯt*.
Sickle: *ṯlṯ ḫrmṯt ṯtm mḫrhm* three sickles whose price is sixty (shekels of copper each), 4.625:1; *(...) ḫrmṯt* (so many) sickles, *passim ibid.*; *ʕl PN (...) ḫrmṯt* to PN's account: (...) one sickle, 4.632:4; *passim ibid.*
Cf. in bkn ctx. *mʕbd ḫrmṯt* work of(with) sickles(?), 1.86:23; 4.670:4.

ḫrn n. m. "gang, caravan" (Akk. *ḫarrānu*, AHw 326f.; CAD Ḫ 106; cf. Watson UF 32 2000 569); ¶ par.: *ʕḏbt*. Forms.: sg. *ḫrn*; cstr. suf. *ḫrnk*.
Gang, caravan: ★a) *ṣḥ ḫrn b bhth* he called together a gang in his house, 1.4 V 36 and par. (*// ʕḏbt*; diff.: Margalit ZAW 99 1987 395 n. 23: 'earth-moving equipment', **ḫrr*); ★b) *bn ḫrn* messenger (Astour AJA 69 1965 258): *bn ḫrnk mġy* your messenger arrived, 2.61:3 (alt.: rdg *bn ḫrn k mġy (...)* as for the messenger: when he arrived (...) (cf. *k (I)*, *k (IV)*; diff. Dijkstra UF 7 1975 565: 'during your journey', Akk. *ḫarrānu*, *mar ḫarrāni*).
Cf. ḫrn(y).

ḫrn(y) PN (etym. unc.; cf. Grøndahl PTU 139; Dietrich - Loretz WO 4 1967/8) 302). Cf. *ġrn*, PN.
PN: 4.33:39 (*ḫbty*); *ḫrny* 4.391:1.

ḫrp "mania" ((?) etym. unc.; cf. De Moor - Spronk UF 16 1984 244: 'insanity', Arab. *ḫaraf*; diff. Caquot SEL 5 1988 39: 'chauve-souris', Aram.). ¶ Forms: sg. *ḫrp*.
Mania(?): in unc. and bkn ctx. *bnt ḫrp* 'crazy(?) creature(s)', 1.82:18.
Cf. ḫrpn, ḫrpnt.

ḫrpn PN (Sem. Cf. Grøndahl PTU 30, 139; Watson AuOr 8 1990 119).
PN: *bn PN*, 4.75 IV 6.

ḫrpnt n. f. "autumn" (cf. Hb. *ḥrp*, HALOT 356; Akk. *ḫarpū* (pl.), AHw 326; CAD Ḫ 106; OSA *ḫrf*, CAME 158; DOSA 210f.; Arab. *ḫarīf*, Lane 720. Cf. De Moor UF 1 1969 175). ¶ Forms: sg. *ḫrpnt*.
Autumn: *dm zt ḫrpnt* juice of an autumn (> early) olive, 1.114:31.
Cf. ḫrp, ḫrpn.

/ḫ-r(-r)/ v. G: "to have spasms (of diarrhoea)" (cf. Akk. *(ḫ)arāru*, cf. AHw 65f., 323; CAD A/2 236. Cf. Dietrich - Loretz - Sanmartín UF 6 1974 39; Cohen - Sivan UHT 18; Cohen UF 28 1996 119f.; Sanmartín AuOr 6 1988 232; diff.: Pardee TH 51f.: 'hennir', Arab. *ḫarra*). G suffc./ptc. *ḫr*.
G. To have spasms (of diarrhoea): *k ḫr śśw* if the horse has spasms (of diarrhoea), 1.85:5 and par.

ḫrs PN (etym. unc.; cf. Watson AuOr 8 1990 119).
PN: *bn PN*, 4.695:5.

ḫrṣ n. m. "gold" (Hb. *ḥrwṣ*, HALOT 352; Ph., Pun. *ḥrṣ*, DNWSI 407; Akk. *ḫurāṣu*, AHw 358; CAD Ḫ 245ff.; Arab. *ḫurṣ*, Lane 723; Gk *khrysós*, Liddell - Scott 2011; Linear B: *ku-ru-so*; cf. Hurr. *ḫiyaruḫḫe*, GLH 105); ¶ **syll. Ug.**: *ḫu-r*[*a-ṣu*], Ug 5 137 II 4'; Huehnergard UVST 130; Van Soldt SAU 304; cf. /ḫarūṣu/, /ḫurāṣu/ in PNN, Sivan GAGl 228, 230; ¶ **RS Akk.**: (kù+gi)GUŠKIN, cf. Huehnergard UVST 403; ¶ **par.**: *iqnu*, *ksp*. ¶ **Forms**: sg. *ḫrṣ*, suff. *ḫrṣm* (encl. *-m*).
Gold: ★**a)** in general: *tblk (...) gbʕm mḥmd ḫrṣ* may (...) the hills bring you the most precious gold, 1.4 V 33 and par. (// *ksp*); *imtḫṣ ksp irtṯ ḫrṣ* I fought (for) the silver, I took possession of the gold, 1.3 III 47 (// *ksp*); *lm ank ksp w yrq ḫrṣ* why should I want silver and yellow gold?, 1.14 III 34 and par. (cf. Qatna Akk. *ḫuraṣu arqu*, Bottéro RA 43 1949 17; Hb. *yrqrq ḥrwṣ*, Ps 68:14); *yṣq ksp yšlḥ ḫrṣ* he smelted silver, melted gold, 1.4 I 26 (// *ksp*); *ḫrṣ yṣq lrbbt* he smelted gold by the myriad (of shekels), 1.4 I 27; *ḫrṣ l ʕbrm kš* (like) gold (were) the dates for the guests, 1.22 I 15 (// *ksp*); *ḫrṣ nsb l lbnt* the gold had been transformed into bricks, 1.4 VI 34 (// *ksp*); in bkn ctx. [*i*]*rš (...)* [*ḫrṣ w aš*]*lḥk* ask (...) (gold and) shall grant it to you, 1.17 VI 18 (// *ksp*); *ẓl ksp w nr ḫrṣ* the reflection of silver and the sheen of gold, 1.4 II 28 (// *ksp*); cf. *ḫrṣ*, 4.738:1, 7; ★**b)** in craftwork: *w bn bbt ksp w ḫrṣ* and build a house of silver and gold, 1.4 V 34 and par. (// *iqnim*); *yṣq (...) b gl ḫrṣ nbt* he poured (...) honey in a cup of gold, 1.14 IV 2 and par. (// *ksp*); *št (...) b ks*(!) *ḫrṣ dm ʕṣm* drink (...) (in) cup of gold juice of vines, 1.4 IV 37 and par.; *kt il (...) šmrg*(!)*t b dm ḫrṣ* a divine podium (...) covered with a 'bath' of gold, 1.4 I 32 (// *ksp*); *nʕl il (...) ʕln yblhm ḫrṣ* a divine palanquin (...) upon its rods of gold, 1.4 I 37; *bnt (...) hkly dtm ḫrṣ* I have built (...) my palace of gold, 1.4 VI 38 (// *ksp*); *ṯlṯ mrkb*[*t*] *spyt b ḫrṣ* three chariots plated with gold, 4.167:2;]*ṣpy b ḫrṣ nʕmm*] covered / embroidered with good quality gold, 2.79:10; cf.]*xṣpy b ḫr*[*ṣ*, 2.83:9; *ššrt ḫrṣ ṯqlm kbd ʕšrt mznh* a chain of gold whose weight is twelve shekels, 4.341:1; ★**c)** as tribute: *šqrb (...) w ḫrṣ* offer (...) and also gold, 1.16 I 45; [*k*]*s mn ḫrṣ*, one cup (and) one mina of gold, 3.1:20 (1 GAL KÙ.GI.MEŠ MA.NA KI.LÁ-*šu*, PRU 4 41 [RS 17.227 and dupl.]: 22; cf. Knoppers BASOR 289 1993 87); *ks ḫrṣ* one cup of gold, 3.1:27, 29 (1 GAL KÙ.GI.MEŠ, PRU 4 42 [RS 17.227 and dupl.]:25, 27); [*ḫ*]*rṣ argmny* the gold of my tribute, 2.36:6 (cf. *ibid.* ln. 12); ★**d)** cultic offering: *ksp w ḫrṣ kmm* silver and gold, ditto, 1.90:4 and par; *ṯql ḫrṣ l špš* a

shekel of gold for DN, 1.43:10, 13; *nskt ksp w ḫrṣ ṯʕ* an offering of silver and gold, the Noble, 1.105:22; ★e) in transactions: (her double in silver) *atn w ṯlṯh ḫrṣm* I will give, and her triple in gold, 1.14 IV 43 (// *k*(!)*spm*); *w atn (...) alp ksp w rbt ḫrṣ* I will pay [...] one thousand (shekels) of silver, ten thousand of gold, 1.24:20-21 (// *ksp*); *qlm ḫrṣ b ṯmnt ksp* two shekels of gold for eight of silver, 4.337:20; *arbʕt ʕšrt ḫrṣ b ṯqlm kbd arbʕm* fourteen (shekels) of gold for forty two (shekels of silver), 4.341:16; *ʕšrt ḫrṣ b arbʕm* ten (shekels of) gold for forty, 4.341:18; ★f) elliptical use, shekel of gold: *ḫrṣ ṯlṯt* of gold three (shekels), 1.43:5 (diff.: Aartun UF 16 1984 30f.: '(Palmen)-Zweig', Arab. *ḫurṣ, ḫarṣ*); *ybl hw mit ḫrṣ* he personally took one hundred (shekels) of gold, 2.72:28; *arbʕ mat ḫrṣ* four hundred (shekels) of gold, 4.172:8; 4.266:7; *mnym ḫrṣ* eighty (shekels) of gold, 4.265:6; *mitm ʕšrm kbd ḫrṣ* two hundred and twenty (shekels) of gold, 4.336:10; *ḫmš ḫrṣ* five (shekels of) gold, 4.341:5 (cf. ln 16, 18); *ṯlṯ*[*m*] *ḫrṣ* thirty (shekels of) gold, 1.164:16.
Bkn: *ht hln ḫrṣ*[..., 2.36:12 (cf. Pardee AfO 29/30 1983/84 325: 'indeed the [or: [your]] gold'); 4.23:3; 4.550:3; 7.135:4; ★g) greenish yellow (a metal / gold): *qḥ ksp w yrq ḫrṣ yd mqmh* take silver and yellow (metal), gold together with the place in which it is found, 1.14 III 22 and par.
Cf. ḫrṣbʕ, ḫrṣn.

ḫrṣbʕ TN (Belmonte RGTC 12/2 133f.: *Ḫur(i)-ṣubūʕi*. Cf. Virolleaud Syria 21 1940 144; Heltzer RCAU 10, 16 n. 24; Astour UF 13 1981 7f. n. 37; RSP 2 289 no. 45, 352 no. 151; Wesselius UF 15 1983 315; Van Soldt UF 28 1996 671; UF 30 1998 723, 727); ¶ syll.: cf. URU *ḫu-ur-ṣu-*<*bu*!>*-i*, Ug 5 102:14'; URU *ḫu-u*[*r*]*-ṣú-*[*bu-i*, Ug 5 104:2'; URU *ḫu-ri-*KIRI$_4$, PRU 3 p. 265; RSOu 7 4:8; URU ḪU, PRU 3 189 (RS 10.044):13'.
TN: 4.73:8; 4.288:5; 4.346:9; 4.355:15; 4. 610 (II) 6; 4.693:56(!); 4.770:3; 4.712:1; RSOu 14 35 [KTU 9.388] I 28. Bkn: cf. 4.235:10; 4.244:33; 4.629:3 (Belmonte RGTC 12/2 134).

ḫrṣn PN (etym. unc. Cf. Ginsberg JAOS 70 1950 160; Grøndahl PTU 30, 136, 140; Lipiński OLA 23 1988 127, 129 n. 26; Watson AuOr 8 1990 119, 245; Bordreuil Fs. Loretz 1998 127ff.); ¶ syll.: cf. *ḫu-ra-ṣa-na*, PRU 3 102 (RS 15.109):13; 118 (RS 15.155):13; PRU 6 83 III 5; cf. DUMU *ḫa-ra-*ZI*-na*, Syria 18 1937 246 (RS 8.145):11; *ḫa-ru-*ZI*-en-ni*, Syria 15 1934 137 (RS [Varia 3]):11, 22; cf. Sivan GAGl 230. Cf. *ḫrzn* PN.
PN: ★a) 6.10:1 (*rb khnm*); ★b) *bn PN*, 4.278:4.

ḫrṣp n. m. "tendon" (Hb. *ḥrṣb*, HALOT 356. Cf. Caquot SDB 9 1412; Pardee AfO 33 1986 134; diff. Dietrich - Loretz MU 125f.: 'Gelenk', but cf. Pardee Fs. Fitzmyer 84f.). ¶ **Forms**: sg. *ḫrṣp*.

Tendon: *w in ḫrṣp b kr*[*ʕ* if it has no tendon in the knuckle, 1.103+:27.

ḫršḫ n. m. 1) "bowl for burning perfume"; 2) "brazier for incense" (< Hurr. *aḫrušḫi-*, cf. Laroche GLH 38; alph. Hurr. cf. *aġrtḫnd* (det., dir.), 1.125:14; Laroche Ug 5 506. Cf. Goetze JCS 22 1968/69 17; De Moor UF 2 1970 321; Dietrich - Loretz - Sanmartín UF 6 1974 28; Heltzer GPOTU 50; Xella TRU 41; > Hitt. *aḫrušhi-*, HW^2 1 46, HEG 5; Watson SEL 6 1989 48ff.; Kammenhuber Or 55 1986 105ff.; Akk. *aḫrušḫu*, CAD A/1 194). ¶ **Forms**: sg. *ḫršḫ*.

1) Bowl (for burning perfume): *mit ḫršḫ b ṯqlm* one hundred (perfume burning) bowls for two shekels, 4.341:19.

2) Large brazier for cultic incense (cf. alph. Hurr.: *aġrtḫnd* ('DN', determ., direct.), 1.125:14; cf. Ug. (DN) *uṯḫt*, 1.47:31; 1.118:30; Akk. RS.: ^{d}DUG.BUR.ZI.NÍG.NA, Ug 5 18:30): *š ṣrp w ṣp ḫršḫ* one ram as a burnt offering and one white ewe, perfumed, 1.105:2.

Cf. **uṯḫt**.

ḫršn (I) n. m. "(divine) mountain", dwelling of the god El (Belmonte RGTC 12/2 135: *Ḫuršanu*. Akk. *plurale tantum*: *ḫuršānu*, AHw 360; CAD Ḫ 253ff. Cf. Clifford CMC 39ff.; Wakemann GBM 90; Van Soldt UBL 11 370 n. 29; cf. Hitt. TN *Ḫuršana*, Del Monte(-Tischler) RGTC 6 128, 6.2 45); **RS Akk.** : cf. ^{d}ḪUR.SAG *ḫa-zi*, Ug 5 18:14; ¶ **par.**: *ġr*. ¶ **Forms**: sg. *ḫršn*.

TN in myth: 1.1 II 23 and par.

ḫršn (II) PN (Sem. Cf. Grøndahl PTU 30, 140; cf. Watson AuOr 11 1993 216); ¶ **syll.**: DUMU *ḫu-ur-ša-na*, PRU 6 135:2.

PN: ★**a**) 4.222:13; ★**b**) *bn PN*, 4.63 III 40; 4.715:17.

ḫrt n. f. "cave, grave" (cf. *ḫr*, cf. Akk. *ḫirītu*, AHw 348; CAD Ḫ 198f.; cf. Emar Akk. *ḫi-ri-TI*, Pentiuc Vocabulary 70. Cf. Gordon Syria 33 1956 102f.; De Moor SP 184; Watson NUS 26 1981 12: Eg. *ḫrt*); ¶ **syll. Ug.**: É : *ḫi-ri-ti*, PRU 3 53f. (RS 15.85):17; Huehnergard UVST 129; Sivan GAGl 229; Van Soldt SAU 304. ¶ **Forms**: sg. *ḫrt*.

Cave, grave: *aštn b ḫrt ilm arṣ* I shall put him in the cave of the underworld gods, 1.5 V 5 and par., formula in myth for the burial of gods and heroes (cf. /q-b-r/, 1.19 III 6 and par.); PN *bʕl ḫr*[*t*] gravedigger, 4.224:6 (cf. *bʕl (I)*).

Unc. ctx.: *l ḫrt* w *riš btn* ... and the head of the snake, 1.175:11.

/ḫ-r-ṭ/ v. G: "to pull out, pull up, pluck" (Arab. *ḫaraṭa*, Lane 723f.; cf. Akk. *ḫarāṭu*, AHw 324; cf. Parpola SAA 1 no. 103:9 note). ¶ Forms: G prefc. *yḫrṭ*.
G. To pull out, pull up, pluck: *yḫrṭ yšt l pḥm* he plucked (it and) placed it on the embers, 1.23:38.

ḫry GN m. "Hurrian" (Cf. Hurr. *ḫurruḫe*, GLH 115; Hb. *ḥry*, HALOT 353; cf. KUR URU ḪUR.RI, Ungnad Subartu 130; Eg. *ḫá-rú*, Helck Bez 269. Cf. Edzard - Kammenhuber RlA 4 508ff.; Astour RSP 2 288f. no. 44); ¶ syll.: cf. KUR *ḫur-ri*, PRU 3 183 (RS 16.146+):10, 11.; ¶ par.: *alṯy*, *ddmy*, *ḫty*, *qṭy*. ¶ Forms: sg. *ḫry*.
GN: *u l p ḫry* or according to the custom of the Hurrian, 1.40:29 and par.; 1.84:4 and par. (// *alṯy*, *ddmy*, *ḫty*, *qṭy*). Bkn: 1.40:37; 1.43:22; 4.11:6.

ḫrẓʕ n. m. "paw" ((?) etym. unc.; cf. Syr. *karsūʕō*, LS 348; Arab. *kursūʕ*, Lane 2999; cf. Akk. *kursinnu* AHw 511. Cf. Pardee AfO 33 1986 132; Marrassini LEM 133f.; diff.: Ginsberg JPOS 16 1936 145 n. 25: Hb. /ḥ-l-ṣ/ + /k-r-ʕ/; Gray LC 78 n. 6: 'haste', rdg *ḫrẓ*, Arab. *ḫaraṭa*; De Moor ARTU 131: 'on tiptoe'; survey in Wyatt RTU 164 n. 13); ¶ par.: *pʕn*. ¶ Forms: sg. suf. *ḫrẓʕh*.
Paw(?): *ngṯhm* [...] *il hd b ḫrẓph* approach them [...] did the god DN on (his) paw(?), 1.12 I 41 (poss. theriomorphic connotation of the god *bʕl*; // *pʕn*).

ḫsn (I) n. m.; a social group ("clientele, dependent(s)" (< Hitt. *ḫaššana-*, Tischler HEG 198. Cf. Kammenhuber HdO 1 2 1/2 189 n. 1; Rainey JNES 24 1965 25: 'in charge of storehouses or other strongholds'; Liverani RSO 44 1969 195; cf. Aartun UF 16 1984 26ff.: 'Erniedrigter (d.h. auf eine tiefere Rangstufe gestellte Person', Arab. *aḫsana*; diff.: Cutler - Macdonald UF 8 1976 33: 'seasoned campaigners', Hb. *ḥsn*); ¶ syll. Ug.: cf. the element /ḫusēn-/ in PNN; cf. Huehnergard UVST 252 n. 165. ¶ Forms: pl. *ḫsnm*.
A social group/class (clientele, dependents): *spr ḫsnm dt b TN* list of 'dependents' present in TN, 4.542:1; listed with other classes: *mdrġlm*, 4.137:10; 4.163:13; 4.173:8; *mrum*, 4.137:8; 4.163:4; 4.173:6; 4.179:7; *ṯnnm*, 4.137:1; 4.163:2; 4.173:1; 4.174:2; 4.179:2. Cf. in bkn ctx. 4.162:1, 2.
Cf. ḫsn (II).

ḫsn (II) PN (Sem. Cf. Grøndahl PTU 28, 140); ¶ syll.: cf. DUMU *ḫu*-ZI-*na*, PRU 6 83 III 3; cf. Huehnergard UVST 252 n. 165. Cf. *ḥsn*, *ḫzn*, PNN.
PN: ★a) (?)1.79:2, 3, 5; ★b) *bn PN*, 4.35 I 23.

/ḫ-s-p/ v. G: "to sink down, wilt" (cf. Ph. *ḥsp*, DNWSI 393; Arab. *ḫasafa*, Lane 738f. Cf. Dijkstra - De Moor UF 7 1975 201 n. 243; Friedrich - Röllig PPG 18 n. 2); ¶ par.: /ḫ-r-b/. ¶ Forms: G prefc. *yḫsp*.

G. To sink down, wilt: *yġly yḫsp ib* the fruit / bud had withered and wilted, 1.19 I 31 (// *yḫrb*).

/ḫ-s-r/ v. G: "to fail, be missing" (Hb., Aram., Palm. *ḥsr*, HALOT 338; DNSWI 394; Arab. *ḫasira*, Lane 736f.; Eth. *ḫasra*, CDG 265f.; cf. Akk. *ḫa/esā/ēru*, AHw 329; CAD Ḫ 176). ¶ Forms: G suffc. *ḫsr*, *ḫsrt*, prefc. *yḫsr*.

G. To fail, be missing, be lacking: *npš ḫsrt bn nšm* vigour is / was lacking to men, 1.6 II 17; *d ḫsrt* what you lack, 2.41:17; *mnm ḫsrt* all that I lack, *ibid.* ln. 20; *d*[*rʕ l*] *adny l yḫsr* may offspring not be lacking to my lord, 2.39:9; *nʕmn yḫsr lh* well-being will be lacking to him, 1.163:13 (cf. Dietrich - Loretz MU 171, 189); *ʕlm mḫsm ḫsr* next the beaters(?) are missing!, 6.48:4 (cf. Dietrich - Loretz ESTU 7). In bkn ctx.: RSOu 14 49 [KTU 9.433]:34.

ḫsr n. m. "deficit" (< /ḫ-s-r/; cf. Hb. *ḥsr(wn)*, HALOT 338). ¶ Forms: sg. *ḫsr*.

Deficit (in the commercial sense): *lṯḥ ḫsr b šbʕ ddm* one *l.* (of flour) in deficit in seven 'cauldronfuls', 4.361:3; *kd šmn ṯʕt ḫsr* a jar of oil from lees, in deficit, 4.778:5; 4.782:8; *kd šmn mlṯḥm ḫsr* a jar of oil of two *m.*, in deficit, 4.778:8; 4.782:12.

Bkn ctx.: ... *mit ḫ*(?)*sr kkrm alpm*, 4.721:5.

Cf. mḫsrn.

/ḫ-s-s/ v. G: "to remember"; D/L: "to arouse, revive" (Akk. *ḫasāsu*, AHw 329f.; CAD Ḫ 122ff.; cf. Arab. *ḥassa*, *aḥassa*, Lane 563f. Cf. Caquot - Sznycer TOu 1 205). G prefc. *tḫss*; D/L prefc. with suff. *yḫssk*.

G. To remember: *w yḫss aṯrt ndrh* DN remembered his vow, 1.15 III 25. In bkn ctx.:]*ṯbr ḫss š*[, 2.31:18.

D/L. To arouse, revive: *hm yd il mlk yḫssk* perhaps the love of DN, the king, has aroused you?, 1.4 IV 39.

ḫss DN, second element in the name of the god of magic and technology *kṯr (w) ḫss* (Akk. *ḫasīsu*, *ḫassu*, AHw 331; CAD Ḫ 127f.; Ebla cf. /ḫasīsu(m)/ in GÈŠTUG = *ḫa-zi-zu-um*, *ḫa-zi-zú*, VE 389; Krebernik ZA 73 1983 15; Fronzaroli EL 142; StEb 7 1984 167. Cf. Pope WbMyth 1 295f.; Van Selms UF 11 1979 741; Lipiński UF 20 1988 138).

DN: ★a) *(kṯr w) ḫss (passim)*; *kṯr ḫss šlm* DN, hail!, 1.123:28; cf. *hlk kṯr (...) tdrq ḫss*, 1.17 V 11; *kṯrm ḥbrk w ḫss dʕtk*, 1.6 VI 50; cf. in bkn ctx.: *kṯ]r w ḫ(!)ss*, RSOu 14 53 [KTU 9.432]:11 (Bordreuil - Pardee RSOu 14 p. 401); ★b) *ql bl ʕm kṯr w ḫss kptrh* take (this) request to DN, in TN, 1.100:46; ★c) cf. *hyn (...) ḫss*, 1.4 I 24. Cf. in bkn ctx. *ḫssm* (1.92:17; suf. encl. *-m*(?)).

ḫs/św(n) n. m.; an edible substance (a kind of "garlic" or "onion"(?), Farber ZA 81 1991 234ff.; Watson SEL 12 1995 227f.; cf. Akk. *azannu*, *ḫazuannu*, Bo. Akk. *azzannu*, AHw 92, 338; CAD A/2 526; Farber ZA 81 1991 238 n. 20a.; Hitt. *ḫazzuwanniš*, Tischler HEG 235; Ebla cf. *ḫa-za-núm*, cf. Civil Biling. 86; Stol BSA 3 1987 58f.; Farber ZA 81 1991 238; *ḫa-sa-nu*, cf. Pettinato Rituale 200; *ḫa-su/zu-wa-an(-nu)*[ki], ARET 1, 3, 4, 7, indexes; Bonechi - Catagnoti NABU 1990 23f.; Astour NuzHur 2 11f., 26. Cf. Segert UF 15 1983 212: /ḫasuwan-/; Rubio JAOS 121 2001 273 n. 29; diff.: Merlis AUL 9ff.: 'a color that often qualifies wool', Akk. *ḫašmānu*, RS Akk. *ḫusmānu*, 'also a fruit or vegetable by virtue of its color'; Hoffner JCS 25 1973 234: 'lettuce', cf. Astour UF 29 1997 40ff.; Tropper UF 27 1995 514). ¶ Forms: sg. *ḫs/św(n)*.

An edible substance: *mit ḫsw<n>*(?) one hundred (of) *ḫ*., 4.60:2; *arbʕ mat* four hundred (of) *ḫ*., 4.14:3,] *ḫśwn*, *ibid*. ln. 11; *ṯlṯm dd*(?) *ḫswn* thirty 'cauldronfuls'(?) of *ḫ*., 4.4:9, 11.

In bkn ctx.: 4.786:9.

Cf. ḫswn.

ḫswn PN (etym. unc. Cf. Grøndahl PTU 30, 141; Dietrich - Loretz (-Sanmartín) UF 5 1973 108; UF 10 1978 431).

PN: ★a) 4.44:26; ★b) *bn PN*, 4.232:32.

ḫsyn PN ((?); cf. Dietrich - Loretz - Sanmartín UF 6 1974 27; Belmonte RGTC 12/2 219: *pdr ḫsyn*).

PN(?), element in the composite toponym *pdr ḫsyn*, 4.19:2.

Cf. pdr (I).

ḫsu,1.164:19; misspelling of *y*(!)*šu*. Cf. /y-ṣ-ʔ/.

/ḫ-ṣ-b/ v. Gt: "to fight" (Hb. *ḥṣb*, HALOT 342?; cf. Akk. *ḫaṣābu*, AHw 331; CAD Ḫ 129); ¶ par.: /m-ḫ-ṣ/. ¶ Forms: Gt prefc. *tḫtṣb*.

Gt. To fight: *tḫtṣb bn qrytm* she fought between (the) two cities, 1.3 II 6 and par. (// *tmtḫṣ*).

Cf. tḫtṣb.

ḫṣt n. f. "half" (Hb. *ḥṣy*, *ḥṣwt*, HALOT 343; Ph., Pun., Aram. *ḥṣy*, DNWSI 399; cf. Akk. *eṣû*, AHw 253; CAD Ḫ 351. Cf. Dietrich - Loretz - Sanmartín UF 7 1975 143). ¶ Forms: sg. *ḫṣt*, suff. *ḫṣth*.

Half: *šnpt ḫsṭh* as a *š.*-offering, half of it, 1.39:10; *ḫsṭ*(!) *kkr*, half a talent, 4.131:5 (cf. Dietrich - Loretz - Sanmartín UF 5 1973 88f.); in bkn ctx.: *l il ḫsṭ*[to DN, half..., 1.136:11.

ḫsṭ, 4.131:5 (*ḫs*[[*ṭ*]]), cf. *ḫsṭ*.

/ḫ-š/ v. G "to tremble, be alarmed" (Hb. *ḥwš*, HALOT 300; Akk. *ḫâšu*, AHw 334f.; CAD Ḫ 146f.; cf. Arab. *ḫāsa*, Hava 191. Cf. Clifford CMC 146 n. 65; Roberts JBL 106 1987 36; diff.: De Moor SP 165; Margalit MLD 64f.: 'to enter, invade', Arab. *ḫašša*; Van Zijl Baal 150f.: 'to hasten', Hb. *ḥwš*, Akk. *ḫāšu*, but cf. Ug. /ḥ-š/). ¶ **Forms**: G prefc. *aḫš*, *aḫšn*, *tḫš*.

G. To tremble, be alarmed: *ib hdd*(!) *lm tḫš* enemies of DN, why are you alarmed?, 1.4 VII 38-39

Cf. in unc. ctx. *ġrm aḫšn*, 1.4 VII 32.

Cf. **/ḥ-š/ (II)**.

ḫš DN / TN, divine mountain, residence of the god Baal (Belmonte RGTC 12/2 127f.: *Ḫazzi*; possibly an allophone of *ks*. Cf. Nougaurol Ug 5 p. 47f.; Dietrich - Loretz - Sanmartín UF 7 1975 524; Del Olmo CR 341 n. 24; AuOr 10 1992 255; Astour UF 29 1997 1ff.; Del Olmo - Sanmartín AuOr 13 1995 259ff.); ¶ **RS Akk.**: ᵈḪUR.SAG *ḫa-zi*, Ug 5 18:14; 170:22'; ᵈIŠKUR ḪUR.SAG *ḫa-zi*, PRU 4 48ff. (RS 17.340+):40'; 63ff. (RS 17.237+):60; 69 (RS 16.276):21; 137f. (RS 18.06+):7'; 227f. (RS 17.429):2'; PRU 6 58:3'; ᵈU ᵈḪUR.SAG *ḫa-zi*, Ug 5 170:19'; ᵈIŠKUR EN(/*be-el*) ḪUR.SAG *ḫa-zi*, PRU 3 76 (16.144):12; 83f. (RS 16.157):27; 107f. (RS 16.238):18; Ug 5 18:4. DN / TN: *il ḫš il add* the god of the divine (mountain) TN, DN, 1.65:9. Cf. DN / GN *ṯṯb ḫzġ*, Hurr. 1.65:9. Cf. **ks**, **ṣpn**.

ḫšm, 1.123:30, here read *ḫšt*. Cf. *ḫšt*.

ḫšt n. f. "sepulchre, mausoleum" (Akk. *ḫaštu*, AHw 334; CAD Ḫ 143. Cf. Sawyer - Strange IEJ 14 1964 97; De Moor UF 1 1969 171 n. 19; Margalit UF 8 1976 148; Sanmartín UF 10 1978 454; diff.: Del Olmo MLC 554: 'pórtico', Arab. *ḫašša*; Watson UF 31 1999 788: 'hearth', Hitt. *ḫešša*; for other opinions cf. Herdner TOu 1 549 n. c; Groddek UF 33 2001 213ff: 'Totentempel'; Lorezt UF 33 2001 377ff.: 'Totenheiligtum'); ¶ **par.**: *bt (II)*. ¶ **Forms**: sg. suf. *ḫštk*.

Sepulchre, mausoleum: *k inr ap ḫštk* like a dog at the entrance to your sepulchre, 1.16 I 3 and par.; *u ḫštk l ntn ʕtq* and your sepulchre has become a perpetual lament(?), 1.16 I 18 and par.; *šlm il ḫšt*, Hail, gods of the mausoleum!, 1.123:30 (cf. Del Olmo CR 344).

ḫt TN (Belmonte RGTC 12/2 120ff.: *Ḫatti*; < Hitt. /ḫatt(i)/, KUR.URU *ḪA-AT-TI* / *ḪAT-TI*, Güterbock RlA 4 373f.; cf. Tischler HEG 223f.;

Hurr. URU *ḫa-at-ti-ni-i/e*, GLH 98. Cf. Astour RSP 2 289f. n. 46, 147f. n. 147); ¶ syll.: KUR(.URU) *ḫa-at-ti*, *ḫa/ḫat-ti*, cf. PRU 3 p. 265; PRU 4 p. 254; PRU 6 p. 146; Ug 5 p. 335; RSOu 7 pg. 137.

TN: *hm ḫt ʕl* if Hatti attacks, 2.30:16; *ṯpllm mlk r[b mlk ḫt* PN the Great King, the King of Hatti, 3.1:16 (thus KTU but cf. Knoppers BASOR 289 1993 83: rdg *ṯpllm mlk r[b* ...). Cf. in bkn ctx. *hmlt ḫt*, 1.83:12; 2.21:22.

Cf. ḫty.

/ḫ-t-ʔ/ v. G: "to grind up, crush, annihilate"; N: "to be ground up, crushed, annihilated" (cf. Akk. *ḫatû*, AHw 336. Cf. Van Zijl Baal 210; Dahood ULx 89; Eg. *ḫtī*, Ward JNES 20 1961 35). ¶ Forms: G inf. *ḫti*; N suffc. *nḫtu*; prefc. *tḫtan*; inf. <*n*>*ḫtu* (rdg *sic* for *ḫtu* in 1.6 II 23).

G. To grind up, crush, annihilate: *ḫti nḫtu* have been overwhelmingly crushed, 2.10:7.

N. To be / remain ground up: *k lli b ṯbrn qnh tḫtan* like a sucking lamb in the opening of his oesophagus you shall remain ground up, 1.4 VIII 20 and par.; *šmʕt ḫti nḫtu ht hm in mm nḫtu* I have heard that they have been overwhelmingly crushed; well, if they have not been crushed..., 2.10:7-10 (cf. diff. Pardee Fs. Pope 1987 67: *ḫti*, "blows" (n. cstr. pl.).

ḫtb PN (etym. unc.; cf. Watson AuOr 8 1990 246). Cf. *ḫtpy*, PN.

PN *bn PN*, 4.356:2.

ḫtm PN (?) (etym. unc. Cf. Grøndahl PTU 276).

PN, in bkn ctx.: *ḫtm rb*[, 2.25:7.

/ḫ-t-n/ v. G/D: "to become a son-in-law, to marry" (< denom. Ug. */ḫatnu/; cf. syll. Ug. PN *ḫa-at-ni* PN, PRU 3 142 [RS 16.136]:5; PRU 3 p. 233; Huehnergard UVST 130; Sivan GAGl 228; Hb., Aram., Nab. *ḥtn*, HALOT 364; DNWSI 414; Syr. *ḥatnō*, LS 264; Arab. *ḫatan*, Lane 704; Akk. and RS Akk. *ḫat(a)nu*, AHw 335f.; CAD Ḫ 148; cf. Emar /ḫuttanu/, Pentiuc Vocabulary 79f. Cf. Herrmann YH 15; Van Zijl Baal 226f.); ¶ par.: /t-r-ḫ/. ¶ Forms: D impv. *ḫtnm* (encl. *-m*); inf. / verb. n. + suff. *ḫtny* (cf. *ḫtn (I)*).

G/D. To become a son-in-law, to marry: *l ḫtnm bʕl* make yourself a son-in-law of DN!, 1.24:25-26 (// *trḫ*).

ḫtn (I) n. m. "relationship by marriage, wedding" (< inf./ n. verb. /ḫ-t-n/); ¶ par.: /t-r-ḫ/. ¶ Forms: sg. suff. *ḫtny*.

Relationship by marriage, wedding: *ʕmn nkl ḫtny* with DN is my wedding, 1.24:32 (// *ytrḫ*).

ḫtn (II) PN (etym. unc.; cf. Grøndahl PTU 27, 276, 301); ¶ syll.: cf. *ḫu-ut-ta*(!)*-na*, Syria 16 1935 196 (RS 6.345):3 (Berger WO 5 1969/70 276; *ḫu-ut-te-nu*, PRU 3 95 (RS 16.246):4 and *passim ibid.*; PRU 6 56 rev. 8'; *ḫu-ud-da-na*, RS 23.22+ VI 14' (Van Soldt SAU 341 n. 185).
PN: 4.269:20, 23, 27.

/ḫ-t(-t)/ v. G: "to break, yield" (Hb. *ḥtt*, HALOT 365); ¶ par.: /l-ʔ-y/w/, /m-t/. ¶ Forms: G suffc. *ḫt*, *ḫtt*.
G. To break, be overcome, yield: *mt dm ḫt* DN, thus, yielded, 1.16 VI 13 and par. (// *laṭ*(!)). In bkn ctx.: *yd*[*y*] *ḫtt* my hand yields, 1.2 IV 1 (// *mtt*).

ḫtt n. m. "terror" ((?); cf. /ḫ-t(-t)/; Hb. *ḥtt*, HALOT 365 Bordreuil - Caquot Syria 57 1980 351). ¶ Forms: sg.(?) *ḫtt*[; suf. *ḫttk*.
Terror(?): in bkn ctx., *al ḫtt* [...] *ḫttk* [, 1.176:26-27.

ḫty (I) GN m. "Hittite" (< *ḫt*, TN; cf. Akk. *ḫattû*, AHw 336; CAD Ḫ 151; Hb. *ḥty*, HALOT 363f.; cf. Hurr. *ḫattuḫi*, GLH 98; Hitt. LÚ/DUMU URU *ḪATTI*, Güterbock RlA 4 373. Cf. Astour RSP 2 289f.); ¶ par.: *alṯy*, *ddmy*, *ḫry*, *qṭy*. ¶ Forms: sg. *ḫty* (f. *ḫtyt* cf. *ḫtyt*).
GN: *u l p ḫty* or according to the custom of the Hittite, 1.40: 29 and par.; *kd l ḫty maḫdh* a jar for 'the Hittite of TN', 4.149:4 (cf. Sanmartín UF 21 1989 341); cf. *kdm l ḫty* two jars for 'the Hittite', 4.216:9.

ḫty (II) PN; cf. *ḫd/ty(n)* PN.

ḫtym PN (etym. unc.; cf. Grøndahl PTU 276); ¶ syll.: cf. DUMU *ḫa*[*-ti-ia-m*]*a*(?), PRU 6 83 III 22.
PN: *bn PN*, 4.687:4.

ḫtyn PN; cf. *ḫd/ty(n)*.

ḫtyt GN f. "Hittite (people(?))" (< *ḫty*). ¶ Forms: sg. *ḫtyt*.
GN: *ḫmš ddm l ḫtyt* five cauldronfuls for the Hittite (people(?), 4.269:3.

/ḫ-ṭ/ v. G: "to wake up, come to" (cf. *ḫiāṭu*, *ḫâṭ/du* AHw 343; CAD Ḫ 159ff. Cf. Dijkstra - De Moor UF 7 1975 209; diff.: Greenfield BSOAS 57 1994 90 n. 23: 'to see', Akk. *ḫâṭu*, Aram. *ḥyṭ*). ¶ Forms: G prefc. *yḫṭ*.
G. To wake up, come to: *krt yḫṭ w ḥlm* PN came to and it was a dream, 1.14 III 50 (diff.: Margalit ZAW 99 1987 399: 'awoke', **ḫṭʔ* + elision of ʔaleph).

ḫṭ n. m. "sceptre, rod, wand, stake" (Arab. *ḫaṭṭ*, Lane 759f.; Akk. *ḫaṭṭu*, AHw 337; CAD Ḫ 153ff. Cf. Tsumura UF 6 1978 408 n. 19; Loretz

MLE 1 1982 40f.; diff. Greenfield BSOAS 57 1994 90 n.3; 'to see', Akk. *ḫâṭu*, Aram. *ḥyṭ*); ¶ par.: *ksu*, *mṭ*. ¶ Forms: sg. *ḫṭ*, suff. *ḫṭk*, *ḫṭh*, *ḫṭm* (encl. *-m*).

Sceptre, rod, wand, stake; ★a) sceptre: *y yṯbr ḫṭ mṯpṭk* no doubt he will break the sceptre of your rule, 1.2 III 18 and par. (// *ksa*); *bdh ḫṭ ṯql* with the sceptre of sterility in his hand, 1.23:9; *il ḫṭh nḥt* DN reached for his sceptre, 1.23:37 (// *mṭ ydh*); *y mt mt nḥtm ḫṭk* oh man, man, you reached for your sceptre!, 1.23:40 and par. (// *mṭ*); ★b) rod, wand: *ylmn ḫṭm* he struck with a rod, 1.114:8 (cf. Dietrich - Loretz UF 25 1993 135; diff.: ʕAjjan NO 12: 'without pity', Arab. *ḫaṭama*); *ḫṭm tʕmt* with a rod he hit him, 1.16 VI 8 (diff.: Margalit UF 8 1976 157: 'string', Hb. *ḥwṭ*, Arab. *ḫayṭ*; Saliba JAOS 92 1972 108f.; Bordreuil - ʕAjjan Semitica 28 1976 5: 'Syrian rose', Arab. *ḫaṭmiyy*; cf. Del Olmo IMC 109); *ḫṭ nqh u qrb ḫṭ* the wand is ready and the wand approaches!, 1.169:5 (diff.: Loretz - Xella MLE 1 1982 37: 'penis', also in ln. 1, rdg *tg ḫṭk*, but cf. /g-ḫ-ṭ/, ln. 14, *ḫṭ + m*; De Moor UF 12 1980 429f.: 'wake up!', /ḫ-ṭ/, the same root in ln. 1, 'he who wakes', rdg *m*(!)*ḫṭ*, and ln. 14, 'one who is awake'; for these and other interpretations cf. Caquot TOu 2 56 n. 131; cf. *ḫṭm*.); ★c) stake: *klb l ḫṭh imḫsh* (like) a dog (tied) to his stake you wounded him, 1.19 I 14 (diff.: Caquot SEL 2 1985 104f.: 'son sceptre'; for this and other interpretations cf. Del Olmo IMC 128 n. 287). Bkn: 1.95:4.

/ḫ-ṭ-ʔ/ v. G: "to make a mistake, sin; to do evil"; Š: "to lead astray" (Hb., Aram., Palm. *ḥṭʔ*, HALOT 305f.; DNWSI 362; Akk. *ḫaṭû*, AHw 337f.; Syr. *ḥṭō*, LS 227; OSA *ḫṭʔ*, DOSA 199; Arab. *ḫaṭiʔa*, Lane 761f.; Eth. *ḫatʔa*, CDG 268); ¶ par.: *šn yp* (cf. /r-š-ʕ/, /š-n-w/. Cf. Dietrich - Loretz - Sanmartín UF 7 1975 157f.). ¶ Forms: G prefc. *tḫṭa*, [*tḫṭu*], *tḫṭin*; Š prefc. with suff. *tšḫḫann*.

G. To make a mistake, sin, do evil: *utḫṭin b apkn (...) u tḫṭin l dbḥm* or whether you have sinned by your anger (...), or whether you have sinned in connection with (/ against) the sacrifices, 1.40:22 and par. (cf. *ušn ypkn*, ln. 36 and par.); *tḫṭa l gbk* do/they do evil to your back(s), 1.169:5 (// *tršʕ*; diff.: Del Olmo CR 385: 'may (your back) suffer evil! [?]; cf. also Verreet Modi 203; Tropper UF 22 1990 388).

Š. To lead astray: *hm (...) tšḫṭann b šnth* if (...) they lead him astray in his sleep, 1.19 III 45 (// *tʕpn*; diff.: Dijkstra - De Moor UF 7 1975 209: 'to awake', /ḫ-ṭ/, assuming it is a mistake for *tšḫṭn*(!)*n*; Margalit ZAW 99 1987 399f.: 'to disturb', */ḫ-ṭ-ʔ/; cf. Verreet Modi 215: 'hindern'; Tropper Kausativstamm 27f.; UF 22 1990 390: 'berauben').

ḫṭm n. m. "nose" (MHb. *ḥwṭm*, Jastrow 431; Arab. *ḫaṭm*, Lane 767f.; cf. Caquot TOu 2 59 n. 151). ¶ Forms: sg. *ḫṭm*.
Nose: *l adm w d ḫṭm* oh man and being that breathes!, 1.169:14 (< 'he of the nose'; for the construction of the syntagm cf. *il d pid*; diff.: Loretz - Xella MLE 1 1982 38: *wd ḫṭm* 'die 'Liebe' seines Penis', cf. *ḫt*; for the various opinions cf. Caquot TOu 2 58 n. 151).

ḫṭm, allograph of *ḥṭm*, 5.22:24; cf. *ḥtt*.

ḫṭpy PN (etym. unc.; cf. Ribichini - Xella RSF 15 1987 9f.).
PN: 4.130:2; 4.635:20 (*adddy*).

ḫṭr n. m.; a tool (Del Olmo MLC 555: 'bieldo'; P.L. Watson MGD 110f.: 'pitchfork'; De Moor SP 210; Dietrich - Loretz - Sanmartín UF 5 1973 89; Stieglitz JCS 33 1981 53; Healey UF 15 1983 51: 'Sieb', 'strainer', 'sieve'; cf. Hb. *ḥšr(h)*, HALOT 363; cf. Aram. *ḥšr*, DJPA 217; Arab. *ḫašara*, Lane 742; diff.: Watson UF 28 1996 702f.: 'a (bladed) weapon' Hurr. *ḫašeri*; but cf. Wyatt RTU 135 n. 82; Watson UF 31 1999 788f.); ¶ par.: *ḥrb*, *rḥm*. ¶ Forms: sg. *ḫṭr*, du. *ḫṭrm*.
A tool: *spr npṣ PN (...) ṯt ḫṭrm* list of the belongings of PN: (...) two *ḫ*., 4.385:2; *b ḫṭr tdrynn* she winnowed him with the *ḫ*., 1.6 II 32 (// *b ḥrb tbqʕnn*, *b rḥm tṭḥnn*).

ḫṭt[, 4.436:3.

ḫym n. m. "canopy" (cf. Arab. *ḫaym*, Lane 837; cf. Van Selms UF 7 1975 471; Dietrich - Loretz UF 10 1978 59; Xella BH 181ff. cf. diff. Caquot - Sznycer TOu 1 195 n. f: 'baldaquin', Akk. *ḫaʔu(m)*); ¶ par.: *kḥṯ*, *kt*. ¶ Forms: sg. *ḫym*.
Canopy: *yṣq ḫym w tbṯḫ* he cast a canopy and a bed, 1.4 I 29. Bkn 4.66:7; 6.39:2.
Cf. ḫm, ḫmn, ḫmt.

ḫyml PN (Anat. Cf. Grøndahl PTU 275, 284); ¶ syll.: DUMU *ḫa-ia-mu-li*, PRU 4 231 (RS 17.244):5.
PN: 4.165:3.

ḫyr MN (Ph. cf. *ḥyr*, KAI III 8; Emar /ḫiyyāru/, Pentiuc Vocabulary 66; cf. Akk. *ayyaru*, AHw 25; CAD A 230; Aram. *ʔyyr*, DJPA 48f.; Arab. *ʔayyār*, Lane 136; cf. Hurro-Akk. *ḫiari*, AHw 342; cf. CAD Ḫ 178f. Cf. Olivier JNSL 1 1971 39ff.; De Tarragon CU 21ff.; Xella UF 13 1981 328f.; Bonechi SEL 7 1990 20; Durand MARI 1 122 n. 9; Vita AoF 27 2000 299: 'Gold', Hurr. *ḫiyari*); ¶ syll. Ug.: cf. *i-na* ITI *ḫi-ya-ri*, RSOu 7 2 (RS 34.169):17'; Huehnergard UVST 128f.; *i-n*]*a* ITI : *ḫi-ya-ri*, RSOu 7 25 (RS 34.167+):10; cf. RS 25.455A+B III 5' (unpubl.); RS 25.132 III 1 (unpubl.); Van Soldt BiOr 46 1989 651; SAU 304; Sivan GAGl 229. ¶ Forms: sg. *ḫyr*.

Month name: *yrḫ ḫyr* in the month of *ḫ.*, 1.105:15 and par.; *b ġb ḫyr* in the *ġ.* of *ḫ.*, 1.105:3; *il ḫyr* gods of (the month of) *ḫ.*, 1.148:23; *b ṯṯ ym ḥdṯ ḫyr* on the sixth of the new moon of MN, 1.78:2.
Cf. **ġyrn, ḫyrn, ḫytr**.

ḫyrn PN (< *ḫyr*, MN. Cf. Grøndahl PTU 21, 30, 138; Sivan GAGl 229; Van Soldt SAU 35, 38; Watson AuOr 11 1993 215; cf. Ward UF 8 1976 355ff. for Eg. [Hyksos] *ḫy3n*); ¶ **syll.**: *ḫi-ia-ra-nu* DUMU *ki-ri-bu-ya*, PRU 3 199 (RS 16.257+) A I 20"; Ug 5 12:42. Allograph *ġyrn* in 4.277:3.
PN: ★**a)** 4.148:2; 4.214 I 17; 4.277:3 (allograph *ġyrn*); 4.307:5 (*bn ʕnt*); 4.332:20; 4.343:8; 4.374:2; 4.378:7; 4.609:4; 4.729:5; ★**b)** *bn PN*: 4.75 III 11, IV 11.

ḫytr MN (?) (cf. Bordreuil - Pardee RSOu 14 p. 377).
Month name (?): *yrḫ ḫytr*, RSOu 14 49 [KTU 9.433]:22.
Cf. **ḫyr**.

ḫzli PN (etym. unc. Cf. Grøndahl PTU 17, 28, 55, 140); ¶ **syll.**: cf. DUMU *ḫu-zi-la-a*, PRU 3 201 (RS 16.257+) A II 48; *ḫa-zi-lu*, PRU 6 86 I 10. Cf. *ḫdl*, PN.
PN: *bt PN*, 4.75 III 6.

ḫzmyn PN; cf. *ḫd/zmyn*.

ḫzn PN (etym. unc.); ¶ **syll.**: cf. DUMU *ḫu*-ZI-*na*, PRU 6 83 III 3. Cf. *ḥsn*, *ḫsn (II)*, PNN.
PN: 4.425:7.

ḫzr n. m. 1) "assistant, auxiliary"; 2) (collect.) "auxiliary personnel" (Akk. *ḫāziru*, AHw 339; CAD Ḫ 166; < */ʕ-ḏ/z-r/; cf. *ḫdrġl*; Dietrich - Loretz WO 3 1966 189f.; Blau - Greenfield BASOR 200 1970 17; Sanmartín UF 21 1989 347 n. 93; diff. Heltzer UF 12 1980 410ff.: 'male', < *ġzr*, cf. Hb. *ʕzr(h)*, HALOT 812; cf. Hurr. *ḫzr*, 1.149:11 [//(?) *tzġ*, cf. Laroche Ug 5 p. 517]); not related to syll. Ug. *ḫu-zi-rù*, Ug 5 137 II 25'; cf. Huehnergard UVST 84, 128; Van Soldt SAU 304; cf. Sivan GAGl 231. ¶ **Forms**: sg. *ḫzr*, pl. *ḫzrm*.
1) Assistant, auxiliary: wine *l ḫzrm* for the assistants, 4.216:6; *ṯṯtm ḫzr dt tbʕln b TN* two auxiliary squads of six who work in TN, 4.141 III 9; *ṯṯtm ḫzr w ʕšt ʕšr ḥrš* two auxiliary squads of six and eleven workers, 4.141 III 7; *ṯmn ḫzr w arbʕ ḥršm* eight assistants and four workers, 4.141 III 4.
2) Auxiliary personnel (coll.): *aḥd kbd arbʕm b ḫzr lqḥ šʕrt* forty one of the auxiliary personnel have received wool, 4.630:2; *ḫzr lqḥ ḥpr* auxiliary personnel who have received the supply, 4.609:51; cf. *ibid.* ln. 52.

Cf. ḫd̲rġl, ḫnzr (I), ḫzrn, ḫzry.

ḫzrn PN (etym. unc. Cf. Grøndahl PTU 22, 28, 140 and cf. *ḫzr*, Dietrich - Loretz - Sanmartín UF 5 1973 107f.).
PN: ★a) 4.632:6; ★b) *bn PN*, 4.69 II 15.

ḫzry PN (etym. unc. Cf. Grøndahl PTU 22, 28, 140 and cf. *ḫzr*, Dietrich - Loretz - Sanmartín UF 5 1973 107f.).
PN: *bn ḫzry*, 4.763:6.

ḫẓ, 1.172:21 (cf. *ḥẓ*, Bordreuil - Caquot Syria 57 1980 345).

k

-k suffixed pronominal morpheme 2nd p. m. and f. sg.: 1) used with nouns, “your(s)”; 2) used with verbs, “you”; 3) used with prepositions, *aṯr, b, bd, l, lpn, ʕd, ʕm, ʕmn* (c.Sem..; cf. Moscati ICGSL 106f.; Gordon UT § 6.7; Segert BGUL 47; Tropper UG 220f.). ¶ Forms: *k*; suff. *km, kn* (encl. *-m, -n*).

1) Used with nouns: *passim*; cf. *anykn dt likt* your ship that you sent, 2.38:10 (*-k* + encl. *-n*; cf. Dietrich - Loretz - Sanmartín UF 5 1973 81); cf. *bn ḫrnk mġy* your messenger arrived (altern.: *bn ḫrn k mġy* as for your messenger, when he arrived ...; cf. *k (I)*).

2) Used with verbs: *aqrbk abh* I shall introduce you to her father, 1.24:27; *tbkyk ab ġr bʕl* for you, father, the mountain of DN weeps, 1.16 I 6 and par.; *ilm tġrk tšlmk tʕzzk* may the gods keep you, bless you, strengthen you, 5.9:3-4 and par. (cf. Cunchillos TOu 2 254ff.); *yblk udr ilqṣm* may they bring you the most noble gems, 1.4 IV 17; *hm l aqryk b ntb pšʕ* if I really go to meet you on the path of rebellion, 1.17 VI 43; *tštk b qrbm asm* may it place you within the granary, 1.19 II 18 and par.; *irš ḥym w atnk blmt w ašlḥk ašsprk (...) šnt* ask life and I shall give it to you, immortality and I shall grant it to you, I shall make you count (...) years, 1.17 VI 27-28 and par.; let *aqht w ypltk (...) w yʕdrk* PN come to save you (...) to help you, 1.18 I 13-14; *ydʕtk bt* I know you, daughter, 1.18 I 16 and par.; *ʕwrt yštk bʕl* may DN leave you blind, 1.19 IV 5; *yštk bʕl ʕnt* did they make you lord of the furrows?, 1.6 IV 2 and par.; *p]ḫrk ygršk qr btk ygršk* [although] your family expel you, the walls of your house expel you, 1.82:40 and par.; *ʕpr btkm ygršk* may the dust of your house evict you!, 1.82:12; *dm rgm iṯ ly w argmk hwt w ṯnyk* since I have a matter that I am going to tell you, a word that I wish to repeat to you, 1.3 III 21-22 and par.; *ʕl aqht ʕbdk* above PN shall I place you, 1.18 IV 22; *tbrkk w ld* bend your knees and give birth, 1.12 I 26; *hm yd il mlk yḫssk ahbt ṯr tʕrrk* perhaps the love of DN, the king, has aroused you, perhaps the love of the Bull has moved you?, 1.4 IV 30; *tispk yd aqht gzr tštk (...)* may the hand of Noble PN gather you, may it place you (...), 1.19 II 17-18 and par.; *ap mṯn rgmm argmk* and another thing I

am going to tell you, 1.4 I 19; *tblk ġrm mid ksp* may the mountains bring you plenty of silver, 1.4 V 31; *šbt dqnk l tsrk* the greyness of your beard truly instructs you, 1.4 V 4; *w yrḫ yark* may DN shine for you!, 1.24:39; *ik al yšmʕk* how, in fact, do you wish that he listens to you?, 1.6 VI 26 and par.; [*ṯ*] *ʕn itʕnk* the attack that I made on you, 1.5 I 26; [*ṯ*]*ṯ mat ʕmn w l atnnk* I have six hundred (shekels) and am prepared to pay them to you, 2.21:16-17; *n*(!)*bšrkm dnil* we are going to impart news to you, PN, 1.19 II 37 (*-k* + encl. *-m*).

3) Used with prepositions: *ʕdk ilm* around you are the gods, 1.6 VI 48-49; *yšlm lk* may it go well for you, 2.34:3 and par. (cf. Cunchillos TOu 2 251ff.); *wn aṯt* [*l*]*k k*[*m ilm*] for you have no wife like the (other) gods, 1.2 III 22; *ʕlk bʕlm pht qlt* because of you DN I have seen prostration, 1.6 V 11 and par.; *ʕlk mḫṣ aqht* upon you (weighs) the death of the hero PN, 1.19 III 52 and par.; *bn bn aṯrk* the sons of (your) sons after you, 1.22 I 3; *alpm aršt lk*he oxen you requested for yourself, 2.45:24; *śśwm nʕmm lk ṯṯm* sixty good horses for you, 2.45:20; *tld šbʕ bnm lk* she shall bear you seven sons, 1.15 II 23s.; *w tld bnt lk* and she shall give birth to daughters, 1.15 III 6; *qḥ (...) ʕmk šbʕt ġlmk* take (...) with you your seven youths, 1.5 V 8, cf. ln. 10-11; *trḫ lk ybrdmy* marry DN, 1.24:29; *ytn bt lk* a house will be given to you, 1.4 V 28; *wn in aṯt* [*l*]*k* for you have no wife, 1.2 III 22; *l rgmt lk* did I not tell you?, 1.4 VII 23 and par., cf. 1.2 IV 8; *lpnk l tšlḥm ytm* in your presence you did not feed the orphan, 1.16 VI 48; *ṯ*]*mn ʕmk* [*m*]*nm šlm* there with you, whatever the situation, 2.65:3 (cf. *ʕm*); *y lk mrrt tġll* woe to you TN!, 1.19 III 51, cf. ln. 46 (*lkm*; *-k* + encl. *-m*), IV 3; *w ylak mlakm lk* and he will send (two) messengers to you, 1.14 III 20; *p ank atn ʕṣm lk* and I am going to distribute the beams to you, 2.26:8; *ašqlk tḥt* [*pʕny*] at [my feet] I shall cast you, 1.17 VI 44; *qḥ rṯt bdk* take a net in your hand, 1.4 II 32; *k l ttn akl lhm* as they did not give them grain, 2.70:22.

Bkn and unc. ctx.: 1.1 IV 27; 1.4 III 6; 1.5 I 5; 1.6 IV 24; 1.16 IV 5; 1.18 I 29; 1.18 IV 17; 1.82:10; 1.101:8; 2.2:8s.; 2.3:21; 2.21:14; 2.31:43; 2.32:7, 10; 2.34:29; 2.50:15; 2.66:3.

k (I) prep., "like" (Hb. *k*, HALOT 453f.; Amor. /ka, ki/, CAAA 22; Ebla *ga* /ka/, *gi* /kī/, Krebernik PET 84, 86; cf. Gelb EDA 70; Akk. *kī*, AHw 468f.; CAD K 322ff.; ESA *k*, DOSA 237; Arab. *ka*, Lane 2998. Cf. Aartun, PU 2 26ff.; 31ff., 92ff.; Gordon UT § 10.9; 12.3; Segert BGUL 78, 102; Tropper UG 760ff.). ¶ Forms: *k*; suff. *km*, *kmt* (*-m* + enc. *-t*); cf. *km*, *kmt*.

Like: *drk*[*t*] *k ab adm* a power like that of the father of mankind, 1.14

I 43; *ṣʕ il dqt k amr sknt k ḫwt yman* a divine platter of manufacture in the TN style, of a form in the TN style, 1.4 I 41-42; he shall bring you a tribute *k ilm (...) k bn qdš* like the (other) gods, (...) like the holy ones, 1.2 I 37; [*a*]*msḫ{.}nn k imr l arṣ* I can pull him like a lamb to the ground, 1.3 V 1 and par.; *k klb b btk nʕtq k inr* like a dog (that) has become old in your house, like a dog, 1.16 I 15-16 and par.; *tḥth k kdrt ri*[*i*] *ʕlh k irbym kp k qṣm* at her feet like balls(?) (rolled) the heads, above her like locusts palms (of hands were flying), 1.3 II 10 and par.; *k irby tškn šd km ḥsn pat mdbr* like locusts they settled in the field, like grasshoppers on the desert fringes, 1.14 II 50; *kbd k iš*[*t*] *tikln* our innards they devour like fire, 1.12 I 10; out she made go *k rḥ npšhm k iṯl brlt* like a breath his soul, like phlegm (his) spirit, 1.19 II 38-39 and par.; *wn in (...) w ḥẓr bt (...) km ilm w ḥẓr k bn aṯrt* but he has no house (...) like the (other) gods, nor a mansion like the sons of DN, 1.4 IV 51 and par.; *wn aṯt* [*l*]*k k*[*m ilm*] for you do not have a wife like the (other) gods, 1.2 III 22; *k bʕl k yḥwh* like DN he certainly gives life to, 1.17 VI 30 (or under *k (II)* 2: 'when'); they attack each other *k gmrm / rumm / bṯnm / lsmm* like champions / wild bulls / snakes / steeds, 1.6 VI 16-21; *k gmn aliyn bʕl* like a funeral offering(?) of DN, the victorious, 1.6 I 19-29; *yḥrṯ k gn ap lb* he ploughed (his) chest like an orchard, 1.5 VI 21; *tšt k yn udmʕt* she drank tears like wine, 1.6 I 10, cf. 1.101:9 and 2.31.65; *k ksp l ʕbrm zt* like silver for the guests (were) the olives, 1.22 I 14; *amrr k kbkb l pnm* DN (went) in front like a star, 1.4 IV 17 (cf. 1.5 III 8); *k lb arḫ l ʕglh k lb ṯat l imrh* like the heart of a cow for her calf, like the heart of a ewe for her lamb, 1.6 II 28; *ṯm tpl k lbnt* there they fell like bricks, 1.13:13; *al tʕdbkm k imr b ph k lli b ṯbrn qnh* he is not to place you like a lamb in his mouth, like a suckling in the opening of his oesophagus, 1.4 VIII 18-19 and par.; *mtqtm k lrmn*[*m*] sweet as pomegranates, 1.23:50; *tirkm yd il k ym (...) k mdb* the member of DN became as long as the sea, (...) as the flood, 1.23:33-34 and par.; *yd ilm p k mtm ʕz mid* here the power of the gods is very strong, very much so, like death / DN, 2.10:12 (cf. Song 8:6; diff.: Cunchillos TOu 2 279: 'plus grand que la force des guerriers', but cf. Pardee Fs. Pope 66ff.; Dietrich - Loretz UF 22 1990 63 n. 41: 'und das (ist) so!', rdg *kmtm*); *k tnḥn udmm* as the two TNN wail, 1.15 I 7; *d k nʕm ʕnt nʕmh* whose grace is like that of DN, 1.14 III 41 and par.; *k apʕ il b gdrt* like a divine viper in a hedge, 1.19 I 13; *k ʕṣm k ʕṣm l ttn k abnm l thggn* like trees, like trees that do not emit (sound), like stones that do not whisper(?), 1.82:43 (cf. Caquot SEL 5 1988 42f.: 'car', *k (II)*); *ḥkmt k ṯr* you are wise like the 'bull', 1.6 IV 2; *tṣu (...) k qṭr*

(II)); *ḥkmt k ṯr* you are wise like the 'bull', 1.6 IV 2; *tṣu (...) k qṭr urbtm k bṯn ʕmdh k yʕlm ẓrh k lbim skh* and out you go (...) like smoke through the skylight, like a snake through the foot of the wall, like mountain goats towards the summit, like a lion towards the den, 1.169:3-4; *ap ab i k mtm tmtn* father, O, like mortals you also die, 1.16 I 3 (cf. 1.16 I 17 and II 40: *k*); *bʕl yṯb k ṯbt ģr* DN sits down as a mountain sits down, 1.101:1 (for other versions cf. Caquot TOu 2 47 n. 98); *nʕmh nšat ẓl k kbkbm* her beauty wore a sheen like the stars, 1.92:27 (Dijkstra UF 26 1994 117); *my k qdš* who is like DN? RSOu 14 53 [KTU 9.432]:14'(?); for *l k* in 1.127:12 cf. *l (I)* 11b). Bkn and unc. ctx.: 1.1 IV 11; 1.5 III 8; 1.10 III 5-6; 1.13:14, 28; 1.17 VI 12; 1.19 I 7; 1.24:10; 1.101:9; 1.133:7 (cf. Dietrich - Loretz UF 23 1991 99); 2.31:65; 2.45:28.
Cf. **km**, **kmt**.

k (II) multiple functor: 1) emphatic "yes", "truly", "already"; 2) subordinating "when", "if", "because", "since, as", "that" (Hb., Moab., Aram., Palm. *ky*, HALOT 470fs.; DNWSI 497f.; Ph., Pun. *k*, DNWSI 497f.; Akk. *kī*, AHw 469; CAD K 316ff., 320ff.; ESA *k*, DOSA 237f., cf. Arab. *kay*, WKAS 1 478f. Cf. Aartun, PU 2 92ff.; Gordon UT § 12.3; Segert BGUL 77, 80; Bandstra SFPK *passim*; Tropper UF 26 1994 460 n. 15, 474 n. 9; UG 809f.). ¶ Forms: *k*; *ky* (*mater lectionis*, 2.16:7; 2.39:19) *km* (encl. *-m*).
1) Emphatic functor, yes, truly (often left untranslated): *k l ṣḥn bʕl ʕm aḫy* yes, surely invite, DN, with my brothers!, 1.5 I 22*l ktp ʕnt k tšth* on the shoulders of DN, yes, she placed him, 1.6 I 15; *hlk bʕl aṯrt k tʕn* the walk of DN did DN contemplate, 1.4 II 14 and par., cf. ln. 27; *ḥkm k ʕm ʕlm* wise, yes, for eternity (?), 1.3 V 30 (but cf. *ḥkmt* 1.4 IV 41); *hlm il k yphnh* as soon as DN saw him, 1.4 IV 27; *il aṯtm k ypt*, DN in fact wished to seduce the two women, 1.23:39; *nʕm aḫ̮h k ysmsm* the comeliness of its brother, handsome as it is, 1.96:3. Unc. ctx.: 1.19 I 8; 1.82:4.
2) Subordinating functor, when, if, because, as, that: ★a) object: *mndʕ k ank aḥš mģy* perhaps I will hurry to come, 2.34:10 and par. (cf. Cunchillos TOu 2 343 n. 13); *passim* with /y-d-ʕ/: *ydʕ[tk] bt k an[št] k in b ilht (...)* I already know, daughter, that you have become livid (with anger), that among the goddesses there is not (...), 1.3 V 27-28 and par.; cf. 1.6 3 8-9 and par.; 1.6 V 17; 1.16 I 33; 2.34:30; *tdʕ ky ʕrbt l pn špš* you should know that she I have entered into the presence of the 'Sun', 2.16:7; *ky likt (...) ky akl b ḫwtk inn* you have written as follows (...):there is no grain in your country, 2.39:19; ★b)

conditional: *k ygʕr śśw* if the horse puffs and blows, 1.85:2 and par.; cf. 1.85:5 and par.; 1.85:9; 1.85:12 and par.; 1.85:18 and par; ★c) explanatory and causal: *k ibr l bʕl yld* for a bull has been born to DN, 1.10 III 35; *k ybky* since / as he is weeping, 1.14 I 39; *k brkm tġll b dm* for she plunged (her) knees in blood, 1.3 II 27 and par.; *k lbš km lpš dm a[ḫh]* for he wore like a garment the blood of his brothers, 1.12 II 46; *k rtqt mrġt* because you tied perversion, 1.13:24 (?); *k mt aliyn bʕl k ḫlq* for DN, the victorious, is dead (...) perished, 1.6 I 41-42 and par.; *k šbʕt l šbʕm aḫh ym[ṯ]* for his seventy-seven brothers (he killed), 1.12 II 48; *k zbyn zb[l]* since our captive was the prince, 1.2 IV 29; *mlbš ṯrmnm k yṯn* as the cloaks of DNN had worn out, 4.168:6; *k ypdd mlbš* as the cloak had worn out, 4.182:61, cf. ln. 63; *k l ttn akl lhm* as they did not give them grain, 2.70:22; ★d) temporal: *mn yrḫ k m[rṣ] mn k dw* how many months since he became sick, how many (since PN) fell ill?, 1.16 II 19-20 and par.; *b ph yrd k ḫrr zt* it will fall into his mouth when the olive tree shrivels, 1 5 II 5; *k tmḫṣ ltn* when you crushed DN, 1.5 I 1 and par.; *k tlakn ġlmm* when the messenger-boys were sent, 1.4 V 42; *k tmzʕ kst dnil* when the garment of PN was ripped, 1.19 I 46; *k ymġy adn ilm rbm*, when the Lord of the great gods approaches, 1.124:1, cf. 2.23:6; *k tʕrb ʕṯtrt šd* when DN of the steppe enters, 1.91:10 and par.; *mʕmsk k šbʕt yn* he who loads himself with you when you are sated with wine, 1.17 II 6 and par.; *k tġḏ arz b ymnh* when the (staff of) cedar is shot from his right, 1.4 VII 41; *k bʕl k yḥwy yʕšr {ḥwy yʕšr}* like DN when (or 'certainly') he gives life to(?) the one he invites, 1.17 VI 30; *k yṯnyn* when he replies, RSOu 14 53 [KTU 9.432]:35'; *km mġy* when he arrived, RSOu 14 51 [KTU 9.425]:15.
3) In compounds, with explamatory function: cf. *kd (II)*.
Bkn ctx.: 1.24:10; 2.8:3, 5; 2.23:6; 2.32:4; 2:33:14, 21; 2.45:28.

k (III) adv., 1) "thus, in this way"; 2) "here"; (Hb. *kh*, HALOT 461; Aram. *kh*, DNWSI 489; cf. Akk. *kīam*, AHw 470; CAD K 325ff.).
¶ Forms: *k*; *ky* (*mater lectionis*, 2.17:13; 2.36:5, 14; 2.39:17; 2.46:9; 2.72:18, 34); suff. *kh* (+ *h*; cf. Aartun, PU 2 165, 167, 175).
1) Thus, in this way: *k rgmt ly* in this way you spoke to me, 2.45:23 (cf. Hoftijzer Fs. Kraus 125 for the possibility that *k* is a relative); *w k rgm špš* and thus says the Sun, 2.23:1; *ky likt bt mlk* in this way did you write to the palace, 2.36:5 (cf. *ibid.* ln. 14; 2.39:17; 2.46:9); *ky tdbr umy* my mother declared thus, 2.72:18 (cf. *ibid.* ln. 34); *gm l ġ[l]mh bʕl k yṣḥ* aloud to his lads DN thus shouted, 1.4 VII 53 and par., cf. 1.17 V 15.

2) Here: *kh lk s̄ls̄t prs̱m b s̄ql* here are: 3 *p.* (of wheat) and one shekel (each), 4.710:5 (Dietrich - Loretz KA 162, 164f.).
In bkn ctx.: 2.17:13.

ki/hdn PN *bn ki/hdn*, 4.715:8.

kb (I) adj. m.; said of a type of cloth or garment ("sewn, scalloped, stuffed"(?); cf. Akk. *kubbû*, AHw 497; CAD K 482; cf. Ribichini - Xella Tessili 40: (?)Akk. *kīpu* 'piece of linen fabric'; Heltzer GPOTU 40, 66 n. 320: 'textiles'; for Akk. *kīpu* cf. diff. Durand MARI 6 660: *kepûm* 'être courbe'; Watson UF 32 2000 569: '(richly) embroided garment', Copt. *kap*). ¶ **Forms**: pl. *kbm*.
Said of a type of cloth or garment ('sewn'(?)): *ṯlṯ* [.]*xxx kbm* three (...) 'sewn'(?), 4.205:8. For 1.4 III 4 (bkn ctx.) cf. Healey DUA 142.

kb (II) n. m. "intestine(s), guts" (cf. Akk. *kippu*, AHw 483; CAD K 399f.; cf. Dietrich - Loretz MU 152ff.). ¶ **Forms**: pl. *kbm*.
Intestine(s), guts: *w i*[*n*] *kbm bh* if it has no guts, 1.103+:55.

kbb "?" (cf. Akk. *kabābu*, AHw 414; CAD K 2f.; alternatively: DN Kubaba, goddess of Karkemiš); in bkn ctx.: 1.81:10.

kbby PN (< DN Kubaba, goddess of Karkemiš; cf. Grøndahl PTU 278; Hawkins RlA 6 257ff.); ¶ **syll.**: [f]*ku-ba-ba*, PRU 3 76 (RS 16.144):6 (cf. Van Soldt SAU 13). Cf. alphab. Hurr. *kbb(d)* DN, 1.116:23.
PN: 4.659:7.

/k-b-d/ vb D: "to honour, to pay homage to, welcome" (Hb., Ph. *kbd*, HALOT 455f.; DNWSI 484; Amor. /k-b-d/, CAAA 22; Emar Akk. cf. /kubbadu/, /kibbadu/, Pentiuc Vocabulary 106f.; Akk. *kabātu* [NA *kabādu*], AHw 416f.; CAD K 14f.; EA Akk. cf. D prefc. *yu-ka-bi-id*, EA 245:39; cf. Sivan, GAGl 237; DNWSI 484; Eth. *kabda*, CDG 273); ¶ **syll. Ug.**: the element /kābid-/, /kabūd-/ in PNN, cf. Sivan GAGl 237; ¶ **par.**: /q-l/ (I). ¶ **Forms**: D prefc. *tkbd*; with suff. *tkbdh*, *tkbdn*, *tkbdnh*, *ykbdnh*; impv. *kbd*.
D. To honour, to pay homage to, welcome: *tšṯḥwy w tkbdh* she prostrated herself and paid him homage, 1.4 IV 26 and par. (prostration formula; cf. Del Olmo MLC 54f.); *sad kbd hmt* comfort (and) welcome them, 1.17 V 20 and par.; *itml ykb*[*d* the previous day will be honoured..., 1.119:19.
In bkn ctx.: *w mlk ykbd* the king pays homage, 1.171:4;]*m kbd*, 2.83:8 (cf. *kbd (I) / (II)*). Cf. **kbd(y)**.

kbd (I) n. usually f. (m. cf. 1.13:31), 1) "liver"; 2) "innards, entrails, womb, mind" 3) > "interior (of)", in prepositional syntagm: "within" (Hb. *kbd*, HALOT 456; Syr. *kabdō*, LS 315; Emar Akk /kabidu/, Pentiuc Vocabulary 93; Akk. *kabattu*, AHw 416; CAD K 11ff.; cf.

g/kabīdu, AHw 272; CAD G 6; Arab. *kabid*, Lane 2584; Eth. *kabd*, CDG 273. Cf. Virolleaud DA 23; Del Olmo AuOr 7 1989 123ff.); ¶ syll. Ug.: cf. [Sum.(?) = Akk.(?) =](Hurr.). *ir-bi* = *ka*-BI[, UF 11 1979 479 (RS 20.189):34; cf. Huehnergard UVST 62, 135; ¶ **par.**: *irt*, *lb*, *p (III)*, *ṯd*. ¶ **Forms**: sg. f. *kbd*; cstr. *kbd*; suff. *kbdk*, *kbdh*, *kbdn*; du. *kbdm*; pl. *kbdt* (1.86:26); pl. suff. *kbdtkm*.

1) Liver: ★**a)** as material for sacrifice: *kbd w š l DN (...) kbd alp w š l DN* one liver one ram to DN (...) one ox liver and one ram to DN, 1.109:8 and par.; *mtntm w kbd alp l DN* two loins and one bull's liver for DN, 1.39:2; in bkn ctx. 1.27:10; *kb*(!)*dm w npš l DN* two livers and one (piece of) offal to DN, 1.109:12; 1.46:16; *kbdm l DNN* two livers to the DNN, 1.130:20; in bkn ctx.]*kbdm*, 1.46:1; *kbd w ššrt l DN* one liver and one 'chainlet' to DN, 1.119:21; ★**b)** in extispicy: *kbd dt PN* liver (examined) for/of PN, 1.143:1; cf. in bkn ctx. 1.155:1; *kbdm tbqrn* two livers are/shall be examined, 1.78:5.

2) Innards, womb, mind: *ygmḏ bm kbd* he rejoiced in (his) liver / innards, 1.12 I 13 (// *lb*); *tdmʕ bm kbd* she shed tears in her liver / innards, 1.19 I 35 (// *lb*); *kbd k iš*<*t*> *tikln* our innards they devour like fire, 1.12 I 10 (// *ṯd*; cf. ln. 9 *kbdn*); *tġdd kbdh b ṣḥq (...) kbd ʕnt tšyt* her liver swelled with laughter (...) with (the satisfaction of the) victory, 1.3 II 25-26 (// *lbh*); *yʕrb* [*b*] *ʕl b kbdh* DN will enter his innards, 1.5 II 4 (// *b ph*); *i/ybqʕ kbdh* I shall open / he opened its innards, 1.19 III 18/24 and par.; (ln. 10 *kbdthm* their innards) *kbdh l ydʕ hrh* whose womb has not known his conception, 1.13:31 (cf. Del Olmo, IMC 100f.); [*ti*]*ḫd d iṯ b kbdk* undertake what you have in your mind, 1.18 I 18 (// *b itrk*).

3) Interior, bosom (of), in syntagm with a preposition > "within": *šk šlm l kbd arṣ arbdd l kbd šdm* pour out peace into the bosom of the earth, rest into the innards of the fields, 1.3 IV 9-10 and par.; cf. Arab. *kabidu-l samāʔi / arḍi*); she scoured (...) *kl ġr l kbd arṣ* every mountain as far as the innards of the earth, 1.6 II 16-17 and par.

In unc. ctx.: *kbdt bnš*[, 1.86:26.

kbd (II) n. m. 1) "total (quantity or price), correct, exact number"; 2) arithmetical functor of addition, 'plus', '+' (< "weight", < /k-b-d/; cf. Hb. *kbwd*, HALOT 457f.; Akk. Mari: *ka/ibittu*, Liverani UF 2 1970 107; *nakbatum*, AHw 721 "Gewicht, Geschlossenheit", cf. CAD N/1 181. Cf. Liverani UF 2 1970 89-108; Wesselius UF 12 1980 450; Bordreuil SEL 2 1985 89-92; Tropper UF 29 1997 661ff.). ¶ Forms: sg. *kbd* (spelling mistake for *kbl* in 4.182:6; rdg *kbd*(!)).

1) Total quantity or price, correct, exact number (in apposition with

a simple numerical amount: *x kbd*; it is semantically redundant); *passim*; cf.]*all iqni arbʕm kbd*(!) (*y*(?)) one] *a.* of violet purple for a total of forty, 4.182:6; *ṯṯm* / *ṯmnym dd dd kbd l mḏrġlm* a total of sixty / eighty 'cauldronfuls', by the 'cauldronful' for the watchmen, 4.387:9, 19; *ʕšrm ddm kbd l alpm mrim* twenty *d.* exactly (of grain) for the fatlings, 4.128:1; *ṯql ksp kbd* exactly one shekel of silver, 1.41:39; 1.87:42; *šbʕm ṯqlm kbd* seventy shekels exactly, 3.10:13; *ḥs*[*p*] *ṯn* of *ḥ*- (wine), two (jars) exactly, 1.91:36; *kdwṯ ṯlṯ kbd* a *k.*-garment for three (shekels) exactly, 4.270:3.
2) Adverbial accus, arithmetical functor of addition, 'plus', '+' (with complex numerical quantities: *(x + y + z)*; it is semantically redundant): ★a) in two-member sets (*y + z*), after the smaller quantity (*z*); *passim*; cf. *šbʕm arbʕ kbd alpm* seventy-four head of cattle, 4.749:4; *tšʕm mrḥ aḥd kbd* ninety-one lances, 4.169:10; *ʕšr ṯn kbd* twelve, 4.270:10; 4.244:21; *ʕšrt ṯqlm kbd* twelve shekels, 4.226:3; 4.755:10; *ṯqlm kbd ʕšrt* twelve shekels, 4.341:1; *mit ṯṯm kbd* one hundred and sixty, 4.280:9; *ṯṯm l mit ṯn kbd* one hundred and sixty-two, 4.173:10; *ṯn ʕšrh mn ʕšrm ṯql kbd* twelve minas twenty shekels, 3.1:20 (cf. RS Akk.: 12 MA.NA 20 GÍN KÙ.GI.MEŠ : *at-ru*, PRU 4 41 (RS 17.227):21; 12 MA.NA.MEŠ KÙ.GI.MEŠ 20 GÍN *at-ra*, PRU 4 44 (RS 17.347):5'); *ṯm*]*nym šbʕ kbd* eighty-six (*ḫrd*), 4.777:2 (cf. *ibid.* ln. 5, 10, 13); *arbʕm ksp ḫmšt kbd* forty-five shekels, 4.778:10 (cf. 4.782:16); *tšʕm ṯlṯt w nṣp kbd* ninety-three and a 'half', 4.779:3; [*ʕ*]*šrm aḥd kbd dd* twenty-one 'cauldronfuls', RSOu 14 39 [KTU 4.790]:10'; ★b) in sets of three or more memebers (x + y + z), after the smaller quantity (*z*), optional and in free position; *passim*; cf. *ṯlṯ mat ḫmšm kbd ḫmš kbd* three hundred and fifty-five, 4.387:12; *mitm arbʕm ṯmn kbd* two hundred and forty-eight, 4.352:5; *ṯmn kkrm alp kbd mitm kbd* eight talents one thousand two hundred (shekels), 4.43:6-7; *kkrm alpm ḫmš mat kbd* two talents two thousand five hundred (shekels), 4.626:9; *arbʕ alpm pḥm ḫmš mat kbd* four thousand five hundred (shekels) of ruby purple, 4.203:4; *alpm pḥm ḫmš mat kbd* two thousand five hundred (shekels) of ruby purple, 4.132:1; *w ṯlṯ ʕšr kbd mitm šmn nḥ* and two hundred and sixteen (units) of *n.*-oil, RSOu 14 37:3; [*m*]*it ṯn ʕšr kbd* one hundred and twelve, RSOu 14 38 [KTU 9.424]:1'.
Rdg *kbd* (spelling mistake for *kdb*) in 4.721:8, 9.
Bkn ctx. 2.77:16; 2.79:8; 2.83:8; RSOu 14 44:9', 10'.

kbd (III), first element of the compound DN *kbd w nr*[(cf. /k-b-d/; cf. Ebla ᵈ*kà-pá-tù*, Mander MROA 2/1 40, 49, 74. Cf. De Moor UF 2

1970 201, 223; De Meyer RTL 11 1980 225ff.; diff.: Del Olmo CR 344 n. 36: com. n. 'glory!').

DN: *kbd w nr*[, 1.123:16; *kbd d il gd*[DN, who is god ..., 1.123:21.

kbd (IV) n. m. "splendour, glory" (?) (cf. Hb. *kbwd*, HALOT 457f.; Pun. *kbd*<*t*>, DNWSI 484; cf. *kbd (III)*. Cf. Dijkstra UF 26 1994 117; ¶ **par.**: *ẓl*. ¶ **Forms**: sg. *kbd*.

Splendour, glory (?): bkn ctx., [*kb*]*d km kbkbt kṯn* [s]plendour(?) like the female stars of TN(?), 1.92:28.

kbdt, pl. of *kbd* in 1.86:26 (bkn ctx.); cf. *kbd (I)*.

kbd(y) PN (Sem. Cf. Grøndahl PTU 148); ¶ **syll.**: DUMU *ka-bu-di-ya*, PRU 3 195 (RS 15.09) A 15 (Sivan GAGl 237); cf. DUGUD-*ia-na*, PRU 3 131 (RS 15.122): 15 and *passim ibid.*; *ka$_4$-bid-na-na*, PRU 3 121 (RS 15.136):4 (cf. Huehnergard UVST 219; AkkUg 399).

PN: ★**a)** 4.75 VI 4; ★**b)** *bn kbdy*, 4.611 (II) 11; in bkn ctx.: *bn kbd*[, 4.432 (II) 19.

kbkb n. m. "heavenly body, star" (Hb., *kwkb*, HALOT 463; Ph. *kkb*, DNSWI 449f.; Aram. *kwkb/p*, DNWSI 4499f.; Syr. *kaukbō*, LS 320; Ebla /kakkab/ in ^{d}MUL = *gag-gáb*, VE 791; Mander MROA 2/1 18; SUD = *ga-ga-bu$_x$*(NI), VE 1185; Krebernik ZA 73 1983 30; Fronzaroli EL 140; Lambert Biling. 397; Xella HSAO 2 351; Amor. /kabkabum/, CAAA 22; Akk. *kakkabu*, AHw 421; CAD K 45ff.; OSA *kwkb*, DOSA 242; Arab. *kawkab*, Lane 2623; Eth. *kokab*, CDG 280); ¶ **par.**: *arṣ*. ¶ **Forms**: sg. *kbkb*; du. *kbkbm*; pl. *kbkbm*, *kbkbt*; assim. *kkbm* (or hapl. for *kbkbm*).

Heavenly body, star, ★**a)** in general: *hlk kbkbm* the course of the stars, 1.19 II 3 and par 1.19 IV 38 (*kbkm*(!)); *tant (...) thmt ʕmn kbkbm* the whispering (...) of the abysses with the stars, 1.3 III 25 and par. (// *arṣ*); *ẓl k kbkbm* [*kb*]*d km kbkbt* sheen like the stars, [sp]lendour like the stars of TN, 1.92:27-28 (cf. De Moor UF 17 1985 228; Dijkstra UF 26 1994 117); *dġṯ hrnmy d kbkbm* the offering of a Harnamite to the stars, 1.19 IV 31 and par.; *qdš yuḫdm šbʕr amrr k kbkb* DN began to shine, DN like a star, 1.4 IV 17; [...] *lšn l kbkbm* [(if he extends)] (his) tongue to the stars, 1.5 II 3; *rbb nskh kbkbm* with drizzle that the stars poured on her, 1.3 IV 44 and par.; [*hm*] *kbkb yql b ṯlṯm ym* [if] a star falls on the thirtieth day, 1.163:7; ★**b)** deities: *pḫr kkbm* the assembly of the stars, 1.10 I 4; *kt* [*k*]*bkbm* the podium of the stars, 1.13:13; *ʕdb l špš rbt w l kbkbm* place (them) next to the Great Lady DN and the stars, 1.23:54; ★**c)** possibly a type of jewel: *b gb bt ilm kbkbm trmt* in the *g.* of the temple of the gods: two 'stars' as an offering, 1.43:3 (diff.: Dietrich - Loretz JA 50:

'Sterngötter', the syntagm *ilm kbkbm*);]*šbʕ kbkbm* seven 'stars', 1.164:15, in bkn ctx. (cf. Van der Toorn BiOr 48 1991 50f.); bkn cf.]*kbkb bʕl w pdry kbkb*, RSOu 14 53 [KTU 9.432]:10.

In bkn ctx., *dk k kbkb*, 1.5 III 8; *ʕl kbkbm nʕm*.[, 1.13:17;]*kl kbkb*, 1.84:25; 7.50:7; *kbkb kbkbm* star of the stars, RSOu 14 53 [KTU 9.432]:8'; *al kbkb*, *ibid.* ln. 8'; *kbkb šmm wthm*, star of sky and ocean, *ibid.* ln. 9'; cf. ln. 10', 11', 12'.

Cf. **kkb (II)**, **kkbn**.

kbl PN; cf. *kb/pl(n)* PN.

kb/pl(n) PN (Hurr.(?). Cf. Grøndahl PTU 148f., 239; Sivan GAGl 237; Watson AuOr 8 1990 120; AuOr 11 1993 216; AuOr 14 1996 100; Van Soldt SAU 120); ¶ **syll.**: cf. DUMU *ka-bu-li*, PRU 3 312 (RS 15.126):3; DUMU.SAL *ka-bu-li*, PRU 6 55:30'; cf. DUG *kap*(?)-*pa-al*(?)-*la-nu re-qu*, PRU 6 158:5 (cf. Nougayrol PRU 6 p. 158 n. 1).

PN: ★**a)** *kbln*, 4.55:5; 4.277:2; 4.317:4; 4.377:17; 4.571:7; 4.705:7; 4.707:13; 4.788:6; ★**b)** *bn kbl*, 4.232:40; *bn kbln*, 4.76:5; 4.112 III 1; *bn kpln*, 4.412 II 12. adj. 4.669:3.

kblbn PN (etym. unc.); ¶ **syll.**: DUMU(?) *ki*]-*bíl-bu-nu*, PRU 3 200 (RS 16.257+) A II 20 (Van Soldt SAU 350 n. 209); *kib-li-bu-na*, PRU 6 54:19 (cf. Huehnergard AkkUg 376); DUMU *ki-bi-il-bu-na*, PRU 6 99:17.

PN: ★**a)** 4.635:57 (*bn x*[]); ★**b)** *bn PN*, 4.335:12. Cf. in bkn ctx. 4.669:1:3; in unc. ctx. 4.149:6.

kbm n. m.; a cult installation (cf. Akk. *kummu*, var. *kūbu*, AHw 498, 506; CAD K 533ff., 488; less probably cf. ESA *kbyt*, DOSA 239. Cf. Xella TRU 84; Del Olmo SEL 3, 1986, 65f. n. 13). ¶ **Forms**: sg. m. suff. *kbmh* (adv. *-h*).

A cult installation: *š kbmh* a ram (will be offered) in the *k*., 1.106:15.

kbn PN (etym. unc.); ¶ **syll.**: cf. *ku*-PI-*na*, PRU 6 43 3; DUMU *ka*-PI-*na* PRU 3 202 (RS 16.257+) III 32. Cf. *kwn*.

PN: *bn kbn*, 4.785:14.

kbr PN (Sem. Cf. Grøndahl PTU 29, 149; Zeeb UF 25 1993 468; Watson AuOr 14 1996 100).

PN: ★**a)** 2.50:14; ★**b)** *bn PN*, 4.309:20; 4.425:14.

kbrt n. f. "sieve" (Hb. *kbrh*, HALOT 459. Cf. De Moor SP 210; Healey UF 15 1983 51); ¶ **par.**: *rḥ*. ¶ **Forms**: sg. f. *kbrt*.

Sieve: *ʕ*[*lk*] *pht* [*dr*]*y b kbrt* on your account I have seen sifting with a sieve, 1.6 V 16 (// *b rḥm*).

kbry TN (Belmonte RGTC 12/2 165: *Kubariyā*); ¶ **syll.**: URU *ku-ba-ri-ia-a*, RS 25.455A+ I 4 (rdg Van Soldt UF 28 1996 674; cf. Arnaud

SMEA 32 1993 128: URU *šu-ma-ri-a*).
TN: RSOu 14 35 [KTU 9.388] II 18.

kbs/ś n. m. "fuller, launderer" (< */k-b-s/š/; Hb. *kwbs*, HALOT 459; Pun. *kbs*, DNWSI 486; Heltzer OH 80; cf. Akk. *kabāsu*, CAD K 7 [2/e]; cf. Akk. *ašlāku*, CAD A/2 445, AHw 81; Tropper UF 27 1995 519); ¶ RS Akk.: cf. LÚ(.MEŠ).TÚG.ME(.MEŠ), PRU 3 204 (RS 16.257+) B IV 37; PRU 3 205 (RS 15.172) A 11; PRU 6 93:17; Van Soldt UF 22 1990 352 n. 217 (cf. diff. Huehnergard AkkUg 406: TÚG.LAL, with Nougayrol); ¶ syll. Ug.: LÚ *ka*$_4$*-bi-s*[*ú*], PRU 6 136:8; Huehnergard UVST 135; cf. PN DUMU *ka-bi*-IZ-ZI, PRU 3 202 (RS 16.257+) B III 39 (Van Soldt SAU 357 n. 224; TN A.ŠÀ.MEŠ *ku-ub-sà-ti*, PRU 3 47 (RS 16.166): 10. ¶ Forms: sg. *kbs/ś*; pl. *kbs/śm*; du.(?) *kbsm*.

Fuller, launderer: *kbśm* fullers, 4.99:7; 4.71 III 5; *kbsm* fullers 4.610:47; *kbsm* (two(?)) fullers, 4.125:19; PN *kbs* fuller, 4.332:13; 4.682:9; *ddm l kbs* two *d.* (of grain) for the fuller, 4.128:6. In bkn ctx.: RSOu 14 34 [KTU 9.436]:10'.

Cf. kpṯ.

kd (I) n. m.; 1) 'jar'; 2) measure of capacity for liquids (Lipiński UF 2 1970 83; cf. Heltzer UF 21 1989 197, 201; UF 22 1990 127: ca. 22 litres, Hb. *bt*, HALOT 166; Hb., Ph., Pun., Aram. *kd*, HALOT 460; DNWSI 4487f.; DJPA 250; cf. Akk. *kandu*, AHw 436; CAD K 148f.; cf. Akk. *kūtu*, CAD K 611f. and Dietrich - Loretz UF 1 1969 63 [Alalakh]; Gk *kádos*, Lat. *cadus*, cf. Amadasi Semitica 38 1990 17ff.; Heltzer NABU 1995, n. 111); ¶ RS Akk.: DUG, *passim*; Huehnergard AkkUg 379; cf. 1 *me-at* 48 DUG GEŠTIN, KTU 4.48:13; cf. Dietrich - Loretz WO 3 1966 222; cf. Akk. Mari: *karpatum*, Finet AfO 25 1974/77 129; ¶ syll. Ug.: DUG *ka-du-ma*^{meš}, PRU 6 147:1 and *passim ibid*; cf. 1 *ka*(?)*-dú*, PRU 6 163:2; cf. Sivan GAGl 235; Huehnergard UVST 136; Van Soldt SAU 304. ¶ Forms: sg. *kd*; suff. *kdh*; pl. *kdm*; du. *kdm* (*passim*; cf. 4.710:12).

1) 'Jar': *kdh l arṣ ṯṯbr* her jar shattered on the ground, 1.16 I 54.

2) Measure of capacity for liquids: ★a) of wine: *arbʕ* [*ʕšr*] *kdm yn* fourteen 'jars' of wine, 1.41:23; *TN kd yn* 1.91:27, *kdm yn*, *ibid.* ln. 26; *kd l* a 'jar' for: 4.149:3, 4, 6, 9; 4.216:5, 6, 7, 11, 12; 4.219:7, 8, 9; 4.230:3, 5, 7, 8, 9; *kdm l* (two) 'jars' for: 4.216:9, 10; 4.219:5, 6; 4.230:2, 4, 6; 4.715:6, 8, 9; PN *kd(m)*: PN ... *w nḥlh kdm*: 4.715:3, 10, 11; *kd yn*, 6.11:1; *passim* in admin. texts (cf. RS Akk.: nn DUG GEŠTIN, 4.48:13; PRU 6 152:2 and *passim*; in 1.112:12 *kbd* mistake for *kd* (*yn*)); *kd mštt mlk*(*t*) a 'jar' for libation by the king / queen,

4.230:5, 8; *alp kd yqḥ b ḫmr* a thousand 'jars' of wine it held, 1.3 I 16; vinegar: *kd(m) ḥmṣ* 'jar(s)' of vinegar, 4.269:27, 28, 35; ★**b)** of oil: 4.41:4, 8, 9, 11, 12; *kd šmn*, 4.131:3; 4.710:3; 4.782:11; *kd šmn ṯʕt ḫsr* one 'jar' of oil less one *ṯ.*, 4.778:5; 4.782:7; *passim* (cf. RS Akk.: nn DUG Ì, PRU 6 122:1 and *passim ibid.*); *kd šmn mr* a 'jar' of myrrh-scented oil, 4.14:2, 8, 15; *kd šmn l nr ilm* a 'jar' of oil for the lamp of the gods, 4.284:6; *kd šmn nr* a 'jar' of lamp oil, 4.786:8; of olives: 4.284:8; 4.429:1-5; *w ṯṯ kd ztm* and six 'jars' of olives, RSOu 14 37:5; *ʕ̱rm s̄ls̄ kd ztm b s̄ls̄t b kdm* twenty three 'jars' of olives at three (shekels) the 'double jar'(?), 4.710:11 (cf. *infra*: 2.b); cf. *kd šmn mlṯḥm* a 'jar' of oil of two *mlṯḥ*, 4.778:7; *kdm šmn / kdm šmn ṭb* two 'jars' of oil / of quality(?) oil, 4.780:5, 8, 10, 13, 16; ★**c)** honey: *kd nbt*, 4.14:2, 8, 15 (cf. RS Akk.: DUG LÀL, PRU 6 159:5'); others: *kdm dġm* two jars of dregs, 4.284:7; ★**d)** elliptical use, *passim* in admin. texts; cf. *kd bt ilm rbm* a 'jar' (of wine) for the temple of the great gods, 4.149:1; *kdm mtḫ l alṯty* two jars (of wine) as a gift for the GN, *ibid.* ln. 7; *kd PN*, 4.283:5; *kd ʕl PN*, *ibid.* ln. 7, 8, 9; *kd ištir ʕm qrt* a 'jar' remains for delivery to the administration, 4.290:3 (Hoftijzer UF 3 1971 363); PN *kd(m)*, 4.761:8-11.

2) Special uses, ★**a)** distributive: *<yn> d nkly {yn} kd w kd* <wine> that was consumed: {} two 'jars' (: one 'jar' and one 'jar', probably a scribal correction), 4.279:1 (for the rdg cf. PRU 2 p. 100); ★**b)** du. *kdm* 'double jar'(?): *ʕ̱rm s̄ls̄ kd ztm b s̄ls̄t b kdm* twenty three 'jars' of olives at three (shekels) the 'double jar'(?), 4.710:12 (or: the 'jar', sg. with encl. *-m*?). In bkn ctx. *kdm*, 1.136:9.

Bkn: 4.373:7; 4.434:2; 4.558:3, 8; 4.717:4 (*kdm*).

kd (II) conj. "anyway, since, as, in case, if" (< *k* + *d*; cf. Hb. *kzh*, HALOT 264; Aram. *kd(y)*, DNWSI 316ff.: *zy* E.f); DJPA 250; Arab. *kaḏa*, Hava 648. Cf. De Moor SP 112). ¶ **Forms:** *kd*.

Anyway, since, as, in case, if: *kd ynaṣn*[since he has scorned us, 1.1 IV 23; *kd ʕl qšt imḫṣh* so for his bow I wounded him, 1.19 I 14; *kd lbšt b ir* as clothed in light, 1.13:25. For the rdg [*k*]*d* in 1.3 V 3 cf. Del Olmo MLC 189. In bkn ctx.: 1.6 II 3, 4.

kd (III) PN (etym. unc.; cf. Grøndahl PTU 149 for Sem.; for possible Hurr. or Anat. elements cf. e.g. AT 139-140: kit=, kid=, kut=, Gelb - Purves - MacRae NPN 224, 231: kat=, kut=, Laroche NH 90f.: kadu=; Grøndahl PTU 279). Cf. *kdy*, *kdn* PNN.

PN: 4.244:25. Cf. in bkn ctx. *bn kd*[, 4.448:2.

kdb, 4.721:8s., rdg *kbd*. Cf. *kbd (II)*.

kdd n. m. "child, young (son), youth/lad" (cf. Akk. *k/gudādu*, AHw

925; cf. CAD Q 293; Aram. /kdādā/, in syll. *ki-da-di-e*, DNWSI 488; /kiddu/ in syll. *-ki-id-du* onom. element, cf. Rainey Or 34 1965 22; Lipiński SAIO 1 110, n. 7; Watson NUS 35 1986 12); ¶ par.: *ġzr*. ¶ Forms: sg. cstr. *kdd*.

Child, young (son), youth/lad: *ydmʕ l kdd dnil* they shed tears for the young boy of PN, 1.19 IV 12 and par. (// *ġzr*).

kdgdl PN (Hurr. Cf. Weippert ZDPV 82 1966 326; cf. Nuzi *Kutuk-katil*, Gelb - Purves - MacRae NPN 93; diff. Grøndahl PTU 44, 149, 425).

PN: *bn PN*, 4.69 VI 7; 4.93 I 13; 4.412 III 4; 4.681:7; 4.769:51. Cf. in bkn ctx. 4.624:11 (cf. Van Soldt SAU 35).

kdkdy TN (Belmonte RGTC 12/2 162: *Kidkidiya*. Cf. Dietrich - Loretz - Sanmartín UF 7 1975 161; Van Soldt SAU 337; UF 28 1996 674; UF 29 1997 693; UF 30 1998 734); ¶ syll.: URU *k*]*i-id-ki-dì-ia*, PRU 4 51 (RS 17.340) rev. 5'; cf. PRU 4 67 (RS 17.62):22'.

TN: 4.696:7.

kd/tln PN (etym. unc.; cf. Grøndahl PTU 268, 279; Dietrich - Loretz OLZ 62 1967 541; Watson AuOr 8 1990 247; for the Hurr. or Anat. elements /kut=/ cf. *kd (III)*); ¶ syll.: cf. DUMU *ku*(?)*-ti-la-na*, PRU 3 204 (RS 16.257+) mg. II 4. Cf. *ktl*, PN.

PN: ★a) 4.307:22; 4.368:21; ★b) *bn PN*, 4.69 VI 14; 4.93 I 15; cf. in bkn ctx. *bn kdl*[, 4.624:11.

kdml PN (etym. unc.).

PN: 4.276:12.

kdn PN (etym. unc. Cf. Grøndahl PTU 28, 149; Weippert ZDPV 82 1966 326; Watson AuOr 13 1995 223; AuOr 14 1996 100; West AOAT 233 32: PN *ka-da-no*, Linear B); ¶ syll.: cf. KU-DU-*na*, PRU 6 137:3; 144:1; KA-TU-*na*, PRU 3 136 (RS 15.168):4 (cf. Huehnergard UVST 215, 220; Van Soldt SAU 320 n. 135); KU-TA-*n*[*a*], PRU 6 49:9'. Cf. *gdn*, *gtn*, *kd (III)*, *ktn*, *qṭn* PNN.

PN: ★a) 4.85:2 (*zlyy*); 4.617:23; ★b) *bn PN*, 4.75 III 3; 4.354:6; 4.432 (II) 8.

kdnt n. f. "she-mule" ((?); cf. Aram., Palm. *kwdn*, DNWSI 492; *kwdntʔ*, Jastrow 617; cf. Akk. *kūdanu*, AHw 498f.; CAD K 491ff.; Arab. *kawdan*, Hava 648). ¶ Forms: sg./pl. *kdnt*.

She-mule(?): cf. in free ctx. *kdnt*, 5.23:8.

kdr n. m.; a type of "trough" (cf. Nuzi Akk.: *kudurru*, CAD K 496; cf. AHw 499: *kudurru* I. Diff.: Dijkstra UF 18 121: 'ball', JAram., MHb; cf. *kdrt*). ¶ Forms: sg. *kdr*.

Type of trough:]*xb kdr* PN(?): a trough, 4.275:8 (cf. *ibid.*: *dqr*, ln. 11,

17); *kdr* trough, 5.22:3, and cf. *kdr*, *ibid.* ln. 10; used in the cult: *kdr w npt* a trough and a sieve, 1.50:10 (diff. Xella TRU 126: 'dono di saluto').
Cf. kdrt.

kdrl PN (Anat. Cf. Grøndahl PTU 311; cf. Weippert ZDPV 82 1966 326).
PN: 4.147:7; 4.264:3.

kdrn PN (Sem. Cf. Grøndahl PTU 28, 149; Weippert ZDPV 82 1966 322, 325f.; Dietrich - Loretz OLZ 62 1967 540; cf. [f]Kutranu AAN 1 88; West AOAT 233 33: PN *ko-do-ro*, Linear B).
PN: *bn PN*, 4.33:22 (*uškny*); 4.55:26 (cf. Van Soldt SAU 33); 4.350:1.

kdrš PN (etym. unc.; cf. Grøndahl PTU 250f., 311; Weippert ZDPV 82 1966 322, 325ff.).
PN: 4.391:5.

kdrt n. f. "ball" ((?); Hb. *kdwr*, HALOT 460; Arab. *kudrat*, *kadarat*, Hava 647. Cf. De Moor SP 90; Oldenburg CBEB 87; Tropper UG 264; for other explanations cf. Sasson RSP 1 421); ¶ par.: *irby*. ¶ Forms: pl.(?) *kdrt*.
Ball(?): *tḥth k kdrt ri*[*š*] at her feet like balls(?) (rolled) the heads, 1.3. II 9 and par. (// *irbym*).

kdt "?"
? : in bkn ctx., *kdt bh x*[, 1.174:3.

kdwṯ n. m.; garment (probl. assimilated var. of *kndpnṯ*: /kindapanṯ-/ > /kiddabaṯṯ-/ > /kiddawaṯ(ṯ)-/; cf. MA *kì-da-pa-še*, Iraq 35 1973 13:1 and AHw 1568; cf. Sanmartín AuOr 10 1992 100; Tropper UF 29 1997 664f.). ¶ Forms: sg. *kdwṯ*; pl. *kdwṯm*.
Garment: *ṯlṯ ʕšr kdwṯm* thirteen *k.*, 4.152:11; *kdwṯ ṯlṯ kbd* a *k.*-garment for three (shekels) precisely, 4.270:3; *arbʕ kdwṯm w ṯt tprtm b ʕšrt ksp* four *k.* and two *t.* for ten (shekels) of silver, 4.341:10; *kdwṯ l* PN one *k.* for PN, 4.337:24; *kdwṯ ḥdṯ bd* PN a new *k.* into the hands of PN, 4.205:19; *ṯlṯ kdwṯm gdlm* three wide *k.*-garments, 4.152:6.
Cf. knd, kndpnṯ.

kdy PN (etym. unc.). Cf. *kd (III)*, *kdn*, PNN.
PN: 4.743:15.

(kḏd), 1.5 I 17 and par.; cf. *ḏd (III)*.

kḏġbr PN (Hurr. Cf. Grøndahl PTU 204, 225, 237; Dietrich - Loretz WO 4 1967/68 302).
PN: *bn PN*, 4.71 III 11. Cf. bkn ctx. 4.725:5.

kḏġdl PN (Hurr. Cf. Grøndahl PTU 204, 221, 237; Dietrich - Loretz

WO 4 1967/68 302).

PN: ★a) 3.5:5 (*bn ušxl*(?)); RSOu 14 46 [KTU 9.469]:9; ★b) *bn PN*, 4.183 II 3. Cf. in bkn ctx. 4.725:5.

kḏyn PN (Hurr. Cf. Grøndahl PTU 238).

PN: 4.635:28; 4.727:16 (cf. *bt (II)*).

(kgmn), 1.6 I 19-29; cf. *gmn*.

kgr, 4.218:4.

kh, cf. *k (III)*.

khn (I) n. m. "priest" (Hb., Ph., Pun., Aram., Nab. *khn*, HALOT 461f.; DNWSI 490ff.; Arab. *kāhin*, Hava 668; Eth. *kāhn*, CDG 278. Cf. Cody AnBib 35 18ff.); ¶ RS Akk.: LÚ.MEŠ SANGA, PRU 3 202 (RS 16.257+) B III 37; PRU 6 93:27; 136:6; cf. PN LÚ.UGULA SANGA, PRU 3 168 (RS 16.186):13'; PRU 6 9:1; PN LÚ.SANGA ^{d}EŠ$_{4}$.DAR URU *zi-in-za-ri*, PRU 4 201 (RS 18.02):3; PN LÚ.MÁŠ. ŠU.GÍD.GÍD LÚ.SANGA ^{d}U, *ibid.* ln. 16; cf. ^{m}DINGIR.SANGA (PN), PRU 3 34 (RS 16.114):14'; cf. Huehnergard AkkUg 380. ¶ Forms: pl. *khnm*.

Priest(s): ★a) *khnm*, 4.36:1; 4.99:9; 4.126:6; 4.410:50; 4.745:5; 4.752:6; RSOu 14 34 [KTU 9.436]:3'; *khnm*: PNN, 4.69 VI 22; 4.633:4; 4.416:6 (nn GÁN.ME fields; diff.: Márquez NABU 1995 63: LÚ.MEŠ); *khnm*, 4.68:72 (cf. *ṭup-pu* ÉRIN.MEŠ *ša* GIŠ.BAN.MEŠ tablet of personnel equipped with bows, *ibid.* l. edge); *khnm* 3 GUR ZÌ.KAL.KAL 6 GÍN KÙ.BABBAR 6 UDU.ḪI.A priests: 3 'kor' of high quality flour, 6 shekels of silver, 6 rams, 4.38:1; *khnm tšʕ bnšm w ḥmr* (for the) priests: nine unskilled labourers and a donkey, 4.29:1; ★b) *rb khnm* high priest, 2.4:1; 6.6:1; 6.7:1; 6.8:1; 6.10:1 (cf. RS Akk.: LÚ.UGULA SANGA, PRU 3 168 (RS 16.186):13'; PRU 6 9:1); *rb khnm rb nqdm* high priest, chief mayor, 1.6 VI 56; *dr khnm* chapter of priests, 4.357:24; cf. in bkn ctx. *ṯllt khn*[, group(?) of priests(?), 1.107:18 (cf. diff. Pardee TPM 230: rdg *k hn*[).

Bkn ctx.: *khnm*[, 4.761:1; 4.481:5.

Cf. khn (II).

khn (II) PN (Sem. Cf. Grøndahl PTU 28, 150).

PN: 4.282:5.

/k-h-p/ vb G: "to droop, become depressed" ((?); cf. Akk. *kâpu*, AHw 445; CAD K 192. Cf. Dietrich - Loretz - Sanmartín UF 6 1974 39; Pardee TH 67; cf. diff. Aartun UF 16 1984 37f.: 'auf dem Boden reiben, scharren' Arab. *kahhafa*; for this and other opinions cf. Cohen - Sivan UHT 39f.; Cohen UF 28 1996 147f.; Renfroe Or 57 1988 189ff.). ¶ Forms: G prefc. *ykhp*.

G. To droop, become depressed(?): *k yraš w ykhp mid* if (the horse) tosses its head and appears to be completely depresssed(?), 1.85:30 and par.

/k-ḥ-d/ vb D: "to hide, deny" ((?); cf. Hb. *kḥd*, HALOT 469; Syr. *kḥad*, LS 320; Ammon. cf. DNWSI 496: *kḥd*. Cf. Dietrich - Loretz UF 16 1984 66). ¶ Forms: D suffc. with suff. *kḥdnn*.
D. To hide, deny(?): *lak lh w kḥdnn* he sent (someone) to tell him, but he had denied it(?), 2.70:13.
Cf. mkḥd.

kḥṯ n. m. "throne" (EA Akk. *kaḫšu*, AHw 420; CAD K 36; Sivan GAGl 235; Hurr. *ke/išḫi*, Laroche GLH 143f. Cf. Dietrich - Loretz UF 10 1978 61; cf. Dahood RSP 2 17); ¶ par.: *ksu*. ¶ Forms: sg. *kḥṯ*; pl. *kḥṯm*.
Throne: *yṯb / yrd l kḥṯ aliyn bʕl* he sat down / came down / from the throne of DN, 1.6 I 58/64; *kḥṯ il* a divine throne, 1.4 I 33; *kḥṯ drkth* the throne of his power, 1.3 IV 3 and par. (// *ksi*); *kḥṯ zblhm* their princely thrones, 1.2 I 23 and par.; *ilm kḥṯm* the throne-gods, 1.4 VI 51.

kkb (I) cf. *kbkb*.

kkb (II) PN (Sem. Cf. Hillers BASOR 173 1964 46f.; Cross BASOR 190 1968 44 n. 21; Dietrich - Loretz KA 251; cf. West AOAT 233 32: PN *ka-ka-po*, Linear B).
PN: 4.767:1.

kkbn PN (etym. unc.; cf. Watson AuOr 11 1993 216; AuOr 14 1996 100; Xella SEL 9 1992 85f.).
PN: 4.734:2.

kkln PN (Anat. Cf. Grøndahl PTU 277; Van Soldt SAU 38; Watson AuOr 14 1996 100); ¶ syll.: cf. *ku-ku-li*, Ug 5 35 obv. 11'. Cf. *qqln* PN.
PN: 4.148:4; 4.352:10; 4.609:5.

kkn PN (etym. unc.; cf. Grøndahl PTU 311; Watson AuOr 5 1987 309ff.).
PN: 4.645:4 ([*bn*] *ubyn*); cf. in bkn ctx. 4.610:69.

kknt n. f. "pot, jar, pitcher" (etym. unc.; (?)< **knkn*; cf. Akk. *kannu*, *kankannu*, AHw 437f.; CAD K 154, G 40f.; cf. De Moor SP 170f.; Margalit UF 8 1976 174 n. 93; UF 11 1979 552 n. 50; Poljakov UF 14 1982 309f.; cf. Watson AuOr 5 1987 309ff.: (?)< Akk. *kukkanītu*, AHw 500; CAD K 498); ¶ syll. Ug.: cf. *ku-ku-na-tu*, RS 19.64 obv. 3' (rdg: Van Soldt SAU 304; PRU 6 163 obv. 3': $^{\text{subat(?)}}$*ka-na-tu*); ¶ par.: *rḥbt*. ¶ Forms: sg. *kknt*.

Pot, jar, pitcher: *tšabn b rḥbt* [...*t*]*šabn b kknt* he draws water with an amphora, [...] draws water with a pitcher, 1.6 I 67 (// *rḥbt*).

kkr "talent" (< "cake, disc", */krkr/; unit of weight = 60 minas = 3000 shekels; cf. Parise IncGr 82 1984 127ff.; Courtois Poids 123; cf. Hb., Pun., Palm. *kkr*, HALOT 473; DNWSI 500; Aram. *knkr*, DNWSI 500; ESA *krkrk*, DOSA 252; Emar Akk. /kakkaru/, Pentiuc Vocabulary 91; Alalakh / EA Akk. *kakkaru*, AHw 422; CAD K 49f. [cf. Akk. *biltu* / GÚ, GUN, Bab. 30 ± 2 kg.; Powell RlA 7 508ff.; Van den Hout RlA 7 525ff.; Karwiese Šiqlu 22f.]); ¶ RS Akk.: GUN, *passim*; GÚ, PRU 6 146:1; Huehnergard AkkUg 364; ¶ syll. Ug.: 2 *ka*$_4$-*ka*$_4$-*r*[*u/a*(?)-*m*]*a* KÙ.BABBAR-*pí*, PRU 3 52 (RS 15.86):23; 1 *ka*$_4$-*ka*$_4$-*ra* GUŠKIN (...) ù *ka*$_4$-*ka*$_4$-*ra* K[Ù.BABBAR], PRU 3 154 (RS 16.205+):20, 22; cf. Nougayrol PRU 3 223, 235; PRU 6 154; Sivan GAGl 235; Huehnergard UVST 136; Van Soldt SAU 319 n. 133. ¶ Forms: sg. *kkr*, pl. *kkrm*, du. *kkrm*.

1) Talent, unit of weight of 3.000 shekels for, ★a) metals: *kkr br* a talent of tin, 4.608:3; *ʕšrm kkr brr* twenty talents of tin, 4.91:11; *(nn) kkr ṯlṯ* (nn) talents of copper, 2.32:5, 6, 11; 4.181:4 (cf. *alpm ṯlṯ* two thousand shekels of copper, *ibid.* ln. 6); 4.280:2, 5; *ḫmš ʕšr kkr ṯlṯ* (ship's cargo of) fifteen talents of copper, 4.390:4; *šbʕ ʕšrm kkr ṯlṯ* twenty seven talents of copper, 4.272:6; *ḫmš kkrm alp kbd ṯlṯ l nskm birtym (...) w ṯṯ mat brr b ṯmnym ksp ṯlṯt kbd* five talents one thousand shekels of copper for the GN smiths (...) and six hundred (shekels) of tin for eighty-three of silver, 4.337:2; *ḫmš kkr brr kkr ḫmš mat kbd ṯlṯ šmn* five talents of tin and one talent five hundred (shekels) of copper (in exchange for) oil, 4.272:3-4 (cf. Sanmartín SEL 5 1988 176f.); *ṯmn kkr ṯlṯ ṯmn kkr brr* eight talents of copper, eight talents of tin, 4.203:1-2; *ṯmn kkrm alp kbd mitm kbd* eight talents one thousand two hundred (shekels), 4.43:5; *ʕšr kkr ṯlṯ ktt* ten talents of powdered copper, 4.721:4; *arbʕ kkr ṯlṯ ktt* four talents of powdered copper, 4.288:8; *kkrm brḏl* two talents of iron, 4.91:6; ★b) minerals and stones: *kkrm alpm ḫmš mat kbd abn ṣrp* two talents (and) two thousand five hundred shekels of alum, 4.626:8; *arbʕ kkr algbṯ arbʕt ksph* four talents of *a.* to the value of four (shekels), 4.158:14; ★c) wool: *ʕšr kkr šʕrt bd PN b arbʕm* ten talents of wool in the hands of PN for forty (shekels), 4.341:15; *ḫṣt*(!) *kkr* half a talent, 4.131:5 (cf. Dietrich - Loretz - Sanmartín UF 5 1973 88f.); *kkr lqḥ PN* PN received a talent, 4.131:6 (cf. *kkrm* two talents *ibid.* ln. 2); *kkr šʕrt nṯkh* its interest is a talent of wool, 4.225:13; (*nn*) *kkr šʕrt l rb*[(nn) talents of wool for the chief(?) / PN[, 4.721:9; *ʕšr kkr šʕrt bd*

PN b arbʕm ten talents of wool ceded to PN for forty (shekels), 4.341:14 (cf. ln. 3); *kkr šʕrt šbʕt ksph* a talent of wool at the price of seven (shekels), 4.158:17; *kkr šʕrt b ṯqlm* a talent of wool for two shekels, 4.707:15; *kkrm šʕrt štt* two talents of spun wool, 4.337:9; ★d) plants: *kkr w mlth tyt* a talent and a *m.* of *t.*, 4.337:26; *ḫmšt kkr tyt* five talents of *t.*, 4.203:17; *arbʕ kkrm ṯmn mat kbd pwt* four talents eight hundred (shekels) of ruby, 4.626:4; *ḫmšm kkr qnm* fifty talents of reeds (?), 4.91:9; *ḫmš kkr qnm* five talents of reeds, 4.158:12; *ḫmš kkrm ṣml*[[*l*]] *ʕšrt ksph* five talents of *ṣ.* for ten shekels, 4.158:10; *ḫmš kkr ṣml b ʕšrt* five talents of *ṣ.* for ten shekels, 4.341:12; ★e) comestibles: [[*drt b kkr*]] [[bran for one talent]], 4.131:4 (text erased; cf. *ibid.* 2, 8, 10, 11, 13); *kkr tznt* a talent in provisions, 4.203:16; *ḫmš kkr ḥlb* five talents of cheese, 4.272:2; *kkr ḥlb* a talent of cheese, 4.707:19; ★f) other items: *ʕšr kkr rtn* ten talents of *r.*, 4.247:32; *ʕšrm kkr kkrm alp ṯṯ mat kbd* twenty-two talents, one thousand six hundred (shekels(?)), 4.353:2. Cf. in bkn ctx.: *w arbʕ kkr ʕl PN* and four talents on PN's account, 4.123:2; *arbʕm kkr x*[forty talents of ...[, 4.342:3-4; ... *mit ḫ*(?)*sr kkrm alpm* 4.721:5.

2) Relative values: *kkr ugrt* Ugaritic talent (: 28·2 kg.), *kkr aḏdd* talent of Ashdod (23·499 kg. = Karkemish(?); ratio 6:5, cf. Parise IncGr 82 1984 129ff.; Courtois Poids 123); cf. *šbʕ kkr šʕrt b kkr aḏdd w b kkr ugrt ḫmš kkrm alp ṯmn mat kbd* seven talents of wool (calculated) by the talent of TN which are, according to the talent of TN, five talents, one thousand eight hundred (shekels) 4.709:1-4.

Bkn: 4.201:3, 5 (rdg?; cf. Tropper AuOr 13 1995 237); 4.206:3; 4.304:3, 5; 4.396:10, 15, 16, 17 (rdg?; cf. Tropper AuOr 13 1995 238); 4.548:1; 4.608:5-13; 4.742:3 (7?).

kkrdn n. m.; a class of "baker" (Hurro-Akk. *kakardinnu*, AHw 421; CAD K 42; < */kakkar= tenn=/, cf. Akk. *kakkaru* "large loaf", AHw 422; CAD K 49f.; Hb. *kkr*, HAL473; Hurr. suff. /=tenn-/ *nomen actoris*; Wilhelm UF 2 1970 280ff. [cf. **tan=* "to make" Laroche GLH 254f.]; Heltzer IOKU 81 n. 8; cf. Aartun SEL 2 1985 81ff.: 'Berufstätige, die das Horn des Nashorns zu Gegenständen verarbeiten', from Indo-Iran). ¶ Forms: pl. *kkrdnm*.

A class of baker: *kkrdnm k.*-bakers, 4.126:27.

kky PN (etym. unc.; cf. Watson AuOr 8 1990 120; Muchiki Loanwords 90).

PN: *bn PN*, 4.321:3.

kl (I) n. m. "totality (of), > all, each, every, the whole, entirety" (cf. Hb., Ammon., Ph., Pun., Aram., Palm., Nab. *kl*, HALOT 474f.;

DNWSI 500ff.; Ebla cf. *gal-iš* /kalîš/, Krebernik PET 86 [and cf. Ug. *klh*]; cf. [*g*]*a-li*, Krebernik QuSe 18 114; Akk. *kalû*, AHw 427; CAD K 87ff.; ESA *kl*, DOSA 247; Arab. *kull*, Lane 3002; Eth. *kʷĕll*, CDG 281; cf. Dietrich - Loretz UF 16 1984 351ff.); ¶ **par.**: *pḫyr*. ¶ Forms: sg. *kl*; suff. *klh*, *klhm*, *klhn*, *klm* (encl. -*m*?).
Totality (of) > all, each, every, the whole, entirety, ★**a**): abs. *mt kl amt* the death of all I also shall die, 1.17 VI 38; *dbḥ kl kl ykly* sacrifice that is completely consumed, 1.127:7-8 (alternatively: 'of which everyone eats'; cf. 1.115:10; Dietrich - Loretz MU 29); *kl d iṯ* [*l špš*] all that the 'Sun' has, 2.81:9; *ank ṯṯ ymm kl lḥmt* as for me, I have fought everyone for six days, 2.82:9; [*yṯ*]*b kmm l kl msp*[*r*] it returns (: it is repeated) once again at / in each recitation, 1.107:14; abs. adv. entirely, completely, in full: *w ḫrṣ l kl* and the gold in full, 1.16 I 45; cf. 1.18 IV 4; 1.124:15 (cf. Del Olmo CR 314 n. 70; cf. *kll*); *b kl ygz ṭ*(!)*bḫ šh* the sacrificer shall shear his sheep completely, 1.80:5; ★**b**) cstr. with noun: *tṣd kl ġr (...) kl gbʕ* she scoured every mountain (...) every height, 1.5 VI 26-27 and par.; *rb tmtt lqḥ kl ḏrʕ b dntm w ank kl ḏrʕhm kl npš kl klhm bd rb tmtt lqḥt* the captain of the (salvage) crew has collected all the seed grain from their containers(?), and I (then) collected all their seed grain, all the persons (and) all their gear, 2.38:17-22; *dbh kl yrḫ* sacrifice of every / each month, 1.127:1; *l kl il alṯy* to all the gods of TN, 2.42:8; *bʕl kl ḫwt* lord of the whole country, 2.81:3 and par., title of the pharaoh; *kl dbrm hmt .... wkl mḫrk* [*d iš*] *tir aštn lk* all the matters ... I will return to you the total amount that I still owe you, 2.32:9 (cf. Dijkstra UF 19 1987 40); *kl šbšlt dg* all types of fish stews, 1.106:21; ★**c**) with suff. pron.: *aṯr ṯlṯ klhm* they go in threes all of them, 1.14 II 42 and par.; *TN il klh* TN that of (one) god it all is, 1.3 VI 14 and par. (diff. Gibson CML 55: 'all broad TN'; De Moor ARTU 19: 'for all Divine TN'; Albright YGC 119 n. 70; Caquot - Sznycer TOu 1 178 n. g: 'car il est à lui'; Cassuto GA 153, 164; Loewenstamm UF 2 1970 33: 'El-Kulla'; Gordon UL 23 44: 'all the gods TN'; Margalit MLD 151: 'the god (who is) its crown', Arab. *kalla*); *w ymlk b arṣ il klh* and he was king in the land (that) of (one) god it all is, 1.6 I 65 (cf. *supra:* 1.3 VI 14 and par.; diff. Loretz UB 223: 'auf der Erde des El'; De Moor UF 18 1986 259: 'all the divine (Egypt)'); *šbʕ pamt l klhm* seven times according to the total (number), 1.43:26 (or "in total"; cf. Dietrich - Loretz UF 16 1984 351f.); *yn l mrynm ḥsk klh* wine for the *m.*: assigned in its entirety, 4.230:1; *gdm klhm*(!) two kids (to) them all, 1.111:7 (for the rdg cf. Del Olmo CR 200 n. 102; cf. different rdg

in KTU *klhn*; cf. Dietrich - Mayer ALASP 7 19: /kullahin(n)a/ 'gänzlich'); *w b klhn špḥ yitbd* and in their entirety the family perished, 1.14 I 24 (// *b pẖryh*).

In bkn ctx.: *kl b kl*, 1.82:26; *kl hw*[, 2.3:4;]*x kl lh*, *ibid.* ln.26; *w l kl*, 2.35:15; *klm ḏrʕ*, 2.81:17; 4.278:12 (Dietrich - Loretz UF 16 1984 352). Cf. 1.9:11. Read *qlh* in 2.31:52 (see *ql (I)*).

Cf. **/k-l-l/**, **kll**, **klyn**, **klt (II)**.

kl (II) n. m. "belonging(s), equipment, gear" (cf. Hb. *kly*, HALOT 478f.; for the idiom *kl (I)* + *kl (II)* cf. Hb. *kl kly*, *passim*; Akk. *mimma šumšu*, *passim* Nuzi, RS, EA Akk.). ¶ **Forms**: pl. cstr. suff. *klhm*.

Belonging(s), equipment, gear: *ank kl ḏrʕhm kl npš kl klhm (...) lqḥt* I (then) collected (...) all his seed grain, all the people (and) all their belongings, 2.38:21; (estate given) *yd* [*k*]*l klh* with all its belongings, 5.3:10. Cf. in bkn ctx. *qštm* [*kl*] *mhrm* the bow(s) (is / are) [the equipment] of warriors, 1.17 VI 40.

/k-l-ʔ/ vb G: "to close" (Hb., Aram. *klʔ*, HALOT 475; DNWSI 508; Syr. *klō*, LS 327; Akk. *kalû*, AHw 428f.; CAD K 95ff.; Arab. *kalaʔa*, Lane 2623f.; Eth. *kalʔa*, CDG 281f.). ¶ **Forms**: G suffc. *klat*.

G. To close: *klat ṯġrt bht* she closed the doors of (her) house, 1.3 II 3 and par. (diff.: Aartun StUL 71f.: 'bewachen', Arab. *kalaʔa*).

kli PN (Hurr. Cf. Dietrich - Loretz OLZ 62 1967 537f.); ¶ **syll.**: *ki-la-ʔe-e*, PRU 4 294 (RS 19.70):3; RSOu 7 19 obv. 3, obv. 3; in bkn ctx. PRU 4 234 (RS 17.112):2; cf. Huehnergard UVST 246. PN: 3.8:3.

klat n. f. "both, both (hands)" (cf. Hb. *klʔym*, HALOT 475f.; Akk. *kilattān*, AHw 475; CAD K 353ff.; Arab. *kilā*, *kiltā*, Hava 664; Eth. *kĕlʔettu*, CDG 282. Cf. De Moor SP 72; Fensham JNSL 4 1975 16); ¶ **par.**: *yd*, *ymn*. ¶ **Forms**: sg. f. *klat*; suff. *klatnm* (*-n-* pron. suff. or emph. [cf. accus. in *-ān-*] + encl. *-m*).

Both, both (hands): *b klat ydh* in both his hands, 1.3 I 11 and par. (// *bdh*); *b klat ydy ilḥm* with both hands I gulped him down, 1.5 I 19; *lqḥ (...) lla klatnm* he took (...) a suckling with both (hands), 1.14 III 57 and par. (// *b ydh*;); *klat tqtnṣn w tldn* both (women) squatted and gave birth, 1.23:57 (diff.: Tsumura UF 10 1978 393: 'completion', cf. /k-l-l/ > *pẖr klat*, 'total completion', Akk. *ina puḫur kullati*).

klb (I) n. m. "dog" (Hb., Ph., Aram. *klb*, HALOT 476; DNWSI 509f.; Akk. *kalbu*, AHw 424f.; CAD K 67; Arab. *kalb*, Lane 2625f.; Eth. *kalb*, CDG 282); ¶ **syll. Ug.**: [UR = *ka-al-bu*(?)] = *ir-bi* = *ka-a*[*l-bu*, UF 11 1979 478:34; Van Soldt UF 21 1989 366; SAU 304; cf. the element /kalb-/in PNN; Sivan GAGl 235; ¶ **par.**: *inr*. ¶ **Forms**: sg. *klb*

(f. cf. *klbt*); pl. *klbm*, suff. *klbh*.
Dog: *k klb* like a dog, 1.16 I 2 and par. (// *inr*); *zġt klb ṣpr* barking of the hunting dog(s), 1.14 III 19 and par. (cf. Sanmartín UF 10 1978 349: 'Windhund'; *pn lm k*(!)*lb tʕdbn nšb* who do not offer a *n.* to a dog, 1.114:12 (// *inr*); *šʕr klb* hair of a dog, 1.114:29; *ṯlṯ klbm* three dogs, 4.54:4; *ḥrṣ klb ilnm* the divine puppy /dog bit, 1.19 I 10 (for other interpretations cf. Del Olmo IMC 129 n. 292; diff.: Margalit UF 16 1984 121: rdg *k lb*; KTU: *k lb*); *klb l ḫṭh* (like) a dog (tied) to its stake, 1.19 I 13-14 (cf. Del Olmo IMC 128 n. 287).
Cf. klb (II), klbt, kalby, klbyn.

klb (II) PN (Sem. Cf. Grøndahl PTU 28, 150; Dietrich - Loretz Fs. Helck 641; Van Soldt SAU 40); ¶ syll.: *kál*(GAL)*-bu/i*, PRU 3 81 (RS 16.239):25-26; 82 (RS 16.143):12, 24; *kal-bi*, PRU 3 82 (RS 16.143):11; cf. Sivan GAGl 235.
PN: ★a) 4.232:44; ★b) *bt PN*, 4.75 III 5.

klbr PN (Hurr. Cf. Grøndahl PTU 211, 225, 236; Dietrich - Loretz OLZ 62 1967 535, 537f.).
PN: 4.391:2.

klbt n. f. "bitch" (< *klb (I)*). ¶ Forms: sg. cstr. *klbt*.
Bitch: *mḫšt klbt ilm* I crushed the Divine Bitch, 1.3 III 45 (written *k.lbt*, see Watson UF 10 1978 397f; cf. West UF 24 1992 369ff.).

klby PN (Sem. Cf. Grøndahl PTU 28, 150; Dietrich - Loretz Fs. Helck 641); ¶ syll.: *kál-be-ia*, Syria 18 246 (RS 8.145):29, 31 (Berger WO 5 1969/70 275); *kál-be-ya*, PRU 3 97f. (RS 16.249), 6 and *passim ibid.*; 155 (RS 16.242):7; *kál-bi-ya*, 121 (RS 15.136):4; 146 (RS 16.139):4; 195 (RS 15.09) B II 10; cf. Sivan GAGl 235; Huehnergard AkkUg 386.
PN: ★a) 2.10:6; 4.63 II 19; 4.69 I 24; 4.75 V 18 (*b*[*n*); 4.76:8; 4.103:36; 4.277:5; 4.357:17; 4.366:7 (*bn iḫy*); 4.609:26, 29; 4.690:2 (*bn ḫdġb*); ★b) *bn PN*, cf. in unc. ctx. *ṯn bn klby*, 4.364:1.

klbyn PN (Sem. Cf. Dietrich - Loretz Fs. Helck 641).
PN: 4.370:20.

kld (I) n. m. "bow" (Hurr. allomorph; < /qalt-/, < Ug. *qšt* /qašt/; cf. AHw 906; CAD Q 147; cf. Hurr. *keltuḫlu*, Mayer Nuzi 186. Cf. Dietrich - Loretz UF 10 1978 429). ¶ Forms: sg. *kld*.
Bow: (list of) *bnš kld* archers, 4.277:1 (cf. *ṭup-pu* ÉRIN.MEŠ *ša* GIŠ.BAN.MEŠ tablet of personnel [equipped] with bows, 4.68:76/l. e.).
Cf. qšt.

kld (II) DN Hurr. ('Health'(?), cf. Hurr. *keldi*, Laroche GLH 141. Cf.

Laroche Ug 5 p. 526; Schwemer NuzHur 7 94f.); ¶ RS Akk.: cf. dSA-*li-mu*, Ug 5 18:33 (// *šlm*, 1.47:34; 1.118:33). ¶ Forms: *kldnd* (1.132:12; Hurr.: DN + det. + dir. /DN=ne=da/).
DN: 1.132:12. In Hurr. ctx. cf. 1.44:10-11; 1.52:10, 14; 1.66:8; 1.128:11, 20.

(klkl), cf. *kl (I)*, *kl (II)*.

/k-l-l/ vb D: "to complete, finish" (denom. < *kl (I)*. Cf. Van Zijl, Baal 113ff.); ¶ syll. Ug.: cf. the element /kallāl/(?) in PNN; Sivan GAGl 235; ¶ par.: /ʕ-m-s/. ¶ Forms: D prefc. with suff. *ykllnh*.
D. To complete, finish: *bt arzm ykllnh* a palace of cedar they shall complete for him, 1.4 V 10 (// *yʕmsnh*).
Cf. škllt.

kll n. m. "totality, whole > all" (< *kl (I)*; cf. Hb. *klyl*, HALOT 479. Cf. Dietrich - Loretz - Sanmartin UF 71975 544). ¶ Forms: sg. *kll*.
Totality, whole, all: *ʕmny šlm kll* with me all is at peace, 2.16:15 (cf. 2.13:10 and par.); *hnny ʕmny kll mid šlm* behold here with me everything is very well, 2.11:11 (cf. 2.34:7 2.36:3; 2.39:3); *š (...) kll ylḥm bh* a ram (...) of which all shall eat, 1.115:10 (cf. *tlḥm at̲t*, *ibid.* ln. 8; cf. Del Olmo CR 266; diff.: Dietrich - Loretz - Sanmartín UF 7 1975 543; Janowski UF 12 1980 247f.: 'gänzlich soll man es essen'; Levine PL 11: '*kalil* (sacrifice)', Hb. *klyl*, Ph. *kll*, but cf. Janowski UF 12 1980 247f.; Dietrich - Loretz - Sanmartín UF 7 1975 561f.; Loretz UF 7 1975 569f.; diff. rdg Dietrich - Loretz UF 13 1981 88: *kl* + *l* + jussive: 'alle sollen von ihm essen'); *l kll* none at all: *l dg w l kl*[*l*] no fish and none at all, 1.124:15 (cf. Del Olmo CR 314 n. 70; cf. diff.: Pardee TPM 180ff.: 'et plus de chien': rdg *kl*[*b*]; cf. Dietrich - Loretz TUAT 2 331). Bkn ctx., *w kll*, 1.173:14; 7.20:2.

kln PN (etym. unc.; cf. Grøndahl PTU 205, 234, 236; Dietrich - Loretz OLZ 62 1967 537f.); ¶ syll.: cf. *ku-la-nu*, PRU 6 54:15; DUMU *kal-la-na*, Ug 5:26. Cf. *gln* PN.
PN: *bn PN*, 4.309:23.

klnmw PN (Anat. Cf. Grøndahl PTU 280, 285).
PN: 4.44:21, 25.

klny adv. "all together, together" (< *kl (I)* + adv. suff. *-ny*; cf. Gordon, UT § 11.3; Aartun, PU 1 44f., 62). ¶ Forms: suff. *klnyy*, *klnyn* (*-y*, *-n* emph. endings, with the same meaning; cf. Tropper UF 26 1994 479f.).
All together, together: *klnyy qšh nbln klnyy nbl ksh* all together we shall carry his tankard, all together we shall carry his cup, 1.3 V 33-34 (cf. 1.4 IV 45-46, *klnyn*: all of us?).

klt (I) n. f. 1) "bride"; 2) "daughter-in-law"(?) (Hb., Palm. *klh*, HALOT 477f.; DNWSI 510; Syr. *kaltō*, LS 326f.; Ebla /kallatu(m)/ in É.GI.A = *gal-la-tum/du*, *gal-tum*, VE 322; ÉxGÌ = *ga-la-tum*, EV 0468; Krebernik ZA 73 1983 14; Fronzaroli EL 140; StEb 7 1984 168; Akk. *kallatu*, AHw 426; CAD K 79ff., also an epithet of goddesses; cf. De Moor SP 82). ¶ Forms: sg./pl. *klt*; suff. *klth*.
1) Bride: *klt knyt* the glorious brides, 1.4 I 15 and par. (epithet of Baal's daughters; diff.: Caquot Fs. Laroche 79ff.: the DN *Kullita*); *PN klt bt špš PN*, the bride, the daughter of the 'Sun' (: Hitt. king), 6.24:2 (cf. Van Soldt UF 21 1989 389ff.). In unc. ctx.: *ššlmt yrḫ l klt* monthly supplementary delivery for the bride(?), 4.786:5.
2) Daughter-in-law(?): in bkn ctx., PN(N) *w klth* and his(their) daughter(s)-in-law(?), 4.80:13 and par.; cf. *yd ṯlṯ kl*[*th* with [his] three daughters[-in-law](?), *ibid.* ln. 4, 19.

klt (II) n. f. "measure, amount, quantity" (< */k-(w)-l/; Hb. *kl*, DNWSI 507f.; Palm. cf. DNWSI 508: kl_3; Arab. *kayl*, *kaylat*, Lane 3005; for Ebla / pre-Sarg. Mari ITU GI.NI cf. Pettinato Ebla[1] 139: rdg *kí-lí* 'mese della misura'; cf. Mander MROA 2/1 96. Cf. Herdner TOu 1 513 n. o; diff.: Aartun UF 16 1984 38: 'festgelegte Portion, Ration', Arab. *kalata*, *kultat*; Gibson CML 149: 'totality, all', /k-l-l/). ¶ Forms: sg. *klt*.
Measure, amount, quantity: *klt lḥmh* a measure of his bread, 1.14 III 58 and par.

klt (III) PN (etym. unc.).
PN: 4.370:38; 4.786:5. Cf. *k/wlt*, 4.34:5.

kltn PN (Hurr. Cf. Grøndahl PTU 236, 260ff.; Dietrich - Loretz OLZ 62 1967 537f.).
PN: *bn PN*, 3.5:13, 18.

klṯṯb PN (Hurr. Cf. Grøndahl PTU 211, 236, 264; Dietrich - Loretz OLZ 62 1967 538; Van Soldt SAU 36).
PN: 4.103:46; 4.357:27; 4.616:12; 4.638:7.

/k-l-y/ vb G: 1) to finish, be finished, to empty, be emptied (out), to consume, be consumed"; 2) "to be liquidated"; N: "to be consumed, used up; to be distributed; to be liquidated"; D: "to finish (off), destroy, drain" (Hb. *klh*, HALOT 476f.; Pun. *kly*, DNWSI 510ff. Cf. Fensham JNSL 7 1949 27ff.; Xella UF 11 1979 835; TRU 341; Milano VO 1 1978 83ff.; Dietrich - Loretz UF 13 1981 294ff.); ¶ par.: /ʔ-k-l/, /m-ḫ̮-ṣ/, /m-ḫ̮-š/, /q-ṯ/, /s-p-ʔ/, /ṣ-m-t/. ¶ Forms: G suffc. *kly*, *klt*; prefc. *ykl*; N suffc. *nkly*; cprf. *ykly*; D suffc. *klt*; cprf. *akly*, *tkly*, *tkl* (jussive), *ykly*; inf. suff. *klyy*, *klyn* (?); part. act. suff. *mkly*.

G. 1) to finish, be finished, to empty, be emptied (out), to consume, be consumed: *yn d ykl bd r*[...] *b dbḥ mlk* wine they deliver (for consumption) into the hands of the *r.*[...] in the royal sacrifice, 1.91:1 (/ N); *kly lḥm (...) kly yn (...) kly šmn* finished was the grain / the wine / the oil, 1.16 III 13-16.
2) To be liquidated, in administrative terminology: *qmḥ d kly b bt skn l PN* flour that has been liquidated for PN in (/ intended for) the house of the prefect, 4.361:1 (cf. Dietrich - Loretz UF 13 1981 296); *qmḥ d kly k ṣḥ PN bd PN* flour that has been liquidated when PN claimed (it) through the mediation of PN, 4.362:1. In bkn ctx.: *dt klt*[, 4.257:3.
N. To be consumed, used up; to be distributed; to be liquidated": *dbḥ kl kl ykly* total sacrifice, that is consumed completely, 1.127:8 (or G 1?; cf. 1.91:1); *yn ḥsp d nkly b dbḥ* decanted wine that has been used up during the sacrifice, 4.213:24; cf.]*nkly l rʕym*]that was distributed to the shepherds, 4.243:45; *tgmr yn d nkly* total of wine distributed, 4.230:15; *<yn> d nkly {yn} kd w kd* <wine> that was used: {} two 'jars' (: one 'jar' and one 'jar'; scribal correction), 4.279:1 (rdg cf. PRU 2 p. 100); *ksp d nkly b šd* money liquidated for a field, 4.280:6. In bkn ctx.:]*d nkly*, 4.227 IV 6.
D. To finish (off), destroy, drain: *klt bt il* I finished off the daughter of DN, 1.3 III 46 (// *ṣmt, mḫšt*); *l klt nhr il rbm* did I not finish off DN, the great god?, 1.3 III 39; *ykly ṯpṭ nhr* he finished off Judge DN, 1.2 IV 27 (// *yqṯ*); *tkly bṯn ʕqltn* you finished off the winding serpent, 1.5 I 2 and par. (// *tmtḫṣ*); *mnth l tkly npr*[*m*] the birds finished (off) his pieces, 1.6 II 36 (// *tikl*); *akly hml*[*t arṣ*] I shall finish off the multitudes [of the land], 1.6 V 24 ((?); altern. transl.: the multitudes of the land shall be my food); *akl<y> mkly* [*ʕ*]*l umty* I am going to finish off the one who finished off my kin, 1.19 IV 34-35 and par. (// *imḫṣ mḫṣ*; cf. 1.4 II 25); *w uḫry ykly ršp* and DN will destroy the descendants, 1.103+:40; *al tkl bn qr ʕnk* do not drain, my son, the springs of your eyes, 1.16 I 26 (jussive); *ytnt (...) bnm umy klyy* you made (...) the sons of my mother my consumption, 1.6 VI 11, 15-16; 1.6 VI 15 (// *spuy*).
In bkn ctx.: cf. *klyn*[, 1.7:18; *d ykl*, 1.104:3; *kly b kpr*, 2.72:43.

kly PN (Hurr. Cf. Grøndahl PTU 205, 236); ¶ **syll.**: *ki-li-ia*, PRU 4 201 (RS 18.02): 3 and *passim ibid.* (Van Soldt SAU 350 n. 209).
PN: ★**a)** PN 4.390:8; 6.43:2; ★**b)** *bn PN*, 4.214 III 6.

klyn PN (Hurr. Cf. Grøndahl PTU 205, 236; Van Soldt SAU 38); ¶ **syll.**: *ki-li-ia-nu*, PRU 3 37 (RS 15.81):1. Cf. *glyn* PN.
PN: ★**a)** 4.80:11 (*apsny*); 4.141 I 17; 4.148:4; 4.609:13, 25; cf. in

bkn ctx. *klyn*[, 1.7:18;]*klyn*, 4.615:5; ★b) *bn PN*, 4.214 III 7.

klyt n. f. "kidneys" (Hb. *klywt*, HALOT 479; Syr. *kūlītō* LS 329; Akk. *kalītu*, AHw 425; CAD K 74ff.; Arab. *kulyat*, Hava 664; Eth. *kʷelīt*, CDG 284). ¶ Forms: pl./du. suff. *klyth*.
Kidneys: *klyth w lbh* his kidneys and his heart, 1.82:3.

-km suffixed pronominal morpheme 2nd p. m. pl.: 1) used with a noun, "your"; 2) used with a verb "you"; 3) used with a preposition, *l*, (C.Sem.. except Akk. and Syr. [*kn*]; cf. Moscati ICGSL 106ff.; Gordon UT § 6.12; Segert BGUL 47; Tropper UG 225). ¶ Forms: pl./du. *-km*.
1) Used with a noun: *passim*.
2) Used with a verb: *b*]*ty aṣḥkm iqra*[*km*] to my house I invite you, I call you, 1.21 II 2-3 and par.; [*l l*]*ḥm l šty ṣḥtkm* to eat and drink I called you, 1.15 IV 27 and par.; *al tʕdbkm k imr* he is not to place you like a lamb in his mouth, 1.4 VIII 16.
3) Used with a preposition: in bkn ctx.: *ank lkm*[, 2.3:16.
Bkn ctx.:]*km rʕy*, 1.21 II 6.

km 1) prep. "like"; 2) conj. "when, in the event of, while"; 3) adv. "thus" (cf. *k (I)* + encl. *-m*; Ph., Pun. *km*, DNWSI 514; Hb. *kmw/h*, HALOT 481; DNWSI 514; Amor. /kama/, CAAA 22; Akk. *kima*, AHw 476f.; CAD K 363; Arab. *kama*, Lane 2989. Cf. Caquot - Sznycer TOu 1 163); ¶ par.: *k*. ¶ Forms: *km*; suff. *kmk*, *kmhm*, *kmm* (encl. *-m (I)* with adverbial meaning; cf. also *kmm*).
1) Prep. like: *d in bn lh km aḫh w šrš km aryh* who has no son like his brothers nor offspring like his kinsmen, 1.17 I 19 and par.; *w in bt l bʕl km ilm* but, evidently, DN has no house like the gods, 1.4 IV 51 and par. (// *k*); *y*[*b*]*n bt lk km aḫk w ḥẓr km aryk* a house will be built for you like (the one of) your brothers, a mansion like (the one of) your kin, 1.4 V 28-29; *k lbš km lpš dm a*[*ḫh*] *km all dm aryh* for he put on like a cloak the blood of his equals, like a cloak the blood of his kinsmen, 1.12 II 46-47; *npl bʕl km ṯr (...) km ibr* DN fell like a bull, (...) like a bull, 1.12 II 54-55; *bhm qrnm km ṯrm w gbṯt km ibrm* they will have horns like bulls and 'a hump' like bulls, 1.12 I 30-31; *km irby tškn šd* like locusts they settled in the field, 1.14 IV 29 (// *k*; cf. II 50, *k irby*); *km ḥsn pat mdbr* (they settled) like grasshoppers in the fringes of the desert, 1.14 III 1 (// *k*; cf. IV 30, *k ḥsn*); *tṣi km rḥ / iṯl / qṭr* may (his soul) go out like a breath / saliva / incense, 1.18 IV 24-25 and par.; *špk km šiy dm km šḫṭ* spill (his) blood like an assassin, like a butcher, 1.18 IV 23-24 and par.; *lbh km bṯn* her heart like a snake('s), 1.19 IV 61, cf. *km bṯn yqr* like a snake

he hissed, 1.17 VI 14; *tḥrṯ km gn ap lb* she ploughed her chest like a garden, 1.6 I 4 (// *k*); *yšql šdmth km gpn* they threw (the sceptre) on the terrace like a vinestock, 1.23:11; *aštk (...) km nšr / diy* I shall place you (...) like an eagle / vulture, 1.18 IV 17-18 (cf. ln. 28, *k nšr*); *bn krt kmhm tdr ap bnt ḥry kmhm* the sons of PN were as many as promised and the daughters of PN as many as them, 1.15 III 23-24; *tntkn udmʕ km ṯqlm / ḫmšt* his tears ran like shekels / like five-shekel weights, 1.14 I 28-29; *w l ytk dmʕt km rbʕt ṯqlm* and truly they poured out tears like quarter-shekels, 1.19 II 33; *km tsm ʕṯtrt tsmh* like the beauty of DN is her beauty, 1.14 III 42 (// *k*); *tn* {*km*} *nḥšm y ḥr*[*n*] *tn km mhry* give me the serpents, O DN, give me (them) as a dowry, 1.100:73 (dittog. of *km*); *ṯdn km mrm tqrṣn* our chests bite us like cubs, 1.12 I 11 (// *k*); *tlu ḥ<m>t km nḫl tplg km plg* the venom remained dried up like a torrent, dried up like a stream, 1.100:68-69; *ybky km nʕr* [*ydmʕ*] *km ṣgr* he weeps like a boy, [pours out tears] like a youngster, 1.107:8 and par.; *trtqṣ (...) km nšr* leapt (...) like an eagle, 1.2 IV 15 and par.; *km ġlmm w ʕrbn* like servants you must enter, 1.3 III 8; *km rgm ṯ*[*rm*] *rgmhm* like the bellow of a bull was their voice, 1.15 VI 6; *km špš d brt kmt br ṣṭqšlm* (?), 2.19:2 (cf. *kmt*); *km klb yqṯqṭ* like a dog he crept, 1.114:5; *km nkyt tġr*[...] *km škllt* like distressed(?) (women) [...] like emaciated (women) (?), 1.16 II 28; *bn km yr* take note(?) how he fires arrows, 1.82:3 (unc. ctx.; cf. De Moor (- Spronk) UF 16 1984 239; ARTU 176); *km dlt tlk km p*[like (a) poor woman she/you shall walk, like [, 1.82:24; *km ṣq* like someone distressed, 1.82:25; [*kb*]*d km kbkbt kṯn* [sp]lendour(?) like the stars of TN, 1.92:28. Bkn ctx.: 1.12 I 7, 8; 1.12 II 39-40; 1.82:11; 1.19 IV 60 (// *km bṯn*); 1.19 I 7 (for the various proposals cf. Del Olmo IMC 128 n. 289; Caquot SEL 2 1985 98f.; Margalit UF 16 1984 120f.; Cooper UF 20 1988 20f.).

2) Conj. when, in the event of, while: *w km iṯ* and when he is (there), 1.41:55 (?); *aqht km yṯb l lḥ*[*m*] when DN sat down to eat, 1.18 IV 29 and par.; *km agrškm b bty* in the event of evicting them from my household, 3.9:6; *km tdd ʕnt ṣd* while DN rushed (off) to hunt, 1.22 I 10. Bkn ctx. 1.20 I 3; *k mġy* when (...) arrived, RSOu 14 51 [KTU 9.425]:15.

3) Adv. thus, likewise: *km lb ʕnt aṯr bʕl* thus the heart of DN (did beat) for DN, 1.6 II 29 and par. (// *k*; cf. *kmt*); *km aḫt ʕrš mdw* thus you have taken to the sickbed, 1.16 VI 35 and par. (diff.: Renfroe AULS 81f., cf. *aḫt*); *km l tudn dbbm kšpm* (...) *yšpk kmm arṣ kšpm dbbm* just as the sorcerers do not listen to the demons... so the

sorcerers spill to the ground the demons, RSOu 14 52 [KTU 9.435]:8, 12. - Unc. ctx.: 1.114:28.
Cf. kmt.

kmġ DN, allograph of *kmṯ*, 1.82:42; cf. *kmṯ*.

kmkty TN (Belmonte RGTC 12/2 151: *Kamkatiya*. Heltzer RCAU 11; Astour UF 13 1981 8; Van Soldt UF 28 1996 674; UF 29 1997 691; UF 30 1998 734); ¶ syll.: URU *kam-ka*$_3$*-ti-ia*, PRU 4 48ff. (RS 17.340+):21' (Belmonte RGTC 12/2 151, 406; URU *kam-ka-ti*$_4$(!)[*ia*, PRU 4 68 (17.339A) A:6'. Cf. PRU 4 66 [RS 17.62]:14'.
TN: 4.648:7, 10, 11, 15.

/k-m-l/ vb G: "to become angry" (cf. Akk. *kamālu*, AHw 430; CAD K 109; cf. De Moor UF 11 1979 653; Dietrich - Mayer ALASP 7 21; diff.: Del Olmo CR 202 n. 115: 'may she unite with him!', rdg *tkm l hy*, **kwm*). ¶ Forms: G prefc. *tkml*.
G. To become angry: *tk*[[*m*]]*ml hy bh* may she be angry with him!, 1.111:22 (diff.: Dietrich - Mayer ALASP 7 19, 21: 'Sie seien auf ihn zornig!').

kmlt adj. f. "anger"(?) (< /k-m-l/; Akk. *kimiltu*, AHw 478; CAD K 372f.; cf. De Moor UF 11 1979 653; Dietrich - Mayer ALASP 7 18; diff.: Del Olmo CR 201 n. 201: 'whole', Arab. *kāmil*). ¶ Forms: sg. *kmlt*.
Anger(?): *šbʕ ṯat l kmlt d ʕṯtr* seven ewes for the anger(?) of PN, 1.111:19.

kmm adv. "ditto, in the same amount" (< *km* + encl. *-m*. Cf. De Moor Fs. Gispen 114; Janowski UF 12 235f.; Dijkstra UF 16 1984 75; for the morpheme. cf. Akk. *kâmma*, *kīamma*, AHw 432; CAD K 325ff.); ¶ RS Akk.: cf. *ka-am-ma-a*, PRU 3 14 (RS 12.33):6; *ka-am-ma*, Ug 5 24:25; cf. Huehnergard AkkUg 198; Van Soldt SAU 466. ¶ Forms: *kmm*.
Ditto, in cultic lists: *bʕlm kmm* (a) DN, ditto (in an offering), 1.148:11 and par.; *w šlmm kmm* and in a communion sacrifice: ditto, 1.109:11 and par., cf. e.g. 1.164:5-8; 1.168:3, 10, 13: *w inš ilm kmm* and (to) the divine people: ditto, 1.132:16, cf. *ibid.* ln. 21, 24. In bkn ctx. cf. *ʕlm kmm* next(?), ditto, 1.49:7; 1.50:6; cf. *ṯlṯ kmm*, 1.16 IV 15.

kmn (I) n. m. "'acre'" (surface measure ≈ *šd (II)* 600 m^2; cf. Hurro-Akk. *kumānu*, AHw 505; CAD K 532; Powell RlA 7 476f., 485. Cf. Dietrich - Loretz UF 1 1969 61f.; Liverani Assur 1 1974 11; Heltzer UF 21 1989 202f. n. 61; diff.: Aartun UF 16 1984 39: 'verborgener Winkel', Arab. *kamīn*); ¶ par.: *šd*. ¶ Forms: sg. *kmn*.

'Acre': *b alp šd rbt kmn* over a thousand hectares, ten thousand acres, 1.3 IV 38 and par., cf. 1.3 VI 6 (distance formula; cf. Del Olmo MLC 40).

kmn (II) n. m. "cumin" (seed of *Cuminum cyminum* L.; Hb., Ph., *kmn*, HALOT 481; DNWSI 515; Aram. *kmwn?*, DJPA 262; Akk. *kamūnu*, AHw 434; CAD K 131f.; Arab. *kammūn*, Hava 686; Eth. *ka/ĕmī/ūn*, CDG 285; Gk *kyminon*, Liddell - Scott 1009; Linear B *ku-mi-no/a*, cf. Sanmartín AuOr 8 1990 98). ¶ Forms: sg. *kmn*.
Cumin seeds : *lth*] *kmn lth sbbyn* a *l.*] of cumin (seeds), a *l.* of black cumin, 4.14:9.

kmn (III) PN (etym. unc.; cf. Grøndahl PTU 311; GLH 154; Watson AuOr 11 1993 216; AuOr 14 1996 100; Muchiki Loanwords 90; cf. West AOAT 233 32: PN *ka-mo-ni-yo*, Linear B). Cf. *gmn* PN.
PN: *bn PN*, 4.377:3; 4.704:2; cf. in bkn ctx. 4.445:3.

kmnt PN (etym. unc. Cf. Watson AuOr 13 1995 223).
PN: *bn PN*, 4.778:11; 4.782:17.

kmrn PN (etym. unc.; cf. Grøndahl PTU 28, 150; Sivan GAGl 238; Gelb - Purves - MacRae NPN 222; Watson AuOr 14 1996 100; cf. ¶ syll. Ug.: *ku₈-um-*[*ru*(?)*-ma*, RS 16.276:22, rdg: Van Soldt SAU 304; PRU 3 p. 70: amil(?) M*ku₈-um-*[*ra-šu*(??)). Cf. *gmrn* PN.
PN: 4.631:8; cf. in unc. ctx. *kmr*[, 4.178:17.

kmrṯn PN (Hurr. Grøndahl PTU 239, 251). Cf. *gmrš* PN.
PN: 4.63 I 3; 4.322:6.

/k-m-s/ vb tD: "to buckle, bend" (Akk. *kamāsu*, AHw 431f.; CAD K 117ff.; Ebla cf. ŠU.KIN.AK = *ga-ma-zu-um*, VE 526; Civil Biling. 88. Cf. Good UF 26 1994 154); ¶ **par.**: /n-p-l/. ¶ **Forms**: tD suffc. *tkms* (for *ktmsm*, 1.6 I 52, cf. Del Olmo IMC 77 n. 151; */m-s(-s)/*).
tD. To buckle, bend: *w tkms hd k ibr* and DN buckled like a bull, 1.12 II 54 (// *npl*; diff.: Sanmartín UF 10 1978 355: 'Sturz', nominal form).

kmsk n. m.; measure (a "bit, small piece"(?); etym. unc.; for the segment *-sk* cf. the use of the Sumerogram SIG in Hitt., Rüster - Neu HZL 255, and cf. the Hitt. measure of length KÙŠ.SIG (/ SIG.KÙŠ), cf. Güterbock Fs. Bittel 206f.; Van den Hout RlA 7 520: 'Halbelle, Spanne' 255. Cf. Liverani UF 2 1970 99 n. 22: 'due, doppio', from the context; Stieglitz JAOS 99 1979 16, 21; Tropper - Vita UF 30 1998 684ff.: '2/3'; Zamora SEL 17 2000 69ff.: 'la metà di una misura'). ¶ **Forms**: sg. *kmsk*.
Measure, ★**a)** of area or length: *(nn) šd w kmsk d PN* (nn) 'strips' and *k.*, of PN, 4.282:2; *kmsk šd PN* one *k.* of a 'strip':PN, *ibid.* ln. 4;

★b) of weight or monetary value: *ʕšr ṣin b ṯṯt w kmsk* ten sheep for six shekels and *k.*, 4.341:9; *kkr ḥlb b ṯql w kmsk* a talent of cheese for one shekel and *k.*, 4.707:20; *(...) k*]*sphn ṯql w kmsk* (...)] whose value is one shekel and *k.*, 4.707:23.

kmt adv.; lengthened form of *km (II)* "like(wise)" (Hb. *kmwt*, HALOT 481. See Tropper UG 748 836: *km* + encl. *t*. Cf. Aartun PU 2 26, 31; Dijkstra - De Moor UF 7 1975 214 n. 345). ¶ Forms: *kmt*.
Like: *km špš d brt kmt br PN b unṯ ʕd ʕlm* like the sun, which is free, likewise PN remains free of debt in perpetuity, 2.19:3. For the rdg *kmt mtm* in 1.20 I 3 cf. Dijkstra - De Moor UF 7 1975 214; for *kmtm* in 2.10.12 cf. Dietrich - Loretz UF 22 1990 63 n. 41: 'und das (ist) so!'; cf. *km*).

kmṯ DN, second element in the DN *⊕ṯ/ẓẓ w kmṯ* (cf. the Moabite deity *kmš*, KAI 181:3 and *passim*; cf. Donner - Röllig KAI 2 172; Röllig WbMyth 1 292; Hb. *kmwš*, HALOT 481; Ebla cf. MN ITU [d]*kà-mi-iš*, Pettinato AfO 25 1974 34f.; Rituale 244; Pomponio UF 15 1983 151; Mander MROA 2/1 94; for MA. [d]*ka-am-muš* and LB [d]*ka-am-mu-uš* in god lists cf. Lambert RlA 5 335: Nergal. Cf. Israel SMSR NS 11 1987 5ff.; Worschech UF 24 1992 397); ¶ syll. Ug.: cf. the element /kamāṯ/ in PN DUMU *ka-ma-ši*, PRU 3 195 (RS 15.09 A):2; Sivan, GAGl 236. ¶ Forms: cf. allograph *kmġ* in 1.82:42; rdg *km*(!)*ṯ* in 1.107:41.
DN: 1.82:42 (*kmġ*); 1.107:41 (*km*(!)*ṯ*); 1.123:5 (*⊕ṯ w*); *ql bl ʕm ẓẓ w kmṯ ḥryth* take (this) request to DN in TN, 1.100:36.
Cf. **gmš**.

kmy PN (etym. unc.; cf. Gelb - Purves - MacRae NPN 222, 227; NH no. 623).
PN: *bn PN*, 4.63 III 43.

-kn suffixed pronominal morpheme: genitive, adnominal, of 3rd p. f. pl. "your" (c.Sem.; cf. Moscati ICGSL 106; Gordon UT § 6.12; Segert BGUL 47; Tropper UG 225f.). ¶ Forms: pl. *kn*.
Your: cf. 1.40:21-22, 38-39 and par. *ypkn / npškn / apkn / ḫbtkn / mdllkn* as opposed to m. *ypkm*, etc.

/k-n/ vb G: "to be (stable), have"; L: "to establish, interpose, bring up"; Š: "to prepare, create" (Hb. *kwn*, HALOT 464f.; Ph., Pun. *kn*, DNWSI 493ff.; Syr. *kon*, LS 321; Ebla G. inf. /kān=u(m)/ in KI.BA$_4$.GAR = *ga-nu/núm*, VE 139, EV 0184; Krebernik ZA 73 1983 6; Conti SQF 84; cf. *ga-wa-nu/núm*, ARET 9 386; Akk. *kânu*, AHw 438ff.; CAD K 159ff.; EA Akk. cf. *ku-na*, EAT 147:36; cf. CAD K 171; Sivan GAGl 239; DNWSI 493; Arab. *kāna*, Lane 3004;

ESA*kwn*, DOSA 242ff.; Eth. *kona*, CDG 299f.); ¶ syll. Ug.: cf. the element /i/ takūn-/, /kūn-/, /yakīn-/ in PNN; Sivan, GAGl 239. ¶ Forms: G suffc. *kn*; prefc. *tkn*, *ykn*; L prefc. *tknn*, *yknn*; suff. *yknnh*. Š prefc. *aškn*; inf. *škn* (?) (other forms come under /š-k-n/; cf. 2.46:13; 2.47:3, 5, etc. and cf. Dietrich - Loretz-Sanmartín UF 6 1974 47ff.).

G. To be (stable), have: *w ykn bnh b bt* and there be a son of his in (his) house, 1.17 I 25 and par. (diff. Wyatt RTU 255 n. 23: 'beget'); *ṯar um tkn lh* for him she was (like) a mother's avenger, 1.14 I 15 (cf. Verreet UF 19 1989 326); *rġbn ykn b ḥwt* there will be hunger in the land, 1.103+:5, cf. ln. 3; *iršn ykn* there will be scarcity, 1.163:10 (cf. Dietrich - Loretz MU 169, 186); *w ln ykn pat* may our borders be / remain (stable), 2.75:7.

L. To establish, interpose, bring up: *il mlk d yknnh* DN, the king who established him, 1.3 V 36, 1.4 IV 48; *k dr{d} d yknn* like the (family) circle of which they established me[, 1.10 III 6; *w mnm šalm dt tknn ʕl ʕrbnm hnhmt tknn* and any claims they bring up, against these guarantors they bring them up, 3.3:5-9 (Hoftijzer - Van Soldt UF 23 1991 190f.).

Š. To prepare, create: *w aškn aškn ydt mrṣ* and I myself shall prepare one who will cast out the illness, 1.16 V 27.

In bkn ctx.:]*ykn*[, 2.43:5.

Cf. kn (I), knʕm, knn, kny, kt (II), kwn, mknt, ttkn, ykn, yknil, yknʕm.

kn (I) adj. m. 1) "fixed, immutable"; 2) "complete, in order" (Hb. *kn*, HALOT 482; Syr. *kēnō* LS 321; Akk. *kī/ēnu*, AHw 481; CAD K 389ff.). ¶ Forms: sg. *kn*; pl. *knm*.

1) Fixed, inmutable, complete: *l špš rbt w l kbkbm knm* next to the Great Lady DN and the immutable stars (?), 1.23.54.

2) Complete, in order: *nqdm dt kn npṣhm* 'chief shepherds' whose military equipment is in order, 4.624:1.

kn (II) adv. "thus" (cf. *k (III)*; Hb., Ph., Pun., Aram. *kn*, HALOT 482f.; DNWSI 516ff.; Syr. *hokan*, *ken*, LS 175, 333; Akk. *(a)kanna*, *kanna/â*, AHw 27, 437; CAD A/1 259f.; cf. EA, Bo., Nuzi Akk. *kinanna*, AHw 479; CAD K 380f. Cf. Aartun PU 1 10). ¶ Forms: *kn*.

Thus: *kn npl bʕl* thus DN fell, 1.12 II 53 (diff.: Dahood ULx 91f.: /k-n/ as a pluperfect as in Phoenician).

Bkn ctx.: *w kn*, 2.31:45; *w ikm kn*, 2.7:10 (or /k-n/).

knʕm PN (Sem. Cf. Grøndahl PTU 43, 63, 109, 153); ¶ syll.: *ku-un-am-mu*, PRU 3 202 (RS 16.257+) III 42 (Van Soldt SAU 34); PRU

6 49:6' and *passim ibid.*; cf. Sivan GAGl 203, 239. Cf. *kn<u>ʕ</u>m* in 4.31:9.
PN: ★a) 4.31:9; 4.96:9 (*šʕrty*); 4.232:41; 4.245 I 7; 4.356:4; 4.366:2 (*bn a*[); 4.370:6, 42; ★b) *bn PN*, 4.309:19.

knʕny GN m. "Canaanite" (cf. Hb. *knʕny*, HALOT 485f.; Mari Akk. LÚ *Ki-na-aḫ-num*[meš/ki], Dossin Syria 50 1973 278f.; Alalakh Akk. LÚ URU *Ki-in-a-nim*[ki], DUMU KUR *Ke-an-a-ni*[ki], AT 48:5; 181:9; Wiseman JCS 8 1954 11; Emar Akk. cf. [d]IM *ša ki-na-i*, Fleming UF 26 1994 127ff.; Eg. *ki-n-ʕ-nu* (*knʕnw*), Edel Stelen 172 n. 122; Helck Bez. 275; cf. TN *Kinaḫni*, *Kinaḫḫ*, Sivan GAGl 237; Weippert RlA 5 352ff.; BN 27 1985 18ff.: */kinaʕan/ [± Hurr. /-ḫi/e/]. Cf. Astour RSP 2 293f. no. 50, 355 no. 158; Pardee AfO 36/37 1989/90 488); ¶ syll.: DUMU.MEŠ KUR *ki-na-ḫi*, Ug 5 36 B 6', 8'. ¶ Forms: sg. *knʕny*.
GN: 4.96:7.

knd n. m.; type of garment or cloth (Akk. cf. *kam/ndu*, AHw 432; CAD K 121; *kimdu*, AHw 478; CAD K 372; Mari Akk.: garment *ša ki-im-di(-im)*, RA 64 1970 25:6; ARMT 18 47:2; 48:2, and p. 133; cf. Merliss AUL 31f.; Ribichini - Xella Tessili 41; Tropper UF 29 1997 664f.); ¶ RS Akk.: cf. TÚG *ki-im-da*, PRU 3 207 (RS 15.135):7; ¶ syll. Ug.: cf. TUG(?) *ka-na-dú*, PRU 6 163 obv. 4'; Huehnergard UVST 137. ¶ Forms: pl. *kndwm* (< /ki/andūma/; Dietrich - Loretz UF 9 1977 340; cf. Sivan UF 21 1989 361).
Type of garment or cloth: *ṯn kndwm adrm* two strong garments (or pieces of) *k*. f, 4.4:2.
Cf. kdwṯ, kndpnṯ.

kndpnṯ n. m.; a garment (woman's underclothes?; cf. Akk. *kindabašše*, AHw 480; CAD K 384; Dietrich - Loretz UF 9 1977 340; Ribichini - Xella Tessili 41; Waetzoldt ZA 77 1987 298; Tropper UF 29 1997 664f.; cf. var. *kdwṯ*). ¶ Forms: sg. *kndpnṯ*.
A garment: *kndpnṯ dq* a fine *k*. (garment), 4.4:3.
Cf. knd, kdwṯ.

knḫ "?" (cf. ¶ RS Akk.: É : *ku-na-ḫi*, Ug 5 5:10, 20; Ribichini - Xella Tessili 41f. refer also to Akk. *kinaḫḫu* 'purple'. Cf. Mari Akk. LÚ *Kinnaḫnim*, Durand MARI 6 660: 'gens de la Beqaʕa'). ¶ Forms: *knḫ*.
? : in bkn ctx.,]*n knḫ*, 4.176:2.

knkny TN, name of divine mountain providing access to the 'underworld' (Belmonte RGTC 12/2 152: *Kankanā(yu)*. Cf. Del Olmo MLC 566 and cf. *knkt*; cf. Poljakov UF 14 1982 309f. and cf. Hoftijzer UF 4 1972 157 n. 17; diff.: De Moor SP 170f.: 'libation-pipe', *knkn* + pn. suff. *-y*, Akk. *kankannu*; Margalit MLD 120: 'my shelter', Arab. *kanna*).

TN: *tk ġr knkny* towards Mount TN, 1.5 V 13.

knkt adj. f. "sealed" (used as a noun, said of a coffin or funerary urn; cf. Akk. *kanāku*, *kaniktu*, *makna/āku*, AHw 434f., 436f., 590; CAD K 136ff., 150, M/1 138. Diff.: cf. Poljakov UF 14 1982 309f. and Hoftijzer UF 4 1972 157 n. 17: < */knkn/, Akk. *kankannu*; De Moor SP 170: 'libation-pipe', rdg *knkn*, Akk. *kankannu*; Margalit UF 8 1976 174; VT 31 1981 373ff.; UR 135ff.; UF 16 1984 145ff.; UF 16 1984 145ff.; UPA 233; De Moor ARTU 258: rdg *knrt*, Hb. TN 'Kinnereth', cf. KTU: *knrt*; for a critique cf. Van Soldt BO 40 1983 696; Dressler VT 34 1984 216ff.). ¶ Forms: sg. *knkt*.

Sealed (used as a noun, said of a coffin or funerary urn): *yqbrnnn b mdgt b knk*(!)*t* and he buried him in a tomb inside a sealed (coffin), 1.19 III 41 (for the rdg *k⌜n⌝kt* cf. Pardee UF 19 1987 200; but cf. Pitard BASOR 293 1994 31ff.).

knn PN (etym. unc.; cf. Grøndahl PTU 51, 153, 278, 286); ¶ syll.: cf.]*ku-un-na-na*, PRU 3 175 (RS 16.311):6'; *ka-an-nu*, PRU 4 203 (RS 18.20+) obv. 8'; *ku-un-n*[*i*], Ug 5 33:28'; cf. Sivan GAGl 239.

PN: ★a) 3.7:14; 4.63 I 15; 4.350:12 (*bn ibrn*); 4.631:19 (*bn ann*); ★b) *bn PN*, 4.63 II 36; 4.69 VI 20; 4.307:18; 4.617:8; 4.635:36; 4.723:9; in bkn ctx.: 4.635:14.

knp n. f. "wing" (Hb. *knp*, HALOT 486; Syr. *kenfō*, LS 334; Arab. *kanaf*, Lane 3004; ESA *knf*, DOSA 250; Eth. *kenf*, CDG 287; Akk. *kappu*, AHw 444; CAD K 185ff.); ¶ syll. Ug.: cf. Huehnergard UVST 101, 138; ¶ par.: *diy*. ¶ Forms: sg. *knp*; pl./du. cstr.(?) *knp*.

Wing: *tšu knp wtr b ʕp* she lifted (her) wing and flew away, 1.10 II 11 and par.; *knp nšrm bʕ yṯbr* the wings of the eagles DN broke, 1.19 III 8 and par.; *knp nšrm ybn bʕl* may DN restore the wings of the eagles, 1.19 III 12 and par.; *bʕl knp g*[*dlt*] (for) 'winged DN': one cow, 1.46:6 (Xella TRU 58; cf. Del Olmo CR 279 n. 72 'shoulder of ram/cow)'.

Cf. knpy, mknpt.

knpy part of the composite toponym *gt knpy* (Belmonte RGTC 12/2 87f., 402: **Gittu-kannāpiyi*. Cf. Heltzer RCAU 11; Kühne UF 7 1975 255f.; De Tarragon CU 1978 n. 21; cf. *knp*); ¶ syll.: cf. A.ŠÀ : *ka-(an)-na-pí-ya*, PRU 3 79 (RS 16.239):7; 85 (RS 16.250):11; cf. Huehnergard UVST 11 n. 51, 138; Van Soldt SAU 304.

Part of the composite toponym *gt knpy*: 4.243:18; 4.271:1; 4.296:10.

knr n. m. 1) "harp, lyre"; 2) DN (Hb. *knwr*, HALOT 484; Aram. *knr*,

DNWSI 520; Syr. *kenorō*, LS 335; Ebla /kinnārum/ in BALAG = *gi-na-rúm/lum(-/ru_{12}-um)*, VE 572; Krebernik ZA 73 1983 21; Fronzaroli EL 141; Sanmartín AuOr 9 1991 190; Mari Akk.: *kinnārātim* (obl. pl.), ARM 13 20 *passim*; cf. AHw 480; CAD K 387; ARM 18 273; ARM 21 368; Emar Akk. /kinnāru/, Pentiuc Vocabulary 98; Arab. *ka/innārat*, Hava 667; cf. Hitt.: *kinirtalla*, Tischler HEG 577f.; Hurro-Akk. *kinnaruḫuli*, Laroche GLH 148; Eg. *ka-n-nù-rú*, WÄS 5 132; Helck Bez. 523 [253]; Sivan - Cochavi WSVES 9. Cf. Parker UF 2 1970 244 n. 9; Kapera FO 13 1971 131ff.; Ivanov ArOr 67 1999 585ff.); ¶ syll. Ug.: ^{d}GIŠ *ki-na-rù*, Ug 5 18:31 (// *knr*, 1.47:32; 1.118:31); Sivan GAGl 237; Huehnergard UVST 138; Van Soldt SAU 304; ¶ par.: *mṣltm*, *rimt*, *tl*, *tp*, *ṯlb*. ¶ Forms: sg. *knr*; suff. *knrh*.

1) Harp, lyre: *tiḫd knr b ydh* he took the lyre in his hand, 1.101:16 (// *rimt*); *k šr knr uṣbʕ<t>h* like a musician (takes hold of) the harp, her fingers (took hold of the weapons), *[n]ša (...) k šr knr uṣbʕ<t>h* she grasped (...) like a singer the harp (with) her fingers, 1.19 I 6-8 (?); // *tlm*; cf. Del Olmo IMC 128 n. 289; diff.: Margalit JNSL 9 1981 106: rdg *k nr* 'like a torch'; De Moor (- Spronk) ARTU 248; CARTU 156: 'musician', rdg *k nr*; cf. KTU: *k nr*); *d yḏmr b knr w b ṯlb* who is celebrated with lyre and flute, 1.108:4 (// *tp*, *mṣltm*).

2) DN *knr*, in lists of DNN: 1.47:32; 1.118:31 (RS Akk.: ^{d}GIŠ *ki-na-rù*, Ug 5 18:31); *[k]nr š*, (to) DN, a ram, 1.148:9.

(knrt), 1.19 III 41; cf. *knkt*.

knt n. f. "continuity" / "constancy" (said of a type of offering; < *kn (I)*, /k-n/; Akk. *kīnu*, *kīnūtu*, AHw 481, 482; CAD K 389ff., 396. Cf. Xella TRU 1 214). ¶ Forms: sg. *knt*.

Continuous offering: *b knt il* in the continuous oblation to DN (we trust), 1.65:17 (cf. *dṯn*, *šrp*, *ibid.* ln. 15, 16; diff.: Healey UF 15 1983 48: 'dais, pedestal', Ug. *kt*).

kny PN (etym. unc.; cf. Grøndahl PTU 51, 153, 278); ¶ syll.: cf. DUMU *ku-ni-ya*, PRU 3 202 (RS 16.257) III 42 (Van Soldt SAU 34); cf. DUMU *ki*(?)*-ni-ya*, PRU 6 53 obv. 9'. Cf. *gny* PN.

PN: 4.171:3.

]knys, 4.431:4.

knyt adj. f. "glorious, of noble ancestry" (cf. Arab. *kanā / kanaya*, *kunyat*, Lane 3004; Akk. *kanūtu*, f. divine epithet, AHw 441; CAD K 171f. Cf. De Moor SP 83f.; cf. Sperling WO 12 1981 13; Watson NUS 35 1986 12; Loretz UF 21 1989 239 n. 16: 'geliebt, gehegt', Akk. *kunnû* AHw 507, CAD K 540). ¶ Forms: pl. *knyt*.

Glorious: *klt knyt* the glorious brides, 1.4 I 15 and par. (epithet of the

daughters of Baal).
Cf. **kny**.

kp n. f. 1) "palm (of the hand)"; 2) "pan (of scales)" (Hb., Aram. *kp*, HALOT 491f.; DNWSI 528; Syr. *kappō* LS 339; Akk. *kappu*, AHw 444; CAD K 185ff.; Arab. *kaff*, Lane 658; Eth. *kaf*, CDG 276; Eg. *ka-pu*, Helck Bez. 522 [249]; Sivan-Cochavi WSVES 28. For a morpho-lexical definition cf. CAD K 189: *kappu B*; Watson UF 10 1978 401 n. 47; cf. AHw 444: *kappu (II)*; cf. Dahood Bib 53 1972 388f.); ¶ **par.**: *mṣb*, *riš*. ¶ **Forms**: sg. *kp*; pl. *kpt*.
1) Palm (of hand): *ʕlh k irbym kp (...) kp mhr* above her like locusts the palm(s) (were flying) (: collect. use) (...) the palm(s) of the warriors, 1.3 II 10-11 and par. (// *r*[*š*]); *šnst kpt b bḫbšh* she girded her belt with palms, 1.3 II 13 and par. (// *rišt*); *bṣr kp* cut off palms, 1.13:6 (// *riš*); *kp ššk* make (her) palms run (with blood), 1.13:6.
2) Pan (of scales): *umh kp mznm* her mother (arranged) the pans of the scales, 1.24:35 (// *mṣb*).
Cf. *mbk kpt* in bkn ctx. 1.82:17-18 (cf. De Moor (- Spronk) ARTU 178, CARTU 176: *kpt* 'palm-frond'). Bkn: *kp mlk mr*[, 1.157:10.

kpḫ n. m.; a group or social stratum ("mitred ones" or entrusted with the "mitre" of Teššub(?); cf. Hurro-Hitt. *kupaḫi=*, Laroche GLH 157; Tischler HEG 640f.). ¶ **Forms**: (collect.(?)) sg. *kpḫ*.
A group or social stratum: *b yrḫ NM (...) arbʕ ddm l kpḫ* in the month of MN (...) four 'cauldronfuls' to the *k*., 4.387:18 (cf. *mdʕ*, ln. 12; *mdrġlm*, ln. 10, 20, 24; *apy TN*, ln. 26-27.

kpln PN; cf. *kb/pl(n)* PN.

kpltn PN (etym. unc.; cf. Grøndahl PTU 150; the element /kapul=/, /kipal=/, Gelb - Purves - MacRae NPN 223, 228).
PN: *bn PN*, 4.71 III 7.

kpr (I) n. m. "village" (cf. Hb., OAram. *kpr*, HALOT 494f.; DNWSI 531; Akk. *kapru*, AHw 444f.; CAD K 189f.; cf. Arab. *kāfir*, Lane 2622, WKAS K 267). ¶ **Forms**: pl. *kprm*.
Village: *kprm ḫlq* 10 villages: missing: 10, 4.611:8. Cf. in bkn ctx. *kly b kpr*, 2:72:43.

kpr (II) n. m. "henna (powder or dye)" (Hb. *kpr*, HALOT 495; Syr. *kūfrō*, LS 340; Gk *kúpros*, Liddell - Scott 1012; cf. Akk. *kupru*, AHw 509; CAD K 553f. Cf. Gaster Thespis 236; De Moor Or 37 1968 212 n. 4, 214; SP 85; UF 17 1985 220f.; diff.: Caquot - Sznycer TOu 1 157: 'essuyer', Akk. *kapāru*; for other options cf. Cassuto GA 113f.; and cf. Erard-Cerceau SMEA 28 1990 261f.: 'le souchet', Myc. *ku-pa-ro*); ¶ **par.**: *rḥ (II)*. ¶ **Forms**: sg. cstr. *kpr*.

Henna (powder or dye): *kpr šbʕ bnt* henna of seven damsels, 1.3 II 2 (// *rḥ*); cf. 1.7:15, 35.
Cf. kprt.

kprt n. f. "henna (plant)" (cf. *kpr (II)*. Cf. Dietrich - Loretz KA 252). ¶ Forms: sg./pl. *kprt*.
Henna plant: *ʕṣ kprt* henna plants, 4.767:2.

kpsln n. m.; a container or measure for liquids (etym. unc.; cf. Hurr. /kapp=/, Neu Or 61 1992 131: 'füllen'; Hitt. DUG *kappi-*, Tischler HEG 491; Haas SMEA 29 1992 107: '(ein Gefäss)' < Akk. *kappu*). ¶ Forms: pl. abs. *kpslnm*; cstr. *kpsln*.
A container or measure for liquids: *ḫmš kpsln yn* five *k.* of wine, 4.786:7; *yn l kpslnm* wine (allotted to fill) the *k.*, 4.274:1, 6.

kptr TN, residence / territory of the god *kṯr w ḫss*, 'Crete' (Belmonte RGTC 12/2 152: *Kaptūru*. *Krētē* [and neighbouring Aegean coasts]; Hb. *kptwr*, HALOT 495f.; NA *Kap-ta-ra*[ki], Weidner AfO 16 1952/53 22 and Taf. I:41; Akk. Mari cf. adj. *Kaptarû*, AHw 445; CAD K 191; Weippert RlA 5 226f.; Groneberg RGTC 3 131; Eg. *kftı͗(w)* (*k(a)-f-tù/tú*), Helck Bez. 258f., 562; BÄBÄ 26ff.; Weippert RlA 6 227ff. Cf. Albright YGC 119; Alt AfO 15 1945/51 71ff.; Eissfeldt FuF 20 1944 26f.; Malamat AS 16 1965 365; Leemans Trade 138; Astour RSP 2 294, 354; Strange Caphtor *passim*); ¶ syll. Ug.: KUR DUGUD(*kaptu*)-*ri*, PRU 3 107 (RS 16.238):10; cf. Van Soldt SEL 12 1995 213; ¶ par.: *ḥ(q)kpt*. ¶ Forms: *kptr*, *kptrh* (adv. *-h*).
TN: 1.3 VI 14 and par.; 1.1 III 18 and par.; 1.100:46.

kpṯ n. m. 1) "floor" (> "firmament, sky"); 2) "gangplank" (cf. Hb. *kbš*, HALOT 460; Akk. *kibšu*, AHw 471; CAD K 336f.; *nakbasu*, AHw 721; CAD N/1 180; cf. Eg. *kú-bu-śá*, Helck Bez. 522 [248]. Cf. Del Olmo AuOr 5 1987 51 n. 49: 'firmament(?)', for semantic par. with Hb. *rqyʕ*; Xella WO 13 1982 34: 'Landungsbrücke'; diff.: Dietrich - Loretz, OLZ 62 1967 541; UF 12 1980 176: 'Turban', Akk. *kubšu*; cf. Ribichini - Xella Tessili 43; Wyatt UF 16, 1984, 330; Waetzoldt ZA 77 1987 298); ¶ par.: *šmm (rmm)*. ¶ Forms: sg. abs. *kpṯ*.
1) Floor (> "Firmament"), in the titles of the goddess Anat: *bʕlt kpṯ* 'Lady of the Firmament', 1.108:8 (// *šmm rmm*); cf. Olyan UF 19 1987 161-174; Wyatt UF 20 1988 383; cf. *bʕlt* ★b).
2) Gangplank (part of naval equipment): *spr npṣ any (...) w kpṯ* list of naval equipment: (...) and a gangplank, 4.689:6.
Cf. kbs/ś.

kpyn PN (etym. unc.).
PN: 4.759:3.

/k-r/ v. G: "to be hot, furious, enraged" (?) (Syr. *kār*, LS 323; Tropper SEL 16 1999 37; UG 647).
G. To be hot, furious, enraged (?): *w kr* (*KTU: w rk*) *bn ilm mt ʕm aliyn bʕl* divine DN_1 was furious(?) with most powerful DN_2, 1.6 V 9.

kr n. m. "ram" (Hb. *kr*, HALOT 496; Akk. *kerru*, AHw 468; CAD K 410f.: *kirru C*. Cf. Sasson RSP 1 423; Del Olmo BSA 7 1993 185f.: 'fatling ram'); ¶ syll. Ug.: cf. the element /karru/ in PNN; Sivan GAGl 236; ¶ par.: *ḫprt*. ¶ Forms: pl. *krm*.
Ram: *špq ilm krm yn* he supplied the ram-gods with wine, 1.4 VI 47. In unc. ctx.: *il kr*, 1.114:14 ((?) Dietrich - Loretz Studien 450: rdg *w l*).

kran PN (etym. unc.; cf. *ku-ra-a-nu*, Cassin - Glassner AAN 1 87); ¶ syll.: cf. *ka(r)-ra-nu*, PRU 3 p. 248; PRU 4 106 (RS 17.137):6'. Cf. *krwn*, *krny* PNN.
PN: [*bn*] *kran*, 4.41:6.

/k-r-ʕ/ vb G: "to prostrate oneself" (Hb. *krʕ*, HALOT 499; cf. Akk. *karû*, AHw 452, CAD K 229, and cf. Von Soden Or 46 1977 537; cf. Arab. *rakaʕa*, Lane 1147, with metathesis. Cf. Van Zijl Baal 248). ¶ Forms: G cprf. *ykrʕ*.
G. To prostrate oneself: *l pʕnh ykrʕ w yql* at her feet he prostrated himself and fell down, 1.10 II 18.

krʕ "knuckle, clavicle" (Hb., Aram. *krʕ*, HALOT 500; DJPA 270; Syr. *krōʕō*, LS 348; Akk. *kurītu*, AHw 510; CAD K 560; ESA *krʕ*, DOSA 252f.; Arab. *kurāʕ*, Hava 651; Eth. *k*^{we}*rmāʕ*, CDG 293). ¶ Forms: sg. *krʕ*.
Knuckle, clavicle: *w in ḫrsp b kr*[*ʕ ydh* and if it has no tendon in the knuckle [of its forepaw, 1.103+:27; *w in krʕ yd*[*h šmal* and if it has no knuckle in its [lef]t forepaw / front hoof, 1.103+:15 (cf. ln. 28).

/k-r-b/ "?" (bkn ctx.; cf. Huehnergard UVST 140: 'twist, curl, bend', Arab. *karaba*, Syr. *ʔekreb*, Eth. *karabā*); ¶ par.: /q-l/ (I). ¶ Forms: G(?) cpref. *tkrb*.
G(?). *tkrb* x[, 1.19 I 2 (// *tql*).

krb PN (etym. unc.; cf. Grøndahl PTU 151, 237; Sivan GAGl 238; Watson AuOr 8 1990 120, 247; AuOr 13 1995 223; AuOr 14 1996 100). Cf. *grb*, *grp*.
PN: 4.357:22.

krd (I) part of the composite toponym *ḫlb krd* (cf. Virolleaud Syria 21 1940 143; GLECS 3 1940 98: 'Ḫalba du héros', Akk. *qarradu*).
Cf. ḫlb krd.

krd (II) PN (etym. unc.; cf. Grøndahl PTU 311; cf. TN *ḫlb krd*). Cf. *qrd* PN.
PN: 4.143:3.

krk (I) n. f. "pick" ((?); cf. the Eg. grapheme *grg*, Gardiner U 17. Cf. Sanmartín AuOr 5 1987 151; cf. diff.: Healey UF 15 1983 51f.: 'a sieve', Hb. *krk*); ¶ syll. Ug.: *ku-re-ku*, PRU 6 157:12; pl. *ku-re-ka-at* [...] URUDU.MEŠ, *ibid.* ln. 3., cf. ln. 2; PRU 6 168:5; Sivan GAGl 239; Huehnergard UVST 140; Van Soldt SAU 304. ¶ Forms: sg. *krk*, du. *krkm*.
Pick(?): *krk mit* a pick(?): a hundred (shekels of copper(?)), 4.625:2; *krk aḥt* one pick, *ibid.* ln. 6 and *passim*; 4.390:8, 13; *ṯt krkm* two picks, 4.184:3.

krk (II) PN (etym. unc.; cf. Grøndahl PTU 151; Dietrich - Loretz BiOr 23 1966 130; Watson AuOr 8 1990 247; cf. the element /kirr=/, PN Kirruke, Gelb - Purves - MacRae NPN 88, 228; AAN 1 84).
PN: *bn PN*, 4.611:12.

/k-r-k-r/ vb G: "to twist, twidddle" (Arab. *karra*, *karkara*, Lane 2600f. Cf. Avishur VT 26 1976 257ff.; Ahlström VT 28 1978 100ff.; Gruber Bib 62 1981 328ff.). ¶ Forms: G prefc. *ykrkr*.
G. To twist, twidddle: *ykrkr uṣbʕth* he twiddled his fingers, 1.4 IV 29-30.

krln n. m.; a container (etym. unc.); ¶ RS Akk.: 1 DUG *ki-ra-li-nu*, PRU 6 158:6; cf. Sivan GAGl 237; Huehnergard UVST 191; Watson UF 30 1998 754: Akk. *kirlammu* etc.). ¶ Forms: du. *krlnm*.
A container: *ṯn krlnm šmn ṭb* two *k.* of good oil, 4.780:14.

krm n. m. "vineyard" (Hb., Ph., Ammon., Aram. *krm*, HALOT 498; DNWSI 536; Ebla cf. ŠE+TIN.DU$_6$= *gú*-LUM, VE 648a; Butz EDA 333; cf. Akk. *karmu*, AHw 449; CAD K 218; *karānu*, AHw 446f.; CAD K 202ff.; for GEŠTIN in Alalakh Akk. cf. Dietrich - Loretz UF 1 1969 63; cf. Arab. *karm*, Wehr 821; Eth. *kĕrm*, CDG 293; cf. Eg. *k3m/n(w)*, WäS 5 106f.; Helck Bez. 505; Van Soldt SAU 36f.); ¶ RS Akk.: cf. GIŠ.GEŠTIN(.NA. MEŠ), *passim*; cf. PRU 3 217, 221; 6 158; Huehnergard AkkUg 375; ¶ syll. Ug.: cf. the element /karmu/ in PNN, Grøndahl PTU 151; Sivan GAGl 236; ¶ par.: *ḥrnq*. ¶ Forms: sg. *krm*, *krmm* (encl. *-m*); pl. *krmm*.
Vineyard: ★a) *krm aḥd* one vineyard, 4.244:5 and *passim ibid.*; *ṯn krm* two vineyards, *ibid.* ln. 26-28; *ṯṯ krm* six vineyards, *ibid.* ln. 11; *ṯmn krm* eight vineyards, *ibid.*; *šbʕ krmm* seven vineyards, *ibid.* ln. 25; *krm PN* the vineyard of PN, *ibid.* ln. 12-13, *passim ibid.*; *PN (...) ytn šd PN* (...) *yd gth yd gnh yd krmh yd klklh w ytn*{.}*nn l PN* (...)

ʕd ʕlm PN (...) has gifted the estate of PN (...) together with its farmstead, its olive-grove(s), its vineyard(s) and everything else and has ceded it to PN (...) in perpetuity, 3.5:9; *akln b grnt l bʕr ap krmm ḫlq* our grain on the threshing floors (has been set on fire), and also the vineyards have been lost, 2.61:10; *krm w šdm* the vineyard and the fields, 4.424:2; *krm PN l PN* the vineyard of PN, for PN, *ibid.* ln. 4, 5, 21, 23; *krm ar* vineyard of TN, 1.92:24; *yġly yḫsp ib krmm* the fruit / bud of the vineyard had withered and wilted, 1.19 I 31; *tn šdh krmm* I shall place (: make) her field a vineyard, 1.24:22; ★b) in a leasing system: *krm ubdy* leased vineyard, 4.244:7; *ṯlṯ krm ubdym l mlkt b* TN three leased vineyards for the queen in TN, *ibid.* ln. 9; ★c) *ṯlṯ šd w krm šir d PN* three 'hectares' and a vineyard of one *s.* (in area), of PN, 4.282:6; *širm šd šd ʕšy w šir šd krm d* PN two *s.* of 'hectare' of cultivated land and a *s.* of 'hectare' of vineyard, of PN, *ibid.* ln. 8; *šir šd krm d PN* a *s.* of 'hectare' of vineyard, of PN, *ibid.* ln. 12; in bkn ctx.]*šir šd kr*[*m* a *s.* of 'hectare', 4.642:3; ★d) *nġr krm* watchman / watchmen of the vineyard, 1.92:23 (cf. Dijkstra UF 26 1994 119); also 4.141 III 17; 4.609:12; ★e) in literary texts: *atn šdh krmm* I shall make her field into a vineyard, 1.24:22 (// *ḥrnqm*; cf. Dahood RSP 1 348; 3 94; De Moor ARTU 144 n. 23).

For *krm yn*, 1.4 VI 47, cf. *kr* (diff.: Heltzer UF 22 1990 120: 'vineyard of wine'). Bkn: 4.292:1; 4.254:5.

Cf. krmn.

krmn PN (Sem. Cf. Grøndahl PTU 18, 30, 151); ¶ syll.: *kar-mu-nu*, PRU 3 193 (RS 12.34):40; cf. Sivan GAGl 236.

PN: ★a) 4.635:50; ★b) *bn PN*, 4.35 I 5; 4.232:10; cf. 4.631:12.

krmpy PN (etym. unc.).

PN: 4.408:4. Cf. *k/wrmp/ṯ*[, 4.364:12, Tropper AuOr 13 1995 238.

krmt PN (etym. unc.; cf. Watson AuOr 11 1993 216).

PN: *bn PN*, 4.687:1; 4.692:2, 4. Cf. *k/wrmp/ṯ*[, 4.364:12, Tropper AuOr 13 1995 238.

krny PN (etym. unc.; cf. Grøndahl PTU 30, 151, 278); ¶ syll.: cf. DUMU *kur-ni-ya*, PRU 6 148:7'; cf. *ki-ir-ru-na*, Syria 28 1951 173ff. 6 (RS 14.16):26; cf. Van Soldt SAU 350; *ku-ra-ni*, PRU 3 76 (RS 16.160):4; cf. also *ka(r)-ra-nu*, PRU 3 p. 248; PRU 4 106 (RS 17.137):6'. Cf. *kran*, PN.

PN: *bn krny*[, 4.335:14; *bn krn*[, 4.611:25.

krpn n. m. "cup, goblet" (Akk. *karpatu*, AHw 449f.; CAD K 219; for Aram. *krpt?* cf. Kaufman AIA 63. Cf. Salonen HAM 49; De Moor SP 72: Akk. *kapparnu*, *kapparinnu*; Ajjan NU 34f.; Watson UF 27 1995

548); ¶ par.: *ks (I)*. ¶ Forms: sg. *krpn*; suff. *krpnm* (encl. *-m*).
Cup, goblet: *št b krpnm yn* drink wine in the cup, 1.4 IV 37 and par. (// *b k<s>*); cf. 1.17 VI 6); *ytn (...) krpnm b klat ydh* he placed (...) a goblet between both hands, 1.3 I 11 and par. (// *ks*); *krpn l tʕn aṯrt* a cup that not even DN saw, 1.13 I 14 (// *ks*); *yiḫd (...) krpn bm* [*ym*]*n* he took (...) a cup in the [righ]t, 1.15 II 17; *krpn ʕl krpn* cup after cup, 1.17 VI 6. Bkn. *tšty krp*[*nm y*]*n* they drank wine in the cup, 1.4 VI 58 and par.; *krpn*, 1.5 IV 18.

krr PN (etym. unc.; cf. Grøndahl PTU 237; Dietrich - Loretz OLZ 62 1967 541; Van Soldt SAU 350 n. 209; Muchiki Loanwords 30; cf. Xella RSF 12 1984 21ff.); ¶ syll.: cf. *ki-ri-ri*, PRU 3 34 (RS 16.114) obv. 5' (Van Soldt SAU 350 n. 209).
PN: cf. the place name *gt krr*, 4.139:9 (Belmonte RGTC 12/2 88: **Gittu-Kiriri*); bkn ctx. *krr*[, 4.75 I 7.

krs PN (etym. unc.; cf Watson AuOr 11 1993 216).
PN: 4.631:13 (*bn ann*); cf. in unc. ctx. 5.2:8.

(krs), 1.5 I 4; rdg *k r<k>s*; cf. *k (I)*.

krs/śu n. f.; a container and measure of capacity (for oil; etym. unc.; cf. Ug. *krś/sn* and *qrsu* < Hitt. (KUŠ) *kurša-*. Cf. Tropper UG 46: 'Teilmenge des *kd*-Masses'; Pardee BASOR 320 2000 58; diff.: Tropper UF 27 1995 516: 'ein Mastfutter / Masttiere', MA *kura/assû*, *kursû*, AHw 514: *kuruštû(m)*; CAD K 582: *ša kuruštê*; cf. Nuzi Akk. *kuruštāʔu*, AHw 514; CAD K 582; Sum. gurušda, Lieberman SLOBA 283). ¶ Forms: sg. nom. *krs/śu*, gen. *krsi*; pl. *krsat*; du. *krsim* (Tropper UG 46, 291).
A container and measure of capacity (for oil): *krsu w ṯʕt šmn* one *k.* and one *ṯ* of oil, RS 94.2600:14; *arbʕm šmn w krsim* forty *(kd)* and two *k.* of oil, RS 94.2392+:4 (both Tropper UG 420); PN [...] *krśu nṯkh* one *k.* is his interest, 4.225:16; in bkn ctx. *k*]*śmm b krsi* s]pelt in exchange for(?) one *k.* (of oil(?)), *ibid.* ln. 17. Cf. pl. *krsat*, RS 94.2392+:12.
Cf. krs/śn, qrsu.

krs/śn n. m. "wineskin, small wineskin" (OAss. *g/ku(r)sā/ an(n)u*, cf. AHw 299, 1557: *gusānu(m)*; CAD G 142f.: *gusānu* and cf. *ibid.* K 567: *kursinnu B*; cf. Hitt. (KUŠ) *kurša-* and *kur(*gu_5*-ur)san(n)u*, HW(1) Erg. 1 41, Erg. 3 21; Tischler HEG 654ff. Cf. Dietrich - Loretz WO 3 1966 222 n. 64; Zamora Vid 470). ¶ Forms: du. *krsnm*, pl.(?) *krśnm*.
Wineskin, small wineskin: *kd yn w krsnm* a jar of wine and two wineskins, 4.279:3. In bkn ctx., PN(?) *krsnm*[, 4.123:13 (cf. *yn*, *ibid.*

ln. 8). Cf. *krśnm*, 5.22:23.
Cf. krs/śu, qrsu.

krt PN, name of the king of *bt ḫbr*, protagonist of the eponymous epic (for the various possible vocalizations cf. Del Olmo MLC 240 n. 6; De Moor - Spronk UF 14 1982 153 n. 4; West AOAT 233 32: PN *ke-re-te-u*, Linear B; Watson UF 26 1994 497ff.; AuOr 14 1996 100f.). ¶ Forms: *krt*; suff. *krtn* (determ. encl. *-n*; cf. Tropper UF 26 1994 468).
PN: *passim* in 1.14-1.16.; cf. *krtn dbḥ dbḥ* PN celebrates a sacrifice, 1.16 I 39 (// *mlk*); royal titles: *krt ṯʕ* PN, the magnificent, 1.15 II 8 and par.

krty PN (etym. unc.; cf. Grøndahl PTU 152; Astour RSP 2 296 no. 54; De Moor-Spronk UF 14 1982 153; Watson UF 26 1994 497ff.). Cf. *krt*.
PN: 4.371:18; 4.617:20, 39; 4.760:1.

krw PN (Anat. Cf. Grøndahl PTU 269, 279; Lemaire Syria 62 1985 32f.; cf. West AOAT 233 33: PN *ke-ro-wo*, Linear B); ¶ syll.: cf. *ku-ru-e*, PRU 6 166 vertical 2.; cf. Van Soldt SAU 358 n. 230.
PN: 4.188:4; 4.261:16 (*šlmy*); 4.385:1.

krwn PN (Anat. Cf. Grøndahl PTU 268, 279; Van Soldt SAU 38f., 103; cf. West AOAT 233 33: PN *ku-ra-no*, Linear B); ¶ syll.: *kur-wa-nu/a*, PRU 3 121f. (RS 15.136):7 and *passim ibid.*; 123 (RS 15.145):14, 17; 124 (RS 15.167+):4 and *passim ibid.*; 199ff. (RS 16.257+) II 2 and *passim ibid.*; PRU 6 49:19'; 82:12; Ug 5 81:44; 83:3; cf. Huehnergard AkkUg 40; *ku-ru-e-na*, PRU 6 138:7, 19; cf. Van Soldt SAU 358 n. 230; *ku-ra-ni*, PRU 3 76 (RS 16.160):4. Cf. *kran*, *krny*, *qrwn* PNN.
PN: ★a) 1.87:60; 4.35 II 20; 4.85:3 (*arty*); 4.97:2 (*bn* [); 4.128:10; 4.141 I 11; 4.175:3; 4.183 II 11; 4.269:19; 4.281:12; 4.282:9; 4.356:11 (cf. *ibid.* ln. 5); 4.370:19; 4.374:11; 4.609:3, 9, 36; 4.754:12; cf. in bkn ctx. 4.367:4; ★b) *bn PN*, 4.69 III 14; 4.77:15; 4.340:4; 4.356:5 (cf. *ibid.* ln. 11); 4.379:6; 4.791:14. Cf. the rdg *krwt*, 4.147:14 (scribal mistake?).

krws PN (Anat. Cf. Grøndahl PTU 268, 279; Watson NUS 39/40 1988 11); ¶ syll.: cf. *kur-wa-zi*, RSOu 7 5:12; cf. Ug 5 98:6.
PN: 4.655:2.

krwt PN (etym. unc.).
PN: 4.147:14 (cf. *krwn* PN; rdg *sic?*)

/k-r-y/ vb G: "to dig, drive in" (Hb. *krh*, HALOT 496; cf. Pun. *kry*, DNWSI 535; Arab. *karā*, Hava 653; Eth. *karaya*, CDG 294f. Cf. Gray

UF 3 1971 63 n. 16; diff.: Schloen JNES 52 1993 216: 'to hire out', Hb. *krh*, Arab. *kry*). ¶ Forms: G impv. *kry*.
G. To dig, drive in: *kry amt ʕpr* dig (your) elbows into the earth, 1.12 I 23.

kry PN (etym. unc.; cf. Grøndahl PTU 28, 151, 236; Astour RSP 2 295f. no. 53; Röllig AuOr 4 1986 56f.; Watson AuOr 13 1995 223).
PN: 4.371:11; 4.647:5.

kryn PN (etym. unc.; cf. Grøndahl PTU 28, 151, 205, 237; Sivan GAGl 236; Van Soldt SAU 40; Watson AuOr 13 1996 223); ¶ syll.: cf. *kar-ia-nu*, PRU 3 37 (RS 15.81):2; *ki-ir-ia-na*, 3 71 (RS 16.295):4 (Van Soldt SAU 350 n. 209).
PN: *bn PN*, 4.110:5.

krzn PN (etym. unc.; cf. Noth ZDPV 65 1942 150 n. 8; Grøndahl PTU 311; Watson AuOr 11 1993 216; Van Soldt SAU 37). Cf. *krs*, PN.
PN: 4.102:1; 4.357:28; 4.391:11; 4.616:6.

ks (I) n. m. "cup, goblet" (Hb. *kws*, HALOT 466; Ph., Aram. *ks*, DNWSI 521; Syr. *kosō*, LS 322; Ebla cf. *gi-šu gi-šu*, ARET 2 2 obv. III 11; Pomponio Biling. 310f.; Akk. *kāsu*, AHw 454f.; CAD K 253ff.; Arab. *kaʔs*, Lane 2581f.; cf. Hurr. /kazi=/, KBo 32 14 I 56, Neu Das Hurritische 28f. [< Akk. *kāsu*]); ¶ RS Akk.: GAL (KÙ.BABBAR, URUDU.MEŠ, ZABAR), cf. Huehnergard AkkUg 386. Cf. Dijkstra - De Moor UF 7 1975 213; Amadasi Semitica 38 1990 16f.; Knoppers BASOR 289 1993 87; ¶ par.: *ḥrb*, *krpn*, *qbʕt*, *qš*, *sʕ*. ¶ Forms: sg. *ks*; allograph *k<u>s</u>* in 6.68:1 (cf. Dietrich - Loretz KA 209); suff. *ksh*; du. *ksm*; cf. unc. *k<u>s</u>t*, 4.710:13 (Dietrich - Loretz KA 166f.: pl.).
Cup, goblet: *ytn ks bdh* he placed a cup in his hand, 1.3 I 10 and par. (// *krpn*); *qḥ ks bdy* take the cup from my hand, 1.19 IV 54 (// *qbʕt*; cf. 1.15 II 16; for the contraposition of both expressions cf. Dijsktra - De Moor UF 7 1975 213); *ks ymsk nhr* he mixes my cup in torrents, 1.5 I 21 and par. (// *sʕ*; cf. Ps 105:41; Del Olmo IMC 70); *ks ḫrṣ / ksp* cup of gold / silver, 3.1:27f. and par.; cf. [*k*]*s mn ḫrṣ* a goblet (and) a mina of gold, 3.1:20 (RS Akk.: 1 GAL KÙ.GI.MEŠ MA.NA KI.LÁ-*šu*, PRU 4 41 [RS 17.227 and dupl.]:22; cf. Knoppers BASOR 289 1993 87); *klnyy nbl ksh* all together we shall carry his cup, 1.3 V 34 and par. (// *qšh*); *l arṣ ksh tšpkm* her cup she spilled on the ground, 1.17 VI 15; *tn ks yn* give / place a cup of wine, 5.9:15; *tšt dmh l bl ks* it drinks its blood without a cup, 1.96:5 (// *ḥrb*); *ks qdš* a holy cup, 1.3 I 13; *štt (...) qlt b ks ištynh* there was put (...) vileness in the cup that I drink, 1.4 III 16;*d škn l ks ilm* that they assigned for

the cup of the gods (?), 4.280:14; *ṯn ksm* two cups, 4.385:2; *ṯn ks yn* give (: put) a cup of wine, 5.9 I 15; *hn ks mḥṯ l mlkt mntn* here is a *m.*-cup for the queen of TN, RSOu 14 53 [KTU 9.432]:39'. Cf. *s̱ls̱t ks̱t*, 4.710:13 (Dietrich - Loretz KA 166f.: 'Becher', pl. of *ks(I)*; cf. also *ks̱t*); *ks̱ PN*, 6.68:1 (Dietrich - Loretz KA 209).
Bkn: *b ks ḫrṣ*, 1.5 IV 16 and par. (cf. ln. 17); 1.16 V 39.

ks (II) TN, divine mountain (possibly an allophone of *ḫš*; < Hurr. ḪUR.SAG *ḫazzi*; Laroche GLH 100; Lat. *Casius*; cf. TN Hitt. *Kasu*, Del Monte RGTC 6 195; Van Soldt UBL 11 370 n. 30. Cf. Pope EUT 96 n. 64; Dietrich - Loretz - Sanmartín UF 5 1973 99 n. 21; Caquot - Sznycer TOu 1 304; Clifford CMC 39; Cross CMHE 38f.; Lipiński UF 2 1970 86ff.: 'montagne de la coupe'; Astour RSP 2 319ff.; Del Olmo - Sanmartín AuOr 13 1995 259ff.; Belmonte RGTC 12/2 127f.: *Ḫazzi*); cf. RS Akk.: DINGIR IM *be-el* ḪUR.SAG *ḫa-zi* Ug 5 18:4; ¶ **par.**: *ḫršn*.
TN in myth: *ġr ks*, 1.1 III 12 (// *ḫršn*).
Cf. **ḫš**, **nny**, **ṣpn**.

ksa DN, second component of the double-barrelled divine name *yrḫ w ksa*, a lunar deity (cf. Hb. *ksʔ*, HALOT 487; Ph. *ksʔ*, DNWSI 522; Akk. *kusīʔu*, AHw 515; cf. CAD K 587; Arab. *kusʔ*, Lane 2608. Cf. De Moor UF 2 1970 314; Xella TRU 220; Del Olmo CR 343 n. 31; Watson UF 30 1998 756).
DN: *yrḫ w ksa*, 1.123:6.

ks/śu n. m./f.(?) "seat, throne, chair" (Hb., Ph. *ksʔ*, HALOT 487; DNWSI 522; Aram. *krsʔ*, DNWSI 536f.; Kaufman AIA 28; Emar Akk. /kissu/, Pentiuc Vocabulary 102f.; Akk. *kussû*, AHw 515; CAD K 587ff.; Ebla cf. *gú-za*, Krebernik PET 88; Arab. *kursiyy*, Lane 2605f.; cf. Sum. gu-zí, Lieberman SLOBA 285f.; ¶ **par.**: *arṣ*, *hdm*, *kḥṯ*, *nḫt*, *ṯbt*, *ṯlḥn*. ¶ **Forms**: sg. *ksu/i/a* (allograph *kśu* in 1.53:7; 1.57:4; Tropper UF 27 1995 516); suff. *ksiy*, *ksih*; pl. *ksat*.
Seat, throne, chair: *ksu ṯbth* the seat of your throne, 1.3 VI 15 and par. (// *arṣ*); *kśu bʕlt bh*[*tm*] the throne of the Lady of the Palace, 1.53:7 and par. (cf. 1.57:4); *grš ym l ksih* drive DN from his throne, 1.2 IV 12 and par. (// *kḥṯ*); *gršh l ksi mlkh*, he drove him from his royal throne, 1.3 IV 2 (// *nḫt*, *kḥṯ*); *tʕdb ksu w yṯṯb* a throne was prepared for them and they sat down, 1.4 V 46; *yʕdb ksa w yṯb* he places a chair and sits down, 1.100:7 and par.; *tḥt ksi* DN at the feet of DN's throne, 1.2 IV 7; *ksu ṯbth* the seat of his throne, 1.4 VIII 12 and par.; *yrd l ksi* he came down from the throne, 1.5 VI 12 (// *hdm*); *yṯb l ksi mlk* he sat on the royal throne, 1.16 VI 23 and par. (// *nḫt*, *kḥṯ*); *l*

yhpk ksa mlkk yes, he will overturn your royal throne, 1.6 VI 28 and par. (cf. KAI 1:2); *ṯṯʕr ksat l mhr* she arranged chairs as (if they were) warriors, 1.3 II 21 and par. (// *ṯlḥn, hdm*); *l ll* [[*l*]] *tʕrk ksu* at night the throne shall be prepared, 1.106:28; *ksi nqmd* throne of PN, 1.161:13; *aṯr bʕlk l ks<i>h* (go down) after(?) your lord, O throne, 1.161:20; (?)DN *špq ilht ksat* [*yn*] she supplied the throne-goddesses with wine, 1.4 VI 52. In bkn ctx. cf. *ksa*[, 1.57:5; x*ṭrd ksat*, 1.151:3; *lksiy* on my throne, 2.31:15; *ksa*[, 4.496:4.
Cf. ksan.

ksan n. m. "stool" (cf. *ksu*. Cf. Gaster Thespis 450; Gray UF 3 1971 62 n. 11, diminutive of *ksu*; diff.: Held SUL 74: 'waterskin", Akk. *g/kušanu*). ¶ Forms: sg. suff. *ksank*.
Stool: *qḥ ksank ḥdgk ḥtlk* take your stool, your chair (for birthing?), your nappies, 1.12 I 17.

ksd (I) n. m.; an occupation or social group (connected with the manufacture of textiles?, cf. Van Soldt UF 22 1990 353; cf. Dietrich - Loretz BiOr 23 1966 130: 'Müller', Sum.-Akk. KA/GAZ.ZÌ.DA / *kaṣṣ/zzidakku*; cf. *id.* TUAT 1 216; Heltzer IOKU 90 n. 37; Cutler - Macdonald UF 8 1976 33 n. 36: 'archers(?)', Sem. *qšt*). ¶ Forms: sg. *ksd*; pl. *ksdm*.
An occupation or social group: *ksdm* PNN, 4.286:1; PN *ksd*, *ibid.* ln. 9; 4.332:18 (after *mḫṣ*); *ksdm*, 4.99:16 (after *mḫṣm*); 4.126:15 (after *kzym*); *ʕšr ksdm yd lmdhm* ten *k.* with their apprentices, 4.125:8 (before *mḫṣm*).
Cf. ksd (II).

ksd (II) PN (etym. unc.).
PN: ★a) *bn PN*, 4.69 II 18; ★b) *gt bn ksd*(?)[, 4.297:7 (Belmonte RGTC 12/2 93).

ksl n. m. 1) "back, shoulder"; 2) "tendon" > sinew, bowstring; 3) "side, sector(?)" (Hb. *ksl*, HALOT 489; Akk. *ka/islu*, AHw 486f.; CAD K 425. Cf. Clifford VT 25 1975 301 n. 7; Gray UF 11 1979 318 n. 20; Held Fs. Landsberger 401f.; De Moor UF 12 1980 425f.; Renfroe AULS 124); for syll. Ug. /kussu/ūlu/ cf. Huehnergard UVST 138; ¶ par.: *pʕn, pn, ẓr*. ¶ Forms: sg. *ksl*; suff. *kslk, kslh*; pl./du. *kslm*.
1) Back, shoulder: *bʕdn ksl ṯṯbr* behind (her) back buckled, 1.3 III 33 and par. (*pʕnm, pnh*); *l tšlḥm (...) bʕd kslk almnt* you have not fed (...) the widow at your back, 1.16 VI 50 (// *l pnk*); *tǵṣ pnt kslh* the joints of her back contracted, 1.3 III 35 and par. (// *ṣrh*).
2) Tendon > sinew, bowstring: *tgrš (...) b ksl qšth* she drove out (...) with the sinew of her bow, 1.3 II 16 (// *mṯm*; cf. Arab. *kisl*); *kslh k*

brq (...) its sinew is like lightning, 1.17 VI 11 (speaking about the bow; but cf. RTU 271 n. 96); *mitm kslm* two hundred sinews / (bow) strings, 4.182:9 (cf. ln. 26; Ribichini - Xella Tessili 81: 'corregge'). 3) Side, sector ((?); said of both horns of the moon): *hm b ṯ]ltt ym yh yrḫ kslm* if on the third day the moon wanes on both sides, 1.163:4 (cf. Dietrich - Loretz MU 169, 174f.; diff.: Bordreuil - Caquot Syria 57 1980 353: 'mois de kislew', Akk. MN *kislīmu*; cf. Dietrich - Loretz TUAT 2 95: 'Kislim').
Cf. ksln.

ksln PN (Sem. Cf. Grøndahl PTU 29, 425).
PN: *bn PN*, 4.12:3; 4.122:5.

ksm (I) n. m. "part, share" (cf. Akk. *kasāmu*, AHw 453; CAD K 240; cf. ARM 27 303: *kismum*. Cf. Van Zijl Baal 271f.; Dietrich - Loretz UF 10 1978 70; diff.: Rainey RSP 2 90: 'ceremonial meal', cf. *ksm (III)*); ¶ par.: *mnt*. ¶ Forms: sg. suff. *ksmy*, *ksmk*, *ksmh*.
Part, share: *spu ksmh bt bʕl* who consumes his share in the temple of DN, 1.17 I 31 and par. (// *mnth*).
Cf. ks/śm(n).

ksm (II) n. m. "limit, edge" (cf. Akk. *kasāmu*, AHw 453; CAD K 240. Cf. Caquot - Sznycer TOu 1 250; Margalit UR 140 n. 35); ¶ par.: *qṣ*. ¶ Forms: sg. *ksm*.
Limit, edge: *l ksm mhyt ʕn* look towards the edge of the meadows, 1.16 III 4 (// *qṣm*); *ʕd ksm mhyt* as far as the limit of the meadow(s), 1.5 VI 5; diff.: Aartun UF 16 1984 39f.: 'Ergiebiges, Fruchtbares', Arab. *kaysūm*).

ksm (III) cf. *ks/śm(n)*.

ks/śm(n) n. m.; grain similar to wheat (*Triticum spelta*, *sativum*, *dicocum* (?); here, by convention: 'spelt'; cf. Hb. *ksmt*, HALOT 490; MHb. *kwsmym/n*, Jastrow 623); ¶ syll. Ug.: cf. [ÁŠ = *ku-na*]-*šu* = *ut-te* = *ku-sú-m*[*u-ma*(?), Ug 5 137 II 45'; Van Soldt RA 75 1981 93; SAU 304; Huehnergard UVST 139; ¶ RS Akk.: ZÍZ.AN.NA, cf. PRU 6 158. ¶ Forms: sg. *ksm*; morph. var. with *-n*: *kśmn* (cf. MHb. and Sanmartín UF 20 1988 270f. n. 23; cf. Tropper UF 27 1995 518); pl. *ks/śmm* (var. spelling *kzmm* in 5.22:25?; cf. Dietrich - Loretz - Sanmartín UF 7 1975 167; Dietrich - Loretz KA 191). Rdg *k smm* in 1.16 III 10 (cf. *smm*) and for 1.17 I 31 cf. *ksm* (De Moor SP 191; Dietrich - Loretz UF 10 1978 424f.; Rainey RSP 2 90).
Grain ('spelt'): ★a) measured in *dd*: *dd kśmn* a 'cauldronful' of spelt, 4.269:4; *dd ksmm* one 'cauldronful' of spelt, 4.608:2; *ddm kśmn l PN* two 'cauldronfuls' of spelt for PN, 4.269:20, and *passim* in admin.

texts; cf. ten 'cauldronfuls' *kśmm* of spelt, 4.691:4; ★b) in accounts: *tgmr kśmm b yrḫ MN* total consumption of spelt in the month of MN, 4.269:30; cf. *kśmn l gzzm* spelt for the shearers, *ibid.* ln. 4; *kśmm b TN* spelt in TN, 4.345:2, 4, 9; 4.400:7, 12, 16; in bkn ctx. *k*]*śmm b krsi* s]pelt in exchange for(?) one *k.* (of oil(?)), 4.225:17; ★c) used as fodder: *ʕšr dd kśmm w ḫmšm* {*ḥmr*} *kśmm* <*ḥmr*> ten 'cauldronfuls' of (normal) spelt and fifty {} of spelt <for donkeys>, 4.691:5 (Sanmartín UF 20 1988 270ff.); offered in the cult: *dṯt w kśm* (an offering of) spring(?) grain and spelt, 1.39:9; 1.41:19; 1.87:20.

In bkn ctx.: *ksmm*, 4.747:2. Cf. *kzmm*, 5.22:25 (Dietrich - Loretz KA 191: 'Emmer').

Cf. ksm (I).

ksn (I) "?" (Ribichini - Xella Tessili 42 mention Akk. *g/kus/šānu*, AHw 299: 'ein Ledersack', and the Arab. garment *kiswa*, Wehr - Cowan 828). ¶ Forms: *ksn.*

? : in bkn ctx., *ksn.*[, 4.10:5.

ksn (II) PN.

PN: *bn PN,* 4.704:1.

ksp n. m. 1) "silver"; 2) "(shekel of) silver"; 3) "money, capital; price, value; payment in cash" (Hb., Ph., Pun., Ammon., Aram., Nab., Palm. *ksp*, HALOT 490f.; DNWSI 524ff.; Ebla cf. KAS-*ba*, *ga-šè-ba*, *ga-ši-bù*, Krebernik PET 93; Akk. *kaspu*, AHw 454; CAD K 245ff.); ¶ RS Akk.: KÙ.BABBAR, *passim*; PRU 3 221, 228f.; PRU 6 156; cf. KÙ.BABBAR *k*[*a-as-pu*(?), Ug 5 133 obv. 14'; GAL KÙ.BABBAR. MEŠ, PRU 4 40ff. (RS 17.227 and dupl.):29 and *passim ibid.*; ¶ syll. Ug.: KÙ = *kaspu*(?) = *uš-ḫ*]*u*(?)-*ni* = *kàs-pu*, [KÙ.BABBAR = *kaspu* = Hurr.: ? =] *ka-as-pu*, Ug 5 137 II 2f.; Sivan, GAGl 236; Huehnergard, UVST 139; UF 15 1983 209; Van Soldt SAU 304; ¶ par.: *iqnu*, *ḫrṣ*, *yrq*. ¶ Forms: sg. *ksp*, suff. *kspy*, *ksph*, *ksphm*, *kspm* (encl. -*m*).

1) Silver, ★a) 4.738:2; *irš ksp w atnk* ask silver and I shall give it to you, 1.17 VI 17 (// *ḫrṣ*); *ṯnh k*(!)*spm atn* double her (weight??) in silver will I give, 1.14 IV 42 (// *ḫrṣm*); *tmtḫṣ ksp* he fought me for the silver, 1.3 III 46 (// *ḫrṣ*); *ẓl ksp aṯrt k tʕn* the reflection of the silver did DN see, 1.4 II 26f. (// *ẓl ksp w n*[; cf. Hb. *ṣl hksp*, Qoh 7:12); *k ksp l ʕbrm zt* like silver for the guests was(were) the olive(s), 1.22 I 14 (// *ḫrṣ*); *qḥ ksp w yrq ḫrṣ* take silver and yellow gold, 1.14 III 22 and par. (Fensham UF 11 1979 268); *tblk ġrm mid ksp* may the mountains bring you plenty of silver, 1.4 V 15 and par. (// *ḫrṣ*); [*kkr*] *ksp* a talent of silver, 4.608 (I) 1; (ritual offering of) *ksp w ḫrṣ* silver

and gold, 1.90:3; 1.168:3, 9; 1.164:4; *w ksp yʕdb* and silver is placed (for the offering), 1.50:11; *adnk šqrb k*[*sp*] *b mgnk w ḫrṣ l kl* to your lord offer si[lver] as your present and gold in full, 1.16 I 44; cf. in bkn ctx. *k*]*sp nʕmm* silver of good quality(?), 2.79:8; ★b) items made of silver: *bn bht ksp w ḫrṣ* build a house of silver and gold, 1.4 V 18 y par. (// *ṯhrm iqnim*); <*b*>*hty bnt dt ksp* my palace is a building of silver, 1.4 VI 37 (// *ḫrṣ*; Sanmartín UF 10 1978 445f.; altern.: mi casa he construido, la de silver, Del Olmo MLC 206 [cf. /b-n-y/]); (for you will be built) *bt kspy* a house with my silver(?). 1.1 IV 21 (Del Olmo IMC 40ff.); *št gpny dt ksp* put on my harnesses of silver, 1.19 II 4 and par. (// *yrq*); *nskt ksp w ḫrṣ* an ingot of silver and (another) of gold, 1.105:22; *ks ksp* cups of silver, 3.1:31 and *passim ibid.* (RS Akk.: GAL KÙ.BABBAR. MEŠ, PRU 4 40ff. (RS 17.227 and duplicates):29 and *passim ibid.*; cf. Knoppers BASOR 289 1993 89); *ks ksp* cups de silver, 5 IV 17 (// *ks ḫrṣ*); ★c) treatment: *nsk ksp* silversmith(s): 4.47:6; 4.68:74; 4.99:14; 4.183 II 23; 4.609:32; 4.745:7; 6.20:1 (cf. RS Akk.: LÚ.MEŠ.KÙ.DÍM, PRU 6 70:4; 131:2); *yṣq ksp* (*l alpm*) he cast silver (by the thousand shekels), 1.4 I 25f. (// *ḫrṣ*); *sb ksp l rqm* the silver had turned into sheets, 1.4 VI 34 (// *ḫrṣ*); *kt il nbt b ksp* a divine platform, a casting in silver, 1.4 I 31 (// *ḫrṣ*). 2) Shekel(s) of silver, *passim*: cf. *rt (...) b ṯql w nṣp ksp* one *r.* (...) for one shekel and a half of silver, 4.337:13; *lqḥ ṯqlm ksp bd amtk* he has collected two shekels of silver from the hands of your handmaid, 2.70:19; *passim* elliptical use *ksp* (shekels) of silver; cf. *šbʕt w nṣp ksp* seven (shekels) and a half of silver, 2.25:6; *ʕšrm ksp ktnt* twenty shekels of silver (in) tunics, 4.771:2; *ʕšrm ksp mškrt ḫr*[twenty (shekels) of silver for a / the skin(s) (...), 4.781:4; *šbʕt w nṣp kbd ksp* seven (shekels) and a half of silver, 4.779:10 (cf. ln. 3); *arbʕm ksp* forty (shekels) of silver, 4.778:2, 9; cf. ln. 13, 16 (*iqni*); *mšq mlkt mitm ṯṯm kbd ksp* {*ksp*} *ṯmnym ḫrṣ* the queen's cup (is worth) two hundred and sixty (shekels) of silver, (that is) eighty of gold, 4.265:3; *ṯṯ mat ksp* six hundred (shekels) of silver, 4.158:1; *(nn) ksp d mkr mlk* (nn) of silver of the king's traders, 4.369:3; cf. *(nn) ksp nqdm* (shekels) of silver of the shepherds, *ibid.* ln. 8; *d PN / (mkr) TN*, *ibid. passim*; *atn* (...) *alp ksp w rbt ḫrṣ* I will pay (...) one thousand (shekels) of silver and ten thousand of gold, 1.24:20; *ṯql ksp ṯt* a shekel of sterling silver, 1.43:12, 15 (cf. Akk. *kaspu*(*m*) *damqu*(*m*)); *ʕšrt ksp b alp* ten (shekels) of silver for one head of cattle, 4.337:21; *pdy*{.}*hm PN mit ksp b yd GN* PN redeemed them for one hundred (shekels) of silver from the power of the GN, 3.4:14; *ṯql ksp* one shekel of silver (as an offering), 1.112:4 and cf. ln. 12; cf. 4.782:1, 19, *pdy{.}hm PN mit ksp b yd GN* PN redeemed them for one hundred (shekels) of silver from the power of the GN, 3.4:14; *ṯql ksp* one shekel of silver (as an offering), 1.112:4 and cf. ln. 12; cf. 4.782:1, 19, 23, 28.

3) Money, capital; value, price; payment in cash: ★a) money, capital: *ksp d šlm PN ʕl bt* capital that PN pays on the palace account, 4.755:1; *PN (nn) ksp (nn) šlm* PN: capital (owing): (nn shekels), he has paid: (nn shekels), 4.226:1-10; *ksp d nkly b šd* capital disbursed for a field, 4.280:6; *atn ksp lhm* I will give them the money, 2.42:20 (cf. Pardee UF 19 1987 208); *ksp ḥbl rišym* money in surety for the GN, 4.778:3; ★b) value, price in cash of a commodity (*ksph*(*m/n*)): *passim*; cf. *arbʕ kkr algbṯ arbʕt ksph* four talents of *a.* for a value of four (shekels), 4.158:16; *ḫmš kkrm ṣml*[[*l*]] *ʕšrt ksph* five talents of *ṣ.* for a value of ten (shekels), 4.158:11; *ḫmš kkr knm ṯlṯt w ṯlṯt ksph* five talents of cane at three plus three (shekels), *ibid.* ln. 13; *ṯt ktnm ḫmšt w nṣp ksphn* two tunics for a value of five (shekels) and a half, 4.132:6; *ktn d TN pḥm bh w ṯqlm ksph* a tunic from TN with (fringes of(?)) ruby purple with a value of two shekels, 4.132:5; *kkr šʕrt šbʕt ksph* a talent of wool at the price of seven (shekels), 4.158:18; *ṯlṯ kkr šʕrt iqnim ṯṯt ʕšrt ksph* three talents of wool in violet purple for a value of ten and six (shekels), 4.341:4; ... *k*]*sphn ṯql w kmsk* its value is one shekel and *k.*, 4.707:23; *tgmr ksp* total value in cash, 4.156:6; 4.341:22; cf. in bkn ctx. *tgmr k*[, 4.333:9; *anyt* (...) ships (...) *arbʕm*(!?) *ksp mḫrhn* their value (per unit) is forty (shekels) of silver, 4.338:17; ★c) payments in cash: *yn d ntn b ksp* wine sold for cash, 4.219:1; *arbʕ mat ʕšrm kbd d*(!) *ntn b*(!) *ksp* four hundred and twenty (jars of wine) sold for cash, 4.274:3; *l ytn ksphm* they have made their contribution in cash, 4.779:4; *ksp d šsʕn* the money that you told me to pay, 2.81:24; as surety, deposits, etc.: *ksp anyt d ʕrb b anyt* ship's deposit as surety for the ships, 4.338:11f. (Dietrich - Loretz - Sanmartín UF 6 1974 473; Pardee JAOS 95 1975 613); *ksp* PN deposit (paid through the mediation) of PN, 3.4:18 (Kienast UF 11 1979 448f.); *l yblt ḫbṯm ap ksphm l yblt* you have not brought the emancipated (men) nor have you brought their deposit, 2.17:2.

In bkn ctx.: *ksp*[, 1.139:18. Unc. ctx.: *wlṯṯyny ksp ṯlṯt*, 5.11:7.

Cf. kspy.

kspy n. m. "treasurer, intendant" ((?); cf. Aram. *kspy*, DNWSI 526; cf. TN *kspyʔ*, HALOT 491). Pl. *kspym*.

Treasurer, intendant(?): *y*]*šlm kspym ṯṯ mat ʕmn* (when) the treasurers(?) pay me the six hundred (shekels), 2.21:15.

kst n. f.; a type of robe or cloak (< /k-s-y/; Akk. *kusītu*, MAD 3 152; AHw 514; CAD K 585ff.; EA Akk. *ku-sí-ti*, EAT 14 III 27 (Egypt); 34:23 (Alašia); Ebla /kusī=t=um/ in *gu-zi-tum* TÚG, Fronzaroli EL 142; StEb 7 1984 168; cf. ARET 2 127; 3 354f.; 4 300; 7 215; MEE 1 285; Sanmartín AuOr 9 1991 191; Hitt. *kušiši*, *kušiti*, HEG 674f.; // Hurr. *alali-*, Neu Das Hurrritische 16f.; cf. Ph., Aram. *kst*, DNWSI 526; Kaufman AIA 65; Hb. *kswt*, HALOT 488f.; Arab. *kiswa*, Wehr - Cowan 828; cf. Akk. *kuššatu*, AHw 517; CAD K 600. Cf. Ribichini - Xella Tessili 42f.; Fronzaroli SEL 7 1984 145ff.); ¶ RS Akk.: cf. TÚG : *ku-u*[*š-ši-ti*], PRU 6 6:26; ¶ par.: *all.* ¶ Forms: sg. *kst*; pl. *kst*; cf. the allograph *kśt*, 1.86:24 (cf. Hb. and cf. Segert UF 15 1983 209; Tropper UF 27 195 519f.).

A type of robe or cloak: *tmzʕ kst* the robe was torn, 1.19 I 36, 47 (// *all*); *ṯlṯm ṯmn kst* 38 *k.*, 4.206:5. Cf. 1.151:6; 2.3:12 (rdg unc.). In bkn ctx. *kst*[, 1.168:7 (as an offering?); cf. var. *kśt*, 1.86:24 (Segert UF 15 1983 209: Hb. *kĕsūt*). For *kṯt*, 4.710:13, cf. *ks (I)*.

Cf. /k-s-y/.

/k-s-y/ vb G: "to cover oneself"; D: "to cover" (Hb. *ksh*, HALOT 487f.; Ph., Aram. *ksy*, DNWSI 523; Syr. *ksō*, LS 337; Arab. *kasā*, Hava 655; ESA *kśw*, DOSA 254; Akk. *kašû*, AHw 463; CAD K 294; Amor. cf. Gelb CAAA 23); ¶ syll. Ug.: cf. KU(?)-U]Z(?)-ZU (inf. abs. D /kussû/?), Ug 5 137 I 21'; cf. Verreet UF 19 1987 340; Sivan GAGl 238; Van Soldt SAU 304; cf. Huehnergard UVST 191. ¶ Forms: G cprf. *tks*, *yks*; D cprf. with suff. *tksynn*.

G. To cover oneself: *lpš yks mizrtm* for clothing he covered himself with a ritual tunic, 1.5 VI 16 and par. (diff.: Dietrich - Loretz UF 18 1986 107: 'schneiden', Akk. *nakāsu*).

D. To cover: bkn ctx. *w tksynn b ṯdh* [...] and she covered him with her udder, 1.10 III 24.

Cf. kst, ksyn, mks.

ksyn PN (Sem. Cf. Grøndahl PTU 51, 152; cf. diff. Dietrich - Loretz OLZ 62 1967 541).

PN: 4.70:9 (*bn lḫsn*).

kṯ, allograph of *ks*, 6.68:1; cf. *ks (I)*.

kśu, allograph of *ksu*, 1.53:7; 1.57:4; cf. *ksu*.

kśt, allograph of *kst*, 1.86:24; cf. *kst*.

kš n. m. "date" ((?); Arab. *kušš*, *kasīs*, Hava 653, 655. Cf. Ribichini - Xella UF 7 1975 153 n. 42; diff.: De Moor ULe 95 n. 3; ARTU 272: 'gourd', Ug. *kṯ*; Gordon PLM 31: 'like *fields*', rdg *k šd*); ¶ par.: *zt*. ¶ Forms: sg. *kš*.

Date(?): *ḫrṣ l ʕbrm kš* (like) gold for the guests were the dates(?), 1.22 I 15 (// *zt*); in bkn ctx.: 1.151:9.

kš[part of a PN (morph. unc.; cf. *ki-iš-ši* and var., NH no. 588); ¶ syll.: cf. *ki-šu*, PRU 195 (RS 15.09) A 21; DUMU *ka-ši-ya*, PRU 3 195 (RS 11.839):22. Cf. *kšt*, *kṯ (II)*, PNN.

PN (part): 4.258:8.

/k-š-d/ vb G: "to search for, reach" (Akk. *kašādu*, AHw 459ff.; CAD K 271ff.; Ebla cf. /G-S-D/, Krebernik PET 46. Cf. Dietrich - Loretz UF 10 1978 435; Pope Maarav 1 1978/79 27 n. 9). ¶ Forms: G prefc. *tkšd*.

G. To search for, reach: *brky tkšd rumm* the pool for which the wild bulls search, 1.5 I 16.

kšp n. m. "conjuror, wizard, sorcerer" (Akk. *kaššāpu*, AHw 463; CAD K 292; Hb. *kšp*, HALOT 503. Cf. Bordreuil - Caquot Syria 57 1980 348). ¶ Forms: pl. *kšpm*.

Conjuror, wizard, sorcerer: *kšpm dbbm ygrš* may the wizards cast out the demons, 1.169:9; *km l tudn dbbm kšpm* (...) *yšpk kmm ar ṣ kšpm dbbm* just as the sorcerers do not listen to the demons... so the sorcerers spill to the ground the demons, RSOu 14 52 [KTU 9.435]:9, 12.

kšt PN (etym. unc.; cf. the element /kašt=/, /kaššut=/, AAN 1 78).

PN: 4.707:15.

kšy PN (etym. unc.).

PN: *bn PN*, RSOu 14 45 [KTU 9.418]:2.

kt (I) n. f. a kind of "pitcher" (Akk. *kūtu*, AHw 519; CAD K 611f.; Ebla cf. *gu-a-ti-iš*, Pettinato Rituale 189. Cf. Dietrich - Loretz - Sanmartín UF 7 1975 560; Dietrich - Loretz UF 19 1987 30ff.; KA 160). ¶ Forms: sg. *kt*.

Pitcher: *kt zt mm kt šmn mr* a pitcher of winter olives (and) a pitcher of myrrh(-scented) oil, 7.786: 13, 14; cf. in bkn ctx. *kt mẓ$_2$k*[a pitcher of mixed drink(?), 1.77:5 (Dietrich - Loretz KA 160). In bkn ctx., cf. 1.147:8; 7.142:1f., 8. For 1.4 I 30f. cf. *kt (II)*; for the syntagm *ṯlṯ ktt* in 4.203:14 and par. cf. *ktt*.

kt (II) n. f. "stage, podium, platform" (Hb. *kn*, HALOT 483; Syr. *kanō*, LS 333; cf. Akk. *kannu*, AHw 437f.; CAD K 154ff.; Salonen HAM 220. Cf. Albright BASOR 91 1943 40 n. 14; Dietrich - Loretz UF 10 1978 60; diff.: Cassuto, BOS II 123 n. 24; Dietrich - Loretz - Sanmartín UF 7 1975 560: 'eine grosse Kanne', Akk. *kūtu* [cf. *kt (I)*]; Dahood UF 1 1969 25: 'beaten work', Hb. *ktt*, *mkwnh*; Margalit MLD 16: 'figure, shape', Akk. *g/kattu*; Rin AE 139: mistake for *ktr*,

Hb. *ktr*); ¶ **par.**: *ḫym*. ¶ **Forms**: sg. *kt*.

Stage, podium, platform: *kt il* a divine platform, 1.4 I 30-31 (// *ḫym*); *kt ġrk ank ydʕt* the podium of your mountain that I have distinguished, 1.13:10; in unc. ctx., [*k*]*t atn an*(!) *mṯbk* the podium I gave (you) as a mansion, 1.13:11; *kt* [*k*]*bkbm* the podium of the stars, 1.13:12.

kt (III) TN "Kition(?)" (Belmonte RGTC 12/2 164; Dietrich - Loretz - Sanmartín UF 7 1975 560; Astour RSP 2 297f.).

TN: *kd bn amht kt* a 'jar' for the servants of TN, 4.230:9.

kt (IV) PN (etym. unc.; cf. Grøndahl PTU 279; Watson AuOr 13 1995 224). Cf. *ktkt* PN.

PN: *bn PN*, 4.141 II 1; 4.425:5. Cf. in unc. ctx.]*m kt tmnm*, 4.734:12.

/k-t-b/ vb G: "to write" (Hb., Ph., Pun., Aram., Nab., Palm. *ktb*, HALOT 503f.; DNWSI 540ff.; Arab. *kataba*, Lane 2589ff.; Eth. *kataba*, CDG 297). ¶ **Forms**: G suffc. *ktb*.

G. To write: *ktb spr hnd* he wrote this document, 2.19:9.

ktkt PN (etym. unc.; cf. Grøndahl PTU 280). Cf. *kt* PN.

PN: *bn PN*, 4.33:16 (*mʕqby*).

ktl PN (etym. unc.; cf. Grøndahl PTU 279; element /=(k)katil/, Gelb - Purves - MacRae NPN 224, 228).

PN: 4.56:3; 4.394:6.

ktln PN; cf. *kd/tln* PN.

ktm "?" (Tsumura UF 22 1990 398; Richardson UBL 11 279: 'gold', Hb. *kétem*, Hoch SWET 501: Akk. *kutimmu*, PhPN *ktm*, OSA *ktm*).

? : in bkn ctx.,]*t ktm*, 7.222:11.

ktmn PN (etym. unc.; cf. Grøndahl PTU 280).

PN: **★a)** 4.15:8; **★b)** *bn PN*, 4.93 IV 14; 4.224:8, 11; 4.571:5.

ktn (I) n. f.; a type of "tunic" (etym. unc.; cf. Hb. *ktnt*, HALOT 505; Aram. *ktn*, DNWSI 548: ktn_2; Kaufman AIA 28; Linear B *ki-to*, Chadwick DMG 320; Linear A *qi-tu-ne*, cf. Best UF 5 1973 57f.; Gk *khitōn*, Liddell - Scott 1993; cf. also Ph., Aram. *ktn*, DNWSI 547f.: ktn_1; Sum. gada; Akk. *kitû(m)*, AHw 495; CAD K 473ff.; Lieberman SLOBA 262f.; OAss. *kutānum*, Garelli AC 288; Veenhof OAT 145ff.; Akk. *qutānu(m)*, AHw 930, 1585; CAD K 607ff.: *k/qutānu*. Cf. Ribichini - Xella Tessili 43f.; Heltzer GPOTU 41f.; Van Soldt UF 22 1990 331f.; Xella UF 22 1990 471); ¶ **RS Akk.**: TÚG.GADA(.MEŠ), *passim*; Van Soldt UF 22 1990 329ff.; cf. PRU 3 181 (RS 11.732) B 1 and *passim*; 184 (RS 16.146+):12 (10 TÚG.GADA.MEŠ 10 TÚG.GÚ.É GADA; cf. *pṯt (I)*); 207 (RS 16.187 A):5' and *passim*;

PRU 4 40ff. (RS 17.227 and dupl.) 23 and *passim*: TÚG.GADA (// KTU 3.1:21 and *passim*: *ktn*(*t*); cf. Dietrich - Loretz, WO 3/2 1966 224ff.); 82 (RS 17.382+):40 and *passim*; TÚG.GADA.MEŠ, PRU 6 14:13 and *passim*. ¶ Forms: sg. *ktn*; pl. *ktnt*; du. *ktnm*.

Type of tunic: 4.206:1; 4.284:1; 4.402:4; 4.738:3; *ṯt ktnm ḫmšt w nṣp ksphn* two tunics for a value of five (shekels) and a half, 4.132:6; *ṯlṯm ḫmš kbd ktnt* a total of thirty five (shekels worth of(?)) tunics, 4.203:7; *arbʕm d ktn* forty (shekels) of (a) tunic(s), 4.779:7; *ʕšrm ksp ktnt* twenty (shekels of) silver in tunics, 4.771:2; *ktnt bd(m)* PN tunics delivered to PN, 4.132:2; 4.337:18; *ktn nʕmm* de luxe tunic, 2.79:9; *ktn d TN pḥm bh (...) bd skn* a tunic from TN with (fringes of(?)) ruby purple (...) in the hands of the prefect, 4.132:4; ritual offering: *lbš w ktn* a garment and a tunic, 1.43:4; tribute: *arbʕ ktnt kt*[*n r*]*b* for (ordinary) tunics (and) a large tunic (// 4 TÚG.GADA 1 TÚG.GADA GAL, PRU 4 40ff. [RS 17.227 and dupl.]: 23; cf. Knoppers BASOR 289 1993 87f.), 3.1:21, cf. *ibid.* ln. 27, 29, 31: cf. *ibid.* ln. 33, 35, 37: *ktn* (// 1 TÚG.GADA, ln. 25, 27, 29). In bkn ctx., [...] *ktnt*, 4.363:1.

ktn (II) PN (etym. unc.); ¶ syll.: cf. KU-UT-TA-*na*, Syria 28 1951 173-179 (RS 14.16):21; KU-TA-*n*[*a*], PRU 6 49:9'; KA-TU-*na*, PRU 3 136 (RS 15.168):4 (cf. Huehnergard UVST 215, 220; Van Soldt SAU 320 n. 135). Cf. *gdn*, *gtn*, *kdn*, *qṭn*, PNN.

PN: 4.607:30.

ktp n. f. 1) "shoulder; 2) "shoulder blade"; 3) "scimitar, *'harpé'*" (Hb. *ktp*, HALOT 505f.; Syr. *katpō*, LS 353; Arab. *katif*, Lane 2998; Eth. *matkaf*, CDG 372; cf. Akk. *katappātu*, AHw 465; CAD K 303. Cf. O'Callaghan Or 21 1952 37ff.; Van Zijl, Baal 35ff. 215f.; Pini OrAnt 15 1976 111f. n. 32; Bordreuil - Pardee MARI 7 68; Del Olmo AuOr 10 1992 256; Vita - Watson AoF 29 2002 146ff.); ¶ par.: *(bn) yd(m)*, *mṣd*, *nṣb*. ¶ Forms: sg. *ktp*; du. *ktpm*.

1) Shoulder: *hlm ktp zbl ym* strike prince DN on the shoulder, 1.2 IV 14 and par. (// *bn ydm*); [...] *mlak bn ktpm* [he had wounded] the (other) messenger on the shoulder, 1.2 I 42; *l ktp ʕnt k tšth* on the shoulders of DN, she did place him, 1.6 I 14.

2) Shoulder blade: *tʕdb (...) lh ʕnt ktp* she held out (...) also to DN a shoulder blade, 1.114:11 and par. (// *nṣb*).

3) Scimitar, *'harpé'*: *rbm ymḫṣ b ktp* the great ones he struck with a scimitar, 1.6 V 2 (// *ṣmd*).

ktr n. m. of a group or profession (etym. unc.; cf. Akk. *kitru*, AHw 494; CAD K 467f.; Hb. *ktr*, HALOT 506: *ktr (I) / (II)*; Aram. cf. *ktr*, DNWSI 548: *ktr*$_1$; 129; cf. also Hitt. SAL *katra*-, Pecchioli Daddi

MPDAI 391ff.; Gk *kithára*, Liddell - Scott 950; Arnaud AuOr 16 1998 169: 'garde', Alal. Akk. *kutturu*). ¶ Forms: pl. *ktrm*.
Group or profession: *ktrm* (listed between *yṣrm* potters and *mṣlm* cymbalists), 4.126:29.
Cf. ktr(y).

ktr(y) PN (etym. unc.; cf. Grøndahl PTU 28, 152f.; Watson AuOr 13 1995 224; West AOAT 233 33: NO *ke-ti-ro*, Linear B).
PN: ★a) *ktr*, 4.141 II 7; ★b) *bn ktry*, 4.638:6.

ktš PN (etym. unc.; Watson AuOr 13 1995 334).
PN: *bn PN*, 4.778:15; 4.782:22.

ktt (I) adj. m. "ground, powdered" (pass. ptc. G */k-t-t/; Hb., Aram. *ktt*, HALOT 507; DJPA 273; Ebla cf. TAR-TAR = *ga-da-tum*, EV 0419; Krebernik QuSe 18 141. Cf. Zaccagnini OrAn 9 1970 320 with n. 36; Collini SEL 4 1987 18f.; Sanmartín SEL 5 1988 175f.). ¶ Forms: sg. *ktt*.
Ground, powdered (said of a stage of copper): *ʕšr kkr ṯlṯ ktt* ten talents of powdered copper, 4.721:4; *arbʕ k*[*kr*] *ṯlṯ ktt* four talents of powdered copper, 4.288:9; *alpm ṯlṯ ktt* two thousand (shekels of) powdered copper, 4.203:14. In bkn ctx.]x*ktt*, 2.33:17 (cf. Pardee AfO 31 1984 219 n. 28).

ktt (II) PN.
PN *bn PN*, 4.382:28.

kṯ (I) n. f. a measure and a container ("flask, bottle, jar"(?); cf. Akk. *kīs/šu*, AHw 487; CAD K 463; *qiššû*, AHw 923; CAD Q 272. Cf. De Moor UF 2 1970 311; Watson UF 30 1998 758 n. 38; Tropper UG 287: 'ein Hohlmass'). ¶ Forms: sg. *kṯ*; pl. *kṯt*; du. *kṯm*.
A measure and a container: *ʕšr kṯt ḫmš ʕšr lg* ten *k*., fifteen *l*., 6.12:2; a container ('flask'(?)), for luxury items: *kṯm ššmn* two flasks(?) of (cream of) sesame, 4.60:8; (offering of) *kṯ ẓrw kṯ nbt* a flask(?) of balsam (and) a flask(?) of honey, 1.148:22 (diff.: Aartun UF 16 1984 41: 'Dick-, Zähflüssiges', Arab. *kaṯṯ*); *ʕšr kṯ*(!)*t ẓrw* ten flasks(?) of balsam, 4.402:10; *kṯm sbbyn* two flasks(?) of (essence of) black cumin, 4.707:8 (diff.: Aartun UF 16 1984 41f.: '(Wieder)anfüllen', Arab. *kṯama*; cf. *kṯ aqḥ*[*r* a *k*. of *a*., 4.61:4. Cf. in unc. ctx. *kṯm r*[*qḥ*(?) two flasks(?) of perfume(?), 4.60:6 (cf. *ṯlṯ kṯt xd h*[, *ibid.* ln. 4). In bkn ctx., 4.594:4; in unc. ctx., 1.101:8: *kṯ*[[*ṯ*]] *ġbt* (cf. De Moor UF 1 1969 182: 'cream' / 'thickness', Arab. *kaṯāt* / *kaṯṯa*; NYCI 2 8: 'desires(?); Dietrich - Loretz UF 17 1985 142; Pardee TPM 147: 'wie zwei (Wolken)', 'comme deux nuées'; cf. Caquot TOu 2 49 n. 112).

/k-š-d/ PN (etym. unc.; cf. Watson AuOr 11 1993 216; *ki-iš-ši* and

1.130:20; *kt*[, 4.754:1.

ktan PN (etym. unc.; cf. the element /kuš(š)=/, Gelb - Purves - MacRae NPN 230, AAN 1 88). Cf. *ktwn*, *ktn* PNN.
PN: *bn PN*, 4.40:8.

ktkn PN (etym. unc.; cf. Grøndahl PTU 302 and cf. *ktky* GN; cf. PN *Kuššakani*, Gelb - Purves - MacRae NPN 92).
PN: 4.245:12; 4.336:5; bkn ctx. 4.574:4.

ktky GN m. "Kaskaean" ((?); cf. Bo. Akk. (LÚ.MEŠ) URU *Ga-aš-ga* and var., Von Schuler Kaškäer 84ff.; RlA 5 460ff.; Del Monte - Tischler RGTC 6 190ff.; cf. Liverani Storia 154f.; cf. Degen WO 4 1967/68 48ff.; Von Schuler Kaskäer 72, 87). ¶ Forms: pl. *ktkym*.
GN: *rb ktkym* sheikh of the GN, 6.3:2; *ktkym*, 4.319:2.
Cf. ktkn.

ktl(y) PN (etym. unc.; cf. Watson AuOr 11 1993 216).
PN: *bn ktl*, 4.309:9; *bn ktly*, 4.55:10; 4.611:5.

ktn (I) PN (etym. unc.; cf. Grøndahl PTU 301; Dijkstra UF 26 1994 120); ¶ syll.: cf. *ki-še-na*, PRU 3 139 (RS 16.131):18, 24; PRU 6 99:14(?); 150:4; *ki-ši-na* RSOu 7 3 obv. 9' (Huehnergard UVST 231 n. 91f.); *ku-ši-nu*, PRU 3 195 (15.09) B I 7.
PN: *bn PN*, 4.335:24; 4.694:4; 4.785:15.

ktn (II) TN (?) (unc. ctx.; cf. Dijkstra UF 26 1994 120: Hb. *kwšn*; Belmonte RGTC 12/2 165: TN).
TN (?): in unc. ctx., *kbkbt ktn* stars de TN(?), 1.92:28.

ktp n. m. "?" (Cf. Pardee TPM 255: 'épaisseurs', Arab. *ktp*). ¶ Forms: pl.(?) *ktpm*.
? : in bkn ctx.,]*xn mšḥt ktpm aktn*[, 1.107:48.

ktr (I) adj. m. "skilful" (cf. Hb., Palm. *kšyr*, DNWSI 539; cf. Hb., Aram. *kšr*, HALOT 503; DNWSI 539f.; Akk. *kašāru*, AHw 461f.; CAD K 284ff. Diff.: Van Selms UF 11 1979 742: 'servant', */k-t-r/). ¶ Forms: pl. *ktrm*.
Skilful: in bkn ctx., *trḥṣn ktrm*[skilful (servants)(?) will wash him, 1.2 III 20.
Cf. ktr (III), ktrt, mktr.

ktr (II) n. m. "vigour, good health" (MHb., Aram. *kwšr*, DJPA 254; Jastrow 626; cf. *ktr (I)*. Cf. Dietrich - Loretz Fs. Elliger 34; Badre *et al.* Syria 53 1976 101; Van Selms UF 11 1979 739ff.; Verreet UF 19 1987 329; diff.: Fensham JNSL 1 1971 19f.: 'while they dine', rdg *k trm*; Van Selms UF 11 1979 742: 'in captivity'; Margalit UF 8 1976 144: 'in (child-)labour', Akk. *šaššurātu*); ¶ par.: *zbln*. ¶ Forms: sg. suff. *ktrm* (encl. *-m*).

Vigour, good health: *mṯlṯt kṯrm tmt* a third died in (full) vigour, 1.14 I 16 (// *zblnm*).

kṯr (III) DN, first element of the name of the god of magic and technology, *kṯr (w) ḫss* (cf. *kṯr (I)*; Ph. *k(y)šr*, *kušor*, in PNN; Pope WbMyth 1 295; for Ebla cf. ᵈ*kà-ša-lu*, Lambert SVT 40 1988 131f.; Mander MROA 2/1 50; > Gk *khousōr*, Cors CPH 116. Cf. Smith KWH 1985; Dahood ADS 81f.; Cooper RSP 3 385ff.; Lipiński UF 20 1988 137ff.; Brown JSS 10 1965 197ff.; Pardee TPM 100 n. 9); ¶ RS Akk.: ᵈ*É-a*, Ug 5 18:15 (cf. *kṯr*, 1.47:16; 1.118:15); ¶ syll. Ug.: cf. ᵈA.A. = *e-ia-an* = *ku-šar-ru*, Ug 5 137 IV a 19, Huehnergard UVST 141; Van Soldt SAU 304; cf. element /kōtar-/ in PNN, Sivan, GAGl 238. ¶ Forms: *kṯr*, *kṯrm* (encl. *-m*).
DN: ★a) *kṯr (w ḫss)*, *passim*; cf. *ḥbr kṯr ẓbm* the good companions of DN, 1.108:5; *kṯr ḫss šlm* DN, hail!, 1.123:28; cf. *hlk kṯr (...) tdrq ḫss*, 1.17 V 10; *kṯrm ḥbrk w ḫss dʕtk*, 1.6 VI 49; ★b) *kṯr* alone in 1.47:16; 1.118:15 (cf. RS Akk.: ᵈ*É-a*, Ug 5 18:15); 1.102:5; 1.2 IV 11, 18; 1.4 VII 15f.; 1.43:8; 1.105:12; 1.148:6; cf. 1.39:14; ★c) *ql bl ʕm kṯr w ḫss kptrh* take (this) message to DN, in TN, 1.100:46.
Cf. kṯrmlk, kṯrn.

kṯrmlk PN (Sem. Cf. Grøndahl PTU 47, 152, 158; Sivan GAGl 238; Huehnergard UVST 219).
PN: 1.87:59 (*bn ytrt*); 4.86:24; 4.188:9; 4.609:32; 4.658:49.

kṯrn PN (Sem. Cf. Grøndahl PTU 52, 152). Cf. *gṯrn* PN.
PN: 4.313:10.

kṯrt DN, goddesses who preside over childbirth (cf. *kṯr (I)*; Emar Akk. /kaṯarātu/, Pentiuc Vocabulary 94; Hb. *kwšrwt*, HALOT 467; Gk *khousarthis*, Cors CPH 116. Cf. Cooper RSP 3 387f.; Margulis JNES 4 1972 55ff.; Du Mesnil EDP 1ff., 9ff.; NE 81ff.; Van Selms UF 11 1979 743f.; Herrmann YN 5f. *and passim*; Del Olmo AuOr 9 1991 74f.; Watson SEL 10 1993 52.); ¶ RS Akk.: ᵈ*sa-sú-ra-tu*$_4$, Ug 5 18:12 (cf. *kṯrt*, 1.47:13; 1.118:12). ¶ Forms: pl. *kṯrt*.
DN, goddesses who preside over childbirth: ★a) *ḥbl kṯrt* the band/flock of the DNN, 1.10 II 30; 1.11:6; *kṯrt bnt hll šnnt* the *k.*, daughters of DN, the swallows, 1.17 II 26f. and par.; ★b) in lists: *kṯrt*, 1.47:13; 1.118:12 (// ᵈ*sa-sú-ra-tu*$_4$, Ug 5 18:12; cf. Nougayrol Ug 5 p. 50; Durand MROA 2/1 184ff.); 1.148:25 (rdg probl. *a*(!)*ṯrt*).

kṯtġlm TN (Belmonte RGTC 12/2 165. Cf. Laroche GLH 139; Dietrich - Loretz - Sanmartín UF 5 1973 110; Kühne UF 6 1974 167 n. 73; Pardee UF 6 1974 280 n. 26; Astour NuzHur 1 14 no. 9; Sanmartín SEL 12 1995 180f.; Del Olmo - Sanmartín AuOr 13 1995 260; Van

Soldt UF 28 1996 674). Cf. *ḫrbġlm*.
TN: 4.310:2; 4.643:25, 26.

kṯwn PN (etym. unc.; cf. *Kašuwa, Kišwa*, NH 89ff.); ¶ syll.: cf. *ku-šá-*PI*-n[i]*, PRU 6 73:11. Cf. *kṯan, kṯy, kṯn* PNN.
PN: 4.339:2.

kṯy (I) GN m. "Kassite" (Akk. *kaššû*, AHw 463; CAD K 293f.; Balkan Kassitenstudien 1 131f.; Nashef RGTC 5 163f.; Brinkman RlA 5 464ff. Cf. Astour JAOS 86 1966 282; Caquot Syria 46 1969 262ff.; De Moor UF 2 1970 314; Dietrich - Loretz - Sanmartín UF 7 1975 143); ¶ syll. Ug.: cf. ᵐ*Ka-ši-ya* LÚ *mur-u*, PRU 3 195 (RS 11.839):22; Grøndahl PTU 301. ¶ Forms: sg. *kṯy*.
Kassite: *yrḫ kṯy* DN Kassite, 1.102:14 and par; cf. *yrḫm k⊕y*, 1.123:7. Cf. kṯy (II).

kṯy (II) PN (etym. unc.; cf. Grøndahl PTU 301; Watson AuOr 14 1996 101 and cf. *kṯy (I)*); ¶ syll.: cf. *ka-ši-ya*, PRU 3 195 (RS 11.839):22; *ku-šá-ya*, PRU 6 72:13' (Huehnergard UVST 231; Huehnergard AkkUg 414). Cf. *gṯy, kṯ (II), kṯwn* PNN.
PN: ★a) 4.63 III 39; 4.170:16; 4.617 (II) 23; ★b) *bn PN*, 4.7:2.

kw n. f.; a container or measure (etym. unc. Cf. Dietrich - Loretz UF 19 1987 29f.: cf. Eg. *qw*, Helck Bez. 402; cf. Emar Akk. /kuʔû/, /kuʔâta/, Pentiuc Vocabulary 105; cf. Tropper UG 54: Akk. *kūtu*; cf. Sanmartín SEL 5 1988 179 n. 27; UF 20 1988 272 n. 32: Eg. *kb*, WäS 5 117, and EA Akk.: *kūbu* [*ku-u/ú-bu/bá*, EAT 14 I 33 and *passim*], CAD K 488; AHw 498; Helck Bez. 402, 409; diff.: Aartun UF 16 1984 34: 'zugebundener Schlauch', Arab. *wikāʔ*). ¶ Forms: sg. *kw*; du. cst. *kwt*.
A container or measure: *ṯt kwt yn* two *k.* of wine, 4.691:6; *kw sʕt* a *k.* of (grain) *s.*, 2.47:17.

kwn PN (etym. unc.; cf. Grøndahl PTU 235, 280; for the element kaw= cf. Gelb - Purves - MacRae NPN 224; cf. West AOAT 233 33: PN *ke-wo-no-yo*, Linear B); ¶ syll.: cf. *ka-ú-a-ni*, PRU 6 73 10 (Huehnergard AkkUg 41; Van Soldt SAU 358); cf. *ku*-PI*-na*, PRU 6 43 3; DUMU *ka*-PI*-na* PRU 3 202 (RS 16.257+) III 32 and *kyn* PN. Cf. *kbn, kwy(n)* PNN.
PN: ★a) 4.307:10; ★b) *bn PN*, 4.692:7, 12.

kwt PN (etym. unc.) Cf. *kwn*.
PN: *bn PN*, 4.93 IV 8.

kwy(n) PN (etym. unc.; cf. Grøndahl PTU 280). Cf. *kwn, kyn, qwy* PNN.
PN: *bn kwy*, 4.313:27; *bn kwyn*, 4.53:6.

ky cf. *k (II)*, *k (III)*.

ky(y) PN (etym. unc.; cf. Grøndahl PTU 277). Cf. *kyn* PN.
PN: *bn ky*, 4.110:6; *bn kyy*, 4.764:5.

kyn PN (Anat. Cf. Grøndahl PTU 277); ¶ syll.: cf. *ki-ia-an-na*, PRU 4 203 (RS 18.20+) obv. 7'; [*ki*](?)*-ia-a-nu*, PRU 6 86 II 2; cf. DUMU *ka*-PI*-na*, PRU 3 202 (RS 16.257+) III 32. Cf. *ky(y)*, *kwn* PNN.
PN: ★a) 4.141 II 21; 4.424:20; ★b) *bn PN*, 4.341:13; 4.611:6.

kzbn PN (etym. unc.; cf. Grøndahl PTU 152); ¶ syll.: cf. DUMU *ki-zi-be*, PRU 6 90 obv. 3'.
PN: *bn PN*, 4.631:17.

kzġb PN (Hurr. Cf. Grøndahl PTU 238, 245; Dietrich - Loretz WO 4 1967 302).
PN: 4.147:17.

kzmm, allograph of *ks/śmm*, 5.22:25; cf. *ks/śm(n)*.

kzn PN (etym. unc.; cf. Grøndahl PTU 277, 280; Dietrich - Loretz - Sanmartín UF 6 1974 40; Watson AuOr 8 1990 246); ¶ syll.: cf. *ki-za-na*, PRU 3 98 (RS 16.249):27; DUMU *ku-za-na*, Ug 5 9:16. Cf. PNN *gsn*, *ksn*.
PN: *bn PN*, 4.69 II 20; 4.340:2; 4.445:4; 5.18:2; cf. in bkn ctx. 4.424:15; 4.445:4.

kzy n. m.; a kind of "groom, squire" (cf. Alalakh Akk. *kizû*, Nuzi Akk., *ka/izû*, AHw 496; CAD K 477f.; Giacumakis 83; Mari *kizûm*, (?)*kazû* (*i-na ka-si-ka*) A 4215:11, Durand Fs. Garelli 58f.; cf. [/ā/ > /ō/(?); Sivan - Cochavi - Rainey WSEVS 86] Eg. *kṯn*, WäS 5 148; Helck Bez. 524 (267): *kú-s`í(-na)*; < EA LÚ $ku_{(8)}$*-sí (ša)* ANŠE. KUR.RA, cf. Rainey EAT 77: *kūsi (ša) sisî*, 'Streitwagenfahrer; groom'; Sivan GAGl 238: /kōsû/, 'stableman'; cf. LÚ.KI.ZI.Ú = *taš-li-šú*(!) *ḫa-ne-gal-<ba>-tum*, MSL 12 226: B VI 145; cf. Hitt. LÚ.IŠ, Kammenhuber FuF 28 1954 121; Hipp. 345; Pecchioli Daddi MPDAI 123ff.; cf. Hurr. */kuz=/, Laroche GLH 157. Cf. Rainey JNES 24 1961 21f.; Dietrich - Loretz - Sanmartín UF 6 1974 30f.; Del Olmo UF 7 1975 101f.; Cutler - Macdonald UF 9 1977 18f.; Heltzer IOKU 124; Beal NABU 1992 n. 48; Vita EU 118ff. ['conductor de carro']; Watson UF 27 1995 545); ¶ RS Akk.: cf. LÚ *ka-zi-i-e ša* É*-ia*, Virolleaud LPD 23 (RS 4.449):6; Cf. Lettinga BiOr 5 1948 112:6; Sivan GAGl 237. ¶ Forms: pl. *kzym*.
Groom, squire: 4.99:10; 4.126:14; 4.68:62 (cf. *ṭup-pu* ÉRIN.MEŠ *ša* GIŠ.BAN.MEŠ tablet of persons with bows, *ibid.* ln. 76/l. edge); *rb kzym* chief groom, 4.222:3 (cf. GAL LÚ(.MEŠ).IŠ, Kammenhuber Hipp. 345).